Enhanced Eighteenth Edition

American Government and Politics Today

M000306675

Enhanced Eighteenth Edition

American Government and Politics Today

Lynne E. Ford
College of Charleston

Barbara A. Bardes
University of Cincinnati

Steffen W. Schmidt
Iowa State University

Mack C. Shelley II
Iowa State University

 CENGAGE

Australia • Brazil • Mexico • Singapore • United Kingdom • United States

American Government and Politics Today, Enhanced Eighteenth Edition

Lynne E. Ford, Barbara A. Bardes, Steffen W. Schmidt, Mack C. Shelley II

Product Manager: Richard Lena

Product Assistant: Haley Gaudreau

Senior Marketing Manager: Valerie Hartmann

Content Manager: David Martinson

Learning Designer: Erika Hayden

IP Analyst: Nancy Dillon

IP Project Manager: Kelli Besse

Production Service and Compositor: SPI Global

Senior Designer: Sarah Cole

Manufacturing Planner: Julio Esperas

Text Designer: Reuter Design

Cover Designer: Sarah Cole

Cover Image:

For product information and technology assistance, contact us at **Cengage Customer & Sales Support, 1-800-354-9706 or support.cengage.com.**

For permission to use material from this text or product, submit all requests online at **www.cengage.com/permissions**.

Library of Congress Control Number: 2018959786

Student Edition:
ISBN: 978-1-337-79035-2

Loose-leaf Edition:
ISBN: 978-0-357-02057-9

Cengage
20 Channel Center Street
Boston, MA 02210
USA

Cengage Learning is a leading provider of customized learning solutions with employees residing in nearly 40 different countries and sales in more than 125 countries around the world. Find your local representative at **www.cengage.com**.

Cengage Learning products are represented in Canada by Nelson Education, Ltd.

To learn more about Cengage platforms and services, register or access your online learning solution, or purchase materials for your course, visit **www.cengage.com**.

Printed in the United States of America
Print Number: 01   Print Year: 2018

Brief Contents

Detailed Contents

PART V Public Policy

A Letter to Instructors

Dear American Politics Instructor:

Americans are often cynical about our national political system. College students in particular are at a loss to know what to do about the polarized politics and policy gridlock occurring within the modern political system, making American Politics a tough course to teach. This edition of *American Government and Politics Today* is designed to help you move your students from the sidelines of politics to full engagement by equipping them with the knowledge and analytical skills needed to shape political decisions at the local, state, and national levels. Based on review feedback, we include a strong emphasis on the power of modern social media and its ability to engage citizens with one another, as well as to connect citizens with political issues and ideas. The solid content on institutions and the processes of government included in previous editions remains. Features such as "Politics in Practice" and "What if...?" will help you bring politics to life in your classroom, while demonstrating to students why politics matters and how it surrounds them each day—at times without their even knowing it. Each chapter has the most up-to-date data and information and includes coverage of current issues and controversies that we believe will engage students and hold their interest.

We believe that part of America's cynicism stems from the growing reality of "two Americas": one with opportunity afforded by privilege and wealth and another whose opportunities, rights, and privileges seem stunted by a lack of wealth. Does the promise of America exist for both groups or only one? How was this theme reflected in the outcome of the 2016 presidential election and in the decision of the Trump administration? How do those who feel they have been left behind as others have prospered regain the promise of the American Dream? What role can political engagement play in doing so? Knowledge is power, and in this edition we try to strike a balance between the content and the skill building necessary for course success, while also presenting students with current controversies in politics and opportunities to engage with those issues. The new "Politics in Practice" feature found in each chapter highlights the ways people engage in politics to make changes. Each chapter begins with the popular feature "What if...?", which presents students with an opportunity to think through a political scenario that for now is a hypothetical, but could actually happen.

These active learning opportunities bring alive the issues that students are confronted with on a daily basis and give students the opportunity to apply their knowledge and skills.

New to This Edition

- This edition has been substantially revised and updated to include the 2016 national elections and recent data, issues, and engaging examples of politics, politicians, and policies. Following the 2016 presidential election, the text has been updated to include issues and examples from the new Trump administration.

- In response to our reviewers, we have substantially revised Chapter 10: "The Media and Politics." This chapter puts a strong emphasis on the way social media connect us to one another and with ideas and political leaders. President Trump's use of Twitter to communicate directly with his supporters and opponents is evaluated in this context.

- Chapter 9 combines material on "Campaigns, Voting, and Elections" in a format that will lead the student seamlessly through the electoral process. The impact of the 2018 midterm elections on the composition of Congress is included.

- In response to reviewers, the features in this edition have been streamlined and the number reduced to three. Each feature has been revised for this edition. "Politics in Practice" is new to this edition and focuses on making politics and people taking political action visible to students by highlighting examples from popular culture and current events. In Chapter 2, the feature highlights the impact of the Broadway musical *Hamilton*, and in Chapter 5 it shows the power of students to change the racial climate on their campus through protest. The feature is designed to enhance student interest by identifying a person or group of people who took on an issue and made a difference.

- A new feature, "Election 2016," has been added to every chapter in the text. Within the context of each chapter's focus, this feature guides students to think about the ways an election can change American politics or reinforce the status quo. Information from the new Trump administration has been added where appropriate.

- Greater attention has been paid to gender issues throughout the text as suggested by reviewers. New material is included on the historic candidacy of Hillary Rodham Clinton, the Equal Pay Act, and the Lilly Ledbetter Act, in addition to updated coverage of women's rights and gender equality, gender and racial discrimination, and the pay gap. The unprecedented number of women running in the 2018 midterm elections is included.

- Care has been taken to reflect the growing political power of Latino/a voters and increasingly diverse communities in the examples used throughout the book.

- Tables and figures have been updated, and the results of the 2016 election are included.

- Recent court decisions on marriage equality and immigration, as well as foreign policy issues like the violence in Syria and the refugee crisis, are integrated into the appropriate chapters in order to ensure that the book addresses the most timely political events and topics.

MindTap

As an instructor, MindTap is here to simplify your workload, organize and immediately grade your students' assignments, and allow you to customize your course as you see fit. Through deep-seated integration with your Learning

Management System, grades are easily exported and analytics are pulled with just the click of a button. MindTap provides you with a platform to easily add in current events videos and RSS feeds from national or local news sources.

Seeing students actively engage with the topics addressed in this book and witnessing an eagerness to learn more about the issues currently facing our nation are some of the most exciting experiences given to any faculty member, particularly when many students will only take one undergraduate course in political science. It is our hope that the revisions to this text will help you reach many students and transform them into thoughtful and engaged citizens for the rest of their lives.

Sincerely,

Lynne E. Ford (FordL@cofc.edu)

Barbara A. Bardes (BardesB@ucmail.uc.edu)

Steffen W. Schmidt

Mack C. Shelley, II

A Letter to Students

Dear Student:

Whether you are a political science major, an international affairs major, or are simply taking this course to fulfill a general requirement, we hope that you will enjoy this book and all of its features. *American Government and Politics Today* is meant to be enjoyed as well as studied. To ensure that the most relevant topics are addressed, the book has been thoroughly revised to include the results of the 2016 national elections, global events and foreign policy, and Supreme Court decisions that affect your life. In every chapter, resources are included to help you go online or use social media to investigate the issues presented in the text that capture your interest. American politics is dynamic, and it is our goal to provide you with clear discussions of the institutions of national government and the political processes so that you can be informed and understand the issues as you participate in our political system.

As a student, the federal government may seem remote from your daily life, but that could not be further from the truth! The issues facing the nation today are serious and require your attention, whether it seems that way upon first glance or not. Decisions made in Washington, DC, and in your state capital can determine, for example, the rate of interest that you will pay on student loans, who must serve in the military, or the level of investment in higher education relative to sustaining pensions and Medicare. You may have heard people talking about the "1 percent" and the "99 percent"—this is a way of capturing the gap between the very rich and everyone else. In what ways does rising wealth inequality matter in America? Is it still possible for everyone to achieve the American Dream? Is political equality possible in the face of economic and social inequality? How did President Trump's election as president reflect a sense that some Americans have been left behind? How will politics change as a result of new groups of political participants? These are just a few of the questions raised by this text. The promise of America is very much alive, but our future is far from certain. Understanding how politics works and knowing your rights as a citizen are critical to shaping the nation's future. Political questions rarely have simple answers. Political issues invite multiple perspectives that can be shaped as much by gender, race, ethnicity, or sexual orientation as by political party or ideology. Throughout this text, we will try to equip you with what you need to develop your own political identity and perspective so that you can fully engage in the national conversation about our shared future.

This edition's interactive features are intended to help you succeed in your coursework as well as to understand the role of politics in the modern world.

- Learning Objectives: These objectives begin each chapter and serve as your "take-aways," highlighting the most important content, concepts, and skills. This will make it easy to check your own learning as you work through each chapter.

- Margin Definitions: These make it easy to double-check your understanding of key terms within the chapters.

- What If: This chapter-opening feature is designed to get you thinking about why politics and government matter to you and your community.

- Politics in Practice: This new feature will help you see politics and popular culture in a new way. In each chapter you will find examples of people using politics to make a change. For example, in Chapter 2 the feature highlights the impact of the Broadway musical *Hamilton* on the public's interest in history, and in Chapter 5 it shows the power of students to change the racial climate on their campus through protest.

- Election 2016: This new feature, appearing in each chapter, will guide you to think about the ways an election can change American politics or reinforce the status quo. Examples from the new Trump administration have been added.

- Social Media Margin Questions: Most chapters include a social media screen capture that poses a critical-thinking question. This feature will challenge you to apply chapter content to the real world.

- Chapter Summaries: Revised for this edition, the end-of-chapter summaries link back to a Learning Objective to better test your understanding of the topics at hand.

- Print, Media, and Online Resources: Each chapter offers a brief list of additional resources that will allow you to explore further the topics that interest you.

The Benefits of Using MindTap as a Student

As a student, the benefits of using MindTap with this book are endless. With automatically graded practice quizzes and activities, an easily navigated learning path, and an interactive eBook, you will be able to test yourself in and outside of the classroom with ease. The accessibility of current events coupled with interactive media makes the content fun and engaging. On your computer, phone, or tablet, MindTap is there when you need it, giving you easy access to flashcards, quizzes, readings, and assignments.

Information is power: when you are well informed, you can participate in discussion with your friends, family, and colleagues and debate ideas with confidence. You can influence events rather than watch as a passive bystander. The future of our republic depends on your full engagement. You are the next generation of leaders, and we wish you well.

Sincerely,

Lynne E. Ford (FordL@cofc.edu)

Barbara A. Bardes (BardesB@ucmail.uc.edu)

Steffen W. Schmidt

Mack C. Shelley, II

Resources

Cengage Unlimited

The first-of-its-kind digital subscription designed specially to lower costs. Students get total access to everything Cengage has to offer on demand—in one place. That's 20,000 eBooks, 2,300 digital learning products, and dozens of study tools across 70 disciplines and over 675 courses. Currently available in select markets. Details at www.cengage.com/unlimited

Students

If you purchased MindTap or CourseReader access with your book, enter your access code and click "Register." You can also purchase the book's resources here separately through the "Study Tools" tab.

Instructors

Access your *American Government and Politics Today* resources via **www.cengage.com/login.**

Log in using your Cengage Learning single sign-on user name and password, or create a new instructor account by clicking on "**New Faculty User**" and following the instructions.

Text Only Edition

ISBN: 9781337790352

This copy of the book does not come bundled with MindTap.

MindTap for *American Government and Politics Today,* Enhanced Eighteenth Edition

Printed Access Card ISBN: 9780357020524

Instant Access Code ISBN: 9780357020494

MindTap for *American Government and Politics Today* is a highly personalized, fully online learning experience built upon Cengage Learning content and correlating to a core set of learning outcomes. MindTap guides students through the course curriculum via an innovative Learning Path Navigator where they will complete reading assignments, challenge themselves with focus activities, and engage with interactive quizzes. Through a variety of gradable activities, MindTap provides students with opportunities to check themselves for where they need extra help, and it allows faculty to measure and assess student progress. Integration with programs like YouTube and Google Drive allows instructors to add and remove content of their choosing with ease, keeping their course current while tracking local and global events through RSS feeds. The product can be used fully online with its interactive eBook for *American Government and Politics Today* Enhanced Eighteenth Edition or in conjunction with the printed text.

CourseReader, Cengage Learning's Powerful, Curated Database of Readings, Is Now Fully Integrated in Every Political Science Mindtap!

Accessed directly from within each MindTap through a new feature called the Instructor's Resource Center, this new tool gives instructors access to readings that were previously exclusively available in a separate digital product. The readings contain primary and secondary sources, are curated by experts, and are designed specifically for use in introductory courses. CourseReader in MindTap is the latest Cengage Learning product to capitalize on the company's unique ability to bring Gale's authoritative library reference content into the classroom.

Instructor Companion Website for Ford/Bardes/ Schmidt/Shelley, *American Government and Politics Today* Enhanced Eighteenth Edition

ISBN: 9780357020487

This Instructor Companion Website is an all-in-one multimedia online resource for class preparation, presentation, and testing. Accessible through Cengage .com/login with your faculty account, you will find available for download: book-specific Microsoft® PowerPoint® presentations; a Test Bank compatible with multiple learning management systems; and an Instructor's Manual.

The Test Bank, offered in Blackboard, Moodle, Desire2Learn, Canvas, and Angel formats, contains learning objective–specific multiple-choice and essay questions for each chapter. Import the test bank into your LMS to edit and manage questions and to create tests.

The Instructor's Manual contains chapter-specific learning objectives, an outline, key terms with definitions, and a chapter summary. Additionally, the Instructor's Manual features a critical thinking question, a lecture launching suggestion, and an in-class activity for each learning objective.

The Microsoft® PowerPoint® presentations are ready-to-use, visual outlines of each chapter. These presentations are easily customized for your lectures.

Cognero for Ford/Bardes/Schmidt/Shelley, *American Government and Politics Today* Enhanced Eighteenth Edition

ISBN: 9780357020555

Cengage Learning Testing Powered by Cognero is a flexible, online system that allows you to author, edit, and manage test bank content from multiple Cengage Learning solutions, create multiple test versions in an instant, and deliver tests from your LMS, your classroom, or wherever you want. The test bank for *American Government and Politics Today* Enhanced Eighteenth Edition contains learning objective–specific multiple-choice and essay questions for each chapter.

Acknowledgments

In preparing this edition of *American Government and Politics Today*, we have received superb guidance and cooperation from a team of publishers and editors at Cengage. We have greatly appreciated the collaboration and encouragement given over the years by Carolyn Merrill, former product team manager. Margaret McAndrew Beasley, our developmental editor, deserves our thanks for keeping us moving toward deadlines and for her well-considered suggestions for improvement. We are also indebted to Megan Garvey, content development manager, and Corinna Dibble, content project manager, for their contributions.

Any errors remain our own. We welcome comments and suggestions from instructors and students alike who are using the book. Their suggestions have helped to strengthen the book and make it more helpful to students and faculty in the changing world of higher education.

Reviewers

We would also like to thank the instructors who have contributed their valuable feedback through reviews of this text:

Brian Dille, *Mesa Community College*

Gerard P. Clock, *Borough of Manhattan Community College*

Katherine A. DeForge, *Marcellus Senior High School*

Anita Falvo, *Watchung Hills Regional High School*

Fred Gordon, *Columbus State University*

Melissa Pivonka, *Quabbin Regional High School*

Michael Vetti, *Seton Catholic Preparatory*

From previous editions:

Krista Ackermann, *Allan Hancock College*

Martin J. Adamian, *California State University, Los Angeles*

Hugh M. Arnold, *Clayton College and State University, Morrow, Georgia*

William Arp III, *Louisiana State University, Baton Rouge*

Louis Battaglia, *Erie Community College*

David S. Bell, *Eastern Washington University, Cheney*

Teri Bengtson, *Elmhurst College*

Dr. Curtis Berry, *Shippensburg University, Shippensburg, Pennsylvania*

John A. Braithwaite, *Coastline Community College, Fountain Valley, California*

Richard G. Buckner, *Santa Fe Community College, New Mexico*

Kenyon D. Bunch, *Fort Lewis College, Durango, Colorado*

Ralph Bunch, *Portland State University, Oregon*

Dewey Clayton, *University of Louisville, Kentucky*

Frank T. Colon, *Lehigh University, Bethlehem, Pennsylvania*

Frank J. Coppa, *Union County College, Cranford, New Jersey*

Irasema Coronado, *University of Texas at El Paso*

Richard D. Davis, *Brigham Young University, Salt Lake City, Utah*

Ron Deaton, *Prince George's Community College, Largo, Maryland*

Marshall L. DeRosa, *Louisiana State University, Baton Rouge*

Jodi Empol, *Montgomery County Community College, Pennsylvania*

Robert S. Getz, *SUNY–Brockport, New York*

Kristina Gilbert, *Riverside Community College, Riverside, California*

William A. Giles, *Mississippi State University, Starkville, Mississippi*

Paul-Henri Gurian, *University of Georgia*

Willie Hamilton, *Mount San Jacinto College, San Jacinto, California*

Matthew Hansel, *McHenry County College, Crystal Lake, Illinois*

David N. Hartman, *Rancho Santiago College, Santa Ana, California*

Robert M. Herman, *Moorpark College, Moorpark, California*

J. C. Horton, *San Antonio College, Texas*

Alice Jackson, *Morgan State University, Baltimore, Maryland*

Robert Jackson, *Washington State University, Pullman*

John D. Kay, *Santa Barbara City College, California*

Bruce L. Kessler, *Shippensburg University, Shippensburg, Pennsylvania*

Samuel Krislov, *University of Minnesota, Minneapolis, Minnesota*

Terence Lenio, *McHenry County College*

Carl Lieberman, *University of Akron, Ohio*

James J. Lopach, *University of Montana, Missoula, Montana*

Jarol B. Manheim, *George Washington University, District of Columbia*

Steve J. Mazurana, *University of Northern Colorado, Greeley*

Jeanine Neher, *Butte Glen Community College*

Keith Nicholls, *University of South Alabama, Mobile, Alabama*

Stephen Osofsky, *Nassau Community College, Garden City, New York*

Neil A. Pinney, *Western Michigan University, Kalamazoo*

Walter V. Powell, *Slippery Rock University, Slippery Rock, Pennsylvania*

Eleanor A. Schwab, *South Dakota State University, Brookings*

Joseph L. Smith, *Grand Valley State University, Allendale, Michigan*

Michael W. Sonnlietner, *Portland Community College, Oregon*

Mark J. Wattier, *Murray State University, Murray, Kentucky*

Stella Webster, *Wayne County Community College—Downtown, Detroit, Michigan*

Lance Widman, *El Camino College, Torrance, California*

Robert D. Wrinkle, *Pan American University, Edinburg, Texas*

About the Authors

Lynne E. Ford is Associate Vice President for the Academic Experience and professor of political science at the College of Charleston in Charleston, South Carolina. She received her B.A. from The Pennsylvania State University and her M.A. and Ph.D. in government and political behavior from the University of Maryland–College Park. Ford's teaching and research interests include women and politics, elections and voting behavior, political psychology, and civic engagement. She has written articles on women in state legislatures, the underrepresentation of women in political office in the American South, and work–family policy in the United States. She has also authored *Women and Politics: The Pursuit of Equality* and *The Encyclopedia of Women and American Politics*. Ford served as Associate Provost for Curriculum and Academic Administration for five years, as department chair for eight years, and she has led a number of campus-wide initiatives, including general education reform, faculty compensation, and civic engagement.

Barbara A. Bardes is professor emerita of political science at the University of Cincinnati. She received her B.A. and M.A. from Kent State University and her Ph.D. from the University of Cincinnati. She served as a faculty member in political science and dean of Mundelein College at Loyola University of Chicago. In 1993, she was appointed dean of the University of Cincinnati Blue Ash, where she served until 2003. She returned to the Political Science Department, where she held the position of graduate director before retiring. Bardes has written articles on public and foreign policy, and women and politics. She also has co-authored *Declarations of Independence: Women and Political Power in 19th Century American Novels*, *Thinking About Public Policy*, *Public Opinion: Measuring The American Mind*, and *American Government and Politics Today*.

Steffen W. Schmidt is a professor of political science at Iowa State University. He grew up in Colombia, South America, and has studied in Colombia, Switzerland, the United States, and France. He has a B.A. from Rollins College and obtained his Ph.D. from Columbia University, New York, in public law and government. Dr. Schmidt has published 14 books and over 130 articles in scholarly journals and major newspapers. He is the recipient of numerous prestigious teaching prizes, including the Amoco Award for Lifetime Career Achievement in Teaching and the Teacher of the Year award. He is a pioneer in the use of web-based and real-time video courses and a founding member of the American Political Science Association's section on Computers and Multimedia. He is known as "Dr. Politics" for his extensive commentary on U.S. politics in both U.S. and international media. He comments on CNN en Español and Univision, as well as CTV Canada Cable TV. Dr. Schmidt is a founding member of the USSTRATCOM academic alliance. He's on Facebook (SteffenWSchmidt) and Twitter (DrPolitics).

Mack C. Shelley, II is a professor of political science and statistics at Iowa State University. After receiving his bachelor's degree from American University in Washington, DC, he went on to graduate studies at the University of Wisconsin–Madison, where he received a master's degree in economics and a Ph.D. in political science. He arrived at Iowa State in 1979. From 1993 to 2002 he served as elected co-editor of the *Policy Studies Journal.* Shelley has also published numerous articles, books, and monographs on public policy, including *The Permanent Majority: The Conservative Coalition in the United States Congress*, *Biotechnology and the Research Enterprise: A Guide to the Literature* (with William F. Woodman and Brian J. Reichel), *American Public Policy: The Contemporary Agenda* (with Steven G. Koven and Bert E. Swanson), and *Quality Research in Literacy and Science Education: International Perspectives and Gold Standards* (with Larry Yore and Brian Hand). He conducts policy research in a number of areas funded by grants and contracts.

Career Opportunites: Political Science

Introduction

It is no secret that college graduates are facing one of the toughest job markets in the past fifty years. Despite this challenge, those with a college degree have done much better than those without since the 2008 recession. One of the most important decisions a student has to make is the choice of a major; many consider future job possibilities when making that call. A political science degree is incredibly useful for a successful career in many different fields, from lawyer to policy advocate, pollster to humanitarian worker. Employer surveys reveal that the skills that most employers value in successful employees—critical thinking, analytical reasoning, and clarity of verbal and written communication—are precisely the tools that political science courses should be helping you develop. This brief guide is intended to help spark ideas for what kinds of careers you might pursue with a political science degree and the types of activities you can engage in now to help you secure one of those positions after graduation.

Careers in Political Science

Law and Criminal Justice

Do you find that your favorite parts of your political science classes are those that deal with the Constitution, the legal system, and the courts? Then a career in law and criminal justice might be right for you. Traditional jobs in the field range from lawyer or judge to police or parole officer. Since 9/11, there has also been tremendous growth in the area of homeland security, which includes jobs in mission support, immigration, travel security, as well as prevention and response.

Public Administration

The many offices of the federal government combined represent one of the largest employers in the United States. Flip to the bureaucracy chapter of this textbook and consider that each federal department, agency, and bureau you see looks to political science majors for future employees. A partial list of such agencies would include the Department of Education, the Department of Health and Human Services, and the Federal Trade Commission. There are also thousands of staffers who work for members of Congress or the Congressional Budget Office, many of whom were political science majors in college. This does not even begin to account for the multitude of similar jobs in state and local governments that you might consider as well.

Campaigns, Elections, and Polling

Are campaigns and elections the most exciting part of political science for you? Then you might consider a career in the growing industry based around political campaigns. From volunteering and interning to consulting, marketing, and fundraising, there are many opportunities for those who enjoy the competitive and high-stakes electoral arena. For those looking for careers that combine political knowledge with statistical skills, there are careers in public opinion polling. Pollsters work for independent national organizations such as Gallup and YouGov, or as part of news operations and campaigns. For those who are interested in survey methodology, there are also a wide variety of non-political career opportunities in marketing and survey design.

Interest Groups, International, and Nongovernmental Organizations

Is there a cause that you are especially passionate about? If so, there is a good chance that there are interest groups out there that are working hard to see some progress made on similar issues. Many of the positions that one might find in for-profit companies also exist in their nonprofit interest group and nongovernmental organization counterparts, including lobbying and high-level strategizing. Do not forget that there are also quite a few major international organizations—such as the United Nations, the World Health Organization, and the International Monetary Fund—where a degree in political science could be put to good use. While competition for those jobs tends to be fierce, your interest in and knowledge about politics and policy will give you an advantage.

Foreign Service

Does a career in diplomacy and foreign affairs, complete with the opportunity to live and work abroad, sound exciting for you? Tens of thousands of people work for the State Department, both in Washington, DC, and in consulates throughout the world. They represent the diplomatic interests of the United States abroad. Entrance into the Foreign Service follows a very specific process, starting with the Foreign Service Officers Test (FSOT)—an exam given three times a year that includes sections on American government, history, economics, and world affairs. Being a political science major is a significant help in taking the FSOT.

Graduate School

While not a career, graduate school may be the appropriate next step for you after completing your undergraduate degree. Being awarded a Ph.D. or master's degree in political science could open additional doors to a career in academia, as well as many of the professions mentioned earlier. If a career as a researcher in political science interests you, you should speak with your advisors about continuing your education.

Preparing While Still on Campus

Internships

One of the most useful steps you can take while still on campus is to visit your college's career center in regard to an internship in your field of interest. Not only does it give you a chance to experience life in the political science realm, it can lead to job opportunities later down the road and add experience to your resume.

Skills

In addition to your political science classes, the following skills will prove useful as a complement to your degree:

Writing: Like anything else, writing improves with practice. Writing is one of those skills that is applicable regardless of where your career might take you. Virtually every occupation relies on an ability to write cleanly, concisely, and persuasively.

Public Speaking: An oft-quoted 1977 survey showed that public speaking was the most commonly cited fear among respondents. And yet oral communication is a vital tool in the modern economy. You can practice this skill in a formal class setting or through extracurricular activities that get you in front of a group.

Quantitative Analysis: The Internet increases exponentially the amount of data gathered, and the nation is facing a drastic shortage of people with basic statistical skills to interpret and use this data. A political science degree can go hand-in-hand with courses in introductory statistics.

Foreign Language: One skill that often helps a student or future employee stand out in a crowded job market is the ability to communicate in a language other than English. Solidify or set the foundation for your verbal and written foreign language communication skills while in school.

Student Leadership

One attribute that many employers look for is "leadership potential," which can be tricky to indicate on a resume or cover letter. One way to do so is to include on your resume and/or cover letter a demonstrated record of involvement in clubs and organizations, preferably in a leadership role. Student government is often listed as the primary source of leadership experience, but most student clubs allow you the opportunity to demonstrate your leadership skills.

Conclusion

We hope that this discussion has sparked your ideas about potential future careers. As a next step, visit your college's career placement office, which is a great place to further explore what you have read here. You might also visit your college's alumni office to connect with graduates who are working in your field of interest. Political science opens the door to a lot of exciting careers. Have fun exploring the possibilities!

Enhanced Eighteenth Edition

American Government and Politics Today

One Republic—
Two Americas?

One World Trade Center, built at Ground Zero of the September 11, 2001 terrorist attacks, was designed to represent the resilience of the American spirit. Including its mast, the building's height is 1,776 feet, making it the tallest building in New York City.

Cameron Davidson/Getty Images

LEARNING OBJECTIVES

After reading this chapter, you will be able to:

■ **1.1** Define the institution of government and the process of politics.

■ **1.2** Identify the political philosophers associated with the "social contract" and explain how this theory shapes our understanding of the purpose of government and the role for individuals and communities in the United States.

■ **1.3** Describe the U.S. political culture and identify the set of ideas, values, and ways of thinking about government and politics shared by all.

■ **1.4** Compare and contrast types of government systems and identify the source of power in each.

■ **1.5** Define political ideology and locate socialism, liberalism, conservatism, and libertarianism along the ideological spectrum.

■ **1.6** Apply understanding of the purpose of government and the U.S. political culture to evaluate government's ability to meet new challenges over time.

What if... Taxes Never Increased and Local Services Disappeared?

Background

The power to tax and spend is a defining function of government. Taxation is a concurrent power, meaning that the federal, state, and local governments can all collect taxes. Taxes on property, goods and services, and income provide revenue for government to operate. Dating back to the earliest days of the republic, the government's power to tax has provoked strong negative reactions. The Boston Tea Party in 1773, the Whiskey Rebellion in 1794, and California's 1978 Proposition 13, known as the "People's Initiative to Limit Property Taxation," are all examples of popular rebellions. More recently, the Tea Party protests have brought attention to questions about the government's power to tax and the appropriate size and role of government. Many fiscally conservative candidates promise to eliminate tax increases and shrink the size of government. In reality, eliminating tax increases means cutting state and local budgets and eliminating services that people have come to expect. How should communities respond? What happens to schools, roads, police and fire protection, and other public services when local governments can no longer afford to pay for them?

Taxes Pay for Local Services We Expect

The tax system allows government to redistribute revenue in a variety of ways. Intergovernmental transfers provide money collected by state and federal governments to local governments, accounting for roughly 40 percent of local operating dollars. Cities and towns make up the rest of their budget through property taxes, local sales taxes, and various user fees. In a recession, people buy fewer goods and services. This means that local governments collect less revenue from sales taxes and need to make up the deficit by other means or cut the budget. Local budget cuts often mean that services to citizens are dramatically reduced or eliminated altogether.

Local governments—counties and cities—usually take responsibility for parks and recreation services, police and fire departments, housing services, emergency medical services, municipal courts, transportation services, and public works (streets, sewers, trash collection, water, snow removal, and signage).

No Taxes, No Services: Tough Choices

In conservative Colorado Springs, Colorado, home of the "Taxpayer's Bill of Rights," voters rejected a tax increase to restore a budget deficit caused by declining sales tax revenues. The city turned off one-third of its streetlights to save electricity costs. The city also locked public restrooms, reduced bus service, and stopped maintaining the city parks.

The city of Flint, Michigan, was placed in state receivership in 2011, and Governor Rick Snyder appointed an emergency manager. At the time, the city was running a $20 million deficit. As a cost-savings measure in 2014, the state decided to temporarily switch Flint's water source from Lake Huron to the Flint River until a new supply line to Lake Huron was ready. Almost immediately, residents began to complain about the color and taste of the water. Testing found dangerously high levels of lead and other toxins caused when caustic Flint River water degraded lead water pipes. City residents were warned against using the water for drinking, cooking, or bathing. Thousands of children have tested positive for elevated lead levels, raising concerns about future health issues and school performance. The National Guard was called in to distribute bottled water to Flint residents. The cost of replacing the damaged pipes is now estimated at more than $55 million.

In New Jersey, Republican governor Chris Christie cut $3 billion from the state budget in his first two years in office. As a result, Trenton, New Jersey, fired one-third of the police force (103 officers). In a single year, gun-related assaults increased by 76 percent, robberies with a firearm increased by 55 percent, car thefts more than doubled, and break-ins more than tripled. The domestic violence unit was eliminated.

In 27 states, municipalities have introduced accident response fees to collect revenue to fund rescue, fire, and ambulance services. Drivers and/or their insurance companies are billed for municipalities' response to traffic accidents. The fees range from about $300 to more than $2,000 per hour per vehicle and are based on the piece of equipment used. Extrication devices, popularly known as "Jaws of Life," are among the most costly. Responding to citizen complaints, many states are reviewing the practice, and 13 states have banned the "crash tax."

For Critical Analysis

1. The U.S. tax system is designed to collect and redistribute revenue. Public goods and services paid for by tax revenue are therefore available to all in most cases (police protection, snow removal) or to those in the community who qualify because of special needs (legal aid to the poor, Medicaid). Some services or facilities are financed with "user fees." In other words, you pay only for what you as an individual use (toll roads, parking meters). Consider the local government services just mentioned. In your view, is it better to pay for each with tax revenue or user fees? What if the services rendered are in response to an accident? How does your answer relate to your perspective on the appropriate role for government?

2. We all live in the same country, but will decisions about who has access to public goods and services mean that we are creating two Americas? What kind of country do you want to live in?

Although it has become popular to complain about government, we could not survive as individuals or as communities without it. The challenge is to become invested enough in the American system and engaged enough in the political process so that the government we have is the government we want and deserve. This is a tremendous challenge because, until you understand how our system works, "the government" can seem as though it belongs to somebody else; it can seem distant, hard to understand, and difficult to use when there is a problem to solve or there are hard decisions to make. Nevertheless, democracies, especially *this* democracy, derive their powers from the people, and this fact provides each of you with a tremendous opportunity. Individuals and groups of like-minded individuals who participate in the system can create change and shape the government to meet their needs. Those who opt not to pay attention or fail to participate must accept what others decide for them—good or bad.

Complicating matters further is the simple truth that although we all live in the same country and share the same political system, we may experience government differently. This leads us to hold different opinions about how big or small government should be, what kind of role government should play in our individual lives, what kinds of issues are appropriate for policymakers to handle, and what should be left to each of us alone.

At the heart of the debate over health care and health insurance is the question of how best to pay for, and provide access to, health care for every citizen. In 2015, this country's federal, state, and local governments, corporations, and individuals spent $3.2 trillion, or about $10,000 for every person, on health care.[1] Health insurance costs are rising faster than wages or inflation. Costs like this are not sustainable and drain the economy of resources needed elsewhere. The Patient Protection and Affordable Care Act (commonly known as the Affordable Care Act) was signed into law in 2010, although many of its provisions will take several years to implement, and several delays and extensions were granted early in its implementation. The act is large and complicated because the issue it addresses is large and complicated.

Several aspects of the law are favored by nearly everyone, such as providing access to insurance for people with preexisting conditions or allowing children to stay on their parents' insurance until age 26. The law also requires people to be insured either through their employer or by purchasing insurance so that the costs and risks are spread across the entire population. Failure to do so results in a penalty. Because young people are typically healthy and rarely incur expensive medical bills, their participation is necessary to offset the costs of caring for others and to maintain the stability of the state and federal health exchanges. As a group, "young invincibles," as they have been labeled by the health insurance industry, have proven difficult to convince of the necessity of health insurance. The law's insurance mandate seems at odds with the value we place on individual responsibility; yet, health care is something everyone requires, and the costs are more manageable if everyone is included.

We resolve these and other conflicting values using the political process, and institutions of government are empowered to make decisions on our behalf. In the case of health care, the conflict has been resolved by the judiciary. The U.S.

did you know?
The Greek philosopher Aristotle favored enlightened despotism over democracy, which to him meant mob rule.

---

1 Centers for Medicare and Medicaid Services, accessed at www.cms.gov.

Supreme Court scheduled an unprecedented six hours of oral arguments over the course of three days in March 2012. The justices faced a number of critical questions, including whether or not the law's requirement that individuals carry health insurance was within the powers granted to Congress by the Constitution. On June 28, 2012, the Supreme Court issued a 5-4 decision upholding nearly all of the health-care law,[2] including the minimum coverage provision. Chief Justice John Roberts wrote the majority opinion. President Obama called the ruling "a victory for people all over this country whose lives will be more secure" because nearly 30 million Americans who currently lack health insurance will eventually be covered as a result of the law. Although in most cases a Supreme Court ruling settles the question, in this case it did not. In September 2013, Senator Ted Cruz (R-TX) controlled the Senate floor for more than 21 hours in what political satirists referred to as a "fauxilibuster" (because a bill was not placed before the body, a true filibuster was not possible). His goal was to attract support to defund implementation of the health-care law. Partisan politics continue to prevent Congress from making performance-enhancing adjustments to the existing law. By some estimates, Republicans in Congress have voted more than 50 times since 2010 to repeal all or part of the Affordable Care Act. Even with Republicans in control of Congress and the White House, multiple attempts to repeal and replace the ACA have failed and the law remains largely intact.

Sir Winston Churchill, British prime minister during World War II, once said, "No one pretends that democracy is perfect or all-wise. Indeed, it has been said that democracy is the worst form of government except all those other forms that have been tried from time to time."[3] Our system is not perfect, but it is more open to change than most. This book offers essential tools to learn about American government and politics today so that you are prepared to change this country for the better.

What are your dreams for the future, and what role do you believe the government can and should play in helping you realize your dreams? There was a time when we all aspired to live the "American Dream" and when we believed that government played an essential role in ensuring that the opportunity to achieve the

---

Twitter Feed ▶ Even with Republicans in control of Congress and the White House following the 2016 elections, multiple attempts to repeal and replace the ACA have failed and the law remains largely intact.

Paul Ryan ✓
@SpeakerRyan

☼ ⚊+ Follow

THIS IS A FIRST → a bill repealing #Obamacare will be sent to the president's desk.

spkrryan.us/1OMvIT1

#OnHisDesk

Bill to Repeal Obamacare

RETWEETS	LIKES
90	**197**

9:26 AM - 6 Jan 2016

Twitter/Paul Ryan

---

2 *National Federation of Independent Business*, et al. v. Sebelius, *Secretary of Health and Human Services, et al.* 567 U.S. (2012).

3 House of Commons speech on November 11, 1947.

American Dream was available to everyone. Members of each successive generation were confident that if they worked hard and followed the rules, they would live richer and more successful lives than the generation before them. Public policy has historically been an effective tool to promote economic growth, educational equity, homeownership, and job security. Is that still true today?

There are some troubling signs, to be sure. Significant inequality in income and wealth exists in the United States, and rather than shrinking, the gap has widened for your generation and your parents' generation. In 1979, the richest 1 percent accounted for 8 percent of all personal income; by 2012, their share had more than doubled, to 19.3 percent, their largest share since 1928.[4] As the economy began to improve, the greatest gains in income share went to the top 10 percent of earners. Hourly wage workers, notably fast food workers, raised awareness of the recovery gap by participating in a series of labor walkouts and demanding an increase to the $7.25 federal minimum hourly wage. To add momentum to the movement, President Obama signed an executive order early in 2014 raising the minimum wage for workers under new federal contracts to $10.10 an hour. In 2016, Oregon lawmakers adopted a series of gradual increases over six years using a unique three-tier geographic system whereby workers in large metro areas would earn more per hour than workers in smaller cities or rural areas.[5] During the same month, legislators in a number of other states considered or passed preemption laws designed to block the development of local wage ordinances. The global economic recession, the unemployment rate, rising home foreclosures, and corporate relocation of jobs overseas all present government with significant challenges. Moreover, people's trust in several institutions (banks, Congress, churches and organized religion) has fallen over the past decade (see Figure 1-1).

Jim West/Alamy Stock Photo

Image 1-1
Hundreds rallied near a Detroit, Michigan, McDonald's restaurant in support of a strike by fast-food workers who were demanding a raise from their current wages of about $7.40 an hour to $15 an hour. Similar strikes for higher wages took place in cities around the country.

4 Facundo Alvaredo, Anthony B. Atkinson, Thomas Piketty, and Emmanuel Saez, "The Top 1 Percent in International and Historical Perspective." *Journal of Economic Perspectives* (2013) 27(3): 3–20.

5 Kristen Hansen, "Oregon's Trailblazing Minimum Wage Has Geographic Tiers, Topped by Portland's $14.75" *San Jose Mercury News*, February 19, 2016.

Native-born citizens know less than ever about the very political system they hope will restore their confidence in the future; one in three failed the civics portion of the naturalization test in a national telephone survey.[6] Can people effectively engage in political activity to change their lives for the better when they know so little about the governmental system?

There are also some hopeful signs. According to the Center for the Study of the American Dream at Xavier University, a majority of Americans surveyed (63 percent) remain confident that they will achieve the American Dream despite the current challenges. More than 75 percent believe they have already achieved some measure of it. Those surveyed defined the American Dream in terms of a good life for their family (45 percent), financial security (34 percent), freedom (32 percent), opportunity (29 percent), the pursuit of happiness (21 percent), a good job (16 percent), and homeownership (7 percent). How does this definition fit with your own? Are you surprised that homeownership is last on the list? How might the mortgage crisis and the persistent economic recession influence how we define our future dreams? As the nation pulls out of the long recession and jobs become more plentiful, will people aspire to own a home again? The U.S. economy added nearly 2.1 million jobs in 2017, dropping the unemployment rate to 4.1 percent. However, five years after the Great Recession, many families still feel financially vulnerable and have doubts about their chances of attaining the American Dream. A 2014 *New York Times* Poll found that only 64 percent of respondents said that they still believed in the American Dream, the lowest result in two decades. In early 2009 as the recession and financial crisis reached its peak, 72 percent of Americans still believed that "hard work could result in riches."[7]

Interestingly, the Xavier study found that Latinos and immigrants are most positive about the possibility of achieving the American Dream and are more optimistic about the future of the country than the population as a whole. Finally, a majority of Americans view immigration as an important part of keeping the American Dream alive and believe that immigration continues to be one of America's greatest strengths. In his 2014 State of the Union address, President Obama said, "What I believe unites the people of this nation, regardless of race or region or party, young or old, rich or poor, is the simple, profound belief in opportunity for all—the notion that if you work hard and take responsibility, you can get ahead."[8]

What is the state of America today? Given the economic and educational disparities evident in the United States today, are we one America or two? Are you confident that your life will be better than that of your parents and grandparents? Can the problems we face as a nation today be addressed by the political system? Voters in 2016 demonstrated their anger at the "establishment" by electing "outsider" Donald J. Trump, believing that he could shake up the political system. President Obama concluded his final State of the Union address by saying, "Fifteen years into this new century, we have picked ourselves up, dusted ourselves off, and begun again the work of

---

6 "U.S. Naturalization Civics Test: National Survey of Native-Born U.S. Citizens, March 2012," conducted by the Center for the Study of the American Dream, Xavier University. http://www.xavier.edu/americandream/programs/National-Civic-Literacy-Survey.cfm

7 Andrew Ross Sorkin and Megan Thee-Brenan, "Many Feel the American Dream Is Out of Reach, Poll Shows," *The New York Times*, December 10, 2014. http://dealbook.nytimes.com/2014/12/10/many-feel-the-american-dream-is-out-of-reach-poll-shows

8 State of the Union Address, January 28, 2014. http://www.whitehouse.gov/the-press-office/2014/01/28/president-barack-obamas-state-union-address

remaking America. We've laid a new foundation. A brighter future is ours to write."[9] Is the American republic up to today's challenges? These will be central questions in our analysis of American government and politics today.

Politics and Government

■ **1.1** Define the institution of government and the process of politics.

Before we can answer any of these provocative questions, we first have to define some terms. What is politics? **Politics** is the process of resolving conflicts and deciding "who gets what, when, and how."[10] Although politics may be found in many places outside of government (for example, in your family or workplace), for the purposes of this book, we refer to conflicts and decisions found at the federal, state, and local levels regarding the selection of decision makers, the structure of institutions, and the creation of public policy. Politics is particularly intense when decisions are made that hit close to home, such as decisions about how to spend local and state tax dollars. Equally intense are political decisions that yield leaders for our country. Elections at the national and state levels attract the most media attention, but thousands of elected and appointed officials make up the government and render decisions that affect our lives.

Government is the term used to describe the formal **institutions** through which decisions about the allocation of resources are made and conflicts are resolved. Government can take many forms, come in many sizes, and perform a variety of functions, but at the core, all governments rule. To govern is to rule. Governments can, as a matter of their authority, force you to comply with laws through taxes, fines, and the power to send you to prison, or worse—to death row. The inherent power of government is what led the founders of the United States to impose limitations on this power relative to the rights of individuals. Likewise, the power of government leads Americans to be wary of too much government when less will do.

Why Is Government Necessary?

■ **1.2** Identify the political philosophers associated with the "social contract" and explain how this theory shapes our understanding of the purpose of government and the role for individuals and communities in the United States.

Americans may not always like government, but they like the absence of government even less. Governments are necessary at a minimum to provide public goods and services that all citizens need but cannot reasonably be expected to provide for themselves. National security and defense are obvious examples. But governments do far more than provide for the common defense. As you will learn in Chapter 2, our founding documents such as the Declaration of Independence and the Constitution are predicated upon and convey through their language a set of shared political values. Government reinforces those values regularly. One of our defining values is belief in the rule of law, which means that laws determined through the political process are enforced uniformly and that no individual, regardless of wealth, privilege,

politics
The process of resolving conflicts and deciding "who gets what, when, and how." More specifically, politics is the struggle over power or influence within organizations or informal groups that can grant or withhold benefits or privileges.

government
The preeminent institution in which decisions are made that resolve conflicts or allocate benefits and privileges. It is unique because it has the ultimate authority within society.

institution
An ongoing organization that performs certain functions for society.

---

9 State of the Union Address, January 12, 2016. http://www.chicagotribune.com/news/nationworld/politics/sns-state-of-the-union-text-story.html
10 Harold Lasswell, *Politics: Who Gets What, When, and How* (New York: McGraw-Hill, 1936).

or position, is above the law. Government includes a system of justice administered by institutions known as the courts to maintain this important value. We will return to this discussion of fundamental values later in this chapter. In addition to providing public goods and services and reinforcing shared values, governments are necessary to provide security so that liberty may flourish.

divine right of kings
A political and religious doctrine that asserts a monarch's legitimacy is conferred directly by God and, as such, a king is not subject to any earthly authority, including his people or the church.

social contract
A theory of politics that asserts that individuals form political communities by a process of mutual consent, giving up a measure of their individual liberty in order to gain the protection of government.

Our contemporary understanding of why government is necessary has been shaped by Enlightenment thinkers from seventeenth- and eighteenth-century Europe. During the Age of Enlightenment, also known as the Age of Reason, philosophers and scientists challenged the **divine right of kings** and argued that the world could be vastly improved through the use of human reason, science, and religious tolerance. Essential to this argument was the belief that all individuals were born free and equal and imbued with natural rights. Individuals were in control of their own destiny, and by working with others, a society could shape a government capable of both asserting and protecting individual rights. English **social contract** theorists such as Thomas Hobbes (1588–1679) and John Locke (1632–1704) were particularly influential in shaping our theory of government. Hobbes was far more pessimistic about human nature than Locke. Hobbes believed that without government and the rule of law, people would revert to a state of nature, and individuals would be left to fight over basic necessities, rendering life "solitary, poor, nasty, brutish, and short."[11] To avoid such a fate, Hobbes argued for a single ruler, a Leviathan, so powerful that the rights of the weak could be protected against intrusion by the strong. By contrast, Locke took basic survival for granted, believing that all humans were endowed with reason—an internal code of conduct. Therefore, individuals are willing to give up a portion of their individual liberty in order to gain the protection of government through the social contract. Government is formed to protect life, liberty, and property; however, if a government compromises its legitimacy by violating the social contract, it is the people's duty to end the abusive government and replace it with a new form.

It is within this theoretical framework that we understand the necessity for government: to provide security, to protect liberty and enforce property rights, and to maintain legitimacy by exercising authority consistent with the fundamental values of those governed. Consent of the governed is the basis for power and legitimacy in American democracy.

Fundamental Values

■ **1.3** Describe the U.S. political culture and identify the set of ideas, values, and ways of thinking about government and politics shared by all.

The authors of the U.S. Constitution believed that the structures they had created would provide for both democracy and a stable political system. They also believed that the nation could be sustained by its **political culture**. A critical question facing America today is to what extent do all citizens continue to share in a single political culture? Does the widening wealth and income gap threaten to undermine our shared political values as well as our confidence in government? We live under one republic, but are we increasingly two Americas? There is considerable consensus among American citizens about

political culture
The set of ideas, values, and ways of thinking about government and politics that is shared by all citizens.

---

11 Thomas Hobbes, *Leviathan:* (Cambridge: Cambridge University Press; Revised Student Edition, 1996).

Beyond Our Borders

Immigrant Workers: Challenging Cultures in Europe

One of the most controversial issues in American politics is the debate over what to do about undocumented immigrants who have come to the United States for employment and a better life. An estimated 12 million individuals reside in the United States without legal status. Some conservatives believe that the best solution is deporting the undocumented people to their respective native countries. Others, including President Obama and moderate leaders of both parties, have argued that the United States should recognize its need for workers and implement a system by which individuals can come to this country to work and someday earn a right to citizenship. Immigration is a major source of population growth and cultural change in the United States. The political focus on undocumented immigrants can overshadow the tremendous benefits of immigration. For example, immigrants are among the founders of many prominent American technology companies, such as Google, Yahoo!, and eBay.

Nations, especially those in Europe, have long admitted immigrants as unskilled and semiskilled workers to fuel their economies and increase their populations. Immigrants make up about 12 percent of the population of Germany and 15 percent of that of Austria. Thirty-seven percent of Luxembourg's populace are immigrants; in Switzerland, that figure is around 23 percent. For many decades, Great Britain has allowed individuals who were subjects of the British Commonwealth to enter the country, and France extended legal residency to many French citizens from its former colonies in North Africa. Germany estimates that it will need to attract up to 1.5 million additional skilled workers through immigration to compensate for an aging population.

All nations face a dilemma in how to balance the cultural energy immigrants bring with the tensions associated with integration and assimilation processes. Immigrants may find limits to employment, education, and housing. Nonwhite and Muslim residents claim they are the subject of unwarranted police attention through racial or religious profiling. Clashes sometimes turn violent. Reports of Syrian refugees raping and groping women during New Year's Eve celebrations in Cologne, Germany, forced German Chancellor Angela Merkel to defend her open-door policy toward Muslim refugees entering the country from terrorism hot spots in the Middle East. Young people rioted in France over the lack of employment opportunities for nonwhite French residents, and the Netherlands has seen outbreaks of violence

Image 1–2 Sergey Brin, co-founder of Google, was born in Moscow, Russia. When Brin was six, his family entered the United States with the assistance of HIAS, the Hebrew Immigrant Aid Society. In honor of the thirtieth anniversary of his family's immigration, Brin gave $1 million to HIAS, which he credits with helping his family escape anti-Semitism in the Soviet Union.

Idealink Photography/Alamy Stock Photo

by Muslim residents against other Dutch citizens. Youth riots in Sweden were particularly surprising, given the nation's reputation for welcoming the world's refugees, most recently people fleeing the civil war in Syria. However, even Sweden adopted tougher measures when the number of asylum seekers topped 80,000 in two months' time. Many of these states are engaged in serious internal discussion about how to socialize new residents to the culture of their new home and how to ensure that immigrants can find economic opportunities for themselves and their children, while at the same time challenging the prejudice and racism sometimes found in the native population.

For Critical Analysis

1. How can the inevitable tensions created when new ideas and customs confront established cultures be resolved? What role is appropriate for government in this process?

2. To what extent should nations ensure that immigrants accept the cultural and political values of their new home? In what specific ways does multiculturalism benefit political, social, and economic development?

concepts basic to the U.S. political system. Given that the population of the United States is made up primarily of immigrants and descendants of immigrants with diverse cultural and political backgrounds, how can we account for this consensus? Primarily, it is the result of **political socialization**—the process by which beliefs and values are transmitted to successive generations. The nation depends on families, schools, houses of worship, and the media to transmit the precepts of our national culture. With fewer people going to church and a widening educational gap that strongly correlates with economic disparities, we may need to reexamine the ways in which our political culture is transmitted. On the other hand, you can find these fundamental values reaffirmed in most major public speeches given by the president and other important officials in American politics. We will return to these important questions throughout the book, but particularly in Chapter 6.

political socialization
The process through which individuals learn a set of political attitudes and form opinions about social issues. Families and the educational system are two of the most important forces in the political socialization process.

liberty
The greatest freedom of individuals that is consistent with the freedom of other individuals in the society.

Liberty As you recall, the advancement and protection of individual liberty is central to the social contract theory of government. **Liberty** is among the natural rights articulated by Locke and later by Thomas Jefferson in the Declaration of Independence ("life, liberty, and the pursuit of happiness"). In the United States, our civil liberties include religious freedom—both the right to believe in whatever religion we choose and freedom from any state-imposed religion. Liberty, as a political value, has two sides to it—one positive (the freedom to) and one negative (the freedom from). The freedom of speech—the right to political expression on all matters, including government actions—is an example of a positive liberty. Freedom of speech is one of our most prized liberties; a democracy could not endure without it. The right to privacy is a more controversial liberty claim. The U.S. Supreme Court has held that the right to privacy can be derived from other rights that are explicitly stated in the Bill of Rights. The Supreme Court has also held that under the right to privacy, the government cannot ban either abortion[12] or private sexual behavior by consenting adults.[13]

Positive freedoms are not absolute, and individual liberty can be limited, such as in times of war. When Americans perceive serious threats, they have supported government actions to limit individual liberties in the name of national security. Such limits were imposed during the Civil War, World War II, and the McCarthy era of the Cold War. Following the terrorist attacks on the World Trade Center and the Pentagon on September 11, 2001, Congress passed legislation designed to provide greater security at the expense of some civil liberties. In particular, the USA PATRIOT (Uniting and Strengthening America by Providing Appropriate Tools Required to Intercept and Obstruct Terrorism) Act gave law enforcement and intelligence-gathering agencies greater latitude to search out and investigate suspected terrorists.

Image 1–3
U.S. Homeland Security
Secretary Kirstjen Nielsen was confirmed by the Senate in December 2017.

Bloomberg/Getty Images

---

12 *Roe v. Wade*, 410 U.S. 113 (1973).
13 *Lawrence v. Texas*, 539 U.S. 558 (2003).

Confidence in Institutions Varies: How Do We Know?

Throughout this book, you will find a number of visual features, including figures, tables, photographs, and political cartoons. These visual features are carefully selected to present information that is critical to your understanding of the content in each chapter. Therefore, you must study the visuals carefully. In addition, you may be tested on this information.

Figure 1-1 presents Gallup polling data on the public's confidence in major institutions at two points in time. Gallup regularly conducts public opinion polls in more than 140 countries around the world. You will often see these polls referenced in news reports. Begin by reading the title of the figure and the descriptive information—the caption—right below the title. Together, the title and caption summarize the information that you need in order to understand the graphic. Captions below photographs and cartoons have a similar function. Figure 1-1 shows two points in time, indicating a change in public attitudes. Other ways to show change over time include line graphs.

This figure communicates a lot of information. On the left vertical axis, you will find the scale indicating the percentage of people who expressed a great deal or quite a lot of confidence in each institution in 2007. To display the magnitude of the change (decline or increase) in confidence, the authors have used four colors. The key for the colors is found on the right, near the top. Black, for example, represents a decline in confidence between 2007 and 2017. Red indicates a modest increase (5% or less), while blue indicates the largest increase in public confidence in an institution. Read the graphic starting on the left and moving to the right, and follow the line connecting the two dots. You will notice that the military enjoys the highest overall levels of public confidence, but small business has experienced the greatest positive change over time.

Like many figures, tables, and photographs, this visual presents you with descriptive data. Descriptive information provides an answer to "what" or "who" questions but does not typically answer "why" or "how" questions. Analysis (determining why or how) is a form of critical thinking. The accompanying text may provide theories or results from other research, and sometimes you will find questions for critical analysis. Other times, as in this case, you are left to ask your own questions based on the data presented. Banks suffered the largest decline in public confidence in the last decade—why? Synthesizing all of the information to create a new explanation or understanding is the most important skill you can develop in college.

Figure 1-1 ▶ Confidence in Institutions Varies

Gallup polling shows gains and losses in public confidence in institutions between 2007 and 2017.

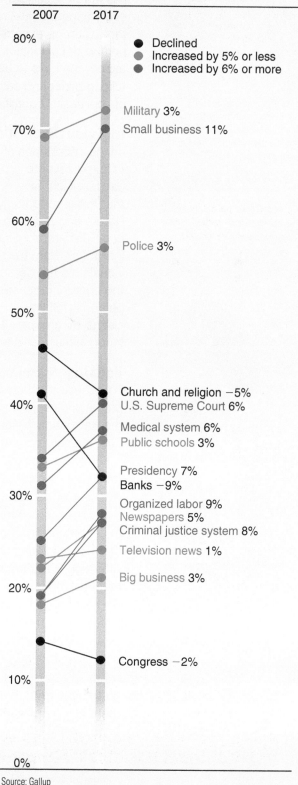

Source: Gallup

Order and the Rule of Law   As noted earlier, individuals and communities create governments to provide stability and order in their lives. Locke justified the creation of governments as a way to protect every individual's property rights and to organize a system of impartial justice. In the United States, laws passed by local, state, and national governments create order and stability in every aspect of life, ranging from traffic to business to a national defense system. Citizens expect these laws to create a society in which individuals can pursue opportunities and live their lives in peace and prosperity. People also expect the laws to be just and to apply to everyone equally. The goal of maintaining **order** and security, however, can sometimes run counter to the values of liberty and equality.

order
A state of peace and security. Maintaining order by protecting members of society from violence and criminal activity is the oldest purpose of government.

Individualism   The Declaration of Independence begins with a statement on the importance of the individual in our political culture: "When in the Course of human events, it becomes necessary for one people to dissolve the political bands which have connected them with one another, and to assume among the Powers of the earth, the separate and equal station to which the Laws of Nature and of Nature's God entitle them . . . ." By a "separate and equal station," Jefferson was distinguishing the belief in the rationality and autonomy of individuals from the traditions of aristocracies and other systems in which individuals did not determine their own destiny. Individualism asserts that one of the primary functions of government is to enable individuals' opportunities for personal fulfillment and development. In political terms, individualism limits claims by groups in favor of the individual. Therefore, it should come as no surprise that a universal right to health care is not a part of the U.S. Constitution.

Equality   Thomas Jefferson wrote in the Declaration of Independence, "We hold these truths to be self-evident, that all men are created equal . . . ." The proper meaning of equality, however, has been disputed by Americans since the Revolution.[14] Much of American history—and world history—is the story of how the value of **equality** has been extended and elaborated.

equality
As a political value, the idea that all people are of equal worth.

Political equality reflects the value that we place on the individual. At our founding, political leaders excluded some people from the broad understanding of a politically autonomous person. African Americans, women, Native Americans, and most men who did not own property were excluded from the equal extension of political rights. Under a social contract theory of government, individuals must freely enter the compact with others on an equal basis. Although Enlightenment philosophers believed in the inherent equality of all persons, they did not define all individuals as full persons. Recall that the Constitution counted slaves as three-fifths of a person. For a period of our history, a married woman was indivisible from her husband and could not act as a full person.[15] Today, of course, we believe all people are entitled to equal political rights as well as the opportunities for personal development provided by equal access to education and employment. In reality, we still have work to do to be sure that opportunities afforded by society and protected by government can be fully realized by everyone in society.

---

14 Gary B. Nash, *The Unknown American Revolution: The Unruly Birth of Democracy and the Struggle to Create America* (New York: Viking, 2005); and Alfred F. Young, ed., *Beyond the American Revolution: Explorations in the History of American Radicalism* (DeKalb, IL: Northern Illinois University Press, 1993).

15 British common law known as "coverture" meant that once married, a woman's identity was "covered" by her husband's, leaving her no independent rights.

Recently, some cultural observers and scholars have begun to question whether political and social equality can coexist with economic inequality. In a book titled *Why Nations Fail*, Massachusetts Institute of Technology (MIT) economist Daron Acemoglu argues that "when economic inequality increases, the people who have become economically more powerful will often attempt to use that power in order to gain even more political power. And once they are able to monopolize political power, they will start using that for changing the rules in their favor."[16] Many people point to the Supreme Court's decision in *Citizens United v. Federal Election Committee*[17] and the growth in super political action committee (PAC) spending in federal elections as evidence of the growing political influence of a few very wealthy individuals and interests. Candidate Bernie Sanders captured the imagination of young people and progressive Democrats in his bid to win the Democratic nomination for president by emphasizing the inordinate power and influence in politics of Wall Street relative to the average person. According to Alan Krueger, former chairman of President Obama's Council of Economic Advisers, the size of the middle class has steadily declined over the last three decades. Whereas in 1970 a little over half of all American households had an income within 50 percent of the median, today the figure is just over 40 percent. Put differently, the share of all income accruing to the top 1 percent increased by 13.5 percent from 1979 to 2007. This is the equivalent of shifting $1.1 trillion of annual income to the top 1 percent of families. More troubling, as income inequality has increased, year to year and generation to generation, economic mobility (the opportunity to improve one's economic standing) has declined. Can the values of political and social equality withstand the significant erosion of economic equality that has accompanied the Great Recession? Civil rights and the value of equality will be discussed further in Chapter 5.

Property

The value of reducing economic inequality is in conflict with the right to **property**. This is because reducing economic inequality typically involves the transfer of property (usually in the form of money) from some people to others. For many people, liberty and property are closely entwined. A capitalist system is based on private property rights. Under **capitalism**, property consists not only of personal possessions but also of wealth-creating assets, such as farms and factories. The investor-owned corporation is in many ways the preeminent capitalist institution. The funds invested by the owners of a corporation are known as *capital*—hence, the very name of the system. Capitalism is also typically characterized by considerable freedom to make binding contracts and by relatively unconstrained markets for goods, services, and investments. Property—especially

OUT OF THE MOUNTAIN OF DESPAIR,
A STONE OF HOPE

Allen Brown/Dbimages/Alamy Stock Photo

Image 1–4
The Martin Luther King, Jr., National Memorial, located on the national mall in Washington, DC, is administered by the National Park Service. The image of Dr. King emerges from a granite "stone of hope" surrounded by a "mountain of despair" reflecting the steadfast resolve of an entire generation to achieve a fair and honest society.

property
Anything that is or may be subject to ownership. As conceived by the political philosopher John Locke, the right to property is a natural right superior to human law (laws made by government).

capitalism
An economic system characterized by the private ownership of wealth-creating assets, free markets, and freedom of contract.

---

16 Daron Acemoglu and James Robinson, *Why Nations Fail: Power, Prosperity, and Poverty* (New York: Crown Publishers, 2012).
17 558 U.S. 08-205 (2010).

wealth-creating property—can be seen as giving its owner political power and the liberty to do whatever he or she wants. At the same time, the ownership of property immediately creates inequality in society. The desire to own property, however, is so widespread among all classes of Americans that egalitarian movements have had a difficult time securing a wide following here.

As with the other values shaping our political culture, even individual property rights are not absolute. **Eminent domain** allows government to take private land for public use in return for just compensation. Weighing the public's interest against the interest of private landowners is a delicate political judgment. Typically, eminent domain is used to acquire land for roads, bridges, and other public works projects. A 2005 Supreme Court ruling, however, allowed the city of New London, Connecticut, to "take" homeowners' property and turn it over to private developers, who built an office park and expensive condominiums.[18] In this atypical case, the majority ruled that economic stimulus and the increase in city tax revenues fulfilled the public use requirement for eminent domain takings. Since the ruling, several state and local governments have passed laws to forbid the kind of takings at issue in this case.

eminent domain
A power set forth in the Fifth Amendment to the U.S. Constitution that allows government to take private property for public use under the condition that just compensation is offered to the landowner.

Why Choose Democracy?

■ **1.4** Compare and contrast types of government systems and identify the source of power in each.

Today, 196 nations exist in the world. Nearly all have some form of government that possesses authority and some degree of legitimacy. Governments vary in their structure and how they govern. The crucial question for every nation is who controls the government. The answer could be a small group, one person—perhaps the monarch or a dictator—or no one.

At one extreme is a society governed by a **totalitarian regime**. In such a political system, a small group of leaders or a single individual—a dictator—makes all political decisions for the society. North Korea is an example of a totalitarian state. Citizens are deprived of the freedom to speak, to dissent, to assemble, and to seek solutions to problems. Individual needs, including food, are subsumed by the interests of the ruler and the regime. Famine, widespread malnutrition, and illness exist as a result of the country's "military first" policy. Running afoul of the regime can often mean imprisonment or death. Kim Jong-il was succeeded by his son, Kim Jong-un, in 2011, continuing an unbroken 63-year reign that began with Kim Jong-il's father, Kim Il-sung. Under Kim Jong-un's rule, North Korea has inflamed relations with South Korea and the United States by developing and testing short-range ballistic missiles and rockets. Totalitarianism is an extreme form of authoritarianism.

totalitarian regime
A form of government that controls all aspects of the political and social life of a nation.

Authoritarianism is also characterized by highly concentrated and centralized power maintained by political repression. Authoritarianism differs from totalitarianism in that only the government is fully controlled by the ruler, leaving social and economic institutions to outside control. The contemporary government of China is often described as authoritarian. China is ruled by a single political party, the Communist Party. Policies are made by Communist Party leaders without input from the general population. The Chinese market

authoritarianism
A type of regime in which only the government is fully controlled by the ruler. Social and economic institutions exist that are not under the government's control.

---

18 *Kelo v. City of New London*, 545 U.S. 469 (2005).

Muzaffar Salman/Reuters

Image 1-5
Demonstrators carry placards and hold a Syrian opposition flag during a protest against Syria's President Bashar al-Assad's regime in Kafranbel in Idlib province, January 18, 2013.

economy is expanding rapidly with little government intrusion or regulations, but signs of political dissent are punished severely. Internet access is monitored and political content restricted.

Many terms for describing the distribution of political power are derived from the ancient Greeks, who were the first Western people to study politics systematically. One form of rule by the few was known as **aristocracy**, literally meaning "rule by the best." In practice, this meant rule by leading members of wealthy families who were, in theory, the best educated and dedicated to the good of the state. The ancient Greeks had another term for rule by the few, **oligarchy**, which means rule by a small group for corrupt and self-serving purposes.

The Greek term for rule by the people was **democracy**, which means that the authority of the government is granted to it from the people as a whole. Within the limits of their culture, some of the Greek city-states operated as democracies. Today, in much of the world, the people will not grant legitimacy to a government unless it is based on democratic principles. Mass protests against the Assad regime in Syria that plunged the country into civil war, as well as continuing unrest in Ukraine, are recent examples.

If totalitarianism is control of all aspects of society by the government, **anarchy** is the complete opposite. It means that there is no government at all. Each individual or family in a society decides for itself how it will behave, and there is no institution with the authority to keep order in any way. As you can imagine, examples of anarchy do not last very long. A state of anarchy may characterize a transition between one form of government (often totalitarian or authoritarian and repressive) and one where people want more power but do not yet have political institutions to structure popular participation. The interim period can be chaotic and violent, as in Somalia and, to a lesser degree in Tunisia, Egypt, Libya, and Yemen following the Arab Spring rebellions. Entire cities have been destroyed in the Syrian uprising and ensuing civil war, leading to a mass exodus of the population as refugees.

aristocracy
Rule by "the best"; in reality, rule by an upper class.

oligarchy
Rule by the few in their own interests.

democracy
A system of government in which political authority is vested in the people. Derived from the Greek words *demos* ("the people") and *kratos* ("authority").

anarchy
The absence of any form of government or political authority.

Direct Democracy as a Model

The system of government in the ancient Greek city-state of Athens is usually considered the purest model of **direct democracy**, because the citizens of that community debated and voted directly on all laws, even those put forward by the ruling council of the city. The most important feature of Athenian democracy was that the **legislature** was composed of all the citizens. Women, foreigners, and slaves, however, were excluded because they were not citizens. This form of government required a high level of participation from every citizen; participation was seen as benefiting the individual and the city-state. The Athenians believed that although a high level of participation might lead to instability in government, citizens, if informed about the issues, could be trusted to make wise decisions. Greek philosophers also believed that debating the issues and participating in making the laws was good for the individual's intellectual and personal development.

Direct democracy has also been practiced in Switzerland and in the United States in New England town meetings. At New England town meetings, which can include all of the voters who live in the town, important decisions—such as levying taxes, hiring city officials, and deciding local ordinances—are made by majority vote. Some states provide a modern adaptation of direct democracy for their citizens; representative democracy is supplemented by the **initiative** or the **referendum**—processes by which the people may vote directly on laws or constitutional amendments. The **recall** process, which is available in many states, allows people to vote to remove an official from state office.

Because of the Internet, Americans have access to more political information than ever before. Voters can go online to examine the record of any candidate. Constituents can contact their congressional representatives and state legislators by sending them email or a text. Individuals can easily find

direct democracy
A system of government in which political decisions are made by the people directly, rather than by their elected representatives; probably attained most easily in small political communities.

legislature
A governmental body primarily responsible for the making of laws.

initiative
A procedure by which voters can propose a law or a constitutional amendment.

referendum
An electoral device whereby legislative or constitutional measures are referred by the legislature to the voters for approval or disapproval.

recall
A procedure allowing the people to vote to dismiss an elected official from state office before his or her term has expired.

Image 1-6
Sen. Marco Rubio (R-FL), an emerging leader within the Republican Party, actively uses social media to promote his ideas and issue positions.

Olivier Douliery/MCT/Newscom

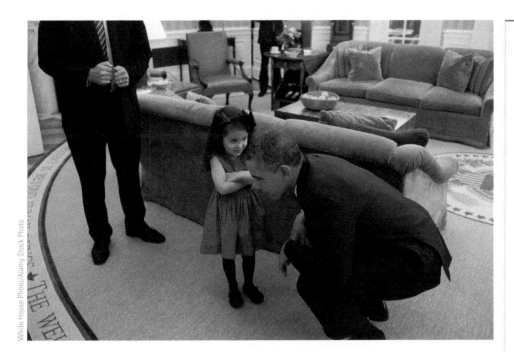

White House Photo/Alamy Stock Photo

Image 1–7
President Barack Obama
was often photographed interacting with children. In this photo, he bends down to listen to the daughter of departing U.S. Secret Service agent in the Oval Office of the White House.

like-minded allies and form political interest groups using social networking sites such as Twitter, Facebook, Google+, and countless others. During the 2008 presidential campaign, the Obama campaign pioneered new uses of the Internet to connect supporters, solicit campaign donations, and maintain nearly constant contact between likely voters and the campaign. By the 2016 presidential contest, a candidacy without a social media relationship with voters would have been unthinkable. Hillary Clinton announced her candidacy in a video and a tweet pointing supporters to her website. Following Republican presidential candidate Donald Trump's campaign announcement, his campaign claimed to have garnered "3.4 million Facebook users in the U.S. who generated 6.4 million interactions regarding the launch of his campaign."[19] Once he was elected president, Donald Trump's prolific use of his personal Twitter account made many Americans uncomfortable.

Social media provides voters with new forms of real-time engagement through breaking campaign news, the debates, and election night returns. President Obama's victory tweet of "Four more years" set a record for retweets. Facebook motivates people to get to the polls; seeing that friends had already voted worked as a form of peer pressure to do likewise. In the last week of the 2012 campaign, Twitter released a political engagement map that allowed users to track tweets about specific candidates or issues around the country. A Republican 2016 campaign manager observed, "Social media is the new coffee shop where neighbors, friends, colleagues and family gather to discuss issues, talk about the candidates and influence others."

There are limits, however, to how much political business people currently want to conduct using technology, largely because of security concerns. Although Colorado offered its citizens the opportunity to vote online in 2000, the experiment was short-lived. The Pentagon canceled a plan for troops overseas to vote online in 2004 due to Internet security concerns. The extent of National

---

19 Andrew O'Reilly, "Candidates, Parties Map Out Social Media Campaigns in Attempt to Reach Latino Voters," Fox Latino News. June 22, 2015.

Security Agency (NSA) surveillance and spying disclosed by Edward Snowden in documents leaked to *The Guardian* and *The Washington Post*, as well as massive personal data breaches reported by retailers, universities, and states, have increased the American people's skepticism about conducting important transactions online. Several states, however, do allow for voter registration online. Three states (Colorado, Oregon, and Washington) mail ballots to all eligible voters for every election.

The Limits of Direct Democracy

Although they were aware of the Athenian model, the framers of the U.S. Constitution had grave concerns about the stability and practicality of direct democracy. During America's colonial period, the idea of government based on the consent of the people gained increasing popularity. Such a government was the main aspiration of the American Revolution, the French Revolution in 1789, and many subsequent revolutions. At the time of the American Revolution, however, the masses were still considered to be too uneducated to govern themselves, too prone to the influence of demagogues (political leaders who manipulate popular prejudices), and too likely to subordinate minority rights to the tyranny of the majority.

James Madison defended the new scheme of government set forth in the U.S. Constitution, while warning of the problems inherent in a "pure democracy":

A common passion or interest will, in almost every case, be felt by a majority of the whole. . . . and there is nothing to check the inducements to sacrifice the weaker party or an obnoxious individual. Hence it is that such democracies have ever been spectacles of turbulence and contention, and have ever been found incompatible with personal security or the rights of property; and have in general been as short in their lives as they have been violent in their deaths.[20]

Like other politicians of his time, Madison feared that direct democracy would deteriorate into mob rule. What would keep the majority of the people, if given direct decision-making power, from abusing the rights of minority groups?

A Democratic Republic

The framers of the U.S. Constitution chose to craft a **republic**. To Americans of the 1700s, the idea of a republic also meant a government based on common beliefs and virtues that would be fostered within small communities. The rulers were to be laypersons—good citizens who would take turns representing their fellow citizens.

The U.S. Constitution created a form of republican government that we now call a **democratic republic**. The people hold the ultimate power over the government through the election process, but policy decisions are made by elected officials. For the founders, even this distance between the people and the government was not sufficient. The Constitution made sure that the Senate and the president would be selected by political elites rather than by the people, although later changes to the Constitution allowed the voters to elect members of the Senate directly.

Despite these limits, the new American system was unique in the amount of power it granted to ordinary citizens. Over the course of the following two

did you know?

The number of Latino voters grew to a record 12.7 million in 2016; however, 14 million Latinos were eligible to vote and did not.

republic
A form of government in which sovereignty rests with the people, as opposed to a king or monarch.

democratic republic
A republic in which representatives elected by the people make and enforce laws and policies.

---

20 James Madison, in Alexander Hamilton, James Madison, and John Jay, *The Federalist Papers, No. 10* (New York: Mentor Books, 1964), p. 81. See Appendix C of this textbook.

Election 2016

A Divided Nation

Going into the general election, Americans were feeling pessimistic about the future. The American Values Survey found that 74 percent of people believed the country was off on the wrong track. White evangelical Protestants perceived the negative change most acutely, with more than 74 percent believing that America is worse off today than in the 1950s. According to exit polls they had a strong showing on Election Day, with 81 percent voting for Donald Trump.

White voters preferred Donald Trump to Hillary Clinton by a 21-point margin—a margin almost identical to Mitt Romney's 20-point advantage with white voters in 2012. However, Trump fared better with African Americans and Hispanics than Romney did, meaning that Hillary Clinton did not attract as strong a following from these core Democratic constituencies. The gender gap, predicted to be historically large, was 12 points. Women did not overwhelmingly support Clinton's bid to become the first woman president—54 percent of women voted for Clinton, but 42 percent voted for Trump. The widest gap in the 2016 election was between those with and those without a college degree. Trump's margin among whites without a college degree was the largest for any candidate in exit polls since 1980 (a 39-point advantage with this group).

For Critical Analysis

1. What accounts for such differences in perception among voters about America's future? How does a college education shape those perceptions?

2. In exit polls, voters were asked to identify the most important quality in a candidate—83 percent of Republicans wanted a candidate who could bring about change. In 2008, candidate Barack campaigned on a promise to bring change. Where does our national desire for change come from?

centuries, democratic values became increasingly popular, at first in the West and then throughout the rest of the world. The spread of democratic principles gave rise to another name for our system of government—**representative democracy**. The term *representative democracy* has almost the same meaning as *democratic republic*, with one exception. In a republic, not only are the people sovereign, but there is no king. What if a nation develops into a democracy but preserves the monarchy as a largely ceremonial institution? This is exactly what happened in Britain. Not surprisingly, the British found the term *democratic republic* to be unacceptable, and they described their system as a representative democracy instead.

representative democracy
A form of government in which representatives elected by the people make and enforce laws and policies; may retain the monarchy in a ceremonial role.

Principles of Democratic Government All representative democracies rest on the rule of the people as expressed through the election of government officials. In the 1790s in the United States, only free white males were able to vote, and in some states they had to be property owners as well. Women did not receive the right to vote in national elections in the United States until 1920, and the right to vote was not secured in practice in all states by African Americans until the 1960s. Today, **universal suffrage** is the rule.

Because everyone's vote counts equally, the only way to make fair decisions is by some form of **majority** will. But to ensure that **majority rule** does not become oppressive, modern democracies also provide guarantees of minority rights. If political minorities were not protected, the majority might violate the fundamental rights of members of certain groups, especially groups that are unpopular or that differ from the majority population, such as religious or ethnic minorities.

universal suffrage
The right of all adults to vote for their representatives.

majority
More than 50 percent.

majority rule
A basic principle of democracy asserting that the greatest number of citizens in any political unit should select officials and determine policies.

To guarantee the continued existence of a representative democracy, there must be free, competitive elections. Thus, the opposition always has the opportunity to win elective office. For such elections to be totally open, freedom of the press and speech must be preserved so that opposition candidates may present their criticisms of the government.

Another key feature of Western representative democracy is the principle of **limited government**. Not only is the government dependent on popular sovereignty, but the powers of the government are also clearly limited, either through a written document or through widely shared beliefs. The U.S. Constitution sets down the fundamental structure of the government and the limits to its activities. Such limits are intended to prevent political decisions based on the ambitions of individuals in government rather than on constitutional principles. Wisely, the founders created constitutional limits on government that actually rely on human nature and ambition. Consider the counsel of Madison in *Federalist Papers* #51:

> *Ambition must be made to counteract ambition. The interest of the man must be connected with the constitutional rights of the place. It may be a reflection on human nature that such devices should be necessary to control the abuses of government. But what is government itself but the greatest of all reflections on human nature? If men were angels, no government would be necessary. If angels were to govern men, neither external nor internal controls on government would be necessary.*[21]

Because neither is the case, constitutional democracy in the United States is based on an intricate set of relationships—federalism, separation of powers, and checks and balances. Each will be discussed in more detail in later chapters.

Who Really Rules in America?

Americans feel free to organize, to call and email their representatives, and to vote candidates in and out of office. We always describe our political system as a democracy or democratic republic. However, do the people of the United States actually hold power today? Political scientists have developed several theories about American democracy, including *majoritarian* theory, *elite* theory, and theories of *pluralism*. Advocates of these theories use them to describe American democracy either as it actually is or as they believe it should be.

Majoritarianism

Many people think that in a democracy, the government ought to do what the majority of the people want. This simple proposition is the heart of majoritarian theory. As a theory of what democracy should be like, **majoritarianism** is popular in concept among ordinary citizens. Majorities, however, can sometimes mobilize around issues with outcomes harmful to minorities. Even if much of the decision making in American government is done on the basis of majorities, it is rarely unchecked. For example, in 2008 a majority of voters (52 percent) in California approved Proposition 8, amending the state constitution to ban same-sex marriage. This action prompted a flurry of actions in state and federal appellate courts. In 2012, a federal appeals court struck down California's ban. The U.S. Supreme Court declined to review the decision in 2013, effectively ending Proposition 8. In 2015, the Supreme Court settled the question for all states by ruling that the fundamental right to marry is guaranteed to same-sex couples by the Due Process Clause and the Equal Protection Clause of the Fourteenth Amendment to the Constitution.

limited government
The principle that the powers of government should be limited, usually by institutional checks.

majoritarianism
A political theory holding that in a democracy, the government ought to do what the majority of the people want.

---

21 James Madison, in Alexander Hamilton, James Madison, and John Jay, *The Federalist Papers, No. 51* (New York: Mentor Books, 1968). See Appendix C.

Many scholars, however, consider majoritarianism to be a surprisingly poor description of how U.S. democracy actually works. In particular, they point to the low level of turnout for elections. Polling data have shown that many Americans are neither particularly interested in politics nor well informed. Few are able to name the persons running for Congress in their districts, and even fewer can discuss the candidates' positions. Despite the court battles and ongoing political rancor over the Affordable Care Act as the enrollment deadline approached in 2014, 42 percent of Americans reported in a Kaiser Health tracking poll that they were unaware of the law.[22]

Elitism

If ordinary citizens do not indicate policy preferences with their votes, then who does? One answer suggests that elites really govern the United States. Rather than opting out of participation, ordinary Americans are excluded. **Elite theory** is usually used simply to describe the American system. Few people today believe it is a good idea for the country to be run by a privileged minority. In the past, however, many people believed that it was appropriate for the country to be run by an elite. Consider the words of Alexander Hamilton, one of the framers of the Constitution:

> *All communities divide themselves into the few and the many. The first are the rich and the wellborn, the other the mass of the people. . . . The people are turbulent and changing; they seldom judge or determine right. Give therefore to the first class a distinct, permanent share in the government. They will check the unsteadiness of the second, and as they cannot receive any advantage by a change, they therefore will ever maintain good government.*[23]

Some versions of elite theory posit a small, cohesive, elite class that makes almost all of the important decisions for the nation, whereas others suggest that voters choose among competing elites.[24] New members are recruited through the educational system so that the brightest children of the masses allegedly have the opportunity to join the elite stratum. One view suggests that the members of the elite are primarily interested in controlling the political system to protect their own wealth and the capitalist system that produces it.[25] Studies of elite opinion, however, have also suggested that elites are more tolerant of diversity, more willing to defend individual liberties, and more supportive of democratic values than are members of the mass public.

elite theory
A perspective holding that society is ruled by a small number of people who exercise power to further their self-interest.

Pluralism

A different school of thought holds that our form of democracy is based on group interests. As early as 1831, French commentator Alexis de Tocqueville noted the American penchant for joining groups: "As soon as the inhabitants of the United States have taken up an opinion or a feeling which they wish to promote in the world, they look out for mutual assistance; and as soon as they have found one another out, they combine. From that moment they are no longer isolated men, but a power seen from afar. . . ."[26]

---

22 Kaiser Health Tracking Poll: April 2013. http://kff.org/health-reform/poll-finding/kaiser-health-tracking-poll-april-2013/
23 Alexander Hamilton, "Speech in the Constitutional Convention on a Plan of Government," in *Writings*, edited by Joanne B. Freeman (New York: Library of America, 2001).
24 Michael Parenti, *Democracy for the Few*, 7th ed. (Belmont, CA: Wadsworth Publishing, 2002).
25 G. William Domhoff, *Who Rules America?* 4th ed. (New York: McGraw-Hill Higher Education, 2002).
26 Alexis de Tocqueville, *Democracy in America*, Volume II, Section 2, Chapter V, "Of the uses which the Americans make of Public Associations" (available in many editions, and as full text in several web locations).

When Passions Mobilize

"We the People" has profound meaning in the twenty-first century. A quick Internet search reveals literally millions of websites with "citizens against" and just as many more with "citizens for" in their titles.

People organize into groups in order to influence the system and effect changes in public policy. Many groups mobilize to keep watch on government power. Some address specific policy problems—the environment, handgun violence, or urban gas well drilling—whereas others have bigger issues, such as reducing taxes or the national debt. Interest groups have mobilized either against the Obama administration's approach to healthcare reform and increased government spending or in support of the president's initiatives, for example. Although such groups may have ties to a political party or to an existing political organization, many people who join do so out of real passion and may have little political experience. Sometimes, the actions of one person result in the mobilization of hundreds or more fellow citizens.

In October 2013, the U.S. federal government closed for 15 days when Congress failed to pass legislation authorizing the government to continue spending money. During the shutdown, approximately 800,000 federal employees were indefinitely furloughed and another 1.3 million who were deemed "essential" were required to report to work without knowing if they would be paid for their time. The shutdown meant that national parks were closed, research funded by the federal government was suspended, the Internal Revenue Service (IRS) warned of delays in processing tax returns and refunds, and services in the District of Columbia were curtailed. One man, watching the news of the shutdown from his home in South Carolina, grew concerned when a reporter observed how vulnerable the national monuments would be to vandals in their unguarded state. Chris Cox threw his bicycle, lawnmower, and a rake into his truck and drove to Washington, DC. According to news accounts, he patrolled the memorials for several days by bicycle to keep watch over them, but when he saw trashcans on the national mall overflowing, he changed his focus. "I realized that I could serve my country better as a custodian," he said. Cox spent ten hours a day as an unofficial, unpaid groundskeeper. Commuters and tourists tweeted photos of him mowing the grass around the Lincoln Memorial carrying a South Carolina flag, earning him the nickname "Lawnmower Man." Cox called his crusade the "Memorial Militia." What motivates a person to drive more than 500 miles to keep national monuments in good order? "I'm not here to point fingers," he said. "I just want to try to get Americans to rally behind these parks. Forget about the party you're in and who you voted for and come together as Americans and make a difference."

Chris Cox wasn't done making a difference once the government reopened. To ensure that monuments, memorials, and all national parks remain open in the event of another government closure, he is now lobbying full-time for The

Image 1-8 Chris Cox rakes leaves near the Lincoln Memorial in Washington, DC, Wednesday, October 9, 2013, while the federal government was closed.

Monuments Protections Act (H.R. 1836) co-sponsored by California Republican Darrel Issa and DC Delegate Eleanor Holmes Norton in the 114th Congress (2015–2016). If adopted as law, state and local governments could pay for the continued operation of memorials, national parks, and wildlife refuges and be reimbursed by the federal government once appropriations were restored. Cox still creates chainsaw art to pay his bills, but his full-time occupation is as an unpaid Capitol Hill lobbyist for the bill. He explains it this way, "So much notoriety came along with the Lawnmower Man stories. I felt that I was responsible for doing something better with it. To make a change."

Source: Susan Bird, "Shutdown's Mystery 'Lawnmower Man' Will Use His Reward to Do More Good Deeds," November 18, 2013. www.care2.com
Rachel Sadon, "Two Years Later, the Lawnmower Man Is Still Fighting to Keep Memorials Open in a Shutdown," August 3, 2015. http://dcist.com/2015/08/lawnmower_guy_story.php

For Critical Analysis

1. What are the issues about which you care most deeply? Would you be willing to drop everything you are doing to take up that cause? How best can you get others to follow your lead?

2. One person, passionate about a cause, can attract attention, but interest groups stand a better chance of mobilizing the thousands of supporters. Veterans were especially angry that the war memorials were closed. How could Chris Cox increase the pressure on Congress to pass The Monuments Protections Act? Besides veterans, what other groups might support this bill?

Pluralist theory proposes that even if the average citizen cannot keep up with political issues or cast a deciding vote in any election, the individual's interests will be protected by groups that represent her or him. Theorists who subscribe to **pluralism** see politics as a struggle among groups to gain benefits for their members.

Many political scientists believe that pluralism works very well as a descriptive theory. As a way to defend the practice of democracy in the United States, however, pluralism has problems. Poor citizens are rarely represented by interest groups. At the same time, rich citizens are often overrepresented, in part because they understand their own interests. As political scientist E. E. Schattschneider observed, "The flaw in the pluralist heaven is that the heavenly chorus sings with a strong upper-class accent."[27] There are also serious doubts as to whether group decision making always reflects the best interests of the nation.

Critics see a danger that groups may become so powerful that all policies become compromises crafted to satisfy the interests of the largest groups. The interests of the public as a whole, then, would not be considered. Critics of pluralism have suggested that a democratic system can be virtually paralyzed by the struggle among interest groups. We will discuss interest groups at greater length in Chapter 7.

Political Ideologies

■ **1.5** Define political ideology and locate socialism, liberalism, conservatism, and libertarianism along the ideological spectrum.

A political **ideology** is a closely linked set of beliefs about politics. Political ideologies offer their adherents well-organized theories that propose goals for the society and the means by which those goals can be achieved. At the core of every political ideology is a set of guiding values. The two ideologies most commonly referred to in discussions of American politics are *liberalism* and *conservatism*. In the scheme of ideologies embraced across the globe, these two, especially as practiced in the United States, are in the middle of the ideological spectrum, as noted in Table 1-1.

27 E. E. Schattschneider, *The Semi-Sovereign People* (Hinsdale, IL: The Dryden Press, 1975 [originally published in 1960]).

pluralism
A theory that views politics as a conflict among interest groups. Political decision making is characterized by bargaining and compromise.

did you know?
The phrase "In God We Trust" was made the national motto on July 30, 1956, but had appeared on U.S. coins as early as 1864.

ideology
A comprehensive set of beliefs about the nature of people and about the role of an institution or government.

Table 1-1 ▶	The Traditional Political Spectrum			
	SOCIALISM	**LIBERALISM**	**CONSERVATISM**	**LIBERTARIANISM**
How much power should the government have over the economy?	Active government control of major economic sectors	Positive government action in the economy	Positive government action to support capitalism	Almost no regulation of the economy
What should the government promote?	Economic equality, community	Economic security, equal opportunity, social liberty	Economic liberty, morality, social order	Total economic and social liberty

The Traditional Political Spectrum

A traditional method of comparing political ideologies is to array them on a continuum from left to right, based primarily on how much power the government should exercise to promote economic equality, as well as the ultimate goals of government activity. Table 1-1 shows how ideologies can be arrayed in a traditional political spectrum. In addition to liberalism and conservatism, the table includes the ideologies of socialism and libertarianism.

Socialism falls on the left side of the spectrum. Socialists play a minor role in the American political arena, although socialist parties and movements are very important in other countries around the world. In the past, socialists typically advocated replacing investor ownership of major businesses with either government ownership or ownership by employee cooperatives. Socialists believed that such steps would break the power of the very rich and lead to an egalitarian society. In more recent times, socialists in Western Europe have advocated more limited programs that redistribute income.

On the right side of the spectrum is **libertarianism**, a philosophy of skepticism toward most government activities. Libertarians strongly support property rights and typically oppose regulation of the economy and redistribution of income. Libertarians support *laissez-faire* capitalism. (*Laissez-faire* is French for "let it be.") Libertarians also tend to oppose government attempts to regulate personal behavior and promote moral values.

In the Middle: Liberalism and Conservatism

The set of beliefs called **liberalism** includes advocacy of government action to improve the welfare of individuals, support for civil rights, and tolerance for social change. American liberals believe that government should take positive action to reduce poverty, to redistribute income from wealthier classes to poorer ones, and to regulate the economy. Those who espouse liberalism may also be more supportive of the rights of historically underrepresented groups including women, the lesbian, gay, bisexual, transgender (LGBT) community, and racial minorities.

The set of beliefs called **conservatism** includes a limited role for the government in helping individuals. Conservatives believe that the private sector can outperform the government in almost any activity. Believing that the individual is primarily responsible for his or her own well-being, conservatives typically oppose government programs to redistribute income. Conservatism may also include support for what conservatives refer to as traditional values regarding individual behavior and the importance of the family. Liberals are often seen as an influential force within the Democratic Party, and conservatives are often regarded as the most influential force in the Republican Party.

The Difficulty of Defining Liberalism and Conservatism

Although political candidates and commentators are quick to label candidates and voters as "liberals" and "conservatives," the meanings of these words have evolved over time. Moreover, each term may represent a different set of ideas to the person or group that uses it.

Liberalism   The word liberal has an odd history. It comes from the same root as *liberty*, and originally it simply meant "free." In that broad sense, the United States as a whole is a liberal country, and all popular American ideologies are variants of liberalism. In a more restricted definition, a liberal was a person who believed in limited government and who opposed religion in politics. A hundred

---

socialism
A political ideology based on strong support for economic and social equality. Socialists traditionally envisioned a society in which major businesses were taken over by the government or by employee cooperatives.

libertarianism
A political ideology based on skepticism or opposition toward almost all government activities.

liberalism
A set of beliefs that includes the advocacy of positive government action to improve the welfare of individuals, support for civil rights, and tolerance for political and social change.

conservatism
A set of beliefs that includes a limited role for the national government in helping individuals, support for traditional values and lifestyles, and a cautious response to change.

years ago, liberalism referred to a philosophy that in some ways resembled modern-day libertarianism. For that reason, many libertarians today refer to themselves as *classical* liberals.

How did the meaning of the word liberal change? In the 1800s, the Democratic Party was seen as the more liberal of the two parties. The Democrats of that time stood for limited government and opposition to moralism in politics. Democrats opposed Republican projects such as building roads, freeing the slaves, and prohibiting the sale of alcoholic beverages. Beginning with Democratic President Woodrow Wilson (served 1913–1921), however, the party's economic policies began to change. President Franklin Delano Roosevelt won a landslide election in 1932 by pledging to take steps to end the Great Depression. Roosevelt and the Democratic Congress quickly passed several measures that increased federal government intervention in the economy and improved conditions for Americans. By the end of Roosevelt's presidency in 1945, the Democratic Party had established itself as standing for positive government action to help the economy. Although Roosevelt stood for new policies, he kept the old language— as Democrats had long done, he called himself a liberal. We will discuss the history of the two parties in greater detail in Chapter 8.

Outside of the United States and Canada, the meaning of the word liberal never changed. For this reason, you might hear a left-of-center European denounce U.S. President Ronald Reagan (served 1981–1989) or British Prime Minister Margaret Thatcher (served 1979–1990) for their "liberalism," meaning that these two leaders were enthusiastic advocates of *laissez-faire* capitalism and limited government.

Conservatism The term *conservatism* suffers from similar identity problems. In the United States and Western Europe, conservatives tended to believe in maintaining traditions and opposing change. Conservatives were more likely to support the continuation of the monarchy, for example. At the end of World War II, Senator Robert A. Taft of Ohio was known as "Mr. Conservative," and he steadfastly opposed the Democratic Party's platform of an active government. He was not, however, a spokesperson for conservative or traditional personal values.

Today, conservatism is often considered to have two quite different dimensions. Some self-identified conservatives are "economic conservatives" who believe in less government, support for capitalism and private property, and allowing individuals to pursue their own route to achievement with little government interference. Recent presidential campaigns have seen great efforts to motivate those individuals who might be called "social conservatives" to support Republican candidates. Social conservatives are much less interested in economic issues than in supporting particular social values, including opposition to abortion, support for the death penalty or the right to own firearms, and opposition to gay marriage. Given these two different dimensions of conservatism, it is not surprising that conservatives are not always united in their political preferences. The Tea Party, for example, emerged out of the divisions among conservatives and the Republican Party. Thus, its followers are neither entirely conservative nor exclusively Republican.

Libertarianism Although libertarians make up a much smaller proportion of the population in the United States than do conservatives or liberals, this ideology shares the more extreme positions of both groups. If the only question is how much power the government should have over the economy, then libertarians can be considered conservatives. However, libertarians advocate the most complete possible freedom in social matters. They oppose government action to promote conservative moral values, although such action is often favored by other groups on the political right. Libertarians' strong support for civil liberties seems to align them more closely with modern liberals than with conservatives. Ron Paul, a congressman from Texas and a candidate for the Republican presidential nomination in 2008 and 2012, is known for his libertarian positions. Although Paul has never won the Republican nomination, he remains popular among college students, most likely because of his positions in favor of personal freedoms, liberalizing drug laws, and bringing home troops serving abroad. His son, Rand Paul, a Republican senator from Kentucky and a 2016 candidate for the Republican presidential nomination, also espouses libertarian positions and often aligns with the Tea Party.

The Challenge of Change

■ **1.6** Apply understanding of the purpose of government and the U.S. political culture to evaluate government's ability to meet new challenges over time.

The United States faces enormous internal and external challenges. In the next 50 years, not only will the face of America change as its citizens age, become more diverse, and generate new needs for laws and policies, but the country will also have to contend with a decline in economic dominance in the world. Other nations, including China and India, have much larger populations than the United States and are assuming new roles in the world. The United States and its citizens will need to meet the challenges of a global economy and mitigate the impact of global environmental change. Technology has transformed the way we live, learn, and work. All of these challenges—demographic change, globalization, ubiquitous technology, and environmental change—will affect how the American political system functions in the future.

Demographic Change in a Democratic Republic

The population of the United States is changing in fundamental ways that will affect the political and social system of the nation. Long a nation of growth, the United States has become a middle-aged nation with a low birth rate and an increasing number of older citizens who want the services from government they were promised. Social Security and Medicare are among the few government entitlements remaining, and any suggestion that either program be changed elicits immediate political action by older citizens and their interest groups. In communities where there is a large elderly population whose children are grown and gone, increasing taxes in support of public education is a difficult proposition. Both the aging of the population and its changing ethnic composition will have significant political consequences.

Like other economically advanced countries, the United States has in recent decades experienced falling birth rate and an increase in the number of older citizens. As you can see in Figure 1-2, the proportion of the population most likely to be in the labor force remains relatively stable even as the percentages of the elderly and young increase or decrease slightly. According to the projections, by 2050 just over half of the population (54 percent) will

Figure 1-2 ▶ The Aging of America

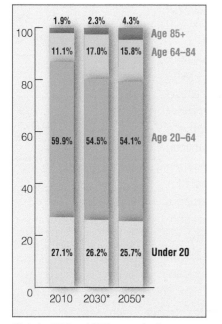

*Data for 2030 and 2050 are projections.
Source: U.S. Census Bureau (Projections and Distribution of the Total Population by Age for the United States: 2010–2050).

fall within prime earning years, whereas a quarter of the population (those under 20) will be considered dependents, and roughly 20 percent will be elderly. The "aging of America" is a weaker phenomenon than in many other wealthy countries, however. Today, the median age of the population is 37.2 in the United States and 40.0 in Europe. By 2050, the median age in the United States is expected to decline slightly to 36.2. In Europe, it is expected to reach 52.7. As is already the case in many European nations, older citizens demand that their need for pensions and health care dominate the political agenda. Young people in the United States, at times apathetic about politics, could use their vote to reorient the policy agenda. In the 2016 presidential contest, people younger than 30 made up a larger share of the electorate than those 65 and older.

Ethnic Change

As a result of differences in fertility rates and immigration, the ethnic character of the United States is also changing. Non-Hispanic white Americans have a fertility rate of just over 1.8 per two people; African Americans have a fertility rate of 2.1; and Hispanic Americans have a current fertility rate of almost 3.0. Figure 1-3 shows the projected changes in the U.S. ethnic distribution in future years.

A large share of all new immigrants is Hispanic. A **Hispanic** or **Latino** is someone who can claim a heritage from a Spanish-speaking country (other than Spain). Today, most individuals who share this heritage prefer to refer to themselves as Latino rather than Hispanic; however, government agencies such as the Census Bureau use the terms *Hispanic* and *non-Hispanic white* for their tables. In this book, *Hispanic* is used when referring to government statistics, and *Latino* is used in other contexts.

Latinos may come from any of about 20 primarily Spanish-speaking countries, and, as a result, they are a highly diverse population. The three largest Hispanic groups are Mexican Americans at 64.1 percent of all Latinos, Puerto Ricans (all of whom are U.S. citizens) at 9.5 percent of the total, and Cuban Americans at 3.7 percent. The diversity among Hispanic Americans results in differing political behavior; however, the majority of Latino Americans vote Democratic.

Hispanic
Someone who can claim a heritage from a Spanish-speaking country other than Spain. This is the term most often used by government agencies to describe this group. Citizens of Spanish-speaking countries do not use this term to describe themselves.

Latino
Preferred term for referring to individuals who claim a heritage from a Spanish-speaking country other than Spain.

Figure 1-3 ▸ Distribution of U.S. Population by Race and Hispanic Origin, 1980–2075

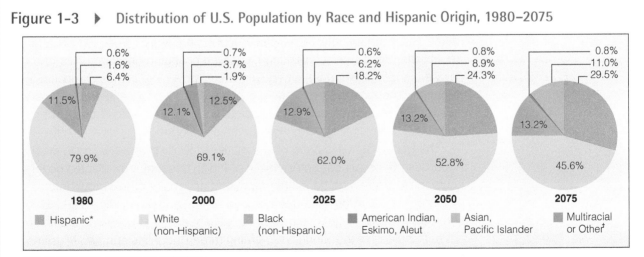

Data for 2025, 2050, and 2075 are projections.
*Persons of Hispanic origin can be of any race.
†The "multiracial or other" category in 2000 was not an official census category, but represents all non-Hispanics who chose either "some other race" or two or more races in the 2000 census.
Source: U.S. Bureau of the Census

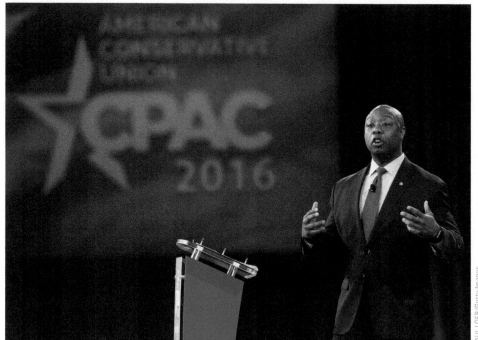

Image 1–9

U.S. Senator Tim Scott (R-SC) is the first African American elected to serve in both the U.S. House of Representatives and the U.S. Senate. Senator Scott, a fiscal and social conservative, speaks at the annual Conservative Political Action Conference (CPAC) in 2016.

SAUL LOEB/Getty Images

Barack Obama captured the majority of the Latino vote in 2008 and in 2012. Between the two presidential elections, the Latino population grew and became more Democratic, particularly in states like Colorado, New Mexico, and Nevada. Nationally, the Latino share of the electorate rose to 10 percent of the whole, and President Obama attracted 71 percent of their support compared with 27 percent for Governor Romney. Similarly, Obama attracted a higher percentage of votes from African Americans (93 percent) and Asian Americans (73 percent) than did the Republican candidate. As the nation's population grows more diverse, political parties and candidates will need to attend carefully to the new demographic reality in America. Republicans, in particular, have signaled their intent to compete for Latino voters, but positions on immigration reform emphasizing border security and enforcement, as well as a significant split within the party over creating a path to citizenship for illegal immigrants, currently makes a shift in support unlikely. Marco Rubio, the Cuban American Republican Senator from Florida and 2016 Republican presidential contender, has called changing demographics one of his party's biggest challenges. When Donald Trump kicked off his campaign for the Republican nomination, he sparked outrage among Mexicans and Latinos when he accused Mexico of sending its rapists and criminals across the border to the United States and calling for a wall to be built along the Mexico–U.S. border.

The United States is becoming a more ethnically diverse nation in every way. Republican Bobby Jindal, an American of Indian descent, was elected governor of Louisiana (even though he did not represent any major ethnic group in that state) by running on a platform of effective government and promising an end to corruption. As a result of the 2012 elections, Tulsi Gabbard (D-HI) became the first member of Congress of the Hindu faith, joining three Buddhists and two Muslims. The election of Jindal—and, even more significantly, of Barack Obama as president of the United States—may signal the end of white dominance in political leadership at state and national levels. Indeed the early Republican field of candidates seeking the 2016 nomination for president was the most diverse in history for either political party. A multiethnic, multiracial society, however, poses challenges to government to balance the needs of each group while keeping in mind the overall interests of the country. If the United States could achieve a higher level of economic equality for all Americans, group differences could be minimized.

Globalization

Globalization of the world economy has advanced rapidly. The power of the American economy and its expansion into other parts of the world spurred similar actions by European, South American, and Asian nations. Huge international corporations produce and market products throughout the world. American soft drinks are produced and sold in China, and Americans buy clothing manufactured in China or the former states of the Soviet Union. Jobs are outsourced from the United States to India, the Philippines, or Vietnam, and other nations outsource jobs to the United States. Companies such as General Electric (GE) employ design teams that collaborate in the design and production of jet engines, with employees working around the clock, across all time zones.

Globalization brings a multitude of challenges to the United States and all other nations, beginning with the fact that no single government can regulate global corporations. Globalization changes employment patterns, reducing jobs in one nation and increasing employment in another. Products produced in low-wage nations are cheaper to buy in the United States, but the result is little control over quality and consumer safety. If you have an Apple iPhone or iPad, chances are that most of its components were manufactured and assembled overseas—most likely in China. When President Obama asked the late Steve Jobs what it would take to make iPhones in the United States, Jobs simply replied "those jobs aren't coming back."[28] Apple is not alone; nearly all U.S. electronics manufacturers rely on factories overseas.

Another challenge of globalization worthy of careful consideration is global conflict. At one time, stability in the world was accomplished by maintaining relative parity between the world superpowers: the United States and the Soviet Union. With the breakup of the Soviet Union and the populist challenges to authoritarian rule around the globe, the United States often finds itself in a quandary over how to confront aggression. When military intervention is not a viable option and diplomatic overtures have proven ineffective, what remains for the United States to do? Take, for example, the case of chemical weapons in Syria. As the Syrian crisis escalated and the world grew concerned over the possibility of chemical weapons being used by Syrian president Bashar al-Assad or perhaps falling into the wrong hands, White House correspondent Chuck Todd asked the president if he envisioned using the U.S. military in this situation. The president responded, "I have, at this point, not ordered military engagement in the situation. But the point that you made about chemical and biological weapons is critical. . . . We have been very clear to the Assad regime, but also to other players on the ground, that a red line for us is we start seeing a whole bunch of chemical weapons moving around or being utilized. That would change my calculus. That would change my equation."[29] The "red line" became a call to action for those who wanted the United States to militarily remove Assad. President Obama pulled back from plans to conduct an airstrike in retaliation for a chemical-weapons attack on civilians. Instead, he accepted a Russian offer to work jointly to remove the chemical weapons. The failure to act called into question the international credibility of the

---

28 Charles Duhigg and Keith Bradsher, "How the US Lost Out on iPhone Work," *New York Times*, January 21, 2012.
29 Presidential Remarks, August 20, 2012. www.whitehouse.gov/the-press-office/2012/08/20/remarks-president-white-house-press-corps

United States and left the president weakened in other instances of aggression, such as Vladimir Putin's incursion into the Crimean peninsula of Ukraine in March 2014. Global conflict and instability pose a grave challenge to U.S. foreign policy and our nation's ability to provide leadership in an uncertain world.

The Technology Revolution

Rapidly changing technology has transformed the way we communicate with one another, where and how we work, and even where and how we learn. You may be reading this book electronically, and you may even be completing this course online. In *The World Is Flat*, author Thomas Friedman claims that globalization and technology are intertwined, each fueling the other. New technologies erase

The World Wide Web at 25 Years Old Is Ubiquitous: How Do We Know?

In 1989, the World Wide Web was introduced in a concept paper written by Sir Tim Berners-Lee proposing an "informational management" system. In 1990, Berners-Lee released to the world the code for his system—for free. Today, 87 percent of adults report using the Internet.*

Describing the Web as "ubiquitous" indicates the breadth and depth of its influence and presence in our lives. *Ubiquitous* means "omnipresent, pervasive, permeating, and everywhere."

The Pew Research Center marked the twenty-fifth birthday of the Web by undertaking a series of studies about its role in American life and in partnership with Elon University; it will continue to explore emerging trends in digital technology by tapping experts in privacy, cybersecurity, and net neutrality.** Of course, you can access all of the surveys, interviews, and research online.

Figure 1-4 and Table 1-2 present data in a graphic format to allow you to assess the dynamic presence of the Web in American life. Figure 1-4 describes how quickly a particular technology was adopted by one-quarter of the population.*** It took just

Figure 1-4 ▶ Technology Adoption

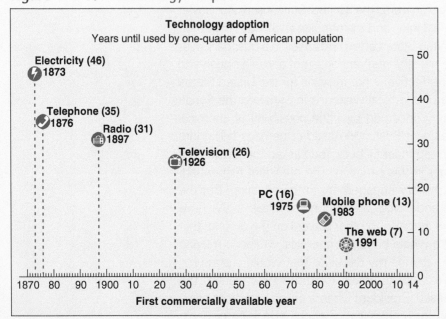

Source: Singularity.com

* Pew Research Center, February 2014, "The Web at 25." Access at: www.pewinternet.org/2014/02/27/the-web-at-25-in-the-u-s/
** Elon University, "Imagining the Internet: A History and Forecast." Access at: http://www.elon.edu/e-web/imagining/
*** "Daily Chart," *The Economist*, March 12, 2014.

Table 1-2 ▶ Technology Dependency

How hard would it be to give up these technologies?

Percent of users of each technology who report how difficult it would be to give up ...

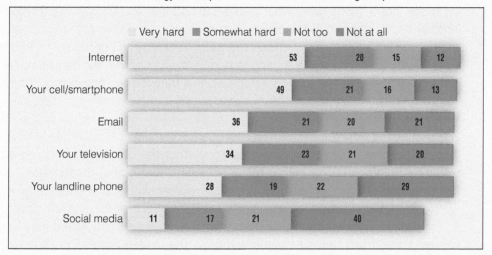

Source: Pew Research Center Internet Project Survey, January 9–12, 2014. N = 1,006 adults; N = 857 Internet users; N = 717 landline owners; N = 928 cell owners.

7 years for the Web to be used by 25 percent of the American population, compared with 46 years for electricity and 26 years for the telephone. What factors might explain the different rates of adoption? Table 1-2 gives you a sense of how difficult it would be for people to give up different types of technology that permeate our lives.**** Interestingly, among Internet users, social media would be the easiest technology to give up. Would you say that is true for you? How well do your opinions match this national sample?

Finally, Figure 1-5 is a reflection of earlier themes in this chapter. U.S. political culture has a strong emphasis on the individual. Although a clear majority of people say that the Internet has been a good thing, 90 percent say it has been good for them as an individual, and 72 percent say the same is true for society. What might account for that difference? In what ways do individuals benefit from Internet-based technology that might differ from society as a whole?

Figure 1-5 ▶ Has the Internet Been a Good Thing or a Bad Thing?

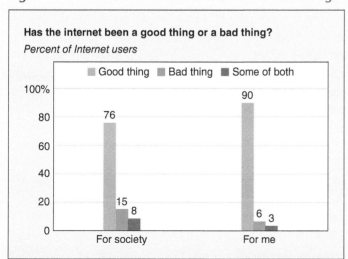

Source: Pew Research Center Internet Project Survey, January 9–12, 2014. N = 857 Internet users.

**** The information was collected by surveying a nationally representative sample of adults by landline and cell phone, in English and in Spanish, over four days in January 2014.

boundaries and connect the previously unconnected, meaning that more people can suddenly compete, connect, and collaborate.[30] In a subsequent book, Friedman observed that when he wrote *The World Is Flat*, "Facebook wasn't even in it. . . . 'Twitter' was just a sound, the 'cloud' was something in the sky, '3G' was a parking space, 'applications' were what you sent to colleges, and 'Skype' was a typo."[31] In other words, the world becomes "flatter" every day. What sort of education and training will tomorrow's workforce require? What role will colleges and universities play in educating and preparing tomorrow's citizens? Will the degree you are earning today enable you to work effectively in a transformed global economy?

Environmental Change

The challenges posed by environmental change are political, technological, and global. The great majority of scientists agree that the climate is changing and global warming is taking place. Many scientists and global organizations are focusing their efforts on measures to reduce humankind's contribution to global warming through carbon emissions and other actions. Whereas the Obama administration signaled strong support for an international treaty to reduce global warming, the Trump administration withdrew the United States from the Paris Climate Accord, a 2015 agreement intended to slash global carbon emissions.

Although many scientists are working on the technologies to slow global warming, others believe that it is more important to concentrate on mitigating the impact of global climate change, whatever the cause. The United States, like many other nations, has a concentration of population on the seacoasts: of the 25 most densely populated U.S. counties, 23 are found along the coast. Scientists estimate that global sea levels rose by seven inches over the twentieth century, and subsiding land exacerbates the problem in low-lying coastal areas such as New Orleans and the communities surrounding the Chesapeake Bay.[32] Scientists at Rutgers University announced in 2016 that the global sea level rose faster in the twentieth century than in any of the 27 previous centuries. In 2012, "Superstorm" Sandy made landfall in New York and New Jersey, killing more than 100 people and displacing thousands from their homes and businesses, with an estimated $65 billion in damages. How should policies change in the face of rising seas and more hurricanes and coastal damage? Climate change is predicted to have more immediate and dire consequences on nations in Africa, where droughts could cause millions to starve. Should the United States play a much greater role in ameliorating these disasters and others caused by human-made climate change in the near future, or should our policy priorities focus on technologies to change our lifestyles years from now?

What will all of these changes mean for you, your generation, and the nation? Is the American government nimble enough to recognize the many challenges we will face in the future in time to meet them? What will doing so mean for the commitments we have made to previous generations and the promises we make to one another as a single nation? Can the United States continue to replicate and embrace a single political culture, or have we become two Americas? These and other questions will guide our exploration of American government and politics today.

---

30 Thomas Friedman, *The World Is Flat: A Brief History of the Twenty-first Century* (New York: Farrar, Straus and Giroux, 2005).

31 Thomas L. Friedman and Michael Mandelbaum, *That Used to Be Us: How America Fell Behind in the World It Invented and How We Can Come Back* (New York: Farrar, Straus and Giroux, 2011).

32 United States Environmental Protection Agency, "Climate Impacts on Coastal Areas," www.epa.gov/climatechange/impacts -adaptation/coasts.html

Key Terms

anarchy 15
aristocracy 15
authoritarianism 14
capitalism 13
conservatism 24
democracy 15
democratic republic 18
direct democracy 16
divine right of kings 8
elite theory 21
eminent domain 14
equality 12
government 7
Hispanic 27

ideology 23
initiative 16
institution 7
Latino 27
legislature 16
liberalism 24
libertarianism 24
liberty 10
limited government 20
majoritarianism 20
majority 19
majority rule 19
oligarchy 15
order 12

pluralism 23
political culture 8
political socialization 10
politics 7
property 13
recall 16
referendum 16
representative democracy 19
republic 18
social contract 8
socialism 24
totalitarian regime 14
universal suffrage 19

Chapter Summary

■ **1.1** Governments are necessary, at a minimum, to provide public goods and services that all citizens need but cannot reasonably be expected to provide for themselves. National security and defense are obvious examples. Our founding documents such as the Declaration of Independence and the Constitution are predicated upon and convey through their language a set of shared political values. Government reinforces those values regularly.

■ **1.1** Politics is the process of resolving conflicts and deciding "who gets what, when, and how." Government is the institution within which decisions are made that resolve conflicts or allocate benefits and privileges. It is unique because it has the ultimate authority within society.

■ **1.2** Political philosophers Thomas Hobbes and John Locke believed governments were formed on the basis of consent. Individuals, all equal and endowed with reason, give up a portion of their individual liberty in order to gain the protection of government through the social contract. Government is formed to provide security and protect life, liberty, and property. Consent to be governed can be withdrawn if government becomes too powerful or abuses fundamental political values such as liberty, equality, individualism, the rule of law, and property rights.

■ **1.3** The authors of the U.S. Constitution believed that the new nation could be sustained by its political culture—the set of ideas, values, and ways of thinking about government and politics that is shared by all citizens. There is considerable consensus among American citizens about concepts basic to the U.S. political system and the fundamental values it embodies, such as liberty, equality, individualism, the rule of law, and property rights. These agreements define our political culture and are transmitted to successive generations through the process of political socialization.

■ **1.4** Governments can vary in form depending on who controls the government. In a democracy, authority is held by the people as a whole. In totalitarian and authoritarian regimes, control is exercised by a single individual or a small group. Greek terms are often used to indicate how widely power is distributed. An aristocracy is "rule by the best," whereas an oligarchy is "rule by a few," and democracy is understood as "rule by the people." The United States is a representative democracy, where the people elect representatives to make the decisions.

■ **1.4** Theories of American democracy include majoritarianism, in which the government does what the majority wants; elite theory, in which the real power lies with one or more elites; and pluralist theory, in which organized interest groups contest for power.

■ **1.5** Popular political ideologies can be arrayed from left (liberal) to right (conservative). We can also analyze economic liberalism and conservatism separately from cultural liberalism and conservatism. Other ideologies on the left (communism) and the right (fascism), however, also exist in the world.

■ **1.6** The United States faces significant change and challenges ahead. Among these are demographic changes in the nation, the impact of economic globalization and the spread of global conflict, technology innovations, and the threats posed by environmental change. This is set against a backdrop of rising economic inequality that may undermine the opportunity for social mobility and progress in ways we have not experienced as a people before.

Selected Resources

PRINT RESOURCES

Acemoglu, Daron, and James Robinson. *Why Nations Fail: The Origins of Power, Prosperity, and Poverty* (New York: Crown Publishers, 2012). The authors, one an economist and the other a political scientist, argue that nations thrive when they develop inclusive political and economic institutions and fail when institutions concentrate power and opportunity in the hands of only a few. Economic growth cannot be sustained in countries with limited political participation, nor can open political systems be maintained when large economic inequalities exist.

Coates, Ta-Nehisi. *Between the World and Me* (New York: Spiegel & Grau, 2015). Framed as a six-chapter letter from Coates to his 15-year-old son, Samori, prompted by his son's reaction to the announcement that no charges would be brought against Ferguson police officer Darren Wilson in the killing of unarmed teenager Michael Brown, he writes "This is your country, this is your world, this is your body, and you must find some way to live within the all of it."

McCall, Leslie. *The Undeserving Rich: American Beliefs about Inequality, Opportunity, and Redistribution* (New York: Cambridge University Press, 2013). An evidence-based examination of the public's knowledge of growing income inequality, the strongly held belief that equality of opportunity is the best counter to income inequality, and deep ambivalence over public policies emphasizing income redistribution.

Obama, Barack. *Dreams from My Father: A Story of Race and Inheritance* (New York: Three Rivers Press, 2004). President Obama's best-selling autobiography ends before his rise to national prominence. He describes the sense of isolation he felt due to his unusual background and his attempts to come to grips with his multiethnic identity.

Packer, George. *The Unwinding: An Inner History of the New America* (New York: Farrar, Straus and Giroux, 2013). A narrative tale of America's "unwinding" told through the lives of everyday Americans and cultural icons with a focus on economic transformation, decline of political institutions, and fraying of the social contract.

MEDIA RESOURCES

All Things Considered—A daily broadcast of National Public Radio (NPR) that provides extensive coverage of political, economic, and social news stories.

American Experience—A Public Broadcasting Service (PBS) documentary series highlighting the people and stories that have shaped America's past and present. Many of the films are available online at www.pbs.org/wgbh/americanexperience/films/.

ONLINE RESOURCES

American Conservative Union—information about conservative positions: www.conservative.org

Americans for Democratic Action—home of one of the nation's oldest liberal political organizations: www.adaction.org

Bureau of the Census—a wealth of information about the changing face of America: www.census.gov

Center for the Study of the American Dream—located at Xavier University, a research center dedicated to the study of the American Dream: past, present, and future: www.xavier.edu/americandream/

Pew Research Center—a nonpartisan repository for facts on the issues, attitudes, and trends shaping America and the world, Pew is a research center and does not take positions on policy: www.pewresearch.org

University of Michigan—a basic "front door" to almost all U.S. government websites: www.lib.umich.edu/govdocs/govweb.html

U.S. Government—access to federal government offices and agencies: www.usa.gov

The Constitution

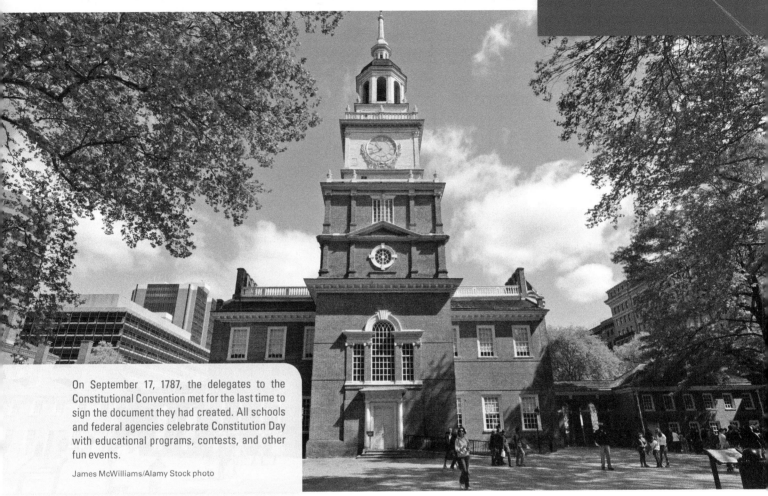

On September 17, 1787, the delegates to the Constitutional Convention met for the last time to sign the document they had created. All schools and federal agencies celebrate Constitution Day with educational programs, contests, and other fun events.

James McWilliams/Alamy Stock photo

LEARNING OBJECTIVES

After reading this chapter, you will be able to:

- **2.1** Explain the theoretical and historical factors that influenced the writers of the U.S. Constitution.

- **2.2** Describe the structure of the Articles of Confederation, and explain why the confederation failed.

- **2.3** Identify and explain the compromises made by the delegates to come to agreement on the U.S. Constitution.

- **2.4** Explain the rationale for, and give examples of, the separation of powers and the checks and balances in the U.S. Constitution.

- **2.5** Explain why some states and their citizens especially wanted the Constitution to include a bill of rights.

- **2.6** Demonstrate understanding of the formal and informal processes for amending the U.S. Constitution.

What if...   The Constitutional Qualification for President Dropped "Natural Born"?

Background

Article II, Section 1, clause 5 of the U.S. Constitution states:

> No person except a natural born citizen, or a citizen of the United States, at the time of the adoption of this Constitution, shall be eligible to the office of President; neither shall any person be eligible to that office who shall not have attained to the age of thirty five years, and been fourteen Years a resident within the United States.

The Twelfth Amendment establishes identical requirements for the vice president, and federal succession law permits only individuals "eligible to the office of President under the Constitution" to act as president in the event that both the president and vice president are unable to fulfill the obligations of office. Members of Congress and justices of the Supreme Court are not required to be "natural born" citizens. Historians attribute this unique limitation on the presidency to the founders' fears of foreign influence over the single most powerful office. "Permit me to hint," John Jay remarked in a letter to George Washington sent during the Constitutional Convention, "whether it would be wise and reasonable to provide a strong check to the admission of Foreigners into the administration of our national Government; and to declare expressly that the Command in Chief of the American army shall not be given to nor evolve on, any but a natural-born Citizen."*

In every state, naturalized citizens are allowed to become governor; should the rules for the presidency follow suit? What if we amended the Constitution to remove "natural born," allowing any citizen to seek the presidency?

Likely Influences on the Founders' Understanding of "Citizen"

Under the English common-law principle of *jus soli* (Latin for "right of the soil"), any person born within the territory of a sovereign state is a citizen from birth. Consequently, persons born within the borders of the United States are "natural born citizens" and eligible to be president. Under the principle of *jus sanguinis* (Latin for "right of blood"), citizenship or nationality is passed from one citizen to another at birth. In 1790, Congress specified that "the children of citizens of the United States that may be born beyond the sea, or out of the limits of the United States shall be considered as natural born citizens." Eight of the eleven members of the committee that proposed the natural-born eligibility requirement to the Convention served in the First Congress, and none objected to a definition of "natural born Citizen" that included persons born abroad to citizen parents. The fact that the founders and early lawmakers were informed by the principles of *jus soli* and *jus sanguinis* leads scholars to conclude that the original meaning of the phrase "natural born citizen" includes both persons born within the U.S. borders and persons born abroad who are citizens from birth based on the citizenship of a birth parent. Thus claims that Ted Cruz, candidate for the Republican nomination for president, is ineligible for the presidency lack foundation. Cruz was born in Canada; his mother was born in Delaware, therefore making him a citizen from birth.

Should We Allow Naturalized Citizens to Be President?

On average, 700,000 people become naturalized citizens every year. In doing so, each takes an oath of allegiance to the United States. Arguments in favor of changing the Constitution to allow naturalized citizens to serve as president take many forms. Some point to the value of equality—all citizens should have an equal right to aspire to the presidency. Others argue that logic and fairness dictate that we make this change. Under our current rule, "An infant born in one of the fifty states but raised in a foreign country by non-United States citizens could serve as President, while a foreign-born child adopted by United States citizens at two months of age and raised in the United States would not be eligible to become President."** Finally, birthright is a poor proxy for loyalty today. An individual has no control over where he or she is born.

Opponents to changing the Constitution argue that as a single executive, the U.S. president makes countless decisions with national security implications, and even the smallest risk of foreign influence should be avoided.

* Letter from John Jay to George Washington (July 25, 1787).
** Sarah Helene Duggin and Mary Beth Collins, "'Natural Born' in the USA," *Boston University Law Review* (2005) 85: 53–154.

How Could It Happen?

In 2003, Senator Orin Hatch proposed to the U.S. Senate the Equal Opportunity to Govern Amendment, which said, "A person who is a citizen of the United States, who has been for 20 years a citizen of the United States, and who is otherwise eligible to the Office of President, is not ineligible to that Office by reason of not being a native born citizen of the United States." If passed by both houses of Congress and ratified by three-quarters of the states, this amendment would make it possible for several well-known politicians to run for the presidency: for example, former Secretary of State Madeline Albright (born in Czechoslovakia, naturalized in 1957) or former governor of Michigan Jennifer Granholm (born in Canada, naturalized in 1980).

For Critical Analysis

1. Would you support a change to the U.S. Constitution to allow naturalized citizens to serve as president? Why or why not? What do you think the likelihood is of such a change being enacted in the next decade?

2. Naturalized citizens swear an oath of allegiance to the United States. Is that a better measure of attachment to our country than place of birth? Explain.

No matter which political party occupies the White House or holds a majority in the Congress, the opposition is likely to claim, sooner or later, that some action taken or law passed violates the Constitution. Groups ranging from the Tea Party to the Occupy movement rally under the banner of the Constitution. Why is this *old* document such an important symbol to Americans? Why hasn't it been changed more drastically or replaced completely since 1789? You may think that the Constitution is not relevant to your life or to modern times, but it continues to define the structure of the national and state governments and to regulate the relationship between the government and each individual citizen.

The Constitution of the United States is a product of the historical period in which it was written, a product of the colonists' experiences with government. Many of its provisions were grounded in the political philosophy of the time, including the writings of Thomas Hobbes and John Locke. The delegates to the Constitutional Convention in 1787 brought with them two important sets of influences: their political culture and their political experience. In the years between the first settlements in the New World and the writing of the Constitution, Americans had developed a political philosophy about how people should be governed and had tried out several forms of government. These experiences gave the founders the tools with which they constructed the Constitution. Milestones in the nation's early political history are shown in Table 2-1.

did you know?

The first U.S. Census, taken in 1790, showed that almost 20 percent of Americans were enslaved people.

The Colonial Background

■ **2.1** Explain the theoretical and historical factors that influenced the writers of the U.S. Constitution.

In 1607, the English government sent a group of farmers to establish a trading post, Jamestown, in what is now Virginia. The Virginia Company of London was the first to establish a permanent English colony in the Americas. The

Table 2-1 ▶ Milestones in Early U.S. Political History

YEAR	EVENT
1607	Jamestown established; Virginia Company lands settlers.
1620	Mayflower Compact signed.
1630	Massachusetts Bay Colony set up.
1639	Fundamental Orders of Connecticut adopted.
1641	Massachusetts Body of Liberties adopted.
1682	Pennsylvania Frame of Government passed.
1701	Pennsylvania Charter of Privileges written.
1732	Last of the 13 colonies (Georgia) established.
1756	French and Indian War declared.
1765	Stamp Act; Stamp Act Congress meets.
1774	First Continental Congress.
1775	Second Continental Congress; Revolutionary War begins.
1776	Declaration of Independence signed.
1777	Articles of Confederation drafted.
1781	Last state (Maryland) signs Articles of Confederation.
1783	"Critical period" in U.S. history begins; weak national government until 1789.
1786	Shays' Rebellion.
1787	Constitutional Convention.
1788	Ratification of Constitution.
1791	Ratification of Bill of Rights.

representative assembly
A legislature composed of individuals who represent the population.

king of England gave the backers of this colony a charter granting them "full power and authority" to make laws "for the good and welfare" of the settlement. The colonists at Jamestown instituted a **representative assembly**, setting a precedent in government that was to be observed in later colonial adventures.

Jamestown was not an immediate success. Of the 105 people who landed, 67 died within the first year. But 800 new arrivals in 1609 added to their numbers. By the spring of the next year, frontier hazards had cut their numbers to 60. This period is sometimes referred to as the "starving time" for Virginia, brought about by a severe drought in the Jamestown area, which lasted from 1607 to 1612.

Separatists, the *Mayflower,* and the Compact

The first New England colony was established in 1620. A group of religious separatists who wished to break with the Church of England came over on the ship *Mayflower* to the New World, landing at Plymouth (Massachusetts). Before going onshore, the adult males—women were not considered to have any political status—drew up the Mayflower Compact, which was signed by 41 of the 44 men aboard the ship on November 21, 1620. This group was outside the jurisdiction of the Virginia Company of London, which had chartered its

The Granger Collection, NYC

Image 2-1
The signing of the compact aboard the *Mayflower*. In 1620, the Mayflower Compact was signed by almost all of the men aboard the *Mayflower* just before they disembarked at Plymouth, Massachusetts. It stated, "We . . . covenant and combine ourselves togeather into a civil body politick. . . ; and by virtue hearof to enact, constitute, and frame such just and equal laws . . . as shall be thought [necessary] for the generall good of the Colonie."

settlement in Virginia, not Massachusetts. The separatist leaders feared that some of the *Mayflower* passengers might conclude that they were no longer under any obligations of civil obedience. Therefore, some form of public authority was imperative. As William Bradford (one of the separatist leaders) recalled in his accounts, there were "discontented and mutinous speeches that some of the strangers amongst them had let fall from them in the ship; That when they came a shore they would use their owne libertie; for none had power to command them."[1]

The compact was a political statement in which the signers agreed to create and submit to the authority of a government, pending the receipt of a royal charter. The Mayflower Compact's historical and political significance is twofold: it depended on the consent of the affected individuals, and it served as a prototype for similar compacts in American history. According to Samuel Eliot Morison, the compact proved the determination of the English immigrants to live under the rule of law, based on the *consent of the people*.[2]

More Colonies, More Government

Another outpost in New England was set up by the Massachusetts Bay Colony in 1630. Then followed other settlements in New England, which became Rhode Island, Connecticut, and New Hampshire, among others. By 1732, the last of the 13 colonies, Georgia, was established. During the colonial period, Americans developed a concept of limited government, which followed from the establishment of the first colonies under Crown charters. Theoretically, London governed the colonies. In practice, due partly to the colonies' distance from London, the colonists exercised a large measure of self-government. The

---

1   John Camp, *Out of the Wilderness: The Emergence of an American Identity in Colonial New England* (Middleton, CT: Wesleyan University Press, 1990).

2   See Morison's "The Mayflower Compact," in Daniel J. Boorstin, ed., *An American Primer* (Chicago: University of Chicago Press, 1966), p. 18.

Image 2-2
King George III
(1738–1820) was king of Great Britain and Ireland from 1760 until his death on January 29, 1820. Under George III, the British Parliament attempted to tax the American colonies. Ultimately, exasperated at repeated attempts at taxation, the colonies proclaimed their independence on July 4, 1776.

King George III, c 1762-64 (oil on canvas), Ramsay, Allan (1713-84)/ National Portrait Gallery, London, UK/Bridgeman Images

colonists were able to make their own laws, as in the Fundamental Orders of Connecticut in 1639. In 1641, the Massachusetts Body of Liberties supported the protection of individual rights and was made a part of colonial law. In 1682, the Pennsylvania Frame of Government was passed. Along with the Pennsylvania Charter of Privileges of 1701, it foreshadowed our modern Constitution and Bill of Rights. All of this legislation enabled the colonists to acquire crucial political experience.

British Restrictions and Colonial Grievances

The conflict between Britain and the American colonies began in the 1760s when the British government decided to raise revenues by imposing taxes on the American colonies. Policy advisers to Britain's young King George III, who ascended to the throne in 1760, decided that it was only logical to require the American colonists to help pay the costs for their defense during the French and Indian War (1756–1763). The colonists, who had grown accustomed to a large degree of self-government and independence from the British Crown, viewed the matter differently.

In 1764, the British Parliament passed the Sugar Act. Many colonists were unwilling to pay the tax imposed by the act. Further regulatory legislation was to come. In 1765, Parliament passed the Stamp Act, providing for internal taxation—or, as the colonists' Stamp Act Congress, assembled in 1765, called it, "taxation without representation." The colonists boycotted the purchase of English commodities in return. The success of the boycott (the Stamp Act was repealed a year later) generated a feeling of unity within the colonies.

The British, however, continued to try to raise revenues in the colonies. When Parliament passed duties (taxes) on glass, lead, paint, and other items in 1767, the colonists again boycotted British goods. The colonists' fury over taxation climaxed in the Boston Tea Party, when colonists disguised themselves as Native Americans of the Mohawk tribe and dumped close to 350 chests of British tea into Boston Harbor as a gesture of protest. In retaliation, Parliament passed the Coercive Acts (the "Intolerable Acts") in 1774, which closed Boston Harbor and placed the government of Massachusetts under direct British control. The colonists were outraged—and they responded.

The Colonial Response

New York, Pennsylvania, and Rhode Island proposed the convening of a colonial congress. The Massachusetts House of Representatives requested that all colonies hold conventions to select delegates to be sent to Philadelphia for such a congress.

The First Continental Congress

The First Continental Congress was held at Carpenters' Hall on September 5, 1774. It was a gathering of delegates from 12 of the 13 colonies (delegates from Georgia did not attend until 1775). At that meeting, there was little talk of independence. The Congress passed a resolution requesting that the colonies send a petition to King George III expressing their grievances. Resolutions were also passed requiring that the colonies raise their own troops and boycott British trade. The British government condemned the Congress's actions, treating them as open acts of rebellion.

The delegates to the First Continental Congress declared that in every county and city, a committee was to be formed whose mission was to spy on the conduct of friends and neighbors and to report to the press any violators of the trade ban. The formation of these committees was an act of cooperation among the colonies, which represented a step toward the creation of a national government.

The Second Continental Congress

By the time the Second Continental Congress met in May 1775 (this time all of the colonies were represented), fighting had already broken out between the British and the colonists. One of the main actions of the Second Continental Congress was to establish an army, naming George Washington as commander in chief. The participants in that Congress still attempted to reach a peaceful settlement with the British Parliament. One declaration of the Congress stated explicitly that "we have not raised armies with ambitious designs of separating from Great Britain, and establishing independent states." But by the beginning of 1776, military encounters had become increasingly frequent.

Public debate was acrimonious. Then Thomas Paine's *Common Sense* appeared in Philadelphia bookstores. The pamphlet was a colonial best seller. (By today's standards, a book would have to sell between 9 and 11 million copies in its first year of publication to equal the success of *Common Sense*.) Paine argued that

> a government of our own is our natural right: and when a man seriously reflects on the precariousness of human affairs, he will become convinced, that it is infinitely wiser and safer, to form a constitution of our own in a cool and deliberate manner, while we have it in our power, than to trust such an interesting event to time and chance.[3]

Students of Paine's pamphlet point out that his arguments were not new— they were common in tavern debates throughout the land. Rather, it was the near poetry of his words—which were at the same time as plain as the alphabet—that struck his readers.

Declaring Independence

On April 6, 1776, the Second Continental Congress voted for free trade at all American ports with all countries except Britain. This act could be interpreted as an implicit declaration of independence. The next month, the Congress suggested that each of the colonies establish a state government unconnected to Britain. Finally, in July, the colonists declared their independence from Britain.

The Resolution of Independence

On July 2, the Resolution of Independence was adopted by the Second Continental Congress:

---

3   *The Political Writings of Thomas Paine*, Vol. 1 (Boston: J. P. Mendum Investigator Office, 1870), p. 46.

RESOLVED, That these United Colonies are, and of right ought to be free and independent States, that they are absolved from allegiance to the British Crown, and that all political connection between them and the state of Great Britain is, and ought to be, totally dissolved.

The actual Resolution of Independence was not legally significant. On the one hand, it was not judicially enforceable, for it established no legal rights or duties. On the other hand, the colonies were already, in their own judgment, self-governing and independent of Britain. Rather, the Resolution of Independence and the subsequent Declaration of Independence were necessary to establish the legitimacy of the new nation in the eyes of foreign governments, as well as in the eyes of the colonists. What the new nation needed most were supplies for its armies and a commitment of foreign military aid. Unless it appeared to the world as a political entity separate and independent from Britain, no foreign government would enter into a contract with its leaders.

July 4, 1776—The Declaration of Independence

By June 1776, Thomas Jefferson (at the age of 33) was writing drafts of the Declaration of Independence in the second-floor parlor of a bricklayer's house in Philadelphia. On adoption of the Resolution of Independence, Jefferson argued that a declaration clearly putting forth the causes that compelled the colonies to separate from Britain was necessary. The Second Congress assigned the task to him, and he completed his work on the declaration, which enumerated the colonists' major grievances against Britain. Some of his work was amended to gain unanimous acceptance (for example, his condemnation of the slave trade was eliminated to satisfy Georgia and North Carolina), but the bulk of it was passed intact on July 4, 1776. On July 19, the modified draft became "the unanimous declaration of the thirteen United States of America." On August 2, it was signed by the members of the Second Continental Congress.

Universal Truths   The Declaration of Independence has become one of the world's most famous and significant documents. The words opening the second paragraph of the Declaration are known most widely:

We hold these Truths to be self-evident, that all Men are created equal, that they are endowed by their Creator with certain unalienable Rights, that among these are Life, Liberty, and the Pursuit of Happiness—That to secure these Rights, Governments are instituted among Men, deriving their just Powers from the Consent of the Governed, that whenever any Form of Government becomes destructive of these Ends, it is the Right of the People to alter or abolish it, and to institute new Government.

natural rights
Rights held to be inherent in natural law, not dependent on governments. John Locke stated that natural law, being superior to human law, specifies certain rights of "life, liberty, and property." These rights, altered to become "life, liberty, and the pursuit of happiness," are asserted in the Declaration of Independence.

Natural Rights and a Social Contract   The assumption that people have **natural rights** ("unalienable Rights"), including the rights to "Life, Liberty, and the Pursuit of Happiness," was a revolutionary concept at that time. Its use by Jefferson reveals the influence of the English philosopher John Locke (1632–1704), whose writings were familiar to educated American colonists.[4] In his *Two Treatises on Government*, published in 1690, Locke argued that all

---

4   Not all scholars believe that Jefferson was truly influenced by Locke. For example, Jay Fliegelman states that "Jefferson's fascination with Homer, Ossian, Patrick Henry, and the violin is of greater significance than his indebtedness to Locke," in Jay Fliegelman, *Declaring Independence: Jefferson, Natural Language, and the Culture of Performance* (Palo Alto, CA: Stanford University Press, 1993).

people possess certain natural rights, including the rights to life, liberty, and property, and that the primary purpose of government was to protect these rights. Furthermore, government was established by the people through a **social contract**—an agreement among the people to form a government and abide by its rules. As you read earlier, such contracts, or compacts, were not new to Americans. The Mayflower Compact was the first of several documents that established governments or governing rules based on the consent of the governed. In citing the "pursuit of happiness" instead of "property" as a right, Jefferson clearly meant to go beyond Locke's thinking.

After setting forth these basic principles of government, the Declaration of Independence goes on to justify the colonists' revolt against Britain. Much of the remainder of the document is a list of what "He" (King George III) had done to deprive the colonists of their rights. (See Appendix A at the end of this book for the complete text of the Declaration of Independence.)

Once it had fulfilled its purpose of legitimating the American Revolution, the Declaration of Independence was all but forgotten for many years. According to scholar Pauline Maier, the Declaration of Independence did not become enshrined as what she calls "American Scripture" until the 1800s.[5]

> **social contract**
> A voluntary agreement among individuals to secure their rights and welfare by creating a government and abiding by its rules.

The Rise of Republicanism

Although the colonists had formally declared independence from Britain, the fight to gain actual independence continued for five more years—until British general Charles Cornwallis surrendered at Yorktown in 1781. In 1783, after Britain formally recognized the independent status of the United States in the Treaty of Paris, Washington disbanded the army. During these years of military struggles, the states faced the additional challenge of creating a system of self-government for an independent United States.

Some colonists had demanded that independence be preceded by the formation of a strong central government. But others, who called themselves Republicans, were against a strong central government. They opposed monarchy, executive authority, and virtually any form of restraint on the power of local groups.

From 1776 to 1780, all of the states adopted written constitutions. Eleven of the constitutions were completely new. Two of them—those of Connecticut and Rhode Island—were old royal charters with minor modifications. Republican sentiment led to increased power for the legislatures. In Pennsylvania and Georgia, **unicameral** (one-body) **legislatures** were unchecked by executive or judicial authority. Basically, the Republicans attempted to maintain the politics of 1776. In almost all states, the legislature was predominant.

> **unicameral legislature**
> A legislature with only one legislative chamber, as opposed to a bicameral (two-chamber) legislature, such as the U.S. Congress. Today, Nebraska is the only state in the Union with a unicameral legislature.

The Articles of Confederation: The First Form of Government

■ **2.2** Describe the structure of the Articles of Confederation, and explain why the confederation failed.

The fear of a powerful central government led to the passage of the Articles of Confederation, which created a weak central government. The term **confederation** is important; it means a voluntary association of *independent*

> **confederation**
> A political system in which states or regional governments retain ultimate authority except for those powers they expressly delegate to a central government. A voluntary association of independent states, in which the member states agree to limited restraints on their freedom of action.

---

5   See Pauline Maier, *American Scripture: Making the Declaration of Independence* (New York: Knopf, 1997).

state
A group of people occupying a specific area and organized under one government; may be either a nation or a subunit of a nation.

states, in which the member states agree to only limited restraints on their freedom of action. As a result, confederations seldom have an effective executive authority.

In June 1776, the Second Continental Congress began the process of drafting what would become the Articles of Confederation. The final form of the Articles was achieved by November 15, 1777. It was not until March 1, 1781, however, that the last state, Maryland, agreed to ratify what was called the Articles of Confederation and Perpetual Union. Well before the final ratification of the Articles, however, many of them were implemented: the Continental Congress and the 13 states conducted American military, economic, and political affairs according to the standards and the form specified by the Articles.[6]

Under the Articles, the 13 original colonies, now states, established on March 1, 1781, a government of the states—the Congress of the Confederation. The Congress was a unicameral assembly of so-called ambassadors from each state, with each state possessing a single vote. Each year, the Congress would choose one of its members as its president (that is, presiding officer), but the Articles did not provide for a president of the United States.

The Congress was authorized in Article X to appoint an executive committee of the states "to execute in the recess of Congress, such of the powers of Congress as the United States, in Congress assembled, by the consent of nine [of the 13] states, shall from time to time think expedient to vest with them." The Congress was also allowed to appoint other committees and civil officers necessary for managing the general affairs of the United States. In addition, the Congress could regulate foreign affairs and establish coinage and weights and measures, but it lacked an independent source of revenue and the necessary executive machinery to enforce its decisions throughout the land. Article II of the Articles of Confederation guaranteed that each state would retain its sovereignty. Figure 2-1 illustrates the structure of the government under the Articles of Confederation; Table 2-2 summarizes the powers—and the lack of powers—of Congress under the Articles of Confederation.

Accomplishments under the Articles

The new government made some accomplishments during its eight years of existence under the Articles of Confederation. Certain states' claims to Western lands were settled. Maryland had objected to the claims of the Carolinas, Connecticut, Georgia, Massachusetts, New York, and Virginia. It was only after these states consented to give up their land claims to the United States as a whole that Maryland signed the Articles of Confederation. Another accomplishment under the Articles was the passage of the Northwest Ordinance of 1787, which established a basic pattern of government for new territories north of the Ohio River. All in all, the Articles represented the first real pooling of resources by the American states.

Figure 2-1 ▶ **The Confederal Government Structure under the Articles of Confederation**

Congress
Congress had one house. Each state had two to seven members, but only one vote. The exercise of most powers required approval of at least nine states. Amendments to the Articles required the consent of all the states.

Committee of the States
A committee of representatives from all the states was empowered to act in the name of Congress between sessions.

Officers
Congress appointed officers to do some of the executive work.

The States

---

6   Robert W. Hoffert, *A Politics of Tensions: The Articles of Confederation and American Political Ideas* (Niwot, CO: University Press of Colorado, 1992).

Table 2-2 ▶ Powers of the Congress of the Confederation

CONGRESS HAD POWER TO	CONGRESS LACKED POWER TO
Declare war and make peace.	Provide for effective treaty-making power and control foreign relations; it could not compel states to respect treaties.
Enter into treaties and alliances.	Regulate interstate and foreign commerce; it left each state free to set up its own tariff system.
Establish and control armed forces.	Compel states to meet military quotas; it could not draft soldiers or demand revenue to support an army or navy.
Requisition men and revenues from states.	Collect taxes directly from the people; it had to rely on states to collect and forward taxes.
Regulate coinage.	Compel states to pay their share of government costs.
Borrow funds and issue bills of credit.	Provide and maintain a sound monetary system or issue paper money; this was left up to the states, and monies in circulation differed tremendously in value.
Fix uniform standards of weight and measurement.	
Create admiralty courts.	
Create a postal system.	
Regulate Indian affairs.	
Guarantee citizens of each state the rights and privileges of citizens in the several states when in another state.	Establish an enforcement division to ensure those rights.
Adjudicate disputes between states on state petition.	

Weaknesses of the Articles

Despite these accomplishments, the Articles of Confederation had many defects. Although Congress had the legal right to declare war and to conduct foreign policy, it did not have the right to demand revenues from the states. It could only *ask* for them. Additionally, the actions of Congress required the consent of nine states. Any amendments to the Articles required the unanimous consent of the Congress and confirmation by every state legislature. Furthermore, the Articles did not create a national system of courts.

Basically, the functioning of the government under the Articles depended on the goodwill of the states. Article III simply established a "league of friendship" among the states—no national government was intended.

The most fundamental weakness of the Articles, and the most basic cause of their eventual replacement by the Constitution, was the lack of power to raise funds for the militia. The Articles contained no language giving Congress coercive power to raise revenues (by levying taxes) to provide adequate

did you know?

The Articles of Confederation specified that Canada could be admitted to the Confederation if it ever wished to join.

support for the military forces controlled by Congress. When states refused to send revenues to support the government (*not one state* met the financial requests made by Congress under the Articles), Congress resorted to selling off Western lands to speculators or issuing bonds that sold for less than their face value. Due to a lack of resources, the Continental Congress was forced to disband the army, even in the face of serious Spanish and British military threats.

Shays' Rebellion and the Need for Revision of the Articles

Because of the weaknesses of the Articles of Confederation, the central government could do little to maintain peace and order in the new nation. The states bickered among themselves and increasingly taxed each other's goods. At times they prevented trade altogether. By 1784, the country faced a serious economic depression. Banks were calling in old loans and refusing to give new ones. People who could not pay their debts were often thrown into prison.

By 1786, in Concord, Massachusetts, three times as many people were in prison for debt as for all other crimes combined. In Worcester County, Massachusetts, the ratio was even higher—20 to 1. Most of the prisoners were small farmers who could not pay their debts because of the economic chaos.

In August 1786, mobs of musket-bearing farmers led by former Revolutionary War captain Daniel Shays seized county courthouses and disrupted the trials of debtors in Springfield, Massachusetts. Shays and his men then launched an attack on the federal arsenal at Springfield, but they were repulsed. Shays' Rebellion demonstrated that the central government could not protect the citizenry from armed rebellion or provide adequately for the public welfare. The rebellion spurred the nation's political leaders to action. As John Jay wrote to Thomas Jefferson,

> *Changes are Necessary, but what they ought to be, what they will be, and how and when to be produced, are arduous Questions. I feel for the Cause of Liberty. . . . If it should not take Root in this Soil[,] Little Pains will be taken to cultivate it in any other.*[7]

Drafting the Constitution

Concerned about the economic turmoil in the young nation, five states called for a meeting to be held at Annapolis, Maryland, on September 11, 1786—ostensibly to discuss commercial problems only. It was evident to those in attendance (including Alexander Hamilton and James Madison) that the national government had serious weaknesses that had to be addressed if it were to survive. Among the important problems to be solved were the relationship between the states and the central government, the powers of the national legislature, the need for executive leadership, and the establishment of policies for economic stability.

Those attending the meeting prepared a petition to the Continental Congress for a general convention to meet in Philadelphia in May 1787 "to consider the exigencies of the union." Congress approved the convention in February 1787. When those who favored a weak central government realized

---

7   Excerpt from a letter from John Jay to Thomas Jefferson written in October 1786, as reproduced in Winthrop D. Jordan et al., *The United States*, combined ed., 6th ed. (Englewood Cliffs, NJ: Prentice Hall, 1987), p. 135.

that the Philadelphia meeting would, in fact, take place, they endorsed the convention. They made sure, however, that the convention would be summoned "for the sole and express purpose of revising the Articles of Confederation." Those in favor of a stronger national government had different ideas.

The designated date for the opening of the convention at Philadelphia, now known as the Constitutional Convention, was May 14, 1787. Because few of the delegates had actually arrived in Philadelphia by that time, however, the convention was not formally opened in the East Room of the Pennsylvania State House until May 25.[8] Fifty-five of the 74 delegates chosen for the convention actually attended, and only about 40 played active roles at the convention. Rhode Island was the only state that refused to send delegates.

Who Were the Delegates?

Who were the 55 delegates to the Constitutional Convention? They certainly did not represent a cross-section of American society in the 1700s. Indeed, most were members of the upper class. Consider the following facts:

- Thirty-three were members of the legal profession.
- Three were physicians.
- Almost 50 percent were college graduates.
- Seven were former chief executives of their respective states.
- Six were owners of large plantations.
- Eight were important businesspersons.

They were also relatively young by today's standards: James Madison was 36, Alexander Hamilton was only 32, and Jonathan Dayton of New Jersey was 26. The venerable Benjamin Franklin, however, was 81 and had to be carried in on a portable chair. Not counting Franklin, the average age was just over 42. What almost all of them shared, however, was prior experience in political office or military service. Most of them were elected members of their own states' legislatures. George Washington, the esteemed commander of the Revolutionary War troops, was named to chair the meeting. There were, however, no women or minorities among this group. Women could not vote anywhere in the confederacy and, although free African Americans played an important part in some Northern states, they were certainly not likely to be political leaders.[9]

The Working Environment

The conditions under which the delegates worked were far from ideal and were made even worse by the necessity of maintaining total secrecy. The framers of the Constitution believed that if public debate took place on particular positions, delegates would have a more difficult time compromising or backing down to reach agreement. Consequently, the windows were usually shut in the East Room of the State House. Summer quickly arrived, and the air became heavy, humid, and hot by noon of each day.

did you know?

The 1776 constitution of New Jersey granted the vote to "all free inhabitants," including women, but the large number of women who turned out to vote resulted in male protests and a new law limiting the right to vote to "free white male citizens."

did you know?

Neither the word *God* nor the word *democracy* appears in the Constitution.

---

8   The State House was later named Independence Hall. This was the same room in which the Declaration of Independence had been signed 11 years earlier.

9   For a detailed look at the delegates and their lively debates, see Carol Berkin, *A Brilliant Solution: Inventing the American Constitution* (New York: Harcourt, 2002).

Alexander Hamilton on Broadway

The Grammys usually feature live performances by nominees, but when the cast of Broadway's musical *Hamilton* was invited to perform at the 58th annual music awards in Los Angeles, they declined an onstage performance, fearing that the magic of their complex production would be lost outside of the Richard Rogers Theatre on Broadway. Instead, the Grammys briefly left L.A. to broadcast *Hamilton*'s opening number "Alexander Hamilton" live from New York City. Not an hour later, the cast was back on stage to receive the Grammy for Best Musical Theater Album. The surprising question most often Googled during the live performance: "Who was Alexander Hamilton?"*

Hamilton, the hip-hop musical biography of Alexander Hamilton, Revolutionary War hero, principal author of the *Federalist Papers*, and the nation's first treasury secretary, was the hottest ticket on Broadway in 2016. Written by and starring Lin-Manuel Miranda as Hamilton himself, *Hamilton* has the potential to shape and reshape our perception of politics in the early American Republic. In Miranda's words, this is "a story about America then, told by America now," a reference to the young, racially diverse cast and the varied genres of music included. "The idea of hip-hop being the music of the Revolution appealed to me immensely; it felt right" Miranda said, but the score also features R&B, choral ballads, and pop. For example, King George III (Jonathan Groff) croons satirically to the colonists, "You'll be back, soon you'll see; you'll remember you belong to me" in an introductory song reminiscent of a Top 40 breakup song.

Hamilton humanizes one of history's best-known villains, Aaron Burr (Leslie Odom, Jr.) and turns one of America's most revered founding fathers, Thomas Jefferson (Daveed Diggs), into the musical's chief antagonist. For nearly two centuries, the founders have been portrayed as quasi-deities. But *Hamilton*'s Jefferson is a petty, cynical manipulator governed by ambition. Alexander Hamilton, long a polarizing historical figure, is given a dynamic personality with a dazzling intellect and knack for being "in the room where it happens." Aaron Burr, the vice president who fatally wounded Hamilton in a duel in 1804, is desperate to be relevant but hesitant to take a stand on anything, earning Hamilton's contempt.

Image 2-3 Anthony Ramos, Lin-Manuel Miranda, Daveed Diggs, and Okieriete Onaodowan in *Hamilton* at the Richard Rodgers Theatre in New York City.

Hamilton manages to tell the inspiring story of the country's founding in the space of three hours without omitting slavery, political corruption, death, or the Reynolds affair that ended Hamilton's chances of becoming president. And, although the story of the founding is largely male-centric, the ebullient Schuyler sisters remind viewers of the women often rendered invisible by history. Miranda asked Ron Chernow, Pulitzer Prize–winning author of the 800-page biography of Alexander Hamilton, to serve as his historical consultant so that historians would take the production seriously. Lin-Manuel first performed the opening song for Chernow sitting on the author's living room couch. Chernow's reaction: "I think that's the most astonishing thing I've ever heard in my life . . . He had accurately condensed the first 40 pages of my book into a four-minute song."**

Hamilton's soundtrack of forty-six songs peaked at #12 on Billboard's Top 200 and became the first Broadway musical to appear on the Billboard rap charts. President Obama has seen the show twice in New York, and the First Lady has invited the cast to the White House to participate in an arts-and-music workshop with schoolchildren. Weekly,

*Madison Malone Kircher, "Tons of People Googled One Question after the 'Hamilton' Grammy Performance," *Tech Insider*, February 16, 2016. http://www.techinsider.io/people-googling-who-is-alexander-hamilton-after-grammys-2016-2
**Jody Rosen, "The American Revolutionary," T-Magazine, *New York Times*, July 8, 2015. www.nytimes.com/interactive/2015/07/08/t-magazine/hamilton-lin-manuel-miranda-roots-sondheim.html

(Continued)

the cast holds a lottery (#Ham4Ham) for $10 seats filling the entire front row. With $1.46 million in support from the Rockefeller Foundation, *Hamilton*'s producer Jeffrey Seller and Miranda have entered into a partnership with the New York City Public Schools enabling 20,000 high school students to see the show for $10 a ticket starting in 2016. "It is a dream come true to have a program like this exist in connection to Hamilton," says Miranda. "I can't wait to perform for a theater full of students who are learning about our Founding Fathers in class and seeing how it still relates to their own lives on stage. They will see Hamilton's story, and I'm hopeful that the stories it will inspire in them will change our lives in ways we can't even anticipate."***

***The Rockefeller Foundation News & Media, October 27, 2015. https://www.rockefellerfoundation.org/about-us/news-media/hamilton-the-musical-and-the-rockefeller-foundation-announce-partnership-to-provide-20000-nyc-public-school-students-with-tickets-to-hamilton-on-broadway-with-1-46-million-grant/
Thank you to Grace Ford-Dirks, a contributing writer.

For Critical Analysis

1. Alexander Hamilton was killed in a duel with Aaron Burr in 1804 at the age of 49, denying him the right to "tell his own story" in a published memoir. Instead his rivals got to shape America's memory of the "ten dollar founding father." How can historians and students of history get the most accurate story of past events? In what ways does it matter who tells the story?

2. The musical *Hamilton* repeatedly emphasizes the role immigrants have played in the nation's founding, growth, and success. Lin-Manuel Miranda's parents are immigrants, and that identity is important to his perspective on history. Why is immigration such a contentious issue in politics today when it has played such an important role in building the country?

Factions among the Delegates

What we know about the actual daily work of the convention comes from the detailed personal journal kept by James Madison. A majority of the delegates were strong nationalists—they wanted a central government with real power, unlike the central government under the Articles of Confederation. George Washington and Benjamin Franklin preferred limited national authority based on a separation of powers. They were apparently willing to accept any type of national government, however, as long as the other delegates approved it. A few advocates of a strong central government, led by Gouverneur Morris of Pennsylvania and John Rutledge of South Carolina, distrusted the ability of the common people to engage in self-government.

Among the nationalists, several went so far as to support monarchy. This group included Alexander Hamilton, who was chiefly responsible for the Annapolis Convention's call for the Constitutional Convention.

Still another faction consisted of nationalists who were less democratic in nature and who would support a central government only if it was founded on very narrowly defined republican principles. Many of the other delegates from Connecticut, Delaware, Maryland, New Hampshire, and New Jersey were concerned about only one thing—claims to Western lands. As long as those lands became the common property of all of the states, they were willing to support a central government.

Finally, there was a group of delegates who were totally against a national authority. Two of the three delegates from New York quit the convention when they saw the nationalist direction of its proceedings.

Politicking and Compromises

■ **2.3** Identify and explain the compromises made by the delegates to come to agreement on the U.S. Constitution.

The debates at the convention started on the first day. James Madison had spent months reviewing European political theory. When his Virginia delegation arrived ahead of most of the others, it got to work immediately. By the time George Washington opened the convention, Governor Edmund Randolph of Virginia was prepared to present 15 resolutions, which set the agenda for the remainder of the convention—even though, in principle, the delegates had been sent to Philadelphia for the sole purpose of amending the Articles of Confederation. They had not been sent to write a new constitution.

The Virginia Plan Randolph's 15 resolutions proposed an entirely new national government under a constitution. It was, however, a plan that favored the large states, including Virginia. Basically, it called for the following:

■ A **bicameral** (two-chamber) **legislature**, with the lower chamber chosen by the people and the smaller upper chamber chosen by the lower chamber from nominees selected by state legislatures. The number of representatives would be proportional to a state's population, thus greatly favoring the states with larger populations, including slaves. The legislature could void any state laws.

■ The creation of an unspecified national executive, elected by the legislature.

■ The creation of a national judiciary, appointed by the legislature.

It did not take long for the smaller states to realize they would fare poorly under the Virginia plan, which would enable Virginia, Massachusetts, and Pennsylvania to form a majority in the national legislature. The debate on the plan dragged on for many weeks. It was time for the small states to come up with their own plan.

The New Jersey Plan On June 15, lawyer William Paterson of New Jersey offered an alternative plan. After all, argued Paterson, under the Articles of Confederation, all states had equality; therefore, the convention had no power to change this arrangement. He proposed the following:

■ The fundamental principle of the Articles of Confederation—one state, one vote—would be retained in a unicameral legislature.

■ Congress would be able to regulate trade and impose taxes.

■ All acts of Congress would be the supreme law of the land.

■ Several people would be elected by Congress to form an executive office.

■ The executive office would appoint a Supreme Court.

Basically, the New Jersey plan was simply an amendment of the Articles of Confederation. Its only notable feature was its reference to the **supremacy doctrine**, which was later included in the Constitution.

bicameral legislature
A legislature made up of two parts, called chambers. The U.S. Congress, composed of the House of Representatives and the Senate, is a bicameral legislature.

supremacy doctrine
A doctrine that asserts the priority of national law over state laws. This principle is rooted in Article VI of the Constitution, which provides that the Constitution, the laws passed by the national government under its constitutional powers, and all treaties constitute the supreme law of the land.

The "Great Compromise" The delegates were at an impasse. Most wanted a strong national government and were unwilling even to consider the New Jersey plan, but when the Virginia plan was brought up again, the small states threatened to leave. The issues involved in the debate included how states and their residents would be represented. Small states feared that the Virginia plan, with its powerful national government, would pass laws that would disadvantage smaller states. The larger states, aware that they would be the economic force in the new nation, absolutely opposed a government in which smaller states had the balance of power. Roger Sherman of Connecticut proposed a solution that gave power to both the small states and the larger states. On July 16, the **Great Compromise** was put forward for debate:

- A bicameral legislature in which the lower chamber, the House of Representatives, would be apportioned according to the number of free inhabitants in each state, plus three-fifths of the slaves.

- An upper chamber, the Senate, which would have two members from each state elected by the state legislatures.

This plan, also called the Connecticut Compromise because of the role of the Connecticut delegates in the proposal, broke the deadlock. It did exact a political price from the larger states, however, because it permitted each state to have equal representation in the Senate. Having two senators represent each state in effect diluted the voting power of citizens living in more heavily populated states and gave the smaller states disproportionate political powers. But the Connecticut Compromise resolved the large-state–small-state controversy. In addition, the Senate acted as part of a checks-and-balances system against the House, which many feared would be dominated by, and responsive to, the masses. Another important piece of the debate, however, needed a resolution: How were slaves to be counted in determining the number of members of Congress allotted to a state?

Great Compromise
The compromise between the New Jersey and Virginia plans that created one chamber of the Congress based on population and one chamber representing each state equally; also called the Connecticut Compromise.

Image 2-4
George Washington presided over the Constitutional Convention of 1787. Although the convention was supposed to start on May 14, 1787, few of the delegates had actually arrived in Philadelphia by that date. The convention formally opened in the East Room of the Pennsylvania State House (later named Independence Hall) on May 25. Only Rhode Island did not send any delegates.

Bettmann/Getty Images

The Three-Fifths Compromise Part of the Connecticut Compromise dealt with this problem. Slavery was still legal in many Northern states, but it was concentrated in the South. Many delegates were opposed to slavery and wanted it banned entirely in the United States. The South wanted slaves to be counted along with free persons in determining representation in Congress. Delegates from the Northern states objected. Sherman's three-fifths proposal was a compromise between Northerners who did not want the slaves counted at all and Southerners who wanted them counted in the same way as free whites. Sherman's Connecticut plan spoke of three-fifths of "all other persons" (and that is the language of the Constitution itself). It is not hard to figure out, though, who those other persons were.

The Three-Fifths Compromise illustrates the power of the Southern states at the convention.[10] The three-fifths rule meant that the House of Representatives and the electoral college would be apportioned in part on the basis of *property*—specifically, property in slaves. Modern commentators have asserted that the three-fifths rule valued African Americans only three-fifths as much as whites. Actually, the additional Southern representatives elected because of the three-fifths rule did not represent the slaves at all. Rather, the additional representatives enhanced the power of the South in Congress.

The Three-Fifths Compromise did not completely settle the slavery issue. There was also the question of the slave trade. Eventually, the delegates agreed that Congress could not ban the importation of slaves until after 1808. The compromise meant that the matter of ending slavery was never addressed directly. Instead, the South won 20 years of unrestricted slave trade and a requirement that escaped slaves in free states be returned to their owners in slave states.

Other Issues The South also worried that the Northern majority in Congress would pass legislation that was unfavorable to its economic interests. Because the South depended on agricultural exports, it feared the imposition of export taxes. In return for acceding to the Northern demand that Congress be able to regulate commerce among the states and with other nations, the South obtained a promise that export taxes would not be imposed. As a result, the United States is among the few countries that do not tax their exports.

There were other disagreements. The delegates could not decide whether to establish only a Supreme Court or to create lower courts as well. They deferred the issue by mandating a Supreme Court and allowing Congress to establish lower courts. They also disagreed over whether the president or the Senate would choose the Supreme Court justices. A compromise was reached with the agreement that the president would nominate the justices and the Senate would confirm the nominations. These compromises, as well as others, resulted from the recognition that if one group of states refused to ratify the Constitution, it was doomed.

Working toward Final Agreement

■ **2.4** Explain the rationale for, and give examples of, the separation of powers and the checks and balances in the U.S. Constitution.

The Connecticut Compromise was reached by mid-July. The makeup of the executive branch and the judiciary, however, was left unsettled. The remaining

---

10 See Garry Wills, *"Negro President": Jefferson and the Slave Power* (New York: Houghton Mifflin, 2003).

work of the convention was turned over to a five-man Committee of Detail, which presented a rough draft of the Constitution on August 6. It made the executive and judicial branches subordinate to the legislative branch.

The Madisonian Model—Separation of Powers

The major issue of **separation of powers** had not yet been resolved. The delegates were concerned with structuring the government to prevent the imposition of tyranny—either by the majority or by a minority. Madison proposed a governmental scheme—sometimes called the **Madisonian model**—to achieve this: the executive, legislative, and judicial powers of government were to be separated so that no one branch had enough power to dominate the others, nor could any one person hold office in two different branches of the government at the same time. The separation of powers was by function, as well as by personnel, with Congress passing laws, the president enforcing and administering laws, and the courts interpreting laws in individual circumstances.

Each of the three branches of government would be independent of the others, but they would have to share power to govern. According to Madison, in Federalist #51 (see Appendix C), "the great security against a gradual concentration of the several powers in the same department consists in giving to those who administer each department the necessary constitutional means and personal motives to resist encroachments of the others."

The Madisonian Model—Checks and Balances

The "constitutional means" Madison referred to is a system of **checks and balances** through which each branch of the government can check the actions of the others. For example, Congress can enact laws, but the president has veto power over congressional acts. The Supreme Court has the power to declare acts of Congress and of the executive branch unconstitutional, but the president appoints the justices of the Supreme Court, with the advice and consent of the Senate. (The Supreme Court's power to declare acts unconstitutional was not mentioned in the Constitution, although arguably the framers assumed that the Court would have this power—see the discussion of judicial review later in this chapter.) Figure 2-2 outlines these checks and balances.

Madison's ideas of separation of powers and checks and balances were not new. The influential French political thinker Baron de Montesquieu (1689–1755) had explored these concepts in his book *The Spirit of the Laws*, published in 1748. Montesquieu not only discussed the "three sorts of powers" (executive, legislative, and judicial) that were necessarily exercised by any government, but also gave examples of how, in some nations, certain checks on these powers had arisen and had been effective in preventing tyranny.

In the years since the Constitution was ratified, the checks and balances built into it have evolved into a sometimes complex give-and-take among the branches of government. Generally, for nearly

separation of powers
The principle of dividing governmental powers among different branches of government.

Madisonian model
A structure of government proposed by James Madison in which the powers of the government are separated into three branches: executive, legislative, and judicial.

checks and balances
A major principle of the American system of government whereby each branch of the government can check the actions of the others.

Image 2-5

James Madison (1751–1836) earned the title "master builder of the Constitution" because of his persuasive logic during the Constitutional Convention. His contributions to the *Federalist Papers* showed him to be a brilliant political thinker and writer.

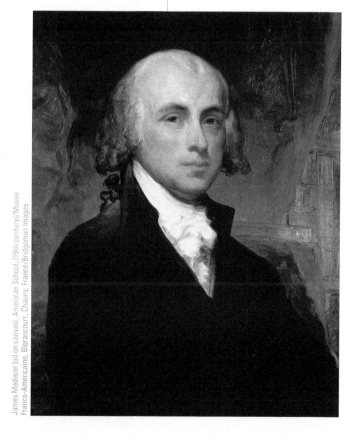

James Madison (oil on canvas), American School, (19th century)/Musee Franco-Americaine, Blerancourt, Chauny, France/Bridgeman Images

Figure 2–2 ▶ Checks and Balances

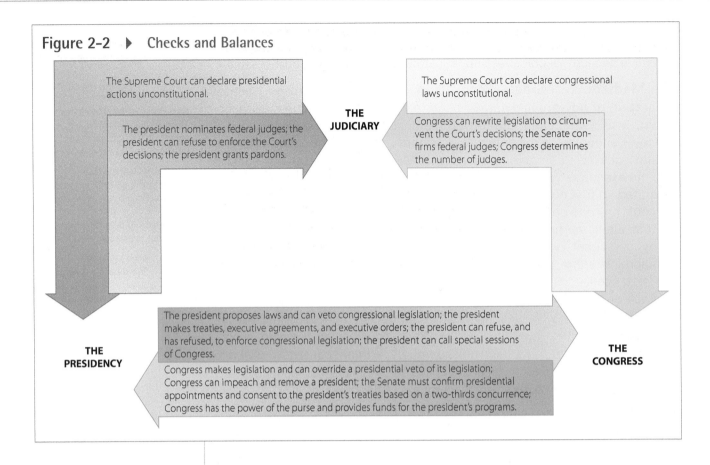

The Supreme Court can declare presidential actions unconstitutional.

The president nominates federal judges; the president can refuse to enforce the Court's decisions; the president grants pardons.

THE JUDICIARY

The Supreme Court can declare congressional laws unconstitutional.

Congress can rewrite legislation to circumvent the Court's decisions; the Senate confirms federal judges; Congress determines the number of judges.

THE PRESIDENCY

THE CONGRESS

The president proposes laws and can veto congressional legislation; the president makes treaties, executive agreements, and executive orders; the president can refuse, and has refused, to enforce congressional legislation; the president can call special sessions of Congress.

Congress makes legislation and can override a presidential veto of its legislation; Congress can impeach and remove a president; the Senate must confirm presidential appointments and consent to the president's treaties based on a two-thirds concurrence; Congress has the power of the purse and provides funds for the president's programs.

every check that one branch has over another, the branch that has been checked has devised a means of circumventing the check. For example, suppose that the president checks Congress by vetoing a bill. Congress can override the presidential veto by a two-thirds vote. Additionally, Congress holds the "power of the purse." If it disagrees with a program endorsed by the executive branch, it can simply refuse to appropriate the funds necessary to operate that program. Similarly, the president can impose a countercheck on Congress if the Senate refuses to confirm a presidential appointment, such as a judicial appointment. The president can simply wait until Congress is in recess and then make what is called a "recess appointment," which does not require the Senate's approval. Recess appointments last until the end of the next session of the Congress.

The Executive Some delegates favored a plural executive made up of representatives from the various regions. This was abandoned in favor of a single chief executive. Some argued that Congress should choose the executive. To make the presidency completely independent of the proposed Congress, however, an electoral college was adopted. Without question, the **electoral college** created a cumbersome presidential election process. The process even made it possible for a candidate who came in second in the popular vote to become president by being the top vote-getter in the electoral college, which happened in 2016 and in four prior contests (1824, 1876, 1888, and 2000). The electoral college insulated the president, however, from direct popular control. The seven-year single term that some of the delegates had proposed was replaced by a four-year term and the possibility of reelection.

electoral college
A group of persons called electors selected by the voters in each state and the District of Columbia; this group officially elects the president and vice president of the United States. The number of electors in each state is equal to the number of each state's representatives in both chambers of Congress.

A Federal Republic The Constitution creates a **federal system** of government that divides the sovereign powers of the nation between the states and the national government. This structure allows for states to make their own laws about many of the issues of direct concern for their citizens while granting the national government far more power over the states and their citizens than under the Articles of Confederacy. As you will read in Chapter 3, the Constitution expressly granted certain powers to the national government.

For example, the national government was given the power to regulate commerce among the states. The Constitution also declared that the president is the nation's chief executive and the commander in chief of the armed forces. Additionally, the Constitution made it clear that laws made by the national government take priority over conflicting state laws. At the same time, the Constitution provided for extensive states' rights, including the right to control commerce within state borders and to exercise those governing powers that were not delegated to the national government.

The Final Document

On September 17, 1787, the Constitution was approved by 39 delegates. Of the 55 who had originally attended, only 42 remained and 3 refused to sign the Constitution.

The Constitution that was to be ratified established the following fundamental principles:

- Popular sovereignty, or control by the people.

- A republican government in which the people choose representatives to make decisions for them.

- Limited government with written laws, in contrast to the powerful British government against which the colonists had rebelled.

- Separation of powers, with checks and balances among branches to prevent any one branch from gaining too much power.

- A federal system that allows for states' rights, because the states feared too much centralized control.

The Difficult Road to Ratification

The founders knew that **ratification** of the Constitution was far from certain. Because it was almost guaranteed that many state legislatures would not ratify it, the delegates agreed that each state should hold a special convention. Elected delegates to these conventions would discuss and vote on the Constitution. Further departing from the Articles of Confederation, the delegates agreed that as soon as 9 states (rather than all 13) approved the Constitution, it would take effect, and Congress could begin to organize the new government.

The federal system created by the founders was a novel form of government at that time—no other country in the world had such a system. It was invented by the founders as a compromise solution to the controversy over whether the states or the central government should have ultimate sovereignty. The debate over where the line should be drawn between states' rights and the powers of the national government has characterized American

federal system
A system of government in which power is divided between a central government and regional, or subdivisional, governments. Each level must have some domain in which its policies are dominant and some genuine political or constitutional guarantee of its authority.

ratification
Formal approval.

politics ever since. The founders did not go into detail about where this line should be drawn, thus leaving it up to scholars and court judges to divine their intentions.

The Federalists Push for Ratification

The two opposing forces in the battle over ratification were the Federalists and the Anti-Federalists. The **Federalists**—those in favor of a strong central government and the new Constitution—had an advantage over their opponents, called the **Anti-Federalists**, who wanted to prevent the Constitution as drafted from being ratified. In the first place, the Federalists had assumed a positive name, leaving their opposition the negative label of *Anti*-Federalist.[11] More important, the Federalists had attended the Constitutional Convention and knew of all the deliberations that had taken place. Their opponents had no such knowledge because those deliberations had not been open to the public. Thus, the Anti-Federalists were at a disadvantage in terms of information about the document. The Federalists also had time, power, and money on their side. Those who had access to the best communications were Federalists—mostly wealthy bankers, lawyers, plantation owners, and merchants living in urban areas, where communications were better. The Federalist campaign was organized relatively quickly and effectively to elect Federalists as delegates to the state ratifying conventions.

The Anti-Federalists, however, had at least one strong point in their favor: they stood for the status quo. In general, the greater burden is always placed on those advocating change.

The *Federalist Papers* In New York, opponents of the Constitution were quick to attack it. Alexander Hamilton answered their attacks in newspaper columns over the signature "Caesar." When the Caesar letters had little effect, Hamilton switched to the pseudonym Publius and secured two collaborators—John Jay and James Madison. In a very short time, those three political figures wrote a series of 85 essays in defense of the Constitution and of a republican form of government. John Jay contributed only 5 essays due to illness, James Madison penned 29 of the *Federalist Papers*, and Hamilton wrote the other 51 essays.

These widely read essays, called the *Federalist Papers*, appeared in New York newspapers from October 1787 to August 1788 and were reprinted in the newspapers of other states. Although we do not know for certain who wrote every one, it is apparent that Hamilton was responsible for about two-thirds of the essays. These included the most important ones, which interpreted the Constitution, explained the various powers of the three branches, and presented a theory of *judicial review*—to be discussed later in this chapter. Madison's Federalist #10 (see Appendix C), however, is considered a classic in political theory; it deals with the nature of groups, or factions, as he called them. Despite the rapidity with which the *Federalist Papers* were written, they are considered by many to be perhaps the best example of political theorizing ever produced in the United States.[12]

Federalist
The name given to one who was in favor of the adoption of the U.S. Constitution and the creation of a federal union with a strong central government.

Anti-Federalist
An individual who opposed the ratification of the new Constitution in 1787. The Anti-Federalists were opposed to a strong central government.

---

11 There is some irony here. At the Constitutional Convention, those opposed to a strong central government pushed for a federal system because such a system would allow the states to retain some of their sovereign rights (see Chapter 3). The label Anti-Federalists thus contradicted their essential views.

12 Some scholars believe that the *Federalist Papers* played only a minor role in securing ratification of the Constitution. Even if this is true, they still have lasting value as an authoritative explanation of the Constitution.

The Anti-Federalist Response The Anti-Federalists used such pseudonyms as Montezuma and Philadelphiensis in their replies. Many of their attacks on the Constitution were also brilliant. The Anti-Federalists claimed that the Constitution was written by aristocrats and would lead to aristocratic tyranny. More important, the Anti-Federalists believed that the Constitution would create an overbearing and overburdening central government hostile to personal liberty. (The Constitution said nothing about freedom of the press, freedom of religion, or any other individual liberty.) They wanted to include a list of guaranteed liberties, or a bill of rights. Finally, the Anti-Federalists decried the weakened power of the states.

The Anti-Federalists cannot be dismissed as unpatriotic extremists. They included such patriots as Patrick Henry and Samuel Adams. They were arguing what had been the most prevalent contemporary opinion. This view derived from the French political philosopher Montesquieu, who believed that liberty was safe only in relatively small societies governed by direct democracy or by a large legislature with small districts. The Madisonian view favoring a large republic, particularly as expressed in Federalist #10 and #51 (see Appendix C), was actually the more *unpopular* view at the time. Madison was probably convincing because citizens were already persuaded that a strong national government was necessary to combat foreign enemies and to prevent domestic insurrections. Still, some researchers believe it was mainly the bitter experiences with the Articles of Confederation, rather than Madison's arguments, that persuaded the state conventions to ratify the Constitution.[13]

The March to the Finish

The struggle for ratification continued. Strong majorities were procured in Delaware, Pennsylvania, New Jersey, Georgia, and Connecticut. After a bitter struggle in Massachusetts, that state ratified the Constitution by a narrow margin on February 6, 1788. By the spring, Maryland and South Carolina had ratified by sizable majorities. Then on June 21, New Hampshire became the ninth state to ratify the Constitution. Although the Constitution was formally in effect, this meant little without Virginia and New York—the latter did not ratify for another month (see Table 2-3).

Did the Majority of Americans Support the Constitution?

In 1913, historian Charles Beard published *An Economic Interpretation of the Constitution of the United States.*[14] This book launched a debate that has continued ever since—the debate over whether the Constitution was supported by a majority of Americans.

Beard's central thesis was that the Constitution had been produced primarily by wealthy property owners who desired a stronger government able to protect their property rights. Beard also claimed that the Constitution had been imposed by undemocratic methods to prevent democratic majorities from exercising real power. He pointed out that there was never any popular vote on whether to hold a constitutional convention in the first place.

13 Of particular interest is the view of the Anti-Federalist position contained in Herbert J. Storing, *What the Anti-Federalists Were For* (Chicago, IL: University of Chicago Press, 1981). Storing also edited seven volumes of the Anti-Federalist writings, *The Complete Anti-Federalist* (Chicago, IL: University of Chicago Press, 1981). See also Josephine F. Pacheco, *Antifederalism: The Legacy of George Mason* (Fairfax, VA: George Mason University Press, 1992).

14 Charles A. Beard, *An Economic Interpretation of the Constitution of the United States* (New York: Macmillan, 1913; New York: Free Press, 1986).

Table 2-3 ▶ Ratification of the Constitution

STATE	DATE	VOTE FOR–AGAINST
Delaware	Dec. 7, 1787	30–0
Pennsylvania	Dec. 12, 1787	43–23
New Jersey	Dec. 18, 1787	38–0
Georgia	Jan. 2, 1788	26–0
Connecticut	Jan. 9, 1788	128–40
Massachusetts	Feb. 6, 1788	187–168
Maryland	Apr. 28, 1788	63–11
South Carolina	May 23, 1788	149–73
New Hampshire	June 21, 1788	57–46
Virginia	June 25, 1788	89–79
New York	July 26, 1788	30–27
North Carolina	Nov. 21, 1789*	194–77
Rhode Island	May 29, 1790	34–32

*Ratification was originally defeated on August 4, 1788, by a vote of 84–184.

Furthermore, even if such a vote had been taken, state laws generally restricted voting rights to property-owning white males, meaning that most people in the country (white males without property, women, Native Americans, and slaves) were not eligible to vote. Finally, Beard pointed out that even the word *democracy* was distasteful to the founders. The term was often used by conservatives to smear their opponents. Beard's explanation for the revolution and constitution prevailed through the 1950s and enjoys some favor even today.

State Ratifying Conventions As for the various state ratifying conventions, the delegates had been selected by only 150,000 of the approximately 4 million citizens. That does not seem very democratic—at least not by today's standards. Some historians have suggested that if a Gallup poll could have been taken at that time, the Anti-Federalists would probably have outnumbered the Federalists.[15]

Support Was Probably Widespread Much has also been made of the various machinations used by the Federalists to ensure the Constitution's ratification (and they did resort to a variety of devious tactics, including purchasing at least one printing press to prevent the publication of Anti-Federalist sentiments). Yet the perception that a strong central government was necessary to keep order and protect the public welfare appears to have been fairly pervasive among all classes—rich and poor alike.

Further, although the need for strong government was a major argument in favor of adopting the Constitution, even the Federalists sought to craft a limited government. Compared with constitutions adopted by other nations in later years, the U.S. Constitution, through its checks and balances, favors limited government over "energetic" government to a marked degree.

did you know?

Not all of the states had ratified the Constitution by April 30, 1789, when George Washington became president of the United States of America.

15 Jim Powell, "James Madison—Checks and Balances to Limit Government Power," *The Freeman*, March 1996, p. 178.

What Makes a Constitution?

When Americans think of the Constitution, most visualize an old handwritten document that is protected in our National Archives. They may also reflect on its basic principles—checks and balances, separation of powers, the Bill of Rights—that structure how the national government carries out its work. The U.S. Constitution, however, was written more than 200 years ago for a relatively small, mostly rural nation. The struggle to write a constitution continues for nations such as Egypt, which has approved two different constitutions within the last few years.

What Should Be Included?

In February 2012, after the overthrow of the repressive Mubarak government, associate justice of the Supreme Court Ruth Bader Ginsburg visited Egypt and gave an interview broadcast on YouTube. Ginsburg's remarks were criticized by some because she suggested that the Egyptians not use our constitution as a model. Although she praised many aspects of the American document, she recommended that the Egyptians look at newer charters such as that of South Africa, the Canadian charter of rights and freedoms, and the Kenyan constitution.

What kinds of models was the justice suggesting? What provisions are included in these new constitutions that make them more appropriate to a nation like Egypt? At the time of her visit, the Egyptian people, who had just ended a repressive military regime, were engaged in the creation of a new constitution. President Morsi immediately implemented the new constitution in 2012. In less than one year, however, protests against the new government erupted. Many Egyptians believed that the Morsi constitution was leading to more Islamist control of society. The military took power in August 2013. A referendum on amendments to the constitution was approved in January 2014. Like other nations writing constitutions after World War II, the Egyptian people must deal with deep religious divisions and serious economic woes. Justice Ginsburg called attention to the South African constitution's bill of rights. It is, in comparison to the U.S. Constitution, very inclusive and modern in its interpretation of human rights. All of the political rights included in the American model are there, but, in addition, citizens are guaranteed the freedom to travel; the right to housing; the right to basic education; the right to food, water, and social assistance from the government; and the right to unionize. The government may not discriminate on the basis of race, gender, sex, pregnancy, religion, ethnic or social origin, sexual orientation, and so on.

Is It a Real Constitution?

During the Cold War between the United States and the Soviet Union, the Soviet republics held elections and called themselves democratic nations. They all had written constitutions to which they strictly adhered. The elections were not contested, and no opposition candidates or political parties emerged. Newspapers and other media were strictly controlled, as was any access to external information. Today, all of the former Soviet republics have new constitutions, and many are democracies with the same freedoms as other nations in Western Europe or the United States.

Similarly, the People's Republic of North Korea has a fairly new constitution (1998) and claims to be democratic. The military and the premier, Kim Jong-un, however, direct all aspects of life there, including limiting the frequencies available on radios and televisions to those approved by the government. So, it seems that just having a written

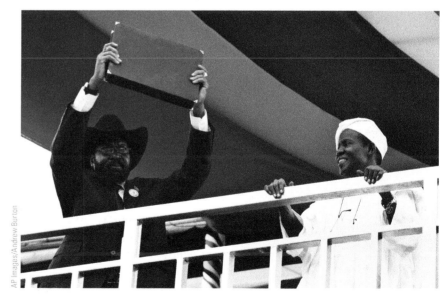

Image 2-6 South Sudan President Salva Kiir lifts South Sudan's new constitution to the crowds of people attending an independence ceremony in Juba, South Sudan, on Saturday July 9, 2011.

(Continued)

(Continued)

document outlining the structures of government and freedoms of the people may not be enough to guarantee any form of democratic government, at least in the sense that we know it. As Justice Ginsburg put it, "The spirit of liberty has to be in the population."* In the United States, the Constitution has lasted, in part, because the people have continued to share the values of those who wrote the document and to transmit those ideas to their children and to those who immigrated to the United States since its founding.

If you would like to read the constitution of any country in the world, go to constituteproject.org.

* "Ruth Bader Ginsburg Talks Constitution, Women and Liberty on Egyptian TV," www.huffingtonpost.com/2012/02/01/justice-ruth-bader-ginsburg-egypt _n_1248527.html. February 1, 2012.

For Critical Analysis

1. Do you think the United States could have survived without a written constitution? Why is it so difficult for countries in transition to draft new constitutions?

2. Do you agree with Justice Ginsburg that modern constitutions should affirm social and economic rights in addition to political rights? If you had the opportunity to add provisions to the U.S. Constitution drawn from the constitutions of other nations, what would you add and why?

The Bill of Rights

■ **2.5** Explain why some states and their citizens especially wanted the Constitution to include a bill of rights.

The U.S. Constitution would not have been ratified in several important states if the Federalists had not assured the states that amendments to the Constitution would be passed to protect individual liberties against incursions by the national government. The idea of including certain rights in the Constitution had been discussed in the convention. There were those who believed that including these rights was simply unnecessary, whereas others suggested that carefully articulating certain rights might encourage the new national government to abuse any that were not specifically defined. Some rights, including the prohibition of *ex post facto lawmaking*, were included in the document. *Ex post facto lawmaking* is passing laws that make one liable for an act that has already taken place. Also prohibited were *bills of attainder*, through which a legislature could pass judgment on someone without legal process. Many of the recommendations of the state ratifying conventions, however, included specific rights that were considered later by James Madison as he labored to draft what became the Bill of Rights.

A "Bill of Limits"

Although called the Bill of Rights, essentially the first 10 amendments to the Constitution were a "bill of limits" because the amendments limited the powers of the national government over the rights and liberties of individuals.

Madison had to cull through more than 200 state recommendations.[16] It was no small task, and in retrospect he chose remarkably well. One of the rights appropriate for constitutional protection that he left out was equal protection under the laws—but that was not commonly regarded as a basic right at that time. Not until 1868 did the states ratify an amendment guaranteeing that no state shall deny equal protection to any person. (The Supreme Court has since applied this guarantee to certain actions of the federal government as well.)

The final number of amendments that Madison and a specially appointed committee came up with was 17. Congress tightened the language somewhat and eliminated five of the amendments. Of the remaining 12, 2—dealing with the apportionment of representatives and the compensation of the members of Congress—were not ratified immediately by the states. Eventually, Supreme Court decisions led to reform of the apportionment process. The amendment on the compensation of members of Congress was ratified 203 years later in 1992, becoming the 27th Amendment.

No Explicit Limits on State Government Powers

On December 15, 1791, the national Bill of Rights was adopted when Virginia agreed to ratify the ten amendments. On ratification, the Bill of Rights became part of the U.S. Constitution. The basic structure of American government had already been established. Now the fundamental rights and liberties of individuals were protected, at least in theory, at the national level. The proposed amendment that Madison characterized as "the most valuable amendment in the whole lot"—which would have prohibited the states from infringing on the freedoms of conscience, press, and jury trial—had been eliminated by the Senate. Thus, the Bill of Rights as adopted did not limit state power, and individual citizens had to rely on the guarantees contained in a particular state constitution or state bill of rights. The country had to wait until the violence of the Civil War before significant limitations on state power in the form of the Fourteenth Amendment became part of the national Constitution.

Altering the Constitution: The Formal Amendment Process

■ **2.6** Demonstrate understanding of the formal and informal processes for amending the U.S. Constitution.

The U.S. Constitution consists of 7,000 words and is shorter than any state constitution except that of Vermont, which has 6,880 words. One of the reasons the U.S. Constitution is relatively short is that the founders intended it to be only a framework for the new government, to be interpreted by succeeding generations. The formal amending procedure does not allow for changes to be made easily, which has kept it short. Article V of the Constitution outlines the ways in which amendments may be proposed and ratified (see Figure 2-3).

---

16 For details on these recommendations, including their sources, see Leonard W. Levy, *Origins of the Bill of Rights* (New Haven, CT: Yale University Press, 1999).

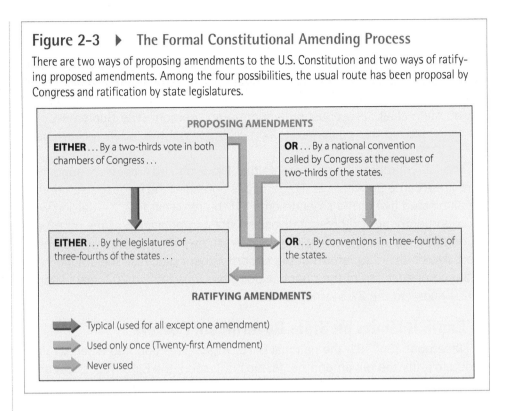

Figure 2–3 ▶ The Formal Constitutional Amending Process

There are two ways of proposing amendments to the U.S. Constitution and two ways of ratifying proposed amendments. Among the four possibilities, the usual route has been proposal by Congress and ratification by state legislatures.

Two formal methods of proposing an amendment to the Constitution are available: (1) a two-thirds vote in each chamber of Congress or (2) a national convention that is called by Congress at the request of two-thirds of the state legislatures (the second method has never been used).

Ratification can occur by one of two methods: (1) by a positive vote in three-fourths of the legislatures of the various states or (2) by special conventions called in the states and a positive vote in three-fourths of them. The second method has been used only once, to repeal Prohibition (the ban on the production and sale of alcoholic beverages). That situation was exceptional because it involved an amendment (the Twenty-first) to repeal an amendment (the Eighteenth, which had created Prohibition). State conventions were necessary for repeal of the Eighteenth Amendment because the "pro-dry" legislatures in the most conservative states would never have passed the repeal. (Note that Congress determines the method of ratification to be used by all states for each proposed constitutional amendment.)

Many Amendments Are Proposed; Few Are Accepted

Congress has considered more than 11,000 amendments to the Constitution. Many proposed amendments have been advanced to address highly specific problems. An argument against such narrow amendments has been that amendments ought to embody broad principles, in the way that the existing Constitution does. For that reason, many people have opposed such narrow amendments as one to prohibit the burning or defacing of the American flag.

Only 33 amendments have been submitted to the states after having been approved by the required two-thirds vote in each chamber of Congress, and only 27 have been ratified—see Table 2-4. (The full annotated text of the U.S. Constitution, including its amendments, is presented in Appendix B at the end of this book.) It should be clear that the amendment process is much more

did you know?

About 11,000 amendments have been proposed to the Constitution. Five hundred of those have been to change the electoral college process used to elect the president.

Table 2-4 ▶ Amendments to the Constitution

AMENDMENT	SUBJECT	YEAR ADOPTED	TIME REQUIRED FOR RATIFICATION
First to Tenth	The Bill of Rights	1791	2 years, 2 months, 20 days
Eleventh	Immunity of states from certain suits	1795	11 months, 3 days
Twelfth	Changes in electoral college procedure	1804	6 months, 3 days
Thirteenth	Prohibition of slavery	1865	10 months, 3 days
Fourteenth	Citizenship, due process, and equal protection	1868	2 years, 26 days
Fifteenth	No denial of vote because of race, color, or previous condition of servitude	1870	11 months, 8 days
Sixteenth	Power of Congress to tax income	1913	3 years, 6 months, 22 days
Seventeenth	Direct election of U.S. senators	1913	10 months, 26 days
Eighteenth	National (liquor) prohibition	1919	1 year, 29 days
Nineteenth	Women's right to vote	1920	1 year, 2 months, 14 days
Twentieth	Change of dates for congressional and presidential terms	1933	10 months, 21 days
Twenty-first	Repeal of the Eighteenth Amendment	1933	9 months, 15 days
Twenty-second	Limit on presidential tenure	1951	3 years, 11 months, 3 days
Twenty-third	District of Columbia electoral vote	1961	9 months, 13 days
Twenty-fourth	Prohibition of tax payment as a qualification to vote in federal elections	1964	1 year, 4 months, 9 days
Twenty-fifth	Procedures for determining presidential disability and presidential succession and for filling a vice presidential vacancy	1967	1 year, 7 months, 4 days
Twenty-sixth	Prohibition of setting minimum voting age above 18 in any election	1971	3 months, 7 days
Twenty-seventh	Prohibition of Congress's voting itself a raise that takes effect before the next election	1992	203 years

difficult than a graphic depiction such as Figure 2-3 can indicate. Because of competing social and economic interests, the requirement that two-thirds of both the House and Senate approve the amendments is difficult to achieve. Thirty-four senators, representing only 17 sparsely populated states, could block any amendment. For example, the Republican-controlled House approved the Balanced Budget Amendment within the first 100 days of the 104th Congress in 1995, but it was defeated in the Senate by one vote.

After approval by Congress, the process becomes even more arduous. Three-fourths of the state legislatures must approve the amendment. Only those amendments that have wide popular support across parties and in all regions of the country are likely to be approved.

Limits on Ratification

A reading of Article V of the Constitution reveals that the framers of the Constitution specified no time limit on the ratification process. The Supreme Court has held that Congress can specify a time for ratification as long as it is "reasonable." Since 1919, most proposed amendments have included a requirement that ratification be obtained within seven years. This was the case with the proposed Equal Rights Amendment, which sought to guarantee equal rights for women. When three-fourths of the states had not ratified in the allotted seven years, however, Congress extended the limit by an additional three years and three months. That extension expired on June 30, 1982, and the amendment still had not been ratified. Another proposed amendment, which would have guaranteed congressional representation to the District of Columbia, fell far short of the 38 state ratifications needed before its August 22, 1985, deadline.

On May 7, 1992, Michigan became the thirty-eighth state to ratify the Twenty-seventh Amendment (on congressional compensation)—one of the two "lost" amendments of the 12 that originally were sent to the states in 1789. Because most of the amendments proposed in recent years have been given a time limit of only seven years by Congress, it was questionable for a time whether the amendment would take effect even if the necessary number of states ratified it. Hundreds of years is apparently not too great a lapse in time, because the amendment was certified as legitimate by archivist Don Wilson of the National Archives on May 18, 1992.

The National Convention Provision

The Constitution provides that a national convention requested by the legislatures of two-thirds of the states can propose a constitutional amendment. Congress has received approximately 400 convention applications since the Constitution was ratified; every state has applied at least once. Fewer than 20 applications were submitted during the Constitution's first hundred years, but more than 150 have been filed in the last two decades. No national convention has been held since 1787, and most national political and judicial leaders are uneasy about the prospect of convening a body that conceivably could do as the Constitutional Convention did—create a new form of government. The state legislative bodies that originate national convention applications, however, do not appear to be uncomfortable with such a constitutional modification process; more than 230 state constitutional conventions have been held.

Informal Methods of Constitutional Change

Formal amendments are one way of changing our Constitution, and, as is obvious from their small number, they have been resorted to infrequently and are very difficult to pass and ratify. If we don't include the first ten amendments (the Bill of Rights), which were adopted soon after the ratification of the Constitution, only 17 formal alterations have been made to the Constitution in the more than 200 years of its existence.

Just looking at the small number of amendments vastly understates the ability of the Constitution to adjust to changing times. The brevity and ambiguity of the original document have permitted great alterations in the Constitution by way of varying interpretations over time. As the United States grew, both in population and territory, new social and political realities emerged. Congress, presidents, and the courts found it necessary to interpret the Constitution's provisions in light of these new realities. The Constitution

A Divergent Election

For the fifth time in U.S. history, and the second time in this century, the winner of the popular vote became president. A divergent election is one in which the winner of the electoral college (and therefore the presidency) does not win the popular vote.

According to analysis by the Pew Research Center, the 2016 mismatch between the electoral and popular votes came about because Donald Trump won several large states by very narrow margins (Florida, Pennsylvania, and Wisconsin) and thus received all of their electoral votes while Hillary Clinton won other large states (California, Illinois, and New York) by much wider margins, adding more votes to the popular vote tally. Even when the same candidate wins both the popular vote and the electoral vote, the system of awarding electoral votes inflates the margin of victory. Historically, the winner's electoral vote share has been 1.36 times his popular vote share. Donald Trump's electoral college victory is likely to be 1.20 times his popular vote share.

According to the National Archives, there have been more proposed constitutional amendments to change the electoral college than any other topic since the founding. When asked by pollsters, only 30 percent of Americans would choose to continue the current system of electing a president. So why hasn't this unique feature of American politics been changed? First, it would require an amendment to the Constitution—a difficult process requiring action by Congress and ratification by 38 states. Following the 2016 election, Republicans control Congress and the executive and legislature in 24 states.

For Critical Analysis

1. The authors of the Constitution made its amendment difficult but not impossible. Is eliminating the electoral college an amendment you would support? Why or why not?

2. In what ways would relying on the popular vote to elect the president be better or worse than the electoral college?

has proved to be a remarkably flexible document, adapting itself repeatedly to new events and concerns.

Congressional Legislation

The Constitution gives Congress broad powers to carry out its duties as the nation's legislative body. For example, Article I, Section 8 of the Constitution gives Congress the power to regulate foreign and interstate commerce. Although the Constitution has no clear definition of foreign commerce or interstate commerce, Congress has cited the *commerce clause* as the basis for passing thousands of laws that have defined the meaning of foreign and interstate commerce.

Similarly, Article III, Section 1 states that the national judiciary shall consist of one supreme court and "such inferior courts, as Congress may from time to time ordain and establish." Through a series of acts, Congress has used this broad provision to establish the federal court system of today, which includes the Supreme Court, the courts of appeal, and district courts. This provision allows Congress to create a court such as the Foreign Intelligence Surveillance Act (FISA) court to review requests for wiretapping suspected terrorists.

In addition, Congress has frequently delegated to federal agencies the legislative power to write regulations. These regulations, numbering in the tens of thousands, become law unless challenged in the court system. Nowhere does the Constitution outline this delegation of legislative authority.

Presidential Actions

Even though the Constitution does not expressly authorize the president to propose bills or even budgets to Congress, presidents since the time of Woodrow Wilson's administration (1913–1921) have proposed hundreds of bills to Congress each year.[17] Presidents have also relied on their Article II authority as commander in chief of the nation's armed forces to send American troops abroad into combat, although the Constitution provides that only Congress has the power to declare war.

The president's powers in wartime have waxed and waned through the course of American history. President Abraham Lincoln instituted a draft and suspended several civil liberties during the Civil War. During World War II, President Franklin Roosevelt approved the internment of thousands of Japanese American citizens. President George W. Bush significantly expanded presidential power in the wake of the terrorist attacks of 2001, especially in regard to the handling of individuals who could be defined as "enemy combatants." The creation of the detention facility at Guantánamo Bay, Cuba, made it possible for those prisoners to be held and interrogated by the military under the full control of the executive branch. After 2010, when President Obama faced a divided Congress, he, too, began to use executive power more liberally on gun control, gay rights, the minimum wage, contraception, and climate change. Obama created the DREAM Act, which allows the children of unauthorized immigrants to stay in the country if they are attending college or in the military. He also raised the minimum wage for federal employees without the authorization of Congress. In addition, presidents have conducted foreign affairs by the use of executive agreements, which are legally binding documents made between the president and a foreign head of state. The Constitution does not mention such agreements.

Judicial Review

Another way of changing the Constitution—or of making it more flexible—is through the power of judicial review. Judicial review refers to the power of U.S. courts to examine the constitutionality of actions undertaken by the legislative and executive branches of government. A state court, for example, may rule that a statute enacted by the state legislature is unconstitutional. Federal courts (and, ultimately, the U.S. Supreme Court) may rule unconstitutional not only acts of Congress and decisions of the national executive branch, but also state statutes, state executive actions, and even provisions of state constitutions.

Not a Novel Concept   The Constitution does not specifically mention the power of judicial review. Those in attendance at the Constitutional Convention, however, probably expected that the courts would have some authority to review the legality of acts by the executive and legislative branches because, under the common-law tradition inherited from England, courts exercised this authority. Alexander Hamilton, in Federalist #78, explicitly outlined the concept of judicial review. Whether the power of judicial review can be justified constitutionally is a question that has been subject to some debate, particularly in recent years. For now, suffice it to say that in 1803, the Supreme Court claimed

---

17 Note, though, that the Constitution, in Article II, Section 3, does state that the president "shall from time to time . . . recommend to [Congress's] consideration such measures as he shall judge necessary and expedient." Some scholars interpret this phrase to mean that the president has the constitutional authority to propose bills and budgets to Congress for consideration.

this power for itself in *Marbury v. Madison*, in which the Court ruled that a particular provision of an act of Congress was unconstitutional.[18]

Allows the Court to Adapt the Constitution   Through the process of judicial review, the Supreme Court adapts the Constitution to modern situations. Electronic technology, for example, did not exist when the Constitution was ratified. Nonetheless, the Supreme Court has used the Fourth Amendment guarantees against unreasonable searches and seizures to place limits on the use of wiretapping and other electronic eavesdropping methods by government officials. The Court has needed to decide whether antiterrorism laws passed by Congress or state legislatures or executive orders declared by the president violate the Fourth Amendment or other constitutional provisions. Additionally, the Supreme Court has changed its interpretation of the Constitution in accordance with changing values. It ruled in 1896 that "separate-but-equal" public facilities for African Americans were constitutional, but by 1954, the times had changed, and the Supreme Court reversed that decision.[19] Woodrow Wilson summarized the Supreme Court's work when he described it as "a constitutional convention in continuous session." Basically, the law is what the Supreme Court says it is at any given time, making the Court's composition very important.

Interpretation, Custom, and Usage

The Constitution has also been changed through interpretation by both Congress and the president. Originally, the president had a staff consisting of personal secretaries and a few others. Today, because Congress delegates specific tasks to the president and the chief executive assumes political leadership, the executive office staff alone has increased to several thousand persons. The executive branch provides legislative leadership far beyond the expectations of the founders.

Changes in the ways of doing political business have also altered the Constitution. The Constitution does not mention political parties, yet these informal, "extraconstitutional" organizations make the nominations for offices, run the campaigns, organize the members of Congress, and in fact change the election system from time to time. The emergence and evolution of the party system, for example, has changed the way the president is elected. The entire nominating process, with its use of primary elections and caucuses to choose delegates to the party's nominating convention, is the creation of the two major political parties. The president is then selected by the electors who are, in fact, chosen by the parties and are pledged to a party's candidate.

A book by Bruce Ackerman argues that the rise of political parties and growth of the executive represent the failure of the Founding Fathers to understand how the government would develop over time. He proposes that the only reason the system has maintained its checks is the development of the Supreme Court into the guarantor of our rights and liberties.[20] Perhaps most striking, the Constitution has been adapted from serving the needs of a small, rural republic to providing a framework of government for an industrial giant with vast geographic, natural, and human resources.

---

18 5 U.S. 137 (1803).

19 *Brown v. Board of Education of Topeka*, 347 U.S. 483 (1954).

20 Bruce Ackerman, *The Failure of the Founding Fathers: Jefferson, Marshall, and the Rise of Presidential Democracy* (Cambridge, MA: The Belknap Press, 2005).

Key Terms

Anti-Federalist 56	**federal system** 55	**separation of powers** 53
bicameral legislature 50	**Great Compromise** 51	**social contract** 43
checks and balances 53	**Madisonian model** 53	**state** 44
confederation 43	**natural rights** 42	**supremacy doctrine** 50
electoral college 54	**ratification** 55	**unicameral legislature** 43
Federalist 56	**representative assembly** 38	

Chapter Summary

■ **2.1** The first permanent English colonies were established at Jamestown in 1607 and Plymouth in 1620. The Mayflower Compact created the first formal government for the British colonists. By the mid-1700s, other British colonies had been established along the Atlantic seaboard from Georgia to Maine.

■ **2.1** In 1763, the British tried to impose a series of taxes and legislative acts on their increasingly independent-minded colonies. The colonists responded with boycotts of British products and protests. Representatives of the colonies formed the First Continental Congress in 1774. The delegates sent a petition to the British king expressing their grievances. The Second Continental Congress established an army in 1775 to defend the colonists against attacks by British soldiers.

■ **2.1** On July 4, 1776, the Second Continental Congress approved the Declaration of Independence. Perhaps the most revolutionary aspects of the Declaration were its assumptions that people have natural rights to life, liberty, and the pursuit of happiness; that governments derive their power from the consent of the governed; and that people have a right to overthrow oppressive governments.

■ **2.1** Based on their understanding of natural rights and the social contract, as well as their experience with an oppressive British regime, all of the colonies adopted written constitutions during the Revolutionary War. Most of these gave great power to their legislatures and restrained the power of the executive branch.

■ **2.2** At the end of the Revolutionary War, the states had signed the Articles of Confederation, creating a weak central government with few powers. In this government, each state had one vote and there was no executive. The Congress had no power to raise revenue and virtually no way to amend the Articles. The Articles proved to be unworkable because the national government had no way to ensure compliance by the states with such measures as securing tax revenues.

■ **2.3** General dissatisfaction with the Articles of Confederation prompted the call for a convention at Philadelphia in 1787. Although the delegates ostensibly convened to amend the Articles, the discussions soon focused on creating a constitution for a new form of government. The Virginia plan and the New Jersey plan did not garner widespread support. The Great Compromise offered by Connecticut helped to break the large-state/small-state disputes dividing the delegates. The Three-Fifths Compromise, which counted slaves as three-fifths of a person for purposes of representation, was adopted to keep the Southern states from leaving the union.

■ **2.4** The final version of the Constitution provided for the separation of powers, checks and balances, and a federal form of government. The principles of separation of powers and checks and balances were intended to prevent any one branch of the government from becoming too powerful. Each branch of government needs to cooperate with the other branches for the government to be effective.

■ **2.5** Fears of a strong central government prompted the addition of the Bill of Rights to the Constitution. The Bill of Rights secured for Americans a wide variety of freedoms, including the freedoms of religion, speech, and assembly. It was initially applied only to the federal government, but amendments to the Constitution following the Civil War made it clear that the Bill of Rights would apply to the states as well.

■ **2.6** An amendment to the Constitution may be proposed either by a two-thirds vote in each house of Congress or by a national convention called by Congress at the request of two-thirds of the state legislatures. Ratification can occur either by a positive vote in three-fourths of the legislatures of the various states or by a positive vote in three-fourths of special conventions called in the states for the specific purpose of ratifying the proposed amendment. The process for amending the Constitution was made very difficult to ensure that most of the states and the majority of both houses agree to the proposed change. Informal methods of constitutional change include congressional legislation, presidential actions, judicial review, and changing interpretations of the Constitution.

Selected Resources

PRINT RESOURCES

Armitage, David. *The Declaration of Independence: A Global History* (Cambridge, MA: Harvard University Press, 2007). The author examines the history of the Declaration of Independence and then looks at its impact on the peoples and governments of other nations.

Bernstein, R. B. *The Founding Fathers Reconsidered* (New York: Oxford University Press, 2011). The author, based on extensive research, presents portraits of the Founding Fathers as real people with flaws, ambitions, rivalries, and ideas of how to build a new nation.

Bilder, Mary Sarah. *Madison's Hand: Revising the Constitutional Convention.* (Boston: Harvard University Press, 2015). Using digital technologies and textual analysis, the author argues that Madison's Notes on the 1787 Constitutional Convention are far from objective observations. Her analysis reveals that Madison revised the Notes to a far greater extent than previously recognized.

Breyer, Stephen G. *Active Liberty: Interpreting Our Democratic Constitution* (New York: Knopf, 2005). Supreme Court Justice Stephen Breyer offers his thoughts on the Constitution as a living document. He argues that the genius of the Constitution rests in the adaptability of its great principles to cope with current problems.

Hamilton, Alexander, et al. *The Federalist: The Famous Papers on the Principles of American Government.* Benjamin F. Wright, ed. (New York: Friedman/Fairfax Publishing, 2002). This is an updated version of the papers written by Alexander Hamilton, James Madison, and John Jay and published in the *New York Packet* in support of the ratification of the Constitution.

Meacham, Jon. *Jefferson: The Pursuit of Power* (New York: Random House, 2012). Meacham presents a biography of Jefferson as a premier politician, power broker, strategist, and managerial president moving the young nation forward.

MEDIA RESOURCES

12 Years a Slave—This 2013 film portrays the true story of Solomon Northup, a free African American who is kidnapped and sold into slavery in the 1830s.

Good Night and Good Luck—In this 2005 feature film, George Clooney plays the famous journalist Edward R. Murrow, who works to discredit the tactics of Senator Joseph McCarthy in the 1950s. As McCarthy tries to ferret out and punish communist sympathizers, Murrow defends aspects of the Bill of Rights: freedom of press, of speech, and of the right to associate with others.

John Adams—An Emmy award–winning mini-series focuses on John Adams's role in starting the Revolutionary War and ends with his actions as the first vice president of the United States. The series aired in 2008.

ONLINE RESOURCES

Avalon Project—provides digital documents relevant to law, history, and diplomacy, including James Madison's notes on the Constitutional Convention debates, taken from his daily journal: http://avalon.law.yale.edu/

FindLaw.com—comprehensive resource for legal information: www.findlaw.com/casecode/state.html

National Constitution Center—offers information on the Constitution, including its history, current debates over constitutional provisions, and news articles: www.constitutioncenter.org

3

Federalism

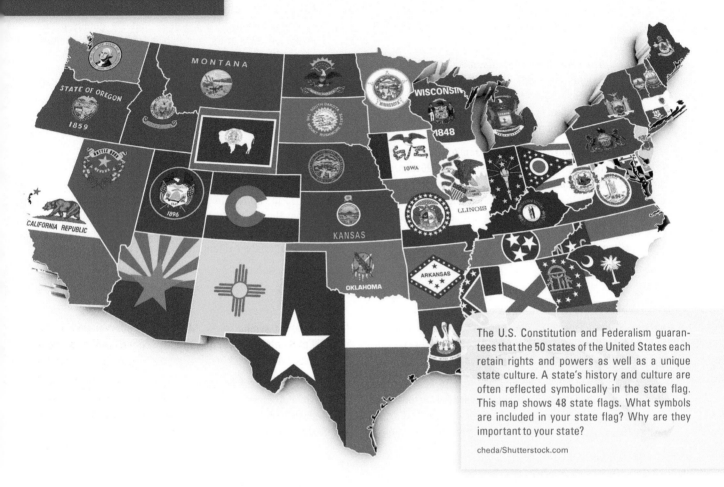

The U.S. Constitution and Federalism guarantees that the **50 states** of the United States each retain rights and powers as well as a unique state culture. A state's history and culture are often reflected symbolically in the state flag. This map shows 48 state flags. What symbols are included in your state flag? Why are they important to your state?

cheda/Shutterstock.com

LEARNING OBJECTIVES

After reading this chapter, you will be able to:

■ **3.1** Define federalism and contrast the federal system of government with the unitary and confederal systems in explaining where governmental power lies.

■ **3.2** Identify two advantages and two disadvantages of the U.S. federal system.

■ **3.3** Locate the sources of federalism in the U.S. Constitution; using the terms *vertical control* and *horizontal control*, explain how the founders intended federalism

and separation of powers to limit the expansion of national power.

■ **3.4** Explain the historical evolution of federalism as a result of the Marshall Court, the Civil War, the New Deal, civil rights, and federal grant making.

■ **3.5** Evaluate immigration policy as a challenge to modern federalism.

What if... What if *Roe v. Wade* Were Overturned?

If the Supreme Court overturned *Roe v. Wade*, the authority to regulate abortion would fall again to the states. Before the case, each state decided whether abortion would be legal within its borders. State legislatures made the laws that covered abortion. Some critics of the constitutional merits of *Roe v. Wade* have argued that allowing the Supreme Court to decide the legality of abortion nationwide is undemocratic because the justices are not elected officials. In contrast, if state legislatures regained the power to create abortion policy, the resulting laws would more closely reflect the majority opinion of each state's voters rather than a national consensus. Researchers find that public opinion regarding abortion has been remarkably stable since the *Roe v. Wade* ruling. Since 1975, Gallup has asked "Should abortion be legal in certain circumstances?" In 1975, 54 percent said yes—the same percentage replying in the affirmative in 2015. Most Americans do not want *Roe* overturned, but they are willing to put significant restrictions on abortion procedures.

The Possibility of State Bans on Abortion

Simply overturning *Roe v. Wade* would not make abortion in the United States illegal overnight. In many states, abortion rights are strongly valued, and the legislatures in those states would not consider measures to ban abortion or to further restrict access to abortion. Some states have laws that would protect abortion rights even if *Roe v. Wade* were overturned. Access to abortions would likely continue in the West Coast states and in much of the Northeast. In much of the South and the Midwest, however, abortion could be seriously restricted or even banned.

State Challenges to *Roe v. Wade*

Texas is the latest state to adopt more stringent regulations on abortion. A statute signed into law in 2013 by then-governor Rick Perry includes a ban on abortion procedures at 20 weeks post-fertilization and articulates a compelling state interest to protect fetuses from pain. The law requires that a doctor who performs abortions have admitting privileges at a nearby hospital and mandates that clinics meet the same standards as other surgical health-care facilities in the state. This last provision has cut the number of clinics providing abortion services in half, with more likely to close because they cannot meet the criteria for surgical centers under the law, leaving only six in the state.

Opposition to the bill came from some within the Texas legislature. Wendy Davis filibustered the bill in an attempt to delay a vote long enough for the legislative session to end. Governor Perry called a second special session, and the bill passed. Ultimately, the Supreme Court ruled (5-3) that the Texas law imposed an unlawful burden on a woman seeking an abortion.

On February 13, 2016, Justice Antonin Scalia, a stalwart conservative and opponent of abortion rights, passed away. Republicans in the Senate vowed not to hold confirmation hearings on anyone President Obama nominated, arguing that the choice should be left to the next president. Regardless of the composition of the Supreme Court, the primary holding in *Roe* is vulnerable due to restrictions imposed by the states. In 2015 alone, states enacted 57 restrictions on abortions, according to the Guttmacher Institute. Under the Affordable Care Act, no private insurer is required to cover abortion services aside from the exceptions permissible under the Hyde Amendment, which restricts federal funding for abortions of pregnancy resulting from incest and rape. As access to legal abortion is restricted, there is evidence that women will find other ways to terminate an unwanted pregnancy. There were more than 700,000 Google searches looking into self-induced abortions in 2015. "This demand is concentrated in the areas where it is most difficult to get an abortion, and it has closely tracked the recent state-level crackdowns on abortion." The state of Mississippi has one abortion clinic and the highest rate of Google searches for self-induced abortions.*

For Critical Analysis

1. Why do you think that abortion remains a contentious topic more than 40 years after the *Roe v. Wade* decision? Whose interests are states protecting by restricting access to abortion?

2. Would you prefer a federal standard apply for abortion rights, or would you prefer states to decide? Explain your choice.

*Seth Stephens-Davidowitz, "The Return of the DIY Abortion," *The New York Times*, March 5, 2016. www.nytimes.com/2016/03/06/opinion/sunday/the-return-of-the-diy-abortion.html

The United States is, as the name implies, a union of states. Unlike in many other nations, the national government does not have all of the authority in the system; rights and powers are reserved to the states by the Tenth Amendment. But the situation is even more complicated because there are more than 89,000 separate governmental units in the United States (see Table 3-1). Distributing authority across multiple levels and throughout many units of government is one of the ways the power of government over individuals is limited, although you can see how it might be interpreted differently.

Visitors from France or Spain are often awestruck by the complexity of our system of government. Consider that a criminal action can be defined by state law, national law, or both. Thus, a criminal suspect can be prosecuted in the state court system or in the federal court system (or both). Think about a routine task such as getting a driver's license. Each state has separate requirements for the driving test, the written test, the number of years between renewals, and the cost for the license. In 2005, Congress passed the REAL ID Act requiring states to include a specified set of information on the license so that it can be used as an identity card for travel and entrance to secure facilities, but the act was opposed by several states that insisted on maintaining their own requirements. If the licenses issued by those states do not meet the new requirements, the IDs will not be accepted at airports for travel starting October 1, 2020. The U.S. Department of Homeland Security has adjusted the implementation plan several times and granted states extensions in meeting the requirements. The U.S. Department of Homeland Security reported that 41 states and the District of Columbia were in compliance by January 1, 2016. Opposition to creating a national identity card remains strong across the political spectrum.

Relations between central governments and local units are structured in various ways around the world. Federalism is one of these ways. Understanding **federalism** and how it differs from other forms of government is important to

federalism
A system of government in which power is divided by a written constitution between a central government and regional or subdivisional governments. Each level must have some domain in which its policies are dominant and some genuine constitutional guarantee of its authority.

Table 3-1 ▶ Governmental Units in the United States

With more than 89,000 separate governmental units in the United States today, it is no wonder that intergovernmental relations in this country are so complicated. Actually, the number of school districts has decreased over time, but the number of special districts created for single purposes, such as flood control, has increased from only about 8,000 during World War II to more than 37,000 today.

Federal government	1
State governments	50
Local governments	89,476
Counties	3,033
Municipalities (mainly cities or towns)	19,492
Townships (less extensive powers)	16,519
Special districts (water, sewer, and so on)	37,381
School districts	13,051
TOTAL UNITS	89,527

Source: U.S. Census Bureau, 2012 Statistical Abstract, Table 428, 2007 data.

understanding the American political system. The impact of policies on the individual would be substantially different if we did not have a federal form of government in which governmental authority is divided between the central government and various subunits.

Three Systems of Government

■ **3.1** Define federalism and contrast the federal system of government with the unitary and confederal systems in explaining where governmental power lies.

Today, there are 196 independent nations in the world. Each of these countries has its own system of government. Relations between central governments and local units typically fit one of three models: (1) the unitary system, (2) the confederal system, or (3) the federal system.

A Unitary System

A **unitary system** of government assigns ultimate governmental authority to the national, or central, government; subnational governments exercise only the powers the central government chooses to delegate. The central government can also withdraw powers previously delegated to local or regional governments. American colonists lived under Great Britain's unitary system, and this experience no doubt contributed to their fear of re-creating an unchecked centralized power. The majority of countries today operate under a unitary form of government.

unitary system
A centralized governmental system in which local or subdivisional governments exercise only those powers given to them by the central government.

A Confederal System

You were introduced to the elements of a **confederal system** of government in Chapter 2, when we examined the Articles of Confederation. A confederation is the opposite of a unitary governing system. It is a league of independent states in which a central government or administration handles only those matters of common concern expressly delegated to it by the member states. The central government has no ability to make laws directly applicable to member states unless the members explicitly support such laws. The United States under the Articles of Confederation was a confederal system. Very few examples of confederal systems are found today; however, Switzerland is one modern example.

confederal system
A system consisting of a league of independent states, each having essentially sovereign powers. The central government created by such a league has only limited powers over the states.

A Federal System

The federal system lies between the unitary and confederal forms of government. In a federal system, authority is divided, usually by a written constitution, between a central government and regional, or subdivisional, governments (often called constituent governments). The central government and the constituent governments both act directly on the people through laws and through the actions of elected and appointed governmental officials. Within each government's sphere of authority, in theory, each is supreme. Thus, a federal system differs sharply from a unitary one, in which the central government is supreme and the constituent governments derive their authority from it. Australia, Brazil, Canada, Germany, India, and Mexico are examples of other nations with federal systems (see Figure 3-1 for a comparison of the three systems).

did you know?
According to the U.S. Census, there were 89,055 units of government in 2016, a significant decline from 1942, when there were 155,116 governmental bodies.

Figure 3-1 ▶ The Flow of Power in the Three Systems of Government

In a unitary system, power flows from the central government to the local and state governments. In a confederal system, power flows in the opposite direction—from the state governments to the central government. In a federal system, the flow of power, in principle, goes both ways.

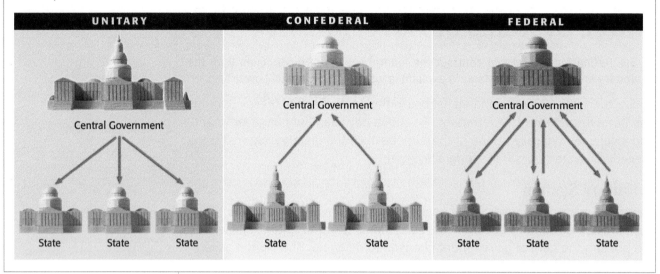

Why Federalism?

■ **3.2** Identify two advantages and two disadvantages of the U.S. federal system.

How best to distribute power in the new government was a question that consumed the founders. Too much power concentrated in any one place posed an unacceptable risk to liberty, but the experience of too little coordinated authority under the Articles of Confederation was sobering. Although not everyone agreed, federalism provided a means to ensure stability while empowering the states to govern in areas closest to the everyday lives of citizens.

A Practical Constitutional Solution

At the Constitutional Convention in Philadelphia, advocates of a strong national government debated states' rights proponents. This debate continued throughout the ratifying conventions in several states. The resulting federal system was therefore one of many compromises.[1] Supporters of the new Constitution were political pragmatists—they realized that without a federal arrangement, the new Constitution would not be ratified. Federalism retained state traditions and local power while establishing a strong national government capable of handling common problems.

Even if colonial leaders had agreed on the desirability of a unitary system, size and regional isolation would have made such a system difficult in practice. At the time of the Constitutional Convention, the 13 colonies were much larger geographically than England or France. Slow travel and communication contributed to the feeling of isolation in many regions within the colonies.

---

1 For a contemporary interpretation of this compromise and how the division of power between the national government and the states has changed, see Edward A. Purcell, *Originalism, Federalism and the American Constitutional Enterprise: A Historical Inquiry* (New Haven, CT: Yale University Press, 2007).

It could take several weeks for all of the colonies to be informed about a particular political decision. A federal form of government that delegates certain functions to the states or provinces made sense. Finally, federalism brings government closer to the people. Not only can local or state governments adopt policies that speak specifically to local or regional needs, the people in those communities have more immediate access to public officials. Alexis de Tocqueville marveled at the stability of public life in America. Government authority shared between the central government and the many states allows the people to exert direct influence over political decisions and indeed to seek political office themselves. There are more than 500,000 elected positions in the United States, and 96 percent of those are at the state or local level.[2]

Benefits for the United States In the United States, federalism has yielded many benefits. State governments long have been a training ground for future national leaders. Many presidents first made their political mark as governors. The states have been testing grounds for new government initiatives. As U.S. Supreme Court Justice Louis Brandeis once observed: "It is one of the happy incidents of the federal system that a single courageous state may, if its citizens choose, serve as a laboratory and try novel social and economic experiments without risk to the rest of the country."[3]

Examples of programs pioneered at the state level include unemployment compensation, begun in Wisconsin, and air pollution control, initiated in California. Statewide health-care plans pioneered in Hawaii and Massachusetts provided models for the Affordable Care Act. Today, states are experimenting with policies initiating education reforms, legalizing recreational marijuana use, and implementing environmental protection measures. States in the West are highly attuned to water politics and drought conditions that affect local economies. The states have employed a variety of different strategies for dealing with the recession and home mortgage crisis—both national problems, but experienced differently across the states. Some states focused on attracting new industries, whereas others invested in education and training opportunities for their residents. Indeed, states have widely different schemes for financing government and provision of public services. As shown in Figure 3-2, seven states do not have an income tax (making them magnets for retirees) and five states do not have a sales tax.

Allowance for Many Political Subcultures The American way of life is characterized by many political subcultures, which divide along the lines of race and ethnic origin, region, wealth, education, and the influence of religion. Regions of the country trend toward conservative or liberal politics, depending on the relative balance of these influences. When the Constitution was written, the diversity of the 13 "states" was seen as an obstacle to the survival of the nation. How could the large, rural, slaveholding states ever coexist with states where slavery was illegal? What would prevent a coalition of the larger states from imposing unfair laws on smaller states and minority groups? In *Federalist Papers* #51 (see Appendix C), Madison argued that adopting a

---

2   Christopher R. Berry and Jacob E. Gersen. June 2007. "The Fiscal Consequences of Electoral Institutions." The Law School, The University of Chicago, The Chicago Working Paper Series Index. www.law.uchicago.edu/Lawecon/index.html
3   *New State Ice Co. v. Liebmann*, 285 U.S. 262 (1932).

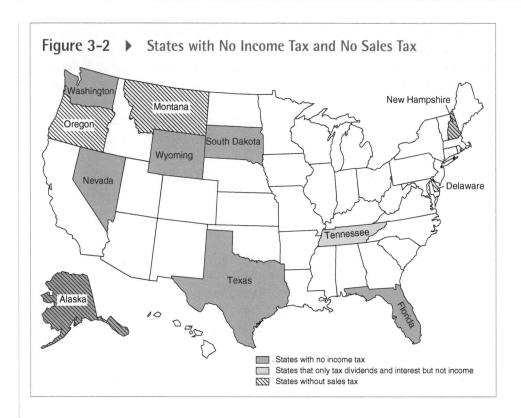

Figure 3-2 ▶ States with No Income Tax and No Sales Tax

- ▓ States with no income tax
- ▒ States that only tax dividends and interest but not income
- ▨ States without sales tax

federal system would protect the people from the absolute power of the national government and the will of an unjust majority. He put it this way:

> In the compound republic of America, the power surrendered by the people is first divided between two distinct governments, and then the portion allotted to each subdivided among distinct and separate departments. Hence a double security arises to the rights of the people. The different governments will control each other, at the same time that each will be controlled by itself.

Had the United States developed into a unitary system, various political subcultures certainly would have been less able to influence government behavior than they have been, and continue to, in our federal system. It is also quite possible that the nation would not have survived, because flourishing political subcultures contribute to the overall political stability of the nation. Lindsey Graham, the conservative Republican senator from South Carolina, for example, would likely be unelectable in New York. Political subcultures both reflect and contribute to the overall diversity of the United States.

Political scientist Daniel Elazar claimed that one of federalism's greatest virtues is that it encourages the development of distinct political subcultures. These political subcultures reflect differing demands and preferences for government. Federalism, he argued, allows for "a unique combination of governmental strength, political flexibility, and individual liberty."[4] The existence of political subcultures allows a wider variety of interests to influence government. As a result, political subcultures have proven instrumental in driving reform even at the national level, as shown by the differing state

---

4   Daniel Elazar, *American Federalism: A View from the States*, 2nd ed. (New York: Crowell, 1972).

approaches to such issues as same-sex marriage, gun laws, and marijuana policy. Handgun regulation runs the gamut from forbidding the ownership of handguns in the city of Chicago to allowing the open carrying of weapons in the state of Virginia. Hawaii limits the sale of cigarettes to those 21 and older. In 2014, Colorado and Washington became the first states in the country to enact a state-legal system of marijuana cultivation and sales to adults 21 years of age and older. Alaska and Oregon have also adopted laws allowing recreational marijuana. Twenty-three states allow legal use of marijuana for medical purposes under a variety of restrictions and regulations.

Arguments against Federalism Some see federalism as a way for powerful state and local interests to block progress and to impede national plans. Smaller political units are more likely to be dominated by a single political interest or group, and at times in our history this influence has limited rights for minority groups. (This was essentially the argument that Madison put forth in *Federalist Papers* #10, provided in Appendix C.) Alternatively, progressive dominant factions in states have pressured the national government for change in many areas, such as the environment, same-sex marriage, and nutrition labels on food.

Critics of federalism also argue that too many Americans suffer as a result of the inequalities that exist across the states. Individual states differ markedly in educational spending and achievement, crime and crime prevention, and even the safety of their buildings. States also differ considerably on women's rights, specifically regarding support for equal pay and free access to safe, legal abortion. Not surprisingly, these critics argue for increased federal legislation and oversight. This involves creating national educational standards, national building code standards, national expenditure minimums for crime control, and so on. The Affordable Care Act expanded the number of people who qualify for Medicaid. Typically, the federal government only covers about half of the cost of Medicaid, but under the new health-care law the federal government agreed to cover the full cost for the first three years. Under the law, all states were initially required to expand Medicaid coverage under threat of losing the federal contribution for all Medicaid. The Supreme Court ruled that the states could not be coerced to participate and thus Medicaid expansion became optional; around half of the states opted out.[5] In those states, the income cutoff to be eligible for Medicaid is generally much lower than what was set in the Affordable Care Act, so fewer people will qualify. Many of the states choosing not to take the federal money to expand Medicaid are led by Republican governors who oppose the Affordable Care Act.

Others see dangers in the expansion of national powers at the expense of the states. President Ronald Reagan (served 1981–1989) said, "The Founding Fathers saw the federalist system as constructed something like a masonry wall. The States are the bricks, the national government is the mortar . . . Unfortunately, over the years, many people have increasingly come to believe that Washington is the whole wall."[6]

did you know?

The state of Alaska is 429 times larger than the state of Rhode Island, but Rhode Island's population is larger than Alaska's.

---

5 *National Federation of Independent Business v. Sebelius*, 567 U.S. (2012), 183 L. Ed. 2d 450, 132 S.Ct. 2566.
6 Text of the address by the president to the National Conference of State Legislatures, Atlanta, Georgia (Washington, DC: The White House, Office of the Press Secretary, July 30, 1981), as quoted in Edward Millican, *One United People: The Federalist Papers and the National Idea* (Lexington, KY: The University Press of Kentucky, 1990).

Image 3-1

Budtender Rob Johnston helps a customer on the first day of legal recreational marijuana sales in Denver, Colorado, January 1, 2014.

The Constitutional Basis for American Federalism

■ **3.3** Locate the sources of federalism in the U.S. Constitution; using the terms *vertical control* and *horizontal control,* explain how the founders intended federalism and separation of powers to limit the expansion of national power.

The term *federal system* is not found in the U.S. Constitution. Nor is it possible to find a systematic division of governmental authority between the national and state governments in that document. Rather, the Constitution sets out different types of powers. These powers can be classified as (1) the powers of the national government, (2) the powers of the states, and (3) prohibited powers. The Constitution also makes it clear that if a state or local law conflicts with a national law, the national law will prevail.

Powers of the National Government

The powers delegated to the national government include both expressed and implied powers, as well as the special category of inherent powers. Most of the powers expressly delegated to the national government are found in Article I, Section 8, of the Constitution. These enumerated powers include coining money, setting standards for weights and measures, making uniform naturalization laws, admitting new states, establishing post offices, and declaring war. Another important enumerated power is the power to regulate commerce among the states—a topic we deal with later in this chapter.

The Necessary and Proper Clause The implied powers of the national government are also based on Article I, Section 8, which states that Congress shall have the power

> [t]o make all Laws which shall be necessary and proper for carrying into Execution the foregoing Powers, and all other Powers vested by this

Constitution in the Government of the United States, or in any Department or Officer thereof.

This clause is sometimes called the **elastic clause**, or **necessary and proper clause**, because it provides flexibility to the U.S. constitutional system. It gives Congress all of those powers that can be reasonably inferred but that are not expressly stated in the brief wording of the Constitution. The clause was first used in the Supreme Court decision of *McCulloch v. Maryland* (discussed later in this chapter) to develop the concept of implied powers.[7] Through this concept, the national government has succeeded in strengthening the scope of its authority to meet the numerous problems that the framers of the Constitution did not, and could not, anticipate.

Inherent Powers A special category of national powers that is not implied by the necessary and proper clause includes the inherent powers of the national government. These powers derive from the fact that the United States is a sovereign power among nations, and so its national government must be the only government that deals with other nations. Under international law, it is assumed that all nation-states, regardless of their size or power, have an *inherent* right to ensure their own survival. To do this, each nation must have the ability to act in its own interest among and with the community of nations.

Note that no specific clause in the Constitution says anything about the acquisition of additional land. Nonetheless, through inherent powers, the federal government made the Louisiana Purchase in 1803 and then went on to acquire Florida, Texas, Oregon, Alaska, Hawaii, and other lands. The United States grew from a mere 13 states to 50 states, plus several "territories."

The national government has these inherent powers whether or not they have been enumerated in the Constitution. Some constitutional scholars categorize inherent powers as a third type of power, completely distinct from the delegated powers (both expressed and implied) of the national government.

Powers of the State Governments

The Tenth Amendment states that the powers not delegated to the United States by the Constitution, nor prohibited by it to the states, are reserved to the states or to the people. These are the reserved powers that the national government cannot deny to the states. States had all the power when the Constitution was written, so it is not surprising that these reserved powers are not more clearly specified, but it does lead to questions about whether a certain power is delegated to the national government or reserved to the states. State powers include each state's right to regulate commerce within its borders and to provide for a state militia. States also have the reserved power to make laws on all matters not prohibited to the states by the U.S. Constitution or state constitutions and not expressly, or by implication, delegated to the national government. Furthermore, the states have **police power**—the authority to legislate for the protection of the health, morals,

elastic clause or **necessary and proper clause**
The clause in Article I, Section 8, that grants Congress the power to do whatever is necessary to execute its specifically delegated powers.

police power
The authority to legislate for the protection of the health, morals, safety, and welfare of the people. In the United States, most police power is reserved to the states.

---

7 4 Wheaton 316 (1819).

Flint, Michigan's Poisoned Water: A Failure at Every Level

"I'm sorry, and I will fix it," Republican Governor Rick Snyder said in his 2016 State of the Union address. "No citizen of this great state should endure this kind of catastrophe. Government failed you—federal, state, and local leaders—by breaking the trust you place in us."*

Flint, Michigan, is a city of fewer than 100,000 people located an hour north of Detroit where more than 40 percent of residents live below the poverty line. Filmmaker and Flint native Michael Moore first directed the nation's attention to Flint in the 1989 documentary *Roger & Me*, a stark portrait of a city abandoned as the auto industry moved jobs elsewhere. A majority (56 percent) of Flint's residents are African American.

From 2011 to 2015 Flint was in state receivership, its finances controlled by a series of four emergency managers appointed by Governor Rick Snyder. In an effort to save money while a new water pipeline was built, Flint's water supply was switched from Lake Huron, provided by Detroit's water utility, to the Flint River. State officials estimated the 2014 water switch would save $5 million over two years. In executing the switch, corrosion-control chemicals were not added to Flint's water supply. Flint River water corroded the city's pipes, allowing lead and other toxins to enter the city's water supply. A chain of subsequent decisions at the state and federal levels contributed to the current public health crisis. According to *The Detroit News*, "The state Department of Environmental Quality failed to ensure the chemicals were added, the federal Environmental Protection Agency didn't alert the public when an employee first raised a red flag."**

Flint residents noticed a difference in their water quality almost immediately after its source changed to the Flint River. The water was brown, smelled like rotten eggs, and tasted bad. People complained of rashes and hair loss, but local and state officials repeatedly assured them that the water was safe to use despite repeated boil advisories and advice to filter the water. LeeAnne Walters, a mother of four, was among the first Flint residents to contact public officials when her four-year old twins developed skin rashes and family members' hair fell out. She complained to city leaders, joining other residents describing vision and memory problems. Her pediatrician warned her not to let her kids consume the water. When city officials finally tested her water months later, they

Image 3-2 LeeAnne Walters, the Flint resident who first alerted officials to the water contamination, holds samples of lead-contaminated brown water drawn from her household faucet.

measured lead levels at 400 parts per billion. There is no safe level of lead in drinking water; the maximum allowed by law is 15 parts per billion.

Walters had also contacted the federal Environmental Protection Agency (EPA). Miguel Del Toral, a groundwater and drinking-water regulations manager for the EPA's Midwest division, reviewed the evidence and wrote an interim report arguing that the agency should take over Flint's water management. In emails released in the investigation, Del Toral is characterized by state officials as a "rogue" employee. However, Del Toral referred Walters to Marc Edwards, a civil engineering professor at Virginia Tech who studies corrosion and lead. Accompanied by student researchers, Professor Edwards travelled to Flint to conduct more tests. He found that Flint's tap water was 19 times more corrosive than Detroit's and estimated that one in six Flint households had lead exposures higher than the threshold required for the EPA to take official action.

The consequences of lead exposure to children and pregnant women are severe, and the neurological and behavioral effects are believed to be irreversible. "A child with lead poisoning presents with nothing. They are completely asymptomatic," says Mona Hanna-Attisha, director of the pediatric residency program at Hurley Children's Hospital at Michigan State University. "But in five years there's an increased likelihood that the kid's going to need

(*Continued*)

special-education services. In ten years, there's an increased likelihood that the kid's going to have ADHD, mental health issues, and behavior issues. And in twenty years, it's going to be a problem with the criminal justice system."***

For residents of Flint, who are still billed monthly by the city for their toxic water, daily life has become about finding clean water for cooking, bathing, and drinking. National attention has filled warehouses with bottled water, but Flint's mayor Karen Weaver estimates it could cost anywhere from $60 million to $1.5 billion to replace the 500 miles of underground, lead-leaching pipes. President Obama declared a state of emergency in early January 2016, authorizing the Federal Emergency Management Agency (FEMA) to coordinate all disaster relief efforts, including $5 million in federal aid to provide water and filters to residents for up to 90 days. Governor Rick Snyder had sought a major disaster declaration, thereby freeing up more federal aid (his request was for $96 million to be expedited), but Flint's crisis does not qualify—it is a manmade disaster. Michael Moore has labeled Flint "Governor Snyder's Katrina" in a reference to the disastrously slow state and federal response to the human crisis in New Orleans following Hurricane Katrina in 2005. In May 2016, President Obama visited Flint to reassure residents of local, state, and federal cooperation in addressing the problem. He drank a glass of filtered Flint tap water. In 2018, pipes in more than 12,000 homes still need to be replaced.

For Critical Analysis:

1. At all levels of government, public officials ignored citizen complaints about Flint's water quality. What factors do you think contributed to this lack of responsiveness by government? Why was government reactive rather than proactive in protecting Flint's water supply?

2. Flint is only one of potentially hundreds of U.S. communities with aging public infrastructure, including pipes, roads, bridges, and waterways. How can local, state, and federal governments work together to maintain our infrastructure? Who should incur the costs for repairs? How should projects be prioritized?

3. Is access to clean water a commodity (something to be purchased) or a basic right? How does your answer to this question shape your responses to questions 1 and 2?

*Julie Bosman and Mitch Smith, "Governor Rick Snyder of Michigan Apologizes in Flint Water Crisis," *The New York Times*, January 19, 2016. www.nytimes.com/2016/01/20/us/obama-set-to-meet-with-mayor-of-flint-about-water-crisis.html

**Jonathan Oosting, Jim Lynch, and Chad Livengood, "Disaster Warning Preceded Flint Water Switch," *The Detroit News*, March 11, 2016. www.detroitnews.com/story/news/politics/2016/03/10/disaster-warning-preceded-flint-water-switch/81629048/

***Susan Cosier, "Unleaded Please" onEarth, November, 2015. http://www.onearth.org/earthwire/flint-michigan-lead-tap-water

safety, and welfare of the people. Their police power enables states to pass laws governing such activities as crimes, marriage, contracts, education, intrastate transportation, and land use.

The ambiguity of the Tenth Amendment has allowed the reserved powers of the states to be defined differently at different times in our history. When widespread support for increased regulation by the national government exists, the Tenth Amendment tends to recede into the background. When the tide turns the other way (in favor of states' rights), the Tenth Amendment is resurrected to justify arguments supporting increased states' rights. The current climate, reflected in Congress and in decisions rendered by the U.S. Supreme Court, favors state prerogatives.

concurrent powers
Powers held jointly by the national and state governments.

Concurrent Powers

In certain areas, the states share **concurrent powers** not specifically listed in the Constitution with the national government. An example is the power to tax. The types of taxation are divided between the levels of government. For example, states may not levy a tariff (a set of taxes on imported goods); only the national government may do this. Neither government may tax the facilities of the other. If the state governments did not have the power to tax, they could not operate independent of the federal government.

Other concurrent powers include the power to borrow funds, to establish courts, and to charter banks and corporations. To a limited extent, the national government exercises police power, and to the extent that it does, police power is also a concurrent power. Concurrent powers exercised by the states are normally limited to the geographic area of each state and to those functions *not* granted by the Constitution exclusively to the national government (such as the coinage of money and the negotiation of treaties).

Prohibited Powers

The Constitution prohibits or denies several powers to the national government. The national government may not impose taxes on goods sold to other countries (exports). Moreover, any power not granted expressly or implicitly to the federal government by the Constitution is prohibited to it. The states are also denied certain powers. No state is allowed to enter into a treaty on its own with another country.

The Supremacy Clause

The supremacy of the national constitution over subnational laws and actions is established in the **supremacy clause** of the Constitution. The supremacy clause (Article VI, Clause 2) states the following:

> *This Constitution, and the Laws of the United States which shall be made in Pursuance thereof; and all Treaties made . . . under the Authority of the United States, shall be the supreme Law of the Land; and the Judges in every State shall be bound thereby, any Thing in the Constitution or Laws of any State to the Contrary notwithstanding.*

In other words, states cannot use their reserved or concurrent powers to prevent or undermine national policies. All national and state officers, including judges, are bound by oath to support the Constitution. Hence, any legitimate exercise of national governmental power supersedes any conflicting state action.[8] Of course, deciding whether a conflict actually exists is a judicial matter, as shown in the case of *McCulloch v. Maryland*.

National government legislation in a concurrent area is said to preempt (take precedence over) conflicting state or local laws or regulations in that area. One of the ways in which the national government has extended its powers is through the preemption of state and local laws by national legislation. In the first decade of the twentieth century, fewer than 20 national laws preempted laws and regulations issued by state and local governments. By the beginning of the twenty-first century, the number had risen to nearly 120.

---

did you know?

Under Article I, Section 10, of the Constitution, no state is allowed to enter into any treaty, alliance, or confederation.

---

supremacy clause
The constitutional provision that makes the Constitution and federal laws superior to all conflicting state and local laws.

---

8   An example of this is President Dwight Eisenhower's disciplining of Arkansas Governor Orval Faubus in 1957 by federalizing the National Guard to enforce the court-ordered desegregation of Little Rock Central High School.

Some political scientists believe that national supremacy is critical for the longevity and smooth functioning of a federal system. Nonetheless, the application of this principle has been a continuous source of conflict. The most extreme example of this conflict was the Civil War.

Vertical and Horizontal Checks and Balances

Recall from Chapter 2 that one of the goals of the founders was to prevent the national government from becoming too powerful. For that reason, they divided the government into three branches: legislative, executive, and judicial. They also created a system of checks and balances that allowed each branch to check the actions of the others. Separation of powers functions as a **horizontal control** when branches of government on the same level (state or national) check one another against the expansion of power. Federalism is also an important form of checks and balances, and it is known as a **vertical control** because the checks and balances involve power-sharing relationships between the states and the national government.

For example, the reserved powers of the states act as a check on the national government. Additionally, the states' interests are represented in the national legislature (Congress), and the citizens of the various states determine who will head the executive branch (the presidency). Finally, national programs and policies are administered by the states. This gives the states considerable control over the ultimate shape of those programs and policies. For example, the states are playing a major role in implementing the Affordable Care Act.

The national government, in turn, can check state policies by exercising its constitutional powers under the clauses just discussed, as well as under the commerce clause (to be examined later). Furthermore, the national government can influence state policies indirectly through federal grants or the federal budget process.

Interstate Relations

So far, we have examined only the relationship between central and state governmental units. The states, however, have constant commercial, social, and other dealings among themselves. The U.S. Constitution imposes certain "rules of the road" on interstate relations. These rules have prevented any one state from setting itself apart from the other states. The three most important clauses governing interstate relations in the Constitution, all derived from the Articles of Confederation, require each state to do the following:

- Give full faith and credit to every other state's public acts, records, and judicial proceedings (Article IV, Section 1).

- Extend to every other state's citizens the privileges and immunities of its own citizens (Article IV, Section 2).

- Agree to return persons who are fleeing from justice in another state back to their home state when requested to do so (Article IV, Section 2).

The Full Faith and Credit Clause This provision of the Constitution protects the rights of citizens as they move from state to state. It provides that "full faith and credit shall be given in each State to the public Acts, Records and judicial Proceedings of every other State." This clause applies only to civil matters. It ensures that rights established under deeds, wills, contracts, and the like will be honored by any other state. It also ensures that any judicial decision with respect to such property rights will be honored, as well as

horizontal control
A check against the expansion of government power that relies on checks and balances between branches of government on the same level.

vertical control
A structural check against the accumulation of too much power in any one level of government (national or state).

full faith and credit clause
This section of the Constitution requires states to recognize one another's laws and court decisions. It ensures that rights established under deeds, wills, contracts, and other civil matters in one state will be honored by other states.

enforced, in all states. The **full faith and credit clause** has contributed to the unity of American citizens, particularly as we have become a more mobile society. Prior to the Supreme Court's ruling in *Obergefell v. Hodges* (2015),[9] marriage between persons of the same sex was legal in some states but not others; same-sex couples residing in states where gay marriage was legal were eligible for all of the federal rights and benefits accruing to any other married persons.[10] In *Obergefell*, the Supreme Court held that the Fourteenth Amendment requires a state to license a marriage between two people of the same sex and to recognize a marriage between two people of the same sex when their marriage was lawfully licensed and performed out of state.

privileges and immunities
Special rights and exceptions provided by law. States may not discriminate against one another's citizens.

Privileges and Immunities **Privileges and immunities** are defined as special rights and exceptions provided by law. Under Article IV, "The Citizens of each State shall be entitled to all Privileges and Immunities of Citizens in the several States." This clause indicates that states are obligated to extend to citizens of other states protection of the laws, the right to work, access to courts, and other privileges they grant their own citizens. If you are a student from Iowa attending college in Ohio, you have the same rights as Ohioans to protest a traffic ticket, to buy a car, to hold a job, and to travel freely throughout the state.

Interstate Extradition The Constitution clearly addressed the issue of how states should cooperate in catching criminals. Article IV, Section 2, states that "[a] person charged in any State with Treason, Felony, or another Crime who shall flee from Justice and be found in another State, shall on Demand of the executive Authority of the State from which he fled, be delivered up, to be removed to the State having jurisdiction of the Crime." Although the language is clear, a federal judge will not order such an action. It is the moral duty of the governor to **extradite** the accused. From time to time, the governor of a state may refuse to do so, either because he or she does not believe in capital punishment, which might be ordered upon conviction, or because the accused has lived a law-abiding life for many years outside the state in which the crime was committed.

extradite
To surrender an accused or convicted criminal to the authorities of the state from which he or she has fled; to return a fugitive criminal to the jurisdiction of the accusing state.

interstate compact
An agreement between two or more states. Agreements on minor matters are made without congressional consent, but any compact that tends to increase the power of the contracting states relative to other states or relative to the national government generally requires the consent of Congress. Such compacts serve as a means by which states can solve regional problems.

Additionally, states may enter into agreements called **interstate compacts**, if consented to by Congress. In reality, congressional consent is necessary only if such a compact increases the power of the contracting states relative to other states (or to the national government). Typical examples of interstate compacts are the establishment of the Port Authority of New York and New Jersey by an interstate compact between those two states in 1921 and the regulation of the production of crude oil and natural gas by the Interstate Oil and Gas Compact of 1935. Regional compacts between states on higher education, climate change, and economic development exist to promote collaboration and to provide resources for innovation. Compacts allow states to work together to address challenges that cross state boundaries. A slightly different form of collaboration can be found in the Common Core State Standards Initiative. The initiative is sponsored by the National Governors Association and the Council of Chief State School Officers, two organizations with a vested interest in raising the quality of educational outcomes. Members of the Common Core State Standards Initiative have agreed to adopt consistent education standards in the areas of math and English language arts to ensure that students are prepared for college or careers no later than the end of high school. Not everyone agrees with this

---

9 *Obergefell v. Hodges*, 576 (2015).
10 *United States v. Windsor*, 570 U.S. (2013).

Beyond Our Borders

Federalism, Fracking, and European Energy Independence

In the United States, the Constitution defines the federal system by laying out the division of powers and authority between the 50 states and the national government. The European Union (EU) is an economic and political union of member states. In many ways, although the subgovernments are not contained within one nation, the EU functions as a federalist system. Energy independence is a goal for both the United States and the European Union. Just as the United States is dependent on foreign oil for about 40 percent of its supply, much of Europe relies on Russian natural gas that flows through pipelines in Ukraine. Global conflict or unrest in the countries that provide oil and gas threaten energy supplies and motivate political leaders to look for alternative sources of energy.

Hydraulic fracturing, popularly known as "fracking," is a drilling process designed to extract natural gas from shale rock layers deep within the earth. Water, sand, and chemicals are injected into the rock at high pressure, allowing the gas to flow out to the head of the well. Horizontal drilling techniques allow oil and gas companies to extract natural gas without necessarily disturbing communities at the surface. Royalty payments from gas companies that extract shale gas have been an economic boom to many rural communities in the Midwest. The increased supply of gas derived from shale has increased the nation's energy security, but not without cost and controversy.

Environmentalists note that fracking uses huge amounts of water that must be transported to the fracking site at significant environmental cost. Potentially carcinogenic chemicals used may escape during the process and contaminate groundwater sources around the fracking site. Methane and other gases are released in the process and contribute to smog and climate change. Finally, fracking may lead to an increase in earthquakes. State legislators and regulators want to protect the environment and public health, but they also recognize the benefits from the revenue the industry brings to state and local economies. Most natural gas–producing states have some form of severance tax that is imposed on resources removed from the ground. The National Council of State Legislatures (NCSL) estimated state revenue as a result of taxes on the oil and gas industry at $18.6 billion.

Fracking is much more prevalent in the United States than in European states. Many Europeans regard the economic boom produced by fracking with trepidation. U.S. natural gas prices, however, have fallen to as little as a quarter of those in Europe as a result of shale gas. The 2014 conflict in Ukraine refocused attention on energy security. When Russia cut off the supply of natural

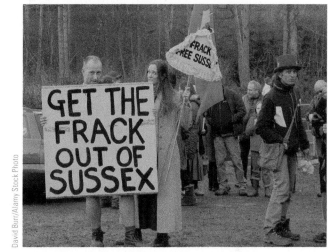

Image 3-3 A protester blocks access to a drilling site in southern England as part of a campaign against the controversial "fracking" process used in shale gas exploration.

gas to Ukraine in 2006 and 2009, prices rose throughout the EU. Yet, efforts to develop shale gas industries have proceeded slowly; there is no commercial shale gas production anywhere in Europe today. Poland, the European country that has been most active in shale gas, has only drilled about 50 exploratory wells to date. Environmental concerns are only part of the explanation. In the United States, property holders own the rights to the minerals under their property, whereas in Europe the subsoil is the property of the state. There is no individual economic incentive for European landowners to promote fracking.

For Critical Analysis

1. All nations have an interest in promoting security through energy independence. How might EU members overcome the lack of individual economic incentives to promote shale gas exploration or continued exploration of other forms of renewable energy?

2. How can nations balance the serious environmental concerns associated with fracking with the need to produce a greater share of their energy supply? Are regulations and policies in this area best handled by states or by the central government? Explain.

coordinated approach. As Governor of South Carolina, Nikki Haley, argued that her state should not "relinquish control of education to the federal government; neither should we cede it to the consensus of other states."[11] South Carolina adopted the Common Core State Standards in 2010, but withdrew from the compact in 2014. Four states never adopted the Common Core State Standards.

Defining Constitutional Powers—The Early Years

■ **3.4** Explain the historical evolution of federalism as a result of the Marshall Court, the Civil War, the New Deal, civil rights, and federal grant making.

To be effective and to endure, constitutional language must have some degree of ambiguity. Certainly, the powers delegated to the national government and the powers reserved to the states contain elements of ambiguity, thus leaving the door open for different interpretations of federalism. Disputes over the boundaries of national versus state powers have characterized this nation from the beginning. In the early 1800s, the most significant disputes arose over differing interpretations of the implied powers of the national government under the necessary and proper clause and over the respective powers of the national government and the states to regulate commerce.

Although political bodies at all levels of government play important roles in the process of settling such disputes, ultimately the Supreme Court casts the final vote. From 1801 to 1835, the Supreme Court was headed by Chief Justice John Marshall, a Federalist who advocated a strong central government. Two cases decided by the Marshall Court are considered milestones in defining the boundaries between federal and state power: *McCulloch v. Maryland*[12] and *Gibbons v. Ogden*.[13]

McCulloch v. Maryland (1819)

Nowhere in the U.S. Constitution does it state that Congress has the power to create a national bank, although Congress is granted the express power to regulate currency. Twice in the history of the nation Congress has chartered banks—the First and Second Banks of the United States—and provided part of their initial capital; thus, they were national banks. The government of Maryland, which intended to regulate its own banks and did not want competition from a national bank, imposed a tax on the Second Bank's Baltimore branch in an attempt to put that branch out of business. The branch's cashier, James William McCulloch, refused to pay the Maryland tax. When Maryland took McCulloch to its state court, the state of Maryland won. The national government appealed the case to the Supreme Court.

The Constitutional Questions   The questions before the Supreme Court were of monumental proportions. The very heart of national power under the Constitution, as well as the relationship between the national government and the states, was at issue. Congress has the authority to make all

---

11 Stephanie Banchero "School-Standards Pushback," *The Wall Street Journal*, May 8, 2012. www.wsj.com/news/articles /SB10001424052702303630404577390431072241906
12 4 Wheaton 316 (1819).
13 9 Wheaton 1 (1824).

laws that are "necessary and proper" for the execution of Congress's expressed powers. Strict Constitution constructionists looked at the word *necessary* and contended that the national government had only those powers *indispensable* to the exercise of its designated powers. To them, chartering a bank and contributing capital to it were not necessary, for example, to coin money and regulate its value.

Loose constructionists disagreed. They believed that the word *necessary* could not be looked at in its strictest sense. As Alexander Hamilton once said, "It is essential to the being of the national government that so erroneous a conception of the meaning of the word *necessary* be exploded." The important issue was, if the national bank was constitutional, could the state tax it?

Marshall's Decision Three days after hearing the case, Chief Justice John Marshall announced the Court's decision. It is true, Marshall said, that Congress's power to establish a national bank was not expressed in the Constitution. He went on to say, however, that if establishing such a national bank aided the government in the exercise of its designated powers, then the authority to set up such a bank could be implied. To Marshall, the necessary and proper clause embraced "all means which are appropriate: to carry out the 'legitimate ends' of the Constitution." Only when such actions are forbidden by the letter and spirit of the Constitution are they thereby unconstitutional. There was nothing in the Constitution, according to Marshall, "which excludes incidental or implied powers; and which requires that everything granted shall be expressly and minutely described." It would be impossible to spell out every action that Congress might legitimately take—the Constitution "would be enormously long and could scarcely be embraced by the human mind."

In perhaps the single most famous sentence ever uttered by a Supreme Court justice, Marshall said, "[W]e must never forget it is a constitution we are expounding." In other words, the Constitution is a living instrument that has to be interpreted to meet the practical needs of government. Having established this doctrine of implied powers, Marshall then answered the other important question before the Court and established the doctrine of national supremacy. Marshall stated that no state could use its taxing power to tax an arm of the national government. If it could, "the declaration that the Constitution . . . shall be the supreme law of the land, is an empty and unmeaning declamation."

Marshall's decision enabled the national government to grow and to meet problems that the Constitution's framers were unable to foresee. Today, practically every expressed power of the national government has been expanded in one way or another by use of the necessary and proper clause.

Gibbons v. Ogden (1824)

One of the most important parts of the Constitution included in Article I, Section 8, is the so-called **commerce clause**, in which Congress is given the power "[t]o regulate Commerce with foreign Nations, and among the several States, and with the Indian Tribes." What exactly does "to regulate commerce" mean? What does "commerce" entail? The issue here is essentially the same as that raised by *McCulloch v. Maryland*: How strict an interpretation should be given to a constitutional phrase? As might be expected given his Federalist loyalties, Marshall used a liberal approach in interpreting the commerce clause in *Gibbons v. Ogden*.

did you know?
The Liberty Bell cracked when it was rung at the funeral of John Marshall in 1835.

commerce clause
The section of the Constitution in which Congress is given the power to regulate trade among the states and with foreign countries.

The Background of the Case Robert Fulton and Robert Livingston secured a monopoly on steam navigation on New York waters from the New York legislature in 1803. They licensed Aaron Ogden to operate steam-powered ferryboats between New York and New Jersey. Thomas Gibbons, who had obtained a license from the U.S. government to operate boats in interstate waters, decided to compete with Ogden, but he did so without New York's permission. Ogden sued Gibbons. The New York state courts prohibited Gibbons from operating in New York waters. Gibbons appealed to the Supreme Court.

Several issues were before the Court in this case. The first was how the term *commerce* should be defined. New York's highest court had defined the term narrowly to mean only the shipment of goods or the interchange of commodities, not navigation or the transport of people. The second was whether the national government's power to regulate interstate commerce extended to commerce within a state (*intra*state commerce) or was limited strictly to commerce among the states (*inter*state commerce). The third was whether the power to regulate interstate commerce was a concurrent power (as the New York court had concluded), meaning a power that could be exercised by both state and national governments, or an exclusive national power. Clearly, if such powers were concurrent, many instances of laws that conflicted with each other would occur.

Marshall's Ruling Marshall defined commerce as all commercial interaction—all business dealings—including navigation and the transport of people. Marshall used this opportunity not only to expand the definition of commerce, but also to validate and increase the power of the national legislature to regulate commerce. Marshall wrote: "What is this power? It is the power . . . to prescribe the rule by which commerce is to be governed. This power, like all others vested in Congress, is complete in itself." Marshall also held that the commerce power of the national government could be exercised in state jurisdictions, even though it cannot reach solely intrastate commerce. Finally, Marshall emphasized that the power to regulate interstate commerce was an exclusive national power. Because Gibbons was duly authorized by the national government to navigate in interstate waters, he could not be prohibited from doing so by a state court.

Marshall's expansive interpretation of the commerce clause in *Gibbons v. Ogden* allowed the national government to exercise increasing authority over all areas of economic affairs throughout the land. In the 1930s and subsequent decades, the commerce clause became the primary constitutional basis for national government regulation.

States' Rights and the Resort to Civil War

In the *McColloch* and *Gibbons* rulings, the Supreme Court expanded and codified national power over states' rights. The question of slavery that led to the Civil War was also a dispute over national government supremacy versus the rights of the separate states. Essentially, the Civil War brought to an ultimate and violent climax the ideological debate that had been outlined by the Federalist and Anti-Federalist parties even before the Constitution was ratified.

Bettmann/Getty Images

Image 3-4
President Lincoln meets with some of his generals and other troops on October 3, 1862. Whereas many believe that the Civil War was fought over the issue of slavery, others point out that it was really a battle over the supremacy of the national government. In any event, once the North won the war, what happened to the size and power of our national government?

The Shift Back to States' Rights

While John Marshall was chief justice of the Supreme Court, he did much to increase the power of the national government and to reduce that of the states. During the Jacksonian era (1829–1837), however, a shift back to states' rights began. The question of the regulation of commerce became one of the major issues in federal–state relations. When Congress passed a tariff in 1828, South Carolina unsuccessfully attempted to nullify the tariff (render it void), claiming that in cases of conflict between a state and the national government, the state should have the ultimate authority over its citizens.

Over the next three decades, the North and South became even more sharply divided over tariffs, which mostly benefited Northern industries, and the issue of slavery. On December 20, 1860, South Carolina formally repealed its ratification of the Constitution and withdrew from the Union. On February 4, 1861, representatives from six Southern states met at Montgomery, Alabama, to form a new government called the Confederate States of America.

War and the Growth of the National Government

The ultimate defeat of the South in 1865 permanently ended any idea that a state could successfully claim the right to secede, or withdraw, from the Union. Contrary to the Southern states' intention, the Civil War resulted in an increase in the national government's political power.

The War Effort Thousands of new employees were hired to run the Union war effort and to deal with the social and economic problems that had to be handled in the aftermath of war. A billion-dollar national government budget was passed for the first time in 1865 to cover the increased government expenditures. The first (temporary) income tax was imposed on citizens to help pay for the war. This tax and the increased national government spending were precursors to the expanded future role of the national government in the American federal system. Civil liberties were curtailed in the Union and in the Confederacy in the name of the wartime emergency. The distribution of pensions and widows' benefits also boosted the national government's social role. Many scholars contend that the North's victory set the nation on the path to a modern industrial economy and society.

The Civil War Amendments The expansion of the national government's authority during the Civil War was reflected in the passage of the Civil War Amendments to the Constitution. Before the war, legislation with regard to slavery was some of the most controversial ever to come before Congress. In fact, in the 1830s, Congress prohibited the submission of antislavery petitions. When new states were admitted into the Union, the primary decision was whether slavery would be allowed. Immediately after the Civil War, at a time when former officers of the Confederacy were barred from voting, the three Civil War Amendments were passed. The Thirteenth Amendment, ratified in 1865, did more than interfere with slavery—it abolished the institution altogether. By abolishing slavery, the amendment also in effect abolished the rule by which three-fifths of the slaves were counted when apportioning seats in the House of Representatives (see Chapter 2). African Americans were now counted in full.

The Fourteenth Amendment (1868) defined who was a citizen of each state. It sought to guarantee equal rights under state law, stating that

> [no] State [shall] deprive any person of life, liberty, or property, without due process of law; nor deny to any person within its jurisdiction the equal protection of the laws.

For a brief time after the ratification of these amendments, the rights of African Americans in the South were protected by the local officials appointed by the Union forces. Within two decades, the Fourteenth Amendment lost much of its power as states reinstituted separate conditions for the former slaves. Decades later, the courts interpreted these words to mean that the national Bill of Rights applied to state governments (see Chapter 4). The Fourteenth Amendment also confirmed the abolition of the three-fifths rule. Finally, the Fifteenth Amendment (1870) gave African Americans the right to vote in all elections, including state elections, although a century would pass before that right was enforced.

The Continuing Dispute over the Division of Power

Although the outcome of the Civil War firmly established the supremacy of the national government and put to rest the idea that a state could secede from the Union, the war by no means ended the debate over the division of powers between the national government and the states. The debate over the division of powers in our federal system can be viewed as progressing through at least two general stages since the Civil War: dual federalism and cooperative federalism.

Dual Federalism and the Retreat of National Authority

During the decades after the Civil War, the prevailing model was what political scientists have called **dual federalism**—a doctrine that emphasizes a distinction

did you know?

Only after the Civil War did people commonly refer to the United States as "it" instead of "they."

dual federalism
A system in which the states and the national government each remains supreme within their own sphere. The doctrine looks on nation and state as coequal sovereign powers. Neither the state government nor the national government should interfere in the other's sphere.

between federal and state spheres of government authority. Dual federalism is commonly depicted as a layer cake, because the state governments and the national government are viewed as separate entities, like separate layers in a cake. The national government is the top layer of the cake; the state government is the bottom layer. Nevertheless, the two layers are physically separate. They do not mix. For the most part, advocates of dual federalism believed that the state and national governments should not exercise authority in the same areas.

A Return to Normal Conditions   The doctrine of dual federalism represented a revival of states' rights following the expansion of national authority during the Civil War. Dual federalism, after all, was a fairly accurate model of the prewar consensus on state–national relations. For many people, it therefore represented a return to normalcy. The national income tax, used to fund the war effort and the reconstruction of the South, was ended in 1872. The most significant step to reverse the wartime expansion of national power, however, took place in 1877, when President Rutherford B. Hayes withdrew the last federal troops from the South. This meant that the national government was no longer in a position to regulate state actions that affected African Americans. Although the black population was now free, it was again subject to the authority of Southern whites.

The Role of the Supreme Court   The Civil War crisis drastically reduced the influence of the U.S. Supreme Court. In the prewar *Dred Scott* decision, the Court had attempted to abolish the power of the national government to restrict slavery in the territories.[14] In so doing, the Court placed itself on the losing side of the impending conflict. After the war, Congress took the unprecedented step of exempting the entire process of the South's reconstruction from judicial review. The Court had little choice but to acquiesce.

In time, the Supreme Court reestablished itself as the legitimate constitutional interpreter. Its decisions tended to support dual federalism, defend states' rights, and limit the powers of the national government. In 1895, for example, the Court ruled that a national income tax was unconstitutional.[15] In subsequent years, the Court gradually backed away from this decision and eventually might have overturned it. In 1913, however, the Sixteenth Amendment explicitly authorized a national income tax.

For the Court, dual federalism meant that the national government could intervene in state activities through grants and subsidies, but for the most part, it was barred from regulating matters that the Court considered to be purely local. The Court generally limited the exercise of police power to the states. In 1918, the Court ruled that a 1916 national law banning child labor was unconstitutional because it attempted to regulate a local problem.[16] In effect, the Court placed severe limits on the ability of Congress to legislate under the commerce clause of the Constitution.

The New Deal and Cooperative Federalism

The doctrine of dual federalism receded into the background in the 1930s as the nation attempted to deal with the Great Depression. President Franklin D. Roosevelt was inaugurated on March 4, 1933. In the previous year, nearly

---

14 *Dred Scott v. Sanford*, 19 Howard 393 (1857).
15 *Pollock v. Farmers' Loan & Trust Co.*, 157 U.S. 429 (1895); *Pollock v. Farmers' Loan & Trust Co.*, 158 U.S. 601 (1895).
16 *Hammer v. Dagenhart*, 247 U.S. 251 (1918). This decision was overruled in *United States v. Darby*, 312 U.S. 100 (1940).

Bettmann/Getty Images

Image 3-5

President Franklin Delano Roosevelt (served 1933–1945). Roosevelt's national approach to addressing the effects of the Great Depression was overwhelmingly popular, although many of his specific initiatives were controversial. How did the Great Depression change the political beliefs of many ordinary Americans?

1,500 banks had failed (and 4,000 more would fail in 1933). Thirty-two thousand businesses had closed down, and almost one-fourth of the labor force was unemployed. The public expected the national government to do something about the disastrous state of the economy. But for the first three years of the Great Depression (1930–1932), the national government did very little.

The "New Deal" President Herbert Hoover (served 1929–1933) clung to the doctrine of dual federalism and insisted that unemployment and poverty were local issues. The states, not the national government, had the sole responsibility for combating the effects of unemployment and providing relief to the poor. Roosevelt, however, did not feel bound by this doctrine, and his new Democratic administration energetically intervened in the economy. Roosevelt's "New Deal" included large-scale emergency antipoverty programs. In addition, the New Deal introduced major new laws regulating economic activity, such as the National Industrial Recovery Act of 1933, which established the National Recovery Administration (NRA). The NRA, initially the centerpiece of the New Deal, provided codes for every industry to restrict competition and regulate labor relations.

The End of Dual Federalism Roosevelt's expansion of national authority was challenged by the Supreme Court, which continued to adhere to the doctrine of dual federalism. In 1935, the Court ruled that the NRA program was unconstitutional.[17]

The NRA had turned out to be largely unworkable and was unpopular. The Court, however, rejected the program on the ground that it regulated intrastate, not interstate, commerce. This position appeared to rule out any alternative recovery plans that might be better designed. Subsequently, the Court struck down the Agricultural Adjustment Act, the Bituminous Coal Act, a railroad retirement plan, legislation to protect farm mortgages, and a municipal bankruptcy act.

In 1937, Roosevelt proposed legislation that would allow him to add up to six new justices to the Supreme Court. Presumably, the new justices would be more amenable to the exercise of national power than were the existing members. Roosevelt's move was widely seen as an assault on the Constitution. Congressional Democrats refused to support the measure, and it failed. Nevertheless, the "court-packing scheme" had its intended effect. Although the membership of the Court did not change, after 1937 the Court ceased its attempts to limit the national government's powers under the commerce clause. For the next half-century, the commerce clause would provide Congress with an unlimited justification for regulating the economic life of the country.

cooperative federalism
The theory that the states and the national government should cooperate in solving problems.

Cooperative Federalism Some political scientists have described the era since 1937 as characterized by **cooperative federalism**, in which the states

17 *Schechter Poultry Corp. v. United States*, 295 U.S. 495 (1935).

and the national government cooperate to solve complex common problems. Roosevelt's New Deal programs, for example, often involved joint action between the national government and the states. The pattern of national–state relationships during these years created a new metaphor for federalism—that of a marble cake. Unlike a layer cake, in a marble cake the two types of cake are intermingled, and any bite contains cake of both flavors. Cooperative federalism in practice often meant that the federal government provided the funding and set the terms for a policy solution at the national level, but left implementation to the states. Examples of this arrangement might include Aid to Families with Dependent Children (AFDC), a form of financial assistance to families in effect from 1935 to 1996, funded by the federal government but administered by the states. Another example might be the interstate highway system. A series of national laws beginning in 1916 provided coordination and funding to establish the vast network of interconnected highways that allow citizens to travel freely and efficiently throughout the country. Interstate highways and their rights of way are owned by the state in which they were built, and maintenance is the responsibility of the state department of transportation.

Methods of Implementing Cooperative Federalism

Even before the Constitution was adopted, the national government gave grants to the states in the form of land to finance education. The national government also provided land grants for canals, railroads, and roads. In the twentieth century, federal grants increased significantly, especially under Roosevelt's administration during the Great Depression and again during the 1960s, when the dollar amount of grants quadrupled. These funds were used for improvements in education, pollution control, recreation, and highways. With this increase in grants, however, came a bewildering number of restrictions and regulations. In the aggregate today, states depend on federal funding for over 35 percent of their income.

Categorical Grants Before the 1960s, most **categorical grants** by the national government were formula grants. These grants take their name from the method used to allocate funds. They fund state programs using a formula based on such variables as the state's needs, population, or willingness to come up with matching funds. Beginning in the 1960s, the national government increasingly offered program grants. This funding requires states to apply for grants for specific programs. The applications are evaluated by the national government, and the applications may compete with one another. Program grants give the national government a much greater degree of control over state activities than do formula grants.

By 1985, categorical grants amounted to more than $100 billion per year. They were spread out across 400 separate programs, but the largest five accounted for more than 50 percent of the revenues spent. These five programs involved Medicaid (health care for the poor), highway construction, unemployment benefits, housing assistance, and welfare programs to assist mothers with dependent children and people with disabilities. In fiscal year 2011, the federal government provided $607 billion in grants to state and local governments. Those funds accounted for 17 percent of federal outlays, 4 percent of gross domestic product (GDP), and a quarter of spending by state and local governments that year.[18]

did you know?

The Morrill Act of 1862, providing for land grants to states to create public institutions of higher education, was the first example of the federal government providing grants to the states.

categorical grant
Federal grant to states or local governments that is for specific programs or projects.

---

18 Congressional Budget Office, "Federal Grants to State and Local Governments," Report. March 5, 2013.

Why have federal grants to the states increased so much? One reason is that Congress has devolved control of some programs to the states while continuing to provide a major part of the funding for them. This allows states to customize implementation of national programs, thereby increasing the overall effectiveness and improving economic efficiencies. Also, Congress continues to use grants as an incentive to persuade states and cities to adopt and operate programs reflecting federal policy priorities. For example, after the September 11, 2001, terrorist attacks, the federal government created new grants to support state and urban security strategies. In 2013, the federal government transferred more than $350 million to states "to address the identified planning, organization, equipment, training, and exercise needs to prevent, protect against, mitigate, respond to, and recover from acts of terrorism and other catastrophic events."[19] Other grants use the broad federal tax base to redistribute resources among communities and individuals. Finally, grants can help foster policy experimentation at the state and local levels that might be lost in a single national program.

Feeling the Pressure—The Strings Attached to Federal Grants No dollars sent to the states are completely free of strings, however; all funds come with requirements that must be met by the states. Often, through the use of grants, the national government has been able to exercise substantial control over matters that traditionally have been under the purview of state governments. When the federal government gives federal funds for highway improvements, for example, it may condition the funds on the state's cooperation with a federal policy. This is exactly what the federal government did in the 1980s and 1990s to force the states to raise their minimum drinking age to 21.

Such carrot-and-stick tactics inevitably include some kind of consequence if a state does not agree to the entire bargain. For example, the No Child Left Behind (NCLB) Act promised billions of dollars to the states to bolster their education budgets. The funds would only be delivered, however, if states agreed to hold schools accountable to new federal achievement benchmarks on standardized tests designed by the federal government. NCLB was replaced with Every Student Succeeds Act (ESSA) in December 2015. ESSA promises to allow states to develop their own school accountability rating systems, providing only rough guidelines for how to identify schools in need of improvement. ESSA focuses on incentivizing state action rather than punishing state inaction.

block grant
Federal program that provides funds to state and local governments for general functional areas, such as criminal justice or mental health programs.

Block Grants **Block grants** lessen the restrictions on federal grants given to state and local governments by grouping several categorical grants under one broad heading. Governors and mayors generally prefer block grants because such grants give the states more flexibility in how the money is spent.

One major set of block grants provides aid to state welfare programs. The Personal Responsibility and Work Opportunity Reconciliation Act of 1996 ended the AFDC program. The Temporary Assistance for Needy Families (TANF) program that replaced AFDC provided a welfare block grant to each state. Each grant has an annual cap. According to some, this is one of the most successful block grant programs. Although state governments prefer block

---

19 Homeland Security Grant Program, Federal Emergency Management Agency. www.fema.gov/fy-2013-homeland-security-grant-program-hsgp-0

grants, Congress generally favors categorical grants, because the expenditures can be targeted according to congressional priorities.

Federal Mandates For years, the federal government has passed legislation requiring that states act to achieve particular national goals—improve environmental conditions and the civil rights of certain groups, for example. Since the 1970s, the national government has enacted literally hundreds of **federal mandates** requiring the states to take some action in areas ranging from the way voters are registered, to ocean-dumping restrictions, to the education of persons with disabilities. The Unfunded Mandates Reform Act of 1995 requires the Congressional Budget Office (CBO) to identify mandates that cost state and local governments more than $50 million to implement. The CBO is tasked with estimating the cost of mandates that would apply to state, local, and tribal governments or to the private sector. Their reports demonstrate that public laws generally contain fewer intergovernmental mandates than private-sector mandates. The National Conference of State Legislatures (NCSL) also closely monitors federal mandates.

One way in which the national government has moderated the burden of federal mandates is by granting *waivers*, which allow individual states to try out innovative approaches to carrying out the mandates. For example, Oregon received a waiver to experiment with a new method of rationing health-care services under the federally mandated Medicaid program.

federal mandate
Requirement in federal legislation that forces states and municipalities to comply with certain rules.

did you know?
State government spending in fiscal year 2016 exceeded $1.6 trillion, the majority of which was directed to five areas: health care, education, pensions, transportation, and assistance to the poor.

The Politics of Federalism

The allocation of powers between the national and state governments continues to be a major issue. The devastation caused by Hurricane Katrina in Louisiana unleashed a heated debate about federalism, as Americans disagreed on which level of government should be held accountable for inadequate preparations and the failures in providing aid afterward. Some 1,300 people died as a result of the storm, and property damage totaled tens of billions of dollars. Many Americans felt that the federal government's response to Katrina was woefully inadequate. Much of their criticism centered on the failures of the Federal Emergency Management Agency (FEMA) in the aftermath of Katrina.

FEMA, the government agency responsible for coordinating disaster preparedness and relief efforts, was disorganized and slow to respond in the days following the storm. On their arrival in the Gulf Coast, FEMA officials often acted counterproductively—on some occasions denying the delivery of storm aid that their agency had not authorized. Some claimed that state and local politicians—including Louisiana Governor Kathleen Blanco and New Orleans Mayor Ray Nagin—were not adequately prepared for the storm. Local officials knew the region and its residents best, yet they failed to make proper provisions for evacuating vulnerable residents.

Although the loss of life and damage to property was significantly lower, Hurricane Sandy confronted major coastal cities in the Northeast and the federal government with the same challenges in the week leading up to the 2012 national election. Storm surge flooded New York City streets, tunnels, and subway lines and cut power in and around the city. New Jersey sustained major damage to its coastal cities and beach communities. Damage amounted to $65 billion. The powerful late-season storm ignited political

Image 3-6

Destroyed beach houses in the aftermath of Hurricane Sandy on November 11, 2012, in Far Rockaway, New York. Politicians debated whether this late-season storm was a result of climate change, but ultimately Congress approved more than $60 billion in emergency relief for the region.

debate over the storm's link to climate change. Congress ultimately authorized nearly $60 billion in emergency relief for the affected states, but not without heated debate over the role and responsibilities of government related to weather disasters. The 2017 U.S. Atlantic hurricane season was the most costly in history, recording more than $202.6 billion in damages. Hurricane Maria devastated Puerto Rico, leaving the island without power for months and sending many residents fleeing to the mainland.

What Has National Authority Accomplished?

Generally speaking, conservatives have favored the states, and liberals have favored the national government. One reason is that throughout American history, the expansion of national authority has typically been an engine of social change. Far more than the states, the national government has been willing to alter the status quo. The expansion of national authority during the Civil War freed the slaves—a major social revolution. During the New Deal, the expansion of national authority meant unprecedented levels of government intervention in the economy. In both the Civil War and New Deal eras, support for states' rights was a method of opposing these changes and supporting the status quo.

Civil Rights and the War on Poverty Another example of the use of national power to change society was the presidency of Lyndon B. Johnson (1963–1969). Johnson oversaw the greatest expansion of national authority since the New Deal. Under Johnson, a series of civil rights acts forced the states to grant African Americans equal treatment under the law. Crucially, these acts included the abolition of all measures designed to prevent African Americans from voting. Johnson's Great Society and War on Poverty programs resulted in major increases in spending by the national government. As before, states' rights were invoked to support the status quo—states' rights meant no action on civil rights and no increase in antipoverty spending.

Why Would the States Favor the Status Quo? When state governments have authority in a particular field, great variations may occur from state to state in how the issues are handled. Inevitably, some states will be more conservative than others. Therefore, bringing national authority to bear on a particular issue may impose national standards on states that, for whatever reason, have not adopted such standards. One example is the voting rights legislation passed under President Johnson. By the 1960s, there was a national consensus that all citizens, regardless of race, should have the right to vote. A majority of the white electorate in former Confederate states, however, did not share this view. National legislation was necessary to impose the national consensus on the recalcitrant states.

Another factor that may make the states more receptive to limited government, especially on economic issues, is competition among the states. It is widely believed that major corporations are more likely to establish new operations in states with a "favorable business climate." Such a climate may mean low taxes and therefore relatively more limited social services. If states compete with one another to offer the best business climate, the competition may force down taxes all around. Competition of this type also may dissuade states from implementing environmental regulations that restrict certain business activities. Those who deplore the effect of such competition often refer to it as a "race to the bottom." National legislation, in contrast, is not constrained by interstate competition.

A final factor that may encourage the states to favor the status quo is the relative power of local economic interests. A large corporation in a small state, for example, may have a substantial amount of political influence. These local economic interests may have less influence at the national level. This observation echoes Madison's point in *Federalist Papers* #10 (see Appendix C of this text). Madison argued that a large federal republic would be less subject to the danger of factions than a small state.

At times, states can be seen pushing the national agenda along—often in progressive directions. Two examples are same-sex marriage and decriminalizing marijuana. The Controlled Substance Act passed by Congress in 1970 makes growing, possessing, and selling marijuana illegal. Twenty states, however, have passed laws decriminalizing marijuana. Typically, decriminalization means no prison time or criminal record for first-time possession of a small amount for personal consumption. The conduct is treated like a minor traffic violation. Thirty states plus the District of Columbia have enacted laws that allow people to use medical marijuana with a doctor's recommendation. Eight states have legalized marijuana for recreational use. All of these state actions remain illegal under the Controlled Substance Act, yet the Obama administration Department of Justice elected to allow states significant leeway in this area as long as they effectively enforce their own regulations and minors are protected. Changing course in 2018, President Trump's attorney general, Jeff Sessions, directed all U.S. Attorneys to enforce the laws enacted by Congress. This action will inevitably result in challenges from affected states. States are also flexing their muscles relative to the federal regulations promulgated under the commerce clause. The Montana Firearms Freedom Act, for example, declares that guns that are manufactured in Montana and remain within the state are not subject to federal regulations, including registration requirements.

Federalism Becomes a Partisan Issue

The **devolution** of power from the national government to the states has become a major ideological theme for the Republican Party. Republicans believe that the increased size and scope of the federal government—which began with the New

devolution
The transfer of powers from a national or central government to a state or local government.

Deal programs of Franklin Roosevelt and continued unabated through Lyndon Johnson's Great Society programs and beyond—pose a threat to individual liberty and to the power of the states. As the Republicans became more conservative in their views regarding the extent of national government power, Democrats have become more liberal and supportive of that power.

The "New Federalism" The architects of Lyndon Johnson's War on Poverty were reluctant to let state governments have a role in the new programs. This reluctance was a response to the resistance of many Southern states to African American civil rights. The Johnson administration did not trust the states to administer antipoverty programs in an impartial and efficient manner.

Republican president Richard Nixon (served 1969–1974), who succeeded Johnson in office, saw political opportunity in the Democrats' suspicion of state governments. Nixon advocated what he called a "New Federalism" that would devolve authority from the national government to the states. In part, the New Federalism involved the conversion of categorical grants into block grants, thereby giving state governments greater flexibility in spending. A second part of Nixon's New Federalism was revenue sharing. Under the revenue-sharing plan, the national government provided direct, unconditional financial support to state and local governments.

Republican President Ronald Reagan was also a strong advocate of New Federalism, but some of his policies withdrew certain financial support from the states. Reagan was more successful than Nixon in obtaining block grants, but Reagan's block grants, unlike Nixon's, were less generous to the states than the categorical grants they replaced. Under Reagan, revenue sharing was eliminated.

New Judicial Federalism In cases where a state's constitution may provide more civil rights and liberties than the minimum standard found in the U.S. Constitution, the U.S. Supreme Court has permitted state judges to base

Image 3–7

Cartoonist Nick Anderson succinctly captures the inherent political tensions involved in the federal system.

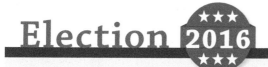

When States Take Policy Questions Directly to Voters

Twenty-six states and the District of Columbia allow for ballot initiatives that place policy decisions directly in the hands of voters. In November 2016, nine states asked voters to decide whether marijuana should be legalized for recreational use (Arizona, Maine, Massachusetts, Nevada and California) or for medical purposes (Montana, North Dakota, Arkansas and Florida). Only the Arizona initiative failed to win approval, meaning that 29 states currently have laws legalizing marijuana in some form. At the federal level, marijuana remains classified as a Schedule I substance under the Controlled Substances Act, making distribution of marijuana a federal criminal offense. The Obama administration responded to this disconnect by directing states to promulgate appropriate regulations on the use and distribution of marijuana and then to enforce the regulations. However, elections have consequences. In 2018, the Trump administration issued new directions requiring all U.S. Attorneys to enforce the laws passed by Congress, meaning that this issue will likely be resolved by the courts. Nearly one-quarter of Americans now live in states that allow recreational use of marijuana.

In other initiatives, states adopted tougher laws on guns and increased the minimum wage beyond the $7.25 required by federal law. State ballot initiative have become more common in the United States. In 2016, voters across the nation were presented with 150 different issues unique to their home state. Many experts attribute this phenomenon to voters filling a void created by congressional inaction.

For Critical Analysis

1. One benefit of a federal system is policy experimentation by states. Is the proliferation of ballot initiatives a sign that federalism is flourishing or that voters are frustrated with federal inaction?

2. In the case of medical marijuana, should Congress follow the lead of 30 states and the District of Columbia and adopt a national policy? The Obama administration allowed states to regulate recreational use of marijuana where legal. How is the Trump administration approaching this issue?

---

their rulings on their state constitution in a practice known as **new judicial federalism**. It reflects a dual-federalism perspective in that states are, if not coequal sovereigns with the federal government, at least sovereign within their own constitutional spheres. This tradition is attributed to Justice William Brennan's call for state courts to step into the breach left by the U.S. Supreme Court's allegedly unsatisfactory protection of individual rights and civil liberties. Scholars have noted the application of this form of federalism in state court rulings on constitutionality of same-sex marriage laws.

new judicial federalism
The increased reliance of state courts of last resort on state constitutions rather than on the federal Constitution for the protection of individual rights.

Federalism in the Twenty-First Century Today, federalism (in the sense of limited national authority) continues to be an important element in conservative ideology. At this point, however, it is not clear whether competing theories of federalism truly divide the Republicans from the Democrats in practice. Consider that under Democratic president Bill Clinton (served 1993–2001), Congress replaced AFDC with the TANF block grants. This change was part of the Welfare Reform Act of 1996, which was perhaps the most significant domestic policy initiative of Clinton's administration. In contrast, a major domestic initiative of Republican president George W. Bush was increased federal funding and control of education—long a preserve of state and local governments. The Affordable Care Act, as the policy was originally designed, included a significant role for states to create and operate health exchanges to enroll individuals in a variety of health insurance options.

Also, in some circumstances, liberals today may benefit from states' rights understood as policy innovation opportunities. States have been incubators for sustainability and green energy initiatives, states primarily in the West have been leaders in developing death with dignity or assisted suicide laws, and still others have legalized marijuana.

Conservatives today also remain active in limiting the scope of federal power. One example is opposition to the Affordable Care Act, particularly the expansion of coverage under Medicaid and the mandate for coverage. The Tea Party emerged in part as a reaction to increased government spending at the start of the 2008 recession.

Federalism and the Supreme Court Today

The U.S. Supreme Court, which normally has the final say on constitutional issues, necessarily plays a significant role in determining the line between federal and state powers. Consider the decisions rendered by Chief Justice Marshall in the cases discussed earlier. Since the 1930s, Marshall's broad interpretation of the commerce clause has made it possible for the national government to justify its regulation of virtually any activity, even when an activity would appear to be purely local in character.

Since the 1990s, however, the Supreme Court has been gradually tailoring the national government's powers under the commerce clause. The Court also has given increased emphasis to state powers under the Tenth and Eleventh Amendments to the Constitution. At the same time, other recent rulings have sent contradictory messages with regard to states' rights and the federal government's power.

Reining in the Commerce Power

In a widely publicized 1995 case, *United States v. Lopez*, the Supreme Court held that Congress had exceeded its constitutional authority under the commerce clause when it passed the Gun-Free School Zones Act in 1990.[20] The Court stated that the act, which banned the possession of guns within 1,000 feet of any school, was unconstitutional because it attempted to regulate an area that had "nothing to do with commerce, or any sort of economic enterprise." This marked the first time in 60 years that the Supreme Court had placed a limit on the national government's authority under the commerce clause.

In 2000, in *United States v. Morrison*, the Court held that Congress had over-reached its authority under the commerce clause when it passed the Violence against Women Act in 1994.[21] The Court invalidated a key section of the act that provided a federal remedy for gender-motivated violence, such as rape. The Court noted that in enacting this law, Congress had extensively documented that violence against women had an adverse "aggregate" effect on interstate commerce: It deterred potential victims from traveling, from engaging in employment, and from transacting business in interstate commerce. It also diminished national productivity and increased medical and other costs. Nonetheless, the Court held that evidence of an aggregate effect on commerce was not enough to justify national regulation of noneconomic, violent criminal conduct.

---

20 514 U.S. 549 (1995).
21 529 U.S. 598 (2000).

One of the central questions in the 2012 challenge to the Affordable Care Act also concerned the commerce power. The most controversial provision of the law, known as the individual mandate, requires individuals to have health insurance either through an employer or by purchasing it through the market. The Obama administration argued that Congress is authorized to enact the individual mandate under two provisions of Article I, Section 8, of the U.S. Constitution—its power to regulate commerce and its power to tax. According to this position, health care falls that health care falls under the heading of commerce because the health-care law addresses a pressing national problem that is economic in nature. Opponents of the law say that the requirement to buy a product or service is unprecedented, regulates inactivity rather than activity, and opens the door to allowing Congress unlimited power to intrude on individual freedom. In the decision issued on June 28, 2012, the Supreme Court upheld the law but did so under Congress's taxing authority and not the commerce clause. Chief Justice Roberts, writing for the 5–4 majority, said the individual mandate "cannot be upheld as an exercise of Congress's power under the commerce clause," which allows Congress to regulate interstate commerce but "not to order individuals to engage in it." He continued, "In this case, however, it is reasonable to construe what Congress has done as increasing taxes on those who have a certain amount of income, but choose to go without health insurance. Such legislation is within Congress's power to tax."[22] In December, 2017, President Trump signed into law a tax reform bill that reduces the individual mandate tax penalty to zero.

State Sovereignty and the Eleventh Amendment

In recent years, the Supreme Court has issued a series of decisions that bolstered the authority of state governments under the Eleventh Amendment to the Constitution. As interpreted by the Court, that amendment in most circumstances precludes lawsuits against state governments for violations of rights established by federal laws unless the states consent to be sued. For example, in a 1999 case, *Alden v. Maine*, the Court held that Maine state employees could not sue the state for violating the overtime pay requirements of a federal act.[23] According to the Court, state immunity from such lawsuits "is a fundamental aspect of the sovereignty which [the states] enjoyed before the ratification of the Constitution, and which they retain today."

In 2000, in *Kimel v. Florida Board of Regents*, the Court held that the Eleventh Amendment precluded employees of a state university from suing the state to enforce a federal statute prohibiting age-based discrimination.[24] In 2003, however, in *Nevada v. Hibbs*, the Court ruled that state employers must abide by the federal Family and Medical Leave Act (FMLA).[25] The reasoning was that the FMLA seeks to outlaw gender bias, and government actions that may discriminate on the basis of gender must receive a "heightened review status" compared with actions that may discriminate on the basis of age or disability. Also, in 2004, the Court ruled that the Eleventh Amendment could not shield states from suits by individuals with disabilities who had been denied access to courtrooms located on the upper floors of buildings.[26]

22 Robert Barnes, "Supreme Court Upholds Obama's Health-Care Law," *The Washington Post*, www.washingtonpost.com /politics/supreme-court-to-rule-thursday-on-health-care-law/2012/06/28/ gJQAarRm8V_story.htm
23 527 U.S. 706 (1999).
24 528 U.S. 62 (2000).
25 538 U.S. 721 (2003).
26 *Tennessee v. Lane*, 541 U.S. 509 (2004).

Tenth Amendment Issues

The Tenth Amendment states: "The powers not delegated to the United States by the Constitution, nor prohibited by it to the States, are reserved to the States respectively, or to the people." In 1992, the Court held that requirements imposed on the state of New York under a federal act regulating low-level radio-active waste were inconsistent with the Tenth Amendment and thus unconstitutional. According to the Court, the act's "take title" provision, which required states to accept ownership of waste or regulate waste following Congress's instructions, exceeded the enumerated powers of Congress. Although Congress can regulate the handling of such waste, "it may not conscript state governments as its agents" in an attempt to enforce a program of federal regulation.[27]

In 1997, the Court revisited this Tenth Amendment issue. In *Printz v. United States*, the Court struck down the provisions of the federal Brady Handgun Violence Prevention Act of 1993 that required state employees to check the backgrounds of prospective handgun purchasers.[28] Said the Court:

> [T]he federal government may neither issue directives requiring the States to address particular problems, nor command the States' officers, or those of their political subdivisions, to administer or enforce a federal regulatory program.

Federalism and State Immigration Policy

■ **3.5** Evaluate immigration policy as a challenge to modern federalism.

Until very recently, immigration policy was widely viewed as falling within the purview of the federal government. Regulating the border would also seem to fall to the federal government because it involves more than one state as well as the United States. Citing inaction or ineffective action by the federal government, however, several states have enacted their own immigration laws that are more restrictive than federal statute requires.

U.S. federal law requires all immigrants over the age of 14 who remain in the United States for more than 30 days to register with the U.S. government and to have registration documents in their possession at all times. Arizona adopted a more restrictive law that makes it a misdemeanor crime for an immigrant to be in Arizona without required documents. The law also requires state law enforcement personnel to attempt to determine an individual's immigration status during a stop, detention, or arrest when "reasonable suspicion" exists that the individual is an illegal immigrant. State and local officials are prohibited from restricting enforcement of immigration law, and stiff penalties are imposed on anyone found to be sheltering, hiring, or transporting illegal immigrants. This approach has been labeled "attrition through enforcement."

On June 25, 2012, the U.S. Supreme Court issued a split decision, upholding part of the Arizona law and rejecting other provisions on the grounds that they interfered with the federal government's role in setting immigration policy. The Court unanimously affirmed the law's requirement that police check the immigration status of people they detain and suspect to be in the country illegally, emphasizing that state law enforcement officials already possessed the discretion to ask about immigration status. The same ruling, however, rejected

---

27 *New York v. United States*, 505 U.S. 144 (1992).
28 521 U.S. 898 (1997).

parts of the Arizona law that it said undermine federal law. Justice Anthony Kennedy, writing for the majority, also indicated that the Court would entertain future challenges to the "show me your papers" provision if there is evidence of illegal racial or ethnic profiling after the law is implemented.

At the federal level, President Obama created, by executive action, the Deferred Action for Childhood Arrivals (DACA) program designed to halt deportation of young people brought to the United States by their parents when they were minors (under 16) and who meet certain criteria (have lived in the United States continuously, are enrolled in school or have graduated from high school, have not been convicted of a felony, and are younger than 30 years old). As the 2014 mid-term elections neared, Obama unveiled the Deferred Action for Parents of Americans and Lawful Permanent Residents (DAPA), along with a number of immigration reform steps, including increased resources for border enforcement, new procedures for high-skilled immigrants, and an expansion of the DACA program. Within a month, Texas and 25 other states filed suit asking the court to stop implementation of DACA and DAPA.[29] The states, all led by Republican governors, claimed that both programs, advanced by executive action rather than legislation, overstepped the bounds of executive authority. A district judge ruled that the states had legal standing to sue and stopped the implementation of the plan—a decision upheld by the U.S. Court of Appeals. An equally divided U.S. Supreme Court (4–4) issued a one-line *per curiam* opinion that leaves in place the lower court's preliminary injunction blocking the program. The Trump administration rescinded DAPA in June 2017. President Trump also announced, in September 2017, the end of DACA but gave Congress until March 5, 2018, to enact legislation to continue the program. Although the deadline passed without congressional action, DACA protections remain in place due to an injunction in federal court blocking the Trump administration from ending DACA pending legal challenges.

Other Federalism Cases

In recent years, the Supreme Court has sent mixed messages in federalism cases. At times the Court has favored states' rights, whereas on other occasions it has backed the federal government's position.

The Supreme Court argued in 2005 that the federal government's power to seize and destroy illegal drugs trumped California's law legalizing the use of marijuana for medical treatment.[30] Yet, less than a year later, the Court favored states' rights in another case rife with federalism issues, *Gonzales v. Oregon*.[31] After a lengthy legal battle, the Court upheld Oregon's controversial "Death with Dignity" law, which allows patients with terminal illnesses to choose to end their lives early and thus alleviate suffering. More recently the Court was presented with the issue of immigration. Control of the country's borders would normally fall within the federal government's jurisdiction; however, the state of Arizona argued that the federal government was not doing enough to control illegal immigration and adopted a controversial new law in 2010. When the Court ruled on the constitutionality of the law in 2012, justices said that a state cannot act to undermine federal authority in immigration law and sided with the administration.

---

29 *Texas v. United States*, 787 F.3d.
30 *Gonzales v. Raich*, 545 U.S. 1 (2005).
31 546 U.S. 243 (2006).

Twitter Feed ▶ **Is refugee resettlement an issue best handled by the states or the national government? Should a state be allowed to refuse to accept refugees legally admitted to the United States?**

Greg Abbott ✔
@GregAbbott_TX

⚙ 👤 Follow

BREAKING: Texas will not accept any Syrian refugees & I demand the U.S. act similarly. Security comes first.

gov.texas.gov/files/press-of …

RETWEETS   LIKES
5,278   5,629

10:24 AM - 16 Nov 2015

Republican candidate Donald J. Trump's promise to build a giant wall along the U.S. southern border and force Mexico to pay for it brought renewed attention to immigration issues in the 2016 primary contests. As President, Trump has asked Congress to pay for the wall. Following coordinated terrorist attacks in Paris in November 2015, several state governors announced that their states would not accept Syrian refugees for resettlement. In a letter to President Obama, the governor of Texas, Greg Abbott, said that he had directed the Texas Health and Human Services Commission's Refugee Resettlement program to stop relocating Syrian refugees. "Given the tragic attacks in Paris and the threats we have already seen, Texas cannot participate in any program that will result in Syrian refugees—any one of whom could be connected to terrorism—being resettled in Texas," Abbott wrote in the letter. "And I urge you, as President, to halt your plans to allow Syrians to be resettled anywhere in the United States."[32] New Jersey governor and former Republican presidential candidate Chris Christie said that his state would not take in any refugees—"not even orphans under the age of five."[33]

According to the U.S. State Department, refugee status gives individuals both legal status in the United States and freedom to move from state to state, making it unclear that states could refuse to take in Syrian refugees. The Obama administration pledged to take 10,000 Syrian refugees, whereas European Union member states agreed to resettle more than 160,000 people. Syrians flown to the United States would be the most heavily vetted group of people currently allowed into the country, according to the State Department. Immigration and refugee resettlement questions illustrate the dynamic tension between national and state interests.

The federal government has provided states with financial resources through direct transfer and various forms of grants-in-aid that have enabled states to experiment with innovative solutions to problems. However, as the federal government has fewer resources to share, how will federalism fare? If the federal government has fewer "carrots" in the form of financial incentives for state policy behavior, will it resort to "sticks" in the form of more unfunded mandates with stiff penalties for noncompliance? How will states and the federal government address ongoing issues such as the opioid epidemic, cybersecurity threats, property damage due to natural disasters, or new technologies such as self-driving cars and drones? How will new initiatives by the Trump administration impact the states? Federalism remains a dynamic force in American politics.

did you know?

About 63 percent of undocumented immigrants have been living in the United States for 10 years or longer.

32 Esther Castillejo, "Growing Number of States Refuse to Accept Syrian Refugees in Wake of Paris Attacks," ABC News, November 16, 2015. http://abcnews.go.com/US/states-refuse-accept-syrian-refugees-wake/

33 Lauren Gambino, "Syrian Refugees in America: Separating Fact from Fiction," *The Guardian*, November 19, 2015. http://www.theguardian.com/us-news/2015/nov/19/syrian-refugees-in-america-fact-from-fiction-congress

Twitter/Greg Abbott

Key Terms

Chapter Summary

■ **3.1** There are three basic models for ordering relations between central governments and local units: (1) a unitary system (in which ultimate power is held by the national government), (2) a confederal system (in which ultimate power is retained by the states), and (3) a federal system (in which governmental powers are divided between the national government and the states).

■ **3.2** Some of the advantages of federalism are that it affords distributed decision making that is effective in large geographic areas, it promotes the development and sustainability of many subcultures within the states, it allows states to serve as incubators for new policies and processes, and it limits the influence of any one group or set of interests. Among the disadvantages of federalism are that powerful states or states controlled by minority interests can limit progress or undermine the rights of minority groups. Federalism also results in inequities across states in terms of policies and spending on services such as education or crime prevention.

■ **3.3** The Constitution expressly delegated certain powers to the national government in Article I, Section 8. In addition to these expressed powers, the national government has implied and inherent powers. Implied powers are those that are reasonably necessary to carry out the powers expressly delegated to the national government. Inherent powers are those held by the national government by virtue of its being a sovereign state with the right to preserve itself. The supremacy clause of the Constitution states that the Constitution, congressional laws, and national treaties are the supreme law of the land. States cannot use their reserved or concurrent powers to override national policies. Vertical checks and balances allow states to influence the national government and vice versa. Horizontal checks and balances provide another form in that governments on the same level—either state or national—may check one another.

■ **3.3** The Tenth Amendment to the Constitution states that powers not delegated to the United States by the Constitution, nor prohibited by it to the states, are reserved to the states, or to the people. In certain areas, the Constitution provides for concurrent powers, such as the power to tax, which are powers that are held jointly by the national and state governments. The Constitution also denies certain powers to both the national government and the states.

■ **3.4** Two landmark Supreme Court cases expanded the constitutional powers of the national government. Chief Justice John Marshall's expansive interpretation of the necessary and proper clause of the Constitution in *McCulloch v. Maryland* (1819) permitted the "necessary and proper" clause to be used to enhance the power of the national government. Additionally, his decision made it clear that no state could tax a national institution. Marshall's broad interpretation of the commerce clause in *Gibbons v. Ogden* (1824) further extended the constitutional regulatory powers of the national government.

■ **3.4** The controversy over slavery that led to the Civil War took the form of a fight over national government supremacy versus the rights of the separate states. Ultimately, the South's desire for increased states' rights and the subsequent Civil War resulted in an increase in the political power of the national government.

■ **3.4** Since the Civil War, federalism has evolved through at least two general phases: dual federalism and cooperative federalism. In dual federalism, each of the states and the federal government remain supreme within their own spheres. The era since the Great Depression has sometimes been labeled one of cooperative federalism, in which states and the national government cooperate in solving complex common problems.

■ **3.4 & 3.5** The U.S. Supreme Court plays a significant role in determining the line between state and federal powers. Since the 1990s, the Court has been nipping at the national government's powers under the commerce clause and has given increased emphasis to state powers under the Tenth and Eleventh Amendments to the Constitution. New challenges to the balance of power between the federal and state governments come from the prolonged economic recession, which limited the federal government's ability to transfer funds to states to promote policy innovation, and from controversial social issues on which public opinion varies widely by state, including immigration policy and refugee resettlement.

Selected Resources

PRINT RESOURCES

Hamilton, Alexander, James Madison and John Jay. *The Federalist Papers.* Clinton Rossiter, editor (New York: Signet Classics, 2003). These essays remain an authoritative exposition of the founders' views on federalism.

Koppel, Ted. *Lights Out: A Cyberattack, A Nation Unprepared, Surviving the Aftermath* (New York: Crown Publishing, 2015). An investigative report of the vulnerability of the nation's power supply to cyber attack and the resulting consequences for a digital-dependent economy. The interconnectivity of the three major regional power grids makes this an interesting challenge to federalism.

Manna, Paul. *School's In: Federalism and the National Education Agenda* (Washington, DC: Georgetown University Press, 2006). The author examines the changing relationship between the federal government and the states with regard to our public education system.

Nugent, John D. *Safeguarding Federalism: How States Protect Their Interests in National Policymaking* (Norman, OK: University of Oklahoma Press, 2009). Tracing the history of federalism, the author proposes that federalism is a vital force in American politics. He shows how the states protect their interest in policy innovation through a number of tactics, including influencing federal legislation.

MEDIA RESOURCES

Borderland: Dispatches from the US-Mexico Boundary—NPR producer Steve Inskeep and a team of broadcast reporters spent two weeks driving through the place where the United States and Mexico meet. The result is a series of stories broadcast on NPR. The website includes video footage, maps, and documents to accompany the audio.

City of Hope—A 1991 movie by John Sayles. The film is a story of life, work, race, and politics in a modern New Jersey city. An African American alderman is one of the several major characters.

The Civil War—The PBS documentary series that made director Ken Burns famous. First shown in 1990, it marked a revolution in documentary technique. Photographs, letters, eyewitness memoirs, and music are used to bring the war to life. The DVD version was released in 2002.

John Adams—John Adams became the second president of the United States (served 1797–1801) after serving two terms as vice president during George Washington's administration. Starring Paul Giamatti as John Adams, the seven-part series aired on HBO in the spring of 2008. It depicts Adams's political life and highlights the role he played in the nation's founding.

The Wire—An HBO series set in Baltimore, Maryland, highlighting issues of state and local collaboration and competition when addressing the illegal drug trade.

When the Levees Broke: A Requiem in Four Acts—A 2006 documentary by Spike Lee that critically examines the federal, state, and local government response to Hurricane Katrina.

ONLINE RESOURCES

Brookings—policy analyses and recommendations on a variety of issues, including federalism: www.brookings.edu

Cato Institute—a libertarian approach to issues relating to federalism: www.cato.org

The Constitution Society—links to U.S. state constitutions, the *Federalist Papers*, and international federations, such as the European Union: www.constitution.org

Council of State Governments—information on state responses to federalism issues: www.csg.org

National Council of State Legislatures—research and resources on issues important to states: http://www.ncsl.org/

National Governors Association—information on issues facing state governments and federal–state relations: www.nga.org

Civil Liberties

Transportation Security Administration (TSA) employees demonstrate a new full-body scanner at Logan Airport in Boston, Massachusetts. Although the flying public has grown accustomed to these security measures, privacy activists warn that civil liberties must remain paramount amid heightened security concerns following the September 11, 2001, terrorist attacks and several subsequent terrorist threats.

epa european pressphoto agency b.v./Alamy Stock Photo

LEARNING OBJECTIVES

After reading this chapter, you will be able to:

■ **4.1** Identify the protection of civil liberties in the Bill of Rights and explain how these protections against government interference were applied to the states.

■ **4.2** Give examples of how the Bill of Rights protects freedom of religion while maintaining a separation between the state and religion, thereby limiting the direct influence of religion in public life.

■ **4.3** Locate the protections of political expression and dissent in the Constitution and explain why freedom of expression is critical to people's participation in politics.

■ **4.4** Discuss the constitutional protection of privacy rights in personal and public life and evaluate the threats to privacy rights posed by technology and security interests.

■ **4.5** Identify the rights of the accused and discuss the role of the Supreme Court in defining criminal due process rights over time.

■ **4.6** Evaluate modern threats to civil liberties posed by spy technology, the transfer of personal information through social media, and heightened security concerns following the September 11, 2001, terrorist attacks.

What if... The Proliferation of Conscience-Clause Laws Undermines Your Civil Liberties?

Background

Conscience-clause laws first appeared in reaction to the U.S. Supreme Court's ruling in *Roe v. Wade*, declaring that a woman's constitutionally protected right to privacy includes the right to have an abortion and limiting the restrictions states could place on abortion services. In the years following *Roe*, several states passed laws that allowed doctors and other health-care providers to refuse to perform or assist in an abortion if doing so would violate their religious principles. Congress enacted the Church Amendment in 1973 that allowed hospitals and other health-care facilities receiving certain types of federal funds to refuse to provide abortion or sterilization if such services were contrary to their religious and moral beliefs. "Right of refusal" laws allow pharmacists to refuse to fill prescriptions for abortifacient drugs, including birth control. In addition to pharmacists, ambulance drivers, cashiers, and prison guards may be covered by state provisions that allow individuals to refuse to sell or provide contraception based on personal religious convictions. Are conscience-clause and right of refusal laws essential protections of religious liberty or a systematic effort to ignore civil liberties protections that should apply to everyone? How can the inherent contradictions be resolved? Can two fundamental constitutional rights conflict yet coexist?

Legal Gay Marriage and the Next Wave of Conscience Laws

Just as *Roe v. Wade* triggered a series of state health-care refusal laws, the Supreme Court's decision in *Obergefell v. Hodges* has resulted in states adopting new right of conscience laws. *Obergefell* established the fundamental right to marry for same-sex couples under the due process clause and the equal protection clause of the Fourteenth Amendment. In particular, states have sought to extend existing religious freedom protections to businesses related to weddings—caterers, florists, photographers, and bakeries. As governor of Indiana Mike Pence signed the Religious Freedom Restoration Act in 2015 allowing individuals and companies to assert that their exercise of religion has been, or is likely to be, substantially burdened as a defense in legal proceedings. Indiana does not have a state wide antidiscrimination law. As one commentator observed, "The irony of gay marriage becoming legal in the United States is that it has made discrimination against LGBT people easier."*

Virginia and other states have laws that extend religious freedom in ways that enable private adoption or foster care agencies to refuse any placement that would violate the agency's written religious or moral convictions or policies. Critics claim these laws allow adoption agencies to refuse placements to same-sex couples, married or unmarried.

Following the *Obergefell* decision, Rowan County Kentucky clerk Kim Davis refused to issue marriage licenses to same-sex couples. When ordered to do so by the courts, she refused, saying that saying she was acting "under God's authority," and spent five days in jail for contempt. As a condition of her release, she agreed not to interfere with her deputies as they issued marriage licenses. Ultimately, Governor Matthew Bevin issued an executive order removing the clerks' names from Kentucky marriage licenses.

Where is the line between freedom of conscience and antidiscrimination protections?

Individuals, Nonprofits, and Corporations: A Distinction without a Difference?

In 2014, the U.S. Supreme Court rendered a decision in *Burwell v. Hobby Lobby Stores, Inc.* recognizing for the first time a for-profit corporation's religious belief. The decision is limited to "for-profit, closely-held corporations," interpreted as private companies (no public stocks are traded) owned and controlled by members of a single family. Although the decision is quite narrow, it opens the door for the protection of religious liberties to be more expansively applied to agencies and businesses rather than being reserved to individuals. It may also make more likely situations in which the religious convictions of an employer (or health-care provider, or retailer) will conflict with the religious convictions of an employee (or a patient, or a customer).

Cases Cited

Roe v. Wade, 410 U.S. 113 (1973).
Obergefell v. Hodges, 576 U.S. (2015).
Burwell v. Hobby Lobby Stores, Inc., 573 U.S. (2014).

For Critical Analysis

1. Are some consciences more important than others? How will courts choose between religious convictions when they conflict? What will be the constitutional criteria for resolving these questions?

2. Is the growing web of state and federal conscience clauses undermining basic civil liberties and laws applicable to all people? Defend your position with examples.

3. In the Hobby Lobby case, the Supreme Court said for the first time that a company can hold religious and moral principles. In practice, what will this mean? If conscience-clause laws allow businesses to pick and choose who they serve, how will you know where you can shop or dine? More importantly, what happens to equal protection and antidiscrimination laws?

*Emma Green, "Can States Protect LGBT Rights without Compromising Religious Freedom?" *The Atlantic*, January 6, 2016. www.theatlantic.com/politics/archive/2016/01/lgbt-discrimination-protection-states-religion/422730/

"The land of the free." Liberty and freedom are fundamental to our understanding of what it means to be an American. Up until this point, when we have talked about liberty or limited government, it has been in the context of the structure and functions of government. **Civil liberties**, on the other hand, are express limits on government's ability to interfere in our individual lives and our ability to exercise popular sovereignty. Without the ability to speak or act freely in politics—especially the ability to express dissenting ideas—we could not claim to be a democracy. Pluralism, the belief that diverse opinions and competing ideas strengthen society, applies to government as well. Because governments small and large might be tempted to quiet dissenting voices, civil liberties exist to put limits on government's power. Civil liberties also include due process considerations, particularly for those accused of a crime. In our system, we embrace the presumption of innocence, and criminal due process protections seek to equalize the power of the individual accused and the government as accuser. The Fourth Amendment protection against unreasonable search and seizure is vital to everyone.

The Bill of Rights articulates many of the civil liberties limitations on the national government. These limits were later applied to prevent state government restrictions of civil liberties. Liberty and freedom are not absolute rights, however, and this chapter explores the ways in which competing liberties and competing political values are resolved by the political system—most often by the U.S. Supreme Court. Our understanding of personal freedoms evolves over time and in reaction to changes in society and the world. Terrorists significantly altered the American view of civil liberties relative to the desire for national security protections. Digital technology has expanded avenues for political expression and action, but it also subjects each of us to increased surveillance and challenges long-held notions of privacy rights.

civil liberties
Those personal freedoms that are protected for all individuals. Civil liberties typically involve restraining the government's actions against individuals.

did you know?
One of the proposed initial constitutional amendments— "No State shall infringe the equal rights of conscience, nor the freedom of speech, nor of the press, nor of the right of trial by jury in criminal cases"—was never sent to the states for approval because the states' rights advocates in the first Congress defeated it.

Civil Liberties and the Bill of Rights

■ **4.1** Identify the protection of civil liberties in the Bill of Rights and explain how these protections against government interference were applied to the states.

Civil liberties are constitutionally guaranteed protections *against* government interference or abuse. The First Amendment reads "Congress shall make no law . . ." meaning that government's actions are restricted when it comes to free speech, religious liberties, and the press. Civil rights, addressed in the next chapter, are different. Civil rights require government to *take action* to protect individuals and their rights. Civil liberties impose limits, and civil rights impose positive obligations on government. Adding the Bill of Rights was necessary to gain ratification of the Constitution in several states. Although several state constitutions contained civil liberties guarantees, the proposed federal constitution did not. Thus, the Federalists promised to take up amendments to the Constitution aimed at limiting government's ability to violate individual liberty. Twelve amendments were proposed and ten were ratified as the Bill of Rights.

The Bill of Rights is relatively brief. The framers set forth broad guidelines, leaving it up to the courts to interpret these constitutional mandates and apply them to specific situations. Thus, judicial interpretations shape the true nature of the civil liberties and rights that we possess. Because judicial interpretations change over time, so do our rights. Conflicts over the meaning of such simple phrases as *freedom of religion* and *freedom of the press* remain unresolved. One important conflict was over the issue of whether the Bill of Rights limited the powers of state governments as well as those of the national government.

Extending the Bill of Rights to State Governments

Many citizens do not realize that, as originally intended, the Bill of Rights limited only the powers of the national government. At the time the Bill of Rights was ratified, the potential of state governments to curb civil liberties caused little concern. State governments were closer to home and easier to control, and most state constitutions already had bills of rights. Rather, the fear was of the potential tyranny of the national government. The Bill of Rights begins with, "Congress shall make no law . . ." It says nothing about *states* making laws.

In 1833, in *Barron v. Baltimore*, the U.S. Supreme Court held that the Bill of Rights did not apply to state laws.[1] The issue was whether a property owner could sue the city of Baltimore for recovery of his losses under the Fifth Amendment to the Constitution. Chief Justice Marshall spoke for a united court, declaring that the Supreme Court could not hear the case because the amendments were meant only to limit the national government.

State bills of rights were similar to the national one. Furthermore, each state's judicial system interpreted the rights differently. Citizens in different states effectively had different sets of civil rights. Remember that the Thirteenth, Fourteenth, and Fifteenth Amendments were passed after the Civil War to guarantee equal rights to the former slaves and free black Americans, regardless of where they lived. It was not until after the Fourteenth Amendment was ratified in 1868 that civil liberties guaranteed by the national Constitution began to be applied to the states. Section 1 of that amendment provides, in part, as follows:

> *No State shall . . . . deprive any person of life, liberty, or property, without due process of law.*

Incorporation of the Fourteenth Amendment

There was no question that the Fourteenth Amendment applied to state governments. For decades, however, the courts were reluctant to define the liberties spelled out in the national Bill of Rights as constituting "due process of law," which was protected under the Fourteenth Amendment. In 1925, in *Gitlow v. New York*, the U.S. Supreme Court held that the Fourteenth Amendment applied the First Amendment, freedom of speech, to the states.[2]

Gradually, but never completely, the Supreme Court accepted the **incorporation theory**—the view that most of the protections of the Bill of Rights are incorporated into the Fourteenth Amendment's protection against state government actions. Table 4-1 shows the rights that the Court has incorporated into the Fourteenth Amendment and the case in which it first applied each protection. The later Supreme Court decisions listed in Table 4-1 require the 50 states to accept for their citizens most of the rights and freedoms that are set forth in the U.S. Bill of Rights.

incorporation theory
The view that most of the protections of the Bill of Rights apply to state governments through the Fourteenth Amendment's due process clause.

---

1 7 Peters 243 (1833).
2 68 U.S. 652 (1925).

Table 4-1 ▶ Incorporating the Bill of Rights into the Fourteenth Amendment

YEAR	ISSUE	AMENDMENT INVOLVED	COURT CASE
1925	Freedom of speech	I	*Gitlow v. New York*, 268 U.S. 652
1931	Freedom of the press	I	*Near v. Minnesota*, 283 U.S. 697
1932	Right to a lawyer in capital punishment cases	VI	*Powell v. Alabama*, 287 U.S. 45
1937	Freedom of assembly and right to petition	I	*De Jonge v. Oregon*, 299 U.S. 353
1940	Freedom of religion	I	*Cantwell v. Connecticut*, 310 U.S. 296
1947	Separation of church and state	I	*Everson v. Board of Education*, 330 U.S. 1
1948	Right to a public trial	VI	*In re Oliver*, 333 U.S. 257
1949	No unreasonable searches and seizures	IV	*Wolf v. Colorado*, 338 U.S. 25
1961	Exclusionary rule	IV	*Mapp v. Ohio*, 367 U.S. 643
1962	No cruel and unusual punishment	VIII	*Robinson v. California*, 370 U.S. 660
1963	Right to a lawyer in all criminal felony cases	VI	*Gideon v. Wainwright*, 372 U.S. 335
1964	No compulsory self-incrimination	V	*Malloy v. Hogan*, 378 U.S. 1
1965	Right to privacy	I, III, IV, V, IX	*Griswold v. Connecticut*, 381 U.S. 479
1966	Right to an impartial jury	VI	*Parker v. Gladden*, 385 U.S. 363
1967	Right to a speedy trial	VI	*Klopfer v. North Carolina*, 386 U.S. 213
1969	No double jeopardy	V	*Benton v. Maryland*, 395 U.S. 784

Freedom of Religion

■ **4.2** Give examples of how the Bill of Rights protects freedom of religion while maintaining a separation between the state and religion, thereby limiting the direct influence of religion in public life.

In the United States, freedom of religion consists of two main principles as presented in the First Amendment. The **establishment clause** prohibits the establishment of a church that is officially supported by the national government, thus guaranteeing a division between church and state. The *free exercise clause* constrains the national government from prohibiting individuals from practicing the religion of their choice. These two precepts can inherently be in tension with one another, however. Public universities must allow religious groups to form on campus under the free exercise clause, but the decision to fund the activities of religious student groups is much more complicated and depends on a number of factors relative to the establishment clause. In the most recent Supreme Court decision on this issue, the majority stipulated that the university may not "silence the expression of selected viewpoints" in making funding decisions.[3]

The Separation of Church and State—The Establishment Clause

The First Amendment to the Constitution states, in part, that "Congress shall make no law respecting an establishment of religion." In the words of Thomas Jefferson, the establishment clause was designed to create a "wall of separation of Church and State."[4]

establishment clause
The part of the First Amendment prohibiting the establishment of a church officially supported by the national government. It is applied to questions of state and local government aid to religious organizations and schools, the legality of allowing or requiring school prayers, and the teaching of evolution versus intelligent design.

did you know?
About half of respondents in the 2015 State of the First Amendment survey believe that the U.S. Constitution establishes a Christian nation.

3 *Rosenberger v. University of Virginia*, 515 U.S. 819 (1995).
4 "Jefferson's Letter to the Danbury Baptists, The Final Letter, as Sent," January 1, 1802, The Library of Congress, Washington, DC.

Perhaps Jefferson was thinking about the religious intolerance that characterized the first colonies. Many of the American colonies were founded by groups that were pursuing religious freedom for their own particular denomination. Nonetheless, the early colonists were quite intolerant of religious beliefs that differed from their own. Established churches, meaning state-protected denominations, existed within 9 of the original 13 colonies.

As interpreted by the U.S. Supreme Court, the establishment clause in the First Amendment means at least the following:

> *Neither a state nor the federal government can set up a church. Neither can pass laws which aid one religion, aid all religions, or prefer one religion over another. Neither can force nor influence a person to go to or to remain away from church against his will or force him to profess a belief or disbelief in any religion. No person can be punished for entertaining or professing religious beliefs or disbeliefs, for church attendance or nonattendance. No tax in any amount, large or small, can be levied to support any religious activities or institutions, whatever they may be called, or whatever form they may adopt to teach or practice religion. Neither a state nor the federal government can, openly or secretly, participate in the affairs of any religious organizations or groups and vice versa.*[5]

The establishment clause is applied to conflicts over state and local government aid to religious organizations and schools, school prayer, evolution versus intelligent design, posting the Ten Commandments in schools or public places, and discrimination against religious groups in publicly operated institutions. The establishment clause's mandate that government can neither promote nor discriminate against religious beliefs raises particularly complex questions.

Aid to Church-Related Schools Throughout the United States, all property owners except religious, educational, fraternal, literary, scientific, and similar

Image 4-1

Students participate in the "See You at the Pole" event outside Old Main at the West Texas A&M University campus in Canyon, Texas. Issues related to prayer in public places, particularly public schools and universities, are far from settled. Students hold a prayer rally around the flag pole (symbolic of government). Social media promotes the event with #neverstoppraying.

nonprofit institutions must pay property taxes. A large part of the proceeds of such taxes goes to support public schools. But not all children attend public schools. Fully 12 percent of school-aged children attend private schools, of which 85 percent have religious affiliations. The Court has tried to draw a fine line between permissible public aid to students in church-related schools and impermissible public aid to religion. These issues have arisen most often at the elementary and secondary levels.

In 1971, in *Lemon v. Kurtzman*, the Court ruled that direct state aid could not be used to subsidize religious instruction.[6] The Court in the *Lemon* case gave its most general statement on the constitutionality of government aid to religious schools, stating that the aid had to be secular (nonreligious) in aim, that it could not have the primary effect of advancing or inhibiting religion, and that the government must avoid "an excessive government entanglement with religion." These three phrases became known as the "three-part *Lemon* test," which has been applied in most of the cases under the establishment clause since 1971. The interpretation of the test, however, has varied over the years.

In several cases, the Supreme Court has held that state programs helping church-related schools are unconstitutional. The Court also has denied state reimbursements to religious schools for field trips and for developing achievement tests. In a series of other cases, however, the Supreme Court has allowed states to use tax funds for lunches, textbooks, diagnostic services for speech and hearing problems, state-required standardized tests, computers, and transportation for students attending church-operated elementary and secondary schools. In some cases, the Court argued that state aid was intended to directly assist the individual child, and in other cases, such as bus transportation, the Court acknowledged the state's goals for public safety.

A Change in the Court's Position Today's Supreme Court has shown a greater willingness to allow the use of public funds for programs in religious schools. In 1985, in *Aguilar v. Felton*, the Supreme Court ruled that state programs providing special educational services for disadvantaged students attending religious schools violated the establishment clause.[7] In 1997, however, when the Supreme Court revisited this decision, the Court reversed its position. In *Agostini v. Felton*, the Court held that *Aguilar* was "no longer good law."[8] What happened to cause the Court to change its mind? Justice Sandra Day O'Connor answered that: What had changed since *Aguilar* was "our understanding" of the establishment clause. Between 1985 and 1997, the Court's makeup had also changed significantly. Six of the nine justices who participated in the 1997 decision were appointed after the 1985 *Aguilar* decision.

School Vouchers Questions about the use of public funds for church-related schools are likely to continue as state legislators search for new ways to improve the educational system. An issue that has come to the forefront is school vouchers. In a voucher system, educational vouchers (state-issued credits) can be used to "purchase" education at any school, public or private. In other words, the public money follows the individual student wherever he or she may enroll. Proponents of these programs argue that vouchers allow

6   403 U.S. 602 (1971).
7   473 U.S. 402 (1985).
8   521 U.S. 203 (1997).

low-income students to escape poorly performing public schools, whereas opponents warn that vouchers take money away from public schools that are already underfunded.

School districts in 13 states and the District of Columbia provide state-funded vouchers to qualifying students. The courts reviewed a case involving Ohio's voucher program in which some $10 million in public funds was spent annually to send 4,300 Cleveland students to 51 private schools, all but 5 of which were Catholic schools. The case presented a straightforward constitutional question: Is it a violation of separation of church and state for public tax money to be used to pay for religious education?

In 2002, the Supreme Court held that the Cleveland voucher program was constitutional.[9] The Court concluded, by a 5–4 vote, that Cleveland's use of taxpayer-paid school vouchers to send children to private schools was constitutional. The Court's majority reasoned that the program did not unconstitutionally entangle church and state because families theoretically could use the vouchers for their children to attend religious schools, secular private academies, suburban public schools, or charter schools, even though few public schools had agreed to accept vouchers. The Court's decision raised a further question—whether religious and private schools that accept government vouchers must comply with disability and civil rights laws, as public schools are required to do. Past decisions by the Supreme Court and recent guidance from the Department of Justice suggest that voucher programs must be administered in nondiscriminatory ways.

Despite the U.S. Supreme Court's decision upholding the Cleveland voucher program, in 2006 the Florida Supreme Court declared Florida's voucher program unconstitutional. The Florida court held that its state constitution bars public funding from being diverted to private schools that are not subject to the uniformity requirements of the state's public school system. The state of Arizona has taken a different approach, passing legislation to allow parents to reduce their state taxes by the amount of tuition paid to a private school. In 2011, the Supreme Court ruled that, because the money was paid directly from the individual to the school and the government did not support the private school, the law could not be challenged by other taxpayers.[10] In 2016, around 141,000 children received school vouchers; however, vouchers remain controversial.

The Issue of School Prayer—*Engel v. Vitale* Do the states have the right to promote religion in general, without making any attempt to establish a particular religion? That is the question raised by school prayer and was the issue in 1962 in *Engel v. Vitale*, the so-called Regents' Prayer case in New York.[11] The State Board of Regents of New York had suggested that a prayer be spoken aloud in the public schools at the beginning of each day. The recommended prayer was as follows:

> *Almighty God, we acknowledge our dependence upon Thee, And we beg Thy blessings upon us, our parents, our teachers, and our Country.*

---

9 *Zelman v. Simmons-Harris*, 536 U.S. 639 (2002).

10 *Arizona School Tuition Organization v. Winn.* 563 US 125 (2011).

11 370 U.S. 421 (1962).

Following implementation, parents of several students challenged the action of the regents, maintaining that it violated the establishment clause of the First Amendment. At trial, the parents lost. The Supreme Court, however, ruled that the regents' action was unconstitutional because "the constitutional prohibition against laws respecting an establishment of a religion must mean at least that in this country it is no part of the business of government to compose official prayers for any group of the American people to recite as part of a religious program carried on by any government." The Court's conclusion was based in part on the "historical fact that governmentally established religions and religious persecutions go hand in hand." In *Abington School District v. Schempp*, the Supreme Court outlawed officially sponsored daily readings of the Bible and recitation of the Lord's Prayer in public schools.[12]

The Debate over School Prayer Continues Although the Supreme Court has ruled repeatedly against officially sponsored prayer and Bible-reading sessions in public schools, other means for bringing some form of religious expression into public education have been attempted. In 1983, the Tennessee legislature passed a bill requiring public school classes to begin each day with a minute of silence. Alabama had a similar law. In 1985, in *Wallace v. Jaffree*, the Supreme Court struck down as unconstitutional the Alabama law authorizing one minute of silence for prayer or meditation in all public schools.[13] Applying the three-part *Lemon* test, the Court concluded that the law violated the establishment clause because it was "an endorsement of religion lacking any clearly secular purpose."

Since then, the lower courts have interpreted the Supreme Court's decision to mean that states can require a moment of silence in the schools as long as they make it clear that the purpose of the law is secular, not religious. Opponents argue that it is an opportunity for prayer in disguise.

Prayer Outside the Classroom The courts have also dealt with cases involving prayer in public schools outside the classroom, particularly during graduation ceremonies. In 1992, in *Lee v. Weisman*, the U.S. Supreme Court held that it was unconstitutional for a school to invite a rabbi to deliver a nonsectarian prayer at graduation.[14] The Court said nothing about *students* organizing and leading prayers at graduation ceremonies and other school events, however, and these issues continue to come before the courts. A particularly contentious question in recent years has been the constitutionality of student-initiated prayers before sporting events, such as football games. In 2000, the Supreme Court held that although school prayer at graduation did not violate the establishment clause, students could not use a school's public-address system to lead prayers at sporting events.[15]

Despite the Court's ruling, students at schools in several states (particularly those in the South) continue to pray over public-address systems prior to sporting events. In other areas, the Court's ruling is skirted by avoiding the use of the public-address system. In North Carolina, a pregame prayer was broadcast over a local radio station and heard by fans who took radios to the game for that purpose. Regardless of the Court's current interpretation, practices

12 374 U.S. 203 (1963).
13 472 U.S. 38 (1985).
14 505 U.S. 577 (1992).
15 *Santa Fe Independent School District v. Doe*, 530 U.S. 290 (2000).

related to prayer outside of the formal school setting vary widely but generally conform to community norms. Only when an individual or group objects is the question subject to the courts' interpretation again.

The Ten Commandments A related church–state issue is whether the Ten Commandments may be displayed in public schools—or on any public property. Supporters of the movement to display the Ten Commandments argue that they embody American values and that they constitute a part of the official and permanent history of American government.

Opponents of such laws claim that they are an unconstitutional government entanglement with the religious life of citizens. Still, various Ten Commandments installations have been found to be constitutional. For example, the Supreme Court ruled in 2005 that a granite monument on the grounds of the Texas state capitol that contained the commandments was constitutional because the monument as a whole was secular in nature.[16] In another 2005 ruling, however, the Court ordered that displays of the Ten Commandments in front of two Kentucky county courthouses had to be removed because they were overtly religious.[17]

Forbidding the Teaching of Evolution For many decades, certain religious groups, particularly in Southern states, have opposed the teaching of evolution in the schools. To these groups, evolutionary theory directly counters their religious belief that human beings did not evolve, but were created fully formed, as described in the biblical story of creation. State and local attempts to forbid the teaching of evolution, however, have not passed constitutional muster in the eyes of the U.S. Supreme Court. In 1968, the Court held in *Epperson v. Arkansas* that an Arkansas law prohibiting the teaching of evolution violated the establishment clause because it imposed religious beliefs on students.[18] The Louisiana legislature passed a law requiring the teaching of the biblical story of the creation alongside the teaching of evolution. In 1987, in *Edwards v. Aguillard*, the Supreme Court declared that this law was unconstitutional, in part because it had as its primary purpose the promotion of a particular religious belief.[19]

Nonetheless, state and local groups around the country continue their efforts against the teaching of evolution. The Cobb County school system in Georgia attempted to include a disclaimer in its biology textbooks that proclaims, "Evolution is a theory, not a fact, regarding the origin of living things." A federal judge later ruled that it must be removed. Other school districts have considered teaching "intelligent design" as an alternative explanation of the origin of life. Proponents of intelligent design contend that evolutionary theory has gaps that can be explained only by the existence of an intelligent creative force (God). Intelligent design, at its essence, proposes an original creator, which is a religious belief that cannot be taught in public schools.

Religious Speech Another controversy in the area of church–state relations concerns religious speech in public schools or universities. In *Rosenberger v. University of Virginia*, the issue was whether the University of Virginia violated

did you know?

The Pew Research Center found that 34 percent of American adults in 2016 rejected evolution, believing instead that "humans and other living things have existed in their present form since the beginning of time."

---

16 *Van Orden v. Perry*, 125 S. Ct. 2854 (2005).
17 *McCreary County v. American Civil Liberties Union*, 125 S. Ct. 2722 (2005).
18 393 U.S. 97 (1968).
19 482 U.S. 578 (1987).

the establishment clause when it refused to fund publication costs related to a Christian magazine, *Wide Awake,* but granted funds collected from student activity fees to more than 100 other student organizations.[20] The university argued that providing funding violated the establishment clause, whereas Robert Rosenberger and other founders of *Wide Awake* argued under a free speech claim that the magazine was designed to promote discussion. The Supreme Court ruled that the university's policy unconstitutionally discriminated against religious speech and that the university may not "silence the expression of selected viewpoints." The Court pointed out that the funds came from student fees, not general taxes, and were used for the "neutral" payment of bills for student groups.

Later, the Supreme Court reviewed a case involving a similar claim of discrimination against a religious group, the Good News Club. The club offers religious instruction to young schoolchildren. The club sued the school board of a public school in Milford, New York, when the board refused to allow the club to meet on school property after the school day ended. The club argued that the school board's refusal to allow the club to meet on school property, when other groups—such as the Girl Scouts and the 4-H Club—were permitted to do so, amounted to discrimination on the basis of religion. Ultimately, the Supreme Court agreed, ruling in *Good News Club v. Milford Central School* that the Milford school board's decision violated the establishment clause.[21]

Public Expression of Religion What kinds of religious expression are protected in public displays? The World Trade Center cross is a configuration of steel beams found in the rubble after the September 11, 2001, terrorist attacks collapsed both towers. The proportions resemble a Christian cross, and once found, the cross became a makeshift memorial and site of reflection. The cross has been installed in the National September 11 Memorial Museum, prompting objections from the group American Atheists. Members of the group are filing a lawsuit arguing that the cross does not belong in a private museum situated on property leased from the government. "It's necessary to fight this because this is inequality on government property," said American Atheists president David Silverman. "If you take the religion away from the cross, you've got scrap metal," Silverman said. "Just like all the other scrap metal that fell on the cross. The only reason that this cross is special is because it is religious."[22]

Blasphemy and Free Speech Rights We have seen a number of instances where fundamental rights collide. In the United States, these conflicts are usually resolved by the Supreme Court, but in other

Image 4-2
This steel beam structure was discovered at ground zero following the collapse of the World Trade Center on September 11, 2001. Resembling a cross, the structure became a memorial and place for reflection during the clean-up and reconstruction. The structure is now housed in the National September 11 Memorial Museum.

Mak/Alamy Stock photo

---

20 515 U.S. 819 (1995).

21 533 U.S. 98 (2001).

22 Scott Stump, "World Trade Center Cross Fight Continues as Atheist Group Appeals Ruling," TODAY News, March 6, 2014. www.today.com/news/world-trade-center-cross-fight-continues-athiest-group-appeals-ruling-2D79328902

nations the means of resolving a clash of fundamental differences is less clear. Take the example of blasphemy—defined as insulting God or any religious or holy person or thing. In some countries, blasphemy is not only illegal but is punishable by death. Although some states have adopted antiblasphemy statutes, such laws violate the U.S. Constitution and, when challenged, have been struck down. On January 7, 2015, armed Islamist terrorists broke into the Paris offices of the French satirical magazine *Charlie Hebdo*, killing 12 people. The gunmen were heard shouting "Allahu akbar" ("God is great" in Arabic) and also "the Prophet is avenged." *Charlie Hebdo* was the target of attacks in 2011 as well—both presumably in response to controversial Muhammad cartoons it published, dubbed "overt provocations" by some. The attack was widely condemned, and those standing in solidarity with the magazine demonstrated their support for free speech and freedom of expression by adopting the phrase *"Je suis Charlie"* (I am Charlie). Offensive, inflammatory, and even blasphemous speech and expression are protected by the First Amendment in the United States. An annual survey of American attitudes about the First Amendment conducted in 2015 found that 63 percent of individuals favor allowing cartoonists to publish images of Muhammad even though those images could be offensive to some religions.[23]

The Free Exercise Clause

free exercise clause
The provision of the First Amendment guaranteeing the free exercise of religion.

The First Amendment constrains Congress from prohibiting the free exercise of religion. Does this **free exercise clause** mean that no type of religious practice can be prohibited or restricted by government? Certainly, a person can hold any religious belief that he or she wants, or have no religious beliefs. When, however, religious *practices* work against public policy and the public welfare, the government can act. For example, regardless of a child's or parent's religious beliefs, the government can require certain types of vaccinations. The sale and use of some controlled substances for religious purposes has been held illegal, because a religion cannot make legal what would otherwise be illegal.

The extent to which government can regulate religious practices has always been a subject of controversy. In 1990, in *Oregon v. Smith*, the U.S. Supreme Court ruled that the state of Oregon could deny unemployment benefits to two drug counselors who had been fired for using peyote, an illegal drug, in their religious services.[24] The counselors had argued that using peyote was part of the practice of a Native American religion. Many criticized the decision, decrying the increased regulation of religious practices.

The Religious Freedom Restoration Act In 1993, Congress responded to the public's criticism by passing the Religious Freedom Restoration Act (RFRA). One of the specific purposes of the act was to overturn the Supreme Court's decision in *Oregon v. Smith*. The act required national, state, and local governments to "accommodate religious conduct" unless the government could show a *compelling* reason not to do so. Moreover, if the government did regulate a religious practice, it had to use the least restrictive means possible.

---

23 Newseum Institute, "The 2015 State of The First Amendment." www.newseuminstitute.org/wp-content/uploads/2015/07/FAC_SOFA15_report.pdf
24 494 U.S. 872 (1990).

Some people believed that the RFRA went too far in the other direction—it accommodated practices that were contrary to the public policies of state governments. Proponents of states' rights complained that the act intruded into an area traditionally governed by state laws, not by the national government. In 1997, in *City of Boerne v. Flores*, the Supreme Court agreed and held that Congress had exceeded its constitutional authority with the RFRA.[25] According to the Court, the act's "sweeping coverage ensures its intrusion at every level of government, displacing laws and prohibiting official actions of almost every description and regardless of subject matter." In response to this ruling, 31 states have adopted Religious Freedom Restoration Acts that apply to state and municipalities.

The Arizona legislature passed a bill in 2014 that would have allowed businesses to deny services to lesbian, gay, bisexual, or transgender (LGBT) customers. Governor Jan Brewer vetoed the law, but that hardly settled the question. Opponents of this and similar bills (pending or adopted) in other states view it as legalizing discrimination. Supporters argue that they should not be compelled by the state to promote views inconsistent with their personal religious beliefs. These divergent opinions were reflected by media tweets announcing the governor's veto—*The Washington Post* referred to it as an antigay bill, whereas *The Wall Street Journal* (a more conservative publication) termed it a religious freedom bill. Most of the cases in this area have arisen when vendors have refused to sell wedding cakes, flowers, or photography services to same-sex couples getting married. Former Indiana Governor Mike Pence signed the RFRA into law, allowing a business owner to cite his or her religious beliefs as a defense in court and banning local governments from making any law "substantially burdening" the free exercise of religion. The law was opposed by many in the business and hospitality community. According to the National Conference of State Legislatures, 21 states have RFRAs in some form.[26] Several other states, including North Carolina and Mississippi, adopted "Religious Liberty" laws in 2016. The reaction from major corporations was swift and negative—PayPal, Inc., withdrew plans to build a new processing facility in North Carolina. Governors in several states including New York and Washington prohibited "nonessential" travel by government employees to North Carolina. In Georgia, Governor Nathan Deal vetoed a similar measure under considerable pressure from major corporations and the Metro Atlanta Chamber.

A similar religious exemption battle took place over the Affordable Care Act's contraception mandate. The Supreme Court heard two cases (*Sebelius v. Hobby Lobby* and *Conestoga Wood Specialties Corp. v. Sebelius*) in which a company claimed its objection to providing mandated contraception coverage stemmed from the owners' religious beliefs. In *Burwell v. Hobby Lobby*, decided by a 5–4 vote in June 2014, the Supreme Court ruled that requiring "closely held" corporations to pay for insurance coverage for contraception violated the Religious Freedom Restoration Act of 1993. Justice Ruth Bader Ginsburg read her dissent from the bench, indicating her strong disagreement with the holding in the majority opinion. Following the *Hobby Lobby* decision, the Obama administration released new rules allowing women to get birth control at no cost, even if they work for employers that do not cover contraception because of religious objections. The Trump administration has pledged to roll back this policy.

---

25 521 U.S. 507 (1997).

26 National Conference of State Legislatures, "2015 State Religious Restoration Legislation." http://www.ncsl.org/research /civil-and-criminal-justice/2015-state-rfra-legislation.aspx

Freedom of Expression

■ **4.3** Locate the protections of political expression and dissent in the Constitution and explain why freedom of expression is critical to people's participation in politics.

Perhaps the most frequently invoked freedom that Americans have is the right to free speech and a free press without government interference. Citizens have the right to have a say, and all of us have the right to hear what others say. For the most part, Americans can criticize public officials and their actions without fear of reprisal by any branch of government.

No Prior Restraint

prior restraint
Restraining an action before the activity has actually occurred. When expression is involved, this means censorship.

Restraining an activity before that activity has actually occurred is called **prior restraint**. When expression is involved, prior restraint means censorship, as opposed to subsequent punishment. Prior restraint of expression would require, for example, that a permit be obtained before a speech could be made, a newspaper article published, a movie shown, or an art exhibition opened. Most, if not all, Supreme Court justices have been very critical of governmental action that imposes prior restraint on expression. The Court clearly displayed this attitude in *Nebraska Press Association v. Stuart*, a case decided in 1976:

> *A prior restraint on expression comes to this Court with a "heavy presumption" against its constitutionality . . . The government thus carries a heavy burden of showing justification for the enforcement of such a restraint.*[27]

One of the most famous cases concerning prior restraint was *New York Times v. United States* in 1971, the so-called Pentagon Papers case.[28] The *Times* and *The Washington Post* were about to publish the Pentagon Papers, an elaborate secret history of the U.S. government's involvement in the Vietnam War (1964–1975) released by Daniel Ellsberg, an employee of the RAND corporation. The government wanted a court order to bar publication of the documents, arguing that national security was threatened and that the documents had been stolen. The documents contained evidence that the U.S. government knew that the Vietnam War was likely "unwinnable" and that continuing the war would result in many more causalities than reported. The newspapers argued that the public had a right to know the information contained in the papers, even if it embarrassed the government, and that the press had the right to inform the public. The Supreme Court ruled 6–3 in favor of the newspapers' right to publish the information. This case affirmed the no prior restraint doctrine.

WikiLeaks, Edward Snowden, and Classified Information on the Internet

An organization known as WikiLeaks, led by Australian Julian Assange, released thousands of documents online leaked from governments around the world in 2010. Most documents had been "classified" by the respective governments as too sensitive to be made public. U.S. military and diplomatic documents were leaked by Chelsea Manning (born Bradley Manning), an Army intelligence officer with access to intelligence databases. Manning was convicted in 2013 on

---

27 427 U.S. 539 (1976). See also *Near v. Minnesota*, 283 U.S. 697 (1931).
28 403 U.S. 713 (1971).

Image 4-3
A supporter of the Anonymous group wearing a Guy Fawkes mask holds up a placard featuring a photo of U.S. intelligence leaker Edward Snowden during a rally in front of Berlin's landmark Brandenburg Gate on November 5, 2013.

espionage charges and sentenced to 35 years in prison. Just prior to leaving office, former president Obama commuted Manning's sentence and she was released in May 2017. Most recently, Edward Snowden, a computer specialist formerly employed by the Central Intelligence Agency (CIA) and a private contractor doing work for the National Security Agency (NSA), leaked thousands of documents detailing the NSA's international Internet surveillance initiatives and a collection of telephone metadata to *The Guardian* and *The Washington Post*. In June 2013, the U.S. government charged Snowden with espionage and revoked his U.S. passport. At the time, Snowden was in flight from Hong Kong to Ecuador with a one-night layover planned in Moscow. Without a passport, he could not continue his travel and remained stranded in the Moscow airport until Russia offered him temporary asylum for one year. Snowden remains in Russia today and makes his living with remote speaking engagements. Snowden is considered a fugitive from justice by the U.S. government, but a hero and patriot by others. Snowden claims that the only motive for his leaks was to "inform the public as to that which is done in their name and that which is done against them."[29] All of these leaks raise questions about the public's right (and possible need) to know what its government is doing, as well as issues of privacy and national security.

The Protection of Symbolic Speech

Not all expression is in words or in writing. Articles of clothing, gestures, movements, and other forms of expressive conduct are considered **symbolic speech**. Such speech is given substantial protection today by our courts. In a landmark decision issued in 1969, *Tinker v. Des Moines School District*, the U.S. Supreme Court held that the wearing of black armbands by students in protest against the Vietnam War was a form of speech protected by the First

symbolic speech
Nonverbal expression of beliefs, which is given substantial protection by the courts.

29 Glenn Greenwald, Ewen MacAskill, and Laura Poitras. "Edward Snowden: The Whistleblower Behind the NSA Surveillance Revelations." *The Guardian*, June 11, 2013. www.theguardian.com/world/2013/jun/09/edward-snowden-nsa-whistleblower -surveillance

Amendment.[30] The case arose after a school administrator in Des Moines, Iowa, issued a regulation prohibiting students in the Des Moines school district from wearing the armbands. The Supreme Court reasoned that the school district was unable to show that the wearing of the armbands had disrupted normal school activities. Furthermore, the school district's policy was discriminatory, as it banned only certain forms of symbolic speech (the black armbands) and not others (such as lapel crosses and fraternity rings).

In 1989, in *Texas v. Johnson*, the Supreme Court ruled that state laws that prohibited the burning of the American flag as part of a peaceful protest also violated the freedom of expression protected by the First Amendment.[31] Congress responded by passing the Flag Protection Act of 1989, which was ruled unconstitutional by the Supreme Court in June 1990.[32] Congress and President George H. W. Bush immediately pledged to work for a constitutional amendment to "protect our flag"—which has yet to be successful.

In 2003, however, the Supreme Court held that a Virginia statute prohibiting the burning of a cross with "an intent to intimidate" did not violate the First Amendment. The Court concluded that a burning cross is an instrument of racial terror so threatening that it does not warrant protection as a form of free expression.[33]

The Protection of Commercial Speech

commercial speech
Advertising statements, which increasingly have been given First Amendment protection.

Commercial speech is defined as advertising statements. Can advertisers use their First Amendment rights to prevent restrictions on the content of commercial advertising? Until the 1970s, the Supreme Court held that such speech was not protected at all by the First Amendment. By the mid-1970s, however, more commercial speech had been brought under First Amendment protection. According to Justice Harry A. Blackmun, "Advertising, however tasteless and excessive it sometimes may seem, is nonetheless dissemination of information as to who is producing and selling what product for what reason and at what price."[34] Nevertheless, the Supreme Court will consider a restriction on commercial speech valid as long as it (1) seeks to implement a substantial government interest, (2) directly advances that interest, and (3) goes no further than necessary to accomplish its objective. An advertisement that makes totally false claims can be restricted.

Political campaign advertising crosses the boundaries between individual free speech and commercial speech. For many years, federal law has prohibited businesses, labor unions, and other organizations from engaging directly in political advertising, but corporations and other groups were allowed to create political action committees to engage in regulated activities. In recent years, new organizational forms were created to campaign for issues. Nonprofit organizations, however, were strictly prohibited from directly campaigning for candidates. In 2009, the Supreme Court overturned decades of law on this issue, declaring in *Citizens United v. FEC* that corporations and other associations were "persons" in terms of the law and had free speech rights. According to the majority decision, Citizens United, an incorporated nonprofit

30 393 U.S. 503 (1969).
31 488 U.S. 884 (1989).
32 *United States v. Eichman*, 496 U.S. 310 (1990).
33 *Virginia v. Black*, 538 U.S. 343 (2003).
34 *Virginia State Board of Pharmacy v. Virginia Citizens Consumer Council, Inc.*, 425 U.S. 748 (1976).

group, was unfairly denied the right to pay for broadcasting a movie about Senator Hillary Clinton, which was intended to harm her presidential campaign. President Obama asked Congress to rewrite the campaign finance laws to restrict such forms of political advertising, but it has not successfully done so.[35]

Permitted Restrictions on Expression

At various times, restrictions on expression have been permitted. After the terrorist attacks of September 11, 2001, periods of perceived foreign threats to the government sometimes led to more repression of speech that is thought to be dangerous to the nation. The Supreme Court changes its view of what might be dangerous speech depending on the times.

Clear and Present Danger When a person's remarks create a clear and present danger to peace or public order, they can be curtailed constitutionally. Justice Oliver Wendell Holmes used this reasoning in 1919 when examining the case of a socialist who had been convicted for violating the Espionage Act by distributing a leaflet that opposed the military draft. Holmes stated:

> The question in every case is whether the words are used in such circumstances and are of such a nature as to create a clear and present danger that they will bring about the substantive evils that Congress has a right to prevent. It is a question of proximity and degree.[36]

According to the **clear and present danger test**, expression may be restricted if evidence exists that such expression would cause a condition, actual or imminent, that Congress has the power to prevent. Commenting on this test, Justice Louis D. Brandeis in 1920 said, "Correctly applied, it will reserve the right of free speech . . . from suppression by tyrannists, well-meaning majorities, and from abuse by irresponsible, fanatical minorities."[37]

clear and present danger test
The test proposed by Justice Oliver Wendell Holmes for determining when government may restrict free speech. Restrictions are permissible, he argued, only when speech creates a clear and present danger to the public order.

Modifications to the Clear and Present Danger Rule Since the clear and present danger rule was first enunciated, the U.S. Supreme Court has modified it. In 1925, when many Americans feared the increasing power of communist and other left-wing parties in Europe, the Supreme Court heard the case *Gitlow v. New York*.[38] In its opinion, the Court introduced the *bad-tendency rule*. According to this rule, speech or other First Amendment freedoms may be curtailed if a possibility exists that such expression might lead to some "evil." In the *Gitlow* case, a member of a left-wing group was convicted of violating New York State's criminal anarchy statute when he published and distributed a pamphlet urging the violent overthrow of the U.S. government. In its majority opinion, the Supreme Court held that although the First Amendment afforded protection against state incursions on freedom of expression, Gitlow could be punished legally because his expression would tend to bring about evils that the state had a right to prevent. If distributed now, Gitlow's publication would likely have been treated as protected political speech.

The Supreme Court again modified the clear and present danger test in a 1951 case, *Dennis v. United States*.[39] During the early years of the Cold War,

---

35 *Citizens United v. Federal Election Commission*, 558 U.S. (2010).
36 *Schenck v. United States*, 249 U.S. 47 (1919).
37 *Schaefer v. United States*, 251 U.S. 466 (1920).
38 268 U.S. 652 (1925).
39 341 U.S. 494 (1951).

Americans were anxious about the activities of communists and the Soviet Union within the United States. Congress passed several laws that essentially outlawed the Communist Party of the United States and made its activities illegal. Twelve members of the American Communist Party were convicted of violating a statute that made it a crime to conspire to teach, advocate, or organize the violent overthrow of any government in the United States. The Supreme Court affirmed the convictions, significantly modifying the clear and present danger test in the process. The Court applied a *grave and probable danger rule*. Under this rule, "the gravity of the 'evil' discounted by its improbability justifies such invasion of free speech as is necessary to avoid the danger." This rule gave much less protection to free speech than did the clear and present danger test.

Six years after the *Dennis* case, the Supreme Court heard another case in which members of the Communist Party in California were accused of teaching and advocating the overthrow of the government of the United States. The ruling of the Court greatly reduced the scope of the law passed by Congress. In *Yates v. United States*, the Court held that there was a difference between "advocacy and teaching of forcible overthrow as an abstract principle" and actually proposing concrete action.[40] The Court overturned the convictions of the party leaders because they were engaging in speech rather than action. This was the beginning of a series of cases that eventually found the original congressional legislation to be unconstitutional because it violated the First and Fourth Amendments.

Some claim that the United States did not achieve true freedom of political speech until 1969, when, in *Brandenburg v. Ohio*, the Supreme Court overturned the conviction of a Ku Klux Klan leader for violating a state statute.[41] The statute prohibited anyone from advocating "the duty, necessity, or propriety of sabotage, violence, or unlawful methods of terrorism as a means of accomplishing industrial or political reform." The Court held that free speech does not permit a state "to forbid or proscribe advocacy of the use of force or of law violation except where such advocacy is directed to inciting or producing imminent lawless actions and is likely to incite or produce such action." The incitement test enunciated by the Court in this case is a difficult one for prosecutors to meet. As a result, the Court's decision significantly broadened the protection given to advocacy speech.

These rulings are several decades old but the principles remain intact. Consider these examples of political speech and expression—are they protected by the First Amendment? In July 2010, an evangelical Christian pastor named Terry Jones threatened to set fire to 200 copies of the Quran on the anniversary of the September 11, 2001, terrorist attacks. Although he did not carry out the act, the threat alone resulted in violent protests in the Middle East and Asia, leading to several deaths. A year later, he put the Quran on trial, found it guilty of crimes against humanity, and burned the book in his church sanctuary. Again, violent reactions in Afghanistan and elsewhere resulted in multiple injuries and deaths. American politicians from both parties condemned the actions as unnecessary provocations. General David Petraeus, then the commander of international forces in Afghanistan, cautioned that Jones's actions would endanger U.S. military forces stationed in Islamic regions around the world.

---

40 354 U.S. 298 (1957).
41 395 U.S. 444 (1969).

Civil Liberties in a Trump Administration

How you voted on November 8, 2016, likely determines whether you anticipate the erosion or expansion of civil liberties civil liberties under the Trump administration. The Bill of Rights specifically limits encroachment by government on individual liberties, but these protections are subject to interpretation.

During the campaign, Donald Trump called for a ban on Muslims entering the country as well as a ban on anyone who comes from any part of the world with a "proven history of terrorism." Restricting immigration is not without historical precedent. New immigrants from China were excluded for 10 years under the Chinese Exclusion Act of 1882, for example. Whether such a ban can be imposed on the basis of a religious test is unknown.

Candidate Donald Trump also imposed limits on press access to his campaign for specific news outlets that he determined were unfriendly in their coverage. Univision, the *Washington Post*, Politico, and the *Des Moines Register* are a few of the news outlets whose press credentials were revoked.

When Donald Trump assumed the presidency, he took this oath: "I do solemnly swear (or affirm) that I will faithfully execute the Office of President of the United States, and will to the best of my ability, preserve, protect and defend the Constitution of the United States."

For Critical Analysis

1. During a transition in political power, people are understandably nervous about what the change will mean. How are civil liberties at the center of those concerns?

2. The history of civil liberties is characterized by the tension between individual liberties and government's responsibility to maintain order. Where will this tension be most evident in the new administration?

At events and funerals for U.S. soldiers killed in Iraq and Afghanistan, religious extremists from Westboro Baptist Church in Topeka, Kansas, picketed with signs reading, "God hates fags," "God hates America," and "Thank God for dead soldiers." The protests were intended to attract attention to the group's anti-gay agenda. Westboro Baptist Church was founded by the late Fred Phelps, and the congregation consists mainly of his extended family. In 2006, Westboro Baptist Church picketed the funeral of Marine Lance Corporal Matthew Snyder killed in Iraq with signs reading "You're Going to Hell," "Semper Fi Fags," and "God Hates You." Snyder's family filed a lawsuit accusing the church and its founders of defamation, invasion of privacy, and the intentional infliction of emotional distress. A U.S. District Court awarded the family $5 million in damages, but the U.S. Court of Appeals for the Fourth Circuit held that the judgment violated the First Amendment's protections on religious expression. The question, "Does the First Amendment protect protesters at a funeral from liability for intentionally inflicting emotional distress on the family of the deceased?" was argued before the U.S. Supreme Court. In an 8–1 decision, the Court ruled in favor of Westboro and Fred Phelps. Chief Justice Roberts, writing for the majority, said in part, the protection of the First Amendment "cannot be overcome by a jury finding that the picketing was outrageous."[42] Samuel Alito cast the lone dissenting vote, writing, "In order to have a society in which public issues can be openly and vigorously debated, it

---

42 *Snyder v. Phelps*, 562 U.S. 443 (2011).

is not necessary to allow the brutalization of innocent victims like the petitioner." In response, several states passed laws limiting pickets at funerals. In 2012, President Obama signed into law a bill restricting demonstrations at military funerals with regard to time and place.

Unprotected Speech: Obscenity

Many state and federal statutes make it a crime to disseminate obscene materials. Generally, the courts have not been willing to extend constitutional protections of free speech to what they consider to be obscene materials. But what is obscenity? Justice Potter Stewart once stated, in *Jacobellis v. Ohio*, a 1964 case, that even though he could not define *obscenity*, "I know it when I see it."[43] The problem is that even if it were agreed on, the definition of *obscenity* changes with the times. The works of Mark Twain and Edgar Rice Burroughs at times have been considered obscene.

Definitional Problems The Supreme Court has grappled at times with the difficulty of specifying an operationally effective definition of *obscenity*. In 1973, in *Miller v. California*, Chief Justice Warren Burger created a formal list of requirements that must be met for material to be considered legally obscene.[44] Material is obscene if (1) the average person finds that it violates contemporary community standards; (2) the work taken as a whole appeals to a prurient interest in sex; (3) the work shows patently offensive sexual conduct; and (4) the work lacks serious redeeming literary, artistic, political, or scientific merit. The problem is that one person's prurient interest is another person's medical interest or artistic pleasure. The Court went on to state that the definition of *prurient interest* would be determined by the community's standards. The Court avoided presenting a definition of *obscenity*, leaving this determination to local and state authorities. Consequently, the *Miller* case has been applied in a widely inconsistent manner.

Protecting Children The Supreme Court has upheld state laws making it illegal to sell materials showing sexual performances by minors. In 1990, in *Osborne v. Ohio*, the Court ruled that states can outlaw the possession of child pornography in the home.[45] The Court reasoned that the ban on private possession is justified because owning the material perpetuates commercial demand for it and for the exploitation of the children involved. At the federal level, the Child Protection Act of 1984 made it a crime to receive knowingly through the mails sexually explicit depictions of children.

Pornography on the Internet A significant problem facing Americans and lawmakers today is how to control obscenity and child pornography disseminated via the Internet. In 1996, Congress first attempted to protect minors from pornographic materials on the Internet by passing the Communications Decency Act (CDA). This made it a crime to make available to minors online any "obscene or indecent" message that "depicts or describes, in terms patently offensive as measured by contemporary community standards, sexual or excretory activities or organs." It was immediately challenged as an unconstitutional infringement on free speech. The Supreme Court held that the act imposed unconstitutional restraints on free speech and was therefore invalid.[46] In the eyes of the Court, the terms *indecent* and *patently offensive* covered

43 378 U.S. 184 (1964).
44 413 U.S. 5 (1973).
45 495 U.S. 103 (1990).
46 *Reno v. American Civil Liberties Union*, 521 U.S. 844 (1997).

large amounts of nonpornographic material with serious educational or other value. Later attempts by Congress to curb pornography on the Internet also encountered stumbling blocks. The Child Online Protection Act (COPA) of 1998 banned the distribution of material "harmful to minors" without an age-verification system to separate adult and minor users. In 2002, the Supreme Court upheld a lower court injunction suspending the COPA, and in 2004, the Court again upheld the suspension of the law on the ground that it was probably unconstitutional.[47] In 2000, Congress enacted the Children's Internet Protection Act (CIPA), which requires public schools and libraries to install filtering software to prevent children from viewing websites with "adult" content.

Should "Virtual" Pornography Be Deemed a Crime? In 2001, the Supreme Court agreed to review a case challenging the constitutionality of the Child Pornography Prevention Act (CPPA) of 1996. This act made it illegal to distribute or possess "any visual depiction, including any photograph, film, video, picture, or computer or computer-generated image or picture" that "is, or appears to be, of a minor engaging in sexually explicit conduct." The Free Speech Coalition, an adult-entertainment trade association, filed suit alleging that the *appears to be* and *conveys the impression* provisions are overbroad, and thus restrain works otherwise protected by the First Amendment. The Supreme Court, in a 6–3 decision, agreed that the two provisions were overbroad and therefore unconstitutional, noting further that the CPPA prohibits speech that records no crime and creates no victims by its production.[48]

Is there a way for government to prevent the sharing of child pornography on the Internet without violating free expression values? Possession and distribution of child pornography has gone underground. A Justice Department study reported that 21 million unique computer Internet Protocol (IP) addresses were identified and tracked sharing child pornography files, more than 9 million of them in the United States. In 2011, authorities in the United States turned over 22 million images of children actively being abused to make child pornography to the National Center for Missing and Exploited Children to try and identify the victims. According to the International Center for Missing and Exploited Children, these images are crime scene photos of child abuse, not child pornography. Robust enforcement of existing laws has moved child pornography off of easily accessible websites and into password-protected private chat rooms, a world sometimes referred to as the "dark web."[49] In 2015 the Federal Bureau of Investigation (FBI) was able to hack into anonymity software and record unique IP addresses for subscribers to Playpen, a site created to advertise and distribute child pornography. Law enforcement officials expect to prosecute more than 1,500 people as a result of this investigation.[50]

Unprotected Speech: Slander

Individuals are protected from **defamation of character**, which is defined as wrongfully hurting a person's good reputation. The law imposes a general duty on all persons to refrain from making false, defamatory statements about others. Breaching this duty orally is the wrongdoing called *slander*. Breaching it in

defamation of character
Wrongfully hurting a person's good reputation. The law imposes a general duty on all persons to refrain from making false, defamatory statements about others.

---

47 *Ashcroft v. American Civil Liberties Union*, 542 U.S. 656 (2004).
48 *Ashcroft v. Free Speech Coalition*, 535 U.S. 234 (2002).
49 Nicholas Kristoff, "He Was Supposed to Take a Photo." *The New York Times*, March 22, 2014. www.nytimes.com/2014/03/23 /opinion/sunday/kristof-he-was-supposed-to-take-a-photo.html
50 Mary-Ann Russon, "FBI Crack Tor and Catch 1,500 Visitors to Biggest Child Pornography Website on the Dark Web," *International Business Times*, January 6, 2016. www.ibtimes.co.uk/fbi-crack-tor-catch-1500-visitors-biggest-child -pornography-website-dark-web-1536417

slander
The public uttering of a false statement that harms the good reputation of another. The statement must be made to, or within the hearing of, persons other than the defamed party.

did you know?

The American Civil Liberties Union (ACLU) opposes hate-speech codes at public universities and calls them government censorship. Instead they argue that more speech and open dialogue is the best antidote to offensive words aimed at individuals or groups based on race, gender, ethnicity, religion, or sexual orientation.

writing is the wrongdoing called *libel*, which we discuss later. The government does not bring charges of slander or libel. Rather, the defamed person may bring a civil suit for damages.

Legally, **slander** is the public uttering of a false statement that harms the good reputation of another. Slanderous public uttering means that the defamatory statements are made to, or within the hearing of, persons other than the defamed party. If one person calls another dishonest, manipulative, and incompetent to his or her face when no one else is around, that does not constitute slander. The message is not communicated to a third party. If, however, a third party accidentally overhears defamatory statements, the courts have generally held that this constitutes a public uttering and therefore slander, which is prohibited.

Campus Speech

Students often face free-speech challenges on college campuses. One issue has to do with whether a student should have to subsidize, through student activity fees, organizations that promote causes that the student finds objectionable.

Student Activity Fees In 2000, this question came before the U.S. Supreme Court in a case brought by several University of Wisconsin students. The students argued that their mandatory student activity fees—which helped to fund liberal causes with which they disagreed, including gay rights—violated their First Amendment rights of free speech, free association, and free exercise of religion. They contended that they should have the right to choose whether to fund organizations that promoted political and ideological views that were offensive to their personal beliefs. To the surprise of many, the Supreme Court rejected the students' claim and ruled in favor of the university. The Court stated that "the university may determine that its mission is well served if students have the means to engage in dynamic discussions of philosophical, religious, scientific, social, and political subjects in their extracurricular life. If the university reaches this conclusion, it is entitled to impose a mandatory fee to sustain an open dialogue to these ends."[51]

Campus Speech and Behavior Codes Another issue is the legitimacy of campus speech and behavior codes. Some state universities have established codes that challenge the boundaries of the protection of free speech provided by the First Amendment. These codes are designed to prohibit so-called hate speech—abusive speech attacking persons on the basis of their ethnicity, race, or other criteria. A University of Michigan code banned "any behavior, verbal or physical, that stigmatizes or victimizes an individual on the basis of race, ethnicity, religion, sex, sexual orientation, creed, national origin, ancestry, age, marital status, handicap" or Vietnam-veteran status. A federal court found that the code violated students' First Amendment rights.[52]

Although the courts generally have held, as in the University of Michigan case, that campus speech codes are unconstitutional restrictions on the right to free speech, such codes continue to exist. Whether hostile speech should be banned on high school campuses has also become an issue. In view of school shootings and other violent behavior in the schools, school officials have become concerned about speech that consists of bullying, veiled threats, or that could lead to violence. Some schools have even prohibited students from wearing clothing, such as T-shirts bearing verbal messages (such as sexist or racist

51 *Board of Regents of the University of Wisconsin System v. Southworth*, 529 U.S. 217 (2000).
52 *Doe v. University of Michigan*, 721 F. Supp. 852 (1989).

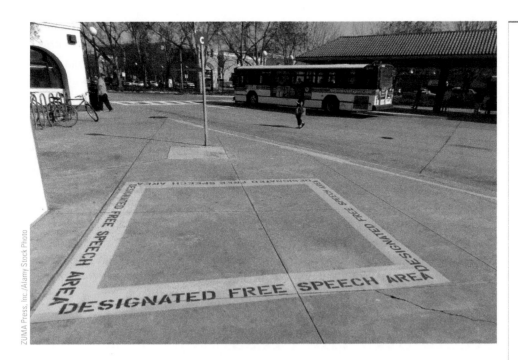

ZUMA Press, Inc./Alamy Stock Photo

Image 4-4
A "designated free speech area" in Modesto, California, raises questions about our First Amendment rights. Should speech be limited to a designated zone on a campus where the exchange of ideas is central to the educational mission? Does your campus have a "designated free speech area"?

comments) or symbolic messages (such as the Confederate flag), that might generate "ill will or hatred." Defenders of campus speech codes argue that they are necessary to prevent violence and to promote equality among different cultural, ethnic, and racial groups on campus and greater sensitivity to the needs and feelings of others in the educational environment.

On some of the nation's top university campuses, a right to speak freely is being challenged by protests loud enough to disrupt lectures, prematurely end events, or lead speakers to be uninvited. Former Secretary of State Condoleezza Rice was convinced by faculty and staff to decline her invitation from Rutgers University to speak at commencement, for example. Sometimes called the "heckler's veto," the courts have consistently ruled that these actions are contrary to freedom of speech protected by the First Amendment.[53] Justice Thurgood Marshall argued that the right to hear is as essential as the right to speak: "[t]he freedom to speak and the freedom to hear are inseparable; they are two sides of the same coin."[54] Speaking in 2015, President Obama encouraged students to engage people they don't agree with, even as they protest and ask tough questions about social justice. However, he continued, "I do think that there have been times on college campuses where I get concerned that the unwillingness to hear other points of view can be as unhealthy on the left as on the right."[55]

Some universities have created "free speech zones" in an attempt to balance the competing interests. On September 17, 2013 (Constitution Day), Robert Van Tuinen, a student at Modesto Junior College in California, was distributing free copies of the U.S. Constitution when he was stopped by campus police and advised that he was in violation of campus policy. The Student Development Office confirmed that distribution of materials could only take place within the "free speech zone." The free speech zone is small and must be scheduled well

---

53 *Terminiello v. Chicago,* 337 U.S. 1 (1949)

54 *Kleindienst v. Mandel,* 408 U.S. 753, 775 (1972) (Marshall, J., dissenting).

55 Sam Sanders, "Obama Warns Campus Protesters Against Urge to 'Shut Up' Opposition," National Public Radio Morning Edition, December 21, 2015. www.npr.org/2015/12/21/460282127/obama-warns-campus-protesters-against-urge-to-shut-up-opposition

in advance. The Foundation for Individual Rights in Education (FIRE) filed a First Amendment lawsuit on the student's behalf. The resulting settlement expanded Modesto Junior College's policy to allow free speech in open areas across campus, and the institution agreed to pay Van Tuinen $50,000.[56]

Hate Speech on the Internet

Extreme hate speech appears on the Internet, including racist materials and denials of the Holocaust (the murder of millions of Jews by the Nazis during World War II). Can the federal government restrict this type of speech? Should it? Content restrictions can be difficult to enforce. Even if Congress succeeded in passing a law prohibiting particular speech on the Internet, an army of "Internet watchers" would be needed to enforce it. Also, what if other countries attempt to impose their laws that restrict speech on U.S. websites? This is not a theoretical issue. In 2000, a French court found Yahoo! in violation of French laws banning the display of Nazi memorabilia. In 2001, however, a U.S. district court held that this ruling could not be enforced against Yahoo! in the United States.[57]

Freedom of the Press

Freedom of the press can be regarded as a special instance of freedom of speech. At the time of the framing of the Constitution, the press meant only newspapers, magazines, and books. As technology has advanced, the laws touching on freedom of the press have been modified. What can and cannot be printed still occupies an important place in constitutional law, however.

Defamation in Writing

libel
A written defamation of a person's character, reputation, business, or property rights.

Libel is defamation in writing (or in pictures, signs, films, or any other communication that has the potentially harmful qualities of written or printed words). As with slander, libel occurs only if the defamatory statements are observed by a third party. If one person writes a private letter to another person wrongfully accusing him or her of embezzling funds, that does not constitute libel. The courts have generally held that dictating a letter to an assistant constitutes communication of the letter's contents to a third party, and therefore, if defamation has occurred, the wrongdoer can be sued.

A 1964 case, *New York Times Co. v. Sullivan*, explored an important question regarding libelous statements made about public officials.[58] The Supreme Court held that only when a statement against a public official was made with **actual malice**—with either knowledge of its falsity or a reckless disregard of the truth—could damages be obtained.

actual malice
Either knowledge of a defamatory statement's falsity or a reckless disregard for the truth.

public figure
A public official or any other person, such as a movie star, known to the public because of his or her position or activities.

The standard set by the Court in the case has since been applied to **public figures** generally. Public figures include not only public officials, but also public employees who exercise substantial governmental power and any persons who are generally in the limelight. Statements made about public figures, especially when they are made through a public medium, usually are related to matters of general public interest. Furthermore, public figures typically have some access to a public medium for answering disparaging falsehoods about themselves, whereas

---

56 Foundation for Individual Rights in Education, "Victory: Modesto Junior College Settles Student's First Amendment Lawsuit," February 25, 2014. www.thefire.org/victory-modesto-junior-college-settles-students-first-amendment-lawsuit/

57 *Yahoo!, Inc. v. La Ligue Contre le Racisme et l'Antisemitisme*, 169 F. Supp. 2d 1181 (N.D. Cal. 2001).

58 376 U.S. 254 (1964).

private individuals do not. For these reasons, public figures must prove that the statements were made with actual malice in defamation cases. Fifty years later, the principles Justice Brennan drew upon in crafting the majority opinion are still vital to a free society. Brennan argued that "debate on public issues should be uninhibited, robust, and wide-open, and that it may well include vehement, caustic, and sometimes unpleasantly sharp attacks on government and public officials."[59]

A Free Press versus a Fair Trial: Gag Orders

Another major issue concerns media coverage of criminal trials. The Sixth Amendment guarantees the right of criminal suspects to a fair trial—the accused have rights. The First Amendment guarantees freedom of the press. What if the two rights appear to be in conflict? Which one prevails?

Jurors may be influenced by reading news stories about the trial in which they are participating. In the 1970s, judges increasingly issued **gag orders**, which restricted the publication of news about a trial in progress or even a pretrial hearing. In a landmark 1976 case, *Nebraska Press Association v. Stuart*, the Supreme Court unanimously ruled that a Nebraska judge's gag order had violated the First Amendment's guarantee of freedom of the press.[60] Chief Justice Warren Burger indicated that even pervasive adverse pretrial publicity did not necessarily lead to an unfair trial and that prior restraints on publication were not justified. Some justices even went so far as to suggest that gag orders are never justified.

Despite the *Nebraska Press Association* ruling, the Court has upheld certain types of gag orders. In *Gannett Co. v. De Pasquale* in 1979, the highest court held that if a judge found a reasonable probability that news publicity would harm a defendant's right to a fair trial, the court could impose a gag rule: "Members of the public have no constitutional right under the Sixth and Fourteenth Amendments to attend criminal trials."[61]

The *Nebraska* and *Gannett* cases, however, involved pretrial hearings. Could a judge impose a gag order on an entire trial, including pretrial hearings? In 1980, in *Richmond Newspapers, Inc. v. Virginia*, the Court ruled that actual trials must be open to the public except under unusual circumstances.[62]

In February 2012, 17-year-old African American Trayvon Martin was shot and killed by George Zimmerman. Zimmerman was acting as a neighborhood watch captain in Sanford, Florida, and had reported Martin to a 911 operator as "a suspicious person" in the neighborhood. The exact circumstances surrounding the altercation were subject to intense scrutiny and disagreement once the case went to trial. The incident attracted international attention, comments from President Obama, and extensive media attention. Zimmerman claimed that he acted in self-defense under Florida's "stand your ground" law. He and his attorneys actively solicited public support and financial contributions using social media and with a dedicated website. Prosecutors sought a gag order, claiming that the website and intense social media campaign could influence potential jurors in the racially charged case. The judge disagreed and refused to grant the order. Prosecutors returned three times to request that parties to the case be prevented from speaking directly to the press or to the public through social media. No gag

gag order
An order issued by a judge restricting the publication of news about a trial or a pretrial hearing to protect the accused's right to a fair trial.

---

59 Roy S. Gutterman, "The Landmark Libel Case, Times v. Sullivan, Still Resonates 50 Years Later," Forbes, March 5, 2014. www
    .forbes.com/sites/realspin/2014/03/05/the-landmark-libel-case-times-v-sullivan-still-resonates-50-years-later/
60 427 U.S. 539 (1976).
61 443 U.S. 368 (1979).
62 448 U.S. 555 (1980).

order was ever issued. Zimmerman was eventually acquitted. The pervasive nature of online communication and the sheer number of 24-hour cable news outlets raise questions about whether gag orders are even possible today.

Information companies, such as Google and Verizon, had been operating under a federal gag order of sorts that prevented the companies from informing clients when a government agency subpoenaed data records. This practice was exposed in the information leaked by Edward Snowden. In January 2014, the Obama administration announced surveillance reforms that have eased these restrictions. Tech companies are now in the position of having to convince business clients and private consumers that they can be trusted with private data and information. Google reacted by creating a video using toy figurines and a game board to explain how it responds to search warrants for client email and other online data. Other companies have adopted the practice of releasing regular government transparency reports detailing the types of user data requests they received from the U.S. government.

Films, Radio, and TV

As noted, only in a few cases has the Supreme Court upheld prior restraint of published materials. The Court's reluctance to accept prior restraint is less evident with respect to motion pictures. In the first half of the twentieth century, films were routinely submitted to local censorship boards. In 1968, the Supreme Court ruled that a film can be banned only under a law that provides for a prompt hearing at which the film is shown to be obscene. Today, few local censorship boards exist. Instead, the film industry regulates itself primarily through the industry's rating system. Video posted to YouTube is not subject to a rating system. YouTube users can flag any video as containing pornography, mature content, or graphic violence; depicting illegal acts; or being racially or ethnically offensive. A video is removed only if a review by the company's customer support department agrees that it is inappropriate or that the video is on its face in violation of the site's terms of use.

Radio and television broadcasting has the least First Amendment protection. In 1934, the national government established the Federal Communications

did you know?

Over 6 billion hours of video are watched each month on YouTube—that's almost an hour for every person on Earth—and 80 percent of YouTube traffic comes from outside the United States.

Image 4-5
Liberty and security are both important values. How does society decide which is more important at any given time? Who is responsible for maintaining the balance?

Commission (FCC) to regulate electromagnetic wave frequencies. The government's position has been that the airwaves and all frequencies that travel through the air belong to the people of the United States. Thus, no broadcaster can monopolize these frequencies, nor can they be abused. The FCC is the authority that regulates the use of the airwaves and grants licenses to broadcast television, radio, satellite transmission, etc. Based on a case decided by the Supreme Court in 1978, the FCC can impose sanctions on radio or TV stations that broadcast "filthy words," even if the words are not legally obscene.[63]

In determining which type of communication enjoys the greatest protection, the Court favors mediums that are broadly available, accessed by all types of people, and used to engage in political discourse. Print media and the Internet are both cheap and readily accessible to all who want to share information or persuade others of their position. Broadcast media—primarily TV, but also radio—remains more closely regulated because it is a "scarce" resource. The profusion of cable networks and Internet companies like Netflix who create original programming challenge this longstanding approach.

The Right to Assemble and to Petition the Government

The First Amendment prohibits Congress from making any law that abridges "the right of the people peaceably to assemble, and to petition the Government for a redress of grievances." Inherent in such a right is the ability of private citizens to communicate their ideas on public issues to government officials, as well as to other individuals. Indeed, the amendment also protects the right of individuals to join interest groups and lobby the government. The Supreme Court has often put this freedom on a par with freedom of speech and freedom of the press. Nonetheless, it has allowed municipalities to require permits for parades, sound trucks, and demonstrations so that public officials can control traffic or prevent demonstrations from turning into riots.

The freedom to demonstrate became a major issue in 1977 when the American Nazi Party sought to march through Skokie, Illinois, a largely Jewish suburb where many Holocaust survivors resided. The Supreme Court let stand a lower court's ruling that the city of Skokie had violated the Nazis' First Amendment guarantees by denying them a permit to march.[64]

More recently, in Charlottesville, Virginia, the city council voted to rename two city parks and remove a statue of Confederate General Robert E. Lee in 2017 (a court injunction has delayed its removal). This action mirrored decisions in several Southern cities to remove Confederate monuments from public property after a self-described white supremacist massacred nine black churchgoers in Charleston, South Carolina, in 2015. Charlottesville is home to the University of Virginia (UVA), founded by Thomas Jefferson. In August 2017, the city issued a permit to organizers of "Unite the Right" to hold a Saturday rally in Emancipation Park (formerly known as Lee Park and home to the Lee statue). The night before the planned event, several hundred white nationalists with flaming torches marched through the UVA campus chanting "Blood and soil!" and "Jews will not replace us!" before clashing with counter-protesters encircling a statue of

---

63 *FCC v. Pacifica Foundation*, 438 U.S. 726 (1978). The phrase "filthy words" refers to a monologue by comedian George Carlin, which became the subject of the court case.

64 *Smith v. Collin*, 439 U.S. 916 (1978).

Thomas Jefferson. Police declared the demonstration illegal (no permit) and dispersed the crowd.

The following day, more people descended on Charlottesville. White nationalists waving Nazi flags and carrying clubs and shields were met by counter-protesters also carrying clubs and shields. Virginia is an open-carry state, so several marchers also carried firearms. Well before the rally was scheduled to begin, Virginia Governor Terry McAuliffe declared a state of emergency and police began moving people out of the city center. Later that afternoon, a man deliberately drove a car into the crowd killing Heather Heyer and injuring 19 others. Two Virginia State Police Troopers were also killed when their helicopter crashed. In the aftermath of the violent weekend, Unite the Right organizers claimed that their First Amendment rights had been violated since the group was not able to rally as planned, while most elected officials expressed horror that white nationalism could be so openly expressed. Rallies in support of Charlottesville were held in cities all over the country under #CharlottesvilleStrong.

Online Assembly

An important question today is whether individuals should have the right to "assemble" online to advocate violence against certain groups (such as physicians who perform abortions) or advocate values that are opposed to our democracy (such as terrorism). Whereas some online advocacy groups promote interests consistent with American political values, other groups aim to destroy those values. Whether First Amendment freedoms should be sacrificed in the interests of national security is a question that will be debated for some time.

Apart from advocating violence or the overthrow of democracy, a number of new tools are available online to create and send petitions of all sorts—Change.org and iPetition, for example. The White House website includes a page titled "We the People: Your Voice in Government," which is dedicated to providing a means for individuals to create a petition or to sign an open petition on an issue they care deeply about.[65] When the number of signatures on a petition reaches a threshold, the administration posts a response. The content of issue petitions is wide ranging—from asking that all single-stall restrooms be made unisex to reforming the postal service.

More Liberties under Scrutiny: Matters of Privacy

■ **4.4** Discuss the constitutional protection of privacy rights in personal and public life and evaluate the threats to privacy rights posed by technology and security interests.

No explicit reference is made anywhere in the Constitution to a person's right to privacy. Until the second half of the twentieth century, the courts did not take a very positive approach toward the right to privacy. During Prohibition, suspected bootleggers' telephones were tapped routinely, and the information obtained was used as a legal basis for prosecution. In *Olmstead v. United States* in 1928, the Supreme

---

65 We the People: Your Voice in Government. https://petitions.whitehouse.gov/

Court upheld such an invasion of privacy.[66] Justice Louis Brandeis strongly dissented from the majority decision in this case. He argued that the framers of the Constitution gave every citizen the right to be left alone. He called such a right "the most comprehensive of rights and the right most valued by civilized men."

In the 1960s, the highest court began to modify the majority view. In 1965, in *Griswold v. Connecticut*, the Supreme Court overturned a Connecticut law that effectively prohibited the use of contraceptives, holding that the law violated the right to privacy.[67] Justice William O. Douglas formulated a unique way of reading this right into the Bill of Rights. He claimed that the First, Third, Fourth, Fifth, and Ninth Amendments created "penumbras [shadows], formed by emanations [things sent out from] those guarantees that help give them life and substance," and he went on to describe zones of privacy that are guaranteed by these rights. When we read the Ninth Amendment, we can see the foundation for his reasoning: "The enumeration in the Constitution, of certain rights, shall not be construed to deny or disparage [belittle] others retained by the people." In other words, just because the Constitution, including its amendments, does not specifically talk about the right to privacy does not mean that this right is denied to the people.

Some of today's most controversial issues relate to the erosion of privacy rights in the information age. Could we be giving away our right to privacy with the volume of personal data we give away online? Other issues concern abortion and the "right to die." The Supreme Court seems content to allow states to take the lead in these areas at the moment. Since the terrorist attacks of September 11, 2001, Americans have faced another crucial question regarding privacy rights: To what extent should Americans sacrifice privacy rights in the interests of national security? To what degree are we prepared to live in a surveillance society in order to feel protected?

Information Privacy

An important privacy issue, created in part by new technology, is the amassing of information on individuals by government agencies and private businesses, such as marketing firms, grocery stores, and casinos. Personal information on the average American citizen is filed away in dozens of agencies—such as the Social Security Administration and the Internal Revenue Service. Because of the threat of indiscriminate use of private information by unauthorized individuals, Congress passed the Privacy Act in 1974. This was the first law regulating the use of federal government information about private individuals. Under the Privacy Act, every citizen has the right to obtain copies of personal records collected by federal agencies and to correct inaccuracies in such records. However, this applies only to government agencies and has no bearing on records collected by private organizations or companies. Other laws are designed to protect the privacy of certain types of information, such as health-care records (Health Insurance Portability and Accountability Act [HIPAA]).

The ease with which personal information can be obtained by using the Internet for marketing and other purposes has led to unique privacy issues. Maybe privacy is something that individuals define for themselves. Portraits on public websites such as Facebook, LinkedIn, or other networking sites are created by the user and can protect personal data or make certain facts *very*

---

66 277 U.S. 438 (1928). This decision was overruled later in *Katz v. United States*, 389 U.S. 347 (1967).
67 381 U.S. 479 (1965).

Satellite Sentinel Project

Actor George Clooney often finds himself the subject of paparazzi attention. The Satellite Sentinel Project is an attempt to redirect this attention to the conflict and humanitarian crisis in Sudan. The project's tag line is, "The world is watching because you are watching."*

The civil war between the north and south in Sudan concluded with a peace agreement in 2005. That conflict, the longest in African history, has also been characterized as the second deadliest global conflict after World War II. Following South Sudan's independence from Sudan as the result of a referendum vote in July 2011, the region has descended into violence, with ongoing deadly border clashes amid a standoff over oil. Sudan Armed Forces (SAF) bomb oil fields in South Sudan; southern militias from the Sudan People's Liberation Army (SPLA) attack oil fields in the North. Civilians are caught in the crossfire. Aid agencies are unable to get into the region, and thousands are seeking to escape. Food relief has become an acute casualty of the conflict.

Sudanese President Omar al-Bashir has been charged with war crimes in connection with armed conflicts between the independent state of South Sudan and Sudan that have killed as many as 400,000 people in the western region of Darfur alone. He is alleged to be responsible for the aerial bombing campaign directed at moving indigenous ethnic groups out of the Nuba Mountains. President al-Bashir's military campaign in the Nuba Mountains has been termed "Starvation Warfare" by Clooney.

Clooney, along with other celebrities including Matt Damon and Brad Pitt, founded Not On Our Watch, a registered nonprofit whose mission is "to focus global attention and resources towards putting an end to mass atrocities around the world." Drawing upon the powerful voices of artists, activists, and cultural leaders, Not On Our Watch generates "lifesaving humanitarian assistance and protection for the vulnerable, marginalized, and displaced."** Sudan is on the organization's watch list, and Clooney has made several trips to Sudan, often with John Prendergast, human rights activist and former Director for African Affairs at the National Security Council. Prendergast is co-founder of the Enough Project, an initiative to end genocide and crimes against humanity. The Enough Project is affiliated with the Center for American Progress.***

Not On Our Watch and the Enough Project have partnered with the Harvard Humanitarian Initiative to use sophisticated private satellite technology to spy on combatants in an active conflict zone with the ultimate goal of protecting civilians.**** The images are analyzed and made public on the project's website, thereby letting combatants know the world is watching. As Clooney said, "We are the antigenocide paparazzi . . . if you

know your actions are going to be covered you tend to behave much differently than when you operate in a vacuum."***** Satellite time is expensive, but DigitalGlobe agreed to donate the images for the start-up of the project. Four staff members and a half-dozen student interns with the Harvard Humanitarian Initiative aggregate the images and coordinate the analysis, searching for clues of impending violence. Soon after the Satellite Sentinel Project began, the Harvard team detected SAF troops gathering near the village of Kurmuk and posted the report and images to the website. As a result, more than 1,500 villagers fled to Ethiopia, leaving fewer targets for the SAF.

In 2016, the Enough Project has turned its digital eye on promoting transparency in the global minerals supply chain and begun to help break links between the minerals trade and violent conflict in the eastern Democratic Republic of Congo (Congo). Known as "conflict minerals," proceeds from tin, tungsten, tantalum, and gold fuel armed conflict and human rights abuses. Section 1502 of the Dodd-Frank Consumer Protection Act requires U.S. companies to identify where minerals used in their products came from. By one estimate, Dodd-Frank has reduced revenue to militias by 65 percent.

For Critical Analysis

1. Satellite surveillance in the "right hands" can promote humanitarian values like those described earlier, but what about satellite surveillance in the "wrong hands"? Which civil liberties are at stake as the number of government and commercial satellites overhead increases?

2. Celebrities use their star power to redirect our attention from them to issues they believe are important. In doing so, they prioritize some crises over others. A free press is an essential civil liberty, but how can we ensure that we are informed about a wide range of issues and not just those attracting the camera's attention at the moment?

* Satellite Sentinel Project http://www.satsentinel.org/
** Not On Our Watch http://notonourwatchproject.org/who_we_are and Enough Project http://www.enoughproject.org/
*** Michael Blanding, "Inside Harvard's Spy Lab." *The Boston Globe Magazine*, April 29, 2012. www.bostonglobe.com/magazine/2012/04/28/inside-george-clooney-harvard-spy-lab/RB6fK8MUYkBn3RvWFZpPqO/ story.html?camp=pm
**** Mark Benjamin, "Clooney's 'Antigenocide Paparazzi: Watching Sudan." *Time*, December 28, 2010. http://content.time.com/time/magazine/article /0,9171,2040211,00.htmlatsentinel.org/
***** Michael Blanding, "Inside Harvard's Spy Lab." *The Boston Globe Magazine*, April 29, 2012. www.bostonglobe.com/magazine/2012/04/28/inside-george-clooney-harvard-spy-lab/RB6fK8MUYkBn3RvWFZpPqO/story.html?camp=pm

public. The person who submits the information gets to decide. Whether privacy rights can survive in an information age is a question that Americans and their leaders continue to confront.

Privacy Rights and Abortion

Historically, abortion was not a criminal offense before the first movement of the fetus in the uterus, usually between the sixteenth and eighteenth weeks of pregnancy. By 1973, however, performing an abortion at any time during pregnancy was a criminal offense in a majority of the states.

Roe v. Wade In 1973, in *Roe v. Wade,* the U.S. Supreme Court accepted the argument that the laws against abortion violated "Jane Roe's" right to privacy under the Constitution.[68] The Court held that during the first trimester (three months) of pregnancy, abortion was an issue solely between a woman and her physician. The state could not limit abortions except to require that they be performed by licensed physicians. During the second trimester, to protect the health of the mother, the state was allowed to specify the conditions under which an abortion could be performed. During the final trimester, the state could regulate or even outlaw abortions, except when necessary to preserve the life or health of the woman.

After *Roe*, the Supreme Court issued decisions in several cases defining and redefining the boundaries of state regulation of abortion. During the 1980s, the Court twice struck down laws that required a woman who wished to have an abortion to undergo counseling designed to discourage abortions. In the late 1980s and early 1990s, however, the Court took a more conservative approach. In *Webster v. Reproductive Health Services* (1989), the Court upheld a Missouri statute that, among other things, banned the use of public hospitals or other taxpayer-supported facilities for performing abortions.[69] In *Planned Parenthood v. Casey* in 1992, the Court upheld a Pennsylvania law that required preabortion counseling; a waiting period of 24 hours; and, for girls under the age of 18, parental or judicial permission.[70] The final decision was a 5–4 vote; Sandra Day O'Connor wrote the opinion. Although the opinion explicitly upheld *Roe*, it changed the grounds on which the states can regulate abortion. The Court found that states could not place an "undue burden" on a woman who sought an abortion. In this case, the Court found that spousal notification was such a burden. Because many other conditions were upheld, abortions continue to be more difficult to obtain in some states than others.

The Controversy Continues Abortion continues to be a divisive issue. "Right-to-life" forces continue to push for laws banning abortion, endorse political candidates who support their views, and organize protests. Because of several episodes of violence attending protests at abortion clinics, in 1994 Congress passed the Freedom of Access to Clinic Entrances Act. The act prohibits protesters from blocking entrances to such clinics. The Supreme Court ruled in 1993 that such protesters can be prosecuted under laws governing racketeering, and in 1998 a federal court in Illinois convicted right-to-life protesters under these laws. In 1997, the Supreme Court upheld the constitutionality

---

68 410 U.S. 113 (1973). Jane Roe was not the real name of the woman in this case. It is a common legal pseudonym used to protect a person's privacy.

69 492 U.S. 490 (1989).

70 505 U.S. 833 (1992).

of prohibiting protesters from entering a 15-foot "buffer zone" around abortion clinics and from giving unwanted counseling to those entering the clinics.[71] In 2006, however, the Supreme Court unanimously reversed its earlier decision that anti-abortion protesters could be prosecuted under laws governing racketeering.[72]

In a 2000 decision, the Court upheld a Colorado law requiring demonstrators to stay at least eight feet away from people entering and leaving clinics unless people consent to be approached. The Court concluded that the law's restrictions on speech-related conduct did not violate the free speech rights of abortion protesters.[73]

That same year, the Supreme Court reviewed a Nebraska law banning "partial-birth" abortions. Similar laws had been passed by at least 27 states. A partial-birth abortion is a procedure that can be used during the second trimester of pregnancy. Abortion-rights advocates claim that in limited circumstances the procedure is the safest way to perform an abortion and that the government should never outlaw specific medical procedures. Opponents argue that the procedure has no medical merit and that it ends the life of a fetus that might be able to live outside the womb. The Supreme Court invalidated the Nebraska law on the grounds that, as written, the law could be used to ban other abortion procedures, and it contained no provisions for protecting the health of the pregnant woman.[74] In 2003, legislation similar to the Nebraska statute was passed by the U.S. Congress and signed into law by President George W. Bush. It was immediately challenged in court. In 2007, the Supreme Court heard several challenges to the partial-birth abortion law and upheld the constitutionality of that legislation, saying that the law was specific enough that it did not "impose an undue burden" on women seeking an abortion.[75]

The abortion debate is now driven entirely by state legislative action restricting access to abortion, and the emphasis on privacy articulated in *Roe* has all but disappeared. In the 43 years since the U.S. Supreme Court handed down *Roe v. Wade*, states have enacted 1,074 abortion restrictions. Of these, 288 (27 percent) have been enacted just since 2010.[76] In 2015 alone, states adopted 57 new restrictions. In 2013, 56 percent of women in the United States lived in one of 27 states characterized as hostile to abortion. The Texas Omnibus Abortion Bill, adopted in 2014, required all abortions (surgical or medical) to be done in an ambulatory surgical center. Further, the law required doctors performing abortions to have admitting privileges at a hospital within 30 miles of the clinic. In a 5–3 decision announced in June 2016, the justices struck down both provisions of the Texas law. "We conclude," Justice Stephen G. Breyer wrote for the majority, "that neither of these provisions offers medical benefits sufficient to justify the burdens upon access that each imposes. Each places a substantial obstacle in the

71 *Schenck v. Pro Choice Network*, 519 U.S. 357 (1997).
72 *Scheidler v. National Organization for Women*, 126 S. Ct. 1264 (2006).
73 *Hill v. Colorado*, 530 U.S. 703 (2000).
74 *Stenberg v. Carhart*, 530 U.S. 914 (2000).
75 *Gonzales v. Carhart*, 550 U.S. (2007) and *Gonzales v. Planned Parenthood*, 550 U.S. (2007).
76 Guttmacher Institute, "Last Five Years Account for More Than One-quarter of All Abortion Restrictions Enacted Since Roe." January 13, 2016. http://www.guttmacher.org/media/inthenews/2016/01/13/

path of women seeking a previability abortion, each constitutes an undue burden on abortion access, and each violates the federal Constitution."[77]

Source for quotation: Adam Liptak, "Supreme Court Strikes Down Texas Abortion Restrictions," New York Times, June 27, 2016. www.nytimes.com/2016/06/28/us/supreme-court-texas-abortion.html

Privacy Rights and the "Right to Die"

A 1976 case was one of the first publicized right-to-die cases.[78] The parents of Karen Ann Quinlan, a young woman who had been in a coma for nearly a year and who had been kept alive during that time by a respirator, wanted her respirator removed. In 1976, the New Jersey Supreme Court ruled that the right to privacy includes the right of a patient to refuse treatment and that patients who are unable to speak can exercise that right through a family member or guardian. In 1990, the Supreme Court took up the issue. In *Cruzan v. Director, Missouri Department of Health*, the Court stated that a patient's life-sustaining treatment can be withdrawn at the request of a family member only if "clear and convincing evidence" exists that the patient did not want such treatment.[79]

What If No Living Will Exists? Since the *Quinlan* decision, most states have enacted laws permitting people to designate their wishes concerning life-sustaining procedures in "living wills" or durable health-care powers of attorney. These laws and the *Cruzan* decision have resolved the right-to-die controversy for situations in which the patient has drafted a living will. Disputes are still possible if there is no living will.

Physician-Assisted Suicide In the 1990s, another issue surfaced: Do privacy rights include the right of terminally ill people to end their lives through physician-assisted suicide? Until 1996, the courts consistently upheld state laws that prohibited this practice, either through specific statutes or under their general homicide statutes. In 1996, after two federal appellate courts ruled that state laws banning assisted suicide were unconstitutional, the issue reached the U.S. Supreme Court. In 1997, in *Washington v. Glucksberg*, the Court stated, clearly and categorically, that the liberty interest protected by the Constitution does not include a right to commit suicide, with or without assistance.[80] In effect, the Supreme Court left the decision in the hands of the states. Oregon adopted the Death with Dignity Act in 1997. In 2006, the Supreme Court upheld Oregon's physician-assisted suicide law against a challenge from the Bush administration.[81]

Assistance with end-of-life choices is now legal in six states and the District of Columbia. Preferring "death with dignity" or "aid in dying," proponents of laws allowing terminally ill patients to choose assistance in dying eschew the term "assisted suicide." In a Gallup Poll conducted in 2017, 73 percent of respondents agreed that when patients and their families wanted it, doctors should be allowed to "end the patient's life by some painless means." Opponents say that actively ending a life, no matter how frail a person is, is a moral violation and that patients might be pushed to die early for the convenience of others.

---

77 Nina Totenberg, "Supreme Court Tests Texas' New Restrictions on Abortion." NPR Morning Edition, March 2, 2016. http://www.npr.org/2016/03/02/468656213/supreme-court-tests-texas-new-restrictions-on-abortion

78 In re Quinlan, 70 N.J. 10 (1976).

79 497 U.S. 261 (1990).

80 521 U.S. 702 (1997).

81 *Gonzales v. Oregon*, 126 S. Ct. 904 (2006).

From the Web ▶ Do you believe community surveillance cameras offer protection or compromise privacy?

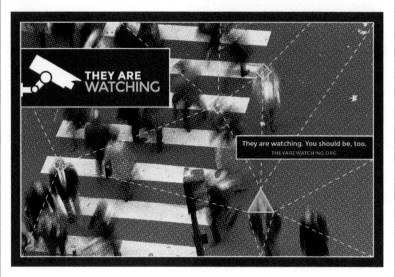

THEY ARE WATCHING

They are watching. You should be, too.
THEYAREWATCHING.ORG

Source: ACLU

Privacy Rights versus Security Issues

As former Supreme Court justice Thurgood Marshall once said, "Grave threats to liberty often come in times of urgency, when constitutional rights seem too extravagant to endure." Not surprisingly, antiterrorist legislation since the attacks on September 11, 2001, has eroded certain basic rights, in particular the Fourth Amendment protections against unreasonable searches and seizures. Several tools previously used against certain types of criminal suspects (for instance, "roving wiretaps" and National Security Letters [NSLs]) have been authorized for use against a broader array of terror suspects. Many civil liberties organizations argue that abuses of the Fourth Amendment are ongoing.

Although it has been possible for a law enforcement agency to gain court permission to wiretap a telephone almost since telephones were invented, a roving wiretap allows an agency to tap all forms of communication used by the named person, including cell phones and email, and it applies across legal jurisdictions. Previously, roving wiretaps could only be requested for persons suspected of one of a small number of serious crimes. Now, if persons are suspected of planning a terrorist attack, they can be monitored no matter what form of electronic communication they use. Such roving wiretaps appear to contravene the Supreme Court's interpretation of the Fourth Amendment, which requires a judicial warrant to describe the *place* to be searched, not just the person, although the Court has not banned them to date. One of the goals of the framers was to avoid *general* searches.

Does a prohibition against general searches extend to surveillance networks now found in many communities near ports, transportation hubs, and other major public attractions? In Washington, residents of Seattle grew concerned enough about a system of 24-hour video cameras trained on a public park overlooking the Puget Sound that they took the issue to the Seattle City Council. Beyond the surveillance, citizens demanded more input and public notice when systems are installed. "What bothers the community," one resident testified, "is that this was never brought to our attention, never discussed. We're concerned about living in a police state. These cameras can potentially look right into our houses—right into my living room."[82] At the same time, people want protection from foreign and domestic attacks—where is the appropriate balance between privacy and law enforcement surveillance?

The USA PATRIOT Act Much of the government's failure to anticipate the attacks of September 11, 2001, has been attributed to a lack of cooperation among

did you know?

The USA PATRIOT Act, enacted following the September 11 terrorist attacks, stands for Uniting and Strengthening America by Providing Appropriate Tools Required to Intercept and Obstruct Terrorism Act of 2001.

82 Jared Friend and Brian Robick, "They Are Watching. Are You?" American Civil Liberties Union Speak Freely Blog, March 4, 2016. www.aclu.org/blog/speak-freely/they-are-watching-are-you

government agencies. At that time, barriers prevented information sharing between the law enforcement and intelligence arms of the government. A major objective of the PATRIOT Act was to eliminate those barriers. Lawmakers claimed that the act would improve lines of communication between agencies such as the FBI and the Central Intelligence Agency (CIA), thereby allowing the government to better anticipate terrorist plots. With improved communication, various agencies could more effectively coordinate their efforts in combating terrorism.

In addition, the PATRIOT Act eased restrictions on the government's ability to investigate and arrest suspected terrorists. Because of the secretive nature of terrorist groups, supporters of the act argue that the government must have greater latitude in pursuing leads on potential terrorist activity. After receiving approval of the Foreign Intelligence Surveillance Act (FISA) Court, the act authorizes law enforcement officials to secretly search a suspected terrorist's home. It also allows the government to monitor a suspect's Internet activities, phone conversations, financial records, and book purchases. Although a number of these search and surveillance tactics have long been a part of criminal investigations, the PATRIOT Act expanded their scope to include individuals as terrorist suspects even if they are not agents of a foreign government.

Civil Liberties Concerns Proponents of the PATRIOT Act insist that ordinary, law-abiding citizens have nothing to fear from the government's increased search and surveillance powers. Groups such as the ACLU have objected to the act, however, arguing that it poses a grave threat to constitutionally guaranteed rights and liberties. Under the PATRIOT Act, FBI agents are required to certify the need for search warrants to the FISA Court. Rarely are such requests rejected.

The FBI has also used the National Security Letter, a form of administrative subpoena, to avoid the procedures required by the FISA Court. The NSL allows the FBI to get records of telephone calls, subscriber information, and other transactions, although it does not give the FBI access to the content of the calls. However, as Congress tightened the requirements for warrants under the PATRIOT Act, the FBI evidently began to use the NSLs as a shortcut. Although the use of NSLs has been legal for more than 20 years, a dramatic increase in the use of this technique has led Congress to consider further restrictions in order to preserve the rights of U.S. citizens.

Opponents of the PATRIOT Act fear that these expanded powers of investigation might be used to silence government critics or to threaten members of interest groups who oppose government polices today or in the future. Congress debated these issues in 2005 and then renewed most of the provisions in 2006. The act has been renewed again as recently as 2015, over the objections of many civil liberties organizations. One of the most controversial aspects of the PATRIOT Act permits the government to eavesdrop on telephone calls with a warrant from the FISA Court. In 2005, it became known that the Bush administration was eavesdropping on U.S. telephone calls without a warrant if the caller was from outside the United States. Congress passed the FISA Amendments Act in June 2008, which regulates such calls and gives immunity from prosecution to telecommunications companies.

The incredible growth of modern wireless technology is an opportunity and a challenge for law enforcement officials, but it also carries potential threats to civil liberties. Modern wireless technology makes it possible to track offenders more easily, but is such tracking legal? Most wireless devices—smartphones, tablets, netbooks—contain wireless receivers that connect with the Internet, and most include a global positioning system (GPS) transmitter. If you lose your telephone, you can call your service provider and be told approximately where it is because it is signaling a nearby tower or satellite. Is this an invasion of your privacy? Fourteen people were killed and many more seriously injured in a mass shooting at the Inland Regional Center in San Bernardino, California, in December 2015. The shooters, a married couple inspired by foreign terrorist groups, fled the scene and were killed by police in a shootout. The investigation found that American-born U.S. citizen Syed Rizwan Farook and his wife Tashfeen Malik, a lawful permanent citizen, had together become radicalized through information obtained from the Internet. The FBI discovered private messages exchanged between husband and wife expressing a commitment to jihadism. A county-issued iPhone 5C phone believed to belong to Farook could not be accessed due to the phone's security features. The FBI asked Apple, Inc., to assist by writing new computer code to disable security features on the device, but Apple declined, citing a number of issues related to consumer security and privacy. Apple also argued that computer code is a form of speech.[83] "This case arises in a difficult context after a terrible tragedy," Apple wrote in a brief filed in U.S. District Court. "But it is in just such highly-charged and emotional cases that the courts must zealously guard civil liberties and the rule of law and reject government overreaching."[84] Apple was joined by other major tech firms in its fight, including Google, Facebook, Twitter, Amazon, and Microsoft. Ultimately in this particular case, the FBI was able to access the phone without Apple's help and the court case was dropped. However, the issues presented in this debate will arise again with broad implications for both privacy and cybersecurity.

As a result of Edward Snowden's leak of top-secret documents, we now know about the NSA's secret operation to mine phone and Internet data. Moreover, intelligence alliances such as "Five Eyes" (involving the United States, Australia, Canada, New Zealand, and the United Kingdom) funnel massive amounts of data to the NSA. Barton Gellman of the *Washington Post* summarized the value of Snowden's information: "Taken together, the revelations have brought to light a global surveillance system that cast off many of its historical restraints after the attacks on September 11, 2001. Secret legal authorities empowered the NSA to sweep in telephone, Internet, and location records of whole populations."[85] President Obama assured the public that there is "no spying on Americans." In January 2014 the nation learned that the NSA had implanted software in nearly 100,000 computers around the world, thereby allowing the United States to conduct surveillance and create a digital highway for launching cyber-attacks. In that same week, President Obama announced that he would accept a series of recommendations for reforms to NSA practices forwarded from an advisory panel. U.S. technology company executives worry that some of the techniques developed by the agency to find flaws in computer systems

83 Steve Lohr, "Analyzing Apple's Argument That First Amendment Applies to Its Code." *The New York Times*, February 25, 2016. http://www.nytimes.com/2016/02/26/technology/in-apple-case-addressing-the-legal-status-of-code.html

84 Mark Berman, "Apple Says the Founding Fathers Would Be 'Appalled' with the Justice Department for iPhone Fight," *The Washington Post*, March 15, 2016. https://www.washingtonpost.com/news/post-nation/wp/2016/03/15/apple-says-the -founding-fathers-would-be-appalled-with-the-justice-dept-for-iphone-fight/

85 Barton Gellman, "Edward Snowden, After Months of NSA Revelations, Says His Mission's Accomplished." *The Washington Post*, December 23, 2013. www.washingtonpost.com/world/national-security/edward-snowden-after-months-of-nsa -revelations-says-his-missions-accomplished/2013/12/23/49fc36de-6c1c-11e3-a523-fe73f0ff6b8d_story.html

undermine global confidence in a range of American-made information products like laptop computers and cloud services. Our total dependence on the Internet and its infrastructure for everything—from our social network to finding the weather or traffic reports to looking for the best deal on a purchase—brings a new set of privacy challenges. Your location is signaled by your wireless device, as is that of your friends as you tweet. Unless the individual puts extensive privacy controls into place, purchase records are sent to advertisers, and Facebook data are sent to friends and to friends of friends and to marketers, leading some to claim that in our data-saturated economy, privacy has become a luxury good.[86] Julia Angwin, a senior reporter for ProPublica, cautions that accessing information, communication, and goods on the Internet for free is not really free—we pay for it with our personal data, which are "spliced and diced and bought and sold." Your Google search results depend on the data provided in the past. Personal data can be used to charge people different prices for goods without their knowledge. Rolling back this information give away will not be easy. With so much of the information given freely by each of us, can we really claim a presumption of privacy? What will happen to your privacy rights in the next few years as you move into the workforce? Can information freely shared prevent you from getting a job? These issues will be important to consider in your lifetime.

The Great Balancing Act: The Rights of the Accused versus the Rights of Society

■ **4.5** Identify the rights of the accused and discuss the role of the Supreme Court in defining criminal due process rights over time.

The United States has one of the highest murder rates in the industrialized world. It is not surprising, therefore, that many citizens have extremely strong opinions about the rights of those accused of crimes. When an accused person, especially one who has confessed to some criminal act, is set free because of an apparent legal technicality, many people opine that the rights of the accused are given more weight than the rights of society and of potential or actual victims. Why, then, give criminal suspects rights? The answer is partly to avoid convicting innocent people, but mostly because all criminal suspects have the right to due process of law and fair treatment. Due process rights are intended to prevent government from abusing its considerable power relative to an individual accused of a crime.

The courts and the police must constantly engage in a balancing act of competing rights. At the basis of all discussions about the appropriate balance is the U.S. Bill of Rights. The Fourth, Fifth, Sixth, and Eighth Amendments deal specifically with the rights of criminal defendants.

The basic rights of criminal defendants are outlined in Table 4-2. When appropriate, the specific constitutional provision or amendment on which a right is based is also given.

---

86 Julia Angwin, "Has Privacy Become a Luxury Good?" *The New York Times*, March 3, 2014. www.nytimes.com/2014/03/04 /opinion/has-privacy-become-a-luxury-good.html

Table 4-2 ▶ Basic Rights of Criminal Defendants

LIMITS ON THE CONDUCT OF POLICE OFFICERS AND PROSECUTORS
No unreasonable or unwarranted searches and seizures (Amend. IV)
No arrest except on probable cause (Amend. IV)
No coerced confessions or illegal interrogation (Amend. V)
No entrapment
On questioning, a suspect must be informed of her or his rights

DEFENDANT'S PRETRIAL RIGHTS
Writ of *habeas corpus* (Article I, Section 9)
Prompt arraignment (Amend. VI)
Legal counsel (Amend. VI)
Reasonable bail (Amend. VIII)
To be informed of charges (Amend. VI)
To remain silent (Amend. V)

TRIAL RIGHTS
Speedy and public trial before a jury (Amend. VI)
Impartial jury selected from a cross-section of the community (Amend. VI)
Trial atmosphere free of prejudice, fear, and outside interference
No compulsory self-incrimination (Amend. V)
Adequate counsel (Amend. VI)
No cruel and unusual punishment (Amend. VIII)
Appeal of convictions
No double jeopardy (Amend. V)

Extending the Rights of the Accused

■ **4.6** Evaluate modern threats to civil liberties posed by spy technology, the transfer of personal information through social media, and heightened security concerns following the September 11, 2001, terrorist attacks.

During the 1960s, the Supreme Court, under Chief Justice Earl Warren, significantly expanded the rights of accused persons. In *Gideon v. Wainwright*, a case decided in 1963, the Court held that if a person is accused of a felony and cannot afford an attorney, an attorney must be made available to the accused person at the government's expense.[87] This case was particularly interesting because Gideon, who was arrested for stealing a small amount of money from a vending machine, was not considered a dangerous man, nor was his intellect in any way impaired. Gideon pursued his own appeal to the Supreme Court because he believed that every accused person who might face prison should be represented.[88] Although the Sixth Amendment to the Constitution provides for the right to counsel, the Supreme Court had established a precedent 21 years earlier in *Betts v. Brady*, when it held that only

---

87 372 U.S. 335 (1963).
88 Anthony Lewis, *Gideon's Trumpet* (New York: Vintage, 1964).

criminal defendants in capital (death penalty) cases automatically had a right to legal counsel.[89]

Miranda v. Arizona In 1966, the Court issued its decision in *Miranda v. Arizona*.[90] The case involved Ernesto Miranda, who was arrested and charged with the kidnapping and rape of a young woman. After two hours of questioning, Miranda confessed and was later convicted. Miranda's lawyer appealed his conviction, arguing that the police had never informed Miranda that he had a right to remain silent and a right to be represented by counsel. The Court, in ruling in Miranda's favor, enunciated the *Miranda* rights that are now familiar to nearly all Americans:

> *Prior to any questioning, the person must be warned that he has a right to remain silent, that any statement he does make may be used against him, and that he has a right to the presence of an attorney, either retained or appointed.*

Two years after the Supreme Court's *Miranda* decision, Congress passed the Omnibus Crime Control and Safe Streets Act of 1968. Section 3501 of the act reinstated a rule that had been in effect for 180 years before *Miranda*—that statements by defendants can be used against them if the statements were made voluntarily. The Justice Department immediately disavowed Section 3501 as unconstitutional and has continued to hold this position. As a result, Section 3501, although it was never repealed, has never been enforced. In 2000, in a surprise move, a federal appellate court held that the all-but-forgotten provision was enforceable, but the Supreme Court held that the *Miranda* warnings were constitutionally based and could not be overruled by a legislative act.[91]

Exceptions to the *Miranda* Rule As part of a continuing attempt to balance the rights of accused persons against the rights of society, the Supreme Court has made several exceptions to the *Miranda* rule. In 1984, for example, the Court recognized a "public-safety" exception to the rule. The need to protect the public warranted the admissibility of statements made by the defendant (in this case, indicating where he had placed a gun) as evidence in a trial, even though the defendant had not been informed of his *Miranda* rights.

In 1985, the Court further held that a confession need not be excluded even though the police failed to inform a suspect in custody that his attorney had tried to reach him by telephone. In an important 1991 decision, the Court stated that a suspect's conviction will not be automatically overturned if the suspect was coerced into making a confession. If the other evidence admitted at trial is strong enough to justify the conviction without the confession, then the fact that the confession was obtained illegally in effect can be ignored. In yet another case, in 1994, the Supreme Court ruled that suspects must unequivocally and assertively state their right to counsel in order to stop police questioning. Saying "Maybe I should talk to a lawyer" during an interrogation after being taken into custody is not enough. The Court held that police officers are not required to decipher the

---

89 316 U.S. 455 (1942).
90 384 U.S. 436 (1966).
91 *Dickerson v. United States*, 530 U.S. 428 (2000).

suspect's intentions in such situations. Most recently, the *Miranda* protections were further narrowed when the Court found that a suspect must expressly announce his or her desire to remain silent, not just sit silently during questioning.

Video Recording of Interrogations In view of the numerous exceptions, there are no guarantees that the *Miranda* rule will survive indefinitely. Increasingly, though, law enforcement personnel are using digital cameras to record interrogations. According to some scholars, the recording of *all* custodial interrogations would satisfy the Fifth Amendment's prohibition against coercion and in the process render the *Miranda* warnings unnecessary. Others argue, however, that recorded interrogations can be misleading.

The Exclusionary Rule

exclusionary rule
A policy forbidding the admission at trial of illegally seized evidence.

At least since 1914, judicial policy has prohibited the admission of illegally seized evidence at trials in federal courts. This is the so-called **exclusionary rule**. Improperly obtained evidence, no matter how telling, cannot be used by prosecutors. This includes evidence obtained by police in violation of a suspect's *Miranda* rights or of the Fourth Amendment. The Fourth Amendment protects against unreasonable searches and seizures and provides that a judge may issue a search warrant to a police officer only on *probable cause* (a demonstration of facts that permit a reasonable belief that a crime has been committed). The question that must be determined by the courts is what constitutes an unreasonable search and seizure.

The reasoning behind the exclusionary rule is that it forces police officers to gather evidence properly, in which case their due diligence will be rewarded by a conviction. Nevertheless, the exclusionary rule has always had critics who argue that it permits guilty persons to be freed because of innocent errors.

This rule was first extended to state court proceedings in a 1961 U.S. Supreme Court decision, *Mapp v. Ohio*.[92] In this case, the Court overturned the conviction of Dollree Mapp for the possession of obscene materials. Police found pornographic books in her apartment after searching it without a search warrant and despite her refusal to let them in.

Over the last several decades, the Supreme Court has diminished the scope of the exclusionary rule by creating some exceptions to its applicability. In 1984, the Court held that illegally obtained evidence could be admitted at trial if law enforcement personnel could prove that they would have obtained the evidence legally anyway. The same year, the Court held that a police officer who used a technically incorrect search warrant form to obtain evidence had acted in good faith and therefore the evidence was admissible at trial. The Court thus created the "good faith" exception to the exclusionary rule.

The Death Penalty

Capital punishment remains one of the most debated aspects of our criminal justice system. Those in favor of the death penalty maintain that it serves as a deterrent to serious crime and satisfies society's need for

---

[92] 367 U.S. 643 (1961).

justice and fair play. Those opposed to the death penalty do not believe it has any deterrent value and hold that it constitutes a barbaric act in an otherwise civilized society.

Cruel and Unusual Punishment?

The Eighth Amendment prohibits cruel and unusual punishment. Throughout history, "cruel and unusual" referred to punishments that were more serious than the crimes—the phrase referred to torture and to executions that prolonged the agony of dying. The Supreme Court never interpreted "cruel and unusual" to prohibit all forms of capital punishment in all circumstances. Indeed, several states had imposed the death penalty for a variety of crimes and allowed juries to decide when the condemned could be sentenced to death. Many believed, however, that the imposition of the death penalty was random and arbitrary, and in 1972 the Supreme Court agreed in *Furman v. Georgia*.[93]

The decision stated that the death penalty, as then applied, violated the Eighth and Fourteenth Amendments. The Court ruled that capital punishment is not necessarily cruel and unusual if the criminal has killed or attempted to kill someone. In its opinion, the Court invited the states to enact more precise laws so that the death penalty would be applied more consistently. By 1976, 25 states had adopted a two-stage, or *bifurcated*, procedure for capital cases. In the first stage, a jury determines the guilt or innocence of the defendant for a crime that has been determined by statute to be punishable by death. If the defendant is found guilty, the jury reconvenes in the second stage and considers all relevant evidence to decide whether the death sentence is, in fact, warranted.

In *Gregg v. Georgia*, the Supreme Court ruled in favor of Georgia's bifurcated process, holding that the state's legislative guidelines had removed the ability of a jury to "wantonly and freakishly impose the death penalty."[94] The Court upheld similar procedures in Texas and Florida, establishing a procedure for all states to follow that would ensure them protection from lawsuits based on Eighth Amendment grounds. On January 17, 1977, Gary Mark Gilmore became the first American to be executed (by Utah) under the new laws.

The Death Penalty Today

Today, 31 states (see Figure 4-1), the military, and the federal government have capital punishment laws based on the guidelines established by the *Gregg* case. State governments are responsible for almost all executions in this country. The execution of Timothy McVeigh in 2001 marked the first death sentence carried out by the federal government since 1963. Only two more have followed. At this time, about 2,817 prisoners are on death row across the nation. The population on death row has been on the decline since 2003. Although California has the largest death row population of any state, Texas has the highest execution rate. The South as a region has executed 1,199

---

93 408 U.S. 238 (1972).
94 428 U.S. 153 (1976).

The Innocence Project

As long as the United States has imposed capital punishment on convicted felons, there have been claims of innocence by those sentenced to die. Although police officers and judges have always known that sometimes the innocent are falsely accused and convicted, they also believe that most of the individuals were correctly prosecuted and convicted of their crimes. New scientific techniques make it possible to recover biological and chemical evidence that was previously inaccessible. Most important of these new tools is the use of DNA. DNA molecules contain all of the information about a person's or an animal's genetic makeup and are unique to each individual. DNA molecules found on a strand of hair or saliva on a handkerchief can be tested many years after they were deposited on that object.

In the early 1990s, law students at the Benjamin N. Cardozo School of Law at Yeshiva University began theorizing that DNA found in old evidence records could be used to establish the innocence of individuals wrongfully convicted of crimes. Led by Barry C. Scheck and Peter J. Neufeld, the students and faculty founded the Innocence Project,* which is dedicated to helping exonerate innocent people and improving the legal system to avoid wrongful convictions. To date, more than 337 people in 36 states have been exonerated through DNA evidence. One-third of the people exonerated by DNA testing were arrested between the ages of 14 and 22.

The Innocence Project identifies a number of reasons why wrongful convictions occur. Witnesses may identify the wrong person as the suspect; individuals who are arrested may feel strongly pressured to make a confession, especially if the prosecution offers a plea bargain for a lesser sentence; forensic science may be faulty in a particular location; the police may have acted out of discriminatory motives or failed to complete an investigation; informants may have given false information; or the defendant's free (or hired) counsel may be incompetent.** The Innocence Project's work has spread throughout the United States and to some foreign countries. Law students provide most of the volunteer investigations into possible cases of wrongful conviction, with guidance from their faculty. Students also research the laws governing criminal procedure in their own state and

Image 4-6 Ronald Cotton was exonerated in 1995 after spending over 10 years in prison for crimes he did not commit. His convictions were based largely on an eyewitness misidentification made by one of the victims, Jennifer Thompson-Cannino. Cotton and Thompson-Cannino are leading advocates for eyewitness identification reform.

then lobby for changes to reduce the chance of wrongful convictions. Based on student research, Ohio adopted a law that requires preservation of DNA evidence forever in serious crimes, strengthens the requirements for police lineups, and gives incentives for the video recording of interrogations in most serious crimes. The legislation is considered groundbreaking for preserving evidence that might prevent wrongful convictions.

For Critical Analysis

1. Elsewhere in this chapter, you read that governors in several states have issued a moratorium on executions pending further study and that some states have eliminated the death penalty entirely. Yet, a majority of states have the death penalty. What impact, if any, do you think initiatives like The Innocence Project have on public attitudes about the death penalty?

2. Wrongful convictions are tragic for everyone involved in the case, but especially for the individual wrongly imprisoned. What, if anything, does the state owe a person wrongfully convicted of a crime? Should restitution be offered? Why or why not?

*Innocence Project http://www.innocenceproject.org/
**Barry Scheck, Peter Neufeld, and Jim Dwyer, *Actual Innocence: When Justice Goes Wrong and How to Make It Right* (New York: New American Library, 2003).

Figure 4-1 ▶ Executions by State: 1976–2015

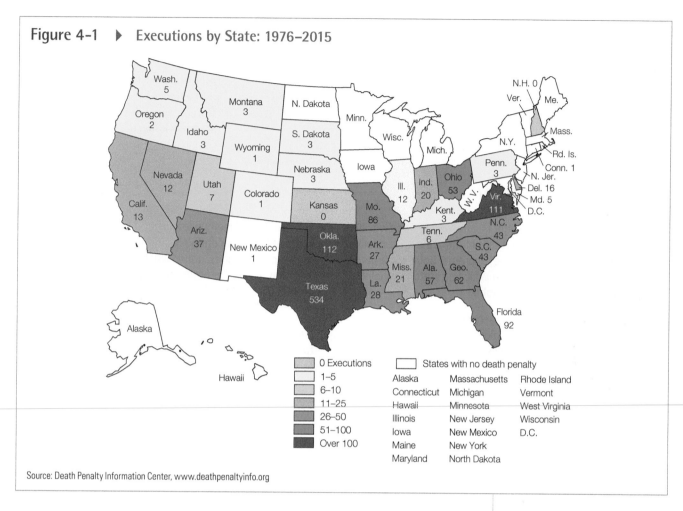

Source: Death Penalty Information Center, www.deathpenaltyinfo.org

people since 1976; in the Northeast, only 4 people have been put to death over the same time period.[95]

The most recent controversy over the death penalty concerns the method by which the punishment is carried out. Most states that have the death penalty use a lethal injection to cause the convicted person's death. A combination of three different drugs is injected intravenously. Several cases have been appealed to the Supreme Court on the basis that this method can cause extreme pain and thus violates the Constitution's ban on cruel and unusual punishment. The Court has upheld the three-drug method, most recently in April 2008, although the justices wrote seven opinions in the case, indicating a lack of consensus among them.[96]

Some believe that the declining number of executions reflects the waning support among Americans for the imposition of the death penalty. In 1994, polls indicated that 80 percent of Americans supported the death penalty. Gallup polling recorded the lowest support for the death penalty in 40 years in its 2018 survey; just 55 percent indicated support. The current era of lower support may be tied to death penalty moratoriums in several states beginning around 2000 after several death row inmates were later proven innocent of the crimes of which they were convicted. Since 2006, six states have repealed death penalty laws outright.

did you know?

According to the Death Penalty Information Center, women represent 2 percent of death row inmates, and 16 women have been executed since 1976.

95 Death Penalty Information Center, Executions by Region. www.deathpenaltyinfo.org/number-executions-state-and-region-1976
96 *Baze v. Rees*, 553 U.S. 35 (2008).

Key Terms

actual malice 130
civil liberties 109
clear and present danger test 123
commercial speech 122
defamation of character 127

establishment clause 111
exclusionary rule 146
free exercise clause 118
gag order 131
incorporation theory 110

libel 130
prior restraint 120
public figure 130
slander 128
symbolic speech 121

Chapter Summary

■ **4.1** Originally, the Bill of Rights limited only the power of the national government, not that of the states. Gradually and selectively, however, the Supreme Court accepted the incorporation theory, under which no state can violate most provisions of the Bill of Rights.

■ **4.2** The First Amendment protects against government interference with freedom of religion by requiring a separation of church and state (under the establishment clause) and by guaranteeing the free exercise of religion. Controversial issues that arise under the establishment clause include aid to church-related schools, school prayer, evolution versus intelligent design, school vouchers, posting the Ten Commandments in public places, and discrimination against religious speech. The government can interfere with the free exercise of religion only when religious practices work against public policy or the public welfare. The government cannot sponsor or support any specific religious belief.

■ **4.3** The First Amendment protects against government interference with freedom of speech, which includes symbolic speech (expressive conduct). The Supreme Court has been especially critical of government actions that impose prior restraint on expression. Commercial speech (advertising) by businesses has received limited First Amendment protection. Restrictions on expression are permitted when the expression creates a clear and present danger to the peace or public order. Speech that has not received First Amendment protection includes expression that is judged to be obscene or slanderous.

■ **4.3** The First Amendment protects against government interference with the freedom of the press, which can be regarded as a special instance of freedom of speech. Libelous statements are not protected by the freedom of the press. Publication of news about a criminal trial may be restricted by a gag order in some circumstances.

■ **4.3** The First Amendment protects the right to assemble peaceably and to petition the government. Permits may be required for parades, sound trucks, and demonstrations to maintain the public order, and a permit may be denied to protect the public safety.

■ **4.4** Under the Ninth Amendment, rights not specifically mentioned in the Constitution are not necessarily denied to the people. Among these unspecified rights is a right to privacy, which has been inferred from the First, Third, Fourth, Fifth, and Ninth Amendments. Major privacy issues today include electronic access to personal data and government surveillance programs. Abortion rights and end-of-life decisions also involve privacy claims.

■ **4.5** The Constitution includes protections for the rights of persons accused of crimes. Under the Fourth Amendment, no one may be subject to an unreasonable search or seizure or be arrested except on probable cause. Under the Fifth Amendment, an accused person has the right to remain silent. Under the Sixth Amendment, an accused person must be informed of the reason for his or her arrest. The accused also has the right to adequate counsel, even if he or she cannot afford an attorney, and the right to a prompt arraignment and a speedy and public trial before an impartial jury selected from a cross-section of the community. The exclusionary rule forbids the admission in court of illegally seized evidence. Under the Eighth Amendment, cruel and unusual punishment is prohibited.

■ **4.6** Civil liberties are not absolute, and the interpretation of the protections against government interference with individual rights is subject to the context of the times. Spy technology, personal information freely disclosed through social media, and heightened geopolitical security concerns present the Supreme Court and society with new challenges.

Selected Resources

PRINT RESOURCES

Herman, Susan N. *Taking Liberties: The War on Terror and the Erosion of American Democracy* (New York: Oxford University Press, 2011). The president of the ACLU analyzes the long- and short-term effects of the USA PATRIOT Act and the new legal practices that have reduced personal liberty.

Lewis, Anthony. *Freedom for the Thought We Hate: Tales of the First Amendment* (New York: Basic Books, 2008). Pulitzer Prize–winning journalist Anthony Lewis writes eloquently on the value of free expression and the resulting need for "activist judges." He provides a series of engaging stories of how the courts came to give real life to the First Amendment.

Lewis, Anthony. *Gideon's Trumpet* (New York: Vintage, 1964). This classic work discusses the background and facts of *Gideon v. Wainwright,* the 1963 Supreme Court case in which the Court held that the state must make an attorney available for any person accused of a felony who cannot afford a lawyer.

Richards, Neil. *Intellectual Privacy: Rethinking Civil Liberties in the Digital Age* (New York: Oxford University Books, 2015). A provocative consideration of privacy and free speech in the digital age. Richards argues that when privacy rights and speech rights conflict, the importance of a free and open society dictates that speech nearly always wins.

Thompson-Cannino, Jennifer, Ronald Cotton, and Erin Roneo. *Picking Cotton: Our Memoir of Injustice and Redemption* (New York: St. Martin's Press, 2009). Jennifer Thompson was raped at knife point, but escaped and identified her attacker as Ronald Cotton. Convicted and sent to prison, Cotton maintained his innocence. DNA evidence ultimately proved him right, and he was released after 10 years. Thompson and Cotton work together on issues of justice, innocence, and memory.

MEDIA RESOURCES

Constitution USA with Peter Sagal—Over the course of the four-hour PBS series first airing in 2013, Sagal travels cross-country on a customized red, white, and blue Harley-Davidson to find out where the Constitution lives, how it works, and how it unites us as a nation. Episode 2, "It's a Free Country," specifically examines the Bill of Rights in everyday life.

Conviction: The Incredible True Story of Betty Anne Waters—A 2010 movie starring Hilary Swank and Sam Rockwell. A working mother puts herself through law school in an effort to represent her brother, who has been wrongfully convicted of murder and has exhausted his chances to appeal his conviction through public defenders.

Gideon's Trumpet—An excellent 1980 movie about the *Gideon v. Wainwright* case. Henry Fonda plays the role of the convicted petty thief Clarence Earl Gideon.

The Lord Is Not on Trial Here Today—A Peabody Award–winning documentary that tells the compelling personal story of Vashti McCollum and how her efforts to protect her 10-year-old son led to one of the most important and landmark First Amendment cases in U.S. Supreme Court history—the case that established the separation of church and state in public schools.

ONLINE RESOURCES

American Civil Liberties Union (ACLU)—the nation's leading civil liberties organization provides an extensive array of information and links concerning civil rights issues: www.aclu.org

The American Library Association—information on free-speech issues, especially issues of free speech on the Internet: www.ala.org

Center for Democracy and Technology—nonprofit institute that monitors threats to the freedom of the Internet, provides a wealth of information about issues involving the Bill of Rights, and focuses on how developments in communications technology are affecting the constitutional liberties of Americans: www.cdt.org

Death Penalty Information Center—national nonprofit organization serving the media and the public with analysis and information on issues concerning capital punishment: www.deathpenaltyinfo.org

Electronic Privacy Information Center—information on digital privacy issues: www.epic.org/privacy

Foundation for Individual Rights in Education (FIRE)—tracks the rights to free speech, press, religion, and assembly at the nation's colleges and universities; find a rating for your own university's speech and conduct codes: www.thefire.org

Freedom Forum—nonpartisan foundation dedicated to free press, free speech, and free spirit for all people; includes history of flag protection and the First Amendment, as well as the status of the proposed flag amendment in Congress: www.freedomforuminstitute.org/freedom-forum/

Legal Information Institute at Cornell University Law School—searchable database of historic Supreme Court decisions: www.law.cornell.edu/

The Oyez Project—provides summaries and the full text of Supreme Court decisions concerning constitutional law, plus a virtual tour of the Supreme Court: www.oyez.org

5

Civil Rights

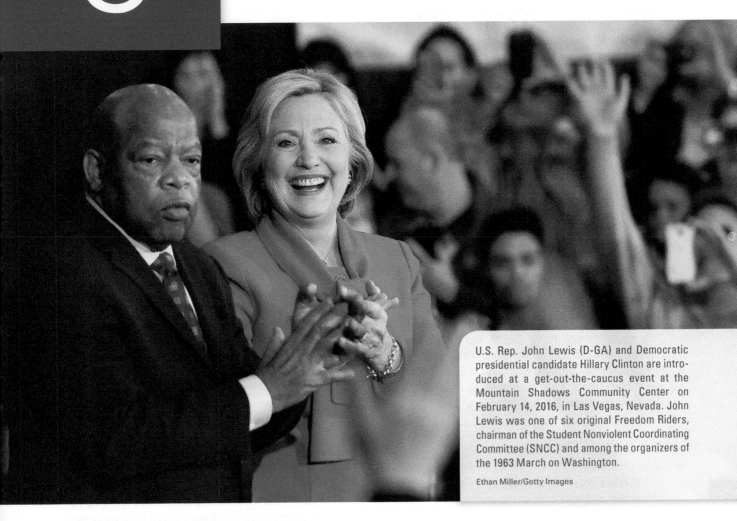

U.S. Rep. John Lewis (D-GA) and Democratic presidential candidate Hillary Clinton are introduced at a get-out-the-caucus event at the Mountain Shadows Community Center on February 14, 2016, in Las Vegas, Nevada. John Lewis was one of six original Freedom Riders, chairman of the Student Nonviolent Coordinating Committee (SNCC) and among the organizers of the 1963 March on Washington.

Ethan Miller/Getty Images

LEARNING OBJECTIVES

After reading this chapter, you will be able to:

■ **5.1** Define civil rights and locate in the U.S. Constitution the obligation of government to guarantee all citizens equal protection of the law.

■ **5.2** Explain why discrimination against individuals and groups exists in the United States today.

■ **5.3** Assess the limits of state and federal law in guaranteeing equality to all people.

■ **5.4** Explain why the U.S. Supreme Court plays such an important role relative to civil rights and identify

at least two significant Supreme Court decisions that advanced civil rights in the United States.

■ **5.5** Identify and explain three significant events related to each of the campaigns for civil rights undertaken by African Americans, women, the Latino community, persons with disabilities, and the LGBTQ community.

■ **5.6** Define the goal of affirmative action and explain why this approach is controversial in the United States.

What if... Birthright Citizenship Were Repealed?

Background

The Fourteenth Amendment (1868) confers citizenship on "all persons born or naturalized in the United States, and subject to the jurisdiction thereof" and was adopted as a repudiation of the U.S. Supreme Court's *Dred Scott* ruling that people of African descent could *never* be American citizens. As a concept, birthright citizenship has its origins in English common law. Until recently, the idea of repealing birthright citizenship had been largely relegated to advocates of severe restrictions on immigration. However, a group of Republican state and national lawmakers has introduced legislation to repeal birthright citizenship. Several well-known legislators are among the supporters of the repeal, including Senators John McCain, Mitch McConnell, Lindsey Graham, Jeff Sessions, and Jon Kyl. Republican candidate for presidential nomination Donald J. Trump reignited the issue during the 2016 campaign by calling for an end to birthright citizenship as a part of a larger immigration plan. According to Trump, birthright citizenship "remains the biggest magnet for illegal immigration."*

Past Challenges

In 1882, the Chinese Exclusion Act (along with other state and federal laws) denied Chinese and other Asians the right to own property, to marry, to return to the United States once they left the country, and to become U.S. citizens. In the case *U.S. v. Wong Kim Ark*, the Supreme Court took up the issue of birthright citizenship. The case involved a man born in San Francisco to Chinese parents who later returned to China. When Wong left the United States to visit his parents, he was denied reentry. The government claimed that Wong had no right to birthright citizenship under the Fourteenth Amendment because his parents remained "subjects of the emperor of China" even while living in California when he was born. In a 7–2 decision, the majority said, "The amendment, in clear words and in manifest intent, includes the children born within the territory of the United States of all other persons, of whatever race or color, domiciled within the United States." This case remains the ruling precedent for challenges to birthright citizenship.

A Political Strategy for Repeal

The process for amending the U.S. Constitution is intentionally difficult, requiring the support of two-thirds of both houses of Congress and three-fourths of the state legislatures. Those advocating the repeal of birthright citizenship avoid this path and have instead proposed a two-pronged strategy. At the federal level, a bill has been introduced to reinterpret the "subject to the jurisdiction thereof" language in the Fourteenth Amendment so that noncitizens and illegal immigrants are not covered. Thus, a student who comes to the United States to attend college would not be "subject to the jurisdiction thereof" for the purposes of citizenship, and any children born to that student would not be citizens of the United States. At the state level, several states working together propose to create two types of birth certificates—one for children born to citizens of the United States and one for those born to noncitizens. Neither of these strategies is likely to pass the test of constitutionality, given the precedent set in *Wong*. Further, a repeal of birthright citizenship is not likely to reduce illegal immigration because most undocumented immigrants are motivated by jobs. Countries without birthright citizenship have not eliminated illegal immigration.

For Critical Analysis

1. In the media, children born to noncitizens are sometimes referred to as "anchor babies" because they presumably tie their parents to this country. This is a misnomer, however, because only the child born here is a citizen. Why do you think opposition exists to granting citizenship to children born to noncitizen parents?

2. Is the concept of birthright citizenship consistent with the values of America? What would be gained and lost by the nation if birthright citizenship were repealed?

*Mark Murray, "Where the GOP 2016 Candidates Stand on Birthright Citizenship," MSNBC, August 18, 2015. www.msnbc.com/msnbc/where-the-gop-2016-candidates-stand-birthright-citizenship

■ **5.1** Define civil rights and locate in the U.S. Constitution the obligation of government to guarantee all citizens equal protection of the law.

Despite the words set forth in the Declaration of Independence that "all Men are created equal," the United States has a long history of discrimination based on race, gender, national origin, religion, and sexual orientation, among others. The majority of the population had few rights at the nation's founding. The framers of the Constitution permitted slavery to continue, thus excluding slaves from the political process. Women also were excluded for the most part, as were Native Americans, African Americans who were not slaves, and white men who did not own property. To the nation's founders, equality required a degree of independent thinking and the capacity for rational action, which they believed members of these groups did not possess. Today we believe that all people are entitled to equal political rights as well as the opportunities for personal development provided by equal access to education and employment. Thus, the story of civil rights in the United States is the struggle to reconcile our ideals as a nation with the realities of discrimination individuals and groups still encounter in daily life.

Equality is at the heart of the concept of civil rights. Generally, the term **civil rights** refers to the rights of all Americans to equal treatment under the law, as provided for by the Fourteenth Amendment to the Constitution and by subsequent acts of Congress. Although the terms *civil rights* and *civil liberties* are sometimes used interchangeably, scholars make a distinction between the two. Civil liberties are limitations on government; they specify what the government *cannot* do. Civil rights, in contrast, specify what the government *must* do to ensure equal protection and freedom from discrimination.

The history of civil rights in America is the story of the struggle of various groups to be free from discriminatory treatment. Ending slavery was a necessary but not sufficient prerequisite to advancing civil rights in America. In this chapter, we first look at two movements with significant consequences: the civil rights movement of the 1950s and 1960s and the women's movement, which began in the mid-1800s and continues today. Each of these movements resulted in legislation that secured important basic rights for all Americans—the right to vote and the right to equal protection under the laws. Each demonstrates how individuals working alone and with others in groups can effect significant change. Today's civil rights activists draw on insights and strategies from these earlier movements in making new claims for political and social equality. We then explore a question with serious implications for today's voters and policymakers: What should the government's responsibility be when equal protection under the law is not enough to ensure truly equal opportunities for Americans? Can political and social equality exist in the face of a widening economic gap?

African Americans and the Consequences of Slavery in the United States

■ **5.2** Explain why discrimination against individuals and groups exists in the United States today.

Before 1863, the Constitution protected slavery and made equality impossible. African American leader Frederick Douglass pointed out that "Liberty and

---

did you know?

At the time of the American Revolution, African Americans made up nearly 25 percent of the American population of about 3 million.

civil rights
All rights rooted in the Fourteenth Amendment's guarantee of equal protection under the law.

Slavery—opposite as Heaven and Hell—are both in the Constitution." Abraham Lincoln stated sarcastically, "All men are created equal, except Negroes."

The constitutionality of slavery was confirmed just a few years before the outbreak of the Civil War in the infamous *Dred Scott v. Sandford* case of 1857. The Supreme Court held that slaves were property, not citizens of the United States, and were not entitled to the rights and privileges of citizenship.[1] The Court also ruled that the Missouri Compromise (1820), which banned slavery in the territories north of 36°30′ latitude (the southern border of Missouri), was unconstitutional. The *Dred Scott* decision had grave consequences. Most observers contend that the ruling contributed to making the Civil War inevitable.

Ending Servitude

With the Emancipation Proclamation in 1863 and ratification of the Thirteenth, Fourteenth, and Fifteenth Amendments during the Reconstruction period following the Civil War, constitutional inequality for African American males ended.

The Thirteenth Amendment (1865) states that neither slavery nor involuntary servitude shall exist within the United States. The Fourteenth Amendment (1868) says that *all* persons born or naturalized in the United States are citizens of the United States. It states, furthermore, that "[n]o State shall make or enforce any law which shall abridge the privileges or immunities of citizens of the United States; nor shall any State deprive any person of life, liberty, or property, without due process of law; nor deny to any person within its jurisdiction the equal protection of the laws." Note the use of the terms *citizen* and *person*. Citizens have political rights, such as the right to vote and run for political office. Citizens also have certain privileges or immunities (see Chapter 4). All *persons*, however, including noncitizens, have a right to due process of law and equal protection under the law.

The Fifteenth Amendment (1870) reads: "The right of citizens of the United States to vote shall not be denied or abridged by the United States or by any State on account of race, color, or previous condition of servitude." Activists in the women's suffrage movements brought pressure on Congress to include in the Fourteenth and Fifteenth Amendments a prohibition against discrimination based on sex, but with no success.

The Civil Rights Acts of 1865 to 1875

At the end of the Civil War, President Lincoln's Republican Party controlled the national government and most state governments, and the so-called radical Republicans, with their strong antislavery stance, controlled the party. From 1865 to 1875, the Republican majority in Congress succeeded in passing a series of civil rights acts that were aimed at enforcing the Thirteenth, Fourteenth, and Fifteenth Amendments even as legislatures in the Southern states moved quickly to pass laws (known as **Black Codes**) intended to limit the civil rights of African Americans and regulate their labor in ways that closely resembled slavery. South Carolina's Black Code (1865) stated that "all persons of color who make contracts for service or labor, shall be known as servants, and those with whom they contract, shall be known as masters."[2] Following the assassination of President Lincoln on April 15, 1865, Andrew Johnson assumed the presidency and oversaw the initial period of Reconstruction.

Black Codes
Laws passed by Southern states immediately after the Civil War denying most legal rights to freed slaves.

---

1   19 Howard 393 (1857).
2   "Acts of the General Assembly of the State of South Carolina Passed at the Sessions of 1864–65," pp. 291–304.

Ku Klux Klan members, late 1860s–70s (engraving) (b/w photo), American School, (19th century)/Private Collection/The Stapleton Collection/Bridgeman Images

Image 5-1
An engraving of Ku Klux Klan members active in the late 1860s as Southerners rebelled against Northern influence during Reconstruction.

Johnson, a Southerner and former slave owner, was viewed by radical Republicans as too conciliatory toward Southern states.

Following the 1866 elections, in which Southern states were not allowed to vote, an emboldened radical Republican majority in Congress moved to take control of Reconstruction. The first Civil Rights Act in the Reconstruction period was passed in 1866 over the veto of President Johnson. That act extended citizenship to anyone born in the United States and gave African Americans full equality before the law. It gave the president authority to enforce the law with military force. Johnson characterized the law as an invasion by federal authority of the rights of the states. It was considered to be unconstitutional, but the ratification of the Fourteenth Amendment two years later ended that concern.

Among the six other civil rights acts passed after the Civil War, one of the most important was the Enforcement Act of 1879, which set out specific criminal sanctions for interfering with the right to vote as protected by the Fifteenth Amendment and by the Civil Rights Act of 1866. Equally important was the Civil Rights Act of 1872, known as the Anti-Ku Klux Klan Act. This act made it a federal crime for anyone to use law or custom to deprive an individual of his or her rights, privileges, and immunities secured by the Constitution or by any federal law.

The last of these early civil rights acts, the Second Civil Rights Act, was passed in 1875. It declared that everyone is entitled to full and equal enjoyment of public accommodations, theaters, and other places of amusement, and it imposed penalties for violators. What is most important about all of the civil rights acts was the belief that congressional power applied to official or government action or to private action. If a state government did not secure rights, then the federal government could do so. Thus, Congress could legislate directly against individuals who were violating the constitutional rights of others. As we will see, these acts were quickly rendered ineffective by law and by custom. They became important in the civil rights struggles of the 1960s, however, 100 years after their passage.

The Limitations of the Civil Rights Laws

■ **5.3** Assess the limits of state and federal law in guaranteeing equality to all people.

The Reconstruction statutes, or civil rights acts, ultimately did little to secure equality for African Americans. Both the *Civil Rights Cases* and *Plessy v. Ferguson* effectively nullified these acts. Rutherford B. Hayes's election in 1877 marked an end to the progressive advance of rights for African Americans during Reconstruction. He withdrew federal forces from states in the former Confederacy. Without direct oversight, Southern and border states created a variety of seemingly race-neutral legal barriers that in reality prevented African Americans from exercising their right to vote; Southern and border states also adopted policies of racial segregation known as **Jim Crow laws**.

Jim Crow laws
Laws enacted by Southern states that enforced segregation in schools, in transportation, and in public accommodations.

The *Civil Rights Cases*   The Supreme Court invalidated the 1875 Civil Rights Act when it held, in the *Civil Rights Cases* of 1883, that the enforcement clause of the Fourteenth Amendment (which states that "[n]o State shall make or enforce any law which shall abridge the privileges or immunities of citizens") was limited to correcting actions by states in their *official* acts; thus, the discriminatory acts of private citizens were not illegal.[3] ("Individual invasion of individual rights is not the subject matter of the Amendment.") The 1883 Supreme Court decision removed the federal government as a forceful advocate for advancing civil rights in all aspects of daily human interaction, and it was met with widespread approval throughout most of the United States.

Twenty years after the Civil War, the white majority was all too ready to forget about the three Civil War amendments and the civil rights legislation of the 1860s and 1870s. The other civil rights laws that the Court did not specifically invalidate became effectively null without any mechanisms of enforcement, although they were never repealed by Congress. At the same time, many former proslavery secessionists had regained political power in the Southern states.

Plessy v. Ferguson: Separate but Equal   A key decision during this period concerned Homer Plessy, a Louisiana resident who was one-eighth African American. In 1892, he boarded a train in New Orleans. The conductor made him leave the car, which was restricted to whites, and directed him to a car for nonwhites. At that time, Louisiana had a statute providing for separate railway cars for whites and African Americans.

Plessy went to court, claiming that such a statute was contrary to the Fourteenth Amendment's equal protection clause. In 1896, the Supreme Court rejected Plessy's contention. The Court concluded that the Fourteenth Amendment "could not have been intended to abolish distinctions based upon color, or to enforce social . . . equality." The Court stated that segregation alone did not violate the Constitution: "Laws permitting, and even requiring, their separation in places where they are liable to be brought into contact do not necessarily imply the inferiority of either race to the other."[4] With this case, the Court announced the **separate but equal doctrine**.

Plessy v. Ferguson became the judicial cornerstone of racial discrimination throughout the United States. Even though *Plessy* upheld segregated facilities in railway cars only, it was assumed that the Supreme Court was upholding segregation everywhere as long as the separate facilities were equal. The result was a system of racial segregation, particularly in the South—supported by laws collectively known as Jim Crow laws—that required separate drinking fountains; separate seats in theaters, restaurants, and hotels; separate public toilets; and separate waiting rooms for the two races. "Separate" was indeed the rule, but "equal" was never enforced, nor was it a reality.

separate but equal doctrine
The 1896 doctrine holding that separate but equal facilities do not violate the equal protection clause.

Voting Barriers   The brief enfranchisement of African Americans ended after 1877, when the federal troops that occupied the South during the Reconstruction era were withdrawn. Southern politicians regained control of state governments and, using everything except race as a formal criterion, passed laws that effectively deprived African Americans of the right to vote. By claiming that political parties were private organizations, the

---

3   109 U.S. 3 (1883).
4   *Plessy v. Ferguson*, 163 U.S. 537 (1896).

white primary
A state primary election that restricts voting to whites only; outlawed by the Supreme Court in 1944.

grandfather clause
A device used by Southern states to disenfranchise African Americans. It restricted voting to those whose grandfathers had voted before 1867.

poll tax
A special tax that must be paid as a qualification for voting. The Twenty-fourth Amendment to the Constitution outlawed the poll tax in national elections, and in 1966, the Supreme Court declared it unconstitutional in all elections.

literacy test
A test administered as a precondition for voting, often used to prevent African Americans from exercising their right to vote.

Democratic Party was allowed to restrict black voters from participating in its primaries. Because most Southern states were dominated by the Democratic Party, the primary prohibition effectively disenfranchised blacks altogether. The **white primary** was upheld by the Supreme Court until 1944 when, in *Smith v. Allwright*, the Court ruled it a violation of the Fifteenth Amendment.[5]

Another barrier to African American voting was the **grandfather clause**, which restricted voting to those who could prove that their grandfathers had voted before 1867. **Poll taxes** required the payment of a fee to vote; thus, poor African Americans—and poor whites—who could not afford to pay the tax were excluded from voting. Not until the Twenty-fourth Amendment was ratified in 1964 was the poll tax eliminated. **Literacy tests** were also used to deny the vote to African Americans. Such tests asked potential voters to read, recite, or interpret complicated texts, such as a section of the state constitution, to the satisfaction of local registrars—who were, of course, never satisfied with the responses of African Americans. Each of these barriers to voting was, on its face, race neutral. Each was vigorously enforced disproportionately against African Americans by government agents and a system of racial intimidation.

Southern states, counties, and towns also passed ordinances and laws to maintain a segregated society and to control the movements and activities of African American residents. In Florida, no "negro, mulatto, or person of color" was permitted to own or carry a weapon, including a knife, without a license. This law did not apply to white residents. Other laws set curfews for African Americans, set limits on the businesses they could own or run and on their rights to assembly, and required the newly freed men and women to find employment quickly or risk penalties. The penalty sometimes meant that the men would be forced into labor at very low wages. Denied the right to register and vote, black citizens were also effectively barred from public office and jury service.

Extralegal Methods of Enforcing White Supremacy The second-class status of African Americans was also a matter of social custom, especially in the South. In their interactions with Southern whites, African Americans were expected to observe an informal but detailed code of behavior that confirmed their inferiority. The most serious violation of the informal code was "familiarity" toward a white woman by an African American man or boy. The code was backed up by the common practice of *lynching*—mob action to murder an accused individual, usually by hanging and sometimes accompanied by torture. Lynching was illegal, but Southern authorities rarely prosecuted these cases, and white juries would not convict. African American women were instrumental in antilynching campaigns, beginning in the 1890s with the work of Ida B. Wells-Barnett. As the owner and editor of *The Free Speech*, a Memphis newspaper, she called attention to the brutality of lynching and argued in editorials that lynching was a strategy to eliminate prosperous, politically active African Americans.

African Americans outside the South were subject to a second kind of violence—race riots. In the early twentieth century, race riots were typically initiated by whites. Frequently, the riots were caused by competition for

---

5 321 U.S. 649 (1944).

employment. For example, several serious riots occurred during World War II (1939–1945), when labor shortages forced Northern employers to hire more black workers.

The End of the Separate-but-Equal Doctrine

■ **5.4** Explain why the U.S. Supreme Court plays such an important role relative to civil rights and identify at least two significant Supreme Court decisions that advanced civil rights in the United States.

The successful attack on the separate-but-equal doctrine began with a series of lawsuits in the 1930s that sought to admit African Americans to state professional schools. In 1909, influential African Americans and progressive whites, including W. E. B. Dubois and Oswald Garrison Villard, joined to form the National Association for the Advancement of Colored People (NAACP) with the express intention of targeting the separate-but-equal doctrine. Although all Southern states maintained a segregated system of elementary and secondary schools as well as colleges and universities, very few offered professional education for African Americans. Thus, the NAACP elected to begin its challenge with law schools, believing in part that it would be too expensive for states to establish an entirely separate system of black professional schools, leaving integration as the best option. To pursue this strategy, the NAACP established the Legal Defense and Education Fund (LDF). As a result of several LDF challenges, law schools in Maryland, Missouri, Oklahoma, and Texas were forced to change their policies regarding admittance or matriculation of law school students, paving the way for *Brown v. Board of Education* (1954).

By 1950, the Supreme Court had ruled that African Americans who were admitted to a state university could not be assigned to separate sections of classrooms, libraries, and cafeterias. In 1951, Oliver Brown attempted to enroll his eight-year-old daughter, Linda Carol Brown, in the third grade of his all-white neighborhood school seven blocks from their home. (The alternative was to have her travel by bus to the segregated school across town.) Although Kansas law did not require schools to be segregated by race, in practice there were separate schools for white and black children. When Linda was denied admission to the all-white school, the Topeka NAACP urged Brown to join a lawsuit against the Topeka Board of Education.

Brown v. Board of Education of Topeka[6] This case established that segregation of races in public schools violates the equal protection clause of the Fourteenth Amendment. First argued in 1952 by NAACP Legal Defense Fund attorney Thurgood Marshall (appointed as the first African American to the U.S. Supreme Court in 1967), the votes were almost evenly split to uphold or strike down *separate-but-equal*; Chief Justice Fred Vinson held the swing vote. In 1953, Vinson died, and President Dwight Eisenhower appointed Earl Warren to replace him. *Brown* was reargued, and Warren wrote a unanimous decision to strike down *separate but equal*, arguing that "separate" is inherently unequal.

---

6   347 U.S. 483 (1954).

Image 5-2

These three lawyers successfully argued in favor of desegregation of the schools in the famous *Brown v. Board of Education of Topeka* case. On the left is George E. C. Hayes; on the right is James Nabrit, Jr.; and in the center is Thurgood Marshall, who later became the first African American Supreme Court justice.

Bettmann/Getty Images

"With All Deliberate Speed" The following year, in *Brown v. Board of Education* (sometimes called the second *Brown* decision), the Court declared that lower courts needed to ensure that African Americans would be admitted to schools on a nondiscriminatory basis "with all deliberate speed."[7] The district courts were to consider devices in their desegregation orders that might include "the school transportation system, personnel, [and] revision of school districts and attendance areas into compact units to achieve a system of determining admission to the public schools on a nonracial basis."

This legal strategy was only one of many African Americans found successful in their struggle for civil rights, and many difficult days lay ahead. The success of civil rights groups in *Brown* was a flashpoint, sparking an enormous backlash among segregationists. They defied the Court, closed public schools rather than integrate them, and vowed to maintain inequality in other areas such as voting. Violence and sometimes death for civil rights activists followed.

Reactions to School Integration

The white South did not let the Supreme Court ruling go unchallenged. Governor Orval Faubus of Arkansas used the state's National Guard to block the integration of Central High School in Little Rock in September 1957. The federal court demanded that the troops be withdrawn. Finally, President Dwight Eisenhower had to federalize the Arkansas National Guard and send in the U.S. Army's 101st Airborne Division to quell the violence. Central High was integrated.

---

7   349 U.S. 294 (1955).

The universities in the South, however, remained segregated. When James Meredith, an African American student, attempted to enroll at the University of Mississippi in 1962, violence flared there, as it had in Little Rock. The white riot was so intense that President John Kennedy was forced to send in 30,000 U.S. combat troops, a larger force than the one then stationed in Korea. There were 375 military and civilian injuries, many from gunfire, and two bystanders were killed. Ultimately, peace was restored, and Meredith began attending classes.[8]

Integration Today

In most parts of the United States, residential concentrations by race have made it difficult to achieve racial balance in schools. This concentration results in **de facto segregation**, as distinct from **de jure segregation**, which results from laws or administrative decisions.

The Resurgence of Minority Schools

Today, schools around the country are becoming segregated again, in large part because changing population demographics result in increased *de facto* segregation. Even as African American and Latino students are becoming more isolated, the typical white child is in a school that is more diverse in large part due to the substantial decline in the number and proportion of white students in the population relative to the increase of nonwhites. In Latino and African American populations, two of every five students attend a school with more than 90 percent minority enrollment. Public school segregation is most severe in the Western states and in New York. In California, the nation's most multiracial state, half of African Americans and Asians attend segregated schools, as do one-quarter of Latino and Native American students.[9] Sixty years after *Brown*, about half of New York State's public school students are white, but during the 2010 school year the average black student in New York went to a school where 17.7 percent of the students were white.[10] Most nonwhite schools are segregated by poverty as well as race. A majority of the nation's dropouts come from nonwhite public schools, leading to large numbers of virtually unemployable young people of color. The Bureau of Labor Statistics reported that in November 2008, the month President Obama was elected, the unemployment rate for African American adult and teen males was nearly twice that for white males—a remarkably persistent gap evident in Figure 5-1.

Generally, Americans are now taking another look at what desegregation means. In 2007, the Supreme Court handed down a decision that would dramatically change the way school districts across the country assigned students to schools. In cases brought by white parents in Seattle and Louisville, the Court, by a narrow 5–4 margin, found that using race to determine which schools students could attend was a violation of the Fourteenth Amendment. White children could not be denied admission to magnet schools or other schools designed to have racially balanced populations on account of their race. Justice Anthony Kennedy was the swing vote in this case. Although he agreed with four justices in striking down voluntary plans that assigned students to schools solely on the basis of race, he also agreed with other justices

de facto segregation
Racial segregation that occurs because of past social and economic conditions and residential racial patterns.

de jure segregation
Racial segregation that occurs because of laws or administrative decisions by public agencies.

---

8 William Doyle, *An American Insurrection: James Meredith and the Battle of Oxford, Mississippi, 1962* (New York: Anchor, 2003).
9 Gary Orfield, *Reviving the Goal of an Integrated Society: A 21st Century Challenge* (Los Angeles, CA: The Civil Rights Project/ Proyecto Derechos Civiles at UCLA, 2009).
10 John Kucsera and Garry Orfeld, "New York State's Extreme School Segregation: Inequality, Inaction, and a Damaged Future," UCLA Civil Rights Project Report, March 26, 2014. http://civilrightsproject.ucla.edu/research/k-12-education/ integration-and-diversity/ny-norflet-report-placeholder/Kucsera-New-York-Extreme-Segregation-2014.pdf

Figure 5-1 ▶ Unemployment Rates by Asians are shown as well or Latino Ethnicity, 1976–2015 Annual Averages

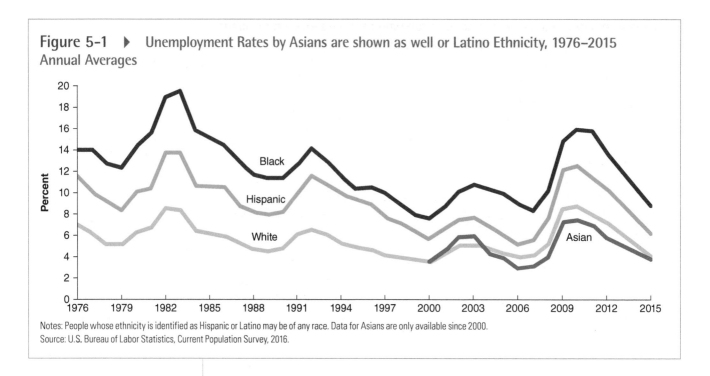

Notes: People whose ethnicity is identified as Hispanic or Latino may be of any race. Data for Asians are only available since 2000.
Source: U.S. Bureau of Labor Statistics, Current Population Survey, 2016.

in holding that integrated education was a compelling educational goal that could be pursued through other methods.[11]

An alternative solution (now implemented in more than 60 school districts across the country) is to integrate schools on the basis of income. A more advantaged school environment translates into higher achievement levels. On the National Assessment of Educational Progress given to all fourth-graders in math, for example, low-income students attending more affluent schools scored almost two years ahead of low-income students attending high-poverty schools. Today more than 3.2 million students live in school districts with some form of socioeconomic integration in place.[12]

The Civil Rights Movement

■ **5.5** Identify and explain three significant events related to each of the campaigns for civil rights undertaken by African Americans, women, the Latino community, persons with disabilities, and the LGBTQ community.

The *Brown* decision applied only to public schools. Not much else in the structure of existing segregation was affected. In December 1955, a 43-year-old African American woman, Rosa Parks, boarded a public bus in Montgomery, Alabama. When the bus became crowded and several white people stepped aboard, Parks was asked to move to the rear of the bus (the "colored" section). She refused, was arrested, and was fined $10, but that was not the end of the matter. For an entire year, African Americans boycotted the Montgomery bus line. The protest was headed by a 27-year-old Baptist minister, Dr. Martin Luther King, Jr. During the protest period, he went to jail and his house was bombed. In the face of overwhelming odds, the protesters won. In 1956, a

---

11 *Parents Involved v. Seattle School District No. 1,* 550 U.S (2007) and *Meredith v. Jefferson County Board of Education,* 550 U.S. (2007).
12 Richard D. Kahlenberg, "Can Separate Be Equal?" *The American Prospect,* September 16, 2009.

federal district court issued an injunction prohibiting the segregation of buses in Montgomery. The era of civil rights protests had begun.

King's Philosophy of Nonviolence

The following year, in 1957, King formed the Southern Christian Leadership Conference (SCLC). King advocated nonviolent **civil disobedience** as a means to achieve racial justice. King's philosophy of civil disobedience was influenced, in part, by the life and teachings of Mahatma Gandhi (1869–1948). Gandhi led resistance to the British colonial system in India from 1919 to 1947, using demonstrations and marches, as well as nonviolent, public disobedience to unjust laws. King's followers successfully used these methods to gain wider public acceptance of their cause.

civil disobedience
A nonviolent, public refusal to obey allegedly unjust laws.

Nonviolent Demonstrations African Americans and sympathetic whites engaged in sit-ins, freedom rides, and freedom marches. Groups including the NAACP, the Congress of Racial Equality (CORE), and the Student Nonviolent Coordinating Committee (SNCC) organized and supported these actions. In the beginning, such demonstrations were often met with violence, and the contrasting image of nonviolent African Americans and violent, hostile whites created strong public support for the civil rights movement. In 1960, when African Americans in Greensboro, North Carolina, were refused service at a Woolworth's lunch counter, they organized a sit-in that was aided day after day by sympathetic whites and other African Americans. Enraged customers threw ketchup on the protesters. Some spat in their faces. The sit-in movement continued to grow, however. Within six months of the first sit-in at the Greensboro Woolworth's, hundreds of lunch counters throughout the South were serving African Americans.

did you know?

The F. W. Woolworth building in Greensboro, North Carolina, the site of the 1960 lunch counter sit-ins, is now the International Civil Rights Center and Museum; the original portion of the lunch counter and stools where the four students sat has never been moved from its original footprint.

The sit-in technique also was successfully used to integrate interstate buses and their terminals, as well as railroads engaged in interstate transportation. Although buses and railroads engaged in interstate transportation were prohibited by law from segregating African Americans from whites, they stopped doing so only after the sit-in protests.

Marches and Demonstrations

One of the most famous of the violence-plagued protests occurred in Birmingham, Alabama, in 1963, when Police Commissioner Eugene "Bull" Connor unleashed police dogs and used electric cattle prods against protesters. People viewed the event with indignation and horror. King was thrown in jail. The media coverage of the Birmingham protest and the violent response by the city government played a key role in ending Jim Crow laws in the United States. The ultimate

Twitter/Barack Obama

Twitter Feed

Barack Obama ✓
@BarackObama

⚙ Following

"If Selma taught us anything, it's that our work is never done." —President Obama #Selma51

RETWEETS
6,578

LIKES
19,244

result was the most important civil rights act in the nation's history, the Civil Rights Act of 1964.

In August 1963, African American leaders A. Philip Randolph and Bayard Rustin organized a massive March on Washington for Jobs and Freedom. Before nearly a quarter-million white and African American spectators and millions watching on television, King told the world: "I have a dream that my four little children will one day live in a nation where they will not be judged by the color of their skin but by the content of their character."

In early 1965, the SCLC made Selma, Alabama, the focus of its efforts to register black voters in the South. In March, protesters attempting to march from Selma to the state capital of Montgomery were met with violent resistance by state and local authorities. As the world watched, the protesters (under the protection of federalized National Guard troops) finally achieved their goal, walking for three days to reach Montgomery. The march to Selma is widely credited with bringing pressure on Congress to finally pass the Voting Rights Act.

Another Approach—Black Power

Not all African Americans agreed with King's philosophy of nonviolence or with the idea that King's strong Christian background represented the core spirituality of African Americans. Black Muslims and other African American separatists advocated a more militant stance and argued that desegregation should not result in cultural assimilation. During the 1950s and 1960s, when King was spearheading nonviolent protests and demonstrations to achieve civil rights for African Americans, Black Power leaders insisted that African Americans should "fight back" instead of turning the other cheek. Some argued that without the fear generated by black militants, a "moderate" such as King would not have garnered such widespread support from white America.

Malcolm Little (who became Malcolm X after joining the Black Muslims in 1952) and other leaders in the Black Power movement believed that African Americans fell into two groups: "Uncle Toms," who peaceably accommodated the white establishment, and "New Negroes," who took pride in their color and culture and who demanded racial separation as well as power. Malcolm X was assassinated in 1965, but he became an important reference point for a new generation of African Americans and a symbol of African American identity.

The Escalation of the Civil Rights Movement

■ **5.3** Assess the limits of state and federal law in guaranteeing equality to all people.

Police dog attacks, cattle prods, high-pressure water hoses, beatings, bombings, the March on Washington, and black militancy—all of these events and developments led to an environment in which Congress felt compelled to act on behalf of African Americans.

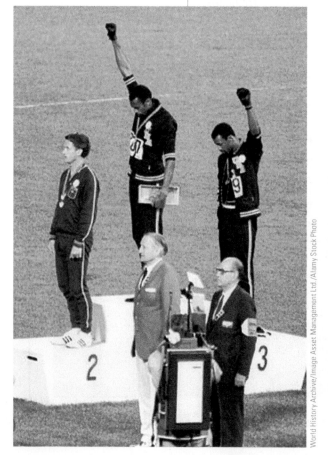

Image 5-3
The Black Power salute was a human rights protest and one of the most overtly political statements in the 110-year history of the civil rights movement.

World History Archive/Image Asset Management Ltd /Alamy Stock Photo

Modern Civil Rights Legislation

Equality before the law became "an idea whose time has come," in the words of then Republican Senate Minority Leader Everett Dirksen. The legislation passed during the Eisenhower administration was relatively symbolic. The Civil Rights Act of 1957 established the Civil Rights Commission and a new Civil Rights Division within the Department of Justice. The Civil Rights Act of 1960 was passed to protect voting rights. Whenever a pattern or practice of discrimination was documented, the Justice Department, on behalf of the voter, could bring suit, even against a state. This act, though, wielded little enforcement power and was relatively ineffective.

The 1960 presidential election pitted Vice President Richard Nixon against Senator John F. Kennedy. Kennedy sought the support of African American leaders, promising to introduce tougher civil rights legislation. When Martin Luther King, Jr., was imprisoned in Georgia after participating in a sit-in in Atlanta, Kennedy called Mrs. King to express his support, and his brother, Robert, made calls to expedite King's release. President Kennedy's civil rights legislation was stalled in the Senate in 1963, however, and his assassination ended the effort in his name. When Lyndon B. Johnson became president in 1963, he committed himself to passing civil rights bills, and the 1964 act was the result.

The Civil Rights Act of 1964 The Civil Rights Act of 1964, the most far-reaching bill on civil rights in modern times, forbade discrimination on the basis of race, color, religion, gender, and national origin. The major provisions of the act were as follows:

1. It outlawed arbitrary discrimination in voter registration.

2. It barred discrimination in public accommodations, such as hotels and restaurants, whose operations affect interstate commerce.

3. It authorized the federal government to sue to desegregate public schools and facilities.

4. It expanded the power of the Civil Rights Commission and extended its life.

5. It provided for the withholding of federal funds from programs administered in a discriminatory manner.

6. It established the right to equality of opportunity in employment.

Title VII of the Civil Rights Act of 1964 is the cornerstone of employment-discrimination law. It prohibits discrimination in employment based on race, color, religion, sex, or national origin. Under Title VII, executive orders were issued that banned employment discrimination by firms that received any federal funding. The act created a five-member commission, the Equal Employment Opportunity Commission (EEOC), to administer Title VII.

The EEOC can issue interpretive guidelines and regulations, but these do not have the force of law. Rather, they give notice of the commission's enforcement policy. The EEOC also has investigatory powers. It has broad authority to require the production of documentary evidence, to hold hearings, and to **subpoena** and examine witnesses under oath.

The equal employment provisions have been strengthened several times since its first passage. In 1965, President Johnson signed an executive order (11246) that prohibited any discrimination in employment by any employer who

subpoena
A legal writ requiring a person's appearance in court to give testimony.

received federal funds, contracts, or subcontracts. It also required all such employers to establish *affirmative action plans*, discussed later in this chapter. A revision of that order extended the requirement for an affirmative action plan to public institutions and medical and health facilities with more than 50 employees. In 1972, the Equal Employment Opportunity Act extended the provisions prohibiting discrimination in employment to the employees of state and local governments and most other not-for-profit institutions.

The Voting Rights Act of 1965 As late as 1960, only 29.1 percent of African Americans of voting age were registered in Southern states, in stark contrast to 61.1 percent of whites. The Voting Rights Act of 1965 addressed this issue. The act had two major provisions. The first one outlawed discriminatory voter-registration tests. The second authorized federal registration of voters and federally administered voting procedures in any political subdivision or state that discriminated electorally against a particular group. In part, the act provided that certain political subdivisions could not change their voting procedures and election laws without federal approval. The act targeted counties, mostly in the South, in which less than 50 percent of the eligible population was registered to vote. Federal voter registrars were sent to these areas to register African Americans who had been kept from voting by local registrars. Within one week after the act was passed, 45 federal examiners were sent to the South. A massive voter-registration drive drew thousands of civil rights activists, many of whom were white college students, to the South over the summer. This effort resulted in a dramatic increase in the proportion of African Americans registered to vote.

Urban Riots Even as the civil rights movement earned its greatest victories, a series of riots swept through African American inner-city neighborhoods. These urban riots were different in character from the race riots described earlier in this chapter. The riots in the first half of the twentieth century were street battles between whites and blacks. The urban riots of the late 1960s and early 1970s, however, were not directed against individual whites—in some instances, whites actually participated in small numbers. The riots were primarily civil insurrections, although these disorders were accompanied by large-scale looting of stores. Inhabitants of the affected neighborhoods attributed the riots to racial discrimination.[13] The riots dissipated much of the goodwill toward the civil rights movement that had been built up earlier in the decade among Northern whites. Together with widespread student demonstrations against the Vietnam War (1964–1975), the riots pushed many Americans toward conservatism.

The Civil Rights Act of 1968 and Other Housing-Reform Legislation Martin Luther King, Jr., was assassinated on April 4, 1968. Despite King's message of peace, his death was followed by far-reaching rioting. Nine days after King's death, President Johnson signed the Civil Rights Act of 1968, which forbade discrimination in most housing and provided penalties for those attempting to interfere with individual civil rights (protecting civil rights workers, among others). Subsequent legislation added enforcement provisions to the federal government's rules against discriminatory mortgage

> *did you know?*
>
> In 2008 and 2012 the black voter turnout rate exceeded the white turnout rate.

---

13 Angus Campbell and Howard Schuman, *ICPSR 3500: Racial Attitudes in Fifteen American Cities, 1968* (Ann Arbor, MI: Inter-University Consortium for Political and Social Research, 1997). Campbell and Schuman's survey documents both white participation and the attitudes of the inhabitants of affected neighborhoods. This survey is available online at www .grinnell.edu/academic/data/sociology/minorityresearch/raceatt1968

Image 5-4
President Lyndon B. Johnson is shown signing the Civil Rights Act of 1968. What are some of the provisions of that far-reaching law?

lending practices. Today, all lenders must report to the federal government the race, gender, and income of all mortgage loan seekers, along with the final decision on their loan applications.

Consequences of Civil Rights Legislation

As a result of the Voting Rights Act of 1965 and its amendments, as well as the large-scale voter-registration drives in the South, the number of African Americans registered to vote climbed dramatically. Subsequent amendments to the act extended its protections to other minorities, including Latinos, Asian Americans, Native Americans, and Native Alaskans. To further protect the voting rights of minorities, the law now provides that states must make bilingual ballots available in counties where 5 percent or more of the population speaks a language other than English.

Some of the provisions in the Voting Rights Act of 1965 were due to "sunset" (expire) in 2007. In July 2006, President George W. Bush signed a 25-year extension of these provisions, following heated congressional debate in which many members, particularly those representing the states and counties still monitored by the Justice Department, argued that the act was no longer needed. In 2013, the U.S. Supreme Court issued a 5–4 decision declaring Section 4 of the Voting Rights Act unconstitutional. Section 4 contains the "coverage formula" that determines which states must receive preclearance from the Justice Department or a federal court in Washington, DC, before making any changes to their voting laws. At the time of the Court's ruling, nine states were subject to the preclearance requirement: Alabama, Alaska, Arizona, Georgia, Louisiana, Mississippi, South Carolina, Texas, and Virginia. Some counties and townships in other states were also covered. These states and counties were identified in the 1965 law on the basis of past discriminatory acts and the consequences of those acts on minority voting rights. Congress last reviewed the basis for preclearance in 2006, but did not make any changes

did you know?

During the Mississippi Summer Project in 1964, organized by students to register African American voters, 1,000 students and voters were arrested, 80 were beaten, 35 were shot, and 6 were murdered; 30 buildings were bombed and 25 churches were burned.

to the formula. Chief Justice Roberts, writing for the majority in *Shelby County v. Holder*, said, "Our country has changed. While any racial discrimination in voting is too much, Congress must ensure that the legislation it passes to remedy that problem speaks to current conditions."[14] Although the Court did not strike Section 5 of the Voting Rights Act (the "preclearance requirement"), without a way to identify which states and localities are subject to prior review, it is largely unenforceable. Justice Ruth Bader Ginsburg summarized her dissenting opinion from the bench to indicate the strength of her disagreement with the majority. She stated that the legacy of Dr. Martin Luther King, Jr., and the nation's commitment to justice had been "disserved by the decision."[15]

Although the Supreme Court specifically invited Congress to create a new formula for identifying areas of the country where voting rights should be carefully scrutinized, Congress has not done so. Seven of the nine preclearance states have enacted new voting restrictions since the Supreme Court's ruling. Some of the changes were under review or had been recently rejected by the Justice Department at the time of the ruling. Just two months after the *Shelby* decision, North Carolina passed a new photo ID requirement, eliminated same-day voter registration, ended a program that allowed high school students to pre-register to vote at age 16, and reduced the number of early voting days. North Carolina led the nation in African American turnout in the 2012 election, with over 80 percent of eligible black voters participating.[16] A study by Dartmouth University scholars found that the changes in North Carolina will have a disproportionate effect on African American voters.[17] In Texas, a voter ID law previously called "the most stringent in the country" by a federal court went into effect along with redistricting maps rejected by the same court for protecting white incumbents while altering districts with minority incumbents.[18] Acceptable forms of identification under the Texas law include a state driver's license or ID card that is not more than 60 days expired at the time of voting, a concealed handgun license, a U.S. passport, a military ID card, or a U.S. citizenship certificate with a photo. The acceptable list is shorter than any other state's. A federal appeals court ruled in July 2016 that the law had a discriminatory effect on blacks and Latinos in violation of the Voting Rights Act. The court did not strike down the law entirely, instead ruling that new procedures must be found to assist potential voters who lack the required credentials.

The *Shelby* ruling does not remove federal scrutiny entirely, but challenges to these and other changes will now occur after the fact and based on evidence of voter disenfranchisement. Thirty-four states have passed laws requiring identification at the polls, and most require a state-issued photo ID. Pivotal swing states under Republican control are embracing significant new electoral restrictions on registering and voting that go beyond the voter identification requirements. In Kansas, the American Civil Liberties Union (ACLU) filed a lawsuit challenging a 2013 voter registration law that requires residents to provide proof of citizenship when they register. Republicans in Ohio and Wisconsin adopted measures

---

14 570 U.S. _(2013).

15 Adam Liptak, "Supreme Court Invalidates Key Part of Voting Rights Act," *The New York Times*, June 25, 2013. http://www .nytimes.com/2013/06/26/us/supreme-court-ruling.html?pagewanted=all

16 Leoneda Inge, "North Carolina Black Turnout Tops in US." North Carolina Public Radio. May 10, 2013. http://wunc.org/post /north-carolina-black-voter-turnout-tops-us

17 Michael C. Herron and Daniel A. Smith, "Race, Shelby County, and the Voter Information Verification Act" February 12, 2014. http://www.dartmouth.edu/~herron/HerronSmithNorthCarolina.pdf

18 Kara Brandeisky and Mike Tigas, "Everything That's Happened Since Supreme Court Ruled on Voting Rights Act," PROPUBLICA, November 1, 2013. http://www.propublica.org/article/voting-rights-by-state-map

limiting the time polls are open, in particular cutting into the weekend voting favored by low-income voters and blacks, who sometimes caravan from churches to polls on the Sunday before the election. Proponents of these new state initiatives argue that they are designed to prevent voter fraud, but most studies find that voter fraud in the United States is rare.[19] By late July and early August prior to the November 2016 election, federal courts began to roll back state restrictions on on voting including those in North Carolina, Texas, Wisconsin, Ohio, North Dakota, and Kansas.

Political Representation by African Americans The movement of African American citizens into high elected office has been steady, if exceedingly slow. African American representatives held 46 of the 435 seats in the House of Representatives (11 percent) and 3 of 100 seats in the Senate in the 114th Congress (through January 2017). South Carolina Republican Tim Scott was appointed to fill the Senate seat following Senator Jim DeMint's resignation and was elected to a full term in 2014. Cory Booker, former Democratic mayor of Newark, won a special election in 2013 to fill the seat of Frank Lautenberg, who passed away. He was also elected to a full term in the 2014 election, marking the first time ever that two African Americans have been elected to the Senate in the same election. Utah voters elected Mia Love to a seat in the House of Representatives in 2014, making her the first African American Republican woman elected to the House. Kamala Harris, elected in 2016, became the first African American to represent California in the U.S. Senate. African American state legislators hold just over 8 percent of seats across the nation. In 2008, Karen Bass was selected as the first female African American assembly speaker in California. At the local level, the Joint Center for Political and Economic Studies estimated that black elected officials held more than 5,700 offices in 2002. In a decisive victory, Barack Obama was elected the first African American president on November 4, 2008. The late Gwen Ifill called his election a breakthrough for black politicians and predicted that his victory would usher in a new age of black political leadership.[20]

To the befuddlement of researchers, Ifill's projected "new age" has not materialized. Why, for example, do so few black House members run for the Senate? Nearly half of the current U.S. Senate is made up of members who previously served in the House, but not one African American House member has ever been elected to a Senate seat. Bruce Oppenheimer, a political scientist at Vanderbilt University, identified a number of possible reasons. First, most African American House members represent districts in large states where competition for Senate seats is fierce, and their name recognition might be low because they represent a small share of the overall population. They are also likely to represent heavily Democratic, liberal districts, which compromises their statewide appeal. Finally, African American House members tend to come from less affluent districts, thus limiting their initial fundraising base for a Senate campaign.[21] Carol Moseley Braun, the first African American woman elected to the Senate, echoes this point. "Without strong fundraising potential," African American politicians "may fail to convince party leaders they can

19 Wendy R. Weiser and Lawrence Norden, "Voting Law Changes in 2012." Brennan Center for Justice at New York University School of Law. http://brennan.3cdn.net/92635ddafbc09e8d88_i3m6bjdeh.pdf

20 Gwen Ifill, *The Breakthrough: Politics and Race in the Age of Obama* (New York: Anchor Books, 2009).

21 Bruce I. Oppenheimer, Gbemende Johnson, and Jennifer Selin. "The House as a Stepping Stone to the Senate: Why Do So Few African-American House Members Run?" Paper presented at Conference on Legislative Elections, Process, and Policy: The Influence of Bicameralism, Vanderbilt University 2009. http://www.vanderbilt.edu/csdi/archived/Bicameralism%20papers/stepping%20stone.pdf

Image 5-5
Former U.S. Attorney General Loretta Lynch (center) speaks during a press conference at the Department of Justice as Principal Deputy Assistant Attorney General Vanita Gupta (left), head of the Civil Rights Division, and U.S. Attorney Zachary T. Fardon (right) of the Northern District of Illinois look on. During the press conference, Lynch announced a Justice Department investigation into the practices of the Chicago Police Department.

win."[22] Nevertheless, Braun remains optimistic that gains in political representation will continue even in the face of structural barriers because President Obama's election and the success of other African Americans in prominent political roles (Condoleezza Rice and Loretta Lynch, for example) will serve to normalize black leadership for voters in statewide or national contests. Although Barack Obama was reelected in 2012, he lost among white voters by a margin greater than any victor in American history. This is compelling evidence that there is still a racial divide in American politics.

The U.S. Census and Civil Rights The census, which calls for a count of the country's population every ten years (next occurring in 2020), is the basis for virtually all demographic information used by policymakers, educators, and community leaders. The census is used to determine representation for the purposes of redistricting. In this sense, the census data also provide an important tool for enforcing the Voting Rights Act, which forbids drawing districts with the intention of diluting the concentration and thus the political power of minority voters. Census data are also used to allocate federal dollars in support of community development, education, crime prevention, and transportation. For these reasons, civil rights leaders urged full participation from within their communities. Being counted in the census equates to political and community empowerment.

Lingering Social and Economic Disparities According to Joyce Ladner of the Brookings Institution, one of the difficulties with the race-based civil rights agenda of the 1950s and 1960s is that it did not envision remedies for cross-racial problems. How should the nation address problems such as poverty and urban violence that affect underclasses in all racial groups? In 1967, when Martin Luther King, Jr., proposed a Poor People's Campaign, he recognized that a civil rights coalition based entirely

22 Jamelle Bouie, "The Other Glass Ceiling," *The American Prospect*, March 14, 2012. http://prospect.org/article/other-glass-ceiling

on race would not be sufficient to address the problem of poverty among whites as well as blacks. During his 1984 and 1988 presidential campaigns, African American Jesse Jackson also acknowledged the inadequacy of a race-based model of civil rights when he attempted to form a "Rainbow Coalition" of minorities, women, and other underrepresented groups, including the poor.[23]

Race-Conscious or Post-Racial Society? Whether we are talking about college attendance, media stereotyping, racial profiling, or academic achievement, the black experience is different from the white one. As a result, African Americans view the nation and many specific issues differently than their white counterparts do.[24] In survey after survey, when blacks are asked whether they have achieved racial equality, few believe that they have. In contrast, whites are five times more likely than blacks to believe that racial equality has been achieved.[25] As a candidate for the Democratic nomination for president, Barack Obama directly addressed race in America in his "A More Perfect Union" speech delivered in Philadelphia in March 2008.[26] After taking office, however, President Obama was criticized by some within the civil rights community for not making the goal of racial equality a higher priority within his administration.

The president addressed racial profiling in ways no previous president could when one of the nation's preeminent African American scholars, Harvard Professor Henry Louis Gates, was arrested in his own home and charged with disorderly conduct for displaying "loud and tumultuous behavior" when he was asked by Cambridge police for identification to prove that he was indeed

By permission of Chris Britt and Creators Syndicate, Inc.

Image 5-6
This cartoon highlights the issue of racial profiling; however, as you know from the description of the incident in the text, Professor Gates was confronted and later arrested in his home during daylight hours. Why would the cartoonist draw this scene at night? How is the fact that neighborhood racial segregation is still prevalent in the United States related to this incident and the way it has been portrayed by the cartoonist?

23 Joyce A. Ladner, "A New Civil Rights Agenda," *The Brookings Review* (Spring 2000) 18 (2): 26–28.

24 Lawrence D. Bobo et al., "Through the Eyes of Black America," *Public Perspective* (May/June 2001): 13.

25 Lawrence D. Bobo et al., "Through the Eyes of Black America," *Public Perspective* (May/June 2001): 13, 15, Figure 2.

26 Barack Obama, "A More Perfect Union," Transcript of speech delivered March 18, 2008, at the Constitution Center in Philadelphia, PA. http://www.npr.org/templates/story/story.php?storyId=88478467

the homeowner. Police said they were responding to a call from a neighbor who reported seeing "two black men with backpacks" trying to enter the house. Professor Gates had returned home from a trip to China to find his front door stuck; he and the taxi driver were trying to get it open. The president, asked at a news conference to comment on the incident, said, "What I think we know, separate and apart from this incident, is that there's a long history in this country of African Americans and Latinos being stopped by law enforcement disproportionately. That's just a fact."[27]

In February 2012, when unarmed 17-year-old African American Trayvon Martin was fatally shot by George Zimmerman, a 28-year-old community watch coordinator in the gated Florida community where the shooting took place, President Obama spoke in highly personal terms in acknowledging the racial overtones of the incident: "Obviously, this is a tragedy; we all have to do some soul searching to find out why something like this happened. But my main message is to the parents of Trayvon Martin. You know, if I had a son, he'd look like Trayvon. And, you know, I think they are right to expect that all of us as Americans are going to take this with the seriousness it deserves and that we're going to get to the bottom of exactly what happened."[28]

#BlackLivesMatter After George Zimmerman was acquitted in 2013 for the shooting death of Trayvon Martin, a new civil rights movement began on social media with #BlackLivesMatter. Co-founded by community organizers Alicia Garza, Patrisse Cullors, and Opal Tometi, Black Lives Matter moved from social media to face-to-face organizing and protest with the shooting death of 18-year-old Michael Brown following an encounter with a white police officer in Ferguson, Missouri. Individuals and organized groups arrived in Ferguson to demonstrate, and clashes with police turned violent. Several nights of arrests, looting, and fires followed. The police response to the shooting and to the

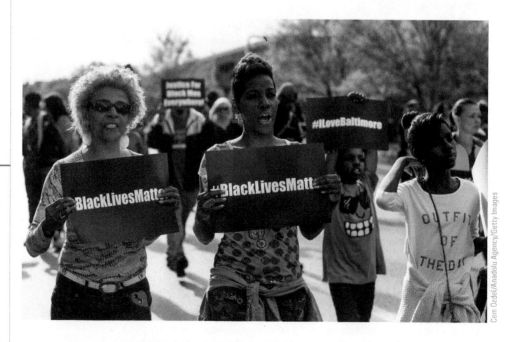

Image 5-7

Black Lives Matter protesters hold placards as they march to the city hall in Baltimore, Maryland, during a demonstration over the death of Freddie Gray. Gray, 25, was arrested for possessing a switchblade knife outside the Gilmor Houses housing project on Baltimore's west side. Gray died from a severe spinal cord injury he allegedly received while in police custody.

Cem Ozdel/Anadolu Agency/Getty Images

27 "Obama Addresses Race and Gates Incident," *Washington Post*, July 23, 2009.
28 Michael D. Shear, "Obama Speaks Out on Trayvon Martin Killing," *The New York Times*, March 23, 2012.

subsequent protests was roundly criticized, leading Missouri Governor Jay Nixon to transfer responsibility for law enforcement to the Missouri State Highway Patrol under the command of Captain Ronald S. Johnson, an African American with roots in the Ferguson community. After months of grand jury testimony, Officer Darren Wilson was not indicted, touching off renewed unrest in the city.

Since the Ferguson protests, participants in the movement have demonstrated against the deaths of numerous other African Americans by police actions or while in police custody, including those of Tamir Rice, Eric Harris, Walter Scott, Jonathan Ferrell, Sandra Bland, Samuel DuBose, Freddie Gray, and Stephon Clark. Black Lives Matter focused attention on other issues with a disparate impact on African Americans, including excessive fines for misdemeanors, mass incarceration and criminal justice reform, and the racial climate on college campuses around the country. Some critics countered with the chant, "All Lives Matter." In the primaries leading up to the 2016 presidential election, Black Lives Matter activists attempted to draw attention to their issues by disrupting campaign events. Democratic candidates Hillary Clinton and Bernie Sanders held several meetings with activists, but at Trump rallies protesters were subject to violence, ejection, and arrest. The Democratic National Committee passed a resolution supporting Black Lives Matter, but the movement disavowed the action and distanced itself from any political party.

Race and Confederate Symbols On June 17, 2015, a white man entered Emanuel AME Church in Charleston, South Carolina, and joined the Bible study for nearly an hour before shooting nine parishioners to death and leaving three survivors. The church's senior pastor, state senator Clementa Pinkney, was among those killed. Police later arrested Dylann Roof, a twenty-one-year-old self-professed white supremacist. Roof expressed a hope that the shootings would ignite a race war, and a website attributed to Roof contained a manifesto as well as photographs of Roof posing with the Confederate flag. Roof faced 9 counts of murder in South Carolina and 33 federal counts, including hate crime charges. A jury convicted Roof and sentenced him to death in 2017.

At Roof's bond hearing, family members of the deceased shocked many by responding with expressions of forgiveness: "You took something really precious from me. I will never talk to her again," the daughter of 70-year-old Ethel Lance, one of nine people killed in the massacre, said. "But I forgive you and have mercy on your soul. You hurt me. You hurt a lot of people. But God forgives you. I forgive you."[29] President Obama delivered the eulogy for state senator Pinkney,

Twitter Feed

President Obama @POTUS — Following

South Carolina taking down the confederate flag - a signal of good will and healing, and a meaningful step towards a better future.

RETWEETS 20,266   LIKES 32,912

10:12 AM - 10 Jul 2015

Twitter/Barack Obama

---

29 Dylan Stableford, "Families of Charleston Shooting Victims to Dylann Roof: We Forgive You." Yahoo! News, June 19, 2015. www.yahoo.com/news/familes-of-charleston-church-shooting-victims-to-dylann-roof--we--forgive-you-185833509.html

calling for action on race in America, not more talk: "None of us can or should expect a transformation in race relations overnight. Every time something like this happens, somebody says, 'We have to have a conversation about race,' . . . We talk a lot about race. There's no shortcut. We don't need more talk."[30]

In July 2015, the South Carolina legislature voted to remove the Confederate flag from the statehouse grounds to a display in the Confederate Relic Room in the South Carolina State Museum. Several retailers, including Walmart and Amazon.com, announced that they would no longer sell Confederate flags or related merchandise. However, the Southern Poverty Law Center estimates that there are at least 1,170 publicly funded Confederate symbols across the country.

Despite the civil rights movement, civil rights legislation, and the election of the first black president, many African Americans continue to feel a sense of injustice in matters of race, and this feeling is often not apparent to, or appreciated by, the majority of white America. There is some evidence that race relations have worsened under the first African American president. In 2009, just after the election, 67 percent of respondents told a *New York Times*/CBS News poll that race relations in the United States were generally good. One year into President Trump's administration, 60 percent of Americans believed race relations had worsened.

Women's Campaign for Equal Rights

Like African Americans and other minorities, women also have had to make a claim for equality. Political citizenship requires personal autonomy (the ability to think and act for oneself), but the prevailing opinion about women was that they were not endowed with reason. During the first phase of this campaign, the primary political goal of women was to obtain the right to vote.

Early Women's Political Movements

The first political cause in which women became actively engaged was the movement to abolish slavery. When the World Antislavery Convention was held in London in 1840, women delegates were barred from active participation. Partly in response to this rebuff, two American delegates, Lucretia Mott and Elizabeth Cady Stanton, returned from that meeting with plans to work for women's rights in the United States.

In 1848, Mott and Stanton organized the first women's rights convention in Seneca Falls, New York. The 300 people who attended the two-day event debated a wide variety of issues important for expanding women's social, civil, and religious rights, including access to education and employment, marriage and divorce reform, and, most controversial of all, **suffrage**. Attendees approved a Declaration of Sentiments modeled in word and spirit on the Declaration of Independence: "We hold these truths to be self-evident: that all men and *women* are created equal." Groups that supported women's rights held similar conventions in cities in the Midwest and East.

With the outbreak of the Civil War, advocates of women's rights were urged to put their support behind the war effort, and women in the North and South

suffrage
The right to vote; the franchise.

---

30 Kevin Liptak, "Obama's Charleston Eulogy: Amazing Grace." CNN Politics, June 29, 2015. http://www.cnn.com/2015/06/26/politics/obama-charleston-eulogy-pastor/

dedicated themselves to their respective causes. In 1866 the American Equal Rights Association (AERA) was formed to advance the cause of universal suffrage, but tensions arose immediately between those whose first priority was black male suffrage and those who were dedicated first to women's suffrage. The failure to include women in the Fifteenth Amendment resulted in the dissolution of the AERA and the formation of two rival women's suffrage organizations.

did you know?
Of all those in attendance at Seneca Falls, only one 19-year-old woman, Charlotte Woodward, lived long enough to exercise her right to vote.

Women's Suffrage Associations

Susan B. Anthony and Elizabeth Cady Stanton formed the National Woman Suffrage Association (NWSA) in 1869 and dedicated themselves almost exclusively to advancing women's suffrage at the federal level by way of a constitutional amendment. In their view, women's suffrage was a means to achieve major improvements in the economic and social situation of women in the United States. Unlike Anthony and Stanton, Lucy Stone, a key founder of the American Woman Suffrage Association (AWSA), continued to support the Fifteenth Amendment (restricted to males) but vowed to support a Sixteenth Amendment dedicated to women's suffrage. The AWSA primarily focused its efforts on the states.

In the November election of 1872, several women attempted to vote under the revolutionary legal reasoning that the Fourteenth Amendment extended citizenship rights to all persons, and voting was among the privilege and immunities of citizenship. In Missouri, Virginia Minor cast her vote and was arrested for illegal voting. In the case of *Minor v. Happersett*, the U.S. Supreme Court ruled that since the federal Constitution did not explicitly grant women the right to vote, the states were free to decide who had the privilege of voting. For suffragists, this left two options—an amendment to the U.S. Constitution or a state-by-state campaign.

For the next 20 years, the two organizations worked along similar paths to educate the public and legislators, testifying before legislative committees, giving public speeches, and conducting public referendum campaigns on women's suffrage with varying degrees of success, as indicated by the map in Figure 5-2. Organizations such as the Women's Christian Temperance Union (WCTU) joined the campaign for suffrage, arguing that only women could be counted on to cast the votes necessary to prohibit the sale and consumption of alcohol. The combination of efforts yielded the movement's first successes. The Western territory of Wyoming granted women the right to vote in 1869, and several state legislatures in other regions outside the South took up legislation granting women the vote. Political scientist Lee Ann Banaszak calculated that between 1870 and 1890, an average of four states a year took up the question of women's suffrage.[31] In 1890, the two organizations joined forces, creating the National American Woman Suffrage Association (NAWSA), with only one goal—the enfranchisement of women—and continued lobbying in the states and Western territories.

Opposition to women's suffrage came from a number of sources, including the liquor industry, big business, and the church. Brewers and distillers were interested in preventing Prohibition, and thus hoped to keep women from the voting booth. Industry was interested in limiting the reach of progressive policy to set wages and improve working conditions (both areas where female activists were heavily involved), and the church opposed suffrage primarily on ideological grounds. However, beginning in about 1880, the most persistent opponents of the suffrage cause emerged: other women. Suffragists at first dismissed the

31 Lynne E. Ford, *Women and Politics: The Pursuit of Equality.* (Boston: Cengage Learning Wadsworth, 2011).

Figure 5-2 ▶ The Suffrage Map, Early August 1920

Source: From "Out of Subjection into Freedom" by Marjorie Shuler, published in *The Woman Citizen*, p. 360, September 4, 1920.

Marjorie Shuler. Courtesy of the Tennessee State Library and Archives

"antis" but later came to understand that they were a powerful, well-organized force dedicated to protecting traditional gender roles as well as women's social and economic privileges as they understood them.[32]

At the turn of the century, an impatient new generation of women introduced direct protest tactics they had observed while working alongside Emmeline Pankhurst in the British suffrage campaign. Harriot Stanton Blatch (Elizabeth Cady Stanton's daughter), Alice Paul, and Lucy Burns urged NAWSA to return to a federal amendment strategy. The new suffragists, as they were called, intended to *demand* their right to vote. They scheduled a massive parade in Washington, DC, for March 3, 1913, to coincide with Woodrow Wilson's inauguration as president, scheduled for the next day. Alice Paul believed that Congress would only be persuaded to move the suffrage amendment forward if prodded to do so by the president. The parade attracted 8,000 marchers and more than half a million spectators.

Alice Paul continued to agitate for women's suffrage in ways that embarrassed NAWSA's leadership. She organized "Silent Sentinels" to stand in front of the White House with banners reading, "Mr. President, What Will You Do for Woman Suffrage?" These women were the first picketers ever to appear before the White House. When the United States joined the war against Germany in 1917, women were urged to set aside their goals in favor of the overall war effort. Paul refused and formed the National Woman's Party (NWP) to bring even greater attention to women's disenfranchisement.

---

32 Susan E. Marshall, *Splintered Sisterhood: Gender and Class in the Campaign Against Women's Suffrage* (Madison, WI: University of Wisconsin Press, 1997).

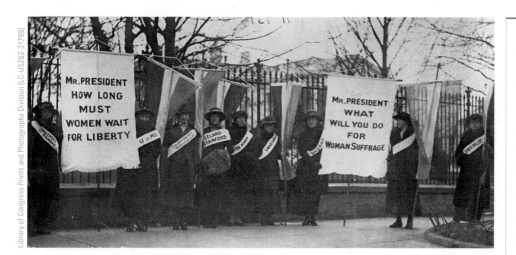

Library of Congress Prints and Photographs Division (LC-USZ62-31799)

Meanwhile, NAWSA members, under the leadership of Carrie Chapman Catt, were pursuing the "winning plan," which entailed a two-pronged lobbying strategy focused on both federal and state legislators. In the end, scholars agree that it was the combination of patient lobbying by NAWSA members and the more militant tactics of the NWP that resulted in Congress passing the suffrage amendment in May 1919. In Tennessee, the last state required to win ratification, the amendment passed by one vote on August 26, 1920. The Nineteenth Amendment reads: "The right of citizens of the United States to vote shall not be denied or abridged by the United States or by any State on account of sex."

The United States was neither the first nor the last to give women the vote. New Zealand introduced universal suffrage in 1893, while Kuwait allowed women to vote and seek public office for the first time in 2005. In 2011, King Abdullah of Saudi Arabia granted women the right to vote and run in municipal elections beginning in 2015 (see Table 5-1). Saudi Arabia permitted women to drive as of June 2018.

The Second Wave of the Women's Movement

■ **5.4** Explain why the U.S. Supreme Court plays such an important role relative to civil rights and identify at least two significant Supreme Court decisions that advanced civil rights in the United States.

After gaining the right to vote in 1920, women did not flock to the polls in large numbers, nor did many of the thousands of women who had lobbied for and against suffrage seek political office. There was little by way of an organized women's movement again until the second wave began in the 1960s. The civil rights movement of that decade resulted in a growing awareness of rights for all groups, including women. Women's increased participation in the workforce and the publication of Betty Friedan's *The Feminine Mystique* in 1963 focused national attention on the unequal status of women in American life.

In 1966, Betty Friedan and others dissatisfied with existing women's organizations, and especially with the failure of

Table 5-1 ▶ WOMEN'S VOTING RIGHTS AROUND THE WORLD, Selected Countries and Year Women's Suffrage Was Granted

Year	Country
1893	New Zealand
1902	Austria
1913	Norway
1918	Canada
1919	Germany
1920	United States
1928	United Kingdom
1930	Turkey
1934	Cuba
1939	El Salvador
1944	France
1945	Japan
1947	Mexico
1948	Israel
1949	China
1950	India
1956	Egypt
1961	Rwanda
1964	Afghanistan
1965	Sudan
1971	Switzerland
1974	Jordan
1980	Iraq
1994	South Africa
2005	Kuwait
2015	Saudi Arabia

Source: Center for the American Woman and Politics

The Campaign for Women's Rights around the World

President Jimmy Carter (served 1977–1981) believes that the most serious and unaddressed worldwide challenge is the deprivation and abuse of women and girls.* He is not alone—Hillary Rodham Clinton calls advancing the rights of women and girls "the great unfinished business of the twenty-first century."** Although women's rights have emerged as a high-priority global issue, progress has been slow. The campaign for women's rights in countries where cultural or legal practices perpetuate the inequality of women is especially difficult. December 2016 marked the 37th anniversary of the United Nations' adoption of the Convention on the Elimination of All Forms of Discrimination against Women (CEDAW), an international treaty to promote the adoption of national laws, policies, and practices to ensure that women and girls live free from violence, have access to high-quality education, and have the right to participate fully in the economic, political, and social sectors of their society. Although the treaty has been ratified by 186 countries, the United States is one of only seven nations that have not ratified. International agreements such as CEDAW convey a set of universal ethical standards and global norms regarding human rights.

The Problem of Violence

Most people consider the right to be free from violence as one of the most basic human rights. Women's rights advocates point out that this right is threatened in societies that do not accept the premise that men and women are equal. Every 10 minutes globally an adolescent girl dies as a result of violence.*** Some parts of India implicitly tolerate the practice of dowry killing. (A dowry is a sum of money given to a husband by the bride's family.) In a number of cases, husbands, dissatisfied with the size of dowries, have killed their wives in order to remarry for a "better deal"—a crime rarely prosecuted.

The Situation in Afghanistan

A startling documentary repeatedly aired on CNN called *Behind the Veil* introduced many Americans to women's rights issues abroad. A courageous female reporter had secretly filmed Afghan women being beaten in the streets, killed in public for trivial offenses, and subjugated in extreme ways. Women's rights became a major issue in our foreign policy. Americans learned that Afghan girls were barred from schools, and by law women were not allowed to work. Women who had lost their husbands

Image 5-9 Malala Yousafzai, education advocate and co-founder of the Malala Fund, speaks during a press conference on girls' education at the United Nations Headquarters in New York City.

during Afghanistan's civil wars were forced into begging and prostitution. Women had no access to medical care. Any woman found with an unrelated man could be executed by stoning, and many were.

Activists for Education

Malala Yousafzai is a Pakistani teenager and education activist. From a very young age, Malala was willing to risk her own life to promote education for girls. A blogger for BBC, she attracted the attention of a documentary filmmaker and multiple international media outlets for her work. On October 9, 2012, Malala was riding the bus home from school when a gunman boarded, asked the children to identify her, then shot Malala in the head. Amazingly, she survived, but even as Malala fought for her life, the Taliban repeated its threats to kill her. The attempt on her life sparked international outrage and action. The United Nations launched "I am Malala," a campaign to enroll all children in school. At 16, Malala was the youngest nominee for the 2013 Nobel Peace Prize. "Girl Rising" is another international project promoting girls' education. The documentary profiles life in the developing world—ordinary girls who confront challenges and overcome nearly impossible odds to pursue their dreams. Prize-winning authors put the girls' stories into words, and renowned actors give them voice.****

Nation Building and Women's Rights: Post-Conflict Challenges

After the collapse of the Taliban regime, the United States and its allies were able to influence the status of Afghan women. The draft constitution of Afghanistan,

(Continued)

adopted in 2004, gave women equality before the law and 20 percent of the seats in the National Assembly. In 2016, women held 27 percent of the legislative seats and ranked fiftieth of 191 nations for the percentage of women serving in the national assembly (the United States ranks ninety-fifth). Much of the country, however, remains outside the control of the national government. Women continue to face abuse, including arson attacks on girls' schools, forced marriages, and reimposition of the all-covering burqa garment.

Women in Iraq had enjoyed greater equality than women in most Arab nations. In line with the secular ideology of the Baath Party, Saddam Hussein's government tended to treat men and women alike. A problem for the U.S.-led Coalition Provisional Authority (CPA) that governed Iraq until June 2004 was ensuring that women did not lose ground under the new regime. The interim Iraqi constitution, adopted in March 2004, allotted 25 percent of the seats in the parliament to women. In 2017, women held 25 percent of the seats in parliament.

For Critical Analysis

1. Is it fair or appropriate for one country to judge the cultural practices of another? Why or why not?

2. Why are so many cultural practices gender based? Can you identify gender-based cultural practices in the United States that might affect women's civil rights?

3. Why is education so critical to the success of women and girls?

*Jimmy Carter, *A Call to Action: Women, Religion, Violence and Power* (New York: Simon and Schuster, 2014).

** Hillary Rodham Clinton, "Helping Women Isn't Just a 'Nice' Thing to Do," Keynote Address, Women in the World Conference, April 5, 2013. www.thedailybeast.com/witw/articles/2013/04/05/hillary-clinton-helpingwomen-isn-t-just-a-nice-thing-to-do.html

*** "16 Reasons to Campaign for Women's Rights in 2016." The Aspen Institute, February 9, 2016. http://www.aspeninstitute.org/about/blog/16-reasons-campaign-womens-rights-2016

**** Girl Rising http://girlrising.com/

the EEOC to address discrimination against women, formed the National Organization for Women (NOW). NOW immediately adopted a blanket resolution designed "to bring women into full participation in the mainstream of American society *now*, exercising all the privileges and responsibilities thereof in truly equal partnership with men."

The second wave gained additional impetus from young women who entered politics to support the civil rights movement or to oppose the Vietnam War. Many found that despite the egalitarian principles of these movements, women remained in second-class positions. In the late 1960s, "women's liberation" organizations began to spring up on college campuses, and women organized "consciousness-raising groups" in which they discussed how gender affected their lives. The new women's movement emerged as a major social force by 1970.

Historian Nancy Cott contends that the word *feminism* first began to be used around 1910.[33] At that time, **feminism** meant, as it does today, political, social, and economic equality for women. It is difficult to measure the support for feminism at present because the word means different things to different people. When the dictionary definition of *feminist*—"someone who supports political, economic, and social equality for women"—was read to respondents in a survey, 67 percent

feminism
The philosophy of political, economic, and social equality for women and the gender consciousness sufficient to mobilize women for change.

33 Nancy F. Cott, *The Grounding of Modern Feminism* (New Haven, CT: Yale University Press, 1987).

labeled themselves as feminists.[34] In the absence of such prompting, however, the term *feminist* (like the term *liberal*) implies radicalism to many people, who therefore shy away from it. Young women have launched a third wave of feminism, embracing a multitude of perspectives on what it means to be a feminist woman.[35]

The Equal Rights Amendment   NOW leaders and other women's rights advocates sought to eradicate gender inequality through a constitutional amendment. The proposed Equal Rights Amendment (ERA), first introduced in Congress in 1923 by leaders of the NWP, states: "Equality of rights under the law shall not be denied or abridged by the United States or by any state on account of sex." For decades the amendment was not even given a hearing in Congress, but finally it was approved by both chambers and sent to the state legislatures for ratification in 1972.

As was noted in Chapter 2, any constitutional amendment must be ratified by the legislatures (or conventions) in three-fourths of the states. Since the early twentieth century, most proposed amendments have required that ratification occur within seven years of Congress's adoption of the amendment. Although states competed to be the first to ratify the ERA, by 1977 only 35 of the necessary 38 states had ratified the amendment. Congress granted a rare extension, but the remaining three states could not be added by the 1982 deadline, even though the ERA was supported by numerous national party platforms, six presidents, and both chambers of Congress.

As with the antisuffrage efforts, the staunchest opponents to the ERA were other women. Many women perceived the goals pursued by feminists as a threat to their way of life. At the head of the countermovement was Republican Phyllis Schlafly and her conservative organization, Eagle Forum. Eagle Forum's "Stop ERA" campaign found significant support among fundamentalist religious groups and other conservative organizations; it was a major force in blocking the ratification of the ERA. Twenty-one states have appended amendments similar to the ERA to their own constitutions.

Three-State Strategy   Had the ERA been ratified by 38 states, it would have become the Twenty-seventh Amendment to the Constitution. Instead, that place is occupied by the "Madison Amendment" governing congressional pay raises, first sent to the states in 1789 and not ratified until 1992. ERA supporters argue that acceptance of the Madison Amendment means that Congress has the power to maintain the legal viability of the ERA and the existing 35 state ratifications. This would leave supporters just three states shy of achieving final ratification. The legal rationale for the three-state strategy was developed by three law students in a law review article published in 1997.[36] Support for constitutional equality remains high in the United States; however, mobilizing support for ratification of the ERA in the future may prove difficult. A poll found that although 96 percent of those polled supported constitutional equality for women and men, 72 percent mistakenly believed that the U.S. Constitution already includes the Equal Rights Amendment.[37]

Challenging Gender Discrimination in the Courts and Legislatures
With the failure of the ERA, feminists turned their attention to national and state laws that would guarantee the equality of women. In 1978, the Civil Rights Act of

did you know?

Seventy-two years passed between the time the Declaration of Independence was signed in 1776 and women first demanded the vote at the Seneca Falls Convention in 1848; it took another 72 years for women to win suffrage via the Nineteenth Amendment, ratified in 1920; and it took another 72 years before more than two women were elected to serve in the U.S. Senate at the same time (1992).

---

34 Nancy E. McGlen and Karen O'Connor, *Women, Politics, and American Society*, 4th ed. (Upper Saddle River, NJ: Prentice Hall, 2004).
35 See, for example, Jessica Valenti, *Full Frontal Feminism: A Young Woman's Guide to Why Feminism Matters* (Emeryville, CA: Seal Press, 2007) and Jennifer Baumgardner and Amy Richards, *Manifesta: Young Women, Feminism, and the Future* (New York: Farrar, Straus and Giroux, 2000).
36 Allison Held, Sheryl Herndon, and Danielle Stager, "The Equal Rights Amendment: Why the ERA Remains Legally Viable and Properly Before the States," *William & Mary Journal of Women and the Law* (Spring 1997): 113–136.
37 *The ERA Campaign*, Issue #5, July 2001, http://eracampaignweb.kishosting.com/newsletter5.html

1964 was amended by the Pregnancy Discrimination Act, which prohibits discrimination in employment against pregnant women. In addition, Title IX of the Education Amendments was passed in 1972; it bans sex discrimination at all levels and in all aspects of education and deals with issues of sexual harassment, pregnancy, parental status, and marital status. Although Title IX is best known for increasing women's access to sports, its impact toward equalizing admissions to professional programs, financial aid, and educational facilities has more practical significance. Prior to Title IX, women's entrance into professional programs in law, medicine, science, and engineering was limited by quotas. In 1996, the Supreme Court held that the state-financed Virginia Military Institute's policy of accepting only males violated the equal protection clause; this finding led to the admission of women at The Citadel, the state-financed military college in South Carolina, as well.[38]

Women's rights organizations challenged discriminatory statutes and policies in the federal courts, contending that **gender discrimination** violated the Fourteenth Amendment's equal protection clause. Since the 1970s, the Supreme Court has tended to scrutinize gender classifications closely and has invalidated a number of such statutes and policies. In 1977, the Court held that police and firefighting units cannot establish arbitrary rules, such as height and weight requirements, that tend to keep women from joining those occupations.[39] In 1983, the Court ruled that life insurance companies cannot charge different rates for women and men.[40]

In 1994, Congress repealed the "risk rule" barring women from all combat situations. As a result, over 90 percent of positions in the military were opened to women. In 2013, Defense Secretary Leon Panetta and the Chairman of the Joint Chiefs of Staff, General Martin Dempsey, announced the rescission of the combat exclusion for women and directed each branch of the military to create a plan to integrate women into the remaining restricted fields by 2016. Although the Marine Corps argued for an exception in some areas (e.g., infantry, machine gunner), Defense Secretary Ash Carter announced that all gender-based restrictions on military service would be lifted. "There will be no exceptions," Secretary Carter said. "They'll be allowed to drive tanks, fire mortars and lead infantry soldiers into combat. They'll be able to serve as Army Rangers and Green Berets, Navy SEALs, Marine Corps infantry, Air Force parajumpers and everything else that was previously open only to men."[41] The end of the combat exclusion may also ultimately mean that women will be included in the draft and required to register with Selective Service. A 1981 Supreme Court decision specifically linked women's exemption from the draft to their ineligibility for combat. In August 2015, the first two women graduated from the elite Army Ranger School. Women make up roughly 15 percent of the 1.4 million active-duty personnel in the U.S. military.

Twitter Feed

U.S. Dept of Defense @DeptofDefense — Follow

#SecDef: Today we proceed with opening all remaining occupations & positions to women. There will be no exceptions.

RETWEETS 790 LIKES 730

12:19 PM - 3 Dec 2015

Twitter/US Department of Defense

gender discrimination
Any practice, policy, or procedure that denies equality of treatment to an individual or to a group because of gender.

did you know?
Congresswoman Tammy Duckworth, elected to the House of Representatives in 2012, is the first female double amputee from the Iraq War.

38 *United States v. Virginia*, 518 U.S. 515 (1996).
39 *Dothard v. Rawlinson*, 433 U.S. 321 (1977).
40 *Arizona v. Norris*, 463 U.S. 1073 (1983).
41 Matthew Rosenberg and Dave Philipps. "All Combat Roles Now Open to Women, Defense Secretary Says," *The New York Times*, December 3, 2015. www.nytimes.com/2015/12/04/us/politics/combat-military-women-ash-carter.html

Twitter Feed

CNN ✓
@CNN   ⚙ 👤 Follow

Only women turned up to work at the Senate after #blizzard2016, @lisamurkowski noted: cnn.it/1SawIMi

RETWEETS   LIKES
466   734

5:43 AM - 27 Jan 2016

Twitter/CNN

Women in Politics Today

Today, women make up just 20.5 percent of the U.S. Congress. The United States ranks 100 of 191 nations by the Inter-Parliamentary Union based on the proportion of seats held by women in the lower house. Rwanda ranks first—in that nation, women hold 56 percent of seats in the Lower House.[42] The efforts of women's rights advocates have helped increase the number of women holding political offices at all levels of government. In 2007 Nancy Pelosi, a Democrat from California, became the first female Speaker of the House, the most powerful member of the majority party and second in the line of succession to the presidency.

When Geraldine Ferraro was selected as the Democratic nominee for vice president in 1984, it was the first time a woman appeared on a major party ticket. In 2008 Hillary Rodham Clinton, senator from New York, became one of two final contenders for the presidential nomination of the Democratic Party, but ultimately lost to Barack Obama. In a surprise move, Senator John McCain chose the Alaskan governor, Sarah Palin, for his running mate. In 2016, former Secretary of State Hillary Clinton won the Democratic nomination for president, making her the first woman to win a major party's nomination for president. Clinton lost to Donald Trump in the general election.

Women are now visible in cabinet posts and high-level administrative posts. Madeleine Albright was the first woman to serve as secretary of state and was followed by Condoleezza Rice (appointed by George W. Bush) and Hillary Clinton (appointed by Barack Obama). President Obama appointed a number of women to high-ranking positions within his first and second administrations. Valerie Jarrett served as his senior adviser, his closest aide. Women served as cabinet secretaries in the Departments of Justice, Interior, Commerce, and Health and Human Services. Loretta Lynch became the first African American woman to serve as attorney general. In the area of foreign policy, Susan Rice was national security adviser, and Samantha Power served as ambassador to the United Nations. Upon the retirement of Ben Bernanke, President Obama appointed (and the Senate confirmed) Janet Yellen as the first woman chair of the Board of Governors of the Federal Reserve System. Yellen served as vice-chair for four years prior to taking the helm of the nation's central banking system in February 2014.

It took nearly 140 years after the federal court system was established in 1789 before the first woman sat on a federal bench. Today, about one-third of all active Article III judges are women. President Ronald Reagan (served 1981–1989) was credited with a historic first when he appointed Sandra Day O'Connor to the Supreme Court in 1981. President Clinton appointed a second woman, Ruth Bader Ginsburg, to the Court. O'Connor retired from the Court in 2006. In 2009 President Obama appointed Federal Appeals

---

42 Inter-Parliamentary Union, "Women in National Parliaments." http://www.ipu.org/wmn-e/classif.htm

Al Drago/CQ Roll Call/Congressional Quarterly/Getty Images

Image 5-10
A record number of women were elected to serve in the 115th Congress, but their underrepresentation was visible in 2016 when President Obama delivered his last State of the Union address in January 2016. In the wake of Trump's election, an unprecedented number of women declared their candidacy for the 2018 midterms. At least 128 women will serve in the 116th Congress; members will include the first Native American women, the first Muslim women, and a record number of women of color. Women are still more likely to be Democrats than Republicans in the House and in the Senate.

Court Judge Sonia Sotomayor to fill the vacancy created by Justice David Souter's retirement. Justice Sotomayor is the first Latina to serve on the U.S. Supreme Court. In April 2010, Justice John Paul Stevens announced his retirement, giving President Obama the chance to make a second appointment to the Court. He selected Elena Kagan, the solicitor general of the United States, to fill the vacancy, thus increasing the number of women currently sitting on the Supreme Court to three. President Obama has appointed 134 female judges—more than any president to date. Upon the death of Justice Antonin Scalia, President Obama nominated Merrick Garland, currently the chief judge of the U.S. Court of Appeals for the D.C. Circuit. Republican leaders in the Senate refused to hold hearings on the nomination until after the 2016 presidential election. In April 2017, the Senate confirmed Trump's nominee, Neil Gorsuch, to fill the vacancy.

Gender-Based Discrimination in the Workplace

Traditional cultural beliefs concerning the proper role of women in society continue to be evident not only in the political arena, but also in the workplace. Since the 1960s, however, women have gained substantial protection against discrimination through laws mandating equal employment opportunities and equal pay.

Title VII of the Civil Rights Act of 1964

Title VII of the Civil Rights Act of 1964 prohibits gender discrimination in employment and has been used to strike down employment policies that discriminate against employees on the basis of gender. Even so-called protective policies violate Title VII if they have a discriminatory effect. In 1991, for example, the Supreme Court held that a fetal protection policy established by Johnson Controls, Inc., the country's largest producer of automobile batteries, violated

Title VII. The policy required all women of childbearing age working in jobs that entailed periodic exposure to lead or other hazardous materials to prove that they were infertile or to transfer to other positions. The same requirement was not applied to men. Women who agreed to transfer often had to accept cuts in pay and reduced job responsibilities. The Court concluded that women who are "as capable of doing their jobs as their male counterparts may not be forced to choose between having a child and having a job."[43]

Sexual Harassment

sexual harassment
Unwanted physical or verbal conduct or abuse of a sexual nature that interferes with a recipient's job performance, creates a hostile work environment, or carries with it an implicit or explicit threat of adverse employment consequences.

The Supreme Court has also held that Title VII's prohibition of gender-based discrimination extends to **sexual harassment** in the workplace. Sexual harassment occurs when job opportunities, promotions, salary increases, and the like are given in return for sexual favors. A special form of sexual harassment, called hostile-environment harassment, occurs when an employee is subjected to sexual conduct or comments that interfere with the employee's job performance or are so pervasive or severe as to create an intimidating, hostile, or offensive environment.

In two 1998 cases, the Supreme Court clarified the responsibilities of employers in preventing sexual harassment. The Court ruled that employers must take reasonable care to prevent and promptly correct any sexually harassing behavior. Claims by the employer that it was unaware of the situation or that the victim suffered no tangible job consequences do not reduce liability.[44] In another 1998 case, *Oncale v. Sundowner Offshore Services, Inc.*, the Supreme Court ruled that Title VII protection extends to same-sex harassment.[45]

Wage Discrimination

Women constitute the majority of U.S. workers today. Although Title VII and other legislation have mandated equal employment opportunities for men and women, women continue to earn less, on average, than men do.

The Equal Pay Act of 1963 The issue of women's wages was first addressed during World War II (1939–1945), when the War Labor Board issued an "equal pay for women" policy to ensure that salaries remained high when men returned from war and reclaimed their jobs. The board's authority ended with the war. Although it was supported by the next three presidential administrations, the Equal Pay Act was not enacted until 1963 as an amendment to the Fair Labor Standards Act of 1938.

The Equal Pay Act requires employers to provide equal pay for substantially equal work. In other words, males cannot legally be paid more than females who perform essentially the same job. The Equal Pay Act did not address occupational segregation, the fact that certain types of jobs traditionally held by women pay lower wages than the jobs usually held by men. For example, more women than men are salesclerks and nurses, whereas more men than women are construction workers and truck drivers. Even if all clerks performing substantially similar jobs for a company earned the same salaries, they typically would still be earning less than the company's truck drivers.

When Congress passed the Equal Pay Act in 1963, a woman, on average, made 59 cents for every dollar earned by a man. Figures recently released by

---

43 *United Automobile Workers v. Johnson Controls, Inc.,* 499 U.S. 187 (1991).
44 524 U.S. 725 (1998) and 524 U.S. 742 (1998).
45 523 U.S. 75 (1998).

the U.S. Department of Labor suggest that women now earn 79 cents for every dollar that men earn—a gap 2.5 times greater than those of other industrialized countries. The wage gap is greater for minority women. In some areas, the wage gap is widening. According to the results of a General Accounting Office survey, female managers in ten industries made less money relative to male managers in 2000 than they did in 1995.[46] A study by the American Association of University Women (AAUW) on the gender pay gap for college graduates found that after one year out of college, women working full-time earn only 80 percent as much as their male peers, even among those men and women graduating with the same major and entering the same occupation. The same study found that women earn only 69 percent of men's wages after ten years out of college.[47]

The first bill President Obama signed after taking office in 2009 was the Lilly Ledbetter Fair Pay Act. The law is an example of congressional action undertaken specifically to overturn a decision by the U.S. Supreme Court. Lilly Ledbetter, an employee of Goodyear Tire and Rubber for 19 years, discovered through an anonymous tip when she retired in 1998 that she was a victim of gender pay discrimination by an anonymous tip when she retired in 1998. She filed a complaint under Title VII, but in a 5–4 ruling the U.S. Supreme Court held that race and gender discrimination claims must be made within 180 days of the employer's discriminatory act.[48] As Justice Ginsburg noted in her dissenting opinion, pay disparities often occur in small increments and over time, making them difficult to discover. The Ledbetter Act amends Title VII of the Civil Rights Act of 1964 by stating that the 180-day statute of limitations for filing an equal-pay lawsuit regarding pay discrimination resets with each new discriminatory paycheck. It does not, however, provide any additional tools to combat wage discrimination or enforce provisions already in effect. Equal Pay Day, typically celebrated in April, indicates how far into the year women must work to "catch up" to men's wages from the previous year. It is an occasion to call attention to the wage gap and to examine progress toward closing the wage gap between women and men (see Figure 5-3). The earlier in April that Equal Pay Day is celebrated, the less poorly women are being compensated relative to men. For example, Equal Pay Day was celebrated on April 8 in 2014, April 12 in 2016, and on April 10 in 2018 indicating a slight improvement in women's wages relative to men's.

On Equal Pay Day 2014, President Obama signed an executive order prohibiting federal contractors from retaliating against employees who choose to discuss their compensation. It does not compel workers to discuss pay, nor does it require employers to publish or otherwise disseminate pay data, but it is one small step toward greater pay transparency, which provides workers a means for discovering violations of equal-pay laws. Using a presidential memorandum, President Obama instructed the secretary of labor to establish new regulations requiring federal contractors to submit summary data on compensation paid to their employees, including data by sex and race, to the Department of Labor. Meanwhile, Senate Republicans blocked debate over the Paycheck Fairness Act, setting up an election-year fight between the parties over whose policies are friendlier to women.

---

46 The results of this survey are online at www.gao.gov/audit.htm. To view a copy of the results, enter "GAO-02-156" in the search box. In 2004, the name of this agency was changed to the "Government Accountability Office."

47 Judy Goldberg Dey and Catherine Hill, "Behind the Pay Gap," AAUW Educational Foundation, April 2007.

48 *Ledbetter v. Goodyear Tire & Rubber Co.,* 550 U.S. 618 (2007).

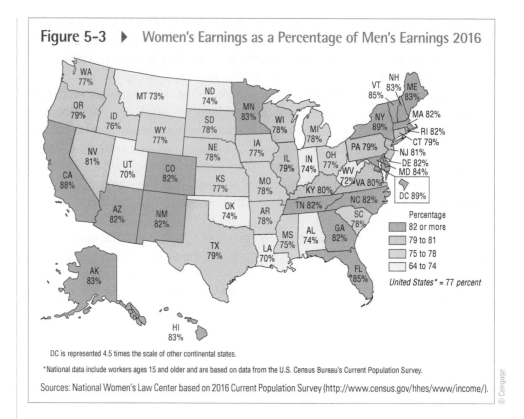

Figure 5-3 ▶ Women's Earnings as a Percentage of Men's Earnings 2016

Percentage

- 82 or more
- 79 to 81
- 75 to 78
- 64 to 74

United States = 77 percent*

DC is represented 4.5 times the scale of other continental states.

*National data include workers ages 15 and older and are based on data from the U.S. Census Bureau's Current Population Survey.

Sources: National Women's Law Center based on 2016 Current Population Survey (http://www.census.gov/hhes/www/income/).

© Cengage

President Obama called on Congress to pass the Paycheck Fairness Act—a revision to the Equal Pay Act of 1963. Among other things, the Paycheck Fairness Act would prohibit employers from retaliating against workers for asking questions about salary and require that employers prove that pay disparities are because of skill and background rather than gender. It also establishes a program through the Department of Labor to train women and girls on negotiating skills. This bill has been introduced in several previous sessions of Congress. The president received a bipartisan standing ovation when he said, "A woman deserves equal pay for equal work. She deserves to have a baby without sacrificing her job. A mother deserves a day off to care for a sick child or sick parent without running into hardship—and you know what, a father does, too. It's time to do away with workplace policies that belong in a *Mad Men* episode."[49]

Economic equality is important to both men and women. President Obama asked Congress to raise the federal minimum wage for all workers from $7.25 per hour to $10.10 per hour by 2015. Women account for 55 percent of minimum wage workers and are largely concentrated in low-wage sectors. Estimates from the President's Council of Economic Advisers suggest that increasing the minimum wage to $10.10 an hour and indexing it to inflation could close about 5 percent of the gender wage gap. Using his executive authority, the president used an executive order to increase the minimum wage for workers on government contracts. Although the increase will not take effect immediately, data suggest it will have an impact. A National Employment Law Project survey of contractors who manufacture military uniforms, provide food and janitorial services in federal agencies, and truck goods found that 75 percent of them earn less than $10 per hour. One in five was dependent on Medicaid for health care, and 14 percent used food stamps.

In January 2016, President Obama again used his authority to issue an executive order that required companies with more than 100 employees to report to the federal government how much they pay employees broken down by race, gender, and ethnicity. The EEOC believes this new transparency will assist individuals filing claims of pay discrimination but also provide employers with data to promote equal pay. "We expect that reporting this data will help employers to evaluate their own pay practices and prevent pay discrimination in their workplaces," said Secretary of Labor Thomas E. Perez.[50]

Although women have made significant progress in the last decade toward equality in politics, education, and the workplace, traditional gender role expectations regarding children and family and the assignment of a disproportionate share of family responsibilities to women make achieving true equality a persistent challenge.

Voting Rights and the Young

The Twenty-sixth Amendment to the Constitution, ratified on July 1, 1971, reads:

> *The right of citizens of the United States, who are eighteen years of age or older, to vote shall not be denied or abridged by the United States or by any State on account of age.*

Before this amendment was ratified, the age at which citizens could vote was 21 in most states. One of the arguments used for granting the right to 18-year-olds was that because they could be drafted to fight in the country's wars, they had a stake in public policy. At the time, the example of the Vietnam War (1964–1975) was paramount. In the first election following ratification, 58 percent of 18- to 20-year-olds were registered to vote, and 48.4 percent reported voting. Only 19.9 percent of 18- to 29-year-olds cast ballots in the 2014 elections. This was the lowest rate of youth turnout recorded in the past 40 years. The proportion of young people who said that they were registered to vote (46.7 percent) was also the lowest over the past 40 years. In contrast, voter turnout among Americans aged 65 or older is very high, usually between 60 and 70 percent. People younger than 30 made up a larger share of the electorate in the 2012 presidential election than those 65 and older, but by 2014 voters under age 30 made up 13 percent of the electorate, whereas voters age 65 and older constituted 22 percent of all voters. The Center for Information and Research on Civic Learning and Engagement (CIRCLE) regularly collects and analyzes data on youth engagement with politics.[51] CIRCLE reported that young people voted in record numbers in the 2016 primary contests and overwhelmingly supported Democrat Bernie Sanders.

---

50 Bouree Lam, "Obama's New Equal-Pay Rules," *The Atlantic*, January 29, 2016. www.theatlantic.com/business/archive/2016 /01/eeoc-pay-discrimination-obama/433926/
51 CIRCLE www.civicyouth.org

Immigration, Latinos, and Civil Rights

■ **5.5** Identify and explain three significant events related to each of the campaigns for civil rights undertaken by African Americans, women, the Latino community, persons with disabilities, and the LGBTQ community.

Time and again, this nation has been challenged, changed, and culturally enriched by immigrant groups. Immigrants have faced challenges associated with living in a new and different political and cultural environment, overcoming language barriers, and often having to deal with discrimination in one form or another. The civil rights legislation passed during and since the 1960s has done much to counter the effects of prejudice against immigrant groups by ensuring that they obtain equal rights under the law.

One of the questions facing Americans and their political leaders today concerns the effect of immigration on American politics and government. This is especially true with regard to the Hispanic American or Latino community. With the influx of individuals from Latin American countries growing exponentially, issues related to immigration and Hispanic Americans will continue to gain greater attention in years to come. Although those in the Latino community did not have to mount a separate campaign to gain access to constitutional suffrage like African Americans and women, they nonetheless have been subject to public and private forms of discrimination.

Mexican American Civil Rights

The history of Mexican Americans spans more than 400 years and varies by region in the United States. Many of the most important challenges to discrimination took place in Texas and California and parallel the claims to rights made by African Americans and women. Mexican American children were forced to attend segregated schools, referred to as "Mexican schools," in California. In a case that preceded *Brown v. Board of Education*, the U.S. Court of Appeals for the Ninth Circuit ruled in 1947 that segregated schools were unconstitutional. In this narrow decision, the court found that although California law provided for separate education for "children of Chinese, Japanese, or Mongolian parentage," the law did not include children of Mexican descent, and therefore it was unlawful to segregate them.[52] California governor Earl Warren, who would later be appointed chief justice of the U.S. Supreme Court and preside over *Brown*, signed a law in 1947 repealing all school segregation statutes.

In 1954, an agricultural worker, Pete Hernandez, was convicted of murder by an all-white jury in Texas. Hernandez maintained that juries could not be impartial unless they included members of other races. The U.S. Supreme Court ruled in *Hernandez v. Texas* that Mexican Americans and other racial groups were entitled to equal protection under the Fourteenth Amendment.[53] The Court ordered that Mr. Hernandez be retried with a jury composed without regard to race or ethnicity.

---

52 *Mendez v. Westminster School District*, 64 F. Supp. 544 (C.D. Cal. 1946), aff'd, 161 F. 2d 744 (9th Cir. 1947) (en banc).
53 *Hernandez v. Texas*, 347 U.S. 475 (1954).

In the realm of voting rights, Mexican Americans were covered under the 1965 Voting Rights Act, but unlike African Americans, they did not enjoy the singular focus of federal registration oversight. Poll taxes (until ended by the Twenty-fourth Amendment in 1964) limited Mexican Americans' electoral participation, particularly in Texas and California. Political organizing in the 1960s and 1970s by groups such as the La Raza Unida Party, founded in Texas but active in other regions, increased minority representation at the local level. Although Mexican Americans potentially constitute a very large voting bloc, they tend to have low voter turnout rates, which scholars attribute to lower income and education rates, as well as recent concerns over immigration status.

The Chicano movement is often characterized as an extension of the Mexican American civil rights movement; it focused on land rights, farmworkers' rights, education, and voting rights, as well as the eradication of ethnic stereotypes and promotion of a positive group consciousness. At first a label with negative connotations, in the 1960s "Chicano" became associated with ethnic pride and self-determination. Movement leaders such as Cesar Chavez and Dolores Huerta were instrumental in founding a number of organizations that, in addition to focusing on labor rights, offered members of the community language classes, assistance in obtaining citizenship, and advocacy for Spanish-language rights. The Chicano movement has galvanized and trained successive generations of community and political activists. Recent campaigns have focused on the plight of immigrant workers in low-wage jobs: janitors, truck drivers, domestic workers, and the like.

The Continued Influx of Immigrants

Every year, about 1 million people immigrate to this country, and those born on foreign soil now constitute more than 12 percent of the U.S. population—twice the percentage of 30 years ago.

Since 1977, more than 80 percent of immigrants have come from Latin America or Asia. Latinos have overtaken African Americans as the nation's largest minority. In 2011, 16 percent of the U.S. population identified itself as Hispanic or Latino, 13 percent as African American or black, and 5 percent as Asian. Non-Latino white Americans made up about 66 percent of the population (see Figure 5-4). If current immigration rates continue, minority groups collectively will constitute the "majority" of Americans by the year 2042, according to estimates by the U.S. Census Bureau. The next census will be taken in 2020. If Latinos, African Americans, and Asians were to form coalitions, they could increase their political strength dramatically and would have the numerical strength to make significant changes. However, as noted in earlier discussions of civil rights campaigns and social movements, coalitions are difficult to form when common interests are not immediately obvious.

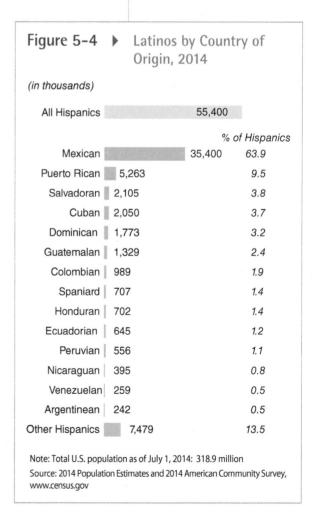

Figure 5-4 ▶ Latinos by Country of Origin, 2014

(in thousands)

		% of Hispanics
All Hispanics	55,400	
Mexican	35,400	63.9
Puerto Rican	5,263	9.5
Salvadoran	2,105	3.8
Cuban	2,050	3.7
Dominican	1,773	3.2
Guatemalan	1,329	2.4
Colombian	989	1.9
Spaniard	707	1.4
Honduran	702	1.4
Ecuadorian	645	1.2
Peruvian	556	1.1
Nicaraguan	395	0.8
Venezuelan	259	0.5
Argentinean	242	0.5
Other Hispanics	7,479	13.5

Note: Total U.S. population as of July 1, 2014: 318.9 million

Source: 2014 Population Estimates and 2014 American Community Survey, www.census.gov

Illegal Immigration

The issue of illegal immigration has become both a hot political issue and a serious policy concern. As many as 12 million undocumented aliens reside and work in the United States. Immigrants typically come to the United States to work, and their labor continues to be in high demand, particularly in construction and farming.

One civil rights question that often surfaces is whether the government should provide services to those who enter the country illegally. Residents of southwestern states complain about the need to shore up border control and perceive that undocumented immigrants place a burden on government-provided social services and the health-care industry. Some schools have become crowded with the children of undocumented immigrants. Often, these children require greater attention because of their inability to speak English, although many are themselves native-born U.S. citizens.

On April 23, 2010, Arizona governor Jan Brewer signed a highly controversial bill on immigration designed to identify, prosecute, and deport illegal immigrants. The law made the failure to carry immigration documents a crime and gave the police broad powers to detain anyone suspected of being in the country illegally. Governor Brewer said the law "represents another tool for our state to use as we work to solve a crisis we did not create and the federal government has refused to fix." On June 25, 2012, the U.S. Supreme Court issued a split decision, upholding part of the Arizona law while rejecting other provisions on the grounds that they interfered with the federal government's

Election 2016

The Uncertain Future of Immigration

President Donald Trump's tough stance against illegal immigration and pledge to enforce immigration laws is largely credited for his victory. Immigration was the most important issue for 64 percent of Republican voters, according to exit polls.

The president has broad authority when it comes to creating and enforcing immigration law. Candidate Trump promised a number of changes to current immigration policy and practice. For example, Trump pledged to build an "impenetrable physical wall on the southern border" and require Mexico to pay for it. He promised to immediately deport immigrants in the country illegally and convicted of crimes, and he promised to end President Obama's executive actions on Deferred Action for Childhood Arrivals (DACA) and Deferred Action for Parents of Americans and Lawful Permanent Residents (DAPA).

Congress has been unable to pass meaningful immigration reform that includes a resolution for the estimated 12 million undocumented immigrants currently living in the United States. Whether President Trump can make good on his campaign promises is uncertain. "Some actions, like

reversing President Obama's immigration executive actions, can be done unilaterally," Cornell Law Professor Stephen W. Yale-Loehr said. "Others, like building a wall and strengthening border security, will require Congress to change current law or to agree to spend the billions of dollars such proposals will require."*

For Critical Analysis

1. The border between the United States and Mexico is 2,000 miles long, and engineers have expressed doubt that a wall is logistically possible. Are there other ways for Trump to honor this promise?

2. What role do you expect the Republican Congress to play in the future of immigration policy with a president of the same party?

*Miriam Valverde, "PolitiFact Sheet: Donald Trump's Immigration Plan," PolitiFact, November 9, 2016.

role in setting immigration policy. The Court unanimously affirmed the law's requirement that police check the immigration status of people they detain and suspect to be in the country illegally, emphasizing that state law enforcement officials already possessed the discretion to ask about immigration status. The Court rejected other portions of the law that criminalized activities such as seeking employment. Leaders in the Latino community maintain that the law will increase racial and ethnic profiling and create a climate of fear among residents of the state. Justice Anthony Kennedy, writing for the majority, left the door open to reconsidering the Arizona law if, after implementation, there is evidence that it leads to illegal racial and ethnic profiling.

The Arizona law offers an opportunity to examine generational differences in attitudes about immigration. A Brookings Institution report found that Arizona has the largest "cultural generation gap" between older Americans, who are largely white (83 percent), and children under 18, who are increasingly members of minorities (57 percent).[54] This gap fuels conflict over policy issues such as immigration and funding allocations for education and health care. Because older people are more likely to vote and less likely to be connected to the perspectives of youth, the gap also has the potential to further alienate young people from direct political participation. A recent poll found that Americans 45 and older were more likely than young people to favor restricting immigration, a finding attributed to the multicultural environment young people today inhabit.

Citizenship Members of Congress from both parties have proposed legislation that would either immediately or gradually extend citizenship to undocumented immigrants now residing in the United States. Although not all Americans agree that citizenship should be extended to illegal immigrants, the greater Latino community in the United States has taken up the cause. Protests and marches calling for citizenship occurred in 2006, with more than a million individuals participating in demonstrations on May 1, 2006, alone. The citizenship question will be an important political topic for the foreseeable future.

One expedited path to citizenship for immigrants with permanent resident status and permission to work (green card holders) is through military service. Noncitizens have served in the military since the Revolutionary War, and today about 29,000 noncitizens serve in uniform. Service members are eligible for expedited citizenship under a July 2002 executive order, an opportunity realized by nearly 43,000 men and women since September 11, 2001.[55]

Accommodating Diversity with Bilingual Education The continuous influx of immigrants into this country presents another ongoing challenge—how to overcome language barriers. Bilingual education programs, first introduced in the 1960s, teach children in their native language while also teaching them English. Congress authorized bilingual education programs in 1968 when it passed the Bilingual Education Act, which was intended primarily to help Hispanic children learn English. In a 1974 case, *Lau v. Nichols*, the Supreme Court bolstered the claim that children have a right to bilingual education.[56] In that case, the Court ordered a California school district to provide special programs for Chinese students with language difficulties if a substantial number of these children attended school in the district. Bilingual programs, however,

54 William H. Frey, *The State of Metropolitan America* (Washington, DC: Brookings Institution, 2010).
55 Department of Defense, MAVNI Fact Sheet, http://www.defense.gov/news/mavni-fact-sheet.pdf
56 414 U.S. 563 (1974).

have more recently come under attack. In 1998, California residents passed a ballot initiative that called for the end of bilingual education programs in that state. The law allowed schools to implement English-immersion programs instead. In these programs, students are given intensive instruction in English for a limited period and then placed in regular classrooms. The law was immediately challenged in court on the grounds that it unconstitutionally discriminated against non–English-speaking groups. A federal district court concluded that the new law did not violate the equal protection clause and allowed the law to stand, thus ending bilingual education efforts in California.

Affirmative Action

■ **5.6** Define the goal of affirmative action and explain why this approach is controversial in the United States.

The Civil Rights Act of 1964 prohibited discrimination against any person on the basis of race, color, national origin, religion, or gender. It also established the right to equal opportunity in employment. A basic problem remained, however: minority groups and women, because of past discrimination, often lacked the education and skills to compete effectively in the marketplace. In 1965, the federal government attempted to remedy this problem by implementing the concept of affirmative action. **Affirmative action** policies attempt to "level the playing field" by giving special preferences in educational admissions and employment decisions to groups that have been discriminated against in the past.

affirmative action
A policy in educational admissions or job hiring that gives special attention or compensatory treatment to traditionally disadvantaged groups in an effort to overcome present effects of past discrimination.

In 1965, President Johnson ordered that affirmative action policies be undertaken to remedy the effects of past discrimination. All government agencies, including those of state and local governments, were required to implement such policies. Additionally, affirmative action requirements were applied to companies that sell goods or services to the federal government and to institutions that receive federal funds. They were also required whenever an employer had been ordered to develop such a plan by a court or by the EEOC because of evidence of past discrimination. Finally, labor unions that had been found to discriminate against women or minorities in the past were required to establish and follow affirmative action plans.

The *Bakke* Case

The first Supreme Court case addressing the constitutionality of affirmative action plans examined a program implemented by the University of California at Davis. Allan Bakke, a white student who had been denied admission to the medical school, discovered that his academic record was better than those of some of the minority applicants who had been admitted to the program. He sued the University of California regents, alleging **reverse discrimination**. The UC Davis Medical School had held 16 places out of 100 for educationally "disadvantaged students" each year and admitted to using race as a criterion for these 16 admissions. Bakke claimed that his exclusion from medical school violated his rights under the Fourteenth Amendment's provision for equal protection of the laws. The trial court agreed. On appeal, the California Supreme Court agreed also. Finally, the regents of the university appealed to the U.S. Supreme Court.

reverse discrimination
The charge that an affirmative action program discriminates against those who do not have minority status.

In 1978, the Supreme Court handed down its decision in *Regents of the University of California v. Bakke*.[57] The Court did not rule against affirmative action

---

57 438 U.S. 265 (1978).

Race @ College—A New Wave of Student Activism

Following California's lead, several states have amended their constitutions to prohibit public universities from using race as a factor in admissions decisions. Minority populations are growing nationwide but shrinking on college campuses. What would it mean to live in a post-racial society? The election of Barack Obama as president signaled a seismic shift in racial attitudes to some; others believe that racism has shape-shifted into less obvious forms of discrimination and prejudice. Students on several U.S. campuses have pushed back against the veneer of campus diversity to highlight their feelings of isolation in the face of declining minority enrollments and call out the "microaggressions" they experience every day on campus. Microaggressions are the subtle ways that racial, ethnic, gender, and other stereotypes find their way into conversations, comments, and questions that cause minority students to stop and wonder, "What did that mean?"

In a nod to the famous Langston Hughes poem "I, Too," students at Harvard have created the "I, too, am Harvard" (#itooamharvard) campaign that includes a play performed on campus written and directed by Kimiko Matsuda-Lawrence, a Harvard sophomore.* The play is based on interviews with 40 Harvard students who identify as black or multiracial. To promote the play, another student took pictures of students holding signs displaying humiliating remarks made by peers such as, "You are really articulate for a black girl" and "Are you all so fast because you spend so much time running from the cops?" Other statements were messages to the university community: "The lack of diversity in this classroom does NOT make me the voice of all black people." The photographs were published on Tumblr, picked up by BuzzFeed, and within a day spread to other campuses and around the world.

Students at the University of Michigan launched a social media campaign called "Being Black at the University of Michigan" (#BBUM) in 2013 in reaction to a fraternity party inviting "rappers, twerkers, gangsters" and others "back to da hood again." Although the party never happened, its promotion exposed simmering racial tensions on campus and highlighted the decline in black undergraduate enrollment since Proposal 2 was adopted in 2006.** Law students at UCLA created the "33/1100" campaign, highlighting the small number of black students in law classes. Gerloni Cotton helped organize the event because she was often the only black woman in a class of 100 students. When issues of race came up in class, she felt called upon to speak to them. "On one hand I felt isolated, but on the other I felt highlighted—invisible but hypervisible," she said.***

"The Black Bruins [spoken word] by Sy Stokes," a video posted to YouTube in November 2013, went viral in a matter of

Image 5-11 Student protesters at the University of Missouri forced the resignation of the university president and Missouri system chancellor over their failure to redress racial bias on campus.

days.**** Sy Stokes, a student at UCLA, created the spoken word performance to demonstrate how small the black population at UCLA is (roughly 4 percent) and put the administration on notice for falling retention rates for black males in particular. The statistics are startling—in fall 2012, a total of 660 graduate and undergraduate African American males were enrolled at UCLA, and 65 percent of them were undergraduate athletes. Stokes also reported that the number of UCLA national championships exceed the number of black male freshmen enrolled. "When every black student in class feels like Rosa Parks on the bus," "when the university refuses to come to our defense," when "our faces are just used to cover up from the public what's really inside," it is clear that UCLA's administration has failed its black community, the students say. The administration claims to share the students' frustrations, but acknowledges that UCLA must do a better job of living up to its commitment to diversity.

In 2015, a number of colleges and universities faced protests by students expressing anger and concern about the racial climate in higher education. Students at more than 60 universities have issued demands aimed at improving campus climate, enhancing student and faculty diversity, diversifying the curriculum, and questioning symbols and practices reminiscent of the past. Triggered by a series of racist incidents at the University of Missouri, student activists tried to confront President Tim Wolfe by blocking his car in the homecoming parade and reciting a list of racial injustices dating back to the school's founding. When Wolfe remained silent and appeared to ignore the students, activists doubled-down. A graduate student engaged in a hunger strike, students and faculty engaged in mass protest, and the university football team

(Continued)

(Continued)

voted to refuse to play for the university until Wolfe resigned. Students organized as Concerned Student 1950, a reference to the year Missouri admitted its first black graduate student. The president and chancellor of the system both resigned.

Other universities were forced by student protesters to make changes as well. Harvard College has replaced the title "house master" with "faculty dean" in its residence halls. Princeton agreed to consider renaming the Woodrow Wilson School of International and Public Affairs but ultimately left the name unchanged. A number of schools have agreed to create and require diversity courses.*****

* Bethonie Butler, "I, Too, Am Harvard: Black Students Show How They Belong," *The Washington Post*, March 4, 2014. www.washingtonpost.com/ blogs/she-the -people/wp/2014/03/05/i-too-am-harvard-black-students-show- they-belong/
** Tanzina Vega, "Colorblind Notion Aside, Colleges Grapple with Racial Tension," *The New York Times*, February 24, 2014. www.nytimes.com/2014/02/25/us /colorblind-notion-aside-colleges-grapple-with-racial-tension.html?_r=0
*** Samantha Tomilowitz and Sam Hoff, "UCLA Students Protest Lack of Diversity," *Daily Bruin*, February 10, 2014.
**** The Black Bruins [spoken word] by Sy Stokes, www.youtube.com /watch?v=BEO3H5BOIFk
*****Alia Wong and Adrienne Green, "Campus Politics: A Cheat Sheet," *The Atlantic*, March 4, 2016. www.theatlantic.com/education/archive/2016/03 /campus-protest-roundup/417570/

For Critical Analysis

1. Students occupy a unique position on college campuses because any one group of students is there for only a short time before graduating and moving on. What gives students power to demand change on a college campus? Is this power similar to or different from other civil rights challenges discussed in this chapter?

2. How does your college or university require students to engage with issues of diversity? Do you have a diversity requirement? How would you characterize the climate on your campus? If you wanted to make changes, how might you go about doing so?

programs. It held that Bakke must be admitted to the UC Davis Medical School because its admissions policy had used race as the sole criterion for the 16 "minority" positions. Justice Lewis Powell, speaking for the Court, indicated that although race can be considered "as a factor" among others in admissions (and presumably hiring) decisions, race cannot be the sole factor. So, affirmative action programs, but not specific quota systems, were upheld as constitutional.

The *Bakke* decision did not end the controversy over affirmative action programs. At issue in the current debate over affirmative action programs is whether favoring one group violates the equal protection clause of the Fourteenth Amendment to the Constitution as it applies to all other groups.

Further Limits on Affirmative Action

Several cases decided during the 1980s and 1990s placed further limits on affirmative action programs by subjecting any federal, state, or local affirmative action program that uses racial or ethnic classifications as the basis for making decisions to "strict scrutiny" by the courts (to be constitutional, a discriminatory law or action must be narrowly tailored to meet a *compelling* government interest).[58] Yet, in two cases involving the University of Michigan, the Supreme Court indicated that limited affirmative action programs continue

---
58 515 U.S. 200 (1995).

to be acceptable and that diversity is a legitimate goal. The Court struck down the affirmative action plan used for undergraduate admissions at the university, which automatically awarded a substantial number of points to applicants based on minority status.[59] At the same time, it approved the admissions plan used by the law school, which took race into consideration as part of a complete examination of each applicant's background.[60]

The Supreme Court again narrowed the scope in which race can be used as one of a number of factors in college admissions in *Fisher v. University of Texas at Austin* (2013).[61] The University of Texas adopted the admissions plan at issue in the case soon after the 2003 ruling in the case of *Grutter v. Bollinger* said that race could be taken into account as one of the factors in helping to achieve racial diversity. In 1997, the Texas legislature passed a law requiring the University of Texas to admit all high school seniors who ranked in the top 10 percent of their high school class. When the University of Texas identified racial and ethnic disparities between the entering class and the state's population, however, it altered its race-neutral admissions policy. For Texas applicants not in the top 10 percent of their class, the university considered race as one of several factors in the admission decision. Abigail Noel Fisher, a student who was not automatically admitted under the top 10 percent rule and was not admitted to the Texas campus, argued that she was denied admission on account of her race whereas minority students with lower grade point averages than hers were admitted under the diversity plan. The district court and the Fifth Circuit Court of Appeals both sided with the University of Texas at Austin, but in a 7–1 decision the U.S. Supreme Court said that the lower courts erred in not applying the standard of "strict judicial scrutiny" to the university's admissions policy. Any policy that takes race into account must be "precisely tailored to serve a compelling governmental interest." University of Texas officials had argued that their policy's use of race was narrowly tailored to pursue greater diversity. (Justice Elena Kagan recused herself because of her involvement in the case while working in the solicitor general's office.) The case returned to the Supreme Court for another hearing in December 2015. In June 2016, the Court issued a 4-3 decision in favor of the University of Texas. Justice Kennedy writing for the majority said courts must give universities leeway in designing admissions programs but noted the need to "reconcile the pursuit of diversity with the constitutional promise of equal treatment and dignity."[62]

State Ballot Initiatives

A ballot initiative passed by California voters in 1996 amended that state's constitution to end all state-sponsored affirmative action programs. The law was challenged immediately by civil rights groups and others, who argued that it violated the Fourteenth Amendment by denying racial minorities and women the equal protection of the laws. In 1997, however, a federal appellate court upheld the constitutionality of the amendment. Thus, affirmative action is now illegal in California in all state-sponsored institutions, including state agencies and educational institutions. In 1998, Washington voters also approved a law banning affirmative action in that state. In 2006, voters in Michigan adopted

59 *Gratz v. Bollinger*, 539 U.S. 244 (2003).
60 *Grutter v. Bollinger*, 539 U.S. 306 (2003).
61 *Fisher v. University of Texas at Austin*, 570 U.S. (2013).
62 *Fisher v. University of Texas at Austin*, 579 U. S. (2016).

Proposal 2 (also known as the Michigan Civil Rights Initiative) effectively ending affirmative action by public institutions based on race, color, sex, or religion. At the University of Michigan, the proportion of African American students fell from 7 percent in 2006 to 4.6 percent in 2014. Student activists argue that it is a result of Proposal 2. University officials have not been able to take race into account in admission decisions or in awarding financial aid packages. Michigan Attorney General Bill Schuette argues that the ban was passed by 58 percent of Michigan voters and therefore represents the will of the citizenry. In *Schuette v. Coalition to Defend Affirmative Action*, decided in April 2014, the Supreme Court upheld the Michigan ban by a 6–2 vote, ruling that policies affecting minorities that do not involve intentional discrimination should be decided at the ballot box rather than in the courtroom.[63] The Court's decision leaves in place state constitutional actions in Arizona, Nebraska, Oklahoma, California, and Washington and could serve as an invitation to other states to enact similar bans.

Making Amends for Past Discrimination through Reparations

reparation
Compensation, monetary or nonmonetary (e.g., formal apology), to make amends for a past transgression or harm.

Whereas affirmative action programs attempt to remedy past discrimination by "leveling the playing field," reparations are a way of apologizing for past discriminatory actions and providing compensation. The legal philosophy of **reparation** requires that victims of a harm be replenished by those who inflicted the harm. In criminal courts, for example, defendants are sometimes sentenced to perform community service or provide restitution to the victim in lieu of jail time. When reparation is used relative to a class of people who experienced discrimination, such as descendants of former slaves or Japanese Americans who were interned during World War II, restitution is made by the government. In 1988, Congress passed legislation that apologized for and admitted that wartime government action against Japanese Americans was based on racial prejudice and war hysteria. Over $1.6 billion has been disbursed to Japanese Americans who were themselves interned or to their heirs.

Proposals for similar forms of restitution for the descendants of slaves in the United States have been under discussion for some time, with little consensus around the issue. On July 29, 2008, the House passed a resolution (with 120 co-sponsors from both parties) apologizing to African Americans for the institution of slavery, Jim Crow laws, and other practices that have denied people equal opportunity under the law. Democrat Steve Cohen from Tennessee introduced the resolution, saying, ". . . only a great country can recognize and admit its mistakes and then travel forth to create indeed a more perfect union."[64] The Senate followed with a similar resolution of apology the following summer. The resolutions did not contain any mention of financial compensation for descendants of slaves.

When President Obama signed into law the 2010 Defense Appropriations Act on December 19, 2009, it included a footnote, entitled Section 8113, otherwise known as an "apology to Native Peoples of the United States." The passage of the apology resolution went largely unnoticed but served as the

---

63 Amy Howe, "Divided Court Upholds Michigan's Ban on Affirmative Action: In Plain English," SCOTUSblog, April 23, 2014. www.scotusblog.com/2014/04/divided-court-upholds-michigans-ban-on-affirmative-action-in-plain-english/
64 "Congress Apologizes for Slavery, Jim Crow," National Public Radio, July 30, 2008.

Library of Congress Prints and Photographs Division [LC-USZ62-113923]

Image 5-12
Asians in America have experienced a long history of discrimination. In 1922, for example, the Supreme Court ruled that Asians were not white and therefore were not entitled to full citizenship rights (*Ozawa v. U.S.*, 1922). Following the Japanese attack on Pearl Harbor in 1941, Executive Order 9066 required the exclusion of all people of Japanese ancestry (including U.S. citizens) from the Pacific coast. Approximately 110,000 people were forcibly relocated to internment camps. In 1944, the Supreme Court upheld the constitutionality of the war relocation camps (*Korematsu v. U.S.*), citing national security concerns during a time of war.

culmination of a five-year attempt by Senator Sam Brownback of Kansas to convince Congress to adopt a formal apology for the government's past treatment of Native Americans. The condensed resolution conveys the nation's regret "for the many instances of violence, maltreatment, and neglect inflicted on Native Peoples by citizens of the United States," as the condensed resolution states. The resolution was not accompanied by monetary reparations or funds for new programs.

Special Protection for Older Americans

Age discrimination is potentially the most widespread form of discrimination because anyone—regardless of race, color, national origin, or gender—could be a victim at some point in life. In an attempt to protect older employees from such discriminatory practices, Congress passed the Age Discrimination in Employment Act (ADEA) in 1967. The act, which applies to employers, employment agencies, and labor organizations and covers individuals over the age of 40, prohibits discrimination against individuals on the basis of age unless age is shown to be a bona fide occupational qualification reasonably necessary to the normal operation of the particular business. To succeed in a suit for age discrimination, an employee must prove that the employer's action, such as a decision to fire the employee, was motivated, at least in part, by age bias. Even if an older worker is replaced by a younger worker who is also over the age of 40, the older worker is entitled to bring a suit under the ADEA.[65] Most states have their own prohibitions against age discrimination in employment, and some are stronger than the federal provisions.

---

65 *O'Connor v. Consolidated Coin Caterers Corp.*, 517 U.S. 308 (1996).

Securing Rights for Persons with Disabilities

Persons with disabilities did not fall under the protective umbrella of the Civil Rights Act of 1964. In 1973, however, Congress passed the Rehabilitation Act, which prohibited discrimination against persons with disabilities in programs receiving federal aid. A 1978 amendment to the act established the Architectural and Transportation Barriers Compliance Board. Regulations for ramps, elevators, and the like in all federal buildings were implemented. Congress passed the Education for All Handicapped Children Act in 1975, guaranteeing that all children with disabilities will receive an "appropriate" education. The most significant federal legislation to protect the rights of persons with disabilities, however, is the Americans with Disabilities Act (ADA), which Congress passed in 1990.

The Americans with Disabilities Act of 1990

The ADA requires that all public buildings and public services be accessible to persons with disabilities. It also mandates that employers must reasonably accommodate the needs of workers or potential workers with disabilities. Physical access means ramps; handrails; wheelchair-accessible restrooms, counters, drinking fountains, telephones, and doorways; and easily accessible mass transit. In addition, other steps must be taken to comply with the act. Car rental companies must provide cars with hand controls for disabled drivers. Telephone companies are required to have operators to pass on messages from speech-impaired persons who use telephones with keyboards.

The ADA requires employers to "reasonably accommodate" the needs of persons with disabilities unless to do so would cause the employer to suffer an "undue hardship." The ADA defines persons with disabilities as persons who have physical or mental impairments that "substantially limit" their everyday activities. Health conditions that have been considered disabilities under federal law

Image 5-13

The Americans with Disabilities Act (ADA) requires that all public buildings and public services be available to persons with disabilities. Universities must enable physical access to facilities and educational programs to persons with disabilities. Similarly, public transportation must be accessible to all.

THIS RAMP IS FOR PERSONS WHO USE WHEELCHAIRS AND OTHER MOBILITY AIDS.

include blindness, alcoholism, heart disease, cancer, muscular dystrophy, cerebral palsy, paraplegia, diabetes, acquired immunodeficiency syndrome (AIDS), and infection with the human immunodeficiency virus (HIV) that causes AIDS. The Affordable Care Act contains a number of provisions that apply to people living with disabilities. For example, insurance companies are no longer able to deny coverage to people with preexisting conditions, such as a disability.

The ADA does not require that *unqualified* applicants with disabilities be hired or retained. If a job applicant or an employee with a disability, with reasonable accommodation, can perform essential job functions, however, then the employer must make the accommodation. Required accommodations may include installing ramps for a wheelchair, establishing more flexible working hours, creating or modifying job assignments, and creating or improving training materials and procedures.

Limiting the Scope and Applicability of the ADA

Beginning in 1999, the Supreme Court has issued a series of decisions that limit the scope of the ADA. In 1999, the Court held in *Sutton v. United Airlines, Inc.*[66] that a condition (in this case, severe nearsightedness) that can be corrected with medication or a corrective device (in this case, eyeglasses) is not considered a disability under the ADA. In other words, the determination of whether a person is substantially limited in a major life activity is based on how the person functions when taking medication or using corrective devices, not on how the person functions without these measures. Since then, the courts have held that plaintiffs with bipolar disorder, epilepsy, diabetes, and other conditions do not fall under the ADA's protections if the conditions can be corrected with medication or corrective devices. The Supreme Court has also limited the applicability of the ADA by holding that lawsuits under the ADA cannot be brought against state government employers.[67]

The Rights and Status of Gays and Lesbians

■ **5.5** Identify and explain three significant events related to each of the campaigns for civil rights undertaken by African Americans, women, the Latino community, persons with disabilities, and the LGBTQ community.

On June 27, 1969, patrons of the Stonewall Inn, a New York City bar popular with gays and lesbians, responded to a police raid by throwing beer cans and bottles because they were angry at what they felt was unrelenting police harassment. In the ensuing riot, which lasted two nights, hundreds of gays and lesbians fought with police. Before Stonewall, the stigma attached to homosexuality and the resulting fear of exposure had tended to keep most gays and lesbians quiescent. In the months immediately after Stonewall, however, "gay power" graffiti began to appear in New York City. The Gay Liberation Front and the Gay Activist Alliance were formed, and similar groups sprang up in other parts of the country. Thus, Stonewall has been called "the shot heard round the homosexual world."

---

66 527 U.S. 471 (1999).
67 *Board of Trustees of the University of Alabama v. Garrett*, 531 U.S. 356 (2001).

hate crime
A crime motivated by racial, sexual, or other prejudice, typically one involving violence.

Progress in the Gay and Lesbian Rights Movement

The Stonewall incident marked the beginning of the movement for gay and lesbian rights. Since then, gays and lesbians have formed thousands of organizations to exert pressure on legislatures, the media, schools, churches, and other organizations to recognize their right to equal treatment.

To a great extent, lesbian and gay groups have succeeded in changing public opinion—and state and local laws—relating to their status and rights. Nevertheless, they continue to struggle against age-old biases against homosexuality, often rooted in deeply held religious beliefs, which allow discrimination to persist. In a widely publicized case involving the Boy Scouts of America, a troop in New Jersey refused to allow gay activist James Dale to be a Scout leader. In 2000, the case came before the Supreme Court, which held that, as a private organization, the Boy Scouts had the right to determine the requirements for becoming a Scout leader.[68] In 1998, a student at the University of Wyoming named Matthew Shepard was brutally beaten, tortured, tied to a fence post, and left to die near Laramie, Wyoming, because he was believed to be gay. His killers could not be charged with a **hate crime** because at the time, the state law did not recognize sexual orientation as a protected class. In 2009, Congress passed the Matthew Shepard Act, expanding the 1969 federal hate crime law to include crimes motivated by the victim's actual or perceived gender, sexual orientation, gender identity, or disability.[69]

State and Local Laws Targeting Gays and Lesbians

Before the Stonewall incident, 49 states had sodomy laws that made various sexual acts, including homosexual acts, illegal (Illinois, which had repealed its sodomy law in 1962, was the only exception). During the 1970s and 1980s, more than half of these laws were either repealed or struck down by the courts. In 2003, the Court reversed an earlier antisodomy position[70] with its decision in *Lawrence v. Texas*.[71] The Court held that laws against sodomy violate the due process clause of the Fourteenth Amendment, stating: "The liberty protected by the Constitution allows homosexual persons the right to choose to enter upon relationships in the confines of their homes and their own private lives and still retain their dignity as free persons." The result of *Lawrence v. Texas* was to invalidate all remaining sodomy laws throughout the country.

Today, 20 states and the District of Columbia have laws protecting lesbians and gays against discrimination in employment, housing, public accommodations, and credit. Several laws at the national level have also been changed over the past two decades. Among other things, the government has lifted a ban on hiring gays and lesbians and voided a 1952 law prohibiting gays and lesbians from immigrating to the United States. Transgender men and women may now serve openly in the military. However, 28 states lack employment nondiscrimination laws covering sexual orientation and gender identity. The U.S. Department of Justice asked a federal judge to block North Carolina from enforcing parts of the state's controversial law requiring people to use public bathrooms corresponding to the sex on their birth certificate. At the same time, Texas and 12 other states filed suit in a different federal court asking a judge to block the federal government from using civil rights

---

68 *Boy Scouts of America v. Dale*, 530 U.S. 640 (2000).
69 "Obama Signs Measure to Widen Hate Crimes Law," PBS NewsHour, October 28, 2009.
70 *Bowers v. Hardwick*, 478 U.S. 186 (1986).
71 539 U.S. 558 (2003).

AP Images/Marcio Jose Sanchez

Image 5-14

Del Martin (L) and Phyllis Lyon (R) are married by San Francisco mayor Gavin Newsom in a private ceremony at San Francisco City Hall on June 16, 2008. Martin and Lyon, a couple since 1953, were active in the gay rights and women's rights movements. Del Martin died on August 27, 2008.

laws to protect transgender individuals, claiming that laws like Title IX prohibit sex-based discrimination and say nothing about gender identity.

Gays and Lesbians in the Military

The U.S. Department of Defense traditionally has viewed homosexuality as incompatible with military service. In 1993 President Clinton announced a new policy, generally characterized as "don't ask, don't tell" (DADT). Enlistees would not be asked about their sexual orientation, and gays and lesbians would be allowed to serve in the military so long as they did not declare that they were gay or lesbian or commit homosexual acts. Military officials endorsed the new policy (after opposing it initially), but supporters of gay rights were not enthusiastic.

As a presidential candidate, Barack Obama promised to help bring an end to the "don't ask, don't tell" policy. In March 2009, Secretary of Defense Robert Gates announced a number of interim steps designed to make it more difficult for the military to discharge openly gay men and women. In December 2010, a bill to repeal DADT was enacted, with the caveat that the policy would remain in place until the president, the secretary of defense, and the chairman of the Joint Chiefs of Staff certified that repeal would not harm military readiness, followed by a 60-day waiting period. The certification was sent to Congress on July 22, 2011, making the date of the law's repeal September 20, 2011. Following the repeal, discharged servicemen and servicewomen were permitted to reenlist, and several have successfully done so. On May 17, 2016, the Senate confirmed Eric Fanning as Secretary of the Army. Fanning is the first openly gay head of a branch of the military.

Same-Sex Marriage

One of the most sensitive political issues with respect to the rights of gay and lesbian couples has been whether they should be allowed to marry, as heterosexual couples are. In 2015, the U.S. Supreme Court settled the question in *Obergefell v. Hodges*,[72] ruling that the Fourteenth Amendment (under the due

---

72 *Obergefell v. Hodges*, 576 U.S. (2015).

process and equal protection clauses) requires a state to license a marriage between two people of the same sex and to recognize a marriage between two people of the same sex when their marriage was lawfully licensed and performed out of state. The Court's decision brought uniformity to a patchwork system of state laws, some allowing and some specifically forbidding gay marriage.

Defense of Marriage Act   The controversy over this issue was fueled in 1993, when the Hawaii Supreme Court ruled that denying marriage licenses to gay couples might violate the equal protection clause of the Hawaii constitution.[73] In the wake of this event, some state legislators grew concerned that they might have to treat gay men or lesbians who were legally married in another state as married couples in their state as well. Opponents of gay rights pushed for state laws banning same-sex marriages, and the majority of states enacted such laws or adopted constitutional amendments. At the federal level, Congress passed the Defense of Marriage Act of 1996 (DOMA), which banned federal recognition of lesbian and gay couples and allowed state governments to ignore same-sex marriages performed in other states.

In 2013, the U.S. Supreme Court declared unconstitutional Section 3 of the law preventing the federal government from recognizing same-sex marriages for the purpose of federal laws or programs even when those couples were legally married in their home state. Justice Anthony Kennedy, writing for the majority in a 5–4 decision, said that the act wrote inequality into federal law and violated the Fifth Amendment's protection of equal liberty. "DOMA's principal effect is to identify a subset of state-sanctioned marriages and make them unequal," he wrote.[74] The decision in *United States v. Windsor* (2013) was issued on June 26, 2013. Almost immediately the federal government changed policy to extend the federal benefits and privileges of marriage to same-sex couples regardless of the law in their home state. Attorney General Eric Holder, the first African American attorney general, has embraced the expansion of civil rights for the lesbian, gay, bisexual, transgender, queer (LGBTQ) community. The government estimated that more than 1,100 federal regulations, rights, and laws touch on, or are affected by, marital status. In court cases and criminal investigations, for example, same-sex couples were covered under spousal privilege—the rule that says spouses cannot be forced to testify against each other. The Bureau of Prisons extended the same visitation rights to married same-sex couples that it does to opposite-sex couples. The Justice Department also recognized same-sex couples when determining eligibility for programs like the September 11th Victim Compensation Fund, which pays people who were injured or made sick by the 2001 terrorist attacks. Same-sex spouses of police killed in the line of duty were made eligible for federal benefits. The Department of Defense changed its definition of *marriage* and *spouse* such that same-sex couples became eligible for all federal military benefits, including access to base housing, health and survivor benefits, and family separation allowances.

Although the *Windsor* decision did not strike down prohibitions on same-sex marriages across the country (that came with *Obergefell*), federal judges used the reasoning to expand equal treatment of gays and lesbians in other

---

73 *Baehr v. Lewin*, 852 P.2d 44 (Hawaii 1993).
74 *United States v. Windsor*, 570 U.S. (2013).

areas of life. In January 2014, the U.S. Court of Appeals for the Ninth Circuit held that gays and lesbians cannot be excluded from juries on the basis of their sexual orientation. Judge Stephen Reinhardt, writing for the unanimous three-judge panel, said that "the Supreme Court's decision was premised on the idea of equal dignity for all, a dignity enhanced by 'responsibilities, as well as rights.'"[75]

A Short History of State Recognition of Gay Marriages Massachusetts was the first state to recognize gay marriage. In November 2003, the Massachusetts Supreme Judicial Court ruled that same-sex couples have a right to civil marriage under the Massachusetts state constitution and that civil unions would not suffice.[76] In 2005, the Massachusetts legislature voted down a proposed ballot initiative that would have amended the state constitution to explicitly state that marriage could only be between one man and one woman (but would have extended civil union status to same-sex couples). Although the highest courts in several states had upheld bans on gay marriage, in 2008 the Supreme Court of California ruled that the state was required to recognize gay marriages. In reaction, opponents immediately prepared petitions to put a constitutional amendment on the ballot in November 2008 to outlaw such marriages. The campaign for and against Proposition 8, which would ban gay marriages in California, cost at least $74 million and was funded by contributions from almost every state. Ultimately, Proposition 8 was approved by a margin of 4 percent. The 18,000 marriages that took place between the California Supreme Court decision and the approval of Proposition 8 remained valid. On August 4, 2010, a federal judge declared California's ban on same-sex marriage unconstitutional, saying that no legitimate state interest justified treating gay and lesbian couples differently from others. The ruling was the first in the country to strike down a marriage ban on federal constitutional grounds rather than on the basis of a state constitution. On the same day the U.S. Supreme Court released the *Windsor* decision, it also ruled that the private-party sponsors of Proposition 8 did not have standing to appeal an adverse federal court ruling. *Hollingsworth v. Perry* (2013) cleared the way for same-sex marriages to resume in California. On October 6, 2014, the Supreme Court said that it would not review a series of U.S. appeals court decisions that struck down state bans paving the way for the *Obergefell* decision in 2015.

Shift in Public Opinion for Marriage Equality

After a period of public opposition to same-sex marriage, President Obama announced an evolution in his thinking in a nationally televised interview in May 2012, saying that he believes same-sex couples should be allowed to marry. His view is supported by a majority of Americans, according to poll data. Polls conducted immediately following the president's statement also found that opposition to gay marriage fell by 11 percentage points among African Americans. The shift in public opinion favoring gay marriage has been rapid and broad. Same-sex marriage is currently accepted in 26 countries. Although international public opinion, like that of the United States, has become more tolerant overall, there are some notable exceptions. Ugandan President Yoweri

75 "The Expanding Power of U.S. v Windsor," *The New York Times*, January 26, 2014. http://www.nytimes.com/2014/01/27/opinion/the-expanding-power-of-us-v-windsor.html
76 *Goodridge v. Department of Public Health*, 798 N.E.2d 941 (Mass. 2003).

Museveni signed a bill criminalizing homosexuality in February 2014. Nigeria banned same-sex unions and arrests people it suspects of being gay. Russia passed a law banning advocacy of gay rights—specifically the propaganda of non-traditional sexual relations to minors. The United Nations estimates that 78 nations ban homosexuality, and seven countries allow the death penalty for those convicted of having consensual homosexual relationships.[77] Homosexuality is defined as a crime in several nations the United States considers allies (Saudi Arabia and India are two examples), but to date no punitive sanctions have been imposed. In all, more than 75 countries have antihomosexuality laws.

Marriage equality represents a major step forward in civil rights for gay and lesbian Americans. The struggle for equality expressed through civil rights for all persons is far from over. Police shootings of African Americans, new state laws intended to limit access to public restrooms by transgender men and women, re-segregated public schools, and access to higher education present Americans with new civil rights challenges.

---

77 Somini Sengupta, "Considering What Can Actually Be Done About Gay Rights Violations," *The New York Times*, March 2, 2014.

Key Terms

affirmative action 192
Black Codes 155
civil disobedience 163
civil rights 154
de facto segregation 161
de jure segregation 161
feminism 179

gender discrimination 181
grandfather clause 158
hate crime 200
Jim Crow laws 156
literacy test 158
poll tax 158
reparation 196

reverse discrimination 192
separate but equal doctrine 157
sexual harassment 184
subpoena 165
suffrage 174
white primary 158

Chapter Summary

■ **5.1** The term *civil rights* refers to the rights of all Americans to equal treatment under the law, as provided for by the Fourteenth Amendment to the Constitution and by subsequent acts of Congress. Although the terms *civil rights* and *civil liberties* are sometimes used interchangeably, scholars make a distinction between the two. Civil liberties are limitations on government; they specify what the government *cannot* do. Civil rights, in contrast, specify what the government *must* do—to ensure equal protection and freedom from discrimination.

■ **5.2** The story of civil rights in the United States is the struggle to reconcile our ideals as a nation with the realities of discrimination individuals and groups may still encounter in daily life. To the nation's founders, political equality required a degree of independent thinking and a capacity for rational action that at the time they believed were limited to a very few white males. Therefore, other groups and individuals were systematically excluded, not only from the exercise of political rights, but also from access to education and employment. Today we believe

that all people are entitled to equal political rights, as well as to the opportunities for personal development provided by equal access to education and employment. However, the roots of past discrimination live on in today's discriminatory practices, including racial profiling, the wage gap, the achievement gap in schools, and the "glass ceiling," which prevents women from rising to the top in business and professional firms.

■ **5.3** Although the government has the power to assert rights and the obligation to protect civil rights, it does not always do so. Individuals and groups then organize to bring pressure on government to act. The civil rights movement started with the struggle by African Americans for equality. Before the Civil War, most African Americans were slaves, and slavery was protected by the Constitution and the Supreme Court. Constitutional amendments after the Civil War legally ended slavery, and African Americans gained citizenship, the right to vote, and other rights through legislation. This legal protection was rendered meaningless in practice by the 1880s, however, and politically and socially, African American inequality continued. Legal guarantees mean little when people's attitudes and practices remain discriminatory.

■ **5.3** Legal segregation was declared unconstitutional by the Supreme Court in *Brown v. Board of Education of Topeka* (1954), in which the Court stated that separation implied inferiority. In *Brown v. Board of Education* (1955), the Supreme Court ordered federal courts to ensure that public schools were desegregated "with all deliberate speed." Also in 1955, the modern civil rights movement began with a boycott of segregated public transportation in Montgomery, Alabama. Of particular impact was the Civil Rights Act of 1964, which banned discrimination on the basis of race, color, religion, sex, or national origin in employment and public accommodations. The act created the Equal Employment Opportunity Commission to administer the legislation's provisions.

■ **5.3** The Voting Rights Act of 1965 outlawed discriminatory voter-registration tests and authorized federal registration of persons and federally administered procedures in any state or political subdivision evidencing electoral discrimination or low registration rates. The Voting Rights Act and other protective legislation passed during and since the 1960s apply not only to African Americans, but to other ethnic groups as well. Minorities have been increasingly represented in national and state politics, although they have yet to gain representation proportionate to their numbers in the U.S. population. Lingering social and economic disparities have led to a new civil rights agenda—one focusing less on racial differences and more on economic differences.

■ **5.4** The Supreme Court is in the best position within the framework of American government to interpret the values and ideals contained in the founding documents and ensure those ideas are reflected in policy and practice. The Court is often in a good position to pull the public along as more progressive ideas are percolating throughout society by issuing rulings that speed up the timetable for social change, as it did in *Brown v. Board of Education* (desegregating schools) and *United States v. Virginia* (opening VMI, the state military college, to women).

■ **5.5** In the early history of the United States, women were considered citizens, but by and large they had no political rights because they were largely viewed as dependents. After the first women's rights convention in 1848, the campaign for suffrage gained momentum, yet not until 1920, when the Nineteenth Amendment was ratified, did women finally obtain the right to vote. The second wave of the women's movement began in the 1960s, and the National Organization for Women (NOW) was formed in 1966 to bring about complete equality for women in all walks of life. Efforts to secure the ratification of the Equal Rights Amendment failed. Women continue to fight gender discrimination in employment. Federal government efforts to eliminate gender discrimination in the workplace include Title VII of the Civil Rights Act of 1964, which prohibits, among other things, gender-based discrimination, including sexual harassment on the job. Wage discrimination also continues to be a problem for women, as does the glass ceiling. Women make up just 20 percent of the U.S. Congress.

■ **5.5** America has always been a land of immigrants and will continue to be so. Today, more than 1 million immigrants enter the United States each year, and more than 12 percent of the U.S. population consists of foreign-born persons. Demographers estimate that the foreign-born will account for 15 percent of the nation sometime between 2020 and 2025. In particular, the Latino community in the United States has experienced explosive growth. In recent years, undocumented immigration has surfaced as a significant issue for border states and the nation. Indeed, one of the pressing concerns facing today's politicians at the state and federal level is how U.S. immigration policy should be reformed.

■ **5.5** The Rehabilitation Act of 1973 prohibited discrimination against persons with disabilities in programs receiving federal aid. Regulations implementing the act provide for ramps, elevators, and the like in federal buildings. The Americans with Disabilities Act of 1990 prohibits job discrimination against persons with physical and mental disabilities, requiring that positive steps be taken to comply with the act. The act also requires expanded access to public facilities, including transportation, and to services offered by such private concerns as car rental and telephone companies.

■ **5.5** Gay and lesbian rights groups work to promote laws protecting gays and lesbians from discrimination and to repeal antigay laws. After 1969, sodomy laws, which criminalized specific sexual practices, were repealed or struck down by the courts in all but 18 states, and in 2003 a Supreme Court decision effectively invalidated all remaining sodomy laws nationwide. Gays and lesbians are no longer barred from federal employment or from immigrating to this country. Twenty states and the District of Columbia outlaw discrimination based on sexual orientation. Hate crimes based on sexual orientation or gender identity are punishable by federal law under the Matthew Shepard Act of 2009. The military's "don't ask, don't tell" policy was repealed effective September 20, 2011. In 2015, the U.S. Supreme Court decision in *Obergefell v. Hodges* relied upon the equal protection and due process clauses of the Fourteenth Amendment to rule that a fundamental right to marry is guaranteed to same-sex couples.

■ **5.6** Affirmative action programs have been controversial because of charges that they can lead to reverse discrimination against majority groups or even other minority groups. Supreme Court decisions have limited affirmative action programs, and voters in California, Michigan, and Washington passed initiatives banning state-sponsored affirmative action in those states.

Selected Resources

PRINT RESOURCES

Kristoff, Nicholas D., and Sheryl WuDunn. *Half the Sky: Turning Oppression into Opportunity for Women Worldwide* (New York: Alfred Knopf, 2009). Written by two Pulitzer Prize–winning journalists, this book demonstrates that the key to solving global poverty is to improve the lives of women around the globe. The book profiles women throughout Asia and Africa who have not only coped with unimaginable forms of brutal discrimination, but also created opportunities for survival for themselves and other women.

Liptak, Adam. *To Have and To Hold: The Supreme Court and the Battle for Same-Sex Marriage* (Kindle Single, 2013). Liptak, a Supreme Court reporter for *The New York Times*, puts the historic *Windsor* decision in social and political context.

Moore, Wes. *The Other Wes Moore: One Name, Two Fates* (New York: Random House, 2010). This memoir tells the story of two boys, both named Wes Moore, who grew up in Baltimore, Maryland, within a few blocks of one another; one became a Rhodes Scholar and one is serving a life sentence in the Jessup Correctional Institution.

Morin, Jose Luis. *Latino/a Rights and Justice in the United States: Perspectives and Approaches* (Durham, NC: Carolina Academic Press, 2009). This book offers a thorough overview of the history and modern incarnation of Latino/a civil rights and experiences within the U.S. justice system. Case studies and a focus on taking action complement the legal analysis.

Phillips, Steve. *Brown Is the New White: How the Demographic Revolution Has Created a New American Majority* (New York: The New Press, 2016). An examination of the role changing demographics play in building electoral coalitions in American politics.

MEDIA RESOURCES

Borderland—A National Public Radio (NPR) series exploring the 2,248-mile border between the United States and Mexico and the lives and stories of the people who cross.

Chisholm '72: Unbought and Unbossed—A documentary about the career of Congresswoman Shirley Chisholm, the first black woman to run for president of the United States. Includes archival footage and contemporary interviews.

Eyes on the Prize: America's Civil Rights Movement 1954–1985—A 14-part *American Experience* documentary (first aired on public television) that features both movement leaders and the stories of average Americans through contemporary interviews and historical footage.

Fight in the Fields: Cesar Chavez and the Farmworkers' Struggle—A 1997 film documenting the first successful drive to organize farmworkers in the United States; described as a social history with Chavez as a central figure, the documentary draws from archival footage, newsreels, and present-day interviews.

Lioness—A documentary film about a group of female army support soldiers who were a part of the first program in American history to send women into direct ground combat against insurgents in Iraq.

Miss Representation—A documentary exploring how the media's misrepresentations of women have led to the underrepresentation of women in positions of power and influence.

Selma—A 2014 film directed by Ava DuVerney depicting the historic events surrounding the fight for voting rights. The film was nominated for Best Picture at the 87th Academy Awards.

ONLINE RESOURCES

National Immigration Forum—established in 1982, the National Immigration Forum is the leading immigrant advocacy organization in the country, with a mission to advocate for the value of immigrants and immigration to the nation: www.immigrationforum.org/

Pew Hispanic Center—founded in 2001, the Pew Hispanic Center is a nonpartisan research organization that seeks to improve understanding of the U.S. Hispanic population and to chronicle Latinos' growing impact on the nation: www.pewhispanic.org/

Reporting Civil Rights—an anthology of the reporters and journalism of the American civil rights movement hosted by Library of America: www.reportingcivilrights.loa.org/

The Great Divide—a *New York Times* blog series on inequality in the United States and around the world and its implications for economics, politics, society, and culture; moderated by Joseph E. Stiglitz, a Nobel laureate in economics: http://opinionator.blogs.nytimes.com/category/the-great-divide/

Women's Rights National Historical Park—operated by the National Park Service, the park preserves the sites associated with the first women's rights convention in 1848: www.nps.gov/wori/index.htm

Public Opinion and Political Socialization

6

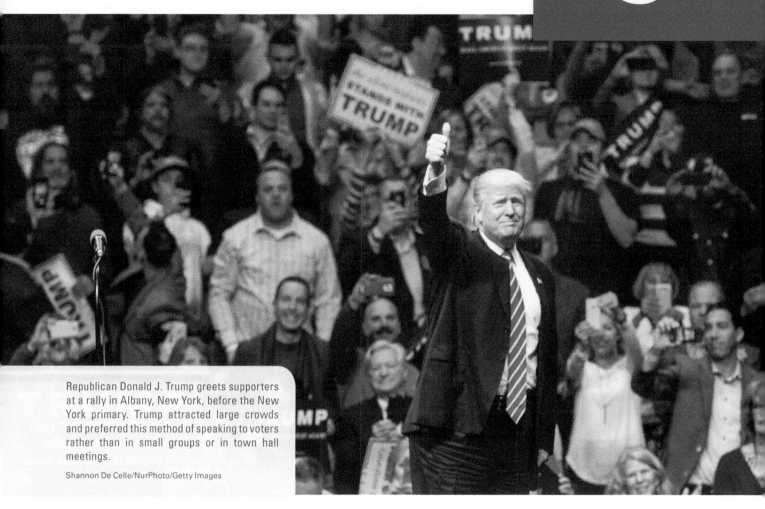

Republican Donald J. Trump greets supporters at a rally in Albany, New York, before the New York primary. Trump attracted large crowds and preferred this method of speaking to voters rather than in small groups or in town hall meetings.

Shannon De Celle/NurPhoto/Getty Images

LEARNING OBJECTIVES

After reading this chapter, you will be able to:

- **6.1** Define public opinion and identify at least two ways public opinion affects government actions.

- **6.2** Evaluate how the political socialization process shapes political attitudes, opinions, and behavior and explain the impact of demographic characteristics on political behavior.

- **6.3** Describe three forms of social media and explain how social media can shape political decisions or events.

- **6.4** Assess the impact that world opinion of the United States has on the government's domestic and foreign policy decisions.

- **6.5** Identify three factors that might distort public opinion results collected through opinion polling.

What if...   Young People Were Required to Serve?

Background

What if the United States adopted a policy that required all persons between the ages of 18 and 22 residing in the country to engage in domestic or military service for a period of at least 18 months? Would this create a stronger bond between young citizens and the nation? How might 18 months of service socialize new generations to politics and political activity?

Young people typically know less about politics, express less interest in politics, and vote less often than their elders. But that can change! In 2012, people under 30 made up a larger share of the electorate than those 65 and older. Thus, young citizens have tremendous potential to shape politics and policy *if* they get involved.

Service as Political Socialization

The United States has a long history of citizens rendering service to their communities, including the Civilian Conservation Corps, the Peace Corps, and Volunteers in Service to America (VISTA). Teach for America recruits college graduates and trains them to teach in America's most challenged schools. During the Clinton administration, AmeriCorps, a large-scale national service program designed to place young people in service positions in communities across the country, was established. The Obama administration significantly expanded both the AmeriCorps and VISTA programs. New initiatives include STEM AmeriCorps (designed to mobilize professionals in science, technology, engineering, and mathematics fields to inspire young people to excel) and FEMACorps (a 1,600-member AmeriCorps program solely devoted to disaster response and recovery).

Would young people be willing to serve their country? This chapter reviews the process of becoming socialized into civic and political life and, as a result, how we develop and express political opinions. Forces such as the family, schools, faith communities, the media, and peers all shape how we understand public life. Likewise, direct personal experience with politics is a developmental force. From national surveys of first-year college students, we know that roughly a third of all students believe that it is important to keep up with political affairs and that roughly a third report a very good chance that they will participate in community service or volunteer work while in college. These individuals are also more likely to remain engaged with their communities after they graduate from college. Those who oppose national service do so for a variety of reasons, including the disruption to education and career, as well as the belief that individual liberty would be violated.

Service as Workforce Preparation

Currently 5.6 million young adults between the ages of 16 and 24 are out of school and not working. By 2020, the United States is projected to experience a shortfall of 5 million workers who have education and training beyond high school. National service offers a strategy to bridge the gap between compulsory education and a robust preparation for work in the new economy. According to a recent report by the Corporation for National and Community Service, service is associated with greater employment outcomes. Service can increase the likelihood of finding employment by 51 percent among volunteers without a high school diploma. Further, every $1 invested in national service returns $4 to society in the form of higher earnings, increased economic output, and savings to taxpayers due to lower spending on government programs.*

Toward a National Policy

What would the nation gain from a service requirement? The U.S. military has been an all-volunteer force since the repeal of the draft in 1973. Representative Charles B. Rangel, a veteran of the Korean conflict, argued in a *New York Times* op-ed essay that the draft should be reinstated to promote the philosophy of shared sacrifice and enforce a greater appreciation of the consequences of war. At any given time in the past decade, less than 1 percent of the American population has been on active military duty, compared with 9 percent of Americans who were in uniform during World War II. When President Bill Clinton proposed AmeriCorps, he said, "Citizen service bridges isolated individuals, local communities, the national community, and ultimately, the community of all people." AmeriCorps members serve in communities across the United States for one or two years in return for an educational stipend.** The nation benefits from a diverse group of committed individuals performing public work that needs doing. Critics charge that national service amounts to forced voluntarism and that the compulsory nature undermines the benefits for individuals and communities. Without any form of compulsory service, about 25 percent of Americans volunteer at least once a year.

* Tracy Ross, Shirley Sagawa, and Melissa Boteach, "Utilizing National Service as a 21st Century Workforce Strategy for Opportunity Youth," American Progress, March 1, 2016. https://www.americanprogress.org/issues/labor/report/2016/03/01/132039 /utilizing-national-service-as-a-21st-century-workforce-strategy-for-opportunity-youth/
** William J. Clinton, "The Duties of Democracy," in E. J. Dionne et al., eds. *United We Serve: National Service and the Future of Citizenship* (Washington, DC: Brookings Institution, 2003).

For Critical Analysis

1. Do you believe a national service requirement would improve young people's connection to politics, to their community, and to the country? Why or why not?

2. Would national service be a good way for young people to gain workforce skills not typically developed through formal education? How might you directly benefit from a service experience in ways that you cannot find in your classroom?

3. You have no doubt heard the phrase, "with rights come responsibilities." What responsibilities do you have as a resident of your community, of your state, and of the nation?

In a democracy, the people express their opinions in many different ways. First and foremost, they express their views in political campaigns and vote for the individuals who will represent their views in government. Between elections, individuals express their opinions in many ways, ranging from writing to the editor to calling their senator's office to responding to a blog. Public opinion is expressed and conveyed to public officials through polls, which are reported daily in the media. Sometimes public opinion is expressed through mass demonstrations, rallies, or protests.

In 2003, when President George W. Bush asked Congress to authorize the use of force against Iraq, 72 percent of the public approved. At that time, more than 80 percent of Americans either believed or considered it possible that Saddam Hussein was building an arsenal of biological and other extremely dangerous weapons. By 2005, support for the use of troops in Iraq had declined to 39 percent and, by mid-2007, had fallen to 36 percent. Senator Barack Obama made withdrawal of American troops from Iraq a priority of his campaign and claimed that if he had been in the Senate at that time, he would not have supported the authorization of the use of force. Senator Hillary Clinton, who had voted for the resolution, no longer supported the Iraqi campaign and claimed that she had been misled at the time of the debate. The approval rating of President Bush, inevitably connected with the unpopular war, fell to 30 percent or less. In the past, public opinion has had a dramatic impact on presidents. In 1968, President Lyndon B. Johnson did not run for reelection because of the intense and negative public reaction to the war in Vietnam. In 1974, President Richard Nixon resigned in the wake of a scandal when it was obvious that public opinion no longer supported him. Although President Obama promised to make health-care reform a top legislative priority, vacillating public opinion made it difficult to pressure even members of his own party in Congress to act. His approval ratings heading into the 2012 campaign were closely tied to the public's perception of the state of the economy, and particularly the unemployment rate. The week of the 2012 election, the percentage of Americans who approved of the job he was doing as president stood at 52 percent (compared with 42 percent who disapproved). At the end of President Trump's first year in office, his approval ratings were quite low for a new president, with less than 40 percent of the people approving his performance. Congress, however, increased its rating to 20 percent, up 9 points. When polls asked about the tax reform law, the signature law for the Republicans, public approval was low at first and then began to rise. Most polling about tax reform suggested that people knew very little about the law and were waiting to see how the policy affected them. Using public opinion to judge the new law will need to wait until its full implementation.

Defining Public Opinion

■ **6.1** Define public opinion and identify at least two ways public opinion affects government actions.

public opinion
The aggregate of individual attitudes or beliefs shared by some portion of the adult population.

consensus
General agreement among the citizenry on an issue.

divisive opinion
Public opinion that is polarized between two quite different positions.

nonopinion
The lack of an opinion on an issue or policy among the majority.

Among the many different publics, no single public opinion exists. In a nation of more than 300 million people, innumerable gradations of opinion on an issue may exist. Thus, we define **public opinion** as the aggregate of individual attitudes or beliefs shared by some portion of the adult population.

Public opinion is distributed among several different positions, and the distribution of opinion tells us how divided the public is on an issue and whether compromise is possible. When a large proportion of the American public appears to express the same view on an issue, a **consensus** exists, at least at the moment the poll was taken. Figure 6-1 shows a pattern of opinion that might be called consensual. In this situation, 61 percent of adults polled by Pew Research Center say U.S. Muslims should not be subject to additional scrutiny solely because of their religion. Issues on which the public holds widely differing attitudes result in **divisive opinion** (see Figure 6-2). For the first time since 9/11, Americans are nearly evenly divided in their assessment of how well the government is doing to reduce the threat of terrorism, with 46 percent reporting that the government is doing well and 52 percent believing otherwise. Sometimes, a poll shows a distribution of opinion indicating that most Americans either have no information about the issue or are not interested enough to formulate a position. This is referred to as **nonopinion** (see Figure 6-3). In September 2014, a referendum took place on Scottish independence (the "no" side won with 55 percent of the vote). It appears that most Americans were not paying attention because when asked whether Scotland should remain in the United Kingdom, 44 percent answered "don't know" and those with an opinion were evenly split. Politicians may believe that the public's lack of knowledge about an issue gives them more room to maneuver, or they may be wary of taking any action for fear that opinion will crystallize after a crisis.

Figure 6-1 ▶ Consensus Opinion

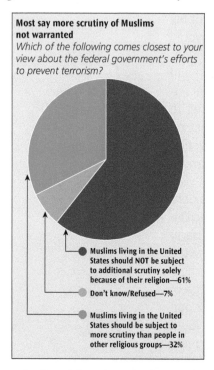

Most say more scrutiny of Muslims not warranted
Which of the following comes closest to your view about the federal government's efforts to prevent terrorism?

● Muslims living in the United States should NOT be subject to additional scrutiny solely because of their religion—61%

● Don't know/Refused—7%

● Muslims living in the United States should be subject to more scrutiny than people in other religious groups—32%

Source: Pew Research Center Access: http://www.people-press.org/files/2015/12/P2-2.png

Public Opinion and Policymaking

Sometimes public officials have a difficult time discerning the public's opinion on a specific issue from the public's expression of general anger or dissatisfaction. The Tea Party protests in 2009 presented just such a dilemma. Rallies began to express opposition to the TARP (Troubled Asset Relief Program) bailout bill passed by Congress. Drawing on themes from the Revolutionary War era and the Boston Tea Party in

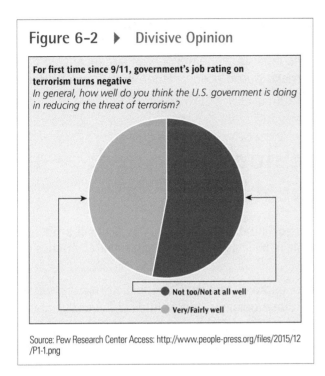

Figure 6-2 ▶ Divisive Opinion

For first time since 9/11, government's job rating on terrorism turns negative
In general, how well do you think the U.S. government is doing in reducing the threat of terrorism?

● Not too/Not at all well
● Very/Fairly well

Source: Pew Research Center Access: http://www.people-press.org/files/2015/12/P1-1.png

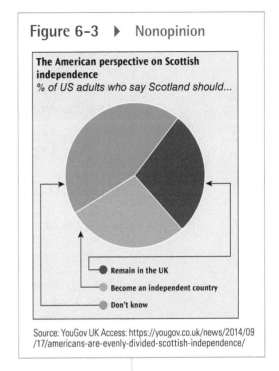

Figure 6-3 ▶ Nonopinion

The American perspective on Scottish independence
% of US adults who say Scotland should...

● Remain in the UK
● Become an independent country
● Don't know

Source: YouGov UK Access: https://yougov.co.uk/news/2014/09/17/americans-are-evenly-divided-scottish-independence/

particular, the protesters often arrived dressed as Patriots and holding handmade placards with anti-tax slogans. Organizers utilized social networking sites and the Internet to call for Tea Party meetings and protests in communities large and small. Tea Party supporters demonstrated against health-care reform and increased government spending. This coalition of disparate groups acting under a single moniker is not "for" or "against" any single policy or program, but is rather an expression of negative opinion directed at incumbents of both parties. As a result, public officials and candidates had a difficult time responding. Many political pundits believe that the popularity of Donald J. Trump as a candidate for president was an extension of the broad dissatisfaction first expressed by Tea Party activists.

If public opinion is important for democracy, are policymakers really responsive to public opinion? A study by political scientists Benjamin I. Page and Robert Y. Shapiro suggests that the national government is very responsive to the public's demands for action.[1] In looking at changes in public opinion poll results over time, research demonstrates that when the public supports a policy change, the following occurs: policy changes in a direction consistent with the change in public opinion 43 percent of the time, policy changes in a direction opposite to the change in opinion 22 percent of the time, and policy does not change at all 33 percent of the time. When public opinion changes dramatically—say, by 20 percentage points rather than by just 6 or 7 percentage points—government policy is more likely to follow changing public attitudes.

Public opinion also serves to limit government. Consider the highly controversial issue of abortion. Most Americans are moderates on this issue; they do not approve of abortion as a means of birth control, but they do feel that it should be available. Yet, sizable groups express very intense feelings for and

---

1   See the extensive work of Page and Shapiro in Benjamin I. Page and Robert Y. Shapiro, *The Rational Public: Fifty Years of Trends in Americans' Policy Preferences* (Chicago: University of Chicago Press, 1992).

against legalized abortion. Given this distribution of opinion, most officials would rather not try to change policy to favor either of the extreme positions. To do so would clearly violate the opinion of the majority of Americans. In this case, public opinion does not make public policy; rather, it restrains officials from taking truly unpopular actions. In this sense, public opinion plays a vital role in the American system.

How Public Opinion Is Formed: Political Socialization

■ **6.2** Evaluate how the political socialization process shapes political attitudes, opinions, and behavior and explain the impact of demographic characteristics on political behavior.

Most Americans are willing to express opinions on political issues when asked. How do people acquire these opinions and attitudes? Typically, views that are expressed as political opinions are acquired through the process of **political socialization**. People acquire their political attitudes, often including their party identification, through relationships with their families, friends, and coworkers.

political socialization
The process by which people acquire political beliefs and attitudes.

Models of Political Socialization

Scholars have long believed that the most important early sources of political socialization are found in the family and the schools. Children learn their parents' views on politics and on political leaders through observation and approval seeking. When parents are strong supporters of a political party, children are very likely to identify with that same party. If parents are alienated from the political system or totally disinterested in politics, children will tend to hold the same attitudes. Other researchers claim that political attitudes (not party identification) are influenced much more heavily by genetics than by parental or environmental socialization.[2] Perhaps most interestingly, in explaining differences in people's tendencies to possess political opinions at all regardless of their ideology, the researchers find that genetics explains one-third of the differences among people, and shared environment is completely inconsequential. Thinking about how nature (genetics) might shape political attitudes is a relatively new area of research, but it complements the nurture approach taken by generations of political socialization researchers, helping to provide answers to long-standing puzzles.

More sources of information about politics are available to Americans today and especially to young people. Although their basic outlook on the political system may be formed by genetics and early family influences, young people are exposed to other sources of information about issues and values through social media and popular culture. It is not unusual for young adults to hold very different views on issues. The exposure of younger Americans to many sources of ideas may also underlie their more progressive views on such issues as immigration and gay rights.

---

2 John Alford, Carolyn Funk, and John R. Hibbing, "Are Political Orientations Genetically Transmitted?" *American Political Science Review* (May 2005) 99 (2): 153–167.

The Family and the Social Environment

Not only do our parents' political attitudes and actions affect our opinions, but family also links us to other factors that affect opinion, such as race, social class, educational environment, and religious beliefs.

Studies suggest that the influence of parents is due to communication and receptivity. Parents communicate their feelings and preferences to children constantly. Because children have such a strong desire for parental approval, they are very receptive to their parents' views. Children are less likely to influence their parents, because parents expect deference from their children.[3]

Other studies show that if children are exposed to political ideas at school and in the media, they will share these ideas with their parents, giving parents what some scholars call a "second chance" at political socialization. Children can also expose their parents to new media, such as Instagram, Snapchat, and Twitter.[4] Facebook has become "social media for adults." The demographics of Facebook users show a 25 percent decline in use among 13- to 17-year-olds coupled with significant increases in the 55-and-up age group (80 percent increase).[5]

did you know?

In February 2016, Twitter had 1.3 billion active registered users and averaged 500 million tweets a day.

Education as a Source of Political Socialization From the early days of the republic, schools were perceived to be important transmitters of political information and attitudes. Children in primary grades learn about their country mostly in patriotic ways. They learn about pilgrims, the flag, some of the nation's presidents, and how to celebrate national holidays. Without much explicit instruction, children easily adopt democratic decision-making tools such as "taking a vote" and democratic procedures such as "the majority wins." In the middle grades, children learn more historical facts and come to understand the structure and functions of government. By high school, students have a more complex understanding of the political system, may identify with a political party, and may take positions on issues. Students may gain some experience in political participation—first, through student elections and activities, and second, through their introduction to registration and voting while still in school.

The more formal education a person receives, the more likely it is that he or she will be interested in politics, be confident in his or her ability to understand political issues, and be an active participant in the political process.

Peers and Peer Group Influence Once a child enters school, the child's friends become an important influence on behavior and attitudes. Friendships and associations in **peer groups** affect political attitudes. We must, however, separate the effects of peer group pressure on opinions and attitudes in general from the effects of peer group pressure on political opinions. For the most part, associations among peers are nonpolitical. Political attitudes are more likely to be shaped by peer groups when peer groups are involved directly in political activities. If you join an interest group based on your passion for the

peer group
Group consisting of members sharing common social characteristics. These groups play an important part in the socialization process, helping to shape attitudes and beliefs.

3   Barbara A. Bardes and Robert W. Oldendick, *Public Opinion: Measuring the American Mind*, 3rd ed. (Belmont, CA: Wadsworth Publishing, 2006), p. 73.
4   For a pioneering study in this area, see Michael McDevitt and Steven H. Chaffee, "Second Chance Political Socialization: 'Trickle-up' Effects of Children on Parents," in Thomas J. Johnson et al., eds., *Engaging the Public: How Government and the Media Can Reinvigorate American Democracy* (Lanham, MD: Rowman & Littlefield, 1998), pp. 57–66.
5   James Brumley, "Facebook Users Are Getting Older . . . And That's a Good Thing." Investor Place, February 4, 2014. http://investorplace.com/2014/02/facebook-users-demographics/#.U0FsYFe9Z8E

First Lady Michelle Obama—Let's Move!

The First Lady of the United States does not have a formal constitutional role within government, but she is a very powerful force in shaping public opinion and social norms. The title was first used when Dolley Madison was eulogized as "America's First lady." Historically, First Ladies have served as the official hostess in the White House and played a supportive role both socially and politically. Today's presidential spouse is much more likely to play a public role of her own design. Michelle Obama graduated from Princeton and earned her law degree at Harvard. Her resume includes practicing law and working with the city of Chicago in launching the youth mentorship program, Public Allies. In the years prior to Barack Obama's election as president in 2008, she served as vice president of community and external affairs for the University of Chicago Hospitals.

The Obamas raised their two daughters, Malia and Sasha, in the White House. They are also the first African American First Family to occupy the White House. The choices made as individuals and as a family are carefully scrutinized by the public. In many ways, the First Family is integral to opinion formation and political socialization. Michelle Obama adopted a public agenda related to promoting healthy habits and the well-being of children. Soon after the Obamas moved into the White House, she planted a vegetable garden on the South Lawn with more than 55 varieties of fruits and vegetables. The produce was used in preparing meals in the White House and a portion was donated to a local soup kitchen.

First Lady Michelle Obama launched the project, Let's Move!, aimed at ending the epidemic of childhood obesity through healthier eating and increased physical activity. Nearly one in three children today is overweight or obese; the numbers are even higher in African American and Hispanic communities, where nearly 40 percent of kids are overweight. Children who are overweight or obese at ages 3 to 5 years old are five times as likely to be overweight or obese as adults. Let's Move! is a comprehensive public health campaign designed to educate people about the causes and consequences of childhood obesity and help everyone make better choices. Nutritional education is combined with practical strategies such as "Supermarket 101," which urges parents to fill the cart with ingredients for healthy meals rather than snack foods. "Chefs Move to Schools" is run through the Department of Agriculture and encourages chefs to adopt a local school. Schools across the country have planted gardens and brought kids into the planning and preparation of healthier school lunches.

Let's Move! urges kids to get at least one hour of physical exercise a day. Let's Move! and NFL's Play 60 program have partnered to promote youth fitness programs of all kinds. Let's Move! involves local governments and nonprofits, school districts, and celebrities. A robust social media campaign invites Americans to contribute to the Let's Move! blog, post to Facebook, and submit YouTube videos. #Letsmove, the Let's Move! Twitter feed, offers advice on eating healthy and featured posts by the First Lady encouraging youth to think about the right nutrition and amount of physical activity needed to stay healthy. In 2016, the Department of the Interior announced Let's Move! Outside, an extension of the Let's Move! campaign aimed at encouraging kids nationwide to be more involved in outdoor activities. As First Lady, Michelle

Twitter Feed

The First Lady ✓
@FLOTUS
Following

In honor of turnips being planted in the Kitchen Garden today, @StephenCurry30 brings back #TurnipForWhat.

RETWEETS 4,380 LIKES 8,574

11:22 AM - 5 Apr 2016

(Continued)

Obama held the nation's attention for eight years and she chose to focus it on improving children's health. The Centers for Disease Control (CDC) reported that the obesity rate for low-income preschool-age children declined between 2008 and 2012 in 19 of 43 states and territories measured and declined overall by 43 percent. The news announcement from the CDC included a remark from Mrs. Obama: "I am thrilled at the progress we've made over the last few years in obesity rates among our youngest Americans."*

*Sabrina Tavernise, "Obesity Rate for Young Children Plummets 43% in a Decade," *The New York Times*, February 25, 2014. http://www.nytimes.com/2014/02/26/health/obesity-rate-for-young-children-plummets-43-in-a-decade.html

For Critical Analysis

1. The role of First Lady is not an elected position, nor is it a paying job. Why then is the First Lady so influential in setting a policy agenda like the one described here? What contributes to the First Lady's power in doing so? Will the power of the role expand or diminish when the presidential spouse is male?

2. In January 2017, Melania Trump became the First Lady and moved into the White House. In a speech prior to the election she signaled that her agenda would include a campaign against cyber-bullying and that she would be an advocate for women and children. Should the president's spouse be expected to enter public life with an agenda of her or his own? Are there any issues that a presidential spouse should avoid? Why or why not?

environment, you are more likely to be influenced by your organizational peers than you are by classmates.

Opinion Leaders' Influence We are all influenced by friends at school, family members and other relatives, and teachers. In a sense, these people are **opinion leaders**, but on an *informal* level; their influence on our political views is not necessarily intentional or deliberate. When President Obama announced a change in his position on gay marriage, a similar positive change in public opinion among African Americans was detected by pollsters. We are also influenced by *formal* opinion leaders, such as presidents, lobbyists, congresspersons, media figures, and religious leaders, who have as part of their jobs the task of shaping people's views. Nicholas Kristof, a prominent *New York Times* reporter and author, has characterized empowerment of women and girls as the twenty-first century's moral imperative.[6] When she was Secretary of State, Hillary Clinton rarely missed an opportunity to urge nations, including the United States, to invest resources to empower women and girls: "[W]ithout providing more rights and responsibilities for women, many of the goals we claim to pursue in our foreign policy are either unachievable or much harder to achieve. . . . Democracy means nothing if half the people can't vote, or if their

opinion leader
Person who is able to influence the opinions of others because of position, expertise, or personality.

Image 6-1
As First Lady, as a U.S. senator, and as secretary of state, Hillary Rodham Clinton urged nations to invest in girls and women. Prior to her candidacy for president, she worked on behalf of global human rights through "No Ceilings: The Full Participation Project," an initiative of the Clinton Foundation.

---

6 Nicholas Kristof and Sheryl WuDunn, "The Women's Crusade," *New York Times Magazine*, August 17, 2009.

vote doesn't count, or if their literacy rate is so low that the exercise of their vote is in question. Which is why when I travel, I do events with women, I talk about women's rights, I meet with women activists, I raise women's concerns with the leaders I'm talking to."[7] The Clinton Foundation partnered with other groups to measure the extent of women's participation across the globe and foster knowledge about women's inequality. As a candidate for president in 2016, Clinton made frequent references to the importance of her candidacy as a role model of achievement for girls and young women. Politicians acting as opinion leaders hope to define the political agenda in such a way that discussions about policy options will take place on their terms.

---

7   Mark Landler, "A New Gender Agenda," *The New York Times*, August 18, 2009.

Beyond Our Borders

World Opinion of the United States

■ **6.4** Assess the impact that world opinion of the United States has on the government's domestic and foreign policy decisions.

In the immediate aftermath of the September 11, 2001, terrorist attacks, most of the world expressed sympathy toward the United States. Few nations objected to the subsequent American invasion of Afghanistan in 2001 to oust the Taliban government or to the Bush administration's vow to hunt down the terrorists responsible for the attacks. When the United States announced plans to invade Iraq in 2003, however, world opinion was not supportive. By 2006, world opinion had become decidedly anti-American, as the United States' ongoing "war on terrorism" continued to offend other nations. There was a brief resurgence attributed to the "Obama Effect" in 2010, but that has largely disappeared. Publics in many nations including our most important allies reacted negatively to the election of Donald Trump as president in 2016.

America's Image Suffers Decline with Trump

The Pew Global Attitudes Project surveyed citizens from more than 40 nations in 2017, a few months after the inauguration of President Trump. The survey found that opinions about the United States and its policies suffered a decline in support in many nations of the world. The median approval rating declined from 69 percent approval in 2015, to 49 percent in 2017. Most notably, some of the United States' strongest allies expressed disapproval of the president and the nation itself. Among our NATO allies, the German public's approval of the United States declined from 57 to 37 percent. Similarly, the French public's approval declined from 63 to 46 percent. Some European allies, including Italy and Poland as well as most of our Asian allies, showed little or no decline in approval. The Canadian approval level plummeted more than 20 points, declining from 65 to 43 percent. Given President Trump's plan to build a wall, it should not be surprising that approval of the United States declined dramatically in Mexico. In the Middle East, the view continued to be negative with the exception of Israel, where more than 80 percent of the public saw the United States favorably. Elsewhere in the region, America's image is largely negative (e.g., in Jordan, Palestine and the Palestinian-occupied territories, Turkey, and Lebanon).

Arab and Muslim Opinion toward America and Its Ideals

Among the majority of Middle Eastern states, approval of the United States is especially low among Muslims. This is true in such states as Egypt, Jordan, Pakistan, and Malaysia. However, divisions exist even among Muslims based on religious views. Sunni Muslims in Lebanon are

(Continued)

much more favorably inclined toward the United States than are their Shia country-men and women. Many Muslim nations and their peoples were opposed to the U.S. action in Iraq and continued aggressive stance toward Iran. Although those nations may not support the current regimes, they are more worried that the United States has destabilized the region, and they continue to see the United States as too supportive of the state of Israel. It is worth noting, however, that most Muslim states in Africa have favorable opinions of the United States.*

Many Arabs and Muslims resent U.S. interventionism in the Middle East. They do not, however, reject all aspects of the United States or its ideals. The majority of Muslims do not support religious extremism or terrorism in their own nations. Nor are Arabs and Muslims dismissive of democracy. There has also been broad support for democracy in the Middle East. Many individuals believe that democracy is a real possibility in their own country. However, many are still suspicious of American motives in the region.

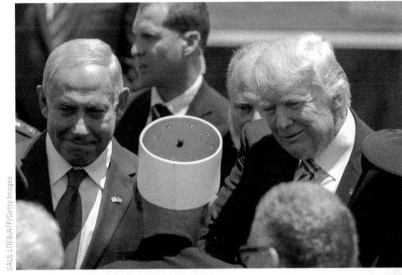

SAUL LOEB/AFP/Getty Images

Image 6-2 Israeli Prime Minister Benjamin Netanyahu and President Trump greet officials at the airport in Tel Aviv, Israel, in June, 2017.

People with a college education hold more favorable views toward America than those without a college degree—a double-digit gap in China, Russia, Pakistan, Venezuela, and Tunisia.

Support for United States Against ISIS

There is extensive support for the U.S. military campaign against ISIS. A median of 62 percent across the 40 nations polled say they support American military efforts against the terrorist militant group in Iraq and Syria, whereas a median of just 24 percent is opposed. This includes support within the Middle East. More than 75 percent of people in Jordan and Lebanon, both of which share a border with Syria, support American military actions.

Young People View United States Most Positively

In many of the nations surveyed by the Global Attitudes Project, people under age 30 are especially likely to have a positive view of America. For example, 59 percent of 18- to 29-year-olds in China have a positive opinion about the United States compared with just 29 percent of those ages 50 and older. Similarly large age gaps are found in Vietnam, Brazil, Mexico, Poland, Ukraine, and Venezuela.

For Critical Analysis

1. Should the U.S. government keep world opinion in mind when making decisions? Why or why not?

2. Some polls have shown that younger Muslims and Arabs have a more positive opinion about the United States. Why might that be the case?

3. World opinion of the United States turned more negative following the U.S. election of President Donald Trump. Why do you think foreign publics reacted to him so negatively? How would a citizen in another country learn about the president and his policies?

* The Pew Global Attitudes Project, 2017 Survey, www.pew.org.

Political Change and Political Socialization The political system is relatively stable in the United States. But what influences might the upheavals and revolutions around the world in recent years have on the political socialization of young people experiencing and witnessing those dramatic changes?[8] How will people who have learned to live under an oppressive regime such as that of Muammar Gaddafi in Libya develop and learn to live in a new regime? The 2014 presidential and provincial council elections in Afghanistan represented only the second time in the nation's history that power has changed hands through popular election. "On behalf of the American people, I congratulate the millions of Afghans who enthusiastically participated in today's historic elections, which promise to usher in the first democratic transfer of power in Afghanistan's history and which represent another important milestone in Afghans taking full responsibility for their country," President Obama declared.[9] The Syrian civil war has presented the world with a tremendous humanitarian challenge. An estimated 4.7 million Syrian refugees have fled to neighboring countries (e.g., Lebanon, Jordan, and Iraq) and another 1 million have applied for asylum in Europe. Within Syria, 6.6 million people remain displaced from their homes and communities by violence. Americans are sometimes puzzled by the slow pace of democratization once a dictator has been removed, but try to imagine the difficulty of building civil society and creating new day-to-day political norms and practices when politics has always meant capriciousness and brutality. New regimes must help people establish important political dispositions such as trust and political efficacy (the belief that your engagement will yield results)—a difficult task when the agents of socialization (education, media, religion) are associated with the old regime. The United Nations Children's Fund estimates that some Syrian children have missed out on as much as two years of education in the midst of their country's ongoing civil struggle.

The Impact of the Media

■ **6.3** Describe three forms of social media and explain how social media can shape political decisions or events.

media
Channels of mass communication.

agenda setting
Determining which public policy questions will be debated or considered.

Clearly, the **media**—newspapers, television, radio, and the Internet—strongly influence public opinion. The media inform the public about the issues and events of our times and thus have an **agenda-setting** effect. To borrow from Bernard Cohen's classic statement about the media and public opinion, the media may not be successful in telling people what to think, but they are "stunningly successful in telling their audience what to think about."[10] During the primary season, the cable news and late-night comedians provided Republican primary candidate Donald Trump with unprecedented media attention. Trump was the subject of late-night jokes three times more than any other candidate. Between the start of his campaign for the Republican nomination (June 16, 2015) and March 2016, Donald Trump earned $1.9 billion in media coverage. Earned media is defined as news and commentary about his campaign on television, in newspapers and magazines, and on social media.

8 Virginia Sapiro, "Not Your Parents' Political Socialization: Introduction for a New Generation," *Annual Review of Political Science* (2004) 7: 1–23.

9 "Obama Hails Afghan Election as Milestone Toward Democracy," FOXNews, April 5, 2014. http://www.foxnews.com/politics/2014/04/05/obama-hails-afghan-elections-as-milestone-toward-democracy/

10 Bernard C. Cohen, *The Press and Foreign Policy* (Princeton, NJ: Princeton University Press, 1963), p. 81.

Trump's earned media was more than twice that of Clinton's and more than that of his 14 Republican rivals combined.[11]

The media also provide a political forum for leaders and the public. Candidates for office use news reporting to sustain interest in their campaigns, and officeholders use the media to gain support for policies or to present an image of leadership. Presidential trips abroad are an outstanding way for the chief executive to get positive and exciting news coverage that makes the president look "presidential." The media also offer ways for citizens to participate in public debate, be it through letters to the editor, televised editorials, or social media. Americans may cherish the idea of an unbiased press, but in the early years of the nation's history, the number of politically sponsored newspapers was significant. The sole reason for the existence of such periodicals was to further the interests of the politicians who paid for their publication. As chief executive of our government during this period, George Washington has been called a "firm believer" in **managed news**. Although acknowledging that the public had a right to be informed, he believed that some matters should be kept secret and that news that might damage the image of the United States should be censored (not published). China announced that it will train and certify "online public opinion management specialists." These specialists, China argues, will be better equipped to meet the challenges of controlling information amid "mass incidents."[12] The Chinese government issued new rules requiring Internet users to provide their real names to service providers while assigning Internet companies greater responsibility for deleting forbidden postings and reporting them to the authorities.

Today, many contend that the media's influence on public opinion has grown to equal that of the family. In her analysis of the role played by the media in American politics, media scholar Doris A. Graber points out that high school students, when asked where they obtain the information on which they base their attitudes, mention the mass media far more than they mention their families, friends, and teachers.[13] Social media platforms give competing candidates and voters immediate access to candidate messaging. Candidates know that each social network attracts a slightly different demographic of potential voters. For example, Instagram has become the most important and most used social network for U.S. teens; 32 percent cite it as their most important social network. For young people between the ages of 18 and 24, Snapchat leads, followed by Vine and Tumblr.[14] The challenge for political parties and candidates is to harness the energy of social media to engage young people in politics. In a Pew Research study, about 35 percent of young people (18 to 24) named a social networking site as their most helpful source for learning about the 2016 presidential election. Overall, based on the Pew study, cable news was the most prevalent source of news about the presidential election.[15]

managed news
Information generated and distributed by the government in such a way as to give government interests priority over candor.

did you know?
The average American spends 5.11 hours a day watching television; that adds up to 9 years over a lifetime.

11 Nicholas Confessore and Karen Yourish, "Measuring Donald Trump's Mammoth Advantage in Free Media," *The New York Times*, March 15, 2016. http://nyti.ms/22ir8te

12 Jonathan Kaiman, "China to Train Leaders to Manage Online Public Opinion." *The Guardian*, March 10, 2014. http://www.theguardian.com/world/2014/mar/10/china-online-opinion-training-programme-sina-weibo

13 See Doris A. Graber, *Mass Media and American Politics*, 7th ed. (Chicago: University of Chicago Press, 2005).

14 Mark Hoelzel, "A Breakdown of the Demographics for Each of the Different Social Networks." *Business Insider*, June 29, 2015. http://www.businessinsider.com/update-a-breakdown-of-the-demographics-for-each-of-the-different-social-networks-2015-6

15 Jeffrey Gottfried et al., "The 2016 Presidential Campaign: A News Event That's Hard to Miss." Pew Research Center, February 4, 2016. http://www.journalism.org/2016/02/04/the-2016-presidential-campaign-a-news-event-thats-hard-to-miss/

Of registered voters who own a cell phone, roughly half used a smart device as a tool for political participation on social networking sites and as a way to fact-check campaign statements in real time. Over 70 percent of Americans have a broadband connection at home, providing high-speed access to the Internet. In 2000, even though about half of all adults reported being online at home, only 3 percent of American households had broadband access.[16] Eighty percent of adults have either broadband access at home or a smartphone today.[17] These trends, combined with the increasing popularity of cable satires such as *The Daily Show*, talk radio, blogs, social networking sites, and the Internet as information sources, may significantly alter the nature of the media's influence on public opinion. A significant difference between this form of media influence and that of the past is that today people are actively creating content through social media rather than simply consuming information produced by others.

The Influence of Political Events

life cycle effect
The concept that people change as they grow older because of age-specific experiences and thus are likely to hold age-specific attitudes.

Older Americans tend to be somewhat more conservative than younger Americans, particularly on social issues and, to some extent, on economic issues. This is known as the **life cycle effect**. People change as they grow older as a result of age-specific experiences like employment, marriage, children, and other responsibilities. Likewise, as new generations of citizens are socialized within a particular social, economic, and political context, individual members' more specific opinions and actions are affected. In other words, political events and environmental conditions have the power to shape the political attitudes of an entire generation. Perhaps you recall what you were doing and where you were on the night the country elected the first African American president or the December 2015 ISIS terrorist attacks in Paris. Although you and your parents witnessed these events, the ways that they have influenced your attitudes about increased airport security measures or progress on civil rights might differ. When events produce such a long-lasting result, we refer to it as a **generational effect** (or *cohort effect*).[18]

generational effect
A long-lasting effect of the events of a particular time on the political opinions of those who came of political age at that time.

Voters who grew up in the 1930s during the Great Depression were likely to form lifelong attachments to the Democratic Party, the party of Franklin D. Roosevelt. In the 1960s and 1970s, the war in Vietnam and the Watergate scandal and subsequent presidential cover-up fostered widespread cynicism toward government. Evidence indicates that the years of economic prosperity under President Reagan during the 1980s led many young people to identify with the Republican Party. More recently, the increase in non–party-affiliated Independents may mean that although young people heavily supported Democrat Barack Obama over Republican John McCain in the 2008 election, Democrats should not count on a lifelong attachment. After a strong showing in the 2008 presidential contest, young voters were largely absent in the 2010 midterm elections, with those under 30 indicating less interest (31 percent compared with 53 percent) and little likelihood of voting (45 percent compared with 76 percent) compared with those over 30 years of age.[19]

---

16 Pew Research Internet Project, "Broadband Technology Fact Sheet." September 2013. http://www.pewinternet.org/fact-sheets/broadband-technology-fact-sheet/

17 John B. Horrigan and Maeve Duggan, "Home Broadband 2015." Pew Research Center, December 21, 2015. http://www.pewinternet.org/2015/12/21/home-broadband-2015/

18 Cliff Zukin, Scott Keeter, Molly Andolina, Krista Jenkins, and Michael X. Delli Carpini, *A New Engagement? Political Participation, Civic Life, and the Changing American Citizen* (New York: Oxford University Press, 2006).

19 "Lagging Youth Enthusiasm Could Hurt Democrats in 2010," Pew Research Center for the People and the Press, October 7, 2010.

Young people returned to the polls in the 2012 election, however, in numbers nearly identical to 2008. The majority of votes went to President Obama, although he pulled a lower share of the youth vote in 2012 than in 2008 (60 percent compared with 68 percent). Researchers characterize this as the "new normal" and expect the positive turnout trend to continue in future elections as young people begin to identify voting as an expression of power. In the 2016 presidential primaries, young people overwhelmingly supported Democrat Bernie Sanders. A data snapshot of young voters in April 2016 (midway through the primaries) found that Bernie Sanders had captured 1.5 million votes from people under 30, well ahead of Hillary Clinton and Donald Trump (1.2 million combined).[20] Pundits labeled these young voters the "gloom and doom" generation: "They grew up in the recession, watched their parents struggle and became anxious about their futures. They are graduating from college with huge debts and gnawing uncertainty about landing jobs and affording homes. They have little faith in government and other institutions they thought they could depend on."[21] Young voters supported Hillary Clinton over Donald Trump by 55 percent to 37 percent, but 8 percent selected a third-party option or voted only in the down-ballot races.

Political Preferences and Voting Behavior

Various socioeconomic and demographic factors appear to influence political preferences. These factors include education, income and **socioeconomic status**, religion, race, gender, geographic region, and similar traits. People who share the same religion, occupation, or any other demographic trait are likely to influence one another and may also have common political concerns that follow from the common characteristic. Other factors, such as party identification, perception of the candidates, and issue preferences, are closely connected to the electoral process.

socioeconomic status
The value assigned to a person due to occupation or income. An upper-class person, for example, has high socioeconomic status.

Demographic Influences

Demographic influences reflect the individual's personal background and place in society. Some factors have to do with the family into which a person was born: race and (for most people) religion. Others may be the result of choices made throughout an individual's life: place of residence, educational achievement, and occupation.

Many of these factors are interrelated. People who have more education are likely to have higher incomes and to hold professional jobs. Similarly, children born into wealthier families are far more likely to complete college than children from poor families. Many other interrelationships are not so immediately obvious; many people might not know that 88 percent of African Americans report that religion is very important in their lives, compared with only 57 percent of whites.[22]

20 Center for Information and Research on Civic Learning and Engagement (CIRCLE), "Estimated Total Youth Votes in Primaries and Caucuses, by Candidate." http://civicyouth.org/total-youth-votes-in-2016-primaries-and-caucuses/

21 John Wagner, "Why Millennials Love Bernie Sanders, and Why That May Not Be Enough," *Washington Post*, October 27, 2015. https://www.washingtonpost.com/politics/in-bernie-sanders-anxious-millennials-find-a-candidate-who-speaks-to-them/2015/10/27/923d0b74-66cc-11e5-9223-70cb36460919_story.html

22 "A Look at Americans and Religion Today," The Gallup Poll, March 23, 2004.

Election 2016

How Did the Polls Get it Wrong?

The results of the 2016 presidential election surprised nearly everyone, since polls consistently predicted that Hillary Clinton would defeat Donald Trump. Forecasters placed the odds of her winning at between 70 and 99 percent. Polls dramatically underestimated Trump's support among voters. What happened?

One likely explanation is nonresponse bias—when certain kinds of people systematically do not respond to surveys despite a pollster's best efforts to reach all parts of the electorate. Less educated voters are typically one of these groups. Combined with the anger and hostility toward "the establishment," including media polling, Trump supporters in general may have refused to respond to polls.

Another hypothesis has to do with socially acceptable response bias. Donald Trump was a highly controversial candidate who seemed to delight in defying conventional political rules by insulting Gold Star families, women, Muslims, Hispanics, and people with disabilities. Some voters may not have wanted anyone to know that they intended to vote for Trump.

Finally, it may be that pollsters themselves had a bias when it came to identifying likely voters. Forecasting elections involves knowing who has reliably voted in the past, but also getting right the new first-time voters. Rust Belt voters in Michigan and Wisconsin turned out in numbers much higher than expected, while a surge of new Hispanic voters in several states failed to materialize. The American Association for Public Opinion Research convened an *ad hoc* committee to study this election.

For Critical Analysis

1. Polling is often viewed as predicting the horse race, but polling also gives voice to the public in ways that elections cannot. What might pollsters do in future elections to encourage people to participate in surveys?

2. Will the failure of polls to accurately predict the outcome of the election make it more or less likely that people will trust survey results in the future?

Education   In the past, having a college education was associated with voting for Republicans. In recent years, however, this correlation has become weaker. In particular, individuals with a postgraduate education (professors, doctors, lawyers, managers) have become increasingly Democratic. Also, a higher percentage of voters with only a high school education, who were likely to be blue-collar workers, voted Republican in 2000 and 2004, compared with the pattern in many previous elections, in which that group of voters tended to favor Democrats. During the 2016 primaries, Republican Donald Trump attracted a majority of his support from white males without a college degree making less than $50,000 a year. Trump attracted 67 percent of the white, non–college educated vote in the general election. Secretary Clinton fared best among those with a college degree and those with post-graduate education. By contrast, voters with a college degree slightly favored Republican Mitt Romney over President Obama (51 percent to 47 percent) in 2012. People with a high school education or less and those with post-graduate or professional degrees favored Obama by much larger margins.

The Influence of Economic Status   Family income is a strong predictor of economic liberalism or conservatism. Those with low incomes tend to favor government action to benefit the poor or to promote economic equality. Historically, voters in union households have voted for the Democratic candidate. Those with high incomes tend to oppose government intervention in the economy or support it only when it benefits business. On economic issues, therefore, the traditional economic spectrum described in Chapter 1 is a useful tool. The rich trend toward the right; the poor trend toward the left.

There are no hard-and-fast rules, however. Some very poor individuals are devoted Republicans, just as some extremely wealthy people support the Democratic Party. Indeed, research indicates that a realignment is occurring among those of higher economic status: professionals now tend to vote Democratic, whereas small-business owners, managers, and corporate executives tend to vote Republican.[23]

The combination of the prolonged economic recession and involvement in multiple conflicts overseas has reshaped the political typology, according to research by the Pew Research Center.[24] The public's political mood is "fractious" and more unpredictable. Pew's typology divides Republicans into "Staunch Republicans" who are conservative on both economic and social issues and "Main Street Republicans"—also conservative, but less so. On the left, Pew identifies "Solid Liberals," predominantly white, who are diametrically opposed to Staunch Republicans on nearly every issue. "New Coalition Democrats" are made up of nearly equal numbers of whites, African Americans, and Hispanics, and "Hard-Pressed Democrats" are highly religious and more socially conservative than Solid Liberals. In the center of the new political typology are the Independents, divided into three categories with little to no overlap: "Libertarians", "Post-Moderns", and "Disaffecteds". The first two are largely white, well educated, and affluent. Those in the Disaffected group are financially stressed and cynical about politics. Groups on the right side of the spectrum prefer elected officials who stick to their positions rather than those who compromise, whereas Solid Liberals overwhelmingly prefer officials who compromise. In short, the political landscape is dynamic and makes establishing electoral coalitions based on partisanship and economic status nearly impossible today.

The 2012 campaign themes emphasized the struggling economy and job creation. Republicans believed they could win votes from Independents who had been negatively affected by the long recession. Even though 45 percent of voters labeled the state of the national economy as "not so good" in exit polls, President Obama won 55 percent of those votes. The president did even better among the 39 percent of the electorate who believed the economy was getting better (88 percent compared to 9 percent for Governor Romney). Although the economy was important to voters, their ultimate decision was based on a far more complex array of issues and factors.

By 2016, voters in both parties remained interested in the economy and jobs, as well as terrorism and national security. Republican candidates focused more on immigration concerns, the federal budget deficit, and the size and efficiency of government. Democrats were specifically interested in the distribution of income and wealth in the United States and on the quality of education. Neither party focused voter attention on climate change and, unlike previous elections, social issues like gay marriage and abortion were not central to debates in either party.

---

23 Thomas B. Edsall, "Voters Thinking Less with Their Wallets," *International Herald Tribune*, March 27, 2001, p. 3.

24 Andrew Kohut, "Beyond Red vs. Blue Political Typology," Pew Research Center for the People and the Press, May 4, 2011.

Religious Influence: Denomination Scholars have examined the impact of religion on political attitudes by dividing the population into such categories as Protestant, Catholic, and Jewish. In recent decades, however, such a breakdown has become less valuable as a means of predicting someone's political preferences. It is true that in the past Jewish voters were notably more liberal than members of other groups on both economic and cultural issues, and they continue to be more liberal today. Persons reporting no religion are likely to be liberal on social issues but have mixed economic views. Northern Protestants and Catholics do not differ that greatly from each other, and neither do Southern Protestants and Catholics. This represents somewhat of a change—in the late 1800s and early 1900s, Northern Protestants were distinctly more likely to vote Republican, and Northern Catholics were more likely to vote Democratic.[25] Between 2004 and 2008, nearly all religious groups moved toward the Democratic candidate Barack Obama, with the largest shifts occurring among Catholics (+7 percentage points) and those unaffiliated with any religion (+8 percentage points).[26] Support among Catholics remained strong even in the face of controversy over contraception coverage and insurer mandates for coverage. By 2016, Catholics and Protestants returned to the Republican Party and supported Donald Trump. Hillary Clinton enjoyed support from Jewish and Muslim voters and those who do not identify with a religion.

Religious Influence: Religiosity and Evangelicals Nevertheless, two factors do turn out to be major predictors of political attitudes among members of the various Christian denominations. One is the degree of *religiosity*, or intensity in practice of beliefs, and the other is whether the person holds fundamentalist or evangelical views. A high degree of religiosity is usually manifested by frequent attendance at church services.

Voters who are more devout, regardless of their church affiliation, tend to vote Republican. In 2008, people who regularly attended church, regardless of denomination, were more likely to support John McCain than Barack Obama (55 percent to 43 percent) compared with those who attended church less often (57 percent voted for Obama, whereas 42 percent voted for McCain). The exception to this trend is that African Americans of all religious backgrounds have been and continue to be strongly supportive of Democrats.

Another distinctive group of voters likely to be very religious are those Americans who hold fundamentalist beliefs or consider themselves part of an evangelical group. They are usually members of a Protestant church, which may be part of a mainstream denomination or may be independent. As voters, these Christians tend to be cultural conservatives but not necessarily economic conservatives. Donald Trump received 81 percent of the white evangelical vote, a share larger than Bush, McCain, or Romney received in previous elections even though questions about Trump's character were pervasive throughout the campaign.

The Influence of Race and Ethnicity Although African Americans are, on average, somewhat conservative on certain cultural issues such as same-sex marriage and abortion, they tend to be more liberal than whites on social welfare matters, civil liberties, and even foreign policy. African Americans

25 John C. Green, *The Faith Factor: How Religion Influences American Elections* (New York: Praeger, 2007).
26 "How the Faithful Voted," The Pew Forum on Religion and Public Life, November 5, 2008.

voted principally for Republicans (the party of Lincoln) until Democrat Franklin Roosevelt's New Deal in the 1930s. Since then, they have strongly supported the Democratic Party. Indeed, Democratic presidential candidates have received, on average, more than 80 percent of the African American vote since 1956. President Obama won 93 percent of the African American vote in 2012, but Hillary Clinton won a smaller share (88 percent) in 2016. Latinos also favor the Democrats. Most Asian American groups lean toward the Democrats, although often by narrow margins. Muslim American immigrants and their descendants are an interesting category.[27] In 2000, a majority of Muslim Americans of Middle Eastern ancestry voted for Republican George W. Bush because they shared his cultural conservatism. In the 2004 and 2008 election campaigns, however, the civil liberties issue propelled many of these voters toward the Democrats.[28] In 2012, the emergence of the Latino vote was the big story. Making up 10 percent of the national electorate, Latino voters overwhelmingly supported Barack Obama (71 percent). Given Donald Trump's divisive rhetoric on illegal immigrants from Mexico, his call for increased deportations, and his promise to build a wall between Mexico and the United States, pundits expected Clinton to receive an overwhelming share of Latino votes. However her 65 percent support was less than Obama's in 2012. Within the Latino electorate, Millennial voters make up the greatest share of eligible voters (44 percent). Between 2012 and 2016, about 3.2 million young Latinos born in the United States turned 18 and became eligible to vote, according to the Pew Research Center. The second-largest source of growth for the Hispanic electorate is adult Hispanic immigrants who decided to become naturalized U.S. citizens.

The Gender Gap Until the 1980s, there was little evidence that men's and women's political attitudes were very different. Following the election of Ronald Reagan in 1980, however, scholars began to detect a **gender gap**. The gender gap has reappeared in subsequent presidential elections, with women being more likely than men to support the Democratic candidate (see Figure 6-4). In 2014, according to the exit polls, men favored Republicans by a 16-point margin (57 percent voted Republican, 41 percent for Democrats), whereas women voted for Democrats by a 4-point margin (51 percent to 47 percent). The first woman presidential candidate attracted only 54 percent of women's votes, with 42 percent of women voting for Trump. Among men, Clinton earned 41 percent to Trump's 53 percent, making the gender gap in 2016 only 12 points. Pundits had predicted a much larger gap given Trump's misogynist statements and the release of a tape on which Trump can be heard boasting about groping women.

Women also appear to hold different attitudes from their male counterparts on a range of issues other than presidential preferences. They are much more likely than men to oppose capital punishment and the use of force abroad. Studies also have shown that women are more concerned about risks to the environment, are more supportive of social welfare, and are more amenable to extending civil rights to gays and lesbians than are men. The contemporary gender gap ranges from about 7 to 12 percent. Obama won about the same

did you know?
Great Britain had a major gender gap for much of the twentieth century—in that women were much more likely than men to support the Conservative Party rather than the more left-wing Labour Party.

gender gap
The difference between the percentage of women who vote for a particular candidate and the percentage of men who vote for the candidate.

27 At least one-third of U.S. Muslims are actually African Americans whose ancestors have been in this country for a long time. In terms of political preferences, African American Muslims are more likely to resemble other African Americans than Muslim immigrants from the Middle East.
28 For up-to-date information on Muslim American issues, see the website of the Council on American-Islamic Relations at www.cair.com.

Figure 6-4 ▶ Gender Gap in Presidential Elections, 1980–2016

The gender gap is defined as the difference in the proportions of women and men voting for the winning candidate. In 2016, the size of the gender gap was expected to be historic, but in reality it was a fairly typical 12 points.

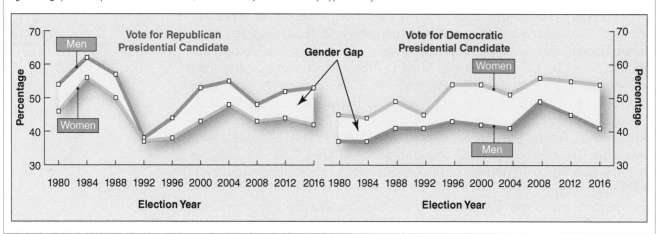

proportion of women voters in 2012 as he did in 2008 (55 percent versus 54 percent), but Governor Romney fared much better among men in 2012 (52 percent) than did Senator McCain in 2008 (48 percent). Because more women are registered to vote and more women vote than men, as a result of the gender gap, female voters can reasonably claim to have delivered victories in many electoral contests. Women did not deliver the 2016 contest for Hillary Clinton as many had predicted.

Reasons for the Gender Gap What is the cause of the gender gap? A number of explanations have been offered, including the increase in the number of working women, feminism, women's concerns over abortion rights and other social issues, and the changing political attitudes of men. Researchers Lena Edlund and Rohini Pande of Columbia University, however, have identified another factor leading to the gender gap—the disparate economic impact on men and women of not being married. In the last three decades, men and women have tended to marry later in life or stay single even after having children. The divorce rate has also risen dramatically. Edlund and Pande argue that, particularly for those in the middle class, this decline in marriage has tended to make men richer and women relatively poorer. Consequently, support for Democrats is higher among single or divorced women.[29]

In 2004, observers noted that women seemed more concerned about homeland security and terrorism than men, so much so that the media coined a new term: *security moms*. The label's origins have been traced to a poll reporting that although only 17 percent of men were personally concerned that a member of their family would be the victim of a terrorist attack, 43 percent of women and 53 percent of mothers with children under 18 expressed the same concern. Further analysis, however, found that although the Democratic candidate, John Kerry, was underperforming among female voters relative to past Democrats, "security moms" did not account for George W. Bush's victory. Researchers Laurel Elder and Steven Greene found

---

29 Lena Edlund and Rohini Pande, "Why Have Women Become Left-Wing? The Political Gender Gap and the Decline in Marriage," *The Quarterly Journal of Economics* (August 2002) 117 (3): 917–961.

that parenthood does not move men or women in a more conservative direction.[30] These studies suggest that labels applied to groups of voters based on demographic characteristics may not always be accurate explanations of voting behavior or political attitudes.

During the Republican presidential primaries in 2012, several issues and candidate statements became known as the "GOP War on Women." Moves to adopt increasingly severe restrictions on abortion services in several Republican-controlled states, initiatives to limit contraception insurance coverage and access, congressional budget cuts to women's health programs, and proposals to weaken the Violence Against Women Act drew lots of media attention. Sandra Fluke, then a Georgetown University law school student, was barred from testifying at a Republican congressional hearing on the Obama administration's policy requiring religiously affiliated institutions to provide free contraception in student health insurance plans. When she appeared before a House Democratic panel and testified to the difficulties female students have when reproductive services are curtailed, conservative talk-radio host Rush Limbaugh accused her of "having so much sex she can't afford the contraception," and called her a slut. Many advertisers immediately dropped his radio show, but he stayed on the air. Senate contests in Indiana and Missouri that had looked like certain wins for Republicans turned into Democratic victories over remarks about pregnancy resulting from rape. Missouri Rep. Todd Aiken claimed that "if it's a legitimate rape, the female body has ways to shut that whole thing down." In a late October debate, Republican candidate Richard Mourdock said that if a woman becomes pregnant from rape it is "something God intended to happen." Although the Romney campaign disavowed both comments, the damage compounded the Republican's image with women voters.

Although nationwide Republican candidates avoided major gender gaffes in the 2016 primaries, candidate Donald Trump reignited the "war on women" with innuendo attacks against party rival Ted Cruz's wife Heidi on Twitter, a Twitter tirade against Fox News's Megyn Kelly after she asked about his history of sexism in an early Republican party primary debate, and attacks on the appearance of female candidate Carly Fiorina. Polling in April 2016 found that Trump was viewed unfavorably by 70 percent of women overall and by 46 percent of Republican women, leaving him with the largest favorability gender gap of any candidate in the race.[31]

Geographic Region Finally, where you live can influence your political attitudes. In one way, regional differences are less important today than just a few decades ago. The formerly solid (Democratic) South has steadily moved toward the Republican Party in national elections. Only 43 percent of the votes from the Southern states went to Democrat Al Gore in 2000, whereas 55 percent went to Republican George W. Bush. Research by a number of scholars suggests there are regional influences, but people also choose to "sort" themselves in neighborhoods of politically like-minded individuals. The "Big Sort," first proposed by Bill Bishop with Robert G. Cushing, finds that polarization between Republicans and Democrats is increasing within regions, states, and counties. Regionally, the coastal regions are becoming more Democratic while the Midwest, Southeast,

---

30 Laurel Elder and Steven Greene, "The Myth of 'Security Moms' and 'NASCAR Dads': Parenthood, Political Stereotypes, and the 2004 Election," *Social Science Quarterly* (March 2007) 88 (1): 1–19.

31 Frank Newport and Lydia Saad, "Seven in Ten Women have Unfavorable Opinion of Trump," Gallup Election 2016, April 1, 2016. http://www.gallup.com/poll/190403/seven-women-unfavorable-opinion-trump.aspx

Figure 6-5 ▶ The Purple Election Map

We have grown used to seeing the national vote portrayed using the electoral college map (see, for example, Figure 8-2 on page 289). Because the states are colored red or blue depending on which party's candidate receives the majority of votes, it appears as if all voters in the state are either Republicans (red) or Democrats (blue). Of course, we know that this is not true. Republican and Democratic voters are in every state, and states are broken down into smaller counties, where the diversity is even more apparent. One way to reveal more accurately the nuance in the vote is to use red, blue, and shades of purple to indicate percentages of votes that each party's candidate receives at the county level. In this way, the diversity of political affiliation within states is more visible. Areas that appear purple represent more balance between Republicans and Democrats.

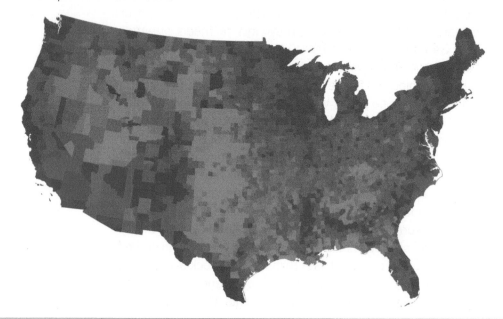

and Southwestern regions are becoming more Republican.[32] Because so much variability exists in political attitudes and partisan affiliation within a single state, a map constructed at the county level looks purple rather than distinctly red (representing Republicans) or blue (representing Democrats) (see Figure 6-5).

Measuring Public Opinion

■ **6.5** Identify three factors that might distort public opinion results collected through opinion polling.

In a democracy, people express their opinions in a variety of ways. One of the most common means of gathering and measuring public opinion on specific issues is, of course, through the use of **opinion polls**.

The History of Opinion Polls

During the 1800s, certain American newspapers and magazines spiced up their political coverage by doing face-to-face straw polls (unofficial polls indicating the trend of political opinion) or mail surveys of their readers' opinions. In the early twentieth century, the magazine *Literary Digest* further developed the technique of opinion polling by mailing large numbers of questionnaires to individuals, many of whom were subscribers, to determine their political opinions. From 1916 to 1936, more than 70 percent of the magazine's election predictions were accurate.

opinion poll
A method of systematically questioning a small, selected sample of respondents who are deemed representative of the total population.

---

32 Bill Bishop with Robert G. Cushing, *The Big Sort: Why the Clustering of Like-Minded Americans is Tearing Us Apart.* (Boston: Houghton Mifflin, 2008).

Literary Digest's polling activities suffered a setback in 1936, however, when the magazine predicted, on the basis of more than 2 million returned questionnaires, that Republican candidate Alfred Landon would win over Democratic candidate Franklin D. Roosevelt. Landon won in only two states. A major problem with the *Digest*'s polling technique was its use of nonrepresentative respondents. In 1936, at possibly the worst point of the Great Depression, the magazine's subscribers were considerably more affluent than the average American. In other words, they did not accurately represent all of the voters in the U.S. population.

Several newcomers to the public opinion poll industry accurately predicted Roosevelt's landslide victory. The Gallup poll founded by George Gallup and the Roper poll founded by Elmo Roper are still active today. Gallup and Roper, along with Archibald Crossley, developed the modern polling techniques of market research. Using personal interviews with small samples of selected voters (fewer than 2,000), they showed that they could predict with accuracy the behavior of the total voting population.

By the 1950s, improved methods of sampling and a new science of survey research had been developed. Survey research centers sprang up throughout the United States, particularly at universities. Some of these survey groups are the American Institute of Public Opinion at Princeton in New Jersey, the National Opinion Research Center at the University of Chicago, and the Survey Research Center at the University of Michigan.

Sampling Techniques

How can interviewing fewer than 2,000 voters tell us what tens of millions of voters will do? Clearly, it is necessary that the sample of individuals be representative of all voters in the population. Consider an analogy: let's say we have a large jar containing 10,000 pennies of various dates, and we want to know how many pennies were minted within certain decades (1960–1969, 1970–1979, and so on).

Representative Sampling One way to estimate the distribution of the dates on the pennies—without examining all 10,000—is to take a representative sample. This sample would be obtained by mixing the pennies up well and then removing a handful of them—perhaps 100 pennies. The distribution of dates might be as follows:

1960–1969: 5 percent
1970–1979: 5 percent
1980–1989: 20 percent
1990–1999: 30 percent
2000–present: 40 percent

If the pennies are very well mixed within the jar, and if you take a large enough sample, the resulting distribution will probably approach the actual distribution of the dates of all 10,000 coins.

The Principle of Randomness The most important principle in sampling, or poll taking, is randomness. Every penny or every person should have a known chance, and especially an *equal chance*, of being sampled. If this happens, then a small sample should be representative of the whole group, both in demographic characteristics (age, religion, race, region, and the like) and in opinions.

The ideal way to sample the voting population of the United States would be to put all voter names into a jar—or a computer—and randomly sample, say, 2,000 of them. Because this is too costly and inefficient, pollsters have developed other ways to obtain good samples. One technique has been simply to choose a random selection of telephone numbers and interview the respective households. Prior to expanded cell phone use, this technique produced a relatively accurate sample at a low cost. In 2014, however, the proportion of people living in households without a landline grew to two in five (43 percent) with another 17 percent mostly using cell phones.[33] Although you might hypothesize that the highest number of cell-only households would be found in large cities, it is actually the opposite. The prevalence of cell-only households is highest in Idaho (52.3 percent) and lowest in New Jersey (19.4 percent). For certain subgroups within the population the proportions are even higher; 60 percent of Latinos are cell-only, as are 54 percent of adults ages 18 to 24 and 66 percent of adults between the ages of 25 and 29. The percentage of households with only a landline continues to decrease but is estimated at about 8 percent. Only 2 percent of the U.S. population cannot be reached by a phone of any kind.

These rapid changes in use of phone technology increase the risk for "coverage error"; that is, the bias introduced when some portion of the population is not covered by the sample. If those missed in the sample differ substantially from those covered, the bias can lead to errors in reporting the results (similar to the *Literary Digest* example). Whereas research in 2006 found that the likelihood of coverage bias in landline phone surveys was very small, a more recent study released by the Pew Research Center indicates that the size of the bias effect is increasing, as well as the likelihood of substantive consequences for social and political research reports.[34] Researchers continue to examine these issues as they develop new techniques such as address-based sampling frames to ensure that every person has a known and equal chance at being sampled. Yet, a majority of households now use either caller ID or some other form of call screening. This has greatly reduced the number of households that polling organizations can reach. Calls may be automatically rejected, or the respondent may not take the call. Even when reached, researchers face additional challenges because fewer adults agree to be interviewed. According to the Pew Research Center, the percentage of households in a sample that are successfully interviewed has fallen dramatically.[35]

To ensure that the random samples include respondents from relevant segments of the population—rural, urban, northeastern, southern, and so on—most survey organizations randomly choose, say, urban areas that they will consider as representative of all urban areas. Then they randomly select their respondents within those areas. A generally less accurate technique is known as *quota sampling*. Here, survey researchers decide how many persons of certain types they need in the survey—such as minorities, women, or farmers—and then send out interviewers to find the necessary number of these types. Not only is this method often less accurate, but it also may be biased if, say, the interviewer refuses to go into certain neighborhoods or will not interview after dark.

---

33 Cliff Zukin, "What's the Matter with Polling?" *The New York Times*, June 20, 2015. http://nyti.ms/1GyPSmU

34 "Assessing the Cell Phone Challenge to Survey Research in 2010," Pew Research Center for the People and the Press, May 20, 2010.

35 "Assessing the Representativeness of Public Opinion Surveys." Pew Research Center for the People and the Press, May 15, 2012. http://www.people-press.org/2012/05/15/assessing-the-representativeness-of-public-opinion-surveys

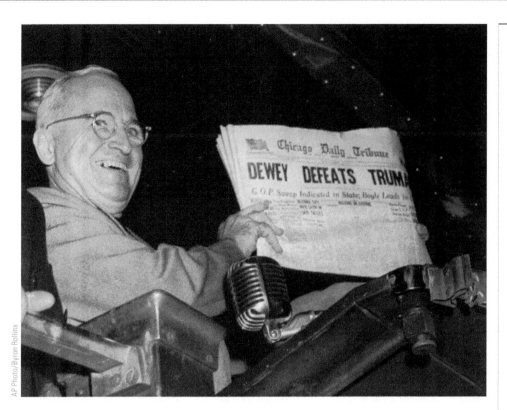

Image 6-3
President Harry Truman holds up the front page of the *Chicago Daily Tribune* issue that predicted his defeat on the basis of a Gallup poll. The poll had indicated that Truman would lose the 1948 contest for his reelection by a margin of 55.5 to 44.5 percent. The Gallup poll was completed more than a week before the election, so it missed a shift by undecided voters to Truman.

Generally, the national survey organizations take great care to select their samples randomly because their reputations rest on the accuracy of their results. The Gallup and Roper polls usually interview about 1,500 individuals, and their results have a very high probability of being correct—within a margin of 3 percentage points.

Problems with Polls

Public opinion polls are snapshots of the opinions and preferences of the people at a specific moment in time and as expressed in response to a specific question. Given that definition, it is fairly easy to imagine situations in which the polls are wrong. Pollsters have been seriously wrong on several recent occasions, which has led to some industry-wide soul searching and, in the case of Gallup, an internal audit following its erroneous prediction that Republican Mitt Romney would defeat incumbent president Obama in 2012. More recently, pollsters misread the 2014 referendum on Scottish independence, underestimated the Republican wave in the 2014 midterms, and predicted that Hillary Clinton would "crush" Bernie Sanders in the Michigan Democratic primary by 21 points (Sanders won by 1.5 percent). What went wrong? Industry experts and academic researchers attribute the problems to two trends: the growth of cell phones and the decline in people willing to answer surveys. Taken together, these trends have made high-quality research more expensive (and thus less plentiful) and have created opportunities for new, less expensive, and less scientifically based forms of polling.

Sampling Errors Polls may also report erroneous results because the pool of respondents was not chosen in a scientific manner; that is, the form of sampling and the number of people sampled may be too small to overcome **sampling error**, the difference between the sample result and the true result

sampling error
The difference between a sample's results and the true result if the entire population had been interviewed.

if the entire population had been interviewed. The sample would be biased, for example, if the poll interviewed people by telephone and did not correct for the fact that more women than men answer the telephone and that some populations (college students and very poor individuals, for example) cannot be found so easily by a landline telephone. Other people are overestimated in samples relying on landline telephone calls (people over 50, likely to be more affluent and more conservative). The rise of cell phone use introduces new complexities. The best survey organizations, like the Pew Research Center, complete about two cell phone interviews for every one on a landline to try and compensate for new challenges. Because cell phone area codes may not correspond to the physical location of the owner, geographic representation in sampling frames is difficult to confirm. Unscientific mail-in polls, telephone call-in polls, Internet polls, and polls completed by the workers in a campaign office are not scientific and do not give an accurate picture of the public's views.

As pollsters get close to Election Day, they become even more concerned about their sample of respondents. Some continue to interview eligible voters (those over age 18 and registered to vote). Many others use a series of questions and other weighting methods to try to identify "likely voters" so that they can be more accurate in their election predictions. According to Cliff Zukin, a Rutgers professor and past president of the American Association for Public Opinion Research, how to identify "likely voters" is one of the greatest challenges pollsters face today. Survey respondents overestimate their likelihood of voting, so when survey coverage shrinks and nonresponse grows, it becomes more difficult to discern who will actually turn out to vote. When a poll changes its method from reporting the views of eligible voters to reporting those of likely voters, the results tend to change dramatically.

Poll Questions It makes sense to expect that the results of a poll will depend on the questions asked. One problem with many polls is the yes/no answer format. Suppose the poll question asks, "Do you favor or oppose the war in Iraq?" Respondents might wish to answer that they favored the war at the beginning but not as it wore on for several years, or that they favor fighting terrorism but not a military occupation. They have no way of indicating their true position with a yes or no answer. Respondents also are sometimes swayed by the inclusion of certain words in a question: more respondents will answer in the affirmative if the question asks, "Do you favor or oppose the war in Iraq as a means of fighting terrorism?" Respondents' answers are also influenced by the order in which questions are asked, by the possible answers from which they are allowed to choose, and, in some cases, by their interaction with the interviewer. To a certain extent, people try to please the interviewer. They answer questions about which they have no information and avoid some answers to try to measure up to the interviewer's expectations.

Push Polls Some campaigns use "push polls," in which the respondents are given misleading information in the questions asked in order to persuade them to vote against a particular candidate. The interviewer might ask, "Do you approve or disapprove of Congressman Smith, who voted to raise your taxes 22 times?" Obviously, the answers given are likely to be influenced by such techniques. Push polls have been condemned by the polling industry and are considered unethical, but they are still used. In the 2000 Republican Party primary in South Carolina, for example, voters were asked, "Would you be more likely or less likely to vote for John McCain for president if you knew he had fathered an illegitimate black child?" Although no basis existed for the substance of the question, and George W. Bush's campaign disavowed any connection to the calls, thousands of Republican primary voters heard a message obviously designed to *push* them away from candidate McCain. In 2008, Jewish voters in Florida and Pennsylvania were targets of a push poll linking Barack Obama to the Palestine Liberation Organization. In the 2016 South Carolina Republican primary, Trump's campaign alleged via Twitter that Ted Cruz was responsible for a push poll sending robocalls to voters. The Cruz campaign denied any involvement. Other than complaining to the media about such efforts, candidates are largely defenseless against this abuse of polling. Because of these problems with polls, you need to be especially careful when evaluating poll results.

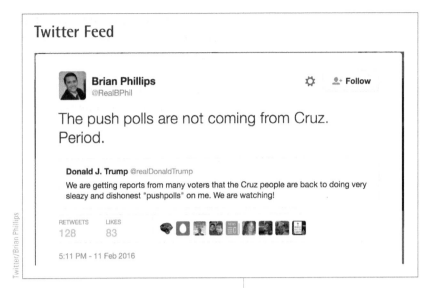

Twitter Feed

Brian Phillips
@RealBPhil   ⚙ ＋ Follow

The push polls are not coming from Cruz. Period.

Donald J. Trump @realDonaldTrump
We are getting reports from many voters that the Cruz people are back to doing very sleazy and dishonest "pushpolls" on me. We are watching!

RETWEETS   LIKES
128   83

5:11 PM - 11 Feb 2016

Twitter/Brian Phillips

Technology, Public Opinion, and the Political Process

Ironically, technological advances in communication have made gathering public opinion data more difficult in some ways. Federal law prohibits any sort of unsolicited calls to cell phones using "automated dialing devices," and because virtually all pollsters now conduct surveys using computerized systems, this presents a problem. Although cell phones make it easier for people to decline to be interviewed, they may also open new avenues to political participation.

Public Opinion and the Political Process

Public opinion affects the political process in many ways. Whether in office or in the midst of a campaign, politicians see public opinion as important to their success. The president, members of Congress, governors, and other elected officials realize that strong public support as expressed in opinion polls is a source of power in dealing with other politicians. It is far more difficult for a senator to say no to the president if the president is immensely popular and if polls show approval of the president's policies. Public opinion also helps candidates identify the most important concerns among the people and may help them shape their campaigns successfully. "Polls give the public an independent voice that's not generally present otherwise in politics and political news coverage," says Michael Traugott, University of Michigan political scientist specializing in polling and public opinion.[36] Thus, the steep decline in people willing to respond to opinion surveys is a

---

36 Joseph P. Williams, "The Problem with Polls." *U.S. News & World Report,* September 28, 2015. http://www.usnews.com /news/the-report/articles/2015/09/28/why-public-opinion-polls-are-increasingly-inaccurate

worrisome trend. In the late 1970s, an 80 percent response rate was considered acceptable. In 2014, response rates hovered around 8 percent, and this significantly affected costs because firms had to work harder to reach respondents.

During the presidential primary contests, polling becomes extremely important. Individuals who would like to make a campaign contribution to their favorite candidate may decide not to if the polls show that the candidate is unlikely to win. Voters do not want to waste their votes on the primary candidates who are doing poorly in the polls. In 2008, the two leading Democratic candidates, Senators Barack Obama and Hillary Clinton, used poll results to try to convince convention delegates of their respective strengths as the party nominee, hoping to influence primaries late in the calendar prior to heading into the party convention. In the 2016 Republican primaries, Donald Trump used his large lead in the polls to create a sense of inevitability in winning the nomination even though by delegate count the race was closer. Polls indicating strong voter support are also helpful in attracting financial contributions to a campaign.

Nevertheless, surveys of public opinion are not equivalent to elections in the United States. Although opinion polls may influence political candidates or elected officials, elections are the major vehicle through which Americans express preferences that can bring about change.

Political Culture and Public Opinion

Given the diversity of American society and the wide range of opinions contained within it, how is it that the political process continues to function without being stalemated by conflict and dissension? One explanation is rooted in the concept of the American political culture, which can be described as a set of attitudes and ideas about the nation and the government. Our political culture is widely shared by Americans of many different backgrounds. The elements of our political culture include certain shared beliefs about the most important values in the American political system, including (1) liberty, equality, and property; (2) support for religious freedom; and (3) community service and personal achievement. The structure of the government—particularly federalism, separation of powers, and popular rule—is also an important value. When people share certain beliefs about the system and a reservoir of good feeling exists toward the institutions of government, the nation will be better able to weather periods of crisis. Such was the case after the 2000 presidential elections when, for several weeks, it was not certain who the next president would be and how that determination would be made. At the time, some argued that the nation was facing a true constitutional crisis. In fact, however, the broad majority of Americans did not believe that the uncertain outcome of the elections had created a constitutional crisis. Polls taken during this time found that, on the contrary, most Americans were confident in our political system's ability to decide the issue peaceably and in a lawful manner.[37]

Political Trust and Support for the Political System
The political culture also helps Americans evaluate their government's performance. At times in our history, **political trust** in government has reached relatively high levels. At other times, political trust in government has fallen to low levels. For

political trust
The degree to which individuals express trust in the government and political institutions, usually measured through a specific series of survey questions.

[37] As reported in Public Perspective, March/April 2002, p. 11, summarizing the results of Gallup/CNN/USA Today polls conducted between November 11 and December 10, 2000.

Figure 6-6 ▶ Reaction to How the Nation Is Being Governed

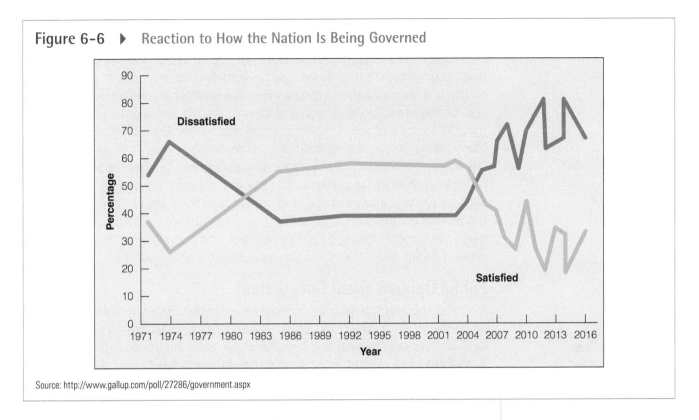

Source: http://www.gallup.com/poll/27286/government.aspx

example, in the 1960s and 1970s, during the Vietnam War and the Watergate scandals, surveys showed that the overall level of political trust in government had declined steeply. Today people are expressing historically high levels of mistrust in government.[38] Americans' satisfaction with the way the nation is being governed is very low, with 67 percent of the public expressing dissatisfaction and only 33 percent of respondents saying they are satisfied (see Figure 6-6). Anger over the government shutdown in October 2013, the repeated trips to the fiscal cliff as lawmakers in Congress argued over raising the debt ceiling, and the botched roll-out of healthcare.gov are all contributing factors. In 2013, civic frustration could be attributed to divided power in Washington, DC—with Democrats controlling the White House and U.S. Senate and Republicans controlling the House of Representatives, very little policy has been accomplished. The 113th Congress (2013–2014) was the least productive in decades. In the first half of the session (2013), Congress enacted only 55 substantive bills and met for the fewest number of hours since 2005, when such records were first filed. Polls show record or near-record criticism of Congress, elected officials, government handling of domestic problems, the scope of government power, and government waste of tax dollars. Fifty-three percent of Americans believe the federal government has become so large and powerful that it poses an immediate threat to the rights and freedoms of ordinary citizens. In May 1995, a little more than a third (36 percent) of the American public expressed this belief.[39] Candidates for president in 2016 from both political parties promised to restore a positive role for government—Republicans promising to shrink the size of government and improve efficiency, and Democrats promising to make government work for the people's interest

38 Gallup's annual Governance survey, updated September 2015. http://www.gallup.com/poll/5392/trust-government.aspx

39 "Majority Says the Federal Government Threatens Their Personal Rights," Pew Research Center for the People and the Press, January 31, 2013. http://www.people-press.org/2013/01/31/majority-says-the-federal-government-threatens-their-personal-rights/

rather than for special interests. What does this indicate about the strength and viability of our shared political culture?

Researchers disagree over exactly how much importance varying levels of trust in government and generalized dissatisfaction with government should be given. Some evidence indicates that the traditional measures of trust bias results negatively (trust is higher than polls show), and some scholars argue that democracy requires healthy skepticism rather than blind trust. Scholar Marc Hetherington demonstrates that declining levels of trust have policy implications. His book *Why Trust Matters* shows that the decline in Americans' political trust explains the erosion in public support for progressive policies such as welfare, food stamps, and health care.[40] As people have lost faith in the federal government, the delivery system for most redistributive policies, they have also lost faith in progressive ideas. The battle over health-care reform offers a recent example of this phenomenon.

Public Opinion about Government

A vital component of public opinion in the United States is the considerable ambivalence with which the public regards many major national institutions. Opinion polls over the last few decades show declining trends in the confidence Americans have in institutions such as government, banks, and the police. The concern is that as confidence in government institutions falls, people will be less likely to embrace a shared political culture and adopt shared norms of political behavior, and as a consequence they will feel less constrained by government decisions. It also means that fewer people will feel compelled to serve in public office. A Gallup poll found that 64 percent of Americans would not like their child to go into politics as a career. Unfortunately, young people express little interest in a career in politics. As Richard Fox and Jennifer Lawless noted in a *Washington Post* opinion essay, "Our political system is built on the premise that running for office is something that a broad group of citizens should want to do . . . [and] if the best and brightest of future generations neither hear nor heed the call to public service, then the quality of U.S. democracy may be compromised."[41] In their survey of high school and college students conducted during the 2012 presidential election, only 11 percent said that they might consider running for political office someday. When presented with choices of careers in business, law, education, sales, and government, government came in last every time. Being a member of Congress was deemed least desirable of all.

Polling organizations regularly ask Americans to name the most important problem facing the country. Figure 6-7 reflects Gallup polls conducted from the years 2001 to 2016. It shows the relative importance Americans place on the economy versus other problems like dissatisfaction with government, health care, and education, among others. In March 2016, noneconomic problems led by a wide margin over economic problems, reflecting the overall improvement in the economy. The public emphasizes problems that are immediate and that have been the subject of many stories in the media. When coverage of a particular problem increases suddenly, the public is more likely to see that as the most important problem. Note the dramatic increase in attention to the economy and

40 Marc J. Hetherington, *Why Trust Matters: Declining Political Trust and the Demise of American Liberalism* (Princeton, NJ: Princeton University Press, 2006).

41 Richard L. Fox and Jennifer L. Lawless, "Turning Off the Next Generation of Politicians," *The Washington Post*, November 22, 2013. http://www.washingtonpost.com/opinions/turning-off-the-next-generation-of-politicians/2013/11/22/b98d1b80-52db-11e3-9e2c-e1d01116fd98_story.html

Figure 6-7 ▶ Perceived Most Important Problem Facing the U.S.

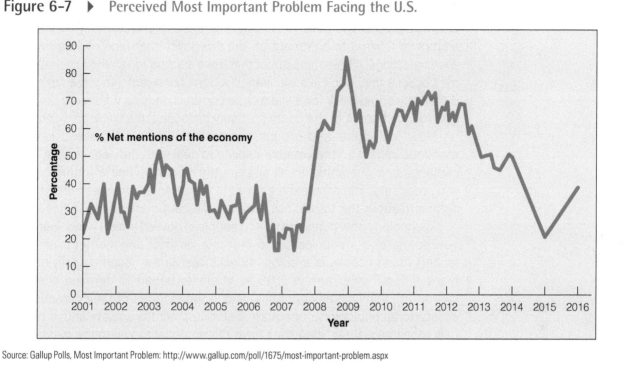

% Net mentions of the economy

Source: Gallup Polls, Most Important Problem: http://www.gallup.com/poll/1675/most-important-problem.aspx

economic issues and corresponding decrease in attention to noneconomic issues that correlates directly with the onset of the global recession in 2008 and 2009. The spike in Figure 6-7 in 2009 indicates that 86 percent of the public perceived that the most important problem facing the United States was the economy.

When government does not respond adequately to a crisis, public reaction is swift and negative. President George W. Bush's approval rating dropped precipitously following Hurricane Katrina because the majority of the public lacked confidence in the government's response to the devastating Gulf Coast hurricane. African Americans, in particular, believed the government would have responded more quickly if those affected by the storm had been wealthy and primarily white.[42] Similarly, as the economy faltered in the latest recession, individuals, businesses, and even the states looked to the federal government for answers and assistance. When an explosion at an offshore drilling rig operated by British Petroleum (BP) dumped unprecedented amounts of oil into the Gulf of Mexico, the Obama administration took action to coordinate relief and cleanup efforts, but still received criticism because it could not plug the leak. Whereas Congress is best suited to investigate the nature of the problem, the president is best able to take action by mobilizing the resources of the federal bureaucracy. The implementation of the Affordable Care Act got off to a very rocky start in October 2013 when the central website designed to connect Americans with health insurance options crashed repeatedly. The president had promised people that if they were happy with their current health-care plans they would be able to keep them, but in many cases that turned out not to be the case because the plans did not meet the minimum coverage criteria in the new law. In November

42 Michael A. Fletcher and Richard Morin, "Bush's Approval Rating Drops to New Low in Wake of Storm," *The Washington Post*, September 13, 2005.

2013, a majority of Americans (54 percent) told pollsters at Quinnipiac University that the president is not honest and trustworthy—a first for President Obama.[43] Obama's drop in the polls in 2013 was especially grave among white voters, prompting Obama to comment on the possibility that race plays a role in his approval ratings: "There's no doubt that there's some folks who just really dislike me because they don't like the idea of a black president. Now the flip side of it is there are some black folks and maybe some white folks who really like me and give me the benefit of the doubt precisely because I'm a black president."[44]

How individuals and groups approach the political process has a tremendous impact on the country's ability to deal with new challenges, resolve conflicts, and guarantee to all citizens the opportunities afforded by peace and prosperity. The material reviewed in this chapter provides some basis for optimism about the future, but raises some caution flags as well.

Technology now connects us as a people in powerful new ways. Harnessing new forms of communication to promote political engagement, particularly among young people, is exciting. #BlackLivesMatter became a rallying cry on many college campuses in 2015 as students began to demand changes in curriculum, administrative policies, and in the cultures of their campuses. Yet access to technology is not equally distributed across society and, if not carefully monitored, these inequities have the potential to widen the gap between the two Americas. On the other hand, as communication technology advances, it becomes cheaper and more ubiquitous. The Arab Spring demonstrated how technology can advance revolutions and coalesce public opinion in support of new leaders and ideas. As oppressive regimes tried to maintain power, they banned mainstream media from reporting on the conflicts. Twitter, Facebook, and YouTube quickly emerged as a much more powerful force in accelerating social protest than traditional media.

Closer to home we find that lots of Americans use social networks and that participants in social networking sites mirror the active and inactive political public in several ways. Those most likely to use social networks to urge political action are found at the farthest ends of the liberal and conservative spectrum—those most activated by their political ideologies—and they tend to be younger. In this respect, they are no different from partisan activists. Political candidates, campaigns, and political organizations are actively reaching out to supporters and likely voters using all of the newest forms of communication technology. Campaign 2012 demonstrated that comfort with social media is key to reaching voters who do not watch television or read newspapers, particularly young voters. Twitter reported that people sent 31 million election-related tweets on Election Day 2012 alone (a 94 percent increase over Election Day 2008). President Obama announced his victory with a tweet that was retweeted more than 714,000 times. Traditional network media outlets cited people's tweets as evidence of voting trends on live television. In the 2016 contests, Facebook was replaced by Snapchat, Vine, Tumblr, and Instagram in extending the candidates' messages and images to voters. As these technologies mature and become more integrated into our daily lives, it remains important to carefully assess their impact on our political culture, shared values, and identity as a nation.

---

43 Ashley Killough, "Poll: Obama Approval Ratings Drop, Americans Say He's Not Trustworthy." CNN Politics, November 12, 2013. http://politicalticker.blogs.cnn.com/2013/11/12/poll-obama-approval-ratings-drop-americans-say-hes-not-trustworthy/

44 David Remnick, "Going the Distance: On and Off the Road with Barack Obama." *The New Yorker*, January 27, 2014. http://www.newyorker.com/reporting/2014/01/27/140127fa_fact_remnick?currentPage=all

Key Terms

agenda setting 218

consensus 210

divisive opinion 210

gender gap 225

generational effect 220

life cycle effect 220

managed news 219

media 218

nonopinion 210

opinion leader 215

opinion poll 228

peer group 213

political socialization 212

political trust 234

public opinion 210

sampling error 231

socioeconomic status 221

Chapter Summary

■ **6.1** Public opinion is defined as the aggregate of individual attitudes or beliefs shared by some portion of the adult population. A consensus exists when a large proportion of the public appears to express the same view on an issue. Divisive opinion exists when the public holds widely different attitudes on an issue. Sometimes, a poll shows a distribution of opinion, indicating that most people either have no information about an issue or are not interested enough in the issue to form a position on it. Public opinion affects government actions by providing support for elected officials to adopt or fail to adopt policies. Public opinion can limit government activity if officials are unclear about the direction a majority of Americans support or if opinion is divided and the safest course of action is no action at all.

■ **6.2** People's opinions are formed through the political socialization process. Important factors in this process are the family, educational experiences, peer groups, opinion leaders, the media, and political events. The influence of the media as a socialization factor may be growing relative to the family. Voting behavior is influenced by demographic factors such as education, economic status, religion, race and ethnicity, gender, and region. It is also influenced by election-specific factors such as party identification, perception of the candidates, and issue preferences.

■ **6.3** Technology is changing the way we communicate with one another. YouTube, Snapchat, Twitter, and Instagram make it possible to share information with millions of people instantly. Social media have the power to shape political events (such as the Arab Spring uprisings and #BlackLivesMatter) and influence support for or opposition to a political candidate.

■ **6.4** Public opinion also plays an important role in domestic and foreign policymaking. Although polling data show that a majority of Americans would like policy leaders to be influenced to a great extent by public opinion, politicians cannot always be guided by opinion polls. This is because the respondents often do not understand the costs and consequences of policy decisions or the trade-offs involved in making such decisions. Similarly, the actions of U.S. government officials can be encouraged or constrained by world opinion.

■ **6.5** Most descriptions of public opinion are based on the results of opinion polls. The accuracy of polls depends on sampling techniques that include a representative sample of the population being polled and ensure randomness in the selection of respondents. Problems with polls include sampling errors (which may occur when the pool of respondents is not chosen in a scientific manner), the difficulty of knowing the degree to which responses are influenced by the type and order of questions asked, the use of a yes/no format for answers, and the interviewer's techniques. Contemporary problems include the rise of cell phone use and the public's unwillingness' to answer surveys. All of these factors make accuracy in polls more difficult.

Selected Resources

PRINT RESOURCES

Dalton, Russell J. *The Good Citizen: How a Younger Generation Is Reshaping American Politics* (Washington, DC: CQ Press, 2009). Despite the conventional wisdom that young people are politically disengaged, this book argues that in many ways today's youth are more engaged than those of previous generations, although the forms of engagement differ. Using public opinion surveys and other empirical research,

Dalton analyzes modern citizenship norms that move away from duty-based engagement toward a more encompassing version of civic engagement.

Lawless, Jennifer L. and Richard Fox. *Running from Office: Why Young Americans Are Turned Off to Politics* (New York: Oxford University Press, 2015). Using an original survey of more than 4,000 high school and college students, Lawless and Fox examine young people's lack of ambition for politics and political office. They find that young people are alienated from politics, but they offer a number of suggestions to turn things around using new technologies, national service, and clever public service announcements.

Newsom, Gavin with Lisa Dickey. *Citizenville: How to Take the Town Square Digital and Reinvent Government* (New York: Penguin Books, 2013). Newsom, the lieutenant governor of California, argues that it is imperative to bring government into the digital age so that citizens can engage and enact change to improve communities.

Sapiro, Virginia. "Not Your Parents' Political Socialization: Introduction for a New Generation." *Annual Review of Political Science* (2004) 7: 1–23. This article reviews the newest research and research questions related to political socialization.

Smith, Christian. *Lost in Transition: The Dark Side of Emerging Adulthood* (New York: Oxford University Press, 2011). Based on over 200 in-depth interviews, this research explores the newest trends in the transition from adolescence to adulthood in the United States. Young people are waiting longer to marry, to have children, and to choose a career direction. The civic and social consequences for these trends are also addressed.

MEDIA RESOURCES

56 Up—The "Up Series" is a British documentary project that in 1964 began chronicling the lives of several 7-year-olds from a variety of economic backgrounds and has reinterviewed them every seven years since. *56 Up* was released in 2013.

Blame It on Fidel—A 2007 French film in which Anna, a 9-year-old girl, must figure out her own beliefs in the confusion created as her parents become increasingly radicalized.

This coming-of-age film explores themes of stereotyping, misinformation, the power of ideologies, and idealism.

Wag the Dog—A 1997 film that provides a very cynical look at the importance of public opinion. The film, which features Dustin Hoffman and Robert De Niro, follows the efforts of a presidential political consultant, who stages a foreign policy crisis to divert public opinion from a sex scandal in the White House.

ONLINE RESOURCES

Corporation for National and Community Service—a federal agency that engages more than 5 million Americans in service through its AmeriCorps, Senior Corps, Social Innovation Fund, and Volunteer Generation Fund programs and leads the president's national call to service initiative, United We Serve: www.NationalService.gov

Fivethirtyeight.com—a blog maintained by Nate Silver, a statistician and writer who analyzes politics, elections, sports, science, and economics to make predictions.

Gallup—a polling organization that has studied human attitudes and behavior for over 75 years. Although some of the data are only available by subscription, the Gallup Daily News

regularly provides information and statistics on a variety of issues and current events: www.gallup.com

Latino Decisions—conducts state-level polls, primarily in states with high Latino populations, to inform candidates and policymakers about concerns in the Latino community: www.latinodecisions.wordpress.com

Pew Forum on Religion and Public Life—part of the Pew Research Center, this forum conducts surveys, demographic analyses, and other social science research on important aspects of religion and public life in the United States and around the world, in addition to providing a neutral venue for discussions of timely issues through roundtables and briefings: www.pewforum.org

Interest Groups

Demonstrators in Chicago protest the death of Laquan McDonald who, was killed by a Chicago police officer. The video of the incident was not released for a year after the shooting.

Scott Olson/Getty Images

LEARNING OBJECTIVES

After reading this chapter, you will be able to:

■ **7.1** Define an interest group and explain the constitutional and political reasons why so many groups are found in the United States.

■ **7.2** Explain why an individual may or may not decide to join an interest group and the benefits that membership can confer.

■ **7.3** Describe different types of interest groups and the sources of their political power.

■ **7.4** Identify the direct and indirect techniques that interest groups use to influence government decisions.

■ **7.5** Describe the legislation that regulates the reporting of lobbying efforts at the federal level and discuss why it is relatively ineffective.

All Interest Groups Were Regulated by the Government?

Background

All it takes to start an interest group is to invite other people who share a common concern to join you to study a given problem or to take action to influence the government on a particular issue. You can meet in your home or at a coffee shop or the public library. You can write letters to your congressperson or the president, or you can start a website promoting your interests. You can collect money for the effort or ask people to donate their time to the cause. All of these activities are protected by the First Amendment to the Constitution and need not involve any level of governmental oversight.

What If the Government Regulated All Interest Groups?

What if, when you started your group, you needed to get a license and report your group to the government? What if, when you contacted the public library to reserve a room, the librarian said, "What is your group's ID number? Do you have a license?" Americans currently join more interest groups than citizens of any other country. Would federal regulations such as these discourage Americans from forming groups and limit their right to express themselves?

Currently, some aspects of interest groups are regulated, primarily through the Internal Revenue Service (IRS) code and the limits placed on campaign contributions. If an interest group wants supporters' donations to be tax deductible for the donor, it must prove that it is a nonprofit group. In that case, the group is severely restricted in its ability to take political action. Such a nonprofit group must file a specific form with the IRS every year, indicating its financial status and how it meets other requirements. Currently, groups that own property are permitted to seek nonprofit status to avoid paying local property taxes. Most religious institutions have this status.

Today, if your new interest group wants to hold a protest, some laws do apply. If your university or local government has a designated free-speech zone, you may be able to speak and hold a protest without permissions needed. Anti-abortion interest groups have regularly protested outside of Planned Parenthood centers. Although institutions and local governments have tried to restrain such protests, generally the Supreme Court has held that only restrictions based on safety concerns can be enforced.

On the other hand, if you want to march down the street or pitch your tents on a public plaza, you will most likely need a permit.

Most interest groups in the United States, whether nonprofit or for profit, exist without much government supervision. What would happen, though, if every interest group with 25 or more members were required to register with the government and report every contribution? Such regulations would require reporting the names of all group members and, most likely, their Social Security numbers, so that the IRS could make sure they were not avoiding taxes on their income. Once the group was registered, it could have access to public spaces for meetings and other public services, much like student groups that form on a campus.

What Would Be the Impact on Democracy?

Regulating interest groups would be a huge, but not impossible, task for the government. Such regulation would have a chilling effect on free speech and the right to assembly in the United States. Individuals whose views are out of the mainstream or who are simply in the minority would be less likely to join groups and to take public action. Fewer groups would form, and there would be a great advantage for the larger, highly organized interest groups in society. James Madison's fear that the majority could override the interests of minorities (*Federalist #10*) might come true. Social scientists have long known that the voices of elites in government and in interest groups get more attention than do the voices of minorities, the poor, and new grassroots groups. As existing groups dominated political decision making, new views would have a difficult time finding a forum, and democratic debate would be diminished.

For Critical Analysis

1. Could the government regulate groups more closely without violating the Constitution and the Bill of Rights?

2. Would you be more or less likely to join a group if your name would be supplied to local or federal government authorities?

Doctors, insurance companies, college students, oil companies, environmentalists, the elderly, African American organizations, Native American tribes, small businesses, unions, gay and lesbian groups, and foreign governments all try to influence the political leaders and policymaking processes of the United States. The structure of American government and the freedoms guaranteed in the Bill of Rights invite the participation of **interest groups** at all stages of the policymaking process. One reason why so many interest groups and other organized institutions attempt to influence our government is the many opportunities for them to do so. Interest groups can hire **lobbyists** to try to influence members of the House of Representatives, the Senate or any of its committees, or the president or any presidential officials. They can file briefs at the Supreme Court or challenge regulations issued by federal agencies. This ease of access to the government is sometimes known as the "multiple cracks" view of our political system. Interest groups can penetrate the political system through many entry points, and, as we will note, their right to do so is protected by the Constitution.

interest group
An organized group of individuals sharing common objectives who actively attempt to influence policymakers.

lobbyist
An organization or individual who attempts to influence legislation and the administrative decisions of government.

Interest Groups: A Natural Phenomenon

■ **7.1** Define an interest group and explain the constitutional and political reasons why so many groups are found in the United States.

Alexis de Tocqueville observed in 1834 that "in no country of the world has the principle of association been more successfully used or applied to a greater multitude of objectives than in America."[1] The French traveler was amazed at the degree to which Americans formed groups to solve civic problems, establish social relationships, and speak for their economic or political interests. James Madison foresaw the importance of having multiple organizations in the political system (see Appendix C). He supported the creation of a large republic with many states to encourage the formation of multiple interests. The multitude of interests, in Madison's view, would protect minority views against the formation of an oppressive majority interest. Madison's belief in the power of groups to protect a democracy was echoed centuries later by the work of Robert A. Dahl, a contributor to the pluralist theory of politics.[2] Pluralism views the political struggle as pitting different groups against each other to reach a compromise vital to the public interest.

Surely, neither Madison nor de Tocqueville foresaw the formation of more than 100,000 associations in the United States or the spending of millions of dollars to influence legislation. Poll data show that more than two-thirds of all Americans belong to at least one group or association. Although the majority of these affiliations could not be classified as interest groups in the political sense, Americans do understand the principles of working in groups.

Today, interest groups range from the small groups, such as local environmental organizations, to national groups, such as the American Civil Liberties

---

1   Alexis de Tocqueville, *Democracy in America*, Vol. 1, edited by Phillips Bradley (New York: Knopf, 1980), p. 191.
2   Robert A. Dahl, *Who Governs? Democracy and Power in an American City* (New Haven, CT: Yale University Press, 1961).

Union and the National Education Association. The continuing increase in the number of groups that lobby governments and the multiple ways in which they are involved in the political process have been seen by some scholars as a detriment to an effective government. Sometimes called *hyperpluralism,* the ability of interest groups to mandate policy or to defeat policies needed by the nation may work against the public good.[3]

Interest Groups and Social Movements

social movement
A movement that represents the demands of a large segment of the public for political, economic, or social change.

Interest groups are often spawned by mass **social movements**. Such movements represent demands by a large segment of the population for change in the political, economic, or social system. Social movements are often the first expression of discontent with the existing system. They may be the authentic voice of weaker or oppressed groups in society that do not have the means or standing to organize as interest groups. For example, most mainstream political and social leaders disapproved of the women's movement of the 1800s. Because women were unable to vote or take an active part in the political system, it was difficult for women who desired greater freedoms to organize formal groups. After the Civil War, when more women became active in professional life, the first real women's rights group, the National Woman Suffrage Association, came into being. One of the best-known groups speaking for the rights of women is NOW, the National Organization for Women. Its website encourages blog postings and donations in order to support women's rights.

African Americans found themselves in an even more disadvantaged situation after the end of the Reconstruction period. They were unable to exercise their political rights in many Southern and border states, and their participation in any form of organization could lead to economic ruin, physical harassment, or even death. The civil rights movement of the 1950s and 1960s was clearly a social movement. Although the movement received support from several formal organizations—including the Southern Christian Leadership Conference, the National Association for the Advancement of Colored People, and the Urban League—only a social movement could generate the kinds of civil disobedience that took place in hundreds of towns and cities across the country. Today, the civil rights movement has added a new component, Black Lives Matter, a nascent social movement that calls attention to the treatment of African Americans by the police and the criminal justice system.

In the mid-twentieth century, Hispanic or Latino Americans became part of a social movement to improve the treatment of immigrant workers. Cesar Chavez, a farmworker,

From the Web ▶ The National Organization for Women has been working for women's equality since the 1960s. This photo symbolizes the organization's push to reach younger women and women of color.

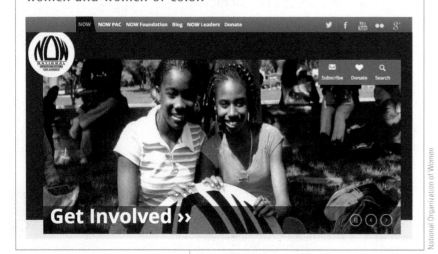

National Organization of Women

---

3   Theodore Lowi, *The End of Liberalism* (New York: W. W. Norton, 1979).

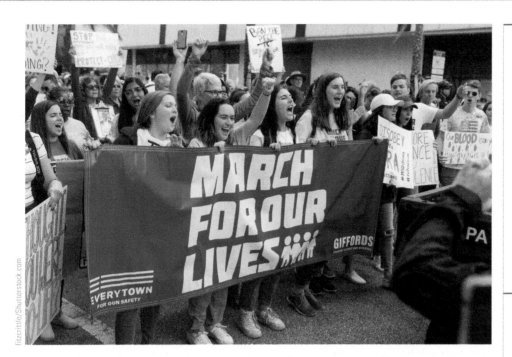

Image 7-1
After the school shooting at Marjorie Stoneman Douglas high school in Florida, students across the country demonstrated for stronger gun laws.

Image 7-2
Cesar Estrada Chavez, leader of the farmworker rights movement. He founded the National Farm Workers Association to secure the rights of migrant farmworkers to better wages and living conditions. One of the tactics he used was a consumer boycott against food producers.

organized the Mexican farm laborers in California and other Western states to demand better working conditions, better treatment, and the right to form a union. At one point, the National Farm Workers Association initiated a strike against the grape growers in California and led a successful national boycott of table grapes for six years. Chavez became a national figure, and his work led to improved conditions for all farmworkers. By the 1960s, other leaders within the Hispanic American community founded the National Council of La Raza to improve educational and employment opportunities for their community. Chavez's social movement became a nationally recognized union, the United Farm Workers, and "La Raza" became recognized as an advocacy group that spoke for Hispanic Americans.

The Stonewall riots in New York City were the beginning of the drive for greater rights and protections for gays and lesbians in the United States. This social movement began in New York City and San Francisco and then spread to gay communities throughout the nation. There is no doubt that lesbian, gay, bisexual, and transgender (LGBT) Americans have become a well-recognized interest group. At the present time, the Human Rights Campaign is the largest lobbying group, with more than 1 million members. The work of LGBT groups has been complicated by the reality that many issues of interest fall under the purview of state law. Thus, many LGBT alliances work at the state and local level. Such groups frequently have chapters on college campuses and, in some areas, within high schools.

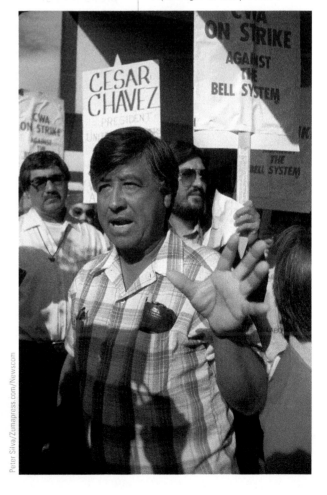

Table 7-1 ▶ Social Movement Interest Groups

NAACP	www.naacp.org
Human Rights Campaign	www.hrc.org
The Urban League	www.nul.org
NOW	www.now.org
League of United Latin American Citizens	www.lulac.org
National LGBTQ Task Force	www.thetaskforce.org

Social movements are often precursors of interest groups, some of which are listed in Table 7-1. It is too soon to know whether the new social movements targeting the justice system or transgender rights in the United States will become more like an interest group. Social movements, including those that support sustainable farming and making high-quality food more accessible to poorer Americans, may yet become interest groups if they find a need to recruit members through group incentives.

Why So Many?

Whether based in a social movement or created to meet an immediate crisis, interest groups continue to form and act in American society. One reason for the multitude of interest groups is that the right to join a group is protected by the First Amendment to the U.S. Constitution (see Chapter 4). Not only are all people guaranteed the right "peaceably to assemble," but they are also guaranteed the right "to petition the Government for a redress of grievances." This constitutional provision encourages Americans to form groups and to express their opinions to the government or to their elected representatives as members of a group.

In addition, our federal system of government provides thousands of "pressure points" for interest group activity. Interest groups and their representatives can lobby legislators for policy changes or attempt to influence the president directly. They can also contact the officials who write regulations and policies. When attempts to influence government through the executive and legislative branches fail, interest groups turn to the courts, filing suit in state or federal courts to achieve their objectives. The Boy Scouts of America has been sued by gay groups because gay men were not allowed to be troop leaders. Pluralist theorists point to the openness of the American political structure as a major factor in the power of groups in American politics.

did you know?

On average, there are now 23 lobbyists for each member of Congress.

From the Web ▶ FIRM, a pro-immigration reform group, publicizes a prayer for justice event at the United States Supreme Court. How would this image build a reputation for FIRM?

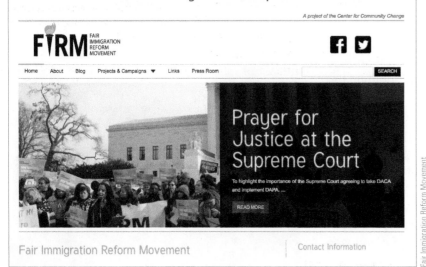

Fair Immigration Reform Movement

Why Do Americans Join Interest Groups?

■ **7.2** Explain why an individual may or may not decide to join an interest group and the benefits that membership can confer.

Why do some people join interest groups, whereas many others do not? Everyone has some interest that could benefit from government action. For many individuals, however, those concerns remain unorganized interests, or **latent interests**.

According to political theorist Mancur Olson, it simply may not be rational for individuals to join most groups.[4] In his classic work on this topic, Olson introduced the idea of the "collective good." This concept refers to any public benefit that, if available to any member of the community, cannot be denied to any other member, whether or not he or she participated in the effort to gain the good.

Although collective benefits are usually thought of as coming from such public goods as clean air or national defense, benefits are also bestowed by the government on subsets of the public. Price subsidies to dairy farmers and loans to college students are examples. Olson used economic theory to propose that it is not rational for interested individuals to join groups that work for group benefits. In fact, it is often more rational for the individual to wait for others to procure the benefits and then share them. How many college students, for example, are aware of the United States Student Association (www.usstudents.org), an organization that lobbies the government for increased financial aid to students? The difficulty interest groups face in recruiting members when the benefits can be obtained without joining is referred to as the **free rider problem**.

Incentives

If so little incentive exists for individuals to join together, why are there thousands of interest groups lobbying in Washington? According to the logic of collective action, if the contribution of an individual *will* make a difference to the effort, then it is worth it to the individual to join. Thus, smaller groups, which seek benefits for only a small proportion of the population, are more likely to enroll members who will give time and funds to the cause. Larger groups, which represent general public interests (the women's movement or the American Civil Liberties Union, for example), will find it relatively more difficult to get individuals to join. People need an incentive—material or otherwise—to participate.

Solidary Incentives Interest groups offer **incentives** for their members. **Solidary incentives** include companionship, a sense of belonging, and the pleasure of associating with others. Although the National Audubon Society was originally founded to save the snowy egret from extinction, today most members join to learn more about birds and to meet and share their pleasure with other birdwatchers. The advent of social media has made the creation of solidary incentives much easier. An individual can make friends and exchange ideas with other members through Facebook or Twitter. Such exchanges make the connection to the organization even more worthwhile to the individual. Even though an individual may "join" a group for free through social media, the interest group benefits from the attention garnered by these "fans." For example, the World Wildlife Fund has 2.4 million friends on Facebook. When the time comes to ask for a financial donation or to take local action, these social media participants will feel an enhanced loyalty to the group and may be willing to take action.

latent interests
Public-policy interests that are not recognized or addressed by a group at a particular time.

free rider problem
The difficulty interest groups face in recruiting members when the benefits they achieve can be gained without joining the group.

incentive
A reason or motive for supporting or participating in the activities of a group based on the desire to associate with others and to share with others a particular interest or hobby.

solidary incentive
A reason or motive having to do with the desire to associate with others and to share with others a particular interest or hobby.

---

4   Mancur Olson, *The Logic of Collective Action* (Cambridge, MA: Harvard University Press, 1965).

material incentive
A reason or motive for supporting or participating in the activities of a group based on economic benefits or opportunities.

Material Incentives For other individuals, interest groups offer direct **material incentives**. A case in point is AARP (formerly the American Association of Retired Persons), which provides discounts, automobile insurance, and organized travel opportunities for its members. The organization even offers free access to a range of computer games on its webpage. After Congress created the prescription drug benefit program supported by AARP, it became one of the larger insurers under that program. Because of its exceptionally low dues ($16 annually) and the benefits gained through membership, AARP has become the largest interest group in the United States, claiming more than 38 million members.

Many other interest groups offer indirect material incentives for their members. Such groups as the American Dairy Association and the National Association of Automobile Dealers do not give discounts or freebies to their members, but they do offer indirect benefits and rewards by, for example, protecting the material interests of their members from government policymaking that is injurious to their industry or business.

purposive incentive
A reason for supporting or participating in the activities of a group based on agreement with the goals of the group. For example, someone with a strong interest in human rights might have a purposive incentive to join Amnesty International.

Purposive Incentives Interest groups also offer the opportunity for individuals to pursue political, economic, or social goals through joint action. **Purposive incentives** offer individuals the satisfaction of taking action when the goals of a group correspond to their beliefs or principles. Although the Black Lives Matter movement is a new and fairly unformed interest, the individuals who took part in the protests and marches expressed very strong feelings about the lack of justice for African Americans in the United States. The individuals who belong to a group focusing on the abortion issue, gun control, or environmental causes, for example, do so because they feel strongly enough about the issues to support the group's work with money and time.

Some scholars have argued that many people join interest groups simply for the discounts, magazine subscriptions, and other tangible benefits and are not really interested in the political positions taken by the groups. According to William P. Browne, however, research shows that people really do care about the policy stance of an interest group. Members of a group seek people who share the group's views and then ask them to join. As one group leader put it, "Getting members is about scaring the hell out of people."[5] People join the group and then feel that they are doing something about a cause that is important to them. Today, the use of social media makes sharing of views and goals even easier for a group.

Types of Interest Groups

■ **7.3** Describe different types of interest groups and the sources of their political power.

Thousands of groups exist to influence government. Among the major types of interest groups are those that represent the main sectors of the economy. Many public-interest organizations have been formed to represent the needs of the general citizenry, including some single-issue groups. The interests of foreign governments and foreign businesses are also represented in the American political arena.

---

5   William P. Browne, *Groups, Interests, and U.S. Public Policy* (Washington, DC: Georgetown University Press, 1998), p. 23.

Economic Interest Groups

More interest groups are formed to represent economic interests than any other set of interests. The variety of economic interest groups mirrors the complexity of the American economy. The major sectors that seek influence in Washington, DC, include business, agriculture, labor unions and their members, government workers, and professionals.

Business Interest Groups Thousands of business groups and trade associations work to influence government policies that affect their respective industries. Umbrella groups represent certain types of businesses or companies that deal in a particular type of product. The U.S. Chamber of Commerce, for example, is an umbrella group that represents businesses, and the National Association of Manufacturers is an umbrella group that represents only manufacturing concerns. These are two of the larger groups listed in Table 7-2.

Some business groups are decidedly more powerful than others. The U.S. Chamber of Commerce, which has more than 300,000 member companies, can bring constituent influence to bear on every member of Congress. Another powerful lobbying organization is the National Association of Manufacturers. With a staff of more than 60 people in Washington, DC, the organization can mobilize dozens of well-educated, articulate lobbyists to work the corridors of Congress on issues of concern to its members.

Although industrial interest groups such as those listed in Table 7-3 are likely to agree on anything that reduces government regulation or taxation, they often do not concur on the specifics of policy, and the sector has been troubled by disagreement and fragmentation within its ranks. Large corporations have been far more concerned with federal regulation of their corporate boards and insider financial arrangements, whereas small businesses lobby for tax breaks for new equipment or new employees. One of the key issues on which businesses have not agreed in the past is immigration reform. Large corporations have found the current visa regulations for bringing in highly skilled employees to be burdensome, whereas small businesses find the government database for checking immigration status unwieldy. By 2013, however, a majority of small and large businesses supported immigration reform, seeing the economic power of immigrants as customers and employees.[6] Furthermore, in January 2014, the American Federation of Labor and Congress of Industrial Organizations (AFL-CIO),

Table 7-2 ▶ Economic Interest Groups—Business

U.S. Chamber of Commerce	www.uschamber.com
Better Business Bureau	www.bbb.org
National Association of Manufacturers	www.nam.com
National Federation of Independent Business	www.nifbonline.com

Table 7-3 ▶ Economic Interest Groups—Industries

American Bankers Association	www.aba.com
National Association of Home Builders	www.nahb.org
National Association of Realtors	www.nar.realtor
National Beer Wholesalers Association	www.nbwa.org
National Restaurant Association	www.restaurant.org
America's Health Insurance Plans	www.ahip.org
Pharmaceutical Research and Manufacturers of America	www.phrma.org
American Hospital Association	www.aha.org

---

6   Kent Hoover, "What business groups like about House Republican immigration reform principles." *The Business Journals*, January 30, 2014. http://www.bizjournals.com/bizjournals/washingtonbureau/2014-01-30-business-groups-welcome-house.html

---

Table 7-4 ▶ Economic Interest Groups—Agriculture

American Farm Bureau Federation	www.fb.org
National Farmers Union	www.nfu.org

---

which has feared that immigrants might be hired in place of union workers, and the U.S. Chamber of Commerce agreed on common principles for immigration reform. The powerful coalition of unions now sees legal immigration and a path to legal residency for workers as an opportunity to provide themselves with new union members.[7]

Agricultural Interest Groups American farmers and their employees represent less than 2 percent of the U.S. population. Nevertheless, farmers' influence on legislation that is beneficial to their interests has been significant. Farmers have succeeded in their aims because they have very strong interest groups. Two of the largest are listed in Table 7-4. These interest groups are geographically dispersed and therefore have many representatives and senators to speak for them.

The American Farm Bureau Federation, established in 1919, has several million members (many of whom are not actually farmers) and is usually considered conservative. It was instrumental in getting government guarantees of "fair" prices during the Great Depression in the 1930s.[8] Another important agricultural interest organization is the National Farmers Union (NFU), which represents smaller family farms. Generally, the NFU holds more progressive policy positions than does the Farm Bureau. As farms have become larger and agribusiness has become a way of life, single-issue farm groups have emerged. The American Dairy Association, the Peanut Growers Group, and the National Cattlemen's Association, for example, work to support their respective farmers and associated businesses. In recent years, agricultural interest groups have become active on many new issues. Among other things, they have opposed immigration restrictions and are very involved in international trade matters as they seek new markets. One of the newest agricultural groups is the American Farmland Trust, which supports policies to conserve farmland and protect natural resources.

labor movement
Generally, the economic and political expression of working-class interests; politically, the organization of working-class interests.

Labor Interest Groups Interest groups representing the **labor movement** date back to at least 1886, when the American Federation of Labor (AFL) was formed. The largest American unions are listed in Table 7-5. In 1955 the AFL joined forces with the Congress of Industrial Organizations (CIO). Today, the combined AFL-CIO is a large union with a membership of nearly 12.4 million workers and an active political arm called the Committee on Political Education. In a sense, the AFL-CIO is a union of unions.

Table 7-5 ▶ Economic Interest Groups—Labor

Change to Win Federation	www.changetowin.org
AFL-CIO	www.aflcio.org
SEIU	www.seiu.org
National Education Association	www.nea.org
International Brotherhood of Teamsters	www.teamster.org

---

7   Steven Greenhouse, "Business and Labor Unite to Try to Alter Immigration Laws," *The New York Times*, February 7, 2014: 1.

8   The Agricultural Adjustment Act of 1933 (declared unconstitutional) was replaced by the 1938 Agricultural Adjustment Act and was later changed and amended several times.

The AFL-CIO experienced severe discord within its ranks during 2005, however, when four key unions left the federation and formed the Change to Win Coalition. The new Change to Win Coalition represents about one-third of the 13 million workers who formerly belonged to the AFL-CIO, including the SEIU, or Service Employees International Union. Formed by unions that were growing, especially in the public sector, the coalition believed that the AFL-CIO was too easily cowed by old-line manufacturing unions and not aggressive enough about organizing new industries. Since its formation in 2005, several members of the coalition have either rejoined the AFL-CIO or became independent. The role of unions in American society has declined in recent decades, as witnessed by the decrease in union membership (see Figure 7-1). In the age of automation and with the rise of the **service sector**, blue-collar workers in basic industries (autos, steel, and the like) represent an increasingly smaller percentage of the total working population. Although there was some growth in union membership in the early 2000s, the economic recession that began in 2008 took its toll on union workers as employees lost their jobs. At the end of 2017, total union membership in the United States stood at 14.8 million workers, or 10.7 percent of the workforce.

With the steady decline in employment in the industrial sector of the economy, national unions are looking to nontraditional areas for their membership, including migrant farmworkers, service workers, and, most recently, public employees—such as police officers, firefighting personnel, and teachers, including college professors and graduate assistants. By 2012 the number of individuals who belonged to public-sector unions outnumbered those in private-sector unions.

service sector
The sector of the economy that provides services—such as health care, banking, and education—in contrast to the sector that produces goods.

Figure 7-1 ▶ Decline in Union Membership, 1948 to Present

As shown in this figure, the percentage of the total workforce that is represented by labor unions has declined precipitously over the last 40 years. Note, however, that in contrast to the decline in union representation in the private sector, the percentage of government workers who are unionized has increased significantly since about 1960.

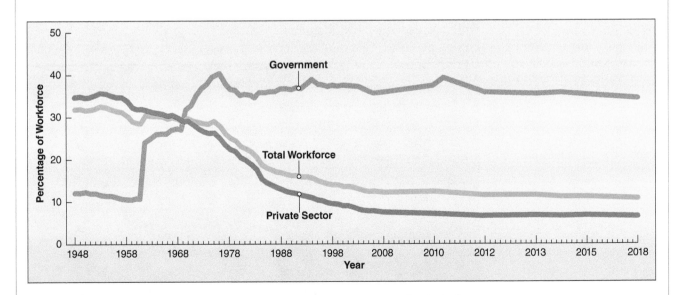

Source: Bureau of Labor Statistics, 2016.

Although the proportion of the workforce that belongs to a union has declined over the years, American labor unions have not given up their efforts to support sympathetic candidates for Congress or for state office. Currently, the AFL-CIO has a large political budget that it uses to help Democratic candidates nationwide. Although interest groups that favor Republicans continue to assist their candidates, the efforts of labor are more sustained and more targeted. Labor offers a candidate (such as Hillary Clinton) a corps of volunteers in addition to campaign contributions. A massive turnout by labor union members in critical elections can significantly increase the final vote totals for Democratic candidates.

Public-Employee Unions The degree of unionization in the private sector has declined since 1965, but this has been partially offset by growth in the unionization of public employees. Figure 7-1 displays the growth in public-sector unionization. With a total membership of more than 7.2 million, public-sector unions are likely to continue expanding.

The American Federation of State, County, and Municipal Employees and the American Federation of Teachers are members of the AFL-CIO's Public Employee Department. Over the years, public-employee unions have become quite militant and are often involved in strikes or protests.

In 2011 the Republican governor and legislature in Wisconsin passed legislation limiting the ability of public-sector union members, including teachers, to bargain for benefits. Teachers, students, and their supporters occupied the Wisconsin statehouse for many weeks, but the law stood. An effort to recall the governor of the state was mounted in 2012. After an intense and expensive campaign, Governor Scott Walker defeated the Democratic challenger in the June 2012 recall election and remained in office.

A powerful interest group lobbying on behalf of public employees is the National Education Association (NEA), a nationwide organization of about 2.8 million teachers and others connected with education. Many NEA locals function as labor unions. The NEA lobbies intensively for increased public funding of education.

Image 7-3
In July 2013, the Bay Area Rapid Transit system was shut down by striking union members who opposed proposed changes in their health-care and pension plans. Thousands of commuters were forced to find other types of transportation during the strike.

Justin Sullivan/Getty Images

Interest Groups of Professionals

Numerous professional organizations exist, including the Association of General Contractors of America and the Institute of Electrical and Electronic Engineers. Some professional groups (see Table 7-6) are more influential than others because of their members' social status. Lawyers have a unique advantage because many members of Congress share their profes-

Table 7-6 ▶ Professional Interest Groups	
American Medical Association	www.ama-assm.org
American Dental Association	www.ada.org
American Bar Association	www.americanbar.org
American Library Association	www.ala.org
American Association for Justice	www.justice.org

sion. Interest groups that represent lawyers include both the American Bar Association and the Association of Trial Lawyers of America, which has renamed itself the American Association for Justice. The trial lawyers have been very active in political campaigns and are usually one of the larger donors to Democratic candidates. In terms of money spent on lobbying, however, one professional organization stands head and shoulders above the rest—the American Medical Association (AMA). Founded in 1847, it is now affiliated with more than 2,000 local and state medical societies and has a total membership of about 300,000.

The Unorganized Poor Some have argued that the system of interest-group politics leaves out poor Americans or those without access to information. Americans who are disadvantaged economically cannot afford to join interest groups; if they are members of the working poor, they may hold two or more jobs just to survive, leaving them no time to participate in interest groups. Other groups in the population—including non-English-speaking groups, resident aliens, single parents, disabled Americans, and younger voters—probably do not have the time or expertise even to find out what group might represent them. Similarly, the millions of Americans affected by the mortgage default crisis, some poor and some middle class, fought their battles against the banks and mortgage companies alone—no interest group exists or has formed to lobby for more effective policies to help these people.

R. Allen Hays examined the plight of poor Americans in his book *Who Speaks for the Poor?*.[9] Hays studied groups and individuals who have lobbied for public housing and other issues related to the poor and concluded that the poor depend largely on indirect representation. Most efforts on behalf of the poor come from a policy network of groups—including public housing officials, welfare workers and officials, religious groups, public-interest groups, and some liberal general-interest groups—that speak loudly and persistently for the poor. More recent studies update this work by suggesting that community-based organizations can survive with a combination of local legitimacy and connections to regional or national organizations.[10] Schlozman, Verba, and Brady completed a comprehensive study of organized interests in 2012 and affirmed the findings of Hays: affluent and upper-middle-class Americans can have their voice heard, whereas poor Americans face tremendous obstacles to participating in the political system and having their interests considered by it.[11]

9 R. Allen Hays, *Who Speaks for the Poor?* (New York: Routledge, 2001).
10 Edward T. Walker and John D. McCarthy, "Legitimacy, Strategy, and Resources in the Survival of Community-Based Organizations," *Social Problems* (2010) 57 (3): 315–340.
11 Kay Lehman Schlozman, Sidney Verba, and Henry Brady, *The Unheavenly Chorus: Unequal Political Voice and the Broken Promise of American Democracy* (Princeton, NJ: Princeton University Press, 2012).

Environmental Groups

Environmental interest groups are not new. We have already mentioned the National Audubon Society, which was founded in 1905 to protect the snowy egret from the commercial demand for hat decorations. The patron of the Sierra Club, John Muir, worked for the creation of national parks more than a century ago. But the blossoming of national environmental groups with mass memberships did not occur until the 1970s. Since the first Earth Day, organized in 1970, many interest groups have sprung up to protect the environment or to save unique ecological niches. The groups, many of which are listed in Table 7-7, range from the National

Politics in Practice

How to Organize a Group

Within the last decade, two very different groups have organized to challenge the political status quo: the Tea Party and the Occupy movement. Although neither of these two groups can be said to have established itself as a true interest group, both have attracted a great deal of attention in the media and many supporters and critics. Both groups have formed and acted using twenty-first-century techniques for organizing.

The Tea Party is a political group that is fairly decentralized and has no top-down administration or bureaucracy. Critics suggest that it is really a faction of the Republican Party that is extremely conservative in its views. Members of Tea Party groups generally dispute that charge, although most of the candidates they back are Republicans. Survey data suggest that some of the members are, in fact, independent voters rather than Republicans.

The Occupy movement arose in the fall of 2011 as a protest movement against the distribution of wealth in the United States and an expression of alienation from corporate values and the current distribution of benefits in society. Occupy camps sprang up across American cities and in European capitals as well. Supporters tended to be young and well educated or current students who were unemployed or underemployed, meaning that they could not find work in the field for which they had trained. The movement challenged local governments by using public spaces for its encampments and accepting the tickets issued by local police. Most camps were eventually disbanded due to public safety concerns, but then warmer weather encouraged them to sprout again.

How could you organize a group to change society or improve your university? First, define your message. Work with a group of like-minded friends to identify your goals. Figure out what kind of a group structure will work and what tasks need to be done. Now, use the Internet to organize: Set up your website, blog, Facebook page, and Twitter account. Generate publicity so that others who agree with you can join your group. You might decide to demonstrate or post signs, or take some symbolic action to get on the news. Maximize the news exposure by posting a video on YouTube. Use any email list available to you. Ask people to join your group by "liking" you on Facebook, following you on Twitter, and perhaps donating to the cause. Use all social media to attract followers and inform them of your mission. Then use the media to let supporters know about your events.

Many organizing methods that seem so obvious to most Americans under 40, such as texting and using social media, did not exist 15 years ago. Of course, getting a group started is one thing, but keeping it going and actually having an impact on public policy require building a more permanent structure and establishing a solid presence in the political arena. It will not be known for some years whether the Occupy movement or the Tea Party has such a future.

For Critical Analysis

1. Can you think of a group or movement that might be threatening to the government or university? Should the formation of such a group require government or university approval?

2. Why do Americans believe that they should form groups to express their views and to lobby governments at every level for their beliefs?

Wildlife Federation, with a membership of more than 5 million and an emphasis on education, to the more elite Environmental Defense Fund, with a membership of 300,000 and a focus on influencing federal policy. The National Resources Defense Council (NRDC) is another very powerful environmental organization, one that has often used the law and lawsuits as part of its strategy. Other groups include the Nature Conservancy, which uses members' contributions to buy up threatened natural areas and either give them to state or local governments or manage them itself, and the more radical Greenpeace Society and Earth First. A more recent entry into the field of environmental groups is the Clean Water Network, which spun off from the National Resources Defense Council in 2008. The Clean Water Action is an alliance of local, state-level, and national groups that works to stop dangerous runoff and protect streams, lakes, and rivers. Many local groups engage in activities such as water sampling and stream monitoring to make sure that water protection standards are followed.

From the Web ▶ The NRDC works around the world to change government policies toward the environment. Here it calls on efforts to save the orcas of the Pacific Northwest coast. Often, NRDC turns to legal action to achieve its goals.

Public-Interest Groups

Public interest is a difficult term to define because there are many publics in our nation of about 323 million. It is almost impossible for one particular public policy to benefit everybody, which makes it practically impossible to define the public interest. Nonetheless, over the past few decades, a variety of lobbying organizations listed in Table 7-8 have been formed "in the public interest."

public interest
The best interests of the overall community; the national good, rather than the narrow interests of a particular group.

Nader Organizations The best-known and perhaps the most effective public-interest groups are those organized under the leadership of consumer activist Ralph Nader. Nader's rise to the top began in 1965 with the publication of his book *Unsafe at Any Speed*, a lambasting critique of General Motors (GM). GM made a clumsy attempt to discredit Nader's background. Nader sued the company, the media exploited the story, and when GM settled out of court for $425,000, Nader became a recognized champion of consumer interests. Since then, Nader has turned over much of his income to the more than 60 public-interest groups that he has formed or sponsored. Nader ran for president in 2000 on the Green Party ticket and again in 2004 and 2008 as an independent.

Other Public-Interest Groups One overarching public interest is an effective political system. One of the first groups seeking

Table 7-7 ▶	Environmental Interest Groups
Sierra Club	www.sierraclub.org
The Nature Conservancy	www.nature.org
National Resources Defense Council	www.nrdc.org
Clean Water Action	www.cleanwateraction.org
The World Wildlife Fund	www.wwf.org
The Audubon Society	www.audubon.org
National Wildlife Federation	www.nwf.org

Table 7-8 ▶	Public-Interest Groups
American Civil Liberties Union	www.aclu.org
League of Women Voters	www.lwv.org
Common Cause	www.commoncause.org
Consumer Federation of America	www.consumerfed.org
Amnesty International	www.amnesty.org

Image 7–4
Young people work together to clean up a creek that has been polluted by runoff and flooding.

Jim West/Alamy Stock Photo

political reform was Common Cause, founded in 1970. Its goals are moving national priorities toward "the public" and making governmental institutions more responsive to the needs of the public. Anyone willing to pay dues of at least $25 per year can become a member. Members are polled regularly to obtain information about local and national issues requiring reassessment. Some of the activities of Common Cause have been (1) helping to ensure the passage of the Twenty-sixth Amendment (giving 18-year-olds the right to vote), (2) achieving greater voter registration in all states, (3) supporting the complete withdrawal of all U.S. forces from South Vietnam in the 1970s, and (4) succeeding in passing campaign finance reform legislation.

Although Common Cause has about 400,000 members and is still working for political reforms at the national and state level, it is not as well known today as MoveOn.org. Founded in 1998 by two entrepreneurs from California, the group's original purpose was to get millions of people to demand that President Clinton be censured instead of impeached and that the country should "move on" to deal with more important problems. What was strikingly different about this organization is that it was—and continues to be—an online interest group. MoveOn (www.moveon.org) has more than 8 million members and is now a family of organizations that are politically active in national campaigns and in pressuring government on specific issues.

The American Civil Liberties Union (ACLU) dates back to World War I (1914–1918), when, under a different name, it defended draft resisters. It generally enters into legal disputes related to Bill of Rights issues. The ACLU website has an excellent discussion of individuals' and groups' rights to express themselves and protest within the law. An international interest group with a strong presence on U.S. college campuses is Amnesty International. This organization, founded in 1961, spans the globe. The mission is to end human rights abuses wherever they are found. Sometimes under fire for its unconventional methods, Amnesty International has compiled an outstanding record of documenting human rights abuses and was awarded the Nobel Prize in 1977.

Other Interest Groups

Single-interest groups, being narrowly focused, may be able to call attention to their causes because they have simple, straightforward goals and because their members tend to care intensely about the issues. Thus, such groups can easily motivate their members to contact legislators or to organize demonstrations in support of their policy goals.

A number of interest groups focus on just one issue. The abortion debate has created various groups opposed to abortion, such as the National Right to Life Committee, and groups in favor of abortion rights, such as NARAL Pro-Choice America (see Table 7-9). Other single-issue groups are the National Rifle Association, the National Right to Work Committee (an anti-union group), and the American Israel Public Affairs Committee (a pro-Israel group).

Table 7-9 ▶ "One-Issue" Interest Groups

National Right to Life Committee	www.nrlc.org
NARAL Pro-Choice America	www.naral.org
National Rifle Association	www.nra.org
Brady Campaign (handgun control)	www.bradycampaign.org
American Society for the Prevention of Cruelty to Animals	www.aspca.org
People for the Ethical Treatment of Animals	www.peta.org
Mothers Against Drunk Driving	www.madd.org
AARP	www.aarp.org

Foreign Governments

Homegrown interests are not the only players in the game. Washington, DC, is also the center for lobbying by foreign governments as well as private foreign interests. The governments of the largest U.S. trading partners, such as Canada, European Union (EU) countries, Japan, and South Korea, maintain substantial research and lobbying staffs. Even smaller nations, such as those in the Caribbean, engage lobbyists when vital legislation affecting their trade interests is considered. Frequently, these foreign interests hire former representatives or former senators to promote their positions on Capitol Hill. To learn more about how foreign interests lobby the U.S. government, see this chapter's Beyond Our Borders feature.

did you know?

At least half of all lobbyists in Washington, DC, are women, but they get paid only 80 percent of what male lobbyists earn.

What Makes an Interest Group Powerful?

At any time, thousands of interest groups are attempting to influence state legislatures, governors, Congress, and members of the executive branch of the U.S. government. What characteristics make some of those groups more powerful than others and more likely to have influence over government policy? Generally, interest groups attain a reputation for being powerful through their membership size, financial resources, leadership, cohesiveness, and, increasingly, their ability to rally public support behind their cause, whether through in-person demonstrations or via social media. Grossmann suggests that certain groups become more powerful than others and more well known through a combination of successful tactics or behaviors and their ability to form an organization that continues these strategies.[12]

---

12 Matt Grossmann, *The Not-So-Special Interests: Interest Groups, Public Representation, and American Governance* (Berkeley, CA: Stanford University Press, 2012).

Figure 7-2 ▶ Profiles of Power—Four Influential Interest Groups

AARP, formerly the American Association of Retired People

Membership: 38 million Americans, mostly over 50

Location: Washington, DC

Website: www.aarp.org

AARP began as an organization of retired teachers and has grown in the last three decades to a mass organization serving more than 38.1 million members. With a membership fee of only $16 per year, members are entitled to magazines and information, lobbying on their behalf, and access to purchase medical insurance, automobile insurance, and travel services. AARP's political power derives from its huge membership, its ability to communicate to its members, and its mission to serve the needs of seniors. The group is now one of the best financed in Washington with an annual revenue base of $1.6 billion. Critics point out that AARP doesn't really offer insurance but lends its name and membership to other corporations, which pay royalties of $880 million a year to AARP. In 2017, AARP spent $9.5 million on lobbying Congress.

Source: Center for Responsive Politics, www.opensecrets.org

The Nature Conservancy

Membership: 1 million through subscriptions to the magazine

Location: Fairfax, Virginia

Website: www.nature.org

The Nature Conservancy is one of the largest and most successful environmental groups in the world, with total lobbying expenditures for 2017 of $25.8 million. The Conservancy is often criticized by other environmental groups because it is very willing to partner with private property owners, corporations, and the states to purchase and save specific tracts of land. It is seen as being more favorable to private ownership and capitalism than many other environmental interest groups. However, it has successfully purchased and preserved millions of acres of land, reefs, and seabed around the world. The organization has net assets of more than $5.7 billion.

Source: The Nature Conservancy 2014 Annual report, Charity Navigator, www.charitynavigator.org

Pharmaceutical Research and Manufacturers of America (PhRMA)

Membership: Only about 50, including all of the major drug-makers in the world. The list is available on PhRMA's website.

Location: Washington, D.C.

Website: PhRMA.org

During the debate over the Patient Protection and Affordabilty Act (the Obama health-care plan), PhRMA was considered one of the most influential players, working on the behalf of its corporate members to keep the government from regulating the cost of drugs. While the overall finances of the association are not public, the not-for-profit arm, PhRMA Foundation, distributes hundreds of thousands of dollars for scholarship and research each year, and the interest group itself spent more than $16.6 million on lobbying in 2014.

Source: Center for Responsive Politics, www.opensecrets.org

Service Employees International Union (SEIU)

Membership: 1.8 million

Location: Washington, DC

Website: www.seiu.org

One of the fastest growing unions in the country, the SEIU played an important role in the election of President Barack Obama. With its growth concentrated among public workers, the union saw the election of a progressive president as essential to the welfare of its members. SEIU has been a major campaign contributor for Democratic party candidates. In the 2016 election cycle, the organization donated $39.4 million to candidates and outside organizations. In addition, the union spent about $24.5 million on "independent" expenditures for advertising and other forms of communication. The organization reported that it spent about $490,000 on lobbying in 2017.

Source: Center for Responsive Politics, www.opensecrets.org

Size and Resources

No legislator can deny the power of an interest group that includes thousands of his or her own constituents among its members. Labor unions and organizations such as AARP and the American Automobile Association (AAA) are able to claim voters in every congressional district. Having a large membership—more than 11 million in the case of the AFL-CIO—carries a great deal of weight with government officials. AARP now has about 38 million members and a budget of approximately $1 billion for its operations. In addition, AARP claims to represent all older Americans, who constitute close to 20 percent of the population, whether they join the organization or not.

Having a large number of members, even if the individual membership dues are relatively small, provides an organization with a strong financial base. Those funds pay for lobbyists, television advertisements, mailings to members, websites, and many other resources that help an interest group make its point to politicians. The business organization with the largest membership is probably the U.S. Chamber of Commerce, which has more than 300,000 members. The Chamber of Commerce uses its members' dues to pay for staff and lobbyists as well as a up-to-date communications network: all members can receive email, use Facebook and Twitter, and check the website to get updates on the latest legislative proposals.

Other organizations may have fewer members but nonetheless be able to muster significant financial resources. The pharmaceutical industry is represented in Washington, DC, by the Pharmaceutical Research Manufacturers of America (PhRMA), sometimes called Big Pharma. In 2009 this lobby poured resources into the fight over health reform legislation, seeking and getting limits on how much the new legislation would cost the pharmaceutical industry. According to Wendell Potter, a former insurance executive turned activist, Big Pharma spent more than $2.6 billion between 1998 and 2012, far more than the gas and oil industry or defense contractors. What do they want for their money? Potter claims that lobbying effort is meant to keep legislators from interfering with the companies' "predatory pricing practices" while they enjoy many years of patent protection.[13]

Leadership

Money is not the only resource that interest groups need to have. Strong leaders who can develop effective strategies are also important. The National Resources Defense Council, formed in 1970 by a group of lawyers and law students who saw the need for a legal approach to environmental problems, is often cited as an outstanding environmental group. The leadership of the NRDC has led strong lobbying efforts for congressional action and planned superb strategies for bringing legal action against polluters and government agencies. Another example is the American Israel Public Affairs Committee (AIPAC), which has long benefited from strong leadership. AIPAC lobbies Congress and the executive branch on issues related to U.S.–Israeli relations, as well as general foreign policy in the Middle East. AIPAC has been successful in facilitating a close relationship between the two nations, which includes the $6 billion to $8 billion in foreign aid that the United States annually bestows on Israel. Despite its modest membership size, AIPAC has won bipartisan support for its agenda and is consistently ranked among the most influential interest groups in America.

Other interest groups, including some with few financial resources, succeed in part because they are led by individuals with charisma and access to power, such as Jesse Jackson of the Rainbow PUSH Coalition. Sometimes, choosing a leader with a particular image can be an effective strategy for an organization. The National Rifle Association (NRA) had more than organizational skills in mind when it elected the late Charlton Heston as its president. The strategy of using an actor who was identified with powerful roles as the spokesperson for the organization worked to improve its national image.

> **did you know?**
> The industry that spends the most on lobbying each year is the pharmaceutical/health industry.

---

13 Wendell Potter, "Big Pharmas' Stranglehold on Washington," Center for Public Integrity, September 13, 2013. http://www.publicintegrity.org/2013/02/11/12175/opinion-big-pharmas-stranglehold-washington

Lobbying and Foreign Interests

Domestic groups are not alone in lobbying the federal government. Many foreign entities hire lobbyists to influence policy and spending decisions in the United States. American lobbying firms are often utilized by foreign groups seeking to advance their agendas. The use of American lobbyists ensures greater access and increases the possibility of success. In 2013 more than 130 countries publicly reported spending more than $300 million lobbying the United States government and promoting their nations through public relations campaigns. With the United States holding such a dominant position in the global economy and world affairs, it is hardly surprising that foreign entities regularly attempt to influence the U.S. government.

Foreign Corporations and the Global Economy

Economic globalization has had an incalculable impact on public policy worldwide. Given the United States' prominence in the global economy, international and multinational corporations have taken a keen interest in influencing the U.S. government. Foreign corporations spend millions of dollars each year on lobbying in an effort to create favorable business and trade conditions.

Consider several examples: In the list of top spenders for lobbying in 2013 is Royal Dutch Shell, the largest oil company in the world. Based in the Netherlands, Shell Oil spent almost $9 million on lobbying in 2013. British Petroleum spent about $8 million, down considerably from the year of the Gulf oil spill, when it spent more than $15 million to assure a settlement in that case. GlaxoSmithKline, one of the world's leading pharmaceutical firms, spent extensively on lobbying in the United States to influence health-care legislation. Toyota Motors, by comparison, spent only about $5 million on lobbying in 2013.*

Influence from Other Nations

Foreign nations also hire firms to represent their interests before Congress and with the executive branch of government. As Congress considers an immigration reform law, many nations will be lobbying to gain higher numbers of visas for their citizens to come to the United States. Ireland, South Korea, Poland, and Canada have already spent millions on this effort.

Poor nations spend some of their budget to lobby Congress for an increase in economic aid, whereas some corrupt regimes hire lobbyists to pursue their interests in Washington, DC, rather than using their own diplomats. For example, Qorvis, a major lobbying firm, has been

Image 7-5 The world headquarters of Royal Dutch Shell in The Hague, Netherlands. The company spends millions of dollars annually to influence U.S. policy.

representing Equatorial Guinea, a very small nation in West Africa. There, the ruling family takes most of the nation's oil money, whereas the majority of its people are impoverished. The nation spent about $70,000 for the U.S. public relations campaign to improve its image in Washington, DC.**

Individuals and firms that lobby as agents of foreign principals must register with the Department of Justice (DOJ). Each year the DOJ sends a report to Congress on the registrants and their clients, data that are available through the Foreign Agents Registration Act (FARA) online list. In recent years, legislation has been introduced to ban lobbying by foreign firms and foreign nations, but it has not become law.

For Critical Analysis

1. Should foreign governments and foreign corporations be permitted to lobby the members of Congress in the same way as American interest groups?

2. Should members of Congress and the executive branch have to report any contacts from a foreign nation or corporation?

For the registration of lobbyists who represent foreign interests, you can go to the database maintained by the Department of Justice at www.fara.gov
**Kessler, Aaron and Wanjohi Kabukuru. "Shadow Diplomacy: African Nations Bypass Embassies, Tap Lobbyists." *Huffington Post*, July 30, 2013. http://www.huffingtonpost.com/2013/07/30/african-lobbyists_n_3676489.html

Cohesiveness

Regardless of an interest group's size or the amount of funds in its coffers, the motivation of its members is a key factor in determining how powerful it is. If the members of a group are committed to their beliefs strongly enough to email or tweet their representatives, join a march on Washington, DC, or work together to defeat a candidate, that group is considered powerful.

In contrast, although groups that oppose abortion rights have had little success in influencing policy, they are considered powerful because their members are vocal and highly motivated. Other measures of cohesion include the ability of a group to get its members to contact Washington, DC, quickly or to give extra money when needed. The NRA can generate hundreds of thousands of messages from its members when gun control legislation is under consideration.

Interest Group Strategies

■ **7.4** Identify the direct and indirect techniques that interest groups use to influence government decisions.

Interest groups employ a wide range of techniques and strategies to promote their policy goals. Although few groups are successful at persuading Congress and the president to completely endorse their programs, many are able to block—or at least weaken—legislation that is injurious to their members. The key to success for interest groups is access to government officials. To gain such access, interest groups and their representatives try to cultivate long-term relationships with legislators and government officials. The best of these relationships are based on mutual respect and cooperation. The interest group provides the officials with excellent sources of information and assistance, and the officials in turn give the group opportunities to express its views.

The techniques used by interest groups can be divided into direct and indirect techniques. With **direct techniques**, the interest group and its lobbyists approach the officials personally to present their case. With **indirect techniques**, in contrast, the interest group uses the general public or individual constituents to influence the government on its behalf.

direct technique
An interest group activity that involves interaction with government officials to further the group's goals.

indirect technique
A strategy employed by interest groups that uses third parties to influence government officials.

did you know?
The lobbying business earns more than $3.3 billion annually.

Direct Techniques

Lobbying, publicizing ratings of legislative behavior, building coalitions, and providing campaign assistance are the four main direct techniques used by interest groups.

Lobbying Techniques The term *lobbying* comes from the activities of private citizens regularly congregating in the lobbies of legislative chambers before a session to petition legislators. In the latter part of the 1800s, railroad and industrial groups openly bribed state legislators to pass legislation beneficial to their interests, giving lobbying a well-deserved bad name. Most lobbyists today are professionals. They are either consultants to a company or interest group or members of one of the Washington, DC, law firms that specialize in providing such services. Specialized law firms based in the capital region provide specialists in every sector of government policy to meet their clients' needs. One of the most successful firms is Akin, Gump, et. al., LLP, which received more than $39 million in fees for its efforts in 2015. Allegiant

Travel, the Denver Airport, Dow Chemicals, and a number of Native American–owned casinos were among Akin, Gump's clients. In addition, the firm represented a number of foreign entities, including Samsung Corporation, the US India Security Council, and Volkswagen AG. Amazon spent more than $600,000 on Akin, Gump, et. al.[14] Among the firm's representatives are several former Representatives and others who have served in government.

Lobbyists engage in an array of activities to influence legislation and government policy. These include the following:

1. Engaging in private meetings with public officials, including the president's advisers, to make known the interests of the lobbyists' clients. Although acting on behalf of their clients, lobbyists often furnish needed information to senators and representatives (and government agency appointees) that these officials could not easily obtain on their own. It is to the lobbyists' advantage to provide accurate information so that policymakers will rely on them as a source in the future.

2. Testifying before congressional committees for or against proposed legislation.

3. Testifying before executive rule-making agencies—such as the Federal Trade Commission (FTC) or the Consumer Product Safety Commission—for or against proposed rules.

4. Assisting legislators or bureaucrats in drafting legislation or prospective regulations. Often, lobbyists furnish advice on the specific details of legislation.

5. Inviting legislators to social occasions, such as cocktail parties, boating expeditions, and other events, including conferences at exotic locations. Most lobbyists believe that meeting legislators in a relaxed social setting is effective.

6. Providing political information to legislators and other government officials. Often, the lobbyists have better information than the party leadership about how other legislators are going to vote. In this case, the political information they furnish may be a key to legislative success.

7. Supplying nominations for federal appointments to the executive branch.

The Ratings Game Many interest groups attempt to influence the overall behavior of legislators through their rating systems. Each year, the interest group selects legislation that it believes is most important to its goals and then monitors how legislators vote on it. Each legislator is given a score based on the percentage of times that he or she voted in favor of the group's position. The usual scheme ranges from 0 to 100 percent. In the ratings scheme of the liberal Americans for Democratic Action, for example, a rating of 100 means that a member of Congress voted with the group on every issue and is, by that measure, very liberal.

Ratings are a shorthand way of describing members' voting records for interested citizens. They can also be used to embarrass members. For example, an environmental group identifies the 12 representatives it believes have the worst voting records on environmental issues and labels them "the

---

14 The full name of this law firm is Akin, Gump, Strauss, Hauer and Feld. The source for the billing information is the Center for Responsive Politics, http://www.opensecrets.org

Dirty Dozen," and a watchdog group describes those representatives who took home the most "pork" for their districts or states as the biggest "pigs."

Building Alliances Another direct technique used by interest groups is to form a coalition with other groups that are concerned about the same legislation. Often, these groups will set up a paper organization with an innocuous name to represent their joint concerns.

Members of such a coalition share expenses and multiply the influence of their individual groups by combining their efforts. Other advantages of forming a coalition are that it blurs the specific interests of the individual groups involved and makes it appear that larger public interests are at stake. These alliances also are efficient devices for keeping like-minded groups from duplicating one another's lobbying efforts.

Campaign Assistance Interest groups have additional strategies to use in their attempts to influence government policies. Groups recognize that the greatest concern of legislators is to be reelected, so they focus on the legislators' campaign needs. Associations with large memberships, such as labor unions, are able to provide workers for political campaigns, including precinct workers to get out the vote, volunteers to put up posters and pass out literature, and people to staff telephone banks for campaign headquarters.

In many states where certain interest groups have large memberships, candidates vie for the groups' endorsements in the campaign. Gaining those endorsements may be automatic, or it may require that the candidates participate in debates or interviews with the interest groups. Endorsements are important because an interest group usually publicizes its choices in its membership publication and because the candidate can use the endorsement in her or his campaign literature. Traditionally, labor unions have endorsed Democratic Party candidates. Republican candidates, however, often try to persuade union locals at least to refrain from any endorsement. Making no endorsement can then be perceived as disapproval of the Democratic Party candidate.

Despite the passage of the Bipartisan Campaign Finance Act in 2002, the 2016 election boasted record campaign spending. The usual array of interest groups—labor unions, professional groups, and business associations—gathered contributions to their political action committees and distributed them to the candidates. Most labor contributions went to Democratic candidates, whereas a

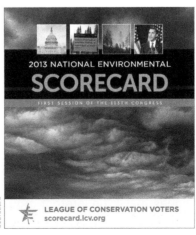

Image 7-6
Interest groups from every imaginable ideological point of view issue scorecards of individual legislators' voting records as they relate to the organization's agenda. Shown here are two such scorecards. How much value can voters place on these kinds of ratings?

Election 2016

Who Decides Endorsements?

In most statewide and national elections, candidates vie for endorsements from interest groups. As noted in the text, an endorsement will bring the candidate free advertising, a connection to a group, and, sometimes, contributions and volunteers. In most cases, interest group endorsements are made in late summer and are fairly easy to predict: unions tend to endorse Democratic candidates, and business groups endorse Republicans. Occasionally a union may decline to endorse any candidate, which is usually read as a negative by the Democratic base.

Who even knows about endorsements? Much of the general public knows very little about endorsements. Only the members of the endorsing organization and strong partisans are aware of endorsements. They may share their information as informed voters with friends, coworkers, and family members. That is exactly what candidates hope for.

In 2016 the presidential primary season occasioned an early scuffle over endorsements. As the expected nominee of the Democratic Party for 2016, Hillary Clinton garnered some endorsements as early as the summer of 2015. When Senator Bernie Sanders entered the race, competition for endorsements began in earnest. By March 2016, the majority of labor unions had endorsed Secretary Clinton, but the Communications Workers of America and several other groups endorsed Sanders.

As the split between the unions became apparent, the process for making endorsements came into question.

Several commentators suggested that unions that held polls of their members were more likely to endorse Sanders, whereas unions that allowed their executive committees to decide all went for Clinton. The AFL-CIO announced that it would not hold an endorsement vote in February, although several of its member unions had already endorsed Secretary Clinton. As the president of the AFL-CIO stated, "I have concluded that there is a broad consensus for the AFL-CIO to remain neutral in the presidential primaries for the time being."* In years past, this major union has sometimes endorsed a candidate early (Al Gore in 1999) and often waited until the primaries were almost over (Barack Obama in 2008). In 2016, the unions united behind Clinton as their candidate for president.

For Critical Analysis

1. Do you think endorsements should be decided by interest group elites or by vote of the group's members?

2. How would you find out if a candidate has received endorsements from interest groups?

*Noam Scheiber, "Unions Say a Majority of Their Members Support Hillary Clinton," *The New York Times*, February 22, 2016.

majority of business contributions went to Republicans. Some groups, such as real estate agents, gave evenly to both parties. At the same time, the newer campaign groups, the so-called 527 organizations—tax-exempt associations focused on influencing political elections—raised more than $800 million in unregulated contributions to support campaign activities, registration drives, and advertising. After seeing the success of these groups in raising and spending funds, hundreds of interest groups, private and nonprofit, have founded their own 527 organizations to spend funds for advertising and other political activities. The 2009 decision of the Supreme Court in *Citizens United v. FEC* makes it possible for unions, interest groups, and corporations to spend money directly on advertising for and against candidates in every election.

Indirect Techniques

Interest groups can also try to influence government policy by working through others, who may be constituents or the general public. Indirect techniques mask the interest group's own activities and make the effort appear to be spontaneous. Furthermore, legislators and government officials are often more impressed by contacts from constituents than from an interest group's lobbyist.

Generating Public Pressure

In some instances, interest groups try to produce a groundswell of public pressure to influence the government. Such efforts may include advertisements in national magazines and newspapers, mass mailings, television publicity, and demonstrations. The Internet, YouTube, Twitter, and Facebook make communication efforts even more effective. "Like" Change to Win Federation or the Sierra Club or Occupy California on Facebook, and you will receive a constant set of tweets, blogs, and links to videos. The Occupy movement gathered almost all of its strength and organizing power through the use of social networks.

Interest groups also may commission polls to find out what the public's sentiments are and then publicize the results. Of course, the questions in the polls are worded to get public responses that support the group's own position. The intent of this activity is to convince policymakers that public opinion overwhelmingly supports the group's position.

Some corporations and interest groups also engage in a practice that might be called **climate control**. With this strategy, public relations efforts are aimed at improving the public image of the industry or group and are not necessarily related to any specific political issue. Contributions by corporations and groups in support of public television programs, sponsorship of special events, and commercials extolling the virtues of corporate research are some ways of achieving climate control. For example, to improve its image in the wake of the 2010 Deepwater Horizon oil spill in the Gulf of Mexico, British Petroleum (BP) launched a set of advertisements featuring individuals who work for the corporation talking about the cleanup, the good work done by BP, and their own pride in working for the corporation. Procter and Gamble (P&G) conceived its "Thank You, Mom" campaign for the 2014 Sochi Winter Olympics to build a warm image in addition to selling products. By building a reservoir of favorable public opinion, groups believe that their legislative goals will be less likely to encounter opposition from the public.

climate control
The use of public relations techniques to create favorable public opinion toward an interest group, industry, or corporation.

Using Constituents as Lobbyists

Interest groups also use constituents to lobby for their goals. In the "shotgun" approach, the interest group tries to mobilize large numbers of constituents to email, tweet, write, or phone their legislators or the president. These efforts are effective on Capitol Hill only with a very large number of responses, however, because legislators know that the voters did not initiate the communications on their own. Artificially manufactured grassroots activity has been aptly labeled *Astroturf lobbying.* A more powerful variation of this technique uses only important constituents. With this approach, known as the "rifle" technique or the "Utah plant manager theory," the interest group might, for example, ask the manager of a local plant in Utah to contact the senator from Utah. Because the constituent is seen as responsible for many jobs or other resources, the legislator is more likely to listen carefully to the constituent's concerns about legislation than to a paid lobbyist.[15]

The importance of the electronic media cannot be understated for indirect lobbying. Whether Yoko Ono is speaking against allowing fracking in her home

---

15 Tim Hyson, "Contrary to Popular Belief, Constituents Trump Lobbyists," Congressional Management Foundation, January 25, 2011. http://www.congressionalfoundation.org/news/blog/866

state, New York, or Beyoncé and a host of other media personalities are organizing for gun control, people recognize these individuals and want to see them, and thus receive a message about a public policy issue.[16]

Unconventional Forms of Pressure Sometimes, interest groups may employ forms of pressure that fall outside the ordinary political process. These can include marches, rallies, civil disobedience, or demonstrations. Such assemblies, as long as they are peaceful, are protected by the First Amendment. Chapter 5 described the civil disobedience techniques of the African American civil rights movement in the 1950s and 1960s. The 1963 March on Washington in support of civil rights was one of the most effective demonstrations ever organized. The women's suffrage movement of the early 1900s also employed marches and demonstrations to great effect.

Demonstrations, however, are not always peaceable. Violent demonstrations have a long history in America, dating back to the anti-tax Boston Tea Party described in Chapter 2. The Vietnam War (1964–1975) provoked many demonstrations, some of which were violent. In 2014 protests against the police and city officials broke out in Ferguson, Missouri. The protests were sparked by the shooting of an unarmed black man by a police officer. Demonstrations became violent, with attacks on property, and the police responded in force. In this case, the accounts of the original shooting and the demonstrations spread across the nation on Twitter and other social media in real time, although not all accounts of the incidents were based in fact. The Ferguson incident became the catalyst for a nationwide social movement, Black Lives Matter, as well as calling attention to the use of military equipment by local authorities. Real policy changes in police behavior and the criminal justice system have resulted from this incident. Another unconventional form of pressure is the **boycott**—a refusal to buy a particular product or deal with a particular business. To be effective, boycotts must command widespread support. One example was the African American boycott of buses in Montgomery, Alabama, during 1955. Another was the boycott of California grapes that were picked by nonunion workers as part of a campaign to organize Mexican American farmworkers. The first grape boycott lasted from 1965 to 1970; a series of later boycotts was less effective. More recently, the Girl Scouts of America faced a cookie boycott from some pastors of the Christian right, who called the scouts pro-abortion and pro-lesbian, and gay and lesbian groups called for a boycott of Russian vodka because of that nation's laws restricting protests or public comment supporting homosexuals.

boycott
A form of pressure or protest—an organized refusal to purchase a particular product or deal with a particular business.

Regulating Lobbyists

■ **7.5** Describe the legislation that regulates the reporting of lobbying efforts at the federal level and discuss why it is relatively ineffective.

Congress made its first attempt to control lobbyists and lobbying activities through Title III of the Legislative Reorganization Act of 1946, otherwise known as the Federal Regulation of Lobbying Act. The act actually provided for public disclosure more than for regulation, and it neglected to specify which agency would enforce its provisions. The 1946 legislation defined a *lobbyist* as any person or organization

---

16 "Demand a Plan PSA: Beyonce, Jessica Alba, Jamie Foxx, Rashida Jones and More Rally for Gun Control (video)." *Huffington Post*, December 21, 2012. www.huffingtonpost.com

that received money to be used principally to influence legislation before Congress. Such persons and individuals were supposed to register their clients and the purposes of their efforts and report quarterly on their activities.

The legislation was tested in a 1954 Supreme Court case, *United States v. Harriss*, and was found to be constitutional.[17] The Court agreed that the lobbying law did not violate due process, freedom of speech or of the press, or the freedom to petition. The Court narrowly construed the act, however, holding that it applied only to lobbyists who were influencing federal legislation *directly*.

The Results of the 1946 Act

The immediate result of the act was that a minimal number of individuals registered as lobbyists. National interest groups, such as the NRA and the American Petroleum Institute, could employ hundreds of staff members who were, of course, working on legislation, but only register one or two lobbyists who were engaged *principally* in influencing Congress. There were no reporting requirements for lobbying the executive branch, federal agencies, the courts, or congressional staff.

According to the Center for Responsive Politics, approximately 11,502 individuals and organizations registered in 2017 as lobbyists, although most experts estimated that 10 times that number were actually employed in Washington, DC, to exert influence on the government.

Whereas lobbying firms and individuals who represent foreign corporations must register with Congress, lobbyists who represent foreign governments must register with the Department of Justice under the Foreign Agent Registration Act of 1938. The Department of Justice publishes an annual report listing the lobbyists and the nations that have reported their activities. That report is available online at the Department of Justice website (www.fara.gov).

The Reforms of 1995

The reform-minded Congress of 1995–1996 overhauled the lobbying legislation, fundamentally changing the ground rules for those who seek to influence the federal government. Lobbying legislation passed in 1995 included the following provisions:

1. A *lobbyist* is defined as anyone who spends at least 20 percent of his or her time lobbying members of Congress, their staffs, or executive branch officials.

2. Lobbyists must register with the clerk of the House and the secretary of the Senate within 45 days of being hired or of making their first contacts. The registration requirement applies to organizations that spend more than $20,000 in one year or to individuals who are paid more than $5,000 annually for lobbying work.

3. Semiannual (now quarterly and electronic) reports must disclose the general nature of the lobbying effort, specific issues and bill numbers, the estimated cost of the campaign, and a list of the branches of government contacted. The names of the individuals contacted need not be reported.

---

17 347 U.S. 612 (1954).

4. Representatives of U.S.-owned subsidiaries of foreign-owned firms and lawyers who represent foreign entities also are required to register.

5. The requirements exempt grassroots lobbying efforts and those of tax-exempt organizations, such as religious groups.

Both the House and the Senate adopted new rules on gifts and travel expenses: The House adopted a flat ban on gifts, and the Senate limited gifts to $50 in value and to no more than $100 in total value from a single source in a year. There are exceptions for gifts from family members and for home-state products and souvenirs, such as T-shirts and coffee mugs. Both chambers banned all-expenses-paid trips, golf outings, and other such junkets. An exception applies for "widely attended" events, however, or if the member is a primary speaker at an event. These gift rules stopped the broad practice of taking members of Congress to lunch or dinner, but the various exemptions and exceptions have caused much controversy as the Senate and House Ethics Committees have considered individual cases.

Lobbying Scandals

The regulation of lobbying activity again surfaced in 2005, when several scandals came to light. At the center of some publicized incidents was a highly influential and corrupt lobbyist, Jack Abramoff. Using his ties with numerous Republican (and a handful of Democratic) lawmakers, Abramoff brokered many deals for the special-interest clients that he represented in return for campaign donations, gifts, and various perks. In January 2006 Abramoff pled guilty to three criminal felony counts related to the defrauding of Native American tribes and the corruption of public officials.

In 2007 both parties claimed that they wanted to reform lobbying legislation and the ethics rules in Congress. The House Democrats tightened the rules in that body early in the year, as did the Senate. The aptly named Honest Leadership and Open Government Act of 2007 was signed by President Bush in September 2007. The law tightened reporting requirements for lobbyists, extended the time period before ex-members can accept lobbying jobs (to two years for senators and one year for House members), set up rules for lobbying by members' spouses, and changed some campaign contribution rules for interest groups. The new rules adopted by the respective houses bar all members from receiving gifts or trips paid for by lobbyists unless preapproved by the Ethics Committee. Within three months after the bill took effect, a loophole was discovered that allows lobbyists to make a campaign contribution to a senator's campaign, for example, and then go to a fancy dinner where the campaign is allowed to pay the bill.[18] As with most other pieces of lobbying legislation, additional loopholes will be discovered and utilized by members and interest groups.

Interest Groups and Representative Democracy

The role played by interest groups in shaping national policy has caused many to question whether we really have a democracy at all. Most interest groups have a middle-class or upper-class bias. Members of interest groups can afford

---

18 Robert Pear, "Ethics Law Isn't Without Its Loopholes," *The New York Times*, April 8, 2008.

to pay the membership fees, are generally well educated, and normally participate in the political process to a greater extent than the "average" American. Furthermore, the majority of Americans do not actually join a group outside of their religious congregation or a recreational group. They allow others who do join to represent them.

Furthermore, leaders of some interest groups may constitute an "elite within an elite," in the sense that they usually are from a different economic or social class than most of their members. Certainly, association executives are highly paid individuals who live in Washington, DC, and associate regularly with the political elites of the country. The most powerful interest groups—those with the most resources and political influence—are primarily business, union, trade, or professional groups. In contrast, public-interest groups or civil rights groups make up only a small percentage of the interest groups lobbying Congress and may struggle to gain enough funds to continue to exist.

Thinking about the relatively low number of Americans who join them and their status as middle class or better leads one to conclude that interest groups are really an elitist phenomenon rather than, as discussed in Chapter 1, a manifestation of pluralism. Pluralist theory proposes that these many groups will try to influence the government and struggle to reach a compromise that will be advantageous to all sides. If most Americans are not represented by a group, say, on the question of farm subsidies or energy imports, however, is there any evidence that the final legislation improves life for ordinary Americans?

Interest Group Influence

The results of lobbying efforts—congressional legislation—do not always favor the interests of the most powerful groups, however. In part, this is because not all interest groups have an equal influence on government. Each group has a different combination of resources to use in the policy-making process. Whereas some groups are composed of members who have high social status and significant economic resources, such as the National Association of Manufacturers, other groups derive influence from their large memberships. AARP's large membership allows it to wield significant power over legislators. Still other groups, such as environmentalist groups, have causes that can claim strong public support even from people who have no direct stake in the issue. Groups such as the NRA are well organized and have highly motivated members. This enables them to channel a stream of mail or electronic messages toward Congress with a few days' effort.

Even the most powerful interest groups do not always succeed in their demands. Whereas the U.S. Chamber of Commerce may understandably have a justified interest in the question of business taxes, many legislators might feel that the group should not engage in the debate over the future of Social Security. In other words, groups are seen as having a legitimate concern about the issues closest to their interests but not necessarily about broader issues. This may explain why some of the most successful groups are those that focus on very specific issues—such as tobacco farming, funding of abortions, or handgun control—and do not get involved in larger conflicts.

Key Terms

boycott 266	**interest group** 243	**purposive incentive** 248
climate control 265	**labor movement** 250	**service sector** 251
direct technique 261	**latent interest** 247	**social movement** 244
free rider problem 247	**lobbyist** 243	**solidary incentive** 247
incentive 247	**material incentive** 248	
indirect technique 261	**public interest** 255	

Chapter Summary

■ **7.1** An interest group is an organization whose members share common objectives and actively attempt to influence government policy. Interest groups proliferate in the United States because they can influence government at many points in the political structure and because their efforts are protected by the First Amendment to the Constitution. Madison believed that having many opportunities for groups to flourish would protect minority rights.

■ **7.2** People join interest groups for solidary or emotional benefits, for material or financial reasons, or for purposive reasons. However, many individuals join no interest groups yet are able to benefit from the work of their members. This reality is called the "free rider" problem. Interest groups often grow from the participation of individuals in social movements.

■ **7.3** Major types of interest groups include business, agricultural, labor, public employee, professional, and environmental groups. Other important groups may be considered public-interest groups. In addition, special-interest groups and foreign governments lobby the government. The relative power of interest groups can be estimated based on the size of their membership, their financial resources, leadership, cohesion, and support among the public.

■ **7.4** Interest groups use direct and indirect techniques to influence government. Direct techniques include testifying

before committees and rulemaking agencies, providing information to legislators, rating legislators' voting records, aiding political campaigns, and building alliances. Indirect techniques to influence government include campaigns to rally public sentiment, use of social media to generate public pressure, efforts to influence the climate of opinion, and the use of constituents to lobby for the group's interests. Unconventional methods of applying pressure include demonstrations and boycotts.

■ **7.5** The 1946 Legislative Reorganization Act was the first attempt to control lobbyists and their activities through registration requirements. The United States Supreme Court narrowly construed the act as applying only to lobbyists who directly seek to influence federal legislation.

■ **7.5** In 1995 Congress approved new legislation requiring anyone who spends 20 percent of his or her time influencing legislation to register. Also, any organization spending $20,000 or more and any individual who is paid more than $5,000 annually for his or her work must register. Quarterly reports must include the names of clients, the bills in which they are interested, and the branches of government contacted. The 2007 lobbying reform law tightened the regulations on lobbyists and imposed other rules on members who wish to become lobbyists after leaving office.

Selected Resources

PRINT RESOURCES

Druter, Lee. *The Business of American Business Is Lobbying* (New York: Oxford University Press, 2015). The author produces a clear picture of corporate lobbying and supports that picture with real data about expenditures on lobbying. He concludes that much of corporate lobbying may not be as effective as CEOs seem to think.

Grossmann, Matt. *The Not-So-Special Interests: Interest Groups, Public Representation, and American Governance*

(Berkeley, CA: Stanford University Press, 2012). The author provides a new framework for analyzing interest groups. His goal is to understand why some groups seem to have a more powerful voice than others.

Leech, Beth. *Lobbyists at Work* (New York: Apress Media LLC, 2013). This volume examines how lobbyists actually assist members of Congress in fundraising and examines how this relationship affects politics in Washington, DC.

Schlozman, Kay Lehman, Sidney Verba, and Henry Brady. *The Unheavenly Chorus: Unequal Political Voice and the Broken Promise of American Democracy* (Princeton, NJ: Princeton University Press, 2012). This superb academic book examines hundreds of organizations and interest groups, as well as public polls, to point out the continuing inequality in political participation in the United States.

Spitzer, Robert. *The Politics of Gun Control*, 5th edition (New York: Paradigm Publishers, 2011). In this updated volume, Spitzer provides a nonpartisan policy analysis of American gun laws and the opposing forces of the NRA and the anti-gun organizations.

MEDIA RESOURCES

Casino Jack and the U.S. of Money—This 2010 documentary takes a scathing look at the machinations of Jack Abramoff and his colleagues. Beginning with Abramoff's days as a college Republican, producer Alex Gibney traces his rise to fame and the tremendous corruption that money brings to Congress.

Inside Job—Winner of the 2010 Oscar for best feature-length documentary, the film reveals the inside influence that kept Congress from regulating the financial industry, thus leading to the housing crash and recession of 2008.

Norma Rae—A 1979 Hollywood movie about an attempt by a Northern union organizer to unionize workers in the Southern textile industry; stars Sally Field, who won an Academy Award for her performance.

Promised Land—This 2012 film stars Matt Damon as an employee of an energy company that specializes in fracking. He is sent to a Pennsylvania farming town to persuade land owners to sign mineral rights leases to allow drilling, where he encounters John Krasinski's character, who is an environmental advocate who starts a grassroots campaign against Damon's company in hopes of preventing drilling.

Syriana—Released in 2005, this thriller follows the trail of a global petroleum corporation and its executives as they use violence abroad and lobbyists at home to get their future assured.

ONLINE RESOURCES

AFL-CIO (American Federation of Labor and Congress of Industrial Organizations—a voluntary federation of 56 national and international labor unions: www.aflcio.org

The Center for Public Integrity—a nonprofit organization dedicated to producing original, responsible investigative journalism on issues of public concern; tracks lobbyists and their expenditures: www.publicintegrity.org

Center for Responsive Politics—a nonpartisan guide to money's influence on U.S. elections and public policy with data derived from Federal Election Commission reports: www.opensecrets.org

National Rifle Association—America's foremost defender of Second Amendment rights and firearms education organization in the world; provides information on the gun control issue: www.nra.org

Sunlight Foundation—A nonpartisan organization that collects and makes available all of the data recorded at the Department of Justice for foreign lobbying registrations: www.sunlightfoundation.com

8 Political Parties

Republican presidential candidates John Kasich, Jeb Bush, Marco Rubio, Donald Trump, Ben Carson, Ted Cruz, Carly Fiorina, and Rand Paul on stage for the Republican presidential debate in Milwaukee, Wisconsin, in November 2015. A total of 17 major candidates competed for the Republican nomination in 2016.

AP Photo/Morry Gash

LEARNING OBJECTIVES

After reading this chapter, you will be able to:

■ **8.1** Define the role political parties play in the U.S. political system.

■ **8.2** Identify the three major components of the political party and describe how each contributes to overall party coherence.

■ **8.3** Explain why political parties formed in the United States and evaluate how their strength and importance have changed over time.

■ **8.4** Compare and contrast the demographics of people who identify as Democrats and Republicans; explain how party positions differ on economic and social issues.

■ **8.5** Summarize the factors that reinforce a two-party system and explain why third parties are rarely successful at winning national elections.

■ **8.6** Discuss the rise of political independents and evaluate how this change might affect American politics.

What if... Political Parties Ended Nominating Conventions?

Background

The question of how to identify qualified candidates for president and vice president was not settled in the U.S. Constitution. Wary of disruptive factions emerging, the founders did not provide any guidance on the mechanisms for nomination. In the first two national elections following ratification, this omission did not matter—George Washington was a consensus candidate and was followed into office by his vice president, John Adams. By 1800, however, nascent political parties were emerging within Congress, and the nominating function naturally fell to these groups. As the country grew and expanded west, congressional caucuses were less likely to naturally agree on a single candidate. In 1831, the Anti-Masonic Party met in Baltimore, Maryland, to select a presidential candidate that would appeal to the entire party in the election of 1832, beginning the tradition of nominating conventions.

Today, the two major parties' quadrennial events are the Democratic National Convention and the Republican National Convention. Each party selects delegates to attend the national meeting and chooses the party's nominee by ballot. Delegates also meet to create the party platform (a statement of principles and policy positions) and determine the rules and procedures that will govern the next election cycle. Speeches allow the parties to audition future candidates. Barack Obama, for example, was the keynote speaker at the Democratic National Convention in 2004. New Jersey Governor Chris Christie delivered the keynote address for Republicans in 2012.

Prior to direct primaries, presidential nominating conventions were exciting events, with choice of the party nominee entirely in the hands of delegates (and the political bosses who influenced their votes). Primaries began in just a handful of states but spread quickly following the chaotic 1968 Democratic National Convention in Chicago. Democrats adopted the direct primary based on the recommendation of the McGovern-Fraser Commission, and Republicans followed suit in 1972. This effectively transferred the power to choose the party's nominee from party delegates to individual voters, who may or may not be party loyalists. By the time the primary season is over in June, the nominee has usually been determined. A pro forma vote by convention delegates makes it official, and the successful nominee announces his or her choice of running mate. Delegates once again endorse that decision with a vote. The presidential nominee's acceptance speech on the last night of the convention marks the first campaign speech on the road to the White House.

Why Cancel the Party? Everyone Is Having So Much Fun!

Even though the nominee is usually not in question going into the national convention, the party uses the mass meeting as an opportunity to celebrate and rally supporters. In July 2016, the Republican National Convention was held in Cleveland, Ohio and the Democratic National Convention met in Philadelphia, Pennsylvania. Each convention involved 50,000 people. In each case, about a third of those involved were representatives of the media. Network television used to provide "gavel-to-gavel" coverage of the conventions but has dropped back to an hour of highlights aired each evening.

Nominating conventions are expensive affairs—the total cost for Democrats was estimated at $127 million and $114 million for Republicans. Congress gave each party $50 million to pay for convention security costs incurred by local and state agencies. Each party covers the shortfall by raising private donations from individuals and corporations. Private and corporate donors provided $67.2 million to Democrats for their convention. Republicans' aimed to raise a similar amount in private support, but they suffered a shortfall when more than two dozen prominent corporations and individuals withdrew financial support following controversial statements made by Donald Trump. In April 2014, President Obama signed a bill redirecting public campaign funds earmarked for conventions to the National Institutes of Health and pediatric medical research, leaving the parties to raise the funds required for conventions from private and corporate donors. This spells the end for Watergate-era public financing, especially as it comes on the heels of the U.S. Supreme Court's decision in *McCutcheon v. Federal Election Commission,* which struck down the cap on total giving to national candidates and political parties.

Would Anybody Miss the Conventions?

In 2016, each party scheduled its convention for July—nearly a month earlier than for previous election cycles. Each national party must select a nominee for president, but if this important choice is substantively accomplished through primaries and party caucuses held in all 50 states and not at the national nominating convention, do delegates still need to meet? There is some value to directing the nation's attention to the presidential selection process when the political parties convene, but the business of conventions could be accomplished another way.

For Critical Analysis

1. Delegates to the presidential nominating conventions are regular people who are hyperengaged with their political party. What might be lost for those people if political parties ended the convention?

2. Conventions, campaigns, and elections are very expensive. Without public money, private donors will play a bigger role in conventions. Will this change who is nominated or the quality of candidates who choose to seek the party's nomination?

3. For months in 2016, the media speculated about brokered conventions. Some pundits warned of chaos, whereas others relished a return to the days when partisan delegates and not primary voters selected the party nominee. In your opinion, who should choose the party nominee and by what process?

faction
A subgroup or bloc within a legislature or political party acting in pursuit of some special interest or position.

D uring national election years, whether for congressional seats, such as 2014, or the presidency, as in 2012 and 2016, political parties are an important feature of the political landscape in the United States. Political parties are made up of people who use the organization, resources, and access to power that the parties provide in order to influence the outcomes of government. Parties play an important coordinating role across institutions and among the local, state, and national levels. The nation's founders worried that political **factions** would destroy the Republic, but in reality political parties are absolutely necessary to make our system function. Identification with a political party links individuals with a group of like-minded people who together recruit candidates for public office, conduct elections, inform voters on issues and policy choices, and organize government. Thus, although it has always been popular in America to speak of parties with disdain and the number of political independents has never been higher, to quote E. E. Schattschneider—"modern democracy is unthinkable save in terms of political parties."[1]

Interestingly, as important as parties are to American politics, affiliation is entirely voluntary and remarkably fluid. To become a "member" of a political party, you do not have to pay dues or swear an oath of allegiance. Individuals and groups switch their allegiance from one party to another between elections; within a single election cycle, an individual might select candidates from different parties for various offices. Also, not everyone within a party agrees on the best path forward, so intraparty debates are common and public. Party soul searching typically follows electoral defeat. Having lost the White House in 2008 and 2012, Republicans set out to review their message and evaluate

---

1 E. E. Schattschneider, *Party Government* (New York: Farrar & Rinehart, 1942).

the demographic changes among voters in preparation for the 2016 contest, but they did not predict the rise in popularity of Donald Trump. President Obama warned Democrats not to be complacent: "During presidential elections, young people vote, women are more likely to vote, blacks, Hispanics are more likely to vote. And suddenly a more representative cross-section of America gets out there and we do pretty well in presidential elections. But in midterms we get clobbered . . . I'm just hoping you all feel the same sense of urgency that I do."[2]

What Is a Political Party and What Do Parties Do?

■ **8.1** Define the role political parties play in the U.S. political system.

A **political party** is a group of political activists who organize to win elections, operate the government, and determine public policy. This definition highlights the difference between an interest group and a political party. Interest groups do not want to operate the government, and they do not put forth political candidates—even though they support candidates who will promote their interests if elected or reelected. Interest groups also tend to be exclusive, attracting people who share their set of interest positions. American political parties, because of our electoral structure where majorities determine most victories, tend to be as inclusive as possible in order to attract every possible voter, while still maintaining their unique "brand."

Political parties in the United States engage in a wide variety of activities, many of which are discussed in this chapter. Through these activities, parties perform several functions in the political system. These functions include the following:

- *Recruiting candidates to run for public office under their party label.* Because a primary goal of parties is to gain control of government, they must work to recruit candidates for all elective offices. If parties did not search out and encourage political hopefuls, far more offices would be uncontested, and voters would have limited choices.

- *Organizing and running elections.* Although elections are a government activity, political parties actually organize the voter-registration drives, recruit the volunteers to work at the polls, provide most of the campaign activity to stimulate interest in the election, and work to increase voter participation.

- *Presenting alternative policies to the electorate.* Political parties are focused on a broad set of issues with specific positions on each. Because political parties are large and complex organizations, there may be smaller constituencies within the party that hold different opinions, but each party reflects a set of principles. The Democrats or Republicans in Congress who vote together do so because they represent constituencies that have similar expectations and demands.

political party
A group of political activists who organize to win elections, operate the government, and determine public policy.

did you know?
In 2018, the number of self-identifying independents grew to 45 percent—just two points shy of the number of Democrats and Republicans combined.

---

2   Tal Kopan, "President Obama: 'In Midterms We Get Clobbered,'" Politico, March 21, 2014. www.politico.com/story/2014/03/obama-democrats-midterm-elections-clobbered-104885.html#ixzz2ylovxAhF

Image 8-1

Donald Trump attracted passionate supporters on the way to securing the Republican nomination in 2016. Trump primary voters tended to be white, more male than female, and lack a college degree. His campaign slogan "Make American Great Again" resonated with people who felt they had been left behind by the global economy and changing demographics at home.

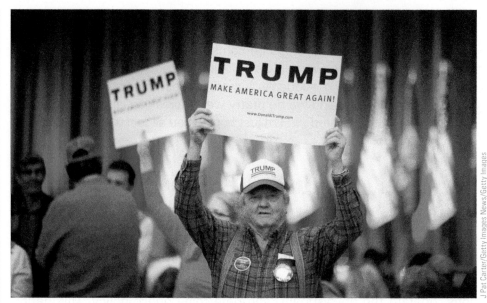

- *Accepting responsibility for operating the government.* When a party elects the president or governor and members of the legislature, it accepts the responsibility for running the government based on the principles it espouses. This includes staffing the executive branch with loyal party supporters and developing linkages among the elected officials to gain support for policies and their implementation.

- *Acting as the organized opposition to the party in power.* The "out" party, or the one not in control, is expected to articulate its own policies and stand in opposition to the winning party when appropriate for the nation. By presenting alternative perspectives to the party in power, the opposition party forces debate on the policy alternatives and ensures that careful scrutiny is paid to policies enacted.

The major functions of American political parties are carried out by a small nucleus of party activists operating at the local, state, and national levels. This arrangement is quite different from the more highly structured, mass-membership party organization typical of many European parties. American parties concentrate on winning elections rather than on signing up large numbers of deeply committed, dues-paying members who believe passionately in the party's program.

Getting Organized: The Three Components of a Party

■ **8.2** Identify the three major components of the political party and describe how each contributes to overall party coherence.

Although American parties are known by a single name, each party really has three major components: party-in-the-electorate, party organization, and party-in-government.

    The first component, the **party-in-the-electorate**, is made up of all of the people who affiliate and identify with the political party. Although they are not required to participate in every election, they are the most likely to do so because they feel a sense of loyalty to the party and use their

party-in-the-electorate
Those members of the general public who identify with a political party or who express a preference for one party over another.

partisanship as a cue to decide who will earn their vote. Party membership might be a rational calculation of which party is most likely to advance their material interest, but for most people, identifying with a party is more analogous to identifying with a geographic region or a major sports team. In this sense, the attachment is emotional, and the affiliation helps us find and make connections with others who share our interests and passions. Some states require you to specify your party affiliation when you register to vote, whereas others do not. In some places, you only have two formal choices when declaring your party—Democrat or Republican—whereas in others, you might be allowed to choose from among many minor parties. Even then, your party preference might not always match your vote choice in a general election. Perhaps you think of yourself as a Libertarian, but because there are few Libertarian candidates standing for election in each race, you select candidates from other parties that match your preferences most closely for a given office or in a given year. Party leaders pay close attention to the affiliation of their members in the electorate because winning a majority of contests is the way to gain control of government and enact the party's policies. Democrats have long enjoyed the support of a majority of African Americans and look to increase their share of the national vote by appealing to the growing number of Hispanic voters. The 2016 electorate was the most diverse in U.S. history.

Party Organization

The second component, the **party organization**, provides the structural framework for the political party by recruiting volunteers to become party leaders; identifying potential candidates; and organizing caucuses, conventions, and election campaigns for its candidates. The party organization and its active workers keep the party functioning between elections, as well as make sure that the party puts forth electable candidates and articulates clear positions in the elections. If the party-in-the-electorate declines in numbers and loyalty, the party organization must try to find a strategy to rebuild the grassroots following.

Each of the American political parties has a parallel structure at the national, state, and local levels. This often leads people to believe that the national party dictates to the state and local parties, but in reality the political parties have a confederal structure in which each unit has significant autonomy and is linked only loosely to the other units. State and local organizations are essential to the party's overall functions, but their influence varies by state. In some states, parties receive significant contributions from individuals and interest groups for their operations, whereas in other states and localities political parties are very weak organizations with very little funding. This is particularly true of the minority party in a state or district where it has little chance to win a seat.

The National Convention The national party organization is responsible for the **national convention**, held every four years and attended by thousands of **convention delegates** from around the country. Delegates are selected by parties at the state level, and the rules for delegate selection in each state vary. The convention is where the presidential and vice

party organization
The formal structure and leadership of a political party, including election committees; local, state, and national executives; and paid professional staff.

> *did you know?*
> Franklin D. Roosevelt was the first person to accept his party's nomination in person, appearing at the 1932 Democratic National Convention in Chicago.

national convention
The meeting held every four years by each major party to select presidential and vice presidential candidates, to write a platform, to choose a national committee, and to conduct party business.

convention delegates
Delegates are individuals chosen to represent their states at their party conventions prior to a presidential election.

party platform
A document drawn up at each national convention outlining the policies, positions, and principles of the party.

national committee
A standing committee of a national political party established to direct and coordinate party activities between national party conventions.

did you know?

The Democrats and Republicans each had exactly one woman delegate at their conventions in 1900.

state central committee
The principal organized structure of each political party within each state. This committee is responsible for carrying out policy decisions of the party's state convention.

presidential candidates are officially nominated and where delegates adopt the **party platform**. The platform is a set of guiding principles and policy positions intended to bring coherence to the party brand. However, the platform is drafted by a committee of loyal party activists who may have supported different candidates for the party's nomination prior to the convention. Compromises are required to reach an agreement on the platform, and the positions articulated in the document are likely to reflect the beliefs of the strongest partisans rather than the average party voter. Republican delegates are more ideologically conservative than the likely Republican voter, just as delegates to the Democratic convention are more liberal than the majority of their party's voters. So, although it is important that the parties detail their core principles for members and voters, the platform is not binding on candidates, officeholders, or even the party itself.

Each of the parties chooses a **national committee**, elected by the individual state parties, to direct and coordinate party activities during the following four years. The Democrats include at least two members (a man and a woman) from each state, from the District of Columbia, and from the several territories. Governors, members of Congress, mayors, and other officials may be included as at-large members of the national committee. The Republicans also include state chairpersons from every state carried by the Republican Party in the preceding presidential, gubernatorial, or congressional elections. The selections of national committee members are ratified by the delegates in attendance. The national committee ratifies the presidential nominee's choice of a national chairperson, who acts as the spokesperson for the party. The national chairperson and the national committee plan the next campaign, as well as the next convention, raise financial contributions, and publicize the national party. The national chairperson is an important face for the party, but his or her power today is less than party leaders enjoyed four decades ago. Robert S. Strauss, former head of the Democratic National Party, died in March 2014. Tributes to his life inevitably commented on the diminished power of political parties and their national leaders and the rise of candidate campaign operations and independent groups "aided by transforming technology that has changed the character of politics."[3]

The State Party Organization The Union has 50 states, plus the District of Columbia and the U.S. territories, and an equal number of party organizations for each major party. Thus, there are more than 100 state parties (and even more if local and minor parties are included. Because every state party is unique, it is impossible to describe what an "average" state political party is like. Nonetheless, state parties have several organizational features in common. Each state party has a chairperson, a committee, and local organizations. In theory, the role of the **state central committee**—the principal organized structure of each political party within each state—is similar in the various states. The committee, usually composed of members who represent congressional districts, state legislative districts, or counties, has responsibility for carrying out the policy decisions of the party's state convention. In some states, the state committee can issue directives to the state chairperson.

---

3 Jonathan Weisman and Jennifer Steinhauer, "Kingmaker's Death Lays Bare Erosion of Parties' Authority," *The New York Times*, March 20, 2014. www.nytimes.com/2014/03/21/us/politics/political-parties-have-seen-shift-in-center-of-power.html

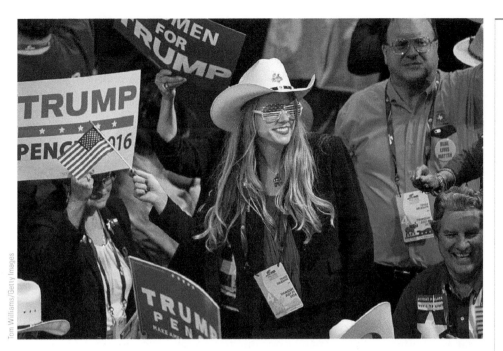

Image 8-2
Texas delegate Erin Swanson dances before Donald Trump, Republican nominee for president, spoke in the Quicken Loans Arena on the final night of the Republican National Convention in Cleveland, Ohio, July 21, 2016. (Photo By Tom Williams/CQ Roll Call)

did you know?
It took 103 ballots before John W. Davis emerged from a field of 15 candidates to win the nomination at the Democratic National Convention in 1924; by comparison, the Republican record for the most ballots needed to select a nominee is 36, set at the 1880 Convention.

Similar to the national committee, the state central committee controls the use of party campaign funds during political campaigns. State parties are also important in national politics because of the **unit rule**, which awards electoral votes in presidential elections as an indivisible bloc (except in Maine and Nebraska). Presidential candidates concentrate their efforts in states in which voter preferences seem to be evenly divided or in which large numbers of electoral votes are at stake.

unit rule
A rule by which all of a state's electoral votes are cast for the presidential candidate receiving a plurality of the popular vote in that state.

Image 8-3
Crowds cheer as Hillary Clinton delivers her address accepting the nomination at the Democratic National Convention in Philadelphia on July 28, 2016.

patronage
Rewarding faithful party workers and followers with government employment and contracts.

Local Party Organizations The lowest level of party machinery is the local organization, supported by district leaders, precinct or ward captains, and party workers. Much of the work is coordinated by county committees and their chairpersons. In the 1800s, the institution of **patronage**—rewarding the party faithful with government jobs or contracts—held the local organization together. For immigrants and the poor, the political machine often furnished important services and protections. The big-city machine was the archetypal example. Tammany Hall, or the Tammany Society, which dominated New York City government for nearly two centuries, was perhaps the most notorious example of this political form.

Today, local political organizations still can contribute a great deal to local election campaigns. These organizations are able to provide the foot soldiers of politics—individuals who pass out literature and get out the vote on Election Day, which can be crucial in local elections. In many regions, local Democratic and Republican organizations still exercise some patronage, such as awarding courthouse jobs, contracts for street repair, and other lucrative construction contracts. Local party organizations are also the most important vehicles for recruiting young adults into political work, because political involvement at the local level offers activists many opportunities to gain experience.

The Party-in-Government

party-in-government
All of the elected and appointed officials who identify with a political party.

The **party-in-government** is the third component of American political parties. The party-in-government consists of elected and appointed officials who identify with a political party. After the election is over and the winners are announced, the focus of party activity shifts to organizing and controlling the government. Partisanship plays an important role in the day-to-day operations of Congress, with party membership determining everything from office space to committee assignments. The political party furnishes to the president the pool of qualified applicants for political appointments to run the government, although the president is free to appoint individuals from any party, and presidential appointment power is limited by the permanent bureaucracy. Judicial appointments, especially nominations to the U.S. Supreme Court, offer the winning party a way to extend its influence far into the future.

divided government
A situation in which one major political party controls the presidency and the other controls the chambers of Congress, or in which one party controls a state governorship and the other controls the state legislature.

ticket splitting
Voting for candidates of two or more parties for different offices. For example, a voter splits her ticket if she votes for a Republican presidential candidate and a Democratic congressional candidate.

Divided Government All of these party appointments suggest that the winning political party at any level has a great deal of control in the American system. Because of the checks and balances and the relative lack of cohesion in American parties, however, such control is an illusion. One reason is that for some time, many Americans have seemed to prefer a **divided government**, with the executive and legislative branches controlled by different parties. The trend toward **ticket splitting**—voting for a president and congressperson of different parties—has increased sharply since 1952. This practice may indicate a lack of trust in government or the relative weakness of party identification among many voters. Voters seem comfortable with having a president affiliated with one party and a Congress controlled by the other.

The Limits of Party Unity The power of the parties is limited in other ways. Consider how major laws are passed in Congress. Traditionally, legislation has rarely been passed by a vote strictly along party lines. Although most Democrats may oppose a bill, for example, some Democrats may vote for it.

did you know?

The political party with the most seats in the House of Representatives chooses the Speaker of the House, makes any new rules it wants, gets a majority of the seats on each important committee, chooses committee chairs, and hires most of the congressional staff.

Their votes, combined with the votes of Republicans, may be enough to pass the bill. Similarly, support from some Republicans may enable a bill sponsored by the Democrats to pass. U.S. elections are "candidate centered," meaning that candidates may choose to run, raise their own funds, build their own organizations, and win elections largely on their own, without significant help from a political party.

Party Polarization When parties in Congress adhere to party loyalty in their votes, the institution becomes polarized. When that happens, little is accomplished, and members dig in and refuse to work across the aisle to reach a compromise. Without the ability to work together, legislative action stalls and the public grows increasingly dissatisfied. One cause of polarization is the ability of the parties to create House districts that are **safe seats** in the redistricting process.[4] In 1992 roughly one-fourth of the House of Representatives was elected from competitive districts (also known as swing districts because the seat could feasibly be won by either party), but today only 32 competitive districts remain—only 7 percent of the institution. Landslide districts, places where one party regularly wins by more than 20 percentage points, have doubled since 1992 and today make up nearly 56 percent of the House. Scholars and pundits differ on whether the polarization cemented in the House through redistricting is a true reflection of divisions within the electorate. Some contend that a majority of Americans are strongly committed to tolerance of opposing political views. Political scientist Morris Fiorina argues that the American people are no more divided over their policy preferences today than they have ever been.[5] Political parties serve to channel the public's energy and divergent opinions into political solutions enacted by government. Parties have played this role in American politics since the founding.

safe seat
A district that returns the legislator with 55 percent of the vote or more.

A History of Political Parties in the United States

■ **8.3** Explain why political parties formed in the United States and evaluate how their strength and importance have changed over time.

Although it is difficult to imagine more than two major political parties in the United States, multiparty systems are quite common in other democracies. Sometimes parties are tied to ideological positions—such as Marxist, socialist, liberal, conservative, and ultraconservative parties. Some nations have political parties representing regional interests born of separate cultural identities, such as the French-speaking and Flemish-speaking regions of Belgium. Some parties are rooted in religious differences. Parties also exist that represent specific economic interests—agricultural, maritime, or industrial—and some, such as monarchist parties, speak for alternative political systems.

---

4   Nate Silver, "As Swing Districts Dwindle, Can a Divided House Stand?" *The New York Times,* December 27, 2012. http://fivethirtyeight.blogs.nytimes.com/2012/12/27/as-swing-districts-dwindle-can-a-divided-house-stand/?_php=true&_type=blogs&_r=0
5   Morris Fiorina, *Culture War? The Myth of a Polarized America* (New York: Longman, 2005).

Politics in Practice

Securing the House of Representatives One State Legislature at a Time

Our constitution is unique in that it gives state legislatures substantial control over how we elect the president and Congress. In many other democracies, the national government runs elections—usually through an impartial commission. In the United States, the party in control of the state legislature draws the lines establishing congressional districts and determines the rules by which national elections are conducted in the state. (Will there be voter ID laws? Early voting? Same-day registration?)

Following the 2008 election, Republicans created the Redistricting Majority Project (REDMAP) aimed at winning seats in state legislative contests. Republican strategist Karl Rove said, "Some of the most important contests [in 2010] will be way down the ballot in . . . state legislative races that will determine who redraws congressional district lines after this year's census, a process that could determine which party controls upwards of 20 seats [in the House of Representatives] and whether many other seats will be competitive."* As Herman Schwartz, constitutional law professor at American University, observes, REDMAP succeeded brilliantly.

Republicans focused on 107 state legislative seats in 16 states where Republican pick-ups of just four or five seats from Democrats would enable the Republican Party to reshape over 190 congressional districts. They succeeded in increasing their share of state house and senate seats by 10 percent, took both legislative chambers in 25 states, and won the legislature and governorship in 21 states. These victories allowed Republicans to remap congressional districts in their favor to great effect in the 2012 elections.

The Republican State Leadership Committee (RSLC) has been largely responsible for carrying out this strategy. By focusing laser-like attention on the states, Republicans have been able to make significant gains in the *national* House of Representatives—gains many describe as "lasting." The Republican State Leadership Committee is described as the largest caucus of Republican state leaders in the country and the only national organization whose mission is to elect down-ballot, state-level Republican officeholders—working since 2002 to elect candidates to the office of lieutenant governor, attorney general, secretary of state and state legislator.** In the 2012 election cycle, the RSLC raised over $39 million to invest in races in 42 states. This organization is classified as a

"527 group"—a tax-exempt political organization created to influence elections.

The RSLC is not a part of the Republican Party, but the direct benefit to the party is very clear in this example. In Virginia and Ohio, the 2012 vote for House of Representatives narrowly favored Republicans (50–48 in Virginia; 51–47 in Ohio), but because of the way the district lines had been drawn, the outcomes in terms of seats was not close: 8–3 in Virginia and 12–4 in Ohio.

The Democratic Party counterpart is the Democratic Legislative Campaign Committee (DLCC), established in 1994.*** Focused on policy coherence at the state level in support of national party action, this group has not strategically focused on winning state elections.

REDMAP illustrates the significant influence exercised by organizations outside of the formal political party structure. Democrats have launched Advantage 2020, a super PAC that hopes to raise $70 million to spend in states where redistricting could lead to Democratic gains.

For Critical Analysis

1. REDMAP is an example of strategic politics at the state level with significant consequences for national politics. As a result of REDMAP's success, fewer congressional districts will feature competitive races between Republican and Democratic candidates at least until 2021 when district lines are redrawn. In your opinion, is there anything wrong with this?

2. In most states the state legislature draws the congressional district lines following the decennial census, but in six states independent commissions draw both state and federal districts, thereby limiting political influence. Given what you know about the success of REDMAP, would you favor independent commissions in all states? Why or why not?

* Herman Schwartz, "Democrats: It's the States, Stupid!" Reuters, July 14, 2013. http://blogs.reuters.com/great-debate/2013/07/14/democrats-its-the-states-stupid/
** Republican State Leadership Committee, www.rslc.com
*** Democratic Legislative Campaign Committee, www.dlcc.org

The United States has had a **two-party system** since about 1800. The function and character of the political parties, as well as the persistence of the two-party system, are largely the result of unique historical forces operating from our country's beginning as an independent nation. James Madison (1751–1836) linked the emergence of political parties to the form of government created by the Constitution. Recall that he attributed factions to human nature—in other words, as long as people are free to form their own opinions, there will always be competing ideas. Federalists and Anti-Federalists differed as to the size and functions of government and ultimately over whether the constitutions should be ratified. Thus, they represent the first signs that America would be shaped by political parties. To understand the evolution of political parties, scholars organize periods of time into party systems. Party systems reflect the number of parties active at a point in time and which party or parties are gaining power and influence, or, conversely, losing power or perhaps even disappearing altogether. The change from one system to another is often signaled by a critical election—one in which a significant transfer of power takes place.

two-party system
A political system in which only two parties have a reasonable chance of winning.

The First-Party System: The Development of Parties, 1789–1828

In September 1796, George Washington, who had served as president for almost two full terms, decided not to run again. In his farewell address, Washington warned that the country might be destroyed by the "baneful effects of the spirit of party." He viewed parties as a threat to both national unity and the concept of popular government. Early in his career, Thomas Jefferson agreed, stating in 1789, "[i]f I could not go to heaven but with a party, I would not go there at all."[6]

Nevertheless, in the years after the ratification of the Constitution, Americans realized that something more permanent than a faction would be necessary to identify candidates for office and represent competing political ideas among the people. The result was two political parties formed around the ideas represented by the Federalists and the Anti-Federalists. One party was called the Federalists and included John Adams, the second president (served 1797–1801). They represented commercial interests such as merchants and large planters and supported a strong national government.

Thomas Jefferson led the other party, which emerged from the thought tradition of the Anti-Federalists and came to be called the Republicans, or Jeffersonian Republicans. (These Republicans should not be confused with the later Republican Party of Abraham Lincoln. To avoid confusion, some scholars refer to Jefferson's party as the Democratic-Republicans, but this name was never used during the time that the party existed.) Jefferson's Republicans represented artisans and farmers. They strongly supported states' rights. In 1800, when Jefferson defeated

Everett Collection Inc/Alamy Stock Photo

Image 8-4
Thomas Jefferson, founder of the first Republican Party. His election to the presidency in 1800 was one of the world's first transfers of power through a free election.

---

6   Letter to Francis Hopkinson written from Paris while Jefferson was minister to France. In John P. Foley, ed., *The Jeffersonian Cyclopedia* (New York: Russell & Russell, 1967), p. 677.

Adams in the presidential contest, one of the world's first peaceful transfers of power from one party to another was achieved.

The Era of Good Feelings

From 1800 to 1820, a majority of U.S. voters regularly elected Republicans to the presidency and to Congress. By 1816, the Federalist Party had virtually collapsed, and two-party competition did not really exist. Even though the Republicans opposed the Federalists' call for a stronger, more active central government, they undertook active government policies such as acquiring the Louisiana Territory and Florida and establishing a national bank. Because the Republicans faced no real political opposition and little political debate was stirred, the administration of James Monroe (served 1817–1825) came to be known as the **era of good feelings**. Because political competition took place among individual Republican aspirants, this period can also be called the *era of personal politics*.

era of good feelings
The years from 1817 to 1825, when James Monroe was president and had, in effect, no political opposition.

The Second-Party System: Democrats and Whigs, 1828–1860

Organized two-party politics returned in 1824. With the election of John Quincy Adams as president, the Democratic-Republican Party split into two entities. The followers of Adams called themselves National Republicans. The followers of Andrew Jackson, who defeated Adams in 1828, formed the **Democratic Party**. Later, the National Republicans took the name **Whig Party**, which had been a traditional name for British liberals. The Whigs stood for federal spending on internal improvements such as roads. The Democrats, the stronger of the two parties, favored personal liberty and opportunity for the "common man." It was understood implicitly that the common man was a white man—the small number of free blacks who could vote identified overwhelmingly as Whigs.[7] Women began to organize during this time period as well. Recall that the Seneca Falls Convention for women's rights was held in 1848 and issued a call for universal suffrage.

Democratic Party
One of the two major American political parties evolving out of the Republican Party of Thomas Jefferson.

Whig Party
A major party in the United States during the first half of the nineteenth century, formally established in 1836. The Whig Party was anti-Jackson and represented a variety of regional interests.

The Jacksonian Democrats' success was linked to superior efforts to involve common citizens in the political process, a philosophy known as populism. Mass participation in politics and elections was a new phenomenon in the 1820s, as the political parties began to appeal to popular enthusiasm and themes. The parties adopted the techniques of mass campaigns, including rallies and parades. Lavishing food and drink on voters at polling places also became a common practice. Perhaps of greatest importance, however, was the push to cultivate party identity and loyalty. In large part, the spirit that motivated the new mass politics was democratic pride in participation. By making citizens feel that they were part of the political process, the parties hoped to win lasting party loyalty at the ballot box.

The Third-Party System: Republicans' Rise to Power and The Civil War, 1860–1896

In the 1850s, hostility between the North and South over slavery divided both parties. The Whigs were the first party to split apart. They had been the party of an active federal government, but Southerners had come to believe that a

---

7   Edward Pessen, *Jacksonian America: Society, Personality, and Politics* (Homewood, IL: Dorsey Press, 1969). See especially pages 246–247.

strong central government might use its power to free their slaves. Southern Whigs therefore ceased to exist as an organized party. Northern Whigs united with antislavery Democrats and members of the radical antislavery Free Soil Party to form the modern **Republican Party**.

After the Civil War, the Democratic Party was able to heal its divisions. Southern resentment of the Republicans' role in defeating the South and fears that the federal government would intervene on behalf of African Americans ensured that the Democrats would dominate the white South for the next century.

"Rum, Romanism, and Rebellion" Northern Democrats feared a strong government for other reasons. The Republicans thought that the government should promote business and economic growth, but many also wanted to use the power of government to impose evangelical Protestant moral values on society. Democrats opposed what they saw as culturally coercive measures. Many Republicans wanted to limit or even prohibit the sale of alcohol. They favored the establishment of public schools—with a Protestant curriculum. As a result, Catholics were strongly Democratic. In 1884, Protestant minister Samuel Burchard described the Democrats as the party of "rum, Romanism, and rebellion." This remark was offensive to Catholics, but as offensive as it may have been, Burchard's characterization of the Democrats contained an element of truth.

The Triumph of the Republicans In this period, the parties were evenly matched in strength. The abolition of the three-fifths rule meant that African Americans would be counted fully when allocating House seats and electoral votes to the South. The Republicans therefore had to carry almost every Northern state to win, and this was not always possible. In the 1890s, however, the Republicans gained a decisive edge. In that decade, the populist movement emerged in the West and South to champion the interests of small farmers, who were often heavily in debt. Populists supported inflation, which benefited debtors by reducing the real value of outstanding debts. In 1896, when William Jennings Bryan became the Democratic candidate for president, the Democrats embraced populism.

As it turned out, the few Western farmers who were drawn to the Democrats by this step were greatly outnumbered by urban working-class voters who believed that inflation would reduce the purchasing power of their paychecks and who therefore became Republicans. William McKinley, the Republican candidate, was elected with a solid majority of the votes. Figure 8-1 shows the states taken by Bryan and McKinley. This pattern of regional support persisted for many years. From 1896 until 1932, the Republicans were successfully able to present themselves as the party that knew how to manage the economy.

The Fourth-Party System: The Progressive Interlude and Republican Dominance, 1896–1932

In the early 1900s, a spirit of political reform arose in both major parties. Called *progressivism*, this spirit was compounded by a fear of the growing power of great corporations and a belief that honest, impartial government could

Republican Party
One of the two major American political parties. It emerged in the 1850s as an antislavery party and consisted of former Northern Whigs and antislavery Democrats.

Bettmann/Getty Images

Image 8-5
Andrew Jackson,
the seventh president of the United States, was known by the name "Old Hickory" for his victories in the War of 1812. This is a painting done by Asher Brown Durand in 1835, during the last years of Jackson's second term.

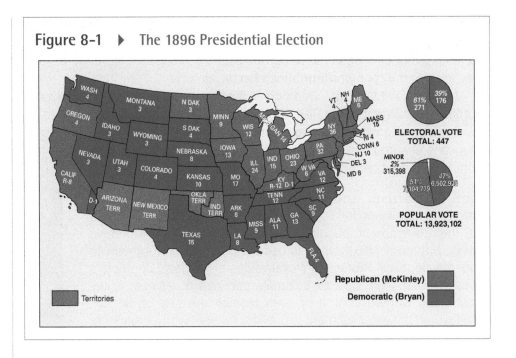

Figure 8-1 ▶ The 1896 Presidential Election

ELECTORAL VOTE TOTAL: 447

61% 271

39% 176

POPULAR VOTE TOTAL: 13,923,102

MINOR 2% 315,398

51% 7,104,779

47% 6,502,925

Republican (McKinley)

Democratic (Bryan)

Territories

regulate the economy effectively. In 1912, the Republican Party temporarily split as former Republican president Theodore Roosevelt campaigned for the presidency on a third-party Progressive, or "Bull Moose," ticket. The Republican split permitted the election of Woodrow Wilson, the Democratic candidate, along with a Democratic Congress.

Like Roosevelt, Wilson considered himself a progressive, although he and Roosevelt did not agree on how progressivism ought to be implemented. Wilson's progressivism marked the beginning of a radical change in Democratic policies. Dating back to its foundation, the Democratic Party had been the party of limited government. Under Wilson, the Democrats became for the first time at least as receptive as the Republicans to government action in the economy.

The Fifth-Party System: The New Deal and Democratic Dominance, 1932–1968

The Republican ascendancy ended with the election of 1932, in the depths of the Great Depression. Republican Herbert Hoover was president when the Depression began in 1929. Although Hoover took some measures to fight the Depression, they fell far short of what the public demanded. Significantly, Hoover opposed federal relief for the unemployed and the destitute. In 1932, Democrat Franklin D. Roosevelt was elected president by an overwhelming margin.

The Great Depression shattered the working-class belief in Republican economic competence. Under Roosevelt, the Democrats began to make major interventions in the economy in an attempt to combat the Depression and to relieve the suffering of the unemployed. Roosevelt's New Deal relief programs were open to all citizens, both black and white. As a result, African Americans began to support the Democratic Party in large numbers—a development that would have stunned any American politician of the 1800s. Women were also actively courted to join the electoral coalition.

Bettmann/Getty Images

Image 8-6

In 1912, Theodore Roosevelt campaigned for the presidency on a third-party Progressive, or Bull Moose, ticket. Here, you see a charter membership certificate showing Roosevelt and his vice presidential candidate, Hiram W. Johnson. What was the main result of Roosevelt's formation of this third party?

Roosevelt's political coalition (the New Deal coalition) was broad enough to establish the Democrats as the new majority party and reelect Franklin D. Roosevelt. (He served an unprecedented four terms as president.) Vice President Harry Truman assumed the presidency upon Roosevelt's death and was elected to a full term in 1948. In the 1950s, Republican Dwight D. Eisenhower, the leading U.S. general during World War II, won two terms as president. Otherwise, with minor interruptions, the Democratic ascendancy lasted until 1968.

The New Deal coalition managed the unlikely feat of including both African Americans and Southern whites who were hostile to African American advancement. This balancing act came to an end in the 1960s, a decade marked by the civil rights movement, several years of race riots in major cities, and increasingly heated protests against the Vietnam War. For many economically liberal, socially conservative voters (especially in the South), social issues had become more important than economic ones, and these voters left the Democrats. These voters outnumbered the new voters who joined the Democrats—newly enfranchised African Americans and former liberal Republicans in New England and the upper Midwest.

The result since 1968 has been an era in which neither party dominates. In presidential elections, the Republicans have had more success than the Democrats. Until 1994, Congress remained Democratic, but official party labels can be misleading. Some of the Democrats were Southern conservatives who normally voted with the Republicans on issues. As these conservative Democrats retired, they were largely replaced by Republicans.

A Post-Party System Era, 1968–Present?

Between the elections of 1968 and 2014, the presidency, the House of Representatives, and the Senate were simultaneously controlled by a single party only about one-third of the time. The Democrats controlled all three institutions during the presidency of Jimmy Carter (1977–1981), the first two years of Bill Clinton's presidency (1992–1994), and the first two years of Barack Obama's presidency (2008–2010). The Republicans controlled all three institutions during the third through sixth years of George W. Bush's presidency.[8]

---

8   The Republicans also were in control of all three institutions for the first four months after Bush's inauguration. This initial period of control ended when Senator James Jeffords of Vermont left the Republican Party, giving the Democrats control of the Senate.

Before the 1992 elections, the electorate seemed to prefer, in most circumstances, to match a Republican president with a Democratic Congress. Under Bill Clinton, that state of affairs was reversed, with a Democratic president serving alongside a Republican Congress. After the 2006 elections, a Republican president again faced a Democratic Congress. In 2008, Americans elected Democrat Barack Obama as president and gave the Democratic Party majorities in both houses of Congress, but the Democrats lost their majority in the House in the 2010 midterm elections and lost their majority in the Senate in the 2014 midterm elections.

Red State, Blue State The pattern of a Republican Congress and a Democratic president would have continued after the election of 2000 if Democratic presidential candidate Al Gore had prevailed. Gore won the popular vote, but he lost the electoral college by a narrow margin. Despite the closeness of the result, most states had voted in favor of either Bush or Gore by a fairly wide margin. To many observers, America had become divided between states that were solidly Republican or Democratic in their leanings, with a handful of "swing states." States that had shown strong support for a Republican candidate were deemed "red states" and so-called Democratic states were labeled "blue states." These labels have now become part of our political culture, and the outcome of any presidential race is portrayed in red and blue.

The outcome of the Bush-Gore contest in 2000 produced lingering bitterness in the political scene and may have increased general distrust of the electoral process. Although President Bush was reelected over his Democratic opponent (John Kerry) in 2004, a combination of Republican scandals, war weariness, and anti-Bush sentiment cost the Republicans their majority in the House in 2006.

In 2008, the nation watched an unprecedented Democratic primary fight between Hillary Rodham Clinton and Barack Obama—each representing a first for the nation with the contest promising a woman or an African American nominee. Although many commentators felt that the party would be weakened by the intense primary fight, Barack Obama easily won the election over Republican John McCain, and the Democrats carried both houses of Congress. Analysts began to talk about a realignment of voters to form a progressive coalition that might last well into the future. However, the economic collapse of the banks and onset of the economic recession that began during the end of the 2008 campaign lingered through much of President Obama's first term. By 2010, opponents of government debt and fears of the economic recession led to the Republicans recapturing the House of Representatives. Republicans coalesced around opposition to the Affordable Care Act and targeted Democrats who helped to pass the law in 2010.

Partisan Trends in the Elections of 2012 and 2016

By the time the votes were all counted, it appeared that there was remarkably little change in the alignment of the voters following the 2012 elections. (See Figure 8-2). The coalition that came together to elect President Obama in 2008 reappeared in 2012: African American voters, women, lower-income voters, union voters, and Latino voters gave the president more than a majority of their votes. These groups reflect changes in the U.S. population that will determine the direction of the nation. The Republican coalition also

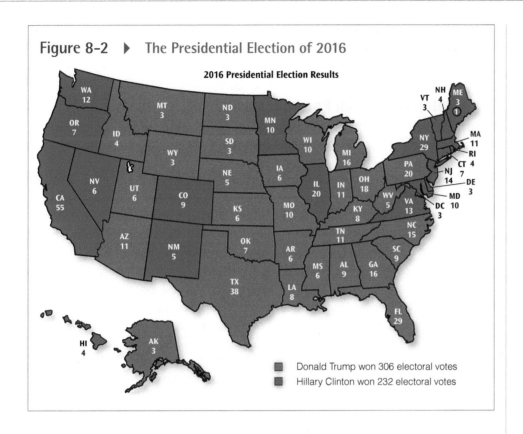

Figure 8-2 ▶ The Presidential Election of 2016

2016 Presidential Election Results

■ Donald Trump won 306 electoral votes
■ Hillary Clinton won 232 electoral votes

remained unchanged: better-educated voters, high-income voters, older voters, white men, and evangelical voters were more likely to vote for the Republicans. The results of the congressional elections were close to those of 2010: Republicans maintained a solid majority in the House of Representatives, and the Democrats gained two seats in the Senate to have a solid 53–45 majority in that chamber. Democrats lost seats in both houses in the 2014 midterm elections and lost control of the U.S. Senate to Republicans. For the first time since 1928, Republicans had convincing control of the Congress.

As a result of the 2016 election, Republicans held a majority of seats in Congress thereby controlling both the executive and legislative branches of government. However, in 2018 voters returned to divided party control by electing a Democratic majority in the House of Representatives and retaining a Republican majority in the Senate. Although the media's prediction of a blue wave did not materialize, the Democrats picked up more than 30 seats in the House.

The Two Major U.S. Parties Today

■ **8.4** Compare and contrast the demographics of people who identify as Democrats and Republicans; explain how party positions differ on economic and social issues.

Sometimes American political parties are likened to Tweedledee and Tweedledum, the twins in Lewis Carroll's *Through the Looking-Glass*. Third-party advocates have an interest in claiming that no difference exists between the two major parties—their chances of gaining support are much greater if the major parties are seen as indistinguishable. Despite such allegations, the major parties do have substantial differences, both in who belongs to each party and in their policy priorities.

Who Belongs to Each Political Party?

Following the Republicans' 2012 loss of the White House, columnist George Will warned that the party was endangered by its failure to grasp that "demography is destiny."[9] Although perhaps an overstatement, this is nevertheless an important reminder that political parties are built by appealing to groups of people and knitting together a coalition based on shared interests. Table 8-1 shows the profiles of partisans and independents among registered voters. In examining Table 8-1, take careful note of the Independent column. In many cases, the largest proportion of people in any demographic category self-identify as independent from Republicans or Democrats. More women identify as Democrats (37 percent) than either Republicans (23 percent) or Independents (35 percent). Democrats have an advantage across nearly every age category, including young people who express a party affiliation. Republicans maintain a slight advantage among white non-Hispanics and those with a high school education. Millennials, between the ages of 18 and 33, lean toward Democrats; people over age 65 tend to identify as Republicans. Nonwhites identify with Democrats, as do those with the least and the most formal education. The wealthiest Americans, those earning in excess of $150,000, typically identify as Republicans, although recently they appear evenly divided as partisans; those at the bottom of the income scale usually identify themselves as the Democrats. Married people, particularly married men, identify with the Republicans; men and women who have never married are more likely to be Democrats. Members of labor unions and those not working are likely Democratic voters as well. Regionally, the South is solidly Republican; the East and West coasts trend toward the Democrats. The starkest differences along religious lines are between white Evangelical protestants (Republicans by nearly 46 points) and those who are religiously unaffiliated (Democrats by a margin of 36 points).

Partisans identifying with each political party differ in their positions on issues as well. For example, in a survey of registered voters leading up to the 2016 primary contests, significantly more Democrats (82 percent) than Republicans (66 percent) viewed health care as an important election issue. Twice as many Democrats (74 percent) than Republicans (37 percent) said the environment would factor into their 2016 voting decisions. Historically, one of the defining differences between the parties is a difference in vision over the size and role of government. Eighty-two percent of Republicans prefer a smaller government providing fewer services (compared to 29 percent of Democrats), whereas a majority (59 percent) of Democrats would choose a bigger government that provided more services (a choice of only 14 percent of Republicans). Registered Republicans favor gun ownership (71 percent), whereas Democrats are more likely to support gun control (75 percent).

9   Mathew Shoenfeld, "For GOP Demographics Are a Concern, But the Party Has a Bigger Problem." HuffPost Politics, June 30, 2013. www.huffingtonpost.com/matthew-schoenfeld/to-republicans-demographi b 3521827.html

Table 8-1 ▶ Who Belongs to Each Political Party?

	PARTY IDENTIFICATION			
	Rep %	Dem %	Ind %	Other/DK %
TOTAL	23	32	39	6
GENDER				
Men	24	26	45	5
Women	23	37	35	6
Race/Ethnicity				
White, non-Hispanic	30	25	40	5
Black, non-Hispanic	5	64	26	5
Hispanic	13	34	44	9
Asian, non-Hispanic	11	37	46	6
Generation				
Millennial (ages 18–33)	18	28	48	6
Generation X (34–49)	22	32	40	6
Baby Boomer (50–68)	25	34	35	5
Silent (69–86)	33	33	29	5
Education				
College graduate +	24	34	39	4
Post-graduate degree	20	38	38	4
College graduate	26	31	39	4
Some college or less	23	31	40	6
Some college	25	30	40	5
High school or less	22	31	40	7
Detailed Family Income				
$150,000+	29	29	38	4
$100,000–$149,999	30	30	37	3
$75,000–$99,999	30	29	38	3
$50,000–$74,999	27	30	38	4
$30,000–$39,999	19	33	43	4
Less than $30,000	17	35	42	7
Employed				
Yes	23	30	40	7
No	22	35	34	9
Marital Status				
Married	28	27	39	6
Unmarried	17	34	43	6
Parent or Guardian				
Yes	21	30	42	7
No	23	31	40	6
Region				
Northeast	20	36	38	6
Midwest	24	31	40	6
South	25	30	39	5
West	22	30	42	7
Community Type				
Urban	18	38	39	6
Suburban	25	29	40	5
Rural	29	26	39	6

Source: Pew Research Center, 2014 merged monthly data

Differences in Party Policy Priorities

Democrats and Republicans differ on policy priorities. Figure 8-3 depicts the top ten issues that partisans believe the president and Congress should deal with in the next year. As you can see, the issue priorities of the parties differ; Democrats' priorities are in the areas of education, poverty, and homelessness; health care; and Social Security and Medicaid; whereas Republicans favor policies related to fighting and preventing terrorism, reducing the federal deficit, reforming immigration, and right-sizing the federal government. Although Republicans and Democrats share issues in common, the magnitude of importance differs across the parties. Differences exist between the parties in the importance of the distribution of wealth, climate change, and gun policy (Democrats) and foreign affairs, taxes, immigration, and world affairs (Republicans).

The 2012 Elections—Shaping the Parties for 2014 and 2016

In addition to the economy, social issues, specifically reproductive rights and abortion issues, were very important in races for the U.S. Senate and persuaded many women to vote for the Democratic ticket at the presidential level.

Figure 8-3 ▶ Top Priority Issues in 2016, by Party Identification

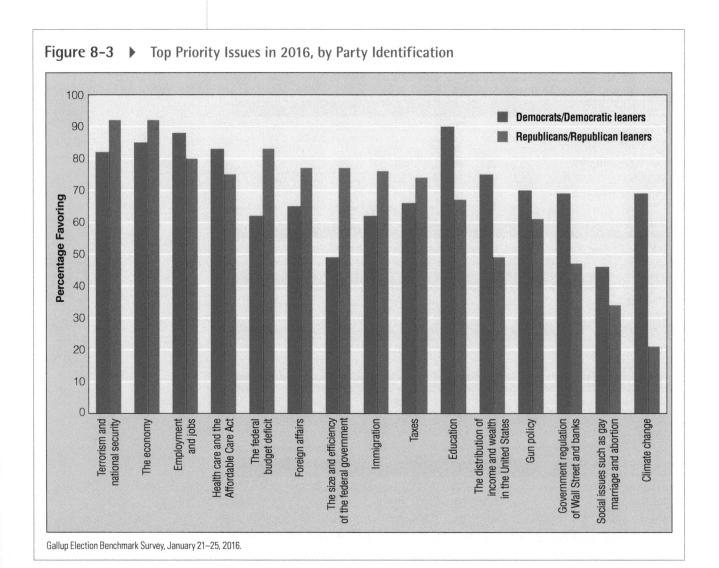

Gallup Election Benchmark Survey, January 21–25, 2016.

Pat Bagley/Cagle Cartoons

Image 8-7
Why aren't the poor represented by a political party in the United States? Does a two-party system make it more or less likely that all interests are reflected in the political debate?

Although economic indicators suggested a very slow and less-than-robust recovery from the major recession of 2008–2009, unemployment rates fell to below 8 percent by October 2012, and there was evidence of growth in the construction of housing. Although the majority of voters still said that the country was going in the wrong direction, the Democratic campaign emphasized the progress that had been made toward recovery. In contrast, the Republican campaign focused on the administration's record and promised a better approach. The Republican position appealed to small-business owners, to Americans who were college educated, and to many independent voters. The Democratic vote was certainly strengthened by the recovery of the automobile industry as a result of the Obama administration's policies, and blue-collar voters kept their loyalty to the Democratic Party.

On issues important to women, the Democratic Party championed reproductive rights for women, health-care initiatives for women, and their support for the right of women to choose an abortion. The Republican Party continued its stance as the party opposed to a woman's right to choose. Their message, which officially allowed abortions under certain conditions, was completely undercut by Senate candidates who would not allow abortion in the case of rape and who made very peculiar statements about rape-caused pregnancies. The publicity accorded to these statements and the Democratic support for women secured a majority of votes for the ticket from women.

Although the politics of immigration was rarely directly addressed in the campaign, it was clear that Latino voters saw the Democratic Party as more likely to pass immigration reform than the Republicans. The Republican ticket moved to the right on this issue, and Latino voters noted this. In 2012, President Obama announced a policy that allows undocumented young people brought to this country before the age of 16 to stay for two years if they meet educational, work, or military service requirements. Undoubtedly Latino voters viewed this action as proof of the Democratic Party's openness.

Because of these electoral outcomes and the reaction of voters to positions and policies adopted by party candidates and the parties, the 2014 midterm elections gained in importance for both parties. The party of the White House typically loses congressional seats in midterm elections, but in 2014 Republicans surged to victories that both increased the size of the GOP majority in the House and gave the party control of the U.S. Senate for the first time since 2006. Republicans were successful in making the elections a national referendum on government competence by raising questions about the U.S. response to international threats such as the Islamic State in Iraq and Syria (ISIS) and Ebola in West Africa and by reminding voters about unresolved issues at home like immigration. As president, Obama was the embodiment of national government. The 2014 midterms set records for spending (an estimated $4 billion in all) and for low turnout (around 36 percent). The demographics of those who stayed home—young people, minority voters, and women—were keys to Democratic victories in 2012.

The 2016 Primaries and the Rise of "Outsiders"

The 2016 Republican nominating season featured the largest and most diverse field of candidates in the history of either party—17 individuals, although 4 withdrew prior to the first contest. The field featured one woman (Carly Fiorina), two Latinos (Ted Cruz and Marco Rubio), one African American (Ben Carson), and one Indian American (Bobby Jindal). The Republican National Committee (RNC) took a number of steps that it believed would produce the strongest general election candidate and limit the damage done to that candidate by fellow Republicans during the primary stage. For one thing, the number of scheduled debates was limited to 12 (down from 20 in 2011–2012). Because of the size of the field, early debates featured top-tier and second-tier debates, assigning candidates based on the latest poll numbers. The Republican National Convention occurred earlier than in previous years. Republicans met in Cleveland, Ohio, July 18–21, 2016. Although early polls featured conventional candidates with experience as legislators or governors, by summer 2015 when Donald Trump announced his candidacy, no single candidate had captured the electorate's attention.

Campaigning on the theme "Make America Great Again," Trump's announcement presaged his campaign's appeal to voters feeling alienated and left behind. In his speech announcing his candidacy, Trump emphasized illegal immigration, saying, "When Mexico sends its people, they're not sending their best . . . They're sending people that have lots of problems, and they're bringing those problems with [them]. They're bringing drugs. They're bringing crime. They're rapists. And some, I assume, are good people."[10] A backlash ensued, but Trump did not retract his statements. In fact, candidate Trump seemed to relish defying conventional wisdom and breaking "the rules" about electability. For example, he took aim at past nominees for their failures to win and specifically questioned the late Senator John McCain's status as a war hero ("He was a war hero because he was captured. I like people who weren't captured."[11]). He promised to build a great wall between Mexico and the United States and make the Mexican government pay for it. After the November 2015

---

10 Reid J. Epstein, "Donald Trump Transcript: 'Our Country Needs a Truly Great Leader,'" *The Wall Street Journal*, June 16, 2015.
11 Catherine Lucey and Steve Peoples, "Trump on John McCain: 'I Like People Who Weren't Captured.'" AP The Big Story, July 18, 2015. http://bigstory.ap.org/article/cde31d2fa3a244d29de77b31a59b799a/gop-candidate-trump-goes-after-sen-john-mccains-war-record

Demographics Are Not Destiny: Republicans and Democrats after Trump

"The forgotten men and women of our country will be forgotten no longer," Donald Trump told supporters when his victory was no longer in doubt. The Trump coalition of voters included many groups Democrats had counted among their longtime loyalists: blue-collar white and working-class voters, and those without a college degree.

Following Mitt Romney's defeat in 2012, Republicans commissioned an autopsy. The report was based on interviews with over 2,600 people as well as individual focus groups and polls with demographics such as Hispanic voters and former Republicans. The recommendations urged the party and its members to listen to minority voters, to change the rhetoric around immigration to avoid handing Democrats Hispanic voters as a permanent constituency, to tone down anti-LGBTQ and anti-gay marriage talk, and to "stop being the rich guys."* So in 2016, the Republicans nominated a thrice-married billionaire who lived in a Manhattan penthouse, and who in announcing his candidacy characterized Mexican immigrants as criminals and rapists. He went on to run an unorthodox campaign and on Election Day his unfavorable ratings topped 60 percent. Headlines asked if the Republican Party could survive a Trump candidacy. Trump won the presidency beating Hillary Clinton and leaving in doubt President Obama's legacy. Headlines asked what remained of the Democratic Party.

Scholars will study this election for decades. Was it a repudiation of "the establishment"? Is this the inevitable backlash against the first African American president by angry whites? Demographics only tell part of the story. Democrats were counting on a changing population to sustain their electoral victories. The Census Bureau projects that the United States will become a majority nonwhite nation by 2050. That explanation ignored the sense among some Americans—many of whom are white, Christian, and rural—that the American Dream is no longer possible for them. Democrats who have benefitted from a political coalition built on identity missed the growing anger and resentment among those who felt left behind. Hillary Clinton also failed to excite the very groups Democrats had been counting on—young people, African Americans, Hispanics, Asian Americans, unions, and even women.

In short, this election reshuffled the knowns and unknowns for both parties. It may be that Donald Trump is an anomaly—evidence that elections are indeed unpredictable. It may be that Hillary Clinton underperformed as a candidate. Few have suggested that 2016 represents a partisan realignment of the electorate—yet. The demographics of Trump's coalition represent a shrinking share of the electorate and as such do not represent a long-term strategy for Republicans. Voters wanted change and elected Republicans to the White House and both houses of Congress to get it done.

For Critical Analysis

1. If ever there was a year for a third party to materialize, this was it. Voters expressed deep dissatisfaction with both mainstream parties. Why didn't a new third way emerge?

2. This was an election characterized by personalities, not policies. What impact, if any, will this have on the future of the two parties? Will this shape future candidate recruitment?

*Benjy Sarlin, "Six Big Takeaways from the RNC's Incredible 2012 Autopsy," TPM, March 18, 2013.

Paris terrorist attacks, Donald Trump called for a "tracking system" for all Muslims in American and later urged "a total and complete shutdown on Muslims entering the United States until our country's representatives can figure out what the hell is going on."[12] These comments, along with countless others, earned Trump widespread condemnation from Republican Party officials and some of his party rivals, but they did not hurt his standing in the polls.

---

12 Jenna Johnson, "Trump Calls for 'Total and Complete Shutdown of Muslims Entering the United States.'" *The Washington Post*, December 7, 2015. https://www.washingtonpost.com/news/post-politics/wp/2015/12/07/donald-trump-calls-for-total-and-complete-shutdown -of-muslims-entering-the-united-states/

Twitter Feed ▶ Campaigns try to attract the attention of voters in a variety of ways.

Women's Policy Inc./Twitter

Trump primary voters tended to be white Republicans who had not completed college and feel that the country's changing demographics and fragile economy have left them on the margins.

Trump preferred large rallies to more intimate campaign appearances, and these rallies attracted thousands of supporters. His sharp rhetoric also attracted protesters in greater numbers. The campaign cancelled a March 2016 rally in Chicago amid fights between supporters and demonstrators, protests in the streets, and concerns that the environment at the event was no longer safe. Trump's popularity and victories steadily winnowed the field of challengers until only Ted Cruz and John Kasich remained heading into the convention (although neither had a chance to win the nomination on the first ballot). Cruz and Kasich withdrew following the Indiana primary in May, leaving Trump the presumptive nominee more than two months before the convention.

On the Democratic side, the field of candidates was much smaller, featuring a total of six declared candidates (three withdrew prior to the Iowa caucuses, and Martin O'Malley withdrew following a third-place finish in Iowa). Although there was some speculation that Vice President Joseph Biden would declare as a candidate, he announced in October 2015 that he would not seek the presidency. The Democratic National Committee held its convention in Philadelphia, Pennsylvania, July 25–28, 2016.

The field was dominated by the presumptive nominee, former Secretary of State Hillary Clinton; however, Vermont Senator Bernie Sanders capitalized on the anti-establishment mood of primary voters and won the New Hampshire primary in a landslide. Clinton suffered from continued negative coverage of her decision to install a private server in her home and use that system for all email communication as Secretary of State. An FBI investigation and the possibility of an indictment hung like a cloud over her candidacy (an indictment was never issued). Although a candidate for the Democratic nomination, Bernie Sanders identifies as a Democratic Socialist. His message about the negative influence of big banks and Wall Street brokerage houses resonated with many in the Democratic Party, as did his stance against international trade agreements. He criticized the influence of big donors and "Super PACs" and focused his fundraising efforts on small donors. In comparison to the raucous Republican debates, the two Democratic candidates appeared cordial to one another through most of the six scheduled debates. Largely as a result of his appeal to young people and disaffected progressives, Sanders did well in predominantly white states and in states with a strong independent tradition (for example, New Hampshire, Colorado, Montana, Vermont, Maine). Attendance at Sanders campaign rallies grew to more than 15,000 people. Hillary Clinton preferred a more retail-style campaign emphasizing local issues. Clinton performed well in states with large minority populations and states in the South (for example, South Carolina, Alabama, Georgia, Texas, Virginia, Florida, Arizona). Both candidates campaigned hard to win contests in New York—a state that Sanders claimed because he was born in Brooklyn and Clinton claimed as her home state, having represented New York in the U.S. Senate for eight years. Secretary Clinton won New York by a large margin and secured her victory as the presumptive nominee following a convincing victory in California in early June. Clinton campaigned on themes that emphasized economic success for the middle class, expanding rights for women, improving school quality, and continuing but improving upon President Obama's legacy.

Why Has the Two-Party System Endured?

■ **8.5** Summarize the factors that reinforce a two-party system and explain why third parties are rarely successful at winning national elections.

There are several reasons why two major parties have dominated the political landscape in the United States for almost two centuries: (1) the historical foundations of the system, (2) political socialization and practical considerations, (3) the winner-take-all electoral system, and (4) state and federal laws favoring the two-party system.

The Historical Foundations of the Two-Party System

As we have seen, many times one preeminent issue or dispute has divided the nation politically. In the beginning, Americans were at odds over ratifying the Constitution. After the Constitution went into effect, the power of the federal government became the major national issue. Thereafter, the dispute over slavery divided the nation by section, North versus South. At times, cultural differences have been important, with advocates of government-sponsored morality (such as banning alcoholic beverages) pitted against advocates of personal liberty.

During much of the 1900s, economic differences were paramount. In the New Deal period, the Democrats became known as the party of the working class, whereas the Republicans became known as the party of the middle and upper classes and commercial interests. When politics is based on an argument between just two opposing points of view, advocates of each viewpoint can mobilize most effectively by forming a single, unified party. The dualist nature of conflict is challenged in conditions of uncertainty or issue complexity when just two positions don't seem to cover the issue. The nature and causes of climate change might be one such issue. The Affordable Care Act is another—nobody really disagrees with the goal of ensuring access to health care for all Americans, but the U.S. health-care system is incredibly complex. Congress adopted one approach to fixing the problem when it passed the Affordable Care Act (ACA), but continuing opposition to the legislation leaves Republicans in the unenviable position of appearing to oppose expanded health insurance coverage. Also, when a two-party system has been in existence for almost two centuries, it becomes difficult to imagine an alternative.

Political Socialization and Practical Considerations

Given that most Americans still tend to lean toward one of the two major political parties even if they identify as an independent, it is not surprising that most children learn at a fairly young age to think of themselves as either Democrats or

Republicans. This generates a built-in mechanism to perpetuate a two-party system. Also, many politically oriented people who aspire to work for social change consider that the only realistic way to capture political power in this country is to be either a Republican or a Democrat. However, the increase in political independents today, particularly among young people, may call into question the continuing power of socialization to maintain the two-party system.

The Winner-Take-All Electoral System

plurality
A number of votes cast for a candidate that is greater than the number of votes for any other candidate, but not necessarily a majority.

At virtually every level of government in the United States, the outcome of elections is based on the **plurality**, winner-take-all principle. The winner is the person who obtains the most votes, even if that person does not receive a majority (more than 50 percent) of the votes. Whoever gets the most votes gets everything. Most legislators in the United States are elected from single-member districts in which only one person represents the constituency. The candidate who finishes second receives nothing for the effort and neither do their supporters. The winner-take-all system also operates in the election of the U.S president. Recall that the voters in each state do not vote for a president directly, but vote for **electoral college** delegates who are committed to the various presidential candidates. These delegates are called *electors*.

electoral college
A group of persons, called electors, who are selected by the voters in each state. This group officially elects the president and the vice president of the United States.

If the electors pledged to a particular presidential candidate receive a plurality of 40 percent of the votes in a state, that presidential candidate will receive all of the state's votes in the electoral college. Minor parties have a difficult time competing under such a system. As shown in Table 8-2, American history has seen a number of national third-party campaigns. Only Theodore Roosevelt, who ran on a third-party ticket, received more than 88 electoral votes. In 1968, George Wallace, the segregationist former governor of Alabama, received 46 electoral votes, all from Deep South states. In recent decades, Ross Perot ran the most successful third-party campaign, garnering 18.9 percent of the popular vote, but no electoral votes at all. Because voters know such candidacies are doomed by the system, it is difficult to convince them to cast their vote for such candidates. Third-party candidate Ralph Nader was accused of siphoning votes away from Democratic candidate Al Gore in 2000, leaving George W. Bush the victor.

Proportional Representation Many other nations use a system of proportional representation with multimember districts. If, during the national election, party X obtains 12 percent of the vote, party Y gets 43 percent of the vote, and party Z gets the remaining 45 percent of the vote, then party X gets 12 percent of the seats in the legislature, party Y gets 43 percent of the seats, and party Z gets 45 percent of the seats. Because even a minor party may still obtain at least a few seats in the legislature, the smaller parties have a greater incentive to organize under such electoral systems than they do in the United States.

The relative effects of proportional representation versus our system of single-member districts are so strong that many scholars have made them one of the few "laws" of political science. Duverger's Law, named after French political scientist Maurice Duverger, states that electoral systems based on single-member districts tend to produce two parties, whereas systems of proportional representation produce multiple parties.[13] Still, many countries with single-member districts have more than two political parties—Britain and Canada are examples.

---

13 As cited in Todd Landman, *Issues and Methods in Comparative Politics* (New York: Routledge, 2003), p. 14.

Table 8-2 ▶ The Most Successful Third-Party Presidential Campaigns since 1864

The following list includes all third-party candidates winning more than 2 percent of the popular vote or any electoral votes since 1864. (We ignore isolated "unfaithful electors" in the electoral college who failed to vote for the candidate to whom they were pledged.)

YEAR	MAJOR THIRD PARTY	THIRD-PARTY PRESIDENTIAL CANDIDATE	PERCENT OF THE POPULAR VOTE	ELECTORAL COLLEGE VOTES	WINNING PRESIDENTIAL CANDIDATE
1892	Populist	James Weaver	8.5	22	Grover Cleveland (D)
1904	Socialist	Eugene Debs	3.0	0	Theodore Roosevelt (R)
1908	Socialist	Eugene Debs	2.8	0	William Howard Taft (R)
1912	Progressive	Theodore Roosevelt	27.4	88	Woodrow Wilson (D)
1912	Socialist	Eugene Debs	6.0	0	Woodrow Wilson (D)
1920	Socialist	Eugene Debs	3.4	0	Warren G. Harding (R)
1924	Progressive	Robert LaFollette	16.6	13	Calvin Coolidge (R)
1948	States' Rights	Strom Thurmond	2.4	39	Harry Truman (D)
1960	Independent Democrat	Harry Byrd	0.4	15*	John Kennedy (D)
1968	American Independent	George Wallace	13.5	46	Richard Nixon (R)
1980	National Union	John Anderson	6.6	0	Ronald Reagan (R)
1992	Independent	Ross Perot	18.9	0	Bill Clinton (D)
1996	Reform	Ross Perot	8.4	0	Bill Clinton (D)
2000	Green	Ralph Nader	2.74	0	George W. Bush (R)
2016	Libertarian	Gary Johnson	3.3	0	Donald Trump (R)

Source: *Dave Leip's Atlas of U.S. Presidential Elections*, www.uselectionatlas.org
*Byrd received 15 electoral votes from unpledged electors in Alabama and Mississippi.

State and Federal Laws Favoring the Two Parties

Many state and federal election laws offer a clear advantage to the two major parties. In some states, the established major parties need to gather fewer signatures to place their candidates on the ballot than do minor parties or independent candidates. The criterion for determining how many signatures will be required is often based on the total party vote in the last general election, thus penalizing a new political party that did not compete in that election.

At the national level, minor parties face different obstacles. The rules and procedures of both houses of Congress divide committee seats, staff members, and other privileges on the basis of party membership. A legislator who is elected on a minor-party ticket, such as the Conservative Party of New York, must choose to be counted with one of the major parties to obtain a committee assignment. The Federal Election Commission (FEC) rules for campaign financing also place restrictions on minor-party candidates. Such candidates are not eligible for federal matching funds in either the primary or the general election. In the 1980 election, John Anderson, running for president as an independent, sued the FEC for campaign funds. The commission finally agreed to repay part of his campaign costs after the election in proportion to the votes he received. Giving funds to a candidate when the campaign is over is, of course, much less helpful than providing funds while the campaign is still under way.

The Role of Minor Parties in U.S. Politics

third party
A political party other than the two major political parties (Republican and Democratic).

Minor parties have a difficult (if not impossible) time competing within the American two-party political system. Nonetheless, minor parties have played an important role in our political life. Parties other than the Republicans or Democrats are usually called **third parties**. (Technically, of course, there could be fourth, fifth, or sixth parties as well, but we use the term *third party* because it has endured.) Third parties can come into existence in three ways: (1) They may be founded from scratch by individuals or groups who are committed to a particular interest, issue, or ideology; (2) they can split off from one of the major parties when a group becomes dissatisfied with the major party's policies; or (3) they can be organized around a particular charismatic leader and serve as that person's vehicle for contesting elections.

Third parties have forced the major parties to recognize new issues or trends in the thinking of Americans. Political scientists believe that third parties have acted as safety valves for dissident groups, preventing major confrontations and political unrest. In some instances, third parties have functioned as way stations for voters en route from one of the major parties to the other. Table 8-2 lists significant third-party presidential campaigns in American history; Table 8-3 provides a brief description of third-party beliefs. No third-party candidate has earned electoral votes since 1968, highlighting the strength of the two main parties.

Table 8-3 ▶ Policies of Selected American Third Parties Since 1864

Populist: This pro-farmer party of the 1890s advocated progressive reforms. It also advocated replacing gold with silver as the basis of the currency in hopes of creating a mild inflation in prices. (It was believed by many that inflation would help debtors and stimulate the economy.)

Socialist: This party advocated a "cooperative commonwealth" based on government ownership of industry. It was pro-labor, often antiwar, and, in later years, anticommunist. It was dissolved in 1972 and replaced by nonparty advocacy groups (Democratic Socialists of America and Social Democrats USA).

Communist: This left-wing breakaway from the socialists was the U.S. branch of the worldwide communist movement. The party was pro-labor and advocated full equality for African Americans. It was also closely aligned with the Communist Party–led Soviet Union, which provoked great hostility among most Americans.

Progressive: This name was given to several successive splinter parties built around individual political leaders. Theodore Roosevelt, who ran in 1912, advocated federal regulation of industry to protect consumers, workers, and small businesses. Robert LaFollette, who ran in 1924, held similar viewpoints.

American Independent: Built around George Wallace, this party opposed any further promotion of civil rights and advocated a militant foreign policy. Wallace's supporters were mostly former Democrats who were soon to be Republicans.

Libertarian: This party believes that the individual and private marketplace will produce the best policies. The national government has a role in defending the nation and little else.

Reform: The Reform Party was initially built around businessman Ross Perot but later was taken over by others. Under Perot, the party was a middle-of the-road group opposed to federal budget deficits. Under Patrick Buchanan, it came to represent right-wing nationalism and opposition to free trade.

Green: The Greens are a left-of-center, pro-environmental party; they are also generally hostile to globalization.

Ideological Third Parties

The longest-lived third parties have been those with strong ideological foundations that are typically at odds with the majority mind-set. The Socialist Party is an example. The party was founded in 1901 and lasted until 1972, when it was finally dissolved. (A smaller party later took up the name.)

Members of a minor party regard themselves as outsiders and look to one another for support; ideology provides great psychological cohesiveness. Second, because the rewards of ideological commitment are partly psychological, these minor parties do not think in terms of immediate electoral success. A poor showing at the polls therefore does not dissuade either the leadership or the grassroots participants from continuing their quest for change in American government (and, ultimately, American society).

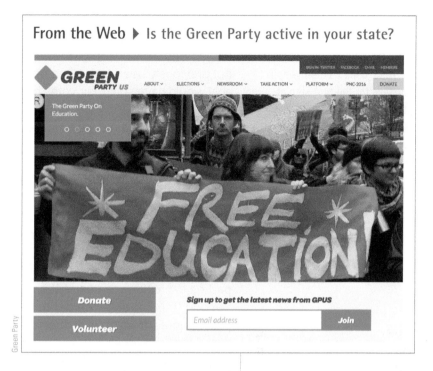

From the Web ▶ Is the Green Party active in your state?

Green Party

Currently active ideological parties include the Libertarian Party and the Green Party. The Libertarian Party supports a laissez-faire ("let it be") capitalist economic program, together with a hands-off policy on regulating matters of moral conduct. The Green Party began as a grassroots environmentalist organization with affiliated political parties across North America and Western Europe. It was established in the United States as a national party in 1996 and nominated Ralph Nader to run for president in 2000. Nader campaigned against what he called "corporate greed," advocated universal health insurance, and promoted environmental concerns.[14] He ran again for president as an independent in 2004 and in 2008. The Green Party's Twitter feed (shown in the screen capture) posts regular videos that champion key themes to the party's platform and encourages fundraising activities.

Splinter Parties

Some of the most successful minor parties have been those that split from major parties. The impetus for these **splinter parties**, or factions, has usually been a situation in which a particular personality was at odds with the major party. The most successful of these splinter parties was the Bull Moose Progressive Party, formed in 1912 to support Theodore Roosevelt for president. The Republican National Convention of that year denied Roosevelt the nomination, although he had won most of the primaries. He therefore left the Republicans and ran against Republican "regular" William Howard Taft in the general election. Although Roosevelt did not win the election, he did split the Republican vote, enabling Democrat Woodrow Wilson to become president.

did you know?

The FreeSoil Party, active in the 1848 and 1852 presidential elections, was organized on a platform opposing the extension of slavery. The slogan of the party was "free soil, free speech, free labor and free men."

splinter party
A new party formed by a dissident faction within a major political party. Often, splinter parties have emerged when a particular personality was at odds with the major party.

---

14 Ralph Nader offers his own entertaining account of his run for the presidency in 2000 in *Crashing the Party: How to Tell the Truth and Still Run for President* (New York: St. Martin's Press, 2002).

Third parties have also been formed to back individual candidates who were not rebelling against a particular party. Ross Perot, for example, who challenged Republican George H. W. Bush and Democrat Bill Clinton in 1992, had not previously been active in a major party. Perot's supporters, likewise, probably would have split their votes between Bush and Clinton had Perot not been in the race. In theory, Perot ran in 1992 as a nonparty independent; in practice, he had to create a campaign organization. By 1996, Perot's organization was formalized as the Reform Party.

The Impact of Minor Parties

Third parties have rarely been able to affect American politics by actually winning elections. (One exception: third-party and independent candidates have occasionally won races for state governorships—for example, Jesse Ventura was elected governor of Minnesota on the Reform Party ticket in 1998.) Instead, the impact of third parties has taken two forms. First, third parties can influence one of the major parties to take up one or more issues. Second, third parties can determine the outcome of a particular election by pulling votes from one of the major-party candidates in what is called the "spoiler effect."

Influencing the Major Parties One of the most clear-cut examples of a major party adopting the issues of a minor party took place in 1896, when the Democratic Party co-opted the Populist demand for "free silver"—that is, a policy of coining enough new money to create inflation. Absorbing the Populists' demands cost the Democrats votes overall.

Affecting the Outcome of an Election The presidential election of 2000 was one instance in which a minor party may have altered the outcome. Green candidate Ralph Nader received almost 100,000 votes in Florida, a majority of which would probably have gone to Democrat Al Gore if Nader had not been in the race. The real question is whether the effect was important.

The problem is that in an election as close as the presidential election of 2000, *any* factor with an impact on the outcome can be said to have determined the results of the election. Discussing his landslide loss to Democrat Lyndon B. Johnson in 1964, Republican Barry Goldwater wrote: "When you've lost an election by that much, it isn't the case of whether you made the wrong speech or wore the wrong necktie. It was just the wrong time."[15] Given that Nader garnered almost 3 million votes nationwide, many people believe that the Nader campaign was an important reason for Gore's loss. Should voters ignore third parties to avoid spoiling the chances of a preferred major-party candidate?

Image 8-8

H. Ross Perot, third-party candidate for president in 1992 and 1996, speaks before a California Senate committee in 2002.

Justin Sullivan/Getty Images

15 Barry Goldwater, *With No Apologies* (New York: William Morrow, 1979).

Mechanisms of Political Change

Support for the two major parties is roughly balanced today. In the future, could one of the two parties decisively overtake the other and become the "natural party of government"? The Republicans held this status from 1896 until 1932, and the Democrats enjoyed it for many years after the election of Franklin D. Roosevelt in 1932. Not surprisingly, political advisers in both parties dream of circumstances that could grant them lasting political dominance.

Realignment

One mechanism by which a party might gain dominance is called **realignment**. Major constituencies shift their allegiance from one party to another, creating a long-term alteration in the political environment. Realignment has often been associated with particular elections, called *realigning elections*. The election of 1896, which established a Republican ascendancy, was clearly a realigning election. So was the election of 1932, which made the Democrats the leading party.

realignment
A process in which a substantial group of voters switches party allegiance, producing a long-term change in the political landscape.

Realignment: The Myth of Dominance Several myths have grown up around the concept of realignment. One is that in realignment, a newly dominant party must replace the previously dominant party. Realignment could easily strengthen an already dominant party. Alternatively, realignment could result in a tie. This has happened—twice. One example was the realignment of the 1850s, which resulted in Abraham Lincoln's election as president in 1860. After the Civil War, the Republicans and the Democrats were almost evenly matched nationally.

The most recent realignment has sometimes been linked to the elections of 1968. The realignment was a gradual process that took place over many years. It is sometimes referred to as a "rolling realignment." In 1968, Democrat Hubert Humphrey, Republican Richard Nixon, and third-party candidate George Wallace of Alabama all vied for the presidency. Following the Republican victory in that election, Nixon adopted a "southern strategy" aimed at drawing dissatisfied Southern Democrats into the Republican Party.[16] At the presidential level, the strategy was an immediate success, although years would pass before the Republicans could gain dominance in the South's delegation to Congress or in state legislatures. Nixon's southern strategy helped create the political environment in which we live today. Another milestone in the progress of the Republicans was Ronald Reagan's sweeping victory in the presidential election of 1980.

Realignment: The Myth of Predictability A second myth concerning realignments is that they take place every 36 years. Supposedly, there were realigning elections in 1860, 1896, 1932, and 1968, and therefore 2004 must have been a year for realignment. No such event took place. In fact, no force could cause political realignments at precise 36-year intervals. Further, realignments are not always tied to particular elections. The most recent realignment, in which conservative Southern Democrats became conservative Southern Republicans, was not closely linked to a particular election. The realignment of the 1850s, following the creation of the modern Republican Party, also took place over a period of years.

---

16 The classic work on Nixon's southern strategy is Kirkpatrick Sales, *The Emerging Republican Majority* (New Rochelle, NY: Arlington House, 1969).

Multiparty Systems: The Rule Rather than the Exception

The United States has a two-party system. Occasionally, a third-party candidate enters the race, but has little chance of winning at the national level. Throughout the world, though, most democracies have multiparty systems.

Some Examples

In its first legislative elections ever, Afghanistan saw the emergence of six major parties and seven minor parties. The 2013 Iraqi provincial council elections had a total of 50 political alliances plus hundreds of other parties competing. India's general election takes place in nine phases across 534 constituencies. India has 6 national parties, another 36 state parties, and more than 100 regional parties.

The latest elections in Germany resulted in a "grand coalition," bringing together two main center-right and center-left parties within a system of five parties. Any given presidential election in France has even more parties. They include several representing the left, center-left, right, and center-right. The National Front represents the extreme right, anti-immigrant part of the electorate. The Socialist Party represents the left.

After the Egyptian popular uprising, which overthrew the authoritarian government of Hosni Mubarak, the leaders of the movement quickly moved to establish an election system. Within weeks, dozens of political parties formed and, as the first presidential election approached, at least 10 of these parties had candidates for that office. Parties ranged from conservative groups that had supported Mubarak to radical leftists to democratic liberals and Islamist groups who wanted a religious-based government.

Proportional Representation and Coalitions

Great Britain has often been described as having a two-and-one-half party system: The major parties, the Labour and Conservative parties, have alternated governing the nation for most of the time since World War II. The Liberal Democrat party, which has a long and distinguished history, usually comes in third, not securing enough votes to make a difference.

In the 2010 parliamentary elections, neither major party won enough seats in Parliament to claim the right to form a government. As soon as the election results were announced, each of the two major parties began to "court" the Liberal Democrats, who had won enough seats to create a coalition. Within a week, Queen Elizabeth asked the head of the Conservative Party to become prime minister and to negotiate a coalition with the Liberal Democrats. In a surprising move, the two parties announced that although

Image 8-9 The House of Commons of the United Kingdom has 650 members known as Members of Parliament (MPs). MPs are seated with the majority party facing the loyal opposition.

David Cameron, head of the Conservative Party, would be prime minister, Nick Clegg, head of the Liberal Democrat Party, would be named deputy prime minister. In the next election, 2012, the relative balance of power between the three parties did not change, although Conservatives lost about 4 percent of their previous vote and a corresponding number of seats—largely due to voter dissatisfaction over the national budget. Following the vote in 2015, the Conservatives gained a majority, and the leaders of the opposition parties resigned prior to forming a new government. David Cameron resigned as Prime Minister following the UK's decision to leave the European Union (known as Brexit). The Conservative Party chose Theresa May in July 2016 as the Leader of the Conservative Party and she was appointed Prime Minister of the United Kingdom.

Coalitions are almost a certainty in a multiparty system because the leading party usually does not have a majority of votes in the legislature. The leading party has to make compromises to obtain votes from other parties. These coalitions

(Continued)

are subject to change due to the pressures of lawmaking. Often, a minor partner in a coalition finds itself unable to support the laws or policies proposed by its larger partners. Either a compromise will be found or the coalition will be ended and new partners may be sought to form a government coalition. If we had a multiparty system in the United States, we might have a green party reflecting environmental interests, a Latino party, a western party, a labor party, and others. To gain support for her or his program, a president would have to build a coalition of several parties by persuading each that its members would benefit from the coalition. The major difficulty in a multiparty system is, of course, that the parties will withdraw from the coalition when they fail to benefit from it. Holding a coalition together for more than one issue is sometimes impossible. Creating such a system in the United States would require significant structural change to our constitutional system.

For Critical Analysis

1. In your view, are multiparty systems more representative than the two-party system in the United States? Why or why not?

2. Could you imagine a coalition of minor parties forming in the United States? Who might be included and what would the common interests be?

3. Given the rise of voters who identify as independents in the United States, might the time be right for a third party to form? Do you see evidence in the data presented in this chapter that independent voters share enough in common to create a party? Why or why not?

Is Realignment Still Possible? The nature of American political parties created the pattern of realignment in American history. The sheer size of the country, combined with the inexorable pressure toward a two-party system, resulted in parties made up of voters with conflicting interests or values. The pre–Civil War party system involved two parties—Whigs and Democrats—with support in both the North and the South. This system could survive only by burying, as deeply as possible, the issue of slavery. We should not be surprised that the structure eventually collapsed. The Republican ascendancy of 1896–1932 united capitalists and industrial workers under the Republican banner, despite serious economic conflicts between the two. The New Deal Democratic coalition after 1932 brought African Americans and ardent segregationists into the same party.

For realignment to occur, a substantial body of citizens must come to believe that their party can no longer represent their interests or values. The problem must be fundamental and not attributable to the behavior of an individual politician. Given the increasing cohesion of each of the parties today, it is unlikely that a realignment is in the offing. The values that unite each party are relatively coherent, and their constituents are reasonably compatible. Therefore, the current party system should be more stable than in the past, and a major realignment is not likely to take place in the foreseeable future. It appears that instead of moving from one major political party to another, voters have simply moved away from both parties, choosing instead to identify as political independents.

Dealignment

■ **8.6** Discuss the rise of political independents and evaluate how this change might affect American politics.

dealignment
A decline in party loyalties that reduces long-term party commitment.

Among political scientists, one common argument has been that realignment is no longer likely because voters are not as committed to the two major parties as they were in the 1800s and early 1900s. In this view, called **dealignment** theory, large numbers of independent voters may result in political volatility, but the absence of strong partisan attachments means that it is no longer easy to "lock in" political preferences for decades.

party identification
Linking oneself to a particular political party.

Independent Voters Figure 8-4 shows trends in **party identification**, as measured by standard polling techniques from 1937 through 2016. The chart displays a rise in the number of independent voters throughout the period, combined with a fall in support for the Democrats from the mid-1960s on. The decline in Democratic identification may be due to the consolidation of Republican support in the South since 1968, a process that by now may be substantially complete. In any event, the traditional Democratic advantage in party identification has vanished.

Not only has the number of independents grown over the last half-century, but voters are also less willing to vote a straight ticket—that is, to vote for all the candidates of one party. In the early 1900s, **straight-ticket voting** was nearly universal. By midcentury, 12 percent of voters engaged in ticket splitting. In recent presidential elections, between 20 and 40 percent of the voters engaged in split-ticket voting. This trend, along with the increase in the number of voters who call themselves independents, suggests that parties have lost much of their hold on the loyalty of the voters.

straight-ticket voting
Voting exclusively for the candidates of one party.

Not-So-Independent Voters A problem with dealignment theory is that many "independent" voters are not all that independent. If "pushed" to pick a

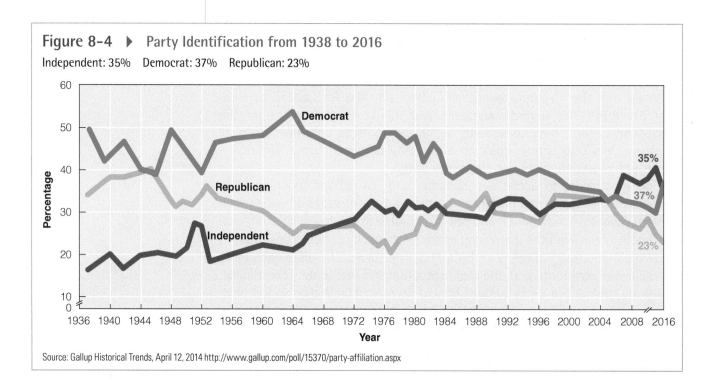

Figure 8-4 ▶ Party Identification from 1938 to 2016

Independent: 35%   Democrat: 37%   Republican: 23%

Source: Gallup Historical Trends, April 12, 2014 http://www.gallup.com/poll/15370/party-affiliation.aspx

party label, Democrats and Republicans pick up about equal shares of voters (18 percent and 17 percent, respectively). The people who are willing to identify if pushed are called "leaners," and sometimes these leaners act like ardent partisans. If these "leaners" are deducted from the independent category, only 10 percent of the voters remain. These true independents are **swing voters**—they can swing back and forth between the parties. These voters are important in deciding elections. Some analysts believe, however, that swing voters are far less numerous today than they were two or three decades ago. Swing voters are only relevant if the district or contest itself is competitive.

swing voters
Voters who frequently swing their support from one party to another.

Tipping

Political transformation can also result from changes in the composition of the electorate. Even when groups of voters never change their party preferences, if one group becomes more numerous over time, it can become dominant for that reason alone. We call this kind of demographically based change **tipping**. Immigration is one cause of this phenomenon.

tipping
A phenomenon that occurs when a group that is becoming more numerous over time grows large enough to change the political balance in a district, state, or country.

Tipping in Massachusetts Consider Massachusetts, where for generations Irish Catholics confronted Protestant Yankees in the political arena. Most of the Yankees were Republican; most of the Irish were Democrats. The Yankees were numerically dominant from the founding of the state until 1928. In that year, for the first time, Democratic Irish voters came to outnumber the Republican Yankees. Massachusetts, which previously had been one of the most solidly Republican states, cast its presidential vote for Democrat Al Smith. Within a few years, Massachusetts became one of the most reliably Democratic states in the nation.

Tipping in California California may have experienced a tipping effect during the 1990s. From 1952 until 1992, California consistently supported Republican presidential candidates, turning Democratic only in the landslide election of Lyndon Johnson in 1964. In 1992, however, the California electorate gave Democrat Bill Clinton a larger percentage of its votes than he received in the country as a whole. Since then, no Republican presidential candidate has managed to carry California.

The improved performance of the Democrats in California is almost certainly a function of demography. In 1999, California became the third state, after Hawaii and New Mexico, in which non-Latino whites do *not* make up a majority of the population. Latinos and African Americans both give most of their votes to the Democrats, but sometimes even though the eligible voting population is more diverse, voters remain older and predominantly white. For the first time, California Latinos, Asian Americans, and African Americans voted in numbers roughly equivalent to their share of registered voters in 2012. About 40 percent of California's electorate is now nonwhite, and ethnic voters made up about 40 percent of those who mailed in their ballots or went to the polls. Mitt Romney won the white vote in California by 8 percentage points while losing the state in a landslide by 22 points. President Obama won among Latinos by 45 points, Asian Americans by 58 points, and African Americans by 93 points, according to the exit poll data.[17]

---

17 Daniel Weintraub, "November Election Was a Tipping Point for Ethnic Voters," *California Health Report*, December 9, 2012. www.healthycal.org/archives/10392

Political Parties of the Future

Despite the erosion of support for Republicans and Democrats, political parties perform vital functions in the American political system. Change is inevitable, but the direction of change is never entirely predictable. Technology, the rise of nonparty organizational support for national candidates, and significant demographic changes in the electorate challenge the current parties.

Democratic strategists hope that the tolerant spirit of many younger voters may work to their advantage. The Democratic Party has worked hard in southwestern states and California to bring Latino voters to the fold, and the Obama administration appealed, in particular, to female voters through its positions on health care and contraceptive coverage. If the Democrats could add a significant majority of female and Latino voters to their numbers, it could offset some losses among blue-collar workers who are concerned about jobs and the economy but persuaded by Republicans on social issues.

Republicans recognize that the current demographic trends are not working in their favor but refuse to accept that "demography is destiny." Following the 2012 defeat for the White House, strategists worked to hone the Republican message to women, Latinos, and young people. However, that was before the 2016 primary contests and Donald Trump's ascendancy. Throughout the primaries Trump was a "plurality front-runner," meaning that he was winning but with a plurality—not a majority—of the votes cast. His unfavorable ratings among millennials, minorities, and college-educated white women did not prevent him from winning the presidency, but may leave a lasting impact on the Republican brand for members of these groups. The results of the 2016 election surprised everyone. Can Mr. Trump pull Republicans together and govern? Will President Trump be able to capitalize on Republican majorities in the House and Senate to effect the change he promised on the campaign trail?

Key Terms

convention delegates 277
dealignment 306
Democratic Party 284
divided government 280
electoral college 298
era of good feelings 284
faction 274
national committee 278
national convention 277
party identification 306

party-in-government 280
party-in-the-electorate 276
party organization 277
party platform 278
patronage 280
plurality 298
political party 275
realignment 303
Republican Party 285
safe seat 281

splinter party 301
state central committee 278
straight-ticket voting 306
swing voters 307
third party 300
ticket splitting 280
tipping 307
two-party system 283
unit rule 279
Whig Party 284

Chapter Summary

■ **8.1** A political party is a group of political activists who organize to win elections, operate the government, and determine public policy. Political parties recruit candidates for public office, organize and run elections, present alternative policies to the voters, assume responsibility for operating the government, and act as the opposition to the party in power.

8.2 A political party consists of three components: the party-in-the-electorate, the party organization, and the party-in-government. The party-in-the electorate is made up of all of the people who affiliate and identify with the political party. Although they are not required to participate in every election, they are the most likely to do so because they feel a sense of loyalty to the party. The party organization provides the structural framework for the political party by recruiting volunteers to become party leaders; identifying potential candidates; and organizing caucuses, conventions, and election campaigns for its candidates. The party-in-government consists of elected and appointed officials who identify with a political party. After the election is over and the winners are announced, the focus of party activity shifts from getting out the vote to organizing and controlling the government.

8.3 The evolution of our nation's political parties can be divided into five party systems: (1) the development of parties, 1789–1828; (2) Democrats and Whigs, 1828–1860; (3) Republicans' rise to power and the Civil War, 1860–1896; (4) the Progressive interlude and Republican dominance, 1896–1932; and (5) the New Deal and Democratic dominance, 1932–1968. Political parties today differ considerably, although sometimes voters do not accurately define the differences or align predictably with a party. Weaker attachment to parties and the rising influence of nonparty organizations in campaigns and elections make a sixth-party system unlikely to emerge.

8.4 Political parties are built by appealing to groups of people and knitting together a coalition based on shared interests. The Democratic and Republican parties appeal to different constituencies and embrace different issue positions. Men, people over the age of 65, the wealthy, married people, and better-educated voters tend to identify with the Republicans. Women, young people, nonwhites, members of labor unions, and the unemployed affiliate with the Democrats. Regionally, the South is solidly Republican, whereas the East and West coasts trend toward the Democrats. The starkest differences along religious lines are between white Evangelical protestants (Republicans) and those who are religiously

unaffiliated (Democrats). Partisans identifying with each political party differ in their positions on issues as well. Historically, one of the defining differences between the parties is a difference in vision over the size and role of government. Republicans prefer a smaller government providing fewer services, whereas a majority of Democrats would choose a bigger government that provided more services.

8.5 Two major parties have dominated the political landscape in the United States for almost two centuries. Reasons for this include (1) the historical foundations of the system, (2) political socialization and practical considerations, (3) the winner-take-all electoral system, and (4) state and federal laws favoring the two-party system. Minor parties find it extremely difficult to win elections. Yet minor (or third) parties have emerged, sometimes as dissatisfied splinter groups from within major parties, and have acted as barometers of changes in the political mood. Third parties can affect the political process (even if they do not win) if major parties adopt their issues or if they determine which major party wins an election.

8.6 The share of voters who describe themselves as independents has grown steadily in each election and today represents the identity (or lack of partisan identity) of over one-third of the electorate. Many independents actually vote as if they were Democrats or Republicans, however, and we call them "leaners." Historically, realigning elections have signaled significant change in public sentiment favoring a new political direction and a new dominant political party (e.g., 1932 and the rise of the New Deal coalition of Democrats). Disaffection with both major parties leads to dealignment, resulting in unpredictable voter behavior for a period of time. Among millennial voters, people between the ages of 18 and 33, half choose not to identify with either party, and only 31 percent see a difference between the major parties. This trend toward greater independence from the major parties, particularly among the young, might signal greater instability in American elections in years to come or perhaps action by the parties to redefine their base constituencies in an effort to reclaim prior dominance.

Selected Resources

PRINT RESOURCES

Abramowitz, Alan I. *The Disappearing Center: Engaged Citizens, Polarization, and American Democracy* (New Haven, CT: Yale University Press, 2011). Abramowitz argues that the number of moderate voters in the nation is decreasing as the two parties become more distant and more ideological, thus increasing the polarization of politics.

DeLuca, Stefani, Susan Clampet-Lundquist, and Kathryn Edin. *Coming of Age in the Other America* (New York: Russell Sage Foundation, 2016). A ten-year study of the impact of impoverished neighborhoods on children and families and the likelihood of upward mobility.

Purdum, Todd S. *An Idea Whose Time Has Come: Two Presidents, Two Parties, and the Battle for the Civil Rights Act of 1964* (New York: Henry Holt and Co., 2014). The political story of the creation of the landmark civil rights bill—a piece of legislation that prompted the longest filibuster in U.S. Senate history, but ultimately passed with overwhelming bipartisan support.

Skocpol, Theda, and Vanessa Williamson. *The Tea Party and the Remaking of the Republican Party* (New York: Oxford University Press, 2011). Two political scientists report on their year-long investigation into the Tea Party. By spending long periods of time talking to these supporters, they are able to describe the goals and beliefs of Tea Party voters.

MEDIA RESOURCES

The American President—A 1995 film starring Michael Douglas as a widowed president who must balance partisanship and friendship (Republicans in Congress promise to approve the president's crime bill only if he modifies an environmental plan sponsored by his liberal girlfriend).

The Best Man—A 1964 drama based on Gore Vidal's play of the same name. The film, which deals with political smear campaigns by presidential party nominees, focuses on political party power and ethics.

The Circus: Inside the Greatest Political Show on Earth—A Showtime documentary series airing on Sunday nights throughout the 2016 presidential election contest characterized in a review as "cheerfully cynical yet with a sincere appetite for the game."

House of Cards—A Netflix political drama featuring, a Southern Democrat in pursuit of political power at any cost.

Ides of March—A 2011 film (starring Ryan Gosling and George Clooney) about the pursuit of the Democratic nomination for president. Features intraparty intrigue and the political horse trading that occur in national campaigns.

ONLINE RESOURCES

Democratic Party—www.democrats.org

Green Party of the United States—a federation of state Green parties committed to environmentalism, nonviolence, social justice, and grassroots organizing: www.gp.org

Libertarian Party—America's third largest and fastest-growing political party; calls itself the party of principle and supports smaller government, lower taxes, and more freedom: www.lp.org

The Pew Research Center for the People & the Press—an independent, nonpartisan public opinion research organization that studies attitudes toward politics, the press, and public policy issues and offers survey data online on how the parties fared during the most recent elections, voter typology, and numerous other issues: www.people-press.org

Republican Party—www.gop.com

Campaigns, Voting, and Elections

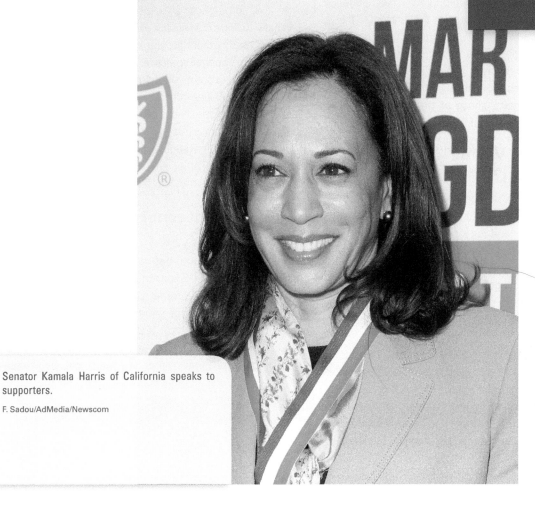

Senator Kamala Harris of California speaks to supporters.

F. Sadou/AdMedia/Newscom

LEARNING OBJECTIVES

After reading this chapter, you will be able to:

■ **9.1** Explain the eligibility requirements for president, senator, and representative; discuss why an individual might choose to become a candidate for office.

■ **9.2** Produce a plan for a modern campaign for the U.S. Senate; include the strategy, staff, and finances necessary for such an endeavor.

■ **9.3** Demonstrate an understanding of the evolution of campaign finance regulation, the development of political action committees (PACs), and the current state of such regulation.

■ **9.4** Describe the general outline of today's campaign for the presidency and discuss the impact of the primary system on the outcome of the nomination process.

■ **9.5** Demonstrate an understanding of the electoral process in the United States and explain how it relates to democratic theory.

■ **9.6** Discuss the factors that influence voter turnout in the United States and compare American voter turnout to that of other nations.

■ **9.7** Describe historical restrictions on the vote in the United States and explain how these restrictions have been ended.

■ **9.8** Discuss the impact of the mechanics and technology of voting on voter turnout, vote fraud, and the ability of citizens to trust the process.

■ **9.9** Demonstrate an understanding of the electoral college and its impact on the presidential election campaign.

Voting on the Internet Became Universal?

Background

Today, you can do just about anything on your smartphone. Why can't you vote using a smartphone or the Internet? This seems to be the logical extension of today's technology. Instead, almost all local governments require the voter to vote in person on a specified day or to seek an absentee ballot in advance. Some states allow advance voting in a specified place up to three weeks ahead of the vote; Oregon, Washington, and Colorado conduct all elections by mail.

What If Internet Voting Became Universal?

Many people would find it very convenient to vote over the Internet, whether via smartphone, desktop computer, or iPad. Travelers would no longer need to request an absentee ballot or to vote in advance of the election. Local governments would not have to invest millions of dollars in voting machines and cover the expense of operating polling places. Even if they felt the need to honor the idea of a polling place, allowing voters to use laptops at polling places would be much less expensive and less trouble than today's voting booths.

Using today's technology for voting would likely increase voter turnout among younger Americans, the group least likely to vote. As you will read in this chapter, younger Americans are less likely to be settled in a community and less likely to have an interest in political issues. But if they received an email alert and could vote instantly, voter turnout would likely increase in society.

Voting via the Internet would end the confusion over whether announcing the voting results of the Eastern states affects turnout in the Western states. A "window" for voting would open at a certain time, either in a state or across the nation, and all polls would open at the same time and close at the same time. Of course, traditional exit polling would cease to exist, as voters would no longer attend a physical location to cast their ballots. Results would be easily calculated and could be announced by a nonpartisan government agency at a specified time. The news would broadcast no more tales of hand-recounted, spoiled ballots and visual inspections of nebulous punch-card markings.

Would Internet Voting Disenfranchise Some Voters?

It is important to remember that not all Americans are "connected" to the Internet. Service does not reach many rural areas of the United States, and many economically disadvantaged individuals are without access to computers or to Internet services. Older Americans who do not have Internet services would likely be discouraged from voting, as would poorer groups. Individuals who value their privacy might prefer not to vote via the Internet because it could be traced back to their computer or smartphone.

What would be the result if older Americans, less well-off Americans, and other groups were disenfranchised by Internet voting? Younger voters tend to be more liberal in their social views and, to some extent, in their views about government action. Increasing turnout among these voters would advantage Democratic Party candidates. Lowering turnout among poorer, urban voters, however, would cost those candidates votes as well. Republicans would work very hard to make sure that their older supporters had access to computers and assistance in voting, to be sure.

Why Hasn't Internet Voting Been Adopted?

The major issue with Internet voting is the security of the vote. In 2003, the U.S. Department of Defense announced that it planned to make Internet voting for the 2004 election available to all members of the armed forces serving overseas. At that time, more than 100,000 members of the military were in Iraq. By early 2004, the Pentagon announced that it had cancelled that plan due to the possibility of voter fraud. Stealing voter identification, hacking into the voting system, submitting thousands of fraudulent votes using hijacked computers—all of these are possibilities. In 2010, the District of Columbia announced the trial of an Internet voting system and invited hackers to try to "break into" the system. Within a few days, University of Michigan students hacked into the system, adding the Michigan fight song as a sound track for voting. The trial was cancelled.*

It is worth noting that the country of Estonia has adopted Internet voting, but it is optional there. Other nations are trying to solve the security problems in various ways. The real question is this: Why do people want to tamper with the vote? The answer is because the stakes in governing are so high.

For Critical Analysis

1. Which groups would be most likely to vote over the Internet and which the least?

2. Would Internet voting increase citizens' trust in the voting process or make them even more suspicious of vote fraud?

---

*Mike DeBonis, "Hacker Infiltration Ends D.C. Online Voting Trial," *Washington Post*, October 12, 2010.

Free elections are the cornerstone of the American political system. Voters choose one or more candidates from a pool of candidates by casting ballots in local, state, and federal elections. Voters are free from intimidation or coercion and able to access information about the election. Voting should be easy, with simple forms or machines, and available at convenient hours. If these conditions are met, voters can have confidence in the election process and, in turn, more confidence in their elected officials. This chapter looks at the process of campaigning for election, as well as voting and elections, in the American context.

Who Wants to Be a Candidate?

■ **9.1** Explain the eligibility requirements for president, senator, and representative; discuss why an individual might choose to become a candidate for office.

Democratic political systems require competitive elections. If there is no competition for any office—president or local school superintendent—then the public has no ability to make a choice about its leadership or policies to be pursued. Who, then, are the people who seek to run for office?

The United States has thousands of elective offices. Political parties strive to provide a slate of candidates for every election. Recruiting candidates is easier for some offices than for others. Offices of high esteem and power have no trouble attracting candidates. In many areas of the country, however, one political party may be considerably stronger than the other. In those situations, the minority party may have more difficulty finding nominees for elections in which victory is unlikely.

Why They Run

People who run for office can be divided into two groups—the self-starters and those who are recruited. The self-starters get involved in political activities to further their careers, to carry out specific political programs, or in response to certain issues or events. Candidates for president from third parties often campaign primarily to gain publicity for their views, knowing they are unlikely to win.

Issues are important, but personal goals—status, career objectives, prestige, and income—are central in motivating some candidates to enter political life. Political office is often seen as the stepping stone to achieving certain career goals. A lawyer or an insurance agent may run for office only once or twice and then return to private life with enhanced status. Other politicians may aspire to long-term political office. Finally, we think of ambition as the desire for ever-more-important offices and higher status. Politicians who run for the state house may well desire to be elected to the U.S. House of Representatives in future years.

The Nomination Process

Individuals become official candidates through the process of nomination. Generally, nominating processes for all offices are controlled by state laws and usually favor the two major political parties. For most minor offices, individuals become candidates by submitting petitions to the local election board. Political parties often help individuals obtain the petitions, pay whatever filing fee is required, and gather signatures. In most states, a candidate from one of the two major parties faces far fewer requirements to get on the ballot than a candidate who is an independent or who represents a minor or new party.

did you know?

Five women received votes for vice president at the Democratic Convention in 1924, the first held after women received the right to vote in 1920.

For higher-level offices, candidates may need to petition and then be nominated by a party convention at the state level. In other jurisdictions, party caucuses are empowered to nominate candidates. Many contenders for office are nominated through a primary election in which two or more individuals contend for the party's nomination.

The American system of nominations and primary elections is one of the most complex in the world. In most European nations, the political party's choice of candidates is final, and no primary elections are ever held.

Who Is Eligible?

There are few constitutional restrictions on who can become a candidate in the United States. As set out in the Constitution, the formal requirements for national office are as follows:

1. *President.* Must be a natural-born citizen, have attained the age of 35 years, and be a resident of the country for 14 years by the time of inauguration. The definition of "natural born" citizen was first fixed by the U.S. Congress in 1790. Generally, any child born abroad to a parent who is a U.S. citizen is a natural-born citizen. From time to time, residency requirements for the parent and/or the child have been instituted, but children born to a citizen are citizens by birth.

2. *Vice president.* Must be a natural-born citizen, have attained the age of 35 years, and not be a resident of the same state as the candidate for president.[1]

3. *Senator.* Must be a citizen for at least nine years, have attained the age of 30 by the time of taking office, and be a resident of the state from which elected.

4. *Representative.* Must be a citizen for at least seven years, have attained the age of 25 by the time of taking office, and be a resident of the state from which elected.

The qualifications for state legislators are set by the state constitutions and likewise include age, place of residence, and citizenship. Usually, the requirements for the upper chamber of a legislature are somewhat more stringent than those for the lower chamber. The legal qualifications for running for governor or other state office are similar.

Who Runs?

Despite these minimal legal qualifications for office at both the national and state levels, a quick look at the slate of candidates in any election—or at the current members of the U.S. House of Representatives—will reveal that not all segments of the population take advantage of these opportunities. Holders of political office in the United States are overwhelmingly white and male. Until the twentieth century, presidential candidates were of northern European origin and Protestant heritage.[2] Laws that effectively denied voting rights made it impossible to elect African American public officials in many areas in which African Americans constituted a significant portion of the population. As a result of the passage of major civil rights legislation in the 1960s, however, the number of African American public officials has increased throughout the United States. By 2013, the number of African American elected officials was

1 Technically, a presidential and vice presidential candidate can be from the same state, but if they are, one of the two must forfeit the electoral votes of his or her home state.
2 A number of early presidents were Unitarian. The Unitarian Church is not Protestant, but it is historically rooted in the Protestant tradition.

Figure 9-1 ▶ Women Running for Congress (and Winning)

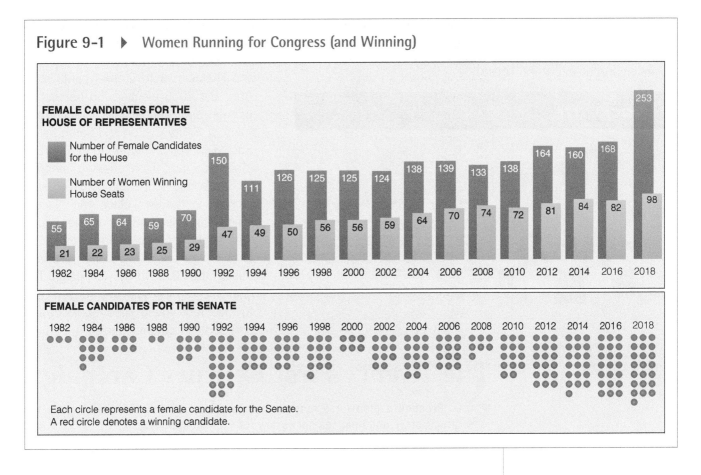

estimated at more than 10,500,[3] and, in 2008, Americans elected Barack Obama to be the first African American president. He was reelected in 2012.

Women as Candidates Until recently, women generally were considered to be appropriate candidates only for lower-level offices, such as state legislator or school board member. It was thought that women would be more acceptable to the voting public if they were either running for an office that allowed them to continue their family duties or were running for an office that focused on local affairs, such as city or school issues. The last 20 years have seen a tremendous increase in the number of women who run for office, not only at the state level but for the U.S. Congress as well. Figure 9-1 shows the increase in female candidates. In 2018, more than 250 women ran for Congress in the general election and more than 110 won. Both Tammy Baldwin, the first openly gay Senator and Maxie Hirono, the first Buddhist Senator were reelected handily.

In the past, women were not recruited because they had not worked their way up through the male-dominated party organization or because they were thought to have no chance of winning. Women also had a more difficult time raising campaign funds. Since the 1970s, there has been a focused effort to increase the number of women candidates. EMILY's List, a group that raises money to recruit and support liberal women candidates, has had a strong impact on the situation for women candidates. Other organizations with more conservative agendas also raise money for women. Recent elections have witnessed women candidates of

did you know?
EMILY's List means Early Money Is Like Yeast, referring both to needing money early in a campaign and to yeast for raising bread.

---

3 Juliet Eilperin, "What's Changed for African Americans since 1963, by the Numbers." http://www.washingtonpost.com /blogs/the-fix/2013/08/22

From the Web ▶ The Rock the Vote organization uses its website to encourage political participation among young Americans of every background.

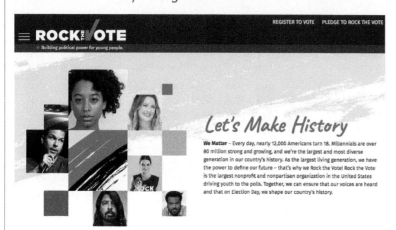

Rock the Vote

either party raising millions of dollars and winning office; however, women voters are more likely to perceive gender bias and a harder path for women candidates. After the 2008 election, 65 percent of women saw gender bias in the treatment of Hillary Clinton and Sarah Palin.[4] Such perceptions work to discourage other women from seeking elective office. To help fight these perceptions of women in the workplace and elected office, Condoleezza Rice, former secretary of state, has partnered with other female business leaders and politicians to start the "Ban Bossy" campaign. The goal is to ban the adjective "bossy" and to encourage young girls to speak up and participate in leadership roles.

The Twenty-First-Century Campaign

■ **9.2** Produce a plan for a modern campaign for the U.S. Senate; include the strategy, staff, and finances necessary for such an endeavor.

After the candidates have been nominated, the most exhausting and expensive part of the election process begins—the general election campaign. Even with the most appealing of candidates, today's campaigns require a strong organization; expertise in political polling and marketing; professional assistance in fundraising, accounting, and financial management; and technological capabilities in every aspect of the campaign.

The Changing Campaign

The goal is the same for all campaigns—to convince voters to choose a candidate or a slate of candidates for office. Part of the reason for the increased intensity of campaigns in the last decade is that they are now centered on the candidate, not on the party. The candidate-centered campaign emerged in response to several developments: changes in the electoral system, the increased importance of television and other forms of electronic media in campaigns, the change in campaign funding, and technological advances in ways to reach potential voters, including social media.

To run a successful and persuasive campaign, the candidate's organization must be able to raise funds for the effort; obtain coverage from the media; produce and pay for advertising, websites, and social media sites; schedule the candidate's time effectively; convey the candidate's position on the issues to the voters; conduct research on the opposing candidate; and get the voters to go to the polls.

Before the advent of candidate-centered politics, political parties provided most of the support for campaigns. Parties provided campaign funding, organized events, registered voters, and turned out the voters on Election Day. Prior

---

4　Jennifer Lawless and Richard L. Fox, "Men Rule: The Continued Underrepresentation of Women in U.S. Politics," Washington, DC: Women and Politics Institute, 2012.

Game Change: An Inside Look at Campaign Decisions

Released in 2012 on HBO, *Game Change* is a look inside the campaign decisions made by the John McCain organization in the 2008 presidential election. Faced with the charismatic Democratic candidate Barack Obama, McCain and his campaign team struggled to find a way to add excitement to his campaign. They decided on Sarah Palin, the untested governor of Alaska (a very small state in terms of voters), as the vice presidential candidate on the Republican ticket. Palin was named as the vice presidential candidate right before the Republican National Convention and completely upended the staid convention with her acceptance speech.

The movie, which stars Woody Harrelson, Ed Harris, and Julianne Moore, tells the story of Palin's rise to stardom and quick fall after some of her "gaffes." Although both Palin and McCain said that they would never see the film and that it is inaccurate, the movie was based on the book *Game Change,* written by two veteran journalists, Mark Halperin and John Heilemann. Some of those who were insiders to the campaign and other journalists who covered the campaign say there is a lot of truth in this fictionalized account of the McCain campaign.

Like other films about political campaigns, *Game Change* underscores the intensity of a campaign and the desperate quality of the decisions that are made in the attempt to win. A wholly fictional treatment of presidential election politics is offered by *House of Cards,* the Netflix original series. Now in its sixth season, the story follows the ascension to the presidency by Frank Underwood, who will lie, cheat, and murder to become president. Although some of the plot turns are farfetched, this fictional account of presidential politics captures the intensity of the political arena and acknowledges the importance of the media.

For Critical Analysis

1. Do social media such as YouTube or made-for-TV movies such as *Game Change, or House of Cards* increase voter cynicism and distrust of government?

2. Does the attention given by social media have a lasting impact on campaigns and elections?

---

to today's media-saturated campaigns, the party label was more important to voters than the candidate's appearance and personality.

Today, with the decline in party identification among American voters, the candidate's campaigns must provide a persuasive case for his or her election to party identifiers and to the growing class of independent voters. Consider the fact that only 20 percent of voters declared themselves independents in 1952 compared with 44 percent in 2018.[5]

The Professional Campaign Staff

Whether a candidate is running for state legislature, the governor's office, U.S. Congress, or the presidency, every campaign has some fundamental tasks to accomplish. Today, in national elections, most of these tasks are handled by paid professionals rather than volunteers or amateur politicians. Volunteers and amateurs are primarily used for the last-minute registration or voter turnout activities.

The most sought-after and possibly the most criticized campaign expert is the **political consultant**, who, for a large fee, devises a campaign strategy,

political consultant
A paid professional hired to devise a campaign strategy and manage a campaign.

---

5 Gallup Poll, January 10, 2018.

creates a campaign theme, oversees the advertising, and possibly chooses the campaign colors and the candidate's official portrait. Political consultants began to displace volunteer campaign managers in the 1960s, about the same time that television became a force in campaigns. The paid consultant and his or her staff monitor the campaign's progress, plan all media appearances, and coach the candidate for debates. The consultants and the firms they represent are not politically neutral; most will work only for candidates from one party. Consultants are on hand constantly to plan rebuttals to the opponent's charges and to recalibrate the campaign.

finance chairperson
The campaign professional who directs fundraising, campaign spending, and compliance with campaign finance laws and reporting requirements.

Under constant pressure to raise more campaign funds and to comply with the campaign finance laws, all campaigns need a **finance chairperson** who plans the fundraising strategy and finds the legal and accounting expertise needed for the organization. Of course, campaigns will either hire an in-house **pollster** or contract with a major polling firm for the tracking polls and focus groups discussed in Chapter 6.

pollster
The person or firm who conducts public opinion polls for the campaign.

Candidates need to have a clear strategy to gain public attention and to respond to attacks by their opponents. The campaign's **communications director** plans appearances, the themes to be communicated by the candidate at specific points in the campaign, and the responses to any attacks. The campaign's **press secretary** is responsible for dealing directly with the press. Perhaps the most famous example of a successful communication strategy was that of Bill Clinton in his 1992 victory. The campaign organized a "War Room" to instantly respond to any attack by his opponents. Today's candidates use Twitter and other social networking sites to respond to charges instantaneously. Counterattacks, a feature of the War Room strategy, can also be launched immediately using social networking sites. At the end of the campaign is the actual election. Campaigns need to find a way to recruit and organize volunteers for the **Get Out the Vote (GOTV)** drive to persuade voters to come to the polls on Election Day.

communications director
A professional specialist who plans the communications strategy and advertising campaign for the candidate.

press secretary
The individual who interacts directly with the journalists covering the campaign.

Get Out the Vote (GOTV)
This phrase describes the multiple efforts expended by campaigns to get voters out to the polls on Election Day.

The Strategy of Winning

In the United States, unlike some European countries, the candidate who comes in second gets no reward. A winner-take-all system is also known as a *plurality voting system.* In most situations, the winning candidate does not need to have a majority of the votes. Given this system, the campaign organization must plan a strategy that maximizes the candidate's chances of winning. Candidates seek to capture all of the votes of their party's supporters, to convince a majority of the independent voters to vote for them, and to gain a few votes from supporters of the other party. To accomplish these goals, candidates must consider their visibility, their message, and their campaign strategy.

Candidate Visibility and Appeal

One of the most important concerns is how well known the candidate is. If she or he is a highly visible incumbent, little campaigning may be needed except to remind the voters of the officeholder's good deeds. If, however, the candidate is an unknown challenger or a largely unfamiliar character running against a well-known public figure, the campaign must devise a strategy to get the candidate before the public.

In the case of the independent candidate or the candidate representing a minor party, the problem of name recognition is serious. Such candidates must present an overwhelming case for the voter to reject the major-party candidates. Both Democratic and Republican candidates use the strategic ploy of labeling third-party candidates as "not serious"—and therefore not worth the voter's time.

Taking the Public Pulse

In addition to measuring name recognition and "feelings" toward a candidate, today's campaigns rely heavily on other ways to find out how the electorate views the candidate and her or his message. Opinion polls are a major source of information for both the media and the candidates. Dozens of public polls are reported in the news. As the election approaches, many candidates and commercial houses use **tracking polls**, which are polls taken almost every day to find out how well they are competing for votes. Tracking polls enable consultants to fine-tune the advertising and the candidate's speeches in the last days of the campaign.

Another tactic is to use a **focus group** to gain insights into public perceptions of the candidate. Professional consultants organize a discussion of the candidate or of certain political issues among 10 to 15 ordinary citizens. The citizens are selected from specific target groups in the population—for example, working women, blue-collar men, senior citizens, or young voters. Recent campaigns have tried to reach groups such as "millennials," "Walmart shoppers," or "NASCAR dads."[6] The group discusses personality traits of the candidate, political advertising, and other candidate-related issues. The conversation is digitally video recorded (and often observed from behind a mirrored wall). Focus groups are expected to reveal more emotional responses to candidates or the deeper anxieties of voters—feelings that consultants believe often are not tapped into by more impersonal telephone surveys.

The Media and Political Campaigns All forms of the media—television, newspapers, radio, magazines, blogs, and podcasts—have a significant political impact on American society, which is most obvious during political campaigns. With the bulk of campaign funds spent on media of one form or another, planning media strategies is one of the most important functions of a campaign. Media strategies include television news and entertainment outlets, social media and web presences, free and paid advertising, and performance in debates. The goal of this activity is for the public to accept and support the image of the candidate created by the campaign.

Financing the Campaign

For any campaign to have a chance at success, it must raise enough funds to be competitive. In a book published in 1932 entitled *Money in Elections,* Louise Overacker had the following to say about campaign financing:

> *The financing of elections in a democracy is a problem which is arousing increasing concern. Many are beginning to wonder if present-day methods of raising and spending campaign funds do not clog the wheels of our elaborately constructed mechanism of popular control, and if democracies do not inevitably become [governments ruled by small groups].*[7]

tracking polls
A poll taken for the candidate on a nearly daily basis as Election Day approaches.

focus group
A small group of individuals who are led in discussion by a professional consultant in order to gather opinions on and responses to candidates and issues.

---

6 NASCAR stands for the National Association of Stock Car Auto Racing.
7 Louise Overacker, *Money in Elections* (New York: Macmillan, 1932), p. vii.

How Short Can a Campaign Be?

Consider the difference between U.S. presidential campaigns and the British system of elections for Parliament and prime minister. In the United States, candidates for president begin traveling the country and building up support about two years before the general election. The primary election season starts just after January 1 of the election year, and the campaigns continue nonstop for almost 11 months.

In the United Kingdom, for more than a century, the prime minister could ask the monarch to dissolve parliament if he or she saw an advantage for their party, although the maximum length of any parliament was set at five years. Beginning in 2011, parliaments now have a fixed term of five years unless a vote of no confidence against the majority is passed. Unlike American elections, however, the British political season is very short. In 2015, the parliament was dissolved on March 30 and the election held six weeks later, on May 7.

In that short period, the political parties assemble their candidates for each constituency, name their leaders as contenders for the prime minister's position, and do all their campaigning, both locally and nationally. With each new election in Great Britain, more American practices have come into play. American political consultants are regularly hired to help with developing party messages and planning the advertising campaign. Survey research and political polling are also well developed in Great Britain, and pre-election polls are widely read. In the 2015 election, the three major-party candidates held a live debate on television, American style, for the first time in British history.

So, how do the parties use that time, and how much money is spent during this short campaign period? British law has focused on spending limits for the campaign rather than on donation limits.* Each party is limited in its expenditures during the year before the election. The spending limits are set on a constituency basis. In 2015, each major party was limited to spending about $56,000 per seat in the House of Commons. Compare that with the United States' average expenditure of more than $1 million for each seat in the House of Representatives. Altogether, the expenditures of the three major parties and more than 35 minor parties were about $44 million—far less than the billions spent in the United States over a similar period.** Although the previous election in 2010 had resulted in a three-way split and a power-sharing agreement between the Conservative and the Liberal Parties, the 2015 election

Image 9-1 Theresa May, a leader within the Conservative Party, was elected by her party as Prime Minister after David Cameron resigned.

was a clear victory for the Conservative Party and its leader, David Cameron, who resigned after the United Kingdom voted to leave the EU.

Could the United States ever face a three-way split in the vote? Conceivably, a third party could win enough seats in Congress to deny the majority to either the Democrats or the Republicans. It is much more difficult in America for a third party to win enough electoral votes to send the presidential election into the House of Representatives.

The larger question is whether the United States could adopt some electoral reforms to reduce the cost of its campaigns (and the possible influence of donors) and shorten the season. Most Americans would like to see a shorter election season and less campaign advertising in their lives.

For Critical Analysis

1. Do you think American campaigns would generate more or less excitement and voter turnout if they were considerably shorter?

2. Is it really possible for candidates and parties to explain their platforms and present their candidates in a couple of weeks?

* See the British Parliament website for more information: www.parliament.uk
** Library of Congress: www.loc.gov/law/help/campaign-finance/uk.php

Figure 9-2 ▶ Growth in Campaign Spending, 1998–2016

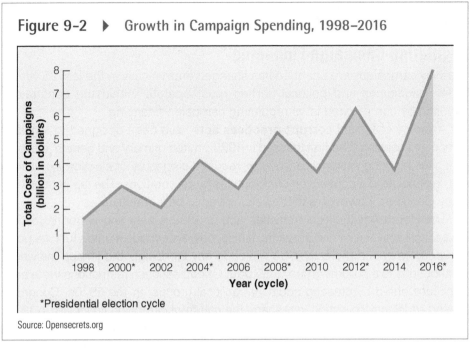

*Presidential election cycle

Source: Opensecrets.org

Although writing more than 70 years ago, Overacker touched on a sensitive issue in American political campaigns—the connection between money and elections. It is difficult to comprehend how quickly spending on political campaigns has risen. Figure 9-2 shows the doubling of campaign spending over the last four presidential elections, with about $8 billion spent at all levels of campaigning during the 2015–2016 election cycle.[8] Total spending by the presidential candidates in 2016 amounted to more than $4 billion. In the North Carolina Senate race in 2014, Kay Hagan and Tom Tillis spent about $113 million in their contest, with $81 million coming from outside spending organizations. Colorado, Iowa, and Kentucky saw Senate races that cost more than $40 million. Traditionally, candidates spend much less to retain or obtain a seat in the House of Representatives because representatives stand for seats in much smaller geographic areas; however, these races are heating up. In 2016, eight races for the House of Representatives saw spending of more than $20 million in each respective district. That would be about $40 for every individual in the congressional district, whether or not they were registered voters. Except for the presidential campaigns, all of these funds had to be provided by the candidates and their families, borrowed, or raised by contributions from individuals, political parties, or *political action committees*, groups to be described later in this chapter. For the presidential campaigns, some of the funds

From the Web ▶ At the OpenSecrets.org website, researchers post data on campaign contributions, lobbying, and campaign spending for anyone to see.

OpenSecrets.org

could come from the federal government, but both candidates in 2016 rejected those funds to raise their own (see the screen capture).

Regulating Campaign Financing

The way campaigns are financed has changed dramatically in the last 25 years. Today, candidates and political parties must operate within the constraints imposed by complicated laws regulating campaign financing.

corrupt practices acts
A series of acts passed by Congress in an attempt to limit and regulate the size and sources of contributions and expenditures in political campaigns.

A variety of federal **corrupt practices acts** have been designed to regulate campaign financing. The first, passed in 1925, limited primary and general election expenses for congressional candidates, required disclosure of election expenses, and, in principle, put controls on contributions by corporations. The restrictions had many loopholes, however, and the acts proved to be ineffective.

Hatch Act
An act passed in 1939 that restricted the political activities of government employees. It also prohibited a political group from spending more than $3 million in any campaign and limited individual contributions to a campaign committee to $5,000.

The **Hatch Act** (Political Activities Act) of 1939 is best known for restricting the political activities of civil servants. It also, however, made it unlawful for a political group to spend more than $3 million in any campaign and limited individual contributions to a political group to $5,000. Of course, such restrictions were easily circumvented by creating additional political groups. In the 1970s, Congress passed additional legislation to reshape the nature of campaign financing. In 1971, it passed the Federal Election Campaign Act to reform the process. Then in 1974, in the wake of the Watergate scandal, Congress enacted further reforms.

The Federal Election Campaign Act

The Federal Election Campaign Act (FECA) of 1971, which became effective in 1972, essentially replaced all past campaign finance laws. This law and all those that have followed are based on three principles: there should be limits placed on individual contributions, there needs to be a disclosure of all contributions to the public, and there should be public funding of presidential campaigns. The act placed no limit on overall spending but restricted the total amount that could be spent on mass-media advertising, including television, if the candidate took public money. It limited the amount that candidates could contribute to their own campaigns (a limit later ruled unconstitutional) and required disclosure of all contributions and expenditures over $100. In principle, the FECA limited the role of labor unions and corporations in political campaigns. It also provided for a voluntary $1 (now $3) checkoff on federal income tax returns for general campaign funds to be used by major-party presidential candidates.

Further Reforms in 1974 For many, the 1971 act did not go far enough. Amendments to the FECA passed in 1974 did the following:

1. *Created the Federal Election Commission (FEC).* This commission consists of six nonpartisan administrators whose duties are to enforce compliance with the requirements of the act.

2. *Provided public financing for presidential primaries and general elections.* Any candidate running for president who is able to obtain sufficient contributions in at least 20 states can obtain a subsidy from the U.S. Treasury to help pay for primary campaigns. The Bush-Kerry race in 2004 was the last time both general election candidates accepted public money for the general election campaign.

3. *Limited presidential campaign spending.* Any candidate accepting federal support must agree to limit campaign expenditures to the amount prescribed by federal law.

4. *Limited contributions.* Under the 1974 amendments, citizens could contribute up to $1,000 to each candidate in each federal election or primary; the total limit on all contributions from an individual to all candidates was $25,000 per year. Groups could contribute a maximum of $5,000 to a candidate in any election. (Some of these limits were changed by the 2002 campaign reform legislation.)

5. *Required disclosure.* Each candidate must file periodic reports with the FEC listing who contributed, how much was spent, and on what the funds were spent.

The 1971 and 1974 laws set in place the principles that have guided campaign finance ever since. The laws and those that have been enacted subsequently are informed by three principles: (1) set limits on what individuals and groups can give to individual candidates and within one election cycle; (2) provide some public funding for the presidential primaries, conventions, and the general election campaign; and (3) make all contributions and reports public. All contributions that are made to candidates under these laws and principles are usually called **hard money**. Individuals and groups that wish to circumvent these principles have been successful in finding ways to do so. Other kinds of campaign donations are referred to as "soft money" or "outside spending."

hard money
This refers to political contributions and campaign spending that is recorded under the regulations set forth in law and by the Federal Election Commission.

Buckley v. Valeo The 1971 act had limited the amount that each individual could spend on his or her own behalf. The Supreme Court declared the provision unconstitutional in the 1976 case *Buckley v. Valeo*, stating that it was unconstitutional to restrict in any way the amount congressional candidates could spend on their own behalf: "The candidate, no less than any other person, has a First Amendment right to engage in the discussion of public issues and vigorously and tirelessly to advocate his own election."[9]

The *Buckley v. Valeo* decision, which has often been criticized, was directly countered by a 1997 Vermont law. The law, known as Act 64, imposed spending limits ranging from $2,000 to $300,000 (depending on the office sought) on candidates for state offices in Vermont. A number of groups, including the American Civil Liberties Union and the Republican Party, challenged the act, claiming that it violated the First Amendment's guarantee of free speech. In a landmark decision in August 2002, a federal appellate court disagreed and upheld the law.[10] In 2006, the U.S. Supreme Court declared that Vermont's campaign spending and donation limits were unconstitutional, thereby reaffirming the *Buckley v. Valeo* decision.

Interest Groups and Campaign Finance: Reaction to New Rules

■ **9.3** Demonstrate an understanding of the evolution of campaign finance regulation, the development of political action committees (PACs), and the current state of such regulation.

In the last two decades, interest groups, individuals, and corporations have worked tirelessly to find ways to support candidates through campaign donations. Candidates, in turn, have become dependent on these donations to run increasingly expensive campaigns. Interest groups and corporations funnel money

---

9 424 U.S. 1 (1976).
10 *Randell v. Vermont Public Interest Research Group*, 300 F.3d 129 (2d Cir. 2002).

political action committee (PAC)
A committee set up by and representing a corporation, labor union, or special-interest group. PACs raise and give campaign donations.

soft money
Campaign contributions unregulated by federal or state law, usually given to parties and party committees to help fund general party activities.

issue advocacy advertising
Advertising paid for by interest groups that support or oppose a candidate or a candidate's position on an issue without mentioning voting or elections.

Super PAC
A political committee that can accept unlimited contributions from individuals and corporations to spend supporting a candidate as long as its efforts are not coordinated with the candidate's own campaign.

did you know?
Abraham Lincoln sold pieces of fence rail that he had split as political souvenirs to finance his campaign.

to political candidates through several devices: **political action committees (PACs)**, **soft money** contributions, 527s, **issue advocacy advertising**, and, after soft money was outlawed, through "**Super PACs**." Every time legislation is passed at the federal or state level, interest groups, corporations, unions, and associations scramble to find new, legally allowable ways to influence campaigns. This activity has prompted commentators to label all campaign finance regulation as "whack the mole" law, meaning for every activity prohibited, another one pops up. Simply put, campaigns tend to net lots of money; some is regulated, some is not.

PACs and Political Campaigns

The 1974 and 1976 amendments to the Federal Election Campaign Act of 1971 allow corporations, labor unions, and other interest groups to set up political action committees, or PACs, to raise funds for candidates. The funds must be raised from at least 50 volunteer donors and must be given to at least five candidates in the federal election. PACs can contribute up to $5,000 to each candidate in each election. Each corporation or each union is limited to one PAC. Corporate PACs obtain contributions from executives and managers in their firms, and unions obtain PAC funds from their members.

The number of PACs has grown significantly since 1976, as has the amount they spend on elections. PACs numbered about 1,000 in 1976; today, the number is more than 4,600. Total spending by PACs grew from $19 million in 1973 to more than $1 billion in 2015–2016. About 35 percent of all campaign funds raised by House candidates in 2016 came from PACs.[11]

Interest groups funnel PAC funds to the candidates they think can do the most good for them. Frequently, they make the maximum contribution of $5,000 per election to candidates who face little or no opposition. Figure 9-3 shows that the great bulk of campaign contributions goes to incumbent candidates rather than to challengers. Table 9-1 shows the amounts contributed by the top 10 PACs during the 2015–2016 election cycle.

As Table 9-1 also shows, many PACs give most of their contributions to candidates of one party. Other PACs, particularly corporate PACs, tend to give funds to Democrats as well as to Republicans because, with both chambers of Congress so closely divided, predicting which party will be in control after an election is almost impossible. Why would members of the National Association of Realtors give to Democrats who may be more liberal than themselves? Interest groups see PAC contributions as a way to ensure *access* to powerful legislators, even though the groups may disagree with the legislators some of the time. PAC contributions are, in a way, an investment in a relationship.

Campaign Financing beyond the Limits

Within a few years after the establishment of the tight limits on contributions, new ways to finance campaigns were developed that skirted the reforms and made it possible for huge sums to be raised, especially by the major political parties.

Contributions to Political Parties Candidates, PACs, and political parties found ways to generate *soft money*—campaign contributions that escaped

11 Center for Responsive Politics, at www.opensecrets.org

Figure 9-3   ▶   PAC Contributions to Congressional Candidates, 1991–2016

PAC Contributions to Congressional Candidates*

Legend: Incumbents   Challengers   Open Seats

Y-axis: Millions of Dollars (0 to 360)

X-axis: 1995–1996, 1997–1998, 1999–2000, 2001–2002, 2003–2004, 2005–2006, 2007–2008, 2009–2010, 2011–2012, 2013–2014, 2015–2016

*Campaign financing regulations clearly limit the amount that a PAC can give to any one candidate, but the amount that a PAC can spend on issue advocacy is limitless, whether on behalf of a candidate or party or in opposition to one.

Source: Center for Responsive Politics, http://www.opensecrets.org

Table 9-1   ▶   The Top Ten PAC Contributors to Federal Candidates, 2015–2016 Election Cycle*

PAC NAME	TOTAL AMOUNT	DEM. (%)	REP. (%)
National Association of Realtors	$3,973,350	42%	58%
National Beer Wholesalers Assn.	$3,322,700	43%	57%
AT&T Inc.	$2,953,750	38%	62%
Honeywell International	$2,861,364	40%	60%
National Auto Dealers Association	$2,659,250	28%	72%
Lockheed Martin	$2,612,750	38%	62%
Blue Cross/Blue Shield	$2,573,398	36%	64%
International Brotherhood of Electrical Workers	$2,570,650	96%	4%
American Bankers Association	$2,444,007	21%	79%
Credit Union National Association	$2,380,350	47%	53%

*Includes subsidiaries and affiliated PACs, if any.
Source: Center for Responsive Politics, 2018.

the limits of federal election law. Although the FECA limited contributions that would be spent on elections, contributions to political parties for activities such as voter education and voter-registration drives had no limits. This loophole enabled the parties to raise millions of dollars from corporations and individuals. Between 1993 and 2002, when soft money was banned, the amount raised for election activities quadrupled, increasing to more than $400 million. The parties spent these funds for their conventions, for registering voters, and for advertising to promote the general party position. The parties also sent a great deal to state and local party organizations, which used the soft money to support their own tickets.

independent expenditures
Nonregulated contributions from PACs, organizations, and individuals. The funds may be spent on advertising or other campaign activities, so long as those expenditures are not coordinated with those of a candidate.

Independent Expenditures Corporations, labor unions, and other interest groups discovered that it was legal to make **independent expenditures** in an election campaign, as long as the expenditures were not coordinated with those of the candidate or political party. Hundreds of unique committees and organizations blossomed to take advantage of this campaign tactic. Although a 1990 U.S. Supreme Court decision, *Austin v. Michigan State Chamber of Commerce,* upheld the right of the states and the federal government to limit independent, direct corporate expenditures (such as for advertisements) on behalf of *candidates*, the decision did not stop businesses and other types of groups from making independent expenditures on *issues.*[12]

Issue Advocacy Indeed, issue advocacy—spending unregulated funds on advertising that promotes positions on issues rather than candidates—has become a common tactic in recent years. Interest groups routinely wage their own issue campaigns. Groups as varied as the AARP and the Environmental Defense Fund sponsor ads on the issues and to promote their agenda. Issue advocacy ads frequently urge voters to contact their senator or representatives and tell him or her how to vote on a specific issue of concern to the interest group sponsoring the ad.

Although promoting issue positions is very close to promoting candidates who support those positions, the courts repeatedly have held, in accordance with the *Buckley v. Valeo* decision mentioned earlier, that interest groups have a First Amendment right to advocate their positions. In a 1996 decision, the Supreme Court clarified this point, stating that political parties may also make independent expenditures on behalf of candidates—as long as the parties do so *independently* of the candidates.[13] In other words, the parties must not coordinate such expenditures with the candidates' campaigns.

The Bipartisan Campaign Reform Act of 2002

Although both Democrats and Republicans argued for campaign reform legislation during the 1990s, the bill cosponsored by Senators John McCain, a Republican, and Russ Feingold, a Democrat, finally became the Bipartisan Campaign Reform Act (BCRA) in 2002. This act, which amended the 1971 FECA, took effect on the day after the congressional elections of November 5, 2002.

12 494 U.S. 652 (1990).
13 *Colorado Republican Federal Campaign Committee v. Federal Election Commission*, 518 U.S. 604 (1996).

Key Elements of the New Law The 2002 law banned the large, unlimited contributions to national political parties termed soft money. It placed curbs on, but did not entirely eliminate, the use of campaign ads by outside special-interest groups advocating the election or defeat of specific candidates. Limits for individual contributions directly to candidates were raised, and the maximum amount that an individual can give to all federal candidates was raised from $25,000 per year to $95,000 over a two-year election cycle. It did not ban soft money contributions to state and local parties. These parties can accept such contributions, as long as they are limited to $10,000 per year per individual. Although the act was challenged by groups that viewed it as a threat to their influence in elections, the Supreme Court, in a series of decisions, upheld most of the law. Remember, however, that the law pertains to direct contributions to candidates and funds spent that are coordinated with the candidate's own campaign.

The Rise of the 527s Interest groups that previously gave soft money to the parties responded to the 2002 BCRA by setting up new groups outside the parties: 527 organizations, so named for the section of the tax code that provides for them. These tax-exempt organizations rely on soft money contributions for their funding and generally must report their contributions and expenditures to the Internal Revenue Service (IRS). What started out as a device to circumvent the campaign finance limits on donations has now grown into a complicated web of unregulated campaign financing. The top names in Table 9-2 might look familiar. EMILY's List has been a long-standing PAC that supports women candidates, mostly Democrats. It still has a PAC that receives regulated contributions and makes direct limited donations to candidates. Yet, it also has a 527 organization that can accept unlimited donations and spend the funds on "uncoordinated advertising." The list of top 2014 groups includes labor unions, groups linked to business, groups headed by well-known politicians, and others that maintain both PACs and 527 organizations. This tactic gives the groups greater ability than a PAC to raise and spend money.

Table 9-2 ▶ Top Ten 527 Committees in Expenditures in 2016

COMMITTEE	2015–2016 EXPENDITURES	VIEWPOINT	AFFILIATION
ActBlue	$45,034,312	Democratic	Democratic Party
American Federation of Teachers	$20,011,672	Democratic	Teacher's Union
New Day for America	$15,817,349	Republican	Support John Kasich
EMILY's List	$15,360,164	Progressive	Support women candidates
New Approach PAC	$13,283,498	Non partisan	Support legalized marijuana
College Republican National Committee	$12,062,395	Republican	Republican Party
International Brotherhood of Electrical Workers	$11,198,505	Democratic	Union
SEIU	$11,048,339	Democratic	Union
Laborer's Union	$10,316,244	Democratic	Union
Our American Revival	$9,228,520	Republican	Conservative Group

Source: Center for Responsive Politics, 2018

Overall, 527 groups, PACs, and Super Pacs spent more than $1 billion in 2016 with at least 20 groups spending more than $20 million apiece. Note the wholesome and patriotic titles of the 527 committees in the table. The vast majority of these groups have a partisan preference, regardless of what they call themselves.

In contrast to the 527s, charities and true not-for-profit organizations are not allowed to participate directly in any type of political activity. If they do so, they risk fines and the loss of their charitable tax-exempt status. In 2005, the IRS reviewed more than 80 churches, charities, and other tax-exempt organizations. The IRS looked for such banned activities as the distribution of printed materials encouraging members to vote for a specific candidate, contributions of cash to candidates' campaigns, and ministers' use of their pulpits to oppose or endorse specific candidates. Of the 82 churches, charities, and other tax-exempt organizations that the IRS examined, more than 75 percent engaged in prohibited political activity during the 2003–2004 election cycle. The IRS proposed to revoke the tax-exempt status of at least three of these organizations.

IRS investigations of churches and other charitable organizations have ceased, due to a 2009 federal court ruling on a case under investigation by the IRS. The court asked the IRS to clarify which level of the organization was responsible for these investigations, noting that administrative changes in the agency no longer met the requirements of the law forbidding political action by churches. The IRS has not clarified these regulations, so no enforcement has occurred; in the interim, the Billy Graham ministry paid for a full-page ad supporting Republican presidential candidate Mitt Romney in the 2012 election and, according to the Pew Research Center, 40 percent of black Protestants said that their pastors urged them to vote for Barack Obama in that same election.[14]

Yet another sort of organization entered the political arena in recent years. Local and statewide groups of political activists have filed to become 504(c)(4) organizations, which are tax-exempt entities that engage in social welfare, educational, or other activities to benefit the

Image 9-2

The Koch brothers, Charles (left) and David (right), have donated millions of dollars to conservative causes and conservative candidates. Originally, the Koch brothers identified themselves as Libertarians, but they support Republicans because Libertarian candidates are unlikely to win office.

14 Rachel Zoll, "Religion and Politics: IRS Not Enforcing Rules on Separation of Church and State," Associated Press, November 3, 2012, reported at www.huffingtonpost.com

community. Local, regional, and statewide Tea Party groups (as well as some pro-Democratic groups) have sought this status from the IRS. Beginning in 2010, such groups reported that their applications were subject to extraordinary scrutiny by the IRS and the decision on their status was delayed for years. Eventually the delay was traced to the Cincinnati office of the agency and to some specific individuals. Although the agency's own investigation has found a bureaucratic problem, Republicans in Congress have continued to investigate the issue.

Citizens United, Freedom Now, and the Future of Campaign Finance Regulation

The Supreme Court decision in *Citizens United v. FEC* shook the political world like no other since *Buckley v. Valeo.*[15] In many ways, the case continued the struggle of outside groups and groups not affiliated with political parties to play a bigger role in political campaigns. Although three decades of campaign finance laws and regulation had been passed to contain the influence of groups on the political process and to limit the contributions of individuals, political action committees, and corporations, the *Citizens United* decision, on its face, lifted many of those restrictions. The decision allows corporations, unions, groups such as Citizens United, and others to spend money in campaign advertising without limit as long as it is not coordinated with a campaign. The restriction against using direct campaign language such as "vote for Mr. Smith" has been lifted as well. President Obama expressed his disagreement with the decision, and most Democrats applauded his remarks. The Democratic leadership of Congress pledged to write new laws to counteract this decision, but no action has yet been taken.

While public attention was focused on the *Citizens United* decision, a federal appeals court granted even more freedom to corporations, unions, individuals, and interest groups to spend money on campaigns. In the case *FreedomNow.org v. FEC*, an interest group that represents conservative economic views charged that the FEC regulations barring individuals and groups from spending as much as they want on campaigns was unconstitutional due to the decision in *Citizens United.* The appeals court agreed, and that decision has opened the doors for the creation of Super PACs, which can raise and spend unlimited amounts of money as long as their campaigns are not coordinated with those of the candidates. Individuals can give unlimited amounts of money to a Super PAC, as can corporations, unions, or other groups. In contrast to the 527 organizations, these campaign PACs must report their donors to the FEC either quarterly or monthly.

With the creation of 527s and Super PACs, what a millionaire or corporation can spend on an election has no limit, which means that campaign spending will soar until some way to regulate this spending can be implemented. Supporters of the Democratic Party claim that certain billionaires such as the Koch brothers and Sheldon Adelson have too much influence through their contributions to Super PACs. Republicans answer that

ITAR-TASS Photo Agency/Alamy Stock Photo

Image 9–3
George Soros, billionaire financier, has donated millions of dollars to liberal causes and candidates. He has donated funds to Moveon.org and was an initial donor to the Center for American Progress, a liberal think tank.

---

15 *Citizens United v. Federal Election Commission,* 558 U.S. (2010).

billionaires such as George Soros and West Coast hedge fund manager Tom Steyer provide every bit as much money to the coffers of the Democratic Party. As noted by Jim Nicholson, a former chairman of the Republican National Committee, "The party can't coordinate with these Super PACs and neither can the campaigns so there's a lot more chaos . . . And the party structure clearly has a diminished role because they don't have the resources they used to have."[16]

Running for President: The Longest Campaign

■ **9.4** Describe the general outline of today's campaign for the presidency and discuss the impact of the primary system on the outcome of the nomination process.

The American presidential election is the culmination of two different campaigns linked by the parties' national conventions. The **presidential primary** campaign lasts from January until June of the election year. Traditionally, the final campaign heats up around Labor Day, although if the nominees are known, it will begin even before the conventions.

Until 1968, however, there were fewer than 20 primary elections for the presidency. They were often **"beauty contests"** in which the candidates competed for popular votes, but the results had little or no impact on the selection of delegates to the national convention. National conventions were meetings of the party elite—legislators, mayors, county chairpersons, and loyal party workers—who were mostly appointed to their delegations. National conventions saw numerous trades and bargains among competing candidates, and the leaders of large blocs of delegates could direct their delegates to support a favorite candidate.

Reforming the Primaries

The character of the primary process and the makeup of the national convention have changed dramatically. The public, rather than party elites, now generally controls the nomination process. In 1968, after President Lyndon B. Johnson declined to run for another term, the Democratic Party nomination race was dominated by candidates who opposed the war in Vietnam. After Robert F. Kennedy was assassinated in June 1968, antiwar Democrats faced a convention that would nominate President Johnson's choice regardless of popular votes. After the extraordinarily disruptive riots outside the doors of the 1968 Democratic Convention in Chicago, many party leaders pushed for serious reforms of the convention process. They saw the general dissatisfaction with the convention, and the riots in particular, as being caused by the inability of the average party member to influence the nomination system.

The Democratic National Committee appointed a special commission to study the problems of the primary system. Called the McGovern-Fraser Commission, the group formulated mandatory new rules on delegate selection for state Democratic parties.

presidential primary
A statewide primary election of delegates to a political party's national convention, held to determine a party's presidential nominee.

"beauty contests"
A presidential primary in which contending candidates compete for popular votes but the results do not control the selection of delegates to the national convention.

---
16 Nicholas Confessore, "Big-Money Donors Demand Larger Say in Campaign Strategy," *The New York Times*, March 1, 2014, p. 1.

The reforms instituted by the Democratic Party, which were imitated in part by the Republicans, revolutionized the nomination process for the presidency. The most important changes require that a majority of the Democratic convention delegates not be nominated by party elites; they must be elected by the voters in primary elections, in caucuses held by local parties, or at state conventions. No delegates can be awarded on a "winner-take-all" basis; all must be proportional to the votes for the contenders. Delegates are normally pledged to a particular candidate, although the pledge is not always formally binding at the convention.

The delegation from each state must also include a proportion of women, younger party members, and representatives of the minority groups within the party. At first, virtually no special privileges were given to elected party officials, such as senators and governors. After the conventions chose candidates who were not as strong as the party hoped for, the Democratic Party invented **superdelegates**, who are primarily elected Democratic officeholders and state leaders. Superdelegates comprise less than 20 percent of the delegate votes.

Front-Loading the Primaries

As soon as politicians and potential presidential candidates realized that winning as many primary elections as possible guaranteed them the party's nomination for president, their tactics changed dramatically. Candidates running in the 2016 primaries, such as Senator Ted Cruz, concentrated on building organizations in states that held early important primary elections. Candidates realized that winning early contests, such as the Iowa caucuses or the New Hampshire primary election (both in February), meant that the media instantly would label the winner as the **front-runner**, thus increasing the candidate's media exposure and escalating the pace of contributions to his or her campaign fund.

The Rush to Be First States and state political parties began to see that early primaries had a much greater effect on the outcome of the presidential election and began to hold their primaries earlier in the season to secure that advantage. Although New Hampshire held on to its claim to be the first primary, other states moved theirs to the following week. A group of mostly Southern states decided to hold their primaries on the same date, known as Super Tuesday, setting a trend for the future. Due to this process of **front-loading** the primaries, in 2000 the presidential nominating process was over in March, with both George W. Bush and Al Gore having enough convention delegate votes to win their nominations.

The 2016 Primary Season

In 2015, it appeared that the Republican primary voter would be able to choose from a number of potential presidential nominees. No one expected the scenario that unfolded in fall 2015 and spring 2016. The early Republican debates featured as many as 18 hopefuls—governors, senators, former candidates, and representatives of American business—plus Donald Trump, celebrity and billionaire. By the beginning of 2016, a number of candidates, faced with raising campaign contributions and aware of polling results, dropped out. However, the Iowa caucus still saw ten contenders, with Ted Cruz narrowly winning the caucus vote over Donald Trump. By March 15, the Republican field

superdelegate
A party leader or elected official who is given the right to vote at the party's national convention. Superdelegates are not elected at the state level.

did you know?
David Leroy Gatchell changed his middle name to "None of the Above," but when he ran for U.S. Senate, representing Tennessee, a court ruled that he could not use his middle name on the ballot.

front-runner
The presidential candidate who appears to be ahead at a given time in the primary season.

front-loading
The practice of moving presidential primary elections to the early part of the campaign to maximize the impact of these primaries on the nomination.

had narrowed to Trump, Cruz, Rubio, and Kasich, with the Republican establishment spending millions of dollars on ads to defeat Trump. However, Trump captured the vote in Rubio's home state, forcing the senator to abandon his campaign and, after Trump posted a solid win in Indiana in May, Cruz and Kasich both suspended their campaigns, leaving the Republican establishment divided over supporting the presumptive nominee, Donald Trump.

As Democratic voters thought about the upcoming election, most assumed that former Secretary of State Hillary Rodham Clinton would be the nominee with a few minor challengers. To the surprise of the commentators and party faithful, Senator Bernie Sanders of Vermont challenged Secretary Clinton from the left. Long an avowed Democratic Socialist, Sanders offered a platform of good jobs, free college tuition, and a national health-care system. Although Clinton amassed far more delegates in the early months of the primary system, Sanders won the Michigan primary, as well as many other states, and pledged to stay in the race until the convention. Clinton entered the primary race with several hundred superdelegates pledged to her candidacy but Sanders challenged them directly, making the point that if a state voted for him, its superdelegates should vote for him also. Clinton and Sanders battled for delegates throughout the primary season but, due, in part, to her lead among superdelegates, Clinton clinched the nomination in early June. Sanders, however, did not endorse her until just before the Democratic convention in July.

On to the National Convention

Presidential candidates have been nominated by the convention method in every election since 1832. Delegates are sent from each state and are apportioned on the basis of state representation. Extra delegates are allowed to attend from states that had voting majorities for the party in the preceding elections. Parties also accept delegates from the District of Columbia, the territories, and certain overseas groups.

credentials committee
A committee used by political parties at their national conventions to determine which delegates may participate. The committee inspects the claim of each prospective delegate to be seated as a legitimate representative of his or her state.

Seating the Delegates Each political party uses a **credentials committee** to determine which delegates may participate. The credentials committee usually prepares a roll of all delegates entitled to be seated. Controversy may arise when rival groups claim to be the official party organization for a county, district, or state. The Mississippi Democratic Party split along racial lines in 1964 at the height of the civil rights movement in the Deep South. Separate all-white and mixed white/African American sets of delegates were selected, and both factions showed up at the national convention. After much debate, the committee decided to seat the pro–civil rights delegates and exclude those who represented the traditional "white" party. Although such a dispute has not occurred in recent years, there could still be controversy over whom the duly elected delegates should be.

Convention Activities The typical convention lasts only a few days. The first day consists of speech making, usually against the opposing party. During the second day, there are committee reports, and during the third day, there is presidential balloting. Because delegates generally arrive at the convention committed to presidential candidates, no convention since 1952 has required more than one ballot to choose a nominee, and since 1972, candidates have usually come into the convention with enough committed delegates to win.

Election 2016

The 2016 Campaign: A Low Point in Campaign History

While the primary campaigns in both the Republican and Democratic parties were bruising, the campaign for the presidency in 2016 was viewed by many voters as a very unpleasant experience. In July, the Republican convention affirmed the nomination of Donald Trump, and his vice presidential running mate, Governor Mike Pence of Indiana. Pence was viewed as bringing a sincerely conservative view and personal integrity to the ticket. In the Democratic convention one week later, former Secretary of State Hillary Rodham Clinton became the first woman ever nominated for the American presidency. She selected for her vice presidential candidate, former governor of Virginia, Tim Kaine. Kaine brought administrative experience to the ticket and a progressive Democratic record.

The campaigning began immediately with personal attacks. Over the course of the campaign and the four debates that were held, each candidate presented their policy positions. Clinton focused on improving the status of women and children, improving Obamacare, and raising taxes to improve social programs. Trump promised to repeal and replace Obamacare, lower taxes, and to "build a wall" to protect our borders. The Democratic Party, including Senator Bernie Sanders and President and First Lady Obama, came together to campaign for Hillary Clinton. In a strange turn of events, many members of the Republican establishment never endorsed Donald Trump while other Republican candidates campaigned with him.

The overriding tone of the two campaigns could be described as "nasty." Each candidate attacked the past behavior, morals, and competency of the other. Added to the mix were a 10-year-old video interview of Trump making lewd remarks about women and the continuing investigation into Mrs. Clinton's emails during her time as Secretary of State. Both candidates had a more than 60 percent disapproval rate, an all-time record low figure. Yet, as the election day drew near, party identifiers remained loyal to their respective candidates and cast their ballots in a very tight race for the presidency.

For Critical Analysis

1. What effect do extremely negative campaigns and personal attacks have on voters and on the general citizenry of the nation?

2. What efforts could be made to focus campaigns more on policy positions and less on personal attacks?

On the fourth day, a vice presidential candidate is usually nominated, and the presidential nominee gives the acceptance speech. In 2016 both the Republican and Democratic conventions were moved earlier in the calendar by more than a month to increase the amount of time spent in the general election period. The Republicans scheduled their convention for the week of July 18 in Cleveland, Ohio, and the Democrats met the following week in Philadelphia, Pennsylvania. Both states have substantial numbers of electoral votes and can be considered battleground states.

On to the General Election

Even though it may seem that the presidential election process lasts years, the general election campaign actually begins after the two party conventions, when the nominees are officially proclaimed. Candidates use media advertising, debates, social media strategies, and Get Out the Vote campaigns. In addition, campaign strategists must constantly plan in order to win enough electoral votes to receive the majority. Campaign managers quickly identify those states where their candidate will almost certainly win the popular vote. Certain states will quickly line up in the Republican or Democratic column. Those states see relatively light campaign activity and advertising. Those states that *are* likely to be close in the popular vote have been tagged **battleground states** and will see intense campaigning up to the very day of the election.

battleground state
A state likely to be so closely fought that the campaigns devote exceptional effort to winning the popular and electoral vote there.

States such as Florida, Ohio, and Wisconsin, which have closely divided electorates, are often in the battleground column. It is important to note, however, that the states that will be closely fought change with every presidential election because the issues and appeals of the two candidates determine race dynamics. In 2016, polls released just before Election Day suggested that the presidential election was too close to predict. The final outcome of the presidential race stunned the Clinton campaign and its supporters. Donald Trump lost the popular vote but won the electoral college vote by carrying Florida and a set of Midwestern states including Wisconsin, which had not voted for a Republican candidate since 1984.

Voting in the United States

■ **9.5** Demonstrate an understanding of the electoral process in the United States and explain how it relates to democratic theory.

In addition to voting for candidates, in some states, people can vote directly on laws. In California, often dozens of referenda are on the ballot at one time. Citizens are often asked to vote three times in one year—in a primary election to choose candidates, in elections for school taxes or other local matters, and in a general election. Americans often elect not only representatives to state and national legislatures and executive officers for the state, but also school superintendents, sheriffs, and even the jailer. In addition, many states have elected judges, which can add 50 more offices in a city as large as Chicago.

Turning Out to Vote

■ **9.6** Discuss the factors that influence voter turnout in the United States and compare American voter turnout to that of other nations.

voter turnout
The percentage of citizens taking part in the election process; the number of eligible voters who actually "turn out" on Election Day to cast their ballots.

In 2016, the voting-age population was more than 251 million people. Fifty-two percent of those people actually went to the polls. When only half of the voting-age population participates in elections, it means, among other things, that the winner of a close presidential election may be voted in by only about one-fourth of the voting-age population (see Table 9-3).

Figure 9-4 shows **voter turnout** for presidential and congressional elections from 1940 to 2016. According to these statistics, the last good year for voter turnout was 1960, when almost 65 percent of the voting-age population actually voted. Each of the peaks in the figure represents voter turnout in a presidential election. Thus, we can also see that turnout for congressional elections is influenced greatly by whether a presidential election occurs in the same year. Whereas voter turnout during the presidential elections of 2012 was more than 50 percent, it was only 42 percent in the midterm elections of 2014.

The same is true at the state level. When there is a race for governor, more voters participate both in the general election for governor and in the election for state representatives. Voter participation rates in gubernatorial elections are also greater in presidential election years. The average turnout

Table 9-3   ▶   Elected by a Majority?

Most presidents have won a majority of the votes cast in the election. We generally judge the extent of their victory by whether they have won more than 51 percent of the votes. Some presidential elections have been proclaimed landslides, meaning that the candidates won by an extraordinary majority of votes cast. As indicated below, however, no modern president has been elected by more than 38 percent of the total voting-age population.

YEAR—WINNER (PARTY)	PERCENTAGE OF TOTAL POPULAR VOTE	PERCENTAGE OF VOTING-AGE POPULATION
1932—Roosevelt (D)	57.4	30.1
1936—Roosevelt (D)	60.8	34.6
1940—Roosevelt (D)	54.7	32.2
1944—Roosevelt (D)	53.4	29.9
1948—Truman (D)	49.6	25.3
1952—Eisenhower (R)	55.1	34.0
1956—Eisenhower (R)	57.4	34.1
1960—Kennedy (D)	49.7	31.2
1964—Johnson (D)	61.1	37.8
1968—Nixon (R)	43.4	26.4
1972—Nixon (R)	60.7	33.5
1976—Carter (D)	50.1	26.8
1980—Reagan (R)	50.7	26.7
1984—Reagan (R)	58.8	31.2
1988—Bush (R)	53.4	26.8
1992—Clinton (D)	43.3	23.1
1996—Clinton (D)	49.2	23.2
2000—Bush (R)	47.8	24.5
2004—Bush (R)	51.0	27.6
2008—Obama (D)	52.6	27.5
2012—Obama (D)	51.0	25.3
2016—Trump (R)	47.4	23.8

Sources: Congressional Quarterly Weekly Report, January 31, 1989, p. 137; *The New York Times*, November 5, 1992; November 7, 1996; November 12, 2004; November 6, 2008; and author's update.

Figure 9-4   ▶   Voter Turnout for Presidential and Congressional Elections, 1940—2018

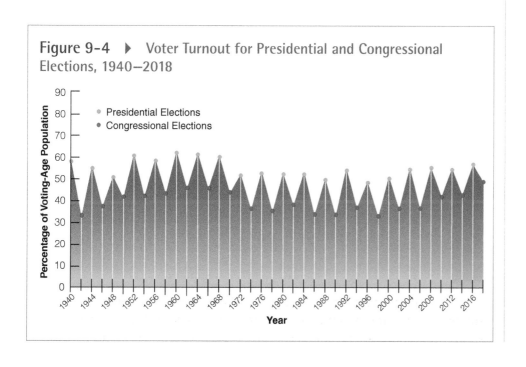

Table 9-4 ▶ Turnout in Selected Countries, Most Recent National Election

COUNTRY	VOTING-AGE POPULATION PERCENTAGE*
Singapore (2015)	93.5
Argentina (2015)	81.4
Iceland (2013)	80.0
Australia (2013)	78.9
Norway (2013)	77.9
France (2012)	71.2
India (2014)	70.2
Mexico (2012)	64.5
United Kingdom (2015)	60.4
Kenya (2013)	55.6
United States (2012)	53.6
Japan (2012)	52.0
Switzerland (2011)	40.0

Source: Institute for Democracy and Electoral Assistance: http://www.idea.int/vt
*These figures are the percentage of the entire voting-age population that voted in the most recent national election.

in state elections is about 14 percentage points higher when a presidential election is held.

In races for mayor, city council, county auditor, and the like, it is fairly common for only 25 percent or less of the electorate to vote. Is something amiss here? It would seem that people should be more likely to vote in elections that directly affect them. At the local level, each person's vote counts more because there are fewer voters. Furthermore, the issues—crime control, school bonds, sewer bonds, and so on—touch the immediate interests of the voters. The facts, however, do not fit democratic theory. Potential voters are most interested in national elections, when a presidential choice is involved. Otherwise, voter participation in our representative government is very low (and is not stellar even in presidential elections).

The Effect of Low Voter Turnout

Some view low voter participation as a threat to representative democratic government. Too few individuals are deciding who wields political power in society. In addition, low voter participation presumably signals apathy or cynicism about the political system in general. It also may signal that potential voters simply do not want to take the time to learn about the issues or that the issues are too complicated. Some suggest that people do not vote because they do not believe that their vote will make any difference.

Others are less concerned about low voter participation. They believe that low voter participation simply indicates more satisfaction with the status quo. Also, they believe that representative democracy is a reality even if a very small percentage of eligible voters vote. If everyone who does not vote believes that the outcome of the election will accord with his or her own desires, then representative democracy is working. The nonvoters are obtaining the type of government—with the type of people running it—that they want to have anyway.

Is Voter Turnout Declining?

During many recent elections, the media have voiced concern that voter turnout is declining. Figure 9-5 appears to show somewhat lower voter turnout in recent years than during the 1960s. Pundits have blamed the low turnout on negative campaigning and broad public cynicism about the political process. But is voter turnout actually as low as it seems?

One problem with widely used measurements of voter turnout is that they compare the number of people who actually vote with the voting-age population, not the population of *eligible voters*. These figures are not the same. The figure for the voting-age population includes felons and ex-felons who have lost the right to vote. Above all, it includes new immigrants who are not yet citizens. Finally, it does not include Americans living abroad, who can cast absentee ballots.

In 2016 the measured voting-age population included 3.2 million ineligible felons and ex-felons and an estimated 21 million noncitizens. It did not include 4.7 million Americans abroad. In 2016, the voting-age population was 250 million people. The number of eligible voters, however, was only 230.3 million. That means that voter turnout in 2016 was not 54.7 percent, but about 59.3 percent of the truly eligible voters.[17]

Factors Influencing Who Votes

A clear association exists between voter participation and the following characteristics: age, educational attainment, minority status, income level, and the existence of two-party competition.

1. *Age.* Examine Figure 9-5, which shows the breakdown of voter participation by age group for the 2016 presidential election. It is very clear that the Americans who have the highest turnout rate are those reaching retirement age. The reported turnout increases with each age group. Greater participation with age is very likely because older voters are more settled in their lives, are already registered, and have had more time to experience voting as an expected activity. Older voters may have more leisure time to learn about the campaign and the candidates; furthermore, communications, especially those from AARP, target this group.

   What is most striking about the turnout figures is that younger voters have the lowest turnout rate. Before 1971, the age of eligibility to vote was 21. Due to the prevailing sentiment that if a man was old enough to be drafted to fight in the Vietnam War, he should be old enough to vote, the U.S. Constitution was amended (via the Twenty-sixth Amendment) to lower the voting age to 18. Young Americans, however, have never exhibited a high turnout rate. In contrast to older Americans, young people are likely to change residences frequently, have fewer ties to the community, and perhaps not perceive election issues as relevant to them.

   Turnout among voters aged 18 to 24 increased significantly between 2000 and 2008, from 36 percent to 48.5 percent in the presidential election. Evidence suggests that the candidates and political parties devoted much more attention to younger voters. Candidates appeared on the television shows watched by younger voters, and campaigns began to utilize the Internet and social media to reach younger voters. Younger voters

---

17 U.S. Elections Project. http://www.gmu.edu/Turnout_2012G.html

Figure 9-5 ▶ Voting in the 2016 Presidential Elections by Age Group

Turnout is given as a percentage of the voting age population. The data in this figure are from the Census Bureau. They have been gathered by polling the American public. The data from the 2016 polls indicate that turnout among older Americans remained high with turnout increasing slightly among the 18- to 29-year old group from 2012.

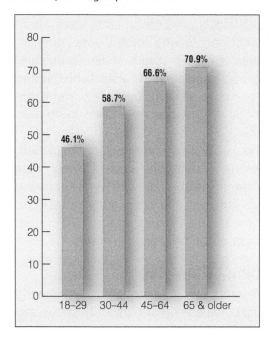

Source: Bureau of the Census: Census Blogs, May 10, 2017

greatly increased their turnout in the 2008 primary elections, with many supporting Barack Obama's campaign for the presidency, although the increase in turnout for the general election was only 1.5 percent above 2004 levels. In 2012, turnout among younger voters declined to 41.2 percent.

2. *Educational attainment.* In general, the more education you have, the more likely you are to vote. This pattern is clearly evident in the 2016 election results, as shown in Figure 9-6. Reported turnout was 30 percentage points higher for those who had some college education than for those who had never been to high school.

3. *Minority status.* Race and ethnicity are also important in determining the level of voter turnout. Non-Latino whites in 2012 voted at a 62.2 percent rate, whereas the non-Latino African American turnout rate was 66.2 percent, up almost 2 percent from 2008. For Latinos, the turnout rate was 48 percent, down slightly from the previous election, and for Asian Americans the rate was 47.3 percent, up slightly from the previous presidential election.[18] These low rates may occur because many Latino and Asian American immigrants are not yet citizens, or they may be attributable to language issues. The fact that turnout increased by 7 percent for African Americans in 2012 was likely due to pride in President Obama's identity as an African American.

18 Michael P. McDonald, "2012 Turnout: Race, Ethnicity and the Youth Vote." May 8, 2013, http://www.huffingtonppost.com /michael-p-mcdonald/

Figure 9-6 ▶ Voting in the 2016 Presidential Elections by Educational Level

Voters with some college are much more likely to vote than voters with less than a high school education. Voters with less education are also less likely to have a high income.

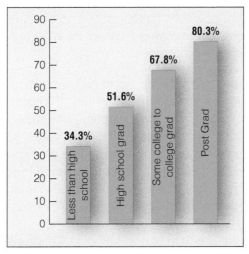

Source: U.S. Elections Project. https://www.electproject.home/voter-turnout/demographics

4. *Income level.* Wealthier people tend to be overrepresented among voters who turn out on Election Day. In the 2016 presidential election, voter turnout for those with the highest annual family incomes was almost twice the turnout for those with the lowest annual family incomes.

5. *Two-party competition.* Another factor in voter turnout is the extent to which elections are competitive within a state. More competitive states generally have higher turnout rates, and turnout increases considerably in states where an extremely competitive race occurs in a particular year. In addition, turnout can be increased through targeted Get Out the Vote drives among minority voters.

Why People Do Not Vote

For many years, political scientists believed that one reason why voter turnout in the United States was so much lower than in other Western nations was that it was very difficult to register to vote. In most states, registration required a special trip to a public office far in advance of elections. Today, all states are required to offer voter registration at a number of sites, including the driver's license bureau. In addition, many states offer advance voting at designated places on a walk-in basis up to three weeks before the election. These two innovations have reduced barriers to registration and voting.

Uninformative Media Coverage and Negative Campaigning Some scholars contend that one of the reasons why some people do not vote has to do with media coverage of campaigns. Many researchers have shown that the news media tend to provide much more news about "the horse race," or

did you know?

Computer software exists that can identify likely voters and likely campaign donors by town, neighborhood, and street.

which candidates are ahead in the polls, than about the actual policy positions of the candidates. Thus, voters are not given the kind of information that would provide them with an incentive to go to the polls on Election Day. Negative campaigning is thought to have an adverse effect on voter turnout. By the time citizens are ready to cast their ballots, most of the information they have heard about the candidates has been so negative that no candidate is appealing. Research on this issue, however, has produced no consensus: voters are able to identify ads as negative and may or may not be influenced by them depending on their own candidate preferences.[19]

The Rational Ignorance Effect Another explanation suggests that citizens are making a logical choice in not voting. If citizens believe that their votes will not affect the outcome of an election, then they have little incentive to seek the information needed to cast intelligent votes. The lack of incentive to obtain costly (in terms of time, attention, and so on) information about politicians and political issues has been called the **rational ignorance effect**. That term may seem contradictory, but it is not. Rational ignorance is a condition in which people purposely and rationally decide not to obtain information—to remain ignorant.[20]

Why, then, do even one-third to one-half of U.S. citizens bother to show up at the polls? One explanation is that most citizens receive personal satisfaction from the act of voting. It makes them feel that they are good citizens and that they are doing something patriotic, even though they are aware that their one vote will not change the outcome of the election. Even among voters who are registered and who plan to vote, if the cost of voting goes up (in terms of time and inconvenience), the number of registered voters who actually vote will fall. In particular, bad weather on Election Day means, on average, a smaller percentage of registered voters at the polls. It also appears that the greater the number of elections that are held, the smaller the turnout for primary and special elections.

Plans for Improving Voter Turnout Mail-in voting in Oregon, Washington, and Colorado and easier access to registration are ideas that have been implemented in the hope of improving voter turnout. Although turnout is somewhat higher in those states, they are also states with higher educational attainment and less economically disadvantaged populations.

Two other ideas seemed promising. The first was to allow voters to visit the polls up to three weeks before Election Day. The second was to allow voters to vote by absentee ballot without having to give any particular reason for doing so. The Committee for the Study of the American Electorate discovered, however, that in areas that had implemented these plans, neither plan increased voter turnout. Indeed, voter turnout actually fell in those jurisdictions. In other words, states that did *not* permit early voting or unrestricted absentee voting had better turnout rates than states that did. Apparently, these two innovations appeal mostly to people who already intended to vote.

What is left? One possibility is to declare Election Day a national holiday or to hold elections on a Sunday, as is done in many other nations. Another is to

rational ignorance effect
An effect produced when people purposely and rationally decide not to become informed on an issue because they believe that their vote on the issue is not likely to be a deciding one; a lack of incentive to seek the necessary information to cast an intelligent vote.

---

19 Ilya Somin, "Democracy and Political Ignorance," October 11, 2013. www.cato-unbound.org/2013/10
20 John Wihbey, "Negative Political Ads, the 2012 Campaign and Voter Effects: Research ROUNDUP," Journalist's Resource, May 6, 2013. http://journalistsresource.org/studies/politics/

adopt a registration method that places the responsibility on the government to make sure all voters are registered. In Canada, a packet of information is mailed to each eligible voter. The citizen then returns the application to a federal office or applies online to be registered. After that act, a citizen is enrolled on the National Register of Electors (or citizens may opt out). This registration activity takes place only once after the first registration—the voter simply apprises the government of any future address changes. By making sure all eligible citizens are registered and informed about the polling place, the burden of registration and voting is lightened.

Legal Restrictions on Voting

■ **9.7** Describe historical restrictions on the vote in the United States and explain how these restrictions have been ended.

Legal restrictions on voter registration have existed since the founding of our nation, when the franchise was granted to free, white males and occasionally to free African Americans. Since that time, groups have struggled to gain the franchise and to overcome voting restrictions in order to be represented at all levels of government.

Historical Restrictions

In most of the American colonies, only white males who owned property with a certain minimum value were eligible to vote, leaving a far greater number of Americans ineligible than eligible to take part in the democratic process.

Property Requirements Many government functions concern property rights and the distribution of income and wealth, and some of the founders of our nation believed it was appropriate that only people who had an interest in property should vote on these issues. The idea of extending the vote to all citizens was, according to Charles Pinckney, a South Carolina delegate to the Constitutional Convention, merely "theoretical nonsense."

The logic behind the restriction of voting rights to property owners was questioned seriously by Thomas Paine in his pamphlet *Common Sense*:

> Here is a man who today owns a jackass, and the jackass is worth $60. Today the man is a voter and goes to the polls and deposits his vote. Tomorrow the jackass dies. The next day the man comes to vote without his jackass and cannot vote at all. Now tell me, which was the voter, the man or the jackass?[21]

The writers of the Constitution allowed the states to decide who should vote. Thus, women were allowed to vote in Wyoming in 1870 but not in the entire nation until the Nineteenth Amendment was ratified in 1920. By about 1850, most white adult males in virtually all the states could vote without any property qualification. North Carolina was the last state to eliminate its property test for voting—in 1856.

Further Extensions of the Franchise Extension of the franchise to black males occurred with the passage of the Fifteenth Amendment in 1870. This

---

21 Thomas Paine, *Common Sense* (London: H. D. Symonds, 1792), p. 28.

enfranchisement was short lived, however, as the "redemption" of the South by white racists had rolled back these gains by the end of the century. African Americans, both male and female, were not able to participate in the electoral process in all states until the 1960s. The most recent extension of the franchise occurred when the voting age was reduced to 18 by the Twenty-sixth Amendment in 1971.

Is the Franchise Still Too Restrictive? Certain classes of people still do not have the right to vote. These include noncitizens and, in most states, convicted felons who have been released from prison. They also include current prison inmates, election law violators, and people who are mentally incompetent. No one under the age of 18 can vote, although an Ohio judge allowed 17-year-olds to vote in the 2016 primary if they would turn 18 before the November general election. Some political activists have argued that some of these groups should be allowed to vote. Most other democracies do not prevent persons convicted of a crime from voting after they have completed their sentences. In the 1800s, many states let noncitizen immigrants vote. In Nicaragua, the minimum voting age is 16.

One discussion concerns the voting rights of convicted felons who have completed their sentence or who were convicted of relatively minor crimes. Some contend that voting should be a privilege, not a right, and we should not want the types of people who commit felonies participating in decision making. Others believe that it is wrong to further penalize those who have paid their debt to society. These people argue that barring felons from the polls injures minority groups because minorities make up a disproportionately large share of former prison inmates.

Current Eligibility and Registration Requirements

Voting generally requires **registration**, and to register, a person must satisfy the following voter qualifications, or legal requirements: (1) citizenship, (2) age (18 or older), and (3) residency—the duration varies widely from state to state and with types of elections. Since 1972, states cannot impose residency requirements of more than 30 days for voting in federal elections.

Each state has different qualifications for voting and registration. In 1993, Congress passed the "motor voter" bill, which requires that states provide voter-registration materials when people receive or renew driver's licenses, that all states allow voters to register by mail, and that voter-registration forms be made available at a wider variety of public places and agencies. In general, a person must register well in advance of an election, although voters in Idaho, Maine, Minnesota, Oregon, Wisconsin, and Wyoming are allowed to register up to, and on, Election Day. North Dakota has no voter registration at all.

Some argue that registration requirements are responsible for much of the nonparticipation in our political process. Since their introduction in the late 1800s, registration laws have reduced the voting participation of African Americans and immigrants. The question arises as to whether registration is really necessary. If it decreases participation in the political process, perhaps it should be dropped altogether. Still, as those in favor of registration requirements argue, such requirements may prevent fraudulent voting practices, such as multiple voting or voting by noncitizens.

In recent years, a number of states have passed stronger voter identification standards, although the actual requirements vary considerably.

Currently, at least eight states have strict photo-ID laws in place, requiring voters to show a government-issued photo ID to be able to vote. Another set of states requires either a photo ID or another nonphoto ID, or that someone at the polling place vouch for the individual personally. About 15 states have lists of acceptable forms of identification and another 19 have no ID requirement to vote. The Supreme Court found Indiana's strict photo-ID law constitutional in 2008, although other states' laws have been found to be discriminatory by lower courts or by the U.S. Department of Justice.[22] A study by the Brennan Center suggested that the stricter photo-ID laws tended to decrease voting turnout in some precincts, whereas they increased turnout among older voters and higher-income voters.[23] The question of whether a voter should have a photo ID is highly partisan: Republicans generally support such requirements as a way to make sure only eligible voters cast ballots; Democrats suggest that strict photo-ID laws are a handicap to poorer voters, elderly voters who do not drive, immigrants, young people, and others who do not have the time to get such an identification card.

Extension of the Voting Rights Act

In the summer of 2006, President Bush signed legislation that extended the Voting Rights Act for 25 more years. As discussed in Chapter 5, the Voting Rights Act was enacted to ensure that African Americans had equal access to the polls. Most of the provisions of the 1965 Voting Rights Act became permanent law. The 2006 act extended certain temporary sections and clarified certain amendments. For example, any new voting practices or procedures in jurisdictions with a history of discrimination in voting had to be approved by the U.S. Department of Justice or the federal district court in Washington, DC, before being implemented. Section 203 of the 2006 act ensured that American citizens with limited proficiency in English can obtain the necessary assistance to enable them to understand and cast a ballot. Further, the act authorized the U.S. attorney general to appoint federal election observers when evidence exists of attempts to intimidate minority voters at the polls.

In 2013, the U.S. Supreme Court struck down the core of the Voting Rights Act of 1965 and all subsequent extensions of the act. The Court voted 5–4 to end the oversight of the nine states in the South that needed to submit their voting laws to the Department of Justice. The majority of the court reasoned that, as Chief Justice Roberts wrote, "Our country has changed. While any racial discrimination in voting is too much, Congress must ensure that the legislation it passes to remedy that problem speaks to current conditions."[24] Civil rights and voting rights advocates were extremely disappointed in the ruling, saying that states would likely move to tighten their registration and voting laws immediately and that discrimination in voting would likely increase. Indeed, Texas announced that its new identification law would go into effect immediately without Justice Department approval.

---

22 *Crawford v. Marion County Election Board,* 553 U.S. 181 (2008).
23 Shelley de Alth, "ID at the Polls: Assessing the Impact of Recent State Voter ID Laws on Voter Turnout," *Harvard Law and Policy Review* (2009) 3(1): 185.
24 Adam Liptak, "Supreme Court Invalidates Key Part of the Voting Rights Act," *The New York Times,* June 25, 2013, p. 1.

Image 9-4

Drew Barrymore speaks at a rally at George Washington University to encourage young people to register and vote.

PixelPro/Alamy Stock Photo

Primary Elections, General Elections, and More

One of the reasons often suggested for low voter turnout in the United States is the quantity of elections that are held. Because the United States has a federal system of government, elections are held at both the state and federal levels. Additionally, most local units of government—towns, cities, counties—are staffed by officials who are elected at the local level. For the sake of convenience, the state organizes the federal elections for the House of Representatives, the Senate, and the presidency, but the county actually sets up and staffs the voting places and counts the vote.

As noted in Chapter 8, political parties in the United States do not have control over the candidates who run under their labels. Individuals who seek political office must be *nominated* in order to have their names placed on the ballot in the general election. The political party may nominate a candidate and endorse her or him, or another individual may submit appropriate petitions to make the nomination competitive. If two or more candidates are contesting the nomination for the party, voters will make the decision in a primary election.

Primary Elections

The purpose of a primary election is to choose a candidate who will become the party's nominee for the general election. This is true whether the primary election is for the nominee for state legislator, city council representative, or president of the United States. Primary elections were first mandated in 1903 in Wisconsin, with the intention of weakening the role of party bosses in the nomination process. Today, all states have primary elections, which, in theory, are organized so that political party members can choose their own preferred candidate for office. There are many different types of primary elections, however, and many are not restricted to party members.

Before discussing the types of primaries, we must first examine how some states use a party **caucus**. A caucus is typically a small, local meeting of party regulars who agree on a nominee. Sometimes the results of caucuses are voted on by a broader set of party members in a primary election. If the party's chosen candidates have no opponents, however, a primary election may not be necessary.

Alternatively, a slate of nominees of loyal party members may be chosen at a local or state party convention. In any event, the resulting primary elections differ from state to state.

caucus
A meeting of party members designed to select candidates and propose policies.

Closed Primary In a **closed primary**, only avowed or declared members of a party can vote in that party's primary. Voters must declare their party affiliation, either when they register to vote or at the primary election. A closed-primary system tries to make sure that registered voters cannot cross over into the other party's primary in order to nominate the weakest candidate of the opposing party or to affect the ideological direction of that party.

closed primary
A type of primary in which the voter is limited to choosing candidates of the party of which he or she is a member.

Open Primary In an **open primary**, voters can vote in either party primary without disclosing their party affiliation. The voter makes the choice in the privacy of the voting booth. The voter must, however, choose one party's list from which to select candidates. Open primaries place no restrictions on independent voters.

open primary
A primary in which any registered voter can vote, but must vote for candidates of only one party.

Blanket Primary In a *blanket primary*, sometimes known as "jungle primary," the voter can vote for candidates of more than one party. Louisiana and Washington have blanket primaries. Blanket-primary campaigns may be much more costly because each candidate for every office is trying to influence all of the voters, not just those in his or her party.

In 2000, the U.S. Supreme Court issued a decision that significantly altered the use of the blanket primary.[25] The case arose when political parties in California challenged the constitutionality of a 1996 ballot initiative authorizing the use of the blanket primary in that state. The parties contended that the blanket primary violated their First Amendment right of association. Because the nominees represent the party, they argued, party members—not the general electorate—should have the right to choose the party's nominee. The Supreme Court ruled in favor of the parties, holding that the blanket primary violated parties' First Amendment associational rights. In a more recent decision, however, the Court upheld the blanket primary approved in the state of Washington.

Runoff Primary Some states have a two-primary system. If no candidate receives a majority of the votes in the first primary, the top two candidates must compete in another primary, called a *runoff primary*.

General and Other Elections

What we commonly think of as "the election" is the general election—the election that finally chooses the winner who will take office. In the United States, all federal general elections are held on the first Tuesday in November unless that is the first day of the month. The earliest date is thus November 2, and the latest is November 8. To keep costs down, almost all states hold their elections on the same day even in years when there are no federal candidates.

---

25 *California Democratic Party v. Jones*, 530 U.S. 567 (2000).

The interval between the primary and the general election may be more than six months or some shorter interval.

In addition to primary and general elections, states and localities often hold other types of elections. In a "special election," candidates vie for an office that has been left vacant due to death, resignation, or elevation to a higher office. Whether or not a special election is held for a representative or senator depends on state law and how much of the term remains. In some years, the nation's attention focuses on "recall elections," which are elections to remove an official from office and replace him or her with another candidate. Recall elections are held in response to petitions by the citizens, much like referenda. In 2012, Governor Scott Walker of Wisconsin, who had championed legislation to limit the bargaining rights of public employees, faced a recall election and successfully defeated the Democratic challenger.

Finally, local elections are held in many states to approve referenda or constitutional amendments. In a state such as Ohio, with a constitution dating back to 1803, almost all local taxes must be approved by the public. What this means is that school districts, park districts, and other public entities are constantly going to the public to get approval for tax increases of any kind. In a less-than-perfect economy or in the face of antitax sentiments, it is not easy to persuade voters to increase their own taxes.

How Are Elections Conducted?

■ **9.8** Discuss the impact of the mechanics and technology of voting on voter turnout, vote fraud, and the ability of citizens to trust the process.

Australian ballot
A secret ballot prepared, distributed, and tabulated by government officials at public expense. Since 1888, all U.S. states have used the Australian ballot rather than an open, public ballot.

The United States uses the **Australian ballot**—a secret ballot that is prepared, distributed, and counted by government officials at public expense. Since 1888, all states have used the Australian ballot. Before that, many states used the alternatives of oral voting and differently colored ballots prepared by the parties. Obviously, knowing which way a person was voting made it easy to apply pressure on the person to change his or her vote, and vote buying was common.

Office-Block and Party-Column Ballots

office-block or Massachusetts ballot
A form of general election ballot in which candidates for elective office are grouped together under the title of each office. It emphasizes voting for the office and the individual candidate, rather than for the party.

Two types of Australian ballots are used in the United States in general elections. The first, called an **office-block ballot**, or sometimes a **Massachusetts ballot**, groups all the candidates for a particular elective office under the title of that office. Parties dislike the office-block ballot because it places more emphasis on the office than on the party; it discourages straight-ticket voting and encourages split-ticket voting.

party-column or Indiana ballot
A form of general election ballot in which all of a party's candidates for elective office are arranged in one column under the party's label and symbol. It emphasizes voting for the party, rather than for the office or individual.

A **party-column ballot** is a form of general election ballot in which all of a party's candidates are arranged in one column under the party's label and symbol. It is also called the **Indiana ballot**. In some states, it allows voters to vote for all of a party's candidates for local, state, and national offices by simply marking a single "X" or by pulling a single lever. Most states use this type of ballot. Because it encourages straight-ticket voting, the two major parties favor this form. When a party has an exceptionally strong presidential or gubernatorial candidate to head the ticket, the use of the party-column ballot increases the **coat-tail effect** (the influence of a popular candidate on the success of other candidates on the same party ticket).

coat-tail effect
The influence of a popular candidate on the electoral success of other candidates on the same party ticket. The effect is increased by the party-column ballot, which encourages straight-ticket voting.

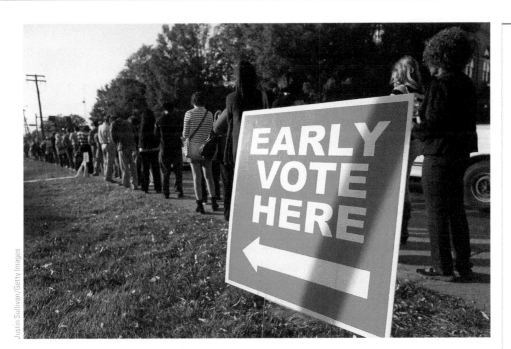

Image 9-5
Citizens of Little Rock, Arkansas, line up for early voting before the 2014 general election.

Vote Fraud

Vote fraud is often suspected but seldom proved. The voting culture of the 1800s, when secret ballots were rare and people had a cavalier attitude toward the open buying of votes, was much more conducive to fraud than are modern elections. Larry J. Sabato and Glenn R. Simpson, however, claim that the potential for vote fraud is high in many states, particularly through the use of phony voter registrations and absentee ballots.[26]

The Danger of Fraud In California, it is very difficult to remove a name from the polling list even if the person has not cast a ballot in the last two years. Thus, many persons are still on the rolls even though they no longer live in California. Enterprising political activists could use these names for absentee ballots. Other states have registration laws meant to encourage easy registration and voting. Such laws can be taken advantage of by those who seek to vote more than once.

After the 2000 elections, Larry Sabato again emphasized the problem of voting fraud. "It's a silent scandal," said Sabato, "and the problem is getting worse with increases in absentee voting, which is the easiest way to commit fraud." In 2000, one-third of Florida's counties found that more than 1,200 votes were cast illegally by felons, and in one county alone nearly 500 votes were cast by unregistered voters. In two precincts, the number of ballots cast was greater than the number of people who voted.[27]

Mistakes by Voting Officials Some observers claim, however, that errors leading to fraud are trivial in number and that a few mistakes are inevitable in a system involving millions of voters. These people argue that an excessive concern with vote fraud makes it harder for minorities and poor people to vote. For example, purging the rolls of thousands of names because addresses are not perfectly correct will likely remove many legitimate voters from the rolls.

---

26 Larry J. Sabato and Glenn R. Simpson, *Dirty Little Secrets: The Persistence of Corruption in American Politics* (New York: Random House, 1996).

27 As cited in "Blind to Voter Fraud," *Wall Street Journal*, March 2, 2001, p. A10.

The Importance of the Voting Machine

The 2000 presidential election spurred a national debate on the mechanics of how people actually cast their ballots on Election Day. The outcome of the 2000 presidential election hinged on Florida's electoral votes. The biggest problem lay in Florida's use of punch-card ballots. Voters slipped their card into the voting book and then "punched" the number next to the name of the candidate they preferred. Because of the layout of the printed book in 2000, names were spread across two pages, resulting in a "butterfly" ballot. Voters could accidentally punch the wrong number and cast their vote for the wrong candidate.

As the election night ended, it was clear that the votes in Florida between George W. Bush and Al Gore were "too close to call." Ballot problems abounded: some voters invalidated their ballots by voting for both candidates; some punch cards were not punched all the way through, resulting in no vote being counted; some had no vote for president at all. The Democratic Party and its candidates went to court to demand a recount of the votes. Republican political leaders in Florida tried to stop recounts in fear of losing the election. After a series of dramatic legal battles, the U.S. Supreme Court settled the election by allowing a Florida decision favoring the Republicans to stand. However, the result was a seriously flawed election process that produced tremendous cynicism about the mechanics of voting.

In 2002, Congress passed the Help America Vote Act, which established the U.S. Election Assistance Commission. The charge of the commission is to set standards for voting machines; to distribute funds to help communities acquire new, easier-to-use machines; and to act as a clearinghouse of information for the states. As expected, several companies began to create new machines for use in the voting booth. Most of these depend on digital recording of votes. Given the mistakes that occurred in Florida, many citizens wanted a record of their votes so that a mistake in tallying votes could be checked against a paper record. Election officials are deeply concerned that recording and transmitting vote counts only digitally may invite hacking and vote fraud. To date, no system, including the use of the Internet, has been devised that is totally immune to some sort of fraud, continuing concern about the security of our election system.

The Electoral College

■ **9.9** Demonstrate an understanding of the electoral college and its impact on the presidential election campaign.

Many people who vote for the president and vice president think that they are voting directly for a candidate. In actuality, they are voting for **electors**, who will cast their ballots in the electoral college. Article II, Section 1, of the Constitution outlines the method of choosing electors for president and vice president. The framers of the Constitution wanted to avoid the selection of president and vice president by the "excitable masses." Rather, they wished the choice to be made by a few supposedly dispassionate, reasonable men (but not women).

The Choice of Electors

Each state's electors are selected during presidential election years, as governed by state laws. After the national party convention, the electors normally

---

did you know?

Each new voting machine costs more than $3,000 for the equipment alone.

---

elector
A member of the electoral college, which selects the president and vice president. Each state's electors are chosen in each presidential election year according to state laws.

are pledged to the candidates chosen. The total number of electors today is 538, equal to 100 senators, 435 members of the House, and three electors for the District of Columbia (the Twenty-third Amendment, ratified in 1961, added electors for the District of Columbia). Each state's number of electors equals that state's number of senators (two) plus its number of representatives. Figure 9-7 shows how the electoral votes are apportioned by state.

The Electors' Commitment

When a plurality of voters in a state chooses a slate of electors—except in Maine and Nebraska, where electoral votes are based on congressional districts—those electors are pledged to cast their ballots on the first Monday after the second Wednesday in December in the state capital for the presidential and vice presidential candidates of their party. The Constitution does not, however, *require* the electors to cast their ballots for the candidates of their party.

The ballots are counted and certified before a joint session of Congress early in January. The candidates who receive a majority of the electoral votes (270) are certified as president-elect and vice president–elect. According to the Constitution, if no candidate receives a majority of the electoral votes, the election of the president is decided in the House from among the candidates with the three highest numbers of votes, with each state having one vote (decided by a plurality of each state delegation). The selection of the vice president is determined by the Senate in a choice between the two candidates with the most votes, each senator having one vote. Congress was required to choose the president and vice president in 1801 (Thomas Jefferson and Aaron Burr), and the House chose the president in 1825 (John Quincy Adams).[28]

It is possible for a candidate to become president without obtaining a majority of the popular vote. Many minority presidents are found in our history, including Abraham Lincoln, Woodrow Wilson, Harry Truman, John F. Kennedy, Richard Nixon (in 1968), Bill Clinton (1992, 1996), and George W. Bush (in 2000). Such an event becomes more likely when there are important third-party candidates.

Perhaps more distressing is the possibility of a candidate's being elected when an opposing candidate receives a plurality of the popular vote. This has occurred on five occasions—in the elections of John Quincy Adams in 1824, Rutherford B. Hayes in 1876, Benjamin Harrison in 1888, George W. Bush in 2000, and Donald Trump in 2016. all of whom won elections in which an opponent received a plurality of the popular vote.

Criticisms of the Electoral College

Besides the possibility of a candidate's becoming president even though an opponent obtains more popular votes, other complaints about the electoral college have emerged. The idea of the Constitution's framers was to have electors use their own discretion to decide who would make the best president. But electors no longer perform the selecting function envisioned by the founders because they are committed to the candidate who has a plurality of popular votes in their state in the general election.[29]

did you know?

Forty-two states do not indicate on the ballot that the voter is casting a ballot for members of the electoral college rather than for the president or vice president directly.

---

[28] For a detailed account of the process, see Michael J. Glennon, *When No Majority Rules: The Electoral College and Presidential Succession* (Washington, DC: Congressional Quarterly Press, 1993), p. 20.

[29] Note, however, that there have been revolts by so-called *faithless electors*—in 1796, 1820, 1948, 1956, 1960, 1968, 1972, 1976, 1988, and 2000.

Figure 9-7 ▶ Electoral Votes by State

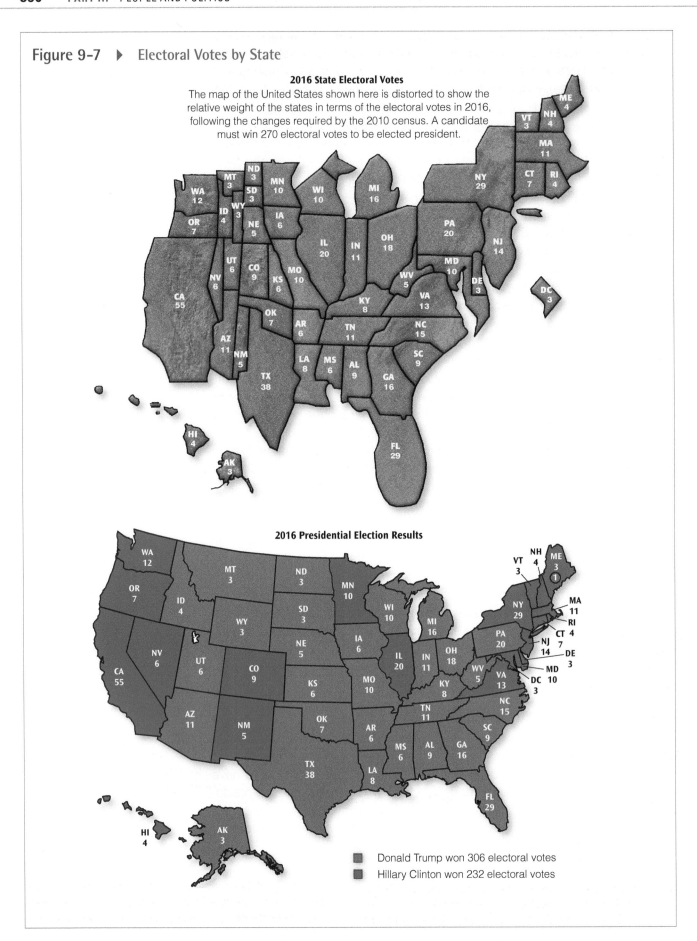

2016 State Electoral Votes

The map of the United States shown here is distorted to show the relative weight of the states in terms of the electoral votes in 2016, following the changes required by the 2010 census. A candidate must win 270 electoral votes to be elected president.

2016 Presidential Election Results

■ Donald Trump won 306 electoral votes
■ Hillary Clinton won 232 electoral votes

One can also argue that the current system, which in most states gives all of the electoral votes to the candidate who has a statewide plurality, is unfair to other candidates and their supporters. The current system of voting also means that presidential campaigning will be concentrated in those states that have the largest number of electoral votes and in the battleground states. Other states may receive little attention from the campaigns. It can also be argued that the system favors states with *smaller* populations, because including Senate seats in the electoral vote total partly offsets the edge of the more populous states in the House. Wyoming (with two senators and one representative) gets an electoral vote for roughly every 164,594 inhabitants (based on the 2000 census), for example, whereas Iowa gets one vote for every 418,046 inhabitants and California has one vote for every 615,848 inhabitants. Note that many of the smallest states have Republican majorities.

Many proposals for reform of the electoral college system have been advanced, particularly after the turmoil resulting from the 2000 elections. The most obvious proposal is to eliminate the electoral college system completely and to elect candidates on a popular-vote basis; in other words, a direct election, by the people, of the president and vice president. Because abolishing the electoral college would require a constitutional amendment, however, the chances of electing the president by a direct vote are remote. The major parties are not in favor of eliminating the electoral college, fearing that this would give minor parties a more influential role. Also, less populous states are not in favor of direct election of the president because they believe they would be overwhelmed by the large-state vote.

Efforts to improve registration systems, to make voting easier and more secure, and to make changes to the electoral college all will work to make elections in the United States more trustworthy for the voters. The explosion in campaign funding, however, especially from unregulated sources, creates new issues for the election process.

Key Terms

Australian ballot 346
battleground state 334
"beauty contest" 330
caucus 345
closed primary 345
coat-tail effect 346
communications director 318
corrupt practices acts 322
credentials committee 332
elector 348
finance chairperson 318
focus group 319

front-loading 331
front-runner 331
Get Out the Vote (GOTV) 318
hard money 323
Hatch Act 322
independent expenditures 326
issue advocacy advertising 324
office-block, or Massachusetts ballot 346
open primary 345
party-column, or Indiana ballot 346
political action committee (PAC) 324

political consultant 317
pollster 318
presidential primary 330
press secretary 318
rational ignorance effect 340
registration 342
soft money 324
Super PAC 324
superdelegate 331
tracking polls 319
voter turnout 334

Chapter Summary

■ **9.1** Eligibility to run for federal office is based on citizenship, residency, and age. Each office has different requirements. Only the president is required to be a natural-born citizen. Candidates for senator and representative could be naturalized citizens. People run for political office to further their careers, to carry out specific political programs, or in response to certain issues or events. Legal qualifications for holding political office are minimal at state and local levels, but office holders remain predominantly white and male and are likely to be from the professional class.

■ **9.2** Political campaigns are lengthy and extremely expensive. In the last decade, they have become more candidate centered rather than party centered due to technological innovations and decreasing party identification. Candidates have begun to rely less on the party and more on paid professional consultants to perform the tasks necessary to wage a political campaign. The crucial task of professional political consultants is image building. The campaign organization devises a campaign strategy to maximize the candidate's chances of winning. Candidates use public opinion polls and focus groups to gauge their popularity and to test the mood of the country.

■ **9.3** The amount of money spent in financing campaigns is increasing steadily. A variety of corrupt practices acts have been passed to regulate campaign finance. The Federal Election Campaign Act of 1971 and its amendments in 1974 and 1976 instituted major reforms by limiting spending and contributions; the acts allowed corporations, labor unions, and interest groups to set up political action committees (PACs) to raise money for candidates. Public matching funds were made available to primary campaigns if certain criteria were met. The intent was to help candidates be competitive in the primaries. New techniques were later developed, including "soft money" contributions to the parties and independent expenditures. The Bipartisan Campaign Reform Act (BCRA) of 2002 banned soft money contributions to the national parties, limited advertising by interest groups, and increased the limits on individual contributions. Since 2008, candidates for president have refused public funding both in the primary campaign and the general election. "Leveling the playing field" for candidates in either the primaries or the general election seemed to be obsolete.

■ **9.4** After the Democratic Convention of 1968, the McGovern-Fraser Commission formulated new rules for primaries, adopted by all Democrats and by Republicans in many states. They opened up the presidential nomination process to all voters. They effectively removed control of the nomination process from the political party members and gave it to the voting public. Sometimes this produces a great party leader, and other years it produces a candidate who is not well supported by party loyalists and who cannot win the election.

■ **9.4** A presidential primary is a statewide election to help a political party determine its presidential nominee at the national convention. Some states use the caucus method of choosing convention delegates. The primary campaign recently has been shortened to the first few months of the election year.

■ **9.4** The party conventions are held to finalize the nomination of a candidate for president. Normally, the convention is used to unite the party and to introduce the winning candidate to the public. It marks the beginning of the general election campaign. Contested conventions have been rare in the last 50 years.

■ **9.4** The general election campaign begins after the national conventions. Presidential candidates and their campaign organizations use advertising, appearances, speeches, and debates to win support from voters. In recent years, attention has been lavished on battleground states where presidential contests were closely fought.

■ **9.5** Free and fair elections are the basis for the continuation of a democratic form of government. Elections should be fairly administered, information about the candidates and issues must be available through a free press, and voters must be free from coercion and intimidation.

■ **9.6** Voter participation in the United States is low compared with that of other countries. Some see this as a threat to representative democracy. Others believe it simply indicates greater satisfaction with the status quo. There is an association between voting and a person's age, education, minority status, and income level. Another factor affecting voter turnout is the extent to which elections are competitive within a state. It is also true that the number of eligible voters is smaller than the number of people of voting age because of ineligible felons and immigrants who are not yet citizens.

■ **9.7** In the United States, only citizens have been allowed to vote. In the early years of the republic, however, only free white male citizens who owned property were eligible to vote. Laws have excluded women, citizens under 18 years of age, felons, ex-slaves, and others. By 1971 suffrage was extended to all citizens, male and female, aged 18 or older. Questions still remain: Should felons be excluded from voting? What about resident noncitizens or people who have difficulty getting registered? Each state has somewhat different registration processes and requirements for identification at the polls. Some claim that these requirements are responsible for much of the nonparticipation in the political process in the United States.

■ **9.8** Because of the federal structure of the United States, citizens vote in federal, state, and local elections. To nominate candidates for office, voters participate in primary elections, which may be restricted to party identifiers (closed), open to all (open), or allow voters to choose between both parties' candidates (blanket). Candidates are elected in the general election. Voters may be asked to cast ballots on referenda, on constitutional amendments at the state level, for tax levies, or in special elections to choose candidates for a vacated office.

■ **9.8** The United States uses the Australian ballot, a secret ballot that is prepared, distributed, and counted by government officials. The office-block ballot groups candidates according to office. The party-column ballot groups candidates according to their party labels and symbols.

■ **9.8** Vote fraud is often charged but not often proven. After the 2000 election, states and local communities adopted new forms of voting equipment, seeking to provide secure voting systems for elections. The federal government established a commission to test new technologies and provide a clearinghouse for information.

■ **9.9** The voter technically does not vote directly but chooses between slates of presidential electors. In most states, the slate that wins the most popular votes throughout the state gets to cast all the electoral votes for the state. The candidate receiving a majority (270) of the electoral votes wins. Both the mechanics and the politics of the electoral college have been sharply criticized. Proposed reforms include a proposal that the president be elected on a popular-vote basis in a direct election.

Selected Resources

PRINT RESOURCES

Berman, Ari. *Give Us the Ballot: The Modern Struggle for Voting Rights in America* (New York: Farrar, Straus and Giroux, 2015). In this well-regarded book, the author traces the 1960s civil rights movement's struggle to extend voting rights to African Americans throughout the nation. He then follows the opposition to expanded voting rights to 2015.

Hasen, Richard L. *Plutocrats United: Campaign Money, the Supreme Court, and the Distortion of American Elections* (New Haven, CT: Yale University Press, 2016). Hasen offers a clear and articulate look at the transformation of campaign financing through Supreme Court decisions such as *Citizens United* and explains why the political leaders really do not want to change the system.

Karpf, David. *The MoveOn Effect: The Unexpected Transformation of American Political Advocacy* (New York: Oxford University Press, 2012). The author examines how today's organizations use the Internet and social media to gain supporters and motivate followers to join others in a common cause. His work addresses the new ways that organizations arise, organize, fundraise, and operate across the country, utilizing the capacity of the Internet to connect their followers.

Leighley, Jan and Jonathan Nagler. *Who Votes Now?: Demographics, Issues, Inequality, and Turnout in the United States* (Princeton, NJ: Princeton University Press, 2013). Using data from the U.S. Census Bureau, the authors examine trends in voting turnout over four decades. They find that the voting gap between black and white Americans has disappeared but that the gap between the wealthy and the poor has not. Among the questions they tackle is whether new practices like same-day registration would erase some of these inequalities in voting.

Piven, Frances Fox, Lori Minnite, and Margaret Groarke. *Keeping Down the Black Vote: Race and Demobilization of American Voters* (New York: The New Press, 2009). The authors claim that under the banner of election reform, leading operatives in the Republican Party have sought to affect elections by suppressing the black vote.

Sides, John and Lynn Vavreck. *The Gamble: Choice and Change in the 2012 Presidential Election* (Princeton, NJ: Princeton University Press, 2013). The authors take an unusual approach to analyzing the 2012 election, using quantitative analysis of the economy, public opinion, the media, and advertising to explain the election results from a social science approach.

MEDIA RESOURCES

American Blackout—A 2005 documentary narrated by former congresswoman Cynthia McKinney from Georgia. She investigates the ways in which African American voters can be challenged at the polls and kept from voting.

The Candidate—A 1972 film (starring Robert Redford) that effectively investigates and satirizes the decisions that a candidate for the U.S. Senate must make. It's a political classic.

Game Change—Released in 2012, this movie portrays the Republican campaign in 2008, with an emphasis on the introduction of Sarah Palin as the vice presidential candidate. It stars Ed Harris, Julianne Moore, and Woody Harrelson.

Hacking Democracy—An HBO production that follows activist Bev Harris of Seattle and others as they take on Diebold, a company that makes electronic voting machines. The documentary argues that security lapses in Diebold's machines are a threat to the democratic process.

Mississippi Burning—This 1988 film, starring Gene Hackman and Willem Dafoe, is a fictional version of the investigation of the deaths of two civil rights workers who came to Mississippi to help register African Americans to vote in 1964.

ONLINE RESOURCES

Ballotpedia—provides an online source for information about voting, state and national issues, ballot measures, and election laws: www.ballotpedia.org

Center for Responsive Politics—a nonpartisan, independent, and nonprofit research group that tracks money in U.S. politics and its effect on elections and public policy: www.opensecrets.org

Federal Election Commission—an independent regulatory agency created by Congress in 1975 to administer and enforce the Federal Election Campaign Act (FECA), the statute that governs the financing of federal elections; contains detailed information about current campaign financing laws and the latest filings of finance reports: www.fec.gov

Institute for Democracy and Electoral Assistance (IDEA)—an intergovernmental organization that supports sustainable democracy worldwide. Provides information about voting and turnout around the world: www.idea.int

Project Vote Smart—investigates voting records and campaign financing information: www.votesmart.org

Rock the Vote—provides tools to "build political power for young people." Its website provides state-level information about registration deadlines, voting requirements, and voting records for elected officials: www.rockthevote.org

The Media and Politics

People attending a rally for candidate Bernie Sanders capture the event using their cell phone cameras. Increasingly, cell phone images and video distributed via social media inform the public and shape the news.

DAVID MCNEW/Getty Images

LEARNING OBJECTIVES

After reading this chapter, you will be able to:

■ **10.1** Briefly describe the evolution of the media's role in U.S. politics.

■ **10.2** Explain the political functions of the media in American society.

■ **10.3** Discuss the impact of all forms of the media on political campaigning.

■ **10.4** Identify ways in which the media influence voters.

■ **10.5** Demonstrate an understanding of the relationship between government and all media sources.

■ **10.6** Critically analyze news stories published by any form of the media.

What if...   Press Freedoms Applied to All of Us?

Background

The Society for Professional Journalists (SPJ) recently adopted a resolution to reject attempts to define a journalist in any way other than someone who commits "acts of journalism." Who is a journalist and what is an act of journalism? Has access to digital media and the ability to instantly distribute images, video, and text around the world changed how we understand journalism? As these definitions change, will the First Amendment and the courts' interpretations of press freedom be able to keep up?

Who Is a Journalist and What Is at Stake?

Journalism and newsrooms have traditionally been governed by a set of ethical standards and behaviors.* The SPJ's Code of Ethics emphasizes four main principles: (1) seek truth and report it; (2) minimize harm; (3) act independently; and (4) be accountable. Dan Gillmor, author of *Mediactive* and director of the Knight Center for Digital Media Entrepreneurship at Arizona State University, outlines five different but complementary principles: thoroughness, accuracy, fairness, independence, and transparency. Gillmor writes, "These are universal principles not just for people who call themselves journalists but for anyone who wants to be trusted for what they say or write."** This new vision of press freedom, one that protects the acts of journalism and not the journalist, may have legal implications. Shield laws have been enacted to protect reporters' ability to gather information without having to reveal confidential information or a confidential source to law enforcement. Without confidential sources and shield laws, we might not have learned about the Watergate scandal that led to President Richard Nixon's resignation in the face of impeachment. *The Guardian* and the *Washington* Post were each awarded a Pulitzer Prize for public service associated with their reporting based on classified documents leaked by former National Security Agency contractor Edward Snowden. The District of Columbia and 49 states have some level of protections from local and state agencies. No statutory protection exists at the federal level.

Today's Journalists? It Could Be You!

According to Pew Research, 64 percent of Americans now own a smartphone; 85 percent of young people between 18 and 29 years of age own a smartphone.*** Your smartphone not only allows you to consume the news, but also to actively create and distribute it. Karina Vargas, 19 years old, stepped off her train in Oakland, California, and saw police arresting a group of young men. She thought the police were using excessive force, so she pulled out her cell phone and started recording. Her footage captured a police officer shooting Oscar Grant in the back while Grant was handcuffed. Similarly, in North Charleston, South Carolina, bystander Feiden Santana watched and recorded police officer Michael Slager shoot Walter Scott in the back as he ran away. Officer Slager's initial account of the incident said that he and Scott struggled over a Taser; Slager felt threatened, and he fired his gun. Only when the video surfaced was he arrested. The images captured by Vargas and by Santana became critical to finding the truth in each incident and contributed to a national dialogue about police violence. Citizen journalism can take other forms as well. Bloggers report regularly on things happening in local communities. Wikinews, similar to the online encyclopedia Wikipedia, allows individuals to contribute to news content. This is especially powerful when an event is still unfolding and eyewitnesses can provide access to information instantly via Twitter and Facebook Go Live.

For Critical Analysis

1. As journalism changes, will our understanding of freedom of the press protected by the First Amendment change as well? What sorts of changes might we anticipate? Will the changes be positive or negative?

2. Shield laws are designed to protect the confidentiality of sources so that informants and whistleblowers will come forward and speak to the press. Does the digital age of media render confidentiality a thing of the past? Why or why not?

*Society of Professional Journalists Code of Ethics. https://www.spj.org/pdf/ethicscode.pdf

**Josh Stearns, "Let's Stop Defining Who Is a Journalist, and Protect All Acts of Journalism." October 28, 2013. http://mediashift.org/2013/10/lets-stop-defining-who-i-a-journalist-and-protect-all-acts-of-journalism/

***Monica Anderson, "6 Facts about Americans and Their Smartphones." Pew Research FactTank, April 1, 2015. http://www.pewresearch.org/fact-tank/2015/04/01/6-facts-about-americans-and-their-smartphones/

We live in a world saturated by media. Twenty-four hours a day, seven days a week, you can access news about American politics, entertainment, sports, world events, science, and the weather. From the car radio or Internet radio first thing in the morning to the opening monologue of a late-night television talk show, media surrounds us. While you watch television, you may be receiving text messages from your friends, reading tweets, or messaging on Instagram. This chapter explores the symbiotic relationship between media and politics in the United States. Media influences politics and government, but politics also influences media.

The term **media** is defined as the means of communication—such as radio, cable television, Internet, and news outlets—that reach or influence people widely. Mainstream media are generally public, available to anyone who wishes to see or read coverage. They can reach millions of individuals around the globe in a matter of seconds. Social media, such as Facebook, Twitter, and Instagram, are also public, but individuals contributing to the sites control access to and distribution of their information. **Social media**'s primary purpose is to connect individuals who want to share information, often of a more personal nature. As we will see in this chapter, politicians, journalists, interest groups, political parties, members of Congress, and even the president have adopted social media as a way to communicate directly with citizens. Social media featured prominently in the 2016 presidential primary and general election campaigns as a way for candidates to respond to one another, communicate with supporters, and mobilize voters. The media have both changed *and* stayed the same throughout the nation's history. Newspapers still report the major news of the day; now, social media allows individuals to report and interact with events in real time.

media
The means of communication—such as radio, television, and news outlets—that reach people widely.

social media
Websites and applications that enable users to create and share content or to participate in social networking.

A Brief History of the Media's Role in United States Politics

■ **10.1** Briefly describe the evolution of the media's role in U.S. politics.

Many years ago, Thomas Jefferson opined: "Were it left to me to decide whether we should have a government without newspapers, or newspapers without a government, I should not hesitate a moment to prefer the latter."[1] Media have played a significant role in politics since the founding of this nation. Political discussion was controlled by a small elite who communicated personally, and before the early 1800s, news traveled slowly. If an important political event occurred in New York, it was not known until five days later in Philadelphia, and not for 10 days later in the capital cities of Connecticut, Maryland, and Virginia. Boston learned of political news 15 days later.

The Rise of the Popular Press

Roughly 3,000 newspapers were being published by 1860. Some of these, such as the *New York Tribune*, were mainly sensationalist outlets that concentrated on crimes, scandals, and social gossip. The *New York Herald* specialized in self-improvement and what today would be called "practical"

---

1   James Madison, "Letter to W. T. Barry" (August 4, 1822), in Gaillard P. Hunt, ed., *The Writings of James Madison* 103 (1910).

news. Although sensational and biased reporting often reinforced political partisanship (this was particularly true during the Civil War), many historians believe that the growth of the print media also played an important role in unifying the country.[2]

Americans may cherish the idea of an unbiased press, but in the early years of the nation's history, the number of politically sponsored newspapers was significant. The sole reason for the existence of such periodicals was to further the interests of the politicians who paid for their publication. As chief executive of our government during this period, George Washington was a firm believer in **managed news**. He believed that some matters should be kept secret and that news that might damage the image of the United States should be censored. Washington, however, made no attempt to control the press.

Mass-Readership Newspapers Two inventions in the nineteenth century led to the development of mass-readership newspapers. The first was the high-speed rotary press; the second was the telegraph. Faster presses meant lower per-unit costs and lower subscription prices. The introduction of the telegraph in 1848 allowed news of an event to reach newsrooms across the nation within hours instead of days.

Along with these technological changes came a growing population and increasing urbanization. A larger, more urban population could support daily newspapers. The burgeoning, diversified economy encouraged the growth of advertising, which meant that newspapers could obtain additional revenues from merchants, who seized the opportunity to promote their wares to a larger public.

Newspaper owners often allowed their editors to engage in sensationalism and what is known as **yellow journalism**. The questionable, or simply personal, activities of a prominent businessperson, politician, or socialite were front-page material. Newspapers, then as now, made their economic way by maximizing readership. Whether the source is the *National Enquirer* at the grocery checkout or tweets from Donald Trump, sensationalism still sells today.

News Delivered over the Airwaves

The first scheduled radio program in the United States featured politicians. On the night of November 2, 1920, KDKA-Pittsburgh transmitted the returns of the presidential election race between Warren G. Harding and James M. Cox. The listeners were a few thousand people tuning in on primitive, homemade sets. By 1924, there were nearly 1,400 radio stations. But it was not until 8 p.m. on November 15, 1926, that the electronic media came into its own in the United States. On that night, the National Broadcasting Company (NBC) made its debut with a four-hour program broadcast by 25 stations in 21 cities. Network broadcasting was born.

Even with the advent of national radio in the 1920s and television in the late 1940s, many politicians were slow to understand the significance of the **electronic media**. The 1952 presidential campaign was the first to feature a role for television. Television coverage of the Republican convention helped

---

managed news
Information generated and distributed by the government in such a way as to give government interests priority over candor.

did you know?
The first successful daily newspaper in the United States was the *Pennsylvania Packet & General Advertiser*, which was initially published on September 21, 1784.

yellow journalism
A term for sensationalistic, irresponsible journalism. Reputedly, the term is an allusion to the cartoon "The Yellow Kid" in the old *New York World*, a newspaper especially noted for its sensationalism.

electronic media
Communication channels that involve electronic transmissions, such as radio, television, and the Internet.

---

2 James L. Baughman, "The Fall and Rise of Partisan Journalism," Center for Journalism Ethics, The University of Wisconsin, April 15, 2011.

Dwight Eisenhower win over delegates and secure the nomination. Without the first televised presidential debate (1960), it is unlikely that John F. Kennedy would have been president. As the story goes, those who listened to the debate on the radio thought Nixon had won, but those watching on television thought Kennedy was the clear winner. Since 88 percent of American households had televisions by 1960, Kennedy's campaign benefited. "Before the television debates most Americans didn't even see the candidates—they read about them, they saw photos of them," says political scientist Larry Sabato. "This allowed the public to judge candidates on a completely different basis."[3]

Although television still plays a dominant role in the campaign strategy of every national politician, all forms of media, including social media, must be leveraged to run a successful campaign.

The Revolution in Electronic Media

Network television news competes now with newspapers, cable TV, and Internet news providers. In 1963 when President John F. Kennedy was assassinated in Dallas, Texas, the event was captured on one or two amateur videos by bystanders. News of the assassination reached Washington, DC, by landline telephone. Millions of Americans rushed to find a television to watch Walter Cronkite report the story as it unfolded on network television. Today, such an event would be captured by hundreds of cell phone cameras, with details immediately uploaded to the Internet and disseminated within seconds as breaking news. With the introduction of Facebook's "Go Live" feature, events can be live-streamed. Everyone—from opposition groups in Syria fighting the government to students protesting a racially hostile campus climate—understands the power of the Internet to get their story out to millions.

In a democracy, a person's ability to gain access to the news quickly is an advantage; direct appeals can persuade the public to be more politically attentive and, in some cases, to more fully participate in public affairs. Researchers have also found that the participatory skills, norms, and networks that develop when social media are used to socialize with friends or to engage with those who share one's interest can and are being transferred to the political realm.[4] During the contentious primaries in 2016, Americans used a variety of news sources to access political information on a weekly basis. Pew researchers found that the source of their information often varied by age, education level, and political party.[5]

Image 10-1

President Dwight Eisenhower shows his discomfort and frustration during a news conference. Worried about the impact of live broadcasts, Eisenhower allowed videotaped versions to be shown after the event ended.

Image 10-2

A Lebanese protester (against Syrian president Assad) photographs a demonstration in Martyrs' Square in Beirut, Lebanon.

3 Kayla Webley, "How the Nixon-Kennedy Debate Changed the World." *TIME*, September 23, 2010. http://content.time.com /time/nation/article/0,8599,2021078,00.html

4 Cathy J. Cohen and Joseph Kahne, "Participatory Politics: New Media and Youth Political Action." Youth and Participatory Politics, 2011. http://ypp.dmlcentral.net/sites/default/files/publications/Participatory_Politics_Report.pdf

5 Amy Mitchell and Rachel Weisel, "The 2016 Presidential Campaign—a News Event That's Hard to Miss." Pew Research Center, February 4, 2016. http://www.journalism.org/2016/02/04/the-2016-presidential-campaign-a-news-event-thats-hard-to-miss/

Social media was named as the most helpful information source for people between the ages of 18 and 29, whereas cable TV news was identified as most helpful by all other age groups (see Figure 10-1). Cable television's popularity is highest among those who are 65 and older and among those who identify as Republicans. Those with a college degree are more likely to name radio, national print newspapers, and news websites or apps as their most helpful news sources. And although people may express a preference for one type of media over another, a majority of Americans get news and information from five or more sources. Likely voters draw their news from more types of media and are more likely to share what they've learned with others in their social networks.

The Special Relationship between the Media and the Executive

The relationship between the media and the president usually is reciprocal: each needs the other to thrive in the political arena. Because of this codependency, both the media and the president work hard to exploit one another. The media need news to report, and the president needs coverage. The political staff of the White House aims for constant and positive

Figure 10-1 ▶ Source for Presidential Campaign News by Age

Where people learned about the presidential campaign varied widely by age in 2016. Young people found social media the most helpful source for campaign news, whereas older voters relied on cable TV news for information.

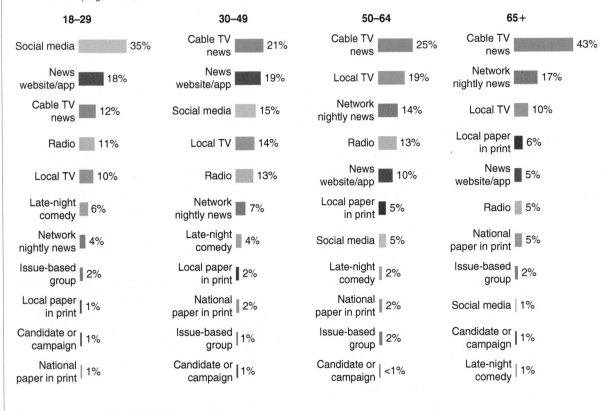

18–29		30–49		50–64		65+	
Social media	35%	Cable TV news	21%	Cable TV news	25%	Cable TV news	43%
News website/app	18%	News website/app	19%	Local TV	19%	Network nightly news	17%
Cable TV news	12%	Social media	15%	Network nightly news	14%	Local TV	10%
Radio	11%	Local TV	14%	Radio	13%	Local paper in print	6%
Local TV	10%	Radio	13%	News website/app	10%	News website/app	5%
Late-night comedy	6%	Network nightly news	7%	Local paper in print	5%	Radio	5%
Network nightly news	4%	Late-night comedy	4%	Social media	5%	National paper in print	5%
Issue-based group	2%	Local paper in print	2%	Late-night comedy	2%	Issue-based group	2%
Local paper in print	1%	National paper in print	2%	National paper in print	2%	Social media	1%
Candidate or campaign	1%	Issue-based group	1%	Issue-based group	2%	Candidate or campaign	1%
National paper in print	1%	Candidate or campaign	1%	Candidate or campaign	<1%	Late-night comedy	1%

Source: Survey conducted Jan.12–27, 2016
PEW RESEARCH CENTER

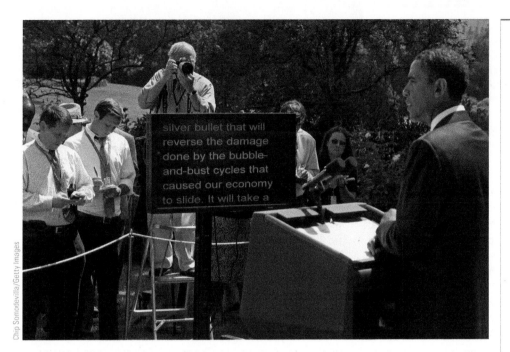

Image 10–3
President Barack Obama reads his prepared remarks from a teleprompter during an event focused on the economic recovery in 2010.

exposure of the president in the media. Presidential events and speeches are planned to the extent that the effort has been nicknamed "the presidential spectacle."

In the United States, the prominence of the president is accentuated by a **White House press corps** that is assigned full-time to cover the presidency. These reporters even have a lounge in the White House where they spend their days, waiting for a story to break. Most of the time, they simply wait for the daily or twice-daily briefings conducted by the president's **press secretary**. Because of the press corps' physical proximity to the president, the chief executive cannot even take a brief stroll around the Rose Garden without it becoming news. Perhaps no other nation allows the press such access to its highest government official. Consequently, no other democratic nation has its airwaves and print media so laden with trivia regarding the personal lives of the chief executive and his or her family.

One of the first presidents to make truly effective use of the media was President Franklin D. Roosevelt. He brought new spirit to a demoralized country and led it through the Great Depression with his radio "fireside chats." In 1933, his announcement on the reorganization of the banks calmed a jittery nation and prevented the collapse of the banking industry. His famous "a day that will live in infamy" Pearl Harbor speech, following the Japanese attack on the U.S. Pacific fleet on December 7, 1941, mobilized the nation for World War II.

Barack Obama's White House revolutionized the use of the media to spread the president's message. Although the Obama was famous for his skill in rhetoric, he favored more intimate and controlled interviews with the major news anchors of virtually every network. The White House website is packed with position papers, speeches, presidential memos, and photo galleries. From the website, citizens can follow the president and his family on Twitter, Snapchat, Facebook, YouTube, and LinkedIn, as well as download speeches and video via iTunes.

White House press corps
The reporters assigned full-time to cover the presidency.

press secretary
The presidential staff member responsible for handling White House media relations and communications.

did you know?
Franklin D. Roosevelt averaged 6 press conferences a month, whereas Barack Obama held an average of just 1.6. Ronald Reagan held fewer than one per month.

Change.org: Internet Activism with Impact

At a time when many traditional news outlets are experiencing a decline in subscribers, Change.org has taken on several functions traditionally associated with mainstream media—informing citizens, calling attention to an issue or problem, serving as a watchdog, and working "to comfort the afflicted and afflict the comfortable."* Change.org is perhaps best known for online petitions designed to produce a specific change—corporate, community, or political—but Change.org is also host to hackathons for social change, a new platform called Change Politics, and a charitable foundation.

Change.org was started in 2007 by Ben Rattray initially to build social networking and fundraising for nonprofits. In 2010, Change.org opened the petition tool. One of the first petitions was created by a woman from a township in South Africa. As a victim of "corrective rape" (a crime intended to "cure" lesbians of their sexual orientation), she wanted the South African government to acknowledge corrective rape as a crime and take action to stop the abuses. Her petition attracted 170,000 signatures, and the South African parliament formed a national task force. For Rattray, this victory demonstrated the power of social media and social networks to connect like-minded citizens across geographic and cultural boundaries and direct their energy toward a specific achievable demand for change. Today, employees at Change.org select "winnable" (a demand for focused action, targeted to a person or institution with the power to take that action) petitions to feature on their website and offer media coaching to petition creators, whose stories attract attention from mainstream news outlets. They write and distribute press releases and publicize winnable petitions by advertising on Facebook.

Notable petitions include one directed at the U.S. Department of Agriculture to eliminate a processed beef product known as "pink slime" from school lunches and another to stop the Illinois state legislature from preempting local ordinances prohibiting the use of plastic grocery bags. The Bank of America dropped its plan to charge debit card holders a $5 monthly fee following a petition with 306,800 signatures. In 2014, Change.org added Decision Maker pages that allow the target of a petition to respond directly to petitioners and provides a "fact check" on the accuracy of petitioners' claims. "We've [built] this incredible megaphone for everyday people to have a voice that is much louder than it was before, but we want to make sure Change.org is more than shouting at decision makers," said Rattray. Change.org claims to have achieved 28,860 victories in 196 countries.

Change.org describes itself as a "mission-driven social enterprise" and is registered as a certified B Corporation, meaning that although it must prioritize social good over profits, it is not a nonprofit operation. In fact, it is a highly profitable source of data collected from petitioners and shared with sponsors. Data analytics allows Change.org to funnel new petition opportunities to individuals based on the petitions they elect to sign. For example, if you sign one on animal rights, you are 2.29 times more likely to sign a criminal justice petition, and if you sign a criminal justice petition, you are 6.3 times more likely to sign an economic justice petition. Change.org makes money by, among other things, connecting users with paying sponsors that you are more likely to give money to. Critics charge that this creates a "Google-like feedback loop that leads us only where we've been before" and "when you consider that petitions in places like California can so easily turn into ballot initiatives, this sort of thing looks even more ominous."** Change.org has developed several offshoots based on its success with the petition platform. Change Politics, launched in January 2016, is intended to "increase citizen participation in campaigns by allowing voters to engage directly with the candidates in the lead up to the election, and shift influence in elections from parties and paid ads, to individuals' trusted personal networks."*** Designed as a mobile application, users can submit questions to political candidates, find endorsements, and create a personalized ballot guide.

Change.org also hosts Hack for Change, a national day of civic hacking. This is a nationwide day of action where developers, government employees, designers, journalists, data scientists, nonprofit employees, and residents come together to design solutions to community problems. In 2016, organizers asked for help to improve digital access to government services.**** For example, make it easier to apply for affordable housing or food stamps or a business license. Hackathons in communities around the nation can set their own challenges.

Change.org has more than 70 million users and adds about 4 million new users each month. Often the media picks up the story resulting from a successful change petition or enhances the coverage of the target issue. In the future Change.org plans to introduce a social media tool similar to those found on news websites: "Instead of just tweeting something, you 'change' it. You go directly from an article that inspired you to Change.org to launch a petition on that same topic."*****

*Greg Beato, "From Petitions to Decisions" Stanford Social Innovation Review, fall 2014. Accessed at http://ssir.org/articles/entry/from_petitions_to_decisions
**Klint Finley, "Meet Change.org, the Google of Modern Politics." WIRED, September 26, 2013. http://www.wired.com/2013/09/change-org/
***http://blog.change.org/post/new-election-app-change-politics-citizen-participation-elections
**** https://www.codeforamerica.org/events/national-day-2016
*****Beato, p. 17.

(Continued)

For Critical Analysis

1. Change.org estimates that more than 25 million people have signed a petition that has led to a victory. Critics have labeled this "clicktivism" or "slacktivism" since the degree of involvement is modest. What do you think? Efficient advocacy or lazy activism?

2. Marketers, nonprofits, and politicians are using a technique called A/B testing to determine which email subject lines and texts are most likely to convince people to open them rather than delete them. Could this lead to oversimplified or extreme messaging? What would the consequences be for politics if it did?

The Internet and Social Media

The use of the Internet and other forms of social media has increased dramatically in the last decade (see Figure 10-2). Political websites were created for the two major-party candidates for president for the first time in 1996 at a time when nonusers outnumbered Internet users. Today candidates drive likely voters to their website to find information and make donations using social media and other forms of electronic communication. Howard Dean and John McCain were early adopters of the Internet to raise money, but Barack Obama became the leader in this practice in 2008. His website encouraged millions of supporters to donate small amounts to his primary campaign and to sign up for monthly charges to their credit cards. By the end of the 2012 campaign, the Obama online fundraising operation had raised $52 million and had added more than 2 million new donors (who had not contributed in 2008).[6] Bernie Sanders, candidate for the Democratic nomination and a big proponent of campaign finance reform, attracted millions of donors through his website, allowing him to claim that he spent very little time on political fundraising events.[7] By the end of March 2016, Sanders had raised as much as Hillary Clinton in total campaign contributions ($182 million).[8] Hillary Clinton and Donald Trump relied less on small donors reached through online fundraising appeals than in previous elections. Trump's advantage in earned media meant that he did not need to raise as much through individual donations. In all, Clinton raised $1.3 billion compared with Trump's $795 million.

After establishing web pages, politicians took the lead from political commentators and began to add blogs to their websites. "**Blog**" comes from "web log," a regular updating of one's ideas at a specific website. Not all of the millions of blogs posted daily are political in nature, but many are, and they can have a dramatic influence on events, giving rise to the term **blogosphere politics**.

did you know?

More than 1,000 new petitions are launched every day on Change.org in the U.S.

blog
A regularly updated website, typically written in a conversational style by an individual or small group.

blogosphere politics
The blogosphere is the collection of blogs often linked to one another within communities of conversation about politics and political issues.

6 Byron Tau, "Obama Campaign Final Fundraising Total: $1.1 Billion." January 19, 2013. http://www.politico.com/story/2013/01/19
7 Fredreka Schouten, "Internet Donations Power Bernie Sanders Ahead of Democratic Primary." *USA Today*, December 20, 2015. http://www.usatoday.com/story/news/politics/elections/2015/12/17/internet-donations-bernie-sanders-hillary-clinton/77496536/
8 Robert Yoon, "$182 Million: Bernie Sanders Equals Hillary Clinton's Campaign Fundraising." CNN, April 21, 2016. www.cnn.com/2016/04/21/politics/2016-bernie-sanders-fundraising-hillary-clinton/

Figure 10-2 ▶ The Growth in Internet Use in the United States

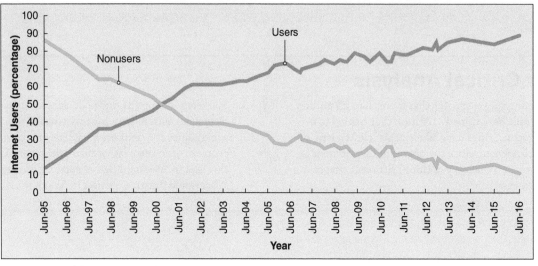

Source: Pew Research Center, Pew Internet Center, 2016.

podcasting
A method of distributing multimedia files, such as audio or video files, for downloading onto mobile devices or personal computers.

did you know?

Facebook has more than 2.19 billion active users.

Blogs can be highly specialized, highly political, and highly entertaining—and they are cheap. The *Washington Post* requires thousands of employees, many reams of paper, and tons of ink to generate its offline product and incurs delivery costs to get its papers to readers. The *Post* also hosts dozens of blogs and hires journalists to create these online columns, just as the official White House blog requires many writers and analysts from the current administration. A small blogging organization such as RealClearPolitics, however, can generate its political commentary with fewer employees.

Blogs have become well established and have expanded into the form of spoken words. Enter **podcasting**, so-called because the first online spoken blogs were downloaded onto iPods. Podcasts, though, can be heard on one's computer or downloaded onto any portable listening device and can also include videos. Hundreds of thousands of podcasts are now being generated every day. News outlets such as National Public Radio (NPR) offer dozens of options for listeners. People may express their views readily on YouTube. The protests in Ukraine could be viewed daily via cell phone videos uploaded to YouTube.

Three-quarters of Americans (77 percent) use social networking sites today.[9] A small proportion of the public remains offline altogether (15 percent). Users are younger, more likely to be female than male, come from higher-income households, and have completed some college. There are no significant differences by racial or ethnic group, but rural communities lag behind urban and suburban communities. The Obama administration pioneered the use of social media to keep in touch with supporters, voters, and the world. The Obama administration pioneered the use of social media to keep in touch with supporters, voters, and the world with Facebook, YouTube, and Twitter. Social media have proven to be effective at mobilizing supporters during the campaign and to turn out voters on Election Day. A study published

9 Percentage of U.S. population with a social media profile from 2008 to 2018." Statistica, March 2018. https://www.statista.com/statistics/273476/percentage-of-us-population-with-a-social-network-profile/

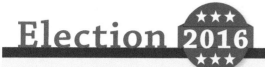

From @realDonaldTrump to @POTUS

Never before has a presidential candidate used Twitter so prodigiously to engage directly with opponents and supporters alike, using the social media platform as one long continuous campaign rally. Trump picked fights with primary rivals, stoked controversies that other candidates would have let die, and generally offered his personal commentary on issues large and small. In the early morning hours of November 9 as his electoral vote total crossed 270 and he became the president-elect, Trump sent a tweet to his 14.3 million followers: "Such a beautiful and important evening! The forgotten man and woman will never be forgotten again. We will all come together as never before."

Barack Obama was the first president to use Twitter. The White House established the @POTUS Twitter account in 2013 to allow the president to engage more directly with the American people. In planning for the transition to a Trump administration, the White House announced a digital transition plan. When Donald Trump was inaugurated as the 45th president, the @POTUS Twitter account was transferred to him. President Obama's tweets as @POTUS will be preserved in the National Archives and Records Administration and he received a new handle, @POTUS44.

For Critical Analysis

1. Donald Trump's Twitter habits did not change when he became president. How will this record impact his legacy?

2. Should tweets be preserved along with all of the other correspondence and documents generated by a presidential administration? What might historians learn from them in the future?

---

in the journal *Nature* confirmed the idea that voting can be significantly influenced by messages on Facebook.[10] Researchers concluded, "First and foremost, online political mobilization works. It induces political self-expression, but it also induces information gathering and real, validated turnout." In addition, the study found that showing Facebook users pictures of friends in their network who had already voted increased the likelihood that they would vote themselves.

The Role of the Media in Our Society

■ **10.2** Explain the political functions of the media in American society.

A democracy can only exist if there are alternative sources of information for citizens. Privately owned media outlets such as the *New York Times* or the *Huffington Post* provide news reports and factual analysis for the public. Citizens must have resources available to them on which to cast an informed ballot.

The Media's Political Functions

The media perform several different functions, including entertainment, but the most important functions are arguably political. The media provide information, identify problems and set the public agenda, investigate and report on

---

10 Robert Bond, et al., "A 61-Million-Person Experiment in Social Influence and Political Mobilization," *Nature* (September 2012); 489 (7415): 295–298.

wrongdoing, socialize new generations, and provide a political forum for dialogue and debate.

Provide Information A primary function of the media—including print, television, radio, and the Internet—is to report news and provide the public with information. The media provide words, pictures, sound, and video about events, facts, personalities, and ideas. The protections of the First Amendment aim to aid the free flow of news because information is an essential part of the democratic process. James Madison delivered incisive insight into the importance of the media when he stated: "A people who mean to be their own governors must arm themselves with the power knowledge gives. A popular government without popular information or the means of acquiring it is but a prologue to a farce or a tragedy or perhaps both."[11]

The ability to provide information and report the news relies on the public's willingness to trust media as a fair and accurate source of reliable information. Gallup polls show a decline in trust and confidence in the media to historic lows in 2016. Only four in ten Americans say that they have "a great deal" or "a fair amount" of trust and confidence in the media to report the news fully, accurately, and fairly. In 1998, 55 percent of Americans indicated a high degree of trust in the media. This decline in trust mirrors the declining confidence in other institutions (refer again to Figure 1-1 in Chapter 1). Levels of trust in the media have declined most sharply among those younger than 50 and among Republicans (32 percent) and Independents (33 percent). Democrats express a higher degree of trust, with 55 percent indicating confidence in the media. One perspective argues that the public trusted the press more when it was less trustworthy. As the press became more aggressive in examining public institutions and more critical of government in general, the public became less trusting of everything. "It only makes sense that the public, exposed to critical thinking in the press, should redirect that critical thinking back onto the press itself. The more people know, the less they trust."[12]

Identify Problems and Set the Public Agenda The power of the media is important not only in revealing what the government is doing, but also in determining what the government *should* do—in other words, in setting the **public agenda**. The mass media identify public issues, such as the danger posed by the shipment of nuclear materials by rail without proper identification or safeguards. Such news stories may lead to government agencies, such as the Environmental Protection Agency (EPA), issuing new rules for such transport, or to Congress holding a hearing on the issue. American journalists have established a long tradition of uncovering and exposing public wrongdoing, corruption, and bribery.

The media raise interest in particular problems, and then public officials begin investigations in order to report back to constituents and the public. **Agenda setting** may also refer to the ability of the media to influence which issues the public thinks are most important. Evidence strongly suggests that the public problems that receive the greatest media treatment will be cited in public opinion surveys as the most important. Agenda setting at the individual level is closely linked with the concept of **priming**, the suggestion of standards to the viewer about the importance of an issue, especially in judging the

public agenda
Issues that are perceived by the political community as meriting public attention and governmental action.

agenda setting
The media's ability to influence the importance of an issue, and thereby add it to the public agenda, by covering it more frequently.

priming
The process by which the media suggest the importance of an issue.

11   James Madison, "Letter to W.T. Barry" (August 4, 1822), in Gaillard P. Hung, ed., *The Writings of James Madison* 103 (1910).
12   Jack Shafer, "The Public's Correct Not to Trust the Media," Politico, September 30, 2015. http://www.politico.com/magazine /story/2015/09/shafer-public-distrust-media-historic-lows-the-public-is-right-chris-cillizza-213208

effectiveness of political officials. If a series of stories shared in various media outlets focuses on an increase in the need for food stamps, readers and viewers will likely first decide to pay more attention to the issue and then to judge whether their elected officials are doing enough to alleviate hunger in their own community. The media may also affect an individual's view of social and political issues through their **framing** of an issue. Framing refers to how the issue is actually presented to the audience: in this example, is hunger presented as a problem mostly affecting children in schools, or is the use of food stamps presented as an example of fraud in government?

framing
The presentation of an issue by the media, which influences how audiences understand it.

Although the media do not make policy decisions, they do influence the policy issues that will be decided—an important part of the political process. Because those who control the media are not elected representatives of the people, the agenda-setting role of the media necessarily is a controversial one. For example, when former Central Intelligence Agency (CIA) and National Security Agency (NSA) contractor Edward Snowden decided to publicize some of the files that he had hacked from the NSA, he did not approach the *New York Times* because he feared that the *Times* would contact the government instead of publishing his releases. Instead, he found a reporter at *The Guardian* in Great Britain who was willing to run the story. Snowden's findings led a number of American news organizations to begin investigating the extent to which the NSA was recording cell phone and email messages of Americans. This put the question of such "eavesdropping" on the agenda of President Obama, who formed a blue-ribbon committee to study the practice.

Because we know that the media can spotlight a political issue and have the power to stimulate the audience to concern and action, the relationship between government and media agenda setting is complex. Officials realize that media coverage can highlight difficult issues and make the officials themselves look less effective. Elected officials and their staffs may also try to control the agenda by identifying problems themselves and trying to frame the issues in a way that benefits their own agendas. Media then need to decide whether to accept a government interpretation of the issue or not.

Investigate and Report on Wrongdoing Investigative reports may lead to a deeper examination of policy alternatives. Public policy is often complex and difficult to make entertaining, but programs devoted to public policy are increasingly being scheduled for prime-time television. Most networks produce shows with a "news magazine" format that include segments on poverty, homelessness, disability claims, or online privacy. Major newspapers and television networks devote resources to investigative reporting. By finding a problem with a public policy or uncovering an official's wrongdoing, the media are alerting the public to important political information. Furthermore, the results of investigative reporting can have a very important impact on officeholders and, in the best case, bring about change for the better. Richard Nixon barely avoided impeachment and resigned from office due to the investigative reporting of Bob Woodward and Carl Bernstein of the *Washington Post*. In 2012, The Associated Press won a Pulitzer Prize for the investigative reporting of Matt Apuzzo, Adam Goldman, Eileen Sullivan, and Chris Hawley and their reporting on the New York City Police Department's undercover surveillance of Muslim mosques and community activities. The secret police program, which was aimed at exposing terrorist activities, had proceeded with neither legal authority nor warrants for its endeavors. ProPublica is an independent,

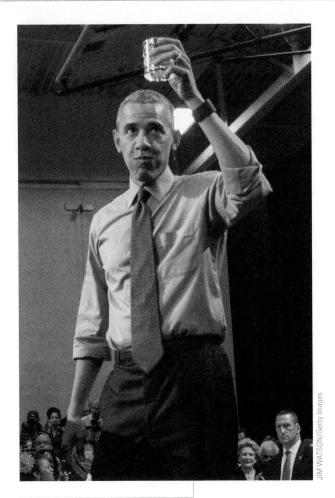

Image 10-4

President Barack Obama visited Flint, Michigan, in May 2016 to assess local, state, and federal efforts to clean up Flint's drinking water. To demonstrate that progress had been made, the president was photographed drinking a glass of Flint tap water. A presidential visit brings media attention, generates public support, and urges governments to act to solve the crisis at hand.

nonprofit newsroom that produces investigative journalism in the public interest. As news organizations have fewer resources to devote to investigative journalism, independent investigations become more important.

Socialize New Generations As mentioned in Chapter 6, the media play a significant role in the political socialization of the younger generation, as well as immigrants to this country. Through the transmission of historical information (which is sometimes fictionalized), the presentation of American culture, and the portrayal of the diverse regions and groups found within the United States, the media teach the nation's youth and immigrants what it means to be an "American." TV talk shows, such as *The Ellen DeGeneres Show*, focus on popular culture, whereas shows such as *Dr. Phil* sometimes focus on more controversial issues such as abortion or assisted suicide. Many children's shows are designed not only to entertain young viewers, but also to instruct them in the traditional moral values of American society. Popular public television programs for children such as *Sesame Street* seek to teach the values of tolerance and respect for others.

As more young Americans turn to the Internet for entertainment, they are also finding an increasing amount of social and political information there. America's youth are the Internet generation. They download movies and music, find information for writing assignments, gather news (perhaps unknowingly), visit social networking sites, and increasingly become involved in political campaigns and interact online with those campaigns.

Providing a Political Forum for Dialogue and Debate As part of their news function, the media also provide a political forum for leaders and the public. Candidates for office use news reporting to sustain interest in their campaigns, whereas officeholders use the media to gain support for their policies or to present an image of leadership. Today, almost all print newspapers also have an online edition where individuals can post comments on the news or on particular columns. Late-night television with Stephen Colbert and Jimmy Fallon or HBO's John Oliver use humor, sarcasm, and superb writing to capture viewers to their respective shows. Distinguishing between news and opinion becomes extremely difficult for the viewer. For example, if President Obama appears on *The View* (with anchors of differing opinions) to announce a new program for the education of preschool children, is that "news" or is it a presidential commercial for his own initiative? Talk radio provides another outlet for opinion and news. The number of radio stations that program only talk shows has increased from about 300 in 1989 to more than 1,200 today. There has been considerable criticism of the political talk shows, especially those hosted by Rush Limbaugh, Glenn Beck, and other conservatives, on the grounds that these shows focus on negative politics rather than policy issues. Recent data from the Pew Research Center show that the audience for talk radio, as well as for television "talk" shows, has sorted it out in a reasonable way. The bulk of Rush Limbaugh's listeners, for example, consider themselves conservative, whereas most of Rachel Maddow's audience is liberal. Pundits worry that television, radio, or social media outlets that emphasize one ideology create a polarizing "filter bubble," exposing people to only a narrow range of opinions. However, research on millennials media use suggests the opposite. Seventy percent of millennials say that their social media feeds are composed of diverse viewpoints evenly mixed between those similar to and different from their own.[13]

The Media's Impact: Political Campaigns

■ **10.3** Discuss the impact of all forms of the media on political campaigning.

Media influence on the political system is most obvious during political campaigns. News coverage of a single event, such as the results of the Iowa caucuses or the New Hampshire primary, may be the most important factor in labeling a candidate as the front-runner in a presidential campaign. Almost all national political figures, starting with the president, plan every public appearance and statement to attract media coverage.

Television has transformed political campaigns. Because television, particularly cable television, is still the primary news source for the majority of Americans, candidates and their consultants spend much of their time devising strategies that use television to their benefit. Three types of TV coverage are generally employed in campaigns for the presidency and other offices: advertising, management of news coverage, and campaign debates. However, with the rise of social media use, "managing" news coverage has become more difficult. The Internet and social media may represent the second major transformation in political campaigns.

Advertising

Perhaps one of the most effective political ads of all time was a 30-second spot created by President Lyndon B. Johnson's media adviser in 1964. In this ad, a little girl stood in a field of daisies. As she held a daisy, she pulled the petals off and quietly counted to herself—when she reached number 10, a deep bass voice cut in and began a countdown. When the voice intoned "zero," the unmistakable mushroom cloud of an atomic bomb began to fill the screen and President Johnson's voice was heard: "These are the stakes. To make a world in which all of God's children can live, or to go into the dark. We must either love each other or we must die." At the end of the commercial, the message read, "Vote for President Johnson on November 3." This ad, which was withdrawn within a few days of its original airing, put a powerful suggestion in the viewer's mind: electing Barry Goldwater might bring us to nuclear war.[14] This spot is an example of negative advertising and also demonstrates how a political ad evokes strong emotions, thus influencing the voter.

Since the daisy girl advertisement, campaign advertising has blossomed. In June 2016 the British people decided by referendum vote to leave the European Union. Experts predicted chaos in the global markets and the value of the British pound plummeted. Donald Trump, the presumptive Republican nominee at the time, responded by flying to Scotland and holding a press conference at the Trump Turnberry resort. Hillary Clinton turned the moment into a negative 30-second ad. "Every president is tested by world events, but Donald Trump thinks about how his

13 American Press Institute, "How Millennials Get News," March 16, 2015. https://www.americanpressinstitute.org/publications/reports/survey-research/millennials-news/

14 As quoted in Kevin Swint, *The Mudslingers: The 25 Dirtiest Campaigns of All Time* (New York: Greenwood Press, 2008), p. 33.

From the Web ▶

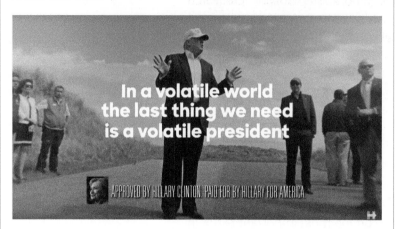

In a volatile world the last thing we need is a volatile president

APPROVED BY HILLARY CLINTON. PAID FOR BY HILLARY FOR AMERICA.

Priorities USA

golf resort can profit from them," a somber voice-over warns. The final message (see screenshot to the left) questions Trump's temperament for the presidency. Negative ads are often sponsored by outside groups rather than by the candidate because the candidate's campaign does not want to appear too negative.

Political advertising can also work to inspire supporters. In 2008, a campaign ad for Barack Obama ran only on YouTube. Rapper will.i.am created an ad based on Obama's concession speech after he lost the New Hampshire primary to Hillary Clinton. The music video, filmed in black and white, became a huge hit on the Internet, with more than 22 million views within a month of its production.[15] Political ads in 2016 took a decidedly negative tone. Donald Trump's paid political ads emphasized America as a country in decline and Trump as an agent of change. Clinton used media to highlight her preparation for office and ran negative ads featuring Trump's caustic comments about women. One particularly effective television ad showed girls looking at their reflection in a mirror while Trump's voice repeated his various insults about womens' physical appearances.

Management of News Coverage

Using political advertising to get a message across to the public is a very expensive tactic. Coverage by the news media, however, is free; it simply demands that the campaign ensure that coverage takes place. In recent years, campaign managers have shown increasing sophistication in creating newsworthy events for journalists to cover. As Doris Graber notes, "[t]o keep a favorable image of their candidates in front of the public, campaign managers arrange newsworthy events to familiarize potential voters with their candidates' best aspects."[16]

The campaign staff uses several methods to try to influence the quantity and type of coverage the campaign receives. First, the campaign staff understands the technical aspects of media coverage—camera angles, necessary equipment, timing, and deadlines—and plans political events to accommodate the press. The campaign organization is aware that political reporters and their sponsors—networks or newspapers—are in competition for the best stories and can be manipulated through the granting of favors, such as a personal interview with the candidate. Campaign managers coordinate events in time for the evening news or the Sunday morning talk shows and work to convince reporters that the event is worth covering.

Today, the art of putting the appropriate **spin** on a story or event is highly developed. Each candidate's or elected official's press advisers, often referred to as **spin doctors**, try to convince journalists that their interpretations of political events are factual. Each political campaign, and the president's own Office of

spin
An interpretation of campaign events or election results that is favorable to the candidate's campaign strategy.

spin doctor
A political campaign adviser who tries to convince journalists of the truth of a particular interpretation of events.

15 Brian Stelter, "Finding Political News Online, the Young Pass It On," *The New York Times*, March 37, 2008.
16 Doris Graber and Johanna Duanway, *Mass Media and American Politics*, 9th ed. (Washington, DC: Congressional Quarterly Press, 2015), p. 320.

Communication, sends information to all the major media, setting out their own version of an event virtually in real time. During the 2016 primaries, candidate Donald Trump was the clear leader in attracting **earned media**. Paul Senatori, a media analytics specialist, said, "Mr. Trump has no weakness in any of the media segments"—in other words, he was strong in every type of earned media, from television to Twitter.[17] CNN's Anderson Cooper described Trump's advantage this way: "News is called news because there's an expectation it'll be *new*—and if the other candidates are offering predictable talking points, then Trump is the only one capable of really making news."[18] By February 2016, Trump had spent $10 million on political advertising, but earned close to $2 billion in free media.

earned media
Sometimes referred to as "free media," earned media is publicity and news coverage attracted without paying for advertising.

Campaign Debates

Debates have been a part of political campaigning in the United States for centuries, but the power of television has greatly amplified their importance, especially for presidential elections. In general, challengers have much more to gain from debating than do incumbents. Challengers hope that the incumbent will make a mistake in the debate and undermine a "presidential" image. Incumbent presidents are loath to debate their challengers because it puts their opponents on an equal footing with them, but the debates have become so widely anticipated that it is difficult for an incumbent to refuse.

Debates can affect the outcome of a race. In 2012, three presidential debates were held along with one vice presidential debate. Sponsored by a nonpartisan national commission, these debates attracted huge audiences. As is the rule in presidential debates, the news media emphasized the demeanor of the candidates in the debates more so than what they actually said about the issues at hand. The Republican nominee Mitt Romney used the first debate to establish himself as a strong, reassuring, yet assertive candidate, whereas President Obama seemed detached from the debate and uncharacteristically subdued. A Gallup poll taken after the debate showed Romney as the victor by a large margin (72 percent to 20 percent).[19] In the second debate both candidates were aggressive and often interrupted each other. President Obama was voted the winner of this debate (51 percent to 38 percent).[20] The final debate saw the president defend his policies and undermine Romney's credentials to be commander in chief. Romney remained assured, but a final Gallup poll declared President Obama the victor (56 percent to 33 percent).[21]

After the debate, each candidate had a room where their spokespeople and surrogates could "spin" the debate and explain in great detail why his or her candidate prevailed. New polls released within a day or two measured whether either candidate had gained an advantage with his performance in the debate. The Romney-Ryan team gained momentum from the debates and benefited from being on equal footing with the president and vice president. The debates also provided extended exposure to a national television audience for the first time.

17 Nicholas Confessore and Karen Yourish, "Measuring Donald Trump's Mammoth Advantage in Free Media," TheUpshot in *The New York Times*, March 15, 2016. http://www.nytimes.com/2016/03/16/upshot/measuring-donald-trumps-mammoth-advantage-in-free-media.html

18 "Anderson Cooper Reveals Key to Trump's 'Earned Media' Lead," 2Paragraphs, April 19, 2016. http://2paragraphs.com/2016/04/anderson-cooper-reveals-key-to-trumps-earned-media-lead/

19 The Gallup Poll, October 8, 2012. http://www.gallup.com/poll/158393/viewers-deem-obama-winner-third-debate.aspx

20 The Gallup Poll, October 12, 2012. http://www.gallup.com/poll/158237/obama-judged-winner-second-debate.aspx

21 The Gallup Poll, October 25, 2012. http://www.gallup.com/poll/158393/viewers-deem-obama-winner-third-debate.aspx

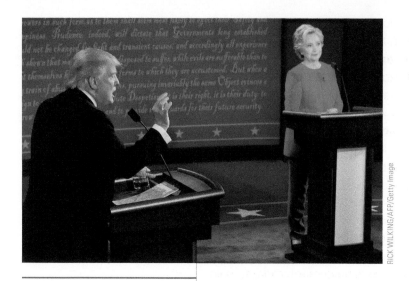

RICK WILKING/AFP/Getty Image

Image 10-5

Republican Donald Trump and Democrat Hillary Clinton in the first presidential debate held at Hofstra University in Hempstead, New York, on September 26, 2016. Over 84 million people watched at home on TV, making it the most-watched televised debate in American history. Livestreaming allowed millions more to watch. Twitter announced that it was "the most tweeted debate ever."

---

did you know?

The average length of a quote, or sound bite, for a candidate has decreased from 49 seconds in 1968 to less than 7 seconds today.

In 2016, the Republican primary field was very large, and debate organizers (media outlets) opted to create a two-tiered system whereby the front-runners debated in prime time and a second group debated in an earlier time slot. Candidates assigned to the second tier (frequently referred to as the "undercard" debate) often tried to argue their way into the main event. Carly Fiorina delivered a strong performance in the first debate even though she was in the second tier and saw her poll numbers rise as potential voters learned more about her. With such a crowded stage, candidates often took to social media to complain about their lack of air time. Donald Trump occupied the center podium and dominated the conversation.

Trump and Clinton debated three times. Polls and pundits agreed that Clinton prevailed each time. In the first debate, Trump appeared unprepared and claimed that his microphone was malfunctioning. The second debate followed the release of an audio recording of Donald Trump bragging to TV host Billy Bush that "when you are a star" you can grab and kiss women without their consent. Trump called the conversation "locker room talk." Indeed, just 90 minutes prior to the second debate, Trump had appeared with four women who had in the past accused Bill Clinton of sexual misconduct. Trump and Clinton did not shake hands before or after the second debate in a breach of political protocol and a sign of the deep rancor between the candidates. In the third and final debate, Trump stunned everyone when he refused to say that he would accept the outcome of the election.

Although debates are justified publicly as an opportunity for the voters to find out how candidates differ on the issues, candidates view the debate as a strategic opportunity to improve their own images or to point out their opponents' failures. Candidates also know that the morning-after interpretation of the debate by the news media may play a crucial role in how the public perceives them.

The Internet and Social Media

Political campaigns began using the Internet for promoting their candidates during the 2004 election campaign. At that time, when two-thirds of all American adults were using the Internet, about 7 percent of those logged onto online campaign activities. By 2008, the Obama campaign perfected the use of the campaign website to contact potential donors, streamlining the process for submitting modest donations. After donating (or merely logging on to Obama's website), supporters were subscribed to an email list; they subsequently received missives from the new president, his campaign manager, and sometimes their own senator.

The Internet was used by both presidential candidates in 2012, not only to advertise the candidates' positions, solicit donations, and offer podcasts of speeches and debates, but also to target messages. Candidates sought email lists sorted by age, gender, and other demographic variables. The 2012 Obama reelection campaign imagined new ways to find voters and encourage them to support the president's campaign. Convinced that using data from voting files could help the campaign hold on to its supporters—while also gaining new voters—the campaign funded a massive data-gathering operation and hired more than 60 analysts to plan the new program. The Obama team, housed in a windowless space known as "The Cave," contracted with data-processing firms, cable TV analysts, and political information brokers to create the plan for the campaign.[22] With a national list of registered voters in hand and a fairly accurate view of who had voted for the president in 2008, the team planned to **microtarget** (focus on specific individuals, types of households, or neighborhoods) voters to assure their votes.

As Election Day approached, both campaigns ramped up their use of the Internet to encourage support for the candidates. The Obama campaign used Facebook to rally supporters to contact their friends in swing states and remind them to vote for the president.[23]

Today, the campaign staff of every candidate running for political office includes a web and social media campaign component—a professional firm hired to create and maintain the campaign website, blog, Facebook page, and Twitter account(s), or else an in-house team. From Hillary Clinton sharing "The Official Hillary 2016 Playlist" on Spotify (featuring such tunes as Katy Perry's "Roar" and Ariana Grande's "Break Free") to Marco Rubio featuring his "Marco Polo" shirt on Instagram, the 2016 presidential candidates learned to diversify their social media portfolios in an effort to raise money, connect with younger voters, and venture onto the virtual campaign trail.

microtarget
To use demographic and consumer data to identify individuals or small groups of people who will receive specific advertising messages.

did you know?
2016 primary candidates Hillary Clinton and Ted Cruz both used social media to announce their candidacies for president.

The Media's Impact: Voters

■ **10.4** Identify ways in which the media influence voters.

The question of exactly how much influence the media have on voting behavior is difficult to answer. Generally, most individuals watch television, read newspapers, or log on to the Internet with certain preconceived ideas about political issues and candidates. These attitudes and opinions act as a kind of perceptual screen that filters out information that makes people feel uncomfortable or that does not fit with their own ideas.

Voters watch campaign commercials and news about political campaigns with "**selective attention**"—that is, they tend to watch those commercials that support the candidates that they already favor and pay more attention to news stories about these candidates. This selectivity also affects their perceptions of the content of a news story or commercial and whether it is remembered. Recent research suggests that for the highly partisan voter, watching his or her preferred political news channel does not enhance partisanship, but watching news from a channel with an opposing view *will* increase the viewer's hostility to that view.[24]

Candidates and their campaign managers have long thought that the media have the most influence on those persons who have not formed an opinion about political candidates or issues. Studies have shown that the flurry of

selective attention
The tendency for individuals to pay attention only to information that reinforces their held beliefs.

22 Sasha Issenberg, "How President Obama's Campaign Used Big Data to Rally Individual Voters, Part I," *MIT Technology Review*, December 16, 2012.

23 Lois Beckett, "Everything We Know (So Far) About Obama's Big Data Tactics," ProPublica, November 29, 2012. http://www .propublica.org/article/everyting-we-knwo-so-far-about-obamas-big-data-operation

24 Kevin Arceneaux and Martin Johnson, *Changing Minds or Changing Channels? Partisan News in an Age of Choice* (Chicago: University of Chicago Press, 2013).

television commercials and debates immediately before Election Day has the greatest impact on those voters who are truly undecided and, for the most part, are not engaged with the political system. Few voters who have already formed their opinions change their minds under the influence of the media.

As Donald Trump's popularity increased and he continued to win delegates in primaries and caucuses around the country, the mainstream media began to reflect on the role they played in his rise. *New York Times* columnist Nicholas Kristoff wrote, "It's not that we shouldn't have covered Trump's craziness, but that we should have aggressively provided context in the form of fact-checks and robust examination of policy proposals. A candidate claiming that his business acumen will enable him to manage America deserved much more scrutiny of his bankruptcies and mediocre investing."[25] The 2016 Republican primaries demonstrated that although media still influence what voters hear and see, they now have to share that role with the far less predictable impact of social media. Trump used social media to recruit and energize supporters, and his use of Twitter to speak directly to his followers has no precedent.

> *did you know?*
>
> Fact checks of inaccurate statements are more persuasive when the consumer and the politician belong to the same political party.

The Government's Regulatory Relationship with Media

■ **10.5** Demonstrate an understanding of the relationship between government and all media sources.

The mass media not only wield considerable power when it comes to political campaigns, but they also, in one way or another, can wield power over the affairs of government and over government officials. Considerable tension exists between the media and government.

Government Regulation of the Media

The United States champions freedom of the press, but regulation of the media does exist, particularly regulation of electronic media.

The First Amendment does not mention electronic media, which did not exist at the time the Bill of Rights was written. The government has assumed much more control over communication via radio, television, and wireless connections than other forms of media, as those connections are made through public airspace via frequencies. The Federal Communications Commission (FCC) was created to distribute and regulate the frequencies, which, in a legal sense, belong to the nation as a whole. As technologies advanced from radio to broadcast television to wireless communications, the FCC has, from time to time, auctioned off more frequencies, even as it held back many frequencies for government use only.

Controlling Ownership of the Media

One of the goals of the FCC (as mandated by Congress) has been to maintain competition in the communications industry. Individuals should have the opportunity to hear or watch many different channels, read more than one newspaper, and access multiple viewpoints. In 1996, Congress passed a piece of legislation that had far-reaching implications for the communications

---

25 John Naughton, "Why Social Media Is the Real Trump Card in the US Election," *The Guardian*, April 3, 2016. http://www.theguardian.com/commentisfree/2016/apr/03/donald-trump-internet-success-twitter-us-election-media

Image 10-6
Savannah Guthrie and Matt Lauer interview 2016 Republican presidential candidate Donald Trump during NBC's Today Trump Town Hall at Rockefeller Plaza in New York City soon after he clinched the Republican nomination. Reporters began referring to him as the "presumptive nominee" since the nomination was not official until after the Republican Convention held in Cleveland, Ohio, in July.

industry: the Telecommunications Act. The act amended the Communications Act of 1934, which created the FCC and transferred regulation of interstate telephone services to the FCC. The Telecommunications Act of 1996 included the Internet within the broadcasting definition and sought to deregulate converging broadcasting and telecommunications markets. A single corporation, such as Time Warner Cable or The Walt Disney Company (which owns the American Broadcasting Company [ABC]), can offer long-distance and local telephone services, cable television, satellite television, and Internet services, as well as libraries of films and entertainment. The act opened the door to competition and led to greater options for consumers, who now can choose among multiple competitors for all of these services delivered to the home. At the same time, it launched a race among competing companies to control media ownership.

Increased Media Concentration

Congress and the FCC have tried to create a communications market that allows for competing voices. One measure of a conglomerate's impact is "audience reach," or the percentage of the national viewing public that has access to the conglomerate's outlets. The FCC places an upper limit on audience reach, known as the "audience-reach cap." In 2004, the FCC raised the national audience-reach cap from 35 percent to 45 percent and allowed a corporation to own a newspaper and a television station in the same market. Congress rebelled against this new rule, however, and pushed the national audience-reach cap back to 39 percent.[26] Nevertheless, a corporation can still own up to three TV stations in its largest market. There are only a few independent news operations left in the entire country.

This concentration has led to the disappearance of localism in the news. Costly locally produced news cannot be shown anywhere except in its local

26 Federal Communications Commission, "Rules Adopted in the Quadrennial Review Order." http://transition.fcc.gov/ownership/rules.html

market. In contrast, the costs of producing a similar show for national broadcast can be amortized over millions and millions of viewers and paid for by higher revenues from national advertisers. Another concern, according to former media mogul Ted Turner, is that the rise of media conglomerates may lead to a decline in democratic debate.[27] The emergence of independent news websites, blogs, and podcasts helps serve to remedy this problem. Consequently, the increased concentration of traditional media news organizations may not seem as worrisome as it did in the not-too-distant past.

Government Control of Content

The U.S. Supreme Court has often been slow to extend free speech and free press guarantees to new media. In 1915, the Court held that "as a matter of common sense," free-speech protections did not apply to cinema. Only in 1952 did the Court find that motion pictures were covered by the First Amendment.[28] In contrast, the Court extended full protection to the Internet almost immediately by striking down provisions of the 1996 Telecommunications Act.[29] Cable TV also received broad protection in 2000.[30]

Control of Broadcasting

Although the Supreme Court has held that the First Amendment is relevant to radio and television, it has never extended full protection to these media. The Court has used several arguments to justify this stance, the first of which was the scarcity of broadcast frequencies. The Court later held that the government could restrict "indecent" programming based on the "pervasive" presence of broadcasting in the home.[31] On this basis, the FCC was granted the authority to fine broadcasters for indecency or profanity.

Indecency in broadcasting became a major issue in 2004. In the first three months of that year, the FCC levied fines that exceeded those imposed in the previous nine years combined. Triggering incidents included the commentary of Howard Stern on the radio and Janet Jackson's infamous "wardrobe malfunction" at the Super Bowl. The FCC asserted its right to regulate indecency even on cable channels. In 2012, the Supreme Court heard two cases from the Fox network and, in both cases, the Court set aside the fines, holding that the FCC had not given fair notice of the change in FCC policy.[32] Although the decision did not limit the power of the FCC to fine stations for indecency, neither did it enhance that power. Most observers believed that the FCC needed to rethink its policies.

Not only does the FCC enforce regulations with regard to indecent language or images in the media, it also has the authority to issue fines for other violations of law or its regulations. In 2014, the FCC fined Viacom, ESPN, and NBCUniversal $1.9 million for broadcasting advertisements for a movie that featured the sound of the Emergency Broadcast Alert System warning siren. FCC policy prohibits the broadcasting of that signal unless it is a test

---

27 Ted Turner, "My Beef with Big Media," *Washington Monthly* (July–August, 2004). http://www.washingtonmonthly.com/features/2004/0407.turner.html
28 *Joseph Burstyn, Inc. v. Wilson*, 343 U.S. 495 (1952).
29 *Reno v. American Civil Liberties Union*, 521 U.S. 844 (1997).
30 *United States v. Playboy Entertainment Group*, 529 U.S. 803 (2000).
31 *FCC v. Pacifica Foundation*, 438 U.S. 230 (1978). In this case, the Court banned seven swear words (famously used by comedian George Carlin) during hours when children could hear them.
32 *FCC v. Fox Television Stations*, 132 U.S. 2307.

or a real emergency. Other fines have been issued in recent years for a station being silent on the air for too long, for stations failing to properly advertise job openings to their community, and for not airing sponsorship identification properly.[33]

Government Control of the Media during the Second Gulf War During the First Gulf War in 1991, the U.S. government was strongly criticized for not providing accurate information to the media. Stung by this criticism, the Bush administration tried a two-pronged strategy during the Second Gulf War in 2003. Every day, reporters at the central command post in Qatar were able to hear briefings from top commanders. (Reporters complained, though, that they did not hear enough about the true progress of the war.) The administration also allowed more than 500 journalists to travel with the combat forces as "embedded" journalists. Reports from the field were very favorable to the military. This was understandable, given that the journalists quickly identified with the troops and their difficulties. The Bush administration, however, was unable to control reports from foreign media.

The Government's Attempt to Control the Media after the September 11, 2001, Attacks Certainly, since September 11, 2001, government secrecy has increased, sometimes (apparently) with the public's acceptance. Senator Patrick Leahy (D-VT) has argued that the First Amendment would have trouble winning ratification today if it were proposed as a constitutional amendment. He based this assertion on a Knight Foundation survey that found that almost 40 percent of 110,000 high school students believed that newspapers should have to get "government approval" of news articles before they are published.

The charter for the Department of Homeland Security, created soon after the September 11 terrorist attacks, includes a provision that allows certain groups to stamp "critical infrastructure information" on the top of documents when they submit information to Homeland Security. This information might include the maps of waterlines or the plans of nuclear power plants. The public has no right to see this information. Additionally, more and more government documents have been labeled "secret" so that they do not have to be revealed to the public. Despite such measures, since the war on terror and the second war in Iraq, there have been numerous intelligence leaks to the press, chief among them Edward Snowden's revelations about NSA surveillance. The tension between needed intelligence secrecy and the public's "right to know" continues to create both legal and military problems.

Net Neutrality **Net neutrality** is the principle that Internet service providers should enable access to all content and applications, regardless of the source, and without favoring or blocking particular products or websites. In December 2017, the FCC voted to repeal its net neutrality rules. In practical terms, this means that we would each experience the Internet differently—some of us could get our information faster than others and the content available to one might not be available to all. Congress could overturn the regulation, but to date they have not. Individual states may try to take action to require net neutrality for providers operating within their borders.

net neutrality
Net neutrality is the movement to keep the Internet "free" (not in monetary terms, but rather in accessibility terms) so that all people can enjoy equal and unfettered access. The Internet's version of "free press."

---

33 For an up-to-date report of FCC fines and penalties, take a look at the Broadcast Law Blog, http://www.broadcast lawblog .com/articles/fcc-fines

Press Freedom and Journalist Safety Abroad

The First Amendment to the Constitution guarantees freedom of expression in the United States by prohibiting Congress from restricting the press or the rights of individuals to speak freely. As a result, there are few restrictions on the press in the United States, and journalists are free to gather and disseminate information. This is not so in many other countries. The Committee to Protect Journalists (CPJ) is an independent nonprofit that promotes freedom of the press worldwide and defends the right of journalists to report the news without fear of reprisal.*

Controlling the News in China

In some nations, the media exist to serve as the government's mouthpiece. Chinese President Xi Jinping explained it this way: "All news media run by the party must work to speak for the party's will and its propositions, and protect the party's authority and unity."** Foreign companies operating in China are no longer allowed to publish and distribute online content. The sweeping ban covers text, video, maps, games, digital books, art, and literature. As a result, Apple's iTunes Books and iTunes Movies were shut down in April 2016. "China must improve management of cyberspace and work to ensure high-quality content with positive voices creating a healthy, positive culture that is a force for good," a report by the state-run news service Xinhua quoted Mr. Xi as saying. Chinese journalist Wan Jing was sentenced in 2016 to prison, convicted of "picking quarrels and provoking trouble" with her writing. According to the CPJ, China is the world's leading jailer of journalists.

The Russians Have Lost Many Press Freedoms, Too

After the end of communism in Russia, a thriving independent press arose. Russians could read or hear all sorts of political views. Since Vladimir Putin reclaimed the office of president, most opposition journalists have been silenced in one way or another. Privately owned television stations have been eliminated, and independent radio stations are often blocked. In early 2014, as Russia began to move into Crimea, an eastern area of Ukraine, the Russian "federal media regulator" blocked several independent online news sources because, in the eyes of the government, they were violating a new law that prohibits any call for an unsanctioned mass gathering.***

The Russian government's control of its nation's media was extended quickly into Crimea. As soon as Russian troops were posted at Ukrainian military bases in that region, all Crimean television station signals were immediately replaced by Russian television broadcasts. The producers, journalists, and technical staff watched in amazement as their signal was replaced by a Russian station.****

Journalists At Risk

Every year, hundreds of journalists are attacked, imprisoned, or killed. Among the most dangerous countries for journalists are Iraq and Syria. Since 1992, the CPJ reports that 1,313 journalists have been killed. CPJ investigates the death of every journalist to confirm that a journalist was murdered in direct reprisal for his or her work. In Syria, CPJ has confirmed 122 journalist killings since 1992. Journalists covering corruption, human rights, war, and politics are at greatest risk. The CPJ also maintains an "Impunity Index," a measure of how often a journalist's killer is allowed to go free. Iraq has the world's worst record on impunity. No convictions have been obtained in 186 journalist slayings in the past decade.

For Critical Analysis

1. In what ways has the evolution of digital media made it both easier and more difficult for a government to control the news?

2. Why are journalists at such risk around the world? What can be done to protect the public's right to free and unfettered access to information and news?

*Committee to Protect Journalists https://cpj.org/about/

** Edward Wong, "Xi Jinping's News Alert: Chinese Media Must Serve the Party," *The New York Times*, February 22, 2016. http://nyti.ms/21aETNm

*** "Kremlin Tightens Censorship as Tensions Over Ukraine Increase," March 14, 2014. http://www.freedomhouse.org/article/kermlin-tightens-censorship-astensions-over-Ukraine-Increase

**** Damien McElroy, "Russian TV Swamps Airwaves in Crimea Propaganda War," *Daily Telegraph*, March 13, 2014. http://www.telegraph.co.uk

The Public's Right to Media Access

Does the public have a right to **media access**? Both the FCC and the courts have gradually taken the stance that citizens do have a right of access to the media, particularly the electronic media. The argument is that because the airwaves are public, the government has the right to dictate how they are used. Congress could, for example, pass a law requiring the broadcast networks to provide free airtime to candidates, as is the case in some European nations. Senator John McCain of Arizona, a major proponent of campaign-finance reform, proposed legislation that would provide such free airtime. Broadcast networks that make bigger profits in election years quietly oppose such a law.

Regardless of the preferences of the government or broadcast corporations, technology has given citizens the tools to make their voices heard. YouTube hosts thousands of videos produced by ordinary citizens: some opine on policy problems, and others document issues such as pollution and dangerous traffic conditions. Cell phone users are the photojournalists of the twenty-first century, and their work is welcomed by television stations. Because cable and satellite operators do not give airtime to individuals, easy access to the Internet has made those media irrelevant for public access.

media access
The public's right of access to the media. The Federal Communications Commission and the courts have gradually taken the stance that citizens do have a right to media access.

Bias in the Media

■ **10.6** Critically analyze news stories published by any form of the media.

Many studies have been undertaken to try to identify the sources and direction of **bias** in the media, and these studies have reached different conclusions. Some claim that the press exhibits a liberal bias. Others conclude that the press shows a conservative bias. Still others do not see any notable partisan bias (see Figure 10–3).

bias
An inclination or a preference that interferes with impartial judgment.

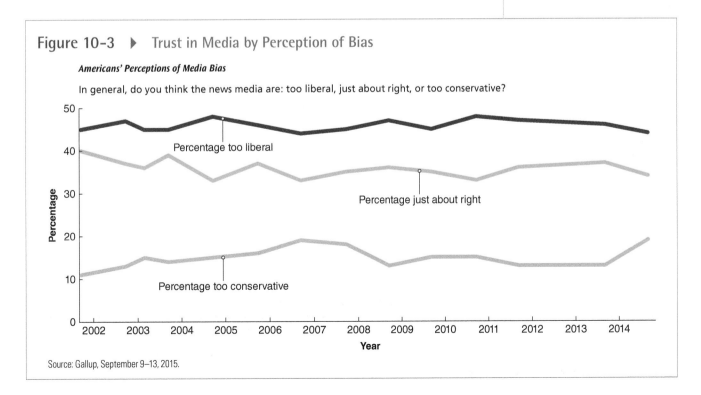

Figure 10-3 ▶ Trust in Media by Perception of Bias

Americans' Perceptions of Media Bias

In general, do you think the news media are: too liberal, just about right, or too conservative?

Source: Gallup, September 9–13, 2015.

Do the Media Have a Partisan Bias?

In a classic study conducted in the 1980s, researchers found that media producers, editors, and reporters (the "media elite") exhibited a notably liberal and "left-leaning" bias in their news coverage.[34] Since then, the contention that the media have a liberal bias has been repeated time and again. In 2005, the University of Connecticut's Department of Public Policy surveyed 300 journalists nationwide about whom they voted for in the 2004 presidential election. The Democratic challenger, John Kerry, received 52 percent of their votes, whereas Bush received only 19 percent (27 percent of those queried either refused to disclose their vote or did not vote).[35] The results are consistent with the surveys done over the last two decades by the Pew Center for the People and the Press. However, even if journalists hold liberal beliefs, those private views should have no bearing on reporting the news due to the standard of objectivity.

The controversy over conservatives' perception of liberal bias in the media has fostered the growth of websites and centers to track bias on the left and on the right. The Media Matters website catalogs the inflammatory statements of conservative talk show hosts and bloggers, and the Media Research Center website tracks supposedly liberal bias in the media. Generally, when surveyed, the public responds to the question of media bias as one would expect: conservatives think there is a liberal bias and liberals find a conservative bias. According to a Pew poll, there has been an increase in the percentage of people who see a great amount of bias, but a decrease in those seeing any bias at all.[36] Such data suggest that most people pay minimal attention to political news and do not see bias in the media (see the screen captures).

A Racial Bias?

racial profiling
Making negative assumptions about a person or class of persons based on racial characteristics.

Racial profiling is the act of routinely making negative assumptions about individuals based on race. The term was first used to describe the behavior of certain police officers who habitually stopped African American motorists more frequently than white ones, often on minor pretexts. African Americans have described these incidents as stops for "driving while black." Some observers have charged that the media—television in particular—engage in racial profiling in their reporting on minority group members. In 2012, for example, the news media covered the shooting of a young African American man, Trayvon Martin, by a civilian neighborhood watch volunteer, George Zimmerman. Initially, Zimmerman was not charged with a crime because he claimed the shooting was in self-defense. Although there were many accusations of bias in the news coverage on all sides, there is little doubt that Trayvon Martin was portrayed as a strong, young black man walking suspiciously in a neighborhood at night.

Those who believe that the media engage in racial profiling point to common stereotypes that journalists often use when illustrating news stories or to the characters portrayed in television drama shows. Critics of racial profiling also argue that African Americans are regularly used to illustrate drug abusers or dealers, even though a majority of users are white, and that images of criminals in general are disproportionately black. A study compared the portrayal of African Americans,

---

34 S. Robert Lichter, Stanley Rothman, and Linda S. Lichter, *The Media Elite* (New York: Adler and Adler, 1986).
35 University of Connecticut, "National Polls of Journalists and the American Public," May 16, 2005.
36 "Perceptions of Bias, News Knowledge," Pew Research Center for the People and the Press, February 7, 2012. http://www.people-press.org.2012/02/07/section-3-perceptions-of-bias-news-knowledge

Hispanics, and whites on prime-time television to a similar study conducted in 2000. The research found that 74 percent of the actors during a two-week time period were Caucasian, 16 percent were African American, and only 5 percent were Latino.[37] Although these proportions underrepresent Hispanics, the more important concern lies in how these actors are characterized. Newer storylines tended to ridicule Hispanics more than those in 2000; Hispanics were often portrayed with heavy accents and as less intelligent, and African American characters were more likely to be immoral than whites or Hispanics.[38]

Greater diversity among newsroom staff members is a goal for most news outlets. The 2012 census of newspapers conducted by the American Society of News Editors (ASNE) showed that about 12.3 percent (4,700 of 38,000) newspaper employees are minorities. According to the ASNE, that percentage has remained steady for about a decade. This organization strives to work until the demographics of the newsroom mirror those of the general population.

A Gender Bias?

Do the media cover men and women differently? Are the guests on the Sunday morning news talk shows more likely to be men? Can presidential candidates expect a more gender-neutral media environment? The answer to all of these questions is yes, a fact that reflects the changing norms of media when it comes to gender bias. At the 2015 White House Correspondents' Association dinner, comedian Cecily Strong asked all members of the press in the ballroom to raise their hands and vow: "I solemnly swear not to talk about Hillary's appearance, because that is not journalism."[39] Researchers have been studying the coverage of female and male political candidates for nearly 25 years. The earliest studies found that media stereotyped female candidates by emphasizing feminine traits and issues, by focusing on appearance over policy positions, and by giving them less coverage overall. Coverage of women in politics has been characterized by the three Hs: hair, husbands, and hemlines. More recent studies, however, have found a trend toward more equitable treatment of men and women seeking public office. This is particularly true when the office is at the local or state level. Presidential politics is a different matter. In 2008 when Hillary Clinton campaigned for the Democratic nomination and Sarah Palin was chosen as Republican John McCain's running mate, the coverage was heavily gendered. Palin, for example, was often portrayed as a sex object, whereas Hillary Clinton was ridiculed for her pantsuits and lack of femininity. In anticipation of 2016, Clinton supporters warned media that they would be looking for "coded sexism" in coverage of the campaign. Words like *ambitious* are often used in a complimentary fashion when applied to men, but negatively when characterizing women. Ironically, 2016 featured plenty of sexism, but it was largely limited to the speeches and Twitter feed of Donald Trump.

Another form of gender bias in the media is found on the Sunday morning television news shows like *Face the Nation* and *Meet the Press*. Media Matters found that male guests greatly outnumbered female guests on such broadcasts

37 Elizabeth Monk-Turner, Mary Heiserman, Crystle Johnson, Vanity Cotton, and Manny Jackson, "The Portrayal of Racial Minorities on Prime Time Television: A Replication of the Mastro and Greenberg Study a Decade Later," *Studies in Popular Culture* (Spring 2010) 32 (2): 101–114.
38 Ibid.
39 Kelly Dittmar, "2016 Outlook: Gender Bias, Media, and the Cause for Concern in Presidential Politics." Presidential Gender Watch 2016, May 1, 2015. http://presidentialgenderwatch.org/2016-outlook-gender-bias-media-and-the-cause-for-concern -in-presidential-politics/

Image 10-7

The media has been criticized for sexualizing female candidates. This picture of Sarah Palin, speaking as a Donald Trump surrogate, is a good example. Without this caption you likely could not identify the former governor of Alaska and Republican vice presidential candidate. Why does the media continue this practice? What are the consequences for women running for public office?

Andrew Harrer/Bloomberg/Getty Images

and on cable political talk shows. More than 70 percent of guests were men on all but MSNBC programs (including on ABC, NBC, CBS, Fox, and CNN). In one-on-one interviews, nearly 90 percent of guests were male.[40] An organization, "Name It. Change It." works to end sexist coverage of women candidates by all members of the press—from bloggers to radio hosts to television pundits—under the slogan "when you attack one woman, you attack all women."[41]

In every election, especially at the national level, candidates charge that they are not getting fair coverage in the media. Every campaign organization has its own vision of what it would consider "fair" and "unbiased" news coverage. Studies of the opposing side's campaign and data will be produced by liberal and conservative think tanks alike, and they will find some source for bias. For journalists, the first goal is to report the news, flattering or not, and to keep their viewers and readers informed. The candidacy of Donald Trump presented the news media with a conundrum. Since the media is a commercial business, the more outrageous Trump behaved, the more viewers tuned in to watch. Megyn Kelly formally of Fox News, one of the few journalists to challenge Trump, claimed that his control of the media is a major advantage. During the latter half March of 2016 the press began to report on itself in articles titled, "How Trump Hacked the Media" (Nate Silver, FiveThirtyEight),[42] "How Donald Trump Bent Television to His Will" (Kyle Blaine, BuzzFeed),[43] and "My Shared Shame: The Media Helped Make Trump" (Nicholas Kristof, the *New York Times*).[44] In each case, the author reflects on tension between media as a business and media as a source of accurate and trusted information. Just what will the public expect from future political journalists as a result of the 2016 election?

40 Media Matters, "Report: Gender Diversity on the 2013 Sunday Morning Political Talk Shows" January 30, 2014. http://mediamatters.org/research/2014/01/30/report-gender-diversity-on-the-2013-sunday-morn/197825

41 http://www.nameitchangeit.org/

42 Nate Silver, "How Trump Hacked the Media," FiveThirtyEight, March 30, 2016. http://fivethirtyeight.com/features/how-donald-trump-hacked-the-media/

43 Kyle Blaine, "How Donald Trump Bent Television to His Will," BuzzFeed, March 18, 2016. https://www.buzzfeed.com/kyleblaine/how-donald-trump-bent-television-to-his-will?utm_term=.srxK0Zqdy#.rpDbXr1Rp

44 Nicholas Kristof, "My Shared Shame: The Media Helped Make Trump," *The New York Times*, March 26, 2016. http://www.nytimes.com/2016/03/27/opinion/sunday/my-shared-shame-the-media-helped-make-trump.html

Key Terms

agenda setting 366	**media** 357	**racial profiling** 380
bias 379	**media access** 379	**selective attention** 373
blog 363	**microtarget** 373	**social media** 357
blogosphere politics 363	**net neutrality** 377	**spin** 370
earned media 371	**podcasting** 364	**spin doctor** 370
electronic media 358	**press secretary** 361	**White House press corps** 361
framing 367	**priming** 366	**yellow journalism** 358
managed news 358	**public agenda** 366	

Chapter Summary

■ **10.1** The media have always played a significant role in American politics. In the 1800s and earlier, however, news traveled slowly, and politics was controlled by small groups whose members communicated personally. The high-speed rotary press and the telegraph led to self-supported newspapers and mass readership.

■ **10.1** Broadcast media (television and radio) have been important means of communication since the early twentieth century. New technologies, such as the Internet, social networking sites, and blogs, offer news organizations more platforms for reaching the public. The public also has access to these platforms.

■ **10.2** The media are enormously important in American politics today. They perform five main political functions: (1) provide information, (2) identify problems and set the public agenda, (3) investigate and report on wrongdoing, (4) socialize new generations, and (5) provide a political forum for dialogue and debate.

■ **10.3** The media exert considerable influence during political campaigns and over the affairs of government and government officials by focusing attention on political actors. Today's political campaigns use political advertising, expert management of news coverage, and social media. For presidential candidates, how they appear in presidential debates is of major importance.

■ **10.4** Today's campaigns rely much more heavily on the Internet to reach potential voters and donors. Candidates and their organizations use email, podcasting, websites, blogs, and downloadable video and audio to involve people in campaigns. The use of these techniques does rely heavily on self-selection by the user, but the techniques are cheap and effective and may work to get the user to feel an attachment to the candidate or public official.

■ **10.5** The relationship between the media and the president is close; each uses the other—sometimes positively, sometimes negatively. The media play an important role in investigating the government, in getting government officials to understand better the needs and desires of American society, and in setting the public agenda.

■ **10.5** The electronic media are subject to government regulation. Many FCC rules pertain to ownership of TV and radio stations. Legislation has removed many rules about co-ownership of several forms of media, although the most recent steps taken by Congress have been to halt any further deregulation.

■ **10.6** Studies of bias in the media have reached different conclusions. Some claim that the press has a liberal bias; others contend that the press shows a conservative bias. Still others conclude that the press is biased toward its own self-interest—the need to gain higher ratings and thus more advertising revenues. Other studies have found other types of biases, such as a bias in favor of the status quo or a bias against losers. Educated consumers of the news should avail themselves of multiple news sources, use fact-checking websites, and ask questions about the motivation for a particular news story.

Selected Resources

PRINT RESOURCES

Arceneaux, Kevin and Martin Johnson. *Changing Minds or Changing Channels? Partisan News in an Age of Choice* (Chicago: University of Chicago Press, 2013). The authors look at the contention that increased selective viewing of television news increases polarization and find that the multiplicity of news sources actually dampens the partisanship of the electorate.

Graber, Doris. *On Media: Making Sense of Politics* (New York: Oxford University Press, 2011). Graber's research focuses on what people actually learn from the news. In this book, she contends that people make sensible decisions about politics based on information that they gain from the news and from their circle of contacts.

Ladd, Jonathan. *Why Americans Hate the Media and How It Matters* (Princeton, NJ: Princeton University Press, 2011). Ladd suggests that the increased competition between media sources has led to more sensationalism in the news. The polarization and increased partisanship of the public can be traced to the rise of the highly competitive news business.

Lehrer, Jim. *Tension City: Inside the Presidential Debates* (New York: Random House Trade Paperbacks, 2012). This volume reveals the background stories of more than 40 years of presidential campaign debates as viewed by a veteran and respected Public Broadcasting Service (PBS) journalist.

McChesney, Robert Waterman and John Nichols. *The Death and Life of American Journalism: The Media Revolution that Will Begin the World Again* (New York: Nation Books, 2011). The authors, two well-regarded journalism scholars, review the technological and social forces that have led to the decline of the print media. They believe, however, that a new future for journalism lies in hybrid forms of news media.

MEDIA RESOURCES

All the President's Men—A 1976 film produced by Warner Brothers and starring Dustin Hoffman and Robert Redford as the two *Washington Post* reporters (Bob Woodward and Carl Bernstein) who broke the story of the Watergate scandal. The film is an excellent portrayal of the *Washington Post* newsroom (at a moment when newsrooms really did set the public agenda) and the decisions that editors make in such situations.

Control Room—A 2004 documentary film about Al Jazeera, the Arab world's most popular news outlet, depicting the international perception of the Iraq War. The film has been criticized by many U.S. officials for presenting a pro-Iraqi bias.

Good Night and Good Luck—The 2005 film, which depicts Edward R. Murrow's work to discredit the communist witch hunts being conducted by Senator Joe McCarthy, is George Clooney's tribute to the early period of television journalism when news anchors like Murrow were the heroes of the media.

Shattered Glass—Released in 2003, the movie details the fall of a journalist who is found to have fabricated the stories in more than half of his articles. This film explores the importance of publishing the truth rather than sensationalism.

The Social Network—The 2010 Oscar-winning film details the founding of Facebook and the ensuing conflicts over the ownership of this blockbuster social media company.

ONLINE RESOURCES

American Journalism Review—includes features from the magazine and original content created specifically for online reading: www.ajr.org

Huffington Post—a leading source of news and opinion on subjects ranging from politics to entertainment, some of the nation's most outstanding columnists are found on the "Huffpost" website: www.huffingtonpost.com

Pew Research Center for the People and the Press—provides up-to-date research on the public and its use of the media,

including an annual State of the Media report: www.people-press.org

Politico—a political journalism outlet covering primarily U.S. politics and a good source for coverage of campaigns and election news: www.politico.com

TED (Technology, Entertainment, Design)—TED talks are short, provocative presentations of ideas and a multitude of topics: www.ted.com/talks

The Congress

Members of the House of Representatives and the Senate assemble for a joint session to count and validate the Electoral College Votes on January 6, 2017.

MIKE THEILER/United Press International (UPI)/NEWSCOM

LEARNING OBJECTIVES

After reading this chapter, you will be able to:

■ **11.1** Describe the major powers of the Congress as granted by the U.S. Constitution.

■ **11.2** Explain the differences between the House of Representatives and the Senate with regard to their constituencies, terms of office, powers, and political processes.

■ **11.3** Describe the processes of reapportionment and redistricting.

■ **11.4** Discuss the importance of committees to the lawmaking process and to the ability of members of Congress to do their jobs.

■ **11.5** Describe the leadership structure in each house of Congress, noting the differences between the House and the Senate.

■ **11.6** Demonstrate how a bill becomes a law and explain how the different processes in the House and the Senate influence legislating.

■ **11.7** Explain how the federal budget is constructed and the legislative process for approving the budget.

What if...   Congress Had Time Limits?

Background

The first year of the 1st Congress, held from 1789 to 1791, members met from March to September, passing necessary legislation and organizing the government. The next year, they met from January to August and then reconvened from December to March. During the next five decades, Congress conducted most of its business in short sessions, with long recess periods for the members to maintain their farms and businesses back home.

Today, the U.S. Congress is still organized as two one-year sessions. The respective houses adjourn at the very end of one year and then reconvene about three weeks later. The House calendar designates the days that members can spend in their districts meeting with constituents and, in many cases, fundraising. Currently, the House works more full weeks than in the past, but it has also given itself more days at home for "district work." Today's House and Senate do not want to adjourn formally because they fear the executive branch will take action while they are not in session. This work pattern allows for difficult issues (such as raising the debt ceiling) to go unresolved for many months. Other measures, such as tax relief or the extension of unemployment benefits, may persist for short periods with no attempt to resolve underlying issues. Congress may, by its own procedures, avoid such unpleasant tasks as finalizing a fiscal-year budget. The government can run on a series of continuing resolutions. The low 2018 public approval ratings of Congress, along with the recent lack of congressional productivity, might make one wonder about an admittedly radical idea.

What If Congress Had Time Limits?

In contrast to Congress, many state constitutions limit the days and weeks that state legislatures can meet. The Kentucky legislature may only meet for 60 "legislative days" in even-numbered years and 30 days in odd-numbered years. In Nevada, the legislature may meet for 120 calendar days. In Missouri, the legislature must conclude its business by May 30. Additionally, most state constitutions require that the state's budget must be balanced and the government cannot continue without a budget for the fiscal year. In some states, if the legislature does not complete the work on a budget, the governor may complete the task.

If the U.S. Congress were limited by a constitutional amendment to meeting for only six months, could the body be effective? Six months to work, followed by six months to be in one's home state, would increase pressure to complete the year's business, including the budget and tax issues, before adjournment. Both political parties might feel pressure to compromise and pass legislation before going home to explain their votes to their constituents. Given the large amount of work to do, members could easily spend as much time in daily floor sessions as

they do now. Communication with their constituents back home could be handled by live conferences over the Internet.

Depending on the wording of the amendment, it would be possible to consider membership in the House or Senate a part-time job, as in many state legislatures. This would mean, perhaps, paying the members a part-time or reduced salary, expecting them to maintain a career in the working world. That change alone would make individuals less likely to see election to Congress as a career. Congress might return to a legislature of citizen-legislators much as the founders envisioned. The expenses of supporting the Congress could be greatly decreased because the large amount of staff on Capitol Hill would no longer be necessary, and congresspersons would not be constantly traveling back and forth to Washington.

Disadvantages of a Part-Time Congress

Obviously, a part-time Congress would have little ability to deal with domestic or international crises. In the states, the governor has the ability to call the legislature back to the capitol in special session. The president can also call Congress into special session to deal with emergencies.

Would making membership a part-time job cost the body in terms of expertise and effectiveness? Scholars who have studied the effects of term limits on state legislatures say that having more frequent turnover of members reduces the knowledge available to make good decisions. It takes several years for a member of Congress to become well versed in public policy in any one specific area or to understand the budget, say, of the Department of Defense. Making their jobs part-time would make it harder to gain the expertise necessary to offset the expertise of either bureaucrats or lobbyists for special interests. Both of those groups would still be engaged in fighting for their interests full time. The executive would likely gain power if the Congress worked only six months a year. The president would be free to make more interim appointments without congressional scrutiny and to dominate the media with his or her agenda. Members of Congress would be playing "catch up" when they returned to Washington after their six months at home.

For Critical Analysis

1. Would forcing members of Congress to adjourn at a specified time motivate them to pass legislation or to leave decisions to the president?

2. Would having a part-time Congress encourage more members to retire earlier and make it possible for more individuals to serve in Congress?

Most Americans view Congress in a less-than-flattering light. In recent years, Congress has appeared to be deeply split, highly partisan in its conduct, and not very responsive to public needs. Polls show that public approval has fallen to record lows. Yet, individual members of Congress often receive much higher approval ratings from the voters in their districts. This is one of the paradoxes of the relationship between the people and Congress. Members of the public hold the institution in relatively low regard compared with the satisfaction they express with their individual representatives.

Part of the explanation for these seemingly contradictory appraisals is that congresspersons spend considerable time and effort serving their **constituents**. If the federal bureaucracy makes a mistake, the senator's or representative's office tries to resolve the issue. Members of Congress spend considerable time and effort developing what is sometimes called a "**homestyle**" to gain the trust and appreciation of their constituents through service, local appearances, and the creation of local offices.

Congress, however, was also created to work for the nation as a whole. The representatives and senators in their Washington work are creating what might be called a "**hillstyle**," which refers to their work on legislation and in party leadership to create laws and policies for our nation.[1] This chapter describes the functions of Congress, including constituent service, representation, lawmaking, and oversight of the government; how the members of Congress are elected; how Congress organizes itself when it meets; and how bills pass through the legislative process.

The Functions of Congress

America's founders believed that the bulk of the power to be exercised by a national government should be in the hands of the legislature because the members were elected by the people or, in the case of the Senate, by the states. The leading role envisioned for Congress is apparent from its primacy in the Constitution. Article I deals with the structure, the powers, and the operation of Congress, beginning in Section 1 with an application of the basic principle of separation of powers: "All legislative Powers herein granted shall be vested in a Congress of the United States, which shall consist of a Senate and House of Representatives." These legislative powers are spelled out in detail in Article I and elsewhere.

The **bicameralism** of Congress—its division into two legislative houses—was in part the result of the Connecticut Compromise, which tried to balance the large-state population advantage, reflected in the House, and the small-state demand for equality in policymaking, satisfied in the Senate. Beyond that, the two chambers of Congress also reflected the social-class biases of the founders. They wished to balance the interests and the numerical superiority of the common citizens with the property interests of the less numerous landowners, bankers, and merchants. They achieved this by providing in Sections 2 and 3 of Article I that members of the House of Representatives should be elected directly by "the People," whereas members of the Senate were to be chosen by the elected representatives sitting in state legislatures, who were more likely to be members of the elite. (In 1913, the passage of the

constituents
One of the persons represented by a legislator or other elected or appointed official.

homestyle
The actions and behaviors of a member of Congress aimed at the constituents and intended to win the support and trust of the voters at home.

hillstyle
The actions and behaviors of a member of Congress in Washington DC, intended to promote policies and the member's own career aspirations.

bicameralism
The division of a legislature into two separate assemblies.

---

1   Richard Fenno, *Home Style: House Members in Their Districts* (Boston: Little, Brown, 1978).

lawmaking
The process of establishing the legal rules that govern society.

logrolling
An arrangement in which two or more members of Congress agree in advance to support each other's bills.

representation
The function of members of Congress as elected officials representing the views of their constituents.

trustee
A legislator who acts according to her or his conscience and the broad interests of the entire society.

Seventeenth Amendment, which provides that senators also are to be elected directly by the people, resulted in the change of the latter provision.) The logic of separate constituencies and separate interests underlying the bicameral Congress was reinforced by differences in length of tenure. Members of the House are required to face the electorate every two years, whereas senators can serve for a much more secure term of six years—even longer than the four-year term provided for the president. Furthermore, the senators' terms are staggered so that only one-third of the senators face the electorate every two years, along with all of the House members.

The bicameral structure of Congress was designed to enable the legislative body and its members to perform certain functions for the political system. These functions include lawmaking, representation, service to constituents, oversight, public education, and conflict resolution. Of these, the two most important and the ones most often in conflict are lawmaking and representation.

The Lawmaking Function

The most obvious function of any legislature is **lawmaking**. Congress is the highest elected body in the country, charged with making binding rules for all Americans. Lawmaking requires decisions about the size of the federal budget, health-care reform and gun control, and the long-term prospects for war or peace. A majority of the bills that Congress acts on originate in the executive branch, and many other bills are traceable to interest groups and political party organizations. Through the processes of compromise and **logrolling** (offering to support a fellow member's bill in exchange for that member's promise to support your bill in the future), as well as debate and discussion, backers of legislation attempt to fashion a winning majority coalition to create policies for the nation.

The Representation Function

Representation includes both representing the desires and demands of the constituents in the member's home district or state and representing larger national interests such as farmers or the environment. Because the interests of constituents in a specific district may be in conflict with the demands of national policy, the representation function is often at variance with the lawmaking function for individual lawmakers and sometimes for Congress as a whole. Although it may be in the interest of the nation to reduce defense spending by closing military bases, such closures are not in the interest of the states and districts that will lose jobs and local spending. Every legislator faces votes that set representational issues against lawmaking realities.

How should the legislators fulfill the representation function? There are several views on how this should be accomplished.

The Trustee View of Representation The first approach to the question of how representation should be achieved is that legislators should act as **trustees** of the broad interests of the entire society. They should vote against the narrow interests of their constituents if their conscience and their perception of national needs so dictate.

Image 11–1
Representative Mia Love of Utah waits with a constituent for the return of his brother from captivity abroad.

Tom Williams/Getty Images

The Instructed-Delegate View of Representation Directly opposed to the trustee view of representation is the notion that the members of Congress should behave as **instructed delegates**; that is, they should mirror the views of the majority of the constituents who elected them to power in the first place. On the surface, this approach is plausible and rewarding. For it to work, however, we must assume that constituents actually have well-formed views on the issues that are decided in Congress and, further, that they have clear-cut preferences about these issues. Neither condition is likely to be satisfied very often.

Generally, most legislators hold neither a pure trustee view nor a pure instructed-delegate view. Typically, they combine both perspectives in a pragmatic mix that is often called the "politico" style.

Service to Constituents

Individual members of Congress are expected to act as brokers between private citizens and the often faceless federal government. This function usually takes the form of **casework**. Legislators make choices about their "hillstyle," deciding how much time they and their staff will spend on casework activities such as tracking down a missing Social Security check, explaining the meaning of particular bills to people who may be affected by them, promoting a local business interest, or interceding with a regulatory agency on behalf of constituents who disagree with proposed agency regulations.

Legislators and many analysts of congressional behavior regard this **ombudsperson** role as an activity that strongly benefits the members of Congress. A government characterized by a large, confusing bureaucracy and complex public programs offers innumerable opportunities for legislators to assist (usually) grateful constituents. Morris P. Fiorina once suggested, somewhat mischievously, that senators and representatives prefer to maintain bureaucratic confusion to maximize their opportunities for performing good deeds on behalf of their constituents:

> Some poor, aggrieved constituent becomes enmeshed in the tentacles of an evil bureaucracy and calls upon Congressman St. George to do battle with the dragon. The constituent who receives aid believes that his congressman and his congressman alone got results.[2]

Although the political parties in Congress disagree on most issues, they find it difficult to vote against benefits for their constituents. As the 2008 recession continued, the administration proposed a reduction in the percentage of wages withheld from workers' paychecks for Social Security as a way to put more money in their pockets. Although Republicans pointed out the long-term consequences of the plan—setting even less money aside for Social Security—they could not vote against a tax cut. Democrats spoke to the benefit of this temporary action for ordinary workers. Both parties chose to ignore the fact that this action makes it likely that Social Security will be insolvent even earlier than has been predicted.

instructed delegate
A legislator who is an agent of the voters who elected him or her and who votes according to the views of constituents regardless of personal beliefs.

did you know?
Less than half of American adults can identify the party that controls either house of Congress.

casework
Personal work for constituents by members of Congress.

ombudsperson
A person who hears and investigates complaints by private individuals against public officials or agencies.

Image 11-2
Housing and Urban Development Secretary Ben Carson testifies before a Congressional committee in 2018.

Mark Wilson/Getty Images

---

2   Morris P. Fiorina, *Congress: Keystone of the Washington Establishment,* 2nd ed. (New Haven, CT: Yale University Press, 1989), pp. 44, 47.

Tweet Your Senator!

To an ordinary citizen, the goings-on of representatives and senators seem extremely uninteresting and difficult to follow. Strange procedural rules and polarized political rhetoric make Capitol Hill look like a miserable place to work. However, the members of the House and the Senate and their staff members do not see life that way. They are deeply immersed in committee hearings, consideration of bills, investigations, and, of course, considering whether they will be reelected. Democrats and Republicans are constantly executing strategies to try to hold on to their current seats and, in the next election, win the majority.

If you want to have a "taste" of what they read and talk about, follow their Twitter accounts and Facebook posts. For a daily look at what is going on in Congress (including video and sound bites), "follow" C-Span on Twitter or log onto C-Span's Facebook page. You can watch congressional hearings in progress, watch candidates give press conferences, and find tweets from all the leading players on Capitol Hill. Other media outlets will also provide news of the Congress and editorial columns discussing what is happening in Washington. Thousands of Washingtonians follow Politico.com (@politico) and The Hill (thehill.com; @the hill) to find out the latest news and gossip. For many years, real insiders in Washington turned first to a blog, The Playbook, for daily tips. Now you can access the Playbook at politico.com/Playbook or @Politico. Media critics have charged Politico with a Republican bias and The Hill with a more Democratic bias, but both are staffed by longtime Washington editors and journalists and are widely respected.

So join the fun and follow the action on Capitol Hill.

For Critical Analysis

1. Why do the mainstream news outlets, both on the major networks and cable channels, spend so little time explaining what is going on in Congress?

2. How could the Congress itself make the workings of the House and Senate more transparent to the voters?

---

oversight
The process by which Congress follows up on laws it has enacted to ensure that they are being enforced and administered in the way Congress intended.

The Oversight Function

Oversight of the bureaucracy is essential if decisions made by Congress are to have any force. **Oversight** is the process by which Congress follows up on the laws it has enacted to ensure that they are being enforced and administered in the way Congress intended. This is done by holding committee hearings and investigations, changing the size of an agency's budget, and cross-examining high-level presidential nominees to head major agencies. Sometimes Congress establishes a special commission to investigate a problem. After finding out that the National Security Agency (NSA) had been gathering and keeping records of all telephone calls and most email in the United States, Congress began a series of hearings on the work of the NSA. Congressional concern about such "eavesdropping" increased when, in 2014, it was revealed that the Central Intelligence Agency (CIA) had been reading the email of members of Congress.[3] Oversight can, of course, be partisan in nature, as when House Republicans grilled State Department administrators about the use of private email accounts by then Secretary of State Clinton and her staff.

---

3   David Horsey, "Dianne Feinstein Outraged that CIA Spied on Her Senate Staff, "*LA Times,* March 13, 2014.

Senators and representatives increasingly see their oversight function as a critically important part of their legislative activities. In part, oversight is related to the concept of constituency service, particularly when Congress investigates alleged arbitrariness or wrongdoing by bureaucratic agencies.

The Public-Education Function

Educating the public is a function that is performed whenever Congress holds public hearings, exercises oversight over the bureaucracy, or engages in committee and floor debate on such major issues and topics as political assassinations, aging, illegal drugs, and the concerns of small businesses. In so doing, Congress presents a range of viewpoints on pressing national questions. In recent years, members of Congress and the committees of Congress have greatly improved access to information through use of the Internet. Congress also decides what issues will come up for discussion and decision; this agenda setting is a major facet of its public-education function.

The Conflict-Resolution Function

Congress is commonly seen as an institution for resolving conflicts within American society. Organized interest groups and representatives of different racial, religious, economic, and ideological interests view Congress as an access point for airing their grievances and seeking help. This puts Congress in the position of trying to resolve the differences among competing points of view by passing laws to accommodate as many interested parties as possible. To the extent that Congress meets pluralist expectations in accommodating competing interests, it tends to build support for the entire political process.

The Powers of Congress

■ **11.1** Describe the major powers of the Congress as granted by the U.S. Constitution.

The Constitution is both highly specific and extremely vague about the powers that Congress may exercise. The first 17 clauses of Article I, Section 8, specify most of the **enumerated powers** of Congress—powers expressly given to that body.

Enumerated Powers

The enumerated powers of Congress include the right to impose taxes and import tariffs; borrow funds; regulate interstate commerce and international trade; establish procedures for naturalizing citizens; make laws regulating bankruptcies; coin (and print) money and regulate its value; establish standards of weights and measures; punish counterfeiters; establish post offices and postal routes; regulate copyrights and patents; establish the federal court system; punish illegal acts on the high seas; declare war; raise and regulate an army and a navy; call up and regulate the state militias to enforce laws, to suppress insurrections, and to repel invasions; and govern the District of Columbia.

The most important of the domestic powers of Congress, listed in Article I, Section 8, are the rights to collect taxes, to spend, and to regulate commerce. The most important foreign policy power is the power to declare war. Other sections of the Constitution allow Congress to establish rules for its own members, to regulate the electoral college, and to override a presidential veto. Congress may also regulate the extent of the Supreme Court's authority to

enumerated powers
Powers specifically granted to the national government by the Constitution. The first 17 clauses of Article I, Section 8, specify most of the enumerated powers of Congress.

review cases decided by the lower courts, regulate relations among states, and propose amendments to the Constitution.

Powers of the Senate   Some functions are restricted to one chamber. The Senate must advise on, and consent to, the ratification of treaties and must accept or reject presidential nominations of ambassadors, Supreme Court justices, and "all other Officers of the United States." During President Obama's first term, two Supreme Court vacancies occurred through the retirements of Justices David Souter in 2009 and John Paul Stevens in 2010. The president nominated Appellate Judge Sonia Sotomayor to fill Souter's seat in 2009. Although the Republicans in the Senate would have liked to object to the appointment, Judge Sotomayor had been confirmed in her appellate seat as an appointee of George W. Bush. In 2010, President Obama made another somewhat controversial appointment, but, given the outstanding qualifications of Solicitor General Elena Kagan, she, too, was confirmed. When Supreme Court Justice Antonin Scalia died suddenly in 2016, President Obama announced his intention to fill that seat, although Republican senators claimed they would not even hold a hearing on a nominee until after the presidential election. Holding firm on this decision, Republicans in the Senate hoped for a Republican president and a Republican-controlled Senate after the 2016 election. With the victory of Donald Trump, they looked forward to his first nominee to the court shortly after his inauguration in January.

Although the Republicans in the Senate slowed the approval process for lower court judges in the first year of the Obama presidency, eventually the majority of his judicial appointments were approved. Republicans in the Senate were particularly angered by the president's decision to make recess appointments to the National Labor Relations Board and the new Consumer Protection Agency during the Christmas holiday in 2011. To prevent such appointments, the Senate did not recess but held symbolic sessions for a few moments each day. When a federal appeals court refused to stop the appointments to the National Labor Relations Board, members of the Senate appealed the case to the Supreme Court in 2014. In a unanimous opinion, the Supreme Court found the president's actions unconstitutional, stating that only the Senate can decide when it is in recess.[4]

Constitutional Amendments   Amendments to the Constitution provide additional powers. Congress must certify the election of a president and a vice president or choose these officers if no candidate has a majority of the electoral vote (Twelfth Amendment). It may levy an income tax (Sixteenth Amendment) and determine who will be acting president in case of the death or incapacity of the president or vice president (Twentieth Amendment and Twenty-fifth Amendment).

The Necessary and Proper Clause

Congress enjoys the right under Article I, Section 8 (the "elastic" or "necessary and proper" clause), "[t]o make all Laws which shall be necessary and proper for carrying into Execution the foregoing Powers [of Article I], and all other Powers vested by this Constitution in the Government of the United States, or in any Department or Officer thereof." This vague statement of congressional responsibilities provided, over time, the basis for a greatly expanded national government. It also constituted, at least in theory, a check on the expansion of presidential powers.

---

4   *National Labor Relations Board v. Noel Canning* U.S. (2014).

Checks on Congress

When you consider all of the powers of Congress and its ability to override a presidential veto, it is undoubtedly the most powerful branch of government. However, given the diversity of interests in the nation, rarely can Congress agree to override a presidential veto. So, one check on Congress is the veto of the president. Another constitutional check is the power of the Supreme Court to hold a law passed by Congress as unconstitutional. Additionally, the members of the House face election every two years. If Congress were to exercise too much power, it is likely that many members would be voted out of office. And on the other side of Capitol Hill sits the Senate, which often curbs the House by not agreeing with proposals from the "other house."

House–Senate Differences

■ **11.2** Explain the differences between the House of Representatives and the Senate with regard to their constituencies, terms of office, powers, and political processes.

Congress is composed of two markedly different—but coequal—chambers. Although the Senate and the House of Representatives exist within the same legislative institution, each has developed certain distinctive features that clearly distinguish it from the other. Table 11-1 summarizes these differences.

Table 11-1 ▶ Differences between the House and the Senate

HOUSE*	SENATE*
Constitutional Differences	
Members chosen from local districts	Members chosen from an entire state
Two-year term	Six-year term
Originally elected by voters	Originally (until 1913) elected by state legislatures
May impeach (indict) federal officials	May convict federal officials of impeachable offenses
Process and Culture	
Larger (435 voting members)	Smaller (100 members)
More formal rules	Fewer rules and restrictions
Debate limited	Debate extended
Less prestige and less individual notice	More prestige and more media attention
More partisan	More individualistic
Specific Powers	
Originates bills for raising revenues	Has power to advise the president on, and to consent to, presidential appointments and treaties

*Some of these differences, such as the term of office, are provided for in the Constitution. Others, such as debate rules, are not.

Size and Rules

The central difference between the House and the Senate is simply that the House is much larger than the Senate. The House has 435 representatives, plus delegates from the District of Columbia, Puerto Rico, Guam, American Samoa, and the Virgin Islands; the Senate has 100 members. This size difference means that a greater number of formal rules are needed to govern activity in the House, whereas looser procedures can be observed in the less crowded Senate.

The effect of the difference in size is most obvious in the rules governing debate on the floors of the two chambers. The House employs an elaborate system to control the agenda and allot time fairly in such a large assembly. For each major bill, the **Rules Committee** normally proposes a **Rule** for debate that includes time limitations, divides the time between the majority and the minority, and specifies whether amendments can be proposed. The House debates and approves the Rule, which will govern the debate on that specific legislation. As a consequence of its stricter time limits on debate, the House, despite its greater size, often is able to act on legislation more quickly than the Senate.

Debate and Filibustering

In the Senate, the rules governing debate are much less restrictive. In fact, for legislation to reach the floor of the Senate, the body must have approved the rules of debate by a **Unanimous Consent Agreement**—the entire body agrees to the rules of debate. The Senate tradition of the **filibuster**, or the use of unlimited debate as a blocking tactic, dates back to 1790, when a proposal to move the U.S. capital from New York to Philadelphia was stalled by such time-wasting maneuvers. This unlimited-debate tradition—which also existed in the House until 1811—is hardly absolute.

Under Senate Rule 22, debate may be ended by invoking *cloture*. Cloture shuts off discussion on a bill. Amended in 1975 and 1979, Rule 22 states that debate may be closed off on a bill if 16 senators sign a petition requesting it and if, after two days have elapsed, three-fifths of the entire membership (60 votes, assuming no vacancies) vote for cloture. After cloture is invoked, each senator may speak on a bill for a maximum of one hour before a vote is taken.

Beginning in 2009, the use of the filibuster became the usual way of doing business in the Senate. At the beginning of the session, the Democratic majority plus the two independent senators (Bernie Sanders of Vermont and Joe Lieberman of Connecticut) could muster 60 votes to support President Obama's initiatives in health-care reform and financial reform. Republicans filibustered many votes but failed to stop the legislation. Beginning in 2013, Republicans controlled 45 seats, rendering their threat of the filibuster even more effective. The Democratic majority in the Senate used a parliamentary tactic to bring a change to the filibuster rule up for a vote. This "nuclear option" allowed a simple majority to change the filibuster rule. The amended rule does not allow the filibuster against any executive or judicial appointments except for Supreme Court nominees. After the vote, Republicans warned Democrats that they will not always hold a majority in the Senate and the rule will be used against them in the future.[5]

The use of such tactics has increased tremendously over the last two decades, leading to the concept of **unorthodox lawmaking**, meaning the use of obscure parliamentary procedures to get laws passed in the face of strong opposition.[6]

Rules Committee
A standing committee of the House of Representatives that provides special rules under which specific bills can be debated, amended, and considered by the House.

Rule
The proposal by the Rules Committee of the House that states the conditions for debate for one piece of legislation.

Unanimous Consent Agreement
An agreement on the rules of debate for proposed legislation in the Senate that is approved by all the members.

filibuster
The use of the Senate's tradition of unlimited debate as a delaying tactic to block a bill.

unorthodox lawmaking
The use of out-of-the-ordinary parliamentary tactics to pass legislation.

---

5   Jeremy Peters, "In Landmark Vote, Senate Limits Use of the Filibuster," *The New York Times*, November 21, 2013, p. 1.
6   Barbara Sinclair, *Unorthodox Lawmaking: New Legislative Processes in the U.S. Congress.* 4th ed. (Washington, DC: CQ Press, 2011).

Such tactics, however, are difficult to explain to the public and certainly undercut trust in the legislative process.

Prestige

As a consequence of the greater size of the House, representatives cannot achieve as much individual recognition and public prestige as can members of the Senate. Senators can more readily gain media exposure and establish careers as spokespersons for large national constituencies. For a House member to become nationally known, he or she must be a member of the leadership or become a recognized expert on a specific policy.

Congresspersons and the Citizenry: A Comparison

Members of Congress are not typical American citizens. They are older than most Americans, partly because of constitutional age requirements and partly because a good deal of political experience normally is an advantage in running for national office. They are also disproportionately white, male, and trained in high-status occupations. Lawyers are by far the largest occupational group among congresspersons, although the proportion of lawyers in the House is lower now than it was in the past. Compared with the average American citizen, members of Congress are well paid. In 2016, annual congressional salaries were $174,000. For the last eight years, members of Congress have voted not to accept an automatic increase scheduled for January 1 of each year. Increasingly, members of Congress are also much wealthier than the average citizen. Whereas less than 1 percent of Americans have assets exceeding $1 million, half of the members of Congress are millionaires. Table 11-2 summarizes selected characteristics of the members of Congress.

Table 11-2 ▶ Characteristics of the 115th Congress, 2017–2019

	U.S. POPULATION, 2018	HOUSE	SENATE
Age (average)	37.8	57.8	61.8
Percent Minority	38%	24%	11
Religion			
Percent Churchgoers	74%	98%	97%
Percent Catholic	21%	33%	24%
Percent Protestant	48%	55%	58%
Percent Jewish	2%	5%	8%
Gender: Percent Female	51%	20%	23%
Lawyers	0.4%	39%	50%
Blue-Collar Occupations	30%	9%	6%
Military veteran/reserves	7.6%	18%	19%
Percent Households earning more than $50,000	42%	100%	100%
Assets more than $1 million	1%	52%	70%

Source: Jennifer E. Manning, "Membership of the 115th Congress: A Profile, Washington, D.C.: Congressional Research Service.

Compared with the composition of Congress over the past 200 years, however, the House and Senate today are significantly more diverse in gender and ethnicity than ever before. In the 115th Congress 2017-2019, there were 88 women in the House of Representatives (20 percent) and 23 women in the U.S. Senate (23 percent). Minority group members filled over 24 percent of the seats in the House; they included 48 African American members, 41 Latino or Hispanic members, 15 Asian or Pacific Islander Americans, and two Native Americans. The Senate has three African American members, five Hispanic members, and three Asian American member. The 115th Congress had significant numbers of members born in 1946 or later, the so-called baby boomers. A majority of House members and senators belong to this postwar generation. This shift in the character of Congress may prompt consideration of the issues that will affect boomers, such as Social Security and Medicare.

Congressional Elections

Congressional elections are conducted by the individual state governments, but the states must conform to the rules established by the U.S. Constitution and by national statutes. Representatives are to be elected every second year by popular ballot, and the number of seats awarded to each state is to be determined every 10 years by the results of the census. The decennial census is viewed as crucial by members of Congress and by the states. If the census is not accurate, perhaps undercounting individuals living in a state, then that state might lose a representative in Congress. Each state has at least one representative, with most congressional districts having about 650,000 residents. Senators are elected by popular vote (the Seventeenth Amendment) every six years; approximately one-third of the seats are chosen every two years. Each state has two senators.

Only states can elect members of Congress. Therefore, territories such as Puerto Rico and Guam are not represented, although they do elect nonvoting delegates who sit in the House. The District of Columbia is also represented only by a nonvoting delegate, but is not represented in the Senate at all. Several proposals have been made to grant congressional representation to our nation's capital. In 1978, Congress approved a constitutional amendment to give the District of Columbia the representation it would have if it were a state, including two senators. The amendment was not ratified, however. Democrats in Congress have generally supported more representation for the district because the majority of its citizens are African American and vote overwhelmingly Democratic. Republicans oppose the initiative for the same reason.

Candidates for Congressional Elections

Candidates for House and Senate seats may be self-selected. Members of the House must be at least 25 years old, a citizen for seven years, and live in the state they will represent. Senators must be 30 years old, a citizen for nine years, and a resident of the state they represent. In congressional districts where one party is very strong, however, there may be a shortage of candidates willing to represent the weaker party. Leaders of the weaker party must often recruit candidates. Candidates may resemble the voters of the district in ethnicity or religion, but are also likely to be very successful individuals previously active in politics. House candidates are especially likely to have local ties to their districts. Candidates usually choose to run because they believe they would enjoy the job and its accompanying status. They also may be thinking of a House seat as a stepping stone to future political office as a senator, governor, or president. Individuals who seek Senate seats may also have plans to run for governor in their home state or be considering a run for the presidency.

Congressional Campaigns and Elections Congressional campaigns have changed considerably in the past two decades. Like all other campaigns, they are much more expensive. Today, the average cost of a winning Senate campaign is $10.5 million; a winning House campaign costs more than $1.7 million.[7] Campaign funds include direct contributions by individuals, contributions by political action committees (PACs), and "soft money" funneled through state party committees. All of these contributions are regulated by laws, including the Federal Election Campaign Act of 1971, as amended, and, most recently, the Bipartisan Campaign Reform Act of 2002.

Most candidates for Congress must win the nomination through a **direct primary**, in which **party identifiers** vote for the candidate who will be on the party ticket in the general election. To win the primary, candidates may take more liberal or more conservative positions to get the votes of party identifiers. In the general election, they may moderate their views to attract the votes of independents and voters from the other party.

Presidential Effects Congressional candidates always hope that a strong presidential candidate will have "coattails" that will sweep in senators and representatives of the same party. Coattail effects have been quite limited, and in recent presidential elections have not materialized at all. One way to measure the coattail effect is to look at the subsequent midterm elections, held in the even-numbered years following the presidential contests—voter turnout falls sharply. In the past, the party controlling the White House normally lost seats in Congress in the midterm elections, in part because the coattail effect ceased to apply. Members of Congress who were from contested districts or who were in their first term were more likely not to be reelected.

Table 11-3 shows the pattern for midterm elections since 1942. The president's party lost seats in every election from 1942 to 1998. In that year, with President Clinton under the threat of impeachment, voters showed displeasure with the Republicans by voting in five more Democrats. In 2002, Republicans bucked the normal slump by winning five more Republican seats in the House. Most commentators believed that these midterm victories were based on public support for the president after the September 11, 2001, attacks. In 2006, the Republicans suffered a fairly normal midterm defeat, comparable to the midterm defeat in 1958, during the Eisenhower presidency.

The 2010 midterm elections were a sweeping win by the Republicans, aided by the newly energized Tea Party movement. Republicans gained more than 60 seats in the House of

direct primary
An intraparty election in which the voters select the candidates who will run on a party's ticket in the subsequent general election.

party identifier
A person who identifies with a political party.

Table 11-3 ▶ Midterm Gains and Losses by the Party of the President, 1942–2018

SEATS GAINED OR LOST BY THE PARTY OF THE PRESIDENT IN THE HOUSE OF REPRESENTATIVES	
1942	−45 (D.)
1946	−55 (D.)
1950	−29 (D.)
1954	−18 (R.)
1958	−47 (R.)
1962	−4 (D.)
1966	−47 (D.)
1970	−12 (R.)
1974	−48 (R.)
1978	−15 (D.)
1982	−26 (R.)
1986	−5 (R.)
1990	−8 (R.)
1994	−52 (D.)
1998	+5 (D.)
2002	+5 (R.)
2006	−30 (R.)
2010	−62 (D.)
2014	−13 (D.)
2018	−33 (R.)

---

7 http://www.opensecrets.org

Representatives, thus gaining majority control in that body. Although it is normal for the "out party" to gain seats in the midterms, the size of the Republican victory was the largest ever in modern times.

The midterm elections of 2018 saw a reversal of the Republicans' fortunes. Although President Trump campaigned hard across the country, his influence was felt only in Senate races where Republicans kept their majority. In the House, Republicans lost more than 30 seats and their majority. The president faced a divided Congress in 2019.

The Power of Incumbency

The power of incumbency in the outcome of congressional elections cannot be overemphasized. Once members are elected and survive the second election, they build considerable loyalty among constituents and are frequently reelected as long as they wish to serve. Table 11-4 shows that more than 90 percent of representatives and a slightly smaller proportion of senators who run for reelection are successful. Several scholars contend that the pursuit of reelection is the strongest motivation behind the activities of members of Congress. Incumbents develop their homestyle, using the mass media, making personal appearances with constituents, and sending newsletters—all to produce a favorable image and to make their name a household word. Members of Congress present themselves as informed, experienced, and responsive to their district's needs. Incumbents can demonstrate the positions that they have taken on key issues by referring to their voting records in Congress.

Table 11-4 ▶ The Power of Incumbency

	1994	1996	1998	2000	2002	2004	2006	2008	2010	2012	2014	2016	2018
House													
Number of incumbent candidates	387	384	402	403	393	404	405	389	393	382	380	385	384
Reelected	349	361	395	394	383	397	382	372	336	345	366	372	357
Percentage of total	90.2	94.0	98.3	97.8	97.5	98.3	94.3	95.6	85.4	90.0	96.0	96.6	92.9
Defeated	38	23	7	9	10	7	23	17	57	37	14	13	27
In primary	3	2	1	3	3	1	2	3	4	5	3	5	5
In general election	34	21	6	6	7	6	21	17	53	32	11	8	22
Senate													
Number of incumbent candidates	26	21	29	29	28	26	29	32	25	22	29	29	32
Reelected	24	19	26	23	24	25	23	23	21	21	26	27	29
Percentage of total	92.3	90.5	89.7	79.3	85.7	96.2	79.3	81.3	84	95.0	89.7	93.1	90.6
Defeated	2	2	3	6	4	1	6	3	4	2	3	2	3
In primary	0	1	0	0	1	0	1*	0	2	1	0	0	0
In general election	2	1	3	6	3	1	6	3	2	1	3	2	3

*Joe Lieberman of Connecticut lost the Democratic primary but won the general election as an independent. He chose to organize with the Senate Democrats.
Sources: Norman Ornstein, Thomas E. Mann, and Michael J. Malbin, *Vital Statistics on Congress, 2001–2002* (Washington, DC: The AEI Press, 2002); and authors' update.

Election 2016

Who Wins Control of the Congress?

For the first nine months of 2016, all media focus was on the presidential primaries, caucuses, and the party conventions. However, at the same time, all 435 members of the House of Representatives and about one-third (34) of the members of the U.S. Senate were consumed with their own professional futures. A number of well-known members announced they would retire from the Capitol. Among them were Barbara Boxer, Democratic Senator from California; and Harry Reid, former Democratic Majority Leader of the Senate.

The Republicans gained a large majority in the House of Representatives during the midterm election of 2014, ending up with 247 seats to the Democrats' 188 members. Due to the redistricting efforts of Republicans after the 2010 Census and the strength they exhibit in rural and suburban areas, Republicans expected to maintain their majority in the 115th Congress. Both Republicans and Democrats were astutely aware that a landslide presidential win would change all the predictions. Presidential candidates who win large majorities across the nation are said to have "coattails" that help members of their party win congressional seats. This is due, in large part, to the larger turnout of voters for the presidential candidate rather than any direct help being given to the congressional candidate.

After the votes were counted in the 2016 election, the Republican majority declined by only six seats. Neither Mr. Trump nor Mrs. Clinton had much effect on the House races. Republicans continue to control the House in 2017-2018.

The Senate presented a much dicier situation for the Republicans in 2016 because they only had a five-seat majority to start with. In addition there were more Republican seats in the "toss-up" category due to retirements and expected challenges in competitive states. Dan Coates's retirement meant that Democrats had a strong chance to win the Indiana Senate seat, especially if Hillary Clinton won the state's electoral votes. Rob Portman, another Republican, faced stiff opposition in Ohio, another highly competitive state. The final election results found the Republicans maintaining control of the Senate by the slender majority of 52 to 48. After Jeff Sessions gave up his seat to become Attorney General, a Democrat replaced him, making the margin 51-49. The midterm elections of 2018 demonstrated the difficulty of holding majorities in both houses. Following a normal pattern, Democrats won more than 30 seats in the House and gained control of the lower house. Republicans held onto a slim majority in the Senate.

For Critical Analysis

1. What are the best conditions for getting legislation passed: one party holding the Congress and the presidency or split control with one party controlling Congress and the other holding the White House?

2. Why are some states and districts so "safe" for one political party?

Congressional Apportionment

■ **11.3** Describe the processes of reapportionment and redistricting.

Two of the most complicated aspects of congressional elections are apportionment issues—**reapportionment** and **redistricting**. In a landmark 6–2 vote in 1962, the U.S. Supreme Court made the apportionment of state legislative districts a **justiciable question** (reviewable).[8] The Court did so by invoking the Fourteenth Amendment principle that no state can deny to any person "the equal protection of the laws." In 1964, the Court held that *both* chambers of a state legislature must be apportioned so that all districts are equal in population.[9] Later that year, the Court applied this "one person, one vote" principle to U.S. congressional districts on the basis of Article I, Section 2, of the Constitution, which requires that members of the House be chosen "by the People of the several States."[10]

reapportionment
The allocation of seats in the House of Representatives to each state after each census.

redistricting
The redrawing of the boundaries of the congressional districts within each state.

justiciable question
A question that may be raised and reviewed in court.

---

8 *Baker v. Carr,* 369 U.S. 186 (1962). The term *justiciable* is pronounced "juhstish-a-buhl."
9 *Reynolds v. Sims,* 377 U.S. 533 (1964).
10 *Wesberry v. Sanders,* 376 U.S. 1 (1964).

Severe malapportionment of congressional districts before 1964 resulted in some districts containing two or three times the populations of other districts in the same state, thereby diluting the effect of a vote cast in the more populous districts. This system generally benefited the conservative populations of rural areas and small towns and harmed the interests of the more heavily populated and liberal cities. Suburban areas have benefited the most from the Court's rulings, as suburbs account for an increasingly larger proportion of the nation's population, whereas cities include a correspondingly smaller segment of the population.

Gerrymandering

Although the general issue of apportionment has been dealt with fairly successfully by the one person, one vote principle, the **gerrymandering** issue has not yet been resolved. This term refers to the legislative boundary-drawing tactics that were used under Elbridge Gerry, the governor of Massachusetts, in the 1812 elections (see Image 11-3). A district is said to have been gerrymandered when its shape is altered substantially by the dominant party in a state legislature to maximize its electoral strength at the expense of the minority party.

In 1986, the Supreme Court heard *Davis v. Bandemer*, a case that challenged gerrymandered congressional districts in Indiana. The Court ruled for the first time that redistricting for the political benefit of one group could be challenged on constitutional grounds. In this specific case, however, the Court did not agree that the districts were drawn unfairly, because it could not be proved that a group of voters would consistently be deprived of influence at the polls as a result of the new districts.[11]

gerrymandering
The drawing of legislative district boundary lines to obtain partisan or factional advantage. A district is said to be gerrymandered when its shape is manipulated by the dominant party in the state legislature to maximize electoral strength at the expense of the minority party.

Image 11-3
The Original Gerrymander
The practice of "gerrymandering"—the excessive manipulation of the shape of a legislative district to benefit a certain incumbent or party—is probably as old as the Republic, but the name originated in 1812. In that year, the Massachusetts legislature carved out of Essex County a district that historian John Fiske said has a "dragonlike contour." When the painter Gilbert Stuart saw the misshapen district, he penciled in a head, wings, and claws and exclaimed, "That will do for a salamander!" Editor Benjamin Russell replied, "Better say a Gerrymander" (after Elbridge Gerry, then-governor of Massachusetts).

Bettmann/Getty Images

---

11 478 U.S. 109 (1986).

Redistricting after the 2010 Census

Republicans won a majority of seats in the House in 2010 and captured a majority of statehouses and governorships—they would have the upper hand in the drawing of new congressional districts after the release of the results of the 2010 Census. Consider Ohio: it lost enough population between 2000 and 2010 to lose two congressional seats. That meant all the districts in the state would be redrawn to adjust for the lower number of congressional districts. Through the "bipartisan" redistricting process, Ohio Republicans managed to put two sitting Democratic members of Congress—Marcy Kaptur and Dennis Kucinich—in one district and, through the drawing of district boundaries, enable Republicans to win 12 of the 16 districts. For an example of a Republican-leaning district, look at Figure 11-1, showing Ohio's First Congressional District. Although this district included half of Hamilton County and half of the city of Cincinnati for many years, it now looks like "crossed signal flags." The district joins the traditional western Hamilton County districts with Warren County to the northeast with an odd-shaped bridge. The intent is to add enough Republican voters to the district to offset the majority Democratic vote in Cincinnati.

Redistricting decisions are often made by a small group of political leaders within a state legislature. Their goal is to shape voting districts to maximize their party's chances of winning state legislative seats as well as seats in

Figure 11-1   ▶   The First Congressional District of Ohio

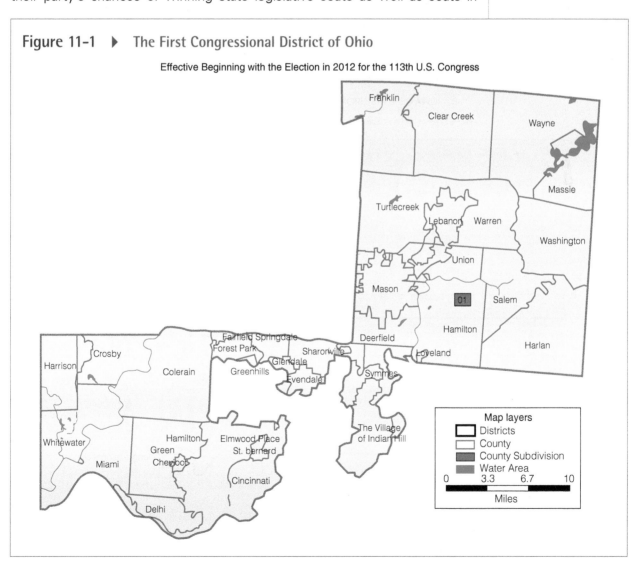

Effective Beginning with the Election in 2012 for the 113th U.S. Congress

Congress. Two of the techniques used are "packing" and "cracking." They *pack* voters supporting the opposing party into as few districts as possible or *crack* the opposing party's supporters into different districts.

Clearly, partisan redistricting aids incumbents. The party that dominates a state's legislature will be making redistricting decisions. Through gerrymandering tactics, districts can be redrawn in such a way as to ensure that party's continued strength in the state legislature or Congress. As noted earlier, some have estimated that only between 30 and 50 of the 435 seats in the House were open for any real competition in the most recent elections.

In 2004, the U.S. Supreme Court reviewed an obviously political redistricting scheme in Pennsylvania. The Court concluded, however, that the federal judiciary would not address purely political gerrymandering claims.[12] Two years later, the Supreme Court reached a similar conclusion with respect to most of the new congressional districts created by the Republicans in the Texas legislature in 2003. Again, the Court largely refused to intervene in what was plainly a political gerrymandering plan, although they did alter one district.[13]

Nonpartisan Redistricting

Several states, including Arizona, Iowa, and Minnesota, have adopted nonpartisan redistricting procedures. As you will see if you compare the First District of Ohio with the map of the Iowa districts (Figure 11-2), nonpartisan districts

Figure 11-2   ▶   Congressional Districts of Iowa

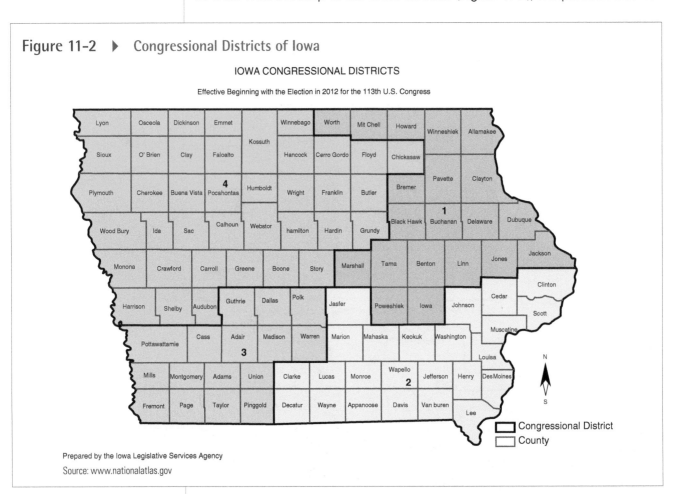

IOWA CONGRESSIONAL DISTRICTS

Effective Beginning with the Election in 2012 for the 113th U.S. Congress

Prepared by the Iowa Legislative Services Agency

Source: www.nationalatlas.gov

---

12 *Vieth v. Jubelirer*, 541 U.S. 267 (2004).
13 *League of United Latin American Citizens v. Perry*, 399 F.Supp. 2nd 756 (2006).

usually respect county lines and divide the state into fairly cleanly shaped districts that share geographic characteristics. Research has shown that nonpartisan districts tend to be more competitive, no doubt because they have not been drawn to favor one party over the other.

"Minority-Majority" Districts

In the early 1990s, the federal government encouraged a type of gerrymandering that facilitated the election of a minority representative from a "minority-majority" area. Under the Voting Rights Act of 1965, the Justice Department issued directives to states after the 1990 Census instructing them to create congressional districts that would maximize the voting power of minority groups—create districts in which minority voters were the majority. The results were several creatively drawn congressional districts—see, for example, the depiction of the Illinois Fourth Congressional District in Figure 11-3, which is commonly described as "a pair of earmuffs."

Constitutional Challenges

Many of these "minority-majority" districts were challenged in court by citizens who claimed that creating districts based on race or ethnicity alone

---

Figure 11-3 ▶ The Fourth Congressional District of Illinois

The Fourth District is outlined here in blue. It stretches from the near north side of Chicago out to the western suburbs and then turns east through the south side of Chicago. Why is the district drawn this way? The district includes a majority of Hispanic Americans and meets the criteria for a "majority-minority" district. However, the northern portion of the district contains many Puerto Rican Americans, and many Mexican Americans live in the southern portion. The western link between the two is a superhighway where no one resides. The question is whether the people in this district have much in common other than Hispanic heritage.

Source: www.nationalatlas.gov

violates the equal protection clause of the Constitution. In 1995, the Supreme Court agreed with this argument when it declared that Georgia's new Eleventh Congressional District was unconstitutional. The district stretched from Atlanta to the Atlantic, splitting eight counties and five municipalities along the way. The Court ruled that when a state assigns voters on the basis of race, "it engages in the offensive and demeaning assumption that voters of a particular race, because of their race, think alike, share the same political interests, and will prefer the same candidates at the polls." The Court also chastised the Justice Department for concluding that race-based districting was mandated under the Voting Rights Act of 1965: "When the Justice Department's interpretation of the Act compels race-based districting, it by definition raises a serious constitutional question."[14] In subsequent rulings, the Court affirmed its position.

Changing Directions

In the early 2000s, the Supreme Court took a new direction on racial redistricting challenges. In a 2000 case, the Court limited the federal government's authority to invalidate changes in state and local elections on the basis that the changes were discriminatory. The case involved a proposed school redistricting plan in Louisiana. The Court held that federal approval for the plan could not be withheld simply because the plan was discriminatory. Rather, the test was whether the plan left racial and ethnic minorities worse off than they were before.[15]

In 2001, the Supreme Court reviewed for a second time a case involving North Carolina's Twelfth District. The district was 165 miles long and largely hewed to Interstate 85. It was drawn to connect most of the urban centers where African American voters lived. In 1996, the Court had held that the district was unconstitutional because race had been the dominant factor in drawing its boundaries. Shortly thereafter, the boundaries were redrawn, but the district was again challenged as a racial gerrymander. In 2001, however, the Supreme Court held that there was insufficient evidence for the lower court's conclusion that race had been the dominant factor when the boundaries were redrawn.[16] The Twelfth District's boundaries remained as drawn.

Perks and Privileges

Legislators have many benefits that are not available to most workers. They are granted generous **franking** privileges permitting them to mail newsletters, surveys, and other correspondence to their constituents. The annual cost of congressional mail rose from $11 million in 1971 to a peak of $70 million. Congress has largely graduated to email and social networks to distribute literature. Today, the franking budget is less than $10 million.

Permanent Professional Staffs

More than 30,000 people are employed in the Capitol Hill bureaucracy. About half of them are personal and committee staff members. Personal staff include office clerks and secretaries; professionals who deal with

franking
A policy that enables members of Congress to send material through the mail by substituting their facsimile signature (frank) for postage.

14 *Miller v. Johnson*, 515 U.S. 900 (1995).
15 *Reno v. Bossier Parish School Board*, 528 U.S. 320 (2000).
16 *Easley v. Cromartie*, 532 U.S. 234 (2001).

media relations, draft legislation, and satisfy constituency requests for service; and staffers who maintain local offices in the member's home district or state.

The average Senate office on Capitol Hill employs about 30 staff members, and twice that number work on the personal staffs of senators from the most populous states. House office staffs are limited to 18 employees. The number of staff members has increased dramatically since 1960. Most increases come in assistants to individual members—some question whether staff members are really advising on legislation or are primarily aiding constituents and gaining votes in the next election.

Congress also benefits from the expertise of the professional staffs of agencies created to produce information for members. The Congressional Research Service, the Government Accountability Office, and the Congressional Budget Office all provide reports, audits, and policy recommendations for review by members of Congress.

Privileges and Immunities under the Law

Members of Congress also benefit from some special constitutional protections. Under Article I, Section 6, of the Constitution, they "shall in all Cases, except Treason, Felony and Breach of the Peace, be privileged from Arrest during their Attendance at the Session of their respective Houses, and in going to and returning from the same; and for any Speech or Debate in either House, they shall not be questioned in any other Place." The arrest immunity clause is not really an important provision today. The "speech or debate" clause, however, means that a member may make any allegations or other statements he or she wishes in connection with official duties and normally not be sued for libel or slander or otherwise be subject to legal action.

Congressional Caucuses: Another Source of Support

All members of Congress are members of one or more caucuses. The most important caucuses are those established by the parties in each chamber. These Democratic and Republican meetings provide information and devise legislative strategy for the party. Other caucuses bring together members who have similar political views, such as the moderate Democratic Study Group, whereas some have a constituency focus, such as the Rust Belt Caucus or the Potato Caucus. Some of the most important and influential caucuses are those for minority and underrepresented groups in Congress.

The Congressional Women's Caucus has long provided support for the women elected to the Congress and has provided a forum for discussing issues that women members find important, including the treatment of women in Afghanistan. Two of the most important minority-based caucuses are the Congressional Black Caucus and the Hispanic Congressional Caucus. Both have grown in the last two decades as the numbers of African American and Hispanic members grew. They are now funded by businesses and special interests, and provide staff assistance and information for members of Congress to help build support among specific groups of voters.

did you know?

Members of Congress have free parking spaces at Reagan National Airport which serves Washington, DC.

did you know?

Jeannette Rankin was elected to the House of Representatives from Montana in 1916, three years before women got the right to vote.

Image 11–4
Former chairman of the Congressional Black Caucus, Representative G. K. Butterfield, speaks to a group while flanked by other members of the caucus.

The Committee Structure

■ **11.4** Discuss the importance of committees to the lawmaking process and to the ability of members of Congress to do their jobs.

Thousands of bills are introduced in every session of Congress, and no single member can possibly be adequately informed on all the issues that arise. The committee system is a way to provide for specialization, or a division of the legislative labor. Members of a committee can concentrate on just one area or topic and develop sufficient expertise to draft appropriate legislation when needed. The flow of legislation through both the House and the Senate is determined largely by the speed with which the members of these committees act on bills and resolutions.

The Power of Committees

Sometimes called "little legislatures," committees usually have the final say on pieces of legislation.[17] Committee actions may be overturned on the floor by the House or Senate, but this rarely happens. Legislators normally defer to the expertise of the chairperson and other members of the committee who speak on the floor in defense of a committee decision. Chairpersons of committees exercise control over the scheduling of hearings and formal action on a bill and decide which subcommittee will act on legislation falling within their committee's jurisdiction.

Committees only rarely are deprived of control over a bill—although this kind of action is provided for in the rules of each chamber. In the House, if a bill has

did you know?

Elmo of Sesame Street is the only nonhuman to testify before Congress.

Image 11–5
Representative Nydia M. Velazquez (D–NY), the first Puerto Rican woman elected to Congress, praises the achievements of Supreme Court Justice Sonia Sotomayor, the first Latina member of the Court.

17 The term *little legislatures* is from Woodrow Wilson, *Congressional Government* (New York: Meridian Books, 1956 [first published in 1885]).

been considered by a standing committee for 30 days, the signatures of a majority (218) of the House membership on a **discharge petition** can pry a bill out of an uncooperative committee's hands. From 1909 to the present, although more than 900 such petitions were initiated, only slightly more than two dozen resulted in successful discharge efforts. Of those, 20 resulted in bills that passed the House.[18]

Types of Congressional Committees

Over the past two centuries, Congress has created several different types of committees, each of which serves the particular needs of the institution.

Standing Committees By far the most important committees in Congress are the **standing committees**—permanent bodies that continue from session to session. A list of the standing committees of the 115th Congress is presented in Table 11-5. In addition, most of the standing committees have created subcommittees to carry out their work. The 115th Congress had 70 subcommittees in the Senate and 104 subcommittees in the House.[19] Each standing committee is given a specific area of legislative policy jurisdiction, and almost all legislative measures are considered by the appropriate standing committees.

discharge petition
Procedure by which a bill in the House of Representatives may be forced (discharged) out of a committee that has refused to report it for consideration by the House. The petition must be signed by an absolute majority (218) of representatives and is used only on rare occasions.

standing committee
A permanent committee in the House or Senate that considers bills within a certain subject area.

Table 11-5 ▶ Standing Committees of the 115th Congress, 2017–2019

HOUSE COMMITTEES	SENATE COMMITTEES
Agriculture	Agriculture, Nutrition, and Forestry
Appropriations	Appropriations
Armed Services	Armed Services
Budget	Banking, Housing, and Urban Affairs
Education and the Workforce	Budget
Energy and Commerce	Commerce, Science, and Transportation
Ethics	Energy and Natural Resources
Financial Services	Environment and Public Works
Foreign Affairs	Finance
Homeland Security	Foreign Relations
House Administration	Health, Education, Labor, and Pensions
Intelligence	Homeland Security and Governmental Affairs
Judiciary	Judiciary
Natural Resources	Rules and Administration
Oversight and Government Reform	Small Business and Entrepreneurship
Rules	Veterans Affairs
Science, Space and Technology	
Small Business	
Transportation and Infrastructure	
Veterans Affairs	
Ways and Means	

---

18 Congressional Quarterly, Inc., *Guide to Congress*, 5th ed. (Washington, DC: CQ Press, 2000); and authors' update.
19 "The Legislature," www.whitehouse.gov

Because of the importance of their work and the traditional influence of their members in Congress, certain committees are considered to be more prestigious than others. Seats on standing committees that handle spending issues are especially desirable because members can use these positions to benefit their constituents. Committees that control spending include the Appropriations Committee in either chamber and the Ways and Means Committee in the House. Members also seek seats on committees that handle matters of special interest to their constituents. A member of the House from an agricultural district, for example, will have an interest in joining the House Agriculture Committee.

Select Committees In principle, a **select committee** is created for a limited time and for a specific legislative purpose. For example, a select committee may be formed to investigate a public problem, such as child nutrition or aging. In practice, a select committee, such as the Select Committee on Intelligence in each chamber, may continue indefinitely. Select committees rarely create original legislation.

Joint Committees A **joint committee** is formed by the concurrent action of both chambers of Congress and consists of members from each chamber. Joint committees, which may be permanent or temporary, have dealt with the economy, taxation, and the Library of Congress.

Conference Committees Special joint committees—**conference committees**—are formed to achieve agreement between the House and the Senate on the exact wording of legislative acts when the two chambers pass legislative proposals in different forms. The bill is reported out of the conference committee if it is approved by the majority of members from both houses who sit on the committee and is returned to the House and Senate for final votes. No bill can be sent to the White House to be signed into law unless it first passes both chambers in identical form. Sometimes called the "third house" of Congress, conference committees are in a position to make significant alterations to legislation and frequently become the focal point of policy debates.

The House Rules Committee Because of its special "gatekeeping" power over the terms on which legislation will reach the floor of the House of Representatives, the House Rules Committee holds a uniquely powerful position. A special committee rule sets the time limit on debate and determines whether and how a bill may be amended. This practice dates back to 1883. The Rules Committee has the unusual power to meet while the House is in session, to have its resolutions considered immediately on the floor, and to initiate legislation on its own.

The Selection of Committee Members

In both chambers, members are appointed to standing committees by the Steering Committee of their party. The majority-party member with the longest term of continuous service on a standing committee can be given preference when the leadership nominates chairpersons. During his time as Speaker of the House, Newt Gingrich restricted chairpersons' terms to six years. Additionally, he bypassed seniority to appoint chairpersons loyal to his own platform.

Respecting seniority is an informal, traditional process, and it applies to other significant posts in Congress as well. The **seniority system**, although it deliberately treats members unequally, provides a predictable means of assigning positions of power within Congress. The most senior member of the minority party is called the *ranking committee member* for that party.

select committee
A temporary legislative committee established for a limited time period and for a special purpose.

joint committee
A legislative committee composed of members from both chambers of Congress.

conference committee
A special joint committee appointed to reconcile differences when bills pass the two chambers of Congress in different forms.

seniority system
A custom followed in both chambers of Congress specifying that the member of the majority party with the longest term of continuous service will be given preference when a committee chairperson (or a holder of some other significant post) is selected.

did you know?
The Constitution does not require that the Speaker of the House of Representatives be an elected member of the House.

The general pattern was that members of the House or Senate who represented **safe seats** would be reelected continually and eventually would accumulate enough years of continuous committee service to enable them to become the chairpersons of their committees. In the 1970s, a number of reforms in the chairperson selection process modified the seniority system. They introduced the use of a secret ballot in electing House committee chairpersons and allowed for the possibility of choosing a chairperson on a basis other than seniority. The Democrats immediately replaced three senior chairpersons who were out of step with the rest of their party. The Republican leadership in the House has also taken more control over the selection of committee chairpersons.

The Formal Leadership

■ **11.5** Describe the leadership structure in each house of Congress, noting the differences between the House and the Senate.

The limited amount of centralized power that exists in Congress is exercised through party-based mechanisms. Congress is organized by party. When the Democratic Party wins a majority of seats in either the House or the Senate, Democrats control the official positions of power in that chamber, and every important committee has a Democratic chairperson and a majority of Democratic members. The same process holds when Republicans are in the majority. For a complete list of the current leadership of both parties in the House of Representatives, go to www.house.gov.

Generally speaking, the leadership organizations in the House and the Senate look alike on paper. Leaders in the House of Representatives, however, have more control over the agenda of the body and, often, over their own party's members. Senate leaders, due to the power of individual members, must work closely with the other party's leaders to achieve success. Although the party leaders in both the House and the Senate are considered to be the most powerful members of the Congress, their powers pale compared to those given to the leaders in true "party government" legislatures. The differences between those legislatures and the U.S. Congress are detailed in the Beyond Our Borders feature.

Leadership in the House

The House leadership is made up of the Speaker, the majority and minority leaders, and the party whips.

The Speaker The foremost power holder in the House of Representatives is the **Speaker of the House**. The Speaker's position is a nonpartisan one, but for the better part of two centuries, has been the official leader of the majority party in the House. When a new Congress convenes, each party nominates a candidate for Speaker. All Democratic members of the House are expected to vote for their party's nominee, and all Republicans are expected to support their candidate. The vote to organize the House is the one vote in which representatives must vote with their party. In a sense, this vote defines a member's partisan status.

The influence of modern-day Speakers is based primarily on their personal prestige, persuasive ability, and knowledge of the legislative process—plus the acquiescence or active support of other representatives. In recent years, both the Republican and Democratic parties in the House have given their

safe seat
A district that returns a legislator with 55 percent of the vote or more.

Speaker of the House
The presiding officer in the House of Representatives. The Speaker is always a member of the majority party and is the most powerful and influential member of the House.

leaders more power in making appointments and controlling the agenda. The major formal powers of the Speaker include the following:

1. Presiding over meetings of the House

2. Appointing members of joint committees and conference committees

3. Scheduling legislation for floor action

4. Deciding points of order and interpreting the rules with the advice of the House parliamentarian

5. Referring bills and resolutions to the appropriate standing committees of the House

A Speaker may take part in floor debate and vote, as can any other member of Congress, but recent Speakers usually have voted only to break a tie. Since 1975, the Speaker, when a Democrat, has also had the power to appoint the Democratic Steering Committee, which determines new committee assignments for House party members.

The powers of the Speaker are related to his or her control over information and communications channels in the House and the degree of support received from members. This is a significant power in a large, decentralized institution in which information is a very important resource. Since the Speakership of Newt Gingrich (R-GA) in 1994, the leadership of the House has held significant power to control the agenda and provide rewards to the members. During the same time period, the degree of polarization between the majority and minority parties has increased, and cohesion within each party has grown stronger. Scholars suggest that this is the result of increased ideological makeup within the congressional delegation of both parties and the election of fewer moderate or centrist members to the House.

The Majority Leader The **majority leader of the House** is elected by a caucus of the majority party to foster cohesion among party members and to act as a spokesperson for the party. The majority leader cooperates with the Speaker and other party leaders to formulate the party's legislative program and to guide it through the legislative process in the House. The Democrats often recruit future Speakers from those who hold that position.

The Minority Leader The **minority leader of the House** is the candidate nominated for Speaker by a caucus of the minority party. Like the majority leader, the leader of the minority party has as her or his primary responsibility the maintaining of cohesion within the party's ranks. The minority leader works for cohesion among the party's members and speaks on behalf of the president if the minority party controls the White House. In relations with the majority party, the minority leader consults with both the Speaker and the majority leader on recognizing members who wish to speak on the floor, on House rules and procedures, and on the scheduling of legislation. Minority leaders have no actual power in these areas, however.

Whips The leadership of each party includes assistants to the majority and minority leaders. **Whips** are members of Congress who assist the party leaders by passing information down from the leadership to party members and by ensuring that members show up for floor debate and cast their votes on important

majority leader of the House
A legislative position held by an important party member in the House of Representatives. The majority leader is selected by the majority party in caucus or conference to foster cohesion among party members and to act as spokesperson for the majority party in the House.

minority leader of the House
The party leader elected by the minority party in the House.

whip
A member of Congress who aids the majority or minority leader of the House or the Senate.

Should Parties Control Legislatures (and Governments)?

The Congress of the United States is a bicameral legislature. The American-style legislature differs from most of the legislatures in the world in several significant ways. Because it is composed of three branches, separate structures sharing powers, we frequently have "divided" government, meaning that the party that controls one or both houses of Congress does not control the presidency. Does this mean that the government is hopelessly deadlocked? Not usually. Members of Congress, especially in the House, frequently support their party leaders but, on many other votes, "cross the aisle" to vote with members of the other side, thinking it best for their constituency or reelection hopes.

Most Americans think that our legislature is modeled on the British parliament. However, the parliament of Great Britain, as well as that of many other Western nations, is based on the idea of "party government." No separation of powers exists between the legislature and the executive branch. When a political party wins a majority of seats in the House of Parliament (the lower and only powerful house), that party then selects the prime minister, who is also the party leader. The prime minister and cabinet members sit in Parliament during debates, playing an active role. The party, which may have promised a better welfare system or to eliminate the armed services, votes the new law into effect, and the prime minister implements the policy.*

Another variation on this type of party government occurs when a nation (Germany, Italy, and Israel are examples) has a multiparty system. In that case, no party wins a majority of seats. The party with the plurality of seats chooses the leader and then negotiates with other parties to form a coalition to constitute a government and pass new legislation. Governing as part of a coalition is much more difficult, however, because if one partner does not agree with the proposed policy, the coalition may fall apart, and new elections may be necessary.

Consider the important relationship between the executive (prime minister or president) and the legislature. In the U.S. system, even if Congress and the president are of the same party, this does not guarantee that the president's agenda will be implemented in full. President Obama, who came into office with a majority in the House, received speedy and cohesive support for his initiatives in his first year, but legislation often bogged down in the Senate due to its procedural rules. Both the Democrats and the Republicans in the House

Image 11-6 Deputy Prime Minister Nick Clegg (fifth from right) and Prime Minister David Cameron of Great Britain respond to members of Parliament during the Question Hour in May 2010.

were so cohesive throughout much of those years that some scholars believed the situation was a form of "conditional party government."** In a true party government system, everything on the Democrats' agenda would become law, and the president would be selected by the Congress.

Although Americans complain bitterly about ineffective Congresses, they generally prefer divided government due to fear that one party will have too much power.

For Critical Analysis

1. Would the United States ever grant the degree of power to the president to achieve his or her agenda that is afforded to the prime minister of Great Britain?

2. What is more important—controlling government power or having a more effective legislature?

3. How would the U.S. Congress be different if three or four parties were represented there?

*For information on the world's legislatures, go to the website of the Inter-Parliamentary Union at www.ipu.org

**The "conditional party government" thesis has been developed by David Rohde, *Parties and Leaders in the Postreform House* (Chicago: University of Chicago Press, 1991).

issues. Whips conduct polls among party members about the members' views on legislation, inform the leaders about whose vote is doubtful and whose is certain, and exert pressure on members to support the leaders' positions. In the House, serving as a whip is the first step toward positions of higher leadership.

Leadership in the Senate

The Senate is less than one-fourth the size of the House. This fact alone explains why a formal, complex, and centralized leadership structure is not as necessary in the Senate as it is in the House. For a list of the current leaders of both parties in the U.S. Senate, go to www.senate.gov.

The two highest-ranking formal leadership positions in the Senate are essentially ceremonial in nature. Under the Constitution, the vice president of the United States is the president of the Senate and may vote to break a tie. The vice president, however, is only rarely present for a meeting of the Senate. Instead, the Senate elects a **president pro tempore** ("pro tem") to preside over the Senate in the vice president's absence. Ordinarily, the president pro tem is the member of the majority party with the longest continuous term of service in the Senate. The president pro tem is mostly a ceremonial position. Junior senators take turns actually presiding over the sessions of the Senate.

The real leadership power in the Senate rests in the hands of the **Senate majority leader**, the **Senate minority leader**, and their respective whips. The Senate majority and minority leaders have the right to be recognized first in debate on the floor and generally exercise the same powers available to the House majority and minority leaders. They control the scheduling of debate on the floor in conjunction with the majority party's Policy Committee, influence the allocation of committee assignments for new members or for senators attempting to transfer to a new committee, influence the selection of other party officials, and participate in selecting members of conference committees. They are expected to mobilize support for partisan legislative initiatives or for the proposals of a president who belongs to their party. The leaders act as liaisons with the White House when the president is of their party, try to obtain the cooperation of

president pro tempore
The temporary presiding officer of the Senate in the absence of the vice president.

Senate majority leader
The chief spokesperson of the majority party in the Senate who directs the legislative program and party strategy.

Senate minority leader
The party officer in the Senate who commands the minority party's opposition to the policies of the majority party and directs the legislative program and strategy of his or her party.

Image 11–7
Mitch McConnell,
Republican Majority Leader of the Senate, shares a moment with Senator Chuck Schumer, Democrat of New York, as they prepare for a taping of *Meet the Press*.

committee chairpersons, and seek to facilitate the smooth functioning of the Senate through the senators' unanimous consent. The majority and minority leaders are elected by their respective party caucuses.

Senate party whips, like their House counterparts, maintain communication within the party on platform positions and try to ensure that party colleagues are present for floor debate and important votes. The Senate whip system is far less elaborate than its counterpart in the House, simply because there are fewer members to track.

How Members of Congress Decide

■ **11.6** Demonstrate how a bill becomes a law and explain how the different processes in the House and the Senate influence legislating.

Each member of Congress casts hundreds of votes in each session and compiles a record of votes during the years that he or she spends in the national legislature. Research shows that the best predictor of a member's vote is party affiliation. Party leadership in each house works hard to build cohesion and agreement among the members through the activities of the party caucuses and conferences.

The Conservative Coalition

Political parties are not always unified. In the 1950s and 1960s, the Democrats in Congress were often split between Northern liberals and Southern conservatives, which gave rise to the **conservative coalition**, a voting bloc made up of conservative Democrats and conservative Republicans. This coalition was able to win many votes over the years. Today, however, most Southern conservatives are Republicans, so the coalition has almost disappeared. Some Democrats in Congress, however, represent more moderate states or districts. The votes of these members, who are known as **Blue Dog Democrats**, are frequently courted by Republican leaders.

Polarization and Gridlock

Over the last two decades, both parties have become more cohesive, both within the halls of Congress and at the state and local level. Almost all of the Democratic members of Congress would now consider themselves to be liberals, whereas almost all Republican members of Congress could be considered conservatives. Numerous voting studies have concluded that both houses of Congress are more polarized than at any time in the last 50 years.[20] This is due, in part, to the ability of the parties to draw congressional districts that are more heavily Democratic or Republican. To win a nomination in such a district, the candidate must gain the votes of the most liberal or most conservative voters. The majority of Democratic representatives are very likely to vote against the majority of Republicans.

Add to this increasing **polarization**—the strong division between groups of people over beliefs. This situation is often termed **divided government**. Divided government can be effective if the parties agree to compromise. When there is a foreign policy crisis, for example, parties typically work well together. Divided government can also lead to a situation where neither side is willing to compromise on public policy, resulting in what is popularly known as

did you know?
The term "Blue Dog Democrat" was coined by a Texas Democratic congressman who said that liberal members were choking some Democrats until they turned blue.

conservative coalition
An alliance of Republicans and Southern Democrats that can form in the House or the Senate to oppose liberal legislation and support conservative legislation.

Blue Dog Democrats
Members of Congress from more moderate states or districts who sometimes "cross over" to vote with Republicans on legislation.

polarization
Strong division between groups of people over beliefs.

divided government
The situation when the presidency and one or more houses of Congress are controlled by different political parties.

---

20 Lynda Saad, "Gridlock Is Top Reason Americans Are Critical of Congress," The Gallup Poll, June 12, 2013.

gridlock. When this happens, major legislation stalls and the only laws that are passed are those which are noncontroversial. Polling over the years shows that the American public is strongly in favor of a productive Congress, regardless of which party is in the majority in either house.[21]

"Crossing Over"

On some votes, individual representatives and senators vote against their party, "crossing over to the other side" because the interests of their states or districts differ from the interests that prevail within the rest of their party. Democratic senators from Western states normally vote with Republicans on agricultural bills. Other voting decisions are based on the members' religious or ideological beliefs. Votes on issues such as abortion or gay rights may be motivated by a member's ideology or personal beliefs.

With so many voting decisions, every member cannot be fully informed on each issue. Research suggests that many voting decisions are based on cues provided by trusted colleagues or the party leadership. A member who sits on the committee that wrote a law may become a reliable source of information about that law. Alternatively, a member may turn to a colleague who represents a district in the same state or one who represents a similar district for cues on voting. Cues may also come from fellow committee members, leaders, and the administration.

Logrolling, Earmarks, and "Pork"

Sometimes, leaders on either side of the aisle will offer incentives to get needed votes for the passage of legislation. Even the president has been known to offer opportunities for the member to better serve his or her district by "bringing home the bacon." When a member "trades" his or her vote on a particular bill with another member in exchange for his or her vote on other legislation, the practice is known as logrolling. Often, members request that special appropriations for projects back home are attached to a bill to gain their votes. If the actual project is named, this is referred to as **earmark**. The term comes from the V-shaped mark that is cut in a pig's ear to identify the animal. These special projects are often referred to as **pork**, as in "bringing home the bacon." Although the Congress passed a moratorium on earmarks in 2011, special projects still find their way into the budget. A close reading of the 2015 appropriation bill found $4.2 billion in earmarks. Efforts have been made to force lawmakers to reveal all of their special projects, but new methods have emerged to hide these special appropriations from the public eye.

Politicians and reformers often rail against the practice of earmarks, and some projects seem ridiculous to everyone except those who will benefit. In some cases, earmarks truly are needed; in others, they are seen as the key to keeping a member of Congress in office. As the late Senator Robert Byrd of West Virginia was known to remark, "One man's pork is another man's job."[22]

How a Bill Becomes Law

Each year, Congress and the president propose and approve many laws. As detailed in Figure 11-4, each law begins as a bill, which must be introduced in

---

did you know?

Did you know that Tammy Baldwin of Wisconsin became the first openly gay member of the U.S. Senate when she was elected in 2012?

---

earmark
Funding appropriation that is specifically designated for a named project in a member's state or district.

pork
Special projects or appropriations that are intended to benefit a member's district or state; slang term for earmarks.

---

21 See the summary of the polarization studies in Thomas Mann and Norman Ornstein, *It's Even Worse Than It Looks: How the American Constitutional System Collided with the New Politics of Extremism* (New York: Basic Books, 2012), pp. 51–58.

22 "Ethan Barton, "They're Back! Congress Snuck $42 Billion Earmarks Despite 2011 Moratorium." *The Daily Caller*, May 13, 2015: http://dailycaller.com/author/ethanbarton/

Figure 11-4 ▶ How a Bill Becomes a Law

This illustration shows the most typical way in which proposed legislation is enacted into law. Most legislation begins as similar bills introduced into the House and the Senate. The process is illustrated here with two hypothetical bills: House bill No. 100 (HR 100) and Senate bill No. 200 (S 200). The path of HR 100 is shown on the left, and that of S 200 on the right.

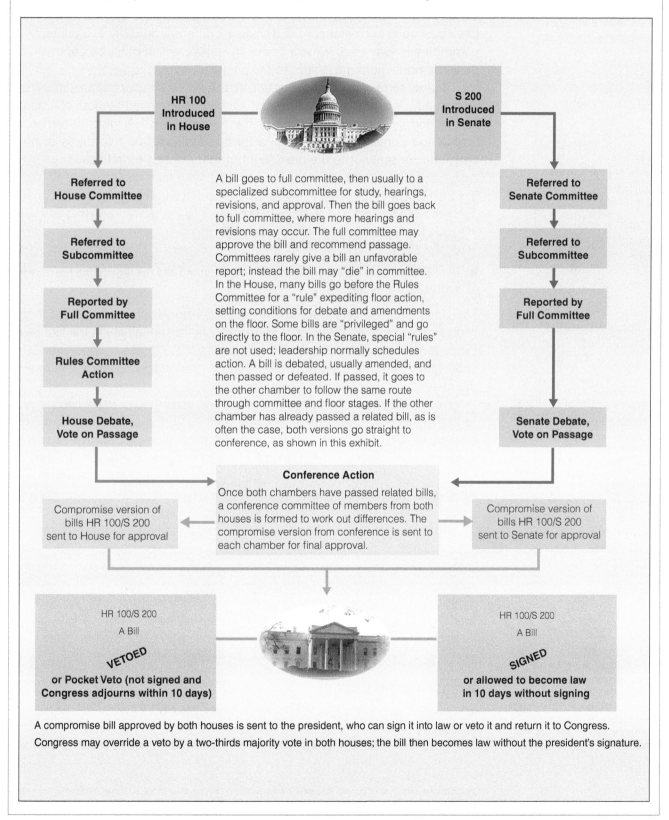

HR 100 Introduced in House

S 200 Introduced in Senate

Referred to House Committee

Referred to Subcommittee

Reported by Full Committee

Rules Committee Action

House Debate, Vote on Passage

A bill goes to full committee, then usually to a specialized subcommittee for study, hearings, revisions, and approval. Then the bill goes back to full committee, where more hearings and revisions may occur. The full committee may approve the bill and recommend passage. Committees rarely give a bill an unfavorable report; instead the bill may "die" in committee. In the House, many bills go before the Rules Committee for a "rule" expediting floor action, setting conditions for debate and amendments on the floor. Some bills are "privileged" and go directly to the floor. In the Senate, special "rules" are not used; leadership normally schedules action. A bill is debated, usually amended, and then passed or defeated. If passed, it goes to the other chamber to follow the same route through committee and floor stages. If the other chamber has already passed a related bill, as is often the case, both versions go straight to conference, as shown in this exhibit.

Referred to Senate Committee

Referred to Subcommittee

Reported by Full Committee

Senate Debate, Vote on Passage

Conference Action

Once both chambers have passed related bills, a conference committee of members from both houses is formed to work out differences. The compromise version from conference is sent to each chamber for final approval.

Compromise version of bills HR 100/S 200 sent to House for approval

Compromise version of bills HR 100/S 200 sent to Senate for approval

HR 100/S 200
A Bill
VETOED
or Pocket Veto (not signed and Congress adjourns within 10 days)

HR 100/S 200
A Bill
SIGNED
or allowed to become law in 10 days without signing

A compromise bill approved by both houses is sent to the president, who can sign it into law or veto it and return it to Congress.

Congress may override a veto by a two-thirds majority vote in both houses; the bill then becomes law without the president's signature.

either the House or the Senate. Often, similar bills are introduced in both chambers. A "money bill," however, must start in the House. In each chamber, the bill follows similar steps. It is referred to a committee and its subcommittees for study, discussion, hearings, and rewriting ("markup"). When the bill is reported out to the full chamber, it must be scheduled for debate (by the Rules Committee in the House and by the leadership in the Senate). After the bill has been passed in each chamber, if it contains different provisions, a conference committee is formed to write a compromise bill, which must be approved by both chambers before it is sent to the president to sign or veto.

Another form of congressional action, the *joint resolution*, differs little from a bill in how it is proposed or debated. Once it is approved by both chambers and signed by the president, it has the force of law.[23] A joint resolution to amend the Constitution, however, after it is approved by two-thirds of both chambers, is sent not to the president but to the states for ratification.

How Much Will the Government Spend?

■ **11.7** Explain how the federal budget is constructed and the legislative process for approving the budget.

The Constitution is very clear about where the power of the purse lies in the national government: all taxing or spending bills must originate in the House of Representatives. Today, much of the business of Congress is concerned with approving government expenditures through the budget process and raising the revenues to pay for government programs.

From 1922, when Congress required the president to prepare and present to the legislature an **executive budget**, until 1974, the congressional budget process was so disjointed that it was difficult to visualize the total picture of government finances. The president presented the executive budget to Congress in January. It was broken down into 13 or more appropriations bills. After all of the bills had been debated, amended, and passed, it was more or less possible to estimate total government spending for the next year.

Frustrated by the president's ability to impound (withhold) funds and dissatisfied with the entire budget process, Congress passed the Budget and Impoundment Control Act of 1974 to regain some control over the nation's spending. The act required the president to spend the funds that Congress had appropriated, ending the president's ability to kill programs by withholding funds. The other major accomplishment was to force Congress to examine total national taxing and spending at least twice in each budget cycle. See Figure 11-5 for a graphic illustration of the budget cycle.

Preparing the Budget

The federal government operates on a **fiscal year (FY)** cycle. The fiscal year runs from October through September, so that fiscal year 2018, or FY18, runs from October 1, 2017, through September 30, 2018. Eighteen months before a

executive budget
The budget prepared and submitted by the president to Congress.

fiscal year (FY)
A 12-month period that is used for bookkeeping, or accounting, purposes. Usually, the fiscal year does not coincide with the calendar year. For example, the federal government's fiscal year runs from October 1 through September 30.

---

23 In contrast, *simple resolutions* and *concurrent resolutions* do not carry the force of law, but rather are used by one or both chambers of Congress, respectively, to express facts, principles, or opinions. For example, a concurrent resolution is used to set the time when Congress will adjourn.

Figure 11-5 ▶ The Budget Cycle

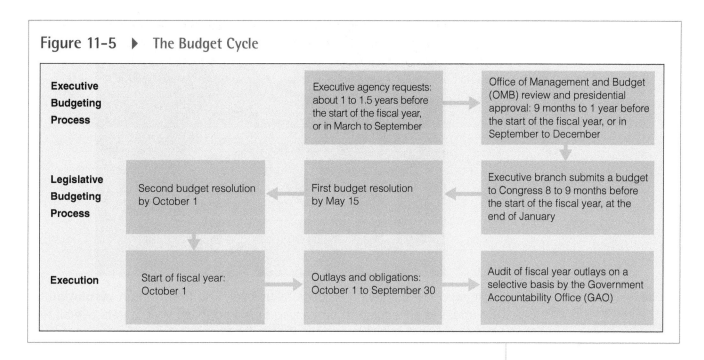

Executive Budgeting Process		Executive agency requests: about 1 to 1.5 years before the start of the fiscal year, or in March to September	Office of Management and Budget (OMB) review and presidential approval: 9 months to 1 year before the start of the fiscal year, or in September to December
Legislative Budgeting Process	Second budget resolution by October 1	First budget resolution by May 15	Executive branch submits a budget to Congress 8 to 9 months before the start of the fiscal year, at the end of January
Execution	Start of fiscal year: October 1	Outlays and obligations: October 1 to September 30	Audit of fiscal year outlays on a selective basis by the Government Accountability Office (GAO)

fiscal year starts, the executive branch begins preparing the budget. The Office of Management and Budget (OMB) outlines the budget and then sends it to the various departments and agencies. Bargaining follows, in which, for example, the Department of Health and Human Services argues for more welfare spending, and the armed forces argue for more defense spending. You can find the federal budget on the official OMB website.

Even though the OMB has only 600 employees, it is one of the most powerful agencies in Washington. It assembles the budget documents and monitors federal agencies throughout each year. Every year, it begins the budget process with a **spring review**, in which it requires all of the agencies to review their programs, activities, and goals. Several months later, the OMB begins the **fall review**. At this time, the OMB looks at budget requests and, in almost all cases, pares them back. Although the OMB works within guidelines established by the president, specific decisions often are left to the OMB director and the director's associates. The budget must be completed by January so that it can be included in the *Economic Report of the President*.

Congress Faces the Budget

In January, nine months before the fiscal year starts, the president takes the OMB's proposed budget, approves it, and submits it to Congress. Then the

From the Web ▶ How important is it that U.S. citizens are aware of where to find the federal budget and other federal documents for reference?

Office of Management Budget

spring review
The annual process in which the Office of Management and Budget requires federal agencies to review their programs, activities, and goals and submit their requests for funding for the next fiscal year.

fall review
The annual process in which the Office of Management and Budget, after receiving formal federal agency requests for funding for the next fiscal year, reviews the requests, makes changes, and submits its recommendations to the president.

Image 11-8
U.S. Secretary of Defense
Secretary of Defense James Mattis testifies before Congress on his department's budget for 2019.

DOD Photo/Alamy Stock Photo

first budget resolution
A resolution passed by Congress in May that sets overall revenue and spending goals for the following fiscal year.

authorization
A formal declaration by a legislative committee that a certain amount of funding may be available to an agency. Some authorizations terminate in a year; others are renewable automatically, without further congressional action.

appropriation
The passage by Congress of a spending bill specifying the amount of authorized funds that actually will be allocated for an agency's use.

second budget resolution
A resolution passed by Congress in September that sets "binding" limits on taxes and spending for the following fiscal year.

continuing resolution
A temporary funding law that Congress passes when an appropriations bill has not been decided by the beginning of the new fiscal year on October 1.

congressional budgeting process takes over. The **first budget resolution** by Congress is scheduled to be passed in May of each year. It sets overall revenue goals and spending targets. During the summer, bargaining among all the concerned parties takes place. Spending and tax laws that are drawn up during this period are supposed to be guided by the May congressional budget resolution. For each departmental budget, Congress must authorize funds to be spent. The **authorization** is a formal declaration by the appropriate congressional committee that a certain amount of funding may be available to an agency. After the funds are authorized, they must be appropriated by Congress. The appropriations committees of both the House and the Senate forward spending bills to their respective bodies. The **appropriation** of funds occurs when the final bill is passed.

Budget Resolutions

By September, Congress is scheduled to pass its **second budget resolution**, one that will set "binding" limits on taxes and spending for the fiscal year beginning October 1. Bills passed before that date that do not fit within the limits of the budget resolution are supposed to be changed.

In actuality, between 1978 and 1996, Congress did not pass a complete budget by October 1. Some years, the Congress has not succeeded in passing a budget at all. In other words, generally, Congress does not follow its own rules. In each fiscal year that starts without a budget, every agency operates on the basis of a **continuing resolution**, which enables the agency to continue its present function with funding equal to that of the previous year. Even continuing resolutions have not always been passed on time.

Key Terms

appropriation 418	**conservative coalition** 413	**earmarks** 414
authorization 418	**constituent** 387	**enumerated powers** 391
bicameralism 387	**continuing resolution** 418	**executive budget** 416
Blue Dog Democrats 413	**direct primary** 397	**fall review** 417
casework 389	**discharge petition** 407	**filibuster** 394
conference committees 408	**divided government** 413	**first budget resolution** 418

Chapter Summary

■ **11.1** The first 17 clauses of Article I, Section 8, of the Constitution specify most of the enumerated, or expressed, powers of Congress, including the right to impose taxes, to borrow money, to regulate commerce, and to declare war. Congress also enjoys the right to "make all Laws which shall be necessary and proper for carrying into Execution the foregoing Powers, and all other Powers vested by this Constitution in the Government of the United States, or in any Department or Officer thereof." This is called the elastic, or necessary and proper, clause.

■ **11.2** The authors of the Constitution believed that the bulk of national power should reside in the legislature because it represents the voters most directly. All legislative power rests in the Congress. The Constitution states that Congress will consist of two chambers. A result of the Connecticut Compromise, this bicameral structure established a balanced legislature, with the membership in the House of Representatives based on population and the membership in the Senate based on the equality of states.

■ **11.2** The functions of Congress include (1) lawmaking, (2) representation, (3) service to constituents, (4) oversight, (5) public education, and (6) conflict resolution. Members of the House and the Senate cultivate votes in their constituencies by representing local interests, providing services, and bringing home federal dollars for projects. At the same time, they must participate in debate and lawmaking for the nation as a whole; this may entail casting votes for legislation that may be of no interest to their constituents or may, in fact, not be beneficial to them. They also participate in committees that allow them to oversee government departments, educate the public, and work to resolve conflicts over policy.

■ **11.2** The House of Representatives has 435 members and the Senate has 100 members. Due to its larger size, the House has more formal rules. The Senate tradition of unlimited debate (filibustering) dates back to 1790 and has been used over the years to frustrate the passage of bills.

Under Senate Rule 22, cloture can be used to halt debate on a bill.

■ **11.2** Members of Congress are older and wealthier than most Americans, disproportionately white and male, and more likely to be trained in professional occupations. Members of the Senate are more likely to be lawyers and to be wealthier than House members. Additionally, there is less diversity in the Senate than in the House of Representatives.

■ **11.3** Congressional elections are operated by the individual state governments, which must abide by rules established by the Constitution and national statutes. Most candidates for Congress must win nomination through a direct primary. The overwhelming majority of incumbent representatives and a smaller proportion of senators who run for reelection are successful. A complicated aspect of congressional elections is apportionment—the allocation of legislative seats to constituencies. The Supreme Court's "one person, one vote" rule has been applied to equalize the populations of congressional and state legislative districts.

■ **11.4** Most of the actual work of legislating is performed by committees and subcommittees within Congress. Legislation introduced into the House or Senate is assigned to the appropriate standing committees for review. Select committees are created for a limited time for a specific purpose. Joint committees are formed by the concurrent action of both chambers and consist of members from each chamber. Conference committees are special joint committees set up to achieve agreement between the House and the Senate on the exact wording of legislative acts passed by both chambers in different forms. The seniority rule, which is usually followed, specifies that the longest-serving member of the majority party will be the chairperson of a committee.

■ **11.5** The foremost power holder in the House of Representatives is the Speaker of the House. Other leaders are the House majority leader, the House minority leader, and the majority and minority whips. Formally, the vice president is the presiding officer of the Senate, with the most senior member of the majority party serving as the president pro tempore to preside when the vice president is absent. Actual leadership in the Senate rests with the majority leader, the minority leader, and their whips.

■ **11.6** A bill becomes law by progressing through both chambers of Congress and their appropriate standing and

joint committees to the president. Members are usually most influenced in their voting decisions by their party affiliation, their constituency's interests, their own interests, and cues given by other legislators.

■ **11.7** The budget process for a fiscal year begins with the preparation of an executive budget by the president. This is reviewed by the Office of Management and Budget and then sent to Congress, which is supposed to pass a final budget by the end of September. Since 1978, Congress generally has not followed its own time rules.

Selected Resources

PRINT RESOURCES

Barone, Michael, and Grant Ujifusa. *The Almanac of American Politics, 2016* (Washington, DC: National Journal, 2016). This book, published biannually, is a comprehensive summary of current political information on each member of Congress, his or her state or congressional district, recent congressional election results, key votes, ratings by various organizations, sources of campaign contributions, and records of campaign expenditures.

Davidson, Roger H., and Walter J. Oleszek. *Congress and Its Members,* 15th ed. (Washington, DC: CQ Press, 2015). This classic looks carefully at the "two Congresses," the one in Washington and the role played by congresspersons at home.

Draper, Robert. *Do Not Ask What Good We Do* (New York: The Free Press, 2012). Draper, a *New York Times* writer, reveals an insider's view of the Congress and some of its colorful members and criticizes both houses for their ineffectiveness.

Golden, Michael. *Unlock Congress: Reform the Rules—Restore the System* (Pacific Grove, CA: Why Not? Books, 2015).

The author, a former journalist, examines the evolution of Congress to the gridlocked institution it is today. He makes clear, nonpartisan recommendations to restore the Congress to an effective legislative body.

Lebovich, Mark, *This Town: Two Parties and a Funeral—Plus Plenty of Valet Parking!—in America's Gilded Capital* (New York: Blue Rider Press, 2013). This outstanding book by a Washington journalist reveals what life in the capital is really like and the sources of information that everyone uses to follow the political life of Washington, DC.

Lott, Trent, and Tom Daschle. *Crisis Point: Why We Must and How We Can Overcome Our Broken Politics in Washington and Across America* (New York: Bloomsbury Press, 2016). Two prominent former senators, Lott, once the majority leader of the Republican Senate, and Daschle, minority leader of the Democrats, present a reasoned discussion of the issues that plague Congress, including campaign finance, media coverage, and the increasing polarization of the members.

MEDIA RESOURCES

Charlie Wilson's War—This hilarious film is based on the true story of how Wilson (Tom Hanks), a hard-living, hard-drinking representative from Texas, almost single-handedly won a billion dollars in funding for the Afghanis, who were fighting a Russian invasion. When equipped with heat-seeking missiles, the Afghanis prevail. Philip Seymour Hoffman steals the show, portraying a rogue CIA operative.

Lincoln—Although this superb 2012 movie is about Lincoln's political leadership, the plot focuses on his dealings with Congress.

House of Cards—This original series by Netflix is praised for its gritty and cynical view of how politics and journalism work in Washington, DC.

Mr. Smith Goes to Washington—A 1939 film in which Jimmy Stewart plays a naïve congressman who is quickly educated in Washington. A true American political classic.

Porked: Earmarks for Profit—A 2008 release from Fox News Channel that investigates congressional earmarks. Fox reporters contend that pork wastes tax dollars. Additionally, the network claims that some members of Congress have funded projects that benefited their own bank accounts.

ONLINE RESOURCES

Congressional Budget Office—provides Congress with nonpartisan analyses for economic and budget decisions and with estimates required for the congressional budget process: www.cbo.gov

Congress—each house's websites are indispensable sources for discovering what committees are doing and the progress of bills: www.house.gov

The Hill—a congressional newspaper that publishes daily when Congress is in session, with a special focus on business and lobbying, political campaigns, and goings-on on Capitol Hill: http://thehill.com

Roll Call—the newspaper of the Capitol that provides an inside view of developments in Washington, DC: www.rollcall.com

Voter Information Services—provides the interest group scorecards of all the members of Congress and allows you to create your own unique scorecard for candidates of interest: www.vis.org

12

The President

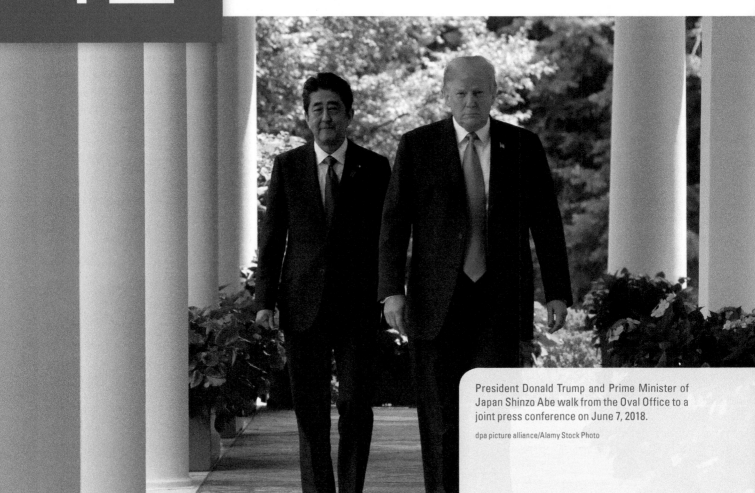

President Donald Trump and Prime Minister of Japan Shinzo Abe walk from the Oval Office to a joint press conference on June 7, 2018.

dpa picture alliance/Alamy Stock Photo

LEARNING OBJECTIVES

After reading this chapter, you will be able to:

■ **12.1** Explain the formal and informal roles played by the president, and discuss the constitutional or political origins of those roles.

■ **12.2** Demonstrate an understanding of the president's powers as commander in chief and the procedures described in the War Powers Act.

■ **12.3** Discuss the president's role in the legislative process; describe executive tools to initiate or block legislation.

■ **12.4** Explain the emergency powers of the president and the executive powers of the president.

■ **12.5** Explain the process by which a president could be impeached and forced to leave office.

■ **12.6** Describe the executive offices that support the president.

■ **12.7** Describe the job of the vice president and explain the circumstances under which the vice president becomes president.

What if... *There Were No Executive Privilege?*

Background

Although executive privilege is not mentioned in the Constitution, all presidents have invoked this privilege in response to perceived encroachments on the executive branch by Congress and by the judiciary. Executive privilege is the claim set forth by the president that certain communications must be kept secret for the good of the nation, whether for domestic interests or national security interests. The trouble begins when other branches suspect the executive is claiming this right to save embarrassment for the president or presidential subordinates. For example, in 2006, when two congressional committees were investigating the federal government's response to Hurricane Katrina, the Bush administration cited the need for confidentiality of executive-branch communications as justification for refusing to turn over certain documents, including email correspondence involving White House staff members. The administration had previously refused to release the names of oil company executives who had advised Vice President Cheney on energy policy.

Nonetheless, Congress could try to prohibit the use of executive privilege by passing a law. Alternatively, the Supreme Court could hold that executive privilege as a right is an unconstitutional exercise of executive power.

If Executive Privilege Were Eliminated

Without executive privilege, a president would have to be aware that all of his or her words, documents, and actions could be made public. We know from twentieth-century history that when a president does not have full executive privilege to protect information, the results can be devastating.

President Richard Nixon (served 1969–1974) tape-recorded hundreds of hours of conversations in the Oval Office. During the Watergate scandal, Congress requested those tapes. Nixon invoked executive privilege and refused to turn them over. Ultimately, the Supreme Court ordered him to comply; the tapes provided damning information about Nixon's role in the purported cover-up of illegal activities. Rather than face impeachment, Nixon resigned the presidency.

If executive privilege were eliminated, it is unlikely that conversations between the president and other members of the executive branch ever would be recorded or otherwise documented. As a result, we would have fewer records of an administration's activities.

Executive Privilege in a World Filled with Terrorism

Following the terrorist attacks on September 11, 2001, Attorney General John Ashcroft advised federal agencies "to lean toward withholding information whenever possible." Often, the Bush administration attempted to withhold information from Congress and the courts, not just the public. In matters of national security, when the president and the president's advisers discuss attacks on terrorist leaders or foreign nuclear plants, claiming executive privilege to prevent leaks to America's enemies would likely be justified. In 2012, the Obama administration claimed executive privilege for communications in the Department of Justice operation known as "Fast and Furious," which involved illegal gun transfers with Mexican drug lords. No details were given, but the operation likely involved relationships with the Mexican government that the president felt could not be disclosed.

Congress itself can be a source of leaks. Although Congress has procedures that can be used to guard sensitive information, it is unaccustomed to keeping secrets and often finds it hard to do so. The very size of Congress and its staff makes it difficult to keep secrets.

Past, Present, and Future Presidential Papers

The Bush administration attempted to control not only its own records, but also those of former presidents. Soon after September 11, 2001, President Bush signed Executive Order 13233, which provided that former presidents' private papers can be released only with the approval of both the former president in question and the current one. Upon taking office in 2009, President Obama rescinded several Bush executive orders, although he did allow former presidents to claim privilege for their own papers. Occasionally, Congress has attempted to place time limits for such claims, although no new laws have been successfully passed.

If executive privilege were eliminated, the White House would have a difficult time regulating the flow of past and present records into the public forum. The behavior of presidents and their administrations would certainly change. They might simply insist that no record of sensitive conversations may exist. If so, future Americans would lose much of the historical background for America's domestic and international actions.

For Critical Analysis

1. The history of executive privilege dates back to 1796, when President George Washington refused a request by the House for certain documents. Given the changes that have taken place since that time, should executive privilege be eliminated—or is it even more necessary today than it was at that time?

2. What would be the costs to the nation if executive privilege were eliminated?

The writers of the Constitution created the presidency of the United States without any models to follow. Nowhere else in the world was there a democratically selected chief executive. What the founders did not want was a king. Given their previous experience with royal governors in the colonies, many Constitutional Convention delegates wanted a very weak executive who could not veto legislation. Other delegates, especially those who had witnessed the need for a strong leader in the Revolutionary army, believed a strong executive was necessary. Overall, however, the delegates did not spend much time discussing actual powers to be granted to the president, leaving those questions to the Committee on Detail. The delegates created a chief executive who had enough powers granted in the Constitution to balance those of Congress.[1]

The power exercised by each president has been scrutinized and judged by historians, political scientists, the media, and the public. The personalities and foibles of each president have also been investigated and judged by many. Indeed, it would seem that Americans are fascinated by presidential power and by the persons who hold the office. In this chapter, after looking at who can become president and at the process involved, we will examine closely the nature and extent of the constitutional powers held by the president, including whether the president can decide which records can be made public and which aides might testify before Congress, as discussed in the opening feature.

Who Can Become President?

The requirements for becoming president, as outlined in Article II, Section 1, of the Constitution, are not overwhelmingly stringent:

> *No person except a natural born Citizen, or a Citizen of the United States, at the time of the Adoption of this Constitution, shall be eligible to the Office of President; neither shall any Person be eligible to that Office who shall not have attained to the Age of thirty-five Years, and been fourteen Years a Resident within the United States.*

The only question that arises about these qualifications relates to the term *natural-born citizen.* Does that mean only citizens born in the United States and its territories? What about a child born to a U.S. citizen (or to a couple who are U.S. citizens) visiting or living in another country? Although the Supreme Court has never directly addressed the question, it is reasonable to expect that someone would be eligible if her or his parents were Americans. The first presidents, after all, were not American citizens at birth, and others were born in areas that did not join the United States until later. These questions were debated when George Romney, who was born in Chihuahua, Mexico, made a serious bid for the Republican presidential nomination in the 1960s.[2] Similar questions were raised about the 2008 Republican candidate, John McCain, who was born in Panama on an American military base. Those questions were quickly dismissed because it is clear that children born abroad to American citizens are considered natural-born Americans. From time to time, movements arise to allow *naturalized* citizens to be eligible to run for the presidency, but these have had no success.

did you know?

Grover Cleveland was the only president to have served as a hangman. He was once sheriff of Erie County, New York, and twice had to spring the trap at a hanging.

---

1 Forrest McDonald, *The American Presidency: An Intellectual History* (Lawrence, KS: University Press of Kansas, 1994), p. 179.
2 George Romney was governor of Michigan from 1963 to 1969. Romney was not nominated for the presidency, and the issue remains unresolved. For a detailed explanation of who qualifies as a natural-born citizen, see "Defining 'Natural Born Citizen,'" James Spurgeon, IVN, August 13, 2013. http://ivn.us/2013.08.13/defining-natural-born-citizen/

Images 12-1 a & b
Harry Truman, left, is shown when he was the proprietor of a Kansas City, Missouri, men's clothing store, about 1920. Ronald Reagan, right, is shown as a frontier marshal in the movie *Law and Order*, released in 1953. Compared to members of Congress, presidents have had more varied backgrounds. How would varied life experiences benefit a president?

The American dream is symbolized by the statement that "anybody can become president of this country." It is true that in modern times, presidents have included a haberdasher (Harry Truman—for a short period), a peanut farmer (Jimmy Carter), and an actor (Ronald Reagan). But if you examine the list of presidents in the appendix, you will see that the most common previous occupation of presidents in this country has been that of lawyer. Out of 43 presidents, 26 have been lawyers, and many have been wealthy. (Fewer lawyers have become president in the last century, in part because senators, who are likely to be lawyers, have had a difficult time being elected president.)

Although the Constitution states that the minimum-age requirement for the presidency is 35 years, most presidents have been much older than that when they assumed office. John F. Kennedy, at the age of 43, was the youngest elected president; the oldest was Donald Trump at age 70. The average age at inauguration has been 54. The selection of presidents reflects a clear demographic bias. Until 2009, all had been white, male, and from the Protestant tradition, except for John F. Kennedy, who was a Roman Catholic. The inauguration of Barack Obama, a man of mixed race—and of Kenyan and American ancestry—was an extraordinary milestone in American history. Presidents have been men of great stature (such as George Washington) and men in whom leadership qualities were not so pronounced (such as Warren Harding). A presidential candidate usually has experience as a vice president, senator, or state governor. Former governors have been especially successful at winning the presidency; they can make the legitimate claims to have executive experience and electability.

did you know?
John F. Kennedy was the youngest elected president, taking office at the age of 43, but Theodore Roosevelt assumed office at the age of 42 after the assassination of President William McKinley.

The Process of Becoming President

Major and minor political parties nominate candidates for president and vice president at national conventions every four years. The nation's voters do not elect a president and vice president directly, but cast ballots for presidential electors, who then vote for president and vice president in the electoral college.

Twelfth Amendment
An amendment to the Constitution, adopted in 1804, that specifies the separate election of the president and vice president by the electoral college.

head of state
The role of the president as ceremonial head of the government.

Image 12-2
President Obama awards the nation's highest honor, the Medal of Honor, to Navy Senior Chief Edward Byers, Jr., for his effort to rescue an American hostage from the Taliban in Afghanistan.

Chip Somodevilla/Getty Images

Twice, the electoral college has failed to give any candidate a majority. At this point, the election is decided in the House of Representatives. The president is then chosen from among the three candidates having the most electoral college votes, as noted in Chapter 9. Thomas Jefferson and Aaron Burr tied in the electoral college in 1800 because the Constitution had not been explicit in indicating which of the two electoral votes were for president and which were for vice president. In 1804, the **Twelfth Amendment** clarified the matter by requiring that the president and vice president be chosen separately. In 1824, the House again had to make a choice, this time among William H. Crawford, Andrew Jackson, and John Quincy Adams. It chose Adams, even though Jackson had more electoral and popular votes.

The Many Roles of the President

■ **12.1** Explain the formal and informal roles played by the president, and discuss the constitutional or political origins of those roles.

The Constitution speaks briefly about the duties and obligations of the president. Based on this brief list of powers and on the precedents of history, the presidency has grown into a very complicated job that requires balancing at least five constitutional roles: (1) head of state, (2) chief executive, (3) commander in chief of the armed forces, (4) chief diplomat, and (5) chief legislator of the United States. It is worth noting that one person plays all these roles simultaneously and that these roles may at times come into conflict. For example, President Obama, in his role as commander in chief, used drones to find and eliminate leaders of al-Qaeda in Pakistan. As leader of the Democratic Party, however, he was critical of former president Bush for his war against terrorists and the creation of the prison at Guantánamo Bay, Cuba.

Head of State

Every nation has at least one ceremonial head of state. In most democratic governments, the role of **head of state** is given to someone other than the chief executive, who leads the executive branch of government. In Britain, the head of state is the queen. In much of Europe, the prime minister is the chief executive, and the head of state is the president. But in the United States, the president is both chief executive and head of state. According to William Howard Taft, as head of state, the president symbolizes the "dignity and majesty" of the American people.

As head of state, the president engages in many activities that are largely symbolic or ceremonial, such as the following:

- Decorating war heroes
- Throwing out the first pitch to open the baseball season
- Dedicating national parks and opening new factories

- Receiving visiting heads of state at the White House

- Representing the nation at times of national mourning, such as after the terrorist attacks of September 11, 2001, after the murder of the school children at Sandy Hook, and after the destruction from Hurricane Sandy in 2012

Some believe that having the president serve as both the chief executive and the head of state drastically limits the time available to do "real" work. Not all presidents have agreed with this conclusion, however—particularly those presidents who have skillfully blended these two roles with their role as politician. Being head of state gives the president tremendous public exposure, which can be an important asset in a campaign for reelection. When that exposure is positive, it helps the president leverage Congress regarding proposed legislation and increases the chances of being relected—or getting the candidates of the president's party elected.

Chief Executive

According to the Constitution, "The executive Power shall be vested in a President of the United States of America. . . . [H]e may require the Opinion, in writing, of the principal Officer in each of the executive Departments, upon any Subject relating to the Duties of their respective Offices . . . and he shall nominate, and by and with the Advice and Consent of the Senate, shall appoint . . . Officers of the United States. . . . [H]e shall take Care that the Laws be faithfully executed."

As **chief executive**, the president is constitutionally bound to enforce the acts of Congress, the judgments of federal courts, and treaties signed by the United States. The duty to "faithfully execute" the laws has been a source of constitutional power for presidents. Is the president allowed to reject certain parts of legislation if he or she believes that they are unconstitutional? For at least 175 years, presidents have used **signing statements**, written declarations made by presidents that accompany legislation, to make substantive constitutional pronouncements on the bill being signed. In 1830, President Andrew Jackson created a controversy when he signed a bill and at the same time sent to Congress a message that restricted the reach of the statute. Presidents Abraham Lincoln, Andrew Johnson, Theodore Roosevelt, Woodrow Wilson, and Franklin Roosevelt all used signing statements.

As for the legality of the practice, the Department of Justice has advised the last four administrations that the Constitution provides the president with the authority to decline to enforce a clearly unconstitutional law. Four justices of the Supreme Court joined in an opinion that the president may resist laws that encroach upon presidential powers by "disregarding them when they're unconstitutional."[3] After George W. Bush took office, he issued signing statements on more than 800 statutes—more than all of the previous presidents combined. He also tended to use the statements for a different purpose. When earlier presidents issued signing statements, they were used to instruct agencies on how to execute the laws or for similar purposes. Many (if not most) of President Bush's signing statements served notice that he believed parts of bills that he signed were unconstitutional or might violate national security. President Obama continued the practice of issuing signing statements to indicate his intentions with regard to legislation, although he used this tool only a few dozen times.

chief executive
The role of the president as head of the executive branch of the government.

signing statement
A written declaration that a president may make when signing a bill into law. Usually, such statements point out sections of the law that the president deems unconstitutional.

---

3 *Freytag v. C.I.R.*, 501 U.S. 868 (1991).

Some members of Congress are not so concerned about presidential signing statements. Senator John Cornyn (R-TX) has predicted that federal courts would be unlikely to consider the statements when interpreting the laws with which they were issued.[4]

The Powers of Appointment and Removal

To assist in the various tasks of the chief executive, the president has a federal bureaucracy (see Chapter 13), which consists of more than 2.7 million federal civilian employees. The president only nominally runs the executive bureaucracy. Most government positions are filled by **civil service** employees, who generally gain government employment through a merit system rather than presidential appointment.[5] Therefore, even though the president has important **appointment power**, it is limited to cabinet and subcabinet jobs, federal judgeships, agency heads, and several thousand lesser jobs. Of the more than 700,000 civilian jobs in the Department of Defense, the president may appoint fewer than 600 (less than one-tenth of 1 percent). Although the president has 555 appointments available in the State Department, some are ambassadorships to important allies, usually given to major donors and supporters of the president. Soon after each presidential election, the government publishes a list of about 8,000 specific jobs in a volume titled "The Plum Book: Policy and Supporting Positions." It is so-called because these have long been considered "plum jobs."

The president's power to remove from office those officials who are not doing a good job or who do not agree with the president is not explicitly granted by the Constitution and has been limited with regard to certain agencies. In 1926, however, a Supreme Court decision prevented Congress from interfering with the president's ability to fire those executive-branch officials whom the president had appointed with Senate approval.[6] The president can remove the heads of ten executive departments, all of the cabinet secretaries, and everyone who works in the Executive Office of the President and the White House Office. Harry Truman spoke candidly of the difficulties a president faces in trying to control the executive bureaucracy. On leaving office, he referred to the problems that Dwight Eisenhower, as a former general of the army, was going to have: "He'll sit here and he'll say do this! do that! and nothing will happen. Poor Ike—it won't be a bit like the Army. He'll find it very frustrating."[7]

The Power to Grant Reprieves and Pardons

Section 2 of Article II of the Constitution gives the president the power to grant **reprieves** and **pardons** for offenses against the United States, except in cases of impeachment. All pardons are administered by the Office of the Pardon Attorney in the Department of Justice. The U.S. Supreme Court upheld the president's power to grant reprieves and pardons in a 1925 case concerning a pardon granted by the president to an individual convicted of contempt of court. The judiciary had contended that only judges had the authority to convict individuals for contempt of court when court orders were violated and that the courts should be free from interference by the executive branch. The Court stated that the president could grant reprieves or pardons for all offenses "either before trial,

civil service
A collective term for the body of employees working for the government. Generally, civil service is understood to apply to all those who gain government employment through a merit system.

appointment power
The authority vested in the president to fill a government office or position. Positions filled by presidential appointment include those in the executive branch and the federal judiciary, commissioned officers in the armed forces, and members of the independent regulatory commissions.

reprieve
A formal postponement of the execution of a sentence imposed by a court of law.

pardon
A release from the punishment for or legal consequences of a crime; a pardon can be granted by the president before or after a conviction.

---

4 Todd Garvey, "Presidential Signing Statements: Constitutional and Institutional Implications" (Washington, DC: Congressional Research Service, January 4, 2012).
5 See Chapter 13 for a discussion of the Civil Service Reform Act.
6 *Meyers v. United States*, 272 U.S. 52 (1926).
7 Bartleby.com, Great Books Online, www.bartleby. Truman may not have considered the amount of politics involved in decision making in the upper echelon of the army.

during trial, or after trial, by individuals, or by classes, conditionally or absolutely, and this without modification or regulation by Congress."[8]

The power to pardon can also be used to apply to large groups of individuals who may be subject to indictment and trial. In 1977, President Jimmy Carter extended amnesty to all Vietnam War resisters who avoided the military draft by fleeing to Canada. More than 50,000 individuals were allowed to come back to the United States, free from the possibility of prosecution. The power to reprieve individuals allows the president to extend clemency to federal prisoners, usually on humanitarian grounds. However, in 1999, President Bill Clinton extended a conditional offer of clemency to a group of Puerto Rican nationalists who had been tried for planning terrorist attacks in the United States. The condition was for them to renounce the use of terrorist tactics and to not associate with other nationalists who advocate violence. Twelve accepted the offer, whereas two refused the conditions.

In a controversial decision, President Gerald Ford pardoned former President Nixon for his role in the Watergate affair before any charges were brought in court. President Obama pardoned 70 individuals by 2016, fewer than most modern presidents. However, he commuted the sentences of more than 200 prisoners, most of whom were serving long sentences for drug-related crimes. The president explained his rationale for these commutations by noting that these individuals would have had much shorter sentences if convicted of the same offense today.[9] **Commutations** do not declare the person innocent but can shorten the individual's sentence.

commutation
The commutation of a criminal sentence means that the sentence can be reduced in length to a specified number of years or to the time served. Commuting a sentence may reflect a change in the laws since the individual was convicted.

Commander in Chief

■ **12.2** Demonstrate an understanding of the president's powers as commander in chief and the procedures described in the War Powers Act.

The president, according to the Constitution, "shall be Commander in Chief of the Army and Navy of the United States, and of the Militia of the several States, when called into the actual Service of the United States." The armed forces are under civilian, rather than military, control.

Wartime Powers Certainly, those who wrote the Constitution had George Washington in mind when they made the president the **commander in chief**. The founders did not, however, expect presidents to lead the country into war without congressional authorization. Remember that Congress is given the power to declare war. As the United States grew in military power and global reach, presidents became much more likely to send troops into armed combat either in crisis situations or with an authorizing resolution short of a declaration of war. The last war to be fought under a congressional declaration was World War II.

Although we do not expect our president to lead the troops into battle, presidents as commanders in chief have wielded dramatic power. President Truman made the difficult decision to drop atomic bombs on Hiroshima and Nagasaki in 1945 to force Japan to surrender and thus bring World War II to an end. President Johnson ordered bombing missions against North Vietnam in the 1960s, and he personally selected some of the targets. President Nixon decided to invade Cambodia in 1970, an action widely condemned as an abuse of his power as commander in chief.

did you know?
Four U.S. presidents have been awarded the Nobel Peace Prize: Theodore Roosevelt, Woodrow Wilson, Jimmy Carter, and Barack Obama.

commander in chief
The role of the president as supreme commander of the military forces of the United States and of the state National Guard units when they are called into federal service.

---

8 *Ex parte Grossman*, 267 U.S. 87 (1925).
9 John Schuppe and Corky Siemaszko, "Obama Commutes Sentences of 61 Prisoners," NBC News, March 30, 2016. http://www.nbcnews.com/news/us~obama-commutes-sentences-61-prisoners-n547956

The president is the ultimate decision maker in military matters and has the final authority to launch a nuclear strike using missiles or bombs. For decades, the nuclear "football"—a briefcase filled with all the codes necessary to order a nuclear attack—accompanied the president. Today, nuclear security codes are uploaded to a website, protected by retinal scan technology, which can only be accessed by the president. Only the president can order the use of nuclear force.

The use of military force by presidents has raised some very thorny issues for the balance between Congress and the presidency. President Truman sent U.S. troops to Korea under a United Nations resolution, and President Johnson escalated the U.S. involvement in Vietnam under the quickly passed Gulf of Tonkin Resolution. President Bush invaded Iraq with congressional authorization. In none of these did Congress and the public expect extended wars with many casualties.

Presidents have also used military force without any congressional authorization, particularly in emergency situations. Ronald Reagan sent troops to Grenada to stop a supposedly communist coup, and Lyndon Johnson invaded the Dominican Republic. George H. W. Bush sent troops to Panama; numerous presidents have ordered quick air strikes on perceived enemies, and Barack Obama ordered the Navy Seal team into Pakistan to capture Osama bin Laden.

The War Powers Resolution   In an attempt to gain more control over such military activities, in 1973 Congress passed the **War Powers Resolution**—over President Nixon's veto—requiring that the president consult with Congress when sending American forces into action. Once they are sent, the president must report to Congress within 48 hours. Unless Congress approves the use of troops within 60 days or extends the 60-day time limit, the forces must be withdrawn. The War Powers Resolution was tested in the fall of 1983, when Reagan requested that troops remain in Lebanon. The resulting compromise was a congressional resolution allowing troops to remain there for 18 months.

Despite the War Powers Resolution, the powers of the president as commander in chief have continued to expand. The attacks of September 11, 2001, were the first on U.S. soil since Pearl Harbor. The imminent sense of threat supported passage of legislation that gave the president and the executive branch powers that had not been seen since World War II. President Bush's use of surveillance powers and other powers granted by the PATRIOT Act have caused considerable controversy. In the face of continued terrorist threats, President Obama signed extensions of the PATRIOT Act and continued many of the actions of the Bush administration. The Obama administration ordered hundreds of drone strikes on terrorist leaders or encampments, skirting the provisions of the War Powers Resolution because no American troops are involved in a combat situation when drones are used.

Chief Diplomat

The Constitution gives the president the power to recognize foreign governments; to make treaties, with the **advice and consent** of the Senate; to make special agreements with other heads of state that do not require congressional approval; and to nominate ambassadors. As **chief diplomat**, the president dominates American foreign policy, a role supported many times by the Supreme Court.

Diplomatic Recognition   An important power of the president as chief diplomat is that of **diplomatic recognition**, or the power to recognize—or refuse to recognize—foreign governments. In the role of ceremonial head of state,

War Powers Resolution
A law passed in 1973 spelling out the conditions under which the president can commit troops without congressional approval.

advice and consent
Terms in the Constitution describing the U.S. Senate's power to review and approve treaties and presidential appointments.

chief diplomat
The role of the president in recognizing foreign governments, making treaties, and effecting executive agreements.

diplomatic recognition
The formal acknowledgment of a foreign government as legitimate.

the president has always received foreign diplomats. In modern times, the simple act of receiving a foreign diplomat has been equivalent to accrediting the diplomat and officially recognizing his or her government. Such recognition of the legitimacy of another country's government is a prerequisite to diplomatic relations or treaties between that country and the United States.

Deciding when to recognize a foreign power is not always simple. The United States did not recognize the Soviet Union until 1933—16 years after the Russian Revolution of 1917. Only after all attempts to reverse the effects of that revolution proved futile—including military invasion of Russia and diplomatic isolation—did Franklin Roosevelt extend recognition to the Soviet government. U.S. presidents faced a similar problem with the Chinese communist revolution. In December 1978, long after the communist victory in China in 1949, Jimmy Carter finally granted official recognition to the People's Republic of China.[10]

After his reelection in 2012, President Obama opened secret negotiations with Cuba aimed at eventually restoring diplomatic relations with the Caribbean nation. The United States closed its embassy and placed an embargo on Cuban goods after Fidel Castro took power in 1959. After several years of meetings, President Obama announced in 2014 that diplomatic relations would be restored and, in 2016, he visited Cuba and proposed stronger economic and social ties to the Cuban people.

When governments are toppled by protests, the president often faces a diplomatic recognition issue. During the "Arab Spring," a new government was put in place in Egypt and recognized by the United States. In countries such as Libya, where the central government is not recognized by many regional leaders, the question becomes "who" to recognize as the official head of government.

Proposal and Ratification of Treaties The president has the sole power to negotiate treaties with other nations. These treaties must be presented to the Senate, where they may be modified and must be approved by a two-thirds vote. After ratification, the president can approve the senatorial version of the treaty. Approval poses a problem when the Senate has added substantive amendments or reservations to a treaty, particularly when such changes may require reopening negotiations with the other signatory governments. A president may decide to withdraw a treaty if changes are too extensive, as Woodrow Wilson did with the Versailles Treaty in 1919. Wilson believed that the senatorial reservations would weaken the treaty so much that it would be ineffective. His refusal to accept the senatorial version of the treaty led to the eventual refusal of the United States to join the League of Nations.

President Carter was successful in lobbying for the treaties that provided for the return of the Panama Canal to Panama by the year 2000 and for neutralizing the canal. President Clinton won a major political and legislative victory in 1993 by persuading Congress to ratify the North American Free Trade Agreement (NAFTA). In so doing, he had to overcome opposition from Democrats and most of organized labor. In 1998, he worked closely with Senate Republicans to ensure Senate approval of a treaty governing the use of chemical weapons. In 2000, he won another major legislative victory when Congress voted to normalize trade relations with China permanently.

---

10 The Nixon administration first encouraged new relations with the People's Republic of China by allowing a cultural exchange of ping-pong teams.

Image 12-3

President Richard Nixon and First Lady Pat Nixon lead the way as they take a tour of China's famed Great Wall, near Beijing, February 21, 1972. Why was Nixon's visit to China so historic?

AP Images

President George W. Bush indicated his intention to steer the United States in a more unilateral direction on foreign policy. He rejected the Kyoto Agreement on global warming and proposed ending the 1972 Anti-Ballistic Missile (ABM) Treaty that was part of the first Strategic Arms Limitation Treaty (SALT I). After the terrorist attacks of September 11, 2001, however, President Bush sought cooperation from U.S. allies in the war on terrorism. Bush's return to multilateralism was exemplified in the signing of a nuclear weapons reduction treaty with Russia in 2002.

The Obama administration quickly signaled a new outlook in foreign policy, with the president making multiple trips overseas, including to Egypt, in his first year in office. President Obama's stated goals in foreign policy included a more cooperative approach to world affairs and the reduction of nuclear weapons for all nations. In 2010, the president signed a treaty with Russia for a joint reduction of long-range nuclear weapons. The new Strategic Arms Reduction Treaty (START) was ratified by the U.S. Senate late in that year and went into force in 2011. The Obama administration used a very different strategy to get approval of an agreement with Iran to limit its development of nuclear weapons. Rather than negotiating a two-nation treaty, negotiations involved a multination team, including Russia, China, the United States, and several European powers. After the agreement with Iran was hammered out, it was sent to the United Nations as a UN treaty and unanimously approved in the Security Council. Early in his term, President Trump threatened to withdraw from the Iran agreement. In 2018, he formally withdrew and reimposed sanctions on the Iranian government.

Executive Agreements Presidential power in foreign affairs is enhanced greatly by the use of **executive agreements** made between the president and other heads of state. Such agreements do not require Senate approval, although the House and Senate may refuse to appropriate the funds necessary to implement them. Whereas treaties are binding on all succeeding administrations, executive agreements require each new president's consent to remain in effect.

Among the advantages of executive agreements are speed and secrecy. The former is essential during a crisis; the latter is important when open senatorial

executive agreement
An international agreement made by the president, without senatorial ratification, with the head of a foreign state.

Lincoln: The President as Legislator

Nominated for Best Picture in 2012, *Lincoln*, produced and directed by Steven Spielberg, examines the last four months of Lincoln's presidency. The film is based in part on Doris Kearns Goodwin's book, *Team of Rivals: The Political Genius of Abraham Lincoln*. Although set in 1865, the role of the president as chief legislator is no different than it was for President Obama; both spar with a contentious and divided Congress.

In the film, Lincoln is determined to persuade Congress to pass the Thirteenth Amendment, which eventually banned slavery in the United States. Although he had issued the Emancipation Proclamation (an executive order), at the time the film is set, he fears that the readmission of the Southern states to the Union at the end of the Civil War will cause the defeat of the amendment. Congress is on the verge of great turnover; many Democratic members have been defeated and are "lame ducks." The president is willing to bribe these defeated members with jobs to get their votes for the amendment. Lincoln is also willing to avoid confirming the presence of Confederate delegates who are approaching Washington to agree to peace terms, knowing that he needs the amendment to pass in order to deal with the Confederate

states. The amendment passes, and Lincoln makes a deal to end the war. A few days later, he is assassinated.

As in Goodwin's book, the president is portrayed as "first among equals" with his Cabinet and the leaders of Congress. He must use all of his resources to get the amendment passed and to make peace with the Confederate states. Some of the deals that are struck are less than principled, but all presidents must, at times, make deals, even with the members of their own party and with their own supporters.

For Critical Analysis

1. Why do you think members of the president's political party in Congress require persuasion and deal making to approve his legislation?

2. Although the Emancipation Proclamation was considered the document that freed the slaves, why did Lincoln feel so strongly that he needed an amendment to the Constitution?

debate may be detrimental to the best interests of the United States or to the interests of the president.[11] Executive agreements (about 13,000) greatly outnumber treaties (about 1,300). Many executive agreements contain secret provisions calling for American military assistance or other support. Franklin Roosevelt used executive agreements to bypass congressional isolationists when he traded American destroyers for British Caribbean naval bases and when he arranged diplomatic and military affairs with Canada and Latin American nations.

Chief Legislator

■ **12.3** Discuss the president's role in the legislative process; describe executive tools to initiate or block legislation.

Constitutionally, presidents must recommend to Congress legislation that they judge necessary and expedient. Not all presidents have wielded their powers as **chief legislator** in the same manner. Some have been almost completely

chief legislator
The role of the president in influencing the making of laws.

---

11 The Case Act of 1972 requires that all executive agreements be transmitted to Congress within 60 days after the agreement takes effect. Secret agreements are transmitted to the foreign relations committees as classified information.

unsuccessful in getting their legislative programs implemented by Congress. Presidents Franklin Roosevelt and Lyndon Johnson, however, saw much of their proposed legislation put into effect. Each year, the *Congressional Quarterly Weekly Review* publishes an analysis of presidential success in terms of legislation passed that the president has publicly supported. As shown in Figure 12-1, presidents tend to have a high success rate at the beginning of their administration, with a steep decline toward the end of their term. George W. Bush had more than a 70 percent success rate during the years he had a Republican-controlled Congress, but it fell to 34 percent after the Democrats won control of Congress in the 2006 elections. President Obama earned the highest success score ever recorded for a president in his first year, 96.7 percent. After the Republicans won the House of Representatives in 2010, his success rate fell to 57 percent and declined further in the later years of his presidency. In his first year, President Trump achieved a success rate of 98.7 percent although he took public positions on only a small number of bills.

Figure 12-1 ▶ Presidential Success Rate by Year of Presidency

The graph illustrates the president's success rate on bills on which he had taken a position. Note that presidents do very well at the beginning of their terms, especially when they have control of Congress. When the other party controls Congress, the presidential success rate falls.

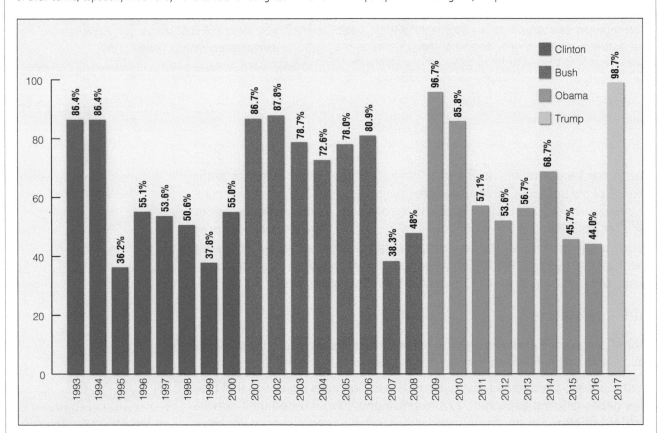

Source: *CQ Weekly*, January 12, 2018.

In modern times, the president has played a dominant role in creating the congressional agenda. In the president's annual **State of the Union message**, which is required by the Constitution (Article II, Section 3) and is usually given in late January, shortly after Congress reconvenes, the president, as chief legislator, presents a program. The message gives a broad, comprehensive view of what the president wishes the legislature to accomplish during its session. Originally, presidents sent a written memo to the Congress, which satisfies the constitutional requirement. In modern times, however, presidents see the State of the Union address as a tool to advance their policy agenda. The president is able to command the media stage and set out his or her goals. President Reagan began the practice of referring to ordinary citizens and bringing the subjects of those stories to sit in the balcony during the speech. Today, the president, the opposition party, and the commentators all recognize the impact of the State of the Union message on public opinion.

Legislation Passed The president can propose legislation, but Congress is not required to pass—or even introduce—any of the administration's bills. How, then, does the president get proposals made into law? One way is by persuasion. The president writes to, telephones, and meets with various congressional leaders; makes public announcements to influence public opinion; and, as head of the party, exercises legislative leadership through the congresspersons of that party. Most presidents also have an Office of Congressional Liaison within the White House Office. Such an office is staffed by individuals with extensive Washington experience, including former members of Congress, who lobby Congress on behalf of the president and monitor the progress of legislation on Capitol Hill. Presidents may also decide to use social events to lobby Congress, inviting the members and their spouses to parties at the White House. A more negative strategy is for the president to threaten to veto legislation if it does not correspond to his or her position.

Saying No to Legislation The president has the power to say no to legislation through use of the veto, by which the White House returns a bill unsigned to Congress with a **veto message** attached.[12] Because the Constitution requires that every bill passed by the House and the Senate be sent to the president before it becomes law, the president must act on each bill.

1. If the bill is signed, it becomes law.

2. If the bill is not sent back to Congress after ten congressional working days, it becomes law without the president's signature.

3. The president can reject the bill and send it back to Congress with a veto message setting forth objections. Congress then can change the bill, hoping to secure presidential approval, and pass it again. Or, Congress can simply reject the president's objections by overriding the veto with a two-thirds roll-call vote of the members present in both the House and the Senate.

4. If the president refuses to sign the bill and Congress adjourns within ten working days after the bill has been submitted to the president, the bill is killed for that session of Congress. This is called a **pocket veto**. If Congress wishes the bill to be reconsidered, the bill must be reintroduced during the following session.

State of the Union message
An annual message to Congress in which the president proposes a legislative program. The message is addressed not only to Congress, but also to the American people and to the world.

veto message
The president's formal explanation of a veto when legislation is returned to Congress.

pocket veto
A special veto exercised by the chief executive after a legislative body has adjourned. Bills not signed by the chief executive die after a specified period of time. If Congress wishes to reconsider such a bill, it must be reintroduced in the following session of Congress.

---

12 *Veto* in Latin means "I forbid."

Table 12-1 ▶ Presidential Vetoes, 1789 to the Present

YEARS	PRESIDENT	REGULAR VETOES	VETOES OVERRIDDEN	POCKET VETOES	TOTAL VETOES
1789–1797	Washington	2	0	0	2
1797–1801	J. Adams	0	0	0	0
1801–1809	Jefferson	0	0	0	0
1809–1817	Madison	5	0	2	7
1817–1825	Monroe	1	0	0	1
1825–1829	J. Q. Adams	0	0	0	0
1829–1837	Jackson	5	0	7	12
1837–1841	Van Buren	0	0	1	1
1841–1841	W. Harrison	0	0	0	0
1841–1845	Tyler	6	1	4	10
1845–1849	Polk	2	0	1	3
1849–1850	Taylor	0	0	0	0
1850–1853	Fillmore	0	0	0	0
1853–1857	Pierce	9	5	0	9
1857–1861	Buchanan	4	0	3	7
1861–1865	Lincoln	2	0	5	7
1865–1869	A. Johnson	21	15	8	29
1869–1877	Grant	45	4	48	93
1877–1881	Hayes	12	1	1	13
1881–1881	Garfield	0	0	0	0
1881–1885	Arthur	4	1	8	12
1885–1889	Cleveland	304	2	110	414
1889–1893	B. Harrison	19	1	25	44
1893–1897	Cleveland	42	5	128	170
1897–1901	McKinley	6	0	36	42
1901–1909	T. Roosevelt	42	1	40	82
1909–1913	Taft	30	1	9	39
1913–1921	Wilson	33	6	11	44
1921–1923	Harding	5	0	1	6
1923–1929	Coolidge	20	4	30	50
1929–1933	Hoover	21	3	16	37
1933–1945	F. Roosevelt	372	9	263	635
1945–1953	Truman	180	12	70	250
1953–1961	Eisenhower	73	2	108	181
1961–1963	Kennedy	12	0	9	21
1963–1969	L. Johnson	16	0	14	30
1969–1974	Nixon	26*	7	17	43
1974–1977	Ford	48	12	18	66
1977–1981	Carter	13	2	18	31
1981–1989	Reagan	39	9	39	78
1989–1993	George H. W. Bush	29	1	15	44
1993–2001	Clinton	37**	2	1	38
2001–2008	George W. Bush	11	4	1	12
2009–2016	Obama	8	0	1	9
2017–2018	Trump	0	0	0	0
TOTAL		**1,503**	**110**	**1,068**	**2,572**

Source: Office of the Clerk.

*Two pocket vetoes by President Nixon, overruled in the courts, are counted here as regular vetoes.

**President Clinton's line-item vetoes are not included.

Do We Need a President *and* a King?

In many democratic societies, the government has a head of government, who actually guides government policy and is the political leader, and a head of state, who is the symbolic head of government. In parliamentary systems, the head of government is actually elected by his or her peers in the majority party in the legislature. In Great Britain, the queen has no political power whatsoever. She cannot refuse to name the leader of the majority party. When she opens the parliamentary session, she reads a speech written for her by the prime minister. Similar political systems with royal families and parliamentary leadership are found in Denmark, Sweden, Spain, and a few smaller European nations. The advantage of this system is that the head of state (the monarch) symbolically represents the nation. Public fascination with royalty means that the prime minister can do his or her job without the gossip and journalistic coverage that surrounds the president of the United States.

Other democracies, including Italy, France, and Germany, have no royal families. The president of the nation is separately elected for a longer term but has little political power. He or she is the head of state and may counsel the head of the government, but political and executive power rests with the prime minister or premier. In some democratic states, the president and the premier are elected, although with different terms.

Until 2008, Vladimir Putin was the president of Russia, but his two terms were limited by the 1993 constitution. After his second term, his chosen successor, Dmitry Medvedev, was elected for one term. Soon after the election, Medvedev named Putin as the premier, still leaving him with considerable power. After Medvedev served one term, Putin was elected to the presidency again because his ability to serve two more terms was constitutional. So, in the case of Russia and some other states, the head of state is the president (who is elected) and who then can name the premier and the cabinet ministers. The intent of this system

Image 12-4 President Vladimir Putin of Russia at the opening of negotiations with other European leaders.

is for the president to be popularly elected and to exercise political leadership, while the premier runs the everyday operations of government and leads the legislative branch. Given the 2014 Russian annexation of Crimea and its threats to Ukraine, it appears that President Putin is not only the leader of the state, but also the political leader and decision maker for the government.

For Critical Analysis

1. Why is it important to separate the roles of head of state and head of government?

2. Can the existence of a symbolic head of state, such as a monarch, make the elected leader more effective?

3. Does the U.S. president, who is both head of state and head of government, carry too heavy a burden?

Presidents employed the veto power infrequently until after the Civil War, but it has been used with increasing vigor since then (see Table 12-1). Millard Fillmore (served 1850–1853) was the last president to serve a full term in office without exercising the veto power. Only nine bills were vetoed by President Obama. When control of Congress was split between the two parties, he issued only two vetoes because most measures opposed by the

Image 12-5

President Dwight D. Eisenhower prepares for a nationwide radio and television address in 1959 in which he called for legislation to stop corruption in labor unions.

line-item veto
The power of an executive to veto individual lines or items within a piece of legislation without vetoing the entire bill.

constitutional powers
Powers vested in the president by Article II of the Constitution.

statutory powers
Powers created for the president through laws enacted by Congress.

expressed powers
Powers of the president that are expressly written into the Constitution or into statutory law.

inherent powers
Powers of the president derived from the statements in the Constitution that "the executive Power shall be vested in a President" and that the president should "take Care that the Laws be faithfully executed"; defined through practice rather than through law.

president did not pass Congress. After the Republicans gained control of both houses in 2015, President Obama vetoed seven more bills.

The Line-Item Veto Ronald Reagan lobbied strenuously for Congress to provide the president with the **line-item veto**, which would allow the president to veto *specific* spending provisions of legislation that were passed by Congress. In 1996, Congress passed the Line Item Veto Act. Signed by President Clinton, the law granted the president the power to rescind any item in an appropriations bill unless Congress passed a resolution of disapproval. The congressional resolution could be, in turn, vetoed by the president. The law did not take effect until after the 1996 election.

The act was soon challenged in court as an unconstitutional delegation of legislative powers to the executive branch. In 1998, by a 6–3 vote, the U.S. Supreme Court agreed and overturned the act. The Court stated that "there is no provision in the Constitution that authorizes the president to enact, to amend or to repeal statutes."[13]

Congress's Power to Override Presidential Vetoes A veto is a clear-cut indication of the president's dissatisfaction with congressional legislation. Congress, however, can override a presidential veto, although it rarely exercises this power. Two-thirds of the members of each chamber who are present must vote to override the president's veto in a roll-call vote. This means that if only one-third plus one of the members voting in the House or Senate do not agree to override the veto, the veto holds. Congress first overrode a presidential veto during the administration of John Tyler (served 1841–1845). Overall, only about 7 percent of all regular vetoes have been overridden.

Other Presidential Powers

The powers of the president just discussed are **constitutional powers**, because their basis lies in the Constitution. In addition, Congress has established by law or statute numerous other presidential powers, such as the ability to declare national emergencies. These are **statutory powers**. Both constitutional and statutory powers have been labeled the **expressed powers** of the president, because they are expressly written into the Constitution or into law.

Presidents also have what have come to be known as **inherent powers**. These depend on the statements in the Constitution that "the executive Power shall be vested in a President" and that the president should "take Care that the Laws be faithfully executed." The most common example of inherent powers are those emergency powers invoked by the president during wartime. Franklin Roosevelt used his inherent powers to move the Japanese and Japanese Americans living in the United States into internment camps for the duration of World War II.

Clearly, modern U.S. presidents have many powers at their disposal. According to some critics, among the powers exercised by modern presidents are certain powers that rightfully belong to Congress but that Congress has yielded to the executive branch.

---

13 *Clinton v. City of New York*, 524 U.S. 417 (1998).

The President as Party Chief and Superpolitician

Presidents are by no means above political partisanship, and one of their many roles is that of chief of party. Although the Constitution says nothing about the function of the president within a political party (the mere concept of political parties was abhorrent to most of the Constitution's authors), today presidents are the actual leaders of their parties.

The President as Chief of Party

As party leader, the president chooses the national committee chairperson and tries to discipline party members who fail to support presidential policies. One way of exerting political power is through **patronage**—appointing political supporters to government or public jobs. This power was more extensive in the past, before the establishment of the civil service in 1883 (see Chapter 13), but the president retains important patronage power. The president can appoint several thousand individuals to jobs in the cabinet, the White House, embassies, and the federal regulatory agencies.

patronage
The practice of rewarding faithful party workers and followers with government employment and contracts.

Perhaps the most important partisan role that the president has played in recent decades is that of fundraiser. The president is able to raise large amounts for the party through appearances at dinners, speaking engagements, and other social occasions. President Clinton may have raised more than half a billion dollars for the Democratic Party during his two terms. President George W. Bush was even more successful than President Clinton. President Barack Obama continued the trend of fundraising for his party, raising money for members of Congress in 2012 and 2016.

The president may also make it known that a particular congressperson's choice for federal judge will not be appointed unless that member of Congress is more supportive of the president's legislative program.[14] The president may agree to campaign for a particular program or for a particular candidate. Presidents also reward loyal members of Congress with support for the funding of local projects, tax breaks for local industries, invitations to fly in *Air Force One*, and other forms of social recognition.

The President's Power to Persuade

According to political scientist Richard E. Neustadt, without the power to persuade, no president can lead well. After all, even though the president is in the news virtually every day, the Constitution gives Congress most of the authority in the U.S. political system. The Constitution does not give the executive branch enough constitutional power to firmly establish the president in a strong leadership position. Therefore, the president must establish a "professional reputation" that will convince Congress, the bureaucracy, and the public to support the president's agenda. As Neustadt argues, "presidential power is the power to persuade."[15]

---

14 "Senatorial courtesy" (see Chapter 14) often puts the judicial appointment in the hands of the Senate, however.
15 Richard E. Neustadt, *Presidential Power and the Modern Presidents: The Politics of Leadership from Roosevelt to Reagan*, rev. ed. (New York: Free Press, 1991).

Constituencies and Public Approval

All politicians worry about their constituencies, presidents included. Presidents with high approval ratings are able to leverage those ratings with members of Congress, who would prefer not to vote against the opinions of their own constituents.

Presidential Constituencies According to Neustadt, presidents have not just one constituency, but many. They are beholden to the entire electorate—the public of the United States—even those who did not vote. They are beholden to their party because its members helped to put them in office. The president's constituencies also include members of the opposing party, whose cooperation the president needs. Finally, the president must take into consideration a constituency that has come to be called the **Washington community**. This community consists of individuals who—whether in or out of political office—are familiar with the workings of government, thrive on gossip, and measure on a daily basis the political power of the president.

Public Approval All of these constituencies are impressed by presidents who maintain a high level of public approval, as this is very difficult to accomplish. Presidential popularity, as measured by national polls, gives the president an extra political resource for persuading legislators or bureaucrats to pass legislation. As you will note from Figure 12-2, patterns for almost all presidents are common. Presidential approval ratings tend to be very high when a new president takes office (the honeymoon period) and decline to a low in the last two years of the second term. Spikes in public approval apart from that cycle tend to occur when the United States sends troops in harm's way. This is the "rally 'round the flag" effect. Look at George H. W. Bush's ratings. Popular approval of the president reached a new high at the beginning of the Persian Gulf War, but that approval had no staying power, and his ratings declined precipitously in the year following the victory. Bill Clinton defied all tradition by having high ratings even while he was fighting impeachment.

Washington community
Individuals regularly involved with politics in Washington, DC.

Figure 12-2 ▶ Public Popularity of Modern Presidents

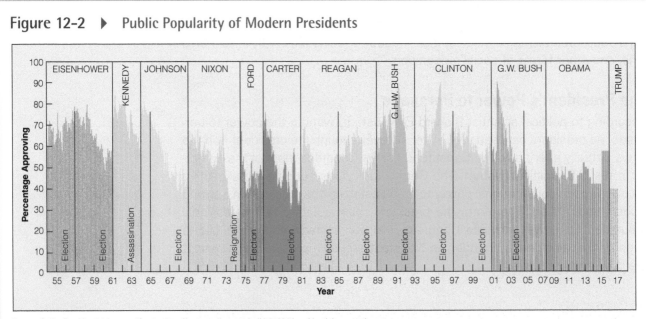

Source: Gallup Presidential Approval Center. http://www.gallup.com/poll/124922/presidential-approval-center.aspx

George W. Bush and the Public Opinion Polls The impact of popular approval on a president's prospects was placed in sharp relief by the experiences of the second President Bush. Immediately after September 11, 2001, Bush had the highest approval ratings ever recorded. His popularity then entered a steep decline that was interrupted only briefly by high ratings during the early phases of the Second Gulf War. During his second term, Bush's approval ratings reached new lows, falling to less than 30 percent by 2008. Without question, the economic crisis of fall 2008 contributed to the final low ebb of his approval ratings.

Obama and Trump: Public Approval

Like most presidents who win office with a substantial margin of victory, President Obama entered office with very high approval ratings. His high standing with the public lasted throughout his first year in office. As the recession deepened, his rating declined to the mid-50s, and he ended his term with an approval rating of 57 percent. At his inaugural, President Trump's public approval rating was just over 40 percent, a significant low for a newly elected president. Throughout his first year in office, his approval ratings hovered around 39 percent, although the public had higher approval for his economic and foreign policies. It is likely that his personal conduct caused the low personal ratings, while the public approved of his policy initiatives.

Image 12-6
President John F. Kennedy discusses the Berlin crisis at a news conference in 1961. Kennedy continues to be considered a master of such events.

AP Images/Bill Chaplis

"Going Public" In the 1800s, only 7 percent of presidential speeches were addressed to the public; since 1900, 50 percent have been addressed to the public. Scholar Samuel Kernell has proposed that the style of presidential leadership has changed since World War II, due partly to the influence of television, with a resulting change in the balance of national politics.[16] Presidents frequently go over the heads of Congress and the political elites, taking their cases directly to the people.

This strategy, which Kernell dubbed "going public," gives the president additional power through the ability to persuade and manipulate public opinion. By identifying their own positions so clearly, presidents weaken the ability of Congress to modify their agenda. Given the increasing importance of the media as the major source of political information for citizens and elites, presidents will continue to use public opinion as part of their arsenal of weapons to gain support from Congress and to achieve their policy goals.

Special Uses of Presidential Power

■ **12.4** Explain the emergency powers of the president and the executive powers of the president.

Presidents have at their disposal a variety of special powers and privileges not available in the other branches of the U.S. government: (1) emergency powers, (2) executive orders, and (3) executive privilege.

Emergency Powers

emergency powers
Inherent powers exercised by the president during a period of national crisis.

The Constitution does not mention additional powers that the executive office may exercise during national emergencies. The Supreme Court has indicated that an "emergency does not create power."[17] But it is clear that presidents have used their inherent powers during times of emergency, particularly concerning foreign affairs. The **emergency powers** of the president were first enunciated in *United States v. Curtiss-Wright Export Corp.*[18] In that case, President Franklin Roosevelt, without congressional authorization, ordered an embargo on the shipment of weapons to two warring South American countries. The Court recognized that the president may exercise inherent powers in foreign affairs and that the national government has primacy in these affairs.

Abraham Lincoln suspended civil liberties at the beginning of the Civil War (1861–1865) and called the state militias into national service. These actions and his subsequent governance of conquered areas, and even of areas of Northern states, were justified by claims that they were essential to preserve the Union. President Truman authorized the federal seizure of steel plants and their operation by the national government in 1952 during the Korean War. Truman claimed that he was using his inherent emergency power as chief executive and commander in chief to safeguard the nation's security, as an ongoing strike by steelworkers threatened the supply of weapons to the armed forces. The Supreme Court did not agree, holding that the president had no authority under the Constitution to seize private property or to legislate such

---

16 Samuel Kernell, *Going Public: New Strategies of Presidential Leadership,* 4th ed. (Washington, DC: Congressional Quarterly Press, 2006).
17 *Home Building and Loan Association v. Blaisdell,* 290 U.S. 398 (1934).
18 299 U.S. 304 (1936).

action.[19] This was the first time a limit was placed on the exercise of the president's emergency powers.

After September 11, 2001, the Bush administration pushed several laws through Congress that granted more power to the Department of Justice and other agencies to investigate possible terrorists. Many of these provisions of the PATRIOT Act and other laws have been reaffirmed by Congress in subsequent years, whereas others have been revised. In 2006, it became clear that President Bush had also authorized federal agencies to eavesdrop on international telephone calls without a court order when the party overseas was suspected of having information about terrorism or might be a suspect in a terrorist plot. This eavesdropping had not been authorized under the legislation. Many scholars claimed that this exercise of presidential power was far beyond what could be claimed an emergency power.[20] The Bush administration claimed that it was entirely within the president's power to make such an authorization, although it did not claim the authorization to be within the Supreme Court's definition of "emergency power." Following these disclosures, the administration pursued an expanded law to allow such wiretapping, but provisions of that new bill proved too controversial to pass in 2008.

President Obama's administration did not attempt to pass any legislation on this matter. In 2013, however, the revelations of Edward Snowden made it clear that the eavesdropping program was still intact and, in fact, the National Security Agency (NSA) was now collecting almost all landline telephone call data, both within the United States and from the United States to other nations.[21] The president, after appointing a commission to make recommendations, announced that some limitations on this program might be possible.

Executive Orders

Congress allows the president (and administrative agencies) to issue **executive orders** that have the force of law. These executive orders can (1) enforce legislative statutes, (2) enforce the Constitution or treaties with foreign nations, and (3) establish or modify rules and practices of executive administrative agencies.

An executive order, then, represents the president's legislative power. The only requirement is that under the Administrative Procedure Act of 1946, all executive orders must be published in the **Federal Register**, a daily publication of the U.S. government. Executive orders have been used to establish procedures, to implement national affirmative action regulations, to restructure the White House bureaucracy, to classify government information as secret, to establish military tribunals for suspected terrorists, and to order federal agencies to provide benefits to legally married same-sex couples.

It is important to note that executive orders can be revoked by succeeding presidents. George H. W. Bush issued an order to ban foreign aid to countries that included abortion in their family planning strategies, because that provision (the Hyde Amendment) could not make it through Congress as legislation. President Clinton revoked the order. The George W. Bush administration revoked many of the thousands of executive orders and regulations issued in the last months of the Clinton administration. Not surprisingly, the Obama administration revoked a

executive order
A rule or regulation issued by the president that has the effect of law. Executive orders can implement and give administrative effect to provisions in the Constitution, to treaties, and to statutes.

Federal Register
A publication of the U.S. government that prints executive orders, rules, and regulations.

---

19 *Youngstown Sheet and Tube Co. v. Sawyer,* 343 U.S. 579 (1952).

20 www.nybooks.com/article/2006/06/22/power-grab/

21 See the chronology of the NSA spying program at the Electronic Frontier Foundation, "NSA Spying FAQ," www.eff .or.nsa-spying number of the Bush orders and issued new orders in support of stronger environmental regulations, food safety, consumer safety, and many other areas. In the last year of his presidency, President Obama and his administration issued a number of orders dealing with the environment.

As soon as President Trump was inaugurated he proceeded to follow up on his promise to repeal many of the Obama executive orders. He signed orders approving the Dakota pipeline, reducing regulations on oil and gas drilling and on coal mining. He also signed a number of orders modifying the Affordable Care Act. Among his most controversial orders were those banning entry visas to citizens of several Muslim-majority nations.

Executive Privilege

Another inherent executive power claimed by presidents concerns the ability to withhold information from, or refuse to appear before, Congress or the courts. This is called **executive privilege**, and it relies on the constitutional separation of powers for its basis.

Presidents have frequently invoked executive privilege to avoid having to disclose information to Congress on actions of the executive branch. Critics of executive privilege believe that it can be used to shield from public scrutiny executive actions that should be open to Congress and to the American citizenry.

Limiting Executive Privilege Limits to executive privilege went untested until the Watergate affair in the early 1970s. Five men broke into the headquarters of the Democratic National Committee and were caught searching for documents that would damage the candidacy of the Democratic nominee, George McGovern. Later investigation showed that the break-in was planned by members of Richard Nixon's campaign committee and that Nixon and his closest advisers had devised a strategy for impeding the investigation of the crime. After it became known that all of the conversations held in the Oval Office had been tape-recorded on a secret system, Nixon was ordered to turn over the tapes to the special prosecutor.

Nixon refused to do so, claiming executive privilege. He argued that "no president could function if the private papers of his office, prepared by his personal staff, were open to public scrutiny." In 1974, in one of the Supreme Court's most famous cases, *United States v. Nixon*, the justices unanimously ruled that Nixon had to hand over the tapes.[22] The Court held that executive privilege could not be used to prevent evidence from being heard in criminal proceedings.

Clinton's Attempted Use of Executive Privilege The claim of executive privilege was also raised by the Clinton administration as a defense against the aggressive investigation of

executive privilege
The right of executive officials to withhold information from or refuse to appear before a legislative committee.

Image 12–7
Richard Nixon says goodbye outside the White House after his resignation on August 9, 1974, as he prepares to board a helicopter for a flight to nearby Andrews Air Force Base. Nixon addressed members of his staff in the East Room prior to his departure. Was Nixon impeached?

AP Images/BOB DAUGHERTY

---

22 318 U.S. 683 (1974).

Clinton's relationship with White House intern Monica Lewinsky by Independent Counsel Kenneth Starr. The Clinton administration claimed executive privilege for several presidential aides who might have discussed the situation with the president. In addition, Clinton asserted that his White House counsel did not have to testify before the Starr grand jury due to attorney-client privilege. The Department of Justice claimed that members of the Secret Service who guard the president could not testify about his activities due to a "protective function privilege" inherent in their duties. The federal judge overseeing the case denied the claims of privilege, however, and the decision was upheld on appeal.

Abuses of Executive Power and Impeachment

■ **12.5** Explain the process by which a president could be impeached and forced to leave office.

Presidents normally leave office either because their first term has expired and they have not sought (or won) reelection or because, having served two full terms, they are not allowed to be elected for a third term (due to the Twenty-second Amendment, passed in 1951). Eight presidents have died in office. But a president may leave office in another way—**impeachment** and conviction. Articles I and II of the Constitution authorize the House and Senate to remove the president, the vice president, or other civil officers of the United States for committing "Treason, Bribery, or other high Crimes and Misdemeanors." According to the Constitution, the impeachment process begins in the House, which impeaches (accuses) the federal officer involved. If the House votes to impeach the officer, it draws up articles of impeachment and submits them to the Senate, which conducts the actual trial.

No president has ever actually been impeached and convicted—and thus removed from office—by means of this process. President Andrew Johnson (served 1865–1869), who succeeded to the office after the assassination of Abraham Lincoln, was impeached by the House but acquitted by the Senate. More than a century later, the House Judiciary Committee approved articles of impeachment against President Nixon for his involvement in the cover-up of the Watergate break-in of 1972. Informed by members of his own party that he would not survive the trial in the Senate, Nixon resigned on August 9, 1974, before the full House voted on the articles. Nixon is the only president to have resigned from office. The second president to be impeached by the House but not convicted by the Senate was President Clinton. In September 1998, Independent Counsel Kenneth Starr submitted the findings of his investigation of the president on the charges of perjury and obstruction of justice. The House approved two charges against Clinton: lying to the grand jury about his affair with Monica Lewinsky and obstruction of justice. The articles of impeachment were then sent to the Senate, which acquitted Clinton.

impeachment
An action by the House of Representatives to accuse the president, vice president, or other civil officers of the United States of committing "Treason, Bribery, or other high Crimes and Misdemeanors."

The Executive Organization

■ **12.6** Describe the executive offices that support the president.

Gone are the days when presidents answered their own mail, as George Washington did. It was not until 1857 that Congress authorized a private secretary for the president, to be paid by the federal government. Woodrow Wilson typed most of his correspondence, even though he did have several

did you know?
President Richard Nixon served 56 days without a vice president, and President Gerald Ford served 132 days without a vice president.

cabinet
An advisory group selected by the president to aid in making decisions. The cabinet includes the heads of 15 executive departments and others named by the president.

kitchen cabinet
The informal advisers to the president.

secretaries. At the beginning of Franklin Roosevelt's tenure in the White House, the entire staff consisted of 37 employees. With the New Deal and World War II, however, the presidential staff became a sizable organization.

Today, the executive organization includes a White House office staff of about 600, including part-time employees and others who are borrowed from their departments by the White House. The more than 460 employees who work in the White House Office are closest to the president. The employees who work for the numerous councils and advisory groups support the president on policy and coordinate the work of departments. Cabinet members, each of whom is the principal officer of a government department, are perhaps the president's most helpful advisors.

The Cabinet

Although the Constitution does not include the word *cabinet*, it does state that the president "may require the Opinion, in writing, of the principal Officer in each of the executive Departments." All presidents have turned to an advisory group, or **cabinet**, for counsel.

Members of the Cabinet Originally, the cabinet consisted of only four officials—the secretaries of state, treasury, and war and the attorney general. Today, the cabinet numbers 14 department secretaries and the attorney general. The cabinet may include others as well. The president can, at his or her discretion, ascribe cabinet rank to the vice president, the head of the Office of Management and Budget, the national security adviser, the ambassador to the United Nations, or others.

Often, a president will use a **kitchen cabinet** to replace the formal cabinet as a major source of advice. The term *kitchen cabinet* originated during the presidency of Andrew Jackson, who relied on the counsel of close friends who often met with him in the kitchen of the White House. A kitchen cabinet is an informal group of advisers—usually, friends with whom the president worked before being elected.

Presidential Use of Cabinets Because neither the Constitution nor statutory law requires the president to consult with the cabinet, its use is purely discretionary. Some presidents have relied on the counsel of their cabinets more than others. Dwight Eisenhower was used to the team approach to solving problems from his military experience, and therefore he frequently turned to his cabinet for advice on a wide range of issues. More often, presidents have solicited the opinions of their cabinets and then done what they wanted to do anyway. After a cabinet meeting in which a vote was seven nays against his one aye, Lincoln supposedly said, "Seven nays and one aye; the ayes have it." In general, few presidents have relied heavily on the advice of their cabinet members.

It is not surprising that presidents tend not to rely on their cabinet members' advice. Often, the departmental heads are more responsive to the wishes of their own staffs or to their own political ambitions than they are to the president. They may be more concerned with obtaining resources for their departments than with achieving the goals of the president. So a strong conflict of interest between presidents and their cabinet members often exists.

The Executive Office of the President

When President Franklin Roosevelt appointed a special committee on administrative management, he knew that the committee would conclude that the president needed help. The committee proposed a major reorganization of the

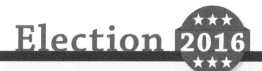
Election 2016

Does It Matter Which Party Holds the Presidency?

Every four years, American citizens go to the polls to elect the president of the United States. There are people who believe that it does not make a difference who is chosen as president, and there are voters who feel that the world will come to an end if their candidate is not elected. The truth lies somewhere in between these views.

American domestic policies—ranging from food stamps to Social Security—have been determined by congressional legislation over the years. Despite their best efforts, Republicans have been unable to dismantle the legislation known as the Affordable Care Act or "Obamacare." A president with a strong agenda can try to alter such policies, but, in fact, is likely to be able to do so only in his or her "honeymoon" period of the first year in office. In addition, many of the president's duties are either ceremonial or required, including making the State of the Union address and preparing a budget for the consideration of Congress. In these areas, changing the party of the president may effect incremental changes.

However, presidents are able to use their executive powers in other ways. As noted in this chapter, Republican presidents are likely to roll back or repeal executive orders issued by more liberal Democratic presidents. Democratic presidents do the same to their Republican predecessors. And, although presidents have relatively few appointments to make in the federal branch, they are able to influence the direction of enforcement in the Justice Department, for example, or the reach of the Environmental Protection Agency (EPA), through their appointments of the executives of these agencies. President Trump's nomination of Scott Pruitt, a strong supporter of carbon fuels to be the director of the EPA signaled a change of direction for that agency.

Perhaps the most important appointments that a president makes are those to the Supreme Court and the lower federal courts. With the sudden death of Antonin Scalia in early 2016, the possibility of an Obama appointment to the court threw the Republicans in the Senate into turmoil. Republicans refused to consider a nominee for the Supreme Court before the presidential election. After Trump became president, he moved quickly to nominate Neil Gorsuch, a conservative jurist, to the Supreme Court. Gorsuch, a highly regarded appellate judge, was confirmed fairly quickly.

In contrast to domestic policy, the president has much more executive discretion to exercise in foreign policy. Whether a Republican president embraces a stronger leadership role for the United States or a Democratic president chooses a partnership role, the position of the United States on issues ranging from our support for the state of Israel, to relationships with China, Russia, North Korea, and Iran will surely depend on the view of the newly elected president. After his inauguration, Trump sought to strengthen the military and took an exceptionally hard line with North Korea.

Critical Analysis Questions

1. Should a newly inaugurated president focus on primary campaign promises or on redirecting the federal bureaucracy?

2. What are the tools of foreign and defense policy available to a new president?

executive branch. Congress did not approve the entire reorganization but did create the **Executive Office of the President (EOP)** to provide staff assistance and to help coordinate the executive bureaucracy. Since then, many agencies have been created within the EOP. These agencies include the following:

- White House Office
- White House Military Office
- Office of the Vice President
- Council of Economic Advisers
- Office of National Drug Control Policy
- Office of Science and Technology Policy
- Office of the United States Trade Representative

Executive Office of the President (EOP)
An organization established by President Franklin D. Roosevelt to assist the president in carrying out major duties.

- Council on Environmental Quality
- President's Critical Infrastructure Protection Board
- Office of Management and Budget
- National Security Council
- President's Foreign Intelligence Advisory Board
- Office of National AIDS Policy

Several of the offices within the EOP are especially important, including the White House Office, the Office of Management and Budget, and the National Security Council.

White House Office
The personal office of the president, which tends to presidential political needs and manages the media.

chief of staff
The person who is named to direct the White House Office and advise the president.

permanent campaign
A coordinated and planned strategy carried out by the White House to increase the president's popularity and support.

The White House Office The **White House Office** includes most of the key personal and political advisers to the president. Among the jobs held by these aides are those of legal counsel to the president, secretary, press secretary, and appointments secretary. In all recent administrations, one member of the White House Office has been named **chief of staff**. This person, who is responsible for coordinating the office, is also one of the president's chief advisers.

Often, the individuals who hold these positions are recruited from the president's campaign staff. Their duties—mainly protecting the president's political interests—are similar to campaign functions. Most observers of the presidency agree that contemporary presidents continue their campaigning after inauguration. The **permanent campaign** is a long-term strategy planned by the White House Office of Communications with the press secretary to keep the president's approval ratings high and to improve support in Congress. The campaign includes staged events, symbolic actions, and controlled media appearances. During the Obama presidency this function rose to a new height with the adoption of all forms of electronic media. Anyone who worked in either of his campaigns or signed up for presidential updates received emails from the president or Joe Biden or the First Lady on a weekly basis with information about the president's initiatives. The White House also sends out tweets and posts information on all social media sites. The president's overall agenda is featured on the official White House website, with links to policy priorities.

The president may establish special advisory units within the White House to address topics the president finds especially important. Under George W. Bush, these units also included the Office of Faith-Based and Community Initiatives and the USA Freedom Corps. The White House Office also includes the staff members who support the First Lady.

The president is also supported by a large number of military personnel, who are organized under the White House Military Office. These members of the military provide communications, transportation, medical care, and food services to the president and the White House staff.

Employees of the White House Office have been both envied and criticized. The White House Office, according to most former staffers, grants its employees access and power. They are able to use the resources of the White House to contact virtually anyone in the world by telephone, text, satellite telephone, or email, as well as to use the influence of the White House to persuade legislators and citizens. Because of this influence, staffers are often criticized for overstepping the bounds of the office. The appointments secretary is able to grant or deny senators, representatives, and cabinet secretaries access to the president.

The press secretary grants the press and television journalists access to any information about the president.

The first year of the Trump White House was characterized by turmoil and staff turnover. The press secretary and chief of staff were replaced. Adding to the general sense of disorder was the Mueller investigation. Attorney General Jeff Sessions recused himself from the investigation because he had been an adviser to the 2016 campaign. Robert Mueller was named a special counsel to investigate possible collusion between the Trump campaign and the Russian attempts to influence the election. Some individuals who might have been part of the president's staff were caught up in the investigation, which continued throughout 2017 into 2018, adding to the stresses of the White House Office.

The Office of Management and Budget The **Office of Management and Budget (OMB)** was originally the Bureau of the Budget, created in 1921 within the Department of the Treasury. Recognizing the importance of this agency, Franklin Roosevelt moved it into the White House Office in 1939. Richard Nixon reorganized the Bureau of the Budget in 1970 and changed its name to reflect its new managerial function. It is headed by a director, who must create the annual federal budget that the president presents to Congress each January for approval. In principle, the director of the OMB has broad fiscal powers in planning and estimating various parts of the federal budget, because all agencies must submit their proposed budget to the OMB for approval. In reality, it is not so evident that the OMB truly can affect the greater scope of the federal budget. Rather, the OMB may be more important as a clearinghouse for legislative proposals initiated in the executive agencies.

The National Security Council The **National Security Council (NSC)** is a link between the president's key foreign and military advisers and the president. Its members consist of the president, the vice president, and the secretaries of state and defense, plus other informal members. Included in the NSC is the president's special assistant for national security affairs. In 2001, Condoleezza Rice became the first woman to serve as a president's national security adviser. In 2013, former Ambassador to the United Nations Susan Rice became the national security adviser.

"Policy Czars" For many decades presidents have created positions within the Executive Office of the President that were focused on one special policy area. Many have been titled "senior policy coordinator" or "senior adviser," and most of them have been appointments that do not require Senate confirmation. In general, these positions last only as long as the president. Each new president decides which domestic or foreign policy issues need special attention from an individual who can report directly to the chief executive. In recent administrations, the nickname "**policy czar**" has been attached to these positions.

Twitter Feed ▶ The President offers a postive comment on relations with North Korea.

Donald J. Trump ✓
@realDonaldTrump

Follow ⌄

I want to thank Chairman Kim for taking the first bold step toward a bright new future for his people. Our unprecedented meeting – the first between an American President and a leader of North Korea – proves that real change is possible!

5:11 PM - 12 Jun 2018

♡ 8.6K   ⟲ 24K   ♡ 111K

Office of Management and Budget (OMB)
A division of the Executive Office of the President. The OMB assists the president in preparing the annual budget, clearing and coordinating departmental agency budgets, and supervising the administration of the federal budget.

National Security Council (NSC)
An agency in the Executive Office of the President that advises the president on national security.

policy czar
A high-ranking member of the Executive Office of the President appointed to coordinate action in one specific policy area.

If the president has special councils on problems such as drugs or the environment and cabinet departments or independent agencies designated to handle an area of government policy, why does the president need yet another individual to supervise government action? Presidents expect a policy czar to focus on the problem, along with coordinating the efforts of all the other government agencies that have authority in that policy area. The individuals named to these positions are often well-regarded experts who can bring an outsider's point of view both to the president and to the agencies involved in dealing with an issue. George W. Bush, over the two terms of his presidency, appointed more than 30 individuals to these positions.

President Obama created more than 40 positions in the Executive Office of the President to advise him on specific issue areas and to coordinate the work of cabinet departments on such topics as health-care reform, climate change, and urban initiatives. Criticism of his decision to create so many special advisers ranged from the cost to the effectiveness of having people in place to oversee the work of cabinet secretaries, but his authority to do so was unquestionable.[23] When Congress managed to defund four of these positions in 2011, Obama noted that he could bypass that provision and appoint the advisers that he needed. Sometimes, an individual who has held one of these positions is then appointed to a regular administrative position.[24]

The Vice Presidency

■ **12.7** Describe the job of the vice president and explain the circumstances under which the vice president becomes president.

The Constitution does not give much power to the vice president. The only formal duty is to preside over the Senate, which is rarely necessary. This obligation is fulfilled when the Senate organizes and adopts its rules and when the vice president is needed to decide a tie vote. In all other cases, the president pro tem manages parliamentary procedures in the Senate. The vice president is expected to participate only informally in senatorial deliberations, if at all.

The Vice President's Job

Vice presidents have traditionally been chosen to balance the ticket to attract groups of voters or appease party factions. If a presidential nominee is from the North, choosing a vice presidential nominee from another region of the country may be a good strategy. If the presidential nominee is from a rural state, perhaps someone with an urban background would be most suitable as a running mate. Presidential nominees who are strongly conservative or strongly liberal would do well to have vice presidential nominees who are more in the middle of the political road.

Strengthening the Ticket In recent presidential elections, vice presidents have often been selected for other reasons. Bill Clinton picked Al Gore to be his running mate in 1992, even though both were Southerners and moderates. The ticket appealed to Southerners and moderates, both of whom were crucial

23 Aaron J. Saiger, "Obama's 'Czar's' for Domestic Policy and the Law of the White House Staff," *Fordham Law Review* (2011) 79: 2576–2616.

24 Bill Piper, "New Drug Czar a Chance to Do Things Right," *HuffPost Politics*, March 24, 2014. http://www.huffingtonpost.com /bill-piper/new-drug-czar_b_5022801.html

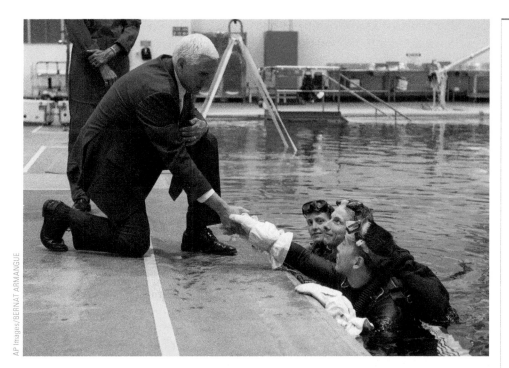

Image 12-8
Vice President Mike
Pence greets NASA astronaut
candidates at the NASA Johnson
Space Center in Houston, Texas.

to the election. In 2000, George W. Bush, who was subject to criticism for his lack of federal government experience and his "lightweight" personality, chose Dick Cheney, a former member of Congress who had also served as secretary of defense. Both presidential candidates in 2008 sought to balance their perceived weaknesses with their vice presidential choices. Barack Obama chose Senator Joseph Biden to add experience and foreign policy knowledge to his ticket, and in 2012, Republican nominee Mitt Romney selected Representative Paul Ryan of Wisconsin to be his running mate. Trump selected Mike Pence, a conservative from Indiana as his vice presidential nominee to gain votes from conservatives in the Republican party.

Supporting the President The job of vice president is not extremely demanding, even when the president gives some specific task to the vice president. Typically, vice presidents spend their time supporting the president's activities. During the Clinton administration (1993–2001), however, Vice President Al Gore did much to strengthen the position by his aggressive support for environmental protection policies on a global basis. He also took a special interest in areas of emerging technology and lobbied Congress to provide subsidies to public schools for Internet use.

Vice President Dick Cheney was clearly was an influential figure in the Bush administration. Although many of the Washington elite were happy to see Dick Cheney as vice president because of his intelligence and wide range of experience, he quickly became a controversial figure due to his outspoken support for a tough foreign and military policy and for having encouraged Bush to attack Iraq.

Vice President Joe Biden, former senator from Delaware, was a popular choice for vice president among Democrats and voters. He had many years of experience in the Senate, thus balancing President's Obama's relative lack of experience on Capitol Hill. Once the Obama administration took office, Biden's role became somewhat clearer. His experiences in the Senate prepared him to be a senior adviser to the president on foreign policy issues, although he was not as controversial a figure as Cheney had been. Of course, the vice presidency takes on more significance if the president becomes disabled or dies in office and the vice president becomes president.

Vice presidents sometimes have become elected presidents in their own right. John Adams and Thomas Jefferson were the first two vice presidents to win the office of president. Richard Nixon was elected president in 1968 after he had served as Dwight D. Eisenhower's vice president from 1953 to 1961. In 1988, George H. W. Bush was elected to the presidency after eight years as Ronald Reagan's vice president.

Presidential Succession

Eight vice presidents have become president upon the death of the president. John Tyler, the first to do so, took over William Henry Harrison's position after only one month. No one knew whether Tyler should simply be a caretaker until a new president could be elected three and a half years later or whether he actually should be president. Tyler assumed that he was supposed to be the chief executive and he acted as such, although he was commonly referred to as "His Accidency." Since then, vice presidents taking over the position of the presidency because of the incumbent's death have assumed the presidential powers.

But what should a vice president do if a president becomes incapable of carrying out necessary duties while in office? When James Garfield was shot in 1881, he survived for two and a half months. What was Vice President Chester Arthur's role? This question was not addressed in the original Constitution. Article II, Section 1, says only that "[i]n Case of the Removal of the President from Office, or of his Death, Resignation, or Inability to discharge the Powers and Duties of the said Office, the same shall devolve on [the same powers shall be exercised by] the Vice President." Many instances of presidential disability have occurred. When Dwight Eisenhower became ill a second time in 1958, he entered into a pact with Richard Nixon specifying that the vice president could determine whether the president was incapable of carrying out his duties if the president could not communicate. John F. Kennedy and Lyndon Johnson entered into similar agreements with their vice presidents. In 1967, the **Twenty-fifth Amendment** was ratified, establishing procedures in case of presidential incapacity.

The Twenty-fifth Amendment

According to the Twenty-fifth Amendment, when a president believes that he or she is incapable of performing the duties of office, the president must inform Congress in writing. Then the vice president serves as acting president until the president can resume normal duties. When the president is unable to communicate, a majority of the cabinet, including the vice president, can declare that fact to Congress. Then the vice president serves as acting president until the president resumes normal duties. If a dispute arises over the return of the president's ability, a two-thirds vote of Congress is required to decide whether the vice president shall remain acting president or whether the president shall resume normal duties.

Twenty-fifth Amendment
A 1967 amendment to the Constitution that establishes procedures for filling presidential and vice presidential vacancies and makes provisions for presidential disability.

AP Images/RON EDMONDS

Image 12-9
An attempted assassination of Ronald Reagan occurred on March 31, 1981. In the foreground, two men bend over Press Secretary James Brady, who lies seriously wounded. In the background, President Reagan is watched over by a U.S. Secret Service agent with an automatic weapon. A Washington, DC, police officer, Thomas Delahanty, lies to the left after also being shot.

In 2002, President George W. Bush formally invoked the Twenty-fifth Amendment for the first time by officially transferring presidential power to Vice President Dick Cheney while the president underwent a colonoscopy, a 20-minute procedure. He commented that he undertook this transfer of power "because we're at war," referring to the war on terrorism. The only other time the provisions of the Twenty-fifth Amendment have been used was during President Reagan's colon surgery in 1985, although Reagan did not formally invoke the amendment.

When the Vice Presidency Becomes Vacant

The Twenty-fifth Amendment also addresses the issue of how the president should fill a vacant vice presidency. Section 2 of the amendment simply states, "Whenever there is a vacancy in the office of the Vice President, the President shall nominate a Vice President who shall take office upon confirmation by a majority vote of both Houses of Congress." This occurred when Richard Nixon's vice president, Spiro Agnew, resigned in 1973 because of his alleged receipt of construction contract kickbacks during his tenure as governor of Maryland. Nixon turned to Gerald Ford as his choice for vice president. After extensive hearings, both chambers of Congress confirmed the appointment. When Nixon resigned on August 9, 1974, Ford automatically became president and nominated Nelson Rockefeller as his vice president, which Congress confirmed. For the first time, neither the president nor the vice president had been elected to either position.

The question of who shall be president if both the president and vice president die is answered by the Succession Act of 1947. If the president and vice president die, resign, or are disabled, the Speaker of the House will become president after resigning from Congress. Next in line is the president pro tem of the Senate, followed by the cabinet officers in the order of the creation of their departments (see Table 12-2).

did you know?
Gerald Ford was the first person to be both vice president and president without being elected by the people. He was appointed vice president when Spiro Agnew resigned, and he succeeded to the presidency when Nixon resigned.

Table 12–2 ▶ Line of Succession to the Presidency of the United States

1.	Vice President
2.	Speaker of the House of Representatives
3.	Senate President Pro Tempore
4.	Secretary of State
5.	Secretary of the Treasury
6.	Secretary of Defense
7.	Attorney General (head of the Justice Department)
8.	Secretary of the Interior
9.	Secretary of Agriculture
10.	Secretary of Commerce
11.	Secretary of Labor
12.	Secretary of Health and Human Services
13.	Secretary of Housing and Urban Development
14.	Secretary of Transportation
15.	Secretary of Energy
16.	Secretary of Education
17.	Secretary of Veterans Affairs
18.	Secretary of Homeland Security

Key Terms

advice and consent 430
appointment power 428
cabinet 446
chief diplomat 430
chief executive 427
chief legislator 433
chief of staff 448
civil service 428
commander in chief 429
commutation 429
constitutional powers 438
diplomatic recognition 430
emergency powers 442
executive agreement 432

Executive Office of the President (EOP) 447
executive order 443
executive privilege 444
expressed powers 438
Federal Register 443
head of state 426
impeachment 445
inherent powers 438
kitchen cabinet 446
line-item veto 438
National Security Council (NSC) 449
Office of Management and Budget (OMB) 449
pardon 428

patronage 439
permanent campaign 448
pocket veto 435
policy czar 449
reprieve 428
signing statement 427
State of the Union message 435
statutory powers 438
Twelfth Amendment 426
Twenty-fifth Amendment 452
veto message 435
War Powers Resolution 430
Washington community 440
White House Office 448

Chapter Summary

■ **12.1** The office of the presidency in the United States, combining as it does the functions of head of state and chief executive, was unique when it was created. The framers of the Constitution were divided over whether the president should be a weak or a strong executive.

■ **12.1** The requirements for the office of the presidency are outlined in Article II, Section 1, of the Constitution and

include both formal and informal duties. The roles of the president include head of state, chief executive, commander in chief, chief diplomat, chief legislator, and party chief.

■ **12.1** As head of state, the president is ceremonial leader of the government. As chief executive, the president is bound to enforce the acts of Congress, the judgments of the federal courts, and treaties. The chief executive has the power of appointment and the power to grant reprieves and pardons.

■ **12.1** Presidents are also the political leaders of their party, naming the leadership of the party and being the chief fundraiser for future elections. To become effective leaders and to gain support for their policies, presidents try to maintain strong approval ratings from the public, as measured by frequent polls. The White House Office works to improve the president's image and reputation through its relationship with the media. Presidents who maintain their popularity are likely to have more success in their legislative programs.

■ **12.2** As commander in chief, the president is the ultimate decision maker in military matters. As chief diplomat, the president recognizes foreign governments, negotiates treaties, signs agreements, and nominates and receives ambassadors.

■ **12.3** The role of chief legislator includes recommending legislation to Congress, lobbying for the legislation, approving laws, and exercising the veto power. The president also has statutory powers written into law by Congress.

■ **12.4** Presidents have a variety of special powers not available to other branches of the government. These include emergency power, most frequently used during war or a national crisis, and the power to issue executive orders and invoke executive privilege.

■ **12.5** Abuses of executive power are addressed by Articles I and II of the Constitution, which authorize the House and Senate to impeach and remove the president, vice president, or other officers of the federal government for committing "Treason, Bribery, or other high Crimes and Misdemeanors."

■ **12.6** The president fulfills the role of chief executive by appointing individuals of his or her choice to positions in the departments and agencies of government, as well as various advisers in the White House Office and the Executive Office of the President. Some of the offices within the EOP were established by law, whereas others are appointed as the president desires. All appointees are supposed to be working for the president's initiatives and making sure that the larger bureaucracy is also supportive of the president's programs.

■ **12.7** The vice president is the constitutional officer assigned to preside over the Senate and to assume the presidency in the event of the death, resignation, removal, or disability of the president. The Twenty-fifth Amendment, passed in 1967, established procedures to be followed in case of presidential incapacity and when filling a vacant vice presidency.

Selected Resources

PRINT RESOURCES

Goldsmith, Jack. *Power and Constraint: The Accountable Presidency After 9/11* (New York: W.W. Norton and Company, 2012). The author takes the position that even though presidents have exercised emergency powers and war powers since September 11, 2001, they are actually more constrained in this era than ever before by courts, Congress, and the media.

Goodwin, Doris Kearns. *The Bully Pulpit: Theodore Roosevelt, William Howard Taft, and the Golden Age of Journalism* (New York: Simon and Shuster, 2013). Goodwin details the presidencies of two men, once friends, but eventually competitors for the White House, at the height of the Progressive era.

Howell, William. *Thinking about the Presidency: The Primacy of Power* (Princeton, NJ: Princeton University Press, 2013). Following on the work of Richard Neustadt, Howell examines how presidents make decisions and finds that the decision making always takes into account presidential power.

Rockman, Bert A., Andrew Rudalevige, and Colin Campbell. *The Obama Presidency: Appraisals and Prospects* (Washington, DC: CQ Press College, 2011). Three of the leading scholars of the presidency examine the successes and failures of the first two years of the Obama presidency.

Toobin, Jeffrey. *The Oath: The Obama White House and the Supreme Court* (New York: Random House, 2012). The author looks closely at the presidency of Barack Obama and the work of the Chief Justice of the Supreme Court, John Roberts. Over the years of the Obama presidency, the chief justice sometimes led the court to support the administration and other times to oppose it.

MEDIA RESOURCES

Bush's War—PBS *Frontline's* documentary delves into the impact of 9/11 on the Bush presidency. It is free to watch at www.pbs.org/wgbh/pages/frontline/bushswar /view/

The Butler—This 2013 award-winning movie follows the life of an African American butler in the White House through the terms of eight presidents and through the battles of the civil rights movement.

Fahrenheit 9/11—Michael Moore's scathing 2004 critique of the Bush administration has been called "one long political attack ad." It is also the highest-grossing documentary ever made. Although the film takes a strong position, it is—like all of Moore's productions—entertaining.

The Guns of October—This film explores the Cuban Missile Crisis of 1962. It portrays the Kennedy decision-making process in deciding against attacking Cuba.

Veep—This comedy, starring Julia Louis-Dreyfus as the vice president of the United States, centers around the White House staff and their arguments, gossip, and interpersonal relationships. The series is a strong satire of politics in Washington, DC, and reminds us that all politicians are human.

ONLINE RESOURCES

The American Presidency Project at the University of California at Santa Barbara—a wonderful collection of presidential photographs, documents, audio, and video: www.presidency.ucsb.edu

Bartleby.com—Internet publisher of literature, reference, and verse providing unlimited access to books and information, including the inaugural addresses of American presidents from George Washington to Donald Trump: www.bartleby.com/124

Dave Leip's Atlas of U.S. Presidential Elections—offers an excellent collection of data and maps describing all U.S. presidential elections: www.uselectionatlas.org

The White House—extensive information on the White House and the presidency: www.whitehouse.gov

The Bureaucracy

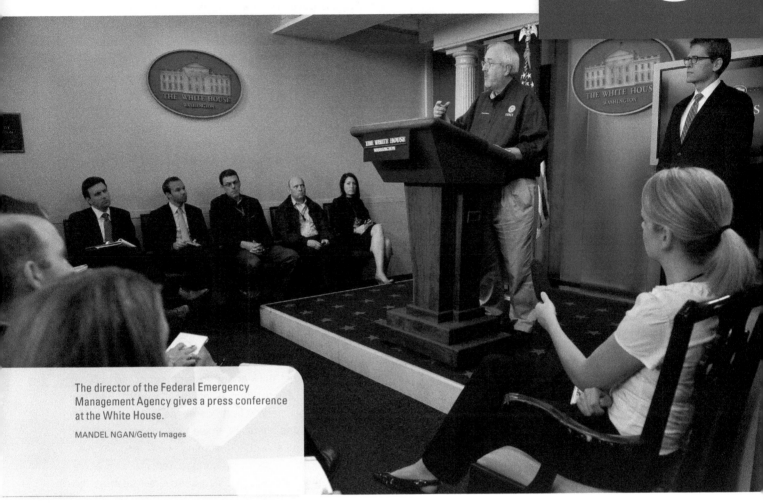

The director of the Federal Emergency Management Agency gives a press conference at the White House.

MANDEL NGAN/Getty Images

LEARNING OBJECTIVES

After reading this chapter, you will be able to:

- **13.1** Define the concept of the bureaucracy, explain why such an organization is necessary, and discuss the various theories of how bureaucracies act.

- **13.2** Compare the structure and function of executive departments, executive agencies, independent regulatory agencies, and government corporations.

- **13.3** Explain how individuals get positions in the federal bureaucracy, and discuss the history of attempts to reform that process.

- **13.4** Discuss some of the critiques of large bureaucracies and describe several types of bureaucratic reform.

- **13.5** Describe the tools and powers that bureaucratic agencies have to shape policies and regulations.

- **13.6** Analyze the relationship among Congress, its committees, interest groups, and the bureaucracy.

Every Federal Agency Reported to the People?

Background

Each year, every federal department, commission, and agency meets with the Office of Management and Budget (OMB) to propose a budget. The General Accountability Office (GAO) may investigate an agency for wrongdoing or simply audit its financial statements. Although Congress approves the budget for every agency, appropriations committees do not have time to look at the work of the entire federal government. Many federal agencies post a great deal of work on the Internet, so why not have every federal agency report directly to the people?

What If Every Federal Agency Reported to the People?

Although most agencies must produce some sort of report to Congress or to the GAO or OMB, no simple report exists showing what the federal government is doing for the people of the United States. Some agencies post their annual reports on the Internet for all to see, but they are glossy presentations that highlight their accomplishments and gloss over their less successful ventures. Other agencies post detailed statistical reports; one example is the Agriculture Department's monthly corn production prediction. The results of other agencies' work turn up in the censuses conducted by the Department of Commerce—the Census of Farm Owners, the Census of Hospitals, or the Census of Small Business, for instance.

What if every agency had to produce on a specified day a five-page report of their work? The contents would be specified by law: What were its revenues and expenses? How many people did it serve? What exactly are its programs, and how were its services delivered? In the case of the U.S. Postal Service, what did it cost to deliver a first-class letter or a heavy catalog, and did the Postal Service make or lose money on each? The reports could be downloaded and printed from the Internet, and each agency's website would be easily navigated, simplifying access to the annual report.

What Would the Reports Accomplish?

Annual reports could make citizens more aware of what their tax dollars purchase in goods and services. Citizens might find that they approve of the services being provided.

Although it is likely to become clear that some services provided by the government are pretty expensive, they will be deemed essential. Consider medical care and rehabilitation for wounded veterans returning from Afghanistan. The extreme cost should surprise no one. On the other hand, public awareness of some of the fraudulent schemes to get Medicare dollars might help citizens stop waste.

Annual reports, produced in very consistent ways, would make agencies more accountable to the president, to the Congress, and to the citizens. Currently, government agencies seek either equal or increased funding each year on the basis that their work is stellar and important. However, most agencies do not need to explain what they do—they assume continued existence. Short, fact-based reports would be nonpolitical, unlike the current glossy brochures. It might be a good idea for a panel of citizens and journalists to draw up the format for the web report and occasionally check that agencies are complying with the reporting requirements.

Annual Reports Could Be a Waste of Time and Money

Few Americans would likely read annual agency reports. Most citizens do not think about government or the political process unless a presidential election looms. Reading through dry bureaucratic reports demands a high interest in government. For the agencies, these new reports would be yet another requirement consuming time and money. Currently Congress requires all sorts of reports from agencies, which tend to produce only controversy, such as the annual report on terrorist groups. Many government workers would likely find it futile to produce an annual report that few would read.

For Critical Analysis

1. What specific items should be included in the annual report of each agency?

2. Name several government organizations that you might be interested in knowing about. Do you think others would have a similar list?

Faceless bureaucrats—this image provokes a negative reaction from many, if not most, Americans. Polls consistently report that the majority of Americans support "less government." The same polls, however, report that the majority of Americans support almost every specific program that the government undertakes. The conflict between the desire for small government and the benefits that only a large government can provide has been a staple of American politics. For example, the goal of preserving endangered species has widespread support. However, many people believe that restrictions imposed under the Endangered Species Act violate the rights of landowners. Helping the elderly pay their medical bills is a popular objective, but hardly anyone enjoys paying the Medicare tax that supports this effort.

Many complain about the inefficiency and wastefulness of government at all levels. The media regularly uncover examples of failures in governmental programs; for example, inadequate, slow, or bungled responses to a crisis such as Hurricane Sandy or the tangled web of governments responsible for the safety of Flint, Michigan's drinking water. This chapter describes the size, organization, and staffing of the federal bureaucracy. We review modern attempts at bureaucratic reform and the process by which Congress exerts ultimate control over the bureaucracy and the bureaucracy's role in making rules and setting policy.

The Nature of Bureaucracy

■ **13.1** Define the concept of the bureaucracy, explain why such an organization is necessary, and discuss the various theories of how bureaucracies act.

Every modern president, at one time or another, has proclaimed that his administration was going to "fix the government." All modern presidents also have put forth plans to end government waste and inefficiency. President Clinton's plan was Reinventing Government, followed by Performance-Based Budgeting under George W. Bush. Within a few months of his inauguration, President Obama issued a call to his departments to "cut what doesn't work."[1] The success of plans such as these has been underwhelming. Presidents generally have been powerless to affect the structure and operation of the federal bureaucracy significantly.

A **bureaucracy** is the name given to a large organization that is structured hierarchically to carry out specific functions. Most bureaucracies are characterized by an organization chart. The units of the organization are divided according to the specialization and expertise of the employees.

bureaucracy
A large organization that is structured hierarchically to carry out specific functions.

Public and Private Bureaucracies

Any large corporation or university can be considered a bureaucratic organization. The handling of complex problems requires a division of labor. Individuals must concentrate their skills on specific, well-defined aspects of a problem and depend on others to solve the rest of it.

Public or government bureaucracies differ from private organizations in some important ways. A private corporation, such as Microsoft, has a board of directors. Public bureaucracies, in contrast, do not have a single set of leaders. Although the president is the chief administrator of the federal system, all bureaucratic agencies are beholden to Congress for their funding, staffing, and continued

---

1   President Barack Obama, Weekly Radio Address, April 25, 2009. http://www.whitehouse.gov

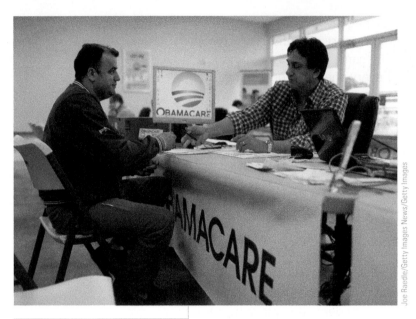

Joe Raedle/Getty Images News/Getty Images

Image 13–1

A representative of a health insurance company counsels a citizen about his options to sign up for insurance before the annual deadline as specified by the Affordable Care Act.

Weberian model
A model of bureaucracy developed by the German sociologist Max Weber, who viewed bureaucracies as rational, hierarchical organizations in which decisions are based on logical reasoning.

acquisitive model
A model of bureaucracy that views top-level bureaucrats as seeking to expand the size of their budgets and staffs to gain greater power.

monopolistic model
A model of bureaucracy that compares bureaucracies to monopolistic business firms. Lack of competition in either circumstance leads to inefficient and costly operations.

existence. Furthermore, public bureaucracies purportedly serve the citizenry.

Government bureaucracies are also not organized to make a profit. They are intended to perform their functions as efficiently as possible to conserve the taxpayers' dollars. Perhaps this ideal makes citizens hostile toward government bureaucracy when they experience inefficiency and red tape.

Models of Bureaucracy

Several theories exist to better understand the ways in which bureaucracies function. Each of these theories focuses on specific features of bureaucracies.

Weberian Model The classic model, or **Weberian model**, of the modern bureaucracy was proposed by German sociologist Max Weber.[2] He argued that the increasingly complex nature of modern life, coupled with the steadily growing demands placed on governments by their citizens, made the formation of bureaucracies inevitable. According to Weber, most bureaucracies—whether public or private—are organized hierarchically and governed by formal procedures. The power flows from the top downward. Decision-making processes are shaped by detailed technical rules that promote similar decisions in similar situations. Bureaucrats are specialists who attempt to resolve problems through logical reasoning and data analysis instead of instinct and guesswork. Individual advancement in bureaucracies is supposed to be based on merit rather than political connections. The modern bureaucracy, according to Weber, should be an apolitical organization.

Acquisitive Model Other theorists do not view bureaucracies in terms as benign as Weber's. Some believe that bureaucracies are acquisitive in nature. Proponents of the **acquisitive model** argue that top-level bureaucrats will always try to expand, or at least to avoid any reductions in, the size of their budgets. Even though public bureaucracies try to be efficient, they have an inevitable desire to expand their mission, adding staff and funding to address policy issues. In the view of most government agencies, if your budget is not increased, your organization is in decline.

Monopolistic Model Because government bureaucracies seldom have competitors, some have suggested that these organizations may be explained best by a **monopolistic model**. The analysis is similar to that used by economists to examine the behavior of monopolistic firms. Monopolistic bureaucracies—like monopolistic firms—essentially have no competitors and act accordingly. Because monopolistic bureaucracies usually are not penalized for chronic inefficiency, they have little reason to adopt cost-saving measures or to use their resources more productively. Some have argued that such problems can be cured only by privatizing certain bureaucratic functions.

---

2 Max Weber, *Theory of Social and Economic Organization*, Talcott Parsons, ed. (New York: Oxford University Press, 1974).

Bureaucracies Compared

The federal bureaucracy in the United States enjoys a greater degree of autonomy than do federal or national bureaucracies in many other nations. Much of the insularity that characterizes the U.S. bureaucracy may stem from the sheer size of the government organizations needed to implement an annual budget that is about $3.8 trillion.

The federal nature of the U.S. government also means that national bureaucracies regularly provide financial assistance to their state counterparts. The Department of Education and the Department of Housing and Urban Development distribute funds to their counterparts at the state level. In contrast, most bureaucracies in European countries have a top-down command structure so that national programs may be implemented directly at the lower level. This is due not only to the unitary government of most European countries but also to the fact that public ownership of such businesses as telephone companies, airlines, railroads, and utilities is far more common in Europe than in the United States.

The fact that the U.S. government owns relatively few enterprises does not mean that its bureaucracies are without resources. Many **administrative agencies** in the federal bureaucracy—such as the Environmental Protection Agency, the Nuclear Regulatory Commission, and the Securities and Exchange Commission—regulate private companies.

administrative agency
A federal, state, or local government unit established to perform a specific function. Administrative agencies are created and authorized by legislative bodies to administer and enforce specific laws.

The Size of the Bureaucracy

In 1789, the new government's bureaucracy was minuscule. There were three departments—State (9 employees), War (2 employees), and Treasury (39 employees)—and the Office of the Attorney General (later, the Department of Justice). The bureaucracy was still small in 1798. At that time, the secretary of state had seven clerks and spent a total of $500 ($10,244.15 in 2018 dollars) on stationery and printing. That same year, the Appropriations Act allocated $1.4 million to the War Department (or $28.7 million in 2018 dollars).[3]

Times have changed, as shown in Figure 13-1, which lists the various federal agencies and the number of civilian employees in each. Excluding the military, the federal bureaucracy includes approximately 2.7 million government employees, which has remained relatively stable for the last several decades. Many other individuals work directly or indirectly for the federal government as subcontractors or consultants and in other capacities. Experts estimate that the number of individuals employed through private contractors for the federal government grew from 4.4 million in 1999 to more than 7.6 million in 2005. During the Obama administration, the number of defense-contracted employees declined as the U.S. role in Iraq diminished. By 2014, the federal government spent about $500 billion annually in service contracts but did not know how many individual employees were working on those contracts. It is not clear whether these contracted services are really less costly than using government employees.[4]

The figures for federal government employment are only part of the story. Figure 13-2 shows the growth in government employment at the federal,

did you know?
The federal government spends more than $1 billion every five hours, every day of the year.

---

3   Leonard D. White, *The Federalists: A Study in Administrative History, 1789–1801* (New York: Free Press, 1948).
4   Scott H. Amey, "Feds vs. Contractors: Federal Employees Often Save Money, But an Advisory Panel Is Needed to Create a Cost Comparison Model," POGO (Project on Government Oversight), April 15, 2013. www.pogo.org/our-work/letters /2013/20130515-feds-vs-contractors-cost-com-arison.html

Figure 13-1 ▶ Federal Agencies and Their Respective Numbers of Civilian Employees

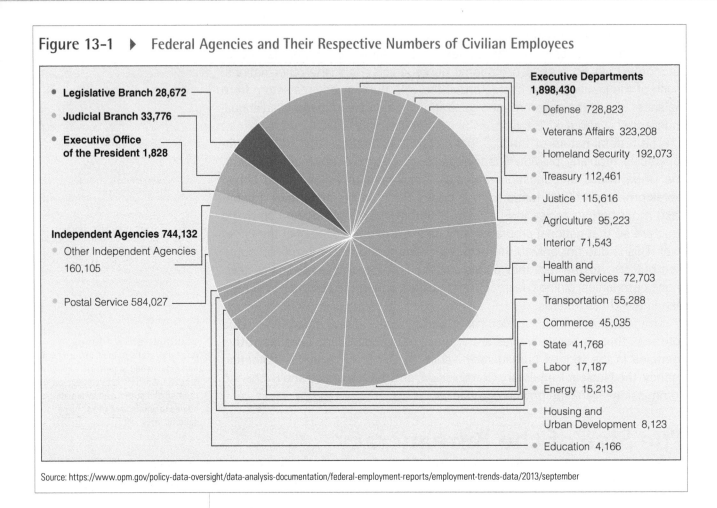

- **Legislative Branch 28,672**
- **Judicial Branch 33,776**
- **Executive Office of the President 1,828**

Independent Agencies 744,132
- Other Independent Agencies 160,105
- Postal Service 584,027

Executive Departments 1,898,430
- Defense 728,823
- Veterans Affairs 323,208
- Homeland Security 192,073
- Treasury 112,461
- Justice 115,616
- Agriculture 95,223
- Interior 71,543
- Health and Human Services 72,703
- Transportation 55,288
- Commerce 45,035
- State 41,768
- Labor 17,187
- Energy 15,213
- Housing and Urban Development 8,123
- Education 4,166

Source: https://www.opm.gov/policy-data-oversight/data-analysis-documentation/federal-employment-reports/employment-trends-data/2013/september

Figure 13-2 ▶ Government-Employment at the Federal, State, and Local Levels

There are more local government employees than federal or state employees combined.

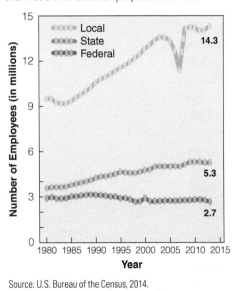

Source: U.S. Bureau of the Census, 2014.

state, and local levels. Since 1970, this growth has occurred mostly at the state and local levels. If all government employees are included, more than 16 percent of all civilian employment is accounted for by government. The costs of the bureaucracy are commensurately high. The share of the gross domestic product accounted for by all government spending was only 8.5 percent in 1929. Today, it has leveled off at about 36 percent. Whether government spending can be reduced without giving up services that citizens desire is an ongoing debate.

The Organization of the Federal Bureaucracy

■ **13.2** Compare the structure and function of executive departments, executive agencies, independent regulatory agencies, and government corporations.

Within the federal bureaucracy are several different types of government agencies and organizations. Figure 13-3 outlines the several bodies within the executive branch, as well as the separate organizations that provide services to Congress, to the courts, and directly to the president.

Figure 13-3 ▶ Organization Chart of the Federal Government

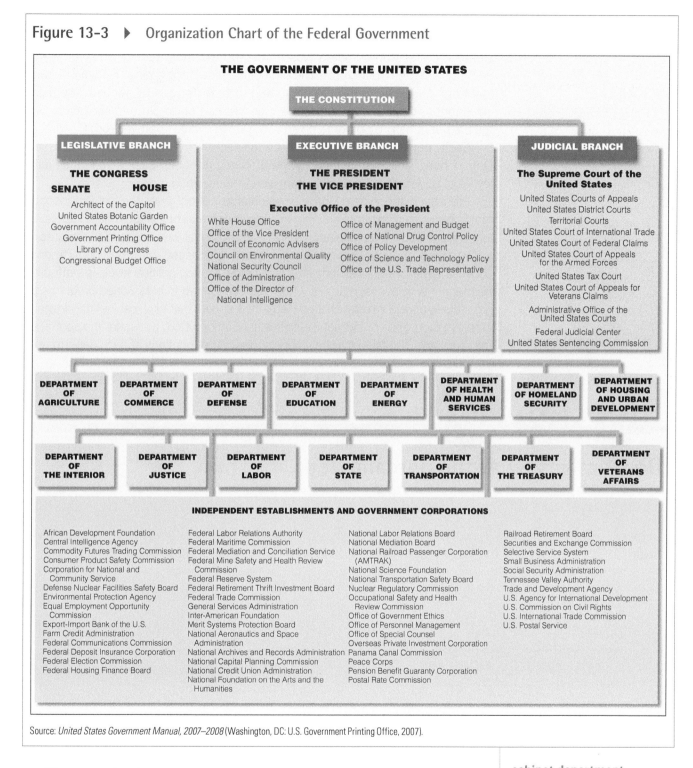

THE GOVERNMENT OF THE UNITED STATES

THE CONSTITUTION

LEGISLATIVE BRANCH

THE CONGRESS
SENATE   HOUSE

Architect of the Capitol
United States Botanic Garden
Government Accountability Office
Government Printing Office
Library of Congress
Congressional Budget Office

EXECUTIVE BRANCH

THE PRESIDENT
THE VICE PRESIDENT

Executive Office of the President

White House Office
Office of the Vice President
Council of Economic Advisers
Council on Environmental Quality
National Security Council
Office of Administration
Office of the Director of
 National Intelligence

Office of Management and Budget
Office of National Drug Control Policy
Office of Policy Development
Office of Science and Technology Policy
Office of the U.S. Trade Representative

JUDICIAL BRANCH

**The Supreme Court of the
United States**

United States Courts of Appeals
United States District Courts
Territorial Courts
United States Court of International Trade
United States Court of Federal Claims
United States Court of Appeals
 for the Armed Forces
United States Tax Court
United States Court of Appeals for
 Veterans Claims
Administrative Office of the
 United States Courts
Federal Judicial Center
United States Sentencing Commission

| DEPARTMENT OF AGRICULTURE | DEPARTMENT OF COMMERCE | DEPARTMENT OF DEFENSE | DEPARTMENT OF EDUCATION | DEPARTMENT OF ENERGY | DEPARTMENT OF HEALTH AND HUMAN SERVICES | DEPARTMENT OF HOMELAND SECURITY | DEPARTMENT OF HOUSING AND URBAN DEVELOPMENT |

| DEPARTMENT OF THE INTERIOR | DEPARTMENT OF JUSTICE | DEPARTMENT OF LABOR | DEPARTMENT OF STATE | DEPARTMENT OF TRANSPORTATION | DEPARTMENT OF THE TREASURY | DEPARTMENT OF VETERANS AFFAIRS |

INDEPENDENT ESTABLISHMENTS AND GOVERNMENT CORPORATIONS

African Development Foundation
Central Intelligence Agency
Commodity Futures Trading Commission
Consumer Product Safety Commission
Corporation for National and
 Community Service
Defense Nuclear Facilities Safety Board
Environmental Protection Agency
Equal Employment Opportunity
 Commission
Export-Import Bank of the U.S.
Farm Credit Administration
Federal Communications Commission
Federal Deposit Insurance Corporation
Federal Election Commission
Federal Housing Finance Board

Federal Labor Relations Authority
Federal Maritime Commission
Federal Mediation and Conciliation Service
Federal Mine Safety and Health Review
 Commission
Federal Reserve System
Federal Retirement Thrift Investment Board
Federal Trade Commission
General Services Administration
Inter-American Foundation
Merit Systems Protection Board
National Aeronautics and Space
 Administration
National Archives and Records Administration
National Capital Planning Commission
National Credit Union Administration
National Foundation on the Arts and the
 Humanities

National Labor Relations Board
National Mediation Board
National Railroad Passenger Corporation
 (AMTRAK)
National Science Foundation
National Transportation Safety Board
Nuclear Regulatory Commission
Occupational Safety and Health
 Review Commission
Office of Government Ethics
Office of Personnel Management
Office of Special Counsel
Overseas Private Investment Corporation
Panama Canal Commission
Peace Corps
Pension Benefit Guaranty Corporation
Postal Rate Commission

Railroad Retirement Board
Securities and Exchange Commission
Selective Service System
Small Business Administration
Social Security Administration
Tennessee Valley Authority
Trade and Development Agency
U.S. Agency for International Development
U.S. Commission on Civil Rights
U.S. International Trade Commission
U.S. Postal Service

Source: *United States Government Manual, 2007–2008* (Washington, DC: U.S. Government Printing Office, 2007).

The executive branch employs most of the government's staff with four major structures: (1) cabinet departments, (2) independent executive agencies, (3) independent regulatory agencies, and (4) government corporations. Each has a distinctive relationship to the president, and some have unusual internal structures, overall goals, and grants of power.

Cabinet Departments

The 15 **cabinet departments** are the major service organizations of the federal government. They can also be described in management terms as **line organizations**. They are directly accountable to the president and perform

cabinet department
One of the 15 departments of the executive branch (State, Treasury, Defense, Justice, Interior, Agriculture, Commerce, Labor, Health and Human Services, Homeland Security, Housing and Urban Development, Education, Energy, Transportation, and Veterans Affairs).

line organization
In the federal government, an administrative unit that is directly accountable to the president.

government functions, such as printing money and securing the border. These departments were created by Congress when the need for each department arose. The first to be created was State, and the most recent was Homeland Security, established in 2003. The difficulties faced in creating that new department are discussed in the "Reorganizing to Stop Terrorism" section. A president might ask that a new department be created or an old one abolished, but the president has no power to do so without legislative approval from Congress.

Each department is headed by a secretary (except for the Justice Department, which is headed by the attorney general). Each also has several levels of undersecretaries, assistant secretaries, and so on.

Presidents theoretically have considerable control over the cabinet departments because presidents are able to appoint or fire all of the top officials, as listed in the Plum Book. Even cabinet departments do not always respond to the president's wishes, though. Presidents are frequently unhappy with their departments because the entire bureaucratic structure below the top political levels is staffed by permanent employees, many of whom are committed to established programs or procedures and who resist change. Table 13-1 shows that each cabinet department employs thousands of individuals, only a handful of whom are under the control of the president. The table also describes some of the functions of each department.

Election 2016

Do Elections Sway the Bureaucracy?

As noted in the beginning of this chapter, bureaucracies, whether private or public, are supposed to be organizations of hard-working individuals who do their jobs as described and carry out the decisions of the leadership. In the United States, the Civil Service was created to maintain a corps of public employees who are politically neutral. However, bureaucratic theory also tells us that such organizations want to maintain their missions and grow in size and budget even when their services may no longer be needed to fulfill the nation's goals.

When a new president is elected, whether Democrat or Republican, the Plum Book will become the guide to appointive jobs in the Executive Office of the President, departments, and independent agencies. A new Democratic president is unlikely to keep very many of President Obama's appointees because she wants to leave her own stamp on the office and bring her trusted advisers to White House. A new Republican president will accept the resignations of all the Obama appointees and seek individuals who support his agenda for those positions. The real question is: Will the new department secretaries and agency directors change policies after the new president is sworn in?

For many departments and agencies the answer is "not very much." The secretary of commerce will continue to oversee the Census Bureau and all of its data gathering. The Department of Agriculture will continue to serve the nation's farmers, and the Social Security Administration will continue to send out benefits to eligible recipients. Most of the federal independent regulatory commissions will see little change in personnel because their boards have staggered terms. However, in the more important departments and agencies, particularly those that are close to the president, change is very likely. The new secretary of state will represent the president to foreign powers and carry his or her message to them. The attorney general will confer with the president about whether to continue policies in regard to domestic terrorism, police procedures, and voting rights violations. The Homeland Security Department will await the new president's initiatives on the status of undocumented residents, and the Environmental Protection Agency may, under a Republican president, pull back its regulations on coal-fired power plants and other sources of carbon emissions. One of the jobs of every agency after the installation of a new administration is to examine the regulations and executive orders from the prior administration and see whether they should be changed or eliminated altogether.

For Critical Analysis

1. Why is it difficult to change the policies and direction of a federal agency?

2. What are the types of issues and policies that a president is most likely to influence through his or her appointments?

Table 13-1 ▶ Executive Departments

DEPARTMENT AND YEAR ESTABLISHED	PRINCIPAL FUNCTIONS
State (1789) (41,768 employees)	Negotiates treaties; develops foreign policy; protects citizens abroad
Treasury (1789) (112,461 employees)	Pays all federal bills; borrows money; collects federal taxes; mints coins and prints paper currency; supervises national banks
Interior (1849) (71,543 employees)	Supervises federally owned lands and parks; supervises Native American affairs
Justice (1870)* (115,616 employees)	Furnishes legal advice to the president; enforces federal criminal laws; supervises federal prisons
Agriculture (1889) (95,223 employees)	Assists farmers and ranchers; conducts agricultural research; works to protect forests
Commerce (1913)** (45,035 employees)	Grants patents and trademarks; conducts national census; monitors weather; protects interests of businesses (Note: The Commerce Department houses the Census Bureau, which increased its workforce from several thousand employees to more than a half million between early 2009 and summer 2010. Most of these workers were short-term temporary employees.)
Labor (1913)** (17,187 employees)	Administers federal labor laws; promotes interests of workers
Defense (1947)** (728,823 employees)	Manages the armed forces; operates military bases; oversees civil defense
Housing and Urban Development (1965) (8,123 employees)	Manages nation's housing needs; develops and rehabilitates urban communities; oversees resale of mortgages
Transportation (1967) (55,288 employees)	Finances improvements in mass transit; develops and administers programs for highways, railroads, and aviation
Energy (1977) (15,213 employees)	Promotes energy conservation; analyzes energy data; conducts research and development
Health and Human Services (1979)*** (72,703 employees)	Promotes public health; enforces pure food and drug laws; conducts and sponsors health-related research
Education (1979)*** (4,166 employees)	Coordinates federal education programs and policies; administers aid to education; promotes educational research
Veterans Affairs (1988) (323,208 employees)	Promotes welfare of U.S. veterans
Homeland Security (2003) (192,073 employees)	Attempts to prevent terrorist attacks within the United States; controls U.S. borders; minimizes damage from natural disasters

Source: https://www.opm.gov/policy-data-oversight/data-analysis-documentation/federal-employment-reports/employment-trends-data/2013/september

*Formed from the Office of the Attorney General (created in 1789).

**Formed from the Department of Commerce and Labor (created in 1903).

***Formed from the Department of War (created in 1789) and the Department of the Navy (created in 1798).

****Formed from the Department of Health, Education, and Welfare (created in 1953). Office of Personnel Management, FedScope database, December 2013.

Independent Executive Agencies

Independent executive agencies are bureaucratic organizations that report directly to the president, who appoints their chief officials. When a new federal agency is created—the Environmental Protection Agency (EPA), for example—Congress decides where it will be located in the bureaucracy. In recent decades, presidents often have asked that a new organization be kept separate or independent rather than added to an existing department, particularly if a

independent executive agency
A federal agency that is not part of a cabinet department but reports directly to the president.

Image 13-2
Education Secretary Betsy DeVos testifies before the Senate Appropriations Committee in June of 2017.

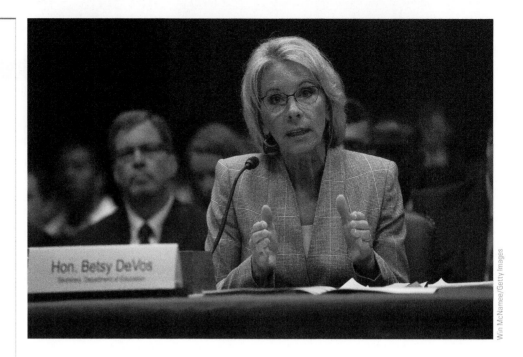

department may be hostile to the agency's creation. One example is the Central Intelligence Agency (CIA). Formed in 1947, the CIA gathers and analyzes political and military information about foreign countries and conducts covert operations outside the United States.

The newest independent agency is the Consumer Financial Protection Bureau, established in 2010 after the financial meltdown of 2008–2009. This agency oversees mortgages, debt collection, student loans, and credit card issuers and protects the interests of ordinary citizens in these financial matters. The creation of this independent executive agency was not without controversy: many believed that this should be an independent regulatory agency with a nonpartisan board of commissioners rather than an agency reporting to the president.

Independent Regulatory Agencies

independent regulatory agency
An agency outside the major executive departments charged with making and implementing rules and regulations.

The **independent regulatory agencies** are responsible for a specific type of public policy and make and implement rules and regulations in a particular sphere of action to protect the public interest. The earliest such agency was the Interstate Commerce Commission (ICC), which was established in 1887 when Americans began to seek some form of government control over the rapidly growing business and industrial sector. This new form of organization, the independent regulatory agency, was supposed to make technical, nonpolitical decisions about rates, profits, and rules that would benefit all and that did not require congressional legislation. After the creation of the ICC, other agencies were formed to regulate communication (the Federal Communications Commission), nuclear power (the Nuclear Regulatory Commission), etc. (The ICC was abolished on December 30, 1995.)

The Purpose and Nature of Regulatory Agencies The regulatory agencies are administered independently of all three branches of government. They were formed because Congress felt it was unable to handle the complexities and technicalities required to carry out specific laws in the public interest. The regulatory commissions combine some functions of all three branches of government. They are legislative in that they make rules that have the force of law, executive in that they enforce those rules, and judicial in that they decide disputes involving the rules they have made.

Members of regulatory agency boards or commissions are appointed by the president with the consent of the Senate but do not report to the president. By law, the members of regulatory agencies cannot all be from the same political party and may be removed by the president only for causes specified in the law creating the agency. Presidents can influence regulatory agency behavior by appointing people of their own parties or individuals who share their political views when vacancies occur—in particular, when the chair is vacant. President George W. Bush placed people on the Federal Communications Commission (FCC) who shared his desire to curb obscene language in the media. Not surprisingly, the FCC soon thereafter started to "crack down" on obscenities on the air. One victim of this regulatory effort was Howard Stern, a nationally syndicated radio and television personality. His response was to switch from commercial radio and TV to unregulated satellite radio.

Agency Capture In recent decades, the true independence of regulatory agencies has been called into question. Some contend that many independent regulatory agencies have been **captured** by the very industries and firms they were supposed to regulate. The results have been less competition rather than more competition, higher prices rather than lower prices, and less choice rather than more choice for consumers. One of the accusations made after the 2010 BP oil spill in the Gulf of Mexico was that the relevant regulatory agency, the Minerals and Mining Administration, had become too lax in enforcing the safety regulations on the drilling rigs because of cozy ties with the oil companies.

capture
The act by which an industry being regulated by a government agency gains direct or indirect control over agency personnel and decision makers.

Deregulation and Reregulation During President Reagan's administration, some significant deregulation (the removal of regulatory restraints) occurred, much of which had already commenced under President Carter. President Carter appointed a chairperson of the Civil Aeronautics Board (CAB) who gradually eliminated regulation of airline fares and routes. Under Reagan, the CAB was eliminated on January 1, 1985.

During the administration of George H. W. Bush, calls for reregulation of many businesses increased. The Americans with Disabilities Act of 1990, the Civil Rights Act of 1991, and the Clean Air Act Amendments of 1991, all of which increased or changed the regulation of many businesses, were passed. Additionally, the Cable Act of 1992, which placed further regulation on that industry, was passed.

Under President Clinton, the ICC was eliminated, and the banking and telecommunications industries, along with many other sectors of the economy, were deregulated. At the same time, extensive regulation protected the environment. In the wake of the mortgage crisis of 2007 and the failure of several large investment houses in 2008, Congress passed the Dodd-Frank bill in 2010, which tightened regulations on banks and almost all financial institutions. In the years that followed, various federal regulatory agencies continued to issue new rules for banks, for financial advisers, for payday lenders, and for stockbrokers.

government corporation
An agency of government that administers a quasi-business enterprise. These corporations are used when activities are primarily commercial.

Government Corporations

Another form of bureaucratic organization in the United States is the **government corporation**. Although the concept is borrowed from the world of business, distinct differences exist between public and private corporations.

A private corporation has shareholders (stockholders) who elect a board of directors, who in turn choose the corporate officers, such as president and vice president. When a private corporation makes a profit, it must pay taxes (unless it avoids them through various legal loopholes). It either distributes part or all of the after-tax profits to shareholders as dividends or plows the profits back into the corporation to make new investments.

A government corporation has a board of directors and managers, but it does not have any stockholders. We cannot buy shares of stock in a government corporation. If the government corporation makes a profit, it does not distribute the profit as dividends. Also, if it makes a profit, it does not have to pay taxes; the profits remain in the corporation.

Two of the best-known government corporations are the U.S. Postal Service and Amtrak, the domestic passenger railroad corporation. Thirty-five years ago, after several private rail companies went bankrupt, Congress created a public railway system called Amtrak. Today, Amtrak links 500 American towns and cities in 46 states with more than 22,000 miles of rail—and has many critics.

During Amtrak's existence, American taxpayers have subsidized it to the tune of more than $25 billion. The rail service, on average, loses about $400 million a year. Harold Rogers, the former chairman of the House Transportation Committee, has long criticized the rail service as inefficient and costly. Those in favor of the Amtrak subsidies argue that Amtrak provides essential transportation for the poor. In 2008, Congress passed legislation to force Amtrak to find alternative funding by sharing costs with the states it serves. Pennsylvania, for example, contracts to pay for specific routes, such as from Pittsburgh to Harrisburg and Philadelphia.[5] Such routes are not profitable, but the state deems it important to its own economy. Although Congress has not yet ended the rail service's subsidy, it has been reduced from more than $1 billion to about $400 million. For many years, critics of this government corporation have said that the benefits of Amtrak, including reducing congestion on the highways, do not outweigh the costs. Some have suggested that the passenger service be privatized—sold to a private corporation. However, as the price of gasoline rose in 2008 and the issue of the future supply of oil became critical, Amtrak became more popular with travelers. It had its best year in decades in 2012, carrying more passengers and having a smaller operating deficit.[6] When gas prices decline, however, people are more likely to drive than buy tickets for the train service.

The U.S. Postal Service, the second largest employer in the United States (after Wal-Mart), has more than 586,000 employees. On paper, the Postal Service appears to be "breaking even" in terms of costs and revenues for its primary business. However, critics note that this government corporation has the right to borrow funds from the federal government at a very low interest

did you know?

The U.S. Postal Service processes 509 million pieces of mail each day.

---

5 Ron Nixon, "Amtrak Subsidy Gone, States Must Pay the Freight to Keep Rail Routes," *The New York Times*, May 2, 2013.
6 Eleanor Randolph, "AMTRAK: Not a Money Pit After All," *New York Times Editorial Blog*, October 16, 2013. http://takingnote .blogs.nytimes.com

rate and has borrowed its statutory limit of $15 billion to support its operations. Recently, the U.S. Postal Service has proposed several strategies for cutting costs; eliminating Saturday delivery and closing large bulk-mail centers are two proposals. Additionally, the post office is collaborating with a private corporation, UPS, to deliver packages to home addresses.

Challenges to the Bureaucracy

With cabinet departments, independent executive agencies, independent regulatory agencies, and government corporations, the federal bureaucracy is both complex and very specialized. Each agency, corporation, or line department has its own mission, its own goals, and, in many cases, its own constituents either at home or, in the case of the State Department, abroad. However, some problems and crises require the attention of multiple agencies. In these cases overlapping jurisdictions can cause confusion, or problems may arise that no agency has the authority to solve.

A famous story about the Carter administration illustrates this point: President Jimmy Carter believed he smelled something dead behind his Oval Office wall—probably a mouse. His staff called the General Services Administration, which has responsibility for the White House, but those bureaucrats claimed it was not their problem. They had fumigated recently, so the mouse must have come in from outside. The Department of the Interior, which has responsibility for the gardens and grounds, refused to help because the mouse was now inside. Eventually, an interagency task force was created to remove the mouse. If solving one small problem was this complicated for the federal bureaucracy, consider larger issues such as terrorism and natural disasters.

Reorganizing to Stop Terrorism

After September 11, 2001, the nation saw that no single agency was responsible for coordinating antiterrorism efforts. Nor was one person able to muster a nationwide response to a terrorist attack. Fighting terrorism involves so many different efforts—screening baggage at airports, inspecting freight shipments, and protecting the border, to name just a few—that coordinating them would be impossible unless all of these functions were combined into one agency.

The creation of the Department of Homeland Security (DHS) in 2003 was the largest reorganization of the U.S. government since 1947. Twenty-two agencies with responsibilities for preventing terrorism were merged into a single department. Congress and the president agreed that combining the Federal Emergency Management Agency (FEMA), Customs and Border Protection, the Coast Guard, the Secret Service, and many other organizations into a single agency would promote efficiency and improve coordination. It now has more than 190,000 employees and a proposed budget of $64 billion for 2016. The department's Twitter feed and website offer helpful suggestions and tips.

Image 13-3
An airline passenger stands in a full-body scanner at the Los Angeles International Airport in 2014. Such scanners transmit an image of the passenger to a secure room where they are checked by Transportation Security Administration (TSA) supervisors. The image cannot be seen by the TSA screeners at the security checkpoint or by other passengers.

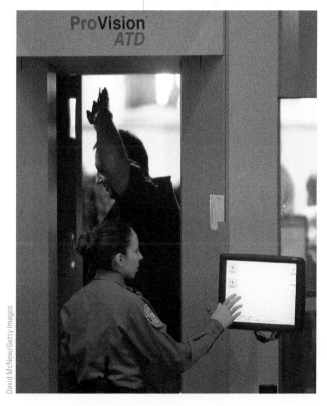

David McNew/Getty Images

It proved difficult to integrate agencies whose missions were very different. Some suggested that the bureaucratic cultures of agencies focused on law enforcement, such as the Secret Service and the Border Patrol, would be difficult to mesh with the agencies that focus on problems faced by citizens in a time of natural disasters, such as FEMA. Indeed, when FEMA became part of the DHS, its funding was reduced and it received less attention because the focus of the DHS has been on fighting terrorism, not on responding to natural disasters. In addition, the DHS did not actually unify all U.S. antiterrorism efforts. The most important antiterrorist agencies are the Federal Bureau of Investigation (FBI) and the CIA, but neither is part of the DHS. Many believe that the number-one problem in addressing terrorism is the failure of the FBI and CIA to exchange information with one another. To address this problem, President Bush created a Terrorist Threat Integration Center in *addition* to the DHS, the FBI, and the CIA. In 2004, Congress established the new Office of the Director of National Intelligence to coordinate the nation's intelligence efforts, and in 2005, President Bush appointed John Negroponte to be the director of national intelligence to try once again to coordinate the nation's intelligence agencies. This position, however, has been difficult to establish. In 2010, President Obama named the fourth director in five years, General James R. Clapper. The authority of the director is often undercut by other appointees who may be closer to the president, including the director of the CIA and the national security advisor, making this a very difficult position to hold.

Dealing with Natural Disasters

As George H. W. Bush faced a tough reelection campaign in 1992, Hurricane Andrew struck southern Florida, destroying many communities south of Miami, Florida, leaving hundreds of thousands of people without power and without homes. Although the total death toll was only 65, the storm cost more than $25 billion in damage and losses. The Bush administration was widely criticized for not getting aid to the victims quickly enough, and the president was chided for not putting in a personal appearance.

Supposedly, FEMA was strengthened and improved after Hurricane Andrew. FEMA dealt competently with hundreds of natural disasters in the years that followed, including tornados, floods, and blizzards. However, in 2005, a year in which five major hurricanes made landfall in the United States, FEMA again proved unable to meet the challenges of a massive natural disaster. When Hurricane Katrina headed toward New Orleans, all authorities warned of a possible flooding situation. No one dreamed of flooding that would trap thousands of residents in their homes for a week or more and destroy whole neighborhoods in New Orleans. No one had planned to evacuate thousands of people with no transportation of their own or to house them for years after the storm. Again, FEMA was criticized for its slow response, as was President George W. Bush. The scope of this disaster was so large and the relationship between the state and federal agencies involved so complex that FEMA could not effectively coordinate the rescue and relief efforts.

Natural and manmade emergencies continue to test the ability of federal agencies to respond. In 2010, an oil-drilling rig in the Gulf of Mexico exploded, triggering a massive oil spill. Again, within days, the media and local government officials were calling for faster and more effective federal government assistance even though the technology for dealing with such a spill is only available in the petroleum industry. President Obama was accused of not visiting the region quickly enough and not demonstrating enough anger at the oil company.

When Hurricane Sandy formed in the Caribbean in October 2012, weather scientists predicted that the very powerful and extraordinarily large storm might come up the east coast of the United States. Mindful of earlier events, FEMA and other local, state, and federal agencies began to plan before the storm came to the United States. Although downgraded to a tropical storm, or "super storm," by the time it came ashore in New York, Sandy took more than 275 lives and caused an estimated $68 billion in damage. Thousands of people lost their homes in New Jersey and New York. FEMA and the other agencies were generally praised for their actions and for warning residents before the storm hit.

Hurricanes Katrina and Sandy illustrate the huge challenge faced by bureaucracies when dealing with natural disasters. So many agencies and levels of government must be coordinated that sometimes responses are delayed and aid does not get to the victims in a timely way. Media coverage of these tragedies focuses on the struggles of citizens, while the struggles of the bureaucrats take place in back rooms as officials strive to find the right equipment and personnel to meet unique disasters. At times, no president can be successful in dealing with the public relations aspect of these events.

Staffing the Bureaucracy

■ **13.3** Explain how individuals get positions in the federal bureaucracy, and discuss the history of attempts to reform that process.

The two categories of bureaucrats are political appointees and civil servants. The president is able to make political appointments to most of the top jobs in the federal bureaucracy and can appoint ambassadors to foreign posts. The rest of the national government's employees belong to the civil service and obtain their jobs through a much more formal process.

Political Appointees

To fill the positions listed in the Plum Book, the president and the president's advisers solicit suggestions from politicians, businesspersons, and other prominent individuals. Appointments offer the president a way to pay off outstanding political debts. But the president must also consider such things as the candidate's work experience, intelligence, political affiliations, and personal characteristics. Presidents have differed in the importance they attach to appointing women and minorities to plum positions. Presidents often use ambassadorships to reward individuals for their campaign contributions.

Even though the president has the power to appoint a government official, this does not mean an appointment will pass muster. Every potential nominee must undergo an FBI investigation and thorough screening. Such a process takes months, and after completing it, the appointees must be confirmed by the Senate. Sometimes, individuals withdraw from the nomination process before confirmation; others prove to be political problems for the administration only after confirmation.

Image 13-4

Secretary of State Mike Pompeo greets the Foreign Minister of China, Wang Yi, before their meeting in Beijing, China.

China News Service/Getty Images

The Aristocracy of the Federal Government Political appointees are in some sense the aristocracy of the federal government. Their powers, although formidable on paper, are often exaggerated. Like the president, a political appointee will occupy her or his position for a comparatively brief time. They often leave office before the president's term actually ends—the average term of service for political appointees is less than two years. Additionally, the professional civil servants who make up the permanent civil service may not feel compelled to carry out their current boss's directives quickly because they know that he or she will not be around for very long.

The Difficulty in Firing Civil Servants This inertia is compounded by the fact that it is very difficult to discharge civil servants. In recent years, less than one-tenth of 1 percent of federal employees have been fired for incompetence. Because discharged employees may appeal their dismissals, many months or even years can pass before the issue is resolved conclusively. The attempt to change the Veterans Administration hospitals was complicated by these rules, and many top-level employees first took administrative leave during the investigative process and then retired with their secure pensions. This occupational rigidity helps ensure that most political appointees, no matter how competent or driven, will not be able to exert much meaningful influence over their subordinates, let alone implement dramatic changes in the bureaucracy itself.

History of the Federal Civil Service

When the federal government was formed in 1789, it boasted no career public servants. Its ranks were composed of amateurs, almost all of them Federalists. When Thomas Jefferson took over as president, few people in his party were holding federal administrative jobs, so he fired more than 100 officials and replaced them with his own supporters. Then, for the next 25 years, as a growing body of federal administrators gained experience and expertise, they developed into professional public servants. These administrators stayed in office regardless of who was elected president. The bureaucracy had become a self-maintaining, long-term element within government.

WASHINGTON, D. C.—THE ATTACK ON THE PRESIDENT'S LIFE—SCENE IN THE LADIES' ROOM OF THE BALTIMORE AND OHIO RAILROAD DEPOT—THE ARREST OF THE ASSASSIN.

Image 13-5

On September 19, 1881, President James A. Garfield was assassinated by a disappointed office seeker, Charles J. Guiteau. The long-term effect of this event was to replace the spoils system with a permanent career civil service. This process began with the passage of the Pendleton Act in 1883, which established the Civil Service Commission.

To the Victor Belong the Spoils When Andrew Jackson took over the White House in 1828, he could not believe how many appointed officials (appointed before he became president, that is) were overtly hostile toward him and his Democratic Party. Because the bureaucracy was reluctant to carry out his programs, Jackson did the obvious: he fired federal officials—more than had all his predecessors combined. The **spoils system**—an application of the principle that to the victor belong the spoils—became the standard method of filling federal positions. Whenever a new president was elected from a different party, the staffing of the federal government would almost completely turn over.

The Civil Service Reform Act of 1883 Jackson's spoils system survived for decades, but it became increasingly corrupt. Also, as the size of the bureaucracy increased by 300 percent between 1851 and 1881, the cry for civil service reform grew louder. Reformers looked to the example of several European countries, Germany in particular, which had established a professional civil service that operated under a **merit system**, in which job appointments were based on competitive examinations.

In 1883, the **Pendleton Act**—or **Civil Service Reform Act**—was passed, placing the first limits on the spoils system. The act established the principle of employment on the basis of open, competitive examinations and created the **Civil Service Commission** to administer the personnel service. Initially, only 10 percent of federal employees were covered by the merit system. Later laws, amendments, and executive orders, however, increased the coverage to more than 90 percent of federal employees. The effects of these reforms were felt at all levels of government.

The Supreme Court strengthened the civil service system in *Elrod v. Burns*[7] in 1976 and *Branti v. Finkel*[8] in 1980. In these cases, the Court used the First

spoils system
The awarding of government jobs to political supporters and friends.

merit system
The selection, retention, and promotion of government employees on the basis of competitive examinations.

Pendleton Act (Civil Service Reform Act)
An act that established the principle of employment on the basis of merit and created the Civil Service Commission to administer the personnel service.

Civil Service Commission
The initial central personnel agency of the national government, created in 1883.

---

7   427 U.S. 347 (1976).
8   445 U.S. 507 (1980).

Amendment to forbid government officials from discharging or threatening to discharge public employees solely for *not* being supporters of the political party in power unless party affiliation is an appropriate requirement for the position. Additional enhancements to the civil service system were added in *Rutan v. Republican Party of Illinois* in 1990.[9] The Court's ruling effectively prevented the use of partisan political considerations as the basis for hiring, promoting, or transferring most public employees. An exception was permitted, however, for senior policymaking positions, which usually go to officials who will support the programs of the elected leaders.

The Civil Service Reform Act of 1978 In 1978, the Civil Service Reform Act abolished the Civil Service Commission and created two new federal agencies to perform its duties. To administer the civil service laws, rules, and regulations, the act created the Office of Personnel Management (OPM), which is empowered to recruit, interview, and test potential government workers and determine who should be hired. The OPM makes recommendations to the individual agencies as to which persons meet the standards (typically, the top three applicants for a position), and the agencies then decide whom to hire. To oversee promotions, employees' rights, and other employment matters, the act created the Merit Systems Protection Board (MSPB), which evaluates charges of wrongdoing, hears employee appeals of agency decisions, and can order corrective action against agencies and employees.

Federal Employees and Political Campaigns In 1933, when President Franklin D. Roosevelt set up his New Deal, a virtual army of civil servants was hired to staff the numerous new agencies that were created. Because the individuals who worked in these agencies owed their jobs to the Democratic Party, it seemed natural for them to campaign for Democratic candidates. The Democrats controlling Congress in the mid-1930s did not object. But in 1938, a coalition of conservative Democrats and Republicans took control of Congress and forced through the Hatch Act—or Political Activities Act—of 1939, which prohibited federal employees from actively participating in the political management of campaigns. It also forbade the use of federal authority to influence nominations and elections and outlawed the use of bureaucratic rank to pressure federal employees to make political contributions.

The Hatch Act created a controversy that lasted for decades. Many contended that the act deprived federal employees of their First Amendment freedoms of speech and association. In 1972, a federal district court declared it unconstitutional. The Supreme Court, however, reaffirmed the challenged portion of the act in 1973, stating that the government's interest in preserving a nonpartisan civil service was so great that the prohibitions should remain.[10] Twenty years later, Congress addressed the criticisms by passing the Federal Employees Political Activities Act of 1993. This act, which amended the Hatch Act, softened the 1939 act in several ways. Among other things, the 1993 act allowed federal employees to run for office in nonpartisan elections, participate in voter-registration drives, make campaign contributions to political organizations, and campaign for candidates in partisan elections.

---

9 497 U.S. 62 (1990).
10 *United States Civil Service Commission v. National Association of Letter Carriers*, 413 U.S. 548 (1973).

Modern Attempts at Bureaucratic Reform

■ **13.4** Discuss some of the critiques of large bureaucracies and describe several types of bureaucratic reform.

As long as the federal bureaucracy exists, attempts to make it more open, efficient, and responsive to the needs of U.S. citizens will continue. The most important actual and proposed reforms in the last several decades include sunshine and sunset laws, privatization, incentives for efficiency, and more protection for so-called whistleblowers.

Sunshine Laws before and after September 11

In 1976, Congress enacted the **Government in the Sunshine Act**. It required for the first time that all multiheaded federal agencies—agencies headed by a committee instead of an individual—hold their meetings regularly in public session. The bill defined *meetings* as almost any gathering, formal or informal, of agency members, including a conference telephone call. The only exceptions to this rule of openness are discussions of matters such as court proceedings or personnel problems, and these exceptions are specifically listed in the bill. Sunshine laws now exist at all levels of government.

Government in the Sunshine Act
A law that requires all committee-directed federal agencies to conduct their business regularly in public sessions.

Information Disclosure Sunshine laws are consistent with the policy of information disclosure supported by the government for decades. Beginning in the 1960s, several consumer protection laws have required that certain information be disclosed to consumers when purchasing homes, borrowing funds, and so on. In 1966, the federal government passed the Freedom of Information Act, which required federal government agencies, with certain exceptions, to disclose to individuals, on their request, any information about them contained in government files.

Curbs on Information Disclosure Since September 11, 2001, the trend toward government in the sunshine and information disclosure has been reversed at both the federal and state levels. Within weeks after September 11, 2001, numerous federal agencies removed hundreds, if not thousands, of documents from websites, public libraries, and reading rooms found in various federal government departments. Information contained in some of the documents included diagrams of power plants and pipelines, structural details on dams, and safety plans for chemical plants. The military also immediately started restricting information about its current and planned activities, as did the FBI. These agencies were concerned that terrorists could use this information to plan attacks.

The federal government pioneered the withdrawal of information from public view, but state and local governments were quick to jump on the bandwagon. State and local governments control and supervise police forces, dams, electricity sources, and water supplies. It is not surprising that many state and local governments followed in the footsteps of the federal government in curbing access to certain public records and information. Most local agencies, however, do involve the public in emergency planning.

Sunset Laws

It has often been suggested that the federal government be subject to **sunset legislation**, which places government programs on a definite schedule for

sunset legislation
Laws requiring that existing programs be reviewed regularly for their effectiveness and be terminated unless specifically extended as a result of these reviews.

Image 13-6

The National Security Agency (NSA) has completed its new data center in Bluffdale, Utah. It may be the largest such facility in the world.

George Frey/Getty Images

congressional consideration. Unless Congress specifically reauthorizes a particular federally operated program at the end of a designated period, it is automatically terminated; that is, its sun sets.

Although this idea was first championed by Franklin D. Roosevelt in the 1930s, it has not been adopted by Congress. Texas and Alabama have sunset laws that affect all state agencies.

Privatization

privatization
The replacement of government services with services provided by private firms.

Another approach to bureaucratic reform is **privatization**, which occurs when government services are replaced by services from the private sector. For example, the government might contract with private firms to operate prisons. Supporters of privatization argue that some services could be provided more efficiently by the private sector. Another scheme is to furnish vouchers to "clients" in lieu of services. For example, instead of supplying housing, the government could offer vouchers that recipients could use to pay for housing in privately owned buildings.

The privatization, or contracting out, strategy has been most successful at the local level. Municipalities can form contracts with private companies for such things as trash collection. This approach is not a cure-all, however, as many functions, particularly on the national level, cannot be contracted out in any meaningful way. The federal government could not contract out most of the Defense Department's functions to private firms. Nonetheless, the U.S. military has contracted out many services in Iraq and elsewhere, as discussed in Beyond Our Borders.

Incentives for Efficiency and Productivity

An increasing number of state governments are beginning to experiment with a variety of schemes to run their operations more efficiently and capably. They focus on maximizing the efficiency and productivity of government workers by providing incentives for improved performance.[11] Some of the most promising

11 See, for example, David Osborne and Ted Gaebler, *Reinventing Government: How the Entrepreneurial Spirit Is Transforming the Public Sector* (Reading, MA: Addison-Wesley, 1992); and David Osborne and Peter Plastrik, *Banishing Bureaucracy: The Five Strategies for Reinventing Government* (Reading, MA: Addison-Wesley, 1997).

measures have included such tactics as permitting agencies that do not spend their entire budgets to keep some of the difference and rewarding employees with performance-based bonuses.

Beyond Our Borders

Bureaucracies around the World Face Ebola

In late 2013, cases of Ebola, a deadly virus, were reported in West Africa. It was not immediately clear whether these were isolated cases or that the disease was being spread across the region. Ebola, which is caused by a virus, is easily spread to those who touch someone with the illness, and is fatal almost 50 percent of the time. Within two years, the reported death total was 11,322 out of possibly 28,000 cases. For the countries involved in the outbreak—Guinea, Liberia, and Sierra Leone—the impact of the disease will be felt for decades in terms of broken families, economic losses, and the loss of a large number of the health-care workers who died of the disease.

Although the first case of the Ebola virus was reported in December 2013, the World Health Organization (WHO) did not declare a health emergency until eight months later, in August 2014. WHO is an agency of the United Nations (UN). Not until that time did the international bureaucracy begin to issue calls for global support in fighting the outbreak. At the same time, medical personnel in the affected countries were trying to deal with a rapidly spreading disease using primitive equipment and facilities. The international organization Doctors Without Borders responded soon after the first cases were reported. Later, the organization described the global response as "lethally inadequate."* The agency's response to the criticism was that "political, cultural, organizational, and financial" factors caused the delay. This suggests that WHO may have been trying to manage the crisis itself without help or that there were political concerns about asking for assistance either from the United Nations' own apparatus or from global powers like the United States.

Almost as soon as WHO declared a global health emergency, the United States began to coordinate its official response. Only one month after the WHO announcement, President Obama released a fact sheet detailing the American response: The Pentagon would establish an African command post; the Public Health Service would

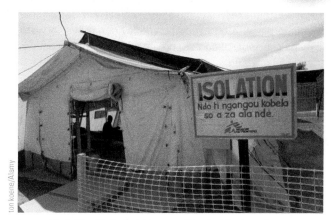

Image 13-7 The Ebola isolation ward in the Mpoko refugee camp.

send 65 doctors; USAID would send care kits to households in Liberia; the Centers for Disease Control (CDC) would help on the ground in Africa; and the United States would send protective gear for the health workers and others in Africa. The federal effort used existing funds, and Congress quickly appropriated more funds. By the time these efforts actually reached West Africa, the epidemic had peaked in some nations and was in retreat in others. One of the American outreach efforts was less than successful. An American field hospital costing $20 million was sent to Liberia and was staffed by military medical personnel. However, this facility was intended to treat foreign health-care professionals and could not be used by Liberian patients.**

The Ebola virus spawned a domestic political crisis as well. As soon as American volunteer health workers were diagnosed with the disease, they were sent home for treatment, which was successful in all cases. However, this raised inevitable bureaucratic problems: Who was in charge of their care and the hospitals where they were treated? What role did the CDC play in decisions about these patients? How did they get access to experimental medicines that were unavailable to patients in Africa? And, finally, with public fear mounting, the Department of

(Continued)

(Continued)

Homeland Security had to devise a quick screening tool for passengers returning from abroad to see if they had any symptoms of the disease.

The Ebola outbreak was only one example of how difficult it is for bureaucracies, whether at the United Nations or in several nations, to put together plans to meet global emergencies. Many commentators suggested that the World Health Organization should have plans in place for the next epidemic. It should also be possible for a global organization to have plans to meet the after-effects of major earthquakes, tsunamis, or nuclear accidents. If a plan is in place, a bureaucratic agency can move forward fairly quickly, but, of course, no emergency actually occurs exactly as planned.

For Critical Analysis

1. If a global institution such as the United Nations plans for global emergencies, how much control over American personnel should be given to the UN?

2. Why does it seem likely that volunteer organizations like Doctors Without Borders can respond more quickly to emergencies such as the Ebola outbreak?

*Denise Roland, "Experts Criticize World Health Organization's 'Slow' Ebola Response," *The Wall Street Journal,* May 12, 2015.

**The White House, "Fact Sheet: U.S. Response to the Ebola Epidemic in West Africa," September 16, 2014. https://www.whitehouse.gove/the-press-office/2014/09/16

Government Performance and Results Act At the federal level, the Government Performance and Results Act of 1997 was designed to improve efficiency in the federal workforce. The act required that all government agencies (except the CIA) describe their new goals and establish methods for determining whether those goals are met.

The performance-based budgeting implemented by President George W. Bush took this results-oriented approach a step further. In the Bush administration, agencies were given specific performance criteria to meet, and the Office of Management and Budget rated each agency to determine how well it performed. Additional efforts to improve efficiency have included bonus pay to employees in some departments of the federal government.

Bureaucracy Has Changed Little Observers disagree over whether the government can meet the demands of a complex economy and diverse nation. Consequently, the government must become more responsive to cope with the increasing demands placed on it. Political scientists Joel Aberbach and Bert Rockman take issue with this contention. They argue that the bureaucracy has changed significantly over time in response to the demands of various presidential administrations. In their opinion, many of the problems attributed to the bureaucracy are, in fact, a result of the political decision-making process. Therefore, attempts to reinvent government by reforming the bureaucracy are misguided.[12]

Others have suggested that the problem lies with the people who run bureaucratic organizations. According to some scholars, what needs to be

---

12 Joel D. Aberbach and Bert A. Rockman, *In the Web of Politics: Three Decades of the U.S. Federal Executive* (Washington, DC: Brookings Institution Press, 2000).

reinvented is not the machinery of government, but public officials. After each election, new appointees to bureaucratic positions may find themselves managing complex, multimillion-dollar enterprises, yet they often are untrained for their jobs. According to these authors, civil service career executives who head federal agencies do a better job than the amateurs appointed by the president.[13]

Saving Costs through E-Government Many contend that the communications revolution brought about by the Internet has not only improved the efficiency with which government agencies deliver services to the public but has also reduced the cost of government. Agencies can now communicate with members of the public, as well as other agencies, via email. Additionally, every federal agency now has a website citizens can access to find information about agency services instead of calling or appearing in person at a regional agency office. Taxes and withholdings are deposited electronically, and payments such as Social Security benefits are transferred electronically. Since 2003, federal agencies have also been required by the Government Paperwork Elimination Act of 1998 to use e-commerce whenever it is practical to do so and will save on costs.

Helping Out the Whistleblowers

The term **whistleblower** as applied to the federal bureaucracy has a special meaning: it is someone who blows the whistle on a gross governmental inefficiency or illegal action. Whistleblowers may be clerical workers, managers, or even specialists, such as scientists.

whistleblower
Someone who brings to public attention gross governmental inefficiency or an illegal action.

Laws Protecting Whistleblowers The 1978 Civil Service Reform Act prohibits reprisals against whistleblowers by their superiors, and it set up the Merit Systems Protection Board as part of this protection. Many federal agencies also have toll-free hotlines that employees can use anonymously to report bureaucratic waste and inappropriate behavior.

Further protection for whistleblowers was provided in 1989, when Congress passed the Whistle-Blower Protection Act. That act established an independent agency, the Office of Special Counsel (OSC), to investigate complaints brought by government employees who have been demoted, fired, or otherwise sanctioned for reporting government fraud or waste.

Some state and federal laws encourage employees to blow the whistle on their employers' wrongful actions by providing monetary incentives to the whistleblowers. At the federal level, the False Claims Act of 1986 allows a whistleblower who has disclosed information about a fraud against the U.S. government to receive a monetary award. If the government chooses to prosecute the case and wins, the whistleblower receives between 15 and 25 percent of the proceeds. If the government declines to intervene, the whistleblower can bring suit on behalf of the government, and if the suit is successful, will receive between 25 and 30 percent of the proceeds.

The Problem Continues Despite these endeavors to help whistleblowers, little evidence indicates that potential whistleblowers truly have received more protection. More than 40 percent of the employees who turned to the OSC for

13 Nick Gallo and David E. Lewis, "The Consequences of Presidential Patronage for Federal Agency Performance," *Journal of Public Administration Research and Theory* (2012) 22 (2): 219–243.

assistance in a recent three-year period stated that they were no longer employees of the government agencies on which they blew the whistle—most have already retired.

The Supreme Court placed restrictions on lawsuits in the 2006 case *Garcetti v. Ceballos*, which involved an assistant district attorney, Richard Ceballos, who wrote a memo asking if a county sheriff's deputy had lied in a search warrant affidavit.[14] Ceballos claimed that he was subsequently demoted and denied a promotion for trying to expose the lie. The outcome of the case turned on an interpretation of an employee's right to freedom of speech—whether it included the right to criticize an employment-related action. In a close (5–4) and controversial decision, the Supreme Court held that when public employees make statements relating to their official duties, they are not speaking as citizens for First Amendment purposes. The Court deemed that when he wrote his memo, Ceballos was speaking as an employee, not a citizen, and was thus subject to his employer's disciplinary actions. The ruling affects millions of governmental employees.

The Obama administration was particularly concerned with the national security implications of information leaked to journalists. Although some federal employees might believe that they are whistleblowers, the Obama administration prosecuted whistleblowers under the Espionage Act of 1917, which makes it a federal crime for federal employees to give "aid to our enemies." This legislation was only used three times between 1917 and 2008, but after President Obama took office, six cases were prosecuted against federal workers, imposing a "chill" on relationships between federal employees and the press.[15]

Bureaucrats as Politicians and Policymakers

■ **13.5** Describe the tools and powers that bureaucratic agencies have to shape policies and regulations.

Because Congress is unable to oversee the day-to-day administration of its programs, it must delegate certain powers to administrative agencies. Congress delegates the power to implement legislation to agencies through **enabling legislation**. For example, the Federal Trade Commission was created by the Federal Trade Commission Act of 1914, the Equal Employment Opportunity Commission was created by the Civil Rights Act of 1964, and the Occupational Safety and Health Administration was created by the Occupational Safety and Health Act of 1970. The enabling legislation generally specifies the name, purpose, composition, functions, and powers of the agency.

In theory, the agencies should administer laws passed by Congress. Laws are often drafted in such vague and general terms, however, that they provide relatively little guidance to agency administrators as to how the laws should be implemented. This means that the agencies must decide how best to carry out the wishes of Congress. This role requires the agency to formulate

enabling legislation
A statute enacted by Congress that authorizes the creation of an administrative agency and specifies the name, purpose, composition, functions, and powers of the agency being created.

---

14 126 S. Ct. 1951 (2006).
15 David Carr, "Blurred Line Between Espionage and Truth," *The New York Times*, February 26, 2012.

administrative rules (regulations). But it also forces the agency to become an unelected policymaker.

The Rule-Making Environment

Rule making does not occur in a vacuum. The EPA might decide to implement the new law through a technical regulation on factory emissions. This proposed regulation is published in the *Federal Register* so that interested parties would have an opportunity to comment on it. Individuals and companies that opposed the rule (or parts of it) might then try to convince the EPA to revise or redraft the regulation. Some parties might try to persuade the agency to withdraw the proposed regulation altogether. In any event, the EPA would consider these comments in drafting the final version of the regulation following the expiration of the comment period.

Waiting Periods and Court Challenges Once the final regulation has been published in the *Federal Register*, the rule can be enforced after a 60-day waiting period. During that period, businesses, individuals, and state and local governments can ask Congress to overturn the regulation. After that 60-day period has lapsed, the regulation can still be challenged in court by a party having a direct interest in the rule, such as a company that expects to incur significant costs in complying with it. The company could argue that the rule misinterprets the applicable law or goes beyond the agency's statutory purview. An allegation by the company that the EPA made a mistake in judgment probably would not be enough to convince the court to throw out the rule. The company instead would have to demonstrate that the rule was "arbitrary and capricious."

Controversies How agencies implement, administer, and enforce legislation has resulted in controversy. Decisions made by agencies charged with administering the Endangered Species Act have led to protests from farmers, ranchers, and others whose economic interests have been harmed. For example, the government decided to cut off the flow of irrigation water from Klamath Lake in Oregon in the summer of 2001. That action, which affected irrigation and water for more than 1,000 farmers in southern Oregon and northern California, was undertaken to save endangered suckerfish and salmon. It was believed that the lake's water level was so low that further use of the water for irrigation would harm these fish. The results of this decision were devastating for many farmers.

One of the agencies that seems to be most sensitive to a change in presidential administration is the Environmental Protection Agency, created by Congress in 1970. Congress has passed several laws to improve air quality in the United States, giving the EPA the authority to carry out this legislation. Presidents differ, however, in how they interpret these congressional mandates. During the George W. Bush administration, the EPA issued decisions that weakened the enforcement of air pollution laws. In 1999, several environmental groups petitioned the EPA to set new standards for automobiles to reduce greenhouse gas emissions. In 2003, during the Bush administration, the EPA refused to do so, claiming that it did not have the legal authority to do this. States that passed laws regulating automobiles in their own areas sued the EPA. In 2007, the Supreme Court ruled that the EPA cannot refuse to assess environmental hazards and issue appropriate regulations. As Justice John Paul Stevens wrote, "This is the Congressional design. EPA has refused

> *did you know?*
>
> Each year, federal administrative agencies produce rules that fill 7,500 pages in the *Code of Federal Regulations.*

to comply with this clear statutory command."[16] This was an unusual situation in that the states actually challenged a regulatory agency to issue stronger regulations. Often, challenges to regulatory agencies are intended to weaken new regulations.

The Obama administration took a much firmer stand on the enforcement of air pollution regulations. While committed to the passage of a new energy bill that would reduce the United States' contribution to greenhouse gases, by spring of 2010 it seemed that major new legislation might not pass quickly. The EPA issued new gas mileage requirements and new rules regulating tail-pipe emissions for cars and trucks in April 2010. A Republican-led attempt in the Senate to veto these new regulations was defeated in June of that year. The EPA also issued new regulations for coal mining and for emissions from coal-burning power plants. With the inauguration of President Trump, support for enhanced enforcement of environmental rules dissipated overnight. Many of the Obama-era rules have been reversed through executive orders, and others are pending further study by the Trump administration.

Negotiated Rule Making

Since 1945, companies, environmentalists, and other special-interest groups have challenged government regulations in court. In the 1980s, however, the sheer wastefulness of attempting to regulate through litigation became more and more apparent. Today, a growing number of federal agencies encourage businesses and public-interest groups to become directly involved in drafting regulations. Agencies hope that such participation may help prevent later courtroom battles over the meaning, applicability, and legal effect of the regulations.

Congress formally approved *negotiated rule making* in the Negotiated Rulemaking Act of 1990. The act authorizes agencies to allow those who will be affected by a new rule to participate in the rule-drafting process. If an agency chooses to engage in negotiated rule making, it must publish in the *Federal Register* the subject and scope of the rule to be developed, the parties affected significantly by the rule, and other information. Representatives of the affected groups and other interested parties then may apply to be members of the negotiating committee. The agency is represented on the committee, but a neutral third party (not the agency) presides over the proceedings. Once the committee members have reached agreement on the terms of the proposed rule, a notice is published in the *Federal Register*, followed by a period for comments by any person or organization interested in the proposed rule. Negotiated rule making often is practiced under the condition that the participants promise not to challenge in court the outcome of any agreement to which they were a party.

Bureaucrats Are Policymakers

Theories of public administration once assumed that bureaucrats do not make policy decisions but only implement the laws and policies promulgated by the president and legislative bodies. A more realistic view now held by most bureaucrats and elected officials is that the agencies and departments of

---

16 *Commonwealth of Massachusetts v. EPA*, 127 S. Ct. 1438 (2007).

government play important roles in policymaking. Many government rules, regulations, and programs are in fact initiated by bureaucrats, based on their expertise and scientific studies. How a law passed by Congress eventually is translated into concrete action—from the forms to be filled out to decisions about who gets the benefits—usually is determined within each agency or department. Even the evaluation of whether a policy has achieved its purpose usually is based on studies commissioned and interpreted by the agency administering the program.

The bureaucracy's policymaking role has often been depicted by what traditionally has been called the "iron triangle." Recently, the concept of an "issue network" has been viewed as a more accurate description of the policymaking process.

Iron Triangles In the past, scholars often described the bureaucracy's role in the policymaking process by using the concept of an **iron triangle**—a three-way alliance among legislators in Congress, bureaucrats, and interest groups. Consider as an example the development of agricultural policy. Congress, as one component of the triangle (see Figure 13-4), includes two major committees concerned with agricultural policy, the House Committee on Agriculture and the Senate Committee on Agriculture, Nutrition, and Forestry. The Department of Agriculture, the second component of the triangle, has more than 95,000 employees, plus thousands of contractors and consultants. Agricultural interest groups, the third component of the iron triangle in agricultural policymaking, include many large and powerful associations, such as the American Farm Bureau Federation, the National Cattlemen's Association, and the Corn Growers Association. These three components of the iron triangle work together, formally or informally, to create policy.

iron triangle
The three-way alliance among legislators, bureaucrats, and interest groups to make or preserve policies that benefit their respective interests.

Figure 13-4 ▶ Iron Triangle

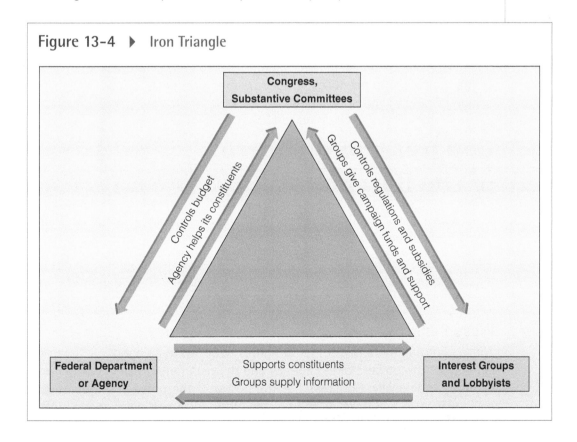

issue network
A group of individuals or organizations—which may consist of legislators and legislative staff members, interest group leaders, bureaucrats, the media, scholars, and other experts—that supports a particular policy position on a given issue.

For example, the various agricultural interest groups lobby Congress to develop policies that benefit their interests. Members of Congress cannot afford to ignore the wishes of interest groups because they are potential sources of voter support and campaign contributions. The legislators in Congress also work closely with the Department of Agriculture, which, in implementing a policy, can develop rules that benefit—or at least do not hurt—certain industries or groups. The Department of Agriculture, in turn, supports policies that enhance the department's budget and powers. In this way, according to theory, agricultural policy is created that benefits all three components of the iron triangle.

Issue Networks This example is a simplified picture of how the iron triangle works. With the growth in the complexity of government, policymaking also has become more complicated. The bureaucracy is larger, Congress has more committees and subcommittees, and interest groups are more powerful than ever. Although iron triangles still exist, often they are inadequate as descriptions of how policy is actually made. Frequently, different interest groups concerned about a certain area of policy have conflicting demands, making agency decisions difficult. Additionally, divided government in some years has meant that departments are sometimes pressured by the president to take one approach and by Congress to take another.

Many scholars now use the term *issue network* to describe the policymaking process. An **issue network** consists of individuals or organizations that support a particular policy position on the environment, taxation, consumer safety, or some other issue. Typically, it includes legislators and/or their staff members, interest groups, bureaucrats, scholars and other experts, and representatives from the media. Members of a particular issue network work together to influence the president, members of Congress, administrative agencies, and the courts to affect public policy on a specific issue. Each policy issue may involve conflicting positions taken by two or more issue networks. During the Trump administration, issue networks concerned with energy policy, trade policy, and tax policy ramped up their efforts to be influential in legislation favored by the president.

Congressional Control of the Bureaucracy

■ **13.6** Analyze the relationship between Congress, its committees, interest groups, and the bureaucracy.

Many political pundits doubt whether Congress can meaningfully control the federal bureaucracy. Nevertheless, Congress does have some means of exerting control.

Ways Congress Does Control the Bureaucracy

These commentators forget that Congress specifies in an agency's "enabling legislation" the powers of the agency and the parameters within which it can operate. Additionally, Congress has the power of the purse and theoretically could refuse to authorize or appropriate funds for a particular agency. After allegations were made that the Internal Revenue Service (IRS) targeted

The Veterans Administration Faces a Scandal

The Department of Veterans Affairs is one of the largest federal organizations, second only to the Defense Department in the number of employees. The three most important functions of the department are dispersing veterans' benefits, providing for burials and memorials, and providing health care to eligible veterans. The Veterans Health Administration oversees a network of hospitals and outpatient clinics that serve veterans from all branches of service and at all ages. In recent years, the veterans of the Vietnam War era have become retirees and their medical needs have increased while, at the same time, thousands of veterans of the Iraq and Afghanistan conflicts have sought care both for physical and psychological needs.

Over the years, there had been a number of complaints about the difficulty of getting appointments with medical personnel at the VA's facilities, but little attention was paid to these issues until 2013. After his retirement, one of the physicians at the Phoenix hospital went public with his allegations that there was an official "wait list" that was reported to Washington, DC, and an unofficial list that showed veterans waiting more than a year for an appointment. Families of veterans reported their loved ones died while waiting for an appointment, and other VA employees came forward to discuss orders to falsify records of appointment times. A preliminary investigation of the Phoenix system found that about 1,700 veterans were "at risk of being lost or forgotten" after being dropped from the waiting list.* At least 18 of the veterans in that group died while waiting for an appointment.

As the various reports became public, it seemed clear that multiple hospitals were involved and multiple employees either ordered the manipulation of the lists or falsified records. Because the VA had offered a monetary bonus for exemplary performance, officials noted that the records were changed so individuals could receive the bonus awards. Although it seemed clear that much of this had gone on for several years, Secretary of Veterans Affairs Eric Shinseki resigned under the pressure of public opinion. The president then nominated Robert McDonald, former CEO of Procter & Gamble, as secretary and he was quickly confirmed. Congress passed legislation making the firing of top officials at the VA easier and other legislation allowing veterans who lived at a distance from a VA facility to get treatment at other facilities.

So, the question became, what changed at the VA after all the scandal. By 2015, the department had removed 14 people (out of more than 300,000) from their jobs, and 16 received other punishments.** Indeed, an investigation by the *New York Times* found that only eight were punished for their part in the scandal, and of that number, one retired and others were suspended with pay. Raymond Kelley, a

From the Web ▶ The VA website encourages veterans to find out what services are available to them but avoids any reference to the recent scandal.

US Department of Veteran Affairs

spokesman for the Veterans of Foreign Wars organization, commented, "The government firing system is so cumbersome bad employees can continue to be paid for years."***

The scandal at the Veterans Administration illustrates the strengths and the weaknesses of the federal employment system. Employees who do excellent jobs have protection from capricious bosses and can commit to their work for a long career. However, those who do not follow the rules, manipulate their records to get rewards, or who are simply waiting out their time to retirement can be fired only with great difficulty. Scandals such as this cause great harm to an administration and its political agenda even though the president has no part in the misbehavior. Civil service protections then keep the president from making appropriate changes to satisfy the public's demands.

For Critical Analysis

1. Do performance bonuses for public employees encourage falsifying records or other illegal actions?

2. Would more public reporting of federal government actions and activities help prevent scandals like that at the VA?

*Katie Zezima, "Everything You Need to Know about the VA—And the Scandals Engulfing It," *The Washington Post*, May 30, 2014.
**Steve Contorno, "VA Secretary Claims 900 Firings, 60 Related to Wait Times, Since He Took Over." *Politifact*, February 20, 2015. http://www.Politifact.com/truth-o-meter/statements/2015/feb/20/Robert-mcdonald-/va-secretary-claims-900-firings-60-related-wait-times/
***Dave Philipps, "Few People Lost Jobs with V.A. in Scandal," *The New York Times*, April 22, 2015.

conservative political groups, funding was reduced for that agency. Congress does have the legal authority to decide whether or not to fund administrative agencies. Congress can also exercise oversight over agencies through investigations and hearings.[17]

Congressional committees conduct investigations and hold hearings to oversee an agency's actions, reviewing them to ensure compliance with congressional intentions. The agency's officers and employees can be ordered to testify before a committee about the details of an action. Through these oversight activities, especially in the questions and comments of members of the House or Senate during the hearings, Congress indicates its positions on specific programs and issues.

Congress can ask the GAO to investigate particular agency actions as well. The Congressional Budget Office (CBO) also conducts oversight studies. The results of a GAO or CBO study may encourage Congress to hold further hearings or make changes in the law. Even if a law is not changed explicitly by Congress, however, the views expressed in any investigations and hearings are taken seriously by agency officials, who often act on those views.

In 1996, Congress passed the Congressional Review Act, which created special procedures that can be employed to express congressional disapproval of particular agency actions. Between 1996 and 2016, the congressional review process was employed only eight times but, in the first year of the Trump administration, it was successfully invoked 15 times.

Reasons Why Congress Cannot Easily Oversee the Bureaucracy

Despite the powers just described, one theory of congressional control over the bureaucracy suggests that Congress cannot possibly oversee all of the bureaucracy. Consider two possible approaches to congressional control—(1) the "police patrol" and (2) the "fire alarm" approach. Certain congressional activities, such as annual budget hearings, fall under the police patrol approach. This regular review occasionally catches *some* deficiencies in a bureaucracy's job performance, but it usually fails to detect most problems.

In contrast, the fire alarm approach is more likely to discover gross inadequacies in a bureaucracy's job performance. In this approach, Congress and its committees react to scandal, citizen disappointment, and massive negative publicity by launching a full-scale investigation into whatever agency is suspected of wrongdoing. In 2014, newspaper reports of veterans who could not get appointments or treatment at Veterans Administration hospitals triggered special investigations and an ongoing congressional hearing. Fire alarm investigations will not catch all problems, but they will alert bureaucracies that they need to clean up their procedures before a problem arises in their own agencies.[18]

17 Walter J. Oleszek, *Congressional Oversight: An Overview* (Washington, D.C.: Congressional Research Service, 2010).

18 Matthew D. McCubbins and Thomas Schwartz, "Congressional Oversight Overlooked: Police Patrols versus Fire Alarms," *American Journal of Political Science*, February 28, 1984: 165–179.

Key Terms

acquisitive model 460	**Government in the Sunshine Act** 475	**Pendleton Act (Civil Service Reform Act)** 473
administrative agency 461	**independent executive agency** 465	**privatization** 476
bureaucracy 459	**independent regulatory agency** 466	**spoils system** 473
cabinet department 463	**iron triangle** 483	**sunset legislation** 475
capture 467	**issue network** 484	**Weberian model** 460
Civil Service Commission 473	**line organization** 463	**whistleblower** 479
enabling legislation 480	**merit system** 473	
government corporation 468	**monopolistic model** 460	

Chapter Summary

■ **13.1** Bureaucracies are hierarchical organizations characterized by a division of labor and extensive procedural rules. Bureaucracy is the primary form of organization of most major corporations and universities as well as governments. These organizations are developed to carry out complex policies and procedures or to deliver multiple services or products in a fair, consistent, and effective manner.

■ **13.1** Several theories have been offered to explain bureaucracies. The Weberian model posits that bureaucracies are rational, hierarchical organizations in which decisions are based on logical reasoning. The acquisitive model views top-level bureaucrats as pressing for ever-larger budgets and staffs to augment their own sense of power and security. The monopolistic model focuses on the environment in which most government bureaucracies operate, stating that bureaucracies are inefficient and excessively costly to operate because they have no competitors.

■ **13.2** Since the founding of the United States, the federal bureaucracy has grown from 50 to about 2.7 million employees (excluding the military). Federal, state, and local employees together make up more than 16 percent of the nation's civilian labor force. The federal bureaucracy consists of 15 cabinet departments, as well as a large number of independent executive agencies, independent regulatory agencies, and government corporations. These entities enjoy varying degrees of autonomy, visibility, and political support.

■ **13.3** A federal bureaucracy of career civil servants was formed during Thomas Jefferson's presidency. Andrew Jackson implemented a spoils system through which he appointed his own political supporters. A civil service based on professionalism and merit was the goal of the Civil Service Reform Act of 1883. Concerns that the civil service be freed from the pressures of politics prompted the passage of the Hatch Act in 1939. Significant changes in the administration of the civil service were made by the Civil Service Reform Act of 1978.

■ **13.4** Bureaucracies, due to their size and complexity, may become inefficient and slow. Presidents try to manage the bureaucracy through political appointments to top positions. Congress also becomes frustrated when it receives reports of corruption or malfeasance in the bureaucracy. To solve some of these problems, many attempts have been made to make the federal bureaucracy more open, efficient, and responsive to the needs of U.S. citizens. The most important reforms have included sunshine and sunset laws, privatization, strategies to provide incentives for increased productivity and efficiency, and protection for whistleblowers.

■ **13.5** The bureaucracy has a complex relationship with the political branches of the government. Although it reports to the president, the Congress oversees the bureaucracy and provides its budget. In addition, Congress delegates much of its authority to federal agencies when it creates new laws. The bureaucrats who run these agencies become important policymakers because Congress has neither the time nor the technical expertise to oversee the administration of its laws. In the agency rule-making process, a proposed regulation is published. A comment period follows, during which interested parties may offer suggestions for changes. Because companies and other organizations have challenged many regulations in court, federal agencies now are authorized to allow parties that will be affected by new regulations to participate in the rule-drafting process.

■ **13.6** Congress exerts ultimate control over all federal agencies because it controls the federal government's purse strings. It also establishes the general guidelines by which regulatory agencies must abide. The appropriations process may provide a way to send messages of approval or disapproval to particular agencies, as do congressional hearings and investigations of agency actions.

Selected Resources

PRINT RESOURCES

Ghattas, Kim. *The Secretary: A Journey with Hillary Clinton from Beirut to the Heart of American Power* (New York: Henry Holt and Company, 2013). The author, a journalist, covered Secretary of State Clinton for four years as she traveled the world. Her book is an inside account of Clinton's work and her reception in the nations she visited.

Government Jobs News, Info Tech Employment, and Partnerships for Community, editors, *Government Jobs in America: Jobs in U.S. States and Cities and U.S. Federal Agencies with Job Titles, Salaries, and Pension Estimates—Why You Want One, What Jobs Are Available, How to Get One* (Washington, DC: Partnerships for Community, 2016). If you are interested in applying for a job with any U.S. government agency, this comprehensive guide will lead you through the process, from reviewing the qualifications necessary to the final interview.

Grisinger, Joanna. *The Unwieldy American State: Administrative Politics Since the New Deal* (New York: Cambridge University Press, 2014). Thinking about the size of American federal government and the vast array of policies that it implements is daunting. Grisinger traces the transformation of the federal government from the New Deal to the mid-1960s, showing how administrative law has come to dominate the policymaking process.

Haymann, Philip, B. *Living the Policy Process* (New York: Oxford University Press, 2008). Haymann uses case studies to examine how policymakers struggle to affect governmental decisions. His detailed accounts range from the cabinet level down to the middle tiers of the federal bureaucracy.

Examples include providing support to anti-Soviet Afghan rebels and attempting to restrict smoking.

Katz, Jonathan M. *The Big Truck That Went By: How the World Came to Save Haiti and Left Behind a Disaster* (New York: St. Martin's Press, 2013). A reporter, Katz is on the scene in Haiti during the earthquake and reports on the misguided and confused efforts of all outsiders to help the Haitian people.

Osborne, David, and Peter Plastrik. *Banishing Bureaucracy: The Five Strategies for Reinventing Government* (San Francisco: David Osborne Publishing, 2006). In 1992, David Osborne (with Ted Gaebler) wrote a best seller entitled *Reinventing Government. Banishing Bureaucracy* is his sequel, which goes one step further—it outlines specific strategies that can help transform public systems and organizations into engines of efficiency. The book focuses on clarifying a bureaucracy's purpose, creating incentives, improving accountability, redistributing power, and nurturing the correct culture.

Workman, Sam. *The Dynamics of Bureaucracy in the U.S. Government: How Congress and Federal Agencies Process Information and Solve Problems* (New York: Cambridge University Press, 2015). Workman's analysis of all of the regulations put forward by the government for 40 years focuses attention on the process of agenda building. He examines how agencies work with Congress to address the most important problems to be solved.

MEDIA RESOURCES

Dallas Buyers Club—In this stark portrayal of the HIV/AIDS epidemic before widespread use of today's life-saving drugs was approved, an infected man decides to bring unapproved drugs into the country from Mexico for the people he knows. The villain of this film is the Food and Drug Administration; that agency tries to prevent the importation of the drugs (2013).

Food, Inc.—In this startling documentary, the filmmakers examine agribusiness and how corporations control food production in the United States (2008).

Parks and Rec—The hit comedy series set in a small town in Indiana chronicles the efforts of a woman to improve her city and the many bureaucratic and personal obstacles she encounters along the way.

Top Secret America—A decade after the September 11 attacks on the World Trade Center, *Frontline* produced a program tracing the efforts of the United States to protect the nation against future attacks. The program is linked to other programs that investigate the National Security Agency (NSA) and other agencies (2011).

When the Levees Broke: A Requiem in Four Acts—A strong treatment of Hurricane Katrina's impact on New Orleans by renowned director Spike Lee. We learn about the appalling performance of authorities at every level and the suffering that could have been avoided. Lee's anger at what he saw adds spice to the 2006 production.

ONLINE RESOURCES

Federal Register—the official publication for executive branch documents: www.federalregister.gov

The Plum Book—lists the bureaucratic positions that can be filled by presidential appointment: www.govinfo.gov/content/pkg/GPO-PLUMBOOK-2016/pdf/GPO-PLUMBOOK-2016.pdf

United States Government Manual—describes the origins, purposes, and administrators of every federal department and agency: www.usgovernmentmanual.gov

USA.gov—the U.S. government's official web portal, which makes it easy for the public to get government information and services on the Web, such as telephone numbers for government agencies and personnel: www.USA.gov

14

The Courts

A line of mourners wait for their chance to pay respects to the late Supreme Court Justice Antonin Scalia in front of the high court's building.

EQRoy/Shutterstock.com

LEARNING OBJECTIVES

After reading this chapter, you will be able to:

■ **14.1** Explain how judges in the American system decide cases and define *stare decisis*.

■ **14.2** Define judicial review and explain the constitutional and judicial origins of this power.

■ **14.3** Produce a graphic illustration of the federal court system and explain how a case moves from the trial court to the highest court of appeals, the Supreme Court.

■ **14.4** Explain how judges are nominated and confirmed for the Supreme Court.

■ **14.5** Compare the concepts of judicial activism and judicial restraint; link these concepts to the decisions of the Supreme Court in the last few decades.

■ **14.6** Discuss the constitutional and political constraints on the Supreme Court.

What if... Supreme Court Justices Had Term Limits?

Background

The nine justices who sit on the Supreme Court are not elected officials. They are appointed by the president and confirmed by the Senate. Barring gross misconduct, they hold office for life. Given the lifespan of Americans, it is common for justices to be actively serving on the court after they turn 80 years old. Would the justices be more in tune with the ideas of Americans and less likely to use their power to make policy if they did not hold permanent seats? One way to make the justices even more responsive to public opinion might be to limit their tenure in office.

What If Supreme Court Justices Had Term Limits?

What should be the length of the term? Perhaps an appropriate one would be the average time on the bench from the founding of our nation until 1970—15 years. After confirmation by the Senate, a person could serve only 15 years on the bench and then would have to retire. The most important result of term limits would be a reduction in the rancor surrounding confirmation hearings. Today, the confirmation of a Supreme Court nominee—one chosen by the president to fit his or her views—is a major political event because that person may be on the Court for the next three decades.

Consider the current chief justice, John Roberts. When he took the Supreme Court bench at age 50, Americans could anticipate that his conservative ideology would influence Supreme Court decisions for as long as 30 years. Knowing this, those who did not share his views or philosophy opposed his confirmation. If term limits had been in existence, less would have been at stake—about half as many years of his influence.

Term Limits Would Put the United States in Line with Other Democracies

In having no term limits for federal judges, the United States is somewhat out of step. Not only does just one state—Rhode Island—appoint state supreme court justices for life, but virtually every other major democratic nation has age or term limits for judges. Thus, term limits in the United States for federal judges would not be an anomaly. Even with term limits, Supreme Court justices would still be independent, which is what the framers of the Constitution desired.

More Infusion of New Blood

With term limits, vacancies would be created on a more or less regular basis. Consequently, Supreme Court justices would have less temptation to time their retirements for political purposes. Thus, liberal-leaning justices would not delay their retirements until a Democratic president was in office, and conservative-leaning justices would not wait for a Republican. Fewer justices would follow the example of Justice Thurgood Marshall, who said that he was determined to hang on to his judicial power until a Democratic president was in office to appoint his successor. After many years on the bench, he joked, "I have instructed my clerks that if I should die, they should have me stuffed—and continue to cast my votes."

Virtually every president, whether he or she was a Republican or Democrat, would get a chance to fill a Supreme Court vacancy every few years. As a result, "new blood" would be infused into the Supreme Court more often. We would no longer face the risk of having Supreme Court justices who become less than enthusiastic about their work and less willing to examine new intellectual arguments. Term limits would also avoid the decrepitude that has occurred with several very old Supreme Court justices. In the last 30 years, some truly have stayed until the last possible minute. The public might prefer at least to have a mandatory retirement age.

For Critical Analysis

1. What are the benefits of having lifetime appointments to the Supreme Court?

2. Just because a president can appoint whomever he or she wishes to the Supreme Court, does that necessarily mean that the successful nominee will always reflect the president's political philosophy? Explain your answer.

As Alexis de Tocqueville, a French commentator on American society in the 1800s, noted, "scarcely any political question arises in the United States that is not resolved, sooner or later, into a judicial question."[1] Our judiciary forms part of our political process. The instant that judges interpret the law, they become actors in the political arena—policymakers working within a political institution. The most important political force within our judiciary is the U.S. Supreme Court.

How do courts make policy? Why do the federal courts play such an important role in American government? The answers to these questions lie, in part, in our colonial heritage. Most of American law is based on the English system, particularly the English *common-law tradition*. The decisions made by judges constitute an important source of law. The Supreme Court has extraordinary power to shape the nation's policies through the practice of **judicial review**, first explicated by Justice Marshall in the *Marbury v. Madison* case in 1803. This chapter opens with an examination of this tradition and of the various sources of American law and then looks at the federal court system.

Sources of American Law

■ **14.1** Explain how judges in the American system decide cases and define *stare decisis*.

In 1066, the Normans conquered England, and William the Conqueror and his successors began the process of unifying the country under their rule by establishing the king's courts. Before the conquest, disputes had been settled according to local custom. The king's courts sought to establish a common or uniform set of rules for the whole country. As the number of courts and cases increased, portions of the most important decisions of each year were compiled in *Year Books*. Judges settling disputes similar to ones that had been decided before used the *Year Books* as the basis for their decisions. If a case was unique, judges had to create new laws, but they based their decisions on the general principles suggested by earlier cases. The body of judge-made law that developed under this system is still used today and is known as the **common law**.

The practice of deciding new cases with reference to former decisions—according to **precedent**—became a cornerstone of the English and American judicial systems and is embodied in the doctrine of *stare decisis* (pronounced *ster*-ay dih-*si*-ses), a Latin phrase that means "to stand on decided cases." The doctrine of ***stare decisis*** obligates judges to follow the precedents set previously by their own courts or by higher courts that have authority over them.

A lower state court in California would be obligated to follow a precedent set by the California Supreme Court. That lower court, however, would not be obligated to follow a precedent set by the supreme court of another state, because each state court system is independent. When the U.S. Supreme Court decides an issue, all of the nation's other courts are obligated to abide by the Court's decision because the Supreme Court is the highest court in the land.

Stare decisis provides a basis for judicial decision making in all countries that have common-law systems. Generally, those countries that were once British colonies, such as Australia, Canada, and India, have retained their English common-law heritage. An alternative legal system based on Muslim *sharia* is discussed in this chapter's Beyond Our Borders feature.

judicial review
The power of the Supreme Court or any court to hold a law or other legal action as unconstitutional.

common law
Judge-made law that originated in England from decisions shaped according to prevailing custom. Decisions were applied to similar situations and gradually became common to the nation.

precedent
A court rule bearing on subsequent legal decisions in similar cases. Judges rely on precedents in deciding cases.

stare decisis
To stand on decided cases; the judicial policy of following precedents established by past decisions.

---

1 Alexis de Tocqueville, *Democracy in America* (New York: Harper & Row, 1966), p. 248.

Beyond Our Borders

The Legal System Based on *Sharia*

Many Muslims throughout the world are governed by a system of law called *sharia*. In this system, religious laws and precepts are combined with practical laws relating to common actions, such as entering into contracts and borrowing funds.

The Authority of *Sharia*

Sharia, or Islamic law, is drawn from the Quran and the specific guidelines laid down in it. The second major source, called *sunnah*, is based on the way the Prophet Muhammad lived his life. The lesser source is called *ijma*; it represents the consensus of opinion in the community of Muslims. *Sharia* law is comprehensive in nature. All possible actions of Muslims are divided into five categories: obligatory, meritorious, permissible, reprehensible, and forbidden.

The Scope of *Sharia* Law

Sharia law covers many aspects of daily life, including:

- Dietary rules
- Relations between married men and women
- Marriage contracts and divorces
- The role of women
- Holidays
- Dress codes, particularly for women
- Speech with respect to the Prophet Muhammad
- Crimes, including adultery, murder, and theft
- Business dealings, including the borrowing and lending of funds

Where *Sharia* Law Is Applied

The degree to which *sharia* is used varies throughout Muslim societies today. Several countries with the largest Muslim populations (e.g., Bangladesh, India, and Indonesia) do not have Islamic law. Other Muslim countries have dual systems of *sharia* courts and secular courts. In the nations of Western Europe and North America, *sharia* courts have been set up by local communities to deal with many issues.

After the terrorist attacks in Paris in 2015 and Brussels in 2016, some commentators suggested that there was a link between Muslim neighborhoods in European cities where *sharia* law is practiced and terrorist activities. Although there are predominately Muslim areas in Belgium and France, there is no link between the practice of *sharia* and terrorist plans because the dictates of this legal practice have nothing to do with the goals of the terrorists.

In Great Britain, there are more than 80 such courts, and the Law Society of that nation has drawn up guidelines for attorneys on some *sharia* practices that may be followed in British secular courts. As the president of the Law Society notes, "There is a wide variety of spiritual, religious and cultural beliefs within our population and the Law Society wants to support its members so they can help clients from all backgrounds."* Other Britons opposed this initiative, fearing that the rights of women may be weakened if there is not one law for everyone in the nation.

Canada, which has a *sharia* arbitration court in Ontario, is the first North American country to establish a *sharia* court. However, *sharia* courts, as such, do not exist in the United States, although the dictates of that legal system do come into play in many cases, particularly in divorce hearings. In a New Jersey divorce case, an Islamic woman asked to have her dowry returned as specified in the couple's religious marriage contract. The New Jersey judge agreed, saying the contract was as valid as any other contract signed between two individuals. The fact that the contract met the conditions of *sharia* law was not at issue in the case.**

For Critical Analysis

1. What benefits derive from integrating religious beliefs and practices with secular laws? What are the disadvantages of doing so?

2. Should the United States allow *sharia* courts in communities with a high Muslim population similar to Canada's practice?

*Sam Webb, "Sharia Law to Be Enshrined in British Legal System as Lawyers Get Guidelines on Drawing Up Documents According to Islamic Rules," Mail online, March 23, 2014. www.dailymail.co.uk/news/article-2587215/Sharia-Law-enshrined-British-legal-lawyers-guidelines-drawing-documents-according-Islamic-rules.html

**Abed Awad, "The True Story of Sharia in American Courts," *The Nation*, July 2–9, 2012, www.thenation.com/article/168378/true-story-sharia-american-courts#

Image 14-1

Justice Tom Colbert is the first African American to be appointed to the Supreme Court of Oklahoma. Prior to that appointment, he served on the Oklahoma Court of Civil Appeals.

case law
Judicial interpretations of common-law principles and doctrines, as well as interpretations of constitutional law, statutory law, and administrative law.

The body of American law includes the federal and state constitutions, statutes passed by legislative bodies, administrative law, and case law—the legal principles expressed in court decisions.

Constitutions

The constitutions of the federal government and the states set forth the general organization, powers, and limits of government. The U.S. Constitution is the supreme law of the land. A law in violation of the Constitution, regardless of source, may be declared unconstitutional and thereafter cannot be enforced. Similarly, the state constitutions are supreme within their respective borders (unless they conflict with the U.S. Constitution or federal laws and treaties made in accordance with it). The Constitution thus defines the political playing field on which state and federal powers are reconciled. The idea that the Constitution should be supreme in certain matters stemmed from widespread dissatisfaction with the weak federal government that had existed under the Articles of Confederation adopted in 1781.

Statutes and Administrative Regulations

Although the English common law provides the basis for both our civil and criminal legal systems, statutes (laws enacted by legislatures) increasingly have become important in defining the rights and obligations of individuals. Federal statutes may relate to any subject that is a concern of the federal government and may apply to areas ranging from hazardous waste to federal taxation. State statutes include criminal codes, commercial laws, and laws covering a variety of other matters. Cities, counties, and other local political bodies also pass statutes, which are called ordinances. These ordinances may deal with such issues as zoning proposals and public safety. Rules and regulations issued by administrative agencies are another source of law. Today, much of the work of the courts consists of interpreting these laws and regulations and applying them to circumstances in cases before the courts.

Case Law

Because we have a common-law tradition, the decisions rendered by the courts also form an important body of law, collectively referred to as **case law**. Case law includes judicial interpretations of common-law principles and doctrines, as well as interpretations of the types of law just mentioned—constitutional provisions, statutes, and administrative agency regulations. It is up to the courts—and particularly the Supreme Court—to decide what a constitutional provision or a statutory phrase means. In doing so, the courts, in effect, establish law.

Judicial Review

■ **14.2** Define judicial review and explain the constitutional and judicial origins of this power.

The process for deciding whether a law is contrary to the mandates of the Constitution is known as judicial review. This power is not mentioned in the U.S. Constitution. Rather, this judicial power was first established in the famous case of *Marbury v. Madison* (as discussed in Politics in Practice). In that case, Chief Justice Marshall insisted that the Supreme Court had the power to decide that a law passed by Congress violated the Constitution:

> *It is emphatically the province and duty of the Judicial Department to say what the law is. Those who apply the rule to a particular case must, of necessity, expound and interpret that rule. If two laws conflict with each other, the courts must decide on the operation of each.*[2]

The Supreme Court has ruled parts or all of certain acts of Congress to be unconstitutional fewer than 200 times in its history. State laws, however, have been declared unconstitutional by the Court much more often—more than 1,000 times. The Court has been more active in declaring federal or state laws unconstitutional since the beginning of the twentieth century.

---

2   5 U.S. (1 Cranch) 137 (1803).

Politics in Practice

Political Court Battles Early in the Republic

Complaints about activist judges are typical in today's political scene and might be a description of politics in the twenty-first century. This also describes the presidential election of 1800, which led to *Marbury v. Madison*, one of the most important Supreme Court cases, the influence of which is still felt today.

Marbury v. Madison established the doctrine of judicial review. It was precipitated by the presidential election of 1800, in which the incumbent president, John Adams, was defeated by his vice president, Thomas Jefferson. Not only did this event mark the first election where issues divided the emerging political parties, but it was also intensely and personally fought. President Adams was a member of the Federalist Party, which had emerged victorious in the fights over ratification of the Constitution. Jefferson was an Anti-Federalist and the leader of the ascendant Jeffersonian Republicans. These two groups disagreed on the power of the federal government. In addition, the two men bitterly disagreed with each other's politics.

Thomas Jefferson eventually won the election but did not take office until March 1801. Between the election and inauguration, the Federalist-controlled Congress passed a series of laws creating additional judicial positions that would be staffed with Federalist appointments. One of these positions was District of Columbia Justice of the Peace, a relatively low-level judicial appointment whose term would expire

in five years. William Marbury was confirmed as an appointment. The day before inauguration, the appointment papers were signed and sealed, but not delivered. John Marshall was to deliver the appointment, but he had his own appointment to become chief justice of the Supreme Court. Upon taking office, President Jefferson ordered his secretary of state, James Madison, not to deliver the commissions. Marbury and two others brought suit to the Supreme Court, asking that the Court force Jefferson to deliver the commissions.

Some accounts argue that Marbury took this action not because he wanted the appointment, but because he wanted to provoke a fight with Jefferson. Marbury was a committed Federalist who believed that the Jeffersonian argument to reduce federal government control and give power back to state governments was deeply flawed. These Federalists were very unhappy with the outcome of the election and were seeking mechanisms to remain influential.

By then, the chief justice of the Supreme Court was John Marshall, a Federalist appointed by the former President Adams. Marshall knew that if he ordered Jefferson to honor the commission, the president would likely ignore the order, resulting in an unacceptably dangerous constitutional crisis for the young country, and the Supreme Court would be weakened. Marshall, writing for the Court, issued a decision that found Marbury's rights had been denied but

(Continued)

(Continued)

that the law passed by Congress that would have granted the Court the power of redress was unconstitutional. In other words, Marshall said that the Supreme Court was not where Marbury should have sought a solution, arguing for the first time that the Court had the power to "say what the law is."*

John Marshall's role and the legal arguments he used in deciding the case have many interpretations.** Without dispute, however, this case marked the formal articulation of judicial review, a power that in the twentieth century would touch Americans' most basic liberties and rights. Even more significantly, the case illustrates that the intense battles waged by groups to make a difference in contemporary politics (e.g., *Roe v. Wade* and *Bush v. Gore)* are as old as the Republic.

For Critical Analysis

1. Should the Supreme Court's power of judicial review be formally defined by the Constitution with a constitutional amendment?

2. When the Court makes a decision, should it take into consideration whether the decision can be implemented?

* *Marbury v. Madison*, 5 U.S. 137 (1803).
** See, for example, Alexander M. Bickel, *The Least Dangerous Branch: The Supreme Court at the Bar of Politics* (New Haven, CT: Yale University Press, 1986); and William E. Nelson, *Marbury v. Madison: The Origins and Legacy of Judicial Review* (Lawrence, KS: University Press of Kansas, 2000).

The Supreme Court can effectively define the separation of powers between the branches. In 1983, the Court outlawed the practice of the legislative veto by which one or both chambers of Congress could overturn decisions made by the president or by executive agencies. Then, in 2006, the Supreme Court ruled that the president had no authority to set up military tribunals at the Guantanamo Bay prison, but Congress did have the authority to create such tribunals by legislation, thus making it clear that the creation of courts is within the prerogative of Congress, not the president.

did you know?

The Supreme Court was not provided with a building of its own until 1935, in the 146th year of its existence.

The Federal Court System

■ **14.3** Produce a graphic illustration of the federal court system and explain how a case moves from the trial court to the highest court of appeals, the Supreme Court.

The United States has a dual court system with state courts and federal courts. Each of the 50 states, as well as the District of Columbia, has its own independent system of courts, for 52 court systems in total. The federal courts derive their power from the U.S. Constitution, Article III, Section 1, and are organized according to congressional legislation. State courts draw authority from state constitutions and laws. Court cases in state court systems reach the Supreme Court only after they have been appealed to the highest possible state court. Figure 14-1 shows the basic components of the state and federal court systems.

Figure 14-1 ▶ Dual Structure of the American Court System

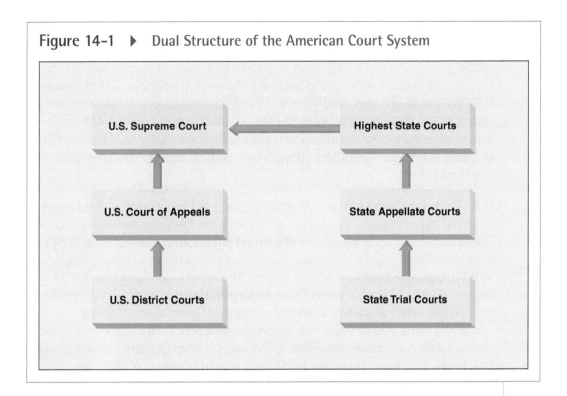

Basic Judicial Requirements

In any court system, state or federal, before a case can be brought before a court, certain requirements must be met. Two important requirements are jurisdiction and standing to sue.

Jurisdiction A state court can exercise **jurisdiction** over the residents of a particular geographic area, such as a county or district. A state's highest court, or supreme court, has jurisdictional authority over all residents within the state. Because the Constitution established a federal government with limited powers, federal jurisdiction is also limited.

Article III, Section 1, of the U.S. Constitution limits the jurisdiction of the federal courts to cases that involve either a federal question or diversity of citizenship. A **federal question** arises when a case is based, at least in part, on the U.S. Constitution, a treaty, or a federal law. A person who claims that her or his rights under the Constitution, such as the right to free speech, have been violated could bring a case in a federal court. **Diversity of citizenship** exists when the parties to a lawsuit are from different states or (more rarely) when the suit involves a U.S. citizen and a government or citizen of a foreign country. The amount in controversy must be at least $75,000 before a federal court can take jurisdiction in a diversity case.

Standing to Sue Another basic judicial requirement is standing to sue, or a sufficient "stake" in a matter to justify bringing suit. The party bringing a lawsuit must have suffered a harm or have been threatened by a harm as a result of the action that led to the dispute in question. Standing to sue also requires that the controversy at issue be a justiciable controversy—real and substantial, as opposed to hypothetical or academic. Although some European courts review laws before they are implemented to see if they are constitutional, no American court will give an opinion on a hypothetical case or a law that has not yet been implemented.

jurisdiction
The authority of a court to decide certain cases. Not all courts have the authority to decide all cases. Two jurisdictional issues are where a case arises as well as its subject matter.

federal question
A question that has to do with the U.S. Constitution, acts of Congress, or treaties. A federal question provides a basis for federal jurisdiction.

diversity of citizenship
The condition that exists when the parties to a lawsuit are citizens of different states, or when citizens of a U.S. state are parties in a lawsuit against citizens (or the government) of a foreign country. Diversity of citizenship can provide a basis for federal jurisdiction.

Types of Federal Courts

As shown in Figure 14-2, the federal court system is basically a three-tiered model consisting of (1) U.S. district courts and various specialized courts of limited jurisdiction (not all of the latter are shown in the figure), (2) intermediate U.S. courts of appeals, and (3) the U.S. Supreme Court. Other specialized courts in the federal system are discussed later. In addition, the U.S. military has its own system of courts, which are established under the Uniform Code of Military Justice. Cases from these other federal courts may also reach the Supreme Court.

trial court
The court in which most cases begin.

general jurisdiction
Exists when a court's authority to hear cases is not significantly restricted. A court of general jurisdiction normally can hear a broad range of cases.

limited jurisdiction
Exists when a court's authority to hear cases is restricted to certain types of claims, such as tax claims or bankruptcy petitions.

appellate court
A court having jurisdiction to review cases and issues that were originally tried in lower courts.

U.S. District Courts The U.S. district courts are trial courts. A **trial court** is what the name implies—a court in which trials are held and testimony is taken. The U.S. district courts are courts of **general jurisdiction**, meaning that they can hear cases involving a broad array of issues. Federal cases involving most matters typically are heard in district courts. The courts on the lower tier of the model in Figure 14-2 are courts of **limited jurisdiction** that can try cases involving only certain types of claims, such as tax claims or bankruptcy petitions.

Every state has at least one federal district court. The number of judicial districts can vary over time due to population changes and corresponding caseloads. Currently, there are 94 federal judicial districts. A party who is dissatisfied with the decision of a district court can appeal the case to the appropriate U.S. court of appeals, or federal **appellate court**. Figure 14-3 shows the jurisdictional boundaries of the district courts (which are state boundaries, unless otherwise indicated by dotted lines within a state) and of the U.S. courts of appeals.

U.S. Courts of Appeals The 13 U.S. courts of appeals are also referred to as U.S. circuit courts of appeals. Twelve of these courts, including the U.S. Court of Appeals for the District of Columbia, hear appeals from the federal district courts located within their respective judicial circuits (geographic areas

Figure 14-2 ▶ The Federal Court System

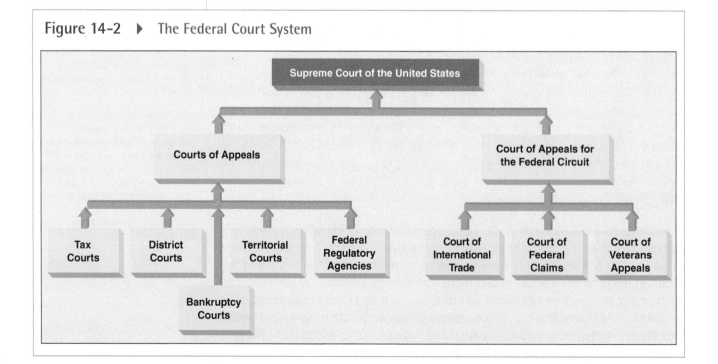

Figure 14-3 ▶ Geographic Boundaries of Federal District Courts and Circuit Courts of Appeals

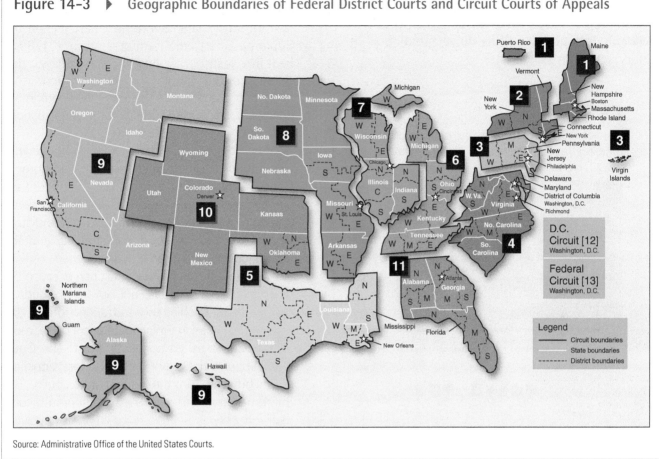

Source: Administrative Office of the United States Courts.

over which they exercise jurisdiction). The Court of Appeals for the Thirteenth Circuit (the Federal Circuit) has national appellate jurisdiction over certain types of cases, such as cases involving patent law and those in which the U.S. government is a defendant. In 2013, when Republicans in the Senate were blocking President Obama's nominations for those courts, the Senate changed its rules to disallow filibusters on such appointments. When a president is able to appoint judges who share his or her viewpoint to the DC appellate courts, he or she is trying to ensure favorable opinions on the administration's regulations for years to come.

When an appellate court reviews a case that was decided in a district court, it does not conduct another trial. A panel of three or more judges reviews the record of the case on appeal, which includes a transcript of the trial proceedings, and determines whether the trial court committed an error. Usually, appellate courts do not look at questions of *fact* (such as whether a party did, in fact, commit a certain action, such as burning a flag) but at questions of *law* (such as whether the act of burning a flag is a form of speech protected by the First Amendment to the Constitution). An appellate court will challenge a trial court's finding of fact only when the finding is clearly contrary to the evidence presented at trial or when no evidence supports the finding.

A party can petition the U.S. Supreme Court to review an appellate court's decision, but the likelihood that the Supreme Court will grant the petition is slim because the Court reviews very few of the cases decided by the appellate courts. Decisions made by appellate judges are usually final.

Twitter Feed ▶ After the Supreme Court decided the case *Foster v. Humphrey*, the ACLU tweeted its position. Why do you think bias in jury selection still exists?

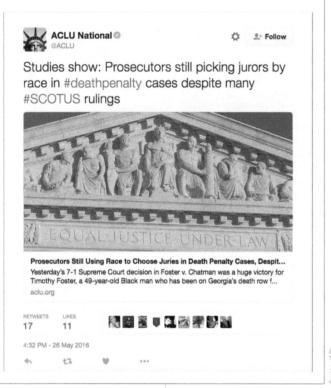

ACLU National ✓
@ACLU
⚙ ▲ Follow

Studies show: Prosecutors still picking jurors by race in #deathpenalty cases despite many #SCOTUS rulings

Prosecutors Still Using Race to Choose Juries in Death Penalty Cases, Despit...
Yesterday's 7-1 Supreme Court decision in Foster v. Chatman was a huge victory for Timothy Foster, a 49-year-old Black man who has been on Georgia's death row f...
aclu.org

RETWEETS LIKES
17   11

4:32 PM - 26 May 2016

Twitter/ACL

The U.S. Supreme Court

The highest level of the three-tiered model of the federal court system is the U.S. Supreme Court. When the Supreme Court held its first session in 1789, it had five justices. Congress passes laws that determine the number of justices and other aspects of the court. In the following years, more justices were added. Since 1869, nine justices have been on the Court at any given time.

According to Article III of the U.S. Constitution, there is only one national Supreme Court. All other courts in the federal system are considered "inferior." Congress is empowered to create other inferior courts such as the district courts, the federal courts of appeals, and the federal courts of limited jurisdiction.

Although the Supreme Court can exercise original jurisdiction (that is, act as a trial court) in certain cases, such as those affecting foreign diplomats and those in which a state is a party, most of its work is as an appellate court. The Court hears appeals not only from the federal appellate courts but also from the highest state courts. The Supreme Court can review a state supreme court decision only if a federal question is involved. Because of its importance in the federal court system, we will look more closely at the Supreme Court in a later section. Modern decisions are posted on the Supreme Court's website and Twitter feed, providing easy access to information and rulings, as shown in the screen capture. Political analysts and political groups use social media to respond to rulings, as shown in the screen capture.

Specialized Federal Courts and the War on Terrorism

The federal court system includes a variety of trial courts of limited jurisdiction, dealing with matters such as tax claims, patent law, Native American claims, bankruptcy, or international trade. The government's attempts to combat terrorism have drawn attention to certain specialized courts that meet in secret.

The FISA Court The federal government created the first secret court in 1978, when Congress passed the Foreign Intelligence Surveillance Act (FISA). This established a court to hear requests for warrants for the surveillance of suspected spies. Officials can request warrants without having to reveal to the suspect or the public the information used to justify the warrant. The FISA court has approved almost all of the thousands of requests for warrants that the U.S. attorney general's office and other officials have submitted. The seven judges on the FISA court (federal district judges from across the nation) meet in secret, with no published opinions or orders. The public has no access to the court's proceedings or records. Hence, when the court authorizes surveillance, most suspects do not even know that they are under scrutiny. Additionally, during the Clinton administration, the court was given the authority to approve physical as well as electronic searches, which means that officials may search

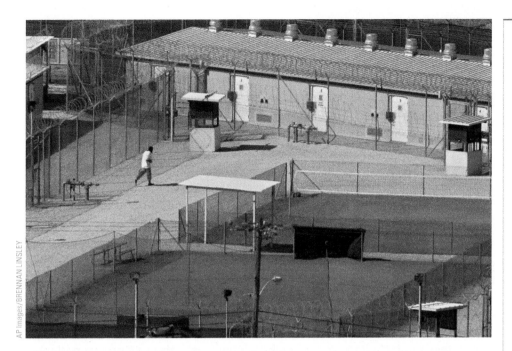

AP Images/BRENNAN LINSLEY

Image 14-2
The prison at Guantánamo Bay, Cuba, where the detainees from the Afghanistan and Iraq wars were held until their military trials or their release to another country. Why did the United States create the prison at Guantánamo Bay?

a suspect's property without obtaining a warrant in open court and without notifying the subject.

In the aftermath of the terrorist attacks on September 11, 2001, the Bush administration expanded the powers of the FISA court. Previously, the FISA allowed secret domestic surveillance only if the target was spying as an agent of another nation. Post–September 11 amendments allow warrants if a "significant purpose" of the surveillance is to gather foreign intelligence and allow surveillance of groups who are not agents of a foreign government.

Alien "Removal Courts" The FISA court is not the only court in which suspects' rights have been reduced. In response to the Oklahoma City bombing in 1995, Congress passed the Anti-Terrorism and Effective Death Penalty Act of 1996. The act included a provision creating an alien "removal court" to hear evidence against suspected "alien terrorists." The judges rule on whether there is probable cause for deportation. If so, a public deportation proceeding is held in a U.S. district court. The prosecution does not need to follow procedures that normally apply in criminal cases, and the defendant cannot see the evidence that the prosecution used to secure the hearing.

In some cases, the U.S. Supreme Court ruled against the George W. Bush administration's efforts to use secret legal proceedings in dealing with suspected terrorists. In 2004, it ruled that enemy combatants who are U.S. citizens and taken prisoner by the United States cannot be denied due process rights. Justice Sandra Day O'Connor wrote that "due process demands that a citizen held in the United States as an enemy combatant be given a meaningful opportunity to contest the factual basis of that detention before a neutral decision maker.... [a] state of war is not a blank check for the president when it comes to the rights of the nation's citizens."[3] The Court also found that noncitizen detainees held at Guantánamo Bay in Cuba were entitled to challenge the grounds for their confinement.[4]

---

3 *Hamdi v. Rumsfeld,* 542 U.S. 507 (2004).
4 Hamdi was eventually released following a settlement with the government under which he agreed to renounce his U.S. citizenship and return to Saudi Arabia.

In response to the Court rulings, the Bush administration asked Congress to enact a law establishing military tribunals to hear the prisoners' cases at Guantánamo. In 2006, the Court held that these tribunals did not meet due process requirements for a fair hearing. The central issue in the case was whether the entire situation at the prison camp violated the prisoners' right of *habeas corpus*—the right of a detained person to challenge the legality of his or her detention before a judge or other neutral party. Congress then passed the Military Commissions Act of 2006, which eliminated federal court jurisdiction over *habeas corpus* challenges by enemy combatants. This law was also tested in court, but the Supreme Court refused to hear the case, so the law, as upheld by an appellate court, stands.[5]

Finally, in 2008, the Supreme Court, by a 5–4 majority, held that enemy combatants have the right to challenge their detention in front of a federal court if they have not been charged with a crime. This ruling essentially grants the detainees at Guantánamo Bay the right of *habeas corpus*, a right that a majority of Congress cannot constitutionally restrict.[6] After President Obama took office in 2009, he announced that the prison at Guantánamo would be closed within a year. Attorney General Eric Holder announced that several of the detainees, including Khalid Sheikh Mohammed, the self-proclaimed mastermind behind the September 11, 2001, terrorist attacks, would be transferred to the United States for trial in New York City. After public outcry about the possible trial, the president announced that military commission trials would continue to be held in Guantánamo. Furthermore, Congress has been unwilling to fund a prison in the United States to hold suspected terrorists. As of 2016, 80 prisoners remain at the Cuban facility: 1 is serving a sentence after convictions, 26 have been cleared for release if a country will accept them, and 28 have been deemed too dangerous for release.[7] Fewer than a dozen commission verdicts have been given.[8]

Parties to Lawsuits

In most lawsuits, the parties are the plaintiff (the person or organization that initiates the lawsuit) and the defendant (the person or organization against whom the lawsuit is brought). Numerous plaintiffs and defendants may appear in a single lawsuit. In the last several decades, many lawsuits have been brought by interest groups (see Chapter 7). Interest groups play an important role in our judicial system, because they **litigate**—bring to trial—or assist in litigating most cases of racial or gender-based discrimination, virtually all civil liberties cases, and more than one-third of the cases involving business matters. Interest groups also file *amicus curiae* (pronounced ah-*mee*-kous *kur*-ee-eye) briefs, or "friend of the court" briefs, in more than 50 percent of these kinds of cases.

Sometimes interest groups or other plaintiffs will bring a **class-action suit**, in which the court decision will stand for all members of a class similarly situated (such as users of a particular product manufactured by the defendant in the lawsuit). The strategy of class-action lawsuits was pioneered by such groups as the National Association for the Advancement of Colored People

litigate
To engage in a legal proceeding or seek relief in a court of law; to carry on a lawsuit.

class-action suit
A lawsuit filed by an individual seeking damages for "all persons similarly situated."

5   *Boumediene v. Bush*, 476 F.3d 981 (D.C. Cir. 2007).

6   *Boumediene v. Bush*, 553 U.S. 723 (2008).

7   https://www.aclu.org/infographic/guantanamo-number, 5/1/2016.

8   "The Guantanamo Trials," Human Rights Watch, www.hrw.org/features/guantanamo, 2014.

(NAACP), the Legal Defense Fund, and the Sierra Club, whose leaders believed that the courts would offer a more sympathetic forum for their views than would Congress.

Procedural Rules

Both the federal and the state courts have established procedural rules that shape the litigation process. These rules are designed to protect the rights and interests of the parties, to ensure that the litigation proceeds in a fair and orderly manner, and to identify the issues that must be decided by the court, thus saving court time and costs. The parties must comply with procedural rules and with any orders given by the judge during the course of the litigation. When a party does not follow a court's order, the court can cite him or her for contempt. A party who commits *civil* contempt (failing to comply with a court's order for the benefit of another party to the proceeding) can be taken into custody, fined, or both until the party complies with the court's order. A party who commits *criminal* contempt (obstructing the administration of justice or bringing the court into disrespect) also can be taken into custody and fined but cannot avoid punishment by complying with a previous order.

The Supreme Court at Work

The Supreme Court begins its regular annual term on the first Monday in October and usually adjourns in late June or early July of the next year. Special sessions may be held after the regular term ends, but only a few cases are decided in this way. More commonly, cases are carried over until the next regular session.

Of the total number of cases that are decided each year, those reviewed by the Supreme Court represent less than one-half of 1 percent. Included in

Image 14-3

Former Solicitor General Donald B. Verrilli, Jr., presents the government's case to the Supreme Court in *King v. Burwell*, 576 U.S. ____ (2015), the case that upheld federal subsidies for health insurance in all states.

AP Images/Dana Verkouteren

Image 14-4

Ruth Bader Ginsburg, associate justice of the Supreme Court. At age 85, Justice Ginsburg shows no signs of leaving the court. She has hired clerks through the 2020 term. Known in some circles as "Notorious RBG," Ginsburg was profiled in a documentary titled "RBG" released in May 2018.

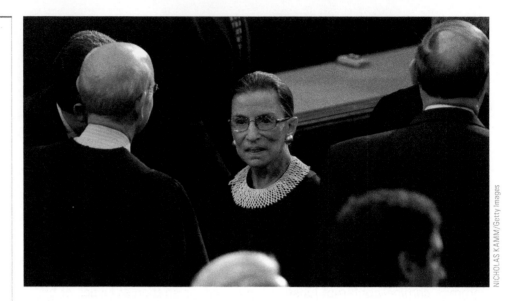

NICHOLAS KAMM/Getty Images

these, however, are decisions that profoundly affect our lives. In recent years, the U.S. Supreme Court has decided issues involving the Affordable Care Act, gay marriage, affirmative action programs, religious freedom, assisted suicide, abortion, property rights, sexual harassment, pornography, states' rights, limits on federal jurisdiction, and many other matters with significant consequences for the nation. Because the Supreme Court exercises a great deal of discretion over the types of cases it hears, it can influence the nation's policies, both by issuing decisions in some types of cases and refusing to hear appeals in others, thereby allowing lower court decisions to stand.

Which Cases Reach the Supreme Court?

Many are surprised to learn that in a typical case, there is no absolute right of appeal to the U.S. Supreme Court. The Court's appellate jurisdiction is almost entirely discretionary; the Court can choose which cases it will decide. The justices never explain their reasons for hearing certain cases and not others, so it is difficult to predict which case or type of case the Court might select. Former Chief Justice William Rehnquist, in his description of the selection process in *The Supreme Court: How It Was, How It Is*, said that the decision of whether to accept a case "strikes me as a rather subjective decision, made up in part of intuition and in part of legal judgment."[9]

Factors That Bear on the Decision Factors that bear on the decision include whether a legal question has been decided differently by various lower courts and needs resolution by the highest court, whether a lower court's decision conflicts with an existing Supreme Court ruling, and whether the issue could have significance beyond the parties to the dispute.

Another factor is whether the solicitor general is pressuring the Court to take a case. The solicitor general, a high-ranking presidential appointee within the Justice Department, represents the national government before the Supreme Court and promotes presidential policies in the federal courts. He or she decides what cases the government should ask the Supreme Court to

---

9 William H. Rehnquist, *The Supreme Court: How It Was, How It Is* (New York: Morrow, 1987).

review and what position the government should take in cases before the Court.

Granting Petitions for Review If the Court decides to grant a petition for review, it will issue a **writ of *certiorari*** (pronounced sur-shee-uh-*rah*-ree). The writ orders a lower court to send the Supreme Court a record of the case for review. More than 90 percent of the petitions for review are denied. A denial is not a decision on the merits of a case, nor does it indicate agreement with the lower court's opinion. (The judgment of the lower court remains in force, however.) Therefore, denial of the writ has no value as a precedent. The Court will not issue a writ unless at least four justices approve of it. This is called the **rule of four**.[10]

Deciding Cases

Once the Supreme Court grants *certiorari* in a particular case, the justices do extensive research on the legal issues and facts involved in the case. Each justice is entitled to four law clerks, who undertake much of the research and preliminary drafting necessary for the justice to form an opinion.[11]

The Court normally does not hear any evidence, as is true with all appeals courts. The Court's consideration of a case is based on the abstracts, the record, and the briefs. The attorneys are permitted to present **oral arguments**. All statements and the justices' questions are recorded during these sessions. Unlike the practice in most courts, lawyers addressing the Supreme Court can be (and often are) questioned by the justices at any time during oral argument.

The justices meet to discuss and vote on cases in conferences held throughout the term. In these conferences, in addition to deciding cases currently before the Court, the justices determine which new petitions for *certiorari* to grant. These conferences take place in the oak-paneled chamber and are strictly private—no stenographers, tape recorders, or video cameras are allowed. Two pages used to be in attendance to wait on the justices while they were in conference, but fear of information leaks caused the Court to stop this practice.[12]

Decisions and Opinions

When the Court has reached a decision, its opinion is written. The **opinion** contains the Court's ruling on the issue or issues presented, the reasons for its decision, the rules of law that apply, and other information. In many cases, the decision of the lower court is **affirmed**, resulting in the enforcement of that court's judgment or decree. If the Supreme Court believes that a reversible error was committed during the trial or that the jury was instructed improperly, however, the decision will be **reversed**. Sometimes the case will be **remanded** (sent back to the court that originally heard the case) for a new trial or other proceeding. Occasionally, the court will issue an unsigned opinion—an opinion *per curiam* (by the court).

writ of *certiorari*
An order issued by a higher court to a lower court to send up the record of a case for review.

rule of four
A U.S. Supreme Court procedure by which four justices must vote to grant a petition for review if a case is to come before the full court.

oral arguments
The verbal arguments presented in person by attorneys to an appellate court. Each attorney presents reasons to the court why the court should rule in her or his client's favor.

opinion
The statement by a judge or a court of the decision reached in a case. The opinion sets forth the applicable law and details the reasoning on which the ruling was based.

affirm
To declare that a court ruling is valid and must stand.

reverse
To annul or make void a court ruling on account of some error or irregularity.

remand
To send a case back to the court that originally heard it.

---

10 The "rule of four" is modified when seven or fewer justices participate, which occurs from time to time. When that happens, as few as three justices can grant *certiorari*.

11 A number of former clerks write about their experiences in Todd C. Peppers and Artemus Ward, eds., *In Chambers: Stories of Supreme Court Law Clerks and Their Justices* (Charlottesville, VA: University of Virginia Press, 2013).

12 It turned out that one supposed information leak came from lawyers making educated guesses.

unanimous opinion
A court opinion or determination on which all judges agree.

majority opinion
A court opinion reflecting the views of the majority of the judges.

concurring opinion
A separate opinion prepared by a judge who supports the decision of the majority of the court but who wants to make or clarify a particular point or to voice disapproval of the grounds on which the decision was made.

dissenting opinion
A separate opinion in which a judge dissents from (disagrees with) the conclusion reached by the majority on the court and expounds his or her own views about the case.

---

did you know?

William Howard Taft is the only person to have served as both president of the United States and chief justice of the Supreme Court.

When all justices unanimously agree on an opinion, the opinion is written for the entire Court (all the justices) and can be deemed a **unanimous opinion**. When there is not a unanimous opinion, a **majority opinion** is written, outlining the views of the majority of the justices involved in the case. Often, one or more justices who feel strongly about making or emphasizing a particular point that is not made or emphasized in the unanimous or majority written opinion will write a **concurring opinion**. That means the justice writing the concurring opinion agrees (concurs) with the conclusion given in the majority written opinion, but for different reasons. Finally, in other than unanimous opinions, one or more **dissenting opinions** are usually written by those justices who do not agree with the majority. The dissenting opinion is important because it often forms the basis of the arguments used years later if the Court reverses the previous decision and establishes a new precedent.

Shortly after the opinion is written, the Supreme Court announces its decision from the bench. At that time, the opinion is made available to the public at the office of the clerk of the Court. The clerk also releases the opinion for online publication. Ultimately, the opinion is published in the *United States Reports*, which is the official printed record of the Court's decisions.

Some have complained that the Court reviews too few cases each term, thus giving the lower courts less guidance on important issues. The number of signed opinions issued by the Court has dwindled notably since the 1980s. In its 1982–1983 term, the Court issued signed opinions in 141 cases. By 2015, this number dropped to less than 50. One reason that the number of opinions has dropped is the Court's ability to group a number of cases into one larger case. Such was the process in the case of the Affordable Care Act challenges by the states.

When There Are Eight Justices

From time to time, there are fewer than nine justices issuing opinions on the cases that come before the court. A justice may recuse herself because she was part of the administration that brought the case to court. Occasionally, a justice may be ill and take a brief leave from the court. However, when a justice dies or resigns from the court, there will be only eight justices hearing cases and writing opinions. When there is a vacancy on the court, the president nominates a candidate and the appointment process goes on as detailed in the next section. However, in 2016, Justice Antonin Scalia, a conservative stalwart, died suddenly while on a vacation trip. The issue of appointing his replacement became highly politicized because the Republican members of the Senate did not want to consider a nominee until after the next presidential election in November 2016 and refused to hold hearings or to take a vote on Obama's nominee, Merrick Garland.

What happens when there are only eight justices? If the court is evenly balanced between liberal or Democrat-appointed justices and conservative or Republican appointees, gridlock can be the result. If the court hears a case and then votes 4–4 on the decision, the court loses its influence on the case. Because there is a tie vote, the decision of the next lowest court, usually a federal appellate court, becomes law. In the case of deciding to hear a case, the "rule of four" is more easily reached with one fewer justice. In any event, cases that result in a tie are likely to return to the Supreme Court with a slightly different legal question after the Court reaches full strength.

Election 2016

A Presidential Opportunity

Most Americans realize that the U.S. Supreme Court can have a significant impact on the laws of the nation, but they are not as attuned to the political nature of the court as strong partisans and political activists. The presidential election is seen by party elites as an opportunity to change the Supreme Court's political direction for decades to come. Most presidents have the opportunity to name at least one justice to the Court and, over the course of two terms, two or more. In addition, a president has the opportunity to name a significant number of lower court judges, who are more likely to share his or her political preferences.

In 2016, the composition of the Supreme Court changed drastically upon the death of Justice Antonin Scalia, a leading conservative voice. With a court that often voted 5–4, the loss of Scalia meant that on many votes the outcome would be 4–4 or no decision. The president quickly nominated Merrick Garland for the vacancy, but the Republican-controlled Senate chose not to act on that nomination. In the absence of the ninth justice, the court responded to cases by either voting 4–4 or finding a consensus that was often a compromise decision. If the court voted 4–4, that meant the last lower court decision would be upheld.

Both political parties saw the election of 2016 as very significant in terms of the Supreme Court. Soon after Donald Trump was sworn in as president, he nominated Colorado federal appeals court judge Neil Gorsuch to fill the vacancy. Gorsuch was confirmed by the Senate in a 54–45 vote on April 7, 2017. Gorsuch pledged to be impartial and independent. "It is the role of judges to apply, not alter, the work of the people's representatives," he said. "A judge who likes every outcome he reaches is very likely a bad judge." Over a year later in June 2018, Justice Anthony Kennedy announced his retirement. Within weeks, Trump nominated Judge Brett Kavanaugh to fill the vacancy.

For Critical Analysis

1. Should a president strive to appoint justices who are more extreme in their political beliefs or more moderate? Which is best for the nation?

2. How would the importance of the presidential election change if the Supreme Court justices were term limited?

The Selection of Federal Judges

■ **14.4** Explain how judges are nominated and confirmed for the Supreme Court.

All federal judges are appointed. The Constitution, in Article II, Section 2, states that the president appoints the justices of the Supreme Court with the advice and consent of the Senate. Congress has provided the same procedure for staffing other federal courts. This means that the Senate and the president jointly decide who shall fill every vacant judicial position, no matter what the level.

Federal judgeships in the United States number more than 870. Once appointed to such a judgeship, a person holds that job for life. Judges serve until they resign, retire voluntarily, or die. Federal judges who engage in blatantly illegal conduct may be removed through impeachment, although such action is rare.

Judicial Appointments

Judicial candidates for federal judgeships are suggested to the president by the Department of Justice, senators, other judges, the candidates, and lawyers' associations and other interest groups. In selecting a candidate to nominate for a judgeship, the president considers not only the person's competence but also other factors, including the person's political philosophy, ethnicity, and gender.

Image 14–5

Sonia Sotomayor, associate justice of the Supreme Court, addresses a crowd at the housing project in New York City where she grew up. The project was renamed in her honor.

The nomination process—no matter how the nominees are obtained—always works the same way. The president makes the actual nomination, transmitting the name to the Senate. The Senate then either confirms or rejects the nomination. To reach a conclusion, the Senate Judiciary Committee (operating through subcommittees) invites testimony, both written and oral, at its various hearings. In 2016, President Obama nominated Merrick Garland to replace the deceased Justice Scalia, hoping that a moderate nominee would be confirmed by the Republican Senate. Although many senators were willing to meet privately with the nominee and all noted his competence, the Senate Judiciary Committee showed no inclination to hold hearings and vote on the nominee. President Obama insisted that the Senate was "shirking its duty," whereas Republican senators noted that the Constitution did not require them to act quickly on the nomination.

A practice used in the Senate, called **senatorial courtesy**, is a constraint on the president's freedom to appoint federal district judges. Senatorial courtesy allows a senator of the president's political party to veto a judicial appointment in her or his state by way of a "blue slip." Traditionally, the senators from the nominee's state are sent a blue form on which to make comments. They may return the "blue slip" with comments or not return it at all. Not returning the blue slip is a veto of the nomination.[13] During much of American history, senators from the "opposition" party (the party to which the president did not belong) also have enjoyed the right of senatorial courtesy, although their veto power has varied over time.

senatorial courtesy
In federal district court judgeship nominations, a tradition allowing a senator to veto a judicial appointment in his or her state.

Federal District Court Judgeship Nominations
Although the president officially nominates federal judges, in the past the nomination of federal district court judges actually originated with a senator or senators of the president's

---

13 Charlie Savage, "Despite Filibuster Limits, a Door Remains Open to Block Judge Nominees," *The New York Times*, November 13, 2013. www.nytimes.com/2013/11/29/us/politics/despite-filibuster-limits-a-door-remains-open-to-block-judge-nominees.html. And for a historical view, see Mitchell A. Sollenberger, "The Blue Slip Process in the Senate Committee on the Judiciary: Background, Issues, and Options," Congressional Research Service, November 21, 2003.

party from the state in which there was a vacancy. In effect, judicial appointments were a form of political patronage. President Jimmy Carter (served 1977–1981) ended this tradition by establishing independent commissions to oversee the initial nomination process. President Ronald Reagan (served 1981–1989) abolished Carter's nominating commissions and established complete presidential control of nominations.

Federal Courts of Appeals Appointments

Appointments to the federal courts of appeals are far less numerous than federal district court appointments but are more important. Federal appellate judges handle more important matters, at least from the point of view of the president, and therefore presidents take a keener interest in the nomination process for such judgeships. Also, the U.S. courts of appeals have become stepping stones to the Supreme Court.

Supreme Court Appointments The president nominates Supreme Court justices. As shown in Table 14-1, which summarizes the background of all Supreme Court justices to 2018, the most common occupational background of the justices at the time of their appointment has been private legal practice or state or federal judgeship. Those nine justices who were in federal executive posts at the time of their appointment held the high offices of secretary of state, comptroller of the treasury, secretary of the navy, postmaster general, secretary of the interior, chairman of the Securities and Exchange Commission, and secretary of labor. In the "Other" category under "Occupational Position before Appointment" in Table 14-1 are two justices who were professors of law (including William H. Taft, a former president) and one justice who was a North Carolina state employee with responsibility for organizing and revising the state's statutes.

The Special Role of the Chief Justice

Although ideology is always important in judicial appointments, when a chief justice is selected for the Supreme Court, other considerations must also be taken into account. The chief justice is not only the head of a group of nine justices who interpret the law, but is also in essence the chief executive

Table 14-1 ▶ Background of U.S. Supreme Court Justices to 2018 (Number of Justices = 113 Total)

OCCUPATIONAL POSITION BEFORE APPOINTMENT	
Private legal practice	25
State judgeship	21
Federal judgeship	32
U.S. attorney general	7
Deputy or assistant U.S. attorney general	2
U.S. solicitor general	3
U.S. senator	6
U.S. representative	2
State governor	3
Federal executive post	9
Other	3
RELIGIOUS BACKGROUND	
Protestant	84
Roman Catholic	14
Jewish	7
Unitarian	7
No religious affiliation	7
AGE ON APPOINTMENT	
Under 40	5
41–50	35
51–60	59
61–70	14
POLITICAL PARTY AFFILIATION	
Federalist (to 1835)	13
Jeffersonian Republican (to 1828)	7
Whig (to 1861)	1
Democrat	46
Republican	45
Independent	1
EDUCATIONAL BACKGROUND	
College graduate	97
Not a college graduate	16
GENDER	
Male	109
Female	4
RACE	
White	110
African American	2
Hispanic American	1

Source: Congressional Quarterly, *Congressional Quarterly's Guide to the U.S. Supreme Court* (Washington, DC: Congressional Quarterly Press, 1996); and authors' updates.

officer (CEO) of a large bureaucracy that includes 1,200 judges with lifetime tenure, more than 850 magistrates and bankruptcy judges, and more than 30,000 staff members.

The chief justice is also the chair of the Judicial Conference of the United States, a policymaking body that sets priorities for the federal judiciary. That means the chief justice also indirectly oversees the $7 billion budget of this group.

Finally, the chief justice appoints the director of the Administrative Office of the United States Courts. The chief justice and this director select judges who sit on judicial committees that examine international judicial relations, technology, and a variety of other topics.

Partisanship and Judicial Appointments

Ideology plays an important role in the president's choices for judicial appointments. In most circumstances, the president appoints judges or justices who belong to the president's own political party.[14] Presidents see their federal judiciary appointments as the one sure way to institutionalize their political views long after they have left office. By 1993, presidents Ronald Reagan and George H. W. Bush together had appointed nearly three-quarters of all federal court judges. This preponderance of Republican-appointed federal judges strengthened the legal moorings of the conservative social agenda on a variety of issues, ranging from abortion to civil rights. Nevertheless, President Bill Clinton had the opportunity to appoint about 200 federal judges, thereby shifting the ideological makeup of the federal judiciary.

During the first two years of his second term, President George W. Bush was able to nominate two relatively conservative justices to the Supreme Court—John Roberts, who became chief justice, and Samuel Alito. During his first term as chief justice, Roberts voted most of the time with the Court's most conservative justices, Antonin Scalia and Clarence Thomas, but was part of the majority that upheld the Affordable Care Act in 2012. Justices can shift views once on the Court. Sandra Day O'Connor, the first female justice and a conservative, gradually shifted to the left on several issues, including abortion. In 1981, during her confirmation hearing before the Senate Judiciary Committee, she said, "I am opposed to it [abortion], as a matter of birth control or otherwise." By 1992, she was part of a 5–4 majority that agreed that the Constitution protects a woman's right to an abortion.

To fill the vacancy left by the retirement of Justice John Paul Stevens, President Obama nominated Solicitor General Elena Kagan, former dean of the law school at Harvard University. His first nominee to the Court, Associate Justice Sonia Sotomayor, who replaced Justice David Souter, became the first Hispanic American to serve on the Court. Both of President Obama's appointments were to seats formerly held by relatively liberal justices, so the balance of ideology on the Supreme Court remained as it had during the George W. Bush administration.

---

14 For a discussion of how the public regards the politics of Supreme Court appointments, see Brandon L. Bartels and Christopher D. Johnston, "Political Justice? Perceptions of Politicization and Public Preferences Toward the Supreme Court Appointment Process," *Public Opinion Quarterly* (Spring, 2012) 76 (1): 105–116.

The Asahi Shimbun/Getty Images

Image 14-6
On April 10, 2017,
Neil Gorsuch was sworn in as the
113th Supreme Court justice. His
appointment fulfilled a Trump
campaign promise to appoint conservative jurists to the bench.

The Senate's Role

Ideology also plays a large role in the Senate's confirmation hearings, and presidential nominees to the Supreme Court have not always been confirmed.
Almost 20 percent of presidential nominations to the Supreme Court have
been either rejected or not acted on by the Senate. Many acrimonious battles
over Supreme Court appointments have occurred when the Senate and the
president have not seen eye to eye on political matters.

The U.S. Senate had a long record of refusing to confirm the president's judicial nominations, extending from the beginning of Andrew Jackson's presidency
in 1829 to the end of Ulysses Grant's presidency in 1877. From 1894 until 1968,
however, only three nominees were not confirmed. Then, from 1968 through
1987, four presidential nominees to the highest court were rejected. One of the
most controversial Supreme Court nominations was that of Clarence Thomas,
who underwent an extremely volatile confirmation hearing in 1991, replete with
charges against him of sexual harassment. He was ultimately confirmed by the
Senate, however, and has been a stalwart voice for conservatism ever since.

President Bill Clinton had little trouble gaining approval for both of his nominees to the Supreme Court: Ruth Bader Ginsburg and Stephen Breyer.
President George W. Bush's nominees faced hostile grilling in their confirmation hearings, and various interest groups mounted intense media advertising
blitzes against them. Bush had to forgo one of his nominees, Harriet Miers,
when he realized that she could not be confirmed by the Senate. President
Obama's two nominations, Sonia Sotomayor and Elena Kagan, seen as too
liberal by some senators, were eminently qualified for the Court and were
approved by the Senate with little incident.

Both Clinton and Bush had trouble securing Senate approval for their judicial nominations to the lower courts. During the late 1990s and early 2000s,
the duel between the Senate and the president aroused considerable concern
about the consequences of the increasingly partisan and ideological tension

did you know?
Jimmy Carter is the only
president who made no
appointments to the Supreme
Court.

over federal judicial appointments. On several occasions, presidents have appointed federal judges using a temporary "recess appointment." This procedure is always used for the same reason—to avoid the continuation of an acrimonious and perhaps futile Senate confirmation process.

Although the confirmation hearings on Supreme Court nominees get all of the media attention, the hearings on nominees for the lower federal courts are equally bitter, leading some to ask whether the politicization of the confirmation process has gone too far. According to Fifth Circuit Court Judge Edith Jones, judicial nominations have turned into battlegrounds because so many federal judges now view the courts as agents of social change. Jones argues that when judge-made law (as opposed to legislature-made law) enters into sensitive topics, it provokes a political reaction. Thus, the ideology and political views of the potential justices should be a matter of public concern and political debate.[15]

Policymaking and the Courts

The partisan battles over judicial appointments reflect an important reality in today's American government: the importance of the judiciary in national politics. Because appointments to the federal bench are for life, the ideology of judicial appointees can affect national policy for years to come. Although the primary function of judges in our system of government is to interpret and apply the laws, inevitably judges make policy when carrying out this task. One of the major policymaking tools of the federal courts is their power of judicial review.

Judicial Review

If a federal court declares that a federal or state law or policy is unconstitutional, the court's decision affects the application of the law or policy only within that court's jurisdiction. For this reason, the higher the level of the court, the greater the impact of the decision on society. Because of the Supreme Court's national jurisdiction, its decisions have the greatest impact. When the Supreme Court held that an Arkansas state constitutional amendment limiting the terms of congresspersons was unconstitutional, laws establishing term limits in 23 other states were also invalidated.[16]

Some claim that the power of judicial review gives judges and justices on federal court benches too much influence over national policy. Others argue that the powers exercised by the federal courts, particularly the power of judicial review, are necessary to protect our constitutional rights and liberties. Built into our federal form of government is a system of checks and balances. If the federal courts did not have the power of judicial review, no governmental body could check Congress's lawmaking authority.

Judicial Activism and Judicial Restraint

■ **14.5** Compare the concepts of judicial activism and judicial restraint; link these concepts to the decisions of the Supreme Court in the last few decades.

Judicial scholars like to characterize different judges and justices as being either "activist" or "restraintist." The doctrine of **judicial activism** rests on the

judicial activism
A doctrine holding that the Supreme Court should take an active role by using its powers to check the activities of governmental bodies when those bodies exceed their authority.

---

15 Cited by John Leo, "A Judge with No Agenda," *Jewish World Review*, July 5, 2005.
16 *U.S. Term Limits v. Thornton*, 514 U.S. 779 (1995).

Joseph Mirachi/The New Yorker Collection/The Cartoon Bank

Image 14-7
"Do you ever have one of those days when everything seems un-Constitutional?"

conviction that the federal judiciary should take an active role by using its powers to check the activities of Congress, state legislatures, and administrative agencies when those governmental bodies exceed their authority. One of the Supreme Court's most activist eras was the period from 1953 to 1969, when the Court was headed by Chief Justice Earl Warren. The Warren Court propelled the civil rights movement forward by holding, among other things, that laws permitting racial segregation violated the equal protection clause.

In contrast, the doctrine of **judicial restraint** rests on the assumption that the courts should defer to the decisions made by the legislative and executive branches because members of Congress and the president are elected by the people, whereas members of the federal judiciary are not. Because administrative agency personnel normally have more expertise than the courts do in the areas regulated by the agencies, the courts likewise should defer to agency rules and decisions. Under the doctrine of judicial restraint, the courts should not thwart the implementation of legislative acts and agency rules unless they are clearly unconstitutional.

Judicial activism sometimes is linked with liberalism, and judicial restraint with conservatism. In fact, though, a conservative judge can be activist, just as a liberal judge can be restraintist. In the 1950s and 1960s, the Supreme Court was activist and liberal. Some believe that the Rehnquist Court, with its conservative majority, became increasingly activist during the early 2000s. Some go even further and claim that the federal courts, including the Supreme Court, wield too much power in our democracy.

Strict versus Broad Construction

Other terms that are often used to describe a justice's philosophy are *strict construction* and *broad construction*. Justices who believe in **strict construction** look to the "letter of the law" when they attempt to interpret the Constitution or a particular statute. Those who favor **broad construction** try to determine the context and purpose of the law.

judicial restraint
A doctrine holding that the Supreme Court should defer to the decisions made by the elected representatives of the people in the legislative and executive branches.

strict construction
A judicial philosophy that looks to the "letter of the law" when interpreting the Constitution or a particular statute.

broad construction
A judicial philosophy that looks to the context and purpose of a law when making an interpretation.

As with the doctrines of judicial restraint and judicial activism, strict construction is often associated with conservative political views, whereas broad construction is often linked with liberalism. These traditional political associations sometimes appear to be reversed, however. Consider the Eleventh Amendment to the Constitution, which forbids lawsuits in federal courts "against one of the United States by Citizens of another State, or by Citizens or Subjects of any Foreign State." Nothing is said about citizens suing their *own* states, and strict construction would therefore find such suits to be constitutional. Conservative justices, however, have construed this amendment broadly to deny citizens the constitutional right to sue their own states in most circumstances. John T. Noonan, Jr., a federal appellate court judge who was appointed by a Republican president, has described these rulings as "adventurous."[17]

Broad construction is often associated with the concept of a "living constitution." As one who strongly opposed that view, Supreme Court Justice Antonin Scalia said that the Constitution "is not a living document, it's a dead document.... It's an enduring document. It is a meaningless document if its meaning changes according to whatever the Supreme Court thinks."[18]

Ideology and the Rehnquist Court

William H. Rehnquist became the sixteenth chief justice of the Supreme Court in 1986, after 14 years as an associate justice. He was a strong anchor of the Court's conservative wing until his death in 2005. With Rehnquist's appointment as chief justice, it seemed that the Court would necessarily become more conservative.

Indeed, that is what happened. The Court began to take a rightward shift shortly after Rehnquist became chief justice, which continued as other conservative appointments to the bench were made during the Reagan and George H. W. Bush administrations. During the late 1990s and early 2000s, three of the justices (William Rehnquist, Antonin Scalia, and Clarence Thomas) were notably conservative in their views. Four of the justices (John Paul Stevens, David Souter, Ruth Bader Ginsburg, and Stephen Breyer) held moderate-to-liberal views. The middle of the Court was occupied by two moderate-to-conservative justices, Sandra Day O'Connor and Anthony Kennedy. O'Connor and Kennedy usually provided the swing votes on the Court in controversial cases.

Although the Court seemed to become more conservative under Rehnquist's leadership, its decisions were not always predictable. Many cases were decided by very close votes, and results varied depending on the issue. The Court ruled in 1995 that Congress had overreached its powers under the commerce clause when it attempted to regulate the possession of guns in schoolyards. According to the Court, the possession of guns in school zones had nothing to do with the commerce clause.[19] Yet in 2005, the Court upheld Congress's power under the commerce clause to ban marijuana use even

---

17 John T. Noonan, Jr., *Narrowing the Nation's Power: The Supreme Court Sides with the States* (Berkeley, CA: University of California Press, 2002).

18 "More quotes from Justice Scalia's Speaking Tour," National Constitution Center, August 21, 2013, http://blog.constitutioncenter.org/2013/08/more-quotes-fro-justice-scalias-speaking-tour/

19 *United States v. Lopez*, 514 U.S. 549 (1995).

when a state's law permitted such use.[20] In other areas such as civil rights, the Court generally issued conservative opinions.

The Roberts Court

In 2006, a new chief justice was appointed to the court. John Roberts had a distinguished career as an attorney in Washington, DC, and served as a clerk to the Supreme Court while in law school. The confirmation process was quite smooth, and many hoped that he would be a moderate leader of the Court.

During John Roberts's first term (2005–2006) as chief justice, the Court ruled on several important issues, but no clear pattern was discernible in the decisions. In the years following his appointment, Roberts was more likely to vote with the conservative justices—Scalia, Thomas, and Alito—than with the moderate-to-liberal bloc. Thus, several important decisions were handed down with close votes. In an important case for environmentalist groups, the Court held that the Environmental Protection Agency (EPA) did have the power under the Clean Air Act to regulate greenhouse gases. The vote was 5–4, with the chief justice on the minority side.[21] Similarly, when the Court upheld the 2003 federal law banning partial-birth abortions, Roberts was on the conservative majority in a 5–4 vote.[22]

Later in 2007, the Supreme Court issued a very important opinion on school integration. By another 5–4 vote, the Court ruled that school district policies that included race as a determining factor in admission to certain schools were unconstitutional on the ground that they violated the equal protection clause of the Constitution.[23] After Justices Sonia Sotomayor and Elena Kagan joined the court, court watchers believed that the Roberts Court would make conservative decisions but that the majority often would be razor thin. Indeed, in 2012, the Court announced two decisions that supported this appraisal: The Court overturned four provisions of Arizona's controversial law regarding illegal immigrants but upheld the central provision allowing police officers to check the immigration status of those individuals who had been arrested or stopped on other charges. A few days later, the Supreme Court upheld the individual mandate to buy health insurance under the Affordable Care Act by a 5–4 margin, with the chief justice supporting the law as legal under the commerce clause of the Constitution.

The Roberts Court continued to issue controversial opinions in 2013 and 2014: in 2013, the court, by a 5–4 vote, struck down the heart of the Voting Rights Act, freeing Southern states to revise voting laws without federal scrutiny. The court continued on its path to complete freedom of speech in political campaigns. In 2014, the court struck down the limits on the total amount an individual can contribute to political campaigns in each election, although it affirmed the limit per gift. In yet another close vote, the Court struck down laws against gay marriage in 2015. In *Obergefell v. Hodges,* 576 U.S. (2015), Justice Roberts wrote the dissenting opinion siding with the conservative bloc

---

20 *Gonzales v. Raich,* 545 U.S. 1 (2005).
21 *Massachusetts v. EPA,* 127 St. Ct. 1438 (2007).
22 *Gonzales v. Carhart,* 127 St. Ct. 1610 (2007).
23 *Parents Involved in Community Schools v. Seattle School District,* N. 1, 127 St. Ct. 2162 (2007).

Image 14-8

Jim Obergefell, the lead plaintiff in the Supreme Court case that established the right of gay Americans to marry, speaks to the crowd outside the Supreme Court after the decision was announced in June 2015.

of justices. Legal scholars Lee Epstein and Andrew Martin have suggested that the Roberts Court is more likely to vote based on policy preferences rather than from a consideration for judicial activism or judicial restraint.[24]

What Checks Our Courts?

■ **14.6** Discuss the constitutional and political constraints on the Supreme Court.

Our judicial system is one of the most independent in the world, but the courts do not have absolute independence as part of the political process. Political checks limit the extent to which courts can exercise judicial review and engage in an activist policy. These checks are exercised by the executive branch, the legislature, the public, and the judiciary.

Executive Checks

judicial implementation
The way in which court decisions are translated into action.

President Andrew Jackson was once supposed to have said, after Chief Justice John Marshall made an unpopular decision, "John Marshall has made his decision; now let him enforce it."[25] This purported remark goes to the heart of **judicial implementation**—the enforcement of judicial decisions in such a way that those decisions are translated into policy. The Supreme Court simply does not have any enforcement powers, and whether a decision will be implemented depends on the cooperation of the other two branches of government. Rarely, though, will a president refuse to enforce a Supreme Court decision, as President Jackson did. To take such an action could mean a significant loss of public support because of the Supreme Court's stature in the eyes of the nation.

---

24 Lee Epstein and Andrew D. Martin, "Is the Roberts Court Especially Activist—A Study of Invalidating (and Upholding) Federal, State, and Local Laws," *Emory Law Journal* 61(2011): 737.

25 The decision referred to was *Cherokee Nation v. Georgia*, 30 U.S. 1 (1831).

Image 14-9
Federal troops were sent by President Eisenhower to guard Little Rock High School and to ensure the safety of the African American students who were going to attend that school.

More commonly, presidents exercise influence over the judiciary by appointing new judges and justices as federal judicial seats become vacant. The U.S. solicitor general plays a significant role in the federal court system, and the person holding this office is a presidential appointee.

Executives at the state level may also refuse to implement court decisions with which they disagree. A notable example of such a refusal occurred in Arkansas after the Supreme Court ordered schools to desegregate "with all deliberate speed" in 1955.[26] Arkansas governor Orval Faubus refused to cooperate with the decision and used the state's National Guard to block the integration of Central High School in Little Rock. Ultimately, President Dwight Eisenhower had to federalize the Arkansas National Guard and send federal troops to Little Rock to quell the violence that had erupted.

Legislative Checks

Courts may make rulings, but often the legislatures at local, state, and federal levels are required to appropriate funds to carry out the courts' rulings. A court, for example, may decide that prison conditions must be improved, but the legislature authorizes the funds necessary to carry out the ruling. When such funds are not appropriated, the court that made the ruling has been checked.

Constitutional Amendments Courts' rulings can be overturned by constitutional amendments at both the federal and state levels. Many of

---

26 *Brown v. Board of Education*, 349 U.S. 294 (1955)—the second *Brown* decision.

the amendments to the U.S. Constitution (such as the Fourteenth, Fifteenth, and Twenty-sixth Amendments) check the state courts' ability to allow discrimination. Proposed constitutional amendments that were created in an effort to reverse courts' decisions on school prayer and abortion have failed.

Rewriting Laws Finally, Congress or a state legislature can rewrite (amend) old laws or enact new ones to overturn a court's rulings if the legislature concludes that the court is interpreting laws or legislative intentions erroneously. Congress passed the Civil Rights Act of 1991 in part to overturn a series of conservative rulings in employment-discrimination cases. In 1993, Congress enacted the Religious Freedom Restoration Act (RFRA), which broadened religious liberties, after Congress concluded that a 1990 Supreme Court ruling restricted religious freedom to an unacceptable extent.[27]

According to political scientist Walter Murphy, "A permanent feature of our constitutional landscape is the ongoing tug and pull between elected government and the courts."[28] Certainly, over the last few decades, the Supreme Court has been in conflict with the other two branches of government. Congress at various times has passed laws that, among other things, made it illegal to burn the American flag and attempted to curb pornography on the Internet. In each instance, the Supreme Court ruled that those laws were unconstitutional. The Court also invalidated the RFRA.

Whenever Congress does not like what the judiciary does, it threatens to censure the judiciary for its activism. One member of the Senate Judiciary Committee, John Cornyn (R-TX), claimed that judges are making "political decisions yet are unaccountable to the public." He went on to say that violence against judges in the courtroom can be explained by the public's distress at such activism.

The states can also negate or alter the effects of Supreme Court rulings, when such decisions allow it. In *Kelo v. City of New London,* the Supreme Court allowed a city to take private property for redevelopment by private businesses. Since that case was decided, a majority of states have passed legislation limiting or prohibiting such actions.[29]

Public Opinion

Public opinion plays a significant role in shaping government policy, and the judiciary is not exempt from this rule. Persons affected by a Supreme Court decision that is noticeably at odds with their views may simply ignore it. Officially sponsored prayers were banned in public schools in 1962, yet it was widely known that the ban was (and still is) ignored in many Southern districts. Unless someone complains about the prayers and initiates a lawsuit, the courts can do nothing. The public can also pressure state and local government officials to refuse to enforce a certain decision. Judicial implementation requires the cooperation of government officials at all levels, and public opinion

---

27 *Employment Division, Department of Human Resources of Oregon v. Smith,* 494 U.S. 872 (1990).

28 As quoted in Neal Devins, "The Last Word Debate: How Social and Political Forces Shape Constitutional Values," *American Bar Association Journal,* October 1997, p. 48.

29 545 U.S. 469 (2005).

in various regions of the country will influence whether such cooperation is forthcoming.

The courts necessarily are influenced by public opinion to some extent. After all, judges are not isolated in our society; their attitudes are influenced by social trends, just as the attitudes and beliefs of all persons are. Courts generally tend to avoid issuing decisions that they know will be noticeably at odds with public opinion.[30] This is because the judiciary prefers to avoid creating divisiveness among the public. Also, a court—particularly the Supreme Court—may lose stature if it decides a case in a way that markedly diverges from public opinion. In 2002, the Supreme Court ruled that the execution of developmentally disabled criminals violates the Eighth Amendment's ban on cruel and unusual punishment. In its ruling, the Court indicated that the standards of what constitutes cruel and unusual punishment are influenced by public opinion and that there is "powerful evidence that today our society views mentally retarded offenders as categorically less culpable than the average criminal."[31]

Judicial Traditions and Doctrines

Supreme Court justices (and other federal judges) typically exercise self-restraint in fashioning decisions. In part, this restraint stems from their knowledge that the other two branches of government and the public can exercise checks on the judiciary. To a large extent, however, this restraint is mandated by various judicially established traditions and doctrines. When reviewing a case, the Supreme Court typically narrows its focus to just one issue or one aspect of an issue involved in the case. The Court rarely makes broad, sweeping decisions on issues. The doctrine of *stare decisis* acts as a restraint because it obligates the courts, including the Supreme Court, to follow established precedents when deciding cases. Only rarely will courts overrule a precedent.

Hypothetical and Political Questions

Other judicial doctrines and practices also act as restraints. The courts will hear only what are called justiciable disputes, which arise out of actual cases—a court will not hear a case that involves a hypothetical issue. Additionally, if a political question is involved, the Supreme Court often will exercise judicial restraint and refuse to rule on the matter. A **political question** is one that the Supreme Court declares should be decided by the elected branches of government—the executive branch, the legislative branch, or those two branches acting together. The Supreme Court has refused to rule on the controversy regarding the rights of gays and lesbians in the military, preferring instead to defer to the executive branch's decisions on the matter. Generally, fewer questions are deemed political questions by the Supreme Court today than in the past.

political question
An issue that a court believes should be decided by the executive or legislative branch.

The Impact of the Lower Courts

Higher courts can reverse the decisions of lower courts and lower courts can act as a check on higher courts. Lower courts can—and have—ignored Supreme Court decisions. Usually, this is done indirectly. A lower court might conclude, for example, that the precedent

---

30 One striking counterexample is the *Kelo v. City of New London* decision mentioned earlier.
31 *Atkins v. Virginia*, 536 U.S. 304 (2002).

set by the Supreme Court does not apply to the exact circumstances in the case before the court; or the lower court may decide that the Supreme Court's decision was ambiguous with respect to the issue before the lower court. The fact that the Supreme Court rarely makes broad and clear-cut statements on any issue makes it easier for the lower courts to interpret the Supreme Court's decisions in a different way.

Key Terms

affirm 505
appellate court 498
broad construction 513
case law 494
class-action suit 502
common law 492
concurring opinion 506
dissenting opinion 506
diversity of citizenship 497
federal question 497
general jurisdiction 498

judicial activism 512
judicial implementation 516
judicial restraint 513
judicial review 492
jurisdiction 497
limited jurisdiction 498
litigate 502
majority opinion 506
opinion 505
oral arguments 505
political question 519

precedent 492
remand 505
reverse 505
rule of four 505
senatorial courtesy 508
stare decisis 492
strict construction 513
trial court 498
unanimous opinion 506
writ of *certiorari* 505

Chapter Summary

■ **14.1** American law is rooted in the common-law tradition, which is part of our heritage from England. Fundamental sources of American law include the U.S. Constitution and state constitutions, statutes enacted by legislative bodies, regulations issued by administrative agencies, and case law. The common-law doctrine of *stare decisis* ("to stand on decided cases") obligates judges to follow precedents established previously by their own courts or by higher courts that have authority over them. Precedents established by the U.S. Supreme Court, the highest court in the land, are binding on all lower courts.

■ **14.2** The most important policymaking tool of the federal courts is the power of judicial review, which allows the Courts to declare unconstitutional any law or regulation in conflict with the Constitution. This power was not mentioned specifically in the Constitution, but John Marshall claimed the power for the Court in his 1803 decision in *Marbury v. Madison.*

■ **14.3** Article III, Section 1, of the U.S. Constitution limits the jurisdiction of the federal courts to cases involving (1) a federal question, which is a question based, at least in part, on the U.S. Constitution, a treaty, or a federal law; or (2) diversity of citizenship, which arises when parties to a lawsuit are from different states or when the lawsuit involves a foreign citizen or government. The federal court system is a three-tiered model consisting of (1) U.S.

district (trial) courts and various lower courts of limited jurisdiction, (2) U.S. courts of appeals, and (3) the U.S. Supreme Court. Cases may be appealed from the district courts to the appellate courts. In most cases, the decisions of the federal appellate courts are final because the Supreme Court hears relatively few cases.

■ **14.3** The Supreme Court's decision to review a case is influenced by many factors, including the significance of the issues involved and whether the solicitor general is pressing the Court to take the case. After a case is accepted, the justices undertake research (with the help of their law clerks) on the issues involved in the case, hear oral arguments from the parties, meet in conference to discuss and vote on the issue, and announce the opinion, which is then released for publication.

■ **14.4** Federal judges are nominated by the president and confirmed by the Senate. Once appointed, they hold office for life, barring gross misconduct. The nomination and confirmation process, particularly for Supreme Court justices, is often extremely politicized. Democrats and Republicans alike realize that justices may occupy seats on the Court for decades and naturally want to have persons appointed who share their basic views.

■ **14.5** Judges who take an active role in checking the activities of the other branches of government sometimes are characterized as "activist" judges, and judges who defer to the other branches' decisions sometimes are regarded as "restraintist" judges. The Warren Court of the 1950s and 1960s was activist in a liberal direction, whereas the Rehnquist Court became increasingly activist in a conservative direction. One of the criticisms of the Court is that it should not "make law," but should defer to the legislative branch in deciding policy issues. However, in the interpretation of previously written laws, it has often fallen to the Supreme Court to make a final determination.

■ **14.6** Checks on the powers of the federal courts include executive checks, legislative checks, public opinion, and judicial traditions and doctrines.

Selected Resources

PRINT RESOURCES

Coyle, Marcia. *The Roberts Court: The Struggle for the Constitution* (New York: Simon and Schuster, 2013). In the view of this constitutional scholar, the Court remains divided between liberals and conservatives. She looks at the justices and their differences in four important cases: the Affordable Care Act, money in elections, gun control, and racial integration of the schools.

Peppers, Todd C., and Artemus Ward, editors. *In Chambers: Stories of Supreme Court Law Clerks and Their Justices* (Charlottesville, VA: University of Virginia Press, 2013). Young attorneys who have completed their positions as "clerks" to the Supreme Court justices write about their experiences and about the everyday life of the Court behind the scenes.

Roosevelt, Kermit. *The Myth of Judicial Activism: Making Sense of Supreme Court Decisions* (New Haven, CT: Yale University Press, 2008). Roosevelt, a University of Pennsylvania professor, defends the Court against charges of undue judicial activism. Roosevelt finds the Court's decisions to be reasonable, although he disagrees with some of them.

Stevens, John Paul. *Five Chiefs: A Supreme Court Memoir* (Boston: Little, Brown and Co., 2011). Retired Justice Stevens comments on his colleagues, the architecture of the building, and legal argument in this well-written and "gentle" memoir of his days on the high court.

Teles, Stephen. *The Rise of the Conservative Legal Movement: The Battle for Control of the Law* (Princeton, NJ: Princeton University Press, 2012). Teles provides an account of how conservative foundations and institutions fostered ways to support the education and later networking of the conservative legal scholars who have challenged liberal policies before the Court.

Urofsky, Melvin. *Dissent and the Supreme Court: Its Role in the Court's History and the Nation's Constitutional Dialogue* (New York: Random House, 2015). The author examines famous dissenting opinions throughout the Court's history and finds that many of these dissents have led to increased individual rights and liberties.

MEDIA RESOURCES

Amistad—A 1997 movie, starring Anthony Hopkins, about a slave-ship mutiny in 1839. Much of the story revolves around the prosecution, ending at the Supreme Court, of the slave who led the revolt.

Gideon's Trumpet—A 1980 film, starring Henry Fonda as the small-time criminal James Earl Gideon, which elucidates the path a case takes to the Supreme Court and the importance of cases decided there.

Marbury v. Madison—A 1987 video on the famous 1803 case that established the principle of judicial review. This is the first in a four-part series, *Equal Justice Under Law: Landmark Cases in Supreme Court History*, produced by the Judicial Conference of the United States.

The Supreme Court—A four-part PBS series that won a 2008 Parents' Choice Gold Award. The series follows the history of the Supreme Court from the first chief justice, John Marshall, to the earliest days of the Roberts Court. Some of the many topics are the Court's dismal performance in the Civil War era, its conflicts with President Franklin D. Roosevelt, its role in banning the segregation of African Americans, and the abortion controversy.

ONLINE RESOURCES

FindLaw—searchable database of Supreme Court decisions since 1970: www.findlaw.com

Legal Information Institute at Cornell University Law School—offers an easily searchable index to Supreme Court opinions, including some important historic decisions: www.law.cornell.edu/supct/index.html

The Oyez Project—multimedia archive devoted to the Supreme Court of the United States and its work: www.oyez.org

Supreme Court of the United States—Supreme Court decisions are available here within hours of their release: supreme-courtus.gov

United States Courts—home page of the federal courts and a good starting point for learning about the federal court system in general; follow the path of a case as it moves through the federal court system: www.uscourts.gov

Wild About Trials—This website covers current trials in the United States as well as breaking headlines in criminal justice cases. Some videos of trials are available in their archives. Most famous trials have some portion of the proceedings here or on YouTube: www.wildabouttrial.com

Domestic Policy

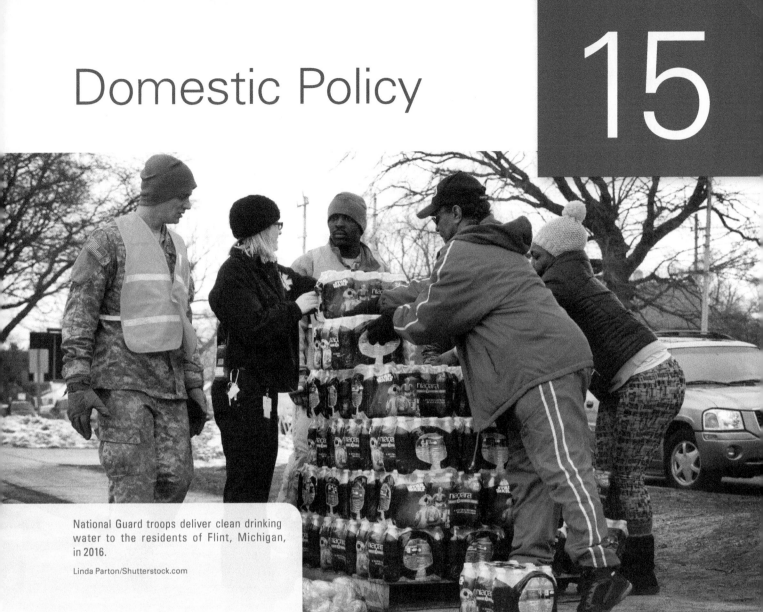

National Guard troops deliver clean drinking water to the residents of Flint, Michigan, in 2016.

Linda Parton/Shutterstock.com

LEARNING OBJECTIVES

After reading this chapter, you will be able to:

■ **15.1** Define *public policy* and describe the policy-making process as it applies to American national government institutions.

■ **15.2** Explain the principles underlying the American health-care system and the issues facing that system.

■ **15.3** Describe the environmental policies of the United States and the role of the Environmental Protection Agency in implementing these policies.

■ **15.4** Analyze American energy policy and discuss how it encourages energy independence.

■ **15.5** Describe the national policies for ending poverty in the United States and alleviating the issues caused by economic downturns.

■ **15.6** Discuss the issues raised by immigration into the United States and the proposed reforms to the immigration system.

Background

In the United States, we have a private health-care system, but around 40 percent of Americans use government programs to pay for health insurance. That includes the senior citizens under Medicare, military veterans, permanently disabled Americans, children insured under the state–federal partnership program, and the poorest Americans who are covered under Medicaid, another joint state–federal program. The Patient Protection and Affordable Care Act, hereafter referred to as the Affordable Care Act (ACA), is a step toward universal health care but maintains the private health-care system. Although it requires that all Americans have health insurance, either purchased privately or through the federal or state government, it does not take control of private physicians, the prescription drug industry, or hospitals. Even after all provisions of the ACA are implemented, the United States will remain the only major industrialized democratic nation without a health-care system that guarantees equal access to basic health care for all citizens.

What If We Had Universal Health Care?

With universal health care, everyone in need of basic medical care would have access to physicians, clinics, and hospital services. Every legal resident of the United States would receive free or nearly free medical examinations, routine physician visits, well-baby care, and required tests. Most likely, prescription drugs would be available at very low cost to all Americans, regardless of their income or where they obtain their insurance. Such a health-care system would likely be paid for by a combination of taxes on workers and their employers and income taxes on all. Such a system might include the option for additional private insurance available for extra cost. Doctors might work for the state or national government, or they could remain as private practitioners.

How Does Universal Health Care Affect the Individual Patient?

The National Audit Office of the United Kingdom (Great Britain, Scotland, and Wales) conducted a study of the health-care systems in ten major industrialized nations in 2011, which underscored the fact that all of these nations except the United States guaranteed universal health care. Different countries utilize various systems: Britain has state-employed doctors and state-run hospitals; France features national health insurance but private physicians who "bill" the state for their services.

Studies of universal systems show that for the average individual, good basic care is available. Infant mortality tends to decrease because all pregnant women have access to prenatal care. People with chronic diseases get more regular care and tend to do better at maintaining their health. Most nations cover the cost of prescriptions so that no individual is denied an expensive but necessary medication. However, in some nations there are long waits for advanced procedures and less availability of some of the more expensive tests and scans performed routinely in the United States. Some procedures that are covered in the United States might not be covered under a national system, but it is difficult to generalize across all nations. Americans have made clear their desire to keep their private physicians, private hospitals, and the right to access very expensive and advanced treatments. Whether Americans will be willing to trade these practices for a universal health-care system is a question yet to be decided.

For Critical Analysis

1. What are the advantages and disadvantages of a universal health-care system?

2. How could the United States implement a universal health-care system and retain some of the features of the current system that are desired by citizens?

domestic policy
Public plans or courses of action that concern internal issues of national importance, such as poverty, health care, and the environment.

Americans expect the federal government to pay attention to the issues that affect the lives of American citizens. The legislation and regulations passed to address these problems are usually called "domestic policy." **Domestic policy** can be defined as all of the laws, government planning, and government actions that affect each individual's daily life in the United States. Consequently, the span of such policies is enormous. Domestic policies range from relatively simple issues, such as what the speed limit should be on interstate highways, to more complex ones, such as how best to reduce our nation's contribution to climate change or how to improve the performance of schools across the nation.

The question of providing health care to all Americans is a consuming national issue. In 2010, the United States adopted a major reform of our health policies, but Congress did not adopt a universal health-care system. The complex nature of the health policy reform legislation and the debate that accompanied that reform effort reflect the fact that the reform will touch virtually all Americans. Like many other domestic policies, this one was formulated and implemented by the federal government but will involve efforts of federal, state, and local governments and the private sector.

This chapter looks at domestic policy issues involving health care, the environment and energy, poverty and welfare, immigration, and others. Before we start our analysis, though, we must look at how public policies are made.

The Policymaking Process

■ **15.1** Define *public policy* and describe the policymaking process as it applies to American national government institutions.

How does any issue get resolved? First, the issue must be identified as a problem. Often, policymakers simply have to turn on the news or look at the Internet or hear from a constituent to discover that a problem is brewing. On rare occasions, a crisis, such as that brought about by the terrorist attacks of September 11, 2001, or the destruction caused by Hurricane Maria in 2017, creates the need to formulate policy. Like most Americans, however, policymakers receive much of their information from the national media. Of course, interest groups are always bringing issues to the attention of Congress in hopes of influencing policy outcomes.

Consider the Affordable Care Act. President Obama made it a priority of his first year in office. The law, which was passed about 14 months later, requires all Americans to have health insurance, whether through their employer, state insurance exchanges, or a federal program such as Medicaid. Some provisions of the law took effect almost immediately, including the one that requires insurance companies to allow parents to keep their children on their policies until age 26. No matter how simple or how complex the problem, those who make policy follow several steps. We can divide the process of policymaking into at least five steps: agenda building, policy formulation, policy adoption, policy implementation, and policy evaluation (see Figure 15-1).

Agenda Building

First, the issue must get on the agenda—Congress must become aware that an issue requires congressional action. Agenda building may occur as the result of a crisis, technological change, or mass media campaigns, as well as through the efforts of strong political personalities and effective lobbying groups.

Advocates for improved health care in this nation had called for a serious reform of the system for years. The Democratic majorities

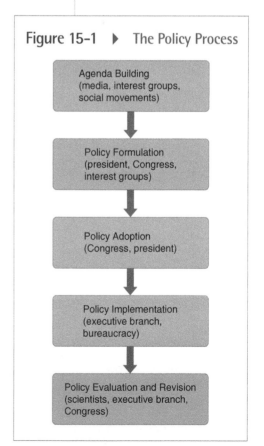

Figure 15-1 ▶ The Policy Process

Agenda Building
(media, interest groups, social movements)

Policy Formulation
(president, Congress, interest groups)

Policy Adoption
(Congress, president)

Policy Implementation
(executive branch, bureaucracy)

Policy Evaluation and Revision
(scientists, executive branch, Congress)

in both the House and the Senate supported President Obama's priority as they, under the leadership of the late Senator Ted Kennedy, had pushed for reform of the health system for many years.

Policy Formulation

During the next step in the policymaking process, various policy proposals are discussed among government officials and the public. Such discussions may take place in the printed media, on television, and in the halls of Congress. Congress holds hearings, the president voices the administration's views, and the topic may even become a campaign issue.

With the Democratic majorities in Congress beginning work on the legislation, Republicans quickly took the position that they opposed the reform bill, but they lacked the votes in either house to change the momentum. Interest groups, seeing that the bill had a chance to become law, offered their own proposals. As the policy was being formulated, groups representing America's doctors, hospitals, pharmacies, medical appliance makers, pharmaceutical manufacturers, and every other part of the medical industry, offered proposals and commented on the draft legislation. In some cases, groups agreed not to oppose the law if their interests were protected.[1] The input of these groups into the policy formulation process is invaluable: they know more about the health-care system than any member of Congress.

Policy Adoption

The third step in the policymaking process involves choosing a specific policy from among the proposals that have been discussed. In the end, the bill passed both houses, although the margin in the Senate was very small. The progress of the bill through Congress revealed some of the intense partisan behavior that has become common in recent years. Republicans put forward alternative proposals and claimed that they were ignored by the administration and the Democrats. Democrats used all parliamentary means to pass the bill, including keeping the Republicans out of the final negotiations between the House and the Senate. This, of course, was exactly how Republicans had treated Democrats in passing the Medicare prescription drug bill in 2006.

Policy Implementation

The fourth step in the policymaking process involves the implementation of the policy alternative chosen by Congress. Government action must be implemented by bureaucrats, the courts, police, and individual citizens. In the example of the Affordable Care Act, the main portion of the legislation was not to come into effect until 2014. For the most part, therefore, implementation did not begin immediately. Some sections of the bill did become effective in 2011, however, including the creation of insurance pools for people with existing conditions, new taxes on wealthier retirees for their prescription drug coverage, dependents' eligibility for their parents' health insurance until up to age 26, and support for the creating of electronic medical records. The actual requirement to have health

---

1 Lawrence R. Jacobs and Theda Skocpol, *Health Care Reform and American Politics: What Everyone Needs to Know, Revised and Updated*, 2nd ed. (New York: Oxford University Press, 2012).

insurance took effect in 2014. The troubled roll-out of the federal health insurance exchange website in the fall of 2013, however, became the most noticed part of the implementation process. Republican opposition to the law did not abate, and it became a major campaign issue in every federal election that has followed. Although Republicans did gain a majority in the House of Representatives in that election, they could not overturn the bill without gaining control of the Senate. However, a number of states elected Republican administrations, and 26 Republican attorneys general filed suit against the bill, challenging the individual mandate to buy insurance and the provision requiring states to expand their Medicaid rolls. The individual mandate was upheld by the Supreme Court in 2012, but the Medicaid mandate to the states was overturned, leaving that part of the law unenforceable.

Policy Evaluation

After a policy has been implemented, it is evaluated. Groups conduct studies to determine what actually happens after a policy has been in place for a given period. Based on this feedback and the perceived success or failure of the policy, a new round of policymaking initiatives will be undertaken to improve on the effort. Because the Affordable Care Act has not been fully implemented, there has been little evaluation of the policy's outcomes. Some health industry economists and the Congressional Budget Office have suggested that the cost will be far higher than originally estimated, whereas other sources predict it will save billions over the long term. Some believe that many small businesses will drop insurance coverage for their employees due to the high cost of the new program, but these are simply predictions for the future. As of 2016, data reveal that many more families and individuals have found health insurance coverage through Medicaid; however, premium increases for those who buy their own insurance through the state exchanges have been significant. With the penalty for not having insurance still being fairly low, many younger and healthier Americans still have no insurance coverage. It will be the job of future legislators and members of the administration to propose reforms to the Affordable Care Act.

Health Care

■ **15.2** Explain the principles underlying the American health-care system and the issues facing that system.

Undoubtedly, one of the most important problems facing the nation is how to guarantee affordable health care for all Americans at a cost the nation can bear. Spending for health care is estimated to account for about 18 percent of the total U.S. economy. In 1965, about 6 percent of our income was spent on health care, and that percentage has been increasing ever since, exceeding 17.5 percent by 2014 and projected to reach 20 percent by 2020. Per capita spending on health care is greater in the United States than almost anywhere else in the world. Measured by the percentage of the gross domestic product (GDP) devoted to health care, America spends almost twice as much as Australia or Canada (see Figure 15-2). (The GDP is the dollar value of all final goods and services produced in a one-year period.)

Figure 15-2 ▶ Costs of Health Care in Economically Advanced Nations

Cost is given as a percentage of total gross domestic product (GDP).

Source: Organization for Economic Cooperation and Development, OECD Health.

The Rising Cost of Health Care

Numerous explanations exist for why health-care costs have risen so much. At least one has to do with changing demographics—the U.S. population is getting older. Life expectancy has gone up, as shown in Figure 15-3. The top 5 percent of those using health care incur more than 50 percent of all health-care costs. The bottom 70 percent of health-care users account for only 10 percent of health-care expenditures. The elderly make up most of the top users of health-care services, including nursing home care and long-term care for those suffering from debilitating diseases.

Advanced Technology Another reason why health-care costs have risen so dramatically is advancing technology. A magnetic resonance imaging (MRI) scanner can cost more than $2 million. A positron emission tomography (PET) scanner costs approximately $4 million. All of these machines have become increasingly available in recent decades and are in demand around the country. The development of new technologies that help physicians and hospitals prolong human life is an ongoing process in an ever-advancing industry. New procedures and drugs that involve even greater costs can be expected in the future. It is also true that these advanced procedures are more readily available in the United States than anywhere else in the world.

The Government's Role in Financing Health Care Currently, government spending on health care constitutes about 43 percent of total health-care spending. Private insurance accounts for about 33 percent of payments for health care. The remainder is paid directly by individuals or by philanthropy.

Figure 15-3 ▶ Life Expectancy in the United States

Along with health-care spending, life expectancy has gone up. More Americans are living longer due, in great part, to advances in medicine. Immunizations have decreased death from many diseases, allowing more children to reach adulthood.

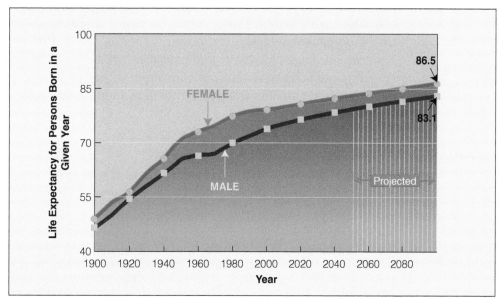

Source: Social Security Administration, Office of the Chief Actuary.

Medicare and Medicaid have been the main sources of hospital and other medical benefits for more than 100 million U.S. residents, including 47 million Americans over 65 and 61 million others.

Medicare is specifically designed to support the elderly, regardless of income. **Medicaid**, a joint state–federal program, is in principle a program to subsidize health care for the poor. In practice, it often provides long-term health care to persons living in nursing homes. (To become eligible for Medicaid, these individuals must first exhaust their financial assets.) Medicare, Medicaid, and private insurance companies are called *third parties*. Caregivers and patients are the two primary parties. When third parties pay for medical care, the demand for such services increases; health-care recipients have no incentive to restrain their use of health care. One result is some degree of wasted resources.

Medicare
A federal health insurance program that covers U.S. residents age 65 and older. The costs are met by a tax on wages and salaries.

Medicaid
A joint state–federal program that provides medical care to the poor (including indigent elderly persons in nursing homes). The program is funded out of general government revenues.

Medicare

The Medicare program, created in 1965 under President Lyndon B. Johnson, pays hospital and physicians' bills for U.S. residents age 65 and older. Beginning in 2006, Medicare also pays for at least part of the prescription drug expenses of the elderly. In return for paying a tax on their earnings (currently set at 2.9 percent of wages and salaries) while in the workforce, retirees are assured that the majority of their hospital and physicians' bills will be paid for with public funds.

Over the past 40 years, Medicare has become the second-largest domestic spending program, after Social Security. Government expenditures on Medicare have routinely turned out to be far in excess of the expenditures forecast at the time the program was put into place or expanded. Chapter 16 discusses Medicare's impact on the current federal budget and the impact it is likely to have in the future. For now, consider only that the total outlays on Medicare are high enough to create substantial demands to curtail its costs.

One response by the federal government to soaring Medicare costs has been to impose reimbursement caps on specific procedures. To avoid going over Medicare's reimbursement caps, however, hospitals have an incentive to discharge patients quickly. The government has also cut rates of reimbursement to individual physicians and physician groups, such as health maintenance organizations (HMOs). One consequence has been a nearly 15 percent reduction in the amount the government pays for Medicare services provided by physicians.

Medicaid

In a few short years, the joint federal–state taxpayer-funded Medicaid program for the "working poor" has generated one of the biggest expansions of government entitlements in the last 50 years. In 1997, Medicaid spending was around $150 billion. By 2014, it tripled to $495 billion. At the end of the last decade, 34 million people were enrolled in the program. Today, there are more than 60 million. The increase in unemployment after the financial crisis of 2008 increased the number by 15 percent. When you add Medicaid coverage to Medicare and the military and federal employee health plans, the government has clearly become the nation's primary health insurer. More than 100 million people—one in three—in the United States has government coverage.

Why Has Medicaid Spending Exploded? The Medicaid program has expanded over time by making more individuals and families eligible for the health insurance. Children of families making up to $46,100 per year are eligible for CHIPs, the health insurance program for children. As the population ages, more senior citizens are being served in nursing homes and assisted living facilities. Almost 10 million senior citizens who have limited means are now Medicaid patients. Medicaid will continue to expand over the next few years as the provisions of the Affordable Care Act take effect. For the states that have chosen to be in the federal program, eligibility for Medicaid now extends to households making 133 percent of the poverty level. The Supreme Court ruling made participation in that part of the Affordable Care Act voluntary, so not all states have this new eligibility level.

Medicaid and the States   On average, the federal government pays almost 60 percent of Medicaid's cost; the states pay the rest. Certain states, particularly in the South, receive even higher reimbursements. For those states that have accepted the new eligibility level under the Affordable Care Act, the expanded enrollment will be reimbursed by the federal government completely for a few years, with a reduction in the federal share to 90 percent by 2020. States that have accepted the new plan are satisfied that the federal reimbursement will help their bottom line. In general, the states have been financially stressed by the increase in Medicaid expenditures over the last two decades. Many states have changed their eligibility rules and their reimbursements to health providers to try to balance their budgets. The federal government, in paying 100 percent of the bill for the new enrollees, is trying to help the states with their Medicaid budget issues.

Image 15-1
A doctor uses his tablet to show test results to the patient. The bedside use of technology is paired with electronic records that can be accessed by the patient's doctors and by the patient herself.

The Uninsured

One of the driving forces for the passage of the Affordable Care Act was the fact that more than 49 million Americans—about 18.5 percent of the population—have not had health insurance. Because about half of all working Americans have health insurance through their employers, the recession of 2008 and the loss of jobs added about 4 million Americans to the ranks of the uninsured. The primary goal of the Affordable Care Act is to make health insurance available through the federal or state exchanges to this population through a combination of incentives (subsidies) and penalties: if a person does not have health insurance, he or she will have part of his or her income tax refund withheld as a penalty. There are, however, a number of ways that an individual or family can request an exemption from the penalty.

Being uninsured has negative health consequences. People without coverage are less likely to get basic preventive care, such as mammograms; less likely to have a personal physician; and more likely to rate their own health as only poor or fair.

A further problem faced by the uninsured is that when they do seek medical care, they must usually pay much higher fees than would be paid on their behalf if they had insurance coverage. Large third-party insurers, private or public, normally strike hard bargains with hospitals and physicians over how much they will pay for procedures and services. The uninsured have less bargaining power. As a result, hospitals attempt to recover from the uninsured the revenues they lost in paying third-party insurers.

In any given year, most people do not require expensive health care. Young, healthy people in particular can be tempted to do without insurance. One benefit of insurance coverage, however, is that it protects the insured against catastrophic costs resulting from unusual events. Medical care for life-threatening accidents or diseases can run into thousands or even hundreds of thousands of dollars. An uninsured person who requires this kind of medical care may be forced into bankruptcy.

The 2010 Health-Care Reform Legislation

On March 23, 2010, after a long and intense battle in Congress, President Obama signed the Patient Protection and Affordable Care Act, the biggest reform of the American health-care and health insurance system since the approval of Medicare in 1965. The new legislation relies on a combination of private insurance, public programs such as Medicare and Medicaid, and new state-based nonprofit health exchanges to provide health insurance coverage to almost all Americans.[2] By 2017, the number of uninsured nonelderly people in the United States dropped from nearly 43 million to 28 million, or about 10.3 percent. The Kaiser Family Foundation reported that about half of the uninsured said the cost was too high.[3] According to their data, the greatest gain in the insured population was among poor and low-income households. Hispanic and African American households were more likely to gain insurance than white households. Most of these gains were due to the increased enrollment of individuals and families in the Medicaid program under the higher income levels. Clearly, the ACA has benefited the less advantaged members of the community. The Trump administration sought repeal of the ACA but Congress did not accomplish this.

The American health-care program as it passed the Congress is not like the types of programs adopted in many European countries or in Canada. Western Europe, Japan, Canada, and Australia all provide systems of universal coverage through **national health insurance**. The government takes over the economic function of providing basic health-care coverage. Private insurers are excluded from this market. The government collects premiums from employers and employees on the basis of their ability to pay and then pays physicians and hospitals for basic services to the entire population. Because the government provides all basic insurance coverage, national health insurance systems are often called **single-payer plans** or *socialized medicine.* Only health insurance is socialized. The government does not employ most physicians, and in many countries the hospitals are largely private as well.[4]

national health insurance
A plan under which the government provides basic health-care coverage to all citizens. Most such plans are funded by taxes on wages or salaries.

single-payer plans
A plan under which one entity has a monopoly on issuing a particular type of insurance. Typically, the entity is the government, and the insurance is basic health coverage.

Environmental Policy

■ **15.3** Describe the environmental policies of the United States and the role of the Environmental Protection Agency in implementing these policies.

Sixty years ago, Rachel Carson published *Silent Spring*, the book that can be credited with starting the contemporary environmental movement in the United States.[5] Carson's book called attention to the consequences of widespread use of pesticides and other chemicals that are dispersed into the waterways and have deadly effects on fish and wildlife. Eight years later, the first Earth Day was celebrated. Later that same year, President Nixon proposed and the Congress approved the creation of the Environmental Protection Agency (EPA), an independent executive agency charged with protecting the environment and human health. Since that time, Americans have paid

---

2   There are many good summaries of the new legislation. Among these is one provided by the Georgetown University Health Institute, http://ccf.georgetown.edu; and the Kaiser Family Foundation, http://kff.org

3   Kaiser Commission on Medicaid and the Uninsured, "Key Facts about the Uninsured Population," Kaiser Family Foundation, November, 2017.

4   Britain is an exception. Under the British "National Health," most (but not all) physicians are employed by the government.

5   Rachel Carson, *Silent Spring* (Boston: Houghton Mifflin, 1962).

increasing attention to environmental issues, and the federal government has enacted a number of specific policies intended to improve our environment.

The Environmental Movement

Environmental issues are not limited to concerns about pollution and its health effects; they include the desire to save and protect natural resources. The environmental movement looks to the early part of the twentieth century for its beginnings, when President Theodore Roosevelt created five national parks and expanded federal protection to a vast area near Yellowstone National Park. The movement to protect the environment has been based on two major strands of thought since its beginnings in the early 1900s. One point of view calls for *conservation*—that is, a policy under which natural resources should be used, but not abused. America's national forests, which are the responsibility of the Department of Agriculture, are an example of conservation in that the forests can be timbered with appropriate permits, hunting and fishing are usually permitted, and, in the West, farmers may obtain licenses to use public lands for their cattle. A second view advocates *preservation*. Under this policy, natural preserves are established that are isolated from the effects of human activity. The national parks and national wilderness areas exemplify this view, with all human activity except hiking and climbing restricted.

In the 1960s, an environmentalist movement arose that was much more focused on pollution issues than the previous conservation movement. The publication of *Silent Spring*; a massive oil spill off the coast of Santa Barbara, California, in 1969; and, in the same year, the fire on the Cuyahoga River caused by flammable chemicals awakened a new movement to control air and water pollution. Established conservation groups like the Audubon Society and the Sierra Club were joined by new groups, including Greenpeace, Friends of the Earth, and the Wilderness Society, to pressure the government to take greater action against pollution and the destruction of our environment.

Photo courtesy of the Environmental Protection Agency

Image 15-2
The Cuyahoga River
in 1969—firefighters extinguish a fire that started on the river and spread to a wooden trestle bridge.

The environmentalist movement focused public attention on the damage that an industrialized society can bring to the environment. In general, people are very supportive of efforts to improve the environment: a Gallup Poll taken in 2018 reported that more than 70 percent of Americans supported higher emission standards for business and industry, 76 percent favored spending more government money on wind and solar power, and 73 percent supported strongly enforcing federal environmental regulations.[6] However, when asked whether they would prioritize environmental protection over economic growth, 57 percent agreed, continuing a trend that began with the recession of 2008. From 1985 until 2009, a majority of Americans prioritized environmental protection over economic growth.[7]

Cleaning Up the Air and Water

The government has been responding to pollution problems since before the American Revolution, when the Massachusetts Bay Colony issued regulations to try to stop the pollution of Boston Harbor. In the 1800s, states passed laws controlling water pollution after scientists and medical researchers convinced most policymakers that dumping sewage into drinking and bathing water caused disease. At the national level, the Federal Water Pollution Control Act of 1948 provided research and assistance to the states for pollution-control efforts, but little was done.

The National Environmental Policy Act The year 1969 marked the start of the most concerted national government involvement in solving pollution problems. The Santa Barbara oil spill occurred that year, resulting in an oil slick covering 800 square miles and killing plant life, birds, and fish. Congress soon passed the National Environmental Policy Act of 1969, which established, among other things, the Council on Environmental Quality. It also mandated that an **environmental impact statement (EIS)** be prepared for all major federal actions that could significantly affect the quality of the environment. The act gave citizens and public-interest groups who were concerned with the environment a weapon against the unnecessary and inappropriate use of natural resources by the government.

environmental impact statement (EIS)
A report that must show the costs and benefits of major federal actions that could significantly affect the quality of the environment.

Curbing Air Pollution Beginning in 1975, the government began regulating tailpipe emissions from cars and light trucks in an attempt to curb air pollution. After years of lobbying by environmentalists, Congress passed the Clean Air Act of 1990. The act established tighter standards for emissions of nitrogen dioxide (NO_2) and other pollutants by newly built cars and light trucks. California was allowed to establish its own stricter standards. By 1994, the maximum allowable NO_2 emissions (averaged over each manufacturer's "fleet" of vehicles) were about one-fifth of the 1975 standard. The "Tier 2" system, phased in between 2004 and 2007, reduced maximum fleet emissions by cars and light trucks to just over 2 percent of the 1975 standard. In 2008–2009, the standards were extended to trucks weighing between 6,000 and 8,500 pounds.

The Obama administration moved swiftly to strengthen fuel efficiency standards for vehicles and to clean up the air pollution caused by cars and trucks. In 2011, the administration issued rules that would improve the fleet

6   Frank Newport, "Americans Want Government to Do More on Environment," March 29, 2018. http://news.gallup.poll/232007/.
7   Dennis Jacobe, "Americans Still Prioritize Economic Growth over Environment," The Gallup Poll, March 29, 2012.

efficiency for medium and heavy duty trucks between 9 and 23 percent. In 2014, the president announced more stringent requirements for heavy trucks and buses. Although the standards will cost the industry about $8 billion for new equipment, it is estimated that the increased fuel efficiency will save the trucking industry up to $50 billion in fuel expenses in the long run.[8] President Obama also directed the EPA to increase its efforts to clean up air pollution by reducing sulfur in gasoline and tightening emission standards for cars.[9] In 2017, President Trump ordered a review of these standards to determine whether a rollback would be ordered.

The United States is making fairly substantial strides in the war on toxic emissions. According to the EPA, in the last 30 years U.S. air pollution has been cut in half. Airborne lead is 3 percent of what it was in 1975, and the lead content of the average American's blood is one-fifth of what it was in that year. Airborne sulfur dioxide concentrations are one-fifth of the levels found in the 1960s. Carbon monoxide concentrations are one-quarter of what they were in 1970. The American public is increasingly aware of the need for environmental protection. To a large extent, this increased awareness has resulted from the efforts of various environmental interest groups, which have also exerted pressure on Congress to take action.

Water Pollution The Clean Water Act of 1972 amended the Federal Water Pollution Control Act of 1948. The Clean Water Act established the following goals: (1) make waters safe for swimming, (2) protect fish and wildlife, and (3) eliminate the discharge of pollutants into the water. The act set specific time schedules, which were subsequently extended by further legislation. Under these schedules, the EPA establishes limits on discharges of types of pollutants based on the technology available for controlling them. The act also required municipal and industrial polluters to apply for permits before discharging wastes into navigable waters. Furthermore, the Clean Water Act also prohibited the filling or dredging of wetlands without a permit from the Army Corps of Engineers.

Perhaps one of the most controversial regulations concerning wetlands was the "migratory-bird rule" issued by the Army Corps of Engineers. Under this rule, any bodies of water that could affect interstate commerce, including seasonal ponds or waters "used or suitable for use by migratory birds" that fly over state borders, were "navigable waters" subject to federal regulation under the Clean Water Act as wetlands. In 2001, after years of controversy, the U.S. Supreme Court struck down the rule. The Court stated that it was not prepared to hold that isolated and seasonal ponds, puddles, and "prairie potholes" become "navigable waters of the United States" simply because they serve as a habitat for migratory birds.[10]

The Endangered Species Act

Inspired by the plight of disappearing species, Congress passed the Endangered Species Preservation Act in 1966. In 1973, Congress passed a completely new Endangered Species Act (ESA), which made it illegal to kill,

did you know?
The federal government owns more than 650 million acres of land, or roughly 30 percent of the United States.

---

8 Juliet Eilperin, "Obama to Tighten Fuel Efficiency Standards for Big Trucks," *The Washington Post*, February 18, 2014.
9 Dina Cappiello, "Obama, EPA to Unveil Proposal to Clean Up Emissions," *U.S. News*, March 28, 2013, www.nbcnews.com /news/us-news
10 *Solid Waste Agency of Northern Cook County v. U.S. Army Corps of Engineers*, 531 U.S. 159 (2001).

harm, or otherwise "take" a species listed as endangered or threatened. The government could purchase habitat critical to the survival of a species or prevent landowners from engaging in development that would harm a listed species.

The ESA proved to be a powerful legal tool for the ecology movement. In a famous example, environmental groups sued to stop the Tennessee Valley Authority from completing the Tellico Dam on the grounds that it threatened habitat critical to the survival of the snail darter, a tiny fish. In 1978, the U.S. Supreme Court ruled in favor of the endangered fish.[11] Further controversy erupted in 1990, when the Fish and Wildlife Service listed the spotted owl as a threatened species. The logging industry blamed the ESA for a precipitous decline in national forest timber sales in subsequent years. Recently, the Fish and Wildlife Service proposed removing the protected status of wolves in some western states. Whereas cattlemen and hunters praised the idea of shooting wolves that preyed on cattle and sheep, environmental groups claimed that the wolf population was not yet strong enough to allow hunting.

The ESA continues to be a major subject of debate. However, signs indicate that the government and environmentalists may be seeking common ground. Both sides are shifting toward incentives for landowners who participate in protection programs. "Regulatory incentives really do result in landowners doing good things for their land," said William Irvin of the World Wildlife Fund.[12]

Sustainability

Before the mid-1980s, environmental politics seemed to be couched in terms of "them against us." "Them" was everyone involved in businesses that cut down rainforests, poisoned rivers, and created oil spills. "Us" was the government, and it was the government's job to stop "them." Today, most Americans support legislation to cut down on pollution, to save green areas, and to encourage the recycling of waste. Around the globe, individuals, governments, and businesses have come to believe that the earth's resources are limited and that the survival of the planet depends on moving toward a sustainable society.

Sustainability means achieving a balance between economic and social activities and nature that will permit the healthy existence of both. In terms of public policy, it means that societies act in such a way as to maintain healthy supplies of air, water, and the natural resources that make modern life possible. The United States adopted a policy of sustainability in 2007, with an executive order requiring all federal agencies to "conduct their environmental, transportation, and energy-related activities . . . in an environmentally sound, economically and fiscally sound, integrated, continuously improving, efficient, and sustainable manner."[13]

At the federal government level, this order directed agencies to buy efficient vehicles, recycle products, and enforce legislation aimed at increasing

sustainability
Achieving a balance between society and nature that will permit both to exist in harmony.

---

11 *Tennessee Valley Authority v. Hill*, 437 U.S. 153 (1978). In 1979, Congress exempted the snail darter from the ESA. In 1980, snail darters were discovered elsewhere, and the species turned out not to be endangered.

12 "Endangered Species Act Turns 30 as Environmental Strategy Shifts," *The Charleston Post and Courier*, Charleston, SC, January 2, 2004.

13 "Sustainability," Environmental Protection Agency statement, www.epa.gov/sustainability/

Election 2016
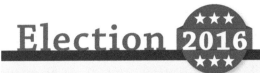

Do Elections Really Mean Policy Changes?

As soon as the president of the United States is inaugurated, he or she can begin issuing executive orders and asking the new cabinet secretaries and directors to enforce or rescind the regulations posted by the prior administration. In the case of the 2016 election, most of these changes will be directed at domestic policies, and there could be large policy swings ahead.

The contrasts between the Republican and Democratic presidential nominees on many important domestic policies were quite striking. Let's take health care, for example. The Democratic nominee for president, Hillary Rodham Clinton, supported the Affordable Care Act as passed in the first two years of the Obama administration. It is likely that she would have continued its implementation with some changes for improvements. She was challenged in the political campaign by Senator Bernie Sanders, who proposed substituting a national health-care plan like those offered by most European nations. Such a plan would cover all Americans. In contrast the Republican nominee, Donald Trump, who campaigned on a platform of "scrapping" Obamacare and substituting individual choice of policies, health savings accounts, and other free-market mechanisms. The difficulty in forecasting exactly how a new president would affect health policies is that the Affordable Care Act is so complex and the financial mechanisms are so deeply embedded in the tax code that changing to a new system is very difficult.

There were similar differences between the Democratic nominee and the Republican nominee in 2016 on environmental policies, tax reform, economic policies, and energy policies. It is important to remember, though, that large changes in policies will require legislation from the Congress which must be negotiated through both houses. Interest groups will lobby intensely against large changes simply because they want to protect the status quo, including benefits and loopholes previously incorporated in laws or regulations. Even with a Republican Congress, President Trump was unable to repeal the ACA. He did roll back regulations in other areas by executive order.

For Critical Analysis

1. Does a "landslide" presidential election automatically give the new president the power to insist on changes in domestic policies?

2. Will the 2020 presidential campaign find the same differences between the Republican and Democratic nominees?

sustainability. The order was reinforced by another in 2009 issued by President Obama to increase efforts to reduce greenhouse emissions. At the state and local level, sustainability means increased recycling efforts, legislation that has banned the use of nonrecyclable plastic bags, efforts to increase composting, and reduction of waste for landfills. Both in Europe and the United States, corporations have responded to the call for a more sustainable society by developing more compostable or degradable products. As shown in the screen capture, the Environmental Defense Fund uses the internet to advertise its platform and gain supporters.

From the Web ▶ The Environmental Defense Fund uses its website to increase public support for its legal actions to protect the environment.

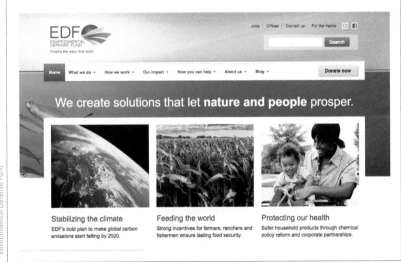

Environmental Defense Fund

Global Climate Change

A major source of concern has been the emission of pollutants into the air and water. Each year, the world atmosphere receives 20 million metric tons of sulfur dioxide, 18 million metric tons of ozone pollutants, and 60 million metric tons of carbon monoxide. A majority of climate scientists believe that these pollutants are the cause of global climate change, and a warming climate will represent a major threat to human survival on the planet. International efforts to limit the output of pollutants, especially carbon dioxide from vehicles and power plants, have been controversial but are widely supported by citizens throughout the world.

The Kyoto Protocol In 1997, delegates from around the world gathered in Kyoto, Japan, for a global climate conference sponsored by the United Nations. The conference issued a proposed treaty aimed at reducing emissions of greenhouse gases to 5.2 percent (below 1990 levels) by 2012. Only 38 developed nations were mandated to reduce their emissions, however—developing nations including China and India faced only voluntary limits. The U.S. Senate voted unanimously in 1997 that it would not accept a treaty that exempted developing countries, and in 2001 President Bush announced that he would not submit the Kyoto protocol to the Senate for ratification. By 2007, 124 nations had ratified the protocol. Its rejection by the United States, however, raised the question of whether it could ever be effective.

Even in those European countries that most enthusiastically supported the Kyoto protocol and signed it, the results have not been overly positive. By 2008, it became clear that 13 of the 15 original European Union signatories would miss their 2010 emission targets. At the same time, two nations that are considered to be "developing nations," China and India, have seen their emissions increase dramatically, but they were not required to abide by the protocol. In May 2011, the potential impact of the Kyoto agreement was severely diminished when Canada, Russia, and France announced that they were withdrawing from the agreement.

COP21: The New Agreement After years of discussion and attempts to forge a replacement agreement for the Kyoto document, representatives of 195 nations agreed to a new regime for addressing climate change. The historic agreement was named COP21 referring to the twenty-first meeting of the Conference of Parties (COP). Rich and poor nations agreed on the overall framework of the plan, including the goal of limiting the increase in global temperatures to less than 2 degrees Celsius.[14] All of the nations who signed the accord committed to public pledges of reducing their carbon emissions and providing data on their progress. Each nation's pledge will be reviewed every five years. Richer nations have committed to providing up to $100 billion per year to poorer nations to help them in this effort, although that pledge is non-binding.[15] Although many of the nations' pledges are subject to their own local issues, the 2015 agreement marked the first time all of the parties agreed that global warming is a serious threat.

---

14 Lynne Peeples, "Historic Climate Change Agreement Adopted in Paris," *Huffington Post*, December 12, 2015. http://www
   .huffingtonpost.com/entry/climate-change-paris_us_566c2048e4b0e292150e169b
15 Jeff Tollefson and Kenneth R. Weiss, "Nations Approve Historic Global Climate Accord," *Nature*, December 12, 2015. http://
   www.nature.com/news/nations-approve-historic-global-climate-accord-1.19021

How Green Is Europe?

The European Community has shown a remarkable ability to agree on energy conservation and environmental goals and to make considerable progress toward attaining these goals. Following the publication of the European Commission's report on sustainable energy in 2006, the European Parliament began considering the situation and acting upon it in 2007. This confederation of nations agreed to cut greenhouse gases by 20 percent by 2020 and to work for a new treaty to follow the Kyoto accords that would further decrease such emissions by 2030. In addition, the European Community has taken a number of steps to help its citizens make "green decisions" to conserve energy in the home and on the road.

Almost every type of appliance sold in Europe is tagged with an Energy Efficiency Rating, which grades the appliance on a scale of A to G on energy efficiency and carbon dioxide impact. The nations agreed that all new buildings and those undergoing substantial remodeling should be more energy efficient and install the most energy-efficient heating and air-conditioning systems available. In future years, Europeans will be able to buy cars and trucks that are increasingly efficient and better for the environment as well. The agreement among the nations sets carbon dioxide emissions standards for all new cars and requires manufacturers to further cut emissions by 1 percent per year, every year, until 2020.

Countries have differing standards, but all of the European Union members have agreed to try to reduce waste and increase recycling. If you live in Germany, for example, your neighbors have strong expectations that you will reuse, recycle, and sort your garbage. Virtually every German neighborhood or apartment building has five different bins outside, all color-coded to help you dispose of your waste properly. You will use the yellow bin for any kind of food packaging, the blue bin for paper and cardboard, the "bio" bin for leftover food waste, and separate bins for clear, brown, and green glass. A black bin is also available for those who are too lazy to separate or have something that does not fit. Switzerland and Denmark also have extremely high rates of recycling waste products from households. In some nations, there are complaints that the government does not provide enough bins for trash or does not pick up the materials properly, whereas in other nations, citizens are fined for not separating their trash.

Image 15-3 These recycling bins in Wales, United Kingdom, are typical of those found in many European countries. Citizens are asked, at a minimum, to sort their waste into paper, plastic, glass, and compostable food items.

Not only do the European nations pride themselves on their "green" habits, but the European Commission makes public everyone's results on the various measures it has adopted. If you go to the website for Europe's Energy Portal (www.energy.eu/), you will find scorecards for gas and oil prices, energy dependency, CO_2 emissions, and renewable energy production for each nation. Imagine a report card on the American states that would give the same kind of measures!

For Critical Analysis

1. Why do you think the European nations have been able to agree on such progressive measures in energy efficiency and environmental protections?

2. Do you think government regulations and fines are the best way to gain citizen compliance with energy and environmental goals?

The Global Warming Debate   Although the majority of scientists who perform research on the world's climate believe that global warming will be significant, there is considerable disagreement as to how much warming will actually occur. It is generally accepted that world temperatures have already increased by at least 0.6 degrees Celsius over the last century. The 2014 report by the United Nations Intergovernmental Panel on Climate Change continued to predict increases ranging from 2.0 to 4.5 degrees Celsius by the year 2100. The latest Intergovernmental Panel on Climate Change (IPCC) raised the risk level for global warming and linked weather-related disasters to climate change, but other scientists are more cautious about the link between climate change and any increase in strong storms, flooding, or tsunamis because comparative historical data is only a few hundred years old.[16]

Global warming has become a major political football to be kicked back and forth by conservatives and liberals. Some conservatives have seized on the work of scientists who believe that global warming does not exist at all. (Some of these researchers work for oil companies.) If this were true, there would be no reason to limit emissions of carbon dioxide and other greenhouse gases. A more sophisticated argument by conservatives is that major steps to limit emissions in the near future would not be cost effective. Bjørn Lomborg, a critic of climate change, believes that the world is spending too much of its resources on combating climate change when there are other much more pressing global problems to solve, including poverty, the spread of disease, and malnutrition.[17]

Energy Policy

■ **15.4** Analyze American energy policy and discuss how it encourages energy independence.

The United States has always had enormous energy resources, whether from coal, oil, natural gas, or alternative sources such as wind or solar power. However, for most of the last 150 years, the American economy has been primarily dependent on fossil fuels, namely oil, coal, and natural gas. It is important to think beyond our cars and our appliance-filled homes. Energy is necessary to power all factories in the United States and to keep all forms of transportation moving. In some cases, fossil fuel is the raw material for objects in our daily lives. Plastics, polystyrene, the case for your iPad—all are made from petroleum products. Although support for alternative sources of energy is very strong across the nation, becoming less dependent on fossil fuel products will require a long-term strategy. If you look at Figure 15-4, you can see the percentage of energy used by the various sectors of the American economy.

energy policy
Laws concerned with how much energy is needed and used.

Energy policy—laws concerned with how much energy is needed and used—and the regulation of energy producers tend to become important only during a crisis. In 1973, the Organization of Petroleum Exporting Countries (OPEC), the cartel of oil-producing nations, instituted an embargo

---

16 Seth Bornstein, "U.N. Scientific Panel Releases Report Sounding Alarm on Climate Change Dangers," *Huffington Post*, March 30, 2014, www.huffingtonpost.com/green/ or, for a different view, Bjorn Lomborg, "Climate Change Misdirection," *The Wall Street Journal*, January 23, 2013. http://www.onlinewsj.com/news/articles

17 See Bjorn Lomborg, *How to Spend $75 Billion to Make the World a Better Place* (Copenhagen, Denmark: Copenhagen Consensus Center, 2014).

Image 15-4
In 2013, a chemical plant in West Virginia along the Kanawha River spilled millions of gallons of waste into the river, forcing hundreds of thousands of residents to find other sources of water for their families.

on shipments of petroleum to the United States because of our support of Israel in the Arab–Israeli conflict of that year. President Nixon declared that the United States would achieve energy independence by reducing speed limits and meeting Corporate Average Fuel Economy (CAFE) standards by a certain time.

In 1977, President Carter also found himself facing shortages of oil and natural gas. The Department of Energy was created, and numerous programs were instituted to assist citizens in buying more energy-efficient appliances and improving the energy profile of their homes. In addition, legislation created the National Petroleum Reserve, and incentives for

Figure 15-4 ▶ U.S. Energy Consumption by Economic Sector, 2017

Transportation 28%

22% Residential

Industrial 32%

18% Commercial

Source: "Energy Consumption Estimates by Sector," U.S. Energy Information Administration, Monthly Energy Review. http://www.eia.gov/consumption/

researching alternative forms of energy were instituted. Over time, Americans sought to replace their smaller, more efficient cars with sport utility vehicles (SUVs) and light trucks. Airline traffic grew. Suburbs were built farther from cities and jobs. America's dependence on foreign oil has grown, as has the nation's overall appetite for energy.

In 2017, the United States consumed about 20 million barrels of petroleum per day, with half of this used as gasoline for transportation. Of those 20 million barrels per day, only 16 percent was imported, an historic low. As has been the case for many decades, the United States is the third largest producer of oil but the largest consumer among the major producers. In fact, the United States has increased domestic production by about 1 million barrels a day over the last three years as prices increased around the world. From the 1970s until about 2003, the price of crude oil averaged less than $40 per barrel. In the last 10 years, the price of crude oil per barrel has reached more than $100 per barrel as demand for the product around the world has grown. When the price of crude rises, it becomes economically feasible for less productive wells in the United States to begin pumping oil again; individual consumers look for ways to cut their use of gasoline and drive down demand for oil; and, most importantly, industries that use oil to produce energy or other products switch to less expensive fuels. Of course, a decrease in the price of oil has the opposite effect. When crude oil prices fell below $40 per barrel in 2015, domestic gasoline dropped to just over $2 and oil production dropped as well. If you look at Figure 15-5, you will see that 31 percent of the nation's energy came from natural gas in 2017. As natural gas has become more abundant due to fracking, the cost has fallen and a number of power-generating plants have switched from burning oil to burning natural gas to produce electricity.

Figure 15-5 ▶ Sources of Electricity Generation, 2017

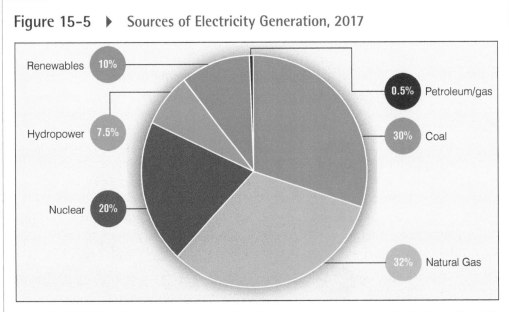

Source: "What Is U.S. Electricity Generation by Energy Source?," U.S. Energy Information Administration, 2016; http://www.eia.gov/tools/faqs/faq.cfm?id=427&t=3

Promised Land: The Politics of Energy

Promised Land, the 2012 film written by Matt Damon and John Krasinski, tells the story of two corporate salespeople who visit a rural Pennsylvania town in an attempt to buy drilling rights from the local residents. Damon stars as one of those salespeople sent by his employer, Global Crosspower Solutions, to quickly and cheaply persuade landowners to sell mineral rights leases that grant drilling rights to his employer. Krasinski stars as an environmental advocate who starts a campaign against the company.

The film was criticized by the energy industry for its portrayal of hydraulic fracking, claiming that it oversimplifies the issue, but it succeeded in starting a conversation about a very real issue. Hydraulic fracking makes it possible to tap into natural gas reservoirs, but only once gas companies have convinced landowners to allow them to drill.

Political films such as *Promised Land* face a difficult road to success. Although *Syriana*, which was produced by and starred George Clooney, received a strong critical response, it also did not gain a huge audience, likely due to its complex exploration of petroleum politics and the global influence of the oil industry. *Promised Land* drew mixed critical reviews, perhaps because it was not a strong enough critique of the energy industry. The movie provides an accurate portrayal of the political process that is occurring across the United States as communities make decisions about natural resource extraction while they are under pressure from economic and environmental groups.

Recently, more issues involving fracking have come to light. The state of Oklahoma, which has welcomed the industry and benefited from energy extraction, has experienced a series of small earthquakes. Scientists are trying to discover whether the deep drilling and injection of salt water into the wells is destabilizing the earth or whether the earthquakes would have occurred without any fracking. The possibility that drilling techniques cause earthquakes could make "selling" energy extraction to communities much more difficult.

For Critical Analysis

1. How can a town judge the trade-off between energy extraction such as fracking and protecting its environment?

2. To what extent is the local debate over fracking, wind farms, or the installation of a field of solar panels made more difficult because the United States has no comprehensive energy policy?

Energy and the Environment

Because of the effects of producing energy and burning fuels, energy policy is deeply entangled with environmental policy.[18] Using gasoline to power a car is the normal practice. However, burning gasoline produces serious emissions that contribute to the buildup of smog in the atmosphere. Through a series of laws passed over the last 20 years, the EPA has forced cities to implement procedures to reduce smog and to require cleaner-burning gasoline. In addition, Congress has mandated that 10 percent of fuels sold in the years to come include ethanol as an ingredient. In response, the production of corn, which is used to make ethanol, has shot up, but still not enough is being grown to overcome the accompanying rise in price.

did you know?
Americans consume 26 percent of the world's energy.

18 For a comprehensive look at all energy resources in the United States, go to the website of the Department of Energy: www.energy.gov/energysources

Philip Scalia/Alamy Stock photo

Image 15–5

In the last ten years, production of natural gas has increased dramatically due to the use of "fracking" to release gas from layers of shale deep beneath the earth's surface. This hydro-fracking well is being drilled in Pennsylvania.

The United States continues to pump oil from existing wells and offshore platforms. However, more areas exist where oil could be found and extracted, but in most cases, environmental risks would be incurred. Following the oil spill in Santa Barbara, California, from an offshore drilling rig, most Americans welcomed laws that forbade drilling in new areas off Florida, Louisiana, Texas, and California. In addition, large areas of the Arctic National Wilderness Reserve (ANWR) have been protected from oil exploration. In 2010, the clash between environmental protection and the need for energy sources came to a head in the Gulf of Mexico at a drilling rig named the Deepwater Horizon. The rig, leased by British Petroleum, was drilling for oil more than a mile deep in the ocean when a "blowout" of oil and gas occurred. The blowout preventer—a multimillion-dollar, five-story apparatus on the sea floor—failed, and the rig exploded. In the weeks and months that followed, millions of gallons of oil and gas spewed from the well as attempts to cap it met limited success. President Obama convinced BP to set aside $20 billion in a fund to compensate Gulf residents for losses in wages and business revenues.

Another dilemma facing the United States involves domestic power production and the need for cleaner air. The majority of electric power generated in the United States comes from coal-fired plants in the Midwest and central regions of the nation. For many years, these plants spewed carbon emissions into the air. As scientists became aware of the impact of these emissions on the environment, new laws required the plants to reduce their emissions by installing scrubbers or, after reaching the legal "cap" on their carbon emissions, buying or trading for the right to produce more. The EPA under the Bush administration issued regulations for coal-burning plants that reduced their burden of meeting the standards. States that felt they received the most damage from some of these emissions sued to make the EPA issue standards that meet the letter of the Clean Air Act. The Supreme Court agreed with these states, and the EPA began to prepare stricter standards. The Obama administration issued draft regulations for existing power plants in 2012. After receiving more than 2 million comments from the industry and the public, the administration announced a revised set of regulations in 2013. The proposed regulations required new gas or coal-fired power plants to meet much higher standards for carbon emissions. Following his campaign promise to aid the coal industry, President Trump ordered the repeal of Obama's Clean Power Act, eliminating many of the new controls on coal-fired power plants.[19]

Nuclear Power—An Unpopular Solution

One strategy for reducing carbon emissions of coal-fired plants and also the environmental and human risks of coal mining is to increase the number of

---

19 Associated Press, "Trump EPA Plan will roll back Obama standards on power plant emissions," *The Guardian*, October 7, 2017.

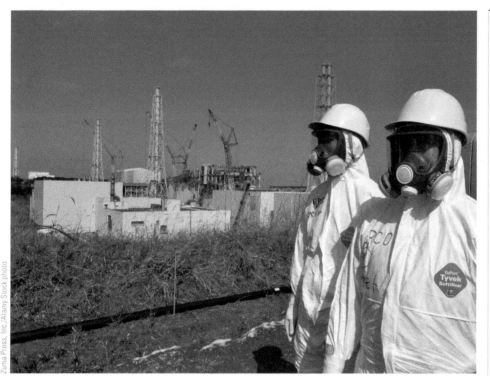

Zuma Press, Inc./Alamy Stock photo

Image 15-6
Japanese journalists inspect the remains of the Fukushima Daiichi nuclear power plant, which was destroyed by the 2011 tsunami. The release of radiation from the plant after its destruction has forced Japan to reconsider its dependency on nuclear energy.

nuclear power plants in the United States. Nuclear power plants are very efficient and emit very low levels of greenhouse gases. The accident at the Three Mile Island plant in Pennsylvania in 1979, followed by the disaster at the Chernobyl, Ukraine, plant in 1986, undermined public confidence in nuclear energy.

The United States for many decades was alone among industrialized nations in its fear of nuclear power, but given the concern about carbon emissions from the coal-fired plants, the United States began to license the construction of new nuclear plants in the early 2000s. However, after a tsunami destroyed a huge coastal area of Japan in 2011 and caused the meltdown of a nuclear plant, the Japanese have begun to have serious concerns about their dependence on nuclear power. Even in Europe and the former Soviet Union, where hundreds of nuclear plants have operated safely for decades, the radiation release from the Japanese plant has renewed the demand to reduce the number of nuclear plants in operation.

Alternative Approaches to the Energy Crisis

Several alternative sources of energy can be used to reduce the nation's dependence on fossil fuels. Huge wind farms in California generate energy for cities there. Research continues on harnessing the power of the ocean waves to produce electricity and the most efficient ways to use geothermal energy from below the surface of the earth.[20] The technology does not yet exist to use any of these sources to produce the quantity of energy needed to replace our coal plants or other current energy sources. And, in some areas, citizens consider wind farms extremely disturbing to the environment and area wildlife.

---

20 For a discussion of these new technologies, see Jay Inslee and Bracken Henricks, *Apollo's Fire* (Washington, DC: Island Press, 2007).

The rising price of gasoline spurred a much greater demand for hybrid automobiles and for smaller, more fuel-efficient cars. In addition, people began to ride motor scooters and bicycles for city commutes and increased their use of mass transit. The Obama administration has sought comprehensive energy legislation from the Congress since the president's inauguration. Members of the administration and of Congress realize that both energy needs and environmental concerns must be addressed in the same legislation. Proponents of a "cap and trade" system want industries to account for their carbon emissions through a market system, as in Europe. The opponents of such a system believe that it will drive up energy costs because costs will be passed down to the ultimate consumer. Energy legislation stalled in the Congress in 2010 and no new plan has been passed.

Poverty and Welfare

■ **15.5** Describe the national policies for ending poverty in the United States and alleviating the issues caused by economic downturns.

Throughout the world, poverty has historically been accepted as inevitable. The United States and other industrialized nations, however, have sustained enough economic growth in the past several hundred years to eliminate mass poverty. Considering the wealth and high standard of living in the United States, the persistence of poverty here appears bizarre and anomalous.

A traditional solution to poverty has been **income transfers**. These are methods of transferring income from relatively upper-income to relatively poor groups in society, and as a nation, we have been using such transfers for a long time. Before we examine these efforts, let us look at the concept of poverty in more detail and at the characteristics of the poor.

income transfer
A transfer of income from some individuals in the economy to others, generally by government action.

The Low-Income Population

We can see in Figure 15-6 that the number of people classified as poor fell steadily from 1961 to 1968—that is, during the presidencies of John Kennedy

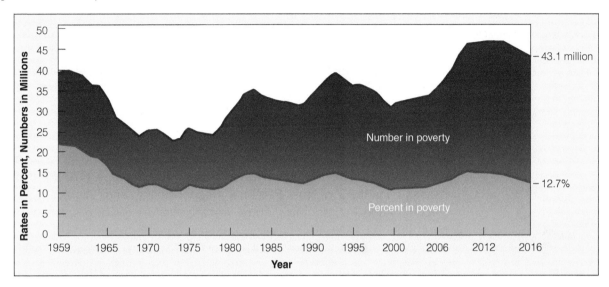

Figure 15-6 ▶ The Official Number of Poor in the United States

The number of individuals classified as poor fell steadily from 1961 through 1968. It then increased during the 1981–1982 recession. After 1994, the number fell steadily until 2000, when it started to rise again. The recession that began in 2008 spurred an increase to a 50-year high in the number of poor Americans.

Note: The data points represent the midpoints of the respective years.

Source: U.S. Census, "Poverty Status of People by Age, Race, and Hispanic Origin, 1959–2014," http://www.census.gov/hhes/www/poverty/data/historical/people.html; U.S. Census, "Income, Poverty and Health Insurance Coverage in the United States, 2014," September, 2017.

and Lyndon Johnson. The number remained level until the recession of 1981–1982, during Ronald Reagan's presidency, when it increased substantially. The number fell during the Internet boom of 1994–2000, but then it started to rise again. The percentage generally has been below 15 percent. In 2014, about 46.7 million Americans, or about 15 percent, were classified as poor. The economic downturn and increase in unemployment sent the rate to the highest it has been since 1997. Even though economists declared that the recession had ended and recovery was beginning, the number of poor increased by more than 6 million between 2009 and 2012. For many of these Americans, family savings were exhausted, unemployment benefits had expired, and the hope of a job was fading. Many Americans who turned 62 applied for early retirement and their reduced Social Security benefits, and others claimed permanent disability.

The threshold income level that is used to determine who falls into the poverty category was originally based on the cost of a nutritionally adequate food plan designed by the U.S. Department of Agriculture in 1963. The poverty level is adjusted each year for changes in the consumer price index. For 2018, for example, the official poverty level for a family of four was about $25,100.

The official poverty level is based on pretax income, including cash but not **in-kind subsidies**—food stamps, housing vouchers, and the like. If we correct poverty levels for such benefits, the percentage of the population that is below the poverty line drops dramatically.

in-kind subsidy
A good or service—such as food stamps, housing, or medical care—provided by the government to low-income groups.

The Antipoverty Budget

It is not always easy to determine how much the government spends to combat poverty. In part, this is because it can be difficult to decide whether a particular program is an antipoverty program. Are grants to foster parents an antipoverty measure? What about job-training programs? Are college scholarships for low-income students an antipoverty measure?

President Trump's 2018 budget allocated a little less than $1 trillion, or about one-third of all federal expenditures, to federal programs that support persons of limited income (scholarships included).[21] Of this amount, $403 billion was for Medicaid, which funds medical services for the poor, as discussed earlier. The states were expected to contribute an additional $150 billion to Medicaid. Medical care is by far the largest portion of the antipoverty budget. Other items include food stamps and housing programs.

Basic Welfare

The program that most people think of when they hear the word *welfare* is now called **Temporary Assistance to Needy Families (TANF)**. With the passage in 1996 of the Personal Responsibility and Work Opportunity Reconciliation Act, popularly known as the Welfare Reform Act, the government created TANF to replace an earlier program known as Aid to Families with Dependent Children (AFDC). The AFDC program provided "cash support for low-income families with dependent children who have been deprived of parental support due to death, disability, continued absence of a parent, or unemployment."

Under TANF, the U.S. government turned over to the states funds targeted for welfare assistance in the form of block grants. The states, not the national government, now bear the burden of any increased welfare spending. If a state wishes to increase the amount of TANF payments over what the national government supports, the state has to pay the additional costs.

One of the aims of the Welfare Reform Act was to reduce welfare spending by limiting most welfare recipients to only two years of assistance at a time and imposing a lifetime limit on welfare assistance of five years. The Welfare Reform Act has largely met its objectives. During the first five years after the act was passed, the number of families receiving welfare payments was cut in half. The 2018 federal budget allocated $15.1 billion to the TANF block grants.

Welfare Controversies

Whether known as AFDC or TANF, the basic welfare program has always been controversial. Conservative and libertarian voters often object to welfare spending as a matter of principle, believing that it reduces the incentive to find paid employment. Because AFDC and TANF have largely supported single-parent households, some also believe that such programs are antimarriage. Finally, certain people object to welfare spending out of a belief that welfare recipients are "not like us." The bulk of TANF recipients, however, are single mothers with children; thus, basic welfare payments in the United States are relatively low when compared with similar payments in other industrialized nations. In 2018, the average monthly TANF payment nationwide was about $700; however, some states have benefits as low as $300 for a family of three.

Temporary Assistance to Needy Families (TANF)
A state-administered program in which grants from the national government are used to provide welfare benefits. The TANF program replaced the Aid to Families with Dependent Children (AFDC) program.

did you know?

The Greenville County Department of Social Services in South Carolina wrote to a food stamp recipient, "Your food stamps will be stopped . . . because we received notice that you passed away. May God bless you. You may reapply if there is a change in your circumstances."

---

21 This sum does not include the earned income tax credit, which is not part of the federal budget.

Other Forms of Government Assistance

The **Supplemental Security Income (SSI)** program was established in 1974 to provide a nationwide minimum income for elderly persons and persons with disabilities who do not qualify for Social Security benefits. The 2018 budget allocated $52 billion to this program.

The government also issues **food stamps**, benefits that can be used to purchase food; they are usually provided electronically through a card similar to a debit card. Food stamps are available to low-income individuals and families. Recipients must prove that they qualify by showing that they have a low income (or no income at all). Food stamps go to a much larger group of people than do TANF payments, including the unemployed and single adults, groups that have expanded during the recession. The number of recipients of food stamps more than doubled since 2003, from 19 million to 45 million, or one out of seven Americans. The food stamp program has become a major part of the welfare system in the United States, although it was started in 1964 mainly to benefit farmers by distributing surplus food through retail channels.

The **earned income tax credit (EITC) program** was created in 1975 to help low-income workers by giving back part or all of their Social Security taxes. Currently, about 15 percent of all taxpayers claim an EITC, and an estimated $56 billion per year is rebated to taxpayers through the program.

Homelessness—Still a Problem

The plight of the homeless remains a problem. Some argue that the Welfare Reform Act of 1996 has increased the number of homeless persons. No hard statistics on the homeless are available, but estimates of the number of people without a home on any given night in the United States range from a low of 230,000 to as many as 750,000.

It is difficult to estimate how many people are homeless because the number depends on how the homeless are defined. There are *street people*—those who sleep in bus stations, parks, and other areas. Many of these people are youthful runaways. There are also the so-called *sheltered homeless*—those who sleep in government-supported or privately funded shelters. Many of these individuals used to live with their families or friends. Whereas street people are almost always single, the sheltered homeless include many families with children. Homeless families are the fastest-growing subgroup of the homeless population. The homeless problem pits liberals against conservatives. Conservatives argue that there are not really that many homeless people and that most of them are alcoholics, drug users, or the mentally ill. In contrast, many liberals argue that homelessness is caused by a reduction in welfare benefits and by expensive housing.

Some cities have "criminalized" homelessness. Many municipalities have outlawed sleeping on park benches and sidewalks, as well as panhandling and leaving personal property on public property. In some cities, police sweeps remove the homeless, who then become part of the criminal justice system. In general, northern cities have assumed a responsibility to shelter the homeless in bad weather. Cities in warmer climates are most concerned with a year-round homeless problem. No new national policies on the homeless have been initiated, in part because of disagreement about the causes of and solutions for the problem.

Supplemental Security Income (SSI)
A federal program established to provide assistance to elderly persons and persons with disabilities.

food stamps
Benefits issued by the federal government to low-income individuals to be used for the purchase of food; originally provided as coupons, but now typically provided electronically through a card similar to a debit card.

earned income tax credit (EITC) program
A government program that helps low-income workers by giving back part or all of their Social Security taxes.

Immigration

■ **15.6** Discuss the issues raised by immigration into the United States and the proposed reforms to the immigration system.

Time and again, this nation has been challenged and changed—and culturally enriched—by immigrant groups. Immigrants have faced the problems involved in living in a new and different political and cultural environment. Most of them have had to overcome language barriers, and many have had to deal with discrimination because of their skin color, their inability to speak English fluently, or their customs. The civil rights legislation passed during and since the 1960s has done much to counter the effects of prejudice against immigrant groups by ensuring that they obtain equal rights under the law.

One of the issues facing Americans and their political leaders today is the effect of immigration on American politics and government. Other issues are whether immigration is having a positive or negative impact on the United States and the form immigration reform should take.

The Continued Influx of Immigrants

Today, immigration rates are among the highest they have been since their peak in the early twentieth century. Every year, more than 1 million people immigrate to this country, and people who were born on foreign soil now constitute more than 10 percent of the U.S. population—twice the percentage of 30 years ago.

Minority Groups' Importance on the Rise Since 1977, four out of five immigrants have come from Latin America or Asia. Hispanics have overtaken African Americans as the nation's largest minority. If current immigration rates continue, by the year 2060, minority groups collectively will constitute the "majority" of Americans. If Hispanics, African Americans, and perhaps Asians were to form coalitions, they could increase their political power dramatically and would have the numerical strength to make significant changes. Many commentators predict that the longtime white majority will no longer dominate American politics.

The Advantages of High Rates of Immigration Some regard the high rate of immigration as a plus for America, because it offsets the low birthrate and aging population. Immigrants expand the workforce and help support through their taxes government programs that benefit older Americans, such as Medicare and Social Security. If it were not for immigration, contend these observers, the United States would be facing even more serious problems than it already does with funding these programs (see Chapter 16). In contrast, nations that do not have high immigration rates, such as Japan, are experiencing serious fiscal challenges due to their aging populations.

Attempts at Immigration Reform

A significant number of U.S. citizens, however, believe that immigration—both legal and illegal—negatively affects America. They argue, among other things, that the large number of immigrants seeking work results in lower wages for Americans, especially those with few skills. They also worry about the cost of providing immigrants with services such as schools and medical care.

Before the 2006 elections, members of Congress were in favor of enacting a sweeping immigration reform bill, but unsurprisingly, the two houses could not agree on what the bill should do. No law passed. Later in the year, however, Congress did pass legislation authorizing the construction of a 700-mile-long fence between the United States and Mexico. The fence is to be a real fence in some areas and a "virtual fence" using cameras and surveillance technologies in other areas. Although a combination of physical fence and "virtual" fence has been completed from San Diego, California, to Yuma, Arizona, President Obama ended any further construction, leaving about 1,450 miles of border without a fence or electronic monitoring.

By 2008, the debate seemed to have changed, with virtually all presidential candidates supporting legislation that would tighten the borders, force employers to check the papers of their workers, and eventually build a path to citizenship. As the recession deepened in 2008 and 2009, many undocumented workers left the United States to return to Central America, and the problem of a "flood" of undocumented workers seemed to dissipate. Comprehensive immigration reform, although supported by President Obama, was not a priority on his first-term agenda. However, a number of states began to pass laws to curtail the activities of undocumented workers. In 2010, Arizona passed a law requiring state and local police and law enforcement officers to check individuals' citizenship or residency papers if they had been stopped on suspicion of an offense. The law, which requires local officials to enforce federal law, sparked a national debate. President Obama ordered the Justice Department to investigate whether the Arizona law was constitutional, and demonstrations against the law took place in many cities. In July 2010, Federal District Court Judge Susan Bolton issued a preliminary injunction blocking the most controversial parts of the law while allowing others to take effect, including one that bans cities from refusing to cooperate with federal immigration officials. The case was appealed by the state of Arizona and reached the Supreme Court in 2011. In June 2012, the Supreme Court held that a number of the provisions of the law were

Jerry Lara/ZUMA Press/Newscom

Image 15–8
The U.S. Border Patrol picks up a group of undocumented immigrants, including adults and children, near McAllen, Texas.

unconstitutional, although the decision upheld the portion of the law allowing police officers who had stopped an individual on suspicion of a crime to ask for proof of citizenship or residency if they suspected the person was undocumented. The Obama administration announced that the federal offices in Arizona might not cooperate with police who made such arrests.

The Obama administration followed a two-pronged approach to dealing with undocumented workers. It stepped up raids on companies suspected of employing a number of such individuals and, if they were found, deported the workers. However, by 2011 the administration announced a policy that suspended deportations of individuals who had not committed crimes. In 2012, the president, by executive order, suspended for one year any deportation of a young adult who had been illegally brought to this country by parents before the child was 16 if that young person had finished high school or was in post-secondary school or the military or gainfully employed. He ordered federal agencies to issue work permits to such individuals if they were under 30 years old and had no serious criminal record.

In 2017, President Trump announced that he was ending this program, known as DACA, in six months. The Congress attempted to write legislation to reform immigration but failed within the six-month window. A federal judge overturned the president's rule and DACA appeared headed for a lengthy legal battle.

The Range of Federal Public Policies

The U.S. government implements policies that have been legislated by Congress across the entire spectrum of American life. Think about federal policies that affect colleges and universities: Title IX programs ensure that women have equal opportunities to play intercollegiate sports, and programs from the Department of Veterans Affairs provide tuition benefits for returning military veterans and for members of the reserves and the National Guard. Almost all aspects of the federal student loan program are regulated by the

Image 15-9
A Newtech Recycling
employee collects e-waste during Somerset County's recycle e-waste program at Newtech Recycling, Inc., in Somerset, New Jersey. The federal government regulates the rare minerals used in the manufacture of electronics such as these.

The Star-Ledger/Patti Sapone/The Image Works

federal government, from eligibility for a subsidized loan to the requirement that colleges keep accurate records of student attendance and dates of withdrawal from class.

The national government implements important policies to support the agricultural industry in this country, to keep the treatment of labor unions fair, to support school systems in their reform efforts, and to assist states to build and maintain highways and bridges. In these times of rising public deficits and seemingly expanding federal programs, a majority of Americans say that government spending and programs should be cut, but the only program a majority of Americans agree should be cut is foreign aid to other nations, one of the smallest government programs in existence.

Key Terms

domestic policy 524
earned income tax credit (EITC) program 549
energy policy 540
environmental impact statement (EIS) 534

food stamps 549
income transfer 546
in-kind subsidy 547
Medicaid 529
Medicare 529
national health insurance 532

single-payer plan 532
Supplemental Security Income (SSI) 549
sustainability 536
Temporary Assistance to Needy Families (TANF) 548

Chapter Summary

■ **15.1** Domestic policy consists of all of the laws, government planning, and government actions that affect the lives of American citizens. Policies are created in response to public problems or public demand for government action. Major policy problems discussed in this chapter relate to health care, poverty and welfare, immigration, the environment, and energy.

■ **15.2** The policymaking process is initiated when policymakers become aware—through the media or from their constituents—of a problem that needs to be addressed by the legislature and the president. The process of policymaking includes five steps: agenda building, policy formulation, policy adoption, policy implementation, and policy evaluation. As the proposed policy is formulated and debated during the adoption process, the views of the public, interest groups, and the government are heard.

■ **15.2** Health-care spending represents about 18 percent of the U.S. economy, and it is growing. Reasons for this growth include the increasing number of elderly persons, advancing technology, and higher demand because costs are picked up by third-party insurers. A major third party is Medicare, the federal program that pays health-care expenses of U.S. residents age 65 and older. The federal government has tried to restrain the growth in Medicare spending, but it has also expanded the program to cover prescription drugs.

■ **15.2** About 15 percent of the population does not have health insurance—a major political issue. Most uninsured adults work for employers that cannot afford to offer health benefits. Hospitals tend to charge the uninsured higher rates than they charge insurance companies or the government. The United States has chosen to adopt a plan that combines government-required health insurance, private and public insurers, and private provision of services. Most Americans prefer this approach because they wish to choose their own medical providers.

■ **15.3** Pollution problems continue to plague the United States and the world. Several significant federal acts have been passed in an attempt to curb the pollution of our environment. The National Environmental Policy Act of 1969 established the Council on Environmental Quality. That act also mandated that environmental impact statements be prepared for all legislation or major federal actions that might significantly affect the quality of the environment. The Clean Water Act of 1972 and the Clean Air Act amendments of 1990 constituted the most significant government attempts at cleaning up our environment.

■ **15.4** Energy policy in the United States has generally sought to stabilize the supply of cheap energy to meet the demands of Americans. When energy sources are threatened, new policies have been adopted, such as increasing efficiency standards for automobiles, funding research on new technologies, and supporting the use of alternative energy. All energy policies are deeply interconnected with environmental issues because the use of fossil fuels contributes to air pollution and climate change. Reducing the use of energy and using new technologies for cleaner energy make all energy more expensive for Americans.

■ **15.5** Despite the wealth of the United States as a whole, a significant number of Americans live in poverty or are homeless. The poverty threshold represents the income needed to maintain a specified standard of living as of 1963, with the purchasing-power value increased year by year based on the general increase in prices. The official poverty level is based on pretax income, including cash, and does not take into consideration in-kind subsidies.

■ **15.5** The 1996 Welfare Reform Act transferred more control over welfare programs to the states, limited the number of years people can receive welfare assistance, and imposed work requirements on welfare recipients. The act succeeded in reducing the number of welfare recipients in the United States by at least 50 percent.

■ **15.6** America has always been a land of immigrants and continues to be so. Today, more than 1 million immigrants from other nations enter the United States each year, and more than 10 percent of the U.S. population consists of foreign-born persons. Civil rights legislation has helped immigrants overcome some of the effects of prejudice and discrimination. Today, the controversy centers on a reform of our immigration legislation that will improve our system for temporary workers and enable undocumented immigrants to have a path to citizenship.

Selected Resources

PRINT RESOURCES

Avery, Samuel and Bill McKibben. *The Pipeline and the Paradigm: Keystone XL, Tar Sands, and the Battle to Defuse the Carbon Bomb* (Washington, DC: Ruka Press, 2013). This book researches the economic, ecological, political, and other issues behind the Keystone XL pipeline. The authors, through scientific evidence, link the proposed pipeline to global climate change.

Desmond, Matthew. *Evicted: Poverty and Profit in the American City* (New York: Crown, 2016). How important is housing policy to ending poverty in the United States? Desmond follows the stories of families who are evicted from their homes in Milwaukee and the issues faced by landlords. The book provides a compelling look at the realities of the lives of poor tenants.

Edelman, Peter. *So Rich, So Poor: Why It's So Hard to End Poverty in America* (New York: The New Press, 2013). A longtime advocate for ending poverty presents the evidence that the poor and people of color in the United States are continuing to fall behind the better-off Americans. He argues that the very structure of the economy leads to this state of affairs.

Emanuel, Ezekiel. *Reinventing American Healthcare: How the Affordable Care Act Will Improve Our Terribly Complex,* *Blatantly Unjust, Outrageously Expensive, Grossly Inefficient, Error Prone System* (New York: Perseus, 2014). Dr. Emanuel, an adviser to the Obama White House and contributor to the writing of the Affordable Care Act, presents his view of how the new health legislation will greatly improve the efficiency and effectiveness of the health-care system.

Gold, Russell. *The Boom: How Fracking Ignited the American Energy Revolution and Changed the World* (New York: Simon and Schuster, 2014). An investigative reporter, Gold traveled to the oil and gas fields and interviewed executives, workers, and environmentalists to describe how the new ways of producing energy are changing the world economy.

Laufer, Peter and Markos Kounalakis. *Calexico: Hope and Hysteria in the California Borderlands* (Sausalito, CA: PoliPointPress, 2009). Calexico is a news-gathering travelogue that explores the California–Mexico border region, a land of its own inhabited by people who experience the immigration crisis in all its dimensions every day. Laufer is a foreign affairs journalist and radio commentator; Kounalakis is the president of the *Washington Monthly*.

MEDIA RESOURCES

Climate of Doubt (PBS 2012)—In this documentary film, the focus is on the competing groups that espouse global warming and the "deniers" who oppose this idea. Economic interests clash with pure activists. https://www.pbs.org/video/frontline-climate-doubt

Escape Fire (2012)—An award-winning documentary examining the inefficiencies and cost of the American health-care system. The film notes, we have a "disease care" system, not a health-care system. http://www.escapefiremovie.com/

Gasland Part II (HBO 2013)—HBO's *Gasland II* presents even more evidence about the dangers of fracking and the false sense of safety and environmentalism that the drillers and industry project. http://www.gaslandthemovie.com/home

Promised Land (2012)—A film starring Matt Damon and John Krasinski that explores a conflict in a small town over fracking.

Sicko—A 2007 Michael Moore film critical of the U.S. healthcare industry. Rather than focusing on the plight of the uninsured, Moore addresses the troubles of those who have been denied coverage by their insurance companies.

In his most outrageous stunt ever, Moore assembles a group of 9/11 rescue workers who have been denied proper care and takes them to Cuba, where the government, perfectly aware of the propaganda implications, is more than happy to arrange for their treatment.

ONLINE RESOURCES

Department of Energy, Energy Information Agency—compiles every possible statistic on energy use, mining, drilling for oil, and the like: www.eia.gov

Environmental Protection Agency—the department charged with implementing the federal regulations regarding air and water pollution, its website documents current programs and gives valuable information about many environmental topics: www.epa.gov

Institute for Research on Poverty—offers information on poverty in the United States and the latest research on this topic: www.ssc.wisc.edu/irp

National Governors Association—bipartisan organization of the nation's governors that promotes visionary state leadership, shares best practices, and speaks with a unified voice on national policy, such as the current status of welfare reform: www.nga.org

U.S. Census Bureau—reports current statistics on poverty in the United States: https://www.census.gov/topics/income-poverty/poverty.html

16

Economic Policy

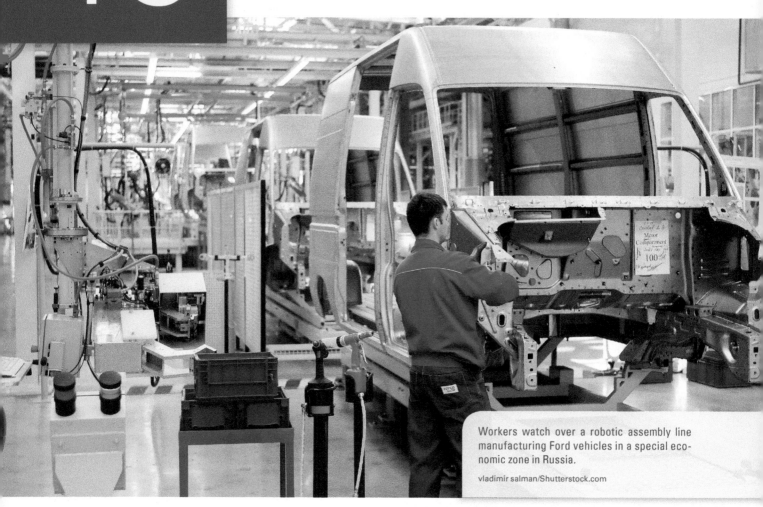

Workers watch over a robotic assembly line manufacturing Ford vehicles in a special economic zone in Russia.

vladimir salman/Shutterstock.com

LEARNING OBJECTIVES

After reading this chapter, you will be able to:

■ **16.1** Explain how the financial crisis that began in 2008 has affected a range of national and state policies and how it is having a long-term impact on the lives of citizens.

■ **16.2** Define fiscal and monetary policy; explain the tools used by the institutions of the national government to shape economic policy.

■ **16.3** Discuss the annual deficit and the total national debt; explain the impact of these two concepts on American life and policies.

■ **16.4** Compare progressive taxes and regressive taxes, and explain the taxation systems used in the United States.

■ **16.5** Define entitlement programs, and describe how these programs are related to economic policies.

■ **16.6** Describe the role of the Federal Reserve Bank and its Board of Governors in influencing the economy.

■ **16.7** Discuss the impact of exports and imports on the American economy and how the World Trade Organization regulates trade.

Background

For most of the history of the United States, the national government operated on a balanced budget. However, during the Civil War and World War II, the government was forced to sell bonds to finance its debt. During the last six decades, the federal government has operated at a deficit in most years. However, all states are required by their constitutions to balance their budgets. Let's assume that an amendment requiring a balanced budget is added to the U.S. Constitution. Initially, the two possible ways to balance the federal budget would be to raise taxes and increase user fees or to reduce the amount of federal government spending. Alternatively, a combination of these two actions could be undertaken.

Increased Taxes

On the revenue side of the equation, one way to balance the budget is to increase taxes on individuals and corporations. If the government increased taxes on individuals, then the tax rates paid by the middle class would have to rise significantly, because the middle class is the source of most federal tax revenues. The rich and the super-rich are currently required to pay a higher tax rate than the middle class, although certain provisions in the tax code may allow them to pay less. Even raising taxes on the rich to 90 percent or more would not balance the federal budget. Thus, taxes would need to be increased among all income groups to raise significantly larger revenues. Middle-class Americans would see their taxes go up rather dramatically. Another way to increase tax revenues is to strengthen economic growth. The more people who are working for good wages, the more tax money is collected at every level of government.

Taxes on corporations could also be increased significantly to raise more revenue in the short run. In a global economy, however, American corporations might decide to move even more of their operations to countries with more advantageous tax structures. This would deprive the government of revenue and Americans of jobs and reduce dividends to stockholders, many of whom depend on that income for their own needs. Finally, increasing taxes on corporations may cause them to raise the cost of their products to recoup that revenue.

It would also be possible to increase user fees for all federal government services, perhaps to keep them more in line with the actual costs of the federal government. The fees to visit national parks would likely be raised, for example.

Reduced Federal Government Spending

On the spending side of the equation, a reduction in federal government spending could mean dramatic changes for many Americans. It seems easy to cut some federal programs, such as the pork-barrel spending projects so beloved by members of Congress. And, of course, particular federal departments are always the target of budget-cutters: the Department of Energy; the Departments of Education, Commerce, and Labor; and the Environmental Protection Agency are among those often mentioned as superfluous by critics. However, these are very small departments with relatively few employees and fairly small budgets.

Many budget critics have suggested that the budget be reduced "across the board" to the levels of the 1990s. Although this is a simple concept to understand, the strategy would require cuts to every budget within the federal government. Would citizens really want a 10 percent reduction in the pay of soldiers in Afghanistan, the reduction of residential mail service to four or five days a week, or increases in spending due to inflation or increased energy costs?

The deepest and most difficult cuts would need to come from entitlements—programs that have promised certain benefits to certain classes of citizens, including Social Security to retired citizens, aid to disabled Americans, pensions to military veterans, and the Medicare health insurance program for seniors. Entitlement programs account for about half of the entire national budget, so these must be cut, but reducing benefits to Social Security recipients or veterans is politically impossible.

The Upside of Balancing the Budget

Although balancing the federal budget every year would be an extremely difficult and painful process, it could be a healthy practice. The government would not need to sell bonds to foreign countries such as China to fund its debt. A reduction in debt would improve the nation's budget status because less interest would need to be paid on the public debt, freeing up those funds for other important programs. However, actually getting to a balanced budget has proved difficult for all modern nations.

For Critical Analysis

1. Of the two methods of reducing the deficit to zero—raising taxes or decreasing government spending—which method do you believe would be perceived by most people to be less painful? Why?

2. How can the federal government spend more than it receives every year, whereas a family would have a hard time doing the same thing year in and year out?

■ **16.1** Explain how the financial crisis that began in 2008 has affected a range of national and state policies and how it is having a long-term impact on the lives of citizens.

The economic recession that began in 2008 is a prime example of how the good intentions of governments, corporations, and citizens can go terribly wrong. The housing bubble and the economic collapse that followed exemplify the ways in which the government affects the economy through laws, regulations, well-intentioned policies, bureaucratic decision making, and sheer politics.

The recession was caused by a complex set of political and economic decisions that came together as a perfect storm of unintended consequences. For the past two decades or so, the federal government had tried to widen opportunities for all Americans to buy homes. Some of the policies were intended to end discrimination by banks against minority or poor borrowers. Other policies aimed to encourage homebuilding and home buying in order to stimulate economic growth. Americans responded by building more homes and condominiums, buying more residences, furnishing them, and borrowing the money to do so. At the same time, assuring lawmakers that they would be responsible and that the crash of 1929 could never happen again, banks pressured Congress to repeal the **Glass-Steagall Act** of 1933, which forbade banks from partnering with investment firms and limited their ability to speculate in stocks and bonds. In 1998, Congress obliged. This change in banking regulation encouraged banks, insurance companies, and all kinds of investment companies to create and invest in forms of credit never before imagined. The riskiest turned out to be "bundles" of home mortgages, a substantial proportion of which were given to people who could not afford the monthly payments when interest rates rose. At the same time, banks and investment firms in the United States traded such bundles to their equals in Europe and throughout the world and they, in turn, invested in U.S. mortgages. When interest rates rose and unemployment began to increase, many homeowners could no longer pay back their loans, and those mortgages went into default. The investment instruments collapsed because there were not enough reserves to cover the losses, and in October 2008, Lehman Brothers, a stalwart Wall Street investment company, failed entirely. Quickly, the Bush administration and Congress realized that other huge banks would fail, and a worldwide economic collapse would follow. The first rescue package was passed before the election of 2008. After the Obama administration came into office, a stimulus bill titled the American Recovery and Reinvestment Act of 2009 was passed, the government assumed control of General Motors and the Chrysler Corporation, and other banks were put under strict federal control until their debts were paid. Although the recession officially ended in 2009, economic recovery was extremely slow, with unemployment remaining above 6 percent for several years. Congress passed and the president signed numerous pieces of legislation to try to encourage growth, but after the 2010 midterm election, the debate over how to do this became even more intensely political. This chapter examines the ways in which the federal government influences the economy and the political differences that underlie all economic policies.

Glass-Steagall Act
A law passed in 1933 to regulate the banking industry, which prohibited banks from engaging in speculative investments or becoming investment houses.

Gambling on a Recession

When the banks and financial houses began to fail in 2008 and 2009, everyone believed that someone—bankers, investors, ordinary pensioners, homeowners—lost money. Even after government bailouts and the insertion of government aid, many people were worse off than before the recession began. However, some investors and financial analysts saw the boom in housing and began to predict the "bust" that followed. Some saw the opportunity to make a great deal of money betting on the falling market.

In the Academy Award–nominated film, *The Big Short,* an all-star cast, including Ryan Gosling, Steve Carell, Christian Bale, and Brad Pitt, portray hedge fund managers who bet against the market. The plot of the film is based on the book *The Big Short: Inside the Doomsday Machine,* written by Michael Lewis, and the characters in the film are modeled on the real-life investors who profited on these schemes.

All four of the main characters in this film construct schemes for their investors, who will profit if the housing bubble bursts. In each case, they succeed, and their investments are doubled or quadrupled by the collapse of the mortgage market in 2008. Although they rejoice as their predictions come true and the wealth piles up, several of the characters realize, to their horror, that people will lose their homes and, in some cases, their lives, in the collapse.

All of the actors and writers involved in making *The Big Short* have commented on how difficult it was to learn and convey the complexities of the financial instruments that were at the base of the collapse. The film itself has been praised for helping the moviegoer begin to understand what was happening in the financial markets in 2007–2008 and why the recession occurred. It was also a box office success, which is unusual for a film on such a serious and complex subject.

For Critical Analysis

1. If individual investors could see the crash coming, why didn't the U.S. government or any other government take action to prevent it?

2. How do you think the government or the banks or the investment houses compensate the "small investors" and homeowners who lost so much in the collapse of the markets?

Prosperity Is the Goal

Democrats and Republicans agree that the goals of the nation's economic policy should be low unemployment, low rates of **inflation** (rising prices and wages), strong growth in the gross domestic product, and increasing incomes for American families. Furthermore, the economy should be stable—not growing too fast and not slowing down too much.

Like any economy that is fundamentally capitalist, the U.S. economy experiences ups and downs. Good times—booms—are followed by lean years. If a slowdown is so severe that the economy actually shrinks for two consecutive quarters, it is a **recession**. Recessions bring increased unemployment, stagnation in household income, and the permanent loss of jobs. Because the consequences of recessions affect individuals directly and therefore influence the voter's view of how well the economy is doing, poor economic conditions disadvantage the sitting president, the president's party, and its members in Congress. Political science research has made clear the importance of economic

inflation
A sustained rise in the general price level of goods and services.

recession
Two or more successive quarters in which the economy shrinks instead of grows.

unemployment
The inability of those who are in the labor force to find a job; defined as the total number of those actively looking for a job but unable to find one.

full employment
An arbitrary level of unemployment that corresponds to "normal" friction in the labor market. In 1986, a 6.5 percent rate of unemployment was considered full employment. Today, it is assumed to be around 5 percent.

perceptions to American voters: Ronald Reagan's campaign in 1980 asked voters, "Are you better off today than you were four years ago?" and the voters replied by denying Jimmy Carter a second term. Incumbent presidents and members of Congress try frequently to influence the economy, although they may not have as much power as the voters believe they do.

Unemployment

One political goal of any administration is to keep the rate of unemployment down. **Unemployment** is the inability of those who are in the workforce to find jobs. Some people enter the labor force for the first time and have to look for a job. Some are fired or laid off and have to look for a job. Others want to change occupations. **Full employment** is defined as a level of unemployment that makes allowances for normal movement between jobs. The Full Employment Act of 1947 set that level at 4 percent. During recessions, unemployment rises well above the full employment level. During the business slowdown of 2001–2002, the rate of unemployment increased from 4 to 6.5 percent. As the financial crisis grew, the stock markets plunged and business activity throughout the world weakened. The average unemployment rate for 2009 was more than 9 percent, and the rate did not begin to decrease until late 2011. The rate continued to decline slowly until 2016 when economic activity accelerated. By the end of 2017, the unemployment rate was at or below 4 percent.

Unemployment Becomes an Issue For much of American history, unemployment was not a problem that the federal government was expected to address. By the late 1800s, many people believed that as a matter of principle, the government should not fight unemployment. This belief followed from an economic philosophy that was dominant in those years—*laissez-faire* economics ("let it be"). Advocates of this philosophy believe that government intervention in the economy is almost always misguided and likely to lead to negative results. A second barrier to any federal government action against unemployment was the doctrine of *dual federalism*, described

Image 16–1
A graduating senior at Pace University speaks with a recruiter at a job fair.

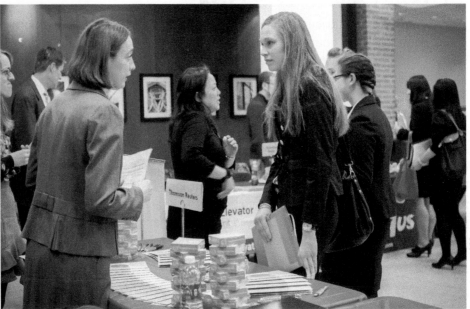

Frances Roberts/AGE Fotostock

in Chapter 3. Under this theory, only state governments had the right to address a problem such as unemployment. For the most part, however, ups and downs in the economy were seen as a consequence of the capitalist system and not a matter for government.

The Great Depression of the 1930s ended popular support for dual federalism and *laissez-faire* economics. Unemployment initially exceeded 25 percent. Relatively high rates of unemployment—more than 15 percent—persisted for more than 10 years. One of the methods that the Franklin D. Roosevelt administration adopted to combat the effects of the Depression was direct government employment of those without jobs through such programs as the Civilian Conservation Corps and the Works Progress Administration.

Since the passage of the Social Security Act of 1935, the federal government has also offered a program of unemployment insurance, which is the government's single most important source of assistance to the jobless. Not all unemployed workers are eligible, however—only about one-third of the unemployed receive benefits. Benefits are not available to employees who quit their jobs voluntarily or are fired for cause (for example, constantly showing up late for work). They are also not paid to workers who are entering the labor force for the first time but cannot find a job. Unemployment insurance is a joint state–federal program, and the state portion is funded by a tax on employers. In 2009 and 2010, facing the highest unemployment rate in decades, Congress extended benefits to 99 weeks from the standard 26 weeks for some of the most affected states and pumped more federal dollars into the fund. That extension ended in 2014.

Measuring Unemployment Estimates of the number of unemployed are prepared by the U.S. Department of Labor. The Bureau of the Census also generates estimates using survey research data. Figure 16-1 shows how unemployment has fluctuated over the course of American history.

Figure 16-1 ▶ More than a Century of Unemployment

Unemployment reached lows during World Wars I and II of less than 2 percent and a high during the Great Depression of more than 25 percent.

Source: U.S. Department of Labor, Bureau of Labor Statistics, http://www.bls.gov/timeseries/LN14000000

Critics of the published unemployment rate believe that it fails to reflect the true numbers of discouraged workers and "hidden unemployed." Although no exact definition of discouraged workers or a way to measure them exists, the Department of Labor defines them as people who have dropped out of the labor force and are no longer looking for a job because they believe that the job market has little to offer them. One of the long-term effects of the 2008 recession was a drop in the labor force participation, meaning that a lower percentage of Americans aged 16 and older are now working as compared to the percentages over the last 40 years.

Inflation

Consumer Price Index (CPI)
A measure of the change in price over time of a specific group of goods and services used by the average household.

Rising prices, or inflation, can also be a serious political problem for any sitting administration, especially if prices are rising quickly. Inflation is a sustained upward movement in the average level of prices. The government measures inflation using the **Consumer Price Index (CPI)**. The Bureau of Labor Statistics (BLS) identifies a market basket of goods and services purchased by the typical consumer and regularly checks the price of that basket. Over a period of many years, inflation can add up. Today's dollar is worth (very roughly) one-twentieth of what a dollar was worth a century ago. Inflation is always a concern for the nation; however, the economic recession and recovery of 2007–2016 has seen very low or negative inflation, mostly due to very low interest rates, which are controlled by the Federal Reserve Bank. Economists worry that a quick recovery would lead to increased inflation. To keep this in perspective, consider the interest rate on a home mortgage. In 2016, rates were extremely low, with some mortgages available at 4 percent. In 1979, the interest rate on a mortgage was more than 12 percent.

The Business Cycle

business cycle
A term that describes fluctuations in the nation's economic activity, including periods of economic expansion and contraction.

The capitalist economy normally passes through times of expansion and contraction known as the **business cycle**. Economies expand in times of growth, creating more jobs and producing more goods and services. The businesses may overexpand and consumers may overspend, and at some point, the economy will cease to grow and enter a period of recession.

An extremely severe recession is called a *depression*, as in the example of the Great Depression. By 1933, actual output was 35 percent below the nation's productive capacity. Between 1929 and 1932, more than 5,000 banks (one out of every five) failed, and their customers' deposits vanished. Most modern recessions have been less severe, in part because the American government and all governments of democratic countries have tried to reduce the effects of recession on their people and encourage growth by every means available.

The Economic Toolkit

When the first signs of a recession appear—say, for example, the unemployment rate ticks up a notch and the stock market falls—the president of the United States turns to the administration's economic team for advice. The president's team consists of the secretary of the Treasury, the Council of Economic Advisers, the budget director, and, possibly, the U.S. trade representative. In the Obama administration, Secretary of the Treasury Timothy Geithner led the effort to meet the economic crisis. The Council of Economic Advisers reviews all the data and suggests strategies to the president and the president's political team. At the same time, the members of Congress, well aware of the political consequences of an economic downturn, begin to investigate ways to stimulate the economy through **fiscal policy**, meaning the use of taxing and spending to affect economic activity. The other major player in this situation is the chairman of the Federal Reserve Bank, Jerome Powell. The Federal Reserve has its own sphere of influence over the economy—**monetary policy**, or the regulation of changes in the supply of money to influence interest rates, credit availability, employment, and the rate of inflation.

As shown in the screen captures of Senator Cory Booker's Twitter feed and President Trump's Twitter feed, the strategies chosen by the president and the Democratic Senator are both economic and political. Whether the sitting administration is Republican or Democratic, presidential team members want to be successful and retain their offices. However, the choices they make to influence economic strategy will likely depend on their political party, their ideological framework—that is, liberal, moderate, or conservative—and which economic theory they believe will generate economic growth.

fiscal policy
The federal government's use of taxation and spending policies to affect overall business activity.

monetary policy
The utilization of changes in the amount of money in circulation to alter credit markets, employment, and the rate of inflation.

Economic Theory Guides Policy

Since the Great Depression of the 1930s, the federal government has grown much larger and taken a much larger role in the economy, and citizens have come to expect that the government will seek to stabilize the economy so that ordinary people can improve their standard of living. Economic theorists argue which strategies are most likely to cushion or reduce the impact of an economic downturn and restart the economy on the road to growth and stability. Policymakers base their recommendations for government intervention and legislation on one or more of these economic theories.

Laissez-Faire Economics

The founders of the American republic did not envision a government that regulated most aspects of the economy. Indeed, John Locke used the example of the small farmer who

Twitter/Paul Ryan

Twitter/Barak Obama

Twitter Feed ▶ How can two leaders have such different views on the impact of tax legislation?

Cory Booker ✓
@CoryBooker

(Follow) ⌄

But instead of trying to work with @SenateDems on any of the bills we've introduced to lower drug costs for Americans, Trump and @SenateGOP passed their tax bill which resulted in the 10 largest drug companies using their windfall to buy back stock, not to lower drug costs.

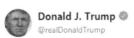

Donald J. Trump ✓
@realDonaldTrump

(Follow) ⌄

Working hard on the biggest tax cut in U.S. history. Great support from so many sides. Big winners will be the middle class, business & JOBS grows enough for himself and then trades or sells for what he needs as the example of a free man who needs little government. Articulated by Adam Smith in *The Wealth of Nations* in 1776, *laissez-faire* theory believes that the actions of each individual person and business will best be regulated through free competition.[1] If an individual prices his or her merchandise too high, it will not sell. A competitor will force the price down. This theory sees government regulation and intervention in the marketplace as mistaken: such interference will upset the free market and will eventually be costly to the economy. Although most modern political leaders support some government regulation of the economy, such as keeping unsafe drugs from the market and prohibiting child labor, libertarians and some conservatives often express the view that the government has no business taking over a company such as General Motors or regulating the compensation of bank executives.

Keynesian Economic Theory

British economist John Maynard Keynes (1883–1946) originated the school of thought called **Keynesian economics**, which supports the use of government spending and taxing to help stabilize the economy. (*Keynesian* is pronounced *kayn*-zee-un.) Keynes believed that a need for government intervention in the economy existed in part because, after falling into a recession or depression, a modern economy may become trapped in an ongoing state of low employment rates.

Keynes developed his fiscal policy theories during the Great Depression. He believed that the forces of supply and demand operated too slowly in such a serious recession. Unemployment meant people had less to spend, leading to more failed businesses, creating additional unemployment. Keynes's idea was simple: in such circumstances, the government should step in and undertake the spending that is needed to return the economy to a more normal state.[2] Since World War II, Keynesian theory has supported the policies of many presidents. The stimulus bill passed in the first months of the Obama administration is a clear example of the government providing funding for infrastructure projects such as roads and bridges to increase employment in the construction sector. The bill also provided billions of dollars in assistance to state and local governments so that they did not need to lay off teachers, police, and fire personnel.

Supply-Side Economics

In 1981, the country was suffering both a recession and extremely high inflation, which hurts the ordinary citizen by requiring higher spending for gas, groceries, clothing, and energy at a time when wages and salaries are not rising at the same rate. The Reagan administration embraced an economic theory called "supply-side economics," which holds that the answer to inflation is to reduce government regulation and cut taxes so that businesses will produce more products and hire more employees. The theory posits that oversupply of production and services will drive down prices through competition. Meanwhile, the theory holds that this increasing growth will produce more government revenue through the increased taxes generated by businesses and individuals. Although Reagan's strategy did

Keynesian economics
A school of economic thought that tends to favor active federal government policymaking to stabilize economy-wide fluctuations, usually by implementing discretionary fiscal policy.

---

1   Adam Smith, *The Wealth of Nations* (London: W. Strahan and T. Cadell, 1776).
2   Robert Skidelsky, *John Maynard Keynes: The Economist as Savior, 1920–1937: A Biography* (New York: Penguin USA, 1994).

curb inflation and stimulate growth, it did not produce the amount of tax revenue that had been predicted, and his administration incurred large budget deficits, as have many others.

Whereas *laissez-faire* economics generally has little role for government in its strategies, both Keynesian theory and supply-side economics envision the president, Congress, and the Federal Reserve System using the tools of fiscal and monetary policy to influence the economy. Democrats tend to subscribe to the "percolate-up" view of the economy, meaning that the government should aid economically disadvantaged citizens, and the improvement of their household income will eventually produce more wealth for everyone. Republicans are said to believe in the "trickle-down" approach to economic policy, meaning that with less government and fewer taxes, the owners of businesses and the rich will do well, and their wealth will generate jobs and income for the poor. The tools of fiscal policy and monetary policy described next can be used to support either approach.

Fiscal Policy

■ **16.2** Define fiscal and monetary policy; explain the tools used by the institutions of the national government to shape economic policy.

To smooth out the ups and downs of the national economy, the government can change the level of taxes or government spending. It can also influence interest rates and the money side of the economy. Fiscal policy is the domain of Congress and the president. Generally, the incumbent president and the president's party are blamed by the public for an economic downturn. However, any real changes in fiscal policy are likely to be initiated by the president and then passed by Congress. In general, these are Keynesian policies.

Discretionary Fiscal Policy

Keynes originally developed his theories as a way of lifting an economy out of a major disaster such as the Great Depression. Beginning with the presidency of John F. Kennedy, however, policymakers have attempted to use Keynesian methods to fine-tune the economy. This is discretionary fiscal policy (*discretionary* means left to the judgment or discretion of a policymaker). Kennedy was the first American president to explicitly adopt Keynesian economics. In 1963, during a mild business slowdown, Kennedy proposed a tax cut. Congress did not actually pass the necessary legislation until early 1964, after Kennedy had been assassinated. The economy picked up—and the tax cut was a success.

President George W. Bush pushed his tax cuts of 2001 and 2003 as a method of stimulating the economy to halt the economic slowdown of those years. During 2006, Bush repeatedly pointed out that since his tax cuts had been put into effect, the economy had grown so much that federal tax revenues had increased more than anticipated, thereby reducing the federal budget deficit below the level predicted. He noted that his proposed 2008 budget submitted to Congress would reduce the budget deficit and produce a surplus by 2012. However, the financial crisis of 2008 intervened and the government increased its deficit spending at a rapid rate, producing the likelihood of unbalanced budgets for the next decade.

did you know?

It cost the U.S. Mint 1.82¢ to make a penny and 6.6¢ to make a nickel as of 2014.

Image 16-2
President Obama greets the Vietnamese president, Tran Dai Quang, at the 2015 Asian economic summit meeting. Nations use different economic tools to stabilize their economies.

The Obama administration consistently followed a Keynesian path as it attempted to speed the economic recovery. Extending unemployment benefits, extending the food stamp program, sending stimulus monies to state and local governments, reducing the Social Security tax paid by workers on their earnings—all qualify as discretionary fiscal policy. Enter Donald Trump, who immediately took a different approach. He pushed for tax cuts and reducing regulation to encourage business growth and job growth. Like President Ronald Reagan, President Trump subscribes to "trickle-down" economic theory.

The Thorny Problem of Timing Attempts to fine-tune the economy face a timing problem. It takes a while to collect and assimilate economic data. There will be a time lag between the recognition of an economic problem and the implementation of policy to solve it. Getting Congress to act can easily take a year or two. Finally, after fiscal policy is enacted, it takes time for the policy to act on the economy. Because fiscal policy time lags are long and variable, a policy designed to combat a recession may not produce results until the economy is already out of the recession.

Government Borrowing

Government spending can be financed in several ways, including by increasing taxes and borrowing. For government spending to have the effect Keynes wanted, however, it is essential that it be financed by borrowing, not taxes. In other words, the government should run a **budget deficit**: it should spend more than it receives. If government spending during a recession is funded by increased taxes, those higher taxes will make the impact of the recession even worse for citizens. During a recession, the government borrows money through debt to spend more on stimulus projects and unemployment. This spending should make up for the reduced spending by businesses and consumers.

The federal government typically borrows by selling **U.S. Treasury bonds**. The sale of these bonds to corporations, private individuals, pension plans, foreign governments, businesses, and individuals adds to the *public debt*. In the last few years, foreigners have increased their holdings of the U.S. public

budget deficit
Government expenditures that exceed receipts.

U.S. treasury bonds
Debt issued by the federal government.

debt to around 35 percent of the total debt. Thirty years ago, the share of the U.S. public debt held by foreigners was only 15 percent.

The Public Debt in Perspective

■ **16.3** Discuss the annual deficit and the total national debt; explain the impact of these two concepts on American life and policies.

Did you know that the federal government has accumulated more than $21 trillion in debt, or $64,552 for each man, woman, and child in the United States? Does that scare you? It certainly would if you thought that we had to pay it back tomorrow, but we do not.[3] As long as the U.S. government can borrow money from its citizens and others and make the interest payments, there is no need to pay off the entire debt.

There are two types of public debt—gross and net. The **gross public debt** includes all federal government interagency borrowings, which really do not matter. This is similar to your taking an IOU ("I owe you") out of your left pocket and putting it into your right pocket. What is important is the **net public debt**—the public debt that does not include interagency borrowing. Figure 16-2 shows the net public debt of the federal government since 1940.

This figure does not consider two very important variables: inflation and increases in population. A better way to examine the relative importance of the public debt is to compare it to the **gross domestic product (GDP)**, as is done in Figure 16-3. (The *gross domestic product* is the dollar value of all final goods and

gross public debt
The net public debt plus interagency borrowings within the government.

net public debt
The accumulation of all past federal government deficits; the total amount owed by the federal government to individuals, businesses, and foreigners.

gross domestic product (GDP)
The dollar value of all final goods and services produced in a one-year period.

Figure 16-2 ▶ Net Public Debt of the Federal Government

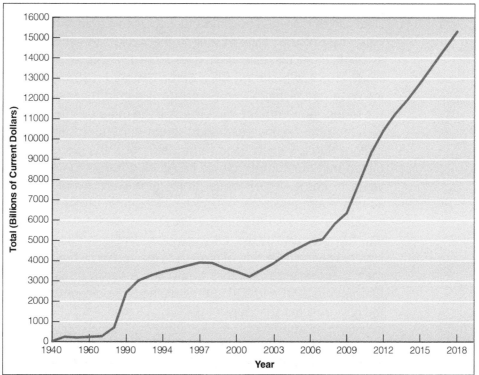

Source: Congressional Budget Office, "An Update to the Budget and Economic Outlook: 2015 to 2025," April 2018.

---

3 If you would like to see the minute-by-minute calculation of the debt as well as other real-time government statistics, go to: www.usdebtclock.org

Figure 16-3 ▶ Net Public Debt as a Percentage of the Gross Domestic Product

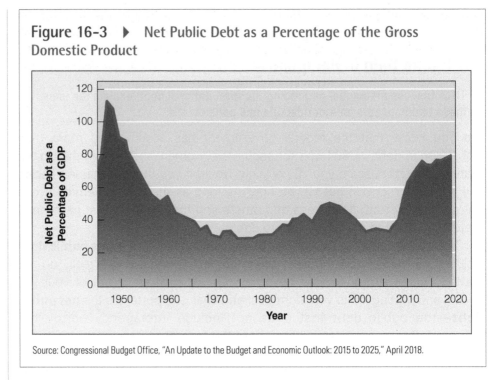

Source: Congressional Budget Office, "An Update to the Budget and Economic Outlook: 2015 to 2025," April 2018.

services produced in a one-year period.) There you see that the public debt reached its peak during World War II and fell thereafter. Since about 1960, the net public debt as a percentage of GDP has ranged between 30 and 50 percent; however, the recent spending to combat the financial crisis and new federal programs have increased the net public debt as a ratio to the GDP to 70-plus percent. Debt can be managed but, in another economic crisis, a high level could lead to a weakening of the nation's credit in the world and serious economic problems similar to those that have been experienced in Greece, Spain, and Portugal.

In 1993, President Bill Clinton (served 1993–2001) brokered a tax increase as the nation emerged from a mild recession. For the first time, the federal government implemented the more painful side of Keynesianism. Between the tax increase and the dot-com boom, the United States had a budget surplus each year from 1998 to 2002. Some commentators predicted that the country would be running federal government surpluses for years to come. All of those projections went by the wayside because of several events.

One event was the dot-com bust, followed by the 2001–2002 recession, which was caused by the terrorist attacks on September 11, 2001. These events lowered not only the rate of growth of the economy but also the federal government's tax receipts. Another event was a series of large tax cuts passed by Congress in 2001 and 2003 at the urging of President George W. Bush. Finally, the government had to pay for the war in Iraq in 2003 and the occupation of that country thereafter, which turned out to be far more costly than ever imagined. The federal budget deficit for 2007 was close to $270 billion. The financial crisis of 2008 plunged the nation into recession and unemployment. Congress reacted by creating bailout funds and passing stimulus spending, thus increasing the debt. The Obama administration, faced with a long-lasting recession and high levels of unemployment, continued to increase government spending on benefits and on programs in hopes the economy would improve. After the Republicans took control of the House of Representatives in 2011, legislative gridlock prevented the passage of either tax increases or serious spending reductions.

By January of 2017 when President Trump took office, the economy had stabilized with relatively slow growth. The president began rolling back regulations on business and, by the end of 2017, succeeded in passing a tax reform package. The GDP had risen to almost 3 percent each quarter and unemployment declined to 4 percent. Still, the two greatest fears are that inflation and interest rates could begin to rise, thus increasing our payments on the debt, and that another recession may occur, requiring the government to step in and issue more debt to sustain the economy.

The Politics of Taxes

■ **16.4** Compare progressive taxes and regressive taxes, and explain the taxation systems used in the United States.

Another major tool to influence economic activity in the United States is taxation. Your state may have changed its tax structure, perhaps by reducing corporate taxes to entice companies to bring their jobs and businesses there. Or, faced with a looming budget deficit, it may have increased income or business taxes. Taxes and tax exclusions and deductions are used by virtually every government body in the United States to give incentives to some sectors of the economy and to discourage other sectors.

Americans pay a variety of different taxes. At the federal level, the income tax is levied on most sources of income. Social Security and Medicare taxes are assessed on wages and salaries. There is an income tax for corporations, and an estate tax is collected from property left behind by wealthy Americans who have died. Excise taxes are paid on gasoline and on certain goods and services at federal, state, and local levels. State and local governments also assess taxes on income, sales, and land. Altogether, the value of all taxes collected by the federal government and by state and local governments is about 35 percent of GDP. This is a substantial sum, but it is far less than many other countries collect.

Federal Income Tax Rates

Individuals and businesses pay taxes based on tax rates. Not all of your income is taxed at the same rate. The first few dollars you make are not taxed at all. The highest rate is imposed on the "last" dollar you make. This highest rate is the *marginal* tax rate. Table 16-1 shows the 2019 marginal tax rates for individuals and married couples. The higher the tax rate, the greater the public's reaction to that tax rate. If the highest tax rate you pay on the income you make is 15 percent, then any method you can use to reduce your taxable income by $1 saves you 15¢ in tax liabilities that you owe the federal government. Individuals paying a 15 percent rate have a relatively small incentive to avoid paying taxes, but consider the individuals who faced a marginal tax rate of 94 percent in the 1940s. They had a tremendous incentive to find legal ways to reduce their taxable incomes. For every $1 of income that was somehow deemed nontaxable, these taxpayers would reduce their tax liability by 94¢.

Table 16-1 ▶ Marginal Tax Rates for Single Persons and Married Couples (2019)

SINGLE PERSONS		MARRIED COUPLES FILING JOINTLY	
Marginal Tax Bracket	Marginal Tax Rate	Marginal Tax Bracket	Marginal Tax Rate
$0–9,525	10%	$0–19,050	10%
$9276–38,700	12%	$19,051–77,400	12%
$38,701–82,500	22%	$77,401–165,000	22%
$82,501–157,500	24%	$165,001–315,000	24%
$157,501–200,000	32%	$315,001–400,000	32%
$200,001–500,000	35%	$400,001–600,000	35%
Over $500,001	37%	Over $600,001	37%

Source: Congressional Budget Office.

Loopholes and Lowered Taxes

loophole
A legal method by which individuals and businesses are allowed to reduce the tax liabilities owed to the government.

Individuals and corporations facing high tax rates will adjust their earning and spending behavior to reduce their taxes. They will also make concerted attempts to get Congress to add **loopholes** to the tax law that allow them to reduce their taxable incomes. When Congress imposed very high tax rates on high incomes, it also provided for more loopholes than it does today. For example, special provisions enabled investors in oil and gas wells to reduce their taxable incomes.

Billionaire Warren Buffet made headlines when he told President Obama that it seemed unfair that he paid a lower rate of taxation than his secretary. Whereas Buffett's secretary earns a six-figure income and thus pays nearly 30 percent per year in federal taxes, Buffett's income comes from dividends on the stock he holds in the corporation. The tax rate on dividend income is 15 percent for most Americans. For households earning more than $400,000, the rate has risen to 20 percent. Like many other very wealthy individuals, Buffett's tax rate is about the same as the average blue-collar household's. Buffett and the president question whether such a tax rate is fair. Many billionaires agree, and the Obama administration and the Democrats made a number of efforts to pass a "Buffett rule" to raise taxes on the wealthiest Americans to at least 30 percent, regardless of the source of their income.

In 2001, George W. Bush persuaded Congress to lower taxes to stimulate the economy. His successor, Barack Obama, raised taxes on the wealthiest Americans. The Trump tax reform legislation eliminated some loopholes and reduced the tax brackets for Americans to those shown in Table 16-1.

Progressive and Regressive Taxation As Table 16-1 shows, the greater your income, the higher the marginal tax rate. Persons with large incomes pay a larger share of their income in income tax. A tax system in which rates go up with income is called a **progressive tax** system. The federal income tax is clearly progressive.

progressive tax
A tax that rises in percentage terms as incomes rise.

The income tax is not the only tax you must pay. The federal Social Security tax is levied on wage and salary income at a flat rate of 6.2 percent. (Employers pay

Table 16-2 ▶ Progressive versus Regressive Taxes

PROGRESSIVE TAXES	REGRESSIVE TAXES
Federal income tax	Social Security tax
State income taxes	Medicare tax
Federal corporate income tax	State sales taxes
Estate tax	Local real estate taxes

another 6.2 percent, making the total effective rate 12.4 percent.) In 2018, however, there was no Social Security tax on wages and salaries in excess of $128,700. (This threshold changes from year to year.) Persons with very high salaries therefore pay no Social Security tax on much of their wages. In addition, the tax is not levied on investment income (including capital gains, rents, some royalties, interest, dividends, or profits from a business). The wealthy receive a much greater share of their income from these sources than do the poor. As a result, the wealthy pay a much smaller portion of their income in Social Security taxes than do the working poor. As Table 16-2 shows, the Social Security tax is therefore a **regressive tax**.

regressive tax
A tax that falls in percentage terms as incomes rise.

Who Pays? The question of whether the tax system should be progressive—and if so, to what degree—is subject to vigorous political debate. Democrats in general and liberals in particular favor a tax system that is significantly progressive. Republicans and conservatives are more likely to prefer a tax system that is proportional or even regressive. President Bush's tax cuts made the federal system somewhat less progressive, largely because they significantly reduced taxes on nonsalary income. Figure 16-4 shows that

Figure 16-4 ▶ Federal Income Tax Burden by Income Group, 2015

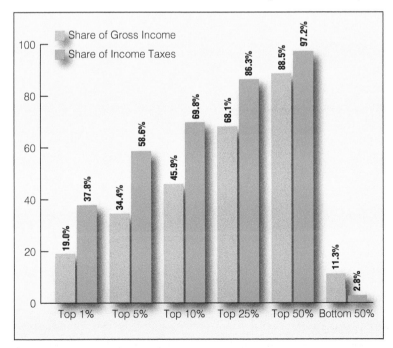

Source: The Tax Foundation, 2015. www.taxfoundation.org.

almost half of all American households pay about 3 percent of federal income taxes, whereas the top 25 percent of all households pay more than 86 percent of all income taxes. Thus, the federal income tax is progressive, but the tax burden overall is much more complicated.

The various taxes Americans pay pull in different directions. The Medicare tax is neither regressive nor progressive, but it has less impact on higher-income workers. Sales taxes are regressive because the wealthy spend a relatively smaller portion of their income on items subject to the sales tax. Table 16-2 lists the characteristics of major taxes. Add everything up, and the tax system as a whole is probably slightly progressive.[4]

Entitlements: The Big Budget Item

■ **16.5** Define entitlement programs, and describe how these programs are related to economic policies.

Lower-income workers are dependent on the programs that have been created to sustain incomes and provide for retirement income. These programs include Social Security, Medicare, unemployment insurance, disability insurance, and medical care and pensions for veterans. All of these programs have broad support from the public and are widely seen as "promises" made to all Americans.

These programs are known as "entitlements"—they are guaranteed to the respective recipients and are not approved through the regular budget process. They are automatically paid and automatically adjusted for cost-of-living increases. All of these programs together amount to almost two-thirds of the federal budget. As shown in Figure 16-5, the taxes collected by the federal government in 2015 amounted to only about two-thirds of what it spent. Therefore, in order to pay these entitlement benefits in the future, we can either eliminate all other federal programs, including defense, or these programs will need to be revised in some way.

> *did you know?*
>
> There are 60 million Americans collecting Social Security; that figure will reach 91 million by 2035.

Figure 16-5 ▶ Federal Income and Outlays for Fiscal Year 2015

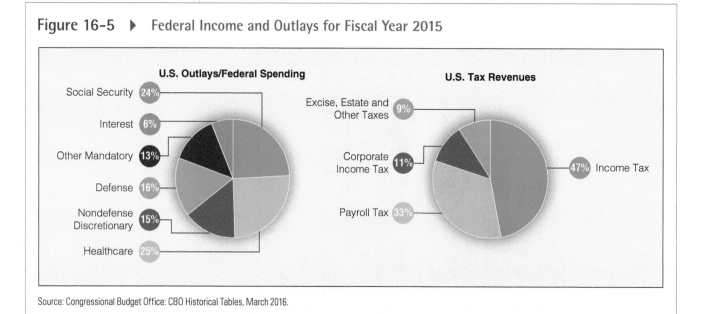

Source: Congressional Budget Office: CBO Historical Tables, March 2016.

---

4 Brian Roach, "GDAE Working Paper No. 03–10: Progressive and Regressive Taxation in the United States: Who's Really Paying (and Not Paying) Their Fair Share?" (Medford, MA: Global Development and Environment Institute, Tufts University, 2003). This paper is available online at www.ase.tufts.edu/gdae/Pubs/wp/03-10-Tax_Incidence.pdf

Social Security and Medicare

Closely related to the question of taxes in the United States is the viability of the Social Security system. Social Security taxes came into existence when the Federal Insurance Contribution Act (FICA) was passed in 1935. Social Security was established as a means of guaranteeing a minimum level of pension benefits to all persons. Today, many people regard Social Security as a kind of "social compact"—a national promise to successive generations that they will receive support in their old age.

To pay for Social Security, as of 2019, a 6.2 percent tax rate is imposed on each employee's wages. Employers must contribute an equal percentage. In addition, a combined employer/employee 2.9 percent tax rate is assessed for Medicare on all wage income, with no upper limit.

Social Security Is Not a Pension Fund

One of the problems with the Social Security system is that people who pay into Social Security think that they are actually paying into a fund, perhaps with their name on it. This is what you do when you pay into a private pension plan. It is not the case, however, with the federal Social Security system, which is basically a pay-as-you-go transfer system in which those who are working are paying benefits to those who are retired.

Currently, the number of people who are working relative to the number of people who are retiring is declining. Therefore, for the system to continue as it is structured now, those who work will have to pay more in Social Security taxes to fund the benefits of those who retire. Projections suggest that by 2030, there will only be two employed workers for every Social Security recipient and, unless there are changes in the system, they will pay a very large part of their paychecks to the federal government to fund the retirement benefits of other Americans.

The Medicare system, which funds health care for those over 65, may experience even more problems. An older population will require greater expenditures on medical care, and medical expenditures *per person* are increasing rapidly. Given continuing advances in medical science, Americans may logically wish to devote an ever greater share of the national income to medical care. This choice puts serious pressure on federal and state budgets, however, because a large part of the nation's medical bill is funded by the government. With the adoption of the 2010 health-care reform legislation and the increase in the number of Americans who will likely be covered either by Medicaid or a state-sponsored program, it is very difficult to predict the future expenditures for these three programs. It is possible that the three combined will total more than 20 percent of the nation's gross domestic product, with a corresponding increase in taxes to fund the benefits provided.

What Will It Take to Salvage Social Security?

These facts illustrate why efforts to reform Social Security and Medicare have begun to dominate the nation's public agenda. What remains to be seen is how the government ultimately will resolve the problem. What, if anything, might be done?

Raise Taxes One option is to raise the combined Social Security and Medicare payroll tax rate. A 2.2 percentage point hike in the payroll tax rate,

How Unequal Is American Society?

In the early days of the American nation, the distribution of wealth among the people was, of course, unequal. Relatively few landholders owned large farms and plantations, and relatively few wealthy merchants owned ships and traded in goods. Most Americans were farmers or craftspeople who owned little except their home, land, and tools. Even in the Southern states, only a small number of landowners were wealthy enough to own slaves. Stratifications of wealth as we know them today developed during the Industrial Age at the end of the nineteenth century.

Many commentators and economists believe that the United States today is a much less equal society than it was only a few decades ago. Due to the recession, the median income today for American families, in inflation-adjusted dollars, is less than it was 10 years ago. Many have lost their savings or their homes due to unemployment, whereas the wealthiest Americans have continued to increase their worth by keeping their tax bills relatively low and earning more wealth through investments, even during a recession. Although it is true that the wealthiest 1 percent of Americans pay a proportionately large share of income taxes—about 38 percent of all taxes paid—their average income is 18 times the median, and their wealth is growing.

The Organization for Economic Cooperation and Development (OECD), an international agency dedicated to improving conditions in all nations, publishes an annual report on income inequality based on a statistic called "the Gini Index," which measures the degree of income equality in a nation by looking at the proportions in different income categories. A Gini Index score of zero means that there is perfect equality among all incomes in a nation. The larger the score, the further the nation is from equality in incomes.

If we compare the score of the United States to those of all other nations, our ranking is not too low: as of 2013, the United States ranked forty-third in income inequality among the 104 nations for which data were available.* The nation with the most inequality was Namibia and that with the least was Denmark. Most of the nations with higher levels of

income inequality were underdeveloped nations that may have a small group of very wealthy households and a multitude of very poor citizens. If we only consider developed Western nations, the United States' degree of income inequality seems more severe. Among these countries, the United States is the most unequal nation, with a Gini coefficient of .47. The issue of income inequality in America has also been the subject of the research of two French economists who currently teach in the United States.** What Emmanuel Saez and Thomas Piketty find in their research is that the United States is quickly becoming more unequal than at any time in its history. Piketty says, "The United States is getting accustomed to a completely crazy level of inequality."*** He continues, "The United States is becoming like Old Europe, which is very strange in historical perspective . . . [it] used to be very egalitarian, not just in spirit but in actuality." He argues that the U.S. middle class is no longer the richest in the world and this state of affairs will only worsen.****

For Critical Analysis

1. Do you think that Americans think of the nation as one of income equality or one of great inequality?

2. What kinds of actions could be taken to increase income equality in the United States?

*Organization for Economic Development and Cooperation, "Income Equality," 2013.
** Emmanuel Saez and Thomas Piketty, cited in "Income Distribution in the U. S.," www.wealthandwant.com/income/income_distribution.html. See also Piketty's new book, *Capital in the 21st Century* (New York: Belknap Press, 2014).
*** Annie Lowry, "French Duo See (Well) Past Tax Rise for the Richest," *The New York Times*, April 17, 2012, A1.
**** See Drew Desilver, "U.S. Middle Class No Longer the World's Richest," Pew Research Center, April 25, 2014, www.pewresearch.org/fact-tank/2014/04/25/chart-of-the-week-u-s-middle-class-no-longer-the-worlds-richest/

to an overall rate of 16.8 percent, would yield an $80 billion annual increase in contributions, which would stabilize the system. Another option is to eliminate the current cap on the level of wages to which the Social Security payroll tax is applied; this measure would also generate about $80 billion per year in additional tax revenues.

Consider Other Options Proposals also suggest increasing the age of full benefit eligibility, perhaps to as high as 70. Many experts believe that increases in immigration offer the best hope of dealing with the tax burdens and workforce shrinkage of the future. Unless Congress changes the existing immigration system to permit the admission of a much larger number of working-age immigrants with useful skills, however, immigration is unlikely to fully relieve the pressure building due to our aging population.

Privatize Social Security Still another proposal calls for partially privatizing the Social Security system in the hope of increasing the rate of return on individuals' retirement contributions. Privatization would allow workers to invest a specified portion of their Social Security payroll taxes in the stock market and possibly in other investment options, such as bonds or real estate. If the economy is good and the stock market grows, then the increased value of these investments would provide more benefits to individuals when they retire. President George W. Bush's proposal that Social Security be partially privatized in this way drew significant support from younger Americans but total opposition from most members of Congress and the AARP.

Obviously, solving the problem of increasing Social Security and Medicare obligations is a task for future presidents and Congresses. Although it will be a controversial issue, most Americans are aware that it must be solved.

Monetary Policy

■ **16.6** Describe the role of the Federal Reserve Bank and its Board of Governors in influencing the economy.

One of the major tools for stabilizing the economy, as noted earlier in the chapter, is *monetary policy*—controlling the rate of growth of the money supply. This policy is the domain of the **Federal Reserve System**, also known simply as **the Fed**. The Fed is the most important regulatory agency in the U.S. monetary system. It regulates the amount of money in circulation, which can be defined loosely as checkable account balances and currency. The Fed also provides a system for transferring checks from one bank to another and holds reserves deposited by most of the nation's banks, savings and loan associations, savings banks, and credit unions.

Federal Reserve System (the Fed)
The most important regulatory agency in the U.S. monetary system. The Fed performs several important functions such as regulating the amount of money in circulation and providing a system for transferring checks from one bank to another.

Organization of the Federal Reserve System

A Board of Governors, consisting of seven full-time members appointed by the president with approval by the Senate, manages the Fed. The most important unit within the Fed is the **Federal Open Market Committee**, which actually determines the future growth of the money supply and other important economy-wide financial variables. This committee is composed of the members of the Board of Governors, the president of the New York Federal Reserve Bank, and presidents of four other Federal Reserve banks, rotated periodically.

The Board of Governors of the Federal Reserve System is independent. The president can attempt to influence the board, and Congress can threaten to merge the Fed into the Treasury Department, but as long as the Fed retains

Federal Open Market Committee
The most important body within the Federal Reserve System. The Federal Open Market Committee decides how monetary policy should be carried out.

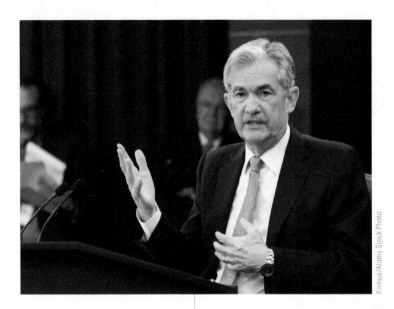

Xinhua/Alamy Stock Photo

Image 16–3

Jerome Powell was sworn in as the Chair of the Board of Governors of the Federal Reserve in 2017.

its independence, its chairperson and governors can do what they please. Hence, any talk about "the president's monetary policy" or "Congress's monetary policy" is inaccurate. To be sure, the Fed has, on occasion, yielded to presidential pressure, and for a while the Fed's chairperson had to observe a congressional resolution requiring him to report monetary targets over each six-month period. But now more than ever before, the Fed remains one of the truly independent sources of economic power in the government.[5]

Loose and Tight Monetary Policies

The Federal Reserve System seeks to stabilize nationwide economic activity by controlling the amount of money in circulation. Changing the amount of money in circulation is a major aspect of monetary policy. If money is "too tight," the Federal Reserve has increased the interest rate that it charges banks, making it more expensive to borrow money. If money is "too loose," the Fed has lowered the interest rate in hopes of stimulating borrowing by businesses and individuals. The businesses will then use that money to invest in new equipment and create new jobs. When the interest rate is lowered, it is easier, theoretically, for businesses and individuals to borrow money, thus stimulating the economy.

How do the actions of the Federal Reserve affect the life of the ordinary citizen? The answer to that question depends on what kinds of loans an individual might have. If you have a 30-year fixed-rate mortgage on your home, for example, nothing the Fed does will change the interest rate of your loan. However, if you have an adjustable-rate mortgage, the rate will increase as the Fed increases the prime rate. This happened to millions of homeowners and investors between 2005 and 2007, with payments increasing so much that many homes were foreclosed on by the banks. Generally, interest on credit cards remains high no matter what the Fed does. It is important to remember that the Fed is more interested in stimulating business activity than it is in stimulating individuals to buy more homes.[6]

Time Lags for Monetary Policy You learned earlier that policymakers who implement fiscal policy—the manipulation of budget deficits and the tax system—experience problems with time lags. The Fed faces similar problems when it implements monetary policy. It must estimate future growth and then make decisions. Policy change takes time to be effective, although the time lag is much less than that of fiscal policy.

Monetary versus Fiscal Policy

A **tight monetary policy** is an effective way of taming inflation. (Some would argue that, ultimately, a tight monetary policy is the only way that inflation can

tight monetary policy
Monetary policy that makes credit expensive in an effort to slow the economy.

---

5   Axel Krause, "The American Federal Reserve System: Functioning and Accountability" (Paris, France: Groupement d'études et de recherches, Notre Europe, Research and Policy Paper No. 7, 1999).

6   For data on Federal Reserve prime rates and mortgage rates, see the Historical Data series from the Federal Reserve Board of Governors at www.federalreserve.gov

be fought.) If interest rates go high enough, people *will* stop borrowing. How effective, though, is a **loose monetary policy** at ending a recession?

Under normal conditions, a loose monetary policy will spur growth in economic activity. At any given time, many businesses are considering whether to borrow. If interest rates are low, they are more likely to do so. Low interest rates also reduce the cost of new houses or cars and encourage consumers to spend. In a serious recession like that of 2008–2009, businesses may not want to borrow, no matter how low the interest rate falls. Likewise, consumers who fear losing their jobs or homes are not going to make major purchases either. In these circumstances, monetary policy is ineffective. Using monetary policy in this situation has been described as "pushing on a string," because the government has no power to *make* people borrow.

loose monetary policy
Monetary policy that makes credit inexpensive and abundant, possibly leading to inflation.

Election 2016

Which Direction for Economic Policy?

Most Americans would agree that the president of the United States needs to keep the nation secure militarily and economically. Indeed, both political parties are astutely aware of the weight that a poor economy puts on their presidential candidate. In 2008, when the economic downturn began, George W. Bush was president and Republicans knew that the "crash" would negatively affect their election chances. Barack Obama was elected president and immediately began to make decisions and request legislation to support economic recovery. He was fortunate to have a Congress controlled by fellow Democrats, and they quickly approved his requests.

What difference does it make if the White House is occupied by a Democrat or a Republican in 2017? Most Democratic presidents are more likely to use Keynesian tools to stimulate economic growth. Government needs to spend more, whether in benefits to the citizens or through job creation programs, to keep the economy steady regardless of the deficit such spending might incur. Republican presidents are more hesitant to use such tools. A fiscally conservative Republican would prefer to cut government spending, reduce the annual deficit, and cut taxes to stimulate more investment in small businesses and jobs. Which approach is "right"? Evidence from the last 50 years is mixed: a government stimulus will help sustain the economy in a recession, but tax cuts also stimulate the economy to grow. Democrats and Republicans simply have different approaches to economic stability.

Whatever the president's approach, there are practical limits to its success. The president will, of course, appoint the secretary of the Treasury and other cabinet officials who share his or her views and try to implement any directives from the President. However, most of the tools of fiscal policy require action by the Congress. If the president faces a Congress where one house is controlled by the other party, such actions may never be approved. The president may also have an opinion about proper monetary policy during an economic downturn, which would require action by the Federal Reserve Board of Governors. The president will have the opportunity to appoint one member of that board every two years when his or her fourteen-year term expires, but it would take eight years for the president to appoint a majority of the seven-member board. The Fed tends to have its own opinion about how to steer the economy and is not subject to political influence. Finally, as mentioned in this chapter, there is the question of timing—whatever action is taken to ensure economic growth, it will take a long time to show any effect, and the party in power may get little credit for its approach.

For Critical Analysis

1. Why do Americans hold the president accountable for the strength of the economy?

2. Should there be more coordination between the president, the Congress, and the Federal Reserve Board in times of economic crisis?

Globalization and World Trade

■ **16.7** Discuss the impact that exports and imports have on the American economy and how the World Trade Organization regulates trade.

Most consumer electronic goods—flat-screen TVs, cell phones, and digital cameras—are made in other countries. Many of the raw materials used in manufacturing in this country are also purchased abroad. Globalization, which means worldwide distribution of production, marketing, and sales of goods and services, has made it possible for many of the corporations that are familiar to Americans (brands such as Coca-Cola, Apple, and Procter & Gamble) to sell their products worldwide, manufacture products in many different nations, and employ hundreds of thousands of people around the globe. When you go into a store to buy clothing or electronics, you do not usually think about where the item was manufactured or whose hands manufactured it. Items appear in-store with English labels and the appropriate price tags and care labels you would expect to see if they were manufactured in the next county. However, they are likely to have been shipped to the United States in a container and composed of parts manufactured in many different nations. Many "American-made" cars and trucks contain parts manufactured in Korea or Mexico or Canada.

World trade has made our lives easier and products cheaper for consumers, but is a controversial topic. Since 1999, meetings of major trade bodies such as the World Trade Organization have been marked by large and sometimes violent demonstrations against globalization. Opponents of globalization often refer to "slave" wages in developing countries as a reason to restrict imports from those nations. Others argue that we should restrict imports from countries that do not enforce the same environmental standards as the United States. There are those who worry that the United States is no longer able to manufacture some products, such as computer monitors, and that this could endanger the nation in a time of war. Most vocal are those

did you know?

The largest car-producing country is China, which produced twice as many vehicles as the United States in 2013.

Image 16-4

Chinese workers assembling Apple products at a factory in Linghua in the Guangdong Province of China. American groups charged Apple with unfair labor practices in such plants, and after an investigation, Apple announced plans to improve the conditions for its workers in China.

who see jobs lost, workers displaced, and towns in economic decline after a factory moves its production overseas. The United States, at one time, had flourishing furniture, textile, and leather industries; most of these goods are now made overseas.

Imports and Exports

Imports are those goods and services that we purchase from outside the United States. Today, imports make up about 16 percent of the goods and services that we buy. Imports include everything from computers to cars to the petroleum that we refine for gasoline.

The United States not only imports goods and services from abroad, but also sells goods and services abroad, called **exports**. Exports include corn, soybeans, wheat, cars, airplanes, tractors, locomotives, and weapons. The United States exports about 14 percent of the GDP. Like our imports, our exports are a relatively small part of our economy compared with many other countries. In world trade, imports are paid for by exports. For a number of years, the United States has run a negative **balance of trade**; it has imported more goods and services (in terms of worth) than it has exported. In 2017, for example, the United States exported $1.5 trillion in goods and service while importing $2.2 trillion, leaving a negative balance of trade of about $737 billion.

The Impact of Import Restrictions on Exports

Import restrictions are often touted as a way to save American jobs, but they may also trigger similar restrictions from other nations. In response to U.S. restrictions and to protect their local agricultural sector, Japan placed severe restrictions on the importation of American beef and other food products, hurting American farmers.

Import restrictions can result in higher prices for American consumers. One example is the automobile industry, where "voluntary" restrictions on Japanese car imports were in place for more than a decade. The United States and Japan entered into a "voluntary agreement" to reduce imports of Japanese cars from 1981 into the late 1990s. The result was more demand for Japanese cars than supply, and their prices went up. Domestic carmakers then increased their prices to match those of the imported cars. The estimated cost in one year to consumers was $6.5 billion, or $250,000 for each of the 26,000 American jobs saved. To become even more competitive, the major Japanese and Korean car companies now assemble cars in the United States, employing thousands of Americans in their plants.

Quotas and Tariffs The U.S. government uses two key tools to restrict foreign trade: import quotas and tariffs, both of which protect American products from competition. An **import quota** is a restriction imposed on the value or number of units of a particular good that can be brought into the United States. **Tariffs** are taxes specifically on imports. Tariffs can be set as a particular dollar amount per unit—say, 10 cents per pound—or as a percentage of the value of the imported commodity.

Free-Trade Areas and Common Markets To lower or even eliminate restrictions on free trade among nations, some nations and groups of nations have created free-trade areas, sometimes called "common markets." The oldest and

imports
Goods and services produced outside a country but sold within its borders.

exports
Goods and services produced domestically for sale abroad.

balance of trade
The difference between the value of a nation's exports of goods and the value of its imports of goods.

did you know?
About 5 million containers of cars, clothing, and other products are aboard ships every day around the world.

import quota
A restriction imposed on the value or number of units of a particular good that can be brought into a country. Foreign suppliers are unable to sell more than the amount specified in the import quota.

tariffs
Taxes on imports.

Image 16–5

Trucks from Mexico cross the border in California and may continue on to Canada under the terms of the NAFTA agreement. President Trump sought to renegotiate the agreement to get better terms for the U.S.

best-known common market is today called the European Union (EU). As of 2016, the EU consisted of 28 member nations. These countries have eliminated almost all restrictions on trade in both goods and services among themselves.

On our side of the Atlantic, the best-known free-trade zone consists of Canada, the United States, and Mexico. This free-trade zone was created by the North American Free Trade Agreement (NAFTA), approved by Congress in 1993. A more recent trade agreement is the Central American–Dominican Republic Free Trade Agreement (CAFTA-DR), which was signed into law by President George W. Bush in 2005. This agreement was formed by Costa Rica, the Dominican Republic, El Salvador, Guatemala, Honduras, Nicaragua, and the United States. CAFTA-DR was implemented on a rolling basis as the trade partners agreed to various provisions. The CAFTA agreement is still opposed by many members of American textile workers' unions, which see it as a threat to their jobs. The United States signed the Trans-Pacific Partnership but participation in the agreement was terminated by President Trump in 2017. The president took the stance that the agreement was not as "fair" as he believed it should be. He also proposed new tariffs on some of the United States trading partners to make trade more profitable to American companies.

The World Trade Organization

Since 1997, the principal institution overseeing tariffs throughout the world has been the World Trade Organization (WTO), designed to lessen trade barriers throughout the world so that all nations can benefit from freer international trade.

What the WTO Does The WTO's many tasks include administering trade agreements, acting as a forum for trade negotiations, settling trade disputes, and reviewing national trade policies. Today, the WTO has more than 164 member nations, accounting for more than 97 percent of world trade. Another 22 countries are negotiating to obtain membership. It has settled many trade disputes between countries. The United States took a case against the European Union to the WTO, charging that the EU imposed unfair tariffs on bananas from the Western

Hemisphere. In that case the WTO ruled in the favor of the United States and its Central American partners. In other cases, the United States has not fared as well.

The WTO continues to work to lower trade barriers across the world, but the negotiations are slow and difficult. Some countries do not want to be flooded with cheap products from other nations that will destroy their own industries. Almost every nation and region works to protect its own agricultural sector and its small farmers. Even within the EU, the winemakers of France and Italy fight over trade policy.

Sending Work Overseas

For hundreds of years, nations have bought goods and services from abroad. Nonetheless, Americans have always perceived the purchase of services from other countries as a way of allowing those countries to "steal" American jobs. Today, such activity is called either *offshoring* or *outsourcing*. During the 2016 presidential campaigns, outsourcing continued to be a hot topic, particularly as factories continued to close in the United States.

Outsourcing diminished during the economic downturn, in part because other nations were experiencing economic problems even greater than those in the United States. At the time of this writing, the U.S. labor market has about 154 million workers and in any one month, roughly 4 million of these workers start new jobs with new employers. However, the Bureau of Labor Statistics has forecast the loss of millions of service-sector jobs in the future due, in part, to increased automation of services. Call centers and computer data centers overseas may replace many technical and service workers in the United States.

Outsourcing is here to stay, but the countries to which jobs are outsourced may change. India and China were the leading "villains" in the outsourcing debate a few years ago, but other countries may soon take their place. Why? Wages for outsourcing services are rising rapidly in both of those countries. This means that other low-wage countries, such as the Philippines and Indonesia, may become larger providers of services.

Facing the Future

Even though American economic growth slowed during the 2008 recession and many Americans lost their jobs, the economy of the United States is still the strongest in the world, and the American dollar remains the currency of world trade. The people of the United States are envied for their freedom, for their access to education, and for their ability to innovate. These qualities will keep the United States a strong economy for many decades in the future.

The economic recession of 2007–2008 and the long economic slowdown that followed will have lasting effects on several generations of Americans. Students who graduated from college during this period may have had a harder time getting a job, paying off their student loans, and moving into their own homes. Many middle-class and middle-aged Americans either lost their homes or saw the value of their homes decline due to the mortgage crisis. Baby boomers saw the value of their retirement savings greatly diminish and must work longer than planned before they can retire. These effects are not only personal: the debt incurred by the government to stimulate the economy and carry people through the recession will need to be repaid over time. To do this, political leaders must come together and work out plans for future sources of revenue and reform spending programs to keep the nation's economy strong.

Key Terms

Chapter Summary

■ **16.1** The recession of 2008 was caused by a multitude of factors, including the relaxing of regulations on banks and investment houses, increasing numbers of mortgages in default, excessive speculation by some investors, and a housing bubble that saw the price of housing reach unsustainable levels. These factors came together as the recession began and caused a crisis in the economic system. The government's attempts to stop a worldwide depression and then to get the economy restarted included bailout funds for financial institutions, stimulus programs, extended unemployment benefits, reductions in Social Security taxes, and an increase in the national debt.

■ **16.2** One of the most important policy goals of the federal government is to maintain economic growth without falling into either excessive unemployment or inflation (rising prices). Inflation is commonly measured using the Consumer Price Index (CPI) published by the U.S. Bureau of Labor Statistics. The regular fluctuations in the economy are called business cycles. If the economy fails to grow for two consecutive quarters, the nation is experiencing a recession. The president, the Congress, and the Federal Reserve System all have tools to help stabilize the economy. Generally, the two major strategies are fiscal policy and monetary policy.

■ **16.3** Fiscal policy is the use of taxes and spending to affect the overall economy. Economist John Maynard Keynes is credited with developing a theory under which the government should run budget deficits during recessions to stimulate the economy. Keynes also advocated budget surpluses in boom times, but political leaders have been reluctant to implement this side of the policy. Time lags in implementing fiscal policy can create serious difficulties.

■ **16.4** The federal government has run a deficit in most years since the 1930s. The deficit is met by U.S. Treasury borrowing. This adds to the public debt of the U.S. government. Although the budget was temporarily in surplus

from 1998 to 2002, deficits now seem likely for many years to come.

■ **16.5** The various types of taxes levied by the federal, state, and local governments have different goals and different impacts on citizens. U.S. taxes amount to about 25 percent of the gross domestic product, which is not particularly high by international standards. Individuals and corporations that pay taxes at the highest rates will try to pressure Congress into creating exemptions and tax loopholes, which allow high-income earners to reduce their taxable incomes. The federal income tax is progressive; that is, tax rates increase as income increases. Some other taxes, such as the Social Security tax and state sales taxes, are regressive—they take a larger share of the income of poorer people. As a whole, the tax system is slightly progressive.

■ **16.6** One of the issues facing the United States is the viability of such entitlement programs as Social Security and Medicare. These programs are actually "promises" of benefits that must be paid to their respective recipients. As the number of people who are retired increases relative to the number of people who are working, those who are working may have to pay more for the benefits of those who retire. Proposed solutions to the problem include raising taxes, reducing benefits, allowing more immigration, and partially privatizing the Social Security system in hopes of obtaining higher rates of return on contributions.

■ **16.7** Monetary policy is controlled by the Federal Reserve System, or the Fed. Monetary policy involves changing the rate of growth of the money supply in an attempt to either stimulate or cool the economy. A loose monetary policy, in which more money is created, encourages economic growth. A tight monetary policy, in which less money is created, may be the only effective way of ending an inflationary spiral. Monetary policy may, however, be ineffectual in pulling the economy out of a severe recession—fiscal policy may be required.

■ **16.8** The United States imports and exports goods as well as services from and to nations around the world. Whereas economists of all persuasions strongly support world trade, the public is less enthusiastic. Restrictions on imports to protect jobs are often popular. Ultimately, however, imports are paid for by exports. Restricting imports restricts exports as well, with resulting loss of employment in export industries. Trade restrictions also increase the cost of the affected goods to consumers.

■ **16.9** Groups of nations have established free-trade blocs to encourage trade among themselves. Examples include the European Union and the North American Free Trade Association (NAFTA). The World Trade Organization (WTO) is an international organization that oversees trade disputes and provides a forum for negotiations to reduce trade restrictions. The WTO has been a source of controversy in American politics.

■ **16.10** The current account balance includes the balance of trade, which is limited to goods, and also the balance in the trade of services and other items. A possible problem for the future is the growing size of the U.S. current account deficit, which is funded by foreign investments in the United States.

Selected Resources

PRINT RESOURCES

Conti-Brown, Peter. *The Power and Independence of the Federal Reserve* (Princeton, NJ: Princeton University Press, 2016). The author gives a clear and complete explanation of the role of the Federal Reserve System in the American economy, dispelling many widely held suppositions about the power of the Fed.

Eberstadt, Nicholas. *A Nation of Takers: America's Entitlement Epidemic* (Templeton Press, W. Consohohocken, PA, 2012). The author, a researcher at the conservative think tank The Heritage Foundation, gives his criticism of increasing government benefit programs.

Mortensen, Gretchen, with Joshua Rosner. *Reckless Endangerment: How Outsized Ambition, Greed and Corruption Led to Economic Armageddon* (New York: Times Books, 2011). Mortenson, a reporter for the *New York Times*, gives a carefully researched account of the conditions leading to the recession in 2008.

Piketty, Thomas. *Capital in the Twenty-first Century* (New York: Belknap Books, 2014). This best-selling book takes a very different view of the relationship between government and capitalism. The author, an economist, proposes new ways to breach inequalities in Western nations.

Taibbi, Matt. *The Divide: American Injustice in the Age of the Wealth Gap* (New York: Speigel and Grau, 2014). While the economy and the wealth of the nation grows, inequality between income groups also grows. The author looks critically at how our economy rewards the very wealthiest Americans.

MEDIA RESOURCES

The Big Short—A star-studded cast depicts the strategies used by financial analysts and investors to gamble on the financial markets and make a great deal of money when the housing market collapsed in 2008.

Enron: The Smartest Guys in the Room—The risk-taking culture of the Enron Corporation led to its fall and the prosecution of many of its executives, even though, as this 2005 documentary shows, they were the smartest guys in the room.

Inside Job—An Academy Award–winning documentary that explains the causes of the recession and the strange financial products that failed.

Margin Call—This film is a very realistic look at the financial industry and the intense pressure placed on analysts to make split-second decisions worth billions of dollars.

Too Big to Fail—An HBO film that portrays the executive decisions at financial institutions that led to the recession. The plot and characters are based on real investors and their decisions.

ONLINE RESOURCES

Federal Reserve Bank of San Francisco—documents actions taken by the Federal Reserve: www.frbsf.org

Office for Management and Budget at the White House—OMB's predominant mission is to assist the president in overseeing the preparation of the federal budget and to supervise its administration in executive branch agencies; OMB's website features recent budgets and budget factsheets: www.whitehouse.gov/omb/budget

Organization for Economic Cooperation and Development—multinational research group that works to increase development and improve the quality of governance among all nations, with statistical reports that are a valuable source of comparative information: www.oecd.org

Tax Foundation—educates taxpayers about sound tax policy and the size of the tax burden borne by Americans at all levels of government; nonpartisan information about federal tax policy and its impact: www.taxfoundation.org

World Trade Organization—provides a set of rules and a negotiating forum for trade between nations at a global or nearly global level: www.wto.org

Foreign Policy and National Security

17

An unmanned aerial vehicle (drone) flies over the aircraft carrier *USS Carl Vinson*.

Everett Collection Inc/Alamy Stock Photo

LEARNING OBJECTIVES

After reading this chapter, you will be able to:

■ **17.1** Define foreign policy, diplomacy, and national security policy; explain how these policies shape the position of the United States in the world.

■ **17.2** Explain the president's role in setting foreign policy and national security policy; compare those powers to the powers of the Congress.

■ **17.3** Trace the evolution of U.S. foreign policy from isolationism to global leadership.

■ **17.4** Explain the origins of the war on terror and how it has influenced domestic policy and relations with other nations.

■ **17.5** Discuss the security and diplomatic challenges facing the United States today.

■ **17.6** Describe the current distribution of nuclear weapons in the world and the efforts to control further proliferation of these weapons.

What if...

The United States Disposed of All of Its Nuclear Weapons?

Background

At the height of the Cold War, both the United States and the Soviet Union possessed more than 10,000 nuclear warheads ready for missile launch. In addition to land-based missiles, both nations had fleets of submarines fully armed with nuclear missiles that could be launched in a matter of minutes. Efforts to limit these weapons began during the Nixon administration and, following the fall of the Soviet Union, several agreements have been signed by the United States and Russia to destroy significant numbers of these weapons.

What If the United States Disposed of All of Its Nuclear Weapons?

According to the Arms Control Association, the United States still maintains about 4,800 active and reserve nuclear warheads and more than 4,000 "retired" warheads waiting for disposal in some form or another. Russia has about 5,500 active and reserve warheads and more than 5,000 "retired" warheads waiting for disposal. What would happen if the United States declared unilaterally that it was proceeding to dismantle and destroy all of its nuclear weapons? It is likely that the other major Western nations that have nuclear weapons—the United Kingdom and France—would do likewise. Russia, which has agreed to a mutual plan for destroying part of its arsenal, might agree, in principle, to do so as well. China, which is estimated to hold 250 warheads, may or may not agree to do so. The nations thought to have nuclear arms but that do not admit to it include Israel, India, and Pakistan. North Korea is suspected of continuing to develop some type of nuclear weapon, and Iran was in an agreement with the United States and its European allies to confine its research to nuclear power until the United States withdrew.

Why wouldn't China, Russia, India, Pakistan, and Israel be quick to dispose of their weapons and thus reduce the possibility of a nuclear war that would threaten the existence of all life on earth? The answer lies in each nation's perception of its most immediate threat. Israel fears attacks from neighboring Arab nations; if the attacks involved a nuclear weapon, the results would be catastrophic. Pakistan, India, China, and Russia share common borders and are concerned about their vulnerability to attack. The nations that are secretly developing weapons are doing so supposedly for self-defense and

protection against their enemies. For these nations to dispose of their weapons requires the establishment of peace in their respective regions of the globe.

Can We Easily Dispose of These Weapons?

In 2010, the United States and Russia agreed to dispose of a large proportion of their stockpiles of nuclear material and reduce their numbers of actual warheads. This agreement followed a 2000 agreement between the nations to get rid of 34 tons of plutonium each, which is enough to make 17,000 bombs. Imagine how much other "spare" nuclear material is available around the world! The material has not been disposed of to date because other nations have not donated the promised $2 billion to help Russia fulfill its end of the bargain. Disposing of nuclear materials and dismantling nuclear warheads is an extremely expensive and difficult business. The 2010 agreement still governs today.

Nuclear material can be destroyed by "burning" it as fuel for energy, diluting it with waste from nuclear power plants, destroying it in accelerators, depositing it in deep holes bored in the earth, burying it beneath the seabed, or sending it to outer space. At the present time, any excess material from the destruction of nuclear warheads is "capsulized" in secure containers for permanent storage. Each method entails enormous problems involving the transport and secure storage of the material at every step. It would take several decades to dismantle and destroy all the material currently owned by the United States alone.

What Are the Politics of This Proposal?

Some arms control advocates have pushed for a nuclear-free world for many decades. In 2007, four prominent American statesmen, including George Shultz and Henry Kissinger, both former secretaries of state, called for increased focus on the global elimination of nuclear weapons. They noted that the "rogue" states and those worried about their own security might be convinced to give up their weapons if the United States and the world's strongest nations agreed to a multilateral approach that reduced the threat of nuclear weapons and provided a secure way to get rid of them together. Arms control advocates agree with the strategy, but suggest that the American nuclear industry and the weapons industry are dragging their feet and slowing down the process of agreeing to the end of the nuclear era because it would destroy their businesses. Conservatives who believe that a strong military posture is essential to American foreign policy point to dangers in the world to the United States and support retaining some nuclear capability. All in all, there does not seem to be enough trust in the world to begin this process.

For Critical Analysis

1. Do you think the United States would be safe from attack if it disposed of its nuclear arsenal?

2. How can the United States and Russia be sure that they have each disposed of all their weapons and that other nations have done so as well?

On any morning, Americans may see the world on their televisions or telephones. They might see President Trump meeting with the Prime Minister of Japan, Syrian refugees fleeing a bombing of their city, a terrorist attack in Europe, or a natural disaster such as a tsunami or earthquake. The world is "smaller" and more accessible to Americans than at any time in history, although Americans are, in general, not better informed about events abroad.

The world has also become an even more complex place for the United States as a nation. It is not clear who might be the enemy or enemies of the United States or what role the United States should play in global affairs. At the end of World War II, the United States was the undisputed leader of the "free world" and a military and economic superpower. Today, the U.S. economy is deeply intertwined with the world economy, our military is not welcome in many nations, and our motives may be suspect to many of the world's freedom fighters. Yet, when a crisis occurs abroad, such as Russia attempting to annex Crimea, formerly part of the nation of Ukraine, the world turns to the United States to intervene.

This chapter examines the tools of foreign policy and national security policy in light of the many challenges facing the United States in the world today, including the threat of nuclear weapons.

Facing the World: Foreign and Defense Policy

■ **17.1** Define foreign policy, diplomacy, and national security policy; explain how these policies shape the position of the United States in the world.

The United States is only one nation in a world with more than 200 independent countries, each of which has its own national goals and interests. What tools does our nation have to deal with the many challenges to its peace and prosperity? One tool is **foreign policy**—the goals the government wants to achieve in the world and the techniques and strategies used to achieve them. If one national goal is to achieve stability in the Middle East and to encourage the formation of pro-American governments there, U.S. foreign policy in

foreign policy
A nation's external goals and the techniques and strategies used to achieve them.

diplomacy
The process by which nations carry on political relations with each other; settling conflicts among nations by peaceful means.

economic aid
Assistance to other nations in the form of grants, loans, or credits to buy the assisting nation's products.

technical assistance
The practice of sending experts in such areas as agriculture, engineering, or business to aid other nations.

foreign policy process
The steps by which foreign policy goals are decided and acted on.

national security policy
Foreign and domestic policy designed to protect the nation's independence and political and economic integrity; policy concerned with the safety and defense of the nation.

defense policy
A subset of national security policies pertaining to the U.S. armed forces.

Image 17–1
To Come

that area may be carried out through **diplomacy**, **economic aid**, **technical assistance**, or military intervention. Sometimes foreign policies are restricted to statements of goals or ideas, such as ending the HIV/AIDS epidemic in Africa, whereas at other times foreign policies are comprehensive efforts to achieve particular objectives, such as changing the regime in Iraq. In the United States, the **foreign policy process** usually originates with the president and those agencies that provide advice on foreign policy matters. Congressional action and national public debate often affect foreign policy formulation.

National Security Policy

As one aspect of overall foreign policy, **national security policy** is designed primarily to protect the independence and the political integrity of the United States. It concerns itself with the defense of the United States against actual or potential (real or imagined) enemies, domestic or foreign.

U.S. national security policy is based on determinations made by the Department of Defense, the Department of State, and many other federal agencies, including the National Security Council (NSC). The NSC acts as an advisory body to the president, but it has increasingly become a rival to the State Department in influencing the foreign policy process.

Defense policy is a subset of national security policy. Generally, defense policy refers to the set of policies that direct the scale and size of the U.S. armed forces. Among the questions defense policymakers must consider is the number of major wars the United States should be prepared to fight simultaneously. Defense policy also considers the types of armed forces units we need to have (Rapid Defense Forces and Marine Expeditionary Forces being two examples) and the types of weaponry that should be developed and maintained for the nation's security. Defense policies are proposed by the leaders of the nation's military forces and the secretary of defense and are greatly influenced by congressional decision makers and by the companies that manufacture weapons, aircraft, and ships.

Diplomacy

Diplomacy is another aspect of foreign policy. Diplomacy includes all of a nation's external relationships, from routine diplomatic communications to summit meetings among heads of state. More specifically, diplomacy refers to the settling of disputes and conflicts among nations by peaceful methods. Diplomacy is the set of negotiating techniques by which a nation attempts to carry out its foreign policy.

Diplomacy can be carried out by individual nations, by groups of nations, or by international organizations. In 2012, after Mohamed Morsi became president following Egypt's first democratic election in decades, Secretary of State Hillary Clinton traveled to Egypt to meet him. Her conversations as the leader of the American diplomatic team

KENA BETANCUR/Getty Images

conveyed American support for the new democratic regime, assurances of continued American assistance, and, most likely, concerns over any attempt to repress the Christian population of that predominantly Muslim nation. When Morsi was removed from office a year later, the United States opened discussions with the military leaders of the country in order to press for democratic elections and equal treatment of all Egyptians.

Over the past 50 years, American presidents have often exercised diplomacy to encourage peace in the Middle East. The most successful example was President Jimmy Carter's efforts in 1978 to get Israel and Egypt to agree to a path to peaceful relations. The Camp David Accords were negotiated in the United States by the leaders of Egypt and Israel with the direct mediation of President Carter. The two countries agreed to work toward peace between them, including mutual recognition.[1] Diplomacy can be successful only if the parties are willing to negotiate. The United States continues to work with European allies to pressure Iran to reject the development of nuclear weapons and—through talks including Russia, China, Japan, South Korea, and North Korea—to persuade North Korea to end its weapons development. In 2018, after years of violating the agreement and a number of long-range missile tests, the North Korean leader agreed to negotiate with the United States and South Korea to end its weapons development.

After months of negotiation, Secretary of State John Kerry and the representatives of many other nations succeeded in getting an agreement with Iran to delay its program to acquire nuclear weapons and to destroy nuclear material and equipment in return for the lifting of economic sanctions by the United States and the European nations. In addition, Iran agreed not to reactivate its program to create nuclear weapons for at least 15 years. After one year of reviewing the agreement, President Trump withdrew the United States from the agreement in 2018 and reimposed sanctions on Iran.

Who Makes Foreign Policy?

■ **17.2** Explain the president's role in setting foreign policy and national security policy; compare those powers to the powers of the Congress.

Given the vast array of challenges in the world, developing a comprehensive U.S. foreign policy is a demanding task. Does this responsibility fall to the president, to Congress, or to both acting jointly? There is no easy answer to this question, because, as constitutional authority Edwin S. Corwin once observed, the U.S. Constitution created an "invitation to struggle" between the president and Congress for control over the foreign policy process.

Constitutional Powers of the President

The Constitution confers on the president broad powers that are either explicit or implied in key constitutional provisions. Article II vests the executive power of the government in the president. The presidential oath of office given in Article II, Section 1, requires that the president "solemnly swear" to "preserve, protect and defend the Constitution of the United States."

---

1   To read the text of the Camp David Accords, go to: www.jimmycarterlibrary.org/documents/campdavid/accords

Image 17-2

President Obama,
Vice President Biden, Secretary of
State Hillary Clinton, and other
members of the national security
team monitor the Navy SEAL raid
on the home of Osama bin Laden
in 2011.

War Powers Perhaps more importantly, Article II, Section 2, designates the president as "Commander in Chief of the Army and Navy of the United States." Beginning with Abraham Lincoln, all presidents have interpreted this authority dynamically and broadly. The United States has been involved in at least 125 undeclared wars conducted under presidential authority. In 1950, Harry Truman ordered U.S. armed forces in the Pacific to counter North Korea's invasion of South Korea. Dwight Eisenhower threatened China and North Korea with nuclear weapons if the Korean peace talks were not successfully concluded. Bill Clinton sent troops to Haiti and Bosnia. In 2001, George W. Bush authorized an attack against the al-Qaeda terrorist network and the Taliban government in Afghanistan. In 2003, after receiving authorization from Congress to use force, Bush sent military forces to Iraq to depose Saddam Hussein.

The president's "war powers" also include the ability to approve covert operations by the military or intelligence agencies and the use of surveillance technologies outside the United States. While a candidate, Barack Obama decried some of President Bush's decisions, including opening the prison at Guantánamo Bay and holding some prisoners abroad in unspecified locations. After only a short time in office, he began using his war powers to make similar decisions. One of the most striking decisions made by President Obama was to increase the use of unmanned drones to assassinate the leadership of al-Qaeda wherever they could be found. According to David Sanger, the president personally approved each target for the drone strikes.[2] Collateral civilian deaths from some of the strikes in Pakistan aggravated U.S.–Pakistan relations, as did the raid on Osama bin Laden's compound in May 2011. Again, the president personally approved the raid, in which Navy SEAL teams were helicoptered into a Pakistani city, attacked bin Laden's compound, killed the al-Qaeda leader, and took the body to a Navy ship for burial at sea.

---

2 David E. Sanger, *Confront and Conceal: Obama's Secret Wars and Surprising Use of American Power* (New York: Crown, 2012).

Treaties and Executive Agreements Article II, Section 2, of the Constitution also grants the president the power to make treaties, provided that two-thirds of the senators present concur. Presidents usually have been successful in getting treaties through the Senate. In addition to this formal treaty-making power, the president uses executive agreements (see Chapter 12). Since World War II, executive agreements have accounted for almost 95 percent of the understandings reached between the United States and other nations.

Executive agreements have a long and important history. During World War II, Franklin Roosevelt reached several agreements with the Soviet Union and other countries on how nations would be treated after the war. One agreement with long-term results was concluded at Yalta in the Soviet Crimea. In all, since 1946, more than 8,000 executive agreements with foreign countries have been made. A relatively small number of these agreements were kept secret due to security concerns. In 1972, however, Congress passed the Case-Zabloki Act, which requires all agreements to be reported to Congress. There are probably several hundred agreements that have never been reported to Congress because the president has considered them "understandings" or "statements of intent" rather than executive agreements.

Election 2016

Becoming Chief Diplomat and Commander in Chief

Whoever is elected president in any election cycle is likely to know very little about the inner working of foreign policy and national security policy. Unless she or he has served as vice president or in a top diplomatic position, the new president must learn quickly to deal with international issues. The president has the opportunity every morning, as early as possible, to meet with the national security advisor or other top officials and be briefed on overnight events around the world. Did a U.S. drone strike accidentally hit a school or, has an earthquake occurred in the Philippines? What does that mean for the United States?

In 2016, the two presidential nominees had vastly different experiences in the international arena: The Democrat, former Secretary of State Hillary Clinton, was very familiar with the role of the president in foreign affairs, although she had no direct experience in military affairs. Republican real estate entrepreneur Donald Trump had no experience in government in either domestic or foreign policy, although he had developed properties in nations around the world.

Has American foreign policy changed under the new president? President Barack Obama began his presidency by visiting the Middle East and pledging a new approach to foreign policy, one that was much less interventionist and more cooperative. Although the president was not able to extract the American military from Afghanistan as he promised, he oversaw a more restrained foreign policy for the United States. Secretary of State Clinton, according to many commentators, was expected to take a more activist role in the world than President Obama, whereas Donald Trump believes in a less active interventionist role. The truth is that the president will face decisions, crises, and situations that are totally unexpected and he will need to adjust personal views to make appropriate decisions just as has President Obama. President Trump is facing the Syrian Civil War, the collapse of the Venezuela economy and a number of other issues unknown at the time of the campaign.

For Critical Analysis

1. How important is military experience to understanding and working with the American military establishment?

2. How does a president develop working relationships with foreign leaders, such as the leaders of China, Russia, Israel, and Saudi Arabia?

Dirck Halstead/Getty Images

Image 17–3
President Carter shakes hands with Panamanian leader General Omar Torrijos after the signing of the Panama Canal Treaties in 1977.

Other Constitutional Powers An additional power conferred on the president in Article II, Section 2, is the right to appoint ambassadors, other public ministers, and consuls. In Section 3 of that article, the president is given the power to recognize foreign governments by receiving their ambassadors. In 2015, President Obama formally recognized the government of Cuba, more than 50 years since Fidel Castro took control of that island nation. The United States reopened its embassy in Havana, and many of the restrictions on travel to Cuba were lifted.

Informal Techniques of Presidential Leadership

Other broad sources of presidential power in the U.S. foreign policy process are tradition, precedent, and the president's personality. The president can employ a host of informal techniques that give the White House overwhelming superiority within the government in foreign policy leadership.

First, the president has access to strategic intelligence provided by the Central Intelligence Agency (CIA) daily in order to make quick decisions and implement those decisions. Second, the president is a legislative leader who can influence the funds that are allocated for different programs. Third, the president can influence public opinion. President Theodore Roosevelt once made the following statement:

People used to say to me that I was an astonishingly good politician and divined what the people are going to think. . . . I did not "divine" how the people were going to think; I simply made up my mind what they ought to think and then did my best to get them to think it.[3]

Presidents are without equal with respect to influencing public opinion, partly because of their ability to command the media. Depending on their skill in appealing to patriotic sentiment (and sometimes fear), they can make people believe that their course in foreign affairs is right and necessary. During his first year in office, President Obama changed the tone of American policy, visiting a number of nations to express support for democracy and signaling that the United States would not intervene militarily in the affairs of other nations. World public opinion responded to these declarations with an increase in approval for the United States in many nations. President George W. Bush's speech to Congress shortly after the September 11, 2001, attacks rallied the nation and brought new respect for his leadership. Presidents normally, although certainly not always, receive the immediate support of the American

---

3   Sidney Warren, *The President as World Leader* (New York: McGraw-Hill, 1964), p. 23.

people in a foreign policy crisis. Political scientists have labeled this "the rally 'round the flag effect."

Finally, the president can commit the nation morally to a course of action in foreign affairs. Because the president is the head of state and the leader of one of the most powerful nations on earth, once the president has made a commitment on behalf of the United States, it is difficult for Congress or anyone else to back down on that commitment.

Other Sources of Foreign Policymaking

In addition to the president, there are at least four foreign policymaking sources within the executive branch: (1) the Department of State, (2) the National Security Council, (3) the intelligence community, and (4) the Department of Defense.

The Department of State   In principle, the State Department is the executive agency that has primary authority over foreign affairs. It supervises U.S. relations with the more than 200 independent nations around the world and with the United Nations and other multinational groups, such as the Organization of American States. It staffs embassies and consulates throughout the world. It has about 24,000 full-time employees in the United States while also employing about 45,000 foreign nationals overseas. This number may sound impressive, but it is small compared with, say, the 86,000 employees of the Department of Health and Human Services. Also, the State Department had an annual budget of only $47.4 billion in fiscal year 2017, one of the smallest budgets of the cabinet departments.

Newly elected presidents usually tell the American public that the new secretary of state is the nation's chief foreign policy adviser. Hillary Clinton was the chief diplomat for the first term of the Obama presidency. Former Senator John Kerry became secretary of state in 2013. Nonetheless, the State Department's preeminence in foreign policy has declined since World War II. Its image within the White House Executive Office and Congress (and even with foreign governments) is quite poor—a slow, plodding, bureaucratic maze of inefficient, indecisive individuals. Reportedly, Premier Nikita Khrushchev of the Soviet Union urged President John F. Kennedy to formulate his own views rather than rely on State Department officials who, according to Khrushchev, "specialized in why something had not worked forty years ago."[4]

It is not surprising that the State Department has been overshadowed in foreign policy. It has no natural domestic constituency as does, for example, the Department of Defense, which can call on defense contractors for support. Instead, the State Department has what might be called **negative constituents**—U.S. citizens who openly oppose the government's policies. One of its major functions, administering foreign aid, often elicits criticisms. There is a widespread belief that the United States spends much more on foreign aid than it actually does. For 2017 Congress approved about $47.4 billion for the State Department and foreign aid, or about 1.5 percent of total federal spending.

negative constituents
Citizens who openly oppose the government's policies.

---

4   Theodore C. Sorensen, *Kennedy* (New York: Harper & Row, 1965), pp. 554–555.

The National Security Council The job of the NSC, created by the National Security Act of 1947, is to advise the president on the integration of "domestic, foreign, and military policies relating to the national security." The role of national security advisor to the president seems to adjust to fit the player. Some advisors have come into conflict with heads of the State Department. Henry A. Kissinger, Nixon's flamboyant and aggressive national security advisor, rapidly gained ascendancy over William Rogers, the secretary of state. Condoleezza Rice played an important role as national security advisor during George W. Bush's first term. Susan Rice, who had been U.S. ambassador to the United Nations, became the national security advisor to President Obama in 2013.

The Intelligence Community No discussion of foreign policy would be complete without some mention of the **intelligence community**, the 40 or more government agencies or bureaus involved in intelligence activities. They include the following:

intelligence community
The government agencies that gather information about the capabilities and intentions of foreign governments or that engage in covert actions.

1. Central Intelligence Agency (CIA)

2. National Security Agency (NSA)

3. Defense Intelligence Agency (DIA)

4. Offices within the Department of Defense

5. Bureau of Intelligence and Research in the Department of State

6. Federal Bureau of Investigation (FBI)

7. Army intelligence

8. Air Force intelligence

9. Drug Enforcement Administration (DEA)

10. Department of Energy

11. Directorate of Information Analysis and Infrastructure Protection in the Department of Homeland Security

12. Office of the Director of National Intelligence

At the time of its creation in 1947, the CIA was intended to be the lead organization in the intelligence community.

did you know?

The budget of the CIA is about $14.7 billion and the agency has about 22,000 employees.

Covert Actions Intelligence activities consist mostly of overt information gathering, but covert actions also are undertaken. Covert actions are carried out in secret, and the American public rarely finds out about them. The CIA covertly aided in the overthrow of the Mossadegh regime of Iran in 1953 and the Árbenz government of Guatemala in 1954. The agency was instrumental in destabilizing the Allende government in Chile from 1970 to 1973.

During the mid-1970s, the "dark side" of the CIA was partly uncovered when the Senate undertook an investigation of its activities. One of the major findings of the Senate Select Committee on Intelligence was that the CIA had routinely spied on American citizens domestically—supposedly a prohibited activity. Consequently, the CIA was scrutinized by oversight committees within Congress, which restricted the scope of its operations. By 1980, however, the CIA had regained much of its lost power to engage in covert activities.

Criticisms of the Intelligence Community By 2001, the CIA had come under fire for several lapses, including the discovery that one of its agents was spying on behalf of a foreign power, the failure to detect the nuclear arsenals of India and Pakistan, and, above all, the failure to obtain advance knowledge about the September 11, 2001, terrorist attacks. With the rise of terrorism as a threat, the intelligence agencies have received more funding and enhanced surveillance powers, but these moves have also provoked fears of civil liberties violations. In 2004, the bipartisan September 11 Commission called for a new intelligence czar to oversee the entire intelligence community, with full control of all agency budgets. Legislation enacted in 2004 established the Office of the Director of National Intelligence to oversee the intelligence community. In 2005, Bush appointed John Negroponte as the first director. In 2009, Obama named the fourth director in five years to the position. It seemed apparent that infighting with the CIA chief and other national security advisors makes this a very difficult position to hold.

Since the terrorist attacks of September 11, 2001, all of the American intelligence agencies have expended considerable effort to stop terrorist plots at home and overseas. Although they were granted enhanced powers for intelligence gathering under the PATRIOT Act and its extensions, most Americans were unaware of the degree to which these agencies use the latest technology to find potential terrorist actors. Edward Snowden, a former contract employee of the National Security Agency, gathered millions of documents from the Internet and, after fleeing the country, made them public. The U.S. government believes that he has endangered the lives of many Americans in the intelligence agency, whereas Snowden sees himself as a whistleblower who has informed his fellow citizens of the extent of NSA spying.[5] Since Snowden's revelations, the intelligence agencies have sought more access to individuals' telephone and Internet records whereas the technology companies have generally resisted granting that access.

The Department of Defense (DOD) The DoD was created in 1947 to bring the various activities of the American military establishment under the jurisdiction of a single department headed by a civilian secretary of defense. The joint chiefs of staff, consisting of the commanders of the various military branches and a chairperson, was created to formulate a unified military strategy.

Although the DoD is larger than any other federal department, it declined in size after the fall of the Soviet Union in 1991. In the subsequent 10 years, the total number of civilian employees was reduced by about 400,000, to about 665,000. Military personnel were also reduced in number. The defense budget remained relatively flat for several years, but with the onset of the war on terrorism and the use of military forces in Afghanistan and Iraq, funding has again been increased.

did you know?

The Pentagon's stockpile of strategic materials includes 1.5 million pounds of quartz crystals used in pre–Great Depression radios and 150,000 tons of tannin for tanning cavalry saddles.

---

5 Snowden's effort to reveal the secret information compiled by the U.S. government and the NSA's use of technology to track terrorists is told by his confidant, journalist Glenn Greenwald, in *No Place to Hide: Edward Snowden, the NSA and the U.S. Surveillance State* (New York: Macmillan, 2014). The documentary *Citizenfour* (2015) includes interviews with Snowden and Greenwald.

Johnny Bivera, U.S. Navy

Image 17-4

An aerial view

of the Pentagon, the headquarters of the U.S. Department of Defense (DoD), located between the Potomac River and Arlington National Cemetery. The Pentagon employs approximately 23,000 military and civilian personnel and is one of the world's largest office buildings, with three times the floor space of the Empire State Building in New York City. In the background, the obelisk of the Washington Monument is visible. When the media refer to the Pentagon, what do they mean?

Congress Balances the Presidency

A new interest in the balance of power between Congress and the president on foreign policy questions developed during the Vietnam War (1964–1975). Sensitive to public frustration over the long and costly war and angry at Richard Nixon for the secret invasion of Cambodia during that war, Congress attempted to establish limits on the power of the president in setting foreign and defense policy. In 1973, Congress passed the War Powers Resolution Act over President Nixon's veto. The act limited the president's use of troops in military action without congressional approval (see Chapter 12). Most presidents, however, have not interpreted the "consultation" provisions of the act as meaning that Congress should be consulted before military action is taken. Instead, presidents Ford, Carter, Reagan, George H. W. Bush, and Clinton ordered troop movements and then informed congressional leaders. It is quite possible for a president to commit troops to a situation from which the nation could not withdraw without incurring heavy losses, whether or not Congress is consulted.

Congress has also exerted its authority by limiting or denying presidential requests for military assistance to various groups (such as Angolan rebels and the government of El Salvador) and requests for new weapons (such as the B-1 bomber). In general, Congress has been hesitant to back a presidential push for military involvement when long-term troop commitment is a possibility. Like most members of the American public, members of Congress do not want to see American troops in harm's way unnecessarily.

Congress has its limits, of course, and often these are based on political considerations about election campaigns. Prior to the 2006 elections, Democrats found that antiwar platforms could be very effective during their campaigns. Certainly, the Iraq War and the future foreign policy direction of the United States were very important issues in the presidential and congressional elections of 2008; however, when the Democratic Party won control of the Congress and the presidency, it then assumed leadership of our national security policy. The party of the president tends to support the commander in chief even when its members may have personal doubts about the use of military force. It is likely that Democrats in Congress would have been very critical of the use of drones to assassinate terrorists if George W. Bush had been the commander in chief.

Domestic Sources of Foreign Policy

The making of foreign policy is often viewed as a presidential prerogative because of the president's constitutional power in that area and the resources of the executive branch that the president controls. Foreign policymaking is also influenced by elite and mass opinion and the *military–industrial complex.*

Elite and Mass Opinion

Public opinion influences the making of U.S. foreign policy through several channels. Elites in American business, education, communications, labor, and religion try to influence presidential decision making through several strategies. A number of elite organizations, such as the Council on Foreign Relations and the Trilateral Commission, work to increase international cooperation and to influence foreign policy through conferences, publications, and research. The members of the American elite establishment also exert influence on foreign policy through the general public by encouraging debate about foreign policy positions, publicizing the issues, and using the media.

Generally, the efforts of the president and the elites are most successful with the segment of the population called the **attentive public**. This sector of the mass public, which probably constitutes 10 to 20 percent of all citizens, is more interested in foreign affairs than are most other Americans, and members of the attentive public are likely to transmit their opinions to the less interested members of the public through conversation and local leadership.

Interest Group Politics in Global Affairs

Civilian fear of the relationship between the defense establishment and arms manufacturers (the **military–industrial complex**) dates back many years. During President Eisenhower's eight years in office, the former five-star army general experienced firsthand the kind of pressure that could be brought against him and other policymakers by arms manufacturers. Eisenhower decided to give the country a solemn and—as he saw it—necessary warning of the consequences of this influence. On January 17, 1961, in his last official speech, he said:

> *In the councils of government, we must guard against the acquisition of unwarranted influence, whether sought or unsought, by the military–industrial complex. The potential for the disastrous rise of misplaced power exists and will persist. . . . Only an alert and knowledgeable citizenry can compel the proper meshing of the huge industrial and military machinery of defense with our peaceful methods and goals, so that security and liberty may prosper together.*[6]

did you know?
A new aircraft carrier costs about $13 billion to build.

attentive public
That portion of the general public that pays attention to policy issues.

military–industrial complex
The mutually beneficial relationship between the armed forces and defense contractors.

---

6   Dwight D. Eisenhower, Farewell Address, Dwight D. Eisenhower Library, Museum and boyhood Home, http://www.eisenhower.archives.gov/research/online_documents/farewell_address.html

The Pentagon has supported a large sector of our economy through defense contracts and has supplied retired army officers as key executives to large defense-contracting firms. The Pentagon's strongest allies have been members of Congress whose districts or states benefit economically from military bases or contracts. After the Cold War ended in the late 1980s, the defense industry looked abroad for new customers. The United States is, at this point in history, the world's largest arms supplier.

Arms suppliers and defense contractors are not the only groups pressing Congress and the president to act on foreign policy issues. Corn and soybean farmers want trade policies that favor the exportation of their products; General Electric, Caterpillar, and John Deere want assistance to sell their machinery overseas; and, at home, Ukrainian Americans, Greek Americans, and many other groups lobby for foreign policies that address their home nation's issues.

The Major Themes of American Foreign Policy

■ **17.3** Trace the evolution of U.S. foreign policy from isolationism to global leadership.

Americans have always felt that their nation had a special destiny. The American experiment in democratic government and capitalism, it was thought, would provide the best possible life for citizens and be a model for other nations. As the United States assumed greater status as a power in world politics, Americans came to believe that the nation's actions on the world stage should be guided by American political and moral principles. As Harry Truman opined, "[t]he United States should take the lead in running the world in the way that it ought to be run." Truman's statement is a classic expression of a **moralist foreign policy**, which bases foreign policy decisions on the morally right decision. George W. Bush defended his invasion of Iraq as a moral decision to rid the world of a bad ruler, and Barack Obama supported the Libyan and Egyptian democracy movements on the moral grounds that democracy is the right of the people. At other times, and sometimes simultaneously, the United States may make decisions based on a **realist foreign policy** perspective, one that puts the nation's economic and security interests ahead of morality. The increased use of drones to track down and dispose of terrorists is an example of a realist decision.

Although some might suggest that U.S. foreign policy is inconsistent, the long view of American diplomatic ventures does reveal major themes underlying foreign policy. In the early years of the nation, presidents and the people generally agreed that the United States should avoid foreign entanglements and concentrate instead on its own development. From the beginning of the twentieth century until today, however, our global engagement has increased. The theme of the post–World War II years was the containment of communism. One of the themes for the first decades of the twenty-first century has been the battle against terrorism and, under President Obama, support for democracy movements in the Middle East.

The Formative Years: Avoiding Entanglements

Foreign policy was largely nonexistent during the formative years of the United States. Remember that the new nation was operating under the Articles of

moralist foreign policy
A foreign policy based on values and moral beliefs.

realist foreign policy
A foreign policy based on an understanding of the nation's economic and security interests.

Confederation. The national government had no right to levy or collect taxes, no control over commerce, no right to make commercial treaties, and no power to raise an army. The government's lack of international power was made clear when Barbary pirates seized American hostages in the Mediterranean. The United States was unable to rescue the hostages and ignominiously had to purchase them in a treaty with Morocco.

The founders had a basic mistrust of European governments. George Washington said it was the U.S. policy "to steer clear of permanent alliances," and Thomas Jefferson echoed this sentiment when he said America wanted peace with all nations but "entangling alliances with none." This was also a logical position at a time when the United States was so weak militarily that it could not influence European affairs directly. Moreover, being protected by oceans that took weeks to traverse certainly allowed the nation to avoid entangling alliances. During the 1800s, therefore, the United States generally stayed out of European conflicts and politics. In this hemisphere, however, the United States pursued an actively **expansionist policy**. The nation purchased Louisiana in 1803, annexed Texas in 1845, gained substantial territory from Mexico in 1848, purchased Alaska in 1867, and annexed Hawaii in 1898.

The Monroe Doctrine President James Monroe, in his message to Congress on December 2, 1823, stated that the United States would not accept foreign intervention in the Western Hemisphere. In return, the United States would not meddle in European affairs. The **Monroe Doctrine** was the underpinning of the U.S. **isolationist foreign policy** toward Europe, which continued throughout the 1800s.

The Spanish–American War and World War I The end of the isolationist policy started with the Spanish–American War in 1898. Winning the war gave the United States possession of Guam, Puerto Rico, and the Philippines (which gained independence in 1946). On the heels of that war came World War I (1914–1918). In his reelection campaign of 1916, President Woodrow Wilson ran on the slogan "He kept us out of war." Nonetheless, the United States declared war on Germany on April 6, 1917, because that country refused to give up its campaign of sinking all ships headed for Britain, including passenger ships. (Large passenger ships of that time commonly held more than a thousand people, so the sinking of such a ship was a disaster comparable to the attack on the World Trade Center.)

In the 1920s, the United States went "back to normalcy," as President Warren G. Harding urged it to do. U.S. military forces were largely disbanded, defense spending dropped to about 1 percent of total annual national income, and the nation returned to a period of isolationism.

The Era of Internationalism

Isolationism was permanently shattered by the bombing of the U.S. naval base at Pearl Harbor, Hawaii, on December 7, 1941. The surprise attack by the Japanese caused the deaths of 2,403 American servicemembers and wounded 1,143 others. Eighteen warships were sunk or seriously damaged, and 188 planes were destroyed at the airfields. The American public was outraged. President Franklin Roosevelt asked Congress to declare war on Japan immediately, and the United States entered World War II. This unequivocal response was certainly due to the nature of the provocation. American soil had not been attacked

expansionist policy
A policy that embraces the extension of American borders as far as possible.

Monroe Doctrine
A policy statement made by President James Monroe in 1823 which set out three principles: (1) European nations should not establish new colonies in the Western Hemisphere; (2) European nations should not intervene in the affairs of independent nations of the Western Hemisphere; and (3) the United States would not interfere in the affairs of European nations.

isolationist foreign policy
A policy of abstaining from an active role in international affairs or alliances, which characterized U.S. foreign policy toward Europe during most of the 1800s.

by a foreign power since the occupation of Washington, DC, by the British in 1814.

The United States was the only major participating country to emerge from World War II with its economy intact, and even strengthened. Britain, France, Germany, Italy, Japan, the Soviet Union, and several minor participants in the war were economically devastated. The United States was also the only country to have control over operational nuclear weapons. President Harry Truman had made the decision to use two atomic bombs, on August 6 and August 9, 1945, to end the war with Japan. (Historians still argue over the necessity of this action, which ultimately killed more than 100,000 Japanese and left an equal number permanently injured.) The United States truly had become the world's superpower.

The Cold War The United States had become an uncomfortable ally of the Soviet Union after Adolf Hitler's invasion of that country. Soon after World War II ended, relations between the Soviet Union and the West deteriorated. The Soviet Union wanted a weakened Germany and insisted that Germany be divided in two, with East Germany becoming a buffer against the West. Little by little, the Soviet Union helped install communist governments in Eastern European countries, which began to be referred to collectively as the **Soviet bloc**. In response, the United States encouraged the re-arming of Western Europe. The **Cold War** had begun.[7]

In Fulton, Missouri, on March 5, 1946, Winston Churchill declared that from the Baltic to the Adriatic Sea "an iron curtain has descended across the [European] continent." The term **iron curtain** became even more appropriate when Soviet-dominated East Germany built a wall separating East Berlin from West Berlin in August 1961.

Containment Policy In 1947, a remarkable article was published in *Foreign Affairs*, signed by "X." The actual author was George F. Kennan, chief of the policy-planning staff for the State Department. The doctrine of **containment** set forth in the article became—according to many—the bible of Western foreign policy. The author, "X," argued that whenever and wherever the Soviet Union could successfully challenge the West, it would do so. He recommended that our policy toward the Soviet Union be "firm and vigilant containment of Russian expansive tendencies."[8]

The containment theory was expressed clearly in the **Truman Doctrine**, which was enunciated by President Truman to Congress on March 12, 1947. In that address, he announced that the United States must help countries in which a communist takeover seemed likely. Later that year, he backed the Marshall Plan, an economic assistance plan for Europe that was intended to prevent the expansion of communist influence there. By 1950, the United States had entered into a military alliance with the European nations commonly called the North Atlantic Treaty Organization (NATO). The combined military power of the United States and the European nations worked to contain Soviet influence over Eastern Europe and to maintain a credible response to any Soviet military attack on Western Europe.

---

did you know?

There are 294 U.S. embassies, consulates, and diplomatic missions around the world.

Soviet bloc
The Soviet Union and the Eastern European countries that installed communist regimes after World War II and were dominated by the Soviet Union.

Cold War
The ideological, political, and economic confrontation between the United States and the Soviet Union following World War II.

iron curtain
The term used to describe the division of Europe between the Soviet bloc and the West; coined by Winston Churchill.

containment
A U.S. diplomatic policy adopted by the Truman administration to contain communist power within its existing boundaries.

Truman Doctrine
The policy adopted by President Harry Truman in 1947 to halt communist expansion in southeastern Europe.

---

7 See John Lewis Gaddis, *The United Nations and the Origins of the Cold War* (New York: Columbia University Press, 1972).
8 X, "The Sources of Soviet Conduct," *Foreign Affairs*, July 1947, p. 575.

Library of Congress Prints and Photographs Division [LC-USZ62-7449]

Image 17-5
British Prime Minister Winston Churchill, U.S. President Franklin Roosevelt, and Soviet leader Joseph Stalin met at Yalta from February 4 to 11, 1945, to resolve their differences over the shape that the international community would take after World War II.

Superpower Relations

During the Cold War, there was never any direct military conflict between the United States and the Soviet Union. Rather, confrontations among "client" nations were used to carry out the policies of the superpowers. Only on occasion did the United States directly enter a conflict in a significant way. Two such occasions were in Korea and in Vietnam.

After the end of World War II, northern Korea was occupied by the Soviet Union, and southern Korea was occupied by the United States. The result was two rival Korean governments. In 1950, North Korea invaded South Korea. Under United Nations authority, the United States entered the war, which prevented an almost certain South Korean defeat. When U.S. forces were on the brink of conquering North Korea, however, China joined the war on the side of the North, resulting in a stalemate. An armistice signed in 1953 led to the two Koreas that exist today. U.S. forces have remained in South Korea ever since.

The Vietnam War also involved the United States in a civil war between a communist North Vietnam and pro-Western South Vietnam. When the French army in Indochina was defeated by the communist forces of Ho Chi Minh and the two Vietnams were created in 1954, the United States assumed the role of supporting the South Vietnamese government against North Vietnam. President Kennedy sent 16,000 "advisers" to help South Vietnam, and after Kennedy's death in 1963, President Johnson greatly increased the scope of that support. More than 500,000 American troops were stationed in Vietnam at the height of the U.S. involvement. More than 58,000 Americans were killed and 300,000 were wounded in the conflict. A peace agreement in 1973 allowed U.S. troops to leave the country, and in 1975 North Vietnam easily occupied Saigon (the South Vietnamese capital) and unified the nation. Opposition to the war and to the military draft was intense.

The Cuban Missile Crisis Perhaps the closest the two superpowers came to a nuclear confrontation was the Cuban missile crisis in 1962. The Soviets installed missiles in Cuba, 90 miles off the U.S. coast, in response to Cuban fears of an American invasion and to try to balance an American nuclear advantage. President Kennedy and his advisers rejected the option of invading Cuba and set up a naval blockade around the island instead. When Soviet vessels appeared near Cuban waters, the tension reached its height. After intense negotiations between Washington and Moscow, the Soviet ships turned around on October 25, and on October 28, the Soviet Union announced the withdrawal of its missile operations from Cuba. In exchange, the United States agreed not to invade Cuba in the future and to remove some of its own missiles that were located near the Soviet border in Turkey.

A Period of *Détente* The French word ***détente*** means "a relaxation of tensions." By the end of the 1960s, it was clear that efforts were needed to reduce the threat of nuclear war between the United States and the Soviet Union. The Soviet Union gradually had begun to catch up in the building of strategic nuclear delivery vehicles in the form of bombers and missiles, thus balancing the nuclear scales between the two countries. Each nation acquired the military capacity to destroy the other with nuclear weapons.

As the result of lengthy negotiations under Secretary of State Henry Kissinger and President Nixon, the United States and the Soviet Union signed the **Strategic Arms Limitation Treaty (SALT I)** in May 1972. That treaty "permanently" limited the development and deployment of antiballistic missiles (ABMs) and limited the number of offensive missiles each country could deploy. To further reduce tensions, new scientific and cultural exchanges were arranged with the Soviets, as well as new opportunities for Jewish emigration out of the Soviet Union.

The policy of *détente* was not limited to the U.S. relationship with the Soviet Union. Seeing an opportunity to capitalize on increasing friction between the Soviet Union and the People's Republic of China, Kissinger secretly began negotiations to establish a new relationship with that nation. President Nixon eventually visited China in 1972. The visit set the stage for the formal diplomatic recognition of that country, which occurred during the Carter administration (1977–1981).

The Reagan–Bush Years President Reagan took a hard line against the Soviet Union during his first term, proposing the strategic defense initiative (SDI), or "Star Wars," in 1983. The SDI was designed to serve as a space-based defense against enemy missiles. Reagan and others in his administration argued that the program would deter nuclear war by shifting the emphasis of defense strategy from offensive to defensive weapons systems.

In November 1985, however, President Reagan and Mikhail Gorbachev, the Soviet leader, began to work on an arms reduction compact. The negotiations resulted in a historic agreement signed by the leaders on December 8, 1987. The terms of the Intermediate-Range Nuclear Force (INF) Treaty, which was ratified by the Senate, required the superpowers to dismantle a total of 4,000 intermediate-range missiles within the first three years of the agreement.

Beginning in 1989, President George H. W. Bush continued the negotiations with the Soviet Union to reduce the number of nuclear weapons and the number of armed troops in Europe. Subsequent events, including developments in Eastern Europe, the unification of Germany, and the dissolution of the Soviet

---

détente
A French word meaning "a relaxation of tensions." The term characterized U.S.–Soviet relations as they developed under President Richard Nixon and Secretary of State Henry Kissinger.

Strategic Arms Limitation Treaty (SALT I)
A treaty between the United States and the Soviet Union to stabilize the nuclear arms competition between the two countries. SALT I talks began in 1969, and agreements were signed on May 26, 1972.

Union (in December 1991), changed the world order. American and other Western leaders now worked to find and control the weapons that had formerly been in the inventory of the Soviet Union. Agreements were signed with Russia and with other former Soviet republics to reduce the weapons threat.

The Dissolution of the Soviet Union After the fall of the Berlin Wall in 1989, many Soviet-controlled states (such as Ukraine) became independent nations. Russia has struggled to become a democratic nation. Vladimir Putin was named acting president in 2000. After completing his terms, Putin became the premier of Russia in 2008 and then, in 2012, was elected president again. Although Putin has publicly declared his faith in a democratic regime, his actions, including unresolved murders of journalists and the jailing of his opponents, have helped him consolidate power.

In 2014, echoes of the Cold War could be heard across Eastern Europe. Ukraine, formerly part of the Soviet Union, negotiated with the European Union about the terms on which it might become a member nation. With a struggling economy, Ukraine needed to finance some of its debt to stabilize its regime. The president of Ukraine rejected the terms of the European Union and turned to Russia, which offered immediate assistance. The majority of citizens in the western part of Ukraine look to Western Europe as a model for their nation. The eastern portion of Ukraine has close ties with Russia. As protests boiled up against the Ukrainian president, Russian troops based in Crimea, a port on the Black Sea, took over buildings and military facilities. Economic sanctions were placed against Russian leaders by the United States and European nations. Within weeks, Crimea declared independence, and the Russian legislature approved its annexation to Russia. The crisis deepened when pro-Russian separatists in eastern Ukraine shot down a Malaysian passenger plane in July 2014. The United States and its European allies called for Russia to denounce this incident and cease supplying arms to the rebels. Russia has also been an active player in Middle Eastern politics, providing armaments and bombing raids to support Syrian president Assad and signing contracts for arms with Iran.

The War on Terror

■ **17.4** Explain the origins of the war on terror and how it has influenced domestic policy and relations with other nations.

In 2001, in a well-coordinated attack, terrorists hijacked four airplanes and crashed three of them into buildings—two into the World Trade Center towers in New York City and one into the Pentagon in Washington, DC The fourth airplane crashed in a field in Pennsylvania after the passengers fought the hijackers. The leaders of the network, including Osama bin Laden, were angered by the presence of U.S. troops on the soil of Saudi Arabia, which they regard as sacred. They also saw the United States as the primary defender of Israel against the Palestinians and as the defender of the royal family that governs Saudi Arabia. The attacks were intended to so frighten and demoralize the American people that they would convince their leaders to withdraw American troops from the Middle East.

After September 11, President Bush implemented stronger security measures to protect homeland security and U.S. facilities and personnel abroad. He sought and received congressional support for heightened airport security,

did you know?
The borders of most the nations in the Middle East were drawn by European nations after World War I.

new laws allowing greater domestic surveillance of potential terrorists, and new funding for the military. The Bush administration also conducted two military efforts as part of the war on terrorism.

The first military response to the attacks was directed against al Qaeda camps in Afghanistan and the Taliban regime, which had ruled that country since 1996. In late 2001, after building a coalition of international allies and anti-Taliban rebels within Afghanistan, the United States defeated the Taliban and fostered the creation of an interim government that did not support terrorism. In 2003, the Bush administration launched a war to remove Saddam Hussein from Iraq that embroiled the United States in a decade-long conflict.

Terrorism has posed a unique challenge for U.S. foreign policymakers. The Bush administration's response was unique. In September 2002, President Bush enunciated what has since become known as the "Bush doctrine," or the doctrine of preemption:

> We will . . . [defend] the United States, the American people, and our interests at home and abroad by identifying and destroying the threat before it reaches our borders. While the United States will constantly strive to enlist the support of the international community, we will not hesitate to act alone, if necessary, to exercise our right of self-defense by acting preemptively against such terrorists, to prevent them from doing harm against our people and our country.[9]

preemptive war
A military engagement fought to stop an enemy before that enemy attacks the United States.

The concept of "**preemptive war**" as a defense strategy was a new element in U.S. foreign policy. The concept is based on the assumption that self-defense must be *anticipatory*. As President Bush stated on March 17, 2003, just before launching the invasion of Iraq, "[r]esponding to such enemies only after they have struck first is not self-defense, it is suicide."

The Bush doctrine was not without its critics. Some pointed out that preemptive wars against other nations have traditionally been waged by dictators and rogue states—not democratic nations. By employing such tactics, the United States would seem to be contradicting its basic values. In his campaign for president, Barack Obama repudiated this approach to national security policy and, in the first year of his presidency, made a number of speeches abroad in which he signaled a new, more conciliatory approach to other nations.

The Iraq and Afghanistan Wars

On August 2, 1990, the Persian Gulf became the setting for a major challenge to the international system set up after World War II (1939–1945). President Saddam Hussein of Iraq sent troops into the neighboring oil sheikdom of Kuwait, occupying that country. This was the most clear-cut case of aggression against an independent nation in half a century.

The Persian Gulf—The First Gulf War At the formal request of the king of Saudi Arabia, American troops were dispatched to set up a defensive line at the Kuwaiti border. After the United Nations approved a resolution authorizing the use of force if Saddam Hussein did not respond to sanctions, the U.S. Congress reluctantly also approved such an authorization. On January 17, 1991, two days after a deadline for Hussein to withdraw, U.S.-led coalition forces launched a massive air attack on Iraq. After several weeks, the ground offensive began. Iraqi troops retreated from Kuwait a few days later, and the

---

9 George W. Bush, "National Strategy for Combating Terrorism," February 2003. https://www.state.gov/documents/organization/60172.pdf

First Gulf War ended, although many Americans criticized President George H. W. Bush for not sending troops to Baghdad to depose Saddam Hussein.

As part of the cease-fire that ended the Gulf War, Iraq agreed to abide by all UN resolutions and to allow UN weapons inspectors to search for and oversee the destruction of its medium-range missiles and all weapons of mass destruction, including any chemical and nuclear weapons, and related research facilities. In 1999, however, Iraq placed so many obstacles in the path of the UN inspectors that they withdrew from the country.

The Iraq War After the terrorist attacks on the United States on September 11, 2001, President George W. Bush called Iraq and Saddam Hussein part of an "axis of evil" that threatened world peace. In 2002 and early 2003, Bush called for a "regime change" in Iraq and began assembling an international coalition to support further military action in Iraq.

Having tried and failed to convince the UN Security Council that the UN should take action to enforce its resolutions, Bush created a coalition of 35 other nations, including Britain, to join the United States to invade Iraq. Within three weeks, the coalition forces had toppled Hussein's decades-old dictatorship and were in control of Baghdad and most of the other major Iraqi cities. After that swift victory, the United States and its allies spent more than ten years trying to establish a democratic government in Iraq.

Occupied Iraq The people of Iraq are divided into three principal groups by ethnicity and religion. The Kurdish-speaking people of the north, who had in practice been functioning as an American-sponsored independent state since the First Gulf War, were overjoyed by the invasion. The Arabs adhering to the Shiite branch of Islam live principally in the south and constitute a majority of the population. Although glad that Hussein had been defeated, Shiites were deeply skeptical of U.S. intentions. Sunnis live in the center of the country, west of Baghdad. Although the Sunnis constituted only a minority of the population, they had controlled the government under Hussein. Figure 17-1 shows the distribution of major ethnic and religious groups in Iraq.

The Situation Worsens Soon after the active military war ended, sectarian violence began between ethnic and religious groups. In 2004, the United States was forced to deal with graphic photographs showing that U.S. guards at Abu Ghraib prison in Baghdad had subjected prisoners to physical and sexual abuse.

Although coalition forces were able to maintain control of the country, they were now suffering monthly casualties comparable to those experienced during the initial invasion. Casualties continued to increase in the years that followed, and the unpopularity of the war among the American people dragged President Bush's approval rating to historic lows.

The Bush Surge By 2007, it was clear that al Qaeda terrorist cells were also participating in the attacks against both coalition forces and the emerging Iraqi government. In spring 2007, President Bush and his commanders in the field requested additional troops for a "surge" of military activity to defeat the insurgency. Although many in Congress and the public did not believe that the surge would be successful, by late 2007, violence in many parts of Iraq had decreased, and the Iraqi military forces were taking the lead in operations against the insurgents. In 2008, the Obama administration scheduled troop withdrawals and began negotiations with the Iraqi government for future assistance and support for democracy. There was increasing violence in Iraq,

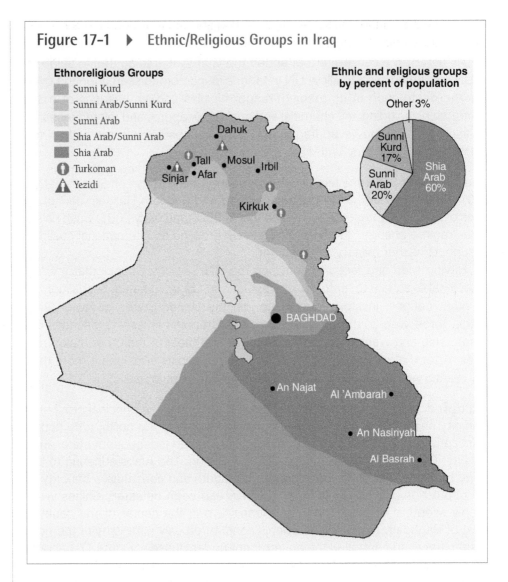

Figure 17-1 ▶ Ethnic/Religious Groups in Iraq

Ethnoreligious Groups
- Sunni Kurd
- Sunni Arab/Sunni Kurd
- Sunni Arab
- Shia Arab/Sunni Arab
- Shia Arab
- 🛈 Turkoman
- ⚠ Yezidi

Ethnic and religious groups by percent of population
- Other 3%
- Sunni Kurd 17%
- Sunni Arab 20%
- Shia Arab 60%

however, after the withdrawal of most of the American troops in 2011. The Office of Security Cooperation–Iraq operated to provide security in Iraq and employed more than 3,500 individuals.[10] As the last troops prepared to leave in 2014, an Islamist force known as Islamic State of Iraq and Syria (ISIS) began attacks on Iraqi cities, capturing Mosul and a number of other towns. ISIS wants the unification of Sunni peoples under one sectarian state. Although the United States has sent some military advisers to Iraq, the battle to retake these cities is being led by the Iraqi military.

The "Necessary" War

In early 2009, it was clear that the situation in Afghanistan was far from resolved. The Taliban regrouped in the provinces, and corruption spread through the government. President Obama had campaigned on the premise that Afghanistan was a "necessary" war, so he was faced with a serious decision on how to proceed with the American mission in that nation. The administration agreed to a type of "surge" in Afghanistan and a planned withdrawal beginning in 2011. Policy seemed to be in disarray, however, in 2010, when the commanding

---

10 Kenneth Katzman, "Iraq: Politics, Governance, and Human Rights," *Congressional Reference Service*, April 23, 2014, http://www.fas.org/sgp/crs/mideast/RS21968.pdf

officer, General Stanley McChrystal, was fired and General David Petraeus was asked to take over the situation in the theater of war.

Petraeus argued that it was necessary to increase troop levels in Afghanistan and to change the American strategy to one in which American troops worked with local tribal leaders to establish stability in their regions. The Obama administration eventually supported the "surge" in Afghanistan. Some Afghani provinces responded well to the new strategy, whereas others remained under the control of the Taliban. By 2012, the difficulty of dealing with Afghan president Hamid Karzai, the challenge of coping with corruption in the government of Afghanistan, and the cost of the war led the Obama administration to begin talks with the Taliban and Karzai about a negotiated settlement of the war. The United States planned to withdraw most of its troops in 2014; however, that remained contingent upon creating an agreement with the Afghan government about future relationships. Karzai refused to sign an agreement, and elections were held in 2014 for a new president. The United States negotiated an agreement with new leadership to allow for NATO and the United States to keep some troops there to help with security.[11] It is clear that the ten years of American presence in Afghanistan did produce progress in the social and economic system of that nation, most notably for Afghani women, who can now attend school and have public careers. Former secretary of state Hillary Clinton, who represented the United States in a conference to develop assistance to Afghanistan in 2012, insisted that maintaining progress for women would be one of the conditions for U.S. troop withdrawal.[12]

As the Iraq and Afghanistan wars wound to an end, many Americans wondered whether they were worth both the financial cost and the cost in American lives. According to a 2014 analysis, the accumulated spending for military operations in these two nations since September 11 was $819.6 billion for Iraq and $743.7 billion for Afghanistan, plus $28 billion for enhanced security and about $91 billion that was unallocated. The grand total was $1.7 trillion over 14 years—about the size of the national deficit in 2012.[13] The U.S. military deaths was about 4,500 deaths in Iraq—3,500 from hostile action—and about 2,400 in Afghanistan. Thanks to advances in medical technology, far more wounded Americans have survived than in the Vietnam conflict, although many need a great deal of rehabilitation to return to productive lives.

Global Policy Challenges

■ **17.5** Discuss the security and diplomatic challenges facing the United States today.

Foreign and national security policies are formulated to deal with world conditions at a particular period in history. Early in its history, the United States was a new nation facing older nations well equipped for world domination. In the twenty-first century, the United States faces different challenges. Now it must

---

11 Carlos Munoz, "Final 32000 American Troops Out of Afghanistan after 2014 Elections," *The Hill*, February 22, 2014. http://thehill.com/policy/defense/284419-panetta-sets-timeline-for-final-drawdown-in-afghanistan.html

12 "Hillary Clinton Puts Conditions on U.S. Portion of $16 Billion Afghan Assistance Pledge," CBS News, July 9, 2012. www.cbsnews.com

13 Amy Belasco, "The Cost of Iraq, Afghanistan and Other Global War on Terror Operations since 9/11," Washington, DC: Congressional Research Service, 2014. A totally different approach to estimating costs was published by Linda J. Bilmes and Josephy E. Stiglitz in *The Three Trillion Dollar War: The True Cost of the Iraq Conflict* (New York: W.W. Norton, 2008).

devise foreign and defense policies that will enhance its security in a world in which it is the global superpower and has no equal. Among the challenges that must be faced are the growth of new economic and military powers, the threat of terrorism, the explosion in technological warfare, the proliferation of nuclear weapons, and numerous regional conflicts, including the ongoing violence in the Middle East.

The Emerging World Order

From 1945 until 1989, the world watched as the United States and the Soviet Union dueled for power in the world. Both nations had their allies and fought wars through their surrogates. They built up arsenals of nuclear weapons and were militarily prepared to destroy each other and the world itself. After the Berlin Wall fell in 1989, the entire Soviet bloc disintegrated with surprising speed. East Germany, one of the strongest allies of the Soviet Union, merged with West Germany to become one nation, democratic and capitalistic. All of the other Eastern bloc nations became truly independent states, and a new Russian state emerged.

After the Persian Gulf War in 1991, it was clear that the American military was the finest in the world and that U.S. advances in technology and weaponry were far superior to those of any other nation—the United States was the sole military global superpower. Under the Clinton administration, the Pentagon tried to plan for a post–Cold War world. What should be the national security objectives of the nation? How should the military be structured? How many wars should the United States be equipped to handle at one time? What kinds of intelligence gathering would be important now that the Soviets were no longer a threat? All of these questions and more needed to be answered in terms of American foreign and national security policy.

The Clinton administration, with the approval of Congress, began to change the size and scope of the American military. By 2001, the active duty military was one-third smaller than it had been in 1990, dropping from 2.1 million in 1989 to 1.4 million in 1999. The number of active duty troops has remained at about 1.4 million since that time, although the Department of Defense's budget request for fiscal year 2015 envisioned further reductions in strength.[14] Fewer appropriations were made to build new ships and acquire new equipment. The CIA was ordered to focus more on economic intelligence and less on military intelligence. The United States has continued to lead NATO and maintain this military alliance of European nations. Although Russia objects to the continued existence of this alliance, many of the former Soviet bloc nations expressed interest in joining NATO. By 2008, the alliance included the 28 members who joined at the beginning of or before the fall of the Soviet Union, as well as the Czech Republic, Hungary, Poland, Bulgaria, Estonia, Latvia, Lithuania, Romania, Slovakia, and Slovenia, all former allies of the Soviet Union. At the same time, other developments in the world challenged American policy. The European Union became a single economic unit, competing with American exports around the world. China began to become an economic force in the world and, a few years later, India followed suit. By 2008, China was a major trading partner of the United States and a major holder of the securities of the U.S.

---

14 Nick Simeone, "Hagel Outlines Budget Reducing Troop Strength, Force Structure," *American Forces Press Service*, February 24, 2014, U.S. Department of Defense, http://www.defense.gov/news/newsarticle.aspx?id=121703

government. China became a major military power as well, with nuclear weapons and missile capabilities. Other nations such as Brazil and Australia became important economic players in the world. As shown in the screen capture, NATO forces have been deployed as preventative measures throughout the world.

By 2012 the United States was focused more on economic growth and economic competition in the world. The U.S. military was prepared for crisis situations and technologically sophisticated warfare, but not for a long engagement on the ground. One of President Trump's top agenda items is the rebuilding of the military following the depletion of the Iraq and Afghanistan wars. While he seems to eschew military involvement, he has directed a number of airstrikes to kill the top leaders of ISIS.

The Threat of Terrorism

Dissident groups, rebels, and other revolutionaries have long engaged in terrorism to gain attention and to force their enemies to the bargaining table. Over the last two decades, however, terrorism has increasingly threatened world peace and the lives of ordinary citizens.

From the Web ▶ Why do you think NATO is advertising the movement of its ships to the Baltic?

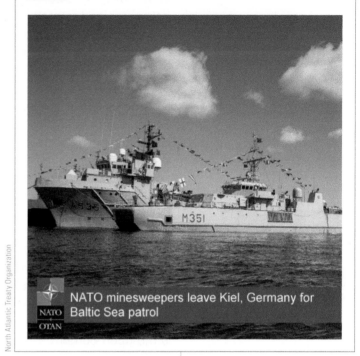

North Atlantic Treaty Organization

NATO minesweepers leave Kiel, Germany for Baltic Sea patrol

Terrorism and Regional Strife Terrorism can be a weapon of choice in regional or domestic strife. In September 2004, terrorists acting on behalf of Chechnya, a breakaway republic of Russia, seized a school at Beslan in the nearby Russian republic of North Ossetia. In the end, at least 330 people—most of them children—were dead. More recently in 2014, a terrorist group in Nigeria responsible for killing many Nigerian citizens kidnapped more than 200 girls from school, holding them hostage for ransom.

Terrorist Attacks against Foreign Civilians Terrorist acts are sometimes planned against civilians traveling abroad to make an international statement. One of the most striking attacks was launched by Palestinian terrorists against Israeli athletes at the Munich Olympics in 1972, during which 11 athletes were murdered. Other attacks have included ship and airplane hijackings, as well as bombings of embassies. In 1998, terrorist bombings of two American embassies in Africa killed 257 people, including 12 Americans, and injured more than 5,500 others.

London Bombings On July 7, 2005, terrorists carried out synchronized bombings of the London Underground (subway) and bus network. Four suicide bombers, believed to have been of Middle Eastern descent, claimed the lives of 52 people and wounded hundreds more in the attacks. On July 21, a second group of bombers attempted to carry out a similar plot, but no one was killed. Following the attacks, security was heightened in Britain and elsewhere, including New York City.

In August 2006, British authorities foiled a plot to bring down ten planes scheduled to leave London's Heathrow Airport for the United States. If successful, it would have been the largest terrorist attack since September 11, 2001. The alleged bombers planned to blow up the airplanes with liquid chemicals combined to make a bomb. Many planned attacks have been thwarted since September 11, 2001. Some perpetrators, such as the underwear bomber on the flight to Detroit and the Times Square bomber in New York, are publicly arrested and tried. Other plots are stopped before execution, and little public knowledge is available. In 2013, two young men with ties to Chechnya planned and carried out a bombing at the finish line of the Boston Marathon, killing 3 people and wounding more than 175 others. One of the bombers was killed in the manhunt that followed the attack. His brother was tried and convicted in Boston.

In the late fall of 2015, another shocking event occurred in Paris, France. This time, the terrorists were linked to the Islamic State or ISIS. A group of terrorists carried out four attacks simultaneously, including one inside a crowded concert hall and another on an open-air café. The death toll reached 138, and more than 300 were injured. Some of the perpetrators fled the city and crossed into Belgium. Four months later, other followers of ISIS conducted three simultaneous attacks in Brussels—two at the international airport and one at the Maelbeek metro station. The death toll was 35, but more than 300 people were injured. One of the obstacles to finding these terrorists in Europe is the open border policy of the European Union (EU). EU citizens can travel freely across borders in Europe without having any identification checked. The search for these terrorists led to closed borders in some places and a tightening of airport security across Europe.

Nuclear Weapons

■ **17.6** Describe the current distribution of nuclear weapons in the world and the efforts to control further proliferation of these weapons.

In 1945, the United States was the only nation to possess nuclear weapons. Several nations quickly joined the "nuclear club," however, including the Soviet Union in 1949, Great Britain in 1952, France in 1960, and China in 1964. Few nations have publicized their nuclear weapons programs since China's successful test of nuclear weapons in 1964. India and Pakistan, however, detonated nuclear devices within a few weeks of each other in 1998, and North Korea conducted an underground nuclear explosion test in October 2006 and more testing in 2009 and 2013. Several other nations are suspected of possessing nuclear weapons or the capability to produce them in a short time.

The United States and the Soviet Union   More than 19,000 nuclear warheads are known to be stocked worldwide, although the exact number is uncertain, because some countries do not reveal the extent of their nuclear stockpiles.[15] Even more troublesome is nuclear proliferation—that is, the development of nuclear weapons by additional nations and the possibility that some nuclear material may be purchased by terrorist groups.

---

15 For current estimates of the number of nuclear devices in the world, see the reports from www.ploughshares.org, the website of the Ploughshares Fund, an organization dedicated to eliminating nuclear weapons worldwide.

Nuclear Proliferation The United States has attempted to influence late arrivals to the nuclear club through a combination of rewards and punishments. In some cases, the United States has promised aid to a nation to gain cooperation. In other cases, such as those of India and Pakistan, it has imposed economic sanctions as a punishment for carrying out nuclear tests. Despite the United States' disagreement with these countries, President Bush signed a new nuclear pact with India in March 2006.

In 1999, President Clinton presented the Comprehensive Nuclear Test Ban Treaty to the Senate for ratification. The treaty, formed in 1996, prohibited all nuclear test explosions worldwide and established a global network of monitoring stations. One hundred eighty-three nations have signed the treaty and 162 have ratified it. Among those that have not are China, Israel, India, and Pakistan. The U.S. Senate rejected the treaty in 1999.

The United States has suspected for some time that nations such as North Korea and Iran might supply nuclear materials to terrorists or to nations that seek nuclear capability. Israel is known to possess more than 100 nuclear warheads. South Africa developed six nuclear warheads in the 1980s but dismantled them in 1990. In 2003, Libya announced that it was abandoning a secret nuclear weapons program. Also, since the dissolution of the Soviet Union in 1991, the security of its nuclear arsenal has declined. There have been reported thefts, smugglings, and illicit sales of nuclear material from the former Soviet Union for 25 years.

For years, the United States, the European Union, and the UN have tried to prevent Iran from becoming a nuclear power. Today, many observers believe that Iran has already developed nuclear capability or is close to doing so. Efforts by the United States and its European allies continue to convince Iran to dismantle its nuclear production facilities.

The United States and Regional Conflicts

The United States has played a role—sometimes alone, sometimes with other powers—in many regional conflicts during the 1990s and 2000s. In other situations, tensions exist between the United States and another nation over trade, weapons acquisition, or political differences. The tense relationships between the United States and Iran and between the United States and North Korea have already been discussed. Both of those states play important roles in their own regions of the globe. The United States is just one player in the situation and often must work with other global powers such as China or Russia.

The Middle East

For many decades, the question of the continued existence and development of the state of Israel has been the predominant issue for the United States in the Middle East. As a longtime supporter of Israel, the United States has undertaken to persuade the Israelis to negotiate with the Palestinian Arabs who live in the territories occupied by the state of Israel. The conflict has been extremely difficult to resolve. The internationally recognized solution is for Israel to yield the West Bank and the Gaza Strip to the Palestinians in return for effective security commitments and abandonment by the Palestinians of any right of return to Israel proper.

ton koene/Alamy Stock Photos

Image 17–6

To protect Israeli civilians from terrorism, Israel has built a wall to separate Palestinian settlements from Jewish neighborhoods.

In December 1988, the United States began talking directly to the Palestine Liberation Organization (PLO), and in 1991, under great pressure from the United States, the Israelis opened talks with representatives of the Palestinians and other Arab states. In 1993, both parties agreed to set up Palestinian self-government in the West Bank and the Gaza Strip. The historic agreement, signed in Cairo on May 4, 1994, put in place a process by which the Palestinians would assume self-rule in the Gaza Strip and in the town of Jericho. In the months that followed, Israeli troops withdrew from much of the occupied territory, the new Palestinian Authority assumed police duties, and many Palestinian prisoners were freed by the Israelis.

President Bush attempted to renew Israeli–Palestinian negotiations in 2003 by sponsoring a "road map" for peace that called for an end to terrorism by the Palestinians. Later, it held out hopes for a Palestinian state alongside Israel. In its weakened condition, however, the Palestinian Authority was unable to make any commitments, and the road map process ground to a halt. In February 2004, Israeli prime minister Ariel Sharon announced a plan under which Israel would withdraw from the Gaza Strip, regardless of whether a deal could be reached with the Palestinians, and ultimately the withdrawal took place.

After the death of Palestinian leader Yasser Arafat in 2004, a moderate prime minister was elected. In January 2006, however, the militant group Hamas won a majority of the seats in the Palestinian legislature. American and European politicians hoped that after it became part of the legitimate government, Hamas would agree to rescind its avowed desire to destroy Israel, but so far, it has not done so. In 2014, after Hamas began launching rockets into Israel, the Israeli military responded by moving into Gaza to destroy the missile sites and the tunnels that are used to move terrorists into Israel. The United States and other nations struggled to get the parties to agree to a cease-fire.

The Arab Spring The situation in the Middle East—including the fate of Israel—has been destabilized by the demands for democracy that arose in 2011 and 2012. Popular movements have replaced the authoritarian regimes in Egypt, Libya, Tunisia, and Yemen. These "Arab Spring" movements could mark very positive change for the United States as new, democratically elected governments come into power (see Figure 17-2). Democratic nations are less likely to go to war and are more stable. The United States has encouraged the development of democracy throughout the world, but, when a movement arises, must decide whether to support the movement with more than words.

The Obama administration encouraged the democracy movement in Egypt through diplomacy and by refusing to offer any assistance to the old regime of Hosni Mubarak. Because it was a peaceful uprising supported by many members of Egypt's military establishment, the United States played no role militarily. After ratifying a new constitution and electing Morsi as president, Egyptians became disillusioned by the movement of his government toward a more Islamist position, and Morsi was ousted in 2013. Military leaders commandeered the government and, after holding elections, installed General Sisi as the head of state. Libya was a very different situation. Buoyed by a burgeoning democracy movement, the United States led a NATO-created military force to provide bombing strikes in aid of the opposition movement. The Libyan leader, Muammar Gaddafi, was captured and killed. The situation in Libya is still unsettled; militia groups still proliferate, including one that attacked the U.S. embassy in September 2012, killing the ambassador and three other Americans. Since that time, Libya has been torn

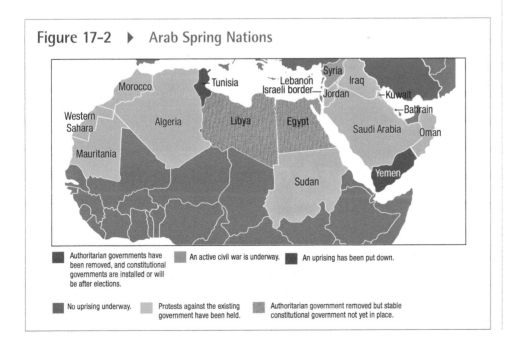

Figure 17-2 ▶ **Arab Spring Nations**

Authoritarian governments have been removed, and constitutional governments are installed or will be after elections.

An active civil war is underway.

An uprising has been put down.

No uprising underway.

Protests against the existing government have been held.

Authoritarian government removed but stable constitutional government not yet in place.

by different political and military factions. The circumstances in Syria are extremely complicated. Opposition to the authoritarian regime of President Assad began to surge in 2013. The United States publicly stated that Assad should resign and that a democratic election should be held in Syria. As opposition movements became more widespread, the Assad regime used chemical weapons, including the deadly gas sarin, on rebel fighters and civilians. Although Russia and the United States did not agree on whether Assad should be removed from office or on how to intervene in the conflict, the two powers agreed that the chemical weapons should be destroyed. The Syrian regime agreed to this provision, and the destruction took place at sea under the authority of NATO. However, the fighting between the various

Politics in Practice

War and Politics in the Movies

It is no secret that Hollywood loves war movies. From the earliest days of film, movies about men and women at war, about submarines, pilots, or the Marines have been the mainstay of the movie industry. However, Hollywood's attitude toward war has undergone a number of changes. During World War II, almost all of the movies about the conflict were patriotic and supported the war effort due to cooperation with the Roosevelt administration. All governmental authorities sought to increase public support for the war effort through movies, radio, and books.

During the Vietnam War, the early movies were also very patriotic. John Wayne starred in *The Green Berets*, a tribute to U.S. Special Forces units. In the years after the war ended, movies became much more critical of the military efforts and, in films such as *The Deerhunter* and *Apocalypse Now*, focused on the plight of the ordinary soldier in an impossible situation.

At this point, the American military has been engaged in the Iraq and Afghanistan efforts for more than 15 years. These have become the "longest wars" ever fought by the United States. Hollywood has made dozens of movies about the two conflicts, some of them very patriotic and supportive and many of them critical. For example, the Academy Award nominee *Zero Dark Thirty* (2012) emphasized the mistreatment of captives by the CIA and the military, and *The Hurt Locker* (2009) follows the life of a soldier whose job is to defuse explosive devices. *American Sniper* (2014), a tribute to Navy SEAL Chris

Kyle's life, presented an extremely supportive view of the men engaged in the Iraq war, showing the degree of brotherhood established by these units. Many of the best films about the Iraq and Afghanistan wars are documentaries: *Restrepo* (2010) is the video diary of a journalist and photographer who are embedded with troops in Afghanistan, and *The War Tapes* (2006) uses footage actually shot by American soldiers during the conflict in Iraq.

Is Hollywood antiwar or prowar? The movie industry's goal is to make excellent films that are box office hits. Many war movies that are released to critical acclaim do not do well at the box office. Others, like *American Sniper*, are financial successes. When the screen writers and directors are focusing on the hardships of war, on unnecessary casualties, or the mistakes of the central command, the underlying theme is the futility of such wars. It is up to the moviegoer to decide whether to buy a ticket to see a point of view, critical or not.

For Critical Analysis

1. Why would movie producers be inclined to take an antiwar position in a film?

2. Do you think that films and television influence the attitudes of Americans toward foreign nations and the use of military force?

rebel groups and the regime has continued. The United States has agreed to supply weapons to groups that appear to have adopted democratic principles. Some of the rebels, however, are supported by terror groups from elsewhere in the Middle East.

With the outbreak of fighting across the most urban parts of Syria, hundreds of thousands of Syrian families and individuals began to move toward Europe. Thousands crossed into Turkey or paid for passage on small boats to one of the Greek Islands. Other sailed for the Italian coast. Led by the German government, the European Union maintained its policy of accepting political refugees and moved thousands of these families to Sweden, Denmark, Germany, and other nations. Some Eastern European nations refused to take a share of the refugees, whereas other nations, such as Sweden, accepted as many as they could. However, over time, there were more refugees than nations could support and integrate into their own societies, and the EU began to negotiate with Turkey to send some immigrants back to that nation. It was hoped that peace would come to Syria eventually and families could go home.

Iranian Ambitions Iran has been a religious state since the overthrow of the former shah and the uprising in support of the Ayatollah Khomeini. After the American embassy was captured and its staff held hostage during the Carter administration, the United States and Iran have had a very difficult relationship. Iran is not a closed society, however, and Iranians travel to Europe frequently and have business relationships with companies throughout the world. The major issue between the United States and Iran is the latter nation's secret development of a nuclear capability. The United States and other nations imposed strong sanctions on Iran to persuade the nation to renounce nuclear weapons. After years of negotiations, some of the sanctions were lifted in 2013, and new business relationships are being developed between Europe and the Iranians. The most recent agreement specifies that Iran will not develop a nuclear weapon, but there are those who believe that secret Iranian nuclear weapon research persists. President Trump cancelled the agreement.

Central and South America

The United States has had a protective attitude toward the rest of the Western Hemisphere since the Monroe Doctrine was announced in 1823. Having stable, democratic governments in Central and South American nations provides the United States with economic partnerships and with a stable "neighborhood." Of course, at many times in the past, the United States has operated under a realist policy of dealing with authoritarians to achieve stability in this region. During the Cold War years, the United States was particularly concerned about the rise of socialist or communist regimes in Central and South America.

Tensions between the United States and Cuba have frequently erupted since Fidel Castro took power in Cuba in 1959. Relations with Cuba continue to be politically important in the United States, because the Cuban American population can influence election outcomes in Florida, a state that all presidential candidates strive to win. When Fidel Castro became seriously ill and underwent surgery in the summer of 2006, his brother, Raul, temporarily assumed power. In 2008, Fidel named his brother as his official successor. Since that time, government regulations on small businesses have been gradually eased, more American tourists have visited the nation, and in 2015, after considerable negotiation, President Obama recognized the nation of Cuba and normal relations have been resumed.

War and HIV/AIDS in Africa

Africa presents many extremely serious challenges to the United States and the rest of the world. Many African nations are still underdeveloped, with enormous health problems and unstable regimes. Tribal rivalries lead to civil wars and, in the worst cases, genocide. The United States has worked with the United Nations to try to end conflicts and improve the situation on the continent.

During the early 2000s, the disease AIDS (acquired immunodeficiency syndrome) spread throughout southern Africa. This disease infects one-fourth of the populations of Botswana and Zimbabwe and is endemic in most other nations in the southernmost part of the continent. Millions of adults have died from AIDS, leaving orphaned children. The epidemic took a huge economic toll on the affected countries because of the cost of caring for patients and the loss of skilled workers. The Bush administration implemented a special aid package directed at treating the disease and curtailing its proliferation. The total aid amounted to $15 billion over five years; by all indications, the program has succeeded in reducing AIDS deaths in Africa. The dedication of resources to this issue continued during the Obama administration.

Revolutions and tribal warfare have occurred in several African nations. In 1994, Rwanda was torn apart by a tribal civil war. Almost a million civilians were massacred during the course of the conflict. France has been deeply involved with Rwanda, a former colony; the United States has had little involvement, despite the humanitarian issues at stake.

In the spring of 2004, Sudan had reached a tenuous agreement with rebels in the southern part of the country, but the agreement did not cover a separate rebellion in Darfur, a western province of Sudan. Government-sponsored militias drove more than a million inhabitants of Darfur from their homes and into refugee camps, where they faced starvation. By 2012, Darfur was subject to somewhat less violence, but groups from Sudan and from the newly formed nation of South Sudan continued to attack Darfur occasionally.

Civil wars have occurred in Zaire and in Angola. Currently, there is unrest in Mali and extreme economic distress in Zimbabwe. Generally, the United States has preferred to work through the United Nations to help bring peace to these African nations. A group called the African Union (AU) has succeeded an earlier organization known as the Organization of African Unity. The African Union has a membership of 54 states and exists to further the economic and political development of all African countries. It has taken action during civil wars and has fielded peacekeeping forces in Darfur, for example. For the United States, supporting the actions of the AU is greatly preferable to intervening directly in African conflicts.

China: A Superpower under the Spotlight

Image 17-7 A satellite photograph of the artificial island constructed by the Chinese government near Spratly Islands on the Mischief Reef in the Pacific Ocean. The ownership of Spratly Islands has been disputed by the Philippines, Malaysia, Vietnam, Brunei, Taiwan, and China for some time.

China is one of the world's great economic powers. Adjusted for purchasing power, China's gross domestic product (GDP) is now equal to that of the United States and is almost double that of Japan. This fact does not mean that all Chinese are rich. Per-capita income in China is well below that of the United States and Europe.

Between 2001 and 2007, China's industrial output increased by almost 50 percent. China now produces more steel than America and Japan combined. Such rapid growth requires massive amounts of raw materials. China consumes 40 percent of the world's output of cement, for example. China's growing demand for raw materials has contributed to dramatic increases in the world prices of many commodities, including oil. Although the worldwide recession of 2008–2009 had some impact on China's economy, mostly because consumers in Western nations purchased fewer Chinese exports, the Chinese economy held steady throughout the entire period.

China's Economic Prospects

For a number of years, China has had the world's second largest economy, second only to the United States. If measured by U.S. dollars, China will remain in second place for many years. However, when measured by the purchasing power of the yuan as compared to the purchasing power of the dollar, China's economy became larger than that of the United States in 2014.

Chinese–American Relations

Since President Nixon's visit to China in 1972, American policy has been to gradually engage the Chinese in diplomatic and economic relationships in the hope of turning the nation in a more pro-Western direction. In 1989, however, when Chinese students engaged in extraordinary demonstrations against the government, the Chinese government crushed the demonstrations, killing several students and protesters and imprisoning others. The result was a distinct chill in Chinese–American relations.

After initially criticizing the administration of George H. W. Bush for not being hard enough on China, President Clinton came around to a policy of diplomatic outreach to the Chinese. An important reason for this change was the large and growing trade ties between the two countries. China was granted most-favored-nation status for tariffs and trade policy on a year-to-year basis. In 2000, Congress granted China permanent **Normal Trade Relations (NTR) status**, thus endorsing China's admission to the World Trade Organization (WTO). For a country that is officially communist, China already permits a striking degree of free enterprise, and the rules China must follow as a WTO member will further increase the role of the private sector in China's economy.

In recent years, China did support the American efforts against terrorists but did not support the war in Iraq. Although the two nations have had diplomatic differences, China has joined the six-party talks, working with the United States, Japan, Russia, South Korea, and North Korea, to negotiate with North Korea to end its pursuit of nuclear weapons. China has not been willing to support the position of the United States with regard to the Ukraine or Syria.

> **Normal Trade Relations (NTR) status**
> A status granted through an international treaty by which each member nation must treat other members at least as well as it treats the country that receives its most favorable treatment. This status was formerly known as most-favored-nation status.

China in the Spotlight

In 2008 China was in the international spotlight due to several events. First, a huge earthquake struck the area near Chengdu, causing thousands of deaths and billions of dollars of destruction. For the first time ever, the Chinese government allowed foreign news agencies to cover the story and accepted international support. Later that same year, the Chinese hosted the 2008 Olympics and showed off their impressive new facilities.

(Continued)

(Continued)

More recently, relationships among China, its nearest neighbors, and the United States have been tense. The Chinese government has claimed as its territory a number of islands in the South China Sea, which have been traditionally claimed by the Philippines. Furthermore, China has constructed an artificial island near the Philippines that appears to be a military base with a runway long enough for most military aircraft. Military maneuvers have been held by the Chinese and by the United States in the region, but the relationship there is tense.

For Critical Analysis

1. How does China's status as an authoritarian state affect relationships with the United States?

2. Why would China want to keep a good relationship with the United States?

Key Terms

attentive public 597
Cold War 600
containment 600
defense policy 588
détente 602
diplomacy 588
economic aid 588
expansionist policy 599
foreign policy 587

foreign policy process 588
intelligence community 594
iron curtain 600
isolationist foreign policy 599
military–industrial complex 597
Monroe Doctrine 599
moralist foreign policy 598
national security policy 588
negative constituents 593

Normal Trade Relations (NTR) status 617
preemptive war 604
realist foreign policy 598
Soviet bloc 600
Strategic Arms Limitation Treaty (SALT I) 602
technical assistance 588
Truman Doctrine 600

Chapter Summary

■ **17.1** Foreign policy includes national goals and the techniques used to achieve them. National security policy is designed to protect the independence and the political and economic integrity of the United States. Diplomacy involves the nation's external relationships and is an attempt to resolve conflict without resorting to arms. U.S. foreign policy is sometimes based on moral idealism and sometimes on political realism.

■ **17.2** The formal power of the president to make foreign policy derives from the U.S. Constitution, which designates the president as commander in chief of the army and navy. The president also has the power to make treaties and executive agreements. In principle, the State Department is the executive agency with primary authority over foreign affairs. The National Security Council also plays a major role. The intelligence community consists of government

agencies engaged in activities varying from information gathering to covert operations. In response to presidential actions in the Vietnam War, Congress attempted to establish some limits on the power of the president to intervene abroad by passing the War Powers Resolution Act in 1973.

■ **17.3** Three major themes have guided U.S. foreign policy. In the early years of the nation, isolationism was the primary strategy. With the start of the twentieth century, isolationism gave way to global involvement. From the end of World War II through the 1980s, the major goal was to contain communism and the influence of the Soviet Union.

■ **17.3** During the 1800s, the United States had little international power and generally stayed out of European conflicts and politics, and so these years have been called the period of isolationism. The Monroe Doctrine of 1823 stated that the United States would not accept foreign intervention in the Western Hemisphere and would not meddle in European affairs. The United States pursued an actively expansionist policy in the Americas and the Pacific area, however.

■ **17.3** The end of the policy of isolationism toward Europe started with the Spanish–American War of 1898. U.S. involvement in European politics became more extensive when the United States entered World War I on April 6, 1917. World War II marked a lasting change in American foreign policy. The United States was the only major country to emerge from the war with its economy intact and the only country with operating nuclear weapons.

■ **17.3** Soon after World War II, the uncomfortable alliance between the United States and the Soviet Union ended, and the Cold War began. A policy of containment, which assumed an expansionist Soviet Union, was enunciated in the Truman Doctrine. Following the frustrations of the Vietnam War and the apparent arms equality of the United States and the Soviet Union, the United States adopted a policy of *détente*. Although President Reagan took a tough stance toward the Soviet Union during his first term, his second term saw serious negotiations toward arms reduction, culminating in the signing of the Intermediate-Range Nuclear Force Treaty in 1987. After the fall of the Soviet Union, Russia emerged as a less threatening state and signed the Strategic Arms Reduction Treaty with the United States in 1992.

■ **17.3** After the dissolution of the Soviet Union, the United States assumed the position of global superpower without a military competitor. However, the United States has maintained the NATO alliance with its European allies and has added several former Soviet bloc states to the alliance. Russia has remained a powerful nation, one that

is becoming increasingly a one-party state. The European Union continues to increase its influence as an economic superpower and competitor to the United States, and the rapidly developing economies of India and China continue to push those nations into the global power structure.

■ **17.4** Terrorism has become a major challenge facing the United States and other nations. The United States waged war on terrorism after the September 11 attacks. U.S. armed forces occupied Afghanistan in 2001 and Iraq in 2003.

■ **17.5** Ethnic tensions and political instability in many regions of the world provide challenges to the United States. Support for Israel has been at the center of U.S. foreign policy in the Middle East, as well as support for the installation of democratic governments in Israel's neighboring countries. Iran has continued to develop nuclear weapons in the face of sanctions imposed by the United Nations. Civil wars have erupted in a number of African states in the last two decades, but the United States has preferred to work through the United Nations or African Union in bringing peace to these nations. In Central and South America, the United States has encouraged economic development and democracy throughout the continent.

■ **17.6** Nuclear proliferation continues to be an issue as a result of the breakup of the Soviet Union and loss of control over its nuclear arsenal, along with the continued efforts of other nations to gain nuclear warheads. More than 18,000 nuclear warheads are known to exist worldwide. The United States is a signatory to the Nuclear Nonproliferation Treaty and the Comprehensive Test Ban Treaty and works actively with other nations to reduce the threat of nuclear arms. In 2010, the United States and Russia signed a treaty to further reduce each nation's supply of nuclear missiles.

Selected Resources

PRINT RESOURCES

Gall, Carlotta. *The Wrong Enemy: America in Afghanistan 2001–2014* (New York: Houghton Mifflin Harcourt, 2014). As a reporter for the *New York Times,* the author writes a startling account of the war in Afghanistan. Her evidence shows that Pakistan was the major supporter of the Taliban throughout this period.

Haass, Richard. *Foreign Policy Begins at Home: The Case for Putting America's House in Order* (New York: Basic Books, 2013). Haass, president of the Council on Foreign Relations, makes the case that the United States must be economically strong and solve its own infrastructure problems before it can resume its place as the world leader. He foresees a time of limited involvement

in conflict, but of having great influence using economic and intellectual power.

Mazzetti, Mark. *The Way of the Knife: The CIA, a Secret Army, and a War at the End of the Earth* (New York: Penguin, 2013). The author explores how the CIA has changed since the end of the Cold War and concludes that, in part, it has become an agency to oversee the assassination of our enemies.

Posen, Barry R. *Restraint: A New Foundation for U.S. Grand Strategy* (New York: Cornell University Press, 2016). The author is a critic of American foreign policy in the sense that our desire to intervene in one instance and not in another situation leads to inconsistency and bad decisions.

He proposes a new strategy for our national security needs that relies on restraint and a well-thought-out plan for the use of U.S. strength.

Sanger, David E. *Confront and Conceal: Obama's Secret Wars and Surprising Use of American Power* (New York: Crown, 2012). The author, a reporter for *The New York Times*, reveals the degree to which President Obama was personally involved in decision making on the U.S. pursuit of terrorists.

Weis, Michael and Hassan Hassan. *ISIS: Inside the Army of Terror* (New York: Simon and Schuster, 2016). Written by a journalist and an expert on jihadist tactics, this book is an inside look at how the Islamic State operates. The authors include data from interviews with military and public officials, Syrians who work for ISIS, and local leaders.

MEDIA RESOURCES

Argo—This fast-paced 2012 film tells the real-life story of how Canadians sheltered Americans who escaped from the embassy in Iran and how they managed to get the Americans back to the United States.

American Sniper—A huge box office hit in 2014, the movie explores the life of Chris Kyle, the most decorated American sniper of the Iraq–Afghanistan wars. The film depicts Kyle as intensely loyal to his fellow soldiers but subject to the same kinds of stress and mental illness that affected so many veterans after coming home.

The Hurt Locker—This 2008 Academy Award–winning film traces the work of an American bomb squad in Iraq and brings home the intensity of these soldiers' work in identifying Iraqi attackers.

Lone Survivor—This 2013 film tells the true story of the memoir of Marcus Luttrell, a U.S. Navy SEAL team soldier who, along with his mission team, is faced with a terrible choice between killing native Afghans or being captured or killed.

This Is What Winning Looks Like—A 2013 documentary, the film uses footage from actual Taliban attacks and interviews with Americans and Britons in Afghanistan to show how difficult the situation is and how hard it would be for Afghans to hold the peace after the NATO withdrawal.

Zero Dark Thirty—The 2012 award-winning film depicting the actions of a female CIA agent whose job is to oversee the interrogation of prisoners to find Osama bin Laden and other terrorist leaders. She is reluctant to use waterboarding and other methods but sees that those tactics work.

ONLINE RESOURCES

Arms Control Association—a national nonpartisan membership organization dedicated to promoting public understanding of and support for effective arms control policies; the website of the ACA lists each country's status in terms of signing arms control treaties and its inventory of weapons: www.armscontrol.org

Brookings—a nonprofit public policy organization based in Washington, DC: www.brookings.edu

Center for Security Studies (CSS)—an academic institute at ETH Zurich specializing in research, teaching, and the provision of services in international and national security policy; provides information about human rights, national security, and other issues from a European point of view: www.css.ethz.ch/index_EN

Central Intelligence Agency—created in 1947 with the signing of the National Security Act by President Harry S Truman; responsible for providing national security intelligence to senior U.S. policymakers: www.cia.gov

U.S. Department of State—provides access to hundreds of websites on foreign and defense policies of the U.S. government and the governments of other nations; includes information about visas, passports, and individual countries: www.state.gov

State and Local Government

Jacob Frey (left), the Mayor of Minneapolis, congratulates Melvin Carter (right) on his election as mayor of St. Paul, Minnesota.

Frazer Harrison/Getty Images

LEARNING OBJECTIVES

After reading this chapter, you will be able to:

- **18.1** Discuss the relationship of state laws and constitutions to the U.S. Constitution and federal law.

- **18.2** Discuss the relationship between governors and state legislatures and the powers associated with each.

- **18.3** Explain why counties, cities, and other units of local government are limited in their power and their autonomy.

- **18.4** Describe the most important sources of revenue for states and local governments and their biggest expenditures, and contrast them with those of the federal government.

What if... All States Offered School Vouchers?

Background

All public education systems in the United States are funded and controlled by local and state governments. These entities set policies, raise taxes and distribute them to schools, and regulate all aspects of the public school system. Many observers argue that the low achievement of American students requires drastic changes, such as making schools compete with each other. Currently, parents are required to send their children to a public school in the particular district where the family's home is located. Generally, only families willing to spend from $3,000 to $10,000 per year for tuition at private schools (in addition to the property taxes they pay to support their local public school districts) have a choice as to which school their children will attend.

What If States Gave Parents Money to Change Schools?

School choice can involve open districts, meaning that parents can choose to send their children to public schools outside of their districts. The type of school choice that generates controversy, however, usually involves giving families vouchers, which represent state funds that can be used at any school, public or private. In other words, a voucher is worth some specified amount of money, such as $5,000, but only if it is redeemed by a bona fide public or private school. Any such plan has to be set up by state or local government, because that is where the responsibility for education currently lies. Today, twenty-six states have approved some type of school voucher system.

Under such a system, parents determine where their children go to school. The children may attend a local public school, a public school in another district, or a private school anywhere. Private schools can accept vouchers as full payment for tuition fees or require that additional fees be paid.

Competition Would Become Evident

If all families received school vouchers, public schools would have to compete not only among themselves (as they currently do in areas that have open districts) but also with private schools. Private schools would have to compete with all schools.

Some critics of school choice, particularly public school teachers and administrators, are uncomfortable with treating public education like a business. Because of the competitive environment that would be created by school choice, some public schools might not be able to keep and attract enough students to survive. These schools, unless further subsidized by state and local governments, would go bankrupt and disappear. Still, in Milwaukee, Wisconsin, where the first voucher program was established in 1990, the program has raised test scores at both private and public schools. School board members and some liberals who formerly opposed the plan now accept it.

The Constitutional Issue

Other critics claim that such programs violate the federal Constitution or state constitutions because they allow state funds to be used for education at religious schools. In Cleveland, Ohio, children from low-income families received state funds in the form of vouchers to attend the schools of their choice. Most of the 4,000 children in the program left public schools to attend Catholic educational institutions. Currently, children with demonstrated economic need or who attend schools rated as failing may apply for vouchers in fourteen states and the District of Columbia.

According to opponents, the use of tax dollars to support religious education violates the establishment clause of the First Amendment to the Constitution, which requires the separation of church and state. In 2002, however, the Supreme Court held that the voucher program was constitutional because families theoretically could use the vouchers to send their children not only to religious schools but also to secular private academies, suburban public schools, or charter schools. Therefore, the program did not unconstitutionally entangle church and state.

For Critical Analysis

1. Why are teachers' unions, such as the National Education Association, so adamantly against vouchers?

2. Do you see school choice as hurtful or helpful to students from low-income families?

For most Americans, state and local governments have the most day-to-day impact on their lives. To get a driver's license, you must complete state-required forms and tests. You probably attended elementary and secondary schools provided by local governmental units, typically called school boards. Local governments determine the cost of a traffic ticket and the day that your street is cleaned. Because they shape the environments in which all Americans live, the more than 90,000 local governmental units in the United States play a vital role in our federal system. However, as you read in Chapter 3, many state government functions are paid for, in part, by federal grants. More and more, federal programs shape or control state programs that directly affect citizens.

From a practical point of view, it is impossible to understand American politics and government today without knowledge of how state and local governments operate. We begin by examining the constitutional powers of the states as set forth by the founders in the U.S. Constitution. As you will see, local governments were not mentioned in the Constitution. The founders left their existence in the hands of state government.

The U.S. Constitution and the State Governments

■ **18.1** Discuss the relationship of state laws and constitutions to the U.S. Constitution and federal law.

We live in a federal system in which there are fifty separate state governments and one national government. The U.S. Constitution reserves a broad range of powers for state governments and prohibits state governments from engaging in certain activities. The U.S. Constitution does not say explicitly what the states actually may do. Rather, state powers are simply reserved, or residual: states may do anything that is not prohibited by the Constitution or anything that is not expressly within the realm of the national government.

The major reserved powers of the states are the powers to tax, spend, and regulate intrastate commerce (commerce within a given state). The states also have general police power, meaning that they can impose their will on their citizens in the areas of safety (traffic laws), health (immunizations), welfare (child abuse laws), and morals (regulation of pornographic materials).

Restrictions on state and local governmental activity are implied by the Constitution in Article VI, Clause 2:

> *This Constitution, and the Laws of the United States which shall be made in Pursuance thereof; and all Treaties made, or which shall be made, under the Authority of the United States, shall be the supreme Law of the Land; and the Judges in every State shall be bound thereby, any Thing in the Constitution or Laws of any State to the Contrary notwithstanding.*

The U.S. Constitution takes precedence over all other laws. No state or local law can be in conflict with the Constitution, with laws made by the national Congress, or with treaties entered into by the national government. State and local governments, however, will create policies that are at odds with federal policies or adopt policies that the federal government has not yet adopted. In recent years, states, especially those along the Mexican border, have passed their own

Image 18–1
Mayor Ivy Taylor of Fort Worth Texas, served in that office from 2014 to 2017.

policies to deal with illegal immigrants, in part because the Congress has not yet agreed on a new immigration policy. Arizona, Alabama, South Carolina, and Utah are among those states that have passed laws to discourage the residency of undocumented immigrants. The Arizona law, signed by Governor Jan Brewer in 2010, required all immigrants to carry their papers, banned immigrants from soliciting work in public places, and required police to ask the immigration status of individuals detained for other crimes if the police suspected that they were illegal immigrants. In a landmark Supreme Court case, many aspects of the Arizona law were found to be unconstitutional, but the provision allowing police officers to ask for proof of legal residency when a suspect is detained was upheld.[1] Alabama passed a law making all contracts signed by undocumented immigrants illegal, including apartment leases and possibly utility contracts. At the same time, other states are passing laws that offer in-state tuition to colleges and universities for undocumented children who have graduated from high school. California now permits undocumented residents to get a driver's license. Of course, these laws and any state laws that affect undocumented residents will be tested against any federal immigration law passed by Congress, because federal law and the Constitution outweigh all state laws.

The U.S. Constitution is a model of brevity, although at the cost of specificity. State constitutions, however, typically are excessively long and detailed. The U.S. Constitution has endured for 200 years and has been amended only 27 times. State constitutions are another matter. Louisiana has had 11 constitutions; Georgia, 9; and Virginia, 7. The number of amendments submitted to voters borders on the absurd. The citizens of Alabama have adopted 856 amendments to their state constitution due to the fact that even local governments must have a state constitutional amendment to engage in certain activities. An amendment might specify the salary for a particular local official or authorize gambling casinos for specified counties.

Why Are State Constitutions So Long?

According to historians, the length and mass of detail of many state constitutions reflect the loss of popular confidence in state legislatures between the end of the Civil War and the early 1900s. During that period, 42 states adopted or revised their constitutions with specific provisions. States seem to believe that a constitution should include items that are usually regulated by statute or legislation. The U.S. Constitution leaves to the legislature the nuts-and-bolts activity of making specific statutory laws.

In all fairness to the states, their courts do not interpret their constitutions as freely as the U.S. Supreme Court interprets the U.S. Constitution. Therefore,

did you know?

The Texas constitution declares that banks may use automated teller machines (ATMs), and the New York constitution specifies the width of ski trails.

---

1 *Arizona v. U.S.,* 567 U.S._ (2012).

the states feel compelled to be more specific in their own constitutions. Additionally, the framers of state constitutions may feel obliged to fill in the gaps left by the very brief federal Constitution.

The Constitutional Convention and the Constitutional Initiative

Two of the several ways to effect constitutional changes are the state constitutional convention and the constitutional initiative. As of 2007, more than 230 state constitutional conventions had been used to write an entirely new constitution or to attempt to amend an existing one. In 18 states, the constitution can be amended by **constitutional initiative**.[2] An initiative allows citizens to place a proposed amendment on the ballot without calling a constitutional convention. The number of signatures required to get a constitutional initiative on the ballot varies from state to state; it is usually between 5 and 10 percent of the total number of votes cast for governor in the last election. The initiative process has been used most frequently in California and Oregon.

> **constitutional initiative**
> An electoral device whereby citizens can propose a constitutional amendment through petitions signed by the required number of registered voters.

The State Executive Branch

All state governments in the United States have executive, legislative, and judicial branches. Here the similarity with the federal government ends. State governments do not always have strong executive branches.

A Weak Executive

During the colonial period, governors were appointed by the Crown and had the power to call the colonial assembly (the colonial legislative body) into session, recommend legislation, exercise veto power, and dissolve the assembly. The colonial governor acted as commander in chief of the colony's military forces and was also the head of the judiciary.

Not surprisingly, the colonies' revolt against British rule centered on the all-powerful colonial governors. When the first states were formed after the Declaration of Independence, hostility toward the governor's office ensured a weak executive branch and an extremely strong legislative branch. By the 1830s, however, governors and other state officers had a greater role to play.

Under the tenets of Jacksonian democracy, the more public officials who are elected (and not appointed), the more democratic (and better) the system will be. Many states have multiple elected officials, including some whose duties are obsolete. Having an elected state treasurer, auditor, and secretary of state prevents the governor from appointing officers of his or her own choosing. If the executive officers are of different political parties, there is likely to be competition rather than collaboration.

A slight majority of the states require that the candidates for governor and lieutenant governor run for election as a team. In some states where this is not required, however, the voters have at times chosen a governor from one political party and a lieutenant governor from another. In a few states, this has actually created a situation in which the governor is unwilling to leave the state in order to prevent the lieutenant governor from exerting power during the governor's absence.

> *did you know?*
> The first woman to become governor of a state was Nellie Taylor Ross, who became governor of Wyoming in 1925.

---

2 These states are Arizona, Arkansas, California, Colorado, Florida, Illinois, Massachusetts, Michigan, Mississippi, Missouri, Montana, Nebraska, Nevada, North Dakota, Ohio, Oklahoma, Oregon, and South Dakota.

Image 18-2
Scott Walker, governor of Wisconsin, talks with the press at a presidential debate in 2015. Walker ran for his third term of governor in 2018.

Zuma Press, Inc./Alamy Stock Photo

Increasing the Governor's Power

In theory, the governor enjoys the same advantage that the president has over Congress in his or her ability to make policy decisions and to embody them in a program on which the state legislative body can act. How the governor exercises this ability often depends on her or his powers of persuasion. A strong personality can make for a strong executive office. Personal skill, the strength of political parties and special-interest groups, and the governor's use of the media can affect how much actual power she or he has.

Despite the fragmentation of executive power and doubts about the concentration of power in an executive's hands, the trend toward modernization has increased the powers of many of the states' highest executives. Based on a governor's ability to make major appointments, formulate a state budget, veto legislation, and exercise other powers, the National Governors Association ranks the governors of at least 25 states as powerful or very powerful executives. Only 11 states are assessed as giving their executives little or very little power.

State governors and legislators are playing increasingly important roles as the states assume more authority over programs, such as welfare, that for decades were controlled by the national government. The trend toward states' rights during the 1990s and 2000s has allowed governors to become models of leadership on several issues affecting national politics, including crime, welfare, and education. A state governorship may also be a stepping-stone to the U.S. presidency. Seventeen of the nation's 45 presidents (39 percent), including several recent presidents (Jimmy Carter, Ronald Reagan, Bill Clinton, and George W. Bush), served as state governors before assuming presidential office. For these reasons, elections to state governorships tend to receive more national attention now than they did in the past. In 2016, the early Republican field of candidates for the presidency included four governors: Chris Christie of New Jersey, Scott Walker of Wisconsin, Bobby Jindal of Louisiana, and John Kasich of Ohio.

The Governor's Veto Power

The mere threat of a presidential veto often means that legislation will not be passed by Congress. In some states, governors have strong veto power, but in others, governors have no veto power at all. Some states give the governor veto power but allow only five days in which to exercise it. Thirteen states give the governor pocket veto power.

In 43 states, the governor has some form of **item veto** power on appropriations, which gives the governor an opportunity to decrease legislative spending. If the governor does not like one item, or line, in an appropriations bill, he or she can veto that item. In 12 states, the governor can reduce the amount of the appropriation but cannot eliminate it altogether. Nineteen states give governors the ability to use the item veto on more than just appropriations.

Twitter Feed ▶ Governor Cuomo of New York uses Twitter to promote his policies on maternal health.

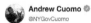

Andrew Cuomo ✔
@NYGovCuomo

(Follow) ⌄

Maternal mortality is not a fear any woman in New York should face in the 21st century.

We are taking aggressive action to address the unacceptable racial disparities in maternal mortality.

New York to Expand Use of Doulas to Reduce Childbirth Deaths
Gov. Andrew Cuomo announced a series of initiatives aimed at addressing a disturbingly high rate of maternal mortality among black women.
nytimes.com

Andrew Cuomo/Twitter, Inc.

item veto
The power exercised by the governors of most states to veto particular sections or items of an appropriations bill while signing the remainder of the bill into law.

The State Legislature

■ **18.2** Discuss the relationship between governors and state legislatures and the powers associated with each.

Although a move in recent years has increased the power of governors, state legislatures are still an important force in state politics and state governmental decision making. The task of these assemblies is to legislate on such matters as taxes; the regulation of business and commerce, highways, and school systems; the funding of education; and welfare payments. Allocation of funds and program priorities are vital issues to local residents and communities; conflicts between regions within the state or between the cities and the rural areas are common.

State legislatures have been criticized for being unprofessional and less than effective. It is true that state legislatures sometimes spend their time considering trivial legislation (such as the official state pie in Florida), and lobbyists often have too much influence in state capitals. At the same time, state legislators are often given few resources with which to work. In many states, legislatures are limited to meeting only part of the year, and in some the pay is a disincentive to real service. In 23 states, state legislators are paid less than $20,000 per year. The National Council of State Legislatures actually categorizes state legislatures as fully professional, hybrid, or volunteer/part time, according to the characteristics discussed here. A complete list of state legislators' salaries, as well as other characteristics of state legislatures, is given in Table 18-1.

Figure 18-1 traces how an idea becomes a law in the Florida legislature. Similar steps are followed in other states (note that Nebraska has a unicameral legislature, however, so it has no second chamber process).

did you know?

In 1999, the Louisiana legislature passed a law requiring students from kindergarten through fifth grade to address teachers as "sir" and "ma'am."

Table 18-1 ▶   Characteristics of State Legislatures 2017

	SEATS IN SENATE	LENGTH OF TERM	SEATS IN HOUSE	LENGTH OF TERM	YEARS SESSIONS ARE HELD	SALARY*
Alabama	35	4	105	4	Annual	$42,830[†]
Alaska	20	4	40	2	Annual	$44,765[†]
Arizona	30	2	60	2	Annual	$24,000[†]
Arkansas	35	4	100	2	Annual	$39,400[†]
California	40	4	80	2	Even**	$104,118[†]
Colorado	35	4	65	2	Annual	$30,000[†]
Connecticut	36	2	151	2	Annual	$28,000
Delaware	21	4	41	2	Annual	$45,291[†]
Florida	40	4	120	2	Annual	$29,697[†]
Georgia	56	2	180	2	Annual	$17,342[†]
Hawaii	25	4	51	2	Annual	$61,390[†]
Idaho	35	2	70	2	Annual	$17,017[†]
Illinois	59	[†]	118	2	Annual	$67,836[†]
Indiana	50	4	100	2	Annual	$24,140[†]
Iowa	50	4	100	2	Annual	$25,000[†]
Kansas	40	4	125	2	Annual	$88.66(d)[†]
Kentucky	38	4	100	2	Annual	$188.20(d)[†]
Louisiana	39	4	105	4	Annual	$16,800[†]
Maine	35	2	151	2	Even	$14,271[§†]
Maryland	47	4	141	4	Annual	$47,769[†]
Massachusetts	40	2	160	2	Biennial**	$62,548[†]
Michigan	38	4	110	2	Annual	$71,865[†]
Minnesota	67	4	134	2	Biennial	$31,140[†]
Mississippi	52	4	122	4	Annual	$10,000[†]
Missouri	34	4	163	2	Annual	$35,915[†]
Montana	50	4	100	2	Odd	$90.64(d)[†]
Nebraska	49	4	–	–	Annual	$12,000[¥]
Nevada	21	4	42	2	Odd	$146.29(d)[†]
New Hampshire	24	2	400	2	Annual	$200(b)
New Jersey	40	4	80	2	Biennial	$49,000
New Mexico	42	4	70	2	Annual	–[†]
New York	62	2	150	2	Annual	$79,500[†]
North Carolina	50	2	120	2	Odd[††]	$13,951[†]
North Dakota	47	4	94	4	Odd	$162(d)[†]
Ohio	33	4	99	2	Biennial	$60,583
Oklahoma	48	4	101	2	Annual	$38,400[†]
Oregon	30	4	0	2	Odd	$24,216[†]
Pennsylvania	50	4	203	2	Odd**	$86,479[†]
Rhode Island	38	2	75	2	Annual	$15,430
South Carolina	46	4	124	2	Biennial	$10,400[†]

Table 18-1 ▶ *(continued)*

	SEATS IN SENATE	LENGTH OF TERM	SEATS IN HOUSE	LENGTH OF TERM	YEARS SESSIONS ARE HELD	SALARY*
South Dakota	35	2	70	2	Annual	$12,000(b)[†]
Tennessee	33	4	99	2	Biennial	$22,667[†]
Texas	31	4	150	2	Odd	$7,200[†]
Utah	29	4	75	2	Annual	$273(d)[†]
Vermont	30	2	150	2	Annual	$707(w)[†]
Virginia	40	4	100	2	Annual	$18,000[††]
Washington	49	4	98	2	Annual	$47,776[†]
West Virginia	34	4	100	2	Annual	$20,000[†]
Wisconsin	33	4	99	2	Biennial	$50,930[†]
Wyoming	30	4	60	2	Biennial	$150(d)[†]

Source: Council of State Governments, *Book of the States* (2015 Edition).

*Salaries annual unless otherwise noted as (d)—per day, (b)—per biennium, or (w)—per week.

[†]Plus *per diem* living expenses.

[‡]Terms vary from two to four years.

[§]For odd year; $9,661 for even year.

[¥]Unicameral legislature.

**Two-year session (that is, it meets every year).

[††]Annual at option of legislature.

[‡‡]Senate; House is $17,640.

Legislative Apportionment

The formulation of legislative districts—state as well as federal—has long been subject to gerrymandering (creative cartography designed to guarantee that one political party maintains control of a particular voting district). Malapportionment is the skewed distribution of voters in a state's legislative districts. The U.S. Supreme Court ruled in 1962 that malapportioned state legislatures violate the equal protection clause of the Fourteenth Amendment.[3] The Court held that legislative districts must be as nearly equal as possible in terms of population, and the grossest examples of state legislative malapportionment were eliminated.[4] The Supreme Court, however, allowed "benevolent, bipartisan gerrymandering" in certain states.

Minority Representation In 1977, the Supreme Court held that a state had an obligation under the 1965 Voting Rights Act to draw district boundaries to maximize minority legislative representation.[5] Thus, each decade, state and federal legislative districts must be redrawn to ensure that every person's vote is roughly equal and that minorities are represented adequately.

By the mid-1990s, the Supreme Court had reversed its position on what has been called "racial gerrymandering." The Court held that voting districts that are redrawn solely with the goal of maximizing the electoral strength and representation of minority groups violate the equal protection clause.[6]

Political Gerrymandering Political gerrymandering that benefits both of the major political parties has become a significant issue. Using sophisticated

3 *Baker v. Carr*, 369 U.S. 186 (1962).
4 *Reynolds v. Sims*, 377 U.S. 533 (1964); and other cases.
5 *United Jewish Organizations of Williamsburg v. Carey*, 430 U.S. 144 (1977).
6 *Miller v. Johnson*, 515 U.S. 900 (1995); *Shaw v. Hunt*, 517 U.S. 899 (1996); and *Bush v. Vera*, 517 U.S. 952 (1996).

Figure 18-1 ▶ How an Idea Becomes a Law

A simplified chart showing the route a bill takes through the Florida legislature. Bills may originate in either house. This bill originated in the House of Representatives.

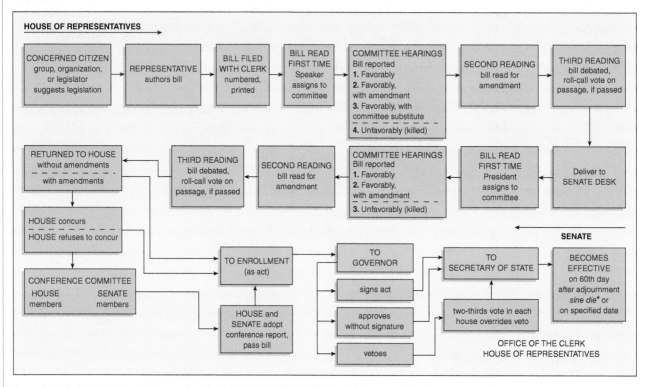

Source: Allen Morris and Joan Perry Morris, compilers, *The Florida Handbook, 2005–2006*, 30th ed. (Tallahassee, FL: Peninsular Books, 2005).
Sine die means "without assigning a day for a further meeting."

computer programs, legislators can draw district lines that virtually guarantee the reelection of incumbents. In many states, Republican and Democratic legislators conspire to ensure the safety of incumbents, regardless of party. Some have said that instead of the voters choosing their legislators, the legislators now choose their voters. The Supreme Court has not blocked this practice. In 1986, the Court did hold that it was at least conceivable that an instance of political gerrymandering might be unconstitutional.[7] In 2004 and 2006, however, the Court in effect withdrew the possibility that it might ever issue such a ruling.[8]

Citizens in states ranging from Massachusetts to California have organized campaigns to create new laws that curb political gerrymandering. Iowa and Arizona already use nonpartisan commissions to draw district lines instead of leaving the job to the legislature and the governor. In 2012, Ohio voters defeated an initiative for a nonpartisan process. Supporters of the reform criticized the language of the initiative for being too complex. The next attempt to create a less partisan commission, in 2015, succeeded, and Ohio will begin using the new process after the 2020 census.[9]

Term Limits for State Legislators

For more than a decade, many states have agreed that a legislator's tenure should be limited. Although the restrictions vary, 15 states have laws

---

7   *Davis v. Bandemer*, 478 U.S. 109 (1986).
8   *Vieth v. Jubelirer*, 541 U.S. 267 (2004); *League of Latin American Citizens v. Perry*, 126 S.Ct. 2594 (2006).
9   J. Siegel, "Voters Approve Issue to Reform Ohio's Redistricting Process," *The Columbus Dispatch*, November 5, 2015, p. 1.

restricting the number of terms a legislator can serve. In four other states—Massachusetts, Oregon, Washington, and Wyoming—term-limit laws were thrown out by the respective state supreme courts, whereas Idaho's and Utah's legislatures repealed their own term-limit laws. Advocates of term limits argue that lawmakers who have not spent years in public office will best represent the interests of voters. Special-interest groups will have less chance to influence a politician who does not have a future campaign to finance. Opponents of term limits argue that the same newly elected lawmakers who are less likely to be swayed by special interests are also more likely to lack the experience required to understand state policy.

Making service in the legislature a part-time job rather than a full-time one is another way states try to keep legislators in tune with their fellow citizens. In some states, especially large states such as California and New York, state legislators receive a salary that is large enough to live on. In these states, service is considered a full-time job, and the members of the statehouse and senate are referred to as professional legislators. In a majority of the states, however, legislative service is considered part-time work, and salaries reflect this expectation. Such states are said to have citizen legislators. The 400 members of New Hampshire's house are paid only $200 per session, with no allowance for expenses. New Hampshire has only about 1.3 million people, so it is relatively easy for a political activist to become part of the legislature.

Those who support a citizen legislature do not believe that states with professional legislators have better laws. They contend that much of the extra time spent by professional legislators is likely to be wasted and that making legislators full-time professionals encourages careerism and a lack of responsiveness to the voters.

Ethics and Campaign Finance Reform in the States

Regulations for campaign contributions and the disclosure of contributors for all federal offices are the result of legislation passed by Congress and rules put forward by the Federal Election Commission. However, regulations that affect candidates for office at the state level are the responsibility of state legislatures and the governor. States differ widely in the degree to which they regulate campaign contributions and the disclosure of donors. Although most states require that all contributions be disclosed to the public through some manner of quarterly reporting system, the amount of information disclosed about the donors varies widely, as does the public's access to the information. Some states require that the donor's name, occupation, address, and employer be disclosed, whereas 14 states do not require either the donor's occupation or employer to be disclosed, thus hiding contributions from those industries that might benefit from legislation. Almost all states require that candidates report expenditures, but several do not require the amount or purpose of the expenditure to be revealed. More than 40 states now post all information that is reported on their websites, but not all require candidates to file electronically, so information is not available to the public quickly.[10]

10 "Grading Campaign Disclosure 2008," The Campaign Disclosure Project, www.campaigndisclosure.org.

Election 2016 ★★★

State Politics and Statehouse Elections

For a number of years, states have been rearranging their election calendars so that major state officeholders do not run for reelection in presidential election years. There are two reasons for this: parties believe they may have a better chance to capture the governorship in a nonpresidential year, and many states have increased their governor's term to four years, beginning in an off-year election. In 2016, of the 50 states, there were only 12 governorships up for election, of which 7 were "open seats," meaning that the incumbent was retiring or was term-limited. These seats were held by eight Democrats and four Republicans. How likely was it that the parties would hold their respective governor's mansions? Some of the states were easy to predict: Indiana, North Dakota, and Utah were very likely to elect Republicans, whereas Delaware, Oregon, and Washington were likely to retain Democratic governors. In 2016, two more governorships were won by Republicans.

Unlike governors, most members of state legislatures hold two-year terms of office. About 80 percent of all state legislative seats were up for reelection in 2016. Recalling the power of incumbency in the Congress, the same is true for state legislators. Incumbents account for about 80 percent of the races and about 40 percent of those face no opposition from the other party. Only about 20 percent of the seats in the legislative elections are open seats.*

The big question looming over all of the 2016 state elections was the impact of the presidential ticket on these races. Commentators and members of the Republican leadership suggested that the nomination of Donald Trump would be disastrous for these state races. Democrats had high hopes that the nomination of Hillary Clinton would bring out their voters and help win these state-level elections. In states that are pretty clearly identified as "red" or "blue," the presidential ticket has little influence due the nature of the state. In states that are difficult to predict, such as North Carolina or Missouri, the top of the ticket may have "coattails" for state elections; however, the popularity of statewide office holders and their positions on issues important to the state are likely to be more important to the voter than the presidential nominee. It is true that a certain nominee may increase turnout and thus affect state elections, but many voters will come out to vote for the presidential ballot and not cast a vote for other offices at all.

For Critical Analysis

1. Why do so many state legislators (40 percent) face no opposition at all?

2. What are some issues at the state level that would be affected if the state legislature changed from Republican to Democrat?

*Ballotpedia, "2016 State Legislative Elections Analyzed Using a Competitive Index," https://ballotpedia.org/2016_state_state_legislative_elections_analyzed _using_a_competitiveness_Index

Similarly, states have struggled to enact and enforce ethics legislation. If a legislature is composed of volunteer legislators meeting, perhaps, for four or five months per year and being paid less than $15,000, it seems unlikely that the legislators depend on their elected position for their livelihood. Most part-time legislators have real careers and earn their livings through those positions. However, there are always questions of conflicts of interest, lobbying gifts and parties, and opportunities for a legislator or the staff to benefit from a particular piece of legislation. There are numerous examples of legislators and governors who have suffered legal action from lapses in ethical decision making. Generally, states have tried to adopt ethics codes that would prohibit legislators and other officeholders from accepting gifts or require them to disclose gifts over a minimum amount. In Tennessee, legislators must disclose any contribution over $250. In addition, states are passing ethics laws that prohibit former legislators from becoming lobbyists at the state capitol for a certain period. Six states have a two-year period before a legislator can become a lobbyist, whereas 20 states require sitting out for only one year.[11] Sometimes, it appears that ethics rules can go too far. A Colorado amendment to the constitution passed by voters in 2006 prevented any state official's child from receiving a college scholarship or any public university professor from accepting the Nobel Prize.[12]

Direct Democracy: The Initiative, Referendum, and Recall

There is a major difference between the legislative process as outlined in the U.S. Constitution and the legislative process as outlined in the various state constitutions. Many states exercise a type of direct democracy through the initiative, the referendum, and the recall—procedures that allow voters to control the government directly.

The Initiative Most states that permit the citizen legislative initiative require that the initiative's backers circulate a petition to place the issue on the ballot and that a certain percentage of the registered voters in the last gubernatorial election sign the petition. Twenty-four states use the legislative initiative, typically those states in which political parties are relatively weak and nonpartisan groups are strong. Legislative initiatives have involved a range of issues, including crime victims' rights, campaign contributions, corporate spending on ballot questions, affirmative action, physician-assisted suicide, and the medical use of marijuana. In some instances, voters have passed state initiatives that are contrary to federal policy—several states passed initiatives legalizing the use of marijuana.

The Referendum The referendum is similar to the initiative, except that the issue (or constitutional change) is proposed first by the legislature and then directed to the voters for their approval. The referendum is most often used for approval of local school bond issues and for amendments to state constitutions. In several states that provide for the referendum, a bill passed by the legislature may be suspended by obtaining the required number of voters' signatures on petitions. A statewide referendum election is then held. If a majority of the voters disapprove of the bill, it is no longer valid.

The referendum was not initially intended for regular use, and it was employed infrequently in the past. Its opponents argue that it is an unnecessary check on representative government and that it weakens legislative responsibility. In recent years, the referendum has become increasingly popular as citizens have attempted to control their state and local governments. Interest groups have been active in sponsoring the petition drives necessary to force a referendum. More than two-thirds of the states provide for the referendum.

The Recall The right of citizens to recall elected officials is not exercised frequently. Recall is a provision written into the constitutions of 15 states. It allows voters to remove elected state officials, including the governor, before the expiration of their terms of office. In the case of judges, the recall can terminate a lifetime appointment.

Citizens begin the recall process by circulating petitions demanding a statewide vote to remove the offending officeholder. The number of signatures needed ranges from 10 to 40 percent of the last vote for the office in question. In some states, the recall election is held concurrently with an

did you know?

The most expensive ballot initiative in history was California's Proposition 94. The opposing sides of the proposition, which expanded the number of casinos on Indian reservations, spent a total of approximately $172 million.

---

11 See the reports of the Center for Ethics in Government sponsored by the National Council of State Legislatures, www. ncsl.org
12 Karl Kurtz, "Colorado Ethics Initiative Blocked by Court," *The Thicket at State Legislatures*, July 1, 2007, http://ncsl.typepad .com/the_thicket

election to pick the official's successor in office. In 2012, Wisconsin held a recall election for Governor Scott Walker, who had proposed and implemented severe changes in the rights of public employees to collectively bargain. Walker became the only American governor to survive a recall election, defeating his opponent handily.

The recall and the initiative are examples of "pure democracy," in which the people as a whole vote directly on important issues. Such measures are distinct in theory and in practice from the norms of "representative democracy," in which the people govern only indirectly through their elected representatives.

The State Judiciary

In addition to the federal courts, each of the 50 states, as well as the District of Columbia, has its own separate court system. Figure 18-2 shows a sample state court system. Like the federal court system, it has several tiers, including trial courts, intermediate courts of appeals, and a supreme court.

Figure 18-2 ▶ A Sample State Court System

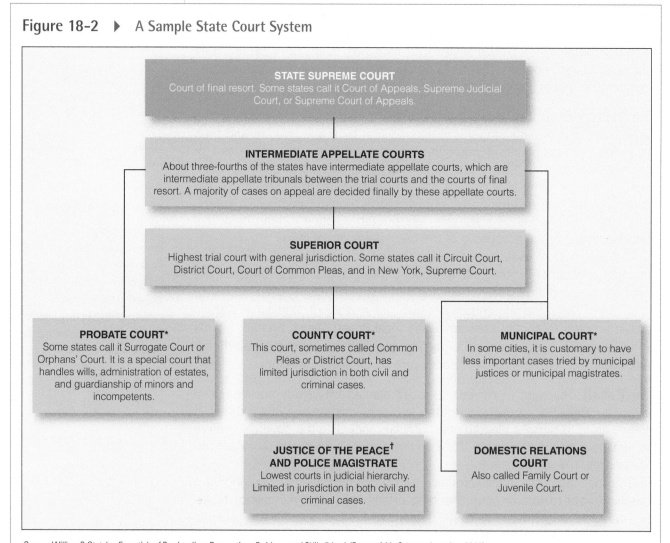

Source: William P. Statsky, *Essentials of Paralegalism: Perspectives, Problems, and Skills,* 5th ed. (Boston, MA: Cengage Learning, 2009).

*Courts of special jurisdiction, such as probate, family, or juvenile courts, and the so-called inferior courts, such as common pleas or municipal courts, may be separate courts or may be part of the trial court of general jurisdiction.

†Justices of the peace do not exist in all states. Their jurisdiction varies greatly from state to state when they do exist.

Trial Courts

All states have major trial courts, commonly called circuit courts, district courts, or superior courts. The number of judges and their terms in office vary widely. As in the federal court system, the trial courts are of two types: those having limited jurisdiction and those having general jurisdiction.[13] Cases heard before these courts can be appealed to the state intermediate appellate court and ultimately to the state supreme court.

Appellate Courts

About three-fourths of the states have intermediate appellate courts between the trial courts of original jurisdiction and the highest state appellate court, or the supreme court. These are usually called courts of appeals. Judges in some states are compensated significantly better than their counterparts in others. Appellate and supreme court members earn a higher salary than the trial judges of their states.

The highest state appellate courts are called supreme courts. Some states use other designations, such as the supreme judicial court (Maine and Massachusetts), the court of appeals (Maryland and New York), the court of criminal appeals (Oklahoma and Texas, which also have separate supreme courts for appeals in noncriminal cases), or the supreme court of appeals (West Virginia). The decisions of each state's highest court on all questions of state law are final. Only when issues of federal law are involved can a decision made by a state's highest court be overruled by the U.S. Supreme Court.

Judicial Elections and Appointments

State court judges are either elected or appointed, depending on the state and (often) on the level of court involved—the procedures vary considerably from state to state. In some states, including Delaware, the procedure is similar to the way federal judges are appointed: the judges are appointed by the governor and confirmed by the upper chamber of the legislature. In other states, all state court judges are elected, either on a partisan ballot (as in Alabama) or on a nonpartisan ballot (as in Kentucky). In several states, judges in some of the lower courts are elected, whereas those in the appellate courts are appointed. Additionally, depending on the state, appointed judges may have to run for reelection if they wish to serve a second term.

In the 38 states that elect judges, many of these elections are turning into hard-fought political battles, even in states with nonpartisan elections. A little-noted Supreme Court decision has changed the old rules for judicial campaigning. In 2002, the Court overturned a state law that barred judicial candidates from commenting on controversies they might have to resolve.[14] Now groups with strong opinions on abortion or same-sex marriage can grill candidates on these issues. The American Bar Association has called for public financing of judicial campaigns so that candidates will not have to seek private contributions.

---

13 See Chapter 14 for a definition of these terms.
14 *Republican Party of Minnesota v. White*, 536 U.S. 765 (2002).

How Local Government Operates

■ **18.3** Explain why counties, cities, and other units of local government are limited in their power and their autonomy.

Local governments are difficult to describe because of their great dissimilarities and because, if we include municipalities, counties, towns, townships, and special districts, there are so many of them. We limit the discussion here to the most important types and features of local governments.

The Legal Existence of Local Government

The U.S. Constitution makes no mention of local governments. Article IV, Section 4, merely states that "[t]he United States shall guarantee to every State in this Union a Republican Form of Government." The states do not even need to have local governments. Consequently, every local government is a creature of the state. The state can create a local government, and the state can terminate the right of a local government to exist. States often have abolished entire counties, school districts, cities, and special districts. Since World War II, almost 20,000 school districts were disbanded and consolidated.

Can the state dictate everything the local government does? For many years, that seemed to be the case. The narrowest possible view of the legal status of local governments follows **Dillon's rule**, outlined by Judge John F. Dillon in his *Commentaries on the Law of Municipal Corporations* in 1872. He stated that municipal corporations may possess only powers "granted in express words . . . [that are] necessarily or fairly implied in or incident to the powers expressly granted."[15] Cities governed under Dillon's rule have sometimes been dominated by the state legislatures, depending on the extent of the authority granted to the cities by the legislatures. Those communities wishing to obtain the status of a municipal corporation have petitioned the state legislature for a **charter**.

In a revolt against state legislative power over municipalities, the home rule movement began, based on **Cooley's rule**, derived from an 1871 decision by Michigan judge Thomas Cooley stating that cities should be able to govern themselves.[16] Since 1900, about four-fifths of the states have allowed **municipal home rule**, but only with respect to local concerns for which no statewide interests are involved. A municipality must choose to become a **home rule city**; otherwise, it operates as a **general law city**. In the latter case, the state makes certain general laws relating to cities of different sizes, which are designated as first-class cities, second-class cities, or towns. Once a city, by virtue of its population, receives such a ranking, it follows the general law established by the state. Only if it chooses to be a home rule city can it avoid such state government restrictions. In many states, only cities with populations of 2,500 or more can choose home rule.

Local Governmental Units

The four major types of local governmental units are municipalities, counties, towns and townships, and special districts.

Municipalities A municipality is a political entity created by the people of a city or town to govern themselves locally. Currently, there are more than

Dillon's rule
The narrowest possible interpretation of the legal status of local governments, outlined by Judge John E. Dillon, who in 1872 stated that a municipal corporation can exercise only those powers expressly granted by state law.

charter
A document issued by a government that grants to a person, a group of persons, or a corporation the right to carry on one or more specific activities. A state government can grant a charter to a municipality.

Cooley's rule
The view that cities should be able to govern themselves, presented in an 1871 Michigan decision by Judge Thomas Cooley.

municipal home rule
The power vested in a local unit of government to draft or change its own charter and to manage its own affairs.

home rule city
A city permitted by the state to let local voters frame, adopt, and amend their own charter.

general law city
A city operating under general state laws that apply to all local governmental units of a similar type.

---

15 John F. Dillon, *Commentaries on the Law of Municipal Corporations*, 5th ed. (Boston, MA: Little, Brown, 1911), Vol. 1, Sec. 237.
16 *People v. Hurlbut*, 24 Mich. 44 (1871).

19,000 municipalities within the 50 states. Almost all municipalities are fairly small cities. Only about 200 cities have populations of more than 100,000, and only 9 cities (Chicago, Dallas, Houston, Los Angeles, New York, Philadelphia, Phoenix, San Antonio, and San Diego) have populations of more than 1 million. City expenditures are primarily for water supply and other utilities, police and fire protection, and education. About three-fourths of municipal tax revenues come from property taxes. Municipalities often rely heavily on financial assistance from both the federal and state governments.

Counties The difference between a **county** and a municipality is that a county is usually not created at the behest of its inhabitants. The state sets up counties on its own initiative to serve as political extensions of the state government. Counties apply state law and administer state business at the local level.

The United States has more than 3,000 counties, which vary greatly in both size and population. San Bernardino County in California is the largest geographically, with 20,102 square miles. New York County in New York is possibly the smallest, with fewer than 22 square miles. County populations within California alone range from millions of residents, as in Los Angeles County, to barely a thousand, as in Alpine County.

County governments' responsibilities include zoning, building regulations, health, hospitals, parks, recreation, highways, public safety, justice, and record-keeping. Typically, when a municipality is established within a county, the county withdraws most of its services from the municipality; the municipal police force takes over from the county police force. County governments are extremely complex entities, a product of the era of Jacksonian democracy and its effort to bring government closer to the people. There is no easy way to describe their operation in summary form. The county has been called by one scholar "the dark continent of American politics."[17]

Towns and Townships A unique governmental creation in the New England states is the **New England town**—not to be confused with the word *town* (meaning a small city). In Connecticut, Maine, Massachusetts, New Hampshire, and Vermont, the unit called the town combines the roles of city and county into one governing unit. A New England town typically consists of one or more urban settlements and the surrounding rural areas. Consequently, counties have little importance in New England. In Connecticut, for example, they are simply geographic units.

From the New England town is derived the tradition of the **town meeting**, an annual meeting at which direct democracy was—and continues to be—practiced. Each resident of a town is summoned to the annual meeting at the town hall. Those who attend levy taxes, pass laws, elect town officers, and appropriate money for different activities.

Normally, few residents show up for town meetings today unless an item of high interest is on the agenda or unless family members want to be elected to office. The town meeting takes a day or more, and few citizens are able to set aside such a large amount of time. Because of the declining interest in town meetings, many New England towns have adopted a **town manager system**: the voters elect three **selectpersons**, who then appoint a professional town manager. The town manager in turn appoints other officials.

county
The chief governmental unit set up by the state to administer state law and business at the local level. Counties are drawn up by area, rather than by rural or urban criteria.

New England town
A governmental unit in the New England states that combines the roles of city and county in one unit.

town meeting
The governing authority of a New England town. Qualified voters may participate in the election of officers and the passage of legislation.

town manager system
A form of town government in which voters elect three selectpersons, who then appoint a professional town manager, who in turn appoints other officials.

selectperson
A member of the governing group of a town.

---

17 Henry S. Gilbertson, *The County, the "Dark Continent of American Politics"* (New York: National Short Ballot Association, 1917).

Everyone Has a Mayor!

As long as humans have lived in communities, there have been community leaders who bear responsibility for the welfare of others or who must bring the members of the community to a decision or lead them into war. Local governments today are the governments closest to the people of a nation. They may have democratically elected leaders, or the leadership may be appointed by the central government. In more primitive societies, the local leader acquires his or her title through birth into a leading family or is named by a religious leader. What services can the town or village provide that a nation cannot?

Although the nation's central government can promise clean water and a sanitary sewer system to every citizen of the country, someone has to make sure that the water and sewers actually reach every individual household. Local governments typically are charged with ensuring the health and safety of the people by providing fire, police, and health services. Standards may be set at the provincial or state level or in unitary states at the national level, but only firefighters at the local firehouse know the neighborhood and the quickest way to reach a fire.

In most European nations, Australia, and New Zealand, local governments are elected. Responsibilities often involve planning, economic development, water, sewer and health issues, and public safety. The terms of local officials may be two, four, or six years. In some nations, such as France, the mayor of a city is not elected directly, but is the choice of the political party that wins the most seats in the city council. Nations with strong central governments (France is such a nation) make policy decisions in the capital, but local services are increasingly decentralized. A large federal nation like India has a variety of local forms of government; they serve both the most modern cities and small villages where basic services are lacking and financial resources are few.

China is a not a democratic government, and local government officials are chosen by regional governments. The Chinese Communist Party carefully monitors the work of local officials to make sure national policies are followed. In recent years, the corruption of local government officials has led to protests and uprisings by local citizens. In Afghanistan, where the United States and North Atlantic Treaty Organization (NATO) allies have worked to bring peace and reduce the influence of the Taliban, most villages are organized by traditional tribal affiliations, and the village chief is chosen by his tribe, not elected. When the United States increased its troop commitment to Afghanistan in 2011, it sought closer collaboration with local leaders to provide support for village needs, with the aim of building more trust between the allied military and Afghani civilians. In the areas where the troop surge was successful, villagelevel tribal councils have continued to thrive and provide leadership for their citizens.*

For Critical Analysis

1. Although most local governments have elected leaders, given the types of services provided by towns, cities, and villages, why shouldn't an appointed leader be just as effective?

2. Discuss whether you think individuals are more likely to know more about their local leaders or their national leaders.

*Kenneth Katzman, "Afghanistan: Politics, Elections, and Government Performance," Congressional Reference Service, February 27, 2014, www.crs.gov

township
A rural unit of government based on federal land surveys of the American frontier in the 1780s. Townships have declined significantly in importance.

Townships operate somewhat like counties, although on a lower level. Where they exist, there may be several dozen within a county. They perform some of the functions that the county would otherwise perform. Most midwestern states have townships, and they are also found in New Jersey, New York, and Pennsylvania. A township is not the same thing as a New England town, because it is meant to be a rural government rather than a city government. Moreover, it is never the principal unit of local government, as are New

England towns. The boundaries of most townships are based on federal land surveys that began in the 1780s, mapping the land into six-square-mile blocks called townships.

Although townships have few functions in many parts of the nation, they are still politically important in others. In some metropolitan areas, townships are the political unit that provides most public services to residents who live in suburban **unincorporated areas**.

Special Districts and School Districts   The most numerous local government units are special districts. Currently, there are more than 38,000 special districts (see Table 18-2). Special districts are one-function governments that usually are created by the state legislature and governed by a board of directors. For example, there are fire protection districts, water districts, sanitation districts, and health districts, some with appointed boards of directors and some with elected directors. Special districts may be called authorities, boards, corporations, or simply districts.

Special districts cut across geographic and governmental boundaries. Sometimes special districts even cut across state lines. The Port Authority of New York and New Jersey was established by an interstate compact between the two states in 1921 to develop and operate the harbor facilities in the area. A mosquito control district may cut across both municipal and county lines. A metropolitan transit district may provide bus service to dozens of municipalities and to several counties.

School districts, although listed separately in Table 18-2, are essentially a type of special district. Except for school districts, the typical citizen is not very aware of most special districts. Most citizens do not know who furnishes their weed control, mosquito abatement, water, or sewage service. Part of the reason for the low profile of special districts is that most special district administrators are appointed, not elected, and therefore receive little public attention.

Consolidation of Governments

With more than 80,000 separate and often overlapping governmental units within the United States, the trend toward consolidation in recent years is understandable. **Consolidation** is the union of two or more governmental units to form a single unit. Typically, a state constitution or a state statute will designate consolidation procedures.

unincorporated area
An area not located within the boundary of a municipality.

consolidation
The union of two or more governmental units to form a single unit.

Table 18-2 ▶ Local Governments in the United States

Counties	3,303
Municipalities (mainly cities and towns)	19,519
Townships (less extensive powers)	16,360
Special districts (water supply, fire protection, hospitals, libraries, parks and recreation, highways, sewers, and the like)	38,266
School districts	12,880
Total	90,056

Source: U.S. Census Bureau, Census of Governments, 2012, "Government Organization Summary Report, 2012."

functional consolidation
Cooperation by two or more units of local government in providing services to their inhabitants. This is generally done by unifying a set of departments (e.g., the police departments) into a single agency.

council of governments (COG)
A voluntary organization of counties and municipalities concerned with area-wide problems.

Consolidation is often recommended for metropolitan-area problems, but few consolidations have occurred within metropolitan areas. The most successful consolidations have been **functional consolidations**, particularly of city and county police, health, and welfare departments. In some situations, functional consolidation is a satisfactory alternative to the complete consolidation of governmental units. One of the most successful examples of functional consolidation was started in 1957 in Dade County, Florida. The county government, now called Miami-Dade, is a union of 26 municipalities. Each municipality has its own governmental entity, but the county government has the authority to furnish water, planning, mass transit, and police services and to set minimum standards of performance. The governing body of Miami-Dade is an elected board of county commissioners, which appoints an executive mayor.

A special type of consolidation is the **council of governments (COG)**, a voluntary organization of counties and municipalities that attempts to deal with area-wide problems. More than 200 COGs have been established, mainly since 1966. The impetus for their establishment was, and continues to be, federal government grants. The power of COGs is advisory only. Each member unit simply selects its council representatives, who report back to the unit after COG meetings. Some COGs are effective, whereas others are not.

How Municipalities Are Governed

We can divide municipal representative governments into four general types of plans: (1) the commission plan, (2) the council-manager plan, (3) the mayor-administrator plan, and (4) the mayor-council plan.

The Commission Plan The commission form of municipal government consists of three to nine members who have both legislative and executive powers. The salient aspects of the commission plan are as follows:

1. Executive and legislative powers are concentrated in a small group of individuals, who are elected at large on a (normally) nonpartisan ballot.

2. Each commissioner is individually responsible for heading a particular municipal department, such as the department of public safety.

3. The commission is collectively responsible for passing ordinances and controlling spending.

4. The mayor (a ceremonial office) is selected from the members of the commission.

The commission plan, originating in Galveston, Texas, in 1901, had its greatest popularity early in the twentieth century. It appealed to municipal government reformers. They looked on it as a type of business organization that would eliminate the problems they believed to be inherent in the long ballot and in partisan municipal politics. Unfortunately, vesting both legislative and executive power in the hands of a small group of individuals means that there are no checks and balances on administration and spending. Also, because the mayoral office is ceremonial, there is no provision for strong leadership. Not surprisingly, only about 100 cities today use the commission plan—Atlantic City, Mobile, Salt Lake City, Topeka, and Tulsa are a few of them.

The Council-Manager Plan In the council-manager form of municipal government, a city council appoints a professional manager, who acts as the chief executive. He or she typically is called the city manager. In principle, the manager is there simply to see that the general directions of the city council are carried out. The important features of the council-manager plan are as follows:

1. A professional, trained manager can hire and fire subordinates and is responsible to the council.

2. The council or commission consists of five to seven members, elected at large on a nonpartisan ballot.

3. The mayor may be chosen from within the council or from outside, but he or she has no executive function. As with the commission plan, the mayor's job may be largely ceremonial, or it may be limited to chairing council meetings. The city manager works for the council, not the mayor (unless, of course, the mayor is part of the council).

Today, more than 3,600 cities use the council-manager plan. About one-third of cities with populations of more than 5,000 and about one-half of cities with populations of more than 25,000 operate with this type of plan. Although the council-manager plan is not prevalent among cities the size of New York City or Chicago, it is commonly found in somewhat smaller cities. More than half of the cities with more than 100,000 citizens use the council-manager plan, including Dallas, San Diego, Phoenix, and Kansas City.

The major defect of the council-manager scheme, as with the commission plan, is that there is no single, strong political executive leader. It is therefore not surprising that large cities rarely use such a plan or that some cities strengthen the mayor's position while keeping a manager.

The Mayor-Administrator Plan The mayor-administrator plan is often used in large cities without a strong mayor. It is similar to the council-manager plan except that the political leadership is vested in the mayor. The mayor is an elected chief executive. She or he appoints an administrative officer, whose function is to free the mayor from routine administrative tasks, such as personnel direction and budget supervision.

The Mayor-Council Plan The mayor-council form of municipal government is the oldest and most widely used. The mayor is an elected chief executive, and the council is the legislative body. Virtually all councils are unicameral. The council typically has five to nine members, except in very large cities. For example, in Chicago, the council has 50 members.

The mayor-council plan can either be a strong mayor type or a weak mayor type. In the *strong mayor-council plan*, the mayor is the chief executive and has virtually complete control over hiring and firing employees, as well as preparing the budget. The mayor exercises strong and positive leadership in the formation of city policies. The *weak mayor-council plan* separates executive and legislative functions completely. The mayor is elected as the chief executive officer; the council is elected as the legislative body. This traditional division of powers allows for checks and balances on spending and administration.

About 50 percent of American cities use some form of the mayor-council plan. Most recently, the mayor-council plan has lost ground to the council-manager plan in small and middle-sized cities.

Politics in Practice

Who Should Run the City, "Professionals" or Politicians?

Who is the mayor of your city or town? Does she or he have executive branch powers such as the ability to make appointments, propose a city budget, and manage day-to-day business? If your mayor is well known and has this kind of authority, your town likely has a strong mayor system. In this type of system, the mayor is elected independently of the town or city council, as opposed to being chosen from the council. Large cities tend to have a strong mayor system, so-called for the executive-type powers the office controls.

Contrast this with a system where the city council is the most powerful elected municipal body. The council members might vie for the mayor's spot, which is usually ceremonial. In this council-manager system, the council will appoint a professional city manager, who will take on the daily management of the municipality.

Cities and towns must make choices about municipal government while considering how best to provide essential services (such as water, police, and waste management) with limited resources. Advocates for the city manager system say it is more economical. They argue that trained professionals are able to hire and fire staff without regard for political patronage and have the educational and vocational background to eliminate waste and inefficiency.*

Many city manager systems were created during the Progressive Era, which fostered a meritocracy over patronage. These Progressive reformers at the turn of the twentieth century valued expertise and skill and formed the modern bureaucracy we see at all levels of government: city, state, and national. A professionalized city management assumed that "scientific management" was superior to political control, which would lead to "cronyism . . . and inferior standards."**

On the other side are proponents of the strong mayor system, where the mayor is elected and has the power to run the day-to-day operations of the municipality, including budget creation, management of personnel, and responsibility for delivery of essential goods and services. Although almost half of all cities with more than 2,500 people use a council-manager system, moderate-sized to large cities with city manager systems sometimes flirt with this strong mayor system.*** Although the larger the city, the greater likelihood of adopting this system, the reasons for success or failure of strong mayor initiatives seem to be specific to the particular city. For example, Miami-Dade, Florida, passed a strong mayor initiative in 2007, moving away from the council-manager system with a weak mayor, despite the strong opposition from some labor groups and city council members.**** The popularity of the then-mayor and general public support paved the way for the change.*****

Advocates of a strong mayor system argue that a political leader, elected by the citizens, is more likely to be attuned to the needs of communities because he or she wants to be reelected. City managers, in contrast, are hired by the council and have no constituents other than the members of council. They are often from "out of town" and have no familiarity with the city's traditional neighborhoods. However, strong mayor systems with highly politicized elections may also be conducive to corruption or favoritism due to political connections. Such were the issues that brought about the Progressive movement in the early twentieth century. So, what has happened to cities that have switched from a weak mayor/council-manager system to a strong mayor form of government? Little systematic evidence of better governance or more efficiency has been gathered. What seems to be more important is the political popularity of the city's leader, regardless of whether he or she is or is not in a strong mayoral system.

For Critical Analysis

1. How do issues such as the delivery of services or road repair become political?

2. Is the trend toward adopting a strong mayor system linked to the increased power of the American president?

---

* www.council-manager.org/index.php, accessed June 5, 2008.
** www.hogriver.org/issues/v02n04/politics.htm, accessed June 5, 2008.
*** www.council-manager.org/index.php, accessed June 5, 2008.
**** "Strong Mayor Isn't a Cure-all," St. Petersburg Times (Florida), February 1, 2007, p. 16A.
***** http://metropolitan.fiu.edu/downloads/HeraldStrongMayor.pdf, accessed June 5, 2008.

Tom Williams/Getty Images

Image 18-3
Michael Ciaravino
(on the far right), the city manager
of Newburgh, New York, discusses
a potential development with
businessmen and other local
officials.

Machine versus Reform in City Politics

For much of the late nineteenth and early twentieth centuries, many major cities were run by "the machine." The machine was an integrated political organization. Each city block within the municipality had an organizer, each neighborhood had a political club, each district had a leader, and all of these parts of the machine had a boss—such as William Tweed in New York, Richard Daley in Chicago, Edward Crump in Memphis, or Tom Pendergast in Kansas City. The machine became a popular form of city political organization in the 1840s, when the first waves of European immigrants came to the United States to work in urban factories. Those individuals, often lacking the ability to communicate in English, needed help—and the machine was created to help them.[18] The urban machine drew on the support of the dominant ethnic groups to forge a strong political institution that was able to keep the boss (usually the mayor) in office year after year. The machine was oiled by patronage—rewarding faithful party workers and followers with government employment and contracts. The party in power was often referred to as the patronage party.[19]

According to sociologist Robert Merton, the machine offered personalized assistance to the needy, helped establish local businesses, opened avenues of upward social mobility for the underprivileged, and afforded a locus of strong political authority and responsibility.[20] Others, however, viewed party machines and the behind-the-scenes government that they often involved as contrary to our principles of government. In their classic work on city politics, Edward Banfield and James Q. Wilson gave a critical appraisal of machine politics:

> [M]achine government is, essentially, a system of organized bribery. The
> destruction of machines . . . permit[s] government on the basis of

---

18 See Harvey W. Zorbaugh, *The Gold Coast and the Slum: A Sociological Study of Chicago's Near North Side* (Chicago, IL: University of Chicago Press, 1929).
19 See, for example, Harold F. Gosnell, *Machine Politics: Chicago Model* (Chicago, IL: University of Chicago Press, 1937).
20 Robert Merton, *Social Theory and Social Structure* (Glencoe, IL: Free Press, 1957), pp. 71–81.

THE "BRAINS"

THAT ACHIEVED THE TAMMANY VICTORY AT THE ROCHESTER DEMOCRATIC CONVENTION.

Library of Congress, Prints & Photographs Division, Reproduction number LC-USZ6-787

Image 18-4
A Thomas Nast cartoon shows Boss Tweed represented as having a money-bag face. The caption reads, "The 'Brains' that achieved the Tammany Victory at the Rochester Democratic Convention." Another identifying feature is a famous $15,500 diamond stickpin. Why are there no true big-city "machine" bosses anymore in the United States?

appropriate motives, that is, public-regarding ones. In fact it has other highly desirable consequences—especially greater honesty, impartiality, and (in routine matters) efficiency.[21]

When the last of the big-city bosses, Mayor Richard Daley of Chicago, died in December 1976, an era died with him. To some extent, machine politics became obsolete when the federal government began to distribute benefits to individuals. Although some argue that the political machine could truly benefit poor citizens, the associated costs of bribery and corruption are too high for most middle-class voters.

Paying for State and Local Government

■ **18.4** Describe the most important sources of revenue for states and local governments and their biggest expenditures, and contrast them with those of the federal government.

Examining the spending habits of a household often gives relevant information about the personalities and priorities of the household members. Examining the expenditure patterns of state and local governments can be similarly illuminating.

State and Local Government Expenditures

Table 18-3 shows state expenditures, by function, in percentages. Table 18-4 shows these data for local governments. Education and highways are major expenses at both the state and local levels. (Most state spending on education is for colleges and universities; most local spending is for elementary and secondary schools.) Because of the growth of Medicaid—the health-care program for the poor—welfare is now the leading expense at the state level. Local governments, in contrast, spend heavily on utilities such as water, electricity, gas, sewers, and garbage collection.

Compare state and local spending on education with spending by the federal government, which allocates only about 4 percent of its budget to education. Despite high expenditures, state and local governments are finding that their educational programs are not always producing well-educated students. The failings of state and local educational systems led Congress to pass President Bush's No Child Left Behind legislation in 2001. Although the law has been much criticized, the Obama administration did not seek to repeal it. Instead, a new program was created, The Race to the Top, which provides grants to states for innovative programs to improve student achievement.

State and Local Government Revenues

State and local expenditures have to be paid for somehow. Until the twentieth century, almost all state and local expenditures were paid for by state and local revenues raised within state borders. Starting in the twentieth century,

21 Edward C. Banfield and James Q. Wilson, *City Politics* (New York: Vintage Books, 1963), p. 12.

Table 18-3 ▶ State Expenditures
(in percentages)

EXPENDITURE	PERCENTAGE
Welfare, including Medicaid	25
Education	30
Employee retirement	10
Highways	6
Governmental administration	3
Health care (includes hospitals)	7
Protection (includes police, fire, prisons)	3
Interest on general debt	2
Other	15

Source: U.S. Census Bureau, 2014, "2012 Survey of State Government Finances."

Table 18-4 ▶ Local Expenditures
(in percentages)

EXPENDITURE	PERCENTAGE
Education	37
Welfare	3
Protection (includes fire and police)	10
Transportation	5
Governmental administration	4
Health care (includes hospitals)	8
Pensions	2
Interest on general debt	4
Other	27

Source: Census of Government 2012.

however, federal grants to state and local governmental units began to pay some of these costs.

Figure 18-3 shows the percentages of revenues in various categories received by state and local governments. The most important tax at the state level is the **general sales tax**. Whereas the federal government obtains about 45 percent of its total revenues from the personal income tax, states obtain only about 16 percent in this way. In 2018 seven states still did not have a personal income tax. Other taxes assessed by states include corporate income

general sales tax
A tax levied as a proportion of the retail price of a commodity at the point of sale.

Figure 18-3 ▶ State and Local Government Revenues 2014

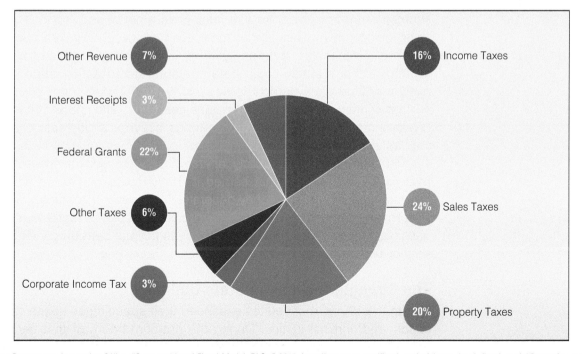

Other Revenue 7%
Interest Receipts 3%
Federal Grants 22%
Other Taxes 6%
Corporate Income Tax 3%
16% Income Taxes
24% Sales Taxes
20% Property Taxes

Source: Government Accounting Office, "State and Local Fiscal Model, FAQs," 2015. http://www.gao.gov/fiscal_outlook/state_local_fiscal_model/interacive_graphic/about_state_local_fiscal_conditions

property tax
A tax on the value of real estate. This tax is a particularly important source of revenue for local governments.

taxes and fees, fees for permits and licenses at both the state and local governmental levels, and inheritance and gift taxes at the state level. At the local level, the most important tax is the **property tax**. More than 95 percent of property tax revenues are raised by local governments.

Because states vary in the types and amounts of taxes collected, there is considerable competition among them to attract businesses or certain populations. States compete to offer a better climate for business by giving incentives such as a 20-year reduction in property taxes to a new employer or creating bonds to help a new business build a facility in the state. Why do states do this? They intend to recoup their investment or lost tax revenue through taxes on the employees' income and on the company in the future. States also compete for new residents. It should be no surprise that many individuals choose Florida as their permanent residence during their retirement years: compare paying no income taxes to paying more than 11 percent of your income in taxes in Hawaii or New York City. Changing residency does not usually mean people must give up their home in their former state of residence; simply being absent from that state for a specified number of days will qualify them as nonresidents, but they may still maintain a home there. States also compete to have the lowest sales tax, gasoline tax, and estate tax. The overall state and local tax burden for an individual can vary from more than 13 percent of income in New York, Washington, DC, and New Jersey to 8 percent in Wyoming.

Nontax revenue includes federal grants to state and local governments. Today, federal grants to state and local governments provide about 22 percent of state government income. The grants are not always without "strings," however. Federal programs in such areas as education, highway construction, health care, and law enforcement may dispense cash subject to certain conditions (see Chapter 3).

Revenues from publicly operated services and businesses are additional sources of income for state and local governments. Publicly operated services include universities and hospitals, as well as municipal utilities such as water, electric power, and bus systems. More than one-third of the states sell liquor at a profit through state-operated stores. Other state-run businesses include Washington's ferries and North Dakota's commercial banks. Further nontax revenue sources include court fines and interest on loans and investments. In the 1980s, state lotteries became an increasingly popular way to raise revenues.

Most revenue from publicly operated services and businesses is earmarked for the services that earned it. Tuition goes only to colleges; state hospitals keep the revenue they generate. A special and rather sizable source of earmarked revenue is the income from state employee retirement plans. In principle, these sums should be used only to pay the pensions of retired state employees.

The Struggle to Balance State Budgets

During the 1990s, most states expanded their spending on health care, education, and criminal justice. During the dot-com boom of that decade, tax revenues were more than sufficient to fund the increases in most states. Some states even cut their tax rates. The dot-com bust of 2001, however, hit state governments hard. In 2002, as a result of the dot-com collapse and the post–September 11 recession, state tax revenue dropped by more than 10 percent by 2003.

State economies recovered from 2004 through mid-2008. But then, the economic crisis of 2008 and the recession that followed sent state tax collections into freefall. By 2010, a number of the larger and wealthier states—Texas, California, New York—found themselves facing huge budget deficits. As the economy slowly began to recover, even more states faced huge budget shortfalls. Remember, except for Vermont, states cannot actually run a budget deficit. By 2012, states' revenues remained more than 5 percent lower than pre-recession levels, whereas their obligations to educate millions of K–12 students and support public universities grew at normal rates. State shortfalls were projected to exceed $540 billion by 2013. What caused these budget deficits? First and foremost, a decline in state revenues of 8.9 percent occurred in 2009 due to the loss of income taxes from workers and businesses. Only five states saw slight increases in their revenues. The situation improved for many states by 2016. Some states raised taxes to increase revenue, whereas others used tax incentives to bring in new industries and create jobs.

Getting into Trouble: Borrowing Too Much Although every state constitution except that of Vermont requires the state to balance its budget, states have shown great ingenuity in evading this requirement. Even if states cannot automatically borrow to meet a budget deficit, their legislatures can still find ways to borrow. Such practices only postpone the problem, though; eventually, the debt must be repaid.

New York is an example of a state that has engaged in what many consider excessive borrowing despite constitutional restrictions. New York's constitution ostensibly requires that voters approve state borrowing. Nevertheless, by 2018, New York's debt had reached $60 billion, or about $3,116 for every inhabitant of the state.

Getting into Trouble: Poor Productivity An additional problem for the states is that the tasks they perform are somewhat resistant to productivity improvements. Over the years, America's farms and factories have posted dramatic improvements in the volume of goods produced by the labor of each individual farmer or worker—these industries have improved their productivity. It is more difficult to attain such improvements in service industries. Some services, notably education and law enforcement, require face-to-face interaction with the public. It is difficult to cut the amount of such interaction without reducing the quality of the service.

Getting into Trouble: Health-Care Costs Increased health-care costs were a major part of the states' budget problems in the early 2000s, and they continue to be a major threat to the solvency of state governments. One problem is the rising cost of health insurance premiums for state and local government employees. Nationwide, the cost of health insurance premiums doubled between 2000 and 2012, and such costs for state employees grew as well. A much greater problem is Medicaid, which provides health-care services to the poor. State Medicaid spending almost doubled between 2000 and 2012. The economic recession sent even more individuals to the Medicaid program, and burdens on the states increased correspondingly. Beginning in 2014, some states started to see large increases in their Medicaid populations due to the provisions of the Affordable Care Act, but states that have accepted the federal program will receive 100 percent of the increased cost from the federal government. States that did not opt into the federal program will see their costs from Medicaid rise in a normal fashion.

States Recover from the Recession

The 2008–2009 recession provided an opportunity for state governments to try different solutions to their recession-caused budget problems. Some states cut their budgets and took a number of austerity measures, whereas other states increased taxes—especially on wealthier citizens—to raise revenue. One analysis found that states with Democratic legislatures and strong unions were more likely to raise taxes than were states with Republican legislatures. Similarly, cuts in personnel were less likely in states with Democratic legislatures.[22] By 2014, many state economies had recovered from the recession, and some had strong economic expansion due to the boom in the petroleum industry. In fact, states that had budget surpluses now faced the problem of what services to restore.[23]

States as Policy Pioneers State budgets are also influenced by the mix of public policies adopted by the state to serve the citizens. Over the past two centuries, states have often pioneered innovative policies that were later adopted by the federal government.

States are also in the forefront of environmental policies, in part because of their unique geographic and demographic situations. California, with its immense population growth and propensity to develop smog in the coastal areas, has been much stricter about emission controls for automobiles than the federal government for more than 30 years. Recently, the California Air Resources Board released a draft plan for reducing greenhouse gas emissions to 1990 levels by creating a carbon credit trading system, using landfills to produce methane, reducing urban sprawl, and changing the law for automobile emissions. The comprehensive plan would affect virtually every industry in California. Although the draft plan needs much more analysis and would need implementation from the legislature, it illustrates the degree to which states can create innovative new policies and experiment with new ways to address public issues.

---

22 Andrea Louise Campbell and Michael W. Sances. "State Fiscal Policy during the Great Recession Budgetary Impacts and Policy Responses," *The ANNALs of The American Academy of Political and Social Science* (2013) 650 (1): 252–273.23.
23 Rick Lyman, "Battle Looms in Many States Over What To Do With Budget Surpluses," *The New York Times*, February 2, 2014.

Key Terms

Chapter Summary

■ **18.1** Under the U.S. Constitution, powers not delegated expressly to the federal government are reserved to the states. The states may exercise taxing, spending, and general police powers. State constitutions are often very long. One reason for their length is that a loss of popular confidence in state legislatures in the late 1800s caused the framers of the constitutions to include many provisions that would normally be considered statutory law. Another reason is state courts' reluctance to interpret state constitutions as freely as the U.S. Supreme Court interprets the U.S. Constitution.

■ **18.2** In colonial America, the governors of the colonies were vested with extensive powers. Following the Revolutionary War, most states established forms of government in which the governor received very limited powers. After Andrew Jackson's presidency, however, all governors (except in South Carolina) were elected directly by the people. Most governors have the right to exercise some sort of veto power; many enjoy item veto power.

■ **18.2** State legislatures deal with matters such as taxes, schools, highways, and welfare. They must also redraw state and federal legislative districts each decade to ensure that every person's vote is roughly equal to that of others and that minorities are adequately represented in both the state legislature and Congress. Voters may exercise some direct control over state government through the use of the initiative, referendum, and recall. Every state has its own court system. Most such systems have several levels of courts, including trial courts, intermediate courts of appeals, and a supreme court.

■ **18.3** The United States has more than 89,000 separate governmental units. State and local governments perform a wide variety of highly visible functions and services, such as education, health care, police and fire protection, parks and recreation, highway safety and maintenance, insurance, and professional licensing. There are more than 19,000 municipalities, most of which are small cities. The more than 3,000 counties in this country are merely extensions of state authority and apply state laws at the local level. In New England, many of the functions of municipalities and counties are combined in towns. Municipalities may be governed by a commission consisting of members with executive and legislative powers, or they may be administered according to a council-manager, mayor-administrator, or mayor-council plan. Most major cities used to be run by political machines, which freely dispensed favors to supporters. In recent decades, however, political machines have become almost completely extinct.

■ **18.4** State spending is funded by sales, property, corporate, and personal income taxes and is concentrated on welfare (including Medicaid), higher education, and highways. Local spending, which is mainly funded by property taxes, goes largely to the public schools and to utility services such as water, electricity, gas, sewers, and garbage collection. States compete for businesses and residents by lowering tax rates or giving rebates. States show considerable variation in their policies and programs. They may have different models of funding their operations, and they may have very different laws and policies. States have long been seen as models of experimentation. If a program works at the state level, it may be copied by other states or enacted into federal law.

Selected Resources

PRINT RESOURCES

Beland, Daniel, Philip Rocco, and Alex Wadda. *Obamacare Wars: Federalism, State Politics, and the Affordable Care Act* (Lawrence, KS: University of Kansas Press, 2016). The authors carefully analyze the relationship between the federal government and the states in the rollout of the Affordable Care Act and document the tensions that have arisen between states and the federal government over this legislation.

Carroll, Susan and Kira Sanbonmatsu. *More Women Can Run: Gender and Pathways to State Legislatures* (New York: Oxford University Press, 2013). More women will be elected to Congress and the presidency if they have a way to begin in politics. The authors offer a strategy for more women to be elected to the state legislature, a first step to higher office.

Ehrenhalt, Alan. *The Great Inversion and the Future of the American City* (New York: Vintage, 2013). A well-known sociologist describes the new urbanism, meaning the movement of young professionals and highly educated people back to the urban core while the economically less well-off citizens are moving to the suburbs. Although this creates new vibrancy for cities, it makes living more expensive for the poor.

Feldman, Daniel and Gerald Benjamin. *Tales from the Sausage Factory: Making Laws in New York State* (New York: Excelsior Editions, 2010). Taking their title from the old adage that like sausage making, you do not want to watch lawmaking, the authors reveal the backroom deals and other political maneuvers in the New York state legislature.

Katz, Bruce. *The Metropolitan Revolution: How Cities and Metros Are Fixing Our Broken Politics and Fragile Economy* (Washington, DC: Brookings, 2013). In this volume, the author points to urban areas and metropolitan regions as the key to solving public problems. Mayors, city councils, and state leaders are creating solutions to unemployment and the lack of job skills.

MEDIA RESOURCES

Bankrupt: How Cronyism and Corruption Brought Down Detroit—Released in 2014, this film analyzes the forces that brought the city of Detroit to bankruptcy in 2013, from the decline of the automotive industry to corruption in city hall.

Boardwalk Empire—An HBO series, the episodes follow the career of Nucky Thompson, the treasurer of Atlantic City, New Jersey, who is as much a criminal as a political leader.

City Hall—A 1996 drama about corruption at city hall in New York and a mayor (Al Pacino) who is willing to break the law to fulfill his presidential aspirations.

The Last Hurrah—A film based, in part, on the career of James Curley (1874–1958) of Massachusetts, who played a leading role in creating and running Boston's political machine in the first half of the twentieth century. When Curley was convicted of mail fraud and sent to prison in 1947, he refused to resign as mayor and maintained his office while in jail.

The United States of ALEC—In this PBS documentary, Bill Moyers examines the role of ALEC, the American Legislative Exchange Council, as it influences the laws adopted by many legislatures. These laws have a strong conservative direction.

ONLINE RESOURCES

The Council of State Governments—region-based forum that fosters the exchange of insights and ideas to help state officials shape public policy; an excellent source for information on state governments: www.csg.org

FindLaw—searchable database of state law codes (statutes) and state court cases: www.findlaw.com/casecode/state.html

National Conference of State Legislatures—bipartisan organization that serves the legislators and staffs of the nation's states, its commonwealths, and territories; provides research, technical assistance, and opportunities for policymakers to exchange ideas on the most pressing state issues: www.ncsl.org

National Governors Association—bipartisan organization of the nation's governors; offers a wide variety of information on issues and data relating to state governments: www.nga.org

Tax Foundation—nonpartisan organization that educates taxpayers about sound tax policy and the size of the tax burden borne by Americans at all levels of government; extensive data on comparative tax collections and revenue expenditures by states and by the federal government: www.taxfoundation.org

Appendix A

The Declaration of Independence

IN CONGRESS, JULY 4, 1776

A Declaration by the Representatives of the United States of America, in General Congress assembled. When in the Course of human Events, it becomes necessary for one People to dissolve the Political Bands which have connected them with another, and to assume among the Powers of the Earth, the separate and equal Station to which the Laws of Nature and of Nature's God entitle them, a decent Respect to the Opinions of Mankind requires that they should declare the causes which impel them to the Separation.

We hold these Truths to be self-evident, that all Men are created equal, that they are endowed by their Creator with certain unalienable Rights, that among these are Life, Liberty, and the Pursuit of Happiness—That to secure these Rights, Governments are instituted among Men, deriving their just Powers from the Consent of the Governed, that whenever any Form of Government becomes destructive of these Ends, it is the Right of the People to alter or to abolish it, and to institute new Government, laying its Foundation on such Principles, and organizing its Powers in such Forms, as to them shall seem most likely to effect their Safety and Happiness. Prudence, indeed, will dictate that Governments long established should not be changed for light and transient Causes; and accordingly all Experience hath shewn, that Mankind are more disposed to suffer, while Evils are sufferable, than to right themselves by abolishing the Forms to which they are accustomed. But when a long Train of Abuses and Usurpations, pursuing invariably the same Object, evinces a Design to reduce them under absolute Despotism, it is their Right, it is their Duty, to throw off such Government, and to provide new Guards for their future Security. Such has been the patient Sufferance of these Colonies; and such is now the Necessity which constrains them to alter their former Systems of Government. The History of the present King of Great-Britain is a History of repeated Injuries and Usurpations, all having in direct Object the Establishment of an absolute Tyranny over these States. To prove this, let Facts be submitted to a candid World.

He has refused his Assent to Laws, the most wholesome and necessary for the public Good.

He has forbidden his Governors to pass Laws of immediate and pressing Importance, unless suspended in their Operation till his Assent should be obtained; and when so suspended, he has utterly neglected to attend to them.

He has refused to pass other Laws for the Accommodation of large Districts of People, unless those People would relinquish the Right of Representation in the Legislature, a Right inestimable to them, and formidable to Tyrants only.

He has called together Legislative Bodies at Places unusual, uncomfortable, and distant from the Depository of their Public Records, for the sole Purpose of fatiguing them into Compliance with his Measures.

He has dissolved Representative Houses repeatedly, for opposing with manly Firmness his Invasions on the Rights of the People.

He has refused for a long Time, after such Dissolutions, to cause others to be elected; whereby the Legislative Powers, incapable of Annihilation, have returned to the People at large for their exercise; the State remaining in the mean time exposed to all the Dangers of Invasion from without, and Convulsions within.

He has endeavoured to prevent the Population of these States; for that Purpose obstructing the Laws for Naturalization of Foreigners; refusing to pass others to encourage their Migrations hither, and raising the Conditions of new Appropriations of Lands.

He has obstructed the Administration of Justice, by refusing his Assent to Laws for establishing Judiciary Powers.

He has made Judges dependent on his Will alone, for the Tenure of their offices, and the Amount and payment of their Salaries.

He has erected a Multitude of new Offices, and sent hither Swarms of Officers to harass our People, and eat out their Substance.

He has kept among us, in Times of Peace, Standing Armies, without the consent of our Legislatures.

He has affected to render the Military independent of, and superior to the Civil Power.

He has combined with others to subject us to a Jurisdiction foreign to our Constitution, and unacknowledged by our Laws; giving his Assent to their Acts of pretended Legislation:

For quartering large Bodies of Armed Troops among us:

For protecting them, by a mock Trial, from Punishment for any Murders which they should commit on the Inhabitants of these States:

For cutting off our Trade with all Parts of the World:

For imposing Taxes on us without our Consent:

For depriving us, in many cases, of the Benefits of Trial by Jury:

For transporting us beyond Seas to be tried for pretended Offences:

For abolishing the free System of English Laws in a neighbouring Province, establishing therein an arbitrary Government, and enlarging its Boundaries, so as to render it at once an Example and fit Instrument for introducing the same absolute Rule into these Colonies:

For taking away our Charters, abolishing our most valuable Laws, and altering fundamentally the Forms of our Governments:

For suspending our own Legislatures, and declaring themselves invested with Power to legislate for us in all Cases whatsoever.

He has abdicated Government here, by declaring us out of his Protection and waging War against us.

He has plundered our Seas, ravaged our Coasts, burnt our towns, and destroyed the Lives of our People.

He is, at this Time, transporting large Armies of foreign Mercenaries to compleat the works of Death, Desolation, and Tyranny, already begun with circumstances of Cruelty and Perfidy, scarcely paralleled in the most barbarous Ages, and totally unworthy the Head of a civilized Nation.

He has constrained our fellow Citizens taken Captive on the high Seas to bear Arms against their Country, to become the Executioners of their Friends and Brethren, or to fall themselves by their Hands.

He has excited domestic Insurrections amongst us, and has endeavoured to bring on the Inhabitants of our Frontiers, the merciless Indian Savages, whose known Rule of Warfare, is an undistinguished Destruction, of all Ages, Sexes and Conditions.

In every state of these Oppressions we have Petitioned for Redress in the most humble Terms: Our repeated Petitions have been answered only by repeated Injury. A Prince, whose Character is thus marked by every act which may define a Tyrant, is unfit to be the Ruler of a free People.

Nor have we been wanting in Attentions to our British Brethren. We have warned them from Time to Time of Attempts by their Legislature to extend an unwarrantable Jurisdiction over us. We have reminded them of the Circumstances of our Emigration and Settlement here. We have appealed to their native Justice and Magnanimity, and we have conjured them by the Ties of our common Kindred to disavow these Usurpations, which, would inevitably interrupt our Connections and Correspondence. They too have been deaf to the Voice of Justice and of Consanguinity. We must, therefore, acquiesce in the Necessity, which denounces our Separation, and hold them, as we hold the rest of Mankind, Enemies in War, in Peace, Friends.

We, therefore, the Representatives of the UNITED STATES OF AMERICA, in General Congress Assembled, appealing to the Supreme Judge of the World for the Rectitude of our Intentions, do, in the Name, and by the Authority of the good People of these Colonies, solemnly Publish and Declare, That these United Colonies are, and of Right ought to be, Free and Independent States; that they are absolved from all Allegiance to the British Crown, and that all political Connection between them and the State of Great-Britain, is and ought to be totally dissolved; and that as Free and Independent States, they have full Power to levy War, conclude Peace, contract Alliances, establish Commerce, and to do all other Acts and Things which Independent States may of right do. And for the support of this declaration, with a firm Reliance on the Protection of divine Providence, we mutually pledge to each other our lives, our Fortunes, and our sacred Honor.

Appendix B

The Constitution of the United States*

THE PREAMBLE

We the People of the United States, in Order to form a more perfect Union, establish Justice, insure domestic Tranquility, provide for the common defence, promote the general Welfare, and secure the Blessings of Liberty to ourselves and our Posterity, do ordain and establish this *Constitution* for the United States of America.

The Preamble declares that "We the People" are the authority for the Constitution (unlike the Articles of Confederation, which derived their authority from the states). The Preamble also sets out the purposes of the Constitution.

ARTICLE I. (*Legislative Branch*)

The first part of the Constitution, Article I, deals with the organization and powers of the lawmaking branch of the national government, the Congress.

Section 1. *Legislative Powers*

All legislative Powers herein granted shall be vested in a Congress of the United States, which shall consist of a Senate and House of Representatives.

Section 2. *House of Representatives*

Clause 1: Composition and Election of Members. The House of Representatives shall be composed of Members chosen every second Year by the People of the several States, and the Electors in each State shall have the Qualifications requisite for Electors of the most numerous Branch of the State Legislature.

Each state has the power to decide who may vote for members of Congress. Within each state, those who may vote for state legislators may also vote for members of the House of Representatives (and, under the Seventeenth Amendment, for U.S. senators). When the Constitution was written, nearly all states limited voting rights to white male property owners or taxpayers at least 21 years old. Subsequent amendments granted voting power to African American men, all women, and everyone at least 18 years old.

Clause 2: Qualifications. No Person shall be a Representative who shall not have attained to the Age of twenty five Years, and been seven Years a Citizen of the United States, and who shall not, when elected, be an Inhabitant of that State in which he shall be chosen.

Each member of the House must be at least 25 years old, a citizen of the United States for at least seven years, and a resident of the state in which she or he is elected.

Clause 3: Apportionment of Representatives and Direct Taxes. Representatives [and direct Taxes][1] shall be apportioned among the several States which may be included within this Union, according to their respective Numbers [which shall be determined by adding to the whole Number of free Persons, including those bound to Service for a Term of Years, and excluding Indians not taxed, three fifths of all other Persons].[2] The actual Enumeration shall be made within three Years after the first Meeting of the Congress of the United States, and within every subsequent Term of ten Years, in such Manner as they shall by Law direct. The Number of Representatives shall not exceed one for every thirty Thousand, but each State shall have at Least one Representative; and until such enumeration shall be made, the State of New Hampshire shall be entitled to chuse three, Massachusetts eight, Rhode Island and Providence Plantations one, Connecticut five, New York six, New Jersey four, Pennsylvania eight, Delaware one, Maryland six, Virginia ten, North Carolina five, South Carolina five, and Georgia three.

A state's representation in the House is based on the size of its population. Population is counted in each decade's census, after which Congress reapportions House seats. Since early in the 20th century, the number of seats has been limited to 435.

Clause 4: Vacancies. When vacancies happen in the Representation from any State, the Executive Authority thereof shall issue Writs of Election to fill such Vacancies.

The "Executive Authority" is the state's governor. When a vacancy occurs in the House, the governor calls a special election to fill it.

Clause 5: Officers and Impeachment. The House of Representatives shall chuse their Speaker and other Officers; and shall have the sole Power of Impeachment.

The power to impeach is the power to accuse. In this case, it is the power to accuse members of the executive or judicial branch of wrongdoing or abuse of power. Once a bill of impeachment is issued, the Senate holds the trial.

Section 3. *The Senate*

Clause 1: Term and Number of Members. The Senate of the United States shall be composed of two Senators from each State [chosen by the Legislature thereof],[3] for six Years; and each Senator shall have one Vote.

Every state has two senators, each of whom serves for six years and has one vote in the upper chamber. Since the Seventeenth

---

* The spelling, capitalization, and punctuation of the original have been retained here. Brackets indicate passages that have been altered by amendments to the Constitution. We have added article titles (in parentheses), section titles, and clause designations. We have also inserted annotations in blue italic type.
1 Modified by the Sixteenth Amendment.
2 Modified by the Fourteenth Amendment.
3 Repealed by the Seventeenth Amendment.

Amendment in 1913, all senators have been elected directly by voters of the state during the regular election.

Clause 2: Classification of Senators. Immediately after they shall be assembled in Consequence of the first Election, they shall be divided as equally as may be into three Classes. The Seats of the Senators of the first Class shall be vacated at the Expiration of the second Year, of the second Class at the Expiration of the fourth Year, and of the third Class at the Expiration of the sixth Year, so that one third may be chosen every second Year; [and if Vacancies happen by Resignation, or otherwise, during the Recess of the Legislature of any State, the Executive thereof may make temporary Appointments until the next Meeting of the Legislature, which shall then fill such Vacancies].[4]

One-third of the Senate's seats are open to election every two years (in contrast, all members of the House are elected simultaneously).

Clause 3: Qualifications. No Person shall be a Senator who shall not have attained to the Age of thirty Years, and been nine Years a Citizen of the United States, and who shall not, when elected, be an Inhabitant of that State for which he shall be chosen.

Every senator must be at least 30 years old, a citizen of the United States for a minimum of nine years, and a resident of the state in which he or she is elected.

Clause 4: The Role of the Vice President. The Vice President of the United States shall be President of the Senate, but shall have no Vote, unless they be equally divided.

The vice president presides over meetings of the Senate but cannot vote unless there is a tie. The Constitution gives no other official duties to the vice president.

Clause 5: Other Officers. The Senate shall chuse their other Officers, and also a President pro tempore, in the Absence of the Vice President, or when he shall exercise the Office of President of the United States.

The Senate votes for one of its members to preside when the vice president is absent. This person is usually called the president pro tempore because of the temporary nature of the position.

Clause 6: Impeachment Trials. The Senate shall have the sole Power to try all Impeachments. When sitting for that Purpose, they shall be on Oath or Affirmation. When the President of the United States is tried, the Chief Justice shall preside: And no Person shall be convicted without the Concurrence of two thirds of the Members present.

The Senate conducts trials of officials that the House impeaches. The Senate sits as a jury, with the vice president presiding if the president is not on trial.

Clause 7: Penalties for Conviction. Judgment in Cases of Impeachment shall not extend further than to removal from Office, and disqualification to hold and enjoy any Office of honor, Trust, or Profit under the United States: but the Party convicted shall nevertheless be liable and subject to Indictment, Trial, Judgment, and Punishment, according to Law.

On conviction of impeachment charges, the Senate can only force an official to leave office and prevent him or her from holding another office in the federal government. The individual, however, can still be tried in a regular court.

Section 4. *Congressional Elections: Times, Manner, and Places*

Clause 1: Elections. The Times, Places and Manner of holding Elections for Senators and Representatives, shall be prescribed in each State by the Legislature thereof; but the Congress may at any time by Law make or alter such Regulations, except as to the Places of chusing Senators.

Congress set the Tuesday after the first Monday in November in even-numbered years as the date for congressional elections. In states with more than one seat in the House, Congress requires that representatives be elected from districts within each state. Under the Seventeenth Amendment, senators are elected at the same places as other officials.

Clause 2: Sessions of Congress. [The Congress shall assemble at least once in every Year, and such Meeting shall be on the first Monday in December, unless they shall by Law appoint a different Day.][5]

Congress has to meet every year at least once. The regular session now begins at noon on January 3 of each year, subsequent to the Twentieth Amendment, unless Congress passes a law to fix a different date. Congress stays in session until its members vote to adjourn. Additionally, the president may call a special session.

Section 5. *Powers and Duties of the Houses*

Clause 1: Admitting Members and Quorum. Each House shall be the Judge of the Elections, Returns, and Qualifications of its own Members, and a Majority of each shall constitute a Quorum to do Business; but a smaller Number may adjourn from day to day, and may be authorized to compel the Attendance of absent Members, in such Manner, and under such Penalties as each House may provide.

Each chamber may exclude or refuse to seat a member-elect.

The quorum rule requires that 218 members of the House and 51 members of the Senate be present to conduct business. This rule normally is not enforced in the handling of routine matters.

Clause 2: Rules and Discipline of Members. Each House may determine the Rules of its Proceedings, punish its Members for disorderly Behaviour, and, with the Concurrence of two thirds, expel a Member.

The House and the Senate may adopt their own rules to guide their proceedings. Each may also discipline its members for conduct that is deemed unacceptable. No member may be expelled without a two-thirds majority vote in favor of expulsion.

Clause 3: Keeping a Record. Each House shall keep a Journal of its Proceedings, and from time to time publish the same, excepting such Parts as may in their Judgment require Secrecy; and the Yeas and Nays of the Members of either

---

4   Modified by the Seventeenth Amendment.
5   Changed by the Twentieth Amendment.

House on any question shall, at the Desire of one fifth of those Present, be entered on the Journal.

The journals of the two chambers are published at the end of each session of Congress.

Clause 4: Adjournment. Neither House, during the Session of Congress, shall, without the Consent of the other, adjourn for more than three days, nor to any other Place than that in which the two Houses shall be sitting.

Congress has the power to determine when and where to meet, provided, however, that both chambers meet in the same city. Neither chamber may recess for more than three days without the consent of the other.

Section 6. *Rights of Members*

Clause 1: Compensation and Privileges. The Senators and Representatives shall receive a Compensation for their services, to be ascertained by Law, and paid out of the Treasury of the United States. They shall in all Cases, except Treason, Felony and Breach of the Peace, be privileged from Arrest during their Attendance at the Session of their respective Houses, and in going to and returning from the same; and for any Speech or Debate in either House, they shall not be questioned in any other Place.

Congressional salaries are to be paid by the U.S. Treasury rather than by the members' respective states. The original salaries were $6 per day; in 1857 they were $3,000 per year. Both representatives and senators were paid $165,200 in 2006.

Treason is defined in Article III, Section 3. A felony is any serious crime. A breach of the peace is any indictable offense less than treason or a felony. Members cannot be arrested for things they say during speeches and debates in Congress. This immunity applies to the Capitol Building itself and not to their private lives.

Clause 2: Restrictions. No Senator or Representative shall, during the Time for which he was elected, be appointed to any civil Office under the Authority of the United States, which shall have been created, or the Emoluments whereof shall have been encreased during such time; and no Person holding any Office under the United States, shall be a Member of either House during his Continuance in Office.

During the term for which a member was elected, he or she cannot concurrently accept another federal government position.

Section 7. *Legislative Powers: Bills and Resolutions*

Clause 1: Revenue Bills. All Bills for raising Revenue shall originate in the House of Representatives; but the Senate may propose or concur with Amendments as on other Bills.

All tax and appropriation bills for raising money have to originate in the House of Representatives. The Senate, though, often amends such bills and may even substitute an entirely different bill.

Clause 2: The Presidential Veto. Every Bill which shall have passed the House of Representatives and the Senate, shall, before it becomes a Law, be presented to the President of the United States; If he approve he shall sign it, but if not he shall return it, with his Objections to the House in which it shall have originated, who shall enter the Objections at large on their

Journal, and proceed to reconsider it. If after such Reconsideration two thirds of that House shall agree to pass the Bill, it shall be sent together with the Objections, to the other House, by which it shall likewise be reconsidered, and if approved by two thirds of that House, it shall become a Law. But in all such Cases the Votes of both Houses shall be determined by Yeas and Nays, and the Names of the Persons voting for and against the Bill shall be entered on the Journal of each House respectively. If any Bill shall not be returned by the President within 10 Days (Sundays excepted) after it shall have been presented to him, the Same shall be a Law, in like Manner as if he had signed it, unless the Congress by their Adjournment prevent its Return in which Case it shall not be a Law.

When Congress sends the president a bill, he or she can sign it (in which case it becomes law) or send it back to the chamber in which it originated. If it is sent back, a two-thirds majority of each chamber must pass it again for it to become law. If the president neither signs it nor sends it back within 10 days, it becomes law anyway, unless Congress adjourns in the meantime.

Clause 3: Actions on Other Matters. Every Order, Resolution, or Vote to which the Concurrence of the Senate and House of Representatives may be necessary (except on a question of Adjournment) shall be presented to the President of the United States; and before the Same shall take Effect, shall be approved by him, or being disapproved by him, shall be repassed by two thirds of the Senate and House of Representatives, according to the Rules and Limitations prescribed in the Case of a Bill.

The president must have the opportunity to either sign or veto everything that Congress passes, except votes to adjourn and resolutions not having the force of law.

Section 8. *The Powers of Congress*

Clause 1: Taxing. The Congress shall have Power to lay and collect Taxes, Duties, Imposts and Excises, to pay the Debts and provide for the common Defence and general Welfare of the United States; but all Duties, Imposts and Excises shall be uniform throughout the United States;

Duties are taxes on imports and exports. Impost is a generic term for tax. Excises are taxes on the manufacture, sale, or use of goods.

Clause 2: Borrowing. To borrow Money on the credit of the United States;

Congress has the power to borrow money, which is normally carried out through the sale of U.S. treasury bonds on which interest is paid. Note that the Constitution places no limit on the amount of government borrowing.

Clause 3: Regulation of Commerce. To regulate Commerce with foreign Nations, and among the several States, and with the Indian Tribes;

This is the commerce clause, which gives to Congress the power to regulate interstate and foreign trade. Much of the activity of Congress is based on this clause.

Clause 4: Naturalization and Bankruptcy. To establish an uniform Rule of Naturalization, and uniform Laws on the subject of Bankruptcies throughout the United States;

Only Congress may determine how aliens can become citizens of the United States. Congress may make laws with respect to bankruptcy.

Clause 5: Money and Standards. To coin Money, regulate the Value thereof, and of foreign Coin, and fix the Standard of Weights and Measures;

Congress mints coins and prints and circulates paper money. Congress can establish uniform measures of time, distance, weight, and so on. In 1838, Congress adopted the English system of weights and measurements as our national standard.

Clause 6: Punishing Counterfeiters. To provide for the Punishment of counterfeiting the Securities and current Coin of the United States;

Congress has the power to punish those who copy American money and pass it off as real. Currently, the fine is up to $5,000 and/or imprisonment for up to 15 years.

Clause 7: Roads and Post Offices. To establish Post Offices and post Roads;

Post roads include all routes over which mail is carried—highways, railways, waterways, and airways.

Clause 8: Patents and Copyrights. To promote the Progress of Science and useful Arts, by securing for limited Times to Authors and Inventors the exclusive Right to their respective Writings and Discoveries;

Authors' and composers' works are protected by copyrights established by copyright law, which currently is the Copyright Act of 1976, as amended. Copyrights are valid for the life of the author or composer plus 70 years. Inventors' works are protected by patents, which vary in length of protection from 14 to 20 years. A patent gives a person the exclusive right to control the manufacture or sale of her or his invention.

Clause 9: Lower Courts. To constitute Tribunals inferior to the supreme Court;

Congress has the authority to set up all federal courts, except the Supreme Court, and to decide what cases those courts will hear.

Clause 10: Punishment for Piracy. To define and punish Piracies and Felonies committed on the high Seas, and Offences against the Law of Nations;

Congress has the authority to prohibit the commission of certain acts outside U.S. territory and to punish certain violations of international law.

Clause 11: Declaration of War. To declare War, grant Letters of Marque and Reprisal, and make Rules concerning Captures on Land and Water;

Only Congress can declare war, although the president, as commander in chief, can make war without Congress's formal declaration. Letters of marque and reprisal authorized private parties to capture and destroy enemy ships in wartime. Since the middle of the 19th century, international law has prohibited letters of marque and reprisal, and the United States has honored the ban.

Clause 12: The Army. To raise and support Armies, but no Appropriation of Money to that Use shall be for a longer Term than two Years;

Congress has the power to create an army; the money used to pay for it must be appropriated for no more than two-year

intervals. *This latter restriction gives ultimate control of the army to civilians.*

Clause 13: Creation of a Navy. To provide and maintain a Navy;

This clause allows for the maintenance of a navy. In 1947, Congress created the U.S. Air Force.

Clause 14: Regulation of the Armed Forces. To make Rules for the Government and Regulation of the land and naval Forces;

Congress sets the rules for the military mainly by way of the Uniform Code of Military Justice, which was enacted in 1950 by Congress.

Clause 15: The Militia. To provide for calling forth the Militia to execute the Laws of the Union, suppress Insurrections and repel Invasions;

The militia is known today as the National Guard. Both Congress and the president have the authority to call the National Guard into federal service.

Clause 16: How the Militia Is Organized. To provide for organizing, arming, and disciplining the Militia, and for governing such Part of them as may be employed in the Service of the United States, reserving to the States respectively, the Appointment of the Officers, and the Authority of training the Militia according to the discipline prescribed by Congress;

This clause gives Congress the power to "federalize" state militia (National Guard). When called into such service, the National Guard is subject to the same rules that Congress has set forth for the regular armed services.

Clause 17: Creation of the District of Columbia. To exercise exclusive Legislation in all Cases whatsoever, over such District (not exceeding ten Miles square) as may, by Cession of particular States, and the Acceptance of Congress, become the Seat of the Government of the United States, and to exercise like Authority over all Places purchased by the Consent of the Legislature of the State in which the Same shall be, for the Erection of Forts, Magazines, Arsenals, dock-Yards, and other needful Buildings;—And

Congress established the District of Columbia as the national capital in 1791. Virginia and Maryland had granted land for the District, but Virginia's grant was returned because it was believed it would not be needed. Today, the District covers 69 square miles.

Clause 18: The Elastic Clause. To make all Laws which shall be necessary and proper for carrying into Execution the foregoing Powers, and all other Powers vested by this Constitution in the Government of the United States, or in any Department or Officer thereof.

This clause—the necessary and proper clause, or the elastic clause—grants no specific powers, and thus it can be stretched to fit different circumstances. It has allowed Congress to adapt the government to changing needs and times.

Section 9. *The Powers Denied to Congress*

Clause 1: Question of Slavery. The Migration or Importation of such Persons as any of the States now existing shall think proper to admit, shall not be prohibited by the Congress prior to the Year one thousand eight hundred and eight, but a Tax or duty may be imposed on such Importation, not exceeding ten dollars for each Person.

"Persons" referred to slaves. Congress outlawed the slave trade in 1808.

Clause 2: Habeas Corpus. The privilege of the Writ of Habeas Corpus shall not be suspended, unless when in Cases of Rebellion or Invasion the public Safety may require it.

A writ of habeas corpus is a court order directing a sheriff or other public officer who is detaining another person to "produce the body" of the detainee so the court can assess the legality of the detention.

Clause 3: Special Bills. No Bill of Attainder or ex post facto Law shall be passed.

A bill of attainder is a law that inflicts punishment without a trial. An ex post facto law is a law that inflicts punishment for an act that was not illegal when it was committed.

Clause 4: Direct Taxes. [No Capitation, or other direct, Tax shall be laid, unless in Proportion to the Census or Enumeration herein before directed to be taken.][6]

A capitation is a tax on a person. A direct tax is a tax paid directly to the government, such as a property tax. This clause was intended to prevent Congress from levying a tax on slaves per person and thereby taxing slavery out of existence.

Clause 5: Export Taxes. No Tax or Duty shall be laid on Articles exported from any State.

Congress may not tax any goods sold from one state to another or from one state to a foreign country. (Congress does have the power to tax goods that are bought from other countries, however.)

Clause 6: Interstate Commerce. No Preference shall be given by any Regulation of Commerce or Revenue to the Ports of one State over those of another: nor shall Vessels bound to, or from, one State, be obliged to enter, clear, or pay Duties in another.

Congress may not treat different ports within the United States differently in terms of taxing and commerce powers. Congress may not give one state's port a legal advantage over the ports of another state.

Clause 7: Treasury Withdrawals. No Money shall be drawn from the Treasury, but in Consequence of Appropriations made by Law; and a regular Statement and Account of the Receipts and Expenditures of all public Money shall be published from time to time.

Federal funds can be spent only as Congress authorizes. This is a significant check on the president's power.

Clause 8: Titles of Nobility. No Title of Nobility shall be granted by the United States: And no Person holding any Office of Profit or Trust under them, shall, without the Consent of the Congress, accept of any present, Emolument, Office,

or Title, of any kind whatever, from any King, Prince, or foreign State.

No person in the United States may hold a title of nobility, such as duke or duchess. This clause also discourages bribery of American officials by foreign governments.

Section 10. *Those Powers Denied to the States*

Clause 1: Treaties and Coinage. No State shall enter into any Treaty, Alliance, or Confederation; grant Letters of Marque and Reprisal; coin Money; emit Bills of Credit; make any Thing but gold and silver Coin a Tender in Payment of Debts; pass any Bill of Attainder, ex post facto Law, or Law impairing the Obligation of Contracts, or grant any Title of Nobility.

Prohibiting state laws "impairing the Obligation of Contracts" was intended to protect creditors. (Shayss' Rebellion—an attempt to prevent courts from giving effect to creditors' legal actions against debtors—occurred only one year before the Constitution was written.)

Clause 2: Duties and Imposts. No State shall, without the Consent of the Congress, lay any Imposts or Duties on Imports or Exports, except what may be absolutely necessary for executing its inspection Laws; and the net Produce of all Duties and Imposts, laid by any State on Imports or Exports, shall be for the Use of the Treasury of the United States; and all such Laws shall be subject to the Revision and Controul of the Congress.

Only Congress can tax imports. Further, the states cannot tax exports.

Clause 3: War. No State shall, without the Consent of Congress, lay any Duty of Tonnage, keep Troops, or Ships of War in time of Peace, enter into any Agreement or Compact with another State, or with a foreign Power or engage in War, unless actually invaded, or in such imminent Danger as will not admit of delay.

A duty of tonnage is a tax on ships according to their cargo capacity. No states may tax ships according to their cargo unless Congress agrees. Additionally, this clause forbids any state to keep troops or warships during peacetime or to make a compact with another state or foreign nation unless Congress so agrees. A state, in contrast, can maintain a militia, but its use has to be limited to disorders that occur within the state—unless, of course, the militia is called into federal service.

ARTICLE II. *(Executive Branch)*

Section 1. *The Nature and Scope of Presidential Power*

Clause 1: Four-Year Term. The executive Power shall be vested in a President of the United States of America. He shall hold his Office during the Term of four Years, and, together with the Vice President, chosen for the same Term, be elected, as follows.

The president has the power to carry out laws made by Congress, called the executive power. He or she serves in office for a four-year term after election. The Twenty-second Amendment limits the number of times a person may be elected president.

---

6   Modified by the Sixteenth Amendment.

Clause 2: Choosing Electors from Each State. Each State shall appoint, in such Manner as the Legislature thereof may direct, a Number of Electors, equal to the whole Number of Senators and Representatives to which the State may be entitled in the Congress; but no Senator or Representative, or Person holding an Office of Trust or Profit under the United States, shall be appointed an Elector.

The "Electors" are known more commonly as the "electoral college." The president is elected by electors—that is, representatives chosen by the people—rather than by the people directly.

Clause 3: The Former System of Elections. [The Electors shall meet in their respective States, and vote by Ballot for two Persons, of whom one at least shall not be an Inhabitant of the same State with themselves. And they shall make a List of all the Persons voted for, and of the Number of Votes for each; which List they shall sign and certify, and transmit sealed to the Seat of the Government of the United States, directed to the President of the Senate. The President of the Senate shall, in the Presence of the Senate and House of Representatives, open all the Certificates, and the Votes shall then be counted. The Person having the greatest Number of Votes shall be the President, if such Number be a Majority of the whole Number of Electors appointed; and if there be more than one who have such Majority, and have an equal Number of Votes, then the House of Representatives shall immediately chuse by Ballot one of them for President; and if no Person have a Majority, then from the five highest on the List the said House shall in like Manner chuse the President. But in chusing the President, the Votes shall be taken by States, the Representation from each State having one Vote; A quorum for this Purpose shall consist of a Member or Members from two thirds of the States, and a Majority of all the States shall be necessary to a Choice. In every Case, after the Choice of the President, the Person having the greater Number of Votes of the Electors shall be the Vice President. But if there should remain two or more who have equal Votes, the Senate shall chuse from them by Ballot the Vice President.][7]

The original method of selecting the president and vice president was replaced by the Twelfth Amendment. Apparently, the framers did not anticipate the rise of political parties and the development of primaries and conventions.

Clause 4: The Time of Elections. The Congress may determine the Time of chusing the Electors, and the Day on which they shall give their Votes; which Day shall be the same throughout the United States.

Congress set the Tuesday after the first Monday in November every fourth year as the date for choosing electors. The electors cast their votes on the Monday after the second Wednesday in December of that year.

Clause 5: Qualifications for President. No person except a natural born Citizen, or a Citizen of the United States, at the time of the Adoption of this Constitution, shall be eligible to the Office of President; neither shall any Person be eligible to that Office who shall not have attained to the Age of thirty five Years, and been fourteen Years a Resident within the United States.

The president must be a natural-born citizen, be at least 35 years of age when taking office, and have been a resident within the United States for at least 14 years.

Clause 6: Succession of the Vice President. [In Case of the Removal of the President from Office, or of his Death, Resignation or Inability to discharge the Powers and Duties of the said Office, the same shall devolve on the Vice President, and the Congress may by Law provide for the Case of Removal, Death, Resignation or Inability, both of the President and Vice President, declaring what Officer shall then act as President, and such Officer shall act accordingly, until the Disability be removed, or a President shall be elected.][8]

This section provided for the method by which the vice president was to succeed to the presidency, but its wording is ambiguous. It was replaced by the Twenty-fifth Amendment.

Clause 7: The President's Salary. The President shall, at stated Times, receive for his Services, a Compensation, which shall neither be encreased nor diminished during the Period for which he shall have been elected, and he shall not receive within that Period any other Emolument from the United States, or any of them.

The president maintains the same salary during each four-year term. Moreover, she or he may not receive additional cash payments from the government. Originally set at $25,000 per year, the salary is currently $400,000 a year plus a $50,000 nontaxable expense account.

Clause 8: The Oath of Office. Before he enter on the Execution of his Office, he shall take the following Oath or Affirmation: "I do solemnly swear (or affirm) that I will faithfully execute the Office of President of the United States, and will to the best of my Ability, preserve, protect and defend the Constitution of the United States."

The president is "sworn in" prior to beginning the duties of the office. The taking of the oath of office occurs on January 20, following the November election. The ceremony is called the inauguration. The oath of office is administered by the chief justice of the United States Supreme Court.

Section 2. *Powers of the President*

Clause 1: Commander in Chief. The President shall be Commander in Chief of the Army and Navy of the United States, and of the Militia of the several States, when called into the actual Service of the United States; he may require the Opinion, in writing, of the principal Officer in each of the executive Departments, upon any Subject relating to the Duties of their respective Offices, and he shall have Power to grant Reprieves and Pardons for Offences against the United States, except in Cases of Impeachment.

The armed forces are placed under civilian control because the president is a civilian but still commander in chief of the military.

---

7 Changed by the Twelfth Amendment.
8 Modified by the Twenty-fifth Amendment.

The president may ask for the help of the head of each of the executive departments (thereby creating the Cabinet). The Cabinet members are chosen by the president with the consent of the Senate, but they can be removed without Senate approval.

The president's clemency powers extend only to federal cases. In those cases, he or she may grant a full or conditional pardon, or reduce a prison term or fine.

Clause 2: Treaties and Appointment. He shall have Power, by and with the Advice and Consent of the Senate, to make Treaties, provided two thirds of the Senators present concur; and he shall nominate, and by and with the Advice and Consent of the Senate, shall appoint Ambassadors, other public Ministers and Consuls, Judges of the supreme Court, and all other Officers of the United States, whose Appointments are not herein otherwise provided for, and which shall be established by Law; but the Congress may by Law vest the Appointment of such inferior Officers, as they think proper, in the President alone, in the Courts of Law, or in the Heads of Departments.

Many of the major powers of the president are identified in this clause, including the power to make treaties with foreign governments (with the approval of the Senate by a two-thirds vote) and the power to appoint ambassadors, Supreme Court justices, and other government officials. Most such appointments require Senate approval.

Clause 3: Vacancies. The President shall have Power to fill up all Vacancies that may happen during the Recess of the Senate, by granting Commissions which shall expire at the end of their next Session.

The president has the power to appoint temporary officials to fill vacant federal offices without Senate approval if the Congress is not in session. Such appointments expire automatically at the end of Congress's next term.

Section 3. *Duties of the President*

He shall from time to time give to the Congress Information of the State of the Union, and recommend to their Consideration such Measures as he shall judge necessary and expedient; he may, on extraordinary Occasions, convene both Houses, or either of them, and in Case of Disagreement between them, with Respect to the Time of Adjournment, he may adjourn them to such Time as he shall think proper; he shall receive Ambassadors and other public Ministers; he shall take Care that the Laws be faithfully executed, and shall Commission all the Officers of the United States.

Annually, the president reports on the state of the union to Congress, recommends legislative measures, and proposes a federal budget. The State of the Union speech is a statement not only to Congress but also to the American people. After it is given, the president proposes a federal budget and presents an economic report. At any time, the president may send special messages to Congress while it is in session. The president has the power to call special sessions, to adjourn Congress when its two chambers do not agree on when to adjourn, to receive diplomatic representatives

of other governments, and to ensure the proper execution of all federal laws. The president further has the ability to empower federal officers to hold their positions and to perform their duties.

Section 4. *Impeachment*

The President, Vice President and all civil Officers of the United States, shall be removed from Office on Impeachment for, and Conviction of, Treason, Bribery, or other high Crimes and Misdemeanors.

Treason denotes giving aid to the nation's enemies. The phrase "high crimes and misdemeanors" is usually considered to mean serious abuses of political power. In either case, the president or vice president may be accused by the House (called an impeachment) and then removed from office if convicted by the Senate. (Note that impeachment does not mean removal but rather refers to an accusation of treason or high crimes and misdemeanors.)

ARTICLE III. (*Judicial Branch*)

Section 1. *Judicial Powers, Courts, and Judges*

The judicial Power of the United States, shall be vested in one supreme Court, and in such inferior Courts as the Congress may from time to time ordain and establish. The Judges, both of the supreme and inferior Courts, shall hold their Offices during good Behaviour, and shall, at stated Times, receive for their Services a Compensation, which shall not be diminished during their Continuance in Office.

The Supreme Court is vested with judicial power, as are the lower federal courts that Congress creates. Federal judges serve in their offices for life unless they are impeached and convicted by Congress. The payment of federal judges may not be reduced during their time in office.

Section 2. *Jurisdiction*

Clause 1: Cases under Federal Jurisdiction. The judicial Power shall extend to all Cases, in Law and Equity, arising under this Constitution, the Laws of the United States, and Treaties made, or which shall be made, under their Authority;—to all Cases affecting Ambassadors, other public Ministers and Consuls;—to all Cases of admiralty and maritime Jurisdiction;—to Controversies to which the United States shall be a Party;—to Controversies between two or more States; [—between a State and Citizens of another State;—][9] between Citizens of different States;—between Citizens of the same State claiming Lands under Grants of different States, [and between a State, or the Citizens thereof, and foreign States, Citizens or Subjects.][10]

The federal courts take on cases that concern the meaning of the U.S. Constitution, all federal laws, and treaties. They also can take on cases involving citizens of different states and citizens of foreign nations.

Clause 2: Cases for the Supreme Court. In all Cases affecting Ambassadors, other public Ministers and Consuls, and those

---

9 Modified by the Eleventh Amendment.
10 Modified by the Eleventh Amendment.

in which a State shall be a Party, the supreme Court shall have original Jurisdiction. In all the other Cases before mentioned, the supreme Court shall have appellate Jurisdiction, both as to Law and Fact, with such Exceptions, and under such Regulations as the Congress shall make.

In a limited number of situations, the Supreme Court acts as a trial court and has original jurisdiction. These cases involve a representative from another country or involve a state. In all other situations, the cases must first be tried in the lower courts and then can be appealed to the Supreme Court. Congress may, however, make exceptions. Today, the Supreme Court acts as a trial court of first instance on rare occasions.

Clause 3: The Conduct of Trials. The Trial of all Crimes, except in Cases of Impeachment, shall be by Jury; and such Trial shall be held in the State where the said Crimes shall have been committed; but when not committed within any State, the Trial shall be at such Place or Places as the Congress may by Law have directed.

Any person accused of a federal crime is granted the right to a trial by jury in a federal court in that state in which the crime was committed. Trials of impeachment are an exception.

Section 3. *Treason*

Clause 1: The Definition of Treason. Treason against the United States, shall consist only in levying War against them, or, in adhering to their Enemies, giving them Aid and Comfort. No Person shall be convicted of Treason unless on the Testimony of two Witnesses to the same overt Act, or on Confession in open Court.

Treason is the making of war against the United States or giving aid to its enemies.

Clause 2: Punishment. The Congress shall have Power to declare the Punishment of Treason, but no Attainder of Treason shall work Corruption of Blood, or Forfeiture except during the Life of the Person attainted.

Congress has provided that the punishment for treason ranges from a minimum of five years in prison and/or a $10,000 fine to a maximum of death. "No Attainder of Treason shall work Corruption of Blood" prohibits punishment of the traitor's heirs.

ARTICLE IV. (*Relations among the States*)

Section 1. *Full Faith and Credit*

Full Faith and Credit shall be given in each State to the public Acts, Records, and judicial Proceedings of every other State. And the Congress may by general Laws prescribe the Manner in which such Acts, Records and Proceedings shall be proved, and the Effect thereof.

All states are required to respect one another's laws, records, and lawful decisions. There are exceptions, however. A state does not have to enforce another state's criminal code. Nor does it have to recognize another state's grant of a divorce if the person obtaining the divorce did not establish legal residence in the state in which it was given.

Section 2. *Treatment of Citizens*

Clause 1: Privileges and Immunities. The Citizens of each State shall be entitled to all Privileges and Immunities of Citizens in the several States.

A citizen of a state has the same rights and privileges as the citizens of another state in which he or she happens to be.

Clause 2: Extradition. A Person charged in any State with Treason, Felony, or other Crime, who shall flee from Justice, and be found in another State, shall on Demand of the executive Authority of the State from which he fled, be delivered up, to be removed to the State having Jurisdiction of the Crime.

Any person accused of a crime who flees to another state must be returned to the state in which the crime occurred.

Clause 3: Fugitive Slaves. [No Person held to Service or Labour in one State, under the Laws thereof, escaping into another, shall, in Consequence of any Law or Regulation therein, be discharged from such Service or Labour, but shall be delivered up on Claim of the Party to whom such Service or Labour may be due.][11]

This clause was struck down by the Thirteenth Amendment, which abolished slavery in 1865.

Section 3. *Admission of States*

Clause 1: The Process. New States may be admitted by the Congress into this Union; but no new State shall be formed or erected within the Jurisdiction of any other State; nor any State be formed by the Junction of two or more States, or Parts of States, without the Consent of the Legislatures of the States concerned as well as of the Congress.

Only Congress has the power to admit new states to the union. No state may be created by taking territory from an existing state unless the state's legislature so consents.

Clause 2: Public Land. The Congress shall have Power to dispose of and make all needful Rules and Regulations respecting the Territory or other Property belonging to the United States; and nothing in this Constitution shall be so construed as to Prejudice any Claims of the United States, or of any particular State.

The federal government has the exclusive right to administer federal government public lands.

Section 4. *Republican Form of Government*

The United States shall guarantee to every State in this Union a Republican Form of Government, and shall protect each of them against Invasion; and on Application of the Legislature, or of the Executive (when the Legislature cannot be convened) against domestic Violence.

Each state is promised a republican form of government—that is, one in which the people elect their representatives. The federal government is bound to protect states against any attack by foreigners or during times of trouble within a state.

---

11 Repealed by the Thirteenth Amendment.

ARTICLE V. (*Methods of Amendment*)

The Congress, whenever two thirds of both Houses shall deem it necessary, shall propose Amendments to this Constitution, or on the Application of the Legislatures of two thirds of the several States, shall call a Convention for proposing Amendments, which, in either Case, shall be valid to all Intents and Purposes, as Part of this Constitution, when ratified by the Legislatures of three fourths of the several States, or by Conventions in three fourths thereof, as the one or the other Mode of Ratification may be proposed by the Congress; Provided that no Amendment which may be made prior to the Year One thousand eight hundred and eight shall in any Manner affect the first and fourth Clauses in the Ninth Section of the First Article; and that no State, without its Consent, shall be deprived of its equal Suffrage in the Senate.

Amendments may be proposed in either of two ways: a two-thirds vote of each chamber (Congress) or at the request of two-thirds of the states. Ratification of amendments may be carried out in two ways: by the legislatures of three-fourths of the states or by the voters in three-fourths of the states. No state may be denied equal representation in the Senate.

ARTICLE VI. (*National Supremacy*)

Clause 1: Existing Obligations. All Debts contracted and Engagements entered into, before the Adoption of this Constitution shall be as valid against the United States under this Constitution, as under the Confederation.

During the Revolutionary War and the years of the Confederation, Congress borrowed large sums. This clause pledged that the new federal government would assume those financial obligations.

Clause 2: Supreme Law of the Land. This Constitution, and the Laws of the United States which shall be made in Pursuance thereof; and all Treaties made, or which shall be made, under the Authority of the United States, shall be the supreme Law of the Land; and the Judges in every State shall be bound thereby, any Thing in the Constitution or Laws of any State to the Contrary notwithstanding.

This is typically called the supremacy clause; it declares that federal law takes precedence over all forms of state law. No government at the local or state level may make or enforce any law that conflicts with any provision of the Constitution, acts of Congress, treaties, or other rules and regulations issued by the president and his or her subordinates in the executive branch of the federal government.

Clause 3: Oath of Office. The Senators and Representatives before mentioned, and the Members of the several State Legislatures, and all executive and judicial Officers, both of the United States and of the several States, shall be bound by Oath or Affirmation, to support this Constitution; but no religious Test shall ever be required as a Qualification to any Office or public Trust under the United States.

Every federal and state official must take an oath of office promising to support the U.S. Constitution. Religion may not be used as a qualification to serve in any federal office.

ARTICLE VII. (*Ratification*)

The Ratification of the Conventions of nine States shall be sufficient for the Establishment of this Constitution between the States so ratifying the Same.

Nine states were required to ratify the Constitution. Delaware was the first and New Hampshire the ninth.

Done in Convention by the Unanimous Consent of the States present the Seventeenth Day of September in the Year of our Lord one thousand seven hundred and Eighty seven and of the Independence of the United States of America the Twelfth. In witness whereof we have hereunto subscribed our Names,

    Go. WASHINGTON
    Presid't.
    and deputy from Virginia
    Attest William Jackson Secretary

Delaware	{	Geo. Read Gunning Bedford jun John Dickinson Richard Bassett Jaco. Broom	New Hampshire	{	John Langdon Nicholas Gilman
Maryland	{	James McHenry Dan of St. Thos. Jenifer Danl. Carroll	Massachusetts	{	Nathaniel Gorham Rufus King
Virginia	{	John Blair James Madison Jr.	Connecticut	{	Wm. Saml. Johnson Roger Sherman
North Carolina	{	Wm. Blount Richd. Dobbs Spaight Hu. Williamson	New York	{	Alexander Hamilton

South Carolina	{ J. Rutledge Charles Cotesworth Pinckney Charles Pinckney Pierce Butler	New Jersey	{ Wh. Livingston David Brearley Wm. Paterson Jona. Dayton
Georgia	{ William Few Abr. Baldwin	Pennsylvania	{ B. Franklin Thomas Mifflin Robt. Morris Geo. Clymer Thos. FitzSimons Jared Ingersoll James Wilson Gouv. Morris

Amendments to the Constitution of the United States (The Bill of Rights)[12]

Articles in addition to, and amendment of, the Constitution of the United States of America, proposed by Congress and ratified by the Legislatures of the several states, pursuant to the Fifth Article of the original Constitution.

AMENDMENT I.
(Religion, Speech, Assembly, and Petition)

Congress shall make no law respecting an establishment of religion, or prohibiting the free exercise thereof; or abridging the freedom of speech, or of the press; or the right of the people peaceably to assemble, and to petition the Government for a redress of grievances.

Congress may not create an official church or enact laws limiting the freedom of religion, speech, the press, assembly, and petition. These guarantees, like the others in the Bill of Rights (the first 10 amendments), are not absolute—each may be exercised only with regard to the rights of other persons.

AMENDMENT II.
(Militia and the Right to Bear Arms)

A well regulated Militia, being necessary to the security of a free State, the right of the people to keep and bear Arms, shall not be infringed.

---

12 On September 25, 1789, Congress transmitted to the state legislatures 12 proposed amendments, two of which, having to do with congressional representation and congressional pay, were not adopted. The remaining 10 amendments became the Bill of Rights. In 1992, the amendment concerning congressional pay was adopted as the Twenty-seventh Amendment.

To protect itself, each state has the right to maintain a volunteer armed force. States and the federal government regulate the possession and use of firearms by individuals.

AMENDMENT III.
(The Quartering of Soldiers)

No Soldier shall, in time of peace be quartered in any house, without the consent of the Owner, nor in time of war, but in a manner to be prescribed by law.

Before the Revolutionary War, it had been common British practice to quarter soldiers in colonists' homes. Military troops do not have the power to take over private houses during peacetime.

AMENDMENT IV.
(Searches and Seizures)

The right of the people to be secure in their persons, houses, papers, and effects, against unreasonable searches and seizures, shall not be violated, and no Warrants shall issue, but upon probable cause, supported by Oath or affirmation, and particularly describing the place to be searched, and the persons or things to be seized.

Here the word warrant *means "justification" and refers to a document issued by a magistrate or judge indicating the name, address, and possible offense committed. Anyone asking for the warrant, such as a police officer, must be able to convince the magistrate or judge that an offense probably has been committed.*

AMENDMENT V.
(Grand Juries, Self-Incrimination, Double Jeopardy, Due Process, and Eminent Domain)

No person shall be held to answer for a capital, or otherwise infamous crime, unless on a presentment or indictment of a Grand Jury, except in cases arising in the land or naval forces, or in the Militia, when in actual service in time of War or public danger; nor shall any person be subject for the same offence to be twice put in jeopardy of life or limb; nor shall be compelled in any criminal case to be a witness against himself, nor be deprived of life, liberty, or property, without due process of law; nor shall private property be taken for public use, without just compensation.

There are two types of juries. A grand jury considers physical evidence and the testimony of witnesses and decides whether there is sufficient reason to bring a case to trial. A petit jury hears the case at trial and decides it. "For the same offence to be twice put in jeopardy of life or limb" means to be tried twice for the same crime. A person may not be tried for the same crime twice or forced to give evidence against herself or himself. No person's right to life, liberty, or property may be taken away except by lawful means, called the due process of law. Private property taken for use in public purposes must be paid for by the government.

AMENDMENT VI.
(Criminal Court Procedures)

In all criminal prosecutions, the accused shall enjoy the right to a speedy and public trial, by an impartial jury of the State and district wherein the crime shall have been committed, which district shall have been previously ascertained by law, and to be informed of the nature and cause of the accusation; to be confronted with the witnesses against him; to have compulsory process for obtaining witnesses in his favor, and to have the Assistance of Counsel for his defence.

Any person accused of a crime has the right to a fair and public trial by a jury in the state in which the crime took place. The charges against that person must be indicated. Any accused person has the right to a lawyer to defend him or her and to question those who testify against him or her, as well as the right to call people to speak in his or her favor at trial.

AMENDMENT VII.
(Trial by Jury in Civil Cases)

In Suits at common law, where the value in controversy shall exceed twenty dollars, the right of trial by jury shall be preserved, and no fact tried by jury, shall be otherwise re-examined in any Court of the United States, than according to the rules of the common law.

A jury trial may be requested by either party in a dispute in any case involving more than $20. If both parties agree to a trial by a judge without a jury, the right to a jury trial may be put aside.

AMENDMENT VIII.
(Bail, Cruel and Unusual Punishment)

Excessive bail shall not be required, nor excessive fines imposed, nor cruel and unusual punishments inflicted.

Bail is that amount of money that a person accused of a crime may be required to deposit with the court as a guaranty that she or he will appear in court when requested. The amount of bail required or the fine imposed as punishment for a crime must be reasonable compared with the seriousness of the crime involved. Any punishment judged to be too harsh or too severe for a crime shall be prohibited.

AMENDMENT IX.
(The Rights Retained by the People)

The enumeration in the Constitution, of certain rights, shall not be construed to deny or disparage others retained by the people.

Many civil rights that are not explicitly enumerated in the Constitution are still held by the people.

AMENDMENT X.
(Reserved Powers of the States)

The powers not delegated to the United States by the Constitution, nor prohibited by it to the States, are reserved to the States respectively, or to the people.

Those powers not delegated by the Constitution to the federal government or expressly denied to the states belong to the states and to the people. This amendment in essence allows the states to pass laws under their "police powers."

AMENDMENT XI.
(Ratified on February 7, 1795—Suits against States)

The Judicial power of the United States shall not be construed to extend to any suit in law or equity, commenced or prosecuted against one of the United States by Citizens of another State, or by Citizens or Subjects of any Foreign State.

This amendment has been interpreted to mean that a state cannot be sued in federal court by one of its own citizens, by a citizen of another state, or by a foreign country.

AMENDMENT XII.
(Ratified on June 15, 1804—Election of the President)

The Electors shall meet in their respective states, and vote by ballot for President and Vice-President, one of whom, at least, shall not be an inhabitant of the same State with themselves; they shall name in their ballots the person voted for as President, and in distinct ballots the person voted for as Vice-President, and they shall make distinct lists of all persons voted for as President, and of all persons voted for as Vice-President, and of the number of votes for each, which lists they shall sign and certify, and transmit sealed to the seat of the government of the United States, directed to the President of the Senate;—The President of the Senate shall, in the presence of the Senate and House of Representatives, open all the certificates and the votes shall then be counted;—The person having the greatest number of votes for President, shall be the President, if such number be a majority of the whole number of Electors appointed; and if no person have such majority, then from the persons having the highest numbers not exceeding three on the list of those voted for as President, the House of Representatives shall choose immediately, by ballot, the President. But in choosing the President, the votes shall be taken by States, the representation from each State having one vote; a quorum for this purpose shall consist of a member or members from two-thirds of the States, and a majority of all States shall be necessary to a choice. [And if the House of Representatives shall not choose a President whenever the right of choice shall devolve upon them, before the fourth day of March next following, then the Vice-President shall act as President, as in the case of the death or other constitutional disability of the President.][13]—The person having the greatest number of votes as Vice-President, shall be the Vice-President, if such number be a majority of the whole number of Electors appointed, and if no person have a majority, then from the two highest numbers on the list, the Senate shall choose the Vice-President; a quorum for the purpose shall consist of two-thirds of the whole number of Senators, and a majority of the whole number shall be necessary to a choice. But no person constitutionally ineligible to the office of President shall be eligible to that of Vice-President of the United States.

The original procedure set out for the election of president and vice president in Article II, Section 1, resulted in a tie in 1800 between Thomas Jefferson and Aaron Burr. It was not until the next year that the House of Representatives chose Jefferson to be president. This amendment changed the procedure by providing for separate ballots for president and vice president.

AMENDMENT XIII.
(Ratified on December 6, 1865—Prohibition of Slavery)

Section 1.

Neither slavery nor involuntary servitude, except as a punishment for crime whereof the party shall have been duly convicted, shall exist within the United States, or any place subject to their jurisdiction.

Some slaves had been freed during the Civil War. This amendment freed the others and abolished slavery.

Section 2.

Congress shall have power to enforce this article by appropriate legislation.

AMENDMENT XIV.
(Ratified on July 9, 1868—Citizenship, Due Process, and Equal Protection of the Laws)

Section 1.

All persons born or naturalized in the United States, and subject to the jurisdiction thereof, are citizens of the United States and of the State wherein they reside. No State shall make or enforce any law which shall abridge the privileges or immunities of citizens of the United States; nor shall any State deprive any person of life, liberty, or property, without due process of law; nor deny to any person within its jurisdiction the equal protection of the laws.

Under this provision, states cannot make or enforce laws that take away rights given to all citizens by the federal government. States cannot act unfairly or arbitrarily toward, or discriminate against, any person.

Section 2.

Representatives shall be apportioned among the several States according to their respective numbers, counting the whole number of persons in each State, excluding Indians not taxed. But when the right to vote at any election for the choice of electors for President and Vice President of the United States, Representatives in Congress, the Executive and Judicial officers of a State, or the members of the Legislature thereof, is denied to any of the male inhabitants of such State, being [twenty-one][14] years of age, and citizens of the United States, or in any way

---

13 Changed by the Twentieth Amendment.
14 Changed by the Twenty-sixth Amendment.

abridged, except for participation in rebellion, or other crime, the basis of representation therein shall be reduced in the proportion which the number of such male citizens shall bear to the whole number of male citizens twenty-one years of age in such State.

Section 3.

No person shall be a Senator or Representative in Congress, or elector of President and Vice President, or hold any office, civil or military, under the United States, or under any State, who having previously taken an oath, as a member of Congress, or as an officer of the United States, or as a member of any State legislature, or as an executive or judicial officer of any State, to support the Constitution of the United States, shall have engaged in insurrection or rebellion against the same, or given aid or comfort to the enemies thereof. But Congress may by a vote of two-thirds of each House, remove such disability.

This provision forbade former state or federal government officials who had acted in support of the Confederacy during the Civil War to hold office again. It limited the president's power to pardon those persons. Congress removed this "disability" in 1898.

Section 4.

The validity of the public debt of the United States, authorized by law, including debts incurred for payment of pensions and bounties for services in suppressing insurrection or rebellion, shall not be questioned. But neither the United States nor any State shall assume or pay any debt or obligation incurred in aid of insurrection or rebellion against the United States, or any claim for the loss or emancipation of any slave, but all such debts, obligations and claims shall be held illegal and void.

Section 5.

The Congress shall have power to enforce, by appropriate legislation, the provisions of this article.

AMENDMENT XV.
(Ratified on February 3, 1870—The Right to Vote)

Section 1.

The right of citizens of the United States to vote shall not be denied or abridged by the United States or by any State on account of race, color, or previous condition of servitude.

No citizen can be refused the right to vote simply because of race or color or because that person was once a slave.

Section 2.

The Congress shall have power to enforce this article by appropriate legislation.

AMENDMENT XVI.
(Ratified on February 3, 1913— Income Taxes)

The Congress shall have power to lay and collect taxes on incomes, from whatever source derived, without apportionment among the several States, and without regard to any census or enumeration.

This amendment allows Congress to tax income without sharing the revenue so obtained with the states according to their population.

AMENDMENT XVII. (Ratified on April 8, 1913—The Popular Election of Senators)

Section 1.

The Senate of the United States shall be composed of two Senators from each State, elected by the people thereof, for six years; and each Senator shall have one vote. The electors in each State shall have the qualifications requisite for electors of the most numerous branch of the State legislatures.

Section 2.

When vacancies happen in the representation of any State in the Senate, the executive authority of such State shall issue writs of election to fill such vacancies: *Provided,* That the legislature of any State may empower the executive thereof to make temporary appointments until the people fill the vacancies by election as the legislature may direct.

Section 3.

This amendment shall not be so construed as to affect the election or term of any Senator chosen before it becomes valid as part of the Constitution.

This amendment modified portions of Article I, Section 3, that related to election of senators. Senators are now elected by the voters in each state directly. When a vacancy occurs, either the state may fill the vacancy by a special election, or the governor of the state involved may appoint someone to fill the seat until the next election.

AMENDMENT XVIII.
(Ratified on January 16, 1919—Prohibition)

Section 1.

After one year from the ratification of this article the manufacture, sale, or transportation of intoxicating liquors within, the importation thereof into, or the exportation thereof from the United States and all territory subject to the jurisdiction thereof for beverage purposes is hereby prohibited.

Section 2.

The Congress and the several States shall have concurrent power to enforce this article by appropriate legislation.

Section 3.

This article shall be inoperative unless it shall have been ratified as an amendment to the Constitution by the legislatures of the several States, as provided in the Constitution, within seven years from the date of the submission hereof to the States by the Congress.[15]

This amendment made it illegal to manufacture, sell, and transport alcoholic beverages in the United States. It was repealed by the Twenty-first Amendment.

---

15 The Eighteenth Amendment was repealed by the Twenty-first Amendment.

AMENDMENT XIX.
(Ratified on August 18, 1920—Women's Right to Vote)

Section 1.
The right of citizens of the United States to vote shall not be denied or abridged by the United States or by any State on account of sex.

Section 2.
Congress shall have power to enforce this article by appropriate legislation.

Women were given the right to vote by this amendment, and Congress was given the power to enforce this right.

AMENDMENT XX.
(Ratified on January 23, 1933—The Lame Duck Amendment)

Section 1.
The terms of the President and Vice President shall end at noon on the 20th day of January, and the terms of Senators and Representatives at noon on the 3d day of January, of the years in which such terms would have ended if this article had not been ratified; and the terms of their successors shall then begin.

This amendment modified Article I, Section 4, Clause 2, and other provisions relating to the president in the Twelfth Amendment. The taking of the oath of office was moved from March 4 to January 20.

Section 2.
The Congress shall assemble at least once in every year, and such meeting shall begin at noon on the 3rd day of January, unless they shall by law appoint a different day.

Congress changed the beginning of its term to January 3. The reason the Twentieth Amendment is called the Lame Duck Amendment is that it shortens the time between when a member of Congress is defeated for reelection and when he or she leaves office.

Section 3.
If, at the time fixed for the beginning of the term of the President, the President elect shall have died, the Vice President elect shall become President. If a President shall not have been chosen before the time fixed for the beginning of his term, or if the President elect shall have failed to qualify, then the Vice President elect shall act as President until a President shall have qualified; and the Congress may by law provide for the case wherein neither a President elect nor a Vice President elect shall have qualified, declaring who shall then act as President, or the manner in which one who is to act shall be selected, and such person shall act accordingly until a President or Vice President shall have qualified.

This part of the amendment deals with problem areas left ambiguous by Article II and the Twelfth Amendment. If the president dies before January 20 or fails to qualify for office, the presidency is to be filled as described in this section.

Section 4.
The Congress may by law provide for the case of the death of any of the persons from whom the House of Representatives may choose a President whenever the rights of choice shall have devolved upon them, and for the case of the death of any of the persons from whom the Senate may choose a Vice President whenever the right of choice shall have devolved upon them.

Congress has never created legislation pursuant to this section.

Section 5.
Sections 1 and 2 shall take effect on the 15th day of October following the ratification of this article.

Section 6.
This article shall be inoperative unless it shall have been ratified as an amendment to the Constitution by the legislatures of three-fourths of the several States within seven years from the date of its submission.

AMENDMENT XXI.
(Ratified on December 5, 1933—The Repeal of Prohibition)

Section 1.
The eighteenth article of amendment to the Constitution of the United States is hereby repealed.

Section 2.
The transportation or importation into any State, Territory, or possession of the United States for delivery or use therein of intoxicating liquors, in violation of the laws thereof, is hereby prohibited.

Section 3.
This article shall be inoperative unless it shall have been ratified as an amendment to the Constitution by conventions in the several States, as provided in the Constitution, within seven years from the date of the submission hereof to the States by the Congress.

The amendment repealed the Eighteenth Amendment but did not make alcoholic beverages legal everywhere. Rather, they remained illegal in any state that so designated them. Many such "dry" states existed for a number of years after 1933. Today, there are still "dry" counties within the United States, in which the sale of alcoholic beverages is illegal.

AMENDMENT XXII.
(Ratified on February 27, 1951—Limitation of Presidential Terms)

Section 1.
No person shall be elected to the office of the President more than twice, and no person who has held the office of President, or acted as President, for more than two years of a term to which some other person was elected President shall be elected to the office of President more than once. But this Article shall not apply to any person holding the office of President when this Article was proposed by the Congress, and shall not

prevent any person who may be holding the office of President, or acting as President, during the term within which this Article becomes operative from holding the office of President or acting as President during the remainder of such term.

Section 2.
This article shall be inoperative unless it shall have been ratified as an amendment to the Constitution by the legislatures of three-fourths of the several States within seven years from the date of its submission to the States by the Congress.

No president may serve more than two elected terms. If, however, a president has succeeded to the office after the halfway point of a term in which another president was originally elected, then that president may serve for more than eight years, but not to exceed 10 years.

AMENDMENT XXIII.
(Ratified on March 29, 1961—Presidential Electors for the District of Columbia)

Section 1.
The District constituting the seat of Government of the United States shall appoint in such manner as the Congress may direct:

A number of electors of President and Vice President equal to the whole number of Senators and Representatives in Congress to which the District would be entitled if it were a State, but in no event more than the least populous State; they shall be in addition to those appointed by the States, but they shall be considered, for the purposes of the election of President and Vice President, to be electors appointed by a State; and they shall meet in the District and perform such duties as provided by the twelfth article of amendment.

Section 2.
The Congress shall have power to enforce this article by appropriate legislation.

Citizens living in the District of Columbia have the right to vote in elections for president and vice president. The District of Columbia has three presidential electors, whereas before this amendment it had none.

AMENDMENT XXIV.
(Ratified on January 23, 1964—The Anti–Poll Tax Amendment)

Section 1.
The right of citizens of the United States to vote in any primary or other election for President or Vice President, for electors for President or Vice President, or for Senator or Representative in Congress, shall not be denied or abridged by the United States, or any State by reason of failure to pay any poll tax or other tax.

Section 2.
The Congress shall have power to enforce this article by appropriate legislation.

No government shall require a person to pay a poll tax to vote in any federal election.

AMENDMENT XXV.
(Ratified on February 10, 1967—Presidential Disability and Vice Presidential Vacancies)

Section 1.
In case of the removal of the President from office or of his death or resignation, the Vice President shall become President.

Whenever a president dies or resigns from office, the vice president becomes president.

Section 2.
Whenever there is a vacancy in the office of the Vice President, the President shall nominate a Vice President who shall take office upon confirmation by a majority vote of both Houses of Congress.

Whenever the office of the vice presidency becomes vacant, the president may appoint someone to fill this office, provided Congress consents.

Section 3.
Whenever the President transmits to the President pro tempore of the Senate and the Speaker of the House of Representatives his written declaration that he is unable to discharge the powers and duties of his office, and until he transmits to them a written declaration to the contrary, such powers and duties shall be discharged by the Vice President as Acting President.

Whenever the president believes she or he is unable to carry out the duties of the office, she or he shall so indicate to Congress in writing. The vice president then acts as president until the president declares that she or he is again able to carry out the duties of the office.

Section 4.
Whenever the Vice President and a majority of either the principal officers of the executive departments or of such other body as Congress may by law provide, transmit to the President pro tempore of the Senate and the Speaker of the House of Representatives their written declaration that the President is unable to discharge the powers and duties of his office, the Vice President shall immediately assume the powers and duties of the office as Acting President.

Thereafter, when the President transmits to the President pro tempore of the Senate and the Speaker of the House of Representatives his written declaration that no inability exists, he shall resume the powers and duties of his office unless the Vice President and a majority of either the principal officers of the executive department or of such other body as Congress may by law provide, transmit within four days to the President pro tempore of the Senate and the Speaker of the House of Representatives their written declaration that the President is unable to discharge the powers and duties of his office. Thereupon Congress shall decide the issue, assembling within forty-eight hours for that purpose if not in session. If the Congress, within twenty-one days after receipt of the latter written declaration, or, if Congress is not in session, within twenty-one days after Congress is required to assemble, determines by two-thirds vote of both Houses that the President is unable to discharge the powers and duties of his office, the Vice President shall continue to discharge the same as Acting President; otherwise, the President shall resume the powers and duties of his office.

Whenever the vice president and a majority of the members of the Cabinet believe that the president cannot carry out her or his duties, they shall so indicate in writing to Congress. The vice president shall then act as president. When the president believes that she or he is able to carry out her or his duties again, she or he shall so indicate to the Congress. However, if the vice president and a majority of the Cabinet do not agree, Congress must decide by a two-thirds vote within three weeks who shall act as president.

AMENDMENT XXVI.
(Ratified on July 1, 1971— The 18-Year-Old Vote)

Section 1.

The right of citizens of the United States, who are eighteen years of age or older, to vote shall not be denied or abridged by the United States or by any State on account of age.

No one 18 years of age or older can be denied the right to vote in federal or state elections by virtue of age.

Section 2.

The Congress shall have power to enforce this article by appropriate legislation.

AMENDMENT XXVII.
(Ratified on May 7, 1992— Congressional Pay)

No law, varying the compensation for the services of the Senators and Representatives, shall take effect, until an election of representatives shall have intervened.

This amendment allows the voters to have some control over increases in salaries for congressional members. Originally submitted to the states for ratification in 1789, it was not ratified until 203 years later, in 1992.

The Federalist Papers Nos. 10 and 51

In 1787, after the newly drafted U.S. Constitution was submitted to the 13 states for ratification, a major political debate ensued between the Federalists (who favored ratification) and the Anti-Federalists (who opposed ratification). Anti-Federalists in New York were particularly critical of the Constitution, and in response to their objections, Federalists Alexander Hamilton, James Madison, and John Jay wrote a series of 85 essays in defense of the Constitution. The essays were published in New York newspapers and reprinted in other newspapers throughout the country.

For students of American government, the essays, collectively known as the Federalist Papers, are particularly important because they provide a glimpse of the founders' political philosophy and intentions in designing the Constitution—and, consequently, in shaping the American philosophy of government.

We have included in this appendix two of these essays: Federalist Papers No. 10 and No. 51. Each essay has been annotated by the authors to indicate its importance in American political thought and to clarify the meaning of particular passages.

FEDERALIST PAPER NO. 10

Federalist Paper No. 10, penned by James Madison, has often been singled out as a key document in American political thought. In this essay, Madison attacks the Anti-Federalists' fear that a republican form of government will inevitably give rise to "factions"—small political parties or groups united by a common interest—that will control the government. Factions will be harmful to the country because they will implement policies beneficial to their own interests but adverse to other people's rights and to the public good. In this essay, Madison attempts to lay to rest this fear by explaining how, in a large republic such as the United States, there will be so many different factions, held together by regional or local interests, that no single one of them will dominate national politics.

Madison opens his essay with a paragraph discussing how important it is to devise a plan of government that can control the "instability, injustice, and confusion" brought about by factions.

Among the numerous advantages promised by a well-constructed Union, none deserves to be more accurately developed than its tendency to break and control the violence of faction. The friend of popular governments never finds himself so much alarmed for their character and fate as when he contemplates their propensity to this dangerous vice. He will not fail, therefore, to set a due value on any plan which, without violating the principles to which he is attached, provides a proper cure for it. The instability, injustice, and confusion introduced into the public councils have, in truth, been the mortal diseases under which popular governments have everywhere perished, as they continue to be the favorite and fruitful topics from which the adversaries to liberty derive their most specious declamations. The valuable improvements made by the American constitutions on the popular models, both ancient and modern, cannot certainly be too much admired; but it would be an unwarrantable partiality to contend that they have as effectually obviated the danger on this side, as was wished and expected. Complaints are everywhere heard from our most considerate and virtuous citizens, equally the friends of public and private faith and of public and personal liberty, that our governments are too unstable, that the public good is disregarded in the conflicts of rival parties, and that measures are too often decided, not according to the rules of justice and the rights of the minor party, but by the superior force of an interested and overbearing majority. However anxiously we may wish that these complaints had no foundation, the evidence of known facts will not permit us to deny that they are in some degree true. It will be found, indeed, on a candid review of our situation, that some of the distresses under which we labor have been erroneously charged on the operation of our governments; but it will be found, at the same time, that other causes will not alone account for many of our heaviest misfortunes; and, particularly, for that prevailing and increasing distrust of public engagements and alarm for private rights which are echoed from one end of the continent to the other. These must be chiefly, if not wholly, effects of the unsteadiness and injustice with which a factious spirit has tainted our public administration.

Madison now defines what he means by the term faction.

By a faction I understand a number of citizens, whether amounting to a majority or minority of the whole, who are united and actuated by some common impulse of passion, or of interest, adverse to the rights of other citizens, or the permanent and aggregate interests of the community.

Madison next contends that there are two methods by which the "mischiefs of faction" can be cured: by removing the causes of faction or by controlling their effects. In the following paragraphs, Madison explains how liberty itself nourishes factions. Therefore, to abolish factions would involve abolishing liberty—a cure "worse than the disease."

There are two methods of curing the mischiefs of faction: the one, by removing its causes; the other, by controlling its effects.

There are again two methods of removing the causes of faction: the one, by destroying the liberty which is essential to its existence; the other, by giving to every citizen the same opinions, the same passions, and the same interests.

It could never be more truly said than of the first remedy that it was worse than the disease. Liberty is to faction what air is to fire, an aliment without which it instantly expires. But it could not be a less folly to abolish liberty, which is essential to political life, because it nourishes faction than it would be to wish the annihilation of air, which is essential to animal life, because it imparts to fire its destructive agency.

The second expedient is as impracticable as the first would be unwise. As long as the reason of man continues fallible, and he is at liberty to exercise it, different opinions will be formed. As long as the connection subsists between his reason and his self-love, his opinions and his passions will have a reciprocal influence on each other; and the former will be objects to which the latter will attach themselves. The diversity in the faculties of men, from which the rights of property originate, is not less an insuperable obstacle to a uniformity of interests. The protection of these faculties is the first object of government. From the protection of different and unequal faculties of acquiring property, the possession of different degrees and kinds of property immediately results; and from the influence of these on the sentiments and views of the respective proprietors ensues a division of the society into different interests and parties.

The latent causes of faction are thus sown in the nature of man; and we see them everywhere brought into different degrees of activity, according to the different circumstances of civil society. A zeal for different opinions concerning religion, concerning government, and many other points, as well of speculation as of practice; an attachment to different leaders ambitiously contending for pre-eminence and power; or to persons of other descriptions whose fortunes have been interesting to the human passions, have, in turn, divided mankind into parties, inflamed them with mutual animosity, and rendered them much more disposed to vex and oppress each other than to co-operate for their common good. So strong is this propensity of mankind to fall into mutual animosities that where no substantial occasion presents itself the most frivolous and fanciful distinctions have been sufficient to kindle their unfriendly passions and excite their most violent conflicts. But the most common and durable source of factions has been the various and unequal distribution of property. Those who hold and those who are without property have ever formed distinct interests in society. Those who are creditors, and those who are debtors, fall under a like discrimination. A landed interest, a manufacturing interest, a mercantile interest, a moneyed interest, with many lesser interests, grow up of necessity in civilized nations, and divide them into different classes, actuated by different sentiments and views. The regulation of these various and interfering interests forms the principal task of modern legislation and involves the spirit of party and faction in the necessary and ordinary operations of government.

No man is allowed to be a judge in his own cause, because his interest would certainly bias his judgment, and, not improbably, corrupt his integrity. With equal, nay with greater reason, a body of men are unfit to be both judges and parties at the same time; yet what are many of the most important acts of legislation but so many judicial determinations, not indeed concerning the rights of single persons, but concerning the rights of large bodies of citizens? And what are the different classes of legislators but advocates and parties to the causes which they determine? Is a law proposed concerning private debts? It is a question to which the creditors are parties on one side and the debtors on the other. Justice ought to hold the balance between them. Yet the parties are, and must be, themselves the judges; and the most numerous party, or in other words, the most powerful faction must be expected to prevail. Shall domestic manufacturers be encouraged, and in what degree, by restrictions on foreign manufacturers? [These] are questions which would be differently decided by the landed and the manufacturing classes, and probably by neither with a sole regard to justice and the public good. The apportionment of taxes on the various descriptions of property is an act which seems to require the most exact impartiality; yet there is, perhaps, no legislative act in which greater opportunity and temptation are given to a predominant party to trample on the rules of justice. Every shilling with which they overburden the inferior number is a shilling saved to their own pockets.

It is in vain to say that enlightened statesmen will be able to adjust these clashing interests and render them all subservient to the public good. Enlightened statesmen will not always be at the helm. Nor, in many cases, can such an adjustment be made at all without taking into view indirect and remote considerations, which will rarely prevail over the immediate interest which one party may find in disregarding the rights of another or the good of the whole.

The inference to which we are brought is that the *causes* of faction cannot be removed and that relief is only to be sought in the means of controlling its *effects*.

Having concluded that "the causes of faction cannot be removed," Madison now looks in some detail at the other method by which factions can be cured—by controlling their effects. This is the heart of his essay. He begins by positing a significant question: How can you have self-government without risking the possibility that a ruling faction, particularly a majority faction, might tyrannize over the rights of others?

If a faction consists of less than a majority, relief is supplied by the republican principle, which enables the majority to defeat its sinister views by regular vote. It may clog the administration, it may convulse the society; but it will be unable to execute and mask its violence under the forms of the Constitution. When a majority is included in a faction, the form of popular government, on the other hand, enables it to sacrifice to its ruling passion or interest both the public good and the rights of other citizens. To secure the public good and private rights against the danger of such a faction, and at the same time to preserve the spirit and the form of popular government, is then the great object to which our inquiries are directed. Let me add that it is the great desideratum by which alone this form of government can be rescued from the opprobrium under which it has so long labored and be recommended to the esteem and adoption of mankind.

Madison now sets forth the idea that one way to control the effects of factions is to ensure that the majority is rendered incapable of acting in concert in order to "carry into effect schemes of oppression." He goes on to state that in a democracy, in which all citizens participate personally in government decision making, there is no way to prevent the majority from communicating with each other and, as a result, acting in concert.

By what means is this object attainable? Evidently by one of two only. Either the existence of the same passion or interest in a majority at the same time must be prevented, or the majority, having such coexistent passion or interest, must be rendered, by their number and local situation, unable to concert and carry into effect schemes of oppression. If the impulse and the opportunity be suffered to coincide, we well know that neither moral nor religious motives can be relied on as an adequate control. They are not found to be such on the injustice and violence of individuals, and lose their efficacy in proportion to the number combined together, that is, in proportion as their efficacy becomes needful.

From this view of the subject it may be concluded that a pure democracy, by which I mean a society consisting of a small number of citizens, who assemble and administer the government in person, can admit of no cure for the mischiefs of faction. A common passion or interest will, in almost every case, be felt by a majority of the whole; a communication and concert results from the form of government itself; and there is nothing to check the inducements to sacrifice the weaker party or an obnoxious individual. Hence it is that such democracies have ever been spectacles of turbulence and contention; have ever been found incompatible with personal security or the rights of property; and have in general been as short in their lives as they have been violent in their deaths. Theoretic politicians, who have patronized this species of government, have erroneously supposed that by reducing mankind to a perfect equality in their political rights, they would at the same time be perfectly equalized and assimilated in their possessions, their opinions, and their passions.

Madison now moves on to discuss the benefits of a republic with respect to controlling the effects of factions. He begins by defining a republic and then pointing out the "two great points of difference" between a republic and a democracy: a republic is governed by a small body of elected representatives, not by the people directly; and a republic can extend over a much larger territory and embrace more citizens than a democracy can.

A republic, by which I mean a government in which the scheme of representation takes place, opens a different prospect and promises the cure for which we are seeking. Let us examine the points in which it varies from pure democracy, and we shall comprehend both the nature of the cure and the efficacy which it must derive from the Union.

The two great points of difference between a democracy and a republic are: first, the delegation of the government, in the latter, to a small number of citizens elected by the rest; secondly, the greater number of citizens and greater sphere of country over which the latter may be extended.

In the following four paragraphs, Madison explains how in a republic, particularly a large republic, the delegation of authority to elected representatives will increase the likelihood that those who govern will be "fit" for their positions and that a proper balance will be achieved between local (factional) interests and national interests. Note how he stresses that the new federal Constitution, by dividing powers between state governments and the national government, provides a "happy combination in this respect."

The effect of the first difference is, on the one hand, to refine and enlarge the public views by passing them through the medium of a chosen body of citizens, whose wisdom may best discern the true interest of their country and whose patriotism and love of justice will be least likely to sacrifice it to temporary or partial considerations. Under such a regulation it may well happen that the public voice, pronounced by the representatives of the people, will be more consonant to the public good than if pronounced by the people themselves, convened for the purpose. On the other hand, the effect may be inverted. Men of factious tempers, of local prejudices, or of sinister designs, may, by intrigue, by corruption, or by other means, first obtain the suffrages, and then betray the interests of the people. The question resulting is, whether small or extensive republics are most favorable to the election of proper guardians of the public weal; and it is clearly decided in favor of the latter by two obvious considerations.

In the first place, it is to be remarked that however small the republic may be the representatives must be raised to a certain number in order to guard against the cabals of a few; and that however large it may be, they must be limited to a certain number in order to guard against the confusion of a multitude. Hence, the number of representatives in the two cases not being in proportion to that of the constituents, and being proportionally greater in the small republic, it follows that if the proportion of fit characters be not less in the large than in the small republic, the former will present a greater option, and consequently a greater probability of a fit choice.

In the next place, as each representative will be chosen by a greater number of citizens in the large than in the small republic, it will be more difficult for unworthy candidates to practice with success the vicious arts by which elections are too often carried; and the suffrages of the people being more free, will be more likely to center on men who possess the most attractive merit and the most diffusive and established characters.

It must be confessed that in this, as in most other cases, there is a mean, on both sides of which inconveniencies will be found to lie. By enlarging too much the number of electors, you render the representative too little acquainted with all their local circumstances and lesser interests; as by reducing it too much, you render him unduly attached to these, and too little fit to comprehend and pursue great and national objects. The federal Constitution forms a happy combination in this respect; the great and aggregate interests being referred to the national, the local and particular to the State legislatures.

Madison now looks more closely at the other difference between a republic and a democracy—namely, that a republic can encompass a larger territory and more citizens than a democracy can. In the remaining paragraphs of his essay, Madison concludes that in a large republic, it will be difficult for factions to act in concert. Although a factious group—religious, political, economic, or otherwise—may control a local or regional government, it will have little chance of gathering a national following. This is because in a large republic, there will be numerous factions whose work will offset the work of any one particular faction ("sect"). As Madison phrases it, these numerous factions will "secure the national councils against any danger from that source."

The other point of difference is the greater number of citizens and extent of territory which may be brought within the compass of republican than of democratic government; and it is this circumstance principally which renders factious combinations less to be dreaded in the former than in the latter. The smaller the society, the fewer probably will be the distinct parties and interests composing it; the fewer the distinct parties and interests, the more frequently will a majority be found of the same party; and the smaller the number of individuals composing a majority, and the smaller the compass within which they are placed, the more easily will they concert and execute their plans of oppression. Extend the sphere and you take in a greater variety of parties and interests; you make it less probable that a majority of the whole will have a common motive to invade the rights of other citizens; or if such a common motive exists, it will be more difficult for all who feel it to discover their own strength and to act in unison with each other. Besides other impediments, it may be remarked that, where there is a consciousness of unjust or dishonorable purposes, communication is always checked by distrust in proportion to the number whose concurrence is necessary.

Hence, it clearly appears that the same advantage which a republic has over a democracy in controlling the effects of faction is enjoyed by a large over a small republic—is enjoyed by the Union over the States composing it. Does this advantage consist in the substitution of representatives whose enlightened views and virtuous sentiments render them superior to local prejudices and to schemes of injustice? It will not be denied that the representation of the Union will be most likely to possess these requisite endowments. Does it consist in the greater security afforded by a greater variety of parties, against the event of any one party being able to outnumber and oppress the rest? In an equal degree does the increased variety of parties comprised within the Union increase this security. Does it, in fine, consist in the greater obstacles opposed to the concert and accomplishment of the secret wishes of an unjust and interested majority? Here again the extent of the Union gives it the most palpable advantage.

The influence of factious leaders may kindle a flame within their particular States but will be unable to spread a general conflagration through the other States. A religious sect may degenerate into a political faction in a part of the Confederacy; but the variety of sects dispersed over the entire face of it must secure the national councils against any danger from that source. A rage for paper money, for an abolition of debts, for an equal division of property, or for any other improper or wicked project, will be less apt to pervade the whole body of the Union than a particular member of it, in the same proportion as such a malady is more likely to taint a particular county or district than an entire State.

In the extent and proper structure of the Union, therefore, we behold a republican remedy for the diseases most incident to republican government. And according to the degree of pleasure and pride we feel in being republicans ought to be our zeal in cherishing the spirit and supporting the character of federalists.

Publius
(James Madison)

FEDERALIST PAPER NO. 51

Federalist Paper No. 51, also authored by James Madison, is another classic in American political theory. Although the Federalists wanted a strong national government, they had not abandoned the traditional American view, particularly notable during the revolutionary era, that those holding powerful government positions could not be trusted to put national interests and the common good above their own personal interests. In this essay, Madison explains why the separation of the national government's powers into three branches—executive, legislative, and judicial—and a federal structure of government offer the best protection against tyranny.

To what expedient, then, shall we finally resort, for maintaining in practice the necessary partition of power among the several departments as laid down in the Constitution? The only answer that can be given is that as all these exterior provisions are found to be inadequate the defect must be supplied, by so contriving the interior structure of the government as that its several constituent parts may, by their mutual relations, be the means of keeping each other in their proper places. Without presuming to undertake a full development of this important idea I will hazard a few general observations which may perhaps place it in a clearer light, and enable us to form a more correct judgment of the principles and structure of the government planned by the convention.

In the next two paragraphs, Madison stresses that for the powers of the different branches (departments) of government to be truly separated, the personnel in one branch should not be dependent on another branch for their appointment or for the "emoluments" (compensation) attached to their offices.

In order to lay a due foundation for that separate and distinct exercise of the different powers of government, which to a certain extent is admitted on all hands to be essential to the preservation of liberty, it is evident that each department should have a will of its own; and consequently should be so constituted that the members of each should have as little agency as possible in the appointment of the members of the others. Were this principle rigorously adhered to, it would require that all the appointments for the supreme executive, legislative, and judiciary magistracies should be drawn from the same fountain of authority, the people, through channels having no communication whatever with one another. Perhaps such a plan of constructing the several departments would be less difficult in practice than it may in contemplation appear. Some difficulties, however, and some additional expense would attend the execution of it. Some deviations, therefore, from the principle must be admitted. In the constitution of the judiciary department in particular, it might be inexpedient to insist rigorously on the principle: first, because peculiar qualifications being essential in the members, the primary consideration ought to be to select that mode of choice which best secures these qualifications; second, because the permanent tenure by which the appointments are held in that department must soon destroy all sense of dependence on the authority conferring them.

It is equally evident that the members of each department should be as little dependent as possible on those of the others for the emoluments annexed to their offices. Were the executive magistrate, or the judges, not independent of the legislature in this particular, their independence in every other would be merely nominal.

In the following passages, which are among the most widely quoted of Madison's writings, he explains how the separation of the powers of government into three branches helps to counter the effects of personal ambition on government. The separation of powers allows personal motives to be linked to the constitutional rights of a branch of government. In effect, competing personal interests in each branch will help to keep the powers of the three government branches separate and, in so doing, will help to guard the public interest.

But the great security against a gradual concentration of the several powers in the same department consists in giving to those who administer each department the necessary constitutional means and personal motives to resist encroachments of the others. The provision for defense must in this, as in all other cases, be made commensurate to the danger of attack. Ambition must be made to counteract ambition. The interest of the man must be connected with the constitutional rights of the place. It may be a reflection on human nature that such devices should be necessary to control the abuses of government. But what is government itself but the greatest of all reflections on human nature? If men were angels, no government would be necessary. If angels were to govern men, neither external nor internal controls on government would be necessary. In framing a government which is to be administered by men over men, the great difficulty lies in this: you must first enable the government to control the governed; and in the next place oblige it to control itself. A dependence on the people is, no doubt, the primary control on the government; but experience has taught mankind the necessity of auxiliary precautions.

This policy of supplying, by opposite and rival interests, the defect of better motives, might be traced through the whole system of human affairs, private as well as public. We see it particularly displayed in all the subordinate distributions of power, where the constant aim is to divide and arrange the several offices in such a manner as that each may be a check on the other—that the private interest of every individual may be a sentinel over the public rights. These inventions of prudence cannot be less requisite in the distribution of the supreme powers of the State.

Madison now addresses the issue of equality between the branches of government. The legislature will necessarily predominate, but if the executive is given an "absolute negative" (absolute veto power) over legislative actions, this also could lead to an abuse of power. Madison concludes that the division of the legislature into two "branches" (parts, or chambers) will act as a check on the legislature's powers.

But it is not possible to give to each department an equal power of self-defense. In republican government, the legislative authority necessarily predominates. The remedy for this inconveniency is to divide the legislature into different branches; and to render them, by different modes of election and different principles of action, as little connected with each other as the nature of their common functions and their common dependence on the society will admit. It may even be necessary to guard against dangerous encroachments by still further precautions. As the weight of the legislative authority requires that it should be thus divided, the weakness of the executive may require, on the other hand, that it should be fortified. An absolute negative on the legislature appears, at first view, to be the natural defense with which the executive magistrate should be armed. But perhaps it would be neither altogether safe nor alone sufficient. On ordinary occasions it might not be exerted with the requisite firmness, and on extraordinary occasions it might be perfidiously abused. May not this defect of an absolute negative be supplied by some qualified connection between this weaker department and the weaker branch of the stronger department, by which the latter may be led to support the constitutional rights of the former, without being too much detached from the rights of its own department?

If the principles on which these observations are founded be just, as I persuade myself they are, and they be applied as a criterion to the several State constitutions, and to the federal Constitution, it will be found that if the latter does not perfectly correspond with them, the former are infinitely less able to bear such a test.

In the remainder of the essay, Madison discusses how a federal system of government, in which powers are divided between the states and the national government, offers "double security" against tyranny.

There are, moreover, two considerations particularly applicable to the federal system of America, which place that system in a very interesting point of view.

First. In a single republic, all the power surrendered by the people is submitted to the administration of a single government; and the usurpations are guarded against by a division of the government into distinct and separate departments. In the compound republic of America, the power surrendered by the people is first divided between two distinct governments, and then the portion allotted to each subdivided among distinct and separate departments. Hence a double security arises to the rights of the people. The different governments will control each other, at the same time that each will be controlled by itself.

Second. It is of great importance in a republic not only to guard the society against the oppression of its rulers, but to guard one part of the society against the injustice of the other part. Different interests necessarily exist in different classes of citizens. If a majority be united by a common interest, the rights of the minority will be insecure. There are but two methods of providing against this evil: the one by creating a will in the community independent of the majority—that is, of the society itself; the other, by comprehending in the society so many separate descriptions of citizens as will render an unjust combination of a majority of the whole very improbable, if not impracticable. The first method prevails in all governments possessing an hereditary or self-appointed authority. This, at best, is but a precarious security; because a power independent of the society may as well espouse the unjust views of the major as the rightful interests of the minor party, and may possibly be turned against both parties. The second method will be exemplified in the federal republic of the United States. Whilst all authority in it will be derived from and dependent on the society, the society itself will be broken into so many parts, interests and classes of citizens, that the rights of individuals, or of the minority, will be in little danger from interested combinations of the majority.

In a free government the security for civil rights must be the same as that for religious rights. It consists in the one case in the multiplicity of interests, and in the other in the multiplicity of sects. The degree of security in both cases will depend on the number of interests and sects; and this may be presumed to depend on the extent of country and number of people comprehended under the same government. This view of the subject must particularly recommend a proper federal system to all the sincere and considerate friends of republican government, since it shows that in exact proportion as the territory of the Union may be formed into more circumscribed Confederacies, or States, oppressive combinations of a majority will be facilitated; the best security, under the republican forms, for the rights of every class of citizen, will be diminished; and consequently the stability and independence of some member of the government, the only other security, must be proportionally increased. Justice is the end of government. It is the end of civil society. It ever has been and ever will be pursued until it be obtained, or until liberty be lost in the pursuit. In a society under the forms of which the stronger faction can readily unite and oppress the weaker, anarchy may as truly be said to reign as in a state of nature, where the weaker individual is not secured against the violence of the stronger; and as, in the latter state, even the stronger individuals are prompted, by the uncertainty of their condition, to submit to a government which may protect the weak as well as themselves; so, in the former state, will the more powerful factions or parties be gradually induced, by a like motive, to wish for a government which will protect all parties, the weaker as well as the more powerful.

It can be little doubted that if the State of Rhode Island was separated from the Confederacy and left to itself, the insecurity of rights under the popular form of government within such narrow limits would be displayed by such reiterated oppressions of factious majorities that some power altogether independent of the people would soon be called for by the voice of the very factions whose misrule had proved the necessity of it. In the extended republic of the United States, and among the great variety of interests, parties, and sects which it embraces, a coalition of a majority of the whole society could seldom take place on any other principles than those of justice and the general good; whilst there being thus less danger to a minor from the will of a major party, there must be less pretext, also, to provide for the security of the former, by introducing into the government a will not dependent on the latter, or, in other words, a will independent of the society itself. It is no less certain than it is important, notwithstanding the contrary opinions which have been entertained, that the larger the society, provided it lie within a practicable sphere, the more duly capable it will be of self-government. And happily for the republican cause, the practicable sphere may be carried to a very great extent by a judicious modification and mixture of the *federal principle*.

Publius

(James Madison)

Glossary

A

Acquisitive model A model of bureaucracy that views stop-level bureaucrats as seeking to expand the size of their budgets and staffs to gain greater power.

Actual malice Either knowledge of a defamatory statement's falsity or a reckless disregard for the truth.

Administrative agency A federal, state, or local government unit established to perform a specific function. Administrative agencies are created and authorized by legislative bodies to administer and enforce specific laws.

Advice and consent Terms in the Constitution describing the U.S. Senate's power to review and approve treaties and presidential appointments.

Affirm To declare that a court ruling is valid and must stand.

Affirmative action A policy in educational admissions or job hiring that gives special attention or compensatory treatment to traditionally disadvantaged groups in an effort to overcome present effects of past discrimination.

Agenda setting The process by which the media identifies the issues the public should be concerned about.

Anarchy The absence of any form of government or political authority.

Anti-Federalist An individual who opposed the ratification of the new Constitution in 1787. The Anti-Federalists were opposed to a strong central government.

Appellate court A court having jurisdiction to review cases and issues that were originally tried in lower courts.

Appointment power The authority vested in the president to fill a government office or position. Positions filled by presidential appointment include those in the executive branch and the federal judiciary, commissioned officers in the armed forces, and members of the independent regulatory commissions.

Appropriation The passage by Congress of a spending bill specifying the amount of authorized funds that actually will be allocated for an agency's use.

Aristocracy Rule by the "best"; in reality, rule by an upper class.

Attentive public That portion of the general public that pays attention to policy issues.

Australian ballot A secret ballot prepared, distributed, and tabulated by government officials at public expense. Since 1888, all U.S. states have used the Australian ballot rather than an open, public ballot.

Authoritarianism A type of regime in which only the government is fully controlled by the ruler. Social and economic institutions exist that are not under the government's control.

Authorization A formal declaration by a legislative committee that a certain amount of funding may be available to an agency. Some authorizations terminate in a year; others are renewable automatically, without further congressional action.

B

Balance of trade The difference between the value of a nation's exports of goods and the value of its imports of goods.

Battleground state A state that is likely to be so closely fought that the campaigns devote exceptional effort to winning the popular and electoral vote there.

"Beauty contest" A presidential primary in which contending candidates compete for popular votes but the results do not control the selection of delegates to the national convention.

Bias An inclination or a preference that interferes with impartial judgment.

Bicameral legislature A legislature made up of two parts, called chambers. The U.S. Congress, composed of the House of Representatives and the Senate, is a bicameral legislature.

Bicameralism The division of a legislature into two separate assemblies.

Black codes Laws passed by Southern states immediately after the Civil War denying most legal rights to freed slaves.

Block grants Federal programs that provide funds to state and local governments for general functional areas, such as criminal justice or mental health programs.

Blog A website or personal online space where an individual makes public his or her opinions, comments, or suggestions.

Blogosphere politics The online arena of politics where the comments of bloggers become news.

Blue Dog Democrats Members of Congress from more moderate states or districts who sometimes "cross over" to vote with Republicans on legislation.

Boycott A form of pressure or protest—an organized refusal to purchase a particular product or deal with a particular business.

Broad construction A judicial philosophy that looks to the context and purpose of a law when making an interpretation.

Budget deficit Government expenditures that exceed receipts.

Bureaucracy A large organization that is structured hierarchically to carry out specific functions.

Business cycle A term that describes fluctuations in the nation's economic activity, including periods of economic expansion and contraction

Busing In the context of civil rights, the transportation of public school students from areas where they live to schools in other areas to eliminate school segregation based on residential racial patterns.

C

Cabinet An advisory group selected by the president to aid in making decisions. The Cabinet includes the heads of 15 executive departments and others named by the president.

Cabinet Department One of the 15 departments of the executive branch (State, Treasury, Defense, Justice, Interior, Agriculture, Commerce, Labor, Health and Human Services, Homeland Security, Housing and Urban Development, Education, Energy, Transportation, and Veterans Affairs).

Capitalism An economic system characterized by the private ownership of wealth-creating assets, free markets, and freedom of contract.

Capture The act by which an industry being regulated by a government agency gains direct or indirect control over agency personnel and decision makers.

Case law Judicial interpretations of common-law principles and doctrines, as well as interpretations of constitutional law, statutory law, and administrative law.

Casework Personal work for constituents by members of Congress.

Categorical grants Federal grants to states or local governments that are for specific programs or projects.

Caucus A meeting of party members designed to select candidates and propose policies.

Charter A document issued by a government that grants to a person, a group of persons, or a corporation the right to carry on one or more specific activities. A state government can grant a charter to a municipality.

Checks and balances A major principle of the American system of government whereby each branch of the government can check the actions of the others.

Chief diplomat The role of the president in recognizing foreign governments, making treaties, and effecting executive agreements.

Chief executive The role of the president as head of the executive branch of the government.

Chief legislator The role of the president in influencing the making of laws.

Chief of staff The person who is named to direct the White House Office and advise the president.

Civil disobedience A nonviolent, public refusal to obey allegedly unjust laws.

Civil liberties Those personal freedoms that are protected for all individuals. Civil liberties typically involve restraining the government's actions against individuals.

Civil rights All rights rooted in the Fourteenth Amendment's guarantee of equal protection under the law.

Civil service A collective term for the body of employees working for the government. Generally, civil service is understood to apply to all those who gain government employment through a merit system.

Civil Service Commission The initial central personnel agency of the national government, created in 1883.

Class-action suit A lawsuit filed by an individual seeking damages for "all persons similarly situated."

Clear and present danger test The test proposed by Justice Oliver Wendell Holmes for determining when government may restrict free speech. Restrictions are permissible, he argued, only when speech creates a *clear and present danger* to the public order.

Climate control The use of public relations techniques to create favorable public opinion toward an interest group, industry, or corporation.

Closed primary A type of primary in which the voter is limited to choosing candidates of the party of which he or she is a member.

Coattail effect The influence of a popular candidate on the electoral success of other candidates on the same party ticket. The effect is increased by the party-column ballot, which encourages straight-ticket voting.

Cold War The ideological, political, and economic confrontation between the United States and the Soviet Union following World War II.

Commander in chief The role of the president as supreme commander of the military forces of the United States and of the state National Guard units when they are called into federal service.

Commerce Clause The section of the Constitution in which Congress is given the power to regulate trade among the states and with foreign countries.

Commercial speech Advertising statements, which increasingly have been given First Amendment protection.

Common law Judge-made law that originated in England from decisions shaped according to prevailing custom. Decisions were applied to similar situations and gradually became common to the nation.

Communications director A professional specialist who plans the communications strategy and advertising campaign for the candidate.

Commutation The commutation of a criminal sentence means that the sentence can be reduced in length to a specified number of years or to the time served. Commuting a sentence may reflect a change in the laws since the individual was convicted.

Concurrent powers Powers held jointly by the national and state governments.

Concurring opinion A separate opinion prepared by a judge who supports the decision of the majority of the court but who wants to make or clarify a particular point or to voice disapproval of the grounds on which the decision was made.

Confederal system A system consisting of a league of independent states, each having essentially sovereign powers. The central government created by such a league has only limited powers over the states.

Confederation A political system in which states or regional governments retain ultimate authority except for those powers they expressly delegate to a central government. A voluntary association of independent states, in which the member states agree to limited restraints on their freedom of action.

Conference committee A special joint committee appointed to reconcile differences when bills pass the two chambers of Congress in different forms.

Consensus General agreement among the citizenry on an issue.

Conservatism A set of beliefs that includes a limited role for the national government in helping individuals, support for traditional values and lifestyles, and a cautious response to change.

Conservative coalition An alliance of Republicans and Southern Democrats that can form in the House or the Senate to oppose liberal legislation and support conservative legislation.

Consolidation The union of two or more governmental units to form a single unit.

Constituent One of the persons represented by a legislator or other elected or appointed official.

Constitutional initiative An electoral device whereby citizens can propose a constitutional amendment through petitions signed by the required number of registered voters.

Constitutional power A power vested in the president by Article II of the Constitution.

Consumer price index (CPI) A measure of the change in price over time of a specific group of goods and services used by the average household.

Containment A U.S. diplomatic policy adopted by the Truman administration to contain communist power within its existing boundaries.

Continuing resolution A temporary funding law that Congress passes when an appropriations bill has not been decided by the beginning of the new fiscal year on October 1.

Cooley's rule The view that cities should be able to govern themselves, presented in an 1871 Michigan decision by Judge Thomas Cooley.

Cooperative Federalism The theory that the states and the national government should cooperate in solving problems.

Corrupt Practices Acts A series of acts passed by Congress in an attempt to limit and regulate the size and sources of contributions and expenditures in political campaigns.

Council of Governments (COG) A voluntary organization of counties and municipalities concerned with area-wide problems.

County The chief governmental unit set up by the state to administer state law and business at the local level. Counties are drawn up by area, rather than by rural or urban criteria.

Credentials committee A committee used by political parties at their national conventions to determine which delegates may participate. The committee inspects the claim of each prospective delegate to be seated as a legitimate representative of his or her state.

D

De facto segregation Racial segregation that occurs because of past social and economic conditions and residential racial patterns.

De jure segregation Racial segregation that occurs because of laws or administrative decisions by public agencies.

Dealignment A decline in party loyalties that reduces long-term party commitment.

Defamation of character Wrongfully hurting a person's good reputation. The law imposes a general duty on all persons to refrain from making false, defamatory statements about others.

Defense policy A subset of national security policies having to do with the U.S. armed forces.

Democracy A system of government in which political authority is vested in the people. Derived from the Greek words *demos* ("the people") and *kratos* ("authority").

Democratic Party One of the two major American political parties evolving out of the Republican Party of Thomas Jefferson.

Democratic Republic A republic in which representatives elected by the people make and enforce laws and policies.

Détente A French word meaning a relaxation of tensions. The term characterized U.S.-Soviet relations as they developed under President Richard Nixon and Secretary of State Henry Kissinger.

Devolution The transfer of powers from a national or central government to a state or local government.

Dillon's rule The narrowest possible interpretation of the legal status of local governments, outlined by Judge John E. Dillon, who in 1872 stated that a municipal corporation can exercise only those powers expressly granted by state law.

Diplomacy The process by which nations carry on political relations with each other; settling conflicts among nations by peaceful means.

Diplomatic recognition The formal acknowledgment of a foreign government as legitimate.

Direct democracy A system of government in which political decisions are made by the people directly, rather than by their elected representatives; probably attained most easily in small political communities.

Direct primary An intraparty election in which the voters select the candidates who will run on a party's ticket in the subsequent general election.

Direct technique An interest group activity that involves interaction with government officials to further the group's goals.

Discharge petition A procedure by which a bill in the House of Representatives may be forced (discharged) out of a committee that has refused to report it for consideration by the House. The petition must be signed by an absolute majority (218) of representatives and is used only on rare occasions.

Dissenting opinion A separate opinion in which a judge dissents from (disagrees with) the conclusion reached by the majority on the court and expounds his or her own views about the case.

Diversity of citizenship The condition that exists when the parties to a lawsuit are citizens of different states, or when citizens of a U.S. state are parties in a lawsuit against citizens (or the government) of a foreign country. Diversity of citizenship can provide a basis for federal jurisdiction.

Divided government A situation in which one major political party controls the presidency and the other controls the chambers of Congress, or in which one party controls a state governorship and the other controls the state legislature.

Divine right of kings A political and religious doctrine that asserts a monarchy's legitimacy is conferred directly by God and as such a king is not subject to any earthly authority, including his people or the church.

Divisive opinion Public opinion that is polarized between two quite different positions.

Domestic policy Public plans or courses of action that concern internal issues of national importance, such as poverty, crime, and the environment.

Dual Federalism A system in which the states and the national government each remains supreme within their own sphere. The doctrine looks on nation and state as coequal sovereign powers. Neither the state government nor the national government should interfere in the other's sphere.

E

Earmarks Funding appropriations that are specifically designated for a named project in a member's state or district.

Earned-Income Tax Credit (EITC) Program A government program that helps low-income workers by giving back part or all of their Social Security taxes.

Economic aid Assistance to other nations in the form of grants, loans, or credits to buy the assisting nation's products.

Elastic Clause, or Necessary and Proper Clause The clause in Article I, Section 8, that grants Congress the power to do whatever is necessary to execute its specifically delegated powers.

Elector A member of the electoral college, which selects the president and vice president. Each state's electors are chosen in each presidential election year according to state laws.

Electoral college A group of persons called *electors* selected by the voters in each state and the District of Columbia; this group officially elects the president and vice president of the United States. The number of electors in each state is equal to the number of each state's representatives in both chambers of Congress.

Electronic media Communication channels that involve electronic transmissions, such as radio, television, and, to an increasing extent, the Internet.

Elite theory A perspective holding that society is ruled by a small number of people who exercise power to further their self-interest.

Emergency power An inherent power exercised by the president during a period of national crisis.

Eminent domain A power set forth in the Fifth Amendment to the U.S. Constitution that allows government to take private property for public use under the condition that compensation is offered to the landowner.

Enabling legislation A statute enacted by Congress that authorizes the creation of an administrative agency and specifies the name, purpose, composition, functions, and powers of the agency being created.

Energy policy Laws concerned with how much energy is needed and used.

Enumerated power A power specifically granted to the national government by the Constitution. The first 17 clauses of Article I, Section 8, specify most of the enumerated powers of Congress.

Environmental Impact Statement (EIS) A report that must show the costs and benefits of major federal actions that could significantly affect the quality of the environment.

Equality As a political value, the idea that all people are of equal worth.

Era of Good Feelings The years from 1817 to 1825, when James Monroe was president and there was, in effect, no political opposition.

Establishment Clause The part of the First Amendment prohibiting the establishment of a church officially supported by the national government.

It is applied to questions of state and local government aid to religious organizations and schools, the legality of allowing or requiring school prayers, and the teaching of evolution versus intelligent design.

Exclusionary rule A policy forbidding the admission at trial of illegally seized evidence.

Executive agreement An international agreement made by the president, without senatorial ratification, with the head of a foreign state.

Executive budget The budget prepared and submitted by the president to Congress.

Executive Office of the President (EOP) An organization established by President Franklin D. Roosevelt to assist the president in carrying out major duties.

Executive order A rule or regulation issued by the president that has the effect of law. Executive orders can implement and give administrative effect to provisions in the Constitution, to treaties, and to statutes.

Executive privilege The right of executive officials to withhold information from or to refuse to appear before a legislative committee.

Expansionist policy A policy that embraces the extension of American borders as far as possible.

Exports Goods and services produced domestically for sale abroad.

Expressed power A power of the president that is expressly written into the Constitution or into statutory law.

Extradite To surrender an accused or convicted criminal to the authorities of the state from which he or she has fled; to return a fugitive criminal to the jurisdiction of the accusing state.

F

Faction A group or bloc in a legislature or political party acting in pursuit of some special interest or position.

Fall review The annual process in which the Office of Management and Budget, after receiving formal federal agency requests for funding for the next fiscal year, reviews the requests, makes changes, and submits its recommendations to the president.

Federal mandate A requirement in federal legislation that forces states and municipalities to comply with certain rules.

Federal Open Market Committee The most important body within the Federal Reserve System. The Federal Open Market Committee decides how monetary policy should be carried out.

Federal question A question that has to do with the U.S. Constitution, acts of Congress, or treaties. A federal question provides a basis for federal jurisdiction.

Federal Register A publication of the U.S. government that prints executive orders, rules, and regulations.

Federal Reserve System (the Fed) The agency created by Congress in 1913 to serve as the nation's central banking organization.

Federal system A system of government in which power is divided between a central government and regional, or subdivisional, governments. Each level must have some domain in which its policies are dominant and some genuine political or constitutional guarantee of its authority.

Federalism A system of government in which power is divided by a written constitution between a central government and regional or subdivisional governments. Each level must have some domain in which its policies are dominant and some genuine constitutional guarantee of its authority.

Federalist The name given to one who was in favor of the adoption of the U.S. Constitution and the creation of a federal union with a strong central government.

Feminism The philosophy of political, economic, and social equality for women and the gender consciousness sufficient to mobilize women for change.

Filibuster The use of the Senate's tradition of unlimited debate as a delaying tactic to block a bill.

Finance chairperson The campaign professional who directs fundraising, campaign spending, and compliance with campaign finance laws and reporting requirements.

First budget resolution A resolution passed by Congress in May that sets overall revenue and spending goals for the following fiscal year.

Fiscal policy The federal government's use of taxation and spending policies to affect overall business activity.

Fiscal year (FY) A 12-month period that is used for bookkeeping or accounting purposes. Usually, the fiscal year does not coincide with the calendar year. For example, the federal government's fiscal year runs from October 1 through September 30.

Focus group A small group of individuals who are led in discussion by a professional consultant in order to gather opinions on and responses to candidates and issues.

Food stamps Benefits issued by the federal government to low-income individuals to be used for the purchase of food; originally provided as coupons, but now typically provided electronically through a card similar to a debit card.

Foreign policy A nation's external goals and the techniques and strategies used to achieve them.

Foreign policy process The steps by which foreign policy goals are decided and acted on.

Framing The presentation of an issue by the media which influences how audiences understand it.

Franking A policy that enables members of Congress to send material through the mail by substituting their facsimile signature (frank) for postage.

Free Exercise Clause The provision of the First Amendment guaranteeing the free exercise of religion.

Free rider problem The difficulty interest groups face in recruiting members when the benefits they achieve can be gained without joining the group.

Front-loading The practice of moving presidential primary elections to the early part of the campaign to maximize the impact of these primaries on the nomination.

Front-runner The presidential candidate who appears to be ahead at a given time in the primary season.

Full employment An arbitrary level of unemployment that corresponds to "normal" friction in the labor market. In 1986, a 6.5 percent rate of unemployment was considered full employment. Today, it is assumed to be around 5 percent.

Full Faith and Credit Clause This section of the Constitution requires states to recognize one another's laws and court decisions. It ensures that rights established under deeds, wills, contracts, and other civil matters in one state will be honored by other states.

Functional consolidation Cooperation by two or more units of local government in providing services to their inhabitants. This is generally done by unifying a set of departments (e.g., the police departments) into a single agency.

G

Gag order An order issued by a judge restricting the publication of news about a trial or a pretrial hearing to protect the accused's right to a fair trial.

Gender discrimination Any practice, policy, or procedure that denies equality of treatment to an individual or to a group because of gender.

Gender gap The difference between the percentage of women who vote for a particular candidate and the percentage of men who vote for the candidate.

General jurisdiction Exists when a court's authority to hear cases is not significantly restricted. A court of general jurisdiction normally can hear a broad range of cases.

General law city A city operating under general state laws that apply to all local governmental units of a similar type.

General sales tax A tax levied as a proportion of the retail price of a commodity at the point of sale.

Generational effect A long-lasting effect of the events of a particular time on the political opinions of those who came of political age at that time.

Gerrymandering The drawing of legislative district boundary lines to obtain partisan or factional advantage. A district is said to be gerrymandered when its shape is manipulated by the dominant party in the state legislature to maximize electoral strength at the expense of the minority party.

Get Out the Vote (GOTV) This phrase describes the multiple efforts expended by campaigns to get voters out to the polls on election day.

Gini index A statistical measure of the distribution of income in a nation. A higher number indicates more inequality in incomes within a nation.

Glass-Steagall Act A law passed in 1933 to regulate the banking industry which prohibited banks from engaging in speculative investments or becoming investment houses.

Government The preeminent institution in which decisions are made that resolve conflicts or allocate benefits and privileges. It is unique because it has the ultimate authority within society.

Government corporation An agency of government that administers a quasi-business enterprise. These corporations are used when activities are primarily commercial.

Government in the Sunshine Act A law that requires all committee-directed federal agencies to conduct their business regularly in public session.

Grandfather clause A device used by Southern states to disenfranchise African Americans. It restricted voting to those whose grandfathers had voted before 1867.

Great Compromise The compromise between the New Jersey and Virginia plans that created one chamber of the Congress based on population and one chamber representing each state equally; also called the Connecticut Compromise.

Gross domestic product (GDP) The dollar value of all final goods and services produced in a one-year period.

Gross public debt The net public debt plus interagency borrowings within the government.

H

Hard money This refers to political contributions and campaign spending that is recorded under the regulations set forth in law and by the Federal Election Commission.

Hatch Act An act passed in 1939 that restricted the political activities of government employees. It also prohibited a political group from spending more than $3 million in any campaign and limited individual contributions to a campaign committee to $5,000.

Hate crime A criminal offense committed against a person or property that is motivated, in whole or in part, by the offender's bias against a race, color, ethnicity, national origin, sex, gender identity or expression, sexual orientation, disability, age, or religion.

Head of state The role of the president as ceremonial head of the government.

Hillstyle The actions and behaviors of a member of Congress in Washington, DC, intended to promote policies and the member's own career aspirations.

Hispanic Someone who can claim a heritage from a Spanish-speaking country other than Spain. This is the term most often used by government agencies to describe this group. Citizens of Spanish-speaking countries do not use this term to describe themselves.

Home rule city A city permitted by the state to let local voters frame, adopt, and amend their own charter.

Homestyle The actions and behaviors of a member of Congress aimed at the constituents and intended to win the support and trust of the voters at home.

I

Ideology A comprehensive set of beliefs about the nature of people and about the role of an institution or government.

Impeachment An action by the House of Representatives to accuse the president, vice president, or other civil officers of the United States of committing "Treason, Bribery, or other high Crimes and Misdemeanors."

Import quota A restriction imposed on the value or number of units of a particular good that can be brought into a country. Foreign suppliers are unable to sell more than the amount specified in the import quota.

Imports Goods and services produced outside a country but sold within its borders.

Income transfer A transfer of income from some individuals in the economy to other individuals. This is generally done by government action.

Incorporation theory The view that most of the protections of the Bill of Rights apply to state governments through the Fourteenth Amendment's due process clause.

Independent A voter or candidate who does not identify with a political party.

Independent executive agency A federal agency that is not part of a Cabinet department but reports directly to the president.

Independent expenditures Nonregulated contributions from political action committees (PACs), organizations, and individuals. The funds may be spent on advertising or other campaign activities, so long as those expenditures are not coordinated with those of a candidate.

Independent regulatory agency An agency outside the major executive departments charged with making and implementing rules and regulations.

Indirect technique A strategy employed by interest groups that uses third parties to influence government officials.

Inflation A sustained rise in the general price level of goods and services.

Inherent power A power of the president derived from the statements in the Constitution that "the executive Power shall be vested in a President" and that the president should "take Care that the Laws be faithfully executed"; defined through practice rather than through law.

Initiative A procedure by which voters can propose a law or constitutional amendment.

In-kind subsidy A good or service—such as food stamps, housing, or medical care—provided by the government to low-income groups.

Institution An ongoing organization that performs certain functions for society.

Instructed delegate A legislator who is an agent of the voters who elected him or her and who votes according to the views of constituents regardless of personal beliefs.

Intelligence community The government agencies that gather information about the capabilities and intentions of foreign governments or that engage in covert actions.

Interest group An organized group of individuals sharing common objectives who actively attempt to influence policy makers.

Interstate compact An agreement between two or more states. Agreements on minor matters are made without congressional consent, but any compact that tends to increase the power of the contracting states relative to other states or relative to the national government generally requires the consent of Congress. Such compacts serve as a means by which states can solve regional problems.

Iron Curtain The term used to describe the division of Europe between the Soviet bloc and the West; coined by Winston Churchill.

Iron Triangle The three-way alliance among legislators, bureaucrats, and interest groups to make or preserve policies that benefit their respective interests.

Isolationist foreign policy A policy of abstaining from an active role in international affairs or alliances, which characterized U.S. foreign policy toward Europe during most of the 1800s.

Issue advocacy advertising Advertising paid for by interest groups that support or oppose a candidate or a candidate's position on an issue without mentioning voting or elections.

Issue network A group of individuals or organizations—which may consist of legislators and legislative staff members, interest group leaders, bureaucrats, the media, scholars, and other experts—that supports a particular policy position on a given issue.

Item veto The power exercised by the governors of most states to veto particular sections or items of an appropriations bill, while signing the remainder of the bill into law.

J

Jim Crow laws Laws enacted by Southern states that enforced segregation in schools, on transportation, and in public accommodations.

Joint committee A legislative committee composed of members from both chambers of Congress.

Judicial activism A doctrine holding that the Supreme Court should take an active role by using its powers to check the activities of governmental bodies when those bodies exceed their authority.

Judicial implementation The way in which court decisions are translated into action.

Judicial restraint A doctrine holding that the Supreme Court should defer to the decisions made by the elected representatives of the people in the legislative and executive branches.

Judicial review The power of the Supreme Court or any court to hold a law or other legal action as unconstitutional.

Jurisdiction The authority of a court to decide certain cases. Not all courts have the authority to decide all cases. Two jurisdictional issues are where a case arises as well as its subject matter.

Justiciable question A question that may be raised and reviewed in court.

K

Keynesian economics A school of economic thought that tends to favor active federal government policy making to stabilize economy-wide fluctuations, usually by implementing discretionary fiscal policy.

Kitchen Cabinet The informal advisers to the president.

L

Labor movement Generally, the economic and political expression of working-class interests; politically, the organization of working-class interests.

Latent interests Public-policy interests that are not recognized or addressed by a group at a particular time.

Latino Preferred term for referring to individuals who claim a heritage from a Spanish-speaking country other than Spain.

Lawmaking The process of establishing the legal rules that govern society.

Legislature A governmental body primarily responsible for the making of laws.

Libel A written defamation of a person's character, reputation, business, or property rights.

Liberalism A set of beliefs that includes the advocacy of positive government action to improve the welfare of individuals, support for civil rights, and tolerance for political and social change.

Libertarianism A political ideology based on skepticism or opposition toward almost all government activities.

Liberty The greatest freedom of individuals that is consistent with the freedom of other individuals in the society.

Life cycle effect People change as they grow older because of age-specific experiences and thus people are likely to hold age-specific attitudes.

Limited government The principle that the powers of government should be limited, usually by constitutional checks.

Limited jurisdiction Exists when a court's authority to hear cases is restricted to certain types of claims, such as tax claims or bankruptcy petitions.

Line organization In the federal government, an administrative unit that is directly accountable to the president.

Line-item veto The power of an executive to veto individual lines or items within a piece of legislation without vetoing the entire bill.

Literacy test A test administered as a precondition for voting, often used to prevent African Americans from exercising their right to vote.

Litigate To engage in a legal proceeding or seek relief in a court of law; to carry on a lawsuit.

Lobbyist An organization or individual who attempts to influence legislation and the administrative decisions of government.

Logrolling An arrangement in which two or more members of Congress agree in advance to support each other's bills.

Loophole A legal method by which individuals and businesses are allowed to reduce the tax liabilities owed to the government.

Loose monetary policy Monetary policy that makes credit inexpensive and abundant, possibly leading to inflation.

M

Madisonian model A structure of government proposed by James Madison in which the powers of the government are separated into three branches: executive, legislative, and judicial.

Majoritarianism A political theory holding that in a democracy, the government ought to do what the majority of the people want.

Majority More than 50 percent.

Majority Leader of the House A legislative position held by an important party member in the House of Representatives. The majority leader is selected by the majority party in caucus or conference to foster cohesion among party members and to act as spokesperson for the majority party in the House.

Majority opinion A court opinion reflecting the views of the majority of the judges.

Majority rule A basic principle of democracy asserting that the greatest number of citizens in any political unit should select officials and determine policy.

Managed news Information generated and distributed by the government in such a way as to give government interests priority over candor.

Material incentive A reason or motive having to do with economic benefits or opportunities.

Media The means of communication, such as radio, television, news outlets, internet, social media that reach people widely.

Media access The public's right of access to the media. The Federal Communications Commission and the courts have gradually taken the stance that citizens do have a right to media access.

Medicaid A joint state–federal program that provides medical care to the poor (including indigent elderly persons in nursing homes). The program is funded out of general government revenues.

Medicare A federal health insurance program that covers U.S. residents age 65 and older. The costs are met by a tax on wages and salaries.

Merit system The selection, retention, and promotion of government employees on the basis of competitive examinations.

Microtarget To use demographic and consumer data to identify individuals or small groups of people who will receive specific advertising messages.

Military-industrial complex The mutually beneficial relationship between the armed forces and defense contractors.

Minority Leader of the House The party leader elected by the minority party in the House.

Monetary policy The utilization of changes in the amount of money in circulation to alter credit markets, employment, and the rate of inflation.

Monopolistic model A model of bureaucracy that compares bureaucracies to monopolistic business firms. Lack of competition in either circumstance leads to inefficient and costly operations.

Monroe Doctrine A policy statement made by President James Monroe in 1823, which set out three principles: (1) European nations should not establish new colonies in the Western Hemisphere; (2) European nations should not intervene in the affairs of independent nations of the Western Hemisphere; and (3) the United States would not interfere in the affairs of European nations.

Moralist foreign policy A foreign policy based on values and moral beliefs.

Municipal home rule The power vested in a local unit of government to draft or change its own charter and to manage its own affairs.

N

Narrowcasting Broadcasting that is targeted to one small sector of the population.

National committee A standing committee of a national political party established to direct and coordinate party activities between national party conventions.

National convention The meeting held every four years by each major party to select presidential and vice presidential candidates, to write a platform, to choose a national committee, and to conduct party business.

National health insurance A plan to provide universal health insurance under which the government provides basic health care coverage to all citizens. In most such plans, the program is funded by taxes on wages or salaries.

National Security Council (NSC) An agency in the Executive Office of the President that advises the president on national security.

National security policy Foreign and domestic policy designed to protect the nation's independence and political and economic integrity; policy that is concerned with the safety and defense of the nation.

Natural rights Rights held to be inherent in natural law, not dependent on governments. John Locke stated that natural law, being superior to human law, specifies certain rights of "life, liberty, and property." These rights, altered to become "life, liberty, and the pursuit of happiness," are asserted in the Declaration of Independence.

Negative constituents Citizens who openly oppose the government's policies.

Net public debt The accumulation of all past federal government deficits; the total amount owed by the federal government to individuals, businesses, and foreigners.

New England town A governmental unit in the New England states that combines the roles of city and county in one unit.

Nonopinion The lack of an opinion on an issue or policy among the majority.

Normal Trade Relations (NTR) status A status granted through an international treaty by which each member nation must treat other members at least as well as it treats the country that receives its most favorable treatment. This status was formerly known as most-favored-nation status.

O

Office of Management and Budget (OMB) A division of the Executive Office of the President. The OMB assists the president in preparing the annual budget, clearing and coordinating departmental agency budgets, and supervising the administration of the federal budget.

Office-block, or Massachusetts, ballot A form of general-election ballot in which candidates for elective office are grouped together under the title of each office. It emphasizes voting for the office and the individual candidate, rather than for the party.

Oligarchy Rule by the few in their own interests.

Ombudsperson A person who hears and investigates complaints by private individuals against public officials or agencies.

Open primary A primary in which any registered voter can vote (but must vote for candidates of only one party).

Opinion leader One who is able to influence the opinions of others because of position, expertise, or personality.

Opinion poll A method of systematically questioning a small, selected sample of respondents who are deemed representative of the total population.

Opinion The statement by a judge or a court of the decision reached in a case. The opinion sets forth the applicable law and details the reasoning on which the ruling was based.

Oral arguments The verbal arguments presented in person by attorneys to an appellate court. Each attorney presents reasons to the court why the court should rule in her or his client's favor.

Order A state of peace and security. Maintaining order by protecting members of society from violence and criminal activity is the oldest purpose of government.

Oversight The process by which Congress follows up on laws it has enacted to ensure that they are being enforced and administered in the way Congress intended.

P

Pardon A release from the punishment for or legal consequences of a crime; a pardon can be granted by the president before or after a conviction.

Party identification Linking oneself to a particular political party.

Party identifier A person who identifies with a political party.

Party organization The formal structure and leadership of a political party, including election committees; local, state, and national executives; and paid professional staff.

Party platform A document drawn up at each national convention outlining the policies, positions, and principles of the party.

Party-column, or Indiana, ballot A form of general-election ballot in which all of a party's candidates for elective office are arranged in one column under the party's label and symbol. It emphasizes voting for the party, rather than for the office or individual.

Party-in-government All of the elected and appointed officials who identify with a political party.

Party-in-the-electorate Those members of the general public who identify with a political party or who express a preference for one party over another.

Patronage The practice of rewarding faithful party workers and followers with government employment and contracts.

Peer group A group consisting of members sharing common social characteristics. These groups play an important part in the socialization process, helping to shape attitudes and beliefs.

Pendleton Act (Civil Service Reform Act) An act that established the principle of employment on the basis of merit and created the Civil Service Commission to administer the personnel service.

Permanent campaign A coordinated and planned strategy carried out by the White House to increase the president's popularity and support.

Picket-fence Federalism A model of federalism in which specific programs and policies (depicted as vertical pickets in a picket fence) involve all levels of government—national, state, and local (depicted by the horizontal boards in a picket fence).

Pluralism A theory that views politics as a conflict among interest groups. Political decision making is characterized by bargaining and compromise.

Plurality A number of votes cast for a candidate that is greater than the number of votes for any other candidate but not necessarily a majority.

Pocket veto A special veto exercised by the chief executive after a legislative body has adjourned. Bills not signed by the chief executive die after a specified period of time. If Congress wishes to reconsider such a bill, it must be reintroduced in the following session of Congress.

Podcasting A method of distributing multimedia files, such as audio or video files, for downloading onto mobile devices or personal computers.

Police power The authority to legislate for the protection of the health, morals, safety, and welfare of the people. In the United States, most police power is reserved to the states.

Policy tsar A high-ranking member of the Executive Office of the President appointed to coordinate action in one specific policy area.

Political Action Committee (PAC) A committee set up by and representing a corporation, labor union, or special-interest group. PACs raise and give campaign donations.

Political consultant A paid professional hired to devise a campaign strategy and manage a campaign.

Political culture The set of ideals, values, and ways of thinking about government and politics that is shared by all citizens.

Political party A group of political activists who organize to win elections, operate the government, and determine public policy.

Political question An issue that a court believes should be decided by the executive or legislative branch.

Political socialization The process through which individuals learn a set of political attitudes and form opinions about social issues. Families and the educational system are two of the most important forces in the political socialization process.

Political trust The degree to which individuals express trust in the government and political institutions, usually measured through a specific series of survey questions.

Politics The process of resolving conflicts and deciding "who gets what, when, and how." More specifically, politics is the struggle over power or influence within organizations or informal groups that can grant or withhold benefits or privileges.

Poll tax A special tax that must be paid as a qualification for voting. The Twenty-fourth Amendment to the Constitution outlawed the poll tax in national elections, and in 1966, the Supreme Court declared it unconstitutional in all elections.

Pollster The person or firm who conducts public opinion polls for the campaign.

Pork Special projects or appropriations that are intended to benefit a member's district or state; slang term for earmarks.

Precedent A court rule bearing on subsequent legal decisions in similar cases. Judges rely on precedents in deciding cases.

Preemptive war A military engagement fought to stop an enemy before that enemy attacks the United States.

President pro tempore The temporary presiding officer of the Senate in the absence of the vice president.

Presidential primary A statewide primary election of delegates to a political party's national convention, held to determine a party's presidential nominee.

Press secretary (1) The individual who interacts directly with the journalists covering the campaign. (2) The presidential staff member responsible for handling White House media relations and communications.

Priming The process by which the media suggest the importance of an issue.

Prior restraint Restraining an action before the activity has actually occurred. When expression is involved, this means censorship.

Privatization The replacement of government services with services provided by private firms.

Privileges and immunities Special rights and exceptions provided by law. States may not discriminate against one another's citizens.

Progressive tax A tax that rises in percentage terms as incomes rise.

Property Anything that is or may be subject to ownership. As conceived by the political philosopher John Locke, the right to property is a natural right superior to human law (laws made by government).

Property tax A tax on the value of real estate. This tax is a particularly important source of revenue for local governments.

Public agenda Issues that are perceived by the political community as meriting public attention and governmental action.

Public figure A public official, movie star, or other person known to the public because of his or her position or activities.

Public interest The best interests of the overall community; the national good, rather than the narrow interests of a particular group.

Public opinion The aggregate of individual attitudes or beliefs shared by some portion of the adult population.

Purposive incentive A reason for supporting or participating in the activities of a group that is based on agreement with the goals of the group. For example, someone with a strong interest in human rights might have a purposive incentive to join Amnesty International.

R

Racial profiling Making negative assumptions about a person or class of persons based on racial characteristics.

Ratification Formal approval.

Rational ignorance effect An effect produced when people purposely and rationally decide not to become informed on an issue because they believe that their vote on the issue is not likely to be a deciding one; a lack of incentive to seek the necessary information to cast an intelligent vote.

Realignment A process in which a substantial group of voters switches party allegiance, producing a long-term change in the political landscape.

Realist foreign policy A foreign policy based on an understanding of the nation's economic and security interests.

Reapportionment The allocation of seats in the House of Representatives to each state after each census.

Recall A procedure allowing people to vote to dismiss an elected official from state office before his or her term has expired.

Recession Two or more successive quarters in which the economy shrinks instead of grows.

Redistricting The redrawing of the boundaries of the congressional districts within each state.

Referendum An electoral device whereby legislative or constitutional measures are referred by the legislature to the voters for approval or disapproval.

Registration The entry of a person's name onto the list of registered voters for elections. To register, a person must meet certain legal requirements of age, citizenship, and residency.

Regressive tax A tax that falls in percentage terms as incomes rise.

Remand To send a case back to the court that originally heard it.

Reparation Compensation, monetary or nonmonetary (e.g., formal apology), to make amends for a past transgression or harm.

Representation The function of members of Congress as elected officials representing the views of their constituents.

Representative assembly A legislature composed of individuals who represent the population.

Representative democracy A form of government in which representatives elected by the people make and enforce laws and policies; may retain the monarchy in a ceremonial role.

Reprieve A formal postponement of the execution of a sentence imposed by a court of law.

Republic A form of government in which sovereignty rests with the people, as opposed to a king or monarch.

Republican Party One of the two major American political parties. It emerged in the 1850s as an antislavery party and consisted of former Northern Whigs and antislavery Democrats.

Reverse discrimination The charge that an affirmative action program discriminates against those who do not have minority status.

Reverse To annul or make void a court ruling on account of some error or irregularity.

Reverse-income effect A tendency for wealthier states or regions to favor the Democrats and for less wealthy states or regions to favor the Republicans. The effect appears paradoxical because it reverses traditional patterns of support.

Rule of four A U.S. Supreme Court procedure by which four justices must vote to grant a petition for review if a case is to come before the full court.

Rule The proposal by the Rules Committee of the House that states the conditions for debate for one piece of legislation.

Rules Committee A standing committee of the House of Representatives that provides special rules under which specific bills can be debated, amended, and considered by the House.

S

Safe seat A district that returns the legislator with 55 percent of the vote or more.

Sampling error The difference between a sample's results and the true result if the entire population had been interviewed.

Second budget resolution A resolution passed by Congress in September that sets "binding" limits on taxes and spending for the following fiscal year.

Select committee A temporary legislative committee established for a limited time period and for a special purpose.

Selective attention The tendency for individuals to only pay attention to information that reinforces their held beliefs.

Selective information processing For an individual, only thinking about the information that is really needed and disregarding the rest of the information presented.

Selectperson A member of the governing group of a town.

Senate Majority Leader The chief spokesperson of the majority party in the Senate, who directs the legislative program and party strategy.

Senate Minority Leader The party officer in the Senate who commands the minority party's opposition to the policies of the majority party and directs the legislative program and strategy of his or her party.

Senatorial courtesy In federal district court judgeship nominations, a tradition allowing a senator to veto a judicial appointment in his or her state.

Seniority system A custom followed in both chambers of Congress specifying that the member of the majority party with the longest term of continuous service will be given preference when a committee chairperson (or a holder of some other significant post) is selected.

Separate-but-equal doctrine The 1896 doctrine holding that separate-but-equal facilities do not violate the equal protection clause.

Separation of powers The principle of dividing governmental powers among different branches of government.

Service sector The sector of the economy that provides services—such as health care, banking, and education—in contrast to the sector that produces goods.

Sexual harassment Unwanted physical or verbal conduct or abuse of a sexual nature that interferes with a recipient's job performance, creates a hostile work environment, or carries with it an implicit or explicit threat of adverse employment consequences.

Signing statement A written declaration that a president may make when signing a bill into law. Usually, such statements point out sections of the law that the president deems unconstitutional.

Single-payer plan A plan under which one entity has a monopoly on issuing a particular type of insurance. Typically, the entity is the government, and the insurance is basic health coverage.

Slander The public uttering of a false statement that harms the good reputation of another. The statement must be made to, or within the hearing of, persons other than the defamed party.

Social contract A theory of politics that asserts that individuals form political communities by a process of mutual consent, giving up a measure of their individual liberty in order to gain the protection of government.

Social media Websites and other online places where people can interact, form social contacts, and share personal or business information.

Social movement A movement that represents the demands of a large segment of the public for political, economic, or social change.

Socialism A political ideology based on strong support for economic and social equality. Socialists traditionally envisioned a society in which major businesses were taken over by the government or by employee cooperatives

Socioeconomic status The value assigned to a person due to occupation or income. An upper-class person, for example, has high socioeconomic status.

Soft money Campaign contributions unregulated by federal or state law, usually given to parties and party committees to help fund general party activities.

Solidary incentive A reason or motive having to do with the desire to associate with others and to share with others a particular interest or hobby.

Soviet bloc The Soviet Union and the Eastern European countries that installed communist regimes after World War II and were dominated by the Soviet Union.

Speaker of the House The presiding officer in the House of Representatives. The Speaker is always a member of the majority party and is the most powerful and influential member of the House.

Spin An interpretation of campaign events or election results that is favorable to the candidate's campaign strategy.

Spin doctor A political campaign adviser who tries to convince journalists of the truth of a particular interpretation of events.

Splinter Party A new party formed by a dissident faction within a major political party. Often, splinter parties have emerged when a particular personality was at odds with the major party.

Spoils system The awarding of government jobs to political supporters and friends.

Spring review The annual process in which the Office of Management and Budget requires federal agencies to review their programs, activities, and goals and submit their requests for funding for the next fiscal year.

Standing Committee A permanent committee in the House or Senate that considers bills within a certain subject area.

Stare decisis To stand on decided cases; the judicial policy of following precedents established by past decisions.

State A group of people occupying a specific area and organized under one government; may be either a nation or a subunit of a nation.

State central committee The principal organized structure of each political party within each state. This committee is responsible for carrying out policy decisions of the party's state convention.

State of the Union message An annual message to Congress in which the president proposes a legislative program. The message is addressed not only to Congress but also to the American people and to the world.

Statutory power A power created for the president through laws enacted by Congress.

Straight-ticket voting Voting exclusively for the candidates of one party.

Strategic Arms Limitation Treaty (SALT I) A treaty between the United States and the Soviet Union to stabilize the nuclear arms competition between the two countries. SALT I talks began in 1969, and agreements were signed on May 26, 1972.

Strict construction A judicial philosophy that looks to the "letter of the law" when interpreting the Constitution or a particular statute.

Subpoena A legal writ requiring a person's appearance in court to give testimony.

Suffrage The right to vote; the franchise.

Sunset legislation Laws requiring that existing programs be reviewed regularly for their effectiveness and be terminated unless specifically extended as a result of these reviews.

Super PAC A political committee that can accept unlimited contributions from individuals and corporations to spend supporting a candidate as long as its efforts are not coordinated with the candidate's own campaign.

Superdelegate A party leader or elected official who is given the right to vote at the party's national convention. Superdelegates are not elected at the state level.

Supplemental Security Income (SSI) A federal program established to provide assistance to elderly persons and persons with disabilities.

Supremacy clause The constitutional provision that makes the Constitution and federal laws superior to all conflicting state and local laws.

Supremacy doctrine A doctrine that asserts the priority of national law over state laws. This principle is rooted in Article VI of the Constitution, which provides that the Constitution, the laws passed by the national government under its constitutional powers, and all treaties constitute the supreme law of the land.

Sustainability Achieving a balance between society and nature that will permit both to exist in harmony.

Swing voters Voters who frequently swing their support from one party to another.

Symbolic speech Nonverbal expression of beliefs, which is given substantial protection by the courts.

T

Tariffs Taxes on imports.

Technical assistance The practice of sending experts in such areas as agriculture, engineering, or business to aid other nations.

Temporary Assistance to Needy Families (TANF) A state-administered program in which grants from the national government are used to provide welfare benefits. The TANF program replaced the Aid to Families with Dependent Children (AFDC) program.

Third party A political party other than the two major political parties (Republican and Democratic).

Ticket splitting Voting for candidates of two or more parties for different offices. For example, a voter splits her ticket if she votes for a Republican presidential candidate and a Democratic congressional candidate.

Tight monetary policy Monetary policy that makes credit expensive in an effort to slow the economy.

Tipping A phenomenon that occurs when a group that is becoming more numerous over time grows large enough to change the political balance in a district, state, or country.

Totalitarian regime A form of government that controls all aspects of the political and social life of a nation.

Town manager system A form of town government in which voters elect three selectpersons, who then appoint a professional town manager, who in turn appoints other officials.

Town meeting The governing authority of a New England town. Qualified voters may participate in the election of officers and the passage of legislation.

Township A rural unit of government based on federal land surveys of the American frontier in the 1780s. Townships have declined significantly in importance.

Tracking poll A poll taken for the candidate on a nearly daily basis as election day approaches.

Trial court The court in which most cases begin.

Truman Doctrine The policy adopted by President Harry Truman in 1947 to halt communist expansion in southeastern Europe.

Trustee A legislator who acts according to her or his conscience and the broad interests of the entire society.

Twelfth Amendment An amendment to the Constitution, adopted in 1804, that specifies the separate election of the president and vice president by the electoral college.

Twenty-fifth Amendment A 1967 amendment to the Constitution that establishes procedures for filling presidential and vice presidential vacancies and makes provisions for presidential disability.

Two-party system A political system in which only two parties have a reasonable chance of winning.

U

U.S. Treasury Bond Debt issued by the federal government.

Unanimous consent agreement An agreement on the rules of debate for proposed legislation in the Senate that is approved by all the members.

Unanimous opinion A court opinion or determination on which all judges agree.

Unemployment The inability of those who are in the labor force to find a job; defined as the total number of those in the labor force actively looking for a job but unable to find one.

Unicameral legislature A legislature with only one legislative chamber, as opposed to a bicameral (two-chamber) legislature, such as the U.S. Congress. Today, Nebraska is the only state in the Union with a unicameral legislature.

Unincorporated area An area not located within the boundary of a municipality.

Unit rule A rule by which all of a state's electoral votes are cast for the presidential candidate receiving a plurality of the popular vote in that state.

Unitary system A centralized governmental system in which local or subdivisional governments exercise only those powers given to them by the central government.

Universal suffrage The right of all adults to vote for their representative.

Unorthodox lawmaking The use of out-of-the-ordinary parliamentary tactics to pass legislation.

V

Veto message The president's formal explanation of a veto when legislation is returned to Congress.

Voter turnout The percentage of citizens taking part in the election process; the number of eligible voters who actually " turn out" on election day to cast their ballots.

W

War Powers Resolution A law passed in 1973 spelling out the conditions under which the president can commit troops without congressional approval.

Washington community Individuals regularly involved with politics in Washington, DC.

Watergate break-in The 1972 illegal entry into the Democratic National Committee offices by participants in President Richard Nixon's reelection campaign.

Weberian model A model of bureaucracy developed by the German sociologist Max Weber, who viewed bureaucracies as rational, hierarchical organizations in which decisions are based on logical reasoning.

Whig Party A major party in the United States during the first half of the nineteenth century, formally established in 1836. The Whig Party was anti-Jackson and represented a variety of regional interests.

Whip A member of Congress who aids the majority or minority leader of the House or the Senate.

Whistleblower Someone who brings to public attention gross governmental inefficiency or an illegal action.

White House Office The personal office of the president, which tends to presidential political needs and manages the media.

White House Press Corps The reporters assigned full-time to cover the presidency.

White primary A state primary election that restricts voting to whites only; outlawed by the Supreme Court in 1944.

Writ of *certiorari* An order issued by a higher court to a lower court to send up the record of a case for review.

Y

Yellow journalism A term for sensationalistic, irresponsible journalism. Reputedly, the term is an allusion to the cartoon "The Yellow Kid" in the old *New York World,* a newspaper especially noted for its sensationalism.

Index

Medvedev, Dmitry, 437
Meredith, James, 161
merit system, 473
Merit Systems Protection Board (MSPB), 474, 479
Merkel, Angela, 9
Merton, Robert, 643
methane, 85
Mexican Americans, civil rights issues, 188–192
Mexico, immigration policy, 550–552
Michigan
  Being Black at the University of Michigan campaign, 193
  Flint, 2, 80–81, 523
  University of Michigan and affirmative action, 194–196
microaggressions, 193
microtargeting, 373
middle class, decline of, 13
Middle East conflicts, foreign policy and, 611–615
midterm elections, 397
Miers, Harriet, 511
migratory-bird rule, 535
military. *See also* national security
  aircraft carrier expense, 597
  China as superpower, 617–618
  Congressional oversight, 596–597
  defense policy, 588
  intelligence community, 594
  intervention, post-Cold War, 29–30
  military-industrial complex, 597–598
  post-Cold War challenges, 608–609
  preemptive war, 604
  President as commander in chief, 429–430
  Veterans Administration scandal, 485
  war on terror, Afghanistan and Iraq, 603–607
  war on terror, costs of, 607
military-industrial complex, 597–598
Miller v. California (1973), 126
minimum wage, 5
Minnesota, redistricting, 402–403
Minor, Virginia, 175
minority groups. *See also* civil rights
  affirmative action, 192–196
  Affordable Care Act and, 532
  bilingual education, 191–192
  California voters, 307
  candidates for office, data on, 314–315
  Congress, members of, 395–396
  gerrymandering and, 403–404
  immigration policy, 550–552
  interest group formation, 244–245
  Latino civil rights issues, 188–192

media bias, 380–381
political party identification, 290–291
reparations, 196–197
school integration, current state of, 161–162
student activism, 193–194
voting behavior, 224–225, 338
voting restrictions, 341–343
Minority Leader of the House, 410
minority-majority districts, 403–404
Minor v. Happersett, 175
Miranda, Lin-Manuel, 48–49
Miranda v. Arizona (1966), 145–146
Missouri
  Ferguson, Michael Brown shooting, 172–173, 266
Missouri Compromise (1820), 155
monetary policy, 575–577
monetary supply, 563
money bill, 416
Money in Elections, 319, 321
monopolistic model of bureaucracy, 460
Monroe, James, 284
Monroe Doctrine, 599, 615
Montana, Jeannette Rankin, 405
Montana Firearms Freedom Act, 97
Montesquieu, Baron de, 53
Moore, Michael, 80–81
moralist foreign policy, 598
Morsi, Mohamed, 588, 613
mortgage lending practices, 166–167
motor voter bills, 342
Mott, Lucretia, 174
Mourdock, Richard, 227
MoveOn.org, 256
Mubarak, Hosni, 304, 613
Mueller, Robert, 449
Muir, John, 254
multiparty systems, 304–305, 411
municipal court, 634–635
municipal home rule, 636
municipalities, 636–637
Murkowski, Lisa, 182
Murphy, Walter, 518
Muslim countries, opinion of U.S., 216–217

N

Nader, Ralph, 255, 301, 302
Nader organizations, 255
Nagin, Ray, 95
Nast, Thomas, 292
National American Woman Suffrage Association (NAWSA), 175
National Association for the Advancement of Colored People (NAACP), 159, 163, 244
National Association of Manufacturers, 249
National Audubon Society, 247, 254
National Cattlemen's Association, 250

national committee, 278
National Conference of State Legislatures (NCSL), 95
national convention, 277–278
  2016 election, 332–333
  argument for ending, 273–274
  electors, selection of, 348–351
  presidential campaigns, 330–331
National Council of La Raza, 245
National Council of State Legislatures, 627
National Education Association (NEA), 252
National Employment Law Project, 186–187
National Environmental Policy Act (1969), 534
National Farmers Union (NFU), 250
National Farm Workers Association, 245
national government. *See also* Congress; judicial branch; President, office of
  accomplishments of, 96–97
  categorical grants, 93–94
  Civil War and states rights, 88–90
  cooperative federalism, 92–93
  dual federalism, 90–91
  interstate relations, 83–86
  powers of, 78–79
  prohibited powers, 82
  supremacy clause, 82–83
National Governors Association, 84, 626
national health insurance, 532
National Industrial Recovery Act (1933), 92
nationalists, 133–134
National Opinion Research Center, 229
National Organization for Women (NOW), 179–180, 244
national parks, 533
National Petroleum Reserve, 541–542
National Recovery Administration (NRA), 92
National Resources Defense Council (NRDC), 255, 259
national security. *See also* military
  alien "removal courts," 501–502
  Congressional oversight, 596–597
  covert actions, 594–595
  Department of Homeland Security, creation of, 469–470
  Foreign Intelligence Surveillance Act (FISA), 500–501
  foreign policy over time, 598–603
  funding for programs, 94
  gender gap and voting decisions, 226–227

information disclosures, curbs on, 475
intelligence community, 594
interest groups, impact on policy, 597–598
National Security Council, 594
national security policy, 588
nuclear weapons disposal, 586–587
nuclear weapons proliferation, 610–611
PATRIOT Act, 430
preemptive war, 604
privacy concerns, 140–143
rights and freedoms, 10
signing statements and, 427
terrorism, continuing challenges, 609–610
war on terror, 603–607
war powers, president, 590
National Security Agency (NSA), 17–18, 142–143, 390, 443, 476, 594, 595
National Security Council (NSC), 448, 449, 588, 594
national security policy, 588
national service requirement, 208
National Wildlife Federation, 254–255
National Woman's Party (NWP), 176
National Woman Suffrage Association (NWSA), 175, 244
Native Americans, 12–13, 196–197
natural born citizen requirement, 36, 424–425
natural disasters, 95–96, 470–471
natural gas, 85
natural rights, 42–43
Nature Conservancy, 255, 258
Near v. Minnesota (1931), 111
Nebraska, abortion laws, 138
Nebraska Press Association v. Stuart (1976), 120, 131
necessary and proper clause, 78–79, 392–393
"necessary" war, Afghanistan, 606–607
negative campaigns, 339–340
negative constituents, 593
Negotiated Rulemaking Act (1990), 482
Negroponte, John, 470
Netanyahu, Benjamin, 217
net neutrality, 377
net public debt, 567–569
Neufeld, Peter J., 148
Neustadt, Richard E., 439, 440
Nevada, legislative calendar, 386
Nevada v. Hibbs, 101
New Deal, 91–93, 286–287, 474
New England Town, 637
New Federalism, 98
New Hampshire, state legislature salaries, 629, 631
New Jersey, tax issues, 2
New Jersey Plan, 50–51
new judicial federalism, 98–99

news media. *See* media
newspapers, history of, 357–358. *See also* media
New York, state legislature salaries, 629, 631
New York Times Co v. Sullivan (1964), 130
New York Times v. United States (1971), 120
Nicholson, Jim, 330
Nielsen, Kirstjen, 10
Nigeria, 609
Nineteenth Amendment, 177
Nixon, Jay, 173
Nixon, Richard
  China policy, 602
  executive privilege, 423
  New Federalism, 98
  Nixon-Kennedy contest (1960), 165, 359
  Office of Management and Budget, creation of, 449
  OPEC embargoes and, 541
  pardon of, 429
  public opinion of, 209
  resignation of, 444, 445
  southern strategy, 303
  as vice president, 452
  War Powers Resolution Act (1973), 590
  Watergate investigation, 367
Nobel Peace Prize, 429
No Child Left Behind (NCLB) Act, 94
nominating conventions. *See* national convention
nomination process, 313–314
nonopinion, 210
nonprofit groups, government regulations and, 242. *See also* interest groups
Noonan, John T., 514
Normal Trade Relations (NTR) status, 617–618
North American Free Trade Agreement (NAFTA) (1993), 431, 580
North Atlantic Treaty Organization (NATO), 600, 608
North Carolina
  lesbian, gay, bisexual or transgender (LGBT) rights, 119
  redistricting, 404
  voter ID laws, 168–169
North Korea, 14, 59–60, 610–611
Norton, Eleanor Holmes, 22
not-for-profit organizations, 328
Not On Our Watch, 136
"nuclear option," filibusters, 394–395
nuclear power, 544–545
Nuclear Regulatory Commission, 466
nuclear weapons, 429, 430
  current challenges, 610–611
  diplomatic negotiations, 589
  disposal of, 586–587
  Intermediate-Range Nuclear Force (INF) Treaty (1987), 602–603